How to Use the Maps in *Western Civilization,* 7th Edition

Here are some basic map concepts that will help you to get the most out of the maps in this textbook.

- Always look at the scale, which allows you to determine the distance in miles or kilometers between locations on the map.

- Examine the legend carefully. It explains the colors and symbols used on the map.

- Note the locations of mountains, rivers, oceans, and other geographic features, and consider how these would affect such human activities as agriculture, commerce, travel, and warfare.

- Read the map caption thoroughly. It provides important information, sometimes not covered in the text itself, and poses a thought question to encourage you to think beyond the mere appearance of the map and make connections across chapters, regions, and concepts.

- Several "spot maps" appear in each chapter, to allow you to view in detail smaller areas that may not be apparent in larger maps. For example a spot map in Chapter 2 zooms in on the Phoenician colonies and trade routes, c. 800 B.C. and one in Chapter 5 shows the city of Rome in detail.

VOLUME C: SINCE 1789
SEVENTH EDITION

WESTERN CIVILIZATION

VOLUME C: SINCE 1789
SEVENTH EDITION

WESTERN CIVILIZATION

JACKSON J. SPIELVOGEL

The Pennsylvania State University

WADSWORTH
CENGAGE Learning™

Australia • Brazil • Japan • Korea • Mexico • Singapore • Spain • United Kingdom • United States

WADSWORTH
CENGAGE Learning™

Western Civilization, Volume C: Since 1789, Seventh Edition
Jackson J. Spielvogel

Publisher: Clark Baxter

Senior Acquisitions Editor: Ashley Dodge

Senior Development Editor:
Margaret McAndrew Beasley

Assistant Editor: Ashley Spicer

Editorial Assistant: Heidi Kador

Associate Development Project Manager:
Lee McCracken

Executive Marketing Manager: Diane Wenckebach

Marketing Assistant: Aimee Lewis

Lead Marketing Communications Manager:
Tami Strang

Senior Production Manager: Michael Burggren

Senior Content Project Manager: Lauren Wheelock

Senior Art Director: Cate Rickard Barr

Manufacturing Manager: Marcia Locke

Permissions Editor: Tim Sisler

Production Service: Orr Book Services

Text Designer: Kathleen Cunningham

Photo Researcher: Abigail Baxter

Copy Editor: Patricia Lewis

Cover Designer: Kathleen Cunningham

Cover Image: Eugene Laloue (1854–1941). Christmas Shopping. Collection Adam Levene, Albourne, UK

Fine Art Photographic Library, London, UK/Art Resource, NY

Cover/Text Printer: Transcontinental Printing

Compositor: International Typesetting and Composition

For product information and technology assistance, contact us at
Cengage Learning Customer & Sales Support, 1-800-354-9706

For permission to use material from this text or product, submit all requests online at **cengage.com/permissions**
Further permissions questions can be e-mailed to
permissionrequest@cengage.com

Library of Congress Control Number: 2007941631

ISBN-13: 978-0-495-50290-6

ISBN-10: 0-495-50290-1

Wadsworth
25 Thomson Place
Boston, MA 02210
USA

Cengage Learning products are represented in Canada by Nelson Education, Ltd.

For your course and learning solutions, visit **academic.cengage.com**

Purchase any of our products at your local college store or at our preferred online store **www.ichapters.com**

Printed in Canada
2 3 4 5 6 7 11 10 09 08

ABOUT THE AUTHOR

JACKSON J. SPIELVOGEL is associate professor emeritus of history at The Pennsylvania State University. He received his Ph.D. from The Ohio State University, where he specialized in Reformation history under Harold J. Grimm. His articles and reviews have appeared in such journals as *Moreana, Journal of General Education, Catholic Historical Review, Archiv für Reformationsgeschichte,* and *American Historical Review.* He has also contributed chapters or articles to *The Social History of the Reformation, The Holy Roman Empire: A Dictionary Handbook,* the *Simon Wiesenthal Center Annual of Holocaust Studies,* and *Utopian Studies.* His work has been supported by fellowships from the Fulbright Foundation and the Foundation for Reformation Research. At Penn State, he helped inaugurate the Western civilization courses as well as a popular course on Nazi Germany. His book *Hitler and Nazi Germany* was published in 1987 (fifth edition, 2005). He is the coauthor (with William Duiker) of *World History,* first published in 1998 (fifth edition, 2007), and *The Essential World History* (third edition, 2008). Professor Spielvogel has won five major university-wide teaching awards. He held the Penn State Teaching Fellowship, the university's most prestigious teaching award, in 1988–1989. In 1996 he won the Dean Arthur Ray Warnock Award for Outstanding Faculty Member and in 2000 the Schreyer Honors College Excellence in Teaching Award.

TO DIANE,
WHOSE LOVE AND SUPPORT MADE IT ALL POSSIBLE

BRIEF CONTENTS

DOCUMENTS xv

MAPS xxi

CHRONOLOGIES xxiii

PHOTO CREDITS xxv

PREFACE xxvii

ACKNOWLEDGMENTS xxxi

INTRODUCTION TO STUDENTS OF WESTERN
  CIVILIZATION xxxv

WESTERN CIVILIZATION TO 1789 xxxvii

19 A REVOLUTION IN POLITICS: THE ERA
    OF THE FRENCH REVOLUTION AND
    NAPOLEON 571

20 THE INDUSTRIAL REVOLUTION AND ITS
    IMPACT ON EUROPEAN SOCIETY 604

21 REACTION, REVOLUTION, AND ROMANTICISM,
    1815–1850 632

22 AN AGE OF NATIONALISM AND REALISM,
    1850–1871 665

23 MASS SOCIETY IN AN "AGE OF PROGRESS,"
    1871–1894 698

24 AN AGE OF MODERNITY, ANXIETY, AND
    IMPERIALISM, 1894–1914 731

25 THE BEGINNING OF THE TWENTIETH-CENTURY
    CRISIS: WAR AND REVOLUTION 768

26 THE FUTILE SEARCH FOR STABILITY: EUROPE
    BETWEEN THE WARS, 1919–1939 803

27 THE DEEPENING OF THE EUROPEAN CRISIS:
    WORLD WAR II 839

28 COLD WAR AND A NEW WESTERN WORLD,
    1945–1965 875

29 PROTEST AND STAGNATION: THE WESTERN
    WORLD, 1965–1985 909

30 AFTER THE FALL: THE WESTERN WORLD IN
    A GLOBAL AGE (SINCE 1985) 935

GLOSSARY 967

PRONUNCIATION GUIDE 975

INDEX 983

DETAILED CONTENTS

DOCUMENTS xv

MAPS xxi

CHRONOLOGIES xxiii

PHOTO CREDITS xxv

PREFACE xxvii

ACKNOWLEDGMENTS xxxi

INTRODUCTION TO STUDENTS OF WESTERN
  CIVILIZATION xxxv

WESTERN CIVILIZATION TO 1789 xxxvii

19 A REVOLUTION IN POLITICS: THE ERA OF THE FRENCH REVOLUTION AND NAPOLEON 571

The Beginning of the Revolutionary Era:
The American Revolution 572
  The War for Independence 572
  Forming a New Nation 573
  Impact of the American Revolution on Europe 574

Background to the French Revolution 575
  Social Structure of the Old Regime 575
  Other Problems Facing the French Monarchy 577

The French Revolution 577
  From Estates-General to a National Assembly 578
  Destruction of the Old Regime 580
  OPPOSING VIEWPOINTS
  THE NATURAL RIGHTS
  OF THE FRENCH PEOPLE: TWO VIEWS 581
  The Radical Revolution 584
  Reaction and the Directory 592

The Age of Napoleon 593
  The Rise of Napoleon 593
  The Domestic Policies of Emperor Napoleon 594
  Napoleon's Empire and the European Response 597
  The Fall of Napoleon 599
  Conclusion 600
  Notes 601
  Suggestions for Further Reading 602

20 THE INDUSTRIAL REVOLUTION AND ITS IMPACT ON EUROPEAN SOCIETY 604

The Industrial Revolution in Great Britain 605
  Origins 605

Technological Changes and New Forms of Industrial
  Organization 607
  Britain's Great Exhibition of 1851 611

The Spread of Industrialization 613
  Limitations to Industrialization 613
  Centers of Continental Industrialization 615
  The Industrial Revolution in the United States 615
  Limiting the Spread of Industrialization in the
  Nonindustrialized World 618

The Social Impact of the Industrial Revolution 618
  Population Growth 618
  The Growth of Cities 619
  New Social Classes: The Industrial Middle Class 622
  New Social Classes: Workers in the Industrial Age 623
  Standards of Living 625
  Efforts at Change: The Workers 627
  Efforts at Change: Reformers and Government 628
  Conclusion 630
  Notes 631
  Suggestions for Further Reading 631

21 REACTION, REVOLUTION, AND ROMANTICISM, 1815–1850 632

The Conservative Order (1815–1830) 633
  The Peace Settlement 633
  The Ideology of Conservatism 635
  Conservative Domination: The Concert of Europe 636
  Conservative Domination: The European States 638

The Ideologies of Change 641
  Liberalism 642
  Nationalism 644
  Early Socialism 644

Revolution and Reform (1830–1850) 646
  Another French Revolution 646
  Revolutionary Outbursts in Belgium, Poland, and Italy 647
  Reform in Great Britain 647
  The Revolutions of 1848 648
  OPPOSING VIEWPOINTS
  RESPONSE TO REVOLUTION:
  TWO PERSPECTIVES 650
  The Maturing of the United States 653

The Emergence of an Ordered Society 654
  New Police Forces 654
  Prison Reform 656

Culture in an Age of Reaction and Revolution:
The Mood of Romanticism   657
   The Characteristics of Romanticism   657
   Romantic Poets   658
   Romanticism in Art   659
   Romanticism in Music   660
   The Revival of Religion in the Age of Romanticism   662
   Conclusion   663
   Notes   663
   Suggestions for Further Reading   663

22   AN AGE OF NATIONALISM AND REALISM, 1850–1871   665

The France of Napoleon III   666
   Louis Napoleon: Toward the Second Empire   666
   The Second Napoleonic Empire   666
   Foreign Policy: The Mexican Adventure   668
   Foreign Policy: The Crimean War   668

National Unification: Italy and Germany   670
   The Unification of Italy   670
   FILM & HISTORY
   THE CHARGE OF THE LIGHT BRIGADE (1936)   671
   The Unification of Germany   673

Nation Building and Reform: The National State
in Midcentury   678
   The Austrian Empire: Toward a Dual Monarchy   678
   Imperial Russia   678
   Great Britain: The Victorian Age   682
   The United States: Slavery and War   683
   The Emergence of a Canadian Nation   684

Industrialization and the Marxist Response   685
   Industrialization on the Continent   685
   Marx and Marxism   686

Science and Culture in an Age of Realism   687
   A New Age of Science   687
   Charles Darwin and the Theory of Organic Evolution   689
   A Revolution in Health Care   689
   Science and the Study of Society   692
   Realism in Literature   693
   Realism in Art   693
   Music: The Twilight of Romanticism   694
   Conclusion   696
   Notes   697
   Suggestions for Further Reading   697

23   MASS SOCIETY IN AN "AGE OF PROGRESS," 1871–1894   698

The Growth of Industrial Prosperity   699
   New Products   699
   New Markets   700
   New Patterns in an Industrial Economy   702
   Women and Work: New Job Opportunities   704
   Organizing the Working Classes   705

The Emergence of a Mass Society   708
   Population Growth   708
   Emigration   709
   Transformation of the Urban Environment   710
   Social Structure of the Mass Society   713
   "The Woman Question": The Role of Women   715
   OPPOSING VIEWPOINTS
   ADVICE TO WOMEN: TWO VIEWS   716
   IMAGES OF EVERYDAY LIFE
   THE MIDDLE-CLASS FAMILY   718
   Education in the Mass Society   719
   Mass Leisure   721

The National State   722
   Western Europe: The Growth of Political Democracy   722
   Central and Eastern Europe: Persistence
     of the Old Order   725
   Conclusion   728
   Notes   729
   Suggestions for Further Reading   729

24   AN AGE OF MODERNITY, ANXIETY, AND IMPERIALISM, 1894–1914   731

Toward the Modern Consciousness: Intellectual and
Cultural Developments   732
   Developments in the Sciences: The Emergence of a New
     Physics   732
   Toward a New Understanding of the Irrational   733
   Sigmund Freud and Psychoanalysis   734
   The Impact of Darwin   735
   The Attack on Christianity   736
   The Culture of Modernity: Literature   737
   Modernism in the Arts   737
   Modernism in Music   741

Politics: New Directions and New Uncertainties   742
   The Movement for Women's Rights   743
   IMAGES OF EVERYDAY LIFE
   THE STRUGGLE FOR THE RIGHT TO VOTE   744
   Jews in the European Nation-State   744
   The Transformation of Liberalism: Great Britain
     and Italy   746
   France: Travails of the Third Republic   748
   Growing Tensions in Germany   748
   Austria-Hungary: The Problem of the
     Nationalities   749
   Industrialization and Revolution in Imperial Russia   749
   The Rise of the United States   750
   The Growth of Canada   751

The New Imperialism   752
   Causes of the New Imperialism   752
   The Scramble for Africa   753
   OPPOSING VIEWPOINTS
   **WHITE MAN'S BURDEN VERSUS
   BLACK MAN'S BURDEN   754**
   Imperialism in Asia   756
   Responses to Imperialism   759
   Results of the New Imperialism   761

International Rivalry and the Coming of War 761
  The Bismarckian System 761
  New Directions and New Crises 762
  Conclusion 765
  Notes 766
  Suggestions for Further Reading 766

25 THE BEGINNING OF THE TWENTIETH-CENTURY CRISIS: WAR AND REVOLUTION 768

The Road to World War I 769
  Nationalism 769
  Internal Dissent 769
  Militarism 770
  The Outbreak of War: The Summer of 1914 770

The War 773
  1914–1915: Illusions and Stalemate 773
  1916–1917: The Great Slaughter 777
  FILM & HISTORY
  PATHS OF GLORY (1957) 779
  The Widening of the War 779
  IMAGES OF EVERYDAY LIFE
  LIFE IN THE TRENCHES 780
  A New Kind of Warfare 783
  The Home Front: The Impact of Total War 783

War and Revolution 789
  The Russian Revolution 789
  The Last Year of the War 795
  Revolutionary Upheavals in Germany and
    Austria-Hungary 795

The Peace Settlement 796
  Peace Aims 796
  OPPOSING VIEWPOINTS
  THREE VOICES OF PEACEMAKING 797
  The Treaty of Versailles 798
  The Other Peace Treaties 799
  Conclusion 800
  Notes 801
  Suggestions for Further Reading 802

26 THE FUTILE SEARCH FOR STABILITY: EUROPE BETWEEN THE WARS, 1919–1939 803

An Uncertain Peace 804
  The Impact of World War I 804
  The Search for Security 804
  The Hopeful Years (1924–1929) 805
  The Great Depression 806

The Democratic States 807
  Great Britain 807
  France 809

The Scandinavian States 810
The United States 810
European States and the World: The Colonial
  Empires 810

The Authoritarian and Totalitarian States 812
  The Retreat from Democracy 812
  Fascist Italy 813
  Hitler and Nazi Germany 816
  The Soviet Union 823
  Authoritarianism in Eastern Europe 826
  Dictatorship in the Iberian Peninsula 827

The Expansion of Mass Culture and Mass
Leisure 828
  Radio and Movies 828
  Mass Leisure 829

Cultural and Intellectual Trends in the Interwar
Years 829
  FILM & HISTORY
  TRIUMPH OF THE WILL (1934) 830
  Nightmares and New Visions: Art and Music 831
  The Search for the Unconscious in Literature 834
  The Unconscious in Psychology: Carl Jung 835
  The "Heroic Age of Physics" 835
  Conclusion 836
  Notes 837
  Suggestions for Further Reading 837

27 THE DEEPENING OF THE EUROPEAN CRISIS: WORLD WAR II 839

Prelude to War (1933–1939) 840
  The Role of Hitler 840
  The "Diplomatic Revolution" (1933–1936) 840
  The Path to War in Europe (1937–1939) 842
  OPPOSING VIEWPOINTS
  THE MUNICH CONFERENCE: TWO VIEWS 845
  The Path to War in Asia 845

The Course of World War II 847
  Victory and Stalemate 847
  The War in Asia 849
  The Turning Point of the War (1942–1943) 851
  The Last Years of the War 854

The New Order 855
  The Nazi Empire 855
  Resistance Movements 857
  The Holocaust 857
  FILM & HISTORY
  EUROPA, EUROPA (1990) 858
  The New Order in Asia 861

The Home Front 862
  The Mobilization of Peoples 862
  Front-Line Civilians: The Bombing of Cities 865
  IMAGES OF EVERYDAY LIFE
  THE IMPACT OF TOTAL WAR 867

Aftermath of the War   868
  The Costs of World War II   868
  The Allied War Conferences   869
  Emergence of the Cold War   870
  Conclusion   872
  Notes   873
  Suggestions for Further Reading   873

28 COLD WAR AND A NEW WESTERN WORLD, 1945–1965   875

Development of the Cold War   876
  Confrontation of the Superpowers   876
  OPPOSING VIEWPOINTS
  WHO STARTED THE COLD WAR? AMERICAN AND SOVIET PERSPECTIVES   877
  FILM & HISTORY
  THE THIRD MAN (1949)   879
  Globalization of the Cold War   880

Europe and the World: Decolonization   883
  Africa: The Struggle for Independence   884
  Conflict in the Middle East   885
  Asia: Nationalism and Communism   888
  Decolonization and Cold War Rivalries   890

Recovery and Renewal in Europe   890
  The Soviet Union: From Stalin to Khrushchev   890
  Eastern Europe: Behind the Iron Curtain   892
  Western Europe: The Revival of Democracy and the Economy   893
  Western Europe: The Move Toward Unity   897

The United States and Canada: A New Era   898
  American Politics and Society in the 1950s   898
  Decade of Upheaval: America in the 1960s   898
  The Development of Canada   899

Postwar Society and Culture in the Western World   899
  The Structure of European Society   900
  Creation of the Welfare State   900
  Women in the Postwar Western World   901
  Postwar Art and Literature   902
  The Philosophical Dilemma: Existentialism   904
  The Revival of Religion   904
  The Explosion of Popular Culture   905
  Conclusion   907
  Notes   907
  Suggestions for Further Reading   908

29 PROTEST AND STAGNATION: THE WESTERN WORLD, 1965–1985   909

A Culture of Protest   910
  A Revolt in Sexual Mores   910
  Youth Protest and Student Revolt   910

IMAGES OF EVERYDAY LIFE
YOUTH CULTURE IN THE 1960S   911
  The Feminist Movement   913
  Antiwar Protests   914

A Divided Western World   914
  Stagnation in the Soviet Union   914
  Conformity in Eastern Europe   915
  Repression in East Germany and Romania   916
  Western Europe: The Winds of Change   917
  The European Community   919
  The United States: Turmoil and Tranquillity   919
  Canada   920

The Cold War: The Move to Détente   920
  The Second Vietnam War   920
  FILM & HISTORY
  DR. STRANGELOVE, OR: HOW I LEARNED TO STOP WORRYING AND LOVE THE BOMB (1964)   921
  China and the Cold War   923
  The Practice of Détente   924
  The Limits of Détente   925

Society and Culture in the Western World   925
  The World of Science and Technology   925
  The Environment and the Green Movements   926
  Postmodern Thought   927
  Trends in Art, Literature, and Music   928
  Popular Culture: Image and Globalization   930
  Conclusion   933
  Notes   933
  Suggestions for Further Reading   933

30 AFTER THE FALL: THE WESTERN WORLD IN A GLOBAL AGE (SINCE 1985)   935

Toward a New Western Order   936
  The Revolutionary Era in the Soviet Union   936
  Eastern Europe: The Revolutions of 1989 and the Collapse of the Communist Order   939
  The Reunification of Germany   941
  The Disintegration of Yugoslavia   942
  Western Europe and the Search for Unity   945
  FILM & HISTORY
  THE LIVES OF OTHERS (2006)   946
  The Unification of Europe   947
  The United States: Move to the Center   949
  Contemporary Canada   949

After the Cold War: New World Order or Age of Terrorism?   949
  The End of the Cold War   949
  An Age of Terrorism?   951
  Terrorist Attack on the United States   951
  The West and Islam   952

New Directions and New Problems in Western Society   953
  Transformation in Women's Lives   953
  Guest Workers and Immigrants   954

Western Culture Today   955
    Varieties of Religious Life   955
    Art and Music in the Age of Commerce: The 1980s
      and 1990s   956

The Digital Age   958
    The Technological World   958
    Music and Art in the Digital Age   958
    Reality in the Digital Age   959

Toward a Global Civilization   960
    The Global Economy   960
    Globalization and the Environmental Crisis   961

The Social Challenges of Globalization   963
New Global Movements and New Hopes   963
Notes   965
Suggestions for Further Reading   965

Glossary   967
Pronunciation Guide   975
Index   983

DOCUMENTS

CHAPTER 19

THE ARGUMENT FOR INDEPENDENCE 574

From *The Federal and State Constitutions*, S.N. Thorpe, compiler and editor, volume 1, pp. 3–4. Washington, D.C., 1909.

THE FALL OF THE BASTILLE 579

From *The Press in the French Revolution: A Selection of Documents Taken from the Press of the Revolution for the Years 1789–1794*. J. Gilchrist and W. J. Murray, eds. (London: Ginn, 1971).

OPPOSING VIEWPOINTS: THE NATURAL RIGHTS OF THE FRENCH PEOPLE: TWO VIEWS 581

Declaration of the Rights of Man and the Citizen. From *The French Revolution* by Paul H. Beik. Copyright © 1970 by Paul H. Beik. Reprinted by permission of Walker & Co.

Declaration of the Rights of Woman and the Female Citizen. From *Women in Revolutionary Paris, 1789–1795: Selected Documents Translated with Notes and Commentary*. Translated with notes and commentary by Darline Gay Levy, Harriet Branson Applewhite, and Mary Durham Johnson. Copyright 1979 by the Board of Trustees of the University of Illinois. Used with permission of the editors and the University of Illinois Press.

JUSTICE IN THE REIGN OF TERROR 588

From J. M. Thompson, *English Witness of the French Revolution* (Oxford: Blackwell, 1938).

ROBESPIERRE AND REVOLUTIONARY GOVERNMENT 589

From *Robespierre*, edited by George Rudé. Copyright © 1967 by Prentice-Hall, Inc.. Reprinted by permission of the publisher.

DE-CHRISTIANIZATION 590

From *The French Revolution* by Paul H. Beik. Copyright © 1970 by Paul H. Beik. Reprinted by permission of Walker & Co.

NAPOLEON AND PSYCHOLOGICAL WARFARE 594

From *A Documentary Survey of the French Revolution* by John Hall Stewart. Copyright © 1951 by Macmillan Publishing Company, renewed 1979 by John Hall Stewart. Reprinted with permission of Prentice-Hall, Inc., a Pearson Education Company.

CHAPTER 20

THE TRAITS OF THE BRITISH INDUSTRIAL ENTREPRENEUR 606

From *The History of the Cotton Manufacture in Great Britain* by Edward Baines (London: Fisher, Fisher, and Jackson, 1835), pp. 195–96.

DISCIPLINE IN THE NEW FACTORIES 611

From *Documents of European Economic History*, Vol. I by Sidney Pollard & Colin Holmes. Copyright © Sidney Pollard and Colin Holmes. Reproduced with permission of Palgrave Macmillan.

"S-T-E-A-M-B-O-A-T A-COMING!" 617

From *Life on the Mississippi* by Mark Twain. New York, Harper and Brothers, 1911.

THE GREAT IRISH FAMINE 619

From *A History of Ireland under the Union* by P. S. O'Hegarty. Copyright © 1952 by Methuen & Co.

CHILD LABOR: DISCIPLINE IN THE TEXTILE MILLS 626

From *Human Documents of the Industrial Revolution in Britain* by E. Royston Pike. London: Unwin & Hyman, 1966.

CHILD LABOR: THE MINES 627

From *Human Documents of the Industrial Revolution in Britain* by E. Royston Pike. London: Unwin & Hyman, 1966.

POLITICAL DEMANDS OF THE CHARTIST MOVEMENT 629

From R. G. Gammage, *History of the Chartist Movement 1837–1854* (Truslove and Hanson, 1894).

CHAPTER 21

THE VOICE OF CONSERVATISM: METTERNICH OF AUSTRIA 635

From Klemens von Metternich, *Memoirs*, Alexander Napler, trans. (London: Richard Bentley & Sons, 1881).

UNIVERSITY STUDENTS AND GERMAN UNITY 641

From *Metternich's Europe*, Mack Walker, ed., copyright © 1968 by Mack Walker. Reprinted by permission of Walker & Co.

THE VOICE OF LIBERALISM: JOHN STUART MILL ON LIBERTY 643

From *Utilitarianism, On Liberty, and Representative Government* by John Stuart Mill. Published by Viking Press, 1914.

OPPOSING VIEWPOINTS: RESPONSE TO THE REVOLUTION: TWO PERSPECTIVES 650

Thomas Babington Macaulay, Speech of March 2, 1831. From *Speeches, Parliamentary and Miscellaneous* by Thomas B. Macaulay (New York: Hurst Co., 1853), vol. 1, pp. 20–21, 25–26.

Carl Schurz, Reminiscences. From *The Reminiscence of Carl Schurz* by Carl Schurz (New York: The McClure Co., 1907), vol. I, pp. 112–13.

THE VOICE OF ITALIAN NATIONALISM: GIUSEPPE MAZZINI AND YOUNG ITALY   653
From *Joseph Mazzini: His Life, Writings, and Political Principles* (New York: Hurd & Houghton, 1872), pp. 62–69, 71–74.

THE NEW BRITISH POLICE: "WE ARE NOT TREATED AS MEN"   656
From Clive Emsley, *Policing and Its Context, 1750–1870* (London: Palgrave Macmillan, 1983).

GOTHIC LITERATURE: EDGAR ALLAN POE   658
From *Selected Prose and Poetry*, Edgar Allan Poe. New York: Holt, Rinehart, and Winston, 1950.

CHAPTER 22

LOUIS NAPOLEON APPEALS TO THE PEOPLE   667
From *The Constitutions and Other Select Documents Illustrative of the History of France 1789–1907*, by Frank Maloy Anderson (Minneapolis: H. W. Wilson, 1904).

GARIBALDI AND ROMANTIC NATIONALISM   674
From the *Times* of London, June 13, 1860.

BISMARCK "GOADS" FRANCE INTO WAR   677
From *Documents of German History*, edited by Louis L. Snyder, ed. (Piscataway: N.J.: Rutgers University Press, 1958).

EMANCIPATION: SERFS AND SLAVES   681
Tsar Alexander II, Imperial Decree, March 3, 1861. From *Annual Register* (New York: Longmans, Green, 1861), p. 207.

President Abraham Lincoln, Emancipation Proclamation, January 1, 1863. From *U. S. Statutes at Large* (Washinton, D.C., Government Printing Office, 1875), vol. 12, pp. 1268–69.

THE CLASSLESS SOCIETY   688
From *The Communist Manifesto* by Karl Marx and Frederick Engels, trans. Samuel Moore, 1888.

DARWIN AND THE DESCENT OF MAN   690
From *The Descent of Man* by Charles Darwin (New York: Appleton, 1876), pp. 606–607, 619.

ANESTHESIA AND MODERN SURGERY   691
From *The History of Medicine in the United States: A Collection of Facts and Figures* by Francis Randolph Packard (Philadelphia: Lippincott, 1901).

REALISM: CHARLES DICKENS AND AN IMAGE OF HELL ON EARTH   694
From Charles Dickens, *The Old Curiosity Shop* (London: Chapman & Hall, 1841).

CHAPTER 23

THE DEPARTMENT STORE AND THE BEGINNINGS OF MASS CONSUMERISM   701
From *Documents of European Economic History*, Vol. I by Sidney Pollard & Colin Holmes. Copyright © Sidney Pollard and Colin Holmes. Reproduced with permission of Palgrave Macmillan.

THE VOICE OF EVOLUTIONARY SOCIALISM: EDUARD BERNSTEIN   707
From Eduard Bernstein, *Evolutionary Socialism*, Edith C. Harney, trans. (New York: B. W. Huebsch, 1911), pp. x–xii, xiv.

THE HOUSING VENTURE OF OCTAVIA HILL   713
From Octavia Hill, *Homes of the London Poor* (New York: Macmillan, 1875), pp. 15–16, 17–18, 23.

OPPOSING VIEWPOINTS: ADVICE TO WOMEN: TWO VIEWS   716
Elizabeth Poole Sanford, *Woman in Her Social and Domestic Character*. From Elizabeth Poole Sanford, *Woman, in Her Social and Domestic Character* (Boston: Otis, Broaders & Co., 1842), pp. 5–7, 15–16.

Henrik Ibsen, *A Doll's House*. Excerpt as appeared in *Roots of Western Civilization* by Wesley D. Camp (Wiley, 1983).

THE FIGHT SONG: SPORTS IN THE ENGLISH PUBLIC SCHOOL   722
From *Athleticism in the Victorian and Edwardian Public School* by J. A. Mangan (Cambridge University Press, 1981).

A LEADER OF THE PARIS COMMUNE   725
From Louise Michel, THE RED VIRGIN: MEMOIRS OF LOUISE MICHEL, pp. 64, 68, trans. by Bullitt Lowry and Elizabeth Ellington Gunter (University of Alabama Press, 1981). Reprinted by permission of University of Alabama Press.

BISMARCK AND THE WELFARE OF THE WORKERS   728
From *Bismarck*, edited by Frederick B. M. Hollyday, pp. 60, 63, 65. Copyright © 1970 by Prentice-Hall, Inc.

CHAPTER 24

FREUD AND THE CONCEPT OF REPRESSION   735
From *Five Lectures on Psycho-analysis* by Sigmund Freud, translated by James Strachey. Copyright © 1961 by James Strachey. Used by permission of W. W. Norton & Company, Inc. and Sigmund Freud Copyrights Ltd.

SYMBOLIST POETRY: ART FOR ART'S SAKE   738
"The Drunken Boat" by Arthur Rimbaud from *Realism, Naturalism, Symbolism: Modes of Thought and Expression in Europe* by Roland Stromberg. English translation copyright © 1968 by Roland Stromberg. Reprinted by permission of the Estate of Roland Stromberg.

THE STRUGGLE FOR THE RIGHT TO VOTE   745
From Emmeline Pankhurst, *My Own Story* (New York: Hearst International Library, 1914).

THE VOICE OF ZIONISM: THEODOR HERZL AND THE JEWISH STATE   747
From Theodor Herzl, *The Jewish State*. Trans. Sylvia d'Avigdor. 3rd edition (New York: Federation of American Zionists, 1917), pp. 7–8, 11, 12.

BLOODY SUNDAY   751
From George Gapon, *The Story of My Life* (New York: Dutton, 1906), pp. 182–85.

OPPOSING VIEWPOINTS: WHITE MAN'S BURDEN VERSUS BLACK MAN'S BURDEN

Rudyard Kipling, *The White Man's Burden*. From *Rudyard Kipling's Verse* (Garden City, N.Y.: Doubleday, 1919), pp. 371–72.

Edward Morel, *The Black Man's Burden*. From E. D. Morel, *The Black Man's Burden: The White Man in Africa from the Fifteenth Century to World War I* (London: National Labour Press, 1920).

THE EMPEROR'S BIG MOUTH   763

From *The Daily Telegraph*, London, October 28, 1908.

CHAPTER 25

"YOU HAVE TO BEAR THE RESPONSIBILITY FOR WAR OR PEACE"   772

From *Diplomatic Documents Relating to the Outbreak of the European War*. Ed. James Brown Scott (New York: Oxford University Press, 1916).

THE EXCITEMENT OF WAR   774

Stefan Zweig, *The World of Yesterday*. From THE WORLD OF YESTERDAY by Stefan Zweig, translated by Helmut Ripperger, copyright 1943 by the Viking Press, Inc. Used by permission of Viking Penguin, a division of Penguin Group (USA) Inc. and by permission of Williams Verlag AG.

Robert Graves, *Goodbye to All That*. From Robert Graves, Good-Bye to All That (London: Jonathan Cape, 1929).

Walter Limmer, *Letter to His Parents*. From Jon E. Lewis, ed., *The Mammoth Book of Eyewitness: World War I* (New York: Caroll and Graf Publishers, an imprint of Avalon Publishing Group, 2003), p. 24.

THE REALITY OF WAR: TRENCH WARFARE   778

All Quiet on the Western Front by Erich Maria Remarque. "Im Westen Nichts Neues," copyright 1928 by Ullstein A.G.; Copyright renewed © 1956 by Erich Maria Remarque. "All Quiet on the Western Front," copyright 1929, 1930 by Little, Brown and Company; Copyright renewed © 1957, 1958 by Erich Maria Remarque. All Rights Reserved.

THE SONGS OF WORLD WAR I   781

"Die Wacht am Rhein (The Watch on the Rhine)," Max Schneckenburger, 1840; "The Old Barbed Wire," lyrics anonymous; "Over There," George M. Cohan, 1917.

WOMEN IN THE FACTORIES   787

From "Munition Work" by Naomi Loughnan, in *Women War Workers*, edited by Gilbert Stone (London: George Harrap and Company, 1917), pp. 25, 35–38.

WAR AND THE FAMILY   788

Personal Letters of Reginald B. Mott family.

SOLDIER AND PEASANT VOICES   792

From *Voices of Revolution, 1917* by Mark D. Steinberg. Copyright © 2001 Yale University Press. Reprinted by permission.

OPPOSING VIEWPOINTS: THREE VOICES OF PEACEMAKING   797

Georges Clemenceau, *Grandeur and Misery of Victory*. From Georges Clemenceau, *Grandeur and Misery of Victory* (New York: Harcourt, 1930), pp. 105, 107, 280.

Pan-African Congress. Excerpts from Resolution from the Pan-African Congress, Paris, 1919.

CHAPTER 26

THE GREAT DEPRESSION: UNEMPLOYED AND HOMELESS IN GERMANY   808

From *Living Age*, Vol. 344, no. 4398 (March 1933), pp. 27–31, 34–38.

THE STRUGGLES OF A DEMOCRACY: UNEMPLOYMENT AND SLUMS IN GREAT BRITAIN   809

Men Without Work: A Report Made to the Pilgrim Trust. From *Men without Work: A Report Made to the Pilgrim Trust* (Cambridge: Cambridge University Press, 1938).

George Orwell, "A Woman in the Slums." From George Orwell, *The Road to Wigan Pier* (London: Victor Gollancz, 1937).

THE VOICE OF ITALIAN FASCISM   816

Reprinted by permission of the publisher from *International Conciliation*, No. 306 (Washington, D.C., Carnegie Endowment for International Peace, 1935), pp. 5–17. www. carnegieendowment.org.

ADOLF HITLER'S HATRED OF THE JEWS   818

From MEIN KAMPF by Adolf Hitler, translated by Ralph Manheim. Copyright © 1943, renewed 1971 by Houghton Mifflin Company. Reprinted by permission of Houghton Mifflin Company and Random House UK. All rights reserved.

PROPAGANDA AND MASS MEETINGS IN NAZI GERMANY   821

From Adolf Hitler, Speech at the Nuremberg Party Rally, 1936.

A Teacher's Impression of a Hitler Rally, 1932. From Louise Solmitz, "Diary," trans. and quoted in Jeremy Noakes and Geoffrey Pridham, *Documents on Nazism, 1919–45* (New York: Viking, 1974), p. 161. Reprinted by permission of Peters Fraser and Dunlop on behalf of Jeremy Noakes and Geoffrey Pridham.

THE FORMATION OF COLLECTIVE FARMS   825

From Fedor Belov, *The History of a Soviet Collective Farm* (New York: Frederick A. Praeger, Inc., 1955). Reproduced with permission of Greenwood Publishing Group, Inc., Westport, CT.

MASS LEISURE: STRENGTH THROUGH JOY   831

From *Nazism 1919–1945: A Documentary Reader, Vol. 2: State, Economy and Society 1933–1939*. Edited by J. Noakes and G. Pridham, new edition, 2000, pp. 158–159. Reprinted by permission of University of Exeter Press.

HESSE AND THE UNCONSCIOUS   835

From *Demian* by Hermann Hesse (New York: Bantam Books, 1966), p. 30.

CHAPTER 27

HITLER'S FOREIGN POLICY GOALS   841

From *Hitler's Secret Book* by Adolf Hitler, translated by Salvator Attanasio. Copyright 1961, 1989 by Grove Press. Used with permission of Grove/Atlantic Inc.

OPPOSING VIEWPOINTS: THE MUNICH CONFERENCE: TWO VIEWS   845

Winston Churchill, Speech to the House of Commons, October 5, 1938. From *Parliamentary Debates, House of*

Commons (London: His Majesty's Stationery Office, 1938), vol. 339, pp. 361–369.

Neville Chamberlain, Speech to the House of Commons, October 6, 1938. From *Neville Chamberlain, In Search of Peace* (New York: Putnam, 1939), pp. 213–215, 217.

A GERMAN SOLDIER AT STALINGRAD 853

From Vaili Chuikov, *The Battle for Stalingrad* (Grafton Books / HarperCollins UK), 1964.

HITLER'S PLANS FOR A NEW ORDER IN THE EAST 856

From *Hitler's Secret Conversations 1941–1944* by Hugh Trevor-Roper (New York: Farrar, Straus & Young, 1953).

THE HOLOCAUST: THE CAMP COMMANDANT AND THE CAMP VICTIMS 862

From *Nazism 1919–1945: A Documentary Reader, Vol. 3: Foreign Policy, War and Racial Extermination*. Edited by J. Noakes and G. Pridham, new edition, 2001, pp. 590–592. Reprinted by permission of University of Exeter Press.

THE BOMBING OF CIVILIANS 866

From John Campbell, ed. *The Experience of World War II* (New York: Oxford University Press, 1989), p. 180.

EMERGENCE OF THE COLD WAR: CHURCHILL AND STALIN 872

From the Congressional Record, 79th Congress, 2nd Session, A (Washington, D.C.: U. S. Government Printing Office), pp. 1145–1147.

CHAPTER 28

OPPOSING VIEWPOINTS: WHO STARTED THE COLD WAR? AMERICAN AND SOVIET PERSPECTIVES 877

From *Origins of the Cold War: The Novikov, Kennan, and Roberts 'Long' Telegrams of 1946*. (Kenneth M. Jensen, editor) Washington, DC: Endowment of the United States Institute of Peace, 1993. pp. 20–21, 28–31, 8, 16. Reprinted by permission of the United States Institute of Peace.

THE TRUMAN DOCTRINE 878

Reprinted from the Congressional Record, 80th Congress, 1st Session (Washington, D.C.: U. S. Government Printing Office), Vol. 93, p. 1981.

THE CUBAN MISSILE CRISIS FROM KHRUSHCHEV'S PERSPECTIVE 884

From *Khrushchev Remembers*, edited and translated by Strobe Talbott (Boston: Little, Brown, 1970).

FRANTZ FANON AND THE WRETCHED OF THE EARTH 887

From *The Wretched of the Earth* by Frantz Fanon, translated by Constance Farrington. Copyright © 1963 by Presence Africaine. Used by permission of Grove/Atlantic, Inc.

KHRUSHCHEV DENOUNCES STALIN 891

Reprinted from the Congressional Record, 84th Congress, 2nd Session (Washington, D.C.: U. S. Government Printing Office), Vol. 102, Part 7, pp. 9389–9402.

SOVIET REPRESSION IN EASTERN EUROPE: HUNGARY, 1956 894

From the Department of State *Bulletin*, Nov. 12, 1956, pp. 746–47.

THE VOICE OF THE WOMEN'S LIBERATION MOVEMENT 903

From THE SECOND SEX by Simone de Beauvior, translated by H. M. Parshley, copyright 1952 and renewed 1980 by Alfred A. Knopf, a division of Random House, Inc. Used by permission of Alfred A. Knopf, a division of Random House, Inc. and by Editions Gallimard.

CHAPTER 29

"THE TIMES THEY ARE A-CHANGIN'": THE MUSIC OF YOUTHFUL PROTEST 912

Copyright © 1963; renewed 1991 by Special Rider Music. All rights reserved. International copyright secured. Reprinted by permission.

1968: THE YEAR OF STUDENT REVOLTS 913

Reprinted from *Student Protest* by Gerald F. McGuigan. Copyright © 1968 by Methuen & Co., Publishers.

THE BREZHNEV DOCTRINE 915

From "A Letter to Czechoslovakia," *Moscow News*, Supplement to No. 30917 (1968), pp. 3–6.

MARGARET THATCHER: ENTERING A MAN'S WORLD 918

Excerpt on "Entering a Man's World" from *The Path to Power* by Margaret Thatcher. Copyright © 1995 by Margaret Thatcher. Reprinted by permission of HarperCollins Publishers, Inc.

THE FURY OF THE RED GUARDS 924

From *Life and Death in Shanghai* by Nien Cheng. Copyright © 1986 by Nien Cheng. Reprinted by permission of Grove/Atlantic, Inc.

THE LIMITS OF MODERN TECHNOLOGY 927

Reuse of excerpt from SMALL IS BEAUTIFUL: ECONOMICS AS IF PEOPLE MATTERED by E.F. SCHUMACHER. Copyright © 1973 by E.F. Schumacher. Reprinted by permission of HarperCollins Publishers.

GRANDMASTER FLASH AND THE FURIOUS FIVE: "THE MESSAGE" 931

"The Message" by Clifton Chase, Edward Fletcher, Melvin Glover, and Sylvia Robinson. Performed by Grandmaster Flash and the Furious Five. Copyright © 1982 E/A Music, Inc. and Grandmaster Flash Publishing Inc. Print rights administered by Sugar Hill Music Publishing, Ltd.

CHAPTER 30

GORBACHEV AND *PERESTROIKA* 938

Excerpt from "New Thinking" from *Perestroika* by Mikhail Gorbachev. Copyright © 1987 by Mikhail Gorbachev. Reprinted by permission of HarperCollins Publishers, Inc.

VACLAV HAVEL: THE CALL FOR A NEW POLITICS 941

From *The Washington Post*, February 22, 1990, p. 28d.

A CHILD'S ACCOUNT OF THE SHELLING OF SARAJEVO 943

From *Zlata's Diary* by Zlata Filipovic, copyright © 1994 by Fixot et editions Robert Laffont. Used by permission of Viking Penguin, a division of Penguin Putnam, Inc.

VIOLENCE AGAINST FOREIGNERS IN GERMANY 956

Published in English in *The German Tribune*, October 6, 1991, pp. 3–5.

POPE JOHN PAUL II: AN APPEAL FOR PEACE   957
From *John Paul II and the Laity,* edited by Leonard Doohan
(The Jesuit Educational Center for Human Development;
published by Le Jacq Publishing, Inc., 1984), pp. 48–50.
Reprinted by permission of Human Development.

A WARNING TO HUMANITY   962
"World Scientists' Warning to Humanity," 1992. Union of
Concerned Scientists. 1992. World Scientists Warning to
Humanity. Excerpt. Cambridge, MA: UCS. Online at
www.ucsusa.org.

"Findings of the IPCC Fourth Assessment Report," 2007.
Union of Concerned Scientists. 2007. Findings of the IPCC
Fourth Assessment Report. Excerpt. Cambridge, MA: UCS.
Online at www.ucsusa.org.

MAPS

MAP 19.1   North America, 1700–1803   573

SPOT MAP   Rebellion in France   585

MAP 19.2   French Expansion During the Revolutionary Wars, 1792–1799   587

SPOT MAP   Revolt in Saint Domingue (Haiti)   591

MAP 19.3   Napoleon's Grand Empire in 1810   598

MAP 20.1   The Industrial Revolution in Britain by 1850   609

MAP 20.2   The Industrialization of Europe by 1850   614

MAP 21.1   Europe After the Congress of Vienna, 1815   634

MAP 21.2   Latin America in the First Half of the Nineteenth Century   637

SPOT MAP   The Balkans by 1830   638

SPOT MAP   Italy, 1815   639

MAP 21.3   The Distribution of Languages in Nineteenth-Century Europe   645

MAP 21.4   The Revolutions of 1848–1849   649

SPOT MAP   The Crimean War   668

MAP 22.1   Decline of the Ottoman Empire   669

MAP 22.2   The Unification of Italy   672

MAP 22.3   The Unification of Germany   676

MAP 22.4   Europe in 1871   679

MAP 22.5   Ethnic Groups in the Dual Monarchy, 1867   680

MAP 22.6   The United States: The West and the Civil War   684

MAP 23.1   The Industrial Regions of Europe at the End of the Nineteenth Century   703

MAP 23.2   Population Growth in Europe, 1820–1900   710

SPOT MAP   Palestine   746

SPOT MAP   Canada, 1871   752

SPOT MAP   The Struggle for South Africa   753

MAP 24.1   Africa in 1914   757

MAP 24.2   Asia in 1914   758

SPOT MAP   Japanese Expansion   760

SPOT MAP   The Balkans in 1878   762

MAP 24.3   The Balkans in 1913   764

MAP 25.1   Europe in 1914   770

SPOT MAP   The Schlieffen Plan   771

MAP 25.2   The Western Front, 1914–1918   775

MAP 25.3   The Eastern Front, 1914–1918   776

MAP 25.4   The Russian Revolution and Civil War   793

SPOT MAP   The Middle East in 1919   799

MAP 25.5   Europe in 1919   800

SPOT MAP   The Little Entente   805

SPOT MAP   Gained Italian Territory   813

SPOT MAP   Eastern Europe After World War I   826

MAP 27.1   Changes in Central Europe, 1936–1939   844

MAP 27.2   World War II in Europe and North Africa   850

MAP 27.3   World War II in Asia and the Pacific   851

MAP 27.4   The Holocaust   860

MAP 27.5   Territorial Changes After World War II   871

SPOT MAP   The Berlin Air Lift   880

MAP 28.1   The New European Alliance Systems in the 1950s and 1960s   881

SPOT MAP   The Korean War   882

MAP 28.2   Decolonization in Africa   886

MAP 28.3   Decolonization in the Middle East   888

MAP 28.4   Decolonization in Asia   889

SPOT MAP   European Economic Community, 1957   897

SPOT MAP   The Vietnam War   922

MAP 30.1   The New Europe   937

SPOT MAP   Chechnya   939

MAP 30.2   The Lands of the Former Yugoslavia, 1995   944

MAP 30.3   European Union, 2007   948

SPOT MAP   Quebec   949

CHRONOLOGIES

The French Revolution   593

The Napoleonic Era, 1799–1815   600

Conservative Domination: The Concert of Europe   638

Reform, Reaction, and Revolution: The European States, 1815–1850   654

The Unification of Italy   673

The Unification of Germany   678

National States at Midcentury   685

National States of Europe, 1871–1894   727

Politics, 1894–1914   752

The New Imperialism: Africa   756

The New Imperialism: Asia   759

European Diplomacy   764

The Road to World War I   771

The Russian Revolution   794

World War I   795

The Democratic States   811

Fascist Italy   817

Nazi Germany   822

The Soviet Union   826

The Authoritarian States   827

Prelude to War, 1933–1939   847

World War II   855

The Cold War to 1962   883

The Soviet Union and Satellite States in Eastern Europe   893

Western Europe After the War   897

The Soviet Bloc   916

Western Europe, 1965–1985   919

The Fall of the Soviet Bloc   942

Western Europe Since 1985   947

PHOTO CREDITS

CHAPTER 19

571 Chateaux de Versailles et de Trianon, Versailles, France//Réunion des Musées Nationaux/Art Resource, NY   **576** © Bettmann/CORBIS   **578** © Musée de la Ville de Paris, Musée Carnavalet, Paris, France//Giraudon/The Bridgeman Art Library   **582** Musée de la Ville de Paris, Musée Carnavalet, Paris, France//Réunion des Musées Nationaux (Bulloz)/Art Resource, NY   **585** The Art Archive/Musée Carnavalet, Paris, France/Marc Charmet   **586** Musée de la Ville de Paris, Musée Carnavalet (f.13), Paris, France//Giraudon/Art Resource, NY   **589** Musée de la Ville de Paris, Musée Carnavalet (f.59), Paris, France//Giraudon/Art Resource, NY   **592** Musée de la Ville de Paris, Musée Carnavalet, Paris, France//Giraudon/Art Resource, NY   **595** Chateaux de Versailles et de Trianon (MV6314), Versailles, France//Réunion des Musées Nationaux (Gérard Blot)/Art Resource, NY   **596** Chateaux de Versailles et de Trianon, Versailles, France//Réunion des Musées Nationaux/Art Resource, NY   **599** Museo del Prado, Madrid, Spain//Erich Lessing/Art Resource, NY

CHAPTER 20

604 © British Library, London, UK//HIP/Art Resource, NY   **607** © Oxford Science Archive, Oxford, UK//HIP/Art Resource, NY   **608** Time & Life Pictures/Getty Images   **610 top** © Ironbridge Gorge Museum, Telford, Shropshire, UK/The Bridgeman Art Library   **610 bottom** © CORBIS   **612 top** © Guildhall Library, City of London, UK/The Bridgeman Art Library   **612 bottom** Victoria & Albert Museum (329–1889), London, UK//Victoria & Albert Museum/Art Resource, NY   **616** Copyright © North Wind/North Wind Picture Archives. All rights reserved.   **620** © Oxford Science Archive, Oxford, UK/HIP/Art Resource, NY   **621** British Museum, London, UK//British Museum/Art Resource, NY   **624** © SSPL/The Image Works   **628** © Trades Union Congress, London, UK/The Bridgeman Art Library

CHAPTER 21

632 Museo del Risorgimento, Milan, Italy//Scala/Art Resource, NY   **633** Maximilianeum Foundation, Munich, Germany//© SuperStock, Inc./SuperStock   **638** The Art Archive/Museo Nacional de Historia, Lima, Peru/Gianni Dagli Orti   **642** © Private Collection/The Bridgeman Art Library   **646** The Art Archive/Eileen Tweedy   **647** Chateaux de Versailles et de Trianon, Versailles, France//Erich Lessing/Art

Resource, NY   **652** Wien Museum Karlsplatz, Vienna, Austria//Erich Lessing/Art Resource, NY   **655** Time & Life Pictures/ Getty Images   **659** Ed Pritchard/Stone/Getty Images   **660 top** Gemaeldegalerie (A II 887), Staatliche Museen zu Berlin, Germany// Bildarchiv Preussischer Kulturbesitz (Jörg P. Anders)/Art Resource, NY   **660 bottom** National Gallery, London, UK//Erich Lessing/Art Resource, NY   **661** Louvre, Paris, France//Erich Lessing/Art Resource, NY

CHAPTER 22

665 Bismarck Museum, Friedrichsruh, Germany//Bildarchiv Preussischer Kulturbesitz/Art Resource, NY   **666** Chateaux de Versailles et de Trianon, Versailles, France//Réunion des Musées Nationaux/Art Resource, NY   **670** Image Select/Art Resource, NY   **671** Warner Bros/The Kobal Collection   **673** The Art Archive/Museo Civico, Modigliana, Italy/Alfredo Dagli Orti   **675** The Art Archive/ Culver Pictures   **681** © Mary Evans Picture Library/The Image Works   **682** Hulton Archive/Getty Images   **686** Bildarchiv Preussischer Kulturbesitz/Art Resource, NY   **687** © Bettmann/ CORBIS   **692** © Jefferson College, Philadelphia, USA/The Bridgeman Art Library   **693** © Oskar Reinhart Collection, Winterthur, Switzerland/ The Bridgeman Art Library   **695** Musée d'Orsay, Paris, France//Erich Lessing/Art Resource, NY

CHAPTER 23

698 Museum of the City of New York/Byron Collection/Getty Images   **700** Photo courtesy private collection   **704** The Art Archive/Private Collection/Laurie Platt Winfrey   **705** © Private Collection//Archives Charmet/The Bridgeman Art Library   **706** Photo courtesy private collection   **711** © Bradford Art Galleries and Museums, West Yorkshire, UK/The Bridgeman Art Library   **712** Topical Press Agency/Getty Images   **718 top** © Harrogate Museums and Art Gallery, North Yorkshire, UK/The Bridgeman Art Library   **718 bottom left** The Art Archive/Bodleian Library (JJ Boy Scouts), Oxford, UK   **718 bottom right** The Art Archive/ Greenaway Collection Keats House, London, UK   **720** © Bettmann/ CORBIS   **723 left & right** Rischgitz/Getty Images   **724** © Scottish National Portrait Gallery, Edinburgh, Scotland/The Bridgeman Art Library   **727** © Bettmann/CORBIS

CHAPTER 24

731 © Bettmann/CORBIS   **733** AP Images   **734** © Oesterreichische Nationalbibliothek, Vienna, Austria//Archives Charmet/The Bridgeman Art Library   **739** Musée Marmottan-Claude Monet, Paris, France//Réunion des Musées Nationaux/Art Resource, NY   **739 bottom** Musée Fabre, Montpellier, France//Erich Lessing/Art Resource, NY   **740 top** Musée d'Orsay, Paris, France//Erich Lessing/ Art Resource, NY   **740 bottom** The Museum of Modern Art, New York, NY, USA//Digital Image © The Museum of Modern Art/Licensed by Scala/Art Resource, NY   **741 top right** © 2004

Artists Rights Society (ARS), New York/ADAGP, Paris//The Museum of Modern Art, New York, NY, USA//Digital Image © The Museum of Modern Art/Licensed by Scala/Art Resource, NY **741 top left** © Dr. Werner Muensterberger Collection, London, UK/The Bridgeman Art Library **741 bottom** © 2004 Artists Rights Society (ARS), New York/ADAGP, Paris//Russian State Museum, St. Petersburg, Russia//Scala/Art Resource, NY **744 top** Hulton Archive/Getty Images **744 bottom** Arthur Barrett/Getty Images **750** © Underwood & Underwood/CORBIS **753** Copyright © North Wind/North Wind Picture Archives. All rights reserved. **761** © Asian Art & Archaeology, Inc./CORBIS

PREFACE

DURING A VISIT to Great Britain, where he studied as a young man, Mohandas Gandhi, the leader of the effort to liberate India from British colonial rule, was asked what he thought of Western civilization. "I think it would be a good idea," he replied. Gandhi's response was as correct as it was clever. Western civilization has led to great problems as well as great accomplishments, but it remains a good idea. And any complete understanding of today's world must take into account the meaning of Western civilization and the role Western civilization has played in history. Despite modern progress, we still greatly reflect our religious traditions, our political systems and theories, our economic and social structures, and our cultural heritage. I have written this history of Western civilization to assist a new generation of students in learning more about the past that has helped create them and the world in which they live.

At the same time, for the seventh edition, as in the sixth, I have added considerable new material on world history to show the impact other parts of the world have made on the West. Certainly, the ongoing struggle with terrorists since 2001 has made clear the intricate relationship between the West and the rest of the world. It is important then to show not only how Western civilization has affected the rest of the world but also how it has been influenced and even defined since its beginnings by contacts with other peoples around the world.

Another of my goals was to write a well-balanced work in which the political, economic, social, religious, intellectual, cultural, and military aspects of Western civilization have been integrated into a chronologically ordered synthesis. I have been especially aware of the need to integrate the latest research on social history and women's history into each chapter of the book rather than isolating it either in lengthy topical chapters, which confuse the student by interrupting the chronological narrative, or in separate sections that appear at periodic intervals between chapters.

Another purpose in writing this history of Western civilization has been to put the *story* back in history. That story is an exciting one; yet many textbooks fail to capture the imagination of their readers. Narrative history effectively transmits the knowledge of the past and is the form that best aids remembrance. At the same time, I have not overlooked the need for the kind of historical analysis that makes students aware that historians often disagree on their interpretations of the past.

Features of the Text

To enliven the past and let readers see for themselves the materials that historians use to create their pictures of the past, I have included in each chapter **primary sources** (boxed documents) that are keyed to the discussion in the text. The documents include examples of the religious, artistic, intellectual, social, economic, and political aspects of Western life. Such varied sources as a Renaissance banquet menu, a student fight song in nineteenth-century Britain, letters exchanged between a husband on the battle front and his wife in World War I, the Declaration of the Rights of Woman and the Female Citizen in the French Revolution, and a debate in the Reformation era all reveal in a vivid fashion what Western civilization meant to the individual men and women who shaped it by their activities. I have added questions at the end of each source to help students in analyzing the documents as well as references to related documents that are available online.

Each chapter has a **lengthy introduction and conclusion** to help maintain the continuity of the narrative and to provide a synthesis of important themes. Anecdotes in the chapter introductions convey more dramatically the major theme or themes of each chapter. **Detailed chronologies** reinforce the events discussed in the text, and **illustrated timelines** at the end of each chapter enable students to review at a glance the chief developments of an era. Many of the timelines also show parallel developments in different cultures or nations. An **annotated bibliography** at the end of each chapter reviews the most recent literature on each period and also gives references to some of the older, "classic" works in each field.

Updated maps and extensive illustrations serve to deepen the reader's understanding of the text. **Detailed map captions** are designed to enrich students' awareness of the importance of geography to history, and numerous **spot maps** enable readers to see at a glance the region or subject being discussed in the text. To facilitate understanding of cultural movements, illustrations of artistic works discussed in the text are placed near the discussions. Throughout the text, illustration captions have been revised and expanded to further students' understanding of the past. **Chapter outlines and focus questions, including critical thinking questions,** at the beginning of each chapter give students a useful overview and guide them to the main subjects of each chapter. The focus questions are then repeated at the beginning of each major section in the chapter. A **glossary**

of **important terms** (now boldfaced in the text when they are introduced and defined) and a **pronunciation guide** are provided at the back of the book to maximize reader comprehension.

New to This Edition

As preparation for the revision of *Western Civilization,* I reexamined the entire book and analyzed the comments and reviews of many colleagues who have found the book to be a useful instrument for introducing their students to the history of Western civilization. In making revisions for the seventh edition, I sought to build on the strengths of the first six editions and, above all, to maintain the balance, synthesis, and narrative qualities that characterized those editions. To keep up with the ever-growing body of historical scholarship, new or revised material has been added throughout the book on many topics, including the Neolithic Age; the Sumerians and their social classes; the Akkadian Empire, especially the role of Naram-Sin; the Amorites; the Babylonian creation epic, *Enuma elish;* the crowns of Egypt's kings; the end of the Old Kingdom in Egypt (**Chapter 1**); the Medes (**Chapter 2**); the Greek way of war (**Chapter 3**); background on Macedonia; Philip's military reforms in Macedonia; Alexander's military skills, including the siege of Tyre (**Chapter 4**); the organization and evolution of the Roman army; the practice of three names in Roman society; Julius Caesar (**Chapter 5**); Romanization in the provinces; trading connections between the Roman Empire and the Han Empire of China; culture and society in the Early Empire; mystery cults in the Roman Empire; Christian martyrs; development of the early Christian church, including the impact of Greek thought on church teachings; the Christian Gospels (**Chapter 6**); the migration of the German tribes and the fusion of Germans and Romans (**Chapter 7**); fiefs (**Chapter 8**); the influence of Asia and the Middle East on Western technological innovations (**Chapter 9**); the Battle of Hastings; Henry I; background to the Crusades and the Peasants' Crusade of Peter the Hermit (**Chapter 10**); the impact of the Black Death on art and women (**Chapter 11**); Hus and Wyclif and their relationship to Luther (**Chapter 12**); the role of popular culture and the role of cities in the spread of Luther's ideas; the Ottoman Empire during the German Reformation; the vibrancy of the Catholic Church in the English Reformation; the Elizabethan religious settlement; the Catholic Reformation (**Chapter 13**); the "military revolution"; Louis XIV's relationship to the Parlements (**Chapter 15**); the relationship between the centralization of European states, larger armies and navies, and international rivalry; causes of population growth; the impact of overseas trade on European cities (**Chapter 18**); the financial crisis in France before the Revolution; the fall of the Bastille; fear of invasion in 1792 and the "Marseillaise"; Girondins and the Mountain and the execution of the king; Robespierre; Napoleon's military campaigns; the response to Napoleon in the German states and Prussia (**Chapter 19**); pollution in cities in the nineteenth century; workhouses in Britain

(**Chapter 20**); a new table on the expansion of the British electorate in the nineteenth century (**Chapter 22**); mass education and upward mobility in the Stalinist era (**Chapter 26**); Germany's union with Austria; Czechoslovakia's pact with France; Chamberlain; the invasion of Poland; the invasion of western Europe; the invasion of the Soviet Union; the Battle of Stalingrad; the Battle of Midway; Normandy; battles in North Africa; industrial mobilization in the United States (**Chapter 27**); the Cold War, including the Truman Doctrine, Berlin Air Lift, creation of West and East Germany, and Korean War (**Chapter 28**); the non-Western world (1965–1985); the Second Vietnam War; antiwar protests in the 1960s (**Chapter 29**); Russia under Yeltsin and Putin; Eastern Europe, Germany, France, Italy, and the United States since 1985; the end of the Cold War; the war in Iraq; and guest workers and immigrants (**Chapter 30**).

Chapters 28 and 29 were reorganized and expanded to create three chapters: Chapter 28: "Cold War and a New Western World, 1945–1965"; Chapter 29: "Protest and Stagnation: The Western World, 1965–1985"; and Chapter 30: "After the Fall: The Western World in a Global Age (Since 1985)." In addition, Chapter 14 was reorganized by placing the section "The Impact of European Expansion" before "Toward a World Economy." New sections were added to a number of chapters: "The Army and Romanization," "Cities and Romanization," "Roman Law and Romanization," and "Christianity and Greco-Roman Culture" in Chapter 6; "The Significance of Charlemagne" in Chapter 8; "Monasticism and Social Services" in Chapter 10; "Calls for Reform" in Chapter 13; "Mercantile Empires and World Trade" in Chapter 18; "Impact of World War I," "Retreat from Democracy," and "German Expressionists" in Chapter 26; "Ongoing Rearmament" (in Germany) and "The Costs of World War II" in Chapter 27; "The First Vietnam War" in Chapter 28; "A Culture of Protest" and "China and the Cold War" in Chapter 29; "Art and Music in the Age of Commerce: The 1980s and the 1990s"; "The Digital Age" with the following subsections: "The Technological World," "Music and Art in the Digital Age," and "Reality in the Digital Age"; and "Toward a Global Civilization" with the following subsections: "The Global Economy," "Globalization and the Environmental Crisis," "The Social Challenges of Globalization," and "New Global Movements and New Hopes" in Chapter 30. The "Suggestions for Further Reading" at the end of each chapter were thoroughly updated and organized under subheadings to make them more useful. New illustrations were added to every chapter.

The enthusiastic response to the primary sources (boxed documents) led me to evaluate the content of each document carefully and add new documents throughout the text, including a new feature called **Opposing Viewpoints,** which presents a comparison of two or three primary sources in order to facilitate student analysis of historical documents. This feature appears in nineteen chapters and includes such topics as "Roman Authorities and a Christian on Christianity," "The Renaissance Prince: The Views of

Machiavelli and Erasmus," "Advice to Women: Two Views," and "Who Started the Cold War? American and Soviet Perspectives." Focus questions are included to help students evaluate the documents.

Two additional new features have also been added to the seventh edition. **Images of Everyday Life** will be found in twelve chapters. This feature combines three or four illustrations with a lengthy caption to provide insight into different aspects of social life, such as "Activities of Athenian Women," "Entertainment in the Middle Ages," "The Aristocratic Way of Life," and "Youth Culture in the 1960s." A third new feature is **Film and History,** which presents a brief analysis of the plot as well as the historical significance, value, and accuracy of sixteen films, including such movies as *Alexander, The Lion in Winter, Marie Antoinette, Triumph of the Will,* and *The Lives of Others.*

Because courses in Western civilization at American and Canadian colleges and universities follow different chronological divisions, a one-volume edition, two two-volume editions, a three-volume edition, and a volume covering events since 1300 are being made available to fit the needs of instructors. Teaching and learning ancillaries include the following:

For the Instructor

Instructor's Manual with Test Bank   Prepared by Eugene Larson, Los Angeles Pierce College. This manual has many features, including chapter outlines, chapter summaries, suggested lecture topics, and discussion questions for the maps and artwork as well as the documents in the text. World Wide Web sites and resources, video collections, a Resource Integration Guide, and suggested student activities are also included. Exam questions include essays, true-false, identifications, and multiple-choice questions. Available in two volumes.

Music of Western Civilization CD   Available free to qualified adopters and for a small fee to students, this CD contains many of the musical selections highlighted in the text and provides a broad sampling of the important musical pieces of Western civilization.

PowerLectures   Includes the Instructor's Manual, Resource Integration Grid, ExamView testing, and PowerPoint® slides with lecture outlines and images that can be used as offered or customized by importing personal lecture slides or other material. It also includes a correlation guide to the music CD. ExamView allows instructors to create, deliver, and customize tests and study guides (both print and online) in minutes via an easy-to-use assessment and tutorial system. Instructors can build tests with as many as 250 questions using up to twelve question types. Using ExamView's complete word-processing capabilities, they can enter an unlimited number of new questions or edit existing ones.

Full-Color Map Acetate Package   Fully revised for this edition of the text. Includes many maps from the text and other

sources. More than one hundred images. Map commentary is provided by James Harrison, Siena College.

Lecture Enrichment Slides   Prepared by George Strong and Dale Hoak, College of William and Mary. These one hundred slides contain images of famous paintings, statues, architectural achievements, and interesting photos. The authors provide commentary for each individual slide.

History Video Library   A completely new selection of videos for this edition, from *Films from the Humanities & Sciences* and other sources. More than fifty titles to choose from, with coverage spanning from "Egypt: A Gift to Civilization" to "Children of the Holocaust." Available to qualified adopters.

Sights and Sounds of History   Prepared by David Redles, Cuyahoga Community College. Short, focused video clips, photos, artwork, animations, music, and dramatic readings are used to bring life to historical topics and events that are most difficult for students to appreciate from a textbook alone. For example, students will experience the grandeur of Versailles and the defeat felt by a German soldier at Stalingrad. The video segments average four minutes in length and make excellent lecture launchers.

For the Student

Study Guide   Prepared by James Baker, Western Kentucky University. Includes new learning objectives, chapter outlines, chapter summaries, glossary terms, and six different types of questions for each chapter. Available in two volumes.

Documents of Western Civilization   Contains a broad selection of carefully chosen documents accompanied by thought-provoking discussion questions. Available in two volumes.

CengageNOW Western Civilization   CengageNOW is a Web-based study system that saves time for students and instructors by providing a complete package of diagnostic quizzes, a personalized study plan, multimedia elements, and a grade book for instructors. CengageNOW uses an intelligent and pedagogically accurate system to help students devise a personalized study plan based on their current understanding of course material. This plan combines testing with interactions and documents to help students master the key concepts of the chapter they have just read. Professors can track their students' progress via a grade book, which is compatible with WebCT and Blackboard course management systems.

Map Exercise Workbook   Prepared by Cynthia Kosso, Northern Arizona University. Includes more than twenty maps and exercises asking students to identify important cities and countries. Available in two volumes.

MapTutor CD-ROM   This interactive map tutorial helps students learn geography by having them locate geographic features, regions, cities, and sociopolitical movements.

Each map exercise is accompanied by questions that test their knowledge and promote critical thinking. Animations vividly show movements such as the conquests of the Romans, the spread of Christianity, invasions, medieval trade routes, and the spread of the Black Death.

Document Exercise Workbook Prepared by Donna Van Raaphorst, Cuyahoga Community College. A collection of exercises based around primary sources. Available in two volumes.

The Journey of Civilization CD-ROM Prepared by David Redles, Cuyahoga Community College. This CD-ROM takes the student on eighteen interactive journeys through history. Enhanced with QuickTime movies, animations, sound clips, maps, and more, the journeys allow students to engage in history as active participants rather than as readers of past events.

History: Hits on the Web Hits on the Web (HOW) is an exciting, class-tested product specially designed to help history students use the Internet for studying, conducting research, and completing assignments. HOW is approximately eighty pages of valuable teaching tools that can be bundled with any Wadsworth textbook at a very affordable price. Available through Cengage Learning Custom Solutions Publishing.

Exploring the European Past: Text and Images A Custom Reader for Western civilization. Written by leading educators and historians, this fully customizable reader of primary and secondary sources is enhanced with an online module of visual sources, including maps, animations, and interactive exercises. Each reading also comes with an introduction and a series of questions. To learn more, visit http://custom.cengage.com/etep or call Cengage Learning Custom Publishing at (800) 355-9983.

Magellan Atlas of Western Civilization Available to bundle with any Western civilization text; contains forty-four full-color historical maps, including "The Conflict in Afghanistan, 2001" and "States of the World, 2001."

Wadsworth Western Civilization Resource Center and Book Companion Web site

http://westernrc.wadsworth.com/
academic.cengage.com/history/spielvogel

Both instructors and students will enjoy the chapter-by-chapter resources for *Western Civilization,* Seventh Edition at the companion Web site available at academic.cengage.com/history/spielvogel. Text-specific content for students includes interactive maps and timelines, tutorial quizzes, glossary, hyperlinks, and Internet activities. Instructors also have access to the Instructor's Manual and PowerPoint slides (access code required). The newly enhanced Wadsworth Western Civilization Resource Center available at http://westernrc.wadsworth.com/ features such resources as documents and links to on-line readings correlated to specific periods in Western civilization, and photos that provide visual connections to events, places, and people covered in a Western civilization course.

ACKNOWLEDGMENTS

I BEGAN TO TEACH at age five in my family's grape arbor. By the age of ten, I wanted to know and understand everything in the world, so I set out to memorize our entire set of encyclopedia volumes. At seventeen, as editor of the high school yearbook, I chose "patterns" as its theme. With that as my early history, followed by many rich years of teaching, writing, and family nurturing, it seemed quite natural to accept the challenge of writing a history of Western civilization as I approached that period in life often described as the age of wisdom. Although I see this writing adventure as part of the natural unfolding of my life, I gratefully acknowledge that without the generosity of many others, it would not have been possible.

David Redles gave generously of his time and ideas, especially for Chapters 28 and 29. Chris Colin provided research on the history of music, while Laurie Batitto, Alex Spencer, Stephen Maloney, Shaun Mason, Peter Angelos, and Fred Schooley offered valuable editorial assistance. I deeply appreciate the valuable technical assistance provided by Dayton Coles. I am deeply grateful to John Soares for his assistance in preparing the map captions and to Charmarie Blaisdell of Northeastern University for her detailed suggestions on women's history. Daniel Haxall of The Pennsylvania State University and Kathryn Spielvogel of SUNY–Buffalo provided valuable assistance with materials on postwar art, popular culture, Postmodern art and thought, the Digital Age, and the new Film and History feature. I am also thankful to the thousands of students whose questions and responses have caused me to see many aspects of Western civilization in new ways.

My ability to undertake a project of this magnitude was in part due to the outstanding European history teachers that I had as both an undergraduate and a graduate student. These included Kent Forster (modern Europe) and Robert W. Green (early modern Europe) at The Pennsylvania State University and Franklin Pegues (medieval), Andreas Dorpalen (modern Germany), William MacDonald (ancient), and Harold J. Grimm (Renaissance and Reformation) at The Ohio State University. These teachers provided me with profound insights into Western civilization and also taught me by their examples that learning only becomes true understanding when it is accompanied by compassion, humility, and open-mindedness.

I would like to thank the many teachers and students who have used the first six editions of my *Western Civilization*. Their enthusiastic response to a textbook that was intended to put the story back in history and capture the imagination of the reader has been very gratifying. I especially thank the many teachers and students who made the effort to contact me personally to share their enthusiasm. Thanks to Wadsworth Cengage Learning comprehensive review process, many historians were asked to evaluate my manuscript and review each edition. I am grateful to the following people for their innumerable suggestions over the course of the first six editions, which have greatly improved my work:

Anne J. Aby
Minnesota West Community and Technical College, Worthington Campus

Paul Allen
University of Utah

Gerald Anderson
North Dakota State University

Susan L. H. Anderson
Campbell University

Letizia Argenteri
University of San Diego

Roy A. Austensen
Illinois State University

James A. Baer
Northern Virginia Community College–Alexandria

James T. Baker
Western Kentucky University

Patrick Bass
Morningside College

John F. Battick
University of Maine

Frederic J. Baumgartner
Virginia Polytechnic Institute

Phillip N. Bebb
Ohio University

Anthony Bedford
Modesto Junior College

F. E. Beemon
Middle Tennessee State University

Leonard R. Berlanstein
University of Virginia

Douglas T. Bisson
Belmont University

Charmarie Blaisdell
Northeastern University

Stephen H. Blumm
Montgomery County Community College

John Bohstedt
University of Tennessee–Knoxville

Hugh S. Bonar
California State University

Werner Braatz
University of Wisconsin–Oshkosh

Alfred S. Bradford
University of Missouri

Janet Brantley
Texarkana College

Maryann E. Brink
College of William & Mary

Jerry Brookshire
Middle Tennessee State University

Daniel Patrick Brown
Moorpark College

Gregory S. Brown
University of Nevada–Las Vegas

Blaine T. Browne
Broward Community College

Kevin W. Caldwell
Blue Ridge Community College

J. Holden Camp Jr.
Hillyer College, University of Hartford

Jack Cargill
Rutgers University

Martha Carlin
University of Wisconsin–Milwaukee

Elizabeth Carney
Clemson University

Susan Carrafiello
Wright State University

Eric H. Cline
Xavier University

Robert G. Clouse
Indiana State University

Robert Cole
Utah State University

William J. Connell
Rutgers University

Nancy Conradt
College of DuPage

Marc Cooper
Southwest Missouri State

Richard A. Cosgrove
University of Arizona

David A. Crain
South Dakota State University

Michael A. Crane Jr. (student)
Everett Community College

Luanne Dagley
Pellissippi State Technical Community College

John Davies
University of Delaware

Michael F. Doyle
Ocean County College

Joseph J. Eble
Burlington County College

James W. Ermatinger
University of Nebraska–Kearney

Porter Ewing
Los Angeles City College

Carla Falkner
Northeast Mississippi Community College

Steven Fanning
University of Illinois–Chicago

Ellsworth Faris
California State University–Chico

Gary B. Ferngren
Oregon State University

Mary Helen Finnerty
Westchester Community College

Jennifer E. Forster
Lakeland Community College

A. Z. Freeman
Robinson College

Marsha Frey
Kansas State University

Frank J. Frost
University of California–Santa Barbara

Frank Garosi
California State University–Sacramento

Laura Gellott
University of Wisconsin–Parkside

Richard M. Golden
University of North Texas

Manuel G. Gonzales
Diablo Valley College

Amy G. Gordon
Denison University

Richard J. Grace
Providence College

Charlotte M. Gradie
Sacred Heart University

Candace Gregory
California State University–Sacramento

Katherine Gribble
Highline Community College

Hanns Gross
Loyola University

John F. Guilmartin
Ohio State University

Jeffrey S. Hamilton
Gustavus Adolphus College

J. Drew Harrington
Western Kentucky University

James Harrison
Siena College

Doina Pasca Harsanyi
Central Michigan University

Jay Hatheway
Edgewood College

A. J. Heisserer
University of Oklahoma

Betsey Hertzler
Mesa Community College

Robert Herzstein
University of South Carolina

Michael C. Hickey
Bloomsburg University

Shirley Hickson
North Greenville College

Martha L. Hildreth
University of Nevada

Boyd H. Hill Jr.
University of Colorado–Boulder

Michael Hofstetter
Bethany College

Donald C. Holsinger
Seattle Pacific University

Frank L. Holt
University of Houston

W. Robert Houston
University of South Alabama

Michael W. Howell
College of the Ozarks

David Hudson
California State University–Fresno

Paul J. L. Hughes
Sussex County Community College

Richard A. Jackson
University of Houston

Fred Jewell
Harding University

Jenny M. Jochens
Towson State University

William M. Johnston
University of Massachusetts

Jeffrey A. Kaufmann
Muscatine Community College

David O. Kieft
University of Minnesota

Patricia Killen
Pacific Lutheran University

William E. Kinsella Jr.
Northern Virginia Community College–Annandale

James M. Kittelson
Ohio State University

Doug Klepper
Santa Fe Community College

Cynthia Kosso
Northern Arizona University

Ed Krzemienski
The Citadel

Paul E. Lambert
Nichols College

Clayton Miles Lehmann
University of South Dakota

Diana Chen Lin
Indiana University, Northwest

Paul Douglas Lockhart
Wright State University

Ursula W. MacAffer
Hudson Valley Community College

Harold Marcuse
University of California–Santa Barbara

Mavis Mate
University of Oregon

Priscilla McArthur
Troy State University–Dothan

T. Ronald Melton
Brewton Parker College

Jack Allen Meyer
University of South Carolina

Eugene W. Miller Jr.
The Pennsylvania State University–Hazleton

David B. Mock
Tallahassee Community College

John Patrick Montano
University of Delaware

Rex Morrow
Trident Technical College

Wyatt S. Moulds
  Jones County Junior College

Kenneth Mouré
  University of California–Santa Barbara

Thomas M. Mulhern
  University of North Dakota

Pierce Mullen
  Montana State University

Frederick I. Murphy
  Western Kentucky University

William M. Murray
  University of South Florida

Otto M. Nelson
  Texas Tech University

Sam Nelson
  Willmar Community College

John A. Nichols
  Slippery Rock University

Lisa Nofzinger
  *Albuquerque Technical Vocational
  Institute*

Chris Oldstone-Moore
  Augustana College

Donald Ostrowski
  Harvard University

James O. Overfield
  University of Vermont

Matthew L. Panczyk
  Bergen Community College

Kathleen A. Parrow
  Black Hills State University

Kathleen Paul
  University of South Florida

Jody Peterson
  Centralia College

Carla Rahn Phillips
  University of Minnesota

Keith Pickus
  Wichita State University

Linda J. Piper
  University of Georgia

Janet Polasky
  University of New Hampshire

Thomas W. Porter
  Randolph-Macon College

Charles A. Povlovich
  California State University–Fullerton

Penne L. Prigge
  Rockingham Community College

Nancy Rachels
  Hillsborough Community College

Norman G. Raiford
  Greenville Technical College

Charles Rearick
  University of Massachusetts–Amherst

Jerome V. Reel Jr.
  Clemson University

Roger Reese
  Texas A&M University

William Roba
  Scott Community College

Joseph Robertson
  Gadsden State Community College

Jonathan Roth
  San Jose State University

Constance M. Rousseau
  Providence College

Beverly J. Rowe
  Texarkana College

Julius R. Ruff
  Marquette University

Geraldine Ryder
  Ocean County College

Richard Saller
  University of Chicago

Magdalena Sanchez
  Texas Christian University

Jack Schanfield
  Suffolk County Community College

Roger Schlesinger
  Washington State University

Joanne Schneider
  Rhode Island College

Thomas C. Schunk
  University of Wisconsin–Oshkosh

Kyle C. Sessions
  Illinois State University

Linda Simmons
  *Northern Virginia Community College–
  Manassas*

Donald V. Sippel
  Rhode Island College

Stuart J. Smyth
  Berkshire Community College

Glen Spann
  Asbury College

Heath A. Spencer
  Seattle University

John W. Steinberg
  Georgia Southern University

Robert P. Stephens
  Virginia Tech

Paul W. Strait
  Florida State University

James E. Straukamp
  California State University–Sacramento

Brian E. Strayer
  Andrews University

Fred Suppe
  Ball State University

Roger Tate
  Somerset Community College

Tom Taylor
  Seattle University

Emily Teipe
  Fullerton College

David Tengewall
  Anne Arundel Community College

Jack W. Thacker
  Western Kentucky University

Thomas Turley
  Santa Clara University

John G. Tuthill
  University of Guam

Maarten Ultee
  University of Alabama

Donna L. Van Raaphorst
  Cuyahoga Community College

J. Barry Vaughn
  University of Alabama

Allen M. Ward
  University of Connecticut

Richard D. Weigel
  Western Kentucky University

Michael Weiss
  Linn-Benton Community College

Arthur H. Williamson
  California State University–Sacramento

Daniel Woods
  Ferrum College

Katherine Workman
  Wright State University

Judith T. Wozniak
  Cleveland State University

Walter J. Wussow
  University of Wisconsin–Eau Claire

Edwin M. Yamauchi
  Miami University

Robert W. Young
  Carroll Community College

The following individuals contributed suggestions for the seventh edition:

Cyriaque Beurtheret
  Salt Lake Community College

Kevin Caldwell
  Blue Ridge Community College

Joseph J. Casino
  St. Joseph's University

Paul Hagenloh
  The University of Alabama

Nicole Jobin
  University of Colorado

Jay Kilroy
  Mesa Community College

Mike Markowski
  Westminster College

Cliona Murphy
  California State University–Bakersfield

Marjorie Plummer
  Western Kentucky University

Norman G. Raiford
  Greenville Technical College

David L. Ruffley
  Pikes Peak Community College

Stuart Smyth
  University at SUNY–Albany

The editors at Wadsworth Cengage Learning Publishing Company have been both helpful and congenial at all times. I especially wish to thank Clark Baxter, whose clever wit, wisdom, gentle prodding, and good friendship have added much depth to our working relationship. Margaret Beasley thoughtfully, wisely, efficiently, and pleasantly guided the overall development of the seventh edition. I also thank Ashley Dodge for her valuable insights. I also want to express my gratitude to John Orr, whose good humor, well-advised suggestions, and generous verbal support made the production process easier. Pat Lewis, a truly outstanding copy editor, continued to teach me much about the fine points of the English language.

Above all, I thank my family for their support. The gifts of love, laughter, and patience from my daughters, Jennifer and Kathryn; my sons, Eric and Christian; my daughters-in-law, Liz and Laurie; and my son-in-law, Daniel, were enormously appreciated. My wife and best friend, Diane, contributed editorial assistance, wise counsel, good humor, and the loving support that made it possible for me to accomplish a project of this magnitude. I could not have written the book without her.

CIVILIZATION, AS HISTORIANS define it, first emerged between five and six thousand years ago when people in different parts of the world began to live in organized communities with distinct political, military, economic, and social structures. Religious, intellectual, and artistic activities assumed important roles in these early societies. The focus of this book is on Western civilization, a civilization that many people identify with the continent of Europe.

Defining Western Civilization

Western civilization itself has evolved considerably over the centuries. Although the concept of the West did not yet exist at the time of the Mesopotamians and Egyptians, their development of writing, law codes, and different roles based on gender all eventually influenced what became Western civilization. Although the Greeks did not conceive of Western civilization as a cultural entity, their artistic, intellectual, and political contributions were crucial to the foundations of Western civilization. The Romans produced a remarkable series of accomplishments that were fundamental to the development of Western civilization, a civilization that came to consist largely of lands in Europe conquered by the Romans, in which Roman cultural and political ideals were gradually spread. Nevertheless, people in these early civilizations viewed themselves as subjects of states or empires, not as members of Western civilization.

With the rise of Christianity during the Late Roman Empire, however, peoples in Europe began to identify themselves as part of a civilization different from others, such as that of Islam, leading to a concept of a Western civilization different from other civilizations. In the fifteenth century, Renaissance intellectuals began to identify this civilization not only with Christianity but also with the intellectual and political achievements of the ancient Greeks and Romans.

Important to the development of the idea of a distinct Western civilization were encounters with other peoples. Between 700 and 1500, encounters with the world of Islam helped define the West. But after 1500, as European ships began to move into other parts of the world, encounters with peoples in Asia, Africa, and the Americas not only had an impact on the civilizations found there but also affected how people in the West defined themselves. At the same time, as they set up colonies, Europeans began to transplant a sense of Western identity to other areas of the world, especially North America and parts of Latin America, that have come to be considered part of Western civilization.

As the concept of Western civilization has evolved over the centuries, so have the values and unique features associated with that civilization. Science played a crucial role in the development of modern Western civilization. The societies of the Greeks, the Romans, and medieval Europeans were based largely on a belief in the existence of a spiritual order; a dramatic departure to a natural or material view of the universe occurred in the seventeenth-century Scientific Revolution. Science and technology have been important in the growth of today's modern and largely secular Western civilization, although antecedents to scientific development also existed in Greek and medieval thought and practice, and religion remains a component of the Western world today.

Many historians have viewed the concept of political liberty, belief in the fundamental value of every individual, and a rational outlook based on a system of logical, analytical thought as unique aspects of Western civilization. Of course, the West has also witnessed horrendous negations of liberty, individualism, and reason. Racism, slavery, violence, world wars, totalitarian regimes—these, too, form part of the complex story of what constitutes Western civilization.

The Dating of Time

In our examination of Western civilization, we also need to be aware of the dating of time. In recording the past, historians try to determine the exact time when events occurred. World War II in Europe, for example, began on September 1, 1939, when Hitler sent German troops into Poland, and ended on May 7, 1945, when Germany surrendered. By using dates, historians can place events in order and try to determine the development of patterns over periods of time.

If someone asked you when you were born, you would reply with a number, such as 1988. In the United States, we would all accept that number without question because it is part of the dating system followed in the Western world (Europe and the Western Hemisphere). In this system, events are dated by counting backward or forward from the birth of Jesus Christ (assumed to be the year 1). An event that took place four hundred years before the birth of Christ would be dated 400 B.C. (before Christ). Dates after the birth of Christ are labeled A.D. These letters stand for the Latin words *anno Domini*, which mean "in the year of the Lord." Thus, an event that took place two hundred years after the birth of Christ is written A.D. 200, or in the year of the Lord 200. It can also be written as 200, just as you would not give your birth year as A.D. 1988, but simply as 1988. Historians also make use of other terms to refer to time. A *decade* is ten years, a *century* is one hundred years, and a *millennium* is one thousand years. Thus, "the fourth century B.C." refers to the fourth period of one hundred years counting backward from 1, the assumed date of the birth of Christ. Since the first century B.C. would be the years 100 B.C. to 1 B.C., the fourth century B.C. would be the years 400 B.C. to 301 B.C. We could say, then, that an event in 350 B.C. took place in the fourth century B.C.

"The fourth century A.D." refers to the fourth period of one hundred years after the birth of Christ. Since the first period of one hundred years would be the years 1 to 100, the fourth period or fourth century would be the years 301 to 400. We could say, then, that an event in 350 took place in the fourth century. Likewise, the first millennium B.C. refers to the years 1000 B.C. to 1 B.C.; the second millennium A.D. refers to the years 1001 to 2000.

Some historians now prefer to use the abbreviations B.C.E. ("before the Common Era") and C.E. ("Common Era") instead of B.C. and A.D. This is especially true of world historians, who prefer to use symbols that are not so Western or Christian oriented. The dates, of course, remain the same. Thus, 1950 B.C.E. and 1950 B.C. would be the same year. In keeping with current usage by many historians of Western civilization, this book uses the terms B.C. and A.D.

The dating of events can also vary from people to people. Most people in the Western world use the Western calendar, also known as the Gregorian calendar after Pope Gregory XIII, who refined it in 1582. The Hebrew calendar uses a different system in which the year 1 is the equivalent of the Western year 3760 B.C., considered to be the date of the creation of the world according to the Bible. Thus, the Western year 2008 is the year 5768 on the Hebrew calendar. The Islamic calendar begins year 1 on the day Muhammad fled Mecca, which is the year 622 on the Western calendar.

ALTHOUGH EARLY CIVILIZATIONS emerged in different parts of the world, the foundations of Western civilization were laid by the Mesopotamians and the Egyptians. They developed cities and struggled with the problems of organized states. They developed writing to keep records and created literature. They constructed monumental architecture to please their gods, symbolize

their power, and preserve their culture. They developed political, military, social, and religious structures to deal with the basic problems of human existence and organization. These first literate civilizations left detailed records that allow us to view how they grappled with three of the fundamental problems that humans have pondered: the nature of human relationships, the nature of the universe, and the role of divine forces in that cosmos. Although later peoples in Western civilization would provide different answers from those of the Mesopotamians and Egyptians, it was they who first posed the questions, gave answers, and wrote them down. Human memory begins with these two civilizations.

By 1500 B.C., much of the creative impulse of the Mesopotamian and Egyptian civilizations was beginning to wane. The entry of new peoples known as Indo-Europeans who moved into Asia Minor and Anatolia (modern Turkey) led to the creation of a Hittite kingdom that entered into conflict with the Egyptians. The invasion of the Sea Peoples around 1200 B.C., however, destroyed the Hittites, severely weakened the Egyptians, and created a power vacuum that allowed a patchwork of petty kingdoms and city-states to emerge, especially in the area of Syria and Palestine. All of them were eventually overshadowed by the rise of the great empires of the Assyrians, Chaldeans, and Persians. The Assyrian Empire was the first to unite almost all of the ancient Near East. Far larger was the empire of the Great Kings of Persia. Although it owed much to the administrative organization developed by the Assyrians, the Persian Empire had its own peculiar strengths. Persian rule was tolerant as well as efficient. Conquered peoples were allowed to keep their own religions, customs, and methods of doing business. The many years of peace that the Persian Empire brought to the Near East facilitated trade and the general well-being of its peoples. Many Near Eastern peoples expressed gratitude for being subjects of the Great Kings of Persia.

The Israelites were one of these peoples. Never numerous, they created no empire and were dominated by the Assyrians, Chaldeans, and Persians. Nevertheless, they left a spiritual legacy that influenced much of the later development of Western civilization. The evolution of Hebrew monotheism (belief in a single god) created in Judaism one of the world's great religions; it influenced the development of both Christianity and Islam. When we speak of the Judeo-Christian heritage of Western

civilization, we refer not only to the concept of monotheism but also to ideas of law, morality, and social justice that have become important parts of Western culture.

On the western fringes of the Persian Empire, another relatively small group of people, the Greeks, were creating cultural and political ideals that would also have an important impact on Western civilization. The first Greek civilization, known as the Mycenaean, took shape around 1600 B.C. and fell to new Greek-speaking invaders five hundred years later. By the eighth century B.C., the *polis* or city-state had become the chief focus of Greek life. Loyalty to the *polis* created a close-knit community but also divided Greece into a host of independent states. Two of them, Sparta and Athens, became the most important. They were very different, however. Sparta created a closed, highly disciplined society, while Athens moved toward an open, democratic civilization.

The Classical Age in Greece (c. 500–338 B.C.) began with a mighty confrontation between the Greeks and the Persian Empire. After their victory over the Persians, the Greeks began to divide into two large alliances, one headed by Sparta and the other by Athens. Athens created a naval empire and flourished during the age of Pericles, but fear of Athens led to the Great Peloponnesian War between Sparta and Athens and their allies. For all of their brilliant accomplishments, the Greeks were unable to rise above the divisions and rivalries that caused them to fight each other and undermine their own civilization.

The accomplishments of the Greeks formed the fountainhead of Western culture. Socrates, Plato, and Aristotle established the foundations of Western philosophy. Our literary forms are largely derived

from Greek poetry and drama. Greek notions of harmony, proportion, and beauty have remained the touchstones for all subsequent Western art. A rational method of inquiry, so important to modern science, was conceived in ancient Greece. Many of our political terms are Greek in origin, and so are our concepts of the rights and duties of citizenship, especially as they were conceived in Athens, the first great democracy. Especially during their Classical period, the Greeks raised and debated fundamental questions about the purpose of human existence, the structure of human society, and the nature of the universe that have concerned Western thinkers ever since.

While the Greek city-states were pursuing their squabbles, to their north a new and powerful kingdom—Macedonia—emerged. Under King Philip II, the Macedonians defeated a Greek allied army in 338 B.C. and then consolidated their control over the Greek peninsula. Although the independent Greek city-states lost their freedom when they were conquered by the Macedonians, Greek culture did not die. Under the leadership of Alexander the Great, son of Philip II, both Macedonians and Greeks invaded and conquered the Persian Empire. In the conquered lands, Greeks and non-Greeks established a series of kingdoms (known as the Hellenistic kingdoms) and inaugurated the Hellenistic era.

The Hellenistic period was, in its own way, a vibrant one. New cities arose and flourished. New philosophical ideas captured the minds of many. Significant achievements occurred in art, literature, and science. Greek culture spread throughout the Near East and made an impact wherever it was carried. In some areas of the Hellenistic world, queens played an active role in political life, and many upper-class women found new avenues for expressing themselves. Although the Hellenistic era achieved a degree of political stability, by the late third century B.C., signs of decline were beginning to multiply, and the growing power of Rome would eventually endanger the Hellenistic world.

Sometime in the eighth century B.C., a group of Latin-speaking people built a small community called Rome on the Tiber River in Italy.

Between 509 and 264 B.C., this city expanded and united almost all of Italy under its control. Even more dramatically, between 264 and 133 B.C., Rome expanded to the west and east and became master of the Mediterranean Sea.

After 133 B.C., however, Rome's republican institutions proved inadequate for the task of ruling an empire. In the breakdown that ensued, ambitious individuals saw opportunities for power unparalleled in Roman history and succumbed to the temptations. After a series of bloody civil wars, peace was finally achieved when Octavian defeated Antony and Cleopatra. Octavian, who came to be known by the title of Augustus, created a new system of government that seemed to preserve the Republic while establishing the basis for a new system that would rule the empire in an orderly fashion.

After a century of internal upheaval, Augustus established a new order that began the Roman Empire, which experienced peace and prosperity between 14 and 180. During this era, trade flourished and the provinces were governed efficiently. In the course of the third century, however, the Roman Empire came near to collapse due to invasions, civil wars, and economic decline. Although the emperors Diocletian and Constantine brought new life to the so-called Late Empire at the beginning of the fourth century, their efforts shored up the empire only temporarily. In the course of the fifth century, the empire divided into western and eastern parts.

The Roman Empire was the largest empire in antiquity. Using their practical skills, the Romans produced achievements in language, law, engineering, and government that were bequeathed to the future. The Romance languages of today (French, Italian, Spanish, Portuguese, and Romanian) are based on Latin. Western practices of impartial justice and trial by jury owe much to Roman law. As great builders, the Romans left monuments to their skills throughout Europe, some of which, such as aqueducts and roads, are still in use today. Aspects of Roman administrative practices survived in the Western world for centuries. The Romans also preserved the intellectual heritage of the ancient world.

During its last two hundred years, the Roman world underwent a slow transformation with the spread of Christianity. The rise of Christianity marked an important break with the dominant values of the Roman world. Christianity began as a small Jewish sect, but under the guidance of Paul of Tarsus it became a world religion that appealed to both Jews and non-Jews. Despite persecution by Roman authorities, Christianity grew and became widely accepted by the fourth century. At the end of that century, it was made the official state religion of the Roman Empire.

The period of late antiquity that saw the disintegration of the western part of the Roman Empire also witnessed the emergence of a new European civilization in the Early Middle Ages. This early medieval civilization was formed by the coalescence of three major elements: the Germanic peoples who moved into the western part of the empire and established new kingdoms, the continuing attraction of the Greco-Roman cultural legacy, and the Christian church. Politically, a new

series of Germanic kingdoms emerged in western Europe. Each fused Roman and Germanic elements to create a new society. The Christian church (or Roman Catholic Church, as it came to be called in the west) played a crucial role in the growth of the new European civilization. The church developed an organized government under the leadership of the pope. It also assimilated the classical tradition and through its clergy brought Christianized civilization to the Germanic tribes. Especially important were the monks and nuns who led the way in converting the Germanic peoples in Europe to Christianity.

At the end of the eighth century, a new kingdom—the Carolingian Empire—came to control much of western and central Europe, especially during the reign of Charlemagne. In the long run, the creation of a western empire fostered the idea of a distinct European identity and marked a shift of power from the south to the north. Italy and the Mediterranean had been the center of the Roman Empire. The lands north of the Alps now became the political center of Europe, and increasingly, Europe emerged as the focus and center of Western civilization.

Building on a fusion of Germanic, classical, and Christian elements, the Carolingian Empire was well gov-

erned but was held together primarily by personal loyalty to the strong king. The economy of the eighth and ninth centuries was based almost entirely on farming, which proved inadequate to maintain a large monarchical system. As a result, a new political and military order—known as fief-holding—subsequently evolved to become an integral part of the political world of the Middle Ages. Fief-holding was characterized by a decentralization of political power, in which lords exercised legal, administrative, and military power. This transferred public power into many private hands and seemed to provide security that the weak central government could not provide.

The new European civilization that had emerged in the ninth and tenth centuries began to come into its own in the eleventh and twelfth centuries, and Europeans established new patterns that reached their high point in the thirteenth century. The High Middle Ages (1000–1300) was a period of recovery and growth for Western civilization, characterized by a greater sense of security and a burst of energy and enthusiasm. Climatic improvements that produced better growing conditions, an expansion of cultivated land, and technological changes combined to enable Europe's food supply to increase significantly after 1000. This increase in agricultural production helped sustain a dramatic rise in population that was physically apparent in the expansion of towns and cities.

The development of trade and the rise of cities added a dynamic new element to the civilization of the High Middle Ages. Trading activities flourished first in northern Italy and Flanders and then spread outward from these centers. In the late tenth and eleventh centuries, this renewal of commercial life led to a revival of cities. Old Roman sites came back to life, and new towns arose at major crossroads or natural harbors favorable to trading activities. By the twelfth and thirteenth centuries, both the urban centers and the urban population of Europe were experiencing a dramatic expansion. The revival of trade, the expansion of towns and cities, and the development of a money economy did not mean the end of a predominantly rural European society, but they did open the door to new ways to make a living and new opportunities for people to ex-

pand and enrich their lives. Eventually, they created the foundations for the development of a predominantly urban industrial society.

During the High Middle Ages, European society was dominated by a landed aristocracy whose primary function was to fight. These nobles built innumerable castles that gave a distinctive look to the countryside. Although lords and vassals seemed forever mired in endless petty conflicts, over time medieval kings began to exert a centralizing authority and inaugurated the process of developing new kinds of monarchical states. By the thirteenth century, European monarchs were solidifying their governmental institutions in pursuit of greater power. The nobles, who rationalized their warlike atti-

tudes by calling themselves the defenders of Christian society, continued to dominate the medieval world politically, economically, and socially. But quietly and surely, within this world of castles and private power, kings gradually began to extend their public powers and developed the machinery of government that would enable them to become the centers of political authority in Europe. The actions of these medieval monarchs laid the foundation for the European kingdoms that in one form or another have dominated the European political scene ever since.

During the High Middle Ages, the power of both nobles and kings was often overshadowed by the authority of the Catholic Church, perhaps the dominant institution of the High Middle Ages. In the Early Middle Ages, the Catholic Church had shared in the challenge of new growth by reforming itself and striking out on a path toward greater papal power, both within the church and over European society. The High Middle Ages witnessed a spiritual renewal that led to numerous and even divergent paths: revived papal leadership, the development of centralized administrative machinery that buttressed papal authority, and new dimensions to the religious life of the clergy and laity. A wave of religious enthusiasm in the twelfth and thirteenth centuries led to the formation of new religious orders that worked to provide for the needs of the people, especially their concern for achieving salvation.

The economic, political, and religious growth of the High Middle Ages also gave European society a new confidence that enabled it to look beyond its borders to the lands and empires of the east. Only a confident Europe could have undertaken the Crusades, a concerted military effort to recover the Holy Land of the Near East from the Muslims.

Western assurance and energy, so crucial to the Crusades, were also evident in a burst of intellectual and artistic activity. New educational institutions known as universities came into being in the twelfth century. New

literature, written in the vernacular language, appealed to the growing number of people in cities or at courts who could read. The study of theology, "queen of the sciences," reached a high point in the work of Thomas Aquinas. At the same time, a religious building spree—especially evident in the great Romanesque and Gothic cathedrals of the age—left the landscape bedecked with churches that were the visible symbols of Christian Europe's vitality.

Growth and optimism seemed to characterize the High Middle Ages, but underneath the calm exterior lay seeds of discontent and change. Dissent from church teaching and practices grew in the thirteenth century, leading to a climate of fear and intolerance as the church responded with inquisitorial instruments to enforce conformity to its teachings. The breakdown of the old agricultural system and the creation of new relationships between lords and peasants led to local peasant uprisings in the late thirteenth century. The Crusades ended ignominiously with the fall of the last crusading foothold in the east in 1291. By that time, more and more signs of ominous troubles were appearing. The fourteenth century would prove to be a time of crisis for European civilization.

In the High Middle Ages, European civilization had developed many of its fundamental features. Monarchical states, capitalist trade and industry, banks, cities, and vernacular literature were all products of that fertile period. During the same time, the Catholic Church, under the direction of the papacy, reached its apogee. Fourteenth-century European society, however, was challenged by an overwhelming number of crises that led to the disintegration of medieval civilization. At midcentury, one of the most destructive natural disasters in history erupted—the Black Death, a devastating plague that wiped out at least one-third of the European population. Economic crises and social upheavals, including a decline in trade and industry, bank failures, and peasant revolts pitting lower classes against the upper classes, followed in the wake of the Black Death. The Hundred Years' War, a long, drawn-out conflict between the English and French, undermined political stability. The Catholic Church, too, experienced a crisis with the absence of the popes from Rome and even the spectacle of two popes condemning each other as the anti-Christ.

The new European society proved remarkably resilient, however. Periods of disintegration are often fertile grounds for change and new developments. Out of the dissolution of medieval civilization came a rebirth of culture that historians have labeled the Renaissance. It was a period of transition that witnessed a continuation of the economic, political, and social trends that had begun in the High Middle Ages. It was also a movement in which artists and intellectuals proclaimed a new vision of humankind and raised fundamental questions about the value and importance of the individual. The humanists or intellectuals of the age called their period (from the mid-fourteenth to the

mid-sixteenth century) an age of rebirth, believing that they had restored arts and letters to new glory after they had been "neglected" or "dead" for centuries. Of course, intellectuals and artists existed only among the upper classes, and the brilliant intellectual, cultural, and artistic accomplishments of the Renaissance were therefore products of and for the elite. The ideas of the Renaissance did not have a broad base among the masses.

The Renaissance did, however, raise new questions about medieval traditions. In advocating a return to the early sources of Christianity and criticizing current religious practices, the humanists raised fundamental issues about the Catholic Church, which was still an important institution. In the sixteenth century, the intellectual revolution of the fifteenth century gave way to a religious renaissance that touched the lives of people, including the masses, in new and profound ways.

When the monk Martin Luther entered the public scene with an attack on the sale of indulgences, few people suspected that he would eventually produce a division of Europe along religious lines. But the yearning for reform of the church and meaningful religious experience caused a seemingly simple dispute to escalate into a powerful movement.

Although Luther felt that this revival of Christianity, based on his interpretation of the Bible, should be acceptable to all, others soon appeared who also read the Bible but interpreted it in different ways. Protestantism split into different sects, which, though united in their dislike of Catholicism, were themselves divided over certain religious beliefs and practices. As reform ideas spread, religion and politics became ever more intertwined.

By 1555, Lutheranism had lost much of its momentum; its energy was largely replaced by the new Protestant form of Calvinism, which had a clarity of doctrine and a fervor that made it attractive to a whole new generation of Europeans. Although Calvinism's militancy enabled it to expand across Europe, Catholicism was also experiencing its own revival and emerged as a militant faith, prepared to do combat for the souls of the faithful. An age of religious passion was followed by an age of religious warfare. That people who were disciples of the Apostle of Peace would kill each other—often in brutal and painful fashion—aroused skepticism about Christianity itself.

Even before the religious upheavals of the sixteenth century, Europeans had burst onto the world scene. Beginning with the seemingly modest ventures of the Portuguese ships that sailed southward along the West African coast in the mid-fifteenth century, the process accelerated with the epoch-making voyages of Columbus to the Americas and Vasco da Gama to the Indian Ocean in the 1490s. Soon a number of other European states had joined in, and by the end of the eighteenth century, they had created a global trade network dominated by Western ships and Western power.

In less than three hundred years, the European "Age of Exploration" changed the shape of the world. In some areas, such as the Americas and the Spice Islands, it led to the

destruction of indigenous civilizations and the establishment of European colonies. In others, as in Africa, India, and mainland Southeast Asia, it left native regimes intact but had a strong impact on local societies and regional trade patterns. Europeans had begun to change the face of the world and would continue on the new path they had started.

In Europe itself, the seventeenth century assumed extraordinary proportions. The concept of a united Christendom, held as an ideal since the Middle Ages, had been irrevocably destroyed by the religious wars, making possible the emergence of a system of nation-states in which power politics assumed increasing significance. The growth of political thought focusing on the secular origins of state power reflected the changes that were going on in seventeenth-century society. Within those states, there

slowly emerged some of the machinery that made possible a growing centralization of power. In those states called absolutist, strong monarchs, with the assistance of their aristocracies, took the lead in creating greater centralization. The best example of absolute monarchy was the France of Louis XIV. But in England, where the landed aristocracy gained power at the expense of the monarchs, the foundations were laid for a constitutional government in which Parliament provided the focus for the institutions of centralized power. In all the major European states, a growing concern for power and dynastic expansion led to larger armies and greater conflict. War remained a basic feature of Western civilization.

At the same time, religious preoccupations and values were losing ground to secular considerations. The seventeenth century was a period of transition to a more secular spirit that has characterized modern Western civilization ever since. No stronger foundation for this spirit could be found than in the new view of the universe that was ushered in by the Scientific Revolution of the seventeenth century.

The Scientific Revolution represents a major turning point in modern Western civilization. In the Scientific Revolution, the Western world overthrew the medieval, Ptolemaic-Aristotelian worldview (in which the earth was at the center of the universe) and arrived at a new conception of the universe: the sun at the center, the planets as material bodies revolving around the sun in elliptical orbits, and an infinite rather than finite world. With the changes in the conception of "heaven" came changes in the conception of "earth." The work of Bacon and Descartes left Europeans with the separation of mind and matter and the belief that by using only reason they could in fact understand and dominate all of nature.

The Scientific Revolution forced Europeans to change their conception of themselves. At first, some were appalled and even frightened by its implications. For centuries, humans on earth had been at the center of the universe. Now the earth was only a tiny planet revolving around a sun that was itself only a speck in a boundless universe. Most people remained optimistic despite the apparent blow to human dignity. After all, had Newton not demonstrated

that the universe was a great machine governed by natural laws? Were there not natural laws governing every aspect of human endeavor that could be found by the new scientific method? Thus, the Scientific Revolution led logically to the Age of Enlightenment of the eighteenth century.

In the eighteenth century, a group of intellectuals known as the philosophes popularized the ideas of the Scientific Revolution and used them to undertake a dramatic reexamination of all aspects of life. Highly influenced by the new worldview created by the Scientific Revolution, the philosophes hoped to create a new society by using reason to discover the natural laws that governed it. They believed that education could produce better human beings and a better human society. By attacking traditional religion as the enemy and creating the new "sciences of man" in economics, politics, justice, and education, the philosophes laid the foundation for a modern worldview based on rationalism and secularism. The ideas of the philosophes had such a widespread impact that historians ever since have called the eighteenth century the Age of Enlightenment.

But the eighteenth century was also an age of tradition. Everywhere in Europe at the beginning of the eighteenth century, the old order remained strong.  Nobles, clerics, towns, and provinces all had privileges, some medieval in origin, others the result of the attempt of monarchies in the sixteenth and seventeenth centuries to gain financial support from their subjects. Everywhere in the eighteenth century, monarchs sought to enlarge their bureaucracies to raise taxes to support the new large standing armies that they needed to compete militarily with the other European states. The existence of these armies made wars more likely. Within the European state system, the nations that would dominate Europe until World War I—Britain, France, Austria, Prussia, and Russia—emerged as the five great powers of Europe. The existence of five great powers, with two of them (France and Britain) in conflict in the East and the New World, initiated a new scale of conflict; the Seven Years' War could legitimately be viewed as the first world war. The wars altered some boundaries on the European continent but were perhaps most significant for the British victories that marked the emergence of Great Britain as the world's greatest naval and colonial power. Everywhere in Europe, increased demands for taxes to support these conflicts led to attacks on the privileged orders and a desire for change not met by the ruling monarchs.

At the same time, sustained population growth, dramatic changes in finance, trade, and industry, and the growth of poverty created tensions that underminded the traditional foundations of European society. The inability of the old order to deal meaningfully with these changes led to a revolutionary outburst at the end of the eighteenth century that marked the beginning of the end for that old order.

CHAPTER 19
A REVOLUTION IN POLITICS: THE ERA OF THE FRENCH REVOLUTION AND NAPOLEON

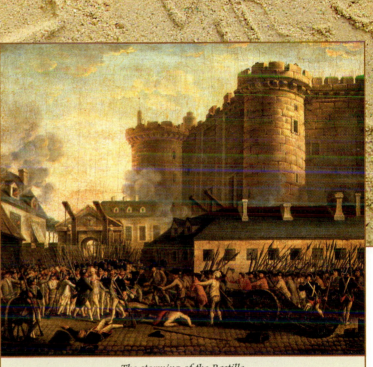

The storming of the Bastille

CHAPTER OUTLINE AND FOCUS QUESTIONS

The Beginning of the Revolutionary Era: The American Revolution

Q What were the causes and results of the American Revolution, and what impact did it have on Europe?

Background to the French Revolution

Q What were the long-range and immediate causes of the French Revolution?

The French Revolution

Q What were the main events of the French Revolution between 1789 and 1799? What role did each of the following play in the French Revolution: lawyers, peasants, women, the clergy, the Jacobins, the sans-culottes, the French revolutionary army, and the Committee of Public Safety?

The Age of Napoleon

Q Which aspects of the French Revolution did Napoleon preserve, and which did he destroy?

CRITICAL THINKING

Q In what ways were the French Revolution, the American Revolution, and the seventeenth-century English revolutions alike? In what ways were they different?

ON THE MORNING OF JULY 14, 1789, a Parisian mob of eight thousand people in search of weapons streamed toward the Bastille, a royal armory filled with arms and ammunition. The Bastille was also a state prison, and although it now contained only seven prisoners, in the eyes of these angry Parisians, it was a glaring symbol of the government's despotic policies. The armory was defended by the marquis de Launay and a small garrison of 114 men. The attack began in earnest in the early afternoon, and after three hours of fighting, de Launay and the garrison surrendered. Angered by the loss of ninety-eight of their members, the victorious mob beat de Launay to death, cut off his head, and carried it aloft in triumph through the streets of Paris. When King Louis XVI was told the news of the fall of the Bastille by the duc de La Roche-foucauld-Liancourt, he exclaimed, "Why, this is a revolt." "No, Sire," replied the duc, "it is a revolution."

Historians have long assumed that the modern history of Europe began with two major transformations—the French Revolution (discussed in this chapter) and the Industrial Revolution (see Chapter 20). Accordingly, the French Revolution has been portrayed as the major turning point in European political and social history, when the institutions of the "old regime" were destroyed and a new order was created based on individual rights, representative institutions, and a concept of loyalty to the nation rather than the monarch. This perspective does have certain limitations, however.

France was only one of a number of areas in the Western world where the assumptions of the old order were challenged. Although some historians have called the upheavals of the eighteenth and early nineteenth centuries a "democratic revolution," it is probably more appropriate to speak of a liberal movement to extend political rights and power to the bourgeoisie in possession of capital—citizens besides the aristocracy who were literate and had become wealthy through capitalist enterprises in trade, industry, and finance. The years preceding and accompanying the French Revolution included attempts at reform and revolt in the North American colonies, Britain, the Dutch Republic, some Swiss cities, and the Austrian Netherlands. The success of the American and French Revolutions makes them the center of attention for this chapter.

Not all of the decadent privileges that characterized the old European regime were destroyed in 1789, however. The revolutionary upheaval of the era, especially in France, did create new liberal and national political ideals, summarized in the French revolutionary slogan, "Liberty, Equality, Fraternity," that transformed France and were then spread to other European countries through the conquests of Napoleon. After Napoleon's defeat, however, the forces of reaction did their best to restore the old order and resist pressures for reform. ◆

The Beginning of the Revolutionary Era: The American Revolution

Q **Focus Question:** What were the causes and results of the American Revolution, and what impact did it have on Europe?

At the end of the Seven Years' War in 1763, Great Britain had become the world's greatest colonial power. In North America, Britain controlled Canada and the lands east of the Mississippi (see Map 19.1). After the Seven Years' War, British policy makers sought to obtain new revenues from the thirteen American colonies to pay for British army expenses in defending the colonists. An attempt to levy new taxes by a stamp act in 1765 led to riots and the law's quick repeal.

The Americans and the British had different conceptions of empire. The British envisioned a single empire with Parliament as the supreme authority throughout. Only Parliament could make laws for all the people in the empire, including the American colonists. The Americans, in contrast, had their own representative assemblies. They believed that neither the king nor Parliament had any right to interfere in their internal affairs and that no tax could be levied without the consent of an assembly whose members actually represented the people.

Crisis followed crisis in the 1770s until 1776, when the colonists decided to declare their independence from the British Empire. On July 4, 1776, the Second Continental Congress approved a declaration of independence written by Thomas Jefferson (see the box on p. 574). A stirring political document, the declaration affirmed the Enlightenment's natural rights of "life, liberty, and the pursuit of happiness" and declared the colonies to be "free and independent states absolved from all allegiance to the British crown." The war for American independence had formally begun.

The War for Independence

The war against Great Britain was a great gamble. Britain was a strong European military power with enormous financial resources. The Second Continental Congress had authorized the formation of a Continental Army under George Washington as commander in chief. Washington, who had had political experience in Virginia and military experience in the French and Indian War, was a good choice for the job. As a southerner, he brought balance to an effort that to that point had been led by New Englanders. Nevertheless, compared to the British forces, the Continental Army consisted of undisciplined amateurs whose terms of service were usually very brief.

Complicating the war effort were the internal divisions within the colonies. Fought for independence, the Revolutionary War was also a civil war, pitting family members and neighbors against one another. The Loyalists, between 15 and 30 percent of the population, questioned whether British policies justified the rebellion. The Loyalists were strongest in New York and Pennsylvania and tended to be wealthy, older, and politically moderate.

Since probably half the colonial population was apathetic at the beginning of the struggle, the patriots, like the Loyalists, constituted a minority of the population. The patriots, however, managed to win over many of the uncommitted, either by persuasion or by force. There were patriots among the rich as well as Loyalists; George Washington owned an estate with 15,000 acres and 150 slaves. But the rich patriots joined an extensive coalition that included farmers and artisans. The wide social spectrum in this coalition had an impact on representative governments in the states after the war. The right to vote was often broadened; Pennsylvania, for example, dropped all property qualifications for voting.

Of great importance to the colonies' cause was the assistance provided by foreign countries that were eager to gain revenge for earlier defeats at the hands of the British. The French supplied arms and money to the rebels from the beginning of the war, and French officers and soldiers also served in Washington's Continental

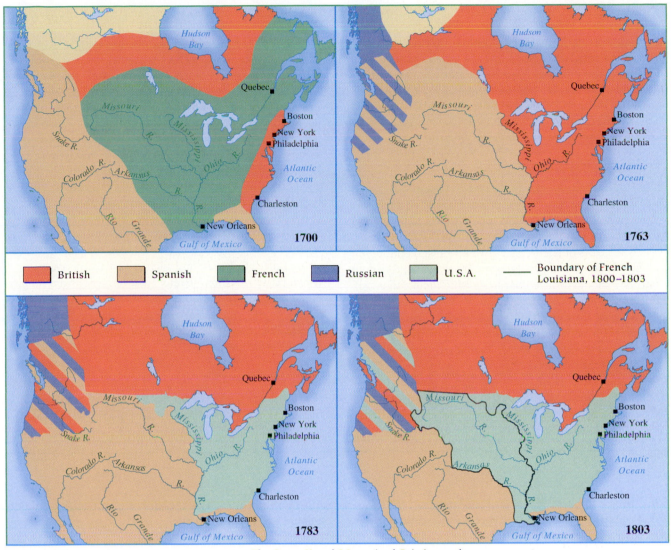

MAP 19.1 **North America, 1700–1803.** The Seven Years' War gained Britain much territory in eastern North America, but asking the American colonies to help pay for the war sparked the American Revolution. The 1803 Louisiana Purchase nearly doubled the size of the United States and spurred westward expansion to the Pacific Ocean.

Q In what periods was the Mississippi River a national boundary, and why was control of the river important for the United States? 🌀 **View an animated version of this map or related maps at** **academic.cengage.com/history/spielvogel**

Army. When the British army of General Cornwallis was forced to surrender to a combined American and French army and French fleet under Washington at Yorktown in 1781, the British government decided to call it quits. The Treaty of Paris, signed in 1783, recognized the independence of the American colonies and granted the Americans control of the western territory from the Appalachians to the Mississippi River.

Forming a New Nation

The thirteen American colonies had gained their independence as the United States of America, but a fear of concentrated power and concern for their own interests caused them to have little enthusiasm for establishing a united nation with a strong central government. The Articles of Confederation, ratified in 1781, did little to provide for a strong central government. A movement for a different form of national government soon arose. In the summer of 1787, fifty-five delegates attended a convention in Philadelphia to revise the Articles of Confederation. The convention's delegates—wealthy, politically experienced, well educated—rejected revision and decided to devise a new constitution.

The proposed constitution created a central government distinct from and superior to the governments of the individual states. The national government was given the power to levy taxes, raise a national army, regulate domestic and foreign trade, and create a national currency. The central or federal government was divided

THE ARGUMENT FOR INDEPENDENCE

On July 2, 1776, the Second Continental Congress adopted a resolution declaring the independence of the American colonies. Two days later, the delegates approved the Declaration of Independence, which gave the reasons for their action. Its principal author was Thomas Jefferson, who basically restated John Locke's theory of revolution (see Chapter 15).

The Declaration of Independence

When in the course of human events it becomes necessary for one people to dissolve the political bands which have connected them with another, and to assume among the Powers of the earth, the separate and equal station to which the Laws of Nature and of Nature's God entitle them, a decent respect to the opinions of mankind requires that they should declare the causes which impel them to the separation.

We hold these truths to be self-evident, that all men are created equal, that they are endowed by their Creator with certain unalienable Rights, that among these are Life, Liberty and the pursuit of Happiness. That to secure these rights, Governments are instituted among Men, deriving their just powers from the consent of the governed, That whenever any Form of Government becomes destructive of these ends, it is the Right of the People to alter or to abolish it and to institute new Government, laying its foundation on such principles and organizing its powers in such form, as to them shall seem most likely to effect their Safety and Happiness. Prudence, indeed, will dictate that Governments long established should not be changed for light and transient causes; and accordingly all experience has shown, that mankind are more disposed to suffer, while evils are sufferable, than to right themselves by abolishing the forms to which they are accustomed. But when a long train of abuses and usurpations, pursuing invariably the same Object evinces a design to reduce them under absolute Despotism, it is their right, it is their duty, to throw off such Government, and to provide new Guards for their future security.—Such has been the patient sufferance of these Colonies; and such is now the necessity which constrains them to alter their former Systems of government. The history of the present King of Great Britain is a history of repeated injuries and usurpations, all having in direct object the establishment of an absolute Tyranny over these States.

Q *What influence did John Locke's theory of revolution have on the American Declaration of Independence? How would a member of the British Parliament have responded to this declaration?*

into three branches, each with some power to check the functioning of the others. A president would serve as the chief executive with the power to execute laws, veto the legislature's acts, supervise foreign affairs, and direct military forces. Legislative power was vested in the second branch of government, a bicameral legislature composed of the Senate, elected by the state legislatures, and the House of Representatives, elected directly by the people. The Supreme Court and other courts "as deemed necessary" by Congress served as the third branch of government. They would enforce the Constitution as the "supreme law of the land."

The United States Constitution was approved by the states—by a slim margin—in 1788. Important to its success was a promise to add a bill of rights to it as the new government's first piece of business. Accordingly, in March 1789, the new Congress proposed twelve amendments to the Constitution; the ten that were ratified by the states have been known ever since as the Bill of Rights. These guaranteed freedom of religion, speech, press, petition, and assembly, as well as the right to bear arms, protection against unreasonable searches and arrests, trial by jury, due process of law, and protection of property rights. Many of these rights were derived from the natural rights philosophy of the eighteenth-century philosophes, which was popular among the American colonists. Is it any wonder that many European intellectuals saw the American Revolution as the embodiment of the Enlightenment's political dreams?

Impact of the American Revolution on Europe

The year 1789 witnessed two far-reaching events, the beginning of a new United States of America and the eruption of the French Revolution. Was there a connection between the two great revolutions of the late eighteenth century?

There is no doubt that the American Revolution had an important impact on Europeans. Books, newspapers, and magazines provided the newly developing reading public with numerous accounts of American events. To many in Europe, it seemed to portend an era of significant changes, including new arrangements in international politics. The Venetian ambassador to Paris astutely observed in 1783 that "if only the union of the [American] provinces is preserved, it is reasonable to expect that, with the favorable effects of time, and of European arts and sciences, it will become the most formidable power in the world."[1] But the American Revolution also meant far more than that. It proved to many Europeans that the liberal political ideas of the Enlightenment were not the vapid utterances of intellectuals. The rights of man, ideas of liberty and equality, popular sovereignty, the separation of powers, and freedom of religion, thought, and press were not utopian ideals. The Americans had created a new social contract, embodied it in a written constitution, and made concepts of liberty and representative government a reality. The premises of the Enlightenment seemed confirmed; a new age and a better world could be achieved. As a Swiss philosophe expressed it, "I am tempted to believe that North America is the country where reason and humanity will develop more rapidly than anywhere else."[2]

Europeans obtained much of their information about America from returning soldiers, especially the hundreds of French officers who had served in the American war. One of them, the aristocratic marquis de Lafayette, had volunteered for service in America in order to "strike a blow against England," France's old enemy. Closely associated with George Washington, Lafayette returned to France with ideas of individual liberties and notions of republicanism and popular sovereignty. He became a member of the Society of Thirty, a club composed of people from the Paris salons. These "lovers of liberty" were influential in the early stages of the French Revolution. The Declaration of the Rights of Man and the Citizen (see "Destruction of the Old Regime" later in this chapter) showed unmistakable signs of the influence of the American Declaration of Independence as well as the American state constitutions. Yet for all of its obvious impact, the American Revolution proved in the long run to be far less important to Europe than the French Revolution. The French Revolution was more complex, more violent, and far more radical in its attempt to construct both a new political order and a new social order. The French Revolution provided a model of revolution for Europe and much of the rest of the world; to many analysts, it remains the political movement that truly inaugurated the modern political world.

Background to the French Revolution

Q **Focus Question:** What were the long-range and immediate causes of the French Revolution?

Although we associate events like the French Revolution with sudden changes, the causes of such events involve long-range problems as well as immediate precipitating forces. **Revolutions,** as has been repeatedly shown, are not necessarily the result of economic collapse and masses of impoverished people hungering for change. In fact, in the fifty years before 1789, France had experienced a period of economic growth due to an expansion of foreign trade and an increase in industrial production, although many people, especially peasants, failed to share in the prosperity. Thus, the causes of the French Revolution must be found in a multifaceted examination of French society and its problems in the late eighteenth century.

Social Structure of the Old Regime

The long-range or indirect causes of the French Revolution must first be sought in the condition of French society. Before the Revolution, French society was grounded in the inequality of rights or the idea of privilege. The population of 27 million was divided, as it had been since the Middle Ages, into legal categories known as the three orders or estates.

The First Estate The First Estate consisted of the clergy and numbered about 130,000 people. The church owned approximately 10 percent of the land. Clergy were exempt from the *taille*, France's chief tax, although the church had agreed to pay a "voluntary" contribution every five years to the state. Clergy were also radically divided, since the higher clergy, stemming from aristocratic families, shared the interests of the nobility while the parish priests were often poor commoners.

The Second Estate The Second Estate was the nobility, composed of no more than 350,000 people who nevertheless owned about 25 to 30 percent of the land. Under Louis XV and Louis XVI, the nobility had continued to play an important and even crucial role in French society, holding many of the leading positions in the government, the military, the law courts, and the higher church offices. Much heavy industry in France was controlled by nobles, either through investment or by ownership of mining and metallurgical enterprises. The French nobility was also divided. The nobility of the robe derived their status from officeholding, a pathway that had often enabled commoners to attain noble rank. These nobles now dominated the royal law courts and important administrative offices. The nobility of the sword claimed to be descendants of the original medieval nobility. As a group, the nobles sought to expand their privileges at the expense of the monarchy—to defend liberty by resisting the arbitrary actions of monarchy, as some nobles asserted—and to maintain their monopolistic control over positions in the military, church, and government. In 1781, in reaction to the ambitions of aristocrats newly arrived from the bourgeoisie, the Ségur Law attempted to limit the sale of military officerships to fourth-generation nobles, thus excluding newly enrolled members of the nobility.

Although there were many poor nobles, on the whole the fortunes of the wealthy aristocrats outstripped those of most others in French society. Generally, the nobles tended to marry within their own ranks, making the nobility a fairly closed group. Although their privileges varied from region to region, the very possession of privileges remained a hallmark of the nobility. Common to all were tax exemptions, especially from the *taille*.

The Third Estate The Third Estate, the commoners of society, constituted the overwhelming majority of the French population. They were divided by vast differences in occupation, level of education, and wealth. The

The Three Estates. This French political cartoon from 1789 reveals a critical view of France's privileged orders. Shown in the cartoon is a naked common man held in chains and being ridden by an aristocrat, a clergyman, and a judge. The message is clear: most ordinary French people (the Third Estate) are suffering horribly as a result of the privileges of the First and Second Estates.

peasants, who alone constituted 75 to 80 percent of the total population, were by far the largest segment of the Third Estate. They owned about 35 to 40 percent of the land, although their landholdings varied from area to area and over half had no or little land on which to survive. Serfdom no longer existed on any large scale in France, but French peasants still had obligations to their local landlords that they deeply resented. These relics of feudalism included the payment of fees for the use of village facilities, such as the flour mill, community oven, and winepress, as well as tithes to the clergy. The nobility also maintained the right to hunt on peasants' land.

Another part of the Third Estate consisted of skilled artisans, shopkeepers, and other wage earners in the cities. Although the eighteenth century had been a period of rapid urban growth, 90 percent of French towns had fewer than 10,000 inhabitants; only nine cities had more than 50,000. In the eighteenth century, consumer prices rose faster than wages, with the result that these urban groups experienced a decline in purchasing power. In Paris, for example, income lagged behind food prices and especially behind a 140 percent rise in rents for working people in skilled and unskilled trades. The economic discontent of

this segment of the Third Estate—and often simply their struggle for survival—led them to play an important role in the Revolution, especially in the city of Paris. Insubordination, one observer noted, "has been visible among the people for some years now and above all among craftsmen." One historian has charted the ups and downs of revolutionary riots in Paris by showing their correlation with changes in bread prices. Ordinary people spent one-third to one-half of their income on bread, which constituted three-fourths of their diet, so sudden increases in the price of bread immediately affected public order. People expected bread prices to be controlled. They grew desperate when prices rose, and their only recourse was mob action to try to change the situation. The towns and cities were also home to large groups of unskilled workers. One magistrate complained that "misery . . . has thrown into the towns people who overburden them with their uselessness, and who find nothing to do, because there is not enough for the people who live there."[3]

About 8 percent, or 2.3 million people, constituted the bourgeoisie or middle class, who owned about 20 to 25 percent of the land. This group included the merchants, industrialists, and bankers who controlled the resources of trade, manufacturing, and finance and benefited from the economic prosperity after 1730. The bourgeoisie also included professional people—lawyers, holders of public offices, doctors, and writers. Many members of the bourgeoisie sought security and status through the purchase of land. They had their own set of grievances because they were often excluded from the social and political privileges monopolized by the nobles. These resentments of the middle class were for a long time assumed to be a major cause of the French Revolution. But although these tensions existed, the situation was not a simple case of a unified bourgeoisie against a unified noble class. As is evident, neither group was monolithic. Nobles were separated by vast differences in wealth and importance. A similar gulf separated wealthy financiers from local lawyers in French provincial towns.

Remarkable similarities existed at the upper levels of society between the wealthier bourgeoisie and the nobility. It was still possible for wealthy middle-class individuals to enter the ranks of the nobility by obtaining public offices and entering the nobility of the robe. In fact, between 1774 and 1789, the not insignificant number of 2,500 wealthy bourgeoisie entered the ranks of the nobility. Over the century as a whole, 6,500 new noble families were created. In addition, as we saw in Chapter 18, the aristocrats were also engaging in capitalist activities on their landed estates, such as mining, metallurgy, and glassmaking, and were even investing in foreign trade. Viewed in terms of economic function, many members of the bourgeoisie and nobility formed a single class. Finally, the new and critical ideas of the Enlightenment proved attractive to both aristocrats and bourgeoisie. Members of both groups shared a common world of liberal political thought. The old view that the French Revolution was the result of the conflict between two rigid orders, the bourgeoisie and the nobility, has been enlarged and revised. Both aristocratic and bourgeois elites, long accustomed to a new socioeconomic reality based on wealth and economic achievement, were increasingly frustrated by a monarchical system resting on privileges and on an old and rigid social order based on the concept of estates. The opposition of these elites to the **old order** ultimately led them to take drastic action against the monarchical regime, although they soon split over the question of how far to proceed in eliminating traditional privileges. In a real sense, the Revolution had its origins in political grievances.

Other Problems Facing the French Monarchy

Although the long-range causes of the French Revolution can thus be found in part in the growing frustration at the monarchy's inability to deal with new social realities and problems, other factors were also present. The failure of the French monarchy was exacerbated by specific problems in the 1780s. Although the country had enjoyed fifty years of growth overall, periodic economic crises still occurred. Bad harvests in 1787 and 1788 and the beginnings of a manufacturing depression resulted in food shortages, rising prices for food and other necessities, and unemployment in the cities. The number of poor, estimated by some at almost one-third of the population, reached crisis proportions on the eve of the Revolution. An English traveler noted the misery of the poor in the countryside: "All the country girls and women are without shoes or stockings; and the plowmen at their work have neither sabots nor stockings to their feet. This is a poverty that strikes at the root of national prosperity."[4]

Ideas of the Philosophes   Increased criticism of existing privileges as well as social and political institutions also characterized the eighteenth century. Although the philosophes did not advocate revolution, their ideas were widely circulated among the literate bourgeois and noble elites of France. The actual influence of the ideas of the philosophes is difficult to prove, but once the Revolution began, the revolutionary leaders frequently quoted Enlightenment writers, especially Rousseau.

Failure to Make Reforms   The French Parlements often frustrated efforts at reform. These thirteen law courts, which were responsible for registering royal decrees, could block royal edicts by not registering them. Although Louis XIV had forced them into submission, the Parlements had gained new strength in the eighteenth century as they and their noble judges assumed the role of defenders of "liberty" against the arbitrary power of the monarchy. As noble defenders, however, they often pushed their own interests as well, especially by blocking new taxes. This last point reminds us that one of the fundamental problems facing the monarchy was financial.

Financial Crisis   The immediate cause of the French Revolution was the near collapse of government finances. At a time when France was experiencing economic crises, the government was drastically short of money. Yet French governmental expenditures continued to grow due to costly wars and royal extravagance. The government responded by borrowing; in the budget of 1788, the interest on the debt alone constituted half of government spending. Total debt had reached 4 billion livres (roughly $800 million). Financial lenders, fearful they would never be repaid, were refusing to lend additional amounts.

The king's finance ministry wrestled with the problem but met with resistance. In 1786, Charles de Calonne, the controller general of finance, finding himself unable to borrow any more, proposed a complete revamping of the fiscal and administrative system of the state. To gain support, Calonne convened an "assembly of notables" early in 1787. This gathering of nobles, prelates, and magistrates refused to cooperate, and the government's attempt to go it alone brought further disaster. On the verge of a complete financial collapse, the government was finally forced to call a meeting of the Estates-General, the French parliamentary body that had not met since 1614. By calling the Estates-General, the government was virtually admitting that the consent of the nation was required to raise taxes.

The French Revolution

Q **Focus Questions:** What were the main events of the French Revolution between 1789 and 1799? What role did each of the following play in the French Revolution: lawyers, peasants, women, the clergy, the Jacobins, the sans-culottes, the French revolutionary army, and the Committee of Public Safety?

In summoning the Estates-General, the government was merely looking for a way to solve the immediate financial crisis. The monarchy had no wish for a major reform of the government, nor did the delegates who arrived at Versailles come with plans for the revolutionary changes that ultimately emerged. Yet over the next years, through the interplay of the deputies meeting in various legislative assemblies, the common people in the streets of Paris and other cities, and the peasants in the countryside, much of the old regime would be destroyed, and Europe would have a new model for political and social change.

From Estates-General to a National Assembly

The Estates-General consisted of representatives from the three orders of French society. In the elections for the Estates-General, the government had ruled that the Third Estate should get double representation (it did, after all, constitute 97 percent of the population). Consequently, while both the First Estate (the clergy) and the Second (the nobility) had about 300 delegates each, the commoners had almost 600 representatives. Two-thirds of the latter were people with legal training, and three-fourths were from towns with over two thousand inhabitants, giving the Third Estate a particularly strong legal and urban representation. Of the 282 representatives of the nobility, about 90 were liberal minded, urban oriented, and interested in the enlightened ideas of the century; half of them were under forty years of age. The activists of the Third Estate and the reform-minded individuals among the First and Second Estates had common ties in their youth, urban background, and hostility to privilege. The *cahiers de doléances,* or statements of local grievances, which were drafted throughout France during the elections to the Estates-General, advocated a regular constitutional government that would abolish the fiscal privileges of the church and nobility as the major way to regenerate the country.

The Estates-General opened at Versailles on May 5, 1789. It was divided from the start over the question of whether voting should be by order or by head (each delegate having one vote). The Parlement of Paris, consisting of nobles of the robe, had advocated voting by order according to the form used in 1614. Each order would vote separately; each would have veto power over the other two, thus guaranteeing aristocratic control over reforms. But opposition to the Parlement's proposal arose from a group of reformers calling themselves patriots or "lovers of liberty." Although they claimed to represent the nation, they consisted primarily of bourgeoisie and nobles. One group of patriots known as the Society of Thirty drew most of its members from the salons of Paris. Some of this largely noble group had been directly influenced by the American Revolution, but all had been affected by the ideas of the Enlightenment and favored reforms made in the light of reason and utility.

The National Assembly   The failure of the government to assume the leadership at the opening of the Estates-General created an opportunity for the Third Estate to push its demands for voting by head. Since it had double representation, with the assistance of liberal nobles and clerics, it could turn the three estates into a single-chamber legislature that would reform France in its own way. One representative, the Abbé Sieyès, issued a pamphlet in which he asked, "What is the Third Estate? Everything. What has it been thus far in the political order? Nothing. What does it demand? To become something." Sieyès's sentiment, however, was not representative of the general feeling in 1789. Most delegates still wanted to make changes within a framework of respect for the authority of the king; revival or reform did not mean the overthrow of traditional institutions. When the First Estate declared in favor of voting by order, the Third Estate felt compelled to respond in a significant fashion. On June 17, 1789, the Third Estate voted to constitute itself a "National Assembly" and decided to draw up a constitution. Three days later, on June 20, the deputies of the Third Estate arrived at their meeting place only to find the doors locked; thereupon they moved to a nearby indoor tennis court and swore (in what has come to be known as the Tennis Court Oath) that they would continue to meet until they had produced a French

The Tennis Court Oath. Finding themselves locked out of their regular meeting place on June 20, 1789, the deputies of the Third Estate met instead in the nearby tennis courts of the Jeu de Paume and committed themselves to continue to meet until they established a new constitution for France. In this painting, the Neoclassical artist Jacques-Louis David presents a dramatic rendering of the Tennis Court Oath.

© Musée de la Ville de Paris, Musée Carnavalet, Paris, France//Giraudon/The Bridgeman Art Library

THE FALL OF THE BASTILLE

On July 14, 1789, Parisian crowds in search of weapons attacked and captured the royal armory known as the Bastille. It had also been a state prison, and its fall marked the triumph of "liberty" over despotism. This intervention of the Parisian populace saved the Third Estate from Louis XVI's attempted counterrevolution.

A Parisian Newspaper Account of the Fall of the Bastille

First, the people tried to enter this fortress by the Rue St.-Antoine, this fortress, which no one has even penetrated against the wishes of this frightful despotism and where the monster still resided. The treacherous governor had put out a flag of peace. So a confident advance was made; a detachment of French Guards, with perhaps five to six thousand armed bourgeois, penetrated the Bastille's outer courtyards, but as soon as some six hundred persons had passed over the first drawbridge, the bridge was raised and artillery fire mowed down several French Guards and some soldiers; the cannon fired on the town, and the people took fright; a large number of individuals were killed or wounded; but then they rallied and took shelter from the fire. . . . Meanwhile, they tried to locate some cannon; they attacked from the water's edge through the gardens of the arsenal, and from there made an orderly siege; they advanced from various directions, beneath a ceaseless round of fire. It was a terrible scene. . . . The fighting grew steadily more intense; the citizens had become hardened to the fire; from all directions they clambered onto the roofs or broke into the rooms; as soon as an enemy appeared among the turrets on the tower, he was fixed in the sights of a hundred guns and mown down in an instant; meanwhile cannon fire was hurriedly directed against the second drawbridge, which it pierced, breaking the chains; in vain did the cannon on the tower reply, for most people were sheltered from it; the fury was at its height; people bravely faced death and every danger; women, in their eagerness, helped us to the utmost; even the children, after the discharge of fire from the fortress, ran here and there picking up the bullets and shot; [and so the Bastille fell and the governor, de Launay, was captured]. . . . Serene and blessed liberty, for the first time, has at last been introduced into this abode of horrors, this frightful refuge of monstrous despotism and its crimes.

Meanwhile, they get ready to march; they leave amidst an enormous crowd; the applause, the outbursts of joy, the insults, the oaths hurled at the treacherous prisoners of war; everything is confused; cries of vengeance and of pleasure issue from every heart; the conquerors, glorious and covered in honor, carry their arms and the spoils of the conquered, the flags of victory, the militia mingling with the soldiers of the fatherland, the victory laurels offered them from every side, all this created a frightening and splendid spectacle. On arriving at the square, the people, anxious to avenge themselves, allowed neither de Launay nor the other officers to reach the place of trial; they seized them from the hands of their conquerors, and trampled them underfoot one after the other. De Launay was struck by a thousand blows, his head was cut off and hoisted on the end of a pike with blood streaming down all sides. . . . This glorious day must amaze our enemies, and finally usher in for us the triumph of justice and liberty. In the evening, there were celebrations.

Q *Why did the fall of the Bastille come to mark the triumph of French "liberty" over despotism? Do you think this Parisian newspaper account might be biased? Why or why not?*

---

constitution. These actions of June 17 and June 20 constituted the first step in the French Revolution, since the Third Estate had no legal right to act as the National Assembly. This revolution, largely the work of the lawyers of the Third Estate, was soon in jeopardy, however, as the king sided with the First Estate and threatened to dissolve the Estates-General. Louis XVI now prepared to use force. The revolution of the lawyers appeared doomed.

Intervention of the Common People The common people, however, in a series of urban and rural uprisings in July and August 1789, saved the Third Estate from the king's attempt to stop the Revolution. From now on, the common people would be mobilized by both revolutionary and counterrevolutionary politicians and used to support their interests. The common people had their own interests as well and would use the name of the Third Estate to wage a war on the rich, claiming that the aristocrats were plotting to destroy the Estates-General and retain its privileges. This war was not what the deputies of the Third Estate had planned.

The most famous of the urban risings was the fall of the Bastille (see the box above). The king's attempt to take defensive measures by increasing the number of troops at the arsenals in Paris and along the roads to Versailles served not to intimidate but rather to inflame public opinion. Increased mob activity in Paris led Parisian leaders to form the so-called Permanent Committee to keep order. Needing arms, they organized a popular force to capture the Invalides, a royal armory, and on July 14 attacked the Bastille, another royal armory. The Bastille had also been a state prison but now held only seven prisoners (five forgers and two insane persons). There were few weapons there except those in the hands of the small group of defenders. The Bastille was an imposing fortress with eight towers connected by 9-foot-thick walls. It was easily defended, but its commander, the marquis de Launay, was more inclined to negotiate. Although fighting erupted, de Launay refused to open fire with his cannon, and the garrison soon surrendered. In the minds of the Parisians who fought there, the fall of the Bastille was a great victory, and it quickly became a popular symbol of triumph over despotism.

Paris was abandoned to the insurgents, and Louis XVI was soon informed that the royal troops were unreliable. Louis's acceptance of that reality signaled the collapse of royal authority; the king could no longer enforce his will. Louis then confirmed the appointment of the marquis de Lafayette as commander of a newly created citizens' militia known as the National Guard. The fall of the Bastille had saved the National Assembly.

At the same time, independently of what was going on in Paris, popular revolutions broke out in numerous cities. In Nantes, permanent committees and national guards were created to maintain order after crowds had seized the chief citadels. This collapse of royal authority in the cities was paralleled by peasant revolutions in the countryside.

Peasant Rebellions and the Great Fear A growing resentment of the entire seigneurial system, with its fees and obligations, greatly exacerbated by the economic and fiscal activities of the great estate holders—whether noble or bourgeois—in the difficult decade of the 1780s, created the conditions for a popular uprising. The fall of the Bastille and the king's apparent capitulation to the demands of the Third Estate now encouraged peasants to take matters into their own hands. From July 19 to August 3, peasant rebellions occurred in five major areas of France. Patterns varied. In some places, peasants simply forced their lay and ecclesiastical lords to renounce dues and tithes; elsewhere they burned charters listing their obligations. The peasants were not acting in blind fury; they knew what they were doing. Many also believed that the king supported their actions. As a contemporary chronicler wrote, "For several weeks, news went from village to village. They announced that the Estates-General was going to abolish tithes, quitrents and dues, that the King agreed but that the peasants had to support the public authorities by going themselves to demand the destruction of titles."[5]

The agrarian revolts served as a backdrop to the Great Fear, a vast panic that spread like wildfire through France between July 20 and August 6. Fear of invasion by foreign troops, aided by a supposed aristocratic plot, encouraged the formation of more citizens' militias and permanent committees. The greatest impact of the agrarian revolts and the Great Fear was on the National Assembly meeting in Versailles. We will now examine its attempt to reform France.

Destruction of the Old Regime

One of the first acts of the National Assembly (also called the Constituent Assembly because from 1789 to 1791 it was writing a new constitution) was to destroy the relics of feudalism or aristocratic privileges. To some deputies, this measure was necessary to calm the peasants and restore order in the countryside, although many urban bourgeois were willing to abolish feudalism as a matter of principle. On the night of August 4, 1789, the National Assembly in an astonishing session voted to abolish seigneurial rights as well as the fiscal privileges of nobles, clergy, towns, and provinces.

The Declaration of the Rights of Man and the Citizen On August 26, the assembly provided the ideological foundation for its actions and an educational device for the nation by adopting the Declaration of the Rights of Man and the Citizen (see the box on p. 581). This charter of basic liberties reflected the ideas of the major philosophes of the French Enlightenment and also owed much to the American Declaration of Independence and American state constitutions. The declaration began with a ringing affirmation of "the natural and imprescriptible rights of man" to "liberty, property, security, and resistance to oppression." It went on to affirm the destruction of aristocratic privileges by proclaiming an end to exemptions from taxation, freedom and equal rights for all men, and access to public office based on talent. The monarchy was restricted, and all citizens were to have the right to take part in the legislative process. Freedom of speech and press were coupled with the outlawing of arbitrary arrests.

The declaration also raised another important issue. Did the proclamation's ideal of equal rights for "all men" include women? Many deputies insisted that it did, at least in terms of civil liberties, provided that, as one said, "women do not aspire to exercise political rights and functions." Olympe de Gouges, a playwright and pamphleteer, refused to accept this exclusion of women from political rights. Echoing the words of the official declaration, she penned a Declaration of the Rights of Woman and the Female Citizen in which she insisted that women should have all the same rights as men (see the box on p. 581). The National Assembly ignored her demands.

The Women's March to Versailles In the meantime, Louis XVI had remained inactive at Versailles. He did refuse, however, to promulgate the decrees on the abolition of feudalism and the declaration of rights, but an unexpected turn of events soon forced the king to change his mind. On October 5, after marching to the Hôtel de Ville, the city hall, to demand bread, crowds of Parisian women numbering in the thousands set off for Versailles, 12 miles away, to confront the king and the National Assembly. One eyewitness was amazed at the sight of "detachments of women coming up from every direction, armed with broomsticks, lances, pitchforks, swords, pistols and muskets." After meeting with a delegation of these women, who tearfully described how their children were starving for lack of bread, Louis XVI promised them grain supplies for Paris, thinking that this would end the protest. But the women's action had forced the Paris

OPPOSING VIEWPOINTS
THE NATURAL RIGHTS OF THE FRENCH PEOPLE: TWO VIEWS

One of the important documents of the French Revolution, the Declaration of the Rights of Man and the Citizen was adopted in August 1789 by the National Assembly. The declaration affirmed that "men are born and remain free and equal in rights," that government must protect these natural rights, and that political power is derived from the people.

Olympe de Gouges (the pen name used by Marie Gouze) was a butcher's daughter who wrote plays and pamphlets. She argued that the Declaration of the Rights of Man and the Citizen did not apply to women and composed her own Declaration of the Rights of Woman and the Female Citizen in 1791.

Declaration of the Rights of Man and the Citizen

The representatives of the French people, organized as a national assembly, considering that ignorance, neglect, and scorn of the rights of man are the sole causes of public misfortunes and of corruption of governments, have resolved to display in a solemn declaration the natural, inalienable, and sacred rights of man, so that this declaration, constantly in the presence of all members of society, will continually remind them of their rights and their duties.... Consequently, the National Assembly recognizes and declares, in the presence and under the auspices of the Supreme Being, the following rights of man and citizen:

1. Men are born and remain free and equal in rights; social distinctions can be established only for the common benefit.
2. The aim of every political association is the conservation of the natural and imprescriptible rights of man; these rights are liberty, property, security, and resistance to oppression.
3. The source of all sovereignty is located in essence in the nation; no body, no individual can exercise authority which does not emanate from it expressly.
4. Liberty consists in being able to do anything that does not harm another person....
6. The law is the expression of the general will; all citizens have the right to concur personally or through their representatives in its formation; it must be the same for all, whether it protects or punishes. All citizens being equal in its eyes are equally admissible to all honors, positions, and public employments, according to their capabilities and without other distinctions than those of their virtues and talents.
7. No man can be accused, arrested, or detained except in cases determined by the law, and according to the forms which it has prescribed....
10. No one may be disturbed because of his opinions, even religious, provided that their public demonstration does not disturb the public order established by law.

11. The free communication of thoughts and opinions is one of the most precious rights of man: every citizen can therefore freely speak, write, and print....
12. The guaranteeing of the rights of man and citizen necessitates a public force; this force is therefore instituted for the advantage of all, and not for the private use of those to whom it is entrusted....
14. Citizens have the right to determine for themselves or through their representatives the need for taxation of the public, to consent to it freely, to investigate its use, and to determine its rate, basis, collection, and duration.
15. Society has the right to demand an accounting of his administration from every public agent.
16. Any society in which guarantees of rights are not assured nor the separation of powers determined has no constitution.
17. Property being an inviolable and sacred right, no one may be deprived of it unless public necessity, legally determined, clearly requires such action, and then only on condition of a just and prior indemnity.

Declaration of the Rights of Woman and the Female Citizen

...Mothers, daughters, sisters and representatives of the nation demand to be constituted into a national assembly. Believing that ignorance, omission, or scorn for the rights of woman are the only causes of public misfortunes and of the corruption of governments, the women have resolved to set forth in a solemn declaration the natural, inalienable, and sacred rights of woman in order that this declaration, constantly exposed before all the members of the society, will ceaselessly remind them of their rights and duties....

Consequently, the sex that is as superior in beauty as it is in courage during the sufferings of maternity recognizes and declares in the presence and under the auspices of the Supreme Being, the following Rights of Woman and of Female Citizens.

1. Woman is born free and lives equal to man in her rights. Social distinctions can be based only on the common utility.
2. The purpose of any political association is the conservation of the natural and imprescriptible rights of woman and man; these rights are liberty, property, security, and especially resistance to oppression.
3. The principle of all sovereignty rests essentially with the nation, which is nothing but the union of woman and man; no body and no individual can exercise any authority which does not come expressly from it [the nation].
4. Liberty and justice consist of restoring all that belongs to others; thus, the only limits on the exercise of the natural rights of woman are perpetual male tyranny;

(continued)

(continued)

these limits are to be reformed by the laws of nature and reason....

6. The law must be the expression of the general will; all female and male citizens must contribute either personally or through their representatives to its formation; it must be the same for all: male and female citizens, being equal in the eyes of the law, must be equally admitted to all honors, positions, and public employment according to their capacity and without other distinctions besides those of their virtues and talents.

7. No woman is an exception; she is accused, arrested, and detained in cases determined by law. Women, like men, obey this rigorous law....

10. No one is to be disquieted for his very basic opinions; woman has the right to mount the scaffold; she must equally have the right to mount the rostrum, provided that her demonstrations do not disturb the legally established public order.

11. The free communication of thought and opinions is one of the most precious rights of woman, since that liberty assured the recognition of children by their fathers....

12. The guarantee of the rights of woman and the female citizen implies a major benefit; this guarantee must be instituted for the advantage of all, and not for the particular benefit of those to whom it is entrusted....

14. Female and male citizens have the right to verify, either by themselves or through their representatives, the necessity of the public contribution. This can only apply to women if they are granted an equal share, not only of wealth, but also of public administration, and in the determination of the proportion, the base, the collection, and the duration of the tax.

15. The collectivity of women, joined for tax purposes to the aggregate of men, has the right to demand an accounting of his administration from any public agent.

16. No society has a constitution without the guarantee of rights and the separation of powers; the constitution is null if the majority of individuals comprising the nation have not cooperated in drafting it.

17. Property belongs to both sexes whether united or separate; for each it is an inviolable and sacred right; no one can be deprived of it, since it is the true patrimony of nature, unless the legally determined public need obviously dictates it, and then only with a just and prior indemnity.

Q *What "natural rights" does the first document proclaim? To what extent was this document influenced by the writings of the philosophes? What rights for women does the second document enunciate? Given the nature and scope of the arguments in favor of natural rights and women's rights in these two documents, what key effects on European society would you attribute to the French Revolution?*

National Guard under Lafayette to follow their lead and march to Versailles. The crowd now insisted that the royal family return to Paris. On October 6, the king complied. As a goodwill gesture, he brought along wagonloads of flour from the palace stores. All were escorted by women armed with pikes (some of which held the severed heads of the king's guards), singing, "We are bringing back the baker, the baker's wife, and the baker's boy" (the king, queen, and their son). The king now accepted the National Assembly's decrees; it was neither the first nor the last occasion when Parisian crowds would affect national politics. The king was virtually a prisoner in Paris, and the National Assembly, now meeting in Paris, would also feel the influence of Parisian insurrectionary politics.

Départ des Héroïnes de Paris pour Versailles le 5 Octobre 1789.

The Women's March to Versailles. On October 5, 1789, thousands of Parisian women marched to Versailles to confront King Louis XVI and to demand bread for their starving children. This contemporary print shows a group of dedicated marchers, some armed with pikes and other weapons while others pull an artillery piece. The aristocratic woman at the far right does not appear to be very enthusiastic about joining the march.

Réunion des Musées Nationaux (Bulloz)/Art Resource, NY

The Catholic Church The Catholic Church was viewed as an important pillar of the old order, and it soon also felt the impact of reform. Because of the need for money, most of the lands of the church were confiscated, and *assignats,* a form of paper money, were issued based on the collateral of the newly nationalized church property. The church was also secularized. In July 1790, the new Civil Constitution of the Clergy was put into effect. Both bishops and priests of the Catholic Church were to be elected by the people and paid by the state. All clergy were also required to swear an oath of allegiance to the Civil Constitution. Since the pope forbade it, only 54 percent of the French parish clergy took the oath, and the majority of bishops refused. This was a critical development because the Catholic Church, still an important institution in the life of the French people, now became an enemy of the Revolution. The Civil Constitution has often been viewed as a serious tactical blunder on the part of the National Assembly, for by arousing the opposition of the church, it gave counterrevolution a popular base from which to operate.

A New Constitution By 1791, the National Assembly had completed a new constitution that established a limited constitutional monarchy. There was still a monarch (now called "king of the French"), but he enjoyed few powers not subject to review by the new Legislative Assembly. The assembly, in which sovereign power was vested, was to sit for two years and consist of 745 representatives chosen by an indirect system of election that preserved power in the hands of the more affluent members of society. A distinction was drawn between active and passive citizens. Although all had the same civil rights, only active citizens (men over the age of twenty-five paying taxes equivalent in value to three days' unskilled labor) could vote. The active citizens probably numbered 4.3 million in 1790. These citizens did not elect the members of the Legislative Assembly directly but voted for electors (men paying taxes equal in value to ten days' labor). This relatively small group of 50,000 electors chose the deputies. To qualify as a deputy, one had to pay at least a "silver mark" in taxes, an amount equivalent to fifty-four days' labor.

The National Assembly also undertook an administrative restructuring of France. In 1789, it abolished all the old local and provincial divisions and divided France into eighty-three departments, roughly equal in size and population. Departments were in turn divided into districts and communes, all supervised by elected councils and officials who oversaw financial, administrative, judicial, and ecclesiastical institutions within their domains. Although both bourgeois and aristocrats were eligible for offices based on property qualifications, few nobles were elected, leaving local and departmental governments in the hands of the bourgeoisie, especially lawyers of various types.

Opposition from Within By 1791, France had moved into a vast reordering of the old regime that had been achieved by a revolutionary consensus that was largely the work of the wealthier members of the bourgeoisie. By mid-1791, however, this consensus faced growing opposition from clerics angered by the Civil Constitution of the Clergy, lower classes hurt by the rise in the cost of living resulting from the inflation of the *assignats,* peasants who remained opposed to dues that had still not been abandoned, and political clubs offering more radical solutions to the nation's problems. The most famous were the Jacobins, who first emerged as a gathering of more radical deputies at the beginning of the Revolution, especially during the events of the night of August 4, 1789. After October 1789, they occupied the former Jacobin convent in Paris. Jacobin clubs also formed in the provinces, where they served primarily as discussion groups. Eventually, they joined together in an extensive correspondence network and by spring 1790 were seeking affiliation with the Parisian club. One year later, there were nine hundred Jacobin clubs in France associated with the Parisian center. Members were usually the elite of their local societies, but they also included artisans and tradespeople.

In addition, by mid-1791, the government was still facing severe financial difficulties due to massive tax evasion. Despite all of their problems, however, the bourgeois politicians in charge remained relatively unified on the basis of their trust in the king. But Louis XVI disastrously undercut them. Quite upset with the whole turn of revolutionary events, he sought to flee France in June 1791 and almost succeeded before being recognized, captured at Varennes, and brought back to Paris. Though radicals called for the king to be deposed, the members of the National Assembly, fearful of the popular forces in Paris calling for a republic, chose to ignore the king's flight and pretended that he had been kidnapped. In this unsettled situation, with a discredited and seemingly disloyal monarch, the new Legislative Assembly held its first session in October 1791.

Because the National Assembly had passed a "self-denying ordinance" that prohibited the reelection of its members, the composition of the Legislative Assembly tended to be quite different from that of the National Assembly. The clerics and nobles were largely gone. Most of the representatives were men of property; many were lawyers. Although lacking national reputations, most had gained experience in the new revolutionary politics and prominence in their local areas through the National Guard, the Jacobin clubs, and the many elective offices spawned by the administrative reordering of France. The king made what seemed to be a genuine effort to work with the new Legislative Assembly, but France's relations with the rest of Europe soon led to Louis's downfall.

Opposition from Abroad Over a period of time, some European countries had become concerned about the French example and feared that revolution would spread to their countries. On August 27, 1791, Emperor Leopold II of Austria and King Frederick William II of Prussia issued the Declaration of Pillnitz, which invited other European monarchs to take "the most effectual means... to put the king of France in a state to strengthen, in the most perfect liberty, the bases of a monarchical government equally becoming to the rights of sovereigns and to the well-being of the French Nation."[6] But European monarchs were too suspicious of each other to undertake such a plan, and in any case, French enthusiasm for war led the Legislative Assembly to declare war on Austria on April 20, 1792. Why take such a step in view of its obvious dangers? Many people in France wanted war. Reactionaries hoped that a preoccupation with war would cool off the Revolution; French defeat, which seemed likely in view of the army's disintegration, might even lead to the restoration of the old regime. Leftists hoped that war would consolidate the Revolution at home and spread it to all of Europe.

The French fared badly in the initial fighting. A French army invaded the Austrian Netherlands (Belgium) but was routed, and Paris now feared invasion by the Austrians and Prussians. In fact, if they had cooperated, they might have seized Paris in May or June. Alarmed by the turn of events, the Legislative Assembly called for 20,000 National Guardsmen from the provinces to come and defend Paris. One such group came from Marseilles singing a rousing war song, soon known as the "Marseillaise," that three years later was made the French national anthem:

> *Arise children of the motherland*
> *The day of glory has arrived.*
> *Against us, tyranny's*
> *Bloody flag is raised.*
> *Don't you hear in our countryside*
> *The roar of their ferocious soldiers?*
> *They are coming into your homes*
> *To butcher your sons and your companions.*
> *To arm, citizens! Form your battalions!*
> *We march, we march!*
> *Let their impure blood water our fields.*

As fears of invasion grew, a frantic search for scapegoats began; as one observer noted, "Everywhere you hear the cry that the king is betraying us, the generals are betraying us, that nobody is to be trusted;... that Paris will be taken in six weeks by the Austrians.... We are on a volcano ready to spout flames."[7] Defeats in war coupled with economic shortages in the spring reinvigorated popular groups that had been dormant since the previous summer and led to renewed political demonstrations, especially against the king. Radical Parisian political groups, declaring themselves an insurrectionary commune, organized a mob attack on the royal palace and Legislative Assembly in August 1792, took the king captive, and forced the Legislative Assembly to suspend the monarchy and call for a national convention, chosen on the basis of universal male suffrage, to decide on the future form of government. The French Revolution was about to enter a more radical stage as power passed from the assembly to the new Paris Commune, composed of many who proudly called themselves the **sans-culottes,** ordinary patriots without fine clothes. Although it has become customary to equate the more radical sans-culottes with working people or the poor, many were merchants and better-off artisans who were often the elite of their neighborhoods and trades.

The Radical Revolution

Before the National Convention met, the Paris Commune dominated the political scene. Led by the newly appointed minister of justice, Georges Danton (1759–1794), the sans-culottes sought revenge on those who had aided the king and resisted the popular will. Fears of treachery were intensified by the advance of a Prussian army on Paris. Thousands of presumed traitors were arrested and then massacred as ordinary Parisian tradespeople and artisans solved the problem of overcrowded prisons by mass executions of their inmates. In September 1792, the newly elected National Convention began its sessions. Although it was called to draft a new constitution, it also acted as the sovereign ruling body of France.

Socially, the composition of the National Convention was similar to that of its predecessors. Dominated by lawyers, professionals, and property owners, it also included for the first time a handful of artisans. Two-thirds of the deputies were under age forty-five, and almost all had had political experience as a result of the Revolution. Almost all were also intensely distrustful of the king and his activities. It was therefore no surprise that the convention's first major step on September 21 was to abolish the monarchy and establish a republic. But that was about as far as members of the convention could agree, and the National Convention soon split into factions over the fate of the king. The two most important were the **Girondins** (so-called because their leaders came from the department of Gironde, located in southwestern France) and the **Mountain** (so-called because its members' seats were on the side of the convention hall where the floor slanted upward). Both were members of the Jacobin club.

Domestic Crises Representing primarily the provinces, the Girondins came to fear the radical mobs in Paris and were disposed to keep the king alive as a hedge against future eventualities. The Mountain represented the interests of the city of Paris and owed much of its strength to the radical and popular elements in the city, although the members of the Mountain themselves were middle class. The Mountain won out at the beginning of 1793 when the National Convention found the king guilty of treason and sentenced him to death. On January 21, 1793, the king was executed, and the destruction of the old regime was complete. Now there could be no turning back. But the execution of the king produced further

Execution of the King. At the beginning of 1793, the National Convention decreed the death of the king, and on January 21 of that year, Louis XVI was executed. As seen in this engraving by Carnavalet, the execution of the king was accomplished by a new revolutionary device, the guillotine.

challenges by creating new enemies for the Revolution both at home and abroad while strengthening those who were already its enemies.

Factional disputes between the Girondins and the Mountain were only one aspect of France's domestic crisis in 1792 and 1793. In Paris, the local government was controlled by the Commune, which drew a number of its leaders from the city's artisans and shopkeepers. The Commune favored radical change and put constant pressure on the National Convention, pushing it to ever more radical positions. As one man warned his fellow deputies, "Never forget that you were sent here by the sans-culottes."[8] At the end of May and the beginning of June 1793, the Commune organized a demonstration, invaded the National Convention, and forced the arrest and execution of the leading Girondins, thereby leaving the Mountain in control of the convention. The National Convention itself still did not rule all of France. The authority of the convention was repudiated in western France, particularly in the department of the Vendée, by peasants who revolted against the new military draft (see "A Nation in Arms" later in this chapter). The Vendéan rebellion soon escalated into a full-blown counterrevolutionary appeal: "Long live the

king and our good priests. We want our king, our priests and the old regime." Some of France's major provincial cities, including Lyons and Marseilles, also began to break away from the central authority. Arguing as Marseilles did that "it is time for the anarchy of a few men of blood to stop,"[9] these cities favored a decentralized republic to free themselves

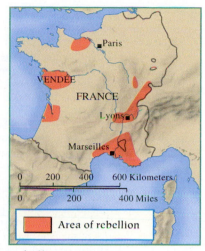

Rebellion in France

from the ascendancy of Paris. In no way did they favor breaking up the "indivisible republic."

Foreign Crisis Domestic turmoil was paralleled by a foreign crisis. Early in 1793, after Louis XVI had been executed, much of Europe—an informal coalition of Austria, Prussia, Spain, Portugal, Britain, and the Dutch Republic—was pitted against France. Carried away by initial successes and their own rhetoric, the French welcomed the struggle. Danton exclaimed to the convention, "They threaten you with kings! You have thrown down your gauntlet to them, and this gauntlet is a king's head, the signal of their coming death."[10] Grossly overextended, the French armies began to experience reverses, and by late spring some members of the anti-French coalition were poised for an invasion of France. If they succeeded, both the Revolution and the revolutionaries would be destroyed and the old regime reestablished. The Revolution had reached a decisive moment.

To meet these crises, the program of the National Convention became one of curbing anarchy and counterrevolution at home while attempting to win the war by a vigorous mobilization of the people. To administer the government, the convention gave broad powers to an executive committee known as the Committee of Public Safety, which was dominated initially by Danton. For the next twelve months, virtually the same twelve members were reelected and gave the country the leadership it needed to weather the domestic and foreign crises of 1793. One of the most important members was Maximilien Robespierre (1758–1794), a small-town lawyer who had moved to Paris as a member of the Estates-General. Politics was his life, and he was dedicated to using power to benefit the people, whom he loved in the abstract though not on a one-to-one basis.

A Nation in Arms To meet the foreign crisis and save the Republic from its foreign enemies, the Committee of

Public Safety decreed a universal mobilization of the nation on August 23, 1793:

> Young men will fight, young men are called to conquer. Married men will forge arms, transport military baggage and guns and will prepare food supplies. Women, who at long last are to take their rightful place in the revolution and follow their true destiny, will forget their futile tasks: their delicate hands will work at making clothes for soldiers; they will make tents and they will extend their tender care to shelters where the defenders of the Patrie [nation] will receive the help that their wounds require. Children will make lint of old cloth. It is for them that we are fighting: children, those beings destined to gather all the fruits of the revolution, will raise their pure hands toward the skies. And old men, performing their missions again, as of yore, will be guided to the public squares of the cities where they will kindle the courage of young warriors and preach the doctrines of hate for kings and the unity of the Republic.[11]

In less than a year, the French revolutionary government had raised an army of 650,000; by September 1794, it numbered 1,169,000. The Republic's army—**a nation in arms**—was the largest ever seen in European history. It now pushed the allies back across the Rhine and even conquered the Austrian Netherlands (see Map 19.2). By May 1795, the anti-French coalition of 1793 was breaking up.

Historians have focused on the importance of the French revolutionary army in the creation of modern nationalism. Previously, wars had been fought between governments or ruling dynasties by relatively small armies of professional soldiers. The new French army, however, was the creation of a "people's" government; its wars were now "people's" wars. The entire nation was to be involved in the war. But when dynastic wars became people's wars, warfare increased in ferocity and lack of restraint. Although innocent civilians had suffered in the earlier struggles, now the carnage became appalling at times. The wars of the French revolutionary era opened the door to the total war of the modern world.

The Committee of Public Safety and the Reign of Terror To meet the domestic crisis, the National Convention and the Committee of Public Safety established the "Reign of Terror." Revolutionary courts were organized to protect the Republic from its internal enemies, "who either by their conduct, their contacts, their words or their writings, showed themselves to be supporters of tyranny or enemies of liberty" or "who have not constantly manifested their attachment to the revolution."[12] Victims of the Terror ranged from royalists, such as Queen Marie Antoinette, to former revolutionary Girondins, including Olympe de Gouges, the chief advocate for political rights for women, and even included thousands of peasants. Many victims were persons who had opposed the radical activities of the sans-culottes. In the course of nine months, 16,000 people were officially killed under the blade of the guillotine, a revolutionary device for the quick and efficient separation of heads from bodies. But the true number of the Terror's victims was probably closer to 50,000 (see the box on p. 588). The bulk of the Terror's executions took place in the Vendée and in cities such as Lyons and Marseilles, places that had been in open rebellion against the authority of the National Convention.

Military force in the form of revolutionary armies was used to bring recalcitrant cities and districts back under the control of the National Convention. Marseilles fell to a revolutionary army in August. Starving Lyons surrendered early in October after two months of bombardment and resistance. Since Lyons was France's second city after Paris and had defied the National Convention during a time when the Republic was in peril, the Committee of Public Safety decided to make an example of it. By April 1794, some 1,880 citizens of Lyons had been executed. When guillotining proved too slow, cannon fire and grapeshot were used to blow condemned men into open graves. A German observed:

> Whole ranges of houses, always the most handsome, [were] burnt. The churches, convents, and all the dwellings of the former patricians were in ruins. When I came to the guillotine, the blood of those who had been executed a few hours beforehand was

Citizens Enlisting in the New French Army. To save the Republic from its foreign enemies, the National Convention created a revolutionary army of unprecedented size. In this painting, citizens hasten to sign up at the recruitment tables set up in the streets. On this occasion, officials are distributing coins to those who have enrolled.

MAP 19.2 **French Expansion During the Revolutionary Wars, 1792–1799.** The conservative rulers of Europe, appalled at the republican character of the French Revolution, took up arms to restore the power of the Bourbon monarchy. The French responded with a people's army, the largest ever seen, which pushed the invaders out of France, annexed the Austrian Netherlands and some Italian territory, and created a number of French satellite states.

Q Why would Austria desire cooperation from the German states if it wanted to wage war on France?

View an animated version of this map or related maps at academic.cengage.com/history/spielvogel

still running in the street. . . . I said to a group of sans-culottes that it would be decent to clear away all this human blood. Why should it be cleared? one of them said to me. It's the blood of aristocrats and rebels. The dogs should lick it up.[13]

In the Vendée, revolutionary armies were also brutal in defeating the rebel armies. After destroying one army on December 12, the commander of the revolutionary army ordered that no quarter be given: "The road to Laval is strewn with corpses. Women, priests, monks, children, all have been put to death. I have spared nobody." The Terror was at its most destructive in the Vendée. Forty-two percent of the death sentences during the Terror were passed in territories affected by the Vendée rebellion. Perhaps the most notorious act of violence occurred in Nantes, where victims were executed by sinking them in barges in the Loire River.

Contrary to popular opinion, the Terror demonstrated no class prejudice. Estimates are that the nobles constituted 8 percent of its victims; the middle classes, 25 percent;

the clergy, 6; and the peasant and laboring classes, 60. To the Committee of Public Safety, this bloodletting was only a temporary expedient. Once the war and domestic emergency were over, "the republic of virtue" would ensue, and the Declaration of the Rights of Man and the Citizen would be fully established. Although theoretically a republic, the French government during the Terror was led by a group of twelve men who ordered the execution of people as national enemies. But how did they justify this? Louis Saint-Just, one of the younger members of the Committee of Public Safety, explained their rationalization in a speech to the convention: "Since the French people has manifested its will, everything opposed to it is outside the sovereign. Whatever is outside the sovereign is an enemy."[14] Clearly, Saint-Just was referring to Rousseau's concept of the general will, but it is equally apparent that these twelve men, in the name of the Republic, had taken upon themselves the right to ascertain the sovereign will of the French people (see the box on p. 589) and to kill their enemies as "outside the sovereign."

JUSTICE IN THE REIGN OF TERROR

The Reign of Terror created a repressive environment in which revolutionary courts often acted quickly to condemn traitors to the revolutionary cause. In this account, an English visitor describes the court, the procession to the scene of execution, and the final execution procedure.

J. G. Milligen, *The Revolutionary Tribunal* (Paris, October 1793)

In the center of the hall, under a statue of Justice, holding scales in one hand, and a sword in the other, sat Dumas, the President, with the other judges. Under them were seated the public accuser, Fourquier-Tinville, and his scribes.... To the right were benches on which the accused were placed in several rows, and *gendarmes* with carbines and fixed bayonets by their sides. To the left was the jury.

Never can I forget the mournful appearance of these funereal processions to the place of execution. The march was opened by a detachment of mounted *gendarmes*—the carts followed; they were the same carts as those that are used in Paris for carrying wood; four boards were placed across them for seats, and on each board sat two, and sometimes three victims; their hands were tied behind their backs, and the constant jolting of the cart made them nod their heads up and down, to the great amusement of the spectators. On the front of the cart stood Samson, the executioner, or one of his sons or assistants; *gendarmes* on foot marched by the side; then followed a hackney, in which was the reporting clerk, whose duty it was to witness the execution, and then return to the public accuser's office to report the execution of what they called the law.

The process of execution was also a sad and heartrending spectacle. In the middle of the Place de la Revolution was erected a guillotine, in front of a colossal statue of Liberty, represented seated on a rock, a cap on her head, a spear in her hand, the other reposing on a shield. On one side of the scaffold were drawn out a sufficient number of carts, with large baskets painted red, to receive the heads and bodies of the victims. Those bearing the condemned moved on slowly to the foot of the guillotine; the culprits were led out in turn, and if necessary, supported by two of the executioner's assistants, but their assistance was rarely required. Most of these unfortunates ascended the scaffold with a determined step—many of them looked up firmly on the menacing instrument of death, beholding for the last time the rays of the glorious sun, beaming on the polished axe: and I have seen some young men actually dance a few steps before they went up to be strapped to the perpendicular plane, which was then tilted to a horizontal plane in a moment, and ran on the grooves until the neck was secured and closed in by a moving board, when the head passed through what was called, in derision, "the republican toilet seat"; the weighty knife was then dropped with a heavy fall; and, with incredible dexterity and rapidity, two executioners tossed the body into the basket, while another threw the head after it.

Q *How were the condemned taken to the executioner? How did this serve to inflame the crowds? How were people executed? Why?*

The "Republic of Virtue" Along with the Terror, the Committee of Public Safety took other steps both to control France and to create a new republican order and new republican citizens. By spring 1793, the committee was sending "representatives on mission" as agents of the central government to all departments to explain the war emergency measures and to implement the laws dealing with the wartime emergency.

The committee also attempted to provide some economic controls, especially since members of the more radical working class were advocating them. It established a system of requisitioning food supplies for the cities enforced by the forays of revolutionary armies into the countryside. The Law of the General Maximum established price controls on goods declared of first necessity, ranging from food and drink to fuel and clothing. The controls failed to work very well because the government lacked the machinery to enforce them.

The Role of Women Women continued to play an active role in this radical phase of the French Revolution. As spectators at sessions of revolutionary clubs and the National Convention, women made the members and deputies aware of their demands. When on Sunday, February 25, 1793, a group of women appealed formally to the National Convention for lower bread prices, the convention reacted by adjourning until Tuesday. The women responded bitterly by accosting the deputies: "We are adjourned until Tuesday; but as for us, we adjourn ourselves until Monday. When our children ask us for milk, we don't adjourn them until the day after tomorrow."[15] In 1793, two women—an actress and a chocolate manufacturer—founded the Society for Revolutionary Republican Women. Composed largely of working-class women, this Parisian group viewed itself as a "family of sisters" and vowed "to rush to the defense of the Fatherland."

Despite the importance of women to the revolutionary cause, male revolutionaries reacted disdainfully to female participation in political activity. In the radical phase of the Revolution, the Paris Commune outlawed women's clubs and forbade women to be present at its meetings. One of its members explained why:

ROBESPIERRE AND REVOLUTIONARY GOVERNMENT

In its time of troubles, the National Convention, under the direction of the Committee of Public Safety, instituted the Reign of Terror to preserve the Revolution from its internal enemies. In this selection, Maximilien Robespierre, one of the committee's leading members, tries to justify the violence to which these believers in republican liberty resorted.

Robespierre, Speech on Revolutionary Government

The theory of revolutionary government is as new as the Revolution that created it. It is as pointless to seek its origins in the books of the political theorists, who failed to foresee this revolution, as in the laws of the tyrants, who are happy enough to abuse their exercise of authority without seeking out its legal justification. And so this phrase is for the aristocracy a mere subject of terror or a term of slander, for tyrants an outrage and for many an enigma. It behooves us to explain it to all in order that we may rally good citizens, at least, in support of the principles governing the public interest.

It is the function of government to guide the moral and physical energies of the nation toward the purposes for which it was established.

The object of constitutional government is to preserve the Republic; the object of the revolutionary government is to establish it.

Revolution is the war waged by liberty against its enemies; a constitution is that which crowns the edifice of freedom once victory has been won and the nation is at peace.

The revolutionary government has to summon extraordinary activity to its aid precisely because it is at war. It is subjected to less binding and less uniform regulations, because the circumstances in which it finds itself are tempestuous and shifting above all because it is compelled to deploy, swiftly and incessantly, new resources to meet new and pressing dangers.

The principal concern of constitutional government is civil liberty; that of revolutionary government, public liberty. Under a constitutional government little more is required than to protect the individual against abuses by the state, whereas revolutionary government is obliged to defend the state itself against the factions that assail it from every quarter.

To good citizens revolutionary government owes the full protection of the state; to the enemies of the people it owes only death.

Q *How did Robespierre justify the violent activities of the French revolutionaries? In your opinion, do his explanations justify his actions? How does this document glorify the state and advance preservation of the state as the highest goal of modern politicians and statesmen?*

It is horrible, it is contrary to all laws of nature for a woman to want to make herself a man. The Council must recall that some time ago these denatured women, these viragos, wandered through the markets with the red cap to sully that badge of liberty and wanted to force all women to take off the modest headdress that is appropriate for them [the bonnet].... Is it the place of women to propose motions? Is it the place of women to place themselves at the head of our armies?[16]

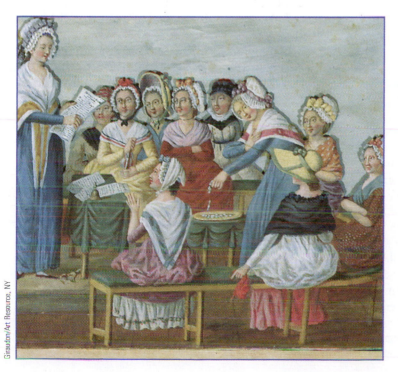

Giraudon/Art Resource, NY

Women Patriots. Women played a variety of roles in the events of the French Revolution. This picture shows a middle-class women's patriotic club discussing the decrees of the National Convention, an indication that some women had become highly politicized by the upheavals of the Revolution. The women are also giving coins to create a fund for impoverished families.

DE-CHRISTIANIZATION

The phenomenon of de-Christianization produced some unusual spectacles during the radical stage of the French Revolution. This selection from the minutes of the National Convention describes how the cathedral of Notre Dame was put to new use as the Temple of Reason.

The Temple of Reason

A member puts in the form of a motion the demand of the citizens of Paris that the metropolitan cathedral [Notre Dame] be henceforth the Temple of Reason.

A member requests that the goddess of Reason place herself at the side of the president.

The attorney of the Commune conducts her to the desk. The president and the secretaries give her the fraternal kiss in the midst of applause.

She sits at the side of the president.

A member demands that the National Convention march in a body, in the midst of the People, to the Temple of Reason to sing the hymn of Liberty there.

This proposal is passed.

The Convention marches with the People to the Temple of Reason in the midst of general enthusiasm and joyful acclamations.

Having entered the Temple of Reason, they sing the following hymn:

> *Descend, O Liberty, daughter of Nature:*
> *The People have recaptured their immortal power;*

> *Over the pompous remains of age-old imposture*
> *Their hands raise thine altar.*
> *Come, vanquisher of kings, Europe gazes upon you;*
> *Come, vanquish the false gods.*
> *Thou, holy Liberty, come dwell in this temple;*
> *Be the goddess of the French.*
> *Thy countenance rejoices the most savage mountain,*
> *Amid the rocks harvests grow:*
> *Embellished by thy hands, the harshest coast,*
> *Embedded in ice, smiles.*
> *Thou doublest pleasures, virtues, genius;*
> *Under thy holy standards, man is always victorious;*
> *Before knowing thee he does not know life;*
> *He is created by thy glance.*
> *All kings make war on the sovereign People;*
> *Let them henceforth fall at thy feet, O goddess;*
> *Soon on the coffins of the world's tyrants*
> *the world's peoples will swear peace.*
> *Warrior liberators, powerful, brave race,*
> *Armed with a human sword, sanctify terror;*
> *Brought down by your blows, may the last slave*
> *Follow the last king to the grave.*

Q What was the purpose of de-Christianization? Based on the ceremony described here, how effective do you think it was?

Most men—radical or conservative—agreed that a woman's place was in the home and not in military or political affairs. As one man asked, "Since when is it considered normal for a woman to abandon the pious care of her home, the cradle of her children, to listen to speeches in the public forum?"[17]

De-Christianization and the New Calendar In its attempt to create a new order, the National Convention also pursued a policy of **de-Christianization.** The word *saint* was removed from street names, churches were pillaged and closed by revolutionary armies, and priests were encouraged to marry. In Paris, the cathedral of Notre-Dame was designated the Temple of Reason (see the box above). In November 1793, a public ceremony dedicated to the worship of reason was held in the former cathedral; patriotic maidens adorned in white dresses paraded before a temple of reason where the high altar once stood. At the end of the ceremony, a female figure personifying Liberty rose out of the temple. As Robespierre came to realize, de-Christianization backfired because France was still overwhelmingly Catholic. In fact, de-Christianization created more enemies than friends.

Yet another manifestation of de-Christianization was the adoption of a new republican calendar on October 5, 1793. Years would no longer be numbered from the birth of Jesus but from September 22, 1792, the day the French Republic was proclaimed. Thus, at the time the calendar was adopted, the French were already living in year II. The calendar contained twelve months; each month consisted of three ten-day weeks (*décades*) with the tenth day of each week a rest day (*décadi*). This eliminated Sundays and Sunday worship services and put an end to the ordering of French lives by a Christian calendar that emphasized Sundays, saints' days, and church holidays and festivals. Religious celebrations were to be replaced by revolutionary festivals. Especially important were the five days (six in leap years) left over in the calendar at the end of the year. These days were to form a half-week of festivals to celebrate the revolutionary virtues—Virtue, Intelligence, Labor, Opinion, and Rewards. The sixth extra day in a leap year would be a special festival day when French citizens would "come from all parts of the Republic to celebrate liberty and equality, to cement by their embraces the national fraternity." Of course, ending church holidays also reduced the number of nonworking holidays from fifty-six to thirty-two, a goal long recommended by eighteenth-century economic theorists.

The anti-Christian purpose of the calendar was reinforced in the naming of the months of the year. The months were given names that were supposed to evoke the seasons, the temperature, or the state of the vegetation: Vendémiaire (harvest—the first month of thirty days beginning September 22), Brumaire (mist), Frimaire (frost), Nivôse (snow), Pluviôse (rain), Ventôse (wind), Germinal (seeding), Floréal (flowering), Prairial (meadows), Messidor (wheat harvest), Thermidor (heat), and Fructidor (ripening).

The new calendar faced intense popular opposition, and the revolutionary government relied primarily on coercion to win its acceptance. Journalists, for example, were commanded to use republican dates in their newspaper articles. But many people refused to give up the old calendar, as one official reported:

> Sundays and Catholic holidays, even if there are ten in a row, have for some time been celebrated with as much pomp and splendor as before. The same cannot be said of *décadi*, which is observed by only a small handful of citizens. The first to disobey the law are the wives of public officials, who dress up on the holidays of the old calendar and abstain from work more religiously than anyone else.[18]

The government could hardly expect peasants to follow the new calendar when government officials were ignoring it. Napoleon later perceived that the revolutionary calendar was politically unpopular, and he simply abandoned it on January 1, 1806 (11 Nivôse XIV).

In addition to its anti-Christian function, the revolutionary calendar had also served to mark the Revolution as a new historical beginning, a radical break in time. Revolutionary upheavals often project millenarian expectations, the hope that a new age is dawning. The revolutionary dream of a new order presupposed the creation of a new human being freed from the old order and its symbols, a new citizen surrounded by a framework of new habits. Restructuring time itself offered the opportunity to forge new habits and create a lasting new order.

Equality and Slavery   Early in the French Revolution, the desire for equality led to a discussion of what to do about slavery. A club called Friends of the Blacks advocated the abolition of slavery, which was achieved in France in September 1791. Nevertheless, French planters in the West Indies, who profited greatly from the use of slaves on their sugar plantations, opposed the abolition of slavery in the French colonies. When the National Convention came into power, the issue was revisited, and on February 4, 1794, guided by ideals of equality, the government abolished slavery in the colonies.

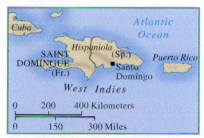

Revolt in Saint Domingue (Haiti)

In one French colony, slaves had already rebelled for their freedom. In 1791, black slaves in the French sugar colony of Saint Domingue (the western third of the island of Hispaniola), inspired by the ideals of the revolution occurring in France, revolted against French plantation owners. Slaves attacked, killing plantation owners and their families and burning their buildings. White planters retaliated with equal brutality. One wealthy French settler reported, "How can we stay in a country where slaves have raised their hands against their masters?"

Eventually, leadership of the revolt was taken over by Toussaint L'Ouverture (1746–1803), a son of African slaves, who seized control of all of Hispaniola by 1801. Although Napoleon had accepted the revolutionary ideal of equality, he did not deny the reports of white planters that the massacres of white planters by slaves demonstrated the savage nature of blacks. In 1802, he reinstated slavery in the French West Indian colonies and sent an army that captured L'Ouverture, who died in a French dungeon within a year. But the French soldiers, weakened by disease, soon succumbed to the slave forces. On January 1, 1804, the western part of Hispaniola, now called Haiti, announced its freedom and became the first independent state in Latin America. Despite Napoleon's efforts to the contrary, one of the French revolutionary ideals had triumphed abroad.

Decline of the Committee of Public Safety   Maintaining the revolutionary ideals in France proved not to be easy. By the Law of 14 Frimaire (passed on December 4, 1793), the Committee of Public Safety sought to centralize the administration of France more effectively and to exercise greater control in order to check the excesses of the Reign of Terror. The activities of both the representatives on mission and the revolutionary armies were scrutinized more carefully, and the campaign against Christianity was also dampened. Finally, in 1794, the Committee of Public Safety turned against its radical Parisian supporters, executed the leaders of the revolutionary Paris Commune, and turned it into a docile tool. This might have been a good idea for the sake of order, but in suppressing the people who had been its chief supporters, the National Convention alienated an important group. At the same time, the French had been successful against their foreign foes. The military successes meant that the Terror no longer served much purpose. But the Terror continued because Robespierre, now its dominant figure, had become obsessed with purifying the body politic of all the corrupt. Only then could the Republic of Virtue follow. Many deputies in the National Convention, however, feared that they were not safe while Robespierre was free to act. An anti-Robespierre coalition in the National Convention, eager now to destroy Robespierre before he destroyed them, gathered enough votes to condemn him. Robespierre was guillotined on July 28, 1794, beginning a reaction that brought an end to this radical stage of the French Revolution.

The National Convention and its Committee of Public Safety had accomplished a great deal. By creating a nation in arms, they preserved the French Revolution and prevented it from being destroyed by its foreign

Robespierre. Maximilien Robespierre eventually came to exercise much control over the Committee of Public Safety. Robespierre and the committee worked to centralize the administration of France and curb the excesses of the Reign of Terror. Fear of Robespierre, however, led many in the National Convention to condemn him, and on July 28, 1794, he was executed.

enemies, who, if they had succeeded, would have reestablished the old monarchical order. Domestically, the Revolution had also been saved from the forces of counterrevolution. The committee's tactics, however, provided an example for the use of violence in domestic politics that has continued to bedevil the Western world to this day.

Reaction and the Directory

After the execution of Robespierre, revolutionary fervor began to give way to the Thermidorean Reaction, named after the month of Thermidor. The Terror began to abate. The National Convention curtailed the power of the Committee of Public Safety, shut down the Jacobin club, and attempted to provide better protection for its deputies against the Parisian mobs. Churches were allowed to reopen for public worship, and a decree of February 21, 1795, gave freedom of worship to all cults. Economic regulation was dropped in favor of *laissez-faire* policies, another clear indication that moderate forces were regaining control of the Revolution. In addition, a new constitution was written in August 1795 that reflected this more conservative republicanism or a desire for a stability that did not sacrifice the ideals of 1789.

To avoid the dangers of another single legislative assembly, the Constitution of 1795 established a national legislative assembly consisting of two chambers: a lower house, known as the Council of 500, whose function was to initiate legislation, and an upper house of 250 members, the Council of Elders, composed of married or widowed members over age forty, which accepted or rejected the proposed laws. The 750 members of the two legislative bodies were chosen by electors who had to be owners or renters of property worth between one hundred and two hundred days' labor, a requirement that limited their number to 30,000, an even smaller base than the Constitution of 1791 had provided. The electors were chosen by the active citizens, now defined as all male taxpayers over the age of twenty-one. The executive authority or Directory consisted of five directors elected by the Council of Elders from a list presented by the Council of 500. To ensure some continuity from the old order to the new, the members of the National Convention ruled that two-thirds of the new members of the National Assembly must be chosen from their ranks. This decision produced disturbances in Paris and an insurrection at the beginning of October that was dispersed after fierce combat by an army contingent under the artillery general Napoleon Bonaparte. This would be the last time in the great French Revolution that the city of Paris would attempt to impose its wishes on the central government. Even more significant and ominous was this use of the army, which made it clear that the Directory from the beginning had to rely on the military for survival.

The period of the Directory was an era of materialistic reaction to the suffering and sacrifices that had been demanded in the Reign of Terror and the Republic of Virtue. Speculators made fortunes in property by taking advantage of the government's severe monetary problems. Elaborate fashions, which had gone out of style because of their identification with the nobility, were worn again. Gambling and roulette became popular once more. Groups of "gilded youth"—sons of the wealthy, with long hair and rumpled clothes—took to the streets to insult former supporters of the Revolution.

The government of the Directory had to contend with political enemies from both ends of the political spectrum. On the right, royalists who dreamed of restoring the monarchy continued their agitation; some still toyed with violent means. On the left, Jacobin hopes of power were revived by continuing economic problems, especially the total collapse in the value of the *assignats*. Some radicals even went beyond earlier goals, especially Gracchus Babeuf, who sneered, "What is the French Revolution? An open war between patricians and plebeians, between rich and poor." Babeuf, who was appalled at the misery of the common people, wanted to abolish private property and eliminate private enterprise. His Conspiracy of Equals was crushed in 1796, and he was executed in 1797.

New elections in 1797 created even more uncertainty and instability. Battered by the left and right, unable to

Assembly of notables	1787
National Assembly (Constituent Assembly)	*1789–1791*
Meeting of Estates-General	May 5, 1789
Formation of National Assembly	June 17, 1789
Tennis Court Oath	June 20, 1789
Fall of the Bastille	July 14, 1789
Great Fear	Summer 1789
Abolition of feudalism	August 4, 1789
Declaration of the Rights of Man and the Citizen	August 26, 1789
Women's march to Versailles; king's return to Paris	October 5–6, 1789
Civil Constitution of the Clergy	July 12, 1790
Flight of the king	June 20–21, 1791
Declaration of Pillnitz	August 27, 1791
Legislative Assembly	*1791–1792*
France declares war on Austria	April 20, 1792
Attack on the royal palace	August 10, 1792
National Convention	*1792–1795*
Abolition of the monarchy	September 21, 1792
Execution of the king	January 21, 1793
Universal mobilization of the nation	August 23, 1793
Execution of Robespierre	July 28, 1794
Directory	*1795–1799*
Constitution of 1795 is adopted	August 22, 1795

find a definitive solution to the country's economic problems, and still carrying on the wars left from the Committee of Public Safety, the Directory increasingly relied on the military to maintain its power. This led to a coup d'état in 1799 in which the successful and popular general Napoleon Bonaparte was able to seize power.

The Age of Napoleon

Q **Focus Question:** Which aspects of the French Revolution did Napoleon preserve, and which did he destroy?

Napoleon dominated both French and European history from 1799 to 1815. The coup that brought him to power occurred exactly ten years after the outbreak of the French Revolution. In a sense, Napoleon brought the Revolution to an end, but he was also its child; he even called himself the Son of the Revolution. The French Revolution had made possible his rise first in the military and then to supreme power in France. Even beyond this,

Napoleon had once said, "I am the Revolution," and he never ceased to remind the French that they owed to him the preservation of all that was beneficial in the revolutionary program.

The Rise of Napoleon

Napoleon was born in Corsica in 1769, only a few months after France had annexed the island. The son of an Italian lawyer whose family stemmed from the Florentine nobility, Napoleone Buonaparte (to use his birth name) grew up in the countryside of Corsica, a willful and demanding child who nevertheless developed discipline, thriftiness, and loyalty to his family. His father's connections in France enabled him to study first at a school in the French town of Autun, where he learned to speak French, and then to obtain a royal scholarship to study at a military school. At that time, he changed his first name to the more French-sounding Napoleon (he did not change his last name to Bonaparte until 1796).

Napoleon's military education led to his commission in 1785 as a lieutenant, although he was not well liked by his fellow officers because he was short, spoke with an Italian accent, and had little money. For the next seven years, Napoleon spent much of his time reading the works of the philosophes, especially Rousseau, and educating himself in military matters by studying the campaigns of great military leaders from the past, including Alexander the Great, Charlemagne, and Frederick the Great. The French Revolution and the European war that followed broadened his sights and presented him with new opportunities.

Napoleon's Military Career Napoleon rose quickly through the ranks. In 1792, he became a captain and in the following year performed so well as an artillery commander in the capture of Toulon that he was promoted to the rank of brigadier general in 1794, when he was only twenty-five. In October 1795, he saved the National Convention from the Parisian mob, for which he was promoted to the rank of major general.

By this time, Napoleon had become a hero in some Parisian social circles, where he met Josephine de Beauharnais, widow of a guillotined general. Six years older than Napoleon, she lived a life of luxury, thanks to gifts from her influential male lovers. Napoleon fell deeply in love with her, married her in 1796, and remained committed to her for many years, despite her well-known affairs with other men.

Soon after his marriage, Napoleon was made commander of the French army in Italy (see the box on p. 594). There he turned a group of ill-disciplined soldiers into an effective fighting force and in a series of stunning victories defeated the Austrians and dictated peace to them in 1797.

Throughout his Italian campaign, Napoleon won the confidence of his men by his energy, charm, and ability to comprehend complex issues quickly and make decisions

NAPOLEON AND PSYCHOLOGICAL WARFARE

In 1796, at the age of twenty-seven, Napoleon Bonaparte was given command of the French army in Italy, where he won a series of stunning victories. His use of speed, deception, and surprise to overwhelm his opponents is well known. In this selection from a proclamation to his troops in Italy, Napoleon also appears to be a master of psychological warfare.

Napoleon Bonaparte, Proclamation to the French Troops in Italy (April 26, 1796)

Soldiers:

In a fortnight you have won six victories, taken twenty-one standards, fifty-five pieces of artillery, several strong positions, and conquered the richest part of Piedmont [in northern Italy]; you have captured 15,000 prisoners and killed or wounded more than 10,000 men.... You have won battles without cannon, crossed rivers without bridges, made forced marches without shoes, camped without brandy and often without bread. Soldiers of liberty, only republican troops could have endured what you have endured. Soldiers, you have our thanks! The grateful Patrie [nation] will owe its prosperity to you....

The two armies which but recently attacked you with audacity are fleeing before you in terror; the wicked men who laughed at your misery and rejoiced at the thought of the triumphs of your enemies are confounded and trembling.

But, soldiers, as yet you have done nothing compared with what remains to be done.... Undoubtedly the greatest obstacles have been overcome; but you still have battles to fight, cities to capture, rivers to cross. Is there one among you whose courage is abating? No.... All of you are consumed with a desire to extend the glory of the French people; all of you long to humiliate those arrogant kings who dare to contemplate placing us in fetters; all of you desire to dictate a glorious peace, one which will indemnify the Patrie for the immense sacrifices it has made; all of you wish to be able to say with pride as you return to your villages, "I was with the victorious army of Italy!"

Q What themes did Napoleon use to play on the emotions of his troops and inspire them to greater efforts? Do you think Napoleon believed these words? Why or why not?

---

rapidly. He was tough on his officers and drove them relentlessly. With rank-and-file soldiers, he took a different approach. He ate with them, provided good food and clothing, and charmed them with his words. "They knew I was their patron," Napoleon once remarked. Throughout the rest of his life, these qualities, combined with his keen intelligence, ease with words, and supreme confidence in himself, enabled Napoleon to influence people and win their firm support. Napoleon liked to see himself as a man of destiny and a great man who mastered luck. He once said:

> A consecutive series of great actions never is the result of chance and luck, it always is the product of planning and genius. Great men are rarely known to fail in their most perilous enterprises.... Is it because they are lucky that they become great? No, but being great, they have been able to master luck.[19]

Napoleon also saw himself as a military genius who had a "touch for leading, which could not be learned from books, nor by practice."

In 1797, Napoleon returned to France as a conquering hero and was given command of an army training to invade England. Believing that the French were unready for such an invasion, he proposed instead to strike indirectly at Britain by taking Egypt and threatening India, a major source of British wealth. But the British controlled the seas and by 1799 had cut off supplies from Napoleon's army in Egypt. Seeing no future in certain defeat, Napoleon did not hesitate to abandon his army and return to Paris, where he participated in the coup d'état that ultimately led to his virtual dictatorship of France. He was only thirty years old at the time.

Napoleon in Control With the coup of 1799, a new form of the Republic was proclaimed with a constitution that established a bicameral legislative assembly elected indirectly to reduce the role of elections. Executive power in the new government was vested in the hands of three consuls, although, as Article 42 of the constitution said, "the decision of the First Consul shall suffice." As first consul, Napoleon directly controlled the entire executive authority of government. He had overwhelming influence over the legislature, appointed members of the bureaucracy, controlled the army, and conducted foreign affairs. In 1802, Napoleon was made consul for life, and in 1804 he returned France to monarchy when he crowned himself Emperor Napoleon I. This step undoubtedly satisfied his enormous ego but also stabilized the regime and provided a permanence not possible in the consulate. The revolutionary era that had begun with an attempt to limit arbitrary government had ended with a government far more autocratic than the monarchy of the old regime. As his reign progressed and the demands of war increased, Napoleon's regime became ever more dictatorial.

The Domestic Policies of Emperor Napoleon

Napoleon often claimed that he had preserved the gains of the Revolution for the French people. The ideal of republican liberty had, of course, been destroyed by

Réunion des Musées Nationaux (Gérard Blot)/Art Resource, NY

Napoleon as a Young Officer. Napoleon rose quickly through the military ranks, being promoted to the rank of brigadier general at the age of twenty-five. This painting of Napoleon by the Romantic painter Baron Gros presents an idealized, heroic image of the young leader.

Napoleon's thinly disguised autocracy. But were revolutionary ideals maintained in other ways? An examination of his domestic policies will enable us to judge the truth or falsehood of Napoleon's assertion.

Napoleon and the Catholic Church   In 1801, Napoleon made peace with the oldest and most implacable enemy of the Revolution, the Catholic Church. Napoleon himself was devoid of any personal faith; he was an eighteenth-century rationalist who regarded religion at most as a convenience. In Egypt, he called himself a Muslim; in France, a Catholic. But Napoleon saw the necessity to come to terms with the Catholic Church in order to stabilize his regime. In 1800, he had declared to the clergy of Milan: "It is my firm intention that the Christian, Catholic, and Roman religion shall be preserved in its entirety. . . . No society can exist without morality; there is no good morality without religion. It is religion alone, therefore, that gives to the State a firm and durable support."[20]   Soon after making this statement, Napoleon opened negotiations with Pope Pius VII to reestablish the Catholic Church in France.

Both sides gained from the Concordat that Napoleon arranged with the pope in 1801. Although the pope gained the right to depose French bishops, this gave him little real control over the French Catholic Church, since the state retained the right to nominate bishops. The Catholic Church was also permitted to hold processions again and reopen the seminaries. But Napoleon gained more than the pope. Just by signing the Concordat, the pope acknowledged the accomplishments of the Revolution. Moreover, the pope agreed not to raise the question of the church lands confiscated during the Revolution. Contrary to the pope's wishes, Catholicism was not reestablished as the state religion; Napoleon was only willing to recognize Catholicism as the religion of a majority of the French people. The clergy would be paid by the state, but to avoid the appearance of a state church, Protestant ministers were also put on the state payroll. As a result of the Concordat, the Catholic Church was no longer an enemy of the French government. At the same time, the agreement reassured those who had acquired church lands during the Revolution that they would not be stripped of them, an assurance that obviously made them supporters of the Napoleonic regime.

A New Code of Laws   Before the Revolution, France did not have a single set of laws but rather some three hundred different legal systems. Efforts were made during the Revolution to codify laws for the entire nation, but it remained for Napoleon to bring the work to completion in seven codes, the most important of which was the Civil Code (also known as the Code Napoléon). This preserved most of the revolutionary gains by recognizing the principle of the equality of all citizens before the law, the right of individuals to choose their professions, religious toleration, and the abolition of serfdom and feudalism. Property rights continued to be carefully protected, while the interests of employers were safeguarded by outlawing trade unions and strikes. The Civil Code clearly reflected the revolutionary aspirations for a uniform legal system, legal equality, and protection of property and individuals.

But the rights of some people were strictly curtailed by the Civil Code. During the radical phase of the French Revolution, new laws had made divorce an easy process for both husbands and wives, restricted the rights of fathers over their children (they could no longer have their children put in prison arbitrarily), and allowed all children (including daughters) to inherit property equally. Napoleon's Civil Code undid most of this legislation. The control of fathers over their families was restored. Divorce was still allowed but was made more difficult for women to obtain. A wife caught in adultery, for example, could be divorced by her husband and even imprisoned. A husband, however, could only be accused of adultery if he moved his mistress into his home. Women were now "less equal than men" in other ways as well. When they married, their property was brought under the control of their husbands. In lawsuits, they were treated as minors, and their testimony was regarded as less reliable than that of men.

Réunion des Musées Nationaux/Art Resource, NY

The Coronation of Napoleon. In 1804, Napoleon restored monarchy to France when he crowned himself emperor. In the coronation scene painted by Jacques-Louis David, Napoleon is shown crowning the empress Josephine while the pope looks on. Shown seated in the box in the background is Napoleon's mother, even though she was not at the ceremony.

The French Bureaucracy Napoleon also worked on rationalizing the bureaucratic structure of France by developing a powerful centralized administrative machine. During the Revolution, the National Assembly had divided France into eighty-three departments and replaced the provincial estates, nobles, and *intendants* with self-governing assemblies. Napoleon kept the departments but eliminated the locally elected assemblies and instituted new officials, the most important of which were the **prefects.** As the central government's agents, appointed by the first consul (Napoleon), the prefects were responsible for supervising all aspects of local government. Yet they were not local men, and their careers depended on the central government.

As part of Napoleon's overhaul of the administrative system, tax collection became systematic and efficient (which it had never been under the old regime). Taxes were now collected by professional collectors employed by the state who dealt directly with each individual taxpayer. No tax exemptions due to birth, status, or special arrangement were granted. In principle, these changes had been introduced in 1789, but not until Napoleon did

they actually work. In 1802, the first consul proclaimed a balanced budget.

Administrative centralization required a bureaucracy of capable officials, and Napoleon worked hard to develop one. Early on, the regime showed its preference for experts and cared little whether that expertise had been acquired in royal or revolutionary bureaucracies. Promotion in civil or military offices was to be based not on rank or birth but only on demonstrated abilities. This was, of course, what many bourgeois had wanted before the Revolution. Napoleon, however, also created a new aristocracy based on merit in the state service. Napoleon created 3,263 nobles between 1808 and 1814; nearly 60 percent were military officers, and the remainder came from the upper ranks of the civil service or were other state and local officials. Socially, only 22 percent of Napoleon's aristocracy came from the nobility of the old regime; almost 60 percent were of bourgeois origin.

Napoleon's Growing Despotism In his domestic policies, then, Napoleon both destroyed and preserved aspects of the Revolution. Although equality was preserved in the law code and the opening of careers to talent, the creation of a new aristocracy, the strong protection accorded to property rights, and the use of conscription for the military make it clear that much equality had been lost. Liberty had been replaced by an initially benevolent despotism that grew increasingly arbitrary. Napoleon shut down sixty of France's seventy-three newspapers and insisted that all manuscripts be subjected to government scrutiny before they were published. Even the mail was opened by government police.

One prominent writer, Germaine de Staël (1766–1817), refused to accept Napoleon's growing despotism. Educated in Enlightenment ideas, she set up a salon in Paris that was a prominent intellectual center by 1800. She wrote novels and political works that denounced Napoleon's rule as tyrannical. Napoleon banned her books in France and exiled her to the German states, where she continued to write, although not without considerable anguish at being absent from France. "The universe is in France," she once wrote; "outside it there is nothing." After the overthrow of Napoleon, Germaine de Staël returned to her beloved Paris, where she died two years later.

Napoleon's Empire and the European Response

When Napoleon became consul in 1799, France was at war with a second European coalition of Russia, Great Britain, and Austria. Napoleon realized the need for a pause. He remarked to a Prussian diplomat "that the French Revolution is not finished so long as the scourge of war lasts. . . . I want peace, as much to settle the present French government as to save the world from chaos."[21] The peace he sought was achieved at Amiens in March 1802 and left France with new frontiers and a number of client territories from the North Sea to the Adriatic. But the peace did not last because the British and French both regarded it as temporary and had little intention of adhering to its terms.

In 1803, war was renewed with Britain, which was soon joined by Austria and Russia in the Third Coalition. At the Battle of Ulm in southern Germany in 1805, Napoleon surrounded an Austrian army, which quickly surrendered. Proceeding eastward from Ulm, Napoleon faced a large Russian army under Tsar Alexander I and some Austrian troops at Austerlitz. The combined allied forces outnumbered Napoleon's forces, but the tsar chose poor terrain for the battle, and Napoleon devastated the allied forces. Austria sued for peace, and Tsar Alexander took his remaining forces back to Russia.

At first, Prussia had refused to join the Third Coalition, but after Napoleon began to reorganize the German states, Prussia reversed course. Acting quickly, Napoleon crushed the Prussian forces in two battles at Jena and Auerstadt in October 1806 and then moved on to defeat the Russians, who had decided to reenter the fray, at Eylau and Friedland in June 1807. Napoleon's Grand Army had defeated the Continental members of the coalition, giving him the opportunity to create a new European order.

Napoleon's Grand Empire The Grand Empire was composed of three major parts: the French empire, a series of dependent states, and allied states (see Map 19.3). The French empire, the inner core of the Grand Empire, consisted of an enlarged France extending to the Rhine in the east and including the western half of Italy north of Rome. Dependent states included Spain, the Netherlands, the kingdom of Italy, the Swiss Republic, the Grand Duchy of Warsaw, and the Confederation of the Rhine (a union of all German states except Austria and Prussia). Allied states were those defeated by Napoleon and forced to join his struggle against Britain; they included Prussia, Austria, and Russia. Although the internal structure of the Grand Empire varied outside its inner core, Napoleon considered himself the leader of the whole: "Europe cannot be at rest except under a single head who will have kings for his officers, who will distribute his kingdom to his lieutenants."

Within his empire, Napoleon demanded obedience, in part because he needed a common front against the British and in part because his growing egotism required obedience to his will. But as a child of the Enlightenment and the Revolution, Napoleon also sought acceptance everywhere of certain revolutionary principles, including legal equality, religious toleration, and economic freedom. As he explained to his brother Jerome, shortly after making him king of the new German state of Westphalia:

> What the peoples of Germany desire most impatiently is that talented commoners should have the same right to your esteem and to public employments as the nobles, that any trace of serfdom and of an intermediate hierarchy between the sovereign and the lowest class of the people should be completely abolished. The benefits of the Code Napoléon, the publicity of judicial procedure, the creation of juries must be so many distinguishing marks of your monarchy. . . . What nation would wish to return under the arbitrary Prussian government once it had tasted the benefits of a wise and liberal administration? The peoples of Germany, the peoples of France, of Italy, of Spain all desire equality and liberal ideas. I have guided the affairs of Europe for many years now, and I have had occasion to convince myself that the buzzing of the privileged classes is contrary to the general opinion. Be a constitutional king.[22]

In the inner core and dependent states of his Grand Empire, Napoleon tried to destroy the old order. Nobility and clergy everywhere in these states lost their special privileges. He decreed equality of opportunity with offices open to talent, equality before the law, and religious toleration. This spread of French revolutionary principles was an important factor in the development of liberal traditions in these countries. These reforms have led

MAP 19.3 Napoleon's Grand Empire in 1810. Napoleon's Grand Army won a series of victories against Britain, Austria, Prussia, and Russia that gave the French emperor full or partial control over much of Europe by 1807.

Q On the Continent, what is the overall relationship between distance from France and degree of French control, and how can you account for this? 🌐 **View an animated version of this map or related maps at** academic.cengage.com/history/spielvogel

some historians to view Napoleon as the last of the enlightened absolutists.

The Problem of Great Britain Like Hitler 130 years later, Napoleon hoped that his Grand Empire would last for centuries; like Hitler's empire, it collapsed almost as rapidly as it had been formed. Two major reasons help explain this: the survival of Great Britain and the force of nationalism. Britain's survival was due primarily to its seapower. As long as Britain ruled the waves, it was almost invulnerable to military attack. Although Napoleon contemplated an invasion of England and even collected ships for it, he could not overcome the British navy's decisive defeat of a combined French-Spanish fleet at Trafalgar in 1805. Napoleon then turned to his **Continental System** to defeat Britain. Put into effect between 1806 and 1807, it attempted to prevent British goods from reaching the European continent in order to weaken Britain economically and destroy its capacity to wage war. But the Continental System failed. Allied states resented the ever-tightening French economic hegemony; some began to cheat and others to resist, thereby opening the door to British collaboration. New markets in the eastern Mediterranean and in Latin America also provided compensation for the British. Indeed, by 1810, British overseas exports were approaching record highs.

Nationalism A second important factor in the defeat of Napoleon was **nationalism.** This political creed had arisen

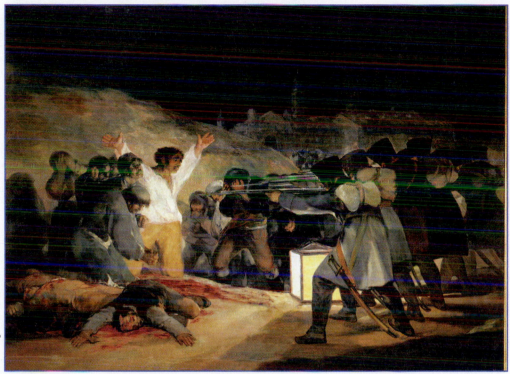

Francisco Goya, *The Third of May 1808*. After Napoleon imposed his brother Joseph on Spain as its king, the Spanish people revolted against his authority, and a series of riots broke out in Madrid. This painting by Francisco Goya shows the French response—a deliberate execution of Spanish citizens to frighten people into submission. Goya portrays the French troops as a firing squad, killing people (including a monk) reacting in terror. The peasant in the middle throws out his arms in a gesture reminiscent of crucifixion. Goya painted many scenes depicting the horrors of war in Napoleonic Spain.

during the French Revolution in the French people's emphasis on brotherhood (*fraternité*) and solidarity against other peoples. Nationalism involved the unique cultural identity of a people based on a common language, religion, and national symbols. The spirit of French nationalism had made possible the mass armies of the revolutionary and Napoleonic eras. But in spreading the principles of the French Revolution beyond France, Napoleon inadvertently brought about a spread of nationalism as well. The French aroused nationalism in two ways: by making themselves hated oppressors, and thus arousing the patriotism of others in opposition to French nationalism, and by showing the people of Europe what nationalism was and what a nation in arms could do. The lesson was not lost on other peoples and rulers. A Spanish uprising against Napoleon's rule, aided by British support, kept a French force of 200,000 pinned down for years.

Nationalist movements also arose in the German states, where a number of intellectuals advocated a cultural nationalism based on the unity of the German people. The philosopher Johann Gottlieb Fichte (1762–1814), who had at first welcomed the French Revolution for freeing the human spirit, soon became a proponent of a German national spirit radically different from that of France. Although philosophical voices like Fichte's did little to overthrow the French, they did awaken a dream of German nationalism that would bear fruit later in the nineteenth century.

In Prussia, feeling against Napoleon led to a serious reform of the old order that had been so easily crushed by the French emperor. As one Prussian officer put it, the Prussians must learn from the French example and "place their entire national energies in opposition to the enemy." Under the direction of Baron Heinrich von Stein and later Prince Karl von Hardenberg, Prussia embarked on a series of political and military reforms, including the abolition of serfdom, election of city councils, and creation of a larger standing army. Prussia's reforms, instituted as a response to Napoleon, enabled it to again play an important role in European affairs.

The Fall of Napoleon

Napoleon once said, "If I had experienced pleasure, I might have rested; but the peril was always in front of me, and the day's victory was always forgotten in the preoccupation with the necessity of winning a new victory on the morrow."[23] Never at rest, Napoleon decided in 1812 to invade Russia. It was the beginning of his downfall, but Russia's defection from the Continental System had left him with little choice. Although aware of the risks in invading such a large country, Napoleon also knew that if the Russians were allowed to challenge the Continental System unopposed, others would soon follow suit. In June 1812, Napoleon's Grand Army of more than 600,000 men entered Russia. Napoleon's hopes for victory depended on quickly meeting and defeating the Russian armies, but the Russian forces refused to give battle and retreated hundreds of miles while torching their own villages and countryside to prevent Napoleon's army from finding food and forage. Heat and disease also took their toll of the army, and the vast space of Russian territory led many troops to desert. When the Russians did stop to fight at Borodino, Napoleon's forces won an indecisive and costly victory. Forty-five thousand Russian troops were killed; the French lost 30,000 men, but they had no replacements nearby. When the remaining troops of the Grand Army arrived in Moscow, they found the city ablaze. Lacking food and supplies, Napoleon abandoned Moscow late in October and made the "Great Retreat" across Russia in terrible winter conditions. Only 40,000 troops managed to straggle back to Poland in January 1813. This military disaster then led to a war of liberation all over Europe, culminating in Napoleon's defeat in April 1814.

The defeated emperor of the French was allowed to play ruler on the island of Elba, off the coast of Tuscany, while the Bourbon monarchy was restored to France in the person of Louis XVIII, brother of the executed king. But the new king had little support, and Napoleon, bored on Elba, slipped back into France. When troops were sent to capture him, Napoleon opened his coat and addressed them: "Soldiers of the fifth regiment, I am your Emperor.... If there is a man among you would kill his Emperor, here I am!" No one fired a shot. Shouting "Vive l'Empéreur! Vive l'Empéreur," the

CHRONOLOGY The Napoleonic Era, 1799–1815	
Napoleon as first consul	1799–1804
Concordat with Catholic Church	1801
Peace of Amiens	1802
Emperor Napoleon I	1804–1815
Battle of Ulm (defeat of Austria)	1805
Battle of Austerlitz (defeat of Russia)	1805
Battle of Trafalgar (naval defeat of Napoleon's forces)	1805
Battles of Jena and Auerstadt (defeat of Prussia)	1806
Continental System established	1806
Battles of Eylau and Friedland (defeat of Russia)	1807
Invasion of Russia	1812
War of liberation	1813–1814
Exile to Elba	1814
Battle of Waterloo; exile to Saint Helena	1815
Death of Napoleon	1821

troops went over to his side, and Napoleon entered Paris in triumph on March 20, 1815.

The powers that had defeated him pledged once more to fight this person they called the "Enemy and Disturber of the Tranquility of the World." Having decided to strike first at his enemies, Napoleon raised yet another army and moved to attack the nearest allied forces stationed in Belgium. At Waterloo on June 18, Napoleon met a combined British and Prussian army under the duke of Wellington and suffered a bloody defeat. This time, the victorious allies exiled him to Saint Helena, a small, forsaken island in the South Atlantic. Only Napoleon's memory would continue to haunt French political life.

CONCLUSION

The late eighteenth century was a time of dramatic political transformation. Revolutionary upheavals, beginning in North America and continuing in France, produced movements for political liberty and equality. The documents created by these revolutions, the Declaration of Independence and the Declaration of the Rights of Man and the Citizen, embodied the fundamental ideas of the Enlightenment and set forth a liberal political agenda based on a belief in popular sovereignty—the people as the source of political power—and the principles of liberty and equality. Liberty, frequently limited in practice, meant, in theory, freedom from arbitrary power as well as the freedom to think, write, and worship as one chose. Equality meant equality in rights and equality of opportunity based on talent rather than birth. In practice, equality remained limited; men who owned property had greater opportunities for voting and officeholding, and there was certainly no equality between men and women.

The leaders of France's liberal revolution, achieved between 1789 and 1791, were men of property, both bourgeois and noble, but they were assisted by commoners, both sans-culottes and peasants. Yet the liberal revolution, despite the hopes of the men of property, was not the end of the Revolution. The decision of the revolutionaries to go to war "revolutionized the Revolution," opening the door to a more radical, democratic, and violent stage. The excesses of the Reign of Terror, however, led to a reaction, first under the Directory and then under

Napoleon, when men of property were willing to give up liberty in exchange for order, security, and economic opportunity. Napoleon, while diminishing freedom by establishing order and centralizing the government, shrewdly preserved equality of rights and the opening of careers to talent and integrated the bourgeoisie and old nobility into a new elite of property owners. For despite the anti-aristocratic revolutionary rhetoric and the loss of their privileges, nobles remained important landowners. Though the nobles lost some of their lands during the Revolution, they were still the largest proprietors in the early 1800s. The great gainers from the redistribution of clerical and noble property, however, had been the bourgeoisie, who also gained dramatically when important government and military positions were opened to men of talent. After 1800, an elite group of property owners, both noble and middle class, dominated French society.

The French Revolution defined the modern revolutionary concept. No one had foreseen or consciously planned the upheaval that began in 1789, but after 1789, "revolutionaries" knew that mass uprisings could succeed in overthrowing unwanted governments. The French Revolution became the classical political and social model for revolution. At the same time, the liberal and national political ideals created by the Revolution and spread through Europe by Napoleon's conquests dominated the political landscape of the nineteenth and early twentieth centuries.

TIMELINE

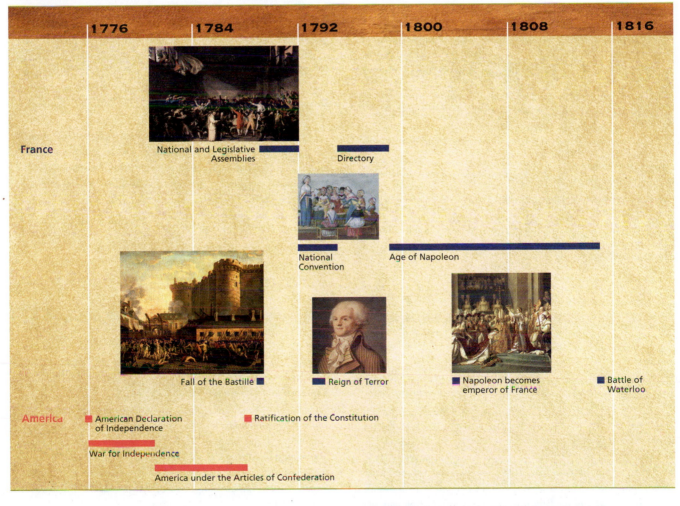

| | 1776 | 1784 | 1792 | 1800 | 1808 | 1816 |

France
National and Legislative Assemblies
Directory
National Convention
Age of Napoleon
Fall of the Bastille ■
■ Reign of Terror
■ Napoleon becomes emperor of France
■ Battle of Waterloo

America
■ American Declaration of Independence
■ Ratification of the Constitution
War for Independence
America under the Articles of Confederation

NOTES

1. Quoted in R. R. Palmer, *The Age of the Democratic Revolutions* (Princeton, N.J., 1959), vol. 1, p. 239.
2. Quoted in ibid., p. 242.
3. Quoted in O. J. Hufton, "Toward an Understanding of the Poor of Eighteenth-Century France," in J. F. Bosher, ed., *French Government and Society, 1500–1850* (London, 1973), p. 152.
4. Arthur Young, *Travels in France During the Years 1787, 1788, and 1789* (Cambridge, 1929), p. 23.

5. Quoted in D. M. G. Sutherland, *France, 1789–1815: Revolution and Counter-Revolution* (New York, 1986), p. 74.

6. Quoted in William Doyle, *The Oxford History of the French Revolution* (Oxford, 1989), p. 156.

7. Quoted in ibid., p. 184.

8. Quoted in J. Hardman, ed., *French Revolution Documents* (Oxford, 1973), vol. 2, p. 23.

9. Quoted in W. Scott, *Terror and Repression in Revolutionary Marseilles* (London, 1973), p. 84.

10. Quoted in H. Morse Stephens, *The Principal Speeches of the Statesmen and Orators of the French Revolution* (Oxford, 1892), vol. 2, p. 189.

11. Quoted in Leo Gershoy, *The Era of the French Revolution* (Princeton, N.J., 1957), p. 157.

12. Quoted in J. M. Thompson, ed., *French Revolution Documents* (Oxford, 1933), pp. 258–259.

13. Quoted in Doyle, *Oxford History of the French Revolution,* p. 254.

14. Quoted in R. R. Palmer, *Twelve Who Ruled* (New York, 1965), p. 75.

15. Quoted in Darline Gay Levy, Harriet Branson Applewhite, and Mary Durham Johnson, eds., *Women in Revolutionary Paris, 1789–1795* (Urbana, Ill., 1979), p. 132.

16. Ibid., pp. 219–220.

17. Quoted in Elizabeth G. Sledziewski, "The French Revolution as the Turning Point," in Geneviève Fraisse and Michelle Perrot, eds., *A History of Women in the West* (Cambridge, 1993), vol. 4, p. 39.

18. Quoted in François Furet and Mona Ozouf, *A Critical Dictionary of the French Revolution,* trans. Arthur Goldhammer (Cambridge, Mass., 1989), p. 545.

19. Quoted in J. Christopher Herold, ed., *The Mind of Napoleon* (New York, 1955), p. 43.

20. Quoted in Felix Markham, *Napoleon* (New York, 1963), pp. 92–93.

21. Quoted in Doyle, *Oxford History of the French Revolution,* p. 381.

22. Quoted in Herold, ed., *The Mind of Napoleon,* pp. 74–75.

23. Quoted in Steven Englund, *Napoleon: A Political Life* (New York, 2004), p. 285.

SUGGESTIONS FOR FURTHER READING

General Works   A well-written introduction to the French Revolution can be found in **W. Doyle, *The Oxford History of the French Revolution,*** 2d ed. (Oxford, 2003). On the entire revolutionary and Napoleonic eras, see **O. Connelly, *The French Revolution and Napoleonic Era,*** 3d ed. (Fort Worth, Tex., 2000). Two brief works are **A. Forrest, *The French Revolution*** (Oxford, 1995), and **J. D. Popkin et al., *A Short History of the French Revolution,*** 4th ed. (Upper Saddle River, N.J., 2005). Three comprehensive reference works are **S. F. Scott and B. Rothaus, eds., *Historical Dictionary of the French Revolution,*** 2 vols. (Westport, Conn., 1985); **F. Furet and M. Ozouf, *A Critical Dictionary of the French Revolution,*** trans. **A. Goldhammer** (Cambridge, Mass., 1989); and **O. Connelly et al., *Historical Dictionary of Napoleonic France, 1799–1815*** (Westport, Conn., 1985). See also **G. Kates, ed., *The French Revolution,*** 2d ed. (London, 2006).

Early Years of the Revolution   The origins of the French Revolution are examined in **W. Doyle, *Origins of the French Revolution,*** 3d ed. (Oxford, 1999), and **P. R. Cambell, ed.,** *Origins of the French Revolution* (New York, 2006), a collection of essays. See also **R. Chartier, *The Cultural Origins of the French Revolution*** (Durham, N.C., 1991). On the early years of the Revolution, see **M. Kennedy, *The Jacobin Clubs in the French Revolution: The First Years*** (Princeton, N.J., 1982); **N. Hampson, *Prelude to Terror*** (Oxford, 1988); **T. Tackett, *Becoming a Revolutionary*** (Princeton, N.J., 1996), on the deputies to the National Assembly; and **J. Markoff, *The Abolition of Feudalism: Peasants, Lords, and Legislators in the French Revolution*** (University Park, Pa., 1996). For interesting insight into Louis XVI and French society, see **T. Tackett, *When the King Took Flight*** (Cambridge, Mass., 2003).

Radical Revolution   Important works on the radical stage of the French Revolution include **D. Andress, *The Terror: The Merciless War for Freedom in Revolutionary France*** (New York, 2005); **A. Soboul, *The Sans-Culottes*** (New York, 1972); **R. R. Palmer, *Twelve Who Ruled*** (New York, 1965), a classic; and **R. Cobb, *The People's Armies*** (London, 1987). For a biography of Robespierre, one of the leading figures of this period, see **D. P. Jordan, *Revolutionary Career of Maximilien Robespierre*** (Chicago, 1989), and **R. Scurr, *Fatal Purity: Robespierre and the French Revolution*** (New York, 2006). The importance of the revolutionary wars in the radical stage of the Revolution is underscored in **T. C. W. Blanning, *The French Revolutionary Wars, 1787–1802*** (New York, 1996). On the Directory, see **M. Lyons, *France Under the Directory*** (Cambridge, 1975), and **R. B. Rose, *Gracchus Babeuf*** (Stanford, Calif., 1978).

Religion and Women   The religious history of the French Revolution is covered in **J. McManners, *The French Revolution and the Church*** (London, 1969). On the role of women in revolutionary France, see **O. J. Hufton, *Women and the Limits of Citizenship in the French Revolution*** (Toronto, 1992); **J. Landes, *Women and the Public Sphere in the Age of the French Revolution*** (Ithaca, N.Y., 1988); and the essays in **G. Fraisse and M. Perrot, eds., *A History of Women in the West,*** vol. 4 (Cambridge, Mass., 1993).

Napoleon   The best biography of Napoleon is **S. Englund, *Napoleon: A Political Life*** (New York, 2004). Also valuable are **G. J. Ellis, *Napoleon*** (New York, 1997); **M. Lyons, *Napoleon Bonaparte and the Legacy of the French Revolution*** (New York, 1994); and the massive biographies by **F. J. McLynn, *Napoleon: A Biography*** (London, 1997), and **A. Schom, *Napoleon Bonaparte*** (New York, 1997). See also **I. Woloch, *Napoleon and His Collaborators: The Making of a Dictatorship*** (New York, 2002), and **A. I. Grab, *Napoleon and the Transformation of Europe*** (New York, 2003), on Napoleon's Grand Empire. On Napoleon's wars, see **O. Connelly, *Blundering to Glory: Napoleon's Military Campaigns,*** 3d ed. (Lanham, Md., 2006), and **D. A. Bell, *The First Total War: Napoleon's Europe and the Birth of Warfare as We Know It*** (Boston, 2007).

American Revolution   A history of the revolutionary era in America can be found in **S. Conway, *The War of American Independence, 1775–1783*** (New York, 1995), and **C. Bonwick, *The American Revolution*** (Charlottesville, Va., 1991). The importance of ideology is treated in **G. Wood, *The Radicalism of the American Revolution*** (New York, 1992).

CengageNOW is an integrated online suite of services and resources with proven ease of use and efficient paths to success, delivering the results you want—NOW!

academic.cengage.com/login/

Enter CengageNOW using the access card that is available with *Western Civilization*. CengageNOW will assist you in understanding the content in this chapter with lesson plans generated for your needs. In addition, you can read the following documents, and many more, online:

Edmund Burke, *Reflections on the Revolution in France*
Thomas Paine, *Common Sense*
King George III, letter on loss of colonies
James Madison, selected Federalist Papers

CHAPTER 20
THE INDUSTRIAL REVOLUTION AND ITS IMPACT ON EUROPEAN SOCIETY

Power looms in an English textile factory

CHAPTER OUTLINE AND FOCUS QUESTIONS

The Industrial Revolution in Great Britain

Q Why was Great Britain the first state to have an Industrial Revolution? Why did it happen in Britain when it did? What were the basic features of the new industrial system created by the Industrial Revolution?

The Spread of Industrialization

Q How did the Industrial Revolution spread from Great Britain to the Continent and the United States, and how did industrialization in those areas differ from British industrialization?

The Social Impact of the Industrial Revolution

Q What effects did the Industrial Revolution have on urban life, social classes, family life, and standards of living? What were working conditions like in the early decades of the Industrial Revolution, and what efforts were made to improve them?

CRITICAL THINKING

Q What role did government and trade unions play in the industrial development of the Western world? Who helped the workers the most?

THE FRENCH REVOLUTION dramatically and quickly altered the political structure of France, and the Napoleonic conquests spread many of the revolutionary principles in an equally rapid and stunning fashion to other parts of Europe. During the late eighteenth and early nineteenth centuries, another revolution—an industrial one—was transforming the economic and social structure of Europe, although more slowly and less dramatically.

The Industrial Revolution caused a quantum leap in industrial production. New sources of energy and power, especially coal and steam, replaced wind and water to build and run machines that dramatically decreased the use of human and animal labor and at the same time increased productivity. This in turn called for new ways of organizing human labor to maximize the benefits and profits from the new machines; factories replaced workshops and home workrooms. Many early factories were dreadful places with difficult working conditions. Reformers, appalled at these conditions, were especially critical of the treatment of married women. One reported, "We have repeatedly seen married females, in the last stage of pregnancy, slaving from morning to night beside these never-tiring machines, and when . . . they were obliged to sit down to take a moment's ease, and being seen by the manager, were fined for the offense." But there were also examples of well-run factories. William Cobbett described one in Manchester in 1830: "In this room, which is lighted in the most convenient and beautiful manner, there were five hundred pairs of looms at work, and five hundred persons attending those looms; and, owing to the goodness of the masters, the whole looking healthy and well-dressed."

During the Industrial Revolution, Europe experienced a shift from a traditional, labor-intensive economy based on farming and handicrafts to a more capital-intensive economy based on manufacturing by machines, specialized labor, and industrial factories. Although the Industrial Revolution took decades to spread, it was truly revolutionary in the way it fundamentally changed Europeans, their society, and their relationship to the rest of the world. The development of large factories encouraged mass movements of people from the countryside to urban areas, where impersonal coexistence replaced the traditional intimacy of rural life. Higher levels of productivity led to a search for new sources of raw materials, new consumption patterns, and a revolution in transportation that allowed raw materials and finished products to be moved quickly around the world. The creation of a wealthy industrial middle class and a huge industrial working class (or proletariat) substantially transformed traditional social relationships. ◇

The Industrial Revolution in Great Britain

Q **Focus Questions:** Why was Great Britain the first state to have an Industrial Revolution? Why did it happen in Britain when it did? What were the basic features of the new industrial system created by the Industrial Revolution?

Although the Industrial Revolution evolved over a long period of time, historians generally agree that it began in Britain sometime after 1750. By 1850, the Industrial Revolution had made Great Britain the wealthiest country in the world; it had also spread to the European continent and the New World. In another fifty years, both Germany and the United States would surpass Britain in industrial production.

Origins

A number of factors or conditions coalesced in Britain to produce the first Industrial Revolution. One of these was the **agricultural revolution** of the eighteenth century. The changes in the methods of farming and stock breeding that characterized this agricultural transformation led to a significant increase in food production. British agriculture could now feed more people at lower prices with less labor. Unlike the rest of Europe, even ordinary British families did not have to use most of their income to buy food, giving them the potential to purchase manufactured goods. At the same time, rapid population growth in the second half of the eighteenth century provided a pool of surplus labor for the new factories of the emerging British industry. Rural workers in cottage industries also provided a potential labor force for industrial enterprises.

Supply of Capital Britain had a ready supply of **capital** for investment in the new industrial machines and the factories that were needed to house them. In addition to profits from trade and cottage industry, Britain possessed an effective central bank and well-developed, flexible credit facilities. Nowhere in Europe were people so accustomed to using paper instruments to facilitate capital transactions. Many early factory owners were merchants and entrepreneurs who had profited from the eighteenth-century cottage industry. Of 110 cotton-spinning mills in operation in the area known as the Midlands between 1769 and 1800, fully 62 were established by hosiers, drapers, mercers, and others involved in some fashion in the cottage textile industry.

Early Industrial Entrepreneurs But capital is only part of the story. Britain had a fair number of individuals who were interested in making profits if the opportunity presented itself (see the box on p. 606). The British were a people, as one historian has said, "fascinated by wealth and commerce, collectively and individually." No doubt the English revolutions of the seventeenth century had helped create an environment in Britain, unlike that of the absolutist states on the Continent, where political power rested in the hands of a progressive group of people who favored innovation in economic matters.

Nevertheless, these early industrial entrepreneurs faced considerable financial hazards. Fortunes were made quickly and lost just as quickly. The structure of early firms was fluid. An individual or family proprietorship was the usual mode of operation, but entrepreneurs also brought in friends to help—and just as easily jettisoned them. John Marshall, who made money in flax spinning, threw his partners out: "As they could neither of them be of any further use, I released them from the firm and took the whole upon myself."[1]

Mineral Resources Britain had ample supplies of important mineral resources, such as coal and iron ore, needed in the manufacturing process. Britain was also small, and the relatively short distances made transportation nonproblematic. In addition to nature's provision of abundant rivers, from the mid-seventeenth century onward, both private and public investment poured into the construction of new roads, bridges, and, beginning in the 1750s and 1760s, canals. By 1780, roads, rivers, and canals linked the major industrial centers of the North, the Midlands, London, and the Atlantic. Unlike the Continental countries, Britain had no internal customs barriers to hinder domestic trade.

THE TRAITS OF THE BRITISH INDUSTRIAL ENTREPRENEUR

Richard Arkwright (1732–1792), inventor of a spinning frame and founder of cotton factories, was a good example of the successful entrepreneur in the early Industrial Revolution in Britain. In this selection, Edward Baines, writing in 1835, discusses the traits that explain the success of Arkwright and presumably other British entrepreneurs.

Edward Baines, *The History of the Cotton Manufacture in Great Britain*

Richard Arkwright rose by the force of his natural talents from a very humble condition in society. He was born at Preston on the 23rd of December, 1732, of poor parents: being the youngest of thirteen children, his parents could only afford to give him an education of the humblest kind, and he was scarcely able to write. He was brought up to the trade of a barber at Kirkham and Preston, and established himself in that business at Bolton in the year 1760. Having become possessed of a chemical process for dyeing human hair, which in that day (when wigs were universal) was of considerable value, he traveled about collecting hair, and again disposing of it when dyed. In 1761, he married a wife from Leigh, and the connections he thus formed in that town are supposed to have afterwards brought him acquainted with Highs's experiments in making spinning machines. He himself manifested a strong bent for experiments in mathematics, which he is stated to have followed with so much devotedness as to have neglected his business and injured his circumstances. His natural disposition was ardent, enterprising, and stubbornly persevering: his mind was as coarse as it was bold and active, and his manners were rough and unpleasing....

The most marked traits in the character of Arkwright were his wonderful ardor, energy, and perseverance. He commonly laboured in his multifarious concerns from five o'clock in the morning till nine at night; and when considerably more than fifty years of age,—feeling that the defects of his education placed him under great difficulty and inconvenience in conducting his correspondence, and in the general management of his business,—he encroached upon his sleep, in order to gain an hour each day to learn English grammar, and another hour to improve his writing and orthography [spelling]! He was impatient of whatever interfered with his favorite pursuits; and the fact is too strikingly characteristic not to be mentioned, that he separated from his wife not many years after their marriage, because she, convinced that he would starve his family [because of the impractical nature of his schemes], broke some of his experimental models of machinery. Arkwright was a severe economist of time; and, that he might not waste a moment, he generally traveled with four horses, and at a very rapid speed. His concerns in Derbyshire, Lancashire, and Scotland were so extensive and numerous, as to [show] at once his astonishing power of transacting business and his all grasping spirit. In many of these he had partners, but he generally managed in such a way, that, whoever lost, he himself was a gainer.

Q *As seen in the life of Richard Arkwright, what traits did Edward Baines think were crucial to being a successful entrepreneur? To what extent are these still considered the necessary traits for a successful entrepreneur?*

Role of Government Britain's government also played a significant role in the process of industrialization. Parliament contributed to the favorable business climate by providing a stable government and passing laws that protected private property. Moreover, Britain was remarkable for the freedom it provided for private enterprise. It placed fewer restrictions on private entrepreneurs than any other European state.

Markets Finally, a supply of markets gave British industrialists a ready outlet for their manufactured goods. British exports quadrupled from 1660 to 1760. In the course of its eighteenth-century wars and conquests, Great Britain had developed a vast colonial empire at the expense of its leading Continental rivals, the Dutch Republic and France. Britain also possessed a well-developed merchant marine that was able to transport goods anywhere in the world. A crucial factor in Britain's successful industrialization was the ability to produce cheaply the articles most in demand abroad. And the best markets abroad were not in Europe, where countries protected their own incipient industries, but in the Americas, Africa, and the East, where people wanted sturdy, inexpensive clothes rather than costly, highly finished luxury items. Britain's machine-produced textiles fulfilled that demand. Nor should we overlook the British domestic market. Britain had the highest standard of living in Europe and a rapidly growing population. As Daniel Defoe noted already in 1728:

> For the rest, we see their Houses and Lodgings tolerably furnished, at least stuff'd well with useful and necessary household Goods: Even those we call poor People, Journeymen, working and Pains-taking People do thus; they lye warm, live in Plenty, work hard, and know no Want. These are the People that carry off the Gross of your Consumption; 'tis for these your Markets are kept open late on Saturday nights; because they usually receive their Week's Wages late.... In a Word, these are the Life of our whole Commerce, and all by their Multitude: Their Numbers are not Hundreds or Thousands, or Hundreds of Thousands, but Millions;... by their Wages they are able to live plentifully, and it is by their expensive, generous, free way of living, that the Home Consumption is rais'd to such a Bulk, as well of our own, as of foreign Production.[2]

This demand from both domestic and foreign markets and the inability of the old system to fulfill it led entrepreneurs to seek and adopt the new methods of manufacturing that a series of inventions provided. In so doing, these individuals initiated the Industrial Revolution.

Technological Changes and New Forms of Industrial Organization

In the 1770s and 1780s, the cotton textile industry took the first major step toward the Industrial Revolution with the creation of the modern factory.

The Cotton Industry   Already in the eighteenth century, Great Britain had surged ahead in the production of cheap cotton goods using the traditional methods of the cottage industry. The development of the flying shuttle had sped the process of weaving on a loom and enabled weavers to double their output. This caused shortages of yarn, however, until James Hargreaves's spinning jenny, perfected by 1768, enabled spinners to produce yarn in greater quantities. Richard Arkwright's water frame spinning machine, powered by water or horse, and Samuel Crompton's so-called mule, which combined aspects of the water frame and the spinning jenny, increased yarn production even more. Edmund Cartwright's power loom, invented in 1787, allowed the weaving of cloth to catch up with the spinning of yarn. Even then, early power looms were grossly inefficient, enabling home-based hand-loom weavers to continue to prosper, at least until the mid-1820s. After that, they were gradually replaced by the new machines. In 1813, there were 2,400 power looms in operation in Great Britain; they numbered 14,150 in 1820, 100,000 in 1833, and 250,000 by 1850. In the 1820s, there were still 250,000 hand-loom weavers in Britain; by 1860, only 3,000 were left.

The water frame, Crompton's mule, and power looms presented new opportunities to entrepreneurs. It was much more efficient to bring workers to the machines and organize their labor collectively in factories located next to rivers and streams, the sources of power for many of these early machines, than to leave the workers dispersed in their cottages. The concentration of labor in the new factories also brought the laborers and their families to live in the new towns that rapidly grew up around the factories.

The early devices used to speed up the processes of spinning and weaving were the products of weavers and spinners—in effect, of artisan tinkerers. But the subsequent expansion of the cotton industry and the ongoing demand for even more cotton goods created additional pressure for new and more complicated technology. The invention that pushed the cotton industry to even greater heights of productivity was the steam engine.

The Steam Engine   The steam engine revolutionized the production of cotton goods and allowed the factory system to spread to other areas of production, thereby securing whole new industries. The steam engine thus ensured the triumph of the Industrial Revolution.

In the 1760s, a Scottish engineer, James Watt (1736–1819), created an engine powered by steam that could pump water from mines three times as quickly as previous engines. In 1782, Watt enlarged the possibilities of the steam engine when he developed a rotary engine that could turn a shaft and thus drive machinery. Steam power could now be applied to spinning and weaving cotton, and before long, cotton mills using steam engines were multiplying across Britain. Because steam engines were fired by coal, they did not need to be located near rivers; entrepreneurs now had greater flexibility in their choice of location.

The new boost given to cotton textile production by technological changes became readily apparent. In 1760, Britain had imported 2.5 million pounds of raw cotton, which was farmed out to cottage industries. In 1787, the British imported 22 million pounds of cotton; most of it was spun on machines, some powered by water in large mills. By 1840, fully 366 million pounds of cotton—now Britain's most important product in value—were imported. By this time, most cotton industry employees worked in factories. The cheapest labor in India could not compete in quality or quantity with Britain. British cotton goods sold everywhere in the world. And in Britain itself, cheap cotton cloth made it possible for millions of poor people to wear undergarments, long a luxury of the rich, who could afford expensive linen cloth. Cotton clothing was tough, comfortable, cheap, and easily washable.

A Boulton and Watt Steam Engine.   Encouraged by his business partner, Matthew Boulton, James Watt developed the first genuine steam engine. Pictured here is a typical Boulton and Watt engine. Steam pressure in the cylinder on the left drives the beam upward and sets the flywheel in motion.

The steam engine proved indispensable. Unlike horses, the steam engine was a tireless source of power and depended for fuel on a substance—coal—that seemed unlimited in quantity. The popular saying that "steam is an Englishman" had real significance by 1850. The success of the steam engine led to a need for more coal and an expansion in coal production; between 1815 and 1850, the output of coal quadrupled. In turn, new processes using coal furthered the development of the iron industry.

The Iron Industry   The British iron industry was radically transformed during the Industrial Revolution. Britain had large resources of iron ore, but at the beginning of the eighteenth century, the basic process of producing iron had changed little since the Middle Ages and still depended heavily on charcoal. In the early eighteenth century, new methods of smelting iron ore to produce cast iron were devised, based on the use of coke derived from coal. Still, a better quality of iron was not possible until the 1780s, when Henry Cort developed a system called puddling in which coke was used to burn away impurities in pig iron to produce an iron of high quality. A boom then ensued in the British iron industry. In 1740, Britain produced 17,000 tons of iron; in the 1780s, almost 70,000 tons; by the 1840s, over 2 million tons; and by 1852, almost 3 million tons, more than the rest of the world combined.

The development of the iron industry was in many ways a response to the demand for the new machines. The high-quality wrought iron produced by the Cort process made it the most widely used metal until the production of cheaper steel in the 1860s. The growing supply of less costly metal encouraged the use of machinery in other industries, most noticeably in new means of transportation.

A Revolution in Transportation   The eighteenth century had witnessed an expansion of transportation facilities in Britain as entrepreneurs realized the need for more efficient means of moving resources and goods. Turnpike trusts constructed new roads, and between 1760 and 1830, a network of canals was built. But both roads and canals were soon overtaken by a new form of transportation that dazzled people with its promise. To many economic historians, railroads were the "most important single factor in promoting European economic progress in the 1830s and 1840s." Again, Britain was the leader in the revolution.

The railways got their start in mining operations in Germany as early as 1500 and in British coal mines after 1600, where small handcarts filled with coal were pushed along parallel wooden rails. The rails reduced friction, enabling horses to haul more substantial loads. By 1700, some entrepreneurs began to replace wooden rails with cast-iron rails, and by the early nineteenth century, railways—still dependent on horsepower—were common in British mining and industrial districts. The development of the steam engine led to a radical transformation of the railways.

In 1804, Richard Trevithick pioneered the first steam-powered locomotive on an industrial rail line in southern Wales. It pulled 10 tons of ore and seventy people at 5 miles per hour. Better locomotives soon followed. The engines built by George Stephenson and his son proved superior, and it was in their workshops in Newcastle-upon-Tyne that the locomotives for the first modern railways in Britain were built. George Stephenson's *Rocket* was used on the first public railway line, which opened in 1830, extending 32 miles from Liverpool to Manchester. *Rocket* sped along at 16 miles per hour. Within twenty years, locomotives had reached 50 miles per hour, an incredible speed to contemporary passengers. During the same period, new companies were formed to build additional railroads as the infant industry proved successful not only technically but also financially. In 1840, Britain had almost 2,000 miles of railroads; by 1850, 6,000 miles of railroad track crisscrossed much of the country (see Map 20.1).

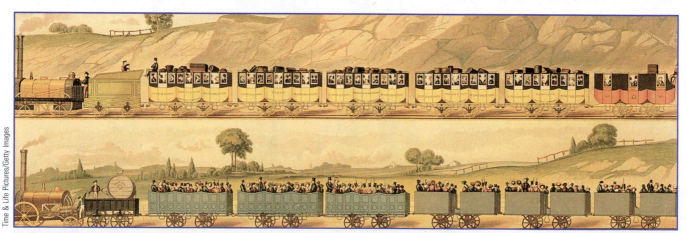

Time & Life Pictures/Getty Images

Railroad Line from Liverpool to Manchester.   The railroad line from Liverpool to Manchester, opened in 1830, relied on steam locomotives. As is evident in this illustration, carrying passengers was the railroad's main business. First-class passengers rode in covered cars; second- and third-class passengers, in open cars.

MAP 20.1 The Industrial Revolution in Britain by 1850. The Industrial Revolution began in the mid-1700s. Increased food production, rapid population growth, higher incomes, plentiful capital, solid banking and financial institutions, an abundance of mineral resources, and easy transport all furthered the process, making Britain the world's wealthiest country by 1850.

Q How well does the railroad system connect important British industrial areas? View an animated version of this map or related maps at academic.cengage.com/history/spielvogel

The railroad contributed significantly to the maturing of the Industrial Revolution. The railroad's demands for coal and iron furthered the growth of those industries. British supremacy in civil and mechanical engineering, so evident after 1840, was in large part based on the skills acquired in railway building. The huge capital demands necessary for railway construction encouraged a whole new group of middle-class investors to invest their money in joint-stock companies (see "Limitations to Industrialization" later in this chapter). Railway construction created new job opportunities, especially for farm laborers and peasants, who had long been accustomed to finding work outside their local villages. Perhaps most important, a cheaper and faster means of transportation had a rippling effect on the growth of an industrial economy. By reducing the price of goods, larger markets were created; increased sales necessitated more factories and more machinery, thereby reinforcing the self-sustaining nature of the Industrial Revolution, which marked a fundamental break with the traditional European economy. The great productivity of the Industrial Revolution enabled entrepreneurs to reinvest their profits in new capital equipment, further expanding the productive capacity of the economy. Continuous, even rapid, self-sustaining economic growth came to be seen as a fundamental characteristic of the new industrial economy.

The railroad was the perfect symbol of this aspect of the Industrial Revolution. The ability to transport goods and people at dramatic speeds also provided visible confirmation of a new sense of power. When railway engineers penetrated mountains with tunnels and spanned chasms with breathtaking bridges, contemporaries experienced a sense of power over nature not felt before in Western civilization.

The Industrial Factory Initially the product of the cotton industry, the factory became the chief means of organizing labor for the new machines. As the workplace shifted from the artisan's shop and the peasant's cottage to the factory, the latter was not viewed as just a larger work unit. Employers hired workers who no longer owned the means of production but were simply paid wages to run the machines.

From its beginning, the factory system demanded a new type of discipline from its employees. Factory owners could not afford to let their expensive machinery stand idle. Workers were forced to work regular hours and in shifts to keep the machines producing at a steady pace for maximum output. This represented a massive adjustment for early factory laborers.

Preindustrial workers were not accustomed to a timed format. Agricultural laborers had always kept irregular hours; hectic work at harvest time might be followed by weeks of inactivity. Even in the burgeoning cottage industry of the eighteenth century, weavers and spinners who worked at home might fulfill their weekly quotas by working around the clock for two or three days and then proceeding at a leisurely pace until the next week's demands forced another work spurt.

Factory owners therefore faced a formidable task. They had to create a system of time-work discipline that would accustom employees to working regular, unvarying hours during which they performed a set number of tasks over and over again as efficiently as possible. One early industrialist said that his aim was "to make such machines of the men as cannot err." Such work, of course,

Opening of the Royal Albert Bridge. This painting by Thomas Robins shows the ceremonies attending the official opening of the Royal Albert Bridge. I. K. Brunel, one of Britain's great engineers, designed this bridge, which carried a railroad line across the Tamar River into Cornwall. As is evident in the picture, the bridge was high enough to allow ships to pass underneath.

tended to be repetitive and boring, and factory owners resorted to tough methods to accomplish their goals. Factory regulations were minute and detailed (see the box on p. 611). Adult workers were fined for a wide variety of minor infractions, such as being a few minutes late for work, and dismissed for more serious misdoings, especially drunkenness. Drunkenness was viewed as particularly offensive because it set a bad example for younger workers and also courted disaster amid dangerous machinery. Employers found that dismissals and fines worked well for adult employees; in a time when great population growth had produced large numbers of unskilled workers, dismissal could be disastrous. Children were less likely to understand the implications of dismissal, so they were sometimes disciplined more directly—by beating.

The efforts of factory owners in the early Industrial Revolution to impose a new set of values were frequently reinforced by the new evangelical churches. Methodism, in particular, emphasized that people

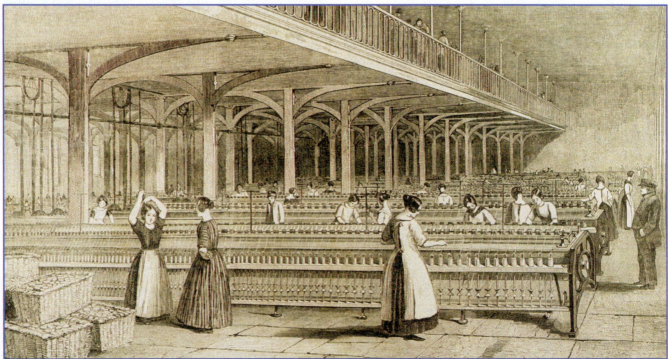

A British Textile Factory. The development of the factory changed the relationship between workers and employers as workers were encouraged to adjust to a new system of discipline that forced them to work regular hours under close supervision. This 1851 illustration shows women working in a British textile factory.

DISCIPLINE IN THE NEW FACTORIES

Workers in the new factories of the Industrial Revolution had been accustomed to a lifestyle free of overseers. Unlike the cottages, where workers spun thread and wove cloth in their own rhythm and time, the factories demanded a new, rigorous discipline geared to the requirements of the machines. This selection is taken from a set of rules for a factory in Berlin in 1844. They were typical of company rules everywhere the factory system had been established.

Factory Rules, Foundry and Engineering Works of the Royal Overseas Trading Company, Berlin

In every large works, and in the co-ordination of any large number of workmen, good order and harmony must be looked upon as the fundamentals of success, and therefore the following rules shall be strictly observed.

1. The normal working day begins at all seasons at 6 A.M. precisely and ends, after the usual break of half an hour for breakfast, an hour for dinner and half an hour for tea, at 7 P.M., and it shall be strictly observed.... Workers arriving 2 minutes late shall lose half an hour's wages; whoever is more than 2 minutes late may not start work until after the next break; or at least shall lose his wages until then. Any disputes about the correct time shall be settled by the clock mounted above the gatekeeper's lodge....

3. No workman, whether employed by time or piece, may leave before the end of the working day, without having first received permission from the overseer and having given his name to the gatekeeper. Omission of these two actions shall lead to a fine of ten silver groschen [pennies] payable to the sick fund.

4. Repeated irregular arrival at work shall lead to dismissal. This shall also apply to those who are found idling by an official or overseer, and refused to obey their order to resume work....

6. No worker may leave his place of work otherwise than for reasons connected with his work.

7. All conversation with fellow-workers is prohibited; if any worker requires information about his work, he must turn to the overseer, or to the particular fellow-worker designated for the purpose.

8. Smoking in the workshops or in the yard is prohibited during working hours; anyone caught smoking shall be fined five silver groschen for the sick fund for every such offense....

10. Natural functions must be performed at the appropriate places, and whoever is found soiling walls, fences, squares, etc., and similarly, whoever is found washing his face and hands in the workshop and not in the places assigned for the purpose, shall be fined five silver groschen for the sick fund....

12. It goes without saying that all overseers and officials of the firm shall be obeyed without question, and shall be treated with due deference. Disobedience will be punished by dismissal.

13. Immediate dismissal shall also be the fate of anyone found drunk in any of the workshops....

14. Every workman is obliged to report to his superiors any acts of dishonesty or embezzlement on the part of his fellow workmen. If he omits to do so, and it is shown after subsequent discovery of a misdemeanor that he knew about it at the time, he shall be liable to be taken to court as an accessory after the fact and the wage due to him shall be retained as punishment.

Q *What impact did factories have on the lives of workers? To what extent have such "rules" determined much of modern industrial life?*

"reborn in Jesus" must forgo immoderation and follow a disciplined path. Laziness and wasteful habits were sinful. The acceptance of hardship in this life paved the way for the joys of the next. Evangelical values paralleled the efforts of the new factory owners to instill laborers with their own middle-class values of hard work, discipline, and thrift. In one crucial sense, the early industrialists proved successful. As the nineteenth century progressed, the second and third generations of workers came to view a regular working week as a natural way of life. It was, of course, an attitude that made possible Britain's incredible economic growth in that century.

Britain's Great Exhibition of 1851

In 1851, the British organized the world's first industrial fair. It was housed at Kensington in London in the Crystal Palace, an enormous structure made entirely of glass and iron, a tribute to British engineering skills. Covering 19 acres, the Crystal Palace contained 100,000 exhibits that showed the wide variety of products created by the Industrial Revolution. Six million people visited the fair in six months. Though most of them were Britons who had traveled to London by train, foreign visitors were also prominent. The Great Exhibition displayed Britain's wealth to the world; it was a gigantic symbol of British success. Even trees were brought inside the Crystal Palace as a visible symbol of how the Industrial Revolution had achieved human domination over nature. Prince Albert, Queen Victoria's husband, expressed the sentiments of the age when he described the exhibition as a sign that "man is approaching a more complete fulfillment of that great and sacred mission which he has to perform in this world... to conquer nature to his use." Not content with that, he also linked British success to

The Great Exhibition of 1851. The Great Exhibition of 1851 was a symbol of the success of Great Britain, which had become the world's first industrial nation and its richest. Over 100,000 exhibits were housed in the Crystal Palace, a giant structure of cast iron and glass. The first illustration shows the front of the palace and some of its numerous visitors. The second shows the opening day ceremonies. Queen Victoria is seen at the center with her family, surrounded by visitors from all over the world. Note the large tree inside the building, providing a visible symbol of how the Industrial Revolution had supposedly achieved human domination over nature.

divine will: "In promoting [the progress of the human race], we are accomplishing the will of the great and blessed God."[3]

By the year of the Great Exhibition, Great Britain had become the world's first industrial nation and its wealthiest. Britain was the "workshop, banker, and trader of the world." It produced one-half of the world's coal and manufactured goods; its cotton industry alone in 1851 was equal in size to the industries of all other European countries combined. The quantity of goods produced was growing at three times the rate in 1780. Britain's certainty about its mission in the world in the nineteenth century was grounded in its incredible material success.

The Spread of Industrialization

Q **Focus Question:** How did the Industrial Revolution spread from Great Britain to the Continent and the United States, and how did industrialization in those areas differ from British industrialization?

Beginning first in Great Britain, industrialization spread to the Continental countries of Europe and the United States at different times and speeds during the nineteenth century. First to be industrialized on the Continent were Belgium, France, and the German states; the first in North America was the new United States. Not until after 1850 did the Industrial Revolution spread to the rest of Europe and other parts of the world.

Limitations to Industrialization

In 1815, the Low Countries, France, and the German states were still largely agrarian. During the eighteenth century, some of the Continental countries had experienced developments similar to those of Britain. They, too, had achieved population growth, made agricultural improvements, expanded their cottage industries, and witnessed growth in foreign trade. But whereas Britain's economy began to move in new industrial directions in the 1770s and 1780s, Continental countries lagged behind because they did not share some of the advantages that had made Britain's Industrial Revolution possible. Lack of good roads and problems with river transit made transportation difficult. Toll stations on important rivers and customs barriers along state boundaries increased the costs and prices of goods. Guild restrictions were also more prevalent, creating impediments that pioneer industrialists in Britain did not have to face. Finally, Continental entrepreneurs were generally less enterprising than their British counterparts and tended to adhere to traditional business attitudes, such as a dislike of competition, a high regard for family security coupled with an unwillingness to take risks in investment, and an excessive worship of thriftiness.

One additional factor also affected most of the Continent between 1790 and 1812: the upheavals associated with the wars of the French revolutionary and Napoleonic eras. Disruption of regular communications between Britain and the Continent made it difficult for Continental countries to keep up with the new British technology. Moreover, the wars wreaked havoc with trade, caused much physical destruction and loss of manpower, weakened currencies, and led to political and social instability. Napoleon's Continental System helped ruin a number of hitherto prosperous ports. The elimination of European markets for British textiles did temporarily revive the woolen industry in France and Belgium and stimulated textile manufacturing along the Rhine and in Silesia. After 1815, however, when cheap British goods again flooded European markets, the European textile industry suffered.

In the long run, the revolutionary and Napoleonic wars created an additional obstacle to rapid industrialization by widening the gap between British and Continental industrial machinery. By 1815, after Napoleon had finally been defeated and normal communication between Britain and the Continent had been restored, British industrial equipment had grown larger and become more expensive. As a result, self-financed family enterprises were either unable or unwilling to raise the amount of capital necessary to modernize by investing in the latest equipment. Instead, most entrepreneurs in France, Belgium, and Germany initially chose to invest in used machines and less productive mills. Consequently, industrialization on the Continent faced numerous hurdles, and as it proceeded in earnest after 1815, it did so along lines that were somewhat different from Britain's.

Borrowing Techniques and Practices Lack of technical knowledge was initially a major obstacle to industrialization. But the Continental countries possessed an advantage here; they could simply borrow British techniques and practices. Of course, the British tried to prevent that. Until 1825, British artisans were prohibited from leaving the country; until 1842, the export of important machinery and machine parts, especially for textile production, was forbidden. Nevertheless, the British were not able to control this situation by legislation. Already by 1825, there were at least two thousand skilled British mechanics on the Continent, and British equipment was also being sold abroad, legally or illegally.

Although many Britons who went abroad to sell their skills were simply skilled mechanics, a number of them were accomplished entrepreneurs who had managerial as well as technical skills. John Cockerill, for example, was an aggressive businessman who established a highly profitable industrial plant at Seraing near Liège in southern Belgium in 1817. Cockerill thought nothing of pirating the innovations of other British industrialists to further his own factories. Aware of their importance, British technicians abroad were often contentious and arrogant, arousing the anger of Continental industrialists. Fritz Harkort, who initiated the engineering industry in Germany, once exclaimed that he could scarcely wait for Germans to be trained "so that the Englishmen could all be whipped out: we must even now tread softly with them, for they're only too quick to speak of quitting if one does so little as not look at them in a friendly fashion."[4]

Gradually, the Continent achieved technological independence as local people learned all the skills their British teachers had to offer. By the 1840s, a new generation of skilled mechanics from Belgium and France was spreading their knowledge east and south, playing

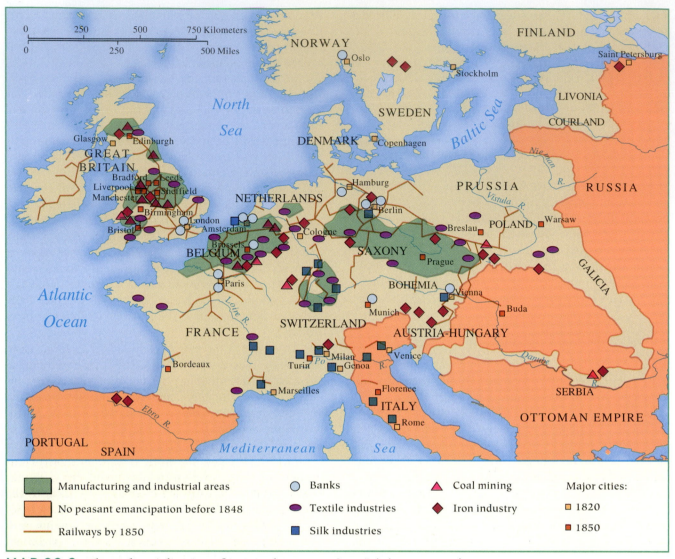

MAP 20.2 **The Industrialization of Europe by 1850.** Great Britain was Europe's first industrialized country; however, by the middle of the nineteenth century, several regions on the Continent, especially in Belgium, France, and the German states, had made significant advances in industrialization.

Q What reasons could explain why coal mining and iron industries are densely clustered in manufacturing and industrial areas? **View an animated version of this map or related maps at** academic.cengage.com/history/spielvogel

the same role that the British had earlier. Even more important, however, Continental countries, especially France and the German states, began to establish a wide range of technical schools to train engineers and mechanics.

Role of Government That government played an important role in this regard brings us to a second difference between British and Continental industrialization. Governments in most of the Continental countries were accustomed to playing a significant role in economic affairs. Furthering the development of industrialization was a logical extension of that attitude. Hence, governments provided for the costs of technical education, awarded grants to inventors and foreign entrepreneurs, exempted

foreign industrial equipment from import duties, and in some places even financed factories. Of equal if not greater importance in the long run, governments actively bore much of the cost of building roads and canals, deepening and widening river channels, and constructing railroads. By 1850, a network of iron rails had spread across Europe, although only Germany and Belgium had completed major parts of their systems by that time (see Map 20.2). Even though European markets did not feel the real impact of the railroad until after 1850, railroad construction itself in the 1830s and 1840s gave great impetus to the metalworking and engineering industries.

Governments on the Continent also used **tariffs** to further industrialization. After 1815, cheap British goods flooded Continental markets. The French responded with high tariffs to protect their fledgling industries. The most systematic argument for the use of tariffs, however, was made by a German writer, Friedrich List (1789–1846), who emigrated to America and returned to Germany as a U.S. consul. In his *National System of Political Economy*, written in 1844, List advocated a rapid and large-scale program of industrialization as the surest path to develop a nation's strength. To assure that path to industrialization, he felt that a nation must use protective tariffs. If countries followed the British policy of free trade, then cheaper British goods would inundate national markets and destroy infant industries before they had a chance to grow. Germany, he insisted, could not compete with Britain without protective tariffs.

Joint-Stock Investment Banks   A third significant difference between British and Continental industrialization was the role of the **joint-stock investment bank** on the Continent. Such banks mobilized the savings of thousands of small and large investors, creating a supply of capital that could then be plowed back into industry. Previously, Continental banks had been mostly merchant or private banks, but in the 1830s two Belgian banks, the Société Générale and the Banque de Belgique, took a new approach. By accepting savings from many depositors, they developed large capital resources that they invested on a large scale in railroads, mining, and heavy industry. Shareholders in these joint-stock corporations had limited liability; they could be held responsible only for the amount of their investment.

Similar institutions emerged in France and in German-speaking lands as well in the 1850s with the establishment of the Crédit Mobilier in France, the Darmstadt Bank in Germany, and the Kreditanstalt in Austria. They, too, took in savings of small investors and bought shares in the new industries. The French consul in Leipzig noted their significance: "Every town and state [in Germany]," he pointed out, "however small it may be, wants its bank and its Crédit Mobilier." These investments were essential to Continental industrialization. By starting with less expensive machines, the British had been able to industrialize largely through the private capital of successful individuals who reinvested their profits. On the Continent, advanced industrial machines necessitated large amounts of capital; joint-stock industrial banks provided it.

Centers of Continental Industrialization

As noted earlier, the Industrial Revolution on the Continent occurred in three major centers between 1815 and 1850—Belgium, France, and the German states. As in Britain, cotton played an important role, although it was not as significant as heavy industry. France was the Continental leader in the manufacture of cotton goods but still lagged far behind Great Britain. In 1849, France used 64,000 tons of raw cotton, Belgium, 11,000, and Germany, 20,000, whereas Britain used 286,000 tons.

Continental cotton factories were older, used less efficient machines, and had less productive labor. In general, Continental technology in the cotton industry was a generation behind Great Britain. But that is not the whole story. With its cheap coal and scarce water, Belgium gravitated toward the use of the steam engine as the major source of power and invested in the new machines. By the mid-1840s, Belgium had the most modern cotton-manufacturing system on the Continent.

The development of cotton manufacturing on the Continent and in Britain differed in two significant ways. Unlike Britain, where cotton manufacturing was mostly centered in Lancashire (in northwestern England) and the Glasgow area of Scotland, cotton mills in France, Germany, and, to a lesser degree, Belgium were dispersed through many regions. Noticeable, too, was the mixture of old and new. The old techniques of the cottage system, such as the use of hand looms, held on much longer. In the French district of Normandy, for example, in 1849, eighty-three mills were still driven by hand or animal power.

As traditional methods persisted alongside the new methods in cotton manufacturing, the new steam engine came to be used primarily in mining and metallurgy on the Continent rather than in textile manufacturing. At first, almost all of the steam engines on the Continent came from Britain; not until the 1820s was a domestic machine industry developed.

In Britain, the Industrial Revolution had been built on the cotton industry; on the Continent, the iron and coal of heavy industry led the way. As in textiles, however, heavy industry on the Continent before 1850 was a mixture of old and new. The adoption of new techniques, such as coke-smelted iron and puddling furnaces, coincided with the expansion of old-type charcoal blast furnaces. Before 1850, Germany lagged significantly behind both Belgium and France in heavy industry, and most German iron manufacturing was still based on old techniques. Not until the 1840s was coke-blast iron produced in the Rhineland. At that time, no one had yet realized the treasure of coal buried in the Ruhr valley. A German official wrote in 1852 that "it is clearly not to be expected that Germany will ever be able to reach the level of production of coal and iron currently attained in England. This is implicit in our far more limited resource endowment." Little did he realize that although the industrial development of Continental Europe was about a generation behind Britain at mid-century, after 1850 an incredibly rapid growth in Continental industry would demonstrate that Britain was not, after all, destined to remain the world's greatest industrial nation.

The Industrial Revolution in the United States

In 1800, the United States was an agrarian society. There were no cities over 100,000, and six out of every seven American workers were farmers. By 1860, however, the

The Steamboat. The steamboat was an important means of transportation for American products and markets. Steamboats like the one shown in this illustration regularly plied the Mississippi River, moving the farm products of the Midwest and the southern plantations to markets in New Orleans. After the American Civil War, railroads began to replace steamboats on many routes.

population had grown from 5 million to 30 million people, larger than Great Britain's. Almost half of them lived west of the Appalachian Mountains. The number of states had more than doubled, from sixteen to thirty-four, and nine American cities had over 100,000 in population. Only 50 percent of American workers were farmers. Between 1800 and the eve of the Civil War, the United States had experienced its own Industrial Revolution and the urbanization that accompanied it.

The initial application of machinery to production was accomplished, as in Continental Europe, by borrowing from Great Britain. A British immigrant, Samuel Slater, established the first textile factory using water-powered spinning machines in Rhode Island in 1790. By 1813, factories with power looms copied from British versions were being established. Soon thereafter, however, Americans began to equal or surpass British technical inventions. The Harpers Ferry arsenal, for example, built muskets with interchangeable parts. Because all the individual parts of the muskets were identical (for example, all triggers were the same), the final product could be put together quickly and easily; this enabled Americans to avoid the more costly system in which skilled workers fitted together individual parts made separately. The so-called American system reduced costs and revolutionized production by saving labor, important to a society that had few skilled artisans.

The Need for Transportation Unlike Britain, the United States was a large country. The lack of a good system of internal transportation seemed to limit American economic development by making the transport of goods prohibitively expensive. This deficiency was gradually remedied, however. Thousands of miles of roads and canals were built linking east and west. The steamboat facilitated transportation on the Great Lakes, Atlantic coastal waters, and rivers. It was especially important to the Mississippi valley; by 1860, one thousand steamboats plied that river (see the box on p. 617). Most important of all in the development of the American transportation system was the railroad. Beginning with 100 miles in 1830, by 1860 more than 27,000 miles of railroad track covered the United States. This transportation revolution turned the United States into a single massive market for the manufactured goods of the Northeast, the early center of American industrialization.

The Labor Force Labor for the growing number of factories came primarily from rural areas. The United States did not possess a large number of craftspeople, but it did have a rapidly expanding farm population; its size in the Northeast soon outstripped the available farmland. While some of this excess population, especially men, went west, others, mostly women, found work in the new textile and shoe factories of New England. Indeed, women

"S-T-E-A-M-BOAT A-COMING!"

Steamboats and railroads were crucial elements in a transportation revolution that enabled industrialists to expand markets by shipping goods cheaply and efficiently. At the same time, these marvels of technology aroused a sense of power and excitement that was an important aspect of the triumph of industrialization. The American novelist Mark Twain captured this sense of excitement in this selection from *Life on the Mississippi*.

Mark Twain, *Life on the Mississippi*

After all these years I can picture that old time to myself now, just as it was then: the white town drowsing in the sunshine of a summer's morning; the streets empty, or pretty nearly so; one or two clerks sitting in front of the Water street stores, with their splint-bottomed chairs tilted back against the walls, chins on breasts, hats slouched over their faces, asleep;...two or three lonely little freight piles scattered about the "levee"; a pile of "skids" on the slope of the stone-paved wharf, and the fragrant town drunkard asleep in the shadow of them;...the great Mississippi, the majestic, the magnificent Mississippi, rolling its mile-wide along, shining in the sun; the dense forest away on the other side; the "point" above the town, and the "point" below, bounding the river glimpse and turning it into a sort of sea, and withal a very still and brilliant and lonely one. Presently a film of dark smoke appears above on those remote "points"; instantly a negro drayman, famous for his quick eye and prodigious voice, lifts up to cry, "S-t-e-a-m-boat a-coming!" and the scene changes! The town drunkard stirs, the clerks wake up, a furious clatter of drays follows, every house and store pours out a human contribution, and all in a twinkling the dead town [Hannibal, Missouri] is alive and moving. Drays, carts, men, boys, all go hurrying from many quarters to a common center, the wharf. Assembled there, the people fasten their eyes upon the coming boat as upon a wonder they are seeing for the first time. And the boat is rather a handsome sight, too. She is long and sharp and trim and pretty; she has two tall, fancy-topped chimneys, with a gilded device of some kind swung between them; a fanciful pilot-house, all glass and "ginger bread," perched on top of the "texas" deck behind them; the paddle-boxes are gorgeous with a picture or with gilded rays above the boat's name; the boiler deck, the hurricane deck, and the texas deck are fenced and ornamented with clean white railings; there is a flag gallantly flying from the jack-staff; the furnace doors are open and the fires glaring bravely; the upper decks are black with passengers; the captain stands by the big bell, calm, imposing, the envy of all; great volumes of the blackest smoke are rolling and tumbling out of the chimneys—a husbanded grandeur created with a bit of pitch pine just before arriving at a town; the crew are grouped on the forecastle; the broad stage is run far out over the port bow, and an envied deck-hand stands picturesquely on the end of it with a coil of rope in his hand; the pent steam is screaming through the gaugecocks; the captain lifts his hand, a bell rings, the wheels stop; then they turn back, churning the water to foam, and the steam is at rest. Then such a scramble as there is to get aboard, and to get ashore, and to take in freight and discharge freight, all at one and the same time; and such a yelling and cursing as the mates facilitate it all with! Ten minutes later the steamer is under way again, with no flag on the jack-staff and no black smoke issuing from the chimneys. After ten more minutes the town is dead again, and the town drunkard asleep by the skids once more.

Q *In what ways does Twain's description illustrate the impact of the transportation revolution on daily life in the United States?*

---

made up more than 80 percent of the laboring force in the large textile factories. In Massachusetts mill towns, company boarding houses provided rooms for large numbers of young women who worked for several years before marriage. Outside Massachusetts, factory owners sought entire families, including children, to work in their mills; one mill owner ran this advertisement in a newspaper in Utica, New York: "Wanted: A few sober and industrious families of at least five children each, over the age of eight years, are wanted at the Cotton Factory in Whitestown. Widows with large families would do well to attend this notice." When a decline in rural births threatened to dry up this labor pool in the 1830s and 1840s, European immigrants, especially poor and unskilled Irish, English, Scots, and Welsh, appeared in large numbers to replace American women and children in the factories.

Women, children, and these immigrants had one thing in common as employees: they were largely unskilled laborers. Unskilled labor pushed American industrialization into a capital-intensive pattern. Factory owners invested heavily in machines that could produce in quantity at the hands of untrained workers. In Britain, the pace of mechanization was never as rapid because Britain's supply of skilled artisans made it more profitable to pursue a labor-intensive economy.

By 1860, the United States was well on its way to being an industrial nation. In the Northeast, the most industrialized section of the country, per capita income was 40 percent higher than the national average. Diets, it has been argued, were better and more varied; machine-made clothing was more abundant. Industrialization did not necessarily lessen economic disparities, however. Despite a growing belief in a myth of social mobility based on equality of economic opportunity, the reality was that the richest 10 percent of the population in the cities held 70 to 80 percent of the wealth, compared to 50 percent in

1800. Nevertheless, American historians generally argue that while the rich got richer, the poor, thanks to an increase in their purchasing power, did not get poorer.

Limiting the Spread of Industrialization in the Nonindustrialized World

Before 1870, the industrialization that had developed in western and central Europe and the United States did not extend in any significant way to the rest of the world. Even in eastern Europe, industrialization lagged far behind. Russia, for example, remained largely rural and agricultural, and its autocratic rulers kept the peasants in serfdom. There was not much of a middle class, and the tsarist regime, fearful of change, preferred to import industrial goods in return for the export of raw materials, such as grain and timber. Russia would not have its Industrial Revolution until the end of the nineteenth century.

The Example of India In other parts of the world where they had established control, newly industrialized European states pursued a deliberate policy of preventing the growth of mechanized industry. A good example is India. In the eighteenth century, India had become one of the world's greatest exporters of cotton cloth produced by hand labor. In the first half of the nineteenth century, much of India fell under the control of the British East India Company (see Chapter 24). With British control came inexpensive British factory-produced textiles, and soon thousands of Indian spinners and hand-loom weavers were unemployed. British policy encouraged Indians to export their raw materials while buying British-made goods. Although some limited forms of industrial factories for making textiles and jute (used in making rope) were opened in India in the 1850s, a lack of local capital and the advantages given to British imports limited the growth of new manufacturing operations. India, then, provides an excellent example of how some of the rapidly industrializing nations of Europe worked to deliberately thwart the spread of the Industrial Revolution to their colonial dominions.

The Social Impact of the Industrial Revolution

Q **Focus Questions:** What effects did the Industrial Revolution have on urban life, social classes, family life, and standards of living? What were working conditions like in the early decades of the Industrial Revolution, and what efforts were made to improve them?

Eventually, the Industrial Revolution radically altered the social life of Europe and the world. Although much of Europe remained bound by its traditional ways, already

in the first half of the nineteenth century, the social impact of the Industrial Revolution was being felt, and future avenues of growth were becoming apparent. Vast changes in the number of people and where they lived were already dramatically evident.

Population Growth

Population increases had already begun in the eighteenth century, but they became dramatic in the nineteenth. They were also easier to discern because record keeping became more accurate. In the nineteenth century, governments began to take periodic censuses and systematically collect precise data on births, deaths, and marriages. In Britain, for example, the first census was taken in 1801, and a systematic registration of births, deaths, and marriages was begun in 1836. In 1750, the total European population stood at an estimated 140 million; by 1800, it had increased to 187 million and by 1850 to 266 million, almost twice its 1750 level.

This population explosion cannot be explained by a higher birthrate, for birthrates were declining after 1790. Between 1790 and 1850, Germany's birthrate dropped from 40 per 1,000 to 36.1; Great Britain's, from 35.4 to 32.6; and France's, from 32.5 to 26.7. The key to the expansion of population was the decline in death rates evident throughout Europe. Historians now believe that two major causes explain this decline. There was a drop in the number of deaths from famines, epidemics, and war. Major epidemic diseases, such as plague and smallpox, declined noticeably, although small-scale epidemics broke out now and then. The ordinary death rate also declined as a general increase in the food supply, already evident in the agricultural revolution of Britain in the late eighteenth century, spread to more areas. More food enabled a greater number of people to be better fed and therefore more resistant to disease. Famine largely disappeared from western Europe, although there were dramatic exceptions in isolated areas, Ireland being the most significant.

Although industrialization itself did not cause population growth, industrialized areas did experience a change in the composition of the population. By 1850, the proportion of the active population involved in manufacturing, mining, or building had risen to 48 percent in Britain, 37 percent in Belgium, and 27 percent in France. But the actual pockets of industrialization in 1850 were small and decentralized; one author characterized them as "islands in an agricultural sea."

This minimal industrialization in light of the growing population meant severe congestion in the countryside, where ever-larger numbers of people divided the same amount of land into ever-smaller plots, and also gave rise to an ever-increasing mass of landless peasants. Overpopulation, especially noticeable in parts of France, northern Spain, southern Germany, Sweden, and Ireland, magnified the already existing problem of rural poverty. In Ireland, it produced the century's greatest catastrophe.

THE GREAT IRISH FAMINE

The Great Irish Famine caused by the potato blight was one of the nineteenth century's worst natural catastrophes, resulting in the decimation of the Irish population. In this selection, an Irish nationalist reported what he had witnessed in Galway in 1847.

John Mitchel, *The Last Conquest of Ireland*

In the depth of winter we traveled to Galway, through the very center of that fertile island, and saw sights that will never wholly leave the eyes that beheld them—cowering wretches, almost naked in the savage weather, prowling in turnip-fields, and endeavoring to grub up roots which had been left, but running to hide as the mail-coach rolled by;—very large fields where small farms had been "consolidated," showing dark bars of fresh mold running through them where the ditches had been leveled;—groups and families, sitting or wandering on the high-road, with failing steps and dim patient eyes, gazing hopelessly into infinite darkness; before them, around them, above them, nothing but darkness and despair—parties of tall brawny men, once the flower of Meath and Galway, stalking by with a fierce but vacant scowl; as if they knew that all this ought not to be, but knew not whom to blame, saw none whom they could rend in their wrath.... Around those farmhouses which were still inhabited were to be seen hardly any stacks of grain; the poor-rate collector, the rent agent, the county-cess collector had carried it off; and sometimes I could see in front of the cottages little children leaning against a fence when the sun shone out—for they could not stand—their limbs fleshless, their bodies half naked, their faces bloated yet wrinkled, and of a pale greenish hue,—children who would never, it was too plain, grow up to be men and women.

Q *What was the impact of the Great Irish Famine on the Irish people and on the broader Atlantic world? How were the industrial revolutions of other nations affected by this disaster?*

The Great Hunger Ireland was one of the most oppressed areas in western Europe. The predominantly Catholic peasant population rented land from mostly absentee British Protestant landlords whose primary concern was collecting their rents. Irish peasants lived in mud hovels in desperate poverty. The cultivation of the potato, a nutritious and relatively easy food to grow that produced three times as much food per acre as grain, gave Irish peasants a basic staple that enabled them to survive and even expand in numbers. As only an acre or two of potatoes was sufficient to feed a family, Irish men and women married earlier than elsewhere and started having children earlier as well. This led to significant growth in the population. Between 1781 and 1845, the Irish population doubled from 4 million to 8 million. Probably half of this population depended on the potato for survival. In the summer of 1845, the potato crop in Ireland was struck by blight due to a fungus that turned the potatoes black. Between 1845 and 1851, the Great Famine decimated the Irish population (see the box above). More than a million died of starvation and disease, and almost 2 million emigrated to the United States and Britain. Of all the European nations, only Ireland had a declining population in the nineteenth century. But other countries, too, faced problems of dire poverty and declining standards of living as their populations exploded.

Emigration The flight of so many Irish to America reminds us that the traditional safety valve for overpopulation has always been emigration. Between 1821 and 1850, the number of emigrants from Europe averaged about 110,000 a year. Most of these emigrants came from places like Ireland and southern Germany, where peasant life had been reduced to marginal existence. Times of agrarian crisis resulted in great waves of emigration. Bad harvests in Europe in 1846–1847 (such as the catastrophe in Ireland) produced massive numbers of emigrants. In addition to the estimated 1.6 million from Ireland, for example, 935,000 people left Germany between 1847 and 1854. More often than emigrating, however, the rural masses sought a solution to their poverty by moving to towns and cities within their own countries to find work. It should not astonish us, then, that the first half of the nineteenth century was a period of rapid urbanization.

The Growth of Cities

Although the Western world would not become a predominantly urban society until the twentieth century, cities and towns had already grown dramatically in the first half of the nineteenth century, a phenomenon related to industrialization. Cities had traditionally been centers for princely courts, government and military offices, churches, and commerce. By 1850, especially in Great Britain and Belgium, cities were rapidly becoming places for manufacturing and industry. With the steam engine, entrepreneurs could locate their manufacturing plants in urban centers where they had ready access to transportation facilities and unemployed people from the country looking for work.

In 1800, Great Britain had one major city, London, with a population of one million, and six cities between 50,000 and 100,000. Fifty years later, London's population had swelled to 2,363,000, and there were nine cities over 100,000 and eighteen cities with populations between 50,000 and 100,000. All together, these twenty-eight cities accounted for 5.7 million, or one-fifth, of the total British

A New Industrial Town. Cities and towns grew dramatically in Britain in the first half of the nineteenth century, largely as a result of industrialization. Pictured here is Saltaire, a model textile factory and town founded near Bradford by Titus Salt in 1851. To facilitate the transportation of goods, the town was built on the Leeds and Liverpool canals.

population. When the populations of cities under 50,000 are added to this total, we realize that more than 50 percent of the British population lived in towns and cities by 1850. Britain was forced to become a food importer rather than an exporter as the number of people involved in agriculture declined to 20 percent of the population.

Urban populations also grew on the Continent, but less dramatically. Paris had 547,000 inhabitants in 1800, but only two other French cities had populations of 100,000: Lyons and Marseilles. In 1851, Paris had grown to a million while Lyons and Marseilles were still under 200,000. German and Austrian lands had only three cities with over 100,000 inhabitants (Vienna had 247,000) in 1800; fifty years later, there were only five, but Vienna had grown to 440,000. As these figures show, urbanization did not proceed as rapidly here as in Britain; of course, neither had industrialization. Even in Belgium, the most heavily industrialized country on the Continent, almost 50 percent of the male workforce was still engaged in agriculture by midcentury.

Urban Living Conditions in the Early Industrial Revolution

The dramatic growth of cities in the first half of the nineteenth century produced miserable living conditions for many of the inhabitants. Of course, this had been true for centuries for many people in European cities, but the rapid urbanization associated with the Industrial Revolution intensified the problems and made these wretched conditions all the more apparent. Wealthy, middle-class inhabitants, as usual, insulated themselves as best they could, often living in suburbs or the outer ring of the city, where they could have individual houses and gardens. In the inner ring of the city stood the small row houses, some with gardens, of the artisans and the lower middle class. Finally, located in the center of most industrial towns were the row houses of the industrial workers. This report on working-class housing in the British city of Birmingham in 1843 gives an idea of the general conditions they faced:

> The courts [of working-class row houses] are extremely numerous; . . . a very large portion of the poorer classes of the inhabitants reside in them. . . . The courts vary in the number of the houses which they contain, from four to twenty, and most of these houses are three stories high, and built, as it is termed, back to back. There is a wash-house, an ash-pit, and a privy at the end, or on one side of the court, and not unfrequently one or more pigsties and heaps of manure. Generally speaking, the privies in the old courts are in a most filthy condition. Many which we have inspected were in a state which renders it impossible for us to conceive how they could be used; they were without doors and overflowing with filth.[5]

Rooms were not large and were frequently overcrowded, as this government report of 1838 revealed: "I entered several of the tenements. In one of them, on the ground floor, I found six persons occupying a very small room, two in bed, ill with fever. In the room above this were two more persons in one bed ill with fever."[6] Another report said, "There were 63 families where there were at least five persons to one bed; and there were some in which even six were packed in one bed, lying at the top and bottom—children and adults."[7]

Sanitary conditions in these towns were appalling. Due to the lack of municipal direction, city streets were often used as sewers and open drains: "In the center of this street is a gutter, into which potato parings, the refuse of animal and vegetable matters of all kinds, the dirty water from the washing of clothes and of the houses, are all poured, and there they stagnate and putrefy."[8] Unable to deal with human excrement, cities in the new industrial era smelled horrible and were extraordinarily unhealthy. The burning of coal blackened towns and cities with soot, as Charles Dickens described in one of his novels: "A long suburb of red brick houses—some with

Slums of Industrial London. Industrialization and rapid urban growth produced dreadful living conditions in many nineteenth-century cities. Filled with garbage and human waste, cities often smelled terrible and were extremely unhealthy. This drawing by Gustave Doré shows a London slum district overshadowed by rail viaducts.

patches of garden ground, where coal-dust and factory smoke darkened the shrinking leaves, and coarse rank flowers; and where the struggling vegetation sickened and sank under the hot breath of kiln and furnace."[9] Towns and cities were fundamentally death traps. As deaths outnumbered births in most large cities in the first half of the nineteenth century, only a constant influx of people from the countryside kept them alive and growing.

Adding to the deterioration of urban life was the adulteration of food. Consumers were defrauded in a variety of ways: alum was added to make bread look white and hence more expensive; beer and milk were watered down; and red lead, despite its poisonous qualities, was substituted for pepper. The government refused to intervene; a parliamentary committee stated that "more benefit is likely to result from the effects of a free competition . . . than can be expected to result from any regulations." It was not until 1875 that an effective food and drug act was passed in Britain.

Our knowledge of the pathetic conditions in the early industrial cities is largely derived from an abundance of social investigations. Such investigations began in France in the 1820s. In Britain, the Poor Law Commission produced detailed reports. The investigators were often struck by the physically and morally debilitating effects of urban industrial life on the poor. They observed, for example, that young working-class men were considerably shorter and scrawnier than the sons of middle-class families and much more subject to disease. They were especially alarmed by what they considered the moral consequences of such living conditions: prostitution, crime, and sexual immorality, all of which they saw as effects of living in such squalor.

Urban Reformers To many of the well-to-do, this situation presented a clear danger to society. Were not these masses of workers, sunk in crime, disease, and immorality, a potential threat to their own well-being? Might not the masses be organized and used by unscrupulous demagogues to overthrow the established order? One of the most eloquent British reformers of the 1830s and 1840s, James Kay-Shuttleworth, described them as "volcanic elements, by whose explosive violence the structure of society may be destroyed." Another observer spoke more contemptuously in 1850:

> They live precisely like brutes, to gratify . . . the appetites of their uncultivated bodies, and then die, to go they have never thought, cared, or wondered whither. . . . Brought up in the darkness of barbarism, they have no idea that it is possible for them to attain any higher condition; they are not even sentient enough to desire to change their situation. . . . They eat, drink, breed, work and die; and . . . the richer and more intelligent classes are obliged to guard them with police.[10]

Some observers were less arrogant, however, and wondered if the workers should be held responsible for their fate.

One of the best of a new breed of urban reformers was Edwin Chadwick (1800–1890). With a background in law, Chadwick became obsessed with eliminating the poverty and squalor of the metropolitan areas. He became a civil servant and was soon appointed to a number of government investigatory commissions. As secretary of the Poor Law Commission, he initiated a passionate search for detailed facts about the living conditions of the working classes. After three years of investigation, Chadwick summarized the results in his *Report on the*

Condition of the Labouring Population of Great Britain, published in 1842. In it, he concluded that "the various forms of epidemic, endemic, and other disease" were directly caused by the "atmospheric impurities produced by decomposing animal and vegetable substances, by damp and filth, and close overcrowded dwellings [prevailing] amongst the population in every part of the kingdom." Such conditions, he argued, could be eliminated. As to the means: "The primary and most important measures, and at the same time the most practicable, and within the recognized province of public administration, are drainage, the removal of all refuse of habitations, streets, and roads, and the improvement of the supplies of water."[11] In other words, Chadwick was advocating a system of modern sanitary reforms consisting of efficient sewers and a supply of piped water. Six years after his report and largely due to his efforts, Britain's first Public Health Act created the National Board of Health, empowered to form local boards that would establish modern sanitary systems.

Many middle-class citizens were quite willing to support the public health reforms of men like Chadwick because of their fear of **cholera.** Outbreaks of this deadly disease had ravaged Europe in the early 1830s and late 1840s and were especially rampant in the overcrowded cities. As city authorities and wealthier residents became convinced that filthy conditions helped spread the disease, they began to support the call for new public health measures.

New Social Classes: The Industrial Middle Class

The rise of industrial capitalism produced a new middle-class group. The bourgeoisie or middle class was not new; it had existed since the emergence of cities in the Middle Ages. Originally, the bourgeois was the burgher or town dweller, active as a merchant, official, artisan, lawyer, or scholar, who enjoyed a special set of rights from the charter of the town. As wealthy townspeople bought land, the original meaning of the word *bourgeois* became lost, and the term came to include people involved in commerce, industry, and banking as well as professionals, such as lawyers, teachers, physicians, and government officials at various levels. At the lower end of the economic scale were master craftspeople and shopkeepers.

The New Industrial Entrepreneurs Lest we make the industrial middle class too much of an abstraction, we need to look at who the new industrial entrepreneurs actually were. These were the people who constructed the factories, purchased the machines, and figured out where the markets were. Their qualities included resourcefulness, single-mindedness, resolution, initiative, vision, ambition, and often, of course, greed. As Jedediah Strutt, the cotton manufacturer, said, the "getting of money . . . is the main business of the life of men."

But this was not an easy task. The early industrial entrepreneurs were called on to superintend an enormous array of functions that are handled today by teams of managers; they raised capital, determined markets, set company objectives, organized the factory and its labor, and trained supervisors who could act for them. The opportunities for making money were great, but the risks were also tremendous. The cotton trade, for example, which was so important to the early Industrial Revolution, was intensely competitive. Only through constant expansion could one feel secure, so early entrepreneurs reinvested most of their initial profits. Fear of bankruptcy was constant, especially among small firms. Furthermore, most early industrial enterprises were small. Even by the 1840s, only 10 percent of British industrial firms employed more than five thousand workers; 43 percent had fewer than one hundred. As entrepreneurs went bankrupt, new people could enter the race for profits, especially since the initial outlay required was not gigantic. In 1816, only one mill in five in the important industrial city of Manchester was in the hands of its original owner.

The new industrial entrepreneurs were from incredibly diverse social origins. Many of the most successful came from a mercantile background. Three London merchants, for example, founded a successful ironworks in Wales that owned eight steam engines and employed five thousand men. In Britain, land and domestic industry were often interdependent. Joshua Fielden, for example, acquired sufficient capital to establish a factory by running a family sheep farm while working looms in the farmhouse. Intelligent, clever, and ambitious apprentices who had learned their trades well could also strike it rich. William Radcliffe's family engaged in agriculture and spinning and weaving at home; he learned quickly how to succeed:

> Availing myself of the improvements that came out while I was in my teens . . . with my little savings and a practical knowledge of every process from the cotton bag to the piece of cloth . . . I was ready to commence business for myself and by the year 1789 I was well established and employed many hands both in spinning and weaving as a master manufacturer.[12]

By 1801, Radcliffe was operating a factory employing a thousand workers.

Members of dissenting religious minorities were often prominent among the early industrial leaders of Britain. The Darbys and Lloyds, who were iron manufacturers; the Barclays and Lloyds, who were bankers; and the Trumans and Perkins, who were brewers, were all Quakers. These were expensive trades and depended on the financial support that coreligionists in religious minorities provided for each other. Most historians believe that a major reason members of these religious minorities were so prominent in business was that they lacked other opportunities. Legally excluded from many public offices, they directed their ambitions into the new industrial capitalism.

It is interesting to note that in Britain in particular, aristocrats also became entrepreneurs. The Lambtons in Northumberland, the Curwens in Cumberland, the Norfolks in Yorkshire, and the Dudleys in Staffordshire all invested in mining enterprises. This close relationship between land and industry helped Britain assume the leadership role in the early Industrial Revolution.

Significance of the Industrial Entrepreneurs By 1850, in Britain at least, the kind of traditional entrepreneurship that had created the Industrial Revolution was declining and was being replaced by a new business aristocracy. This new generation of entrepreneurs stemmed from the professional and industrial middle classes, especially as sons inherited the successful businesses established by their fathers. It must not be forgotten, however, that even after 1850, a large number of small businesses existed in Britain, and some were still being founded by people from humble backgrounds. Indeed, the age of large-scale corporate capitalism did not begin until the 1890s (see Chapter 23).

Increasingly, the new industrial entrepreneurs—the bankers and owners of factories and mines—came to amass much wealth and play an important role alongside the traditional landed elites of their societies. The Industrial Revolution began at a time when the preindustrial agrarian world was still largely dominated by landed elites. As the new bourgeois bought great estates and acquired social respectability, they also sought political power, and in the course of the nineteenth century, their wealthiest members would merge with those old elites.

New Social Classes: Workers in the Industrial Age

At the same time that the members of the industrial middle class were seeking to reduce the barriers between themselves and the landed elite, they also were trying to separate themselves from the laboring classes below them. The working class was actually a mixture of groups in the first half of the nineteenth century. Factory workers would eventually form an industrial proletariat, but in the first half of the century, they did not constitute a majority of the working class in any major city, even in Britain. According to the 1851 census in Britain, there were 1.8 million agricultural laborers and 1 million domestic servants but only 811,000 workers in the cotton and woolen industries. And one-third of these were still working in small workshops or at home.

In the cities, artisans or craftspeople remained the largest group of urban workers during the first half of the nineteenth century. They worked in numerous small industries, such as shoemaking, glovemaking, bookbinding, printing, and bricklaying. Some craftspeople formed a kind of aristocracy of labor, especially those employed in such luxury trades as coach building and clock making, who earned higher wages than others. Artisans were not factory workers; they were traditionally organized in guilds, where they passed on their skills to apprentices. But guilds were increasingly losing their power, especially in industrialized countries. Fearful of losing out to the new factories that could produce goods more cheaply, artisans tended to support movements against industrialization. Industrialists welcomed the decline of skilled craftspeople, as one perceptive old tailor realized in telling his life story:

> It is upwards of 30 years since I first went to work at the tailoring trade in London.... I continued working for the honorable trade and belonging to the Society [for tailors] for about 15 years. My weekly earnings then averaged £1 16s. a week while I was at work, and for several years I was seldom out of work.... No one could have been happier than I was.... But then, with my sight defective...I could get no employment at the honorable trade, and that was the ruin of me entirely; for working there, of course, I got "scratched" from the trade society, and so lost all hope of being provided for by them in my helplessness. The workshop...was about seven feet square, and so low, that as you [sat] on the floor you could touch the ceiling with the tip of your finger. In this place seven of us worked. [The master] paid little more than half the regular wages, and employed such men as myself—only those who couldn't get anything better to do.... I don't think my wages there averaged above 12s. a week.... I am convinced I lost my eyesight by working in that cheap shop.... It is by the ruin of such men as me that these masters are enabled to undersell the better shops.... That's the way, sir, the cheap clothes is produced, by making blind beggars of the workmen, like myself, and throwing us on [the benevolence of] the parish [church] in our old age.[13]

Servants also formed another large group of urban workers, especially in major cities like London and Paris. Many were women from the countryside who became utterly dependent on their upper- and middle-class employers.

Working Conditions for the Industrial Working Class Workers in the new industrial factories also faced wretched working conditions. We have already observed the psychological traumas workers experienced from their employers' efforts to break old preindustrial work patterns and create a well-disciplined labor force. But what were the physical conditions of the factories?

Unquestionably, in the early decades of the Industrial Revolution, "places of work," as early factories were called, were dreadful. Work hours ranged from twelve to sixteen hours a day, six days a week, with a half hour for lunch and for dinner. There was no security of employment and no minimum wage. The worst conditions were in the cotton mills, where temperatures were especially debilitating. One report noted that "in the cotton-spinning work, these creatures are kept, fourteen hours in each day, locked up, summer and winter, in a heat of from eighty to

Women and Children in the Mines. Women and children were often employed in the factories and mines of the early nineteenth century. These illustrations are from the Report of the Children's Employment Commission in Great Britain in 1842. The top image shows a woman dragging a cart loaded with coal behind her. The image below shows a boy walking backwards in a mine, pulling a cart also filled with coal. Both images show the trying conditions under which both women and children worked in the early Industrial Revolution. In 1842, the Coal Mines Act forbade the use of boys younger than ten and women in the mines.

© SSPL/The Image Works

eighty-four degrees." Mills were also dirty, dusty, and unhealthy:

> Not only is there not a breath of sweet air in these truly infernal scenes, but...there is the abominable and pernicious stink of the gas to assist in the murderous effects of the heat. In addition to the noxious effluvia of the gas, mixed with the steam, there are the dust, and what is called cotton-flyings or fuz, which the unfortunate creatures have to inhale; and...the notorious fact is that well constitutioned men are rendered old and past labor at forty years of age, and that children are rendered decrepit and deformed, and thousands upon thousands of them slaughtered by consumptions [lung diseases], before they arrive at the age of sixteen.[14]

Thus ran a report on working conditions in the cotton industry in 1824.

Conditions in the coal mines were also harsh. The introduction of steam power meant only that steam-powered engines mechanically lifted coal to the top. Inside the mines, men still bore the burden of digging the coal out while horses, mules, women, and children hauled coal carts on rails to the lift. Dangers abounded in coal mines; cave-ins, explosions, and gas fumes (called "bad air") were a way of life. The cramped conditions—tunnels often did not exceed 3 or 4 feet in height—and constant dampness in the mines resulted in deformed bodies and ruined lungs.

Both children and women were employed in large numbers in early factories and mines. Children had been an important part of the family economy in preindustrial times, working in the fields or carding and spinning wool at home with the growth of the cottage industry. In the Industrial Revolution, however, child labor was exploited more than ever and in a considerably more systematic fashion (see the boxes on pp. 626–627). The owners of cotton factories appreciated certain features of child labor. Children had an especially delicate touch as spinners of cotton. Their smaller size made it easier for them to crawl under machines to gather loose cotton. Moreover, children were more easily broken to factory work. Above all, children represented a cheap supply of labor. In 1821, just about half of the British population was under twenty years of age. Hence, children made up a particularly abundant supply of labor, and they were paid only about one-sixth to one-third of what a man was paid. In the cotton factories in 1838, children under eighteen made up 29 percent of the total workforce; children as young as seven worked twelve to fifteen hours per day, six days a week, in cotton mills.

Especially terrible in the early Industrial Revolution was the use of so-called pauper apprentices. These were orphans or children abandoned by their parents who had wound up in the care of local parishes. To save on their upkeep, parish officials found it convenient to apprentice them to factory owners looking for a cheap source of labor. These children worked long hours under strict discipline and received inadequate food and recreation; many became deformed from being kept too long in contorted positions. Although economic liberals and some industrialists were against all state intervention in economic matters, Parliament eventually remedied some of the worst ills of child abuse in factories and mines (see "Efforts at Change: Reformers and Government" later in this chapter). The legislation of the 1830s and 1840s, however, primarily affected child labor in textile factories and mines. It did not touch the use of children in small workshops or the nonfactory trades that were not protected. As these trades were in competition with the new factories, conditions there were often even worse. Pottery works, for example, were not investigated until the 1860s, when it was found that 17 percent of the workers were under eleven years of age. One investigator reported what he found:

> The boys were kept in constant motion throughout the day, each carrying from thirty to fifty dozen of molds into the stoves, and remaining . . . long enough to take the dried earthenware away. The distance thus run by a boy in the course of a day . . . was estimated at seven miles. From the very nature of this exhausting occupation children were rendered pale, weak and unhealthy. In the depth of winter, with the thermometer in the open air sometimes below zero, boys, with little clothing but rags, might be seen running to and fro on errands or to their dinners with the perspiration on their foreheads, "after laboring for hours like little slaves." The inevitable result of such transitions of temperature were consumption, asthma and acute inflammation.[15]

Little wonder that child labor legislation enacted in 1864 included pottery works.

By 1830, women and children made up two-thirds of the cotton industry's labor. As the number of children employed declined under the Factory Act of 1833, however, their places were taken by women, who came to dominate the labor forces of the early factories. Women made up 50 percent of the labor force in textile (cotton and woolen) factories before 1870. They were mostly unskilled labor and were paid half or less of what men received. Excessive working hours for women were outlawed in 1844, but only in textile factories and mines; not until 1867 were they outlawed in craft workshops.

The employment of children and women in large part represents a continuation of a preindustrial kinship pattern. The cottage industry had always involved the efforts of the entire family, and it seemed perfectly natural to continue this pattern. Men migrating from the countryside to industrial towns and cities took their wives and children with them into the factory or into the mines. Of 136 employees in Robert Peel's factory at Bury in 1801, 95 were members of the same twenty-six families. The impetus for this family work often came from the family itself. The factory owner Jedediah Strutt was opposed to child labor under age ten but was forced by parents to take children as young as seven.

The employment of large numbers of women in factories did not produce a significant transformation in female working patterns, as was once assumed. Studies of urban households in France and Britain, for example, have revealed that throughout the nineteenth century, traditional types of female labor still predominated in the women's work world. In 1851, fully 40 percent of the female workforce in Britain consisted of domestic servants. In France, the largest group of female workers, 40 percent, worked in agriculture. In addition, only 20 percent of female workers in Britain labored in factories, and only 10 percent did so in France. Regional and local studies have also found that most of the workers were single women. Few married women worked outside the home.

The factory acts that limited the work hours of children and women also began to break up the traditional kinship pattern of work and led to a new pattern based on a separation of work and home. Men came to be regarded as responsible for the primary work obligations as women assumed daily control of the family and performed low-paying jobs such as laundry work that could be done in the home. Domestic industry made it possible for women to continue their contributions to family survival.

Historians have also reminded us that if the treatment of children in the mines and factories seems particularly cruel and harsh, contemporary treatment of children in general was often brutal. Beatings, for example, had long been regarded, even by dedicated churchmen and churchwomen, as the best way to discipline children.

The problem of poverty among the working classes was also addressed in Britain by government action in the form of the Poor Law Act of 1834, which established workhouses where jobless poor people were forced to live. The intent of this policy, based on the assumption that the poor were responsible for their own pitiful conditions, was "to make the workhouses as like prisons as possible . . . to establish therein a discipline so severe and repulsive as to make them a terror to the poor." Within a few years, despite sporadic opposition, more than 200,000 poor people were locked up in workhouses, where family members were separated, forced to live in dormitories, given work assignments, and fed dreadful food. Children were often recruited from parish workhouses as cheap labor in factories.

Standards of Living

One of the most heated debates on the Industrial Revolution concerns the standard of living. Most historians assume that in the long run, the Industrial Revolution increased living standards dramatically in the form of higher per capita incomes and greater consumer choices. But did the first generation of industrial workers experience a decline in their living standards and suffer unnecessarily? Some historians have argued that early industrialization required huge profits to be reinvested in new and ever more expensive equipment; thus, to make the requisite profits, industrialists had to keep wages low. Others have questioned that argument, pointing out that initial investments in early machinery were not necessarily large, nor did they need to be. What certainly did occur in the first half of the nineteenth century was a widening gap

CHILD LABOR: DISCIPLINE IN THE TEXTILE MILLS

Child labor was not new, but in the early Industrial Revolution, it was exploited more systematically. These selections are taken from the Report of Sadler's Committee, a report that was commissioned by the government in 1832 to inquire into the condition of child factory workers.

Keeping the Children Awake

It is a very frequent thing at Mr. Marshall's [at Shrewsbury] where the least children were employed (for there were plenty working at six years of age), for Mr. Horseman to start the mill earlier in the morning than he formerly did; and provided a child should be drowsy, the overlooker walks round the room with a stick in his hand, and he touches that child on the shoulder, and says, "Come here." In a corner of the room there is an iron cistern; it is filled with water; he takes this boy, and takes him up by the legs, and dips him over head in the cistern, and sends him to work for the remainder of the day....

What means were taken to keep the children to their work?—Sometimes they would tap them over the head, or nip them over the nose, or give them a pinch of snuff, or throw water in their faces, or pull them off where they were, and job them about to keep them waking.

The Sadistic Overlooker

Samuel Downe, age 29, factory worker living near Leeds; at the age of about ten began work at Mr. Marshall's mills at Shrewsbury, where the customary hours when work was brisk were generally 5 A.M. to 8 P.M., sometimes from 5:30 A.M. to 8 or 9:

What means were taken to keep the children awake and vigilant, especially at the termination of such a day's labor as you have described?—There was generally a blow or a box, or a tap with a strap, or sometimes the hand.

Have you yourself been strapped?—Yes, most severely, till I could not bear to sit upon a chair without having pillows, and through that I left. I was strapped both on my own legs, and then I was put upon a man's back, and then strapped and buckled with two straps to an iron pillar, and flogged, and all by one overlooker; after that he took a piece of tow, and twisted it in the shape of a cord, and put it in my mouth, and tied it behind my head.

He gagged you?—Yes; and then he orders me to run round a part of the machinery where he was overlooker, and he stood at one end, and every time I came there he struck me with a stick, which I believe was an ash plant, and which he generally carried in his hand, and sometimes he hit me, and sometimes he did not; and one of the men in the room came and begged me off, and that he let me go, and not beat me any more, and consequently he did.

You have been beaten with extraordinary severity?—Yes, I was beaten so that I had not power to cry at all, or hardly speak at one time. What age were you at that time?— Between 10 and 11.

Q *What kind of working conditions did children face in the textile mills during the early Industrial Revolution? Why were they beaten?*

---

between rich and poor. One estimate, based on income tax returns in Britain, is that the wealthiest 1 percent of the population increased its share of the national product from 25 percent in 1801 to 35 percent in 1848.

Wages, prices, and consumption patterns are some of the criteria used for measuring the standard of living. Between 1780 and 1850, as far as we can determine from the available evidence, both wages and prices fluctuated widely. Most historians believe that during the Napoleonic wars, the increase in prices outstripped wages. Between 1815 and 1830, a drop in prices was accompanied by a slight increase in wages. From 1830 to the late 1840s, real wages seem to have improved, although regional variations make generalizations difficult.

When we look at consumption patterns, we find, on the one hand, that in Britain in 1850, tea, sugar, and coffee were still semiluxuries consumed primarily by the upper and middle classes and better-off artisans. Meat consumption per capita was less in 1840 than in 1780. On the other hand, a mass market had developed in the cheap cotton goods so important to the Industrial Revolution. As a final note on the question of the standard of living, some historians who take a positive view of the early Industrial Revolution have questioned what would have happened to Britain's growing population without the Industrial Revolution. Would it have gone the way of Ireland's in the Great Hunger of the mid-nineteenth century? No one really knows.

No doubt the periodic crises of overproduction that haunted industrialization from its beginnings caused even further economic hardship. Short-term economic depressions brought high unemployment and increased social tensions. Unemployment figures could be astronomical. During one of these economic depressions in 1842, for example, 60 percent of the factory employees in Bolton were laid off. Cyclical depressions were particularly devastating in towns whose prosperity rested on one industry.

Overall we can say that some evidence exists for an increase in real wages for the working classes between 1790 and 1850, especially in the 1840s. But can standards of living be assessed only in terms of prices, wages, and consumption patterns? No doubt those meant little to people who faced dreadful housing, adulterated food, public health hazards, and the physical and psychological traumas of work life. The real gainers in the early Industrial Revolution were members of the middle class—and some

CHILD LABOR: THE MINES

After examining conditions in British coal mines, a government official commented that "the hardest labour in the worst room in the worst-conducted factory is less hard, less cruel and less demoralizing than the labour in the best of coal-mines." Yet it was not until 1842 that legislation was passed eliminating the labor of boys under ten from the mines. This selection is taken from a government report on the mines in Lancashire.

The Black Holes of Worsley

Examination of Thomas Gibson and George Bryan, witnesses from the coal mines at Worsley:

Have you worked from a boy in a coal mine?—(Both) Yes.

What had you to do then?—Thrutching the basket and drawing. It is done by little boys; one draws the basket and the other pushes it behind. Is that hard labor?—Yes, very hard labor.

For how many hours a day did you work?—Nearly nine hours regularly; sometimes twelve; I have worked about thirteen. We used to go in at six in the morning, and took a bit of bread and cheese in our pocket, and stopped two or three minutes; and some days nothing at all to eat.

How was it that sometimes you had nothing to eat?—We were over-burdened. I had only a mother, and she had nothing to give me. I was sometimes half starved....

Do they work in the same way now exactly?—Yes, they do; they have nothing more than a bit of bread and cheese in their pocket, and sometimes can't eat it all, owing to the dust and damp and badness of air; and sometimes it is as hot as an oven; sometimes I have seen it so hot as to melt a candle.

What are the usual wages of a boy of eight?—They used to get 3d or 4d a day. Now a man's wages is divided into eight eighths; and when a boy is eight years old he gets one of those eighths; at eleven, two eighths; at thirteen, three eighths; at fifteen, four eighths; at twenty, man's wages.

What are the wages of a man?—About 15s if he is in full employment, but often not more than 10s, and out of that he has to get his tools and candles. He consumes about four candles in nine hours' work, in some places six; 6d per pound, and twenty-four candles to the pound.

Were you ever beaten as a child?—Yes, many a score of times; both kicks and thumps.

Are many girls employed in the pits?—Yes, a vast of those. They do the same kind of work as the boys till they get about 14 years of age, when they get the wages of half a man, and never get more, and continue at the same work for many years.

Did they ever fight together?—Yes, many days together. Both boys and girls; sometimes they are very loving with one another.

Q *What kind of working conditions did children face in the mines during the early Industrial Revolution? Why did entrepreneurs permit such conditions and such treatment of children?*

---

skilled workers whose jobs were not eliminated by the new machines. But industrial workers themselves would have to wait until the second half of the nineteenth century to reap the benefits of industrialization.

Efforts at Change: The Workers

Before long, workers looked to the formation of labor organizations to gain decent wages and working conditions. The British government, reacting against the radicalism of the French revolutionary working classes, had passed the Combination Acts in 1799 and 1800 outlawing associations of workers. The legislation failed to prevent the formation of **trade unions,** however. Similar to the craft societies of earlier times, these new associations were formed by skilled workers in a number of new industries, including the cotton spinners, ironworkers, coal miners, and shipwrights. These unions served two purposes. One was to preserve their own workers' position by limiting entry into their trade; the other was to gain benefits from the employers. These early trade unions had limited goals. They favored a working-class struggle against employers, but only to win improvements for the members of their own trades.

The Trade Union Movement Some trade unions were even willing to strike to attain their goals. Bitter strikes were carried out by hand-loom weavers in Glasgow in 1813, cotton spinners in Manchester in 1818, and miners in Northumberland and Durham in 1810. Such blatant illegal activity caused Parliament to repeal the Combination Acts in 1824, accepting the argument of some members that the acts themselves had so alienated workers that they had formed unions. Unions were now tolerated, but other legislation enabled authorities to keep close watch over their activities.

In the 1820s and 1830s, the union movement began to focus on the creation of national unions. One of the leaders in this effort was a well-known cotton magnate and social reformer, Robert Owen (1771–1858). Owen came to believe in the creation of voluntary associations that would demonstrate to others the benefits of cooperative rather than competitive living (see Chapter 21). Although Owen's program was not directed specifically to trade unionists, his ideas had great appeal to some of their leaders. Under Owen's direction, plans emerged for the Grand National Consolidated Trades Union, which was formed in February 1834. As a national federation of trade unions, its primary purpose was to coordinate a general strike for the

A Trade Union Membership Card. Skilled workers in a number of new industries formed trade unions in an attempt to gain higher wages, better working conditions, and special benefits. The scenes at the bottom of this membership card for the Associated Shipwright's Society illustrate some of the medical and social benefits it provided for its members.

eight-hour working day. Rhetoric, however, soon outpaced reality, and by the summer of that year, the lack of real working-class support led to the federation's total collapse, and the union movement reverted to trade unions for individual crafts. The largest and most successful of these unions was the Amalgamated Society of Engineers, formed in 1850. Its provision of generous unemployment benefits in return for a small weekly payment was precisely the kind of practical gains these trade unions sought. Larger goals would have to wait.

Luddites   Trade unionism was not the only type of collective action by workers in the early decades of the Industrial Revolution. The Luddites were skilled crafts-people in the Midlands and northern England who in 1812 attacked the machines that they believed threatened their livelihoods. These attacks failed to stop the industrial mechanization of Britain and have been viewed as utterly naive. Some historians, however, have also seen them as an intense eruption of feeling against unrestrained industrial capitalism. The inability of 12,000 troops to find the culprits provides stunning evidence of the local support they received in their areas.

Chartism   A much more meaningful expression of the attempts of British workers to improve their condition developed in the movement known as Chartism—the "first important political movement of working men organized during the nineteenth century." Its aim was to achieve political democracy. Chartism took its name from the People's Charter, a document drawn up in 1838, by the London Working Men's Association. The charter demanded universal male suffrage, payment for members of Parliament, the elimination of property qualifications for members of Parliament, and annual sessions of Parliament (see the box on p. 629).

Two national petitions incorporating these demands gained millions of signatures and were presented to Parliament in 1839 and 1842. Chartism attempted to encourage change through peaceful, constitutional means, although there was an underlying threat of force, as is evident in the Chartist slogan, "Peacefully if we can, forcibly if we must." In 1842, Chartist activists organized a general strike on behalf of their goals, but it had little success.

Despite the pressures exerted by the Chartists, both national petitions were rejected by the members of Parliament, who were not at all ready for political democracy. As one member said, universal suffrage would be "fatal to all the purposes for which government exists" and was "utterly incompatible with the very existence of civilization." After 1848, Chartism as a movement had largely played itself out. It had never really posed a serious threat to the British establishment, but it had not been a total failure either. Its true significance stemmed from its ability to arouse and organize millions of working-class men and women, to give them a sense of working-class consciousness that they had not really possessed before. This political education of working people was important to the ultimate acceptance of all the points of the People's Charter in the future.

Efforts at Change: Reformers and Government

Efforts to improve the worst conditions of the industrial factory system also came from outside the ranks of the working classes. From its beginning, the Industrial Revolution had drawn much criticism. Romantic poets like William Wordsworth (see Chapter 21) decried the destruction of the natural world:

> I grieve, when on the darker side
> Of this great change I look; and there behold
> Such outrage done to nature as compels
> The indignant power to justify herself.

Reform-minded individuals, be they factory owners who felt twinges of conscience or social reformers in

POLITICAL DEMANDS OF THE CHARTIST MOVEMENT

In the late 1830s and early 1840s, working-class protest centered on achieving a clear set of political goals, particularly universal male suffrage, as the means to obtain economic and social improvements. This selection is taken from one of the national petitions presented to Parliament by the Chartist movement. Although the petition failed, Chartism helped arouse and organize millions of workers.

National Petition (1839)

To the Honorable the Commons of the United Kingdom of Great Britain and Ireland, in Parliament assembled, the Petition of the undersigned, their suffering countrymen, HUMBLY SHOWS,—

The energies of a mighty kingdom have been wasted in building up the power of selfish and ignorant men, and its resources squandered for their aggrandizement. The good of a part has been advanced at the sacrifice of the good of the nation. The few have governed for the interest of the few, while the interests of the many have been sottishly neglected, or insolently...trampled upon.... We come before your honorable house to tell you, with all humility, that this state of things must not be permitted to continue. That it cannot long continue, without very seriously endangering the stability of the throne, and the peace of the kingdom, and that if, by God's help, and all lawful and constitutional appliances, an end can be put to it, we are fully resolved that it shall speedily come to an end.... Required, as we are universally, to support and obey the laws, nature and reason entitle us to demand that in the making of the laws the universal voice shall be implicitly listened to. We perform the duties of freemen; we must have the privileges of freemen. Therefore, we demand universal suffrage.

The suffrage, to be exempt from the corruption of the wealthy and the violence of the powerful, must be secret.... To public safety, as well as public confidence, frequent elections are essential. Therefore, we demand annual parliaments. With power to choose, and freedom in choosing, the range of our choice must be unrestricted. We are compelled, by existing laws, to take for our representatives men who are incapable of appreciating our difficulties, or have little sympathy with them; merchants who have retired from trade and no longer feel its harassings; proprietors of land who are alike ignorant of its evils and its cure; lawyers by whom the notoriety of the senate is courted only as a means of obtaining notice in the courts.... We demand that in the future election of members of your...house, the approbation of the constituency shall be the sole qualification, and that to every representative so chosen, shall be assigned out of the public taxes, a fair and adequate remuneration for the time which he is called upon to devote to the public service.... Universal suffrage will, and it alone can, bring true and lasting peace to the nation; we firmly believe that it will also bring prosperity. May it therefore please your honorable house, to take this our petition into your most serious consideration, and to use your utmost endeavours, by all constitutional means, to have a law passed, granting to every male of lawful age, sane mind, and unconvicted of crime, the right of voting for members of parliament, and directing all future elections of members of parliament to be in the way of secret ballot, and ordaining that the duration of parliament, so chosen, shall in no case exceed one year, and abolishing all property qualifications in the members, and providing for their due remuneration while in attendance on their parliamentary duties.

Q *What political demands did the Chartists make? Judging by this document, how did the Industrial Revolution shape the political ambitions and interests of the laboring classes in Britain?*

Parliament, campaigned against the evils of the industrial factory, especially condemning the abuse of children. One hoped for the day "that these little ones should once more see the rising and setting of the sun."

Government Action As it became apparent that the increase in wealth generated by the Industrial Revolution was accompanied by ever-increasing numbers of poor people, more and more efforts were made to document and deal with the problems. As reports from civic-minded citizens and parliamentary commissions intensified and demonstrated the extent of poverty, degradation, and suffering, the reform efforts began to succeed.

Their first success was a series of factory acts passed between 1802 and 1819 that limited labor for children between the ages of nine and sixteen to twelve hours a day; the employment of children under nine years old was forbidden. Moreover, the laws stipulated that children were to receive instruction in reading and arithmetic during working hours. But these acts applied only to cotton mills, not to factories or mines where some of the worst abuses were taking place. Just as important, no provision was made for enforcing the acts through a system of inspection.

In the reform-minded decades of the 1830s and 1840s, new legislation was passed. The Factory Act of 1833 strengthened earlier labor legislation. All textile factories were now included. Children between nine and thirteen could work only eight hours a day; those between thirteen and eighteen, twelve hours. Factory inspectors were appointed with the power to fine those who broke the law. Another piece of legislation in 1833 required that children between nine and thirteen have at least two hours of elementary education during the working day. In 1847, the Ten Hours Act reduced the workday for children between thirteen and eighteen to ten hours. Women were also now included in the ten-hour limitation. In 1842, the Coal Mines Act eliminated the employment of boys under ten and women in mines. Eventually, men too would benefit from the move to restrict factory hours.

TIMELINE

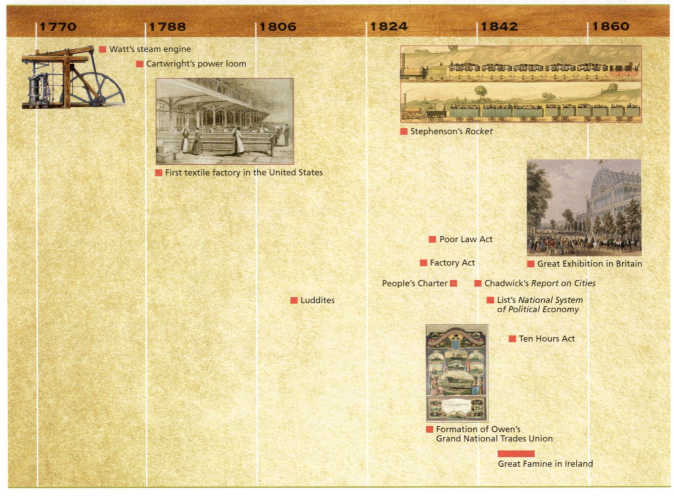

| 1770 | 1788 | 1806 | 1824 | 1842 | 1860 |

- Watt's steam engine
- Cartwright's power loom
- First textile factory in the United States
- Stephenson's *Rocket*
- Poor Law Act
- Factory Act
- Great Exhibition in Britain
- People's Charter
- Chadwick's *Report on Cities*
- Luddites
- List's *National System of Political Economy*
- Ten Hours Act
- Formation of Owen's Grand National Trades Union
- Great Famine in Ireland

CONCLUSION

The Industrial Revolution was one of the major forces of change in the nineteenth century as it led Western civilization into the machine-dependent modern world. Beginning in Britain, its spread to the Continent and the new American nation ensured its growth and domination of the Western world.

The Industrial Revolution seemed to prove to Europeans the underlying assumption of the Scientific Revolution of the seventeenth century—that human beings were capable of dominating nature. By rationally manipulating the material environment for human benefit, people could attain new levels of material prosperity and produce machines not dreamed of in their wildest imaginings. Lost in the excitement of the Industrial Revolution were the voices that pointed to the dehumanization of the workforce and the alienation from one's work, one's associates, oneself, and the natural world.

The Industrial Revolution also transformed the social world of Europe. The creation of an industrial proletariat produced a whole new force for change. The development of a wealthy industrial middle class presented a challenge to the long-term hegemony of landed wealth. Though that wealth had been threatened by the fortunes of commerce, it had never been overturned. But the new bourgeoisie were more demanding. How, in some places, these new industrial bourgeoisie came to play a larger role in the affairs of state will become evident in the next chapter.

NOTES

1. Quoted in W. Gordon Rimmer, *Marshall's of Leeds, Flax-Spinners, 1788–1886* (Cambridge, 1960), p. 40.
2. Daniel Defoe, *A Plan of the English Commerce* (Oxford, 1928), pp. 76–77.
3. Quoted in Albert Tucker, *A History of English Civilization* (New York, 1972), p. 583.
4. Quoted in David Landes, *The Unbound Prometheus: Technological Change and Industrial Development in Western Europe from 1750 to the Present* (Cambridge, 1969), pp. 149–150.
5. Quoted in E. Royston Pike, *Human Documents of the Industrial Revolution in Britain* (London, 1966), p. 320.
6. Ibid., p. 314.
7. Ibid., p. 343.
8. Ibid., p. 315.
9. Charles Dickens, *The Old Curiosity Shop* (New York, 2000), p. 340.
10. Quoted in A. J. Donajgrodzi, ed., *Social Control in Nineteenth-Century Britain* (London, 1977), p. 141.
11. Quoted in Pike, *Human Documents*, pp. 343–344.
12. Quoted in Eric J. Evans, *The Forging of the Modern State: Early Industrial Britain, 1783–1870* (London, 1983), p. 113.
13. Henry Mayhew, *London Labour and the London Poor* (London, 1851), vol.1, pp. 342–343.
14. Quoted in Pike, *Human Documents*, pp. 60–61.
15. Quoted in Evans, *Forging of the Modern State*, p. 124.

SUGGESTIONS FOR FURTHER READING

General Works The well-written work by **D. Landes**, *The Unbound Prometheus: Technological Change and Industrial Development in Western Europe from 1750 to the Present* (Cambridge, 1969), is a good introduction to the Industrial Revolution. Although more technical, also of value are **C. Trebilcock**, *The Industrialization of the Continental Powers, 1780–1914* (London, 1981), and **S. Pollard**, *Peaceful Conquest: The Industrialization of Europe, 1760–1970* (Oxford, 1981). There are good collections of essays in **P. Mathias and J. A. Davis, eds.**, *The First Industrial Revolutions* (Oxford, 1989), and **M. Teich and R. Porter, eds.**, *The Industrial Revolution in National Context: Europe and the USA* (Cambridge, 1996). See also **D. Fisher**, *The Industrial Revolution* (New York, 1992). For a broader perspective, see **P. Stearns**, *The Industrial Revolution in World History* (Boulder, Colo., 1993). On the Industrial Revolution in Britain, see **K. Morgan**, *The Birth of Industrial Britain: Social Change, 1750–1850* (New York, 2004); **P. Mathias**, *The First Industrial Nation: An Economic History of Britain, 1700–1914*, 3d ed. (New York, 2001); and **R. Brown**, *Society and Economy in Modern Britain, 1700–1850* (London, 1991). On the spread of industrialization to the Continent, see **T. Kemp**, *Industrialization in Nineteenth-Century Europe*, 2d ed. (London, 1985).

Britain in the Industrial Revolution Given the importance of Great Britain in the Industrial Revolution, a number of books are available that place it in a broader context. See **E. J. Evans**, *The Forging of the Modern State: Early Industrial Britain, 1783–1870*, 3d ed. (London, 2001), and **P. K. O'Brien and R. Quinault, eds.**, *The Industrial Revolution and British Society* (New York, 1993).

Industrialization in the United States The early industrialization of the United States is examined in **B. Hindle and S. Lubar**, *Engines of Change: The American Industrial Revolution, 1790–1860* (Washington, D.C., 1986). On the economic ties between Great Britain and the United States, see **D. Jeremy**, *Transatlantic Industrial Revolution: The Diffusion of Textile Technology Between Britain and America, 1790–1830* (Cambridge, Mass., 1981).

Social Impact of Industrialization A general discussion of population growth in Europe can be found in **T. McKeown**, *The Modern Rise of Population* (London, 1976). For an examination of urban growth, see the classic work of **A. F. Weber**, *The Growth of Cities in the Nineteenth Century: A Study in Statistics* (Ithaca, N.Y., 1963); **J. G. Williamson**, *Coping with City Growth During the British Industrial Revolution* (Cambridge, 2002); and **L. D. Schwarz**, *London in the Age of Industrialization* (New York, 1992). **C. Kinealy**, *A Death-Dealing Famine: The Great Hunger in Ireland* (Chicago, 1997), is a good account of the great Irish tragedy, but see also **J. S. Donnelly**, *The Great Irish Potato Famine* (London, 2001). Many of the works cited here have much information on the social impact of the Industrial Revolution, but additional material is available in **F. Crouzet**, *The First Industrialists: The Problems of Origins* (Cambridge, 1985), on British entrepreneurs; **J. Merriman**, *The Margins of City Life* (New York, 1991), on French cities; **P. Pilbeam**, *The Middle Classes in Europe, 1789–1914* (Basingstoke, England, 1990); and **T. Koditschek**, *Class Formation and Urban Industrial Society* (New York, 1990). **G. Himmelfarb**, *The Idea of Poverty: England in the Early Industrial Age* (New York, 1984), traces the concepts of poverty and the poor from the mid-eighteenth century to the mid-nineteenth century. **M. J. Maynes**, *Taking the Hard Road* (Chapel Hill, N.C., 1995), offers a glimpse into the lives of workers. A classic work on female labor patterns is **L. A. Tilly and J. W. Scott**, *Women, Work, and Family* (New York, 1978). See also **J. Lown**, *Women and Industrialization: Gender at Work in Nineteenth-Century England* (Minneapolis, Minn., 1990); **J. Rendall**, *Women in an Industrializing Society: England, 1750–1880* (Oxford, 2002); and **K. Honeyman**, *Women, Gender, and Industrialization in England, 1700–1870* (New York, 2000).

CENGAGENOW CengageNOW is an integrated online suite of services and resources with proven ease of use and efficient paths to success, delivering the results you want—NOW! academic.cengage.com/login/

Enter CengageNOW using the access card that is available with *Western Civilization*. CengageNOW will assist you in understanding the content in this chapter with lesson plans generated for your needs. In addition, you can read the following documents, and many more, online:

Adam Smith, selected chapters from *The Wealth of Nations*

Charles Dickens, excerpts from *Hard Times*

Alexis de Tocqueville, excerpts from *Democracy in America*

WESTERN CIVILIZATION RESOURCES

Visit the *Western Civilization* Companion Web site for resources specific to this book:

academic.cengage.com/history/spielvogel

For a variety of tools to help you succeed in this course, visit the Western Civilization Resource Center. Enter the Resource Center using either your *CengageNOW* access card or your standalone access card for the *Wadsworth Western Civilization Resource Center*. Organized by topic, this Web site includes quizzes; images; primary source documents; interactive simulations, maps, and timelines; movie explorations; and a wealth of other resources.

http://westernrc.wadsworth.com/

CHAPTER 21
REACTION, REVOLUTION, AND ROMANTICISM, 1815–1850

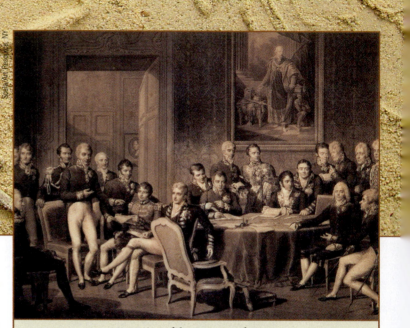

A meeting of the Congress of Vienna

CHAPTER OUTLINE AND FOCUS QUESTIONS

The Conservative Order (1815–1830)

Q What were the goals of the Congress of Vienna and the Concert of Europe, and how successful were they in achieving those goals?

The Ideologies of Change

Q What were the main tenets of conservatism, liberalism, nationalism, and utopian socialism, and what role did each ideology play in Europe in the first half of the nineteenth century?

Revolution and Reform (1830–1850)

Q What forces for change were present in France and Great Britain between 1830 and 1848, and how did each nation respond? What were the causes of the revolutions of 1848, and why did the revolutions fail?

The Emergence of an Ordered Society

Q How did Europe respond to the need for order in society in the first half of the nineteenth century?

Culture in an Age of Reaction and Revolution: The Mood of Romanticism

Q What were the characteristics of Romanticism, and how were they reflected in literature, art, and music?

CRITICAL THINKING

Q In what ways were intellectual and artistic developments related to the political and social forces of the age?

IN SEPTEMBER 1814, hundreds of foreigners began to converge on Vienna, the capital city of the Austrian Empire. Many were members of European royalty—kings, archdukes, princes, and their wives—accompanied by their diplomatic advisers and scores of servants. Their congenial host was the Austrian emperor, Francis I, who never tired of regaling Vienna's guests with concerts, glittering balls, sumptuous feasts, and countless hunting parties. One participant remembered, "Eating, fireworks, public illuminations. For eight or ten days, I haven't been able to work at all. What a life!" Of course, not every waking hour was spent in pleasure during this gathering of notables, known to history as the Congress of Vienna. These people were also representatives of all the states that had fought Napoleon, and their real business was to arrange a final peace settlement after almost a decade of war. On June 8, 1815, they finally completed their task.

The forces of upheaval unleashed during the French revolutionary and Napoleonic wars were temporarily quieted in 1815 as rulers sought to restore stability by reestablishing much of the old order to a Europe ravaged by war. Kings, landed aristocrats, and bureaucratic elites regained their control over domestic governments, and internationally the forces of conservatism tried to maintain the new status quo; some states even used military force to intervene in the internal affairs of other countries in their desire to crush revolutions.

But the Western world had been changed, and it would not readily go back to the old system. New ideologies, especially liberalism and nationalism, both products of the revolutionary upheaval initiated in France, had become too powerful to be contained. Not content with the status quo, the forces of change gave rise first to the revolts and revolutions that periodically shook Europe in the 1820s and 1830s and then to the widespread revolutions of 1848. Some of the revolutions and revolutionaries were successful; most were not. Although the old order usually appeared to have prevailed, by 1850 it was apparent that its days were numbered. This perception was reinforced by the changes wrought by the Industrial Revolution. Together the forces unleashed by the dual revolutions—the French Revolution and the Industrial Revolution—made it impossible to return to prerevolutionary Europe. Nevertheless, although these events ushered in what historians like to call the modern European world, remnants of the old remained amid the new. ◇

The Conservative Order (1815–1830)

Q **Focus Question:** What were the goals of the Congress of Vienna and the Concert of Europe, and how successful were they in achieving those goals?

The immediate response to the defeat of Napoleon was the desire to contain revolution and the revolutionary forces by restoring much of the old order.

The Peace Settlement

In March 1814, even before Napoleon had been defeated, his four major enemies—Great Britain, Austria, Prussia, and Russia—had agreed to remain united, not only to defeat France but also to ensure peace after the war. After Napoleon's defeat, this Quadruple Alliance restored the Bourbon monarchy to France in the person of Louis XVIII and agreed to meet at a congress in Vienna in September 1814 to arrange a final peace settlement.

The leader of the Congress of Vienna was the Austrian foreign minister, Prince Klemens von Metternich (1773–1859). An experienced diplomat who was also conceited and self-assured, Metternich described himself in his memoirs in 1819: "There is a wide sweep about my mind. I am always above and beyond the preoccupation of most public men; I cover a ground much vaster than they can see. I cannot keep myself from saying about twenty times a day: 'How right I am, and how wrong they are.'"[1]

The Principle of Legitimacy Metternich claimed that he was guided at Vienna by the **principle of legitimacy.** To reestablish peace and stability in Europe, he considered it necessary to restore the legitimate monarchs who would preserve traditional institutions. This had already been done in the restoration of the Bourbons in France and Spain, as well as in the return of a number of rulers to their thrones in the Italian states. Elsewhere, however, the principle of legitimacy was largely ignored and completely overshadowed by more practical considerations of power. The congress's treatment of Poland, to which Russia, Austria, and Prussia all laid claim, illustrates this approach. Prussia and Austria were allowed to

Metternich and the Congress of Vienna. Prince Klemens von Metternich, the foreign minister of Austria, played a major role at the Congress of Vienna as the chief exponent of the principle of legitimacy. This painting by Engelbert Seibertz shows a group of the statesmen who participated in the discussions at Vienna. From left to right, they are Talleyrand, the French representative; Montgelas, the Bavarian minister; Hardenberg, the Prussian minister; Metternich, who appears to be the focus of attention in the group; and von Gentz, a German political theorist.

MAP 21.1 **Europe After the Congress of Vienna, 1815.** The Congress of Vienna imposed order on Europe based on the principles of monarchical government and a balance of power. Monarchs were restored in France, Spain, and other states recently under Napoleon's control, and much territory changed hands, often at the expense of small and weak states.

Q How did Europe's major powers manipulate territory to decrease the probability that France could again threaten the Continent's stability? 🌐 **View an animated version of this map or related maps at** academic.cengage.com/history/spielvogel

keep some Polish territory. A new, nominally independent Polish kingdom, about three-quarters of the size of the duchy of Warsaw, was established, with the Romanov dynasty of Russia as its hereditary monarchs. Although Poland was guaranteed its independence, the kingdom's foreign policy (and the kingdom itself) remained under Russian control. As compensation for the Polish lands it lost, Prussia received two-fifths of Saxony, the Napoleonic German kingdom of Westphalia, and the left bank of the Rhine. Austria was compensated for its loss of the Austrian Netherlands by being given control of two northern Italian provinces, Lombardy and Venetia (see Map 21.1).

A New Balance of Power In making these territorial rearrangements, the diplomats at Vienna believed they were forming a new **balance of power** that would prevent any one country from dominating Europe. For example, to balance Russian gains, Prussia and Austria had been strengthened. According to Metternich, this arrangement had clearly avoided a great danger: "Prussia and Austria are completing their systems of defense; united, the two monarchies form an unconquerable barrier against the enterprises of any conquering prince who might perhaps once again occupy the throne of France or that of Russia."[2]

Considerations of the balance of power also dictated the allied treatment of France. France had not been significantly weakened; it remained a great power. The fear that France might again upset the European peace remained so strong that the conferees attempted to establish major defensive barriers against possible French expansion. To the north of France, they created a new enlarged kingdom of the Netherlands composed of the former Dutch Republic and the Austrian Netherlands (Belgium) under a new ruler, King William I of the house of Orange. To the southeast, Piedmont (officially part of the kingdom of Sardinia) was enlarged. On France's eastern frontier, Prussia was strengthened by giving it control of the territory along the east bank of the Rhine. The British at least expected Prussia to be the major bulwark against French expansion in central Europe, but the Congress of Vienna also created a new league of German states, the Germanic Confederation, to replace the Napoleonic Confederation of the Rhine.

Napoleon's escape from Elba and his return to France for one hundred days in the midst of the Congress of Vienna delayed the negotiations but did not significantly alter the overall agreement. It was decided, however, to punish the French people for their enthusiastic response to Napoleon's return. France's borders were pushed back

THE VOICE OF CONSERVATISM: METTERNICH OF AUSTRIA

There was no greater symbol of conservatism in the first half of the nineteenth century than Prince Klemens von Metternich of Austria. Metternich played a crucial role at the Congress of Vienna and worked tirelessly for thirty years to repress the "revolutionary seed," as he called it, that had been spread to Europe by the "military despotism of Bonaparte."

Klemens von Metternich, *Memoirs*

We are convinced that society can no longer be saved without strong and vigorous resolutions on the part of the Governments still free in their opinions and actions.

We are also convinced that this may be, if the Governments face the truth, if they free themselves from all illusion, if they join their ranks and take their stand on a line of correct, unambiguous, and frankly announced principles.

By this course the monarchs will fulfill the duties imposed upon them by Him who, by entrusting them with power, has charged them to watch over the maintenance of justice, and the rights of all, to avoid the paths of error, and tread firmly in the way of truth....

If the same elements of destruction which are now throwing society into convulsions have existed in all ages—for every age has seen immoral and ambitious men, hypocrites, men of heated imaginations, wrong motives, and wild projects—yet ours, by the single fact of the liberty of the press, possesses more than any preceding age the means of contact, seduction, and attraction whereby to act on these different classes of men.

We are certainly not alone in questioning if society can exist with the liberty of the press, a scourge unknown to the world before the latter half of the seventeenth century, and restrained until the end of the eighteenth, with

scarcely any expectations but England—a part of Europe separated from the continent by the sea, as well as by her language and by her peculiar manners.

The first principle to be followed by the monarchs, united as they are by the coincidence of their desires and opinions, should be that of maintaining the stability of political institutions against the disorganized excitement which has taken possession of men's minds; the immutability of principles against the madness of their interpretation; and respect for laws actually in force against a desire for their destruction....

The first and greatest concern for the immense majority of every nation is the stability of the laws, and their uninterrupted action—never their change. Therefore, let the Governments govern, let them maintain the groundwork of their institutions, both ancient and modern; for if it is at all times dangerous to touch them, it certainly would not now, in the general confusion, be wise to do so....

Let them maintain religious principles in all their purity, and not allow the faith to be attacked and morality interpreted according to the social contract or the visions of foolish sectarians.

Let them suppress Secret Societies, that gangrene of society....

To every great State determined to survive the storm there still remain many chances of salvation, and a strong union between the States on the principles we have announced will overcome the storm itself.

Q *Based on Metternich's discussion, how would you define conservatism? What experiences conditioned Metternich's ideas? Based on this selection, what policies do you think Metternich would have wanted his government to pursue?*

---

to those of 1790, and the nation was forced to pay an indemnity and accept an army of occupation for five years. The order established by the Congress of Vienna managed to avoid a general European conflict for almost a century.

The Ideology of Conservatism

The peace arrangements of 1815 were the beginning of a conservative reaction determined to contain the liberal and nationalist forces unleashed by the French Revolution. Metternich and his kind were representatives of the **ideology** known as **conservatism** (see the box above). As a modern political philosophy, conservatism dates from 1790 when Edmund Burke (1729–1797) wrote his *Reflections on the Revolution in France* in reaction to the French Revolution, especially its radical republican and democratic ideas. Burke maintained that society was a contract, but "the state ought not to be considered as nothing better than a partnership agreement in a trade of

pepper and coffee, to be taken up for a temporary interest and to be dissolved by the fancy of the parties." The state was a partnership but one "not only between those who are living, but between those who are living, those who are dead and those who are to be born."[3] No one generation has the right to destroy this partnership; each generation has the duty to preserve and transmit it to the next. Burke advised against the violent overthrow of a government by revolution, but he did not reject the possibility of change. Sudden change was unacceptable but that did not eliminate gradual or evolutionary improvements.

Burke's conservatism, however, was not the only kind. The Frenchman Joseph de Maistre (1753–1821) was the most influential spokesman for a counterrevolutionary and authoritarian conservatism. De Maistre espoused the restoration of hereditary monarchy, which he regarded as a divinely sanctioned institution. Only absolute monarchy could guarantee "order in society" and avoid the chaos generated by movements like the French Revolution.

Despite their differences, most conservatives held to a general body of beliefs. They favored obedience to political authority, believed that organized religion was crucial to social order, hated revolutionary upheavals, and were unwilling to accept either the liberal demands for civil liberties and representative governments or the nationalistic aspirations generated by the French revolutionary era. The community took precedence over individual rights; society must be organized and ordered, and tradition remained the best guide for order. After 1815, the political philosophy of conservatism was supported by hereditary monarchs, government bureaucracies, landowning aristocracies, and revived churches, be they Protestant or Catholic. The conservative forces appeared dominant after 1815, both internationally and domestically.

Conservative Domination: The Concert of Europe

The European powers' fear of revolution and war led them to develop the Concert of Europe as a means to maintain the new status quo they had constructed. This accord grew out of the reaffirmation of the Quadruple Alliance in November 1815. Great Britain, Russia, Prussia, and Austria renewed their commitment against any attempted restoration of Bonapartist power and agreed to meet periodically in conferences to discuss their common interests and examine measures that "will be judged most salutary for the repose and prosperity of peoples, and for the maintenance of peace in Europe."

In accordance with the agreement for periodic meetings, four congresses were held between 1818 and 1822. The first, held in 1818 at Aix-la-Chapelle, was by far the most congenial. "Never have I known a prettier little congress," said Metternich. The four great powers agreed to withdraw their army of occupation from France and to add France to the Concert of Europe. The Quadruple Alliance became a quintuple alliance.

The next congress proved far less pleasant. This session, at Troppau, was called in the autumn of 1820 to deal with the outbreak of revolution in Spain and Italy. The revolt in Spain was directed against Ferdinand VII, the Bourbon king who had been restored to the throne in 1814. In southern Italy, the restoration of another Bourbon, Ferdinand I, as king of Naples and Sicily sparked a rebellion that soon spread to Piedmont in northern Italy.

The Principle of Intervention

Metternich was especially disturbed by the revolts in Italy because he saw them as a threat to Austria's domination of the peninsula. At Troppau, he proposed a protocol that established the **principle of intervention.** It read:

> States which have undergone a change of Government due to revolution, the results of which threaten other states, *ipso facto* cease to be members of the European Alliance, and remain excluded from it until their situation gives guarantees for legal order and stability. If, owing to such situations, immediate

danger threatens other states, the Powers bind themselves, by peaceful means, or if need be by arms, to bring back the guilty state into the bosom of the Great Alliance.[4]

The principle of intervention meant that the great powers of Europe had the right to send armies into countries where there were revolutions to restore legitimate monarchs to their thrones. Britain refused to agree to the principle, arguing that it had never been the intention of the Quadruple Alliance to interfere in the internal affairs of other states, except in France. Ignoring the British response, Austria, Prussia, and Russia met in a third congress at Laibach in January 1821 and authorized the sending of Austrian troops to Naples. These forces crushed the revolt, restored Ferdinand I to the throne, and then moved north to suppress the rebels in Piedmont. At the fourth postwar conference, held at Verona in October 1822, the same three powers authorized France to invade Spain to crush the revolt against Ferdinand VII. In the spring of 1823, French forces restored the Bourbon monarch.

This success for the policy of intervention came at a price, however. The Concert of Europe had broken down when the British rejected Metternich's principle of intervention. And although the British had failed to thwart allied intervention in Spain and Italy, they were successful in keeping the Continental powers from interfering with the revolutions in Latin America.

The Revolt of Latin America

Although much of North America had been freed of European domination in the eighteenth century by the American Revolution, Latin America remained in the hands of the Spanish and Portuguese. Napoleon's Continental wars at the beginning of the nineteenth century, however, soon had repercussions in Latin America. When the Bourbon monarchy of Spain was toppled by Napoleon, Spanish authority in its colonial empire was weakened. By 1810, the disintegration of royal power in Argentina had led to that nation's independence. In Venezuela, a bitter struggle for independence was led by Simón Bolívar (1783–1830), hailed as "the Liberator." His forces freed Colombia in 1819 and Venezuela in 1821. A second liberator was José de San Martín (1778–1850), who freed Chile in 1817 and then in 1821 moved on to Lima, Peru, the center of Spanish authority. He was soon joined by Bolívar, who assumed the task of crushing the last significant Spanish army in 1824. Mexico and the Central American provinces also achieved their freedom, and by 1825, after Portugal had recognized the independence of Brazil, almost all of Latin America had been freed of colonial domination (see Map 21.2).

The Continental powers, however, flushed by their success in crushing the rebellions in Spain and Italy, favored the use of troops to restore Spanish control in Latin America. This time, British opposition to intervention prevailed. Eager to gain access to an entire continent for investment and trade, the British proposed joint action

MAP 21.2 Latin America in the First Half of the Nineteenth Century. Latin American colonies took advantage of Spain's weakness during the Napoleonic wars to fight for independence, beginning with Argentina in 1810 and spreading throughout the region over the next decade with the help of leaders like Simón Bolívar and José de San Martín. The dates in parentheses show the years in which the countries received formal recognition.

Q How many South American countries are sources of rivers that feed the Amazon, and roughly what percentage of the continent is contained within the Amazon's watershed?

🐾 **View an animated version of this map or related maps at** academic.cengage.com/history/spielvogel

with the United States against European interference in Latin America. Distrustful of British motives, President James Monroe acted alone in 1823, guaranteeing the independence of the new Latin American nations and warning against any further European intervention in the New World in the famous Monroe Doctrine. Actually, British ships were more important to Latin American independence than American words. Britain's navy stood between Latin America and any European invasion force, and the Continental powers were extremely reluctant to challenge British naval power.

Although political independence brought economic independence to Latin America, old patterns were quickly reestablished. Instead of Spain and Portugal, Great Britain now dominated the Latin American economy. British merchants moved in in large numbers, while British investors poured in funds, especially in the mining industry. Old trade patterns soon reemerged. Because Latin America served as a source of raw materials and foodstuffs for the industrializing nations of Europe and the United States, exports—especially of wheat, tobacco, wool, sugar, coffee, and hides—to the North Atlantic

José de San Martín. José de San Martín of Argentina was one of the famous leaders of the Latin American independence movement. His forces liberated Argentina, Chile, and Peru from Spanish authority. In this painting by Theodore Gericault, San Martín is shown leading his troops at the Battle of Chacabuco in Chile in 1817.

countries increased noticeably. At the same time, finished consumer goods, especially textiles, were imported in increasing quantities, causing a decline in industrial production in Latin America. The emphasis on exporting raw materials and importing finished products ensured the ongoing domination of the Latin American economy by foreigners.

The Greek Revolt The principle of intervention proved to be a double-edged sword. Designed to prevent revolution, it could also be used to support revolution if the great powers found it in their interest to do so. In 1821, the Greeks revolted against their Ottoman Turkish masters. Although subject to Muslim control for four hundred years, the Greeks had been allowed to maintain their language and their Greek Orthodox faith. A revival of Greek national sentiment at the beginning of the nineteenth century added to the growing desire for liberation "from the terrible yoke of Turkish oppression." The Greek revolt was soon transformed into a noble cause by an outpouring of European sentiment for the Greeks' struggle.

In 1827, a combined British and French fleet went to Greece and defeated a large Ottoman armada. A year later,

Russia declared war on the Ottoman Empire and invaded its European provinces of Moldavia and Wallachia. By the Treaty of Adrianople in 1829, which ended the Russian-Turkish war, the Russians received a protectorate over the two provinces. By the same treaty, the Ottoman Empire agreed to allow Russia, France, and Britain to decide the fate of Greece. In 1830, the three powers declared Greece an independent kingdom, and two years later, a new royal dynasty was established. The revolution had been successful only because the great

The Balkans by 1830

powers themselves supported it. Until 1830, the Greek revolt was the only successful one in Europe; the conservative domination was still largely intact.

Conservative Domination: The European States

Between 1815 and 1830, the conservative domination of Europe evident in the Concert of Europe was also apparent in domestic affairs as conservative governments throughout Europe worked to maintain the old order.

Great Britain: Rule of the Tories In 1815, Great Britain was governed by the aristocratic landowning classes that dominated both houses of Parliament. Suffrage for elections to the House of Commons, controlled by the landed gentry, was restricted and unequal, especially in light of the changing distribution of the British population due to the Industrial Revolution. Large new industrial cities such as Birmingham and Manchester had no representatives, while landowners used pocket and rotten boroughs (see Chapter 18) to control seats in the House of Commons. Although the monarchy was not yet powerless, in practice the power of the crown was largely in the hands of the ruling party in Parliament.

There were two political factions in Parliament, the Tories and the Whigs. Both were still dominated by members of the landed classes, although the Whigs were beginning to receive support from the new industrial middle class. Tory ministers largely dominated the government until 1830 and had little desire to change the existing political and electoral system.

Popular discontent grew after 1815 because of severe economic difficulties. The Tory government's response to falling agricultural prices was the Corn Law of 1815, a measure that imposed extraordinarily high tariffs on foreign grain. Though the tariffs benefited the landowners, the price of bread rose substantially, making conditions for the working classes more difficult. Mass protest meetings took a nasty turn when a squadron of cavalry attacked a crowd of 60,000 demonstrators at Saint Peter's Fields in Manchester in 1819. The deaths of eleven people, called the Peterloo Massacre by government detractors, led Parliament to take even more repressive measures. The government restricted large public meetings and the dissemination of pamphlets among the poor. At the same time, by making minor reforms in the 1820s, the Tories managed to avoid meeting the demands for electoral reforms—at least until 1830 (see "Reform in Great Britain" later in this chapter).

Restoration in France

In 1814, the Bourbon family was restored to the throne of France in the person of Louis XVIII (1814–1824). Louis understood the need to accept some of the changes brought to France by the revolutionary and Napoleonic eras. He accepted Napoleon's Civil Code with its recognition of the principle of equality before the law (see Chapter 19). The property rights of those who had purchased confiscated lands during the Revolution were preserved. A bicameral (two-house) legislature was established, consisting of the Chamber of Peers, chosen by the king, and the Chamber of Deputies, chosen by an electorate restricted to slightly fewer than 100,000 wealthy people.

Louis's grudging moderation, however, was opposed by liberals eager to extend the revolutionary reforms and by a group of **ultraroyalists** who criticized the king's willingness to compromise and retain so many features of the Napoleonic era. The ultras hoped to return to a monarchical system dominated by a privileged landed aristocracy and to restore the Catholic Church to its former position of influence.

The initiative passed to the ultraroyalists in 1824 when Louis XVIII died and was succeeded by his brother, the count of Artois, who became Charles X (1824–1830). In 1825, Charles granted an indemnity to aristocrats whose lands had been confiscated during the Revolution. Moreover, the king pursued a religious policy that encouraged the Catholic Church to reestablish control over the French educational system. Public outrage, fed by liberal newspapers, forced the king to compromise in 1827 and even to accept the principle of **ministerial responsibility**—that the ministers of the king were responsible to the legislature. But in 1829, he violated his commitment. A protest by the deputies led the king to dissolve the legislature in 1830 and call for new elections. France was on the brink of another revolution.

Intervention in the Italian States and Spain

The Congress of Vienna had established nine states in Italy, including Piedmont (part of the kingdom of Sardinia) in the north, ruled by the house of Savoy; the kingdom of the Two Sicilies (Naples and Sicily); the Papal States; a handful of small duchies ruled by relatives of the Austrian emperor; and the important northern provinces of Lombardy and Venetia, which were now part of the Austrian Empire.

Italy, 1815

Much of Italy was under Austrian domination, and all the states had extremely reactionary governments eager to smother any liberal or nationalist sentiment. Nevertheless, secret societies motivated by nationalistic dreams and known as the Carbonari ("charcoal burners") continued to conspire and plan for revolution.

In Spain, another Bourbon dynasty had been restored in the person of Ferdinand VII in 1814. Ferdinand (1814–1833) had agreed to observe the liberal constitution of 1812, which allowed for the functioning of an elected parliamentary assembly known as the Cortes. But the king soon reneged on his promises, tore up the constitution, dissolved the Cortes, and persecuted its members, which led a combined group of army officers, upper-middle-class merchants, and liberal intellectuals to revolt. The king capitulated in March 1820 and promised once again to restore the constitution and the Cortes. But Metternich's policy of intervention came to Ferdinand's rescue. In April 1823, a French army moved into Spain and forced the revolutionary government to flee Madrid.

By August of that year, the king had been restored to his throne.

Repression in Central Europe

After 1815, the forces of reaction were particularly successful in central Europe. The Habsburg empire and its chief agent, Prince Klemens von Metternich, played an important role. Metternich boasted, "You see in me the chief Minister of Police in Europe. I keep an eye on everything. My contacts are such that nothing escapes me."[5] Metternich's spies were everywhere, searching for evidence of liberal or nationalist plots. Although both liberalism and nationalism emerged in the German states and the Austrian Empire, they were initially weak as central Europe tended to remain under the domination of aristocratic landowning classes and autocratic, centralized monarchies.

The Vienna settlement in 1815 had recognized the existence of thirty-eight sovereign states in what had once been the Holy Roman Empire. Austria and Prussia were the two great powers; the other states varied considerably in size. Together these states formed the Germanic Confederation, but the confederation had little power. It had no real executive, and its only central organ was the federal diet, which needed the consent of all member states to take action, making it virtually powerless. Nevertheless, it also came to serve as Metternich's instrument to repress revolutionary movements within the German states.

Initially, Germans who favored liberal principles and German unity looked to Prussia for leadership. During the Napoleonic era, King Frederick William III (1797–1840), following the advice of his two chief ministers, Baron Heinrich von Stein and Prince Karl von Hardenberg, instituted political and institutional reforms in response to Prussia's defeat at the hands of Napoleon. The reforms included the abolition of serfdom, municipal self-government through town councils, the expansion of primary and secondary schools, and universal military conscription to form a national army. The reforms, however, did not include the creation of a legislative assembly or representative government as Stein and Hardenberg wished. After 1815, Frederick William grew more reactionary and was content to follow Metternich's lead. Though reforms had made Prussia strong, it remained largely an absolutist state with little interest in German unity.

Liberal and national movements in the German states seemed largely limited to university professors and students. The latter began to organize **Burschenschaften,** student societies dedicated to fostering the goal of a free, united Germany (see the box on p. 641). Their ideas and their motto, "Honor, Liberty, Fatherland," were in part inspired by Friedrich Ludwig Jahn, who had organized gymnastic societies during the Napoleonic wars to promote the regeneration of German youth. Jahn encouraged Germans to pursue their Germanic heritage and urged his followers to disrupt the lectures of professors whose views were not nationalistic.

From 1817 to 1819, the *Burschenschaften* pursued a variety of activities that alarmed German governments.

At an assembly held at the Wartburg Castle in 1817, marking the three-hundredth anniversary of Luther's Ninety-Five Theses, the crowd burned books written by conservative authors. When a deranged student assassinated a reactionary playwright, Metternich had the diet of the Germanic Confederation draw up the Karlsbad Decrees of 1819. These closed the *Burschenschaften,* provided for censorship of the press, and placed the universities under close supervision and control. Thereafter, except for a minor flurry of activity from 1830 to 1832, Metternich and the cooperative German rulers maintained the conservative status quo.

The Austrian Empire was a multinational state, a collection of different peoples under the Habsburg emperor, who provided a common bond. The empire contained eleven peoples of different national origin, including Germans, Czechs, Magyars (Hungarians), Slovaks, Romanians, Slovenes, Poles, Serbians, and Italians. The Germans, though only a quarter of the population, were economically the most advanced and played a leading role in governing Austria. Essentially, the Austrian Empire was held together by the dynasty, the imperial civil service, the imperial army, and the Catholic Church. But its national groups, especially the Hungarians, with their increasing desire for autonomy, acted as forces to break the empire apart.

Still Metternich managed to hold it all together. His antipathy to liberalism and nationalism was understandably grounded in the realization that these forces threatened to tear the empire apart. The growing liberal belief that each national group had the right to its own system of government could only mean disaster for the multinational Austrian Empire. While the forces of liberalism and nationalism grew, the Austrian Empire largely stagnated.

Russia: Autocracy of the Tsars

At the beginning of the nineteenth century, Russia was overwhelmingly rural, agricultural, and autocratic. The Russian tsar was still regarded as a divine-right monarch. Alexander I (1801–1825) had been raised in the ideas of the Enlightenment and initially seemed willing to make reforms. With the aid of his liberal adviser Michael Speransky, he relaxed censorship, freed political prisoners, and reformed the educational system. He refused, however, to grant a constitution or free the serfs in the face of opposition from the nobility. After the defeat of Napoleon, Alexander became a reactionary, and his government reverted to strict and arbitrary censorship. Soon opposition to Alexander arose from a group of secret societies.

One of these societies, known as the Northern Union, was composed of young aristocrats who had served in the Napoleonic wars and had become aware of the world outside Russia as well as intellectuals alienated by the censorship and lack of academic freedom in Russian universities. The Northern Union favored the establishment of a constitutional monarchy and the abolition of serfdom. The sudden death of Alexander in 1825 offered them their opportunity.

UNIVERSITY STUDENTS AND GERMAN UNITY

In the early nineteenth century, university students and professors were the chief supporters of German nationalism. Especially important were the *Burschenschaften*, student societies that espoused the cause of German unity. In this selection, the liberal Heinrich von Gagern explains the purpose of the *Burschenschaften* to his father.

Heinrich von Gagern, Letter to His Father

It is very hard to explain the spirit of the student movement to you, but I shall try, even though I can only give you a few characteristics.... It speaks to the better youth, the man of heart and spirit and love for all this good, and gives him nourishment and being. For the average student of the past, the university years were a time to enjoy life, and to make a sharp break with his own background in defiance of the philistine world, which seemed to him somehow to foreshadow the tomb. Their pleasures, their organizations, and their talk were determined by their *status* as students, and their university obligation was only to avoid failing the examination and scraping by adequately— bread-and-butter learning. They were satisfied with themselves if they thought they could pass the examination. There are still many of those nowadays, indeed the majority over-all. But at several universities, and especially here, another group—in my eyes a better one—has managed to get the upper hand in the sense that it sets the mood. I prefer really not to call it a mood; rather, it is something that presses hard and tried to spread its ideas....

Those who share in this spirit have then quite another tendency in their student life, Love of Fatherland is their guiding principle. Their purpose is to make a better future for the Fatherland, each as best he can, to spread national consciousness, or to use the much ridiculed and maligned Germanic expression, more folkishness, and to work for better constitutions....

We want more sense of community among the several states of Germany, greater unity in their policies and in their principles of government; no separate policy for each state, but the nearest possible relations with one another; above all, we want Germany to be considered *one* land and the German people *one* people. In the forms of our student comradeship we show how we want to approach this as nearly as possible in the real world. Regional fraternities are forbidden, and we live in a German comradeship, one people in spirit, as we want it for all Germany in reality. We give our selves the freest of constitutions, just as we should like Germany to have the freest possible one, insofar as that is suitable for the German people. We want a constitution for the people that fits in with the spirit of the times and with the people's own level of enlightenment, rather than what each prince gives his people according to what he likes and what serves his private interest. Above all, we want the princes to understand and to follow the principle that they exist for the country and not the country for them. In fact, the prevailing view is that the constitution should not come from the individual states at all. The main principles of the German constitution should apply to all states in common, and should be expressed by the German federal assembly. This constitution should deal not only with the absolute necessities, like fiscal administration and justice, general administration and church and military affairs and so on; this constitution ought to be extended to the education of the young, at least at the upper age levels, and to many other such things.

Q *Would you call Heinrich von Gagern a nationalist? Why or why not? As seen in this selection, why were the forces of nationalism and liberalism allies during the first half of the nineteenth century?*

Although Alexander's brother Constantine was the legal heir to the throne, he had renounced his claims in favor of his brother Nicholas. Constantine's abdication had not been made public, however, and during the ensuing confusion in December 1825, the military leaders of the Northern Union rebelled against the accession of Nicholas. This so-called Decembrist Revolt was soon crushed by troops loyal to Nicholas, and its leaders were executed.

The revolt transformed Nicholas I (1825–1855) from a conservative into a reactionary determined to avoid another rebellion. He strengthened both the bureaucracy and the secret police. The political police, known as the Third Section of the tsar's chancellery, were given sweeping powers over much of Russian life. They deported suspicious or dangerous persons, maintained close surveillance of foreigners in Russia, and reported regularly to the tsar on public opinion.

Matching Nicholas's fear of revolution at home was his fear of revolution abroad. There would be no revolution in Russia during the rest of his reign; if he could help it, there would be none in Europe either. Contemporaries called him the Policeman of Europe because of his willingness to use Russian troops to crush revolutions.

The Ideologies of Change

Q **Focus Question:** What were the main tenets of conservatism, liberalism, nationalism, and utopian socialism, and what role did each ideology play in Europe in the first half of the nineteenth century?

Although the conservative forces were in the ascendancy from 1815 to 1830, powerful movements for change were

© Private Collection/The Bridgeman Art Library

Portrait of Nicholas I. Tsar Nicholas I was a reactionary ruler who sought to prevent rebellion in Russia by strengthening the government bureaucracy, increasing censorship, and suppressing individual freedom by the use of political police. One of his enemies remarked about his facial characteristics: "The sharply retreating forehead and the lower jaw were expressive of iron will and feeble intelligence."

also at work. These depended on ideas embodied in a series of political philosophies or ideologies that came into their own in the first half of the nineteenth century.

Liberalism

One of these ideologies was **liberalism,** which owed much to the Enlightenment of the eighteenth century and to the American and French Revolutions at the end of that century. In addition, liberalism became even more significant as the Industrial Revolution made rapid strides because the developing industrial middle class largely adopted the doctrine as its own. There were divergences of opinion among people classified as liberals, but all began with the belief that people should be as free from restraint as possible. This opinion is evident in both economic and political liberalism.

Economic Liberalism Also called classical economics, economic liberalism had as its primary tenet the concept of *laissez-faire,* the belief that the state should not interrupt the free play of natural economic forces, especially supply and demand. Government should not restrain the economic liberty of the individual and should restrict

itself to only three primary functions: defense of the country, police protection of individuals, and the construction and maintenance of public works too expensive for individuals to undertake. If individuals were allowed economic liberty, ultimately they would bring about the maximum good for the maximum number and benefit the general welfare of society.

The case against government interference in economic matters was greatly enhanced by Thomas Malthus (1766–1834). In his major work, *Essay on the Principles of Population,* Malthus argued that population, when unchecked, increases at a geometric rate while the food supply correspondingly increases at a much slower arithmetic rate. The result will be severe overpopulation and ultimately starvation for the human race if this growth is not held in check. According to Malthus, nature imposes a major restraint: "Unwholesome occupations, severe labor and exposure to the seasons, extreme poverty, bad nursing of children, great towns, excesses of all kinds, the whole train of common disease, and epidemics, wars, plague and famine." Thus, misery and poverty were simply the inevitable result of the law of nature; no government or individual should interfere with its operation.

Malthus's ideas were further developed by David Ricardo (1772–1823). In *Principles of Political Economy,* written in 1817, Ricardo developed his famous "iron law of wages." Following Malthus, Ricardo argued that an increase in population means more workers; more workers in turn cause wages to fall below the subsistence level. The result is misery and starvation, which then reduce the population. Consequently, the number of workers declines, and wages rise above the subsistence level again, which in turn encourages workers to have larger families as the cycle is repeated. According to Ricardo, raising wages arbitrarily would be pointless since it would accomplish little but perpetuate this vicious circle.

Political Liberalism Politically, liberals came to hold a common set of beliefs. Chief among them was the protection of civil liberties or the basic rights of all people, which included equality before the law; freedom of assembly, speech, and press; and freedom from arbitrary arrest. All of these freedoms should be guaranteed by a written document, such as the American Bill of Rights or the French Declaration of the Rights of Man and the Citizen. In addition to religious toleration for all, most liberals advocated separation of church and state. The right of peaceful opposition to the government in and out of parliament and the making of laws by a representative assembly (legislature) elected by qualified voters constituted two other liberal demands. Many liberals believed, then, in a constitutional monarchy or constitutional state with limits on the powers of government to prevent despotism and in written constitutions that would help guarantee these rights.

THE VOICE OF LIBERALISM: JOHN STUART MILL ON LIBERTY

John Stuart Mill was one of Britain's most famous philosophers of liberalism. Mill's essay *On Liberty* is viewed as a classic statement of the liberal belief in the unfettered freedom of the individual. In this excerpt, Mill defends freedom of opinion from both government and the coercion of the majority.

John Stuart Mill, *On Liberty*

The object of this Essay is to assert one very simple principle, as entitled to govern absolutely the dealings of society with the individual in the way of compulsion and control, whether the means used by physical force in the form of legal penalties, or the moral coercion of public opinion. That principle is, that the sole end for which mankind are warranted, individually or collectively, interfering with the liberty of action of any of their number, is self-protection. That the only purpose for which power can be rightfully exercised over any member of a civilized community, against his will, is to prevent harm to others. His own good, either physical or moral, is not a sufficient warrant.... These are good reasons for remonstrating with him, or reasoning with him, or persuading him, or entreating him, but not for compelling him, or visiting him with any evil in case he do otherwise. To justify that, the conduct from which it is desired to deter him, must be calculated to produce evil to some one else. The only part of the conduct of any one, for which he is amenable to society, is that which concerns others. In the part which merely concerns himself, his independence is, of right, absolute. Over himself, over his own body and mind, the individual is sovereign....

Society can and does execute its own mandates: and if it issues wrong mandates instead of right, or any mandates at all in things with which it ought not to meddle, it practices a social tyranny more formidable than many kinds of political oppression, since, though not usually upheld by such extreme penalties, it leaves fewer means of escape, penetrating more deeply into the details of life, and enslaving the soul itself. Protection, therefore, against the tyranny of the magistrate is not enough: there needs protection also against the tyranny of prevailing opinion and feeling, against the tendency of society to impose, by other means than civil penalties, its own ideas and practices as rules of conduct on those who dissent from them....

But there is a sphere of action in which society, as distinguished from the individual has, if any, only an indirect interest; comprehending all that portion of a person's life and conduct which affects only himself, or if it also affects others, only with their free, voluntary and undeceived consent and participation.... This then is the appropriate region of human liberty. It comprises, first, the inward domain of consciousness; demanding liberty of conscience in the most comprehensive sense; liberty of thought and feeling; absolute freedom of opinion and sentiment on all subjects, practical or speculative, scientific, moral, or theological....

Let us suppose, therefore, that the government is entirely at one with the people, and never thinks of exerting any power of coercion unless in agreement with what it conceives to be their voice. But I deny the right of the people to exercise such coercion, either by themselves or by their government. The power itself is illegitimate. The best government has no more title to it than the worst. It is as noxious, or more noxious, when exerted in accordance with public opinion, than when in opposition to it. If all mankind minus one were of one opinion, and only one person were of the contrary opinion, mankind would be no more justified in silencing that one person, than he, if he had the power, would be justified in silencing mankind.... The peculiar evil of silencing the expression of an opinion is, that it is robbing the human race; posterity as well as the existing generation; those who dissent from the opinion, still more than those who hold it. If the opinion is right, they are deprived of the opportunity of exchanging error for truth: if wrong, they lose, what is almost as great a benefit, the clearer perception and livelier impression of truth, produced by its collision with error.

Q *Based on the principles outlined here, how would you define liberalism? How do Mill's ideas fit into the concept of democracy? Which is more important in his thought: the individual or society?*

Many liberals also advocated ministerial responsibility, a system in which the king's ministers were responsible to the legislature rather than to the king, giving the legislative branch a check on the power of the executive. Liberals in the first half of the nineteenth century also believed in a limited suffrage. Although all people were entitled to equal civil rights, they should not have equal political rights. The right to vote and hold office would be open only to men who met certain property qualifications. As a political philosophy, liberalism was tied to middle-class men, especially industrial middle-class men who favored the extension of voting rights so that they could share power with the landowning classes. They had little desire to let the lower classes share that power. Liberals were not democrats.

One of the most prominent advocates of liberalism in the nineteenth century was the English philosopher John Stuart Mill (1806–1873). *On Liberty,* his most famous work, published in 1859, has long been regarded as a classic statement on the liberty of the individual (see the box above). Mill argued for an "absolute freedom of opinion and sentiment on all subjects" that needed to be protected from both government censorship and the tyranny of the majority.

Mill was also instrumental in expanding the meaning of liberalism by becoming an enthusiastic supporter of women's rights. When his attempt to include women in the voting reform bill of 1867 failed, Mill published an essay titled *On the Subjection of Women*, which he had written earlier with his wife, Harriet Taylor. He argued that "the legal subordination of one sex to the other" was wrong. Differences between women and men, he claimed, were due not to different natures but simply to social practices. With equal education, women could achieve as much as men. *On the Subjection of Women* would become an important work in the nineteenth-century movement for women's rights.

Nationalism

Nationalism was an even more powerful ideology for change in the nineteenth century. Nationalism arose out of an awareness of being part of a community that has common institutions, traditions, language, and customs. This community constitutes a "nation," and it, rather than a dynasty, city-state, or other political unit, becomes the focus of the individual's primary political loyalty. Nationalism did not become a popular force for change until the French Revolution. From then on, nationalists came to believe that each nationality should have its own government. Thus, a divided people such as the Germans wanted national unity in a German nation-state with one central government. Subject peoples, such as the Hungarians, wanted national self-determination, or the right to establish their own autonomy rather than be subject to a German minority in a multinational empire.

Nationalism threatened to upset the existing political order, both internationally and nationally (see Map 21.3). A united Germany or united Italy would upset the balance of power established in 1815. By the same token, an independent Hungarian state would mean the breakup of the Austrian Empire. Because many European states were multinational, conservatives tried hard to repress the radical threat of nationalism.

At the same time, in the first half of the nineteenth century, nationalism and liberalism became strong allies. Most liberals believed that liberty could be realized only by peoples who ruled themselves. One British liberal said, "It is in general a necessary condition of free institutions that the boundaries of governments should coincide in the main with those of nationalities." Many nationalists believed that once each people obtained its own state, all nations could be linked together into a broader community of all humanity.

Early Socialism

In the first half of the nineteenth century, the pitiful conditions found in the slums, mines, and factories of the Industrial Revolution gave rise to another ideology for change known as **socialism.** The term eventually became

associated with a Marxist analysis of human society (see Chapter 22), but early socialism was largely the product of political theorists or intellectuals who wanted to introduce equality into social conditions and believed that human cooperation was superior to the competition that characterized early industrial capitalism. To later Marxists, such ideas were impractical dreams, and they contemptuously labeled the theorists **utopian socialists.** The term has endured to this day.

The utopian socialists were against private property and the competitive spirit of early industrial capitalism. By eliminating these things and creating new systems of social organization, they thought that a better environment for humanity could be achieved. Early socialists proposed a variety of ways to accomplish that task.

Fourier   One group of early socialists sought to create voluntary associations that would demonstrate the advantages of cooperative living. Charles Fourier (1772–1838) proposed the creation of small model communities called phalansteries. These were self-contained cooperatives, each consisting ideally of 1,620 people. Communally housed, the inhabitants of the **phalanstery** would live and work together for their mutual benefit. Work assignments would be rotated frequently to relieve workers of undesirable tasks. Fourier was unable to gain financial backing for his phalansteries, however, and his plan remained untested.

Owen   Robert Owen (1771–1858), the British cotton manufacturer, also believed that humans would reveal their true natural goodness if they lived in a cooperative environment. At New Lanark in Scotland, he was successful in transforming a squalid factory town into a flourishing, healthy community. But when he attempted to create a self-contained cooperative community at New Harmony, Indiana, in the United States in the 1820s, bickering within the community eventually destroyed his dream. One of Owen's disciples, a wealthy woman named Frances Wright, bought slaves in order to set up a model community at Nashoba, Tennessee. The community failed, but Wright continued to work for women's rights.

Blanc   The Frenchman Louis Blanc (1813–1882) offered yet another early socialist approach to a better society. In *The Organization of Work*, he maintained that social problems could be solved by government assistance. Denouncing competition as the main cause of the economic evils of his day, he called for the establishment of workshops that would manufacture goods for public sale. The state would finance these workshops, but the workers would own and operate them.

Female Supporters   With their plans for the reconstruction of society, utopian socialists attracted a

MAP 21.3 **The Distribution of Languages in Nineteenth-Century Europe.**
Numerous languages were spoken in Europe. People who used the same language often had a shared history and culture, which laid the seeds for growing nationalism in the nineteenth century. Such nationalism eventually led to unification for Germany and Italy but spelled trouble for the polyglot Habsburg empire.

Q Look at the distribution of Germanic, Latin, and Slavic languages. What patterns emerge, and how can you explain them? **View an animated version of this map or related maps at** academic.cengage.com/history/spielvogel

number of female supporters who believed that only a reordering of society would help women. Zoé Gatti de Gamond, a Belgian follower of Fourier, established her own phalanstery, which was supposed to provide men and women with the same educational and job opportunities. As part of collective living, men and women were to share responsibilities for child care and housecleaning. The ideas of the comte de Saint-Simon, which combined Christian values, scientific thought, and socialist utopianism, proved especially attractive to a number of women who participated in the growing

activism of women in politics that had been set in motion during the French Revolution. Saint-Simon's ideal cooperative society recognized the principle of equality between men and women, and a number of working-class women, including Suzanne Voilquin, Claire Démar, and Reine Guindorf, published a newspaper dedicated to the emancipation of women.

Tristan One female utopian socialist, Flora Tristan (1803–1844), even attempted to foster a "utopian synthesis of socialism and feminism." She traveled through France

Children at New Lanark. Robert Owen created an early experiment in utopian socialism by establishing a model industrial community at New Lanark, Scotland. In this illustration, the children of factory workers are shown dancing the quadrille.

preaching the need for the liberation of women. Her *Worker's Union,* published in 1843, advocated the application of Fourier's ideas to reconstruct both family and work:

> Workers, be sure of it. If you have enough equity and justice to inscribe into your Charter the few points I have just outlined, this declaration of the rights of women will soon pass into custom, from custom into law, and before twenty-five years pass you will then see inscribed in front of the book of laws which will govern French society: THE ABSOLUTE EQUALITY of man and woman. Then, my brothers, and only then, will human unity be constituted.[6]

She envisioned this absolute equality as the only hope to free the working class and transform civilization.

Flora Tristan, like the other utopian socialists, was largely ignored by her contemporaries. Although criticized for their impracticality, the utopian socialists at least laid the groundwork for later attacks on capitalism that would have a far-reaching result. In the first half of the nineteenth century, however, socialism remained a fringe movement largely overshadowed by liberalism and nationalism.

Revolution and Reform (1830–1850)

Q Focus Questions: What forces for change were present in France and Great Britain between 1830 and 1848, and how did each nation respond? What were the causes of the revolutions of 1848, and why did the revolutions fail?

Beginning in 1830, the forces of change began to break through the conservative domination of Europe, more successfully in some places than in others. Finally, in 1848, a wave of revolutionary fervor moved through Europe, causing liberals and nationalists everywhere to think that they were on the verge of creating a new order.

Another French Revolution

The new elections Charles X had called in 1830 produced another victory for the French liberals; at this point, the king decided to seize the initiative. On July 26, 1830, Charles issued a set of edicts (the July Ordinances) that imposed rigid censorship on the press, dissolved the legislative assembly, and reduced the electorate in preparation for new elections. Charles's actions produced an immediate rebellion—the July Revolution. Barricades went up in Paris as a provisional government led by a group of moderate, propertied liberals was hastily formed and appealed to Louis-Philippe, the duke of Orléans, a cousin of Charles X, to become the constitutional king of France. Charles X fled to Britain; a new monarchy had been born.

Louis-Philippe (1830–1848) was soon called the bourgeois monarch because political support for his rule came from the upper middle class. Louis-Philippe even dressed like a member of the middle class in business suits and hats. Constitutional changes that favored the interests of the upper bourgeoisie were instituted. Financial qualifications for voting were reduced yet remained sufficiently high that the number of voters only increased from 100,000 to barely 200,000, guaranteeing that only the wealthiest people would vote.

To the upper middle class, the bourgeois monarchy represented the stopping place for political progress.

Erich Lessing/Art Resource, NY

The Revolution of 1830. In 1830, the forces of change began to undo the conservative domination of Europe. In France, the reactionary Charles X was overthrown and replaced by the constitutional monarch Louis-Philippe, a liberal and former revolutionary soldier. In this painting by Gustave Wappers, Louis-Philippe is seen riding to the Hôtel de Ville, the city hall, preceded by a man holding the French revolutionary tricolor flag, which had not been seen in France since 1815.

To the lesser bourgeoisie and the Parisian working class, who had helped overthrow Charles X in 1830, it was a severe disappointment because they had been completely excluded from political power. The rapid expansion of French industry in the 1830s and 1840s gave rise to an industrial working class concentrated in certain urban areas. Terrible working and living conditions and the periodic economic crises that created high levels of unemployment led to worker unrest and sporadic outbursts of violence.

Even in the legislature—the Chamber of Deputies—there were differences of opinion about the bourgeois monarchy and the direction it should take. Two groups rapidly emerged, both composed of upper-middle-class representatives. The Party of Movement, led by Adolphe Thiers, favored ministerial responsibility, the pursuit of an active foreign policy, and limited expansion of the franchise. The Party of Resistance was led by François Guizot, who believed that France had finally reached the "perfect form" of government and needed no further institutional changes. After 1840, the Party of Resistance dominated the Chamber of Deputies. Guizot cooperated with Louis-Philippe in suppressing ministerial responsibility and pursuing a policy favoring the interests of the wealthier manufacturers and tradespeople.

Revolutionary Outbursts in Belgium, Poland, and Italy

Supporters of liberalism played a primary role in the July Revolution in France, but nationalism was the crucial force in three other revolutionary outbursts in 1830. In an effort to create a stronger, larger state on France's northern border, the Congress of Vienna had added the area once known as the Austrian Netherlands (Belgium) to the Dutch Republic. The merger of Catholic Belgium into the Protestant Dutch Republic never sat well with the Belgians, however, and in 1830, they rose up against the Dutch and succeeded in convincing the major European powers to accept their independence. Leopold of Saxe-Coburg, a minor German prince, was designated to be the new king, and a Belgian national congress established a constitutional monarchy for the new state.

The revolutionary scenarios in Italy and Poland were much less successful. Metternich sent Austrian troops to crush revolts in three Italian states. Poland, too, had a nationalist uprising in 1830 when revolutionaries tried to end Russian control of their country. But the Polish insurgents failed to get hoped-for support from France and Britain, and by September 1831, the Russians had crushed the revolt and established an oppressive military dictatorship over Poland.

Reform in Great Britain

In 1830, new parliamentary elections brought the Whigs to power in Britain. At the same time, the successful July Revolution in France served to catalyze change in Britain. The Industrial Revolution had led to an expanding group of industrial leaders who objected to the corrupt British electoral system, which excluded them from political power. The Whigs, though also members of the landed classes, realized that concessions to reform were superior to revolution; the demands of the wealthy industrial middle class could no longer be ignored. In 1830, the Whigs introduced an election reform bill that was enacted in 1832 after an intense struggle (see the box on p. 650).

The Reform Act of 1832

The Reform Act gave explicit recognition to the changes wrought in British life by the Industrial Revolution. It disenfranchised fifty-six rotten boroughs and enfranchised forty-two new towns and cities and reapportioned others. This gave the new industrial urban communities some voice in government. A property qualification (of £10 annual rent) for voting was retained, however, so the number of voters increased only from 478,000 to 814,000, a figure that still meant that only one in every thirty people was represented in Parliament. Thus, the Reform Act of 1832 primarily benefited the upper middle class; the lower middle class, artisans, and industrial workers still had no vote. Moreover, the change did not significantly alter the composition of the House of Commons. One political leader noted that the Commons chosen in the first election after the Reform Act seemed "to be very much like every other Parliament." Nevertheless, a significant step had been taken. The industrial middle class had been joined to the landed interests in ruling Britain.

New Reform Legislation

The 1830s and 1840s witnessed considerable reform legislation. The aristocratic landowning class was usually (but not always) the driving force for legislation that halted some of the worst abuses in the industrial system by instituting government regulation of working conditions in the factories and mines. The industrialists and manufacturers now in Parliament opposed such legislation and were usually (but not always) the driving forces behind legislation that favored the principles of economic liberalism. The Poor Law of 1834 was based on the theory that giving aid to the poor and unemployed only encouraged laziness and increased the number of paupers. The Poor Law tried to remedy this by making paupers so wretched they would choose to work. Those unable to support themselves were crowded together in workhouses where living and working conditions were intentionally miserable so that people would be encouraged to find profitable employment.

Another piece of liberal legislation involved the repeal of the Corn Laws. This was primarily the work of the manufacturers Richard Cobden and John Bright, who formed the Anti–Corn Law League in 1838 to help workers by lowering bread prices. But abolishing the Corn Laws would also aid the industrial middle classes, who, as economic liberals, favored the principles of free trade. Repeal came in 1846 when Robert Peel (1788–1850), leader of the Tories, persuaded some of his associates to support free trade principles and abandon the Corn Laws.

The year 1848, which witnessed revolutions in most of Europe, ended without a major crisis in Britain. On the Continent, middle-class liberals and nationalists were at the forefront of the revolutionary forces. In Britain, however, the middle class had been largely satisfied by the Reform Act of 1832 and the repeal of the Corn Laws in 1846.

The Revolutions of 1848

Despite the successes of revolutions in France, Belgium, and Greece, the conservative order remained in control of much of Europe. But liberalism and nationalism continued to grow. In 1848, these forces of change erupted once more. Yet again, revolution in France provided the spark for other countries, and soon most of central and southern Europe was ablaze with revolutionary fires (see Map 21.4). Tsar Nicholas I of Russia lamented to Queen Victoria in April 1848, "What remains standing in Europe? Great Britain and Russia."

Yet Another French Revolution

A severe industrial and agricultural depression beginning in 1846 brought great hardship to the French lower middle class, workers, and peasants. One-third of the workers in Paris were unemployed by the end of 1847. Scandals, graft, and corruption were rife, and the government's persistent refusal to extend the suffrage angered the disenfranchised members of the middle class.

As Louis-Philippe's government continued to refuse to make changes, opposition grew. Radical republicans and socialists, joined by the upper middle class under the leadership of Adolphe Thiers, agitated for the dismissal of Guizot. Since they were forbidden by law to stage political rallies, they used the political banquet to call for reforms. Almost seventy such banquets were held in France during the winter of 1847–1848; a grand culminating banquet was planned for Paris on February 22. When the government forbade it, people came anyway; students and workers threw up barricades in Paris. Although Louis-Philippe now proposed reform, he was unable to form another ministry and abdicated on February 24 and fled to Britain. A provisional government was established by a group of moderate and radical republicans; the latter even included the socialist Louis Blanc. The provisional government ordered that representatives for a constituent assembly convened to draw up a new constitution be elected by universal manhood suffrage.

The provisional government also established national workshops under the influence of Louis Blanc. As Blanc envisioned them, the workshops were to be cooperative factories run by the workers. In fact, the workshops primarily provided unskilled jobs, such as leaf raking and ditch digging, for unemployed workers. The cost of the program became increasingly burdensome to the government.

The result was a growing split between the moderate republicans, who had the support of most of France, and the radical republicans, whose main support came from the Parisian working class. In the elections for the National Assembly, five hundred seats went to moderate republicans and three hundred to avowed monarchists, while the radicals gained only one hundred. From March to June, the number of

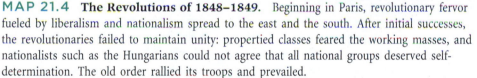

MAP 21.4   The Revolutions of 1848–1849.   Beginning in Paris, revolutionary fervor fueled by liberalism and nationalism spread to the east and the south. After initial successes, the revolutionaries failed to maintain unity: propertied classes feared the working masses, and nationalists such as the Hungarians could not agree that all national groups deserved self-determination. The old order rallied its troops and prevailed.

Q Which regions saw a great deal of revolutionary activity in 1848–1849, and which did not?

View an animated version of this map or related maps at academic.cengage.com/history/spielvogel

unemployed enrolled in the national workshops rose from 10,000 to almost 120,000, emptying the treasury and frightening the moderates, who responded by closing the workshops on June 23. The workers refused to accept this decision and poured into the streets. Four days of bitter and bloody fighting by government forces crushed the working-class revolt. Thousands were killed, and four thousand prisoners were deported to the French colony of Algeria in North Africa.

The new constitution, ratified on November 4, 1848, established a republic (the Second Republic) with a unicameral (one-house) legislature of 750 elected by universal male suffrage for three years and a president, also elected by universal male suffrage, for four years. In the elections for the presidency held in December 1848, four republicans who had been associated with the early months of the Second Republic were resoundingly

defeated by Charles Louis Napoleon Bonaparte, the nephew of Napoleon Bonaparte. Within four years, President Napoleon would become Emperor Napoleon (see Chapter 22).

Revolution in the Germanic States   News of the revolution in Paris in February 1848 triggered upheavals in central Europe as well (see the box on p. 650). Revolutionary cries for change caused many German rulers to promise constitutions, a free press, jury trials, and other liberal reforms. In Prussia, concessions were also made to appease the revolutionaries. King Frederick William IV (1840–1861) agreed to abolish censorship, establish a new constitution, and work for a united Germany. This last promise had its counterpart throughout all the German states as governments allowed elections by universal male suffrage for deputies to an all-German parliament to

OPPOSING VIEWPOINTS
RESPONSE TO REVOLUTION: TWO PERSPECTIVES

Based on their political beliefs, Europeans responded differently to the specter of revolution that haunted Europe in the first half of the nineteenth century. The first excerpt is taken from a speech given by Thomas Babington Macaulay (1800–1859), a historian and a Whig member of Parliament. Macaulay spoke in Parliament on behalf of the Reform Act of 1832, which extended the right to vote to the industrial middle classes of Britain. The Revolution of 1830 in France had influenced his belief that it was better to reform than to have a political revolution.

The second excerpt is taken from the *Reminiscences* of Carl Schurz (1829–1906). Like many liberals and nationalists in Germany, Schurz received the news of the February Revolution of 1848 in France with much excitement and great expectations for revolutionary change in the German states. After the failure of the German revolution, Schurz made his way to the United States and eventually became a U.S. senator.

Thomas Babington Macaulay, Speech of March 2, 1831

My hon. friend the member of the University of Oxford tells us that, if we pass this law, England will soon be a Republic. The reformed House of Commons will, according to him, before it has sat ten years, depose the King, and expel the Lords from their House. Sir, if my hon. friend could prove this, he would have succeeded in bringing an argument for democracy infinitely stronger than any that is to be found in the works of Paine. His proposition is, in fact, this—that our monarchical and aristocratical institutions have no hold on the public mind of England; that these institutions are regarded with aversion by a decided majority of the middle class.... Now, sir, if I were convinced that the great body of the middle class in England look with aversion on monarchy and aristocracy, I should be forced, much against my will, to come to this conclusion, that monarchical and aristocratical institutions are unsuited to this country. Monarchy and aristocracy, valuable and useful as I think them, are still valuable and useful as means, and not as ends. The end of government is the happiness of the people; and I do not conceive that, in a country like this, the happiness of the people can be promoted by a form of government in which the middle classes place no confidence, and which exists only because the middle classes have no organ by which to make their sentiments known. But, sir, I am fully convinced that the middle classes sincerely wish to uphold the royal prerogatives, and the constitutional rights of the Peers....

But let us know our interest and our duty better. Turn where we may—within, around—the voice of great events is proclaiming to us, "Reform, that you may preserve." Now,

therefore, while everything at home and abroad forebodes ruin to those who persist in a hopeless struggle against the spirit of the age; now, while the crash of the proudest throne of the Continent is still resounding in our ears; ... now, while the heart of England is still sound; now, while the old feelings and the old associations retain a power and a charm which may too soon pass away; now, in this your accepted time; now, in this your day of salvation, take counsel, not of prejudice, not of party spirit, not of the ignominious pride of a fatal consistency, but of history, of reason, of the ages which are past, of the signs of this most portentous time. Pronounce in a manner worthy of the expectation with which this great debate has been anticipated, and of the long remembrance which it will leave behind. Renew the youth of the State. Save property divided against itself. Save the multitude, endangered by their own ungovernable passions. Save the aristocracy, endangered by its own unpopular power. Save the greatest, and fairest, and most highly civilized community that ever existed, from calamities which may in a few days sweep away all the rich heritage of so many ages of wisdom and glory. The danger is terrible. The time is short. If this Bill should be rejected, I pray to God that none of those who concur in rejecting it may ever remember their votes with unavailing regret, amidst the wreck of laws, the confusion of ranks, the spoliation of property, and the dissolution of social order.

Carl Schurz, *Reminiscences*

One morning, toward the end of February, 1848, I sat quietly in my attic-chamber, working hard at my tragedy of "Ulrich von Hutten" [a sixteenth-century German knight] when suddenly a friend rushed breathlessly into the room, exclaiming: "What, you sitting here! Do you not know what has happened?"

"No; what?"

"The French have driven away Louis Philippe and proclaimed the republic."

I threw down my pen—and that was the end of "Ulrich von Hutten." I never touched the manuscript again. We tore down the stairs, into the street, to the market-square, the accustomed meeting-place for all the student societies after their midday dinner. Although it was still forenoon, the market was already crowded with young men talking excitedly. There was no shouting, no noise, only agitated conversation. What did we want there? This probably no one knew. But since the French had driven away Louis Philippe and proclaimed the republic, something of course must happen here, too.... We were dominated by a vague feeling as if a great outbreak of elemental forces had begun, as if an earthquake was impending of which we had felt the first shock, and we instinctively crowded together....

(continued)

(continued)

The next morning there were the usual lectures to be attended. But how profitless! The voice of the professor sounded like a monotonous drone coming from far away. What he had to say did not seem to concern us. The pen that should have taken notes remained idle. At last we closed with a sigh the notebook and went away, impelled by a feeling that now we had something more important to do—to devote ourselves to the affairs of the fatherland. And this we did by seeking as quickly as possible again the company of our friends, in order to discuss what had happened and what was to come. In these conversations, excited as they were, certain ideas and catchwords worked themselves to the surface, which expressed more or less the feelings of the people. Now had arrived in Germany the day for the establishment of "German Unity," and the founding of a great, powerful national German Empire. In the first line the convocation of a national parliament. Then the demands for civil rights and liberties, free speech, free press, the right of free assembly, equality before the law, a freely elected representation of the people with legislative power, responsibility of ministers, self-government of the communes, the right of the people to carry arms, the formation of a civic guard with elective officers, and so on—in short, that which was called a "constitutional form of government on a broad democratic basis." Republican ideas were at first only sparingly expressed. But the word democracy was soon on all tongues, and many, too, thought it a matter of course that if the princes should try to withhold from the people the rights and liberties demanded, force would take the place of mere petition. Of course the regeneration of the fatherland must, if possible, be accomplished by peaceable means.... Like many of my friends, I was dominated by the feeling that at last the great opportunity had arrived for giving to the German people the liberty which was their birthright and to the German fatherland its unity and greatness, and that it was now the first duty of every German to do and to sacrifice everything for this sacred object.

Q *What arguments did Macaulay use to support the Reform Bill of 1832? Was he correct? Why or why not? Why was Carl Schurz so excited when he heard the news about the revolution in France? Do you think being a university student helps to explain his reaction? Why or why not? What differences do you see in the approaches of these two writers? What do these selections tell you about the development of politics in the German states and Britain in the nineteenth century?*

meet in Frankfurt, the seat of the Germanic Confederation. Its purpose was to fulfill a liberal and nationalist dream—the preparation of a constitution for a new united Germany.

This Frankfurt Assembly was dominated by well-educated, articulate, middle-class delegates, many of them professors, lawyers, and bureaucrats. When it came to nationalism, many were ahead of the times and certainly ahead of the governments of their respective states. From the beginning, the assembly aroused controversy by claiming to be the government for all of Germany. Then it became embroiled in a sticky debate over the composition of the new German state. Supporters of a *Grossdeutsch* ("Big German") solution wanted to include the German province of Austria, while proponents of a *Kleindeutsch* ("Small German") solution favored excluding Austria and making the Prussian king the emperor of the new German state. The problem was solved when the Austrians withdrew, leaving the field to the supporters of the *Kleindeutsch* solution. Their victory was short-lived, however, as Frederick William IV gruffly refused the assembly's offer of the title of "emperor of the Germans" in March 1849 and ordered the Prussian delegates home.

The Frankfurt Assembly soon disbanded. Although some members spoke of using force, they had no real means of compelling the German rulers to accept the constitution they had drawn up. The attempt of the German liberals at Frankfurt to create a German state had failed.

Upheaval in the Austrian Empire The Austrian Empire also had its social, political, and nationalist grievances and needed only the news of the revolution in Paris to encourage it to erupt in flames in March 1848. The Hungarian liberals under Louis Kossuth agitated for "commonwealth" status; they were willing to keep the Habsburg monarch but wanted their own legislature. In March, demonstrations in Buda, Prague, and Vienna led to Metternich's dismissal, and the archsymbol of the conservative order fled abroad. In Vienna, revolutionary forces, carefully guided by the educated and propertied classes, took control of the capital and insisted that a constituent assembly be summoned to draw up a liberal constitution. Hungary was granted its wish for its own legislature, a separate national army, and control over its foreign policy and budget. Allegiance to the Habsburg dynasty was now Hungary's only tie to the Austrian Empire. In Bohemia, the Czechs began to demand their own government as well.

Although Emperor Ferdinand I (1835–1848) and Austrian officials had made concessions to appease the revolutionaries, they awaited an opportunity to reestablish their firm control. As in the German states, the conservatives were increasingly encouraged by the divisions between radical and moderate revolutionaries and played on the middle-class fear of a working-class social revolution. Their first success came in June 1848 when a military force under General Alfred Windischgrätz ruthlessly suppressed the Czech rebels in

Erich Lessing/Art Resource, NY

Austrian Students in the Revolutionary Civil Guard. In 1848, revolutionary fervor swept the European continent and toppled governments in France, central Europe, and Italy. In the Austrian Empire, students joined the revolutionary civil guard in taking control of Vienna and forcing the Austrian emperor to call a constituent assembly to draft a liberal constitution.

Prague. In October, the death of the minister for war at the hands of a Viennese mob gave Windischgrätz the pretext for an attack on Vienna. By the end of the month, the radical rebels there had been crushed. In December, the feebleminded Ferdinand I agreed to abdicate in favor of his nephew, Francis Joseph I (1848–1916), who worked vigorously to restore the imperial government in Hungary. The Austrian armies, however, were unable to defeat Kossuth's forces, and it was only through the intervention of Nicholas I, who sent a Russian army of 140,000 men to aid the Austrians, that the Hungarian revolution was finally crushed in 1849. The revolutions in Austria had also failed. Autocratic government was restored; emperor and propertied classes remained in control, and the numerous nationalities were still subject to the Austrian government.

Revolts in the Italian States The failure of revolutionary uprisings in Italy in 1830–1831 had encouraged the Italian movement for unification to take a new direction. The leadership of Italy's *risorgimento* ("resurgence") passed into the hands of Giuseppe Mazzini (1805–1872), a dedicated Italian nationalist who founded an organization known as Young Italy in 1831 (see the box on p. 653). This group set as its goal the creation of a united Italian republic. In *The Duties of Man,* Mazzini urged Italians to dedicate their lives to the Italian nation: "O my Brother! Love your Country. Our Country is our home." A number of Italian women also took up Mazzini's call. Especially notable was Cristina Belgioioso, a wealthy aristocrat who worked to bring about Italian unification. Pursued by the Austrian

authorities, she fled to Paris and started a newspaper espousing the Italian cause.

The dreams of Mazzini and Belgioioso seemed on the verge of fulfillment when a number of Italian states rose in revolt in 1848. Beginning in Sicily, rebellions spread northward as ruler after ruler granted a constitution to his people. Citizens in Lombardy and Venetia also rebelled against their Austrian overlords. The Venetians declared a republic in Venice. The king of the northern Italian state of Piedmont, Charles Albert (1831–1849), took up the call and assumed the leadership for a war of liberation from Austrian domination. His invasion of Lombardy proved unsuccessful, however, and by 1849, the Austrians had reestablished complete control over Lombardy and Venetia. Counterrevolutionary forces also prevailed throughout Italy. French forces helped Pope Pius IX regain control of Rome. Elsewhere Italian rulers managed to recover power on their own. Only Piedmont was able to keep its liberal constitution.

The Failures of 1848 Throughout Europe in 1848, popular revolts had initiated revolutionary upheavals that had led to the formation of liberal constitutions and liberal governments. But how could so many immediate successes in 1848 be followed by so many disasters only months later? Two reasons stand out. The unity of the revolutionaries had made the revolutions possible, but divisions soon shattered their ranks. Except in France, moderate liberals from the propertied classes failed to extend suffrage to the working classes who had helped achieve the revolutions. But as radicals pushed for universal male suffrage, liberals everywhere

THE VOICE OF ITALIAN NATIONALISM: GIUSEPPE MAZZINI AND YOUNG ITALY

After the failure of the uprisings in Italy in 1830–1831, Giuseppe Mazzini emerged as the leader of the Italian *risorgimento*—the movement for Italian nationhood. In 1831, he founded an organization known as Young Italy whose goal was the creation of a united Italian republic. This selection is from the oath that the members of Young Italy were required to take.

Giuseppe Mazzini, *The Young Italy Oath*

Young Italy is a brotherhood of Italians who believe in a law of Progress and Duty, and are convinced that Italy is destined to become one nation,—convinced also that she possesses sufficient strength within herself to become one, and that the ill success of her former efforts is to be attributed not to the weakness, but to the misdirection of the revolutionary elements within her,—that the secret of force lies in constancy and unity of effort. They join this association in the firm intent of consecrating both thought and action to the great aim of reconstituting Italy as one independent sovereign nation of free men and equals....

Each member will, upon his initiation into the association of Young Italy, pronounce the following form of oath, in the presence of the initiator: In the name of God and of Italy;

In the name of all the martyrs of the holy Italian cause who have fallen beneath foreign and domestic tyranny;

By the duties which bind me to the land wherein God has placed me, and to the brothers whom God has given me;

By the love—innate in all men—I bear to the country that gave my mother birth, and will be the home of my children....

By the sufferings of the millions,—

I,...believing in the mission intrusted by God to Italy, and the duty of every Italian to strive to attempt its fulfillment; convinced that where God has ordained that a nation shall be, He has given the requisite power to create it; that the people are the depositaries of that power, and that in its right direction for the people, and by the people, lies the secret of victory; convinced that virtue consists in action and sacrifice, and strength in union and constancy of purpose: I give my name to Young Italy, an association of men holding the same faith, and swear:

To dedicate myself wholly and forever to the endeavor with them to constitute Italy one free, independent, republican nation; to promote by every means in my power—whether by written or spoken word, or by action—the education of my Italian brothers toward the aim of Young Italy; toward association, the sole means of its accomplishment, and to virtue, which alone can render the conquest lasting; to abstain from enrolling myself in any other association from this time forth; to obey all the instructions, in conformity with the spirit of Young Italy, given me by those who represent with me the union of my Italian brothers; and to keep the secret of these instructions, even at the cost of my life; to assist my brothers of the association both by action and counsel—NOW AND FOREVER.

Q *Based on the principles outlined here, define nationalism. Why have some called nationalism a "secular religion"?*

---

pulled back. Concerned about their property and security, they rallied to the old ruling classes for the sake of order and out of fear of social revolution by the working classes. All too soon, established governments were back in power.

In 1848, nationalities everywhere had also revolted in pursuit of self-government. But here too, frightfully little was achieved as divisions among nationalities proved utterly disastrous. Though the Hungarians demanded autonomy from the Austrians, at the same time they refused the same to their minorities—the Slovenes, Croats, and Serbs. Instead of joining together against the old empire, minorities fought each other. No wonder that one Czech could remark in April 1848, "If the Austrian state had not already existed for so long, it would have been in the interests of Europe, indeed of humanity itself, to endeavor to create it as soon as possible."[7] The Austrians' efforts to recover the Hungarian provinces met with little success until they began to play off Hungary's rebellious minority nationalities against the Hungarians.

The Maturing of the United States

The U.S. Constitution, ratified in 1789, committed the United States to two of the major forces of the first half of the nineteenth century, liberalism and nationalism. Initially, this constitutional commitment to national unity was challenged by divisions over the power of the federal government vis-à-vis the individual states. Bitter conflict erupted between the Federalists and the Republicans. Led by Alexander Hamilton (1757–1804), the Federalists favored a financial program that would establish a strong central government. The Republicans, guided by Thomas Jefferson (1743–1826) and James Madison (1751–1836), feared centralization and its consequences for popular liberties. These divisions were intensified by European rivalries because the Federalists were pro-British and the Republicans pro-French. The successful conclusion of the War of 1812 brought an end to the Federalists, who had opposed the war, while the surge of national feeling generated by the war served to heal the nation's divisions.

Another strong force for national unity came from the Supreme Court while John Marshall (1755–1835) was

CHRONOLOGY Reform, Reaction, and Revolution: The European States, 1815–1850

Great Britain

Peterloo Massacre	1819
Reform Act	1832
Poor Law	1834
Repeal of Corn Laws	1846

France

Louis XVIII	1814–1824
Charles X	1824–1830
July Revolution	1830
Louis-Philippe	1830–1848
Abdication of Louis-Philippe; formation of provisional government	1848 (February 22–24)
June Days: workers' revolt in Paris	1848 (June)
Establishment of Second Republic	1848 (November)
Election of Louis Napoleon as French president	1848 (December)

Low Countries

Union of Netherlands and Belgium	1815
Belgian independence	1830

German States

Frederick William III of Prussia	1797–1840
Germanic Confederation established	1815
Karlsbad Decrees	1819
Frederick William IV of Prussia	1840–1861
Revolution in Germany	1848
Frankfurt Assembly	1848–1849

Austrian Empire

Emperor Ferdinand I	1835–1848
Revolt in Austrian Empire; Metternich dismissed	1848 (March)
Austrian forces under General Windischgrätz crush Czech rebels	1848 (June)
Viennese rebels crushed	1848 (October)
Francis Joseph I	1848–1916
Defeat of Hungarians with help of Russian troops	1849

Italian States

Revolts in southern Italy and Sardinia crushed	1821
King Charles Albert of Piedmont	1831–1849
Revolutions in Italy	1848
Charles Albert attacks Austrians	1848
Austrians reestablish control in Lombardy and Venetia	1849

Russia

Tsar Alexander I	1801–1825
Decembrist Revolt	1825
Tsar Nicholas I	1825–1855
Polish uprising	1830
Suppression of Polish revolt	1831

chief justice from 1801 to 1835. Marshall made the Supreme Court into an important national institution by asserting the right of the Court to overrule an act of Congress if the Court found it to be in violation of the Constitution. Under Marshall, the Supreme Court contributed further to establishing the supremacy of the national government by curbing the actions of state courts and legislatures.

The election of Andrew Jackson (1767–1845) as president in 1828 opened a new era in American politics, the era of mass democracy. The electorate was expanded by dropping traditional property qualifications; by the 1830s, suffrage had been extended to almost all adult white males. During the period from 1815 to 1850, the traditional liberal belief in the improvement of human beings was also given concrete expression. Americans developed detention schools for juvenile delinquents and new penal institutions, both motivated by the liberal belief that the right kind of environment would rehabilitate those in need of it.

The Emergence of an Ordered Society

Q **Focus Question:** How did Europe respond to the need for order in society in the first half of the nineteenth century?

Everywhere in Europe, the revolutionary upheavals of the late eighteenth and early nineteenth centuries made the ruling elite nervous about social disorder and the potential dangers to their lives and property. At the same time, the influx of large numbers of people from the countryside into rapidly growing cities had led to horrible living conditions, poverty, unemployment, and great social dissatisfaction. The first half of the nineteenth century witnessed a significant increase in crime, especially against property, in Britain, France, and Germany. The rise in property crimes caused a severe reaction among middle-class urban inhabitants, who feared that the urban poor posed a threat to their security and possessions. New police forces soon appeared to defend the propertied classes from criminals and social misfits.

New Police Forces

The first major contribution of the nineteenth century to the development of a disciplined or ordered society in Europe was a regular system of police. A number of European states established civilian police forces—groups of well-trained law enforcement officers who were to preserve property and lives, maintain domestic order, investigate crime, and arrest offenders. It was hoped that their very presence would prevent crime. That the new police existed to protect citizens eventually made them acceptable, and by the end of the nineteenth century, many Europeans viewed them approvingly.

The London Police. One response to the revolutionary upheavals of the late eighteenth and early nineteenth centuries was the development of civilian police forces that would be responsible for preserving property, arresting criminals, and maintaining domestic order. This early photograph shows a group of London policemen, who came to be known as bobbies after Sir Robert Peel, the man responsible for introducing the legislation that initiated the London police force.

French Police This new approach to policing made its first appearance in France in 1828 when Louis-Maurice Debelleyme, the prefect of Paris, proclaimed, "The essential object of our municipal police is the safety of the inhabitants of Paris. Safety by day and night, free traffic movement, clean streets, the supervision of and precaution against accidents, the maintenance of order in public places, the seeking out of offenses and their perpetrators."[8] In March 1829, the new police, known as *serjents,* became visible on Paris streets. They were dressed in blue uniforms to make them easily recognizable by all citizens. They were also lightly armed with a white cane during the day and a saber at night, underscoring the fact that they made up a civilian, not a military, body. Initially, there were not many of the new police officers. Paris had eighty-five by August 1829 and only five hundred in 1850. Before the end of the century, their number had increased to four thousand.

British Bobbies The British, fearful of the powers exercised by military or secret police in authoritarian Continental states, had long resisted the creation of a professional police force. Instead, Britain depended on a system of unpaid constables recruited by local authorities. Often these local constables were incapable of keeping order, preventing crimes, or apprehending criminals. Such jobs could also be dangerous and involve incidents like the one reported by a man passing by a local pub in 1827:

> I saw Thomas Franklin [constable of the village of Leighton Buzzard] coming out backwards. John Brandon . . . was opposite and close to the constable. I saw the said John Brandon strike the said constable twice "bang full in the face" the blows knocked the constable down on his back. John Brandon fell down with him. Sarah Adams . . . got on top of the constable and jostled his head against the ground. . . . The constable appeared very much hurt and his face was all over blood.[9]

The failure of the local constables led to a new approach. Between September 1829 and May 1830, three thousand uniformed police officers appeared on the streets of London. They came to be known as bobbies after Sir Robert Peel, who had introduced the legislation that created the force.

As is evident from the first instruction book for the new British police, their primary goal was to prevent crime: "Officers and police constables should endeavour to distinguish themselves by such vigilance and activity as may render it impossible for any one to commit a crime within that portion of the town under their charge."[10] The municipal authorities soon found, however, that the police were also useful for imposing order on working-class urban inhabitants. On Sundays, they were called on to clean up after Saturday night's drinking bouts. As demands for better pay and treatment led to improved working conditions, British police began to develop a sense of professionalism (see the box on p. 656).

Spread of Police Systems Police systems were reorganized throughout the Western world during the nineteenth century. After the revolutions of 1848 in Germany, a state-financed police force called the *Schutzmannschaft,* modeled after the London police, was established for the city of Berlin. The *Schutzmannschaft* began as a civilian body, but already by 1851, the force had become organized more along military lines and was used for political purposes. Its military nature was reinforced by the force's weaponry, which included swords, pistols, and brass knuckles. One observer noted that "a German policeman on patrol is armed as if for war."[11]

Other Approaches to the Crime Problem Although the new police alleviated some of the fears about the increase in crime, contemporary reformers approached the problem in other ways. Some of them believed that the increase in crime was related to the dramatic increase in poverty.

The New British Police: "We Are Not Treated as Men"

The new British police forces, organized first in London in 1829, were well established throughout much of Britain by the 1840s. As professionalism rose in the ranks of the forces, so did demands for better pay and treatment. In these two selections, police constables make clear their demands and complaints.

Petition for Higher Pay by a Group of Third-Class Constables (1848)

Men joining the Police service as 3rd Class Constables and having a wife and 3 children to support on joining, are not able properly to do so on the pay of 16/8d. Most of the married men on joining are somewhat in debt, and are unable to extricate themselves on account of rent to pay and articles to buy which are necessary for support of wife and children. We beg leave to state that a married man having a wife and 2 children to support on joining, that it is as much as he can do upon 16/8d per week, and having to remain upon that sum for the first 12 to 18 months.

Complaints from Constables of D Division of the London Metropolitan Police

We are not treated as men but as slaves we englishmen do not like to be terrorized by a set of Irish Sergeants who are only lenient to their own countrymen we the D division of Paddington are nearly all ruled by these Irish Sergeants after we have done our night-Duty may we not have the privilege of going to Church or staying at home to Suit our own inclination when we are ordered by the Superintendent to go to church in our uniform on wednesday we do not object to the going to church we like to go but we do not like to be ordered there and when we go on Sunday nights we are asked like so many schoolboys have we been to church should we say no let reason be what it may it does not matter we are forthwith ordered from Paddington to Marylebone lane the next night—about 2 hours before we go to Duty that is 2 miles from many of our homes being tired with our walk there and back we must either loiter about the streets or in some public house and there we do not want to go for we cannot spare our trifling wages to spend them there but there is no other choice left—for us to make our time out to go on Duty at proper time on Day we are ordered there for that offense another Man may faultlessly commit—the crime of sitting 4 minutes during the night—then we must be ordered there another to Shew his old clothes before they are given in even we must go to the expense of having them put in repair we have indeed for all these frightful crimes to walk 3 or 4 miles and then be wasting our time that makes our night 3 hours longer than they ought to be another thing we want to know who has the money that is deducted out of our wages for fines and many of us will be obliged to give up the duty unless we can have fair play as to the stationing of us on our beats why cannot we follow round that may all and each of us go over every beat and not for the Sergeants to put their favorites on the good beats and the others kept back their favorites are not the best policemen but those that will spend the most with them at the public house there are a great many of these things to try our temper.

Q *What were the complaints of the British constables? What was the main issue that the complaints raised? Why might it be said that the development of police forces is a defining characteristic of Western civilization in modern times?*

As one commented in 1816, "Poverty, misery are the parents of crime." Strongly influenced by the middle-class belief that unemployment was the result of sheer laziness, European states passed poor laws that attempted to force paupers to either find work on their own or enter workhouses designed to make people so utterly uncomfortable that they would choose to reenter the labor market.

Meanwhile, another group of reformers was arguing that poor laws failed to address the real problem, which was that poverty was a result of the moral degeneracy of the lower classes, increasingly labeled the "dangerous classes" because of the perceived threat they posed to middle-class society. This belief led one group of secular reformers to form institutes to instruct the working classes in the applied sciences in order to make them more productive members of society. The London Mechanics' Institute, established in Britain, and the Society for the Diffusion of Useful Knowledge in the Field of Natural Sciences, Technical Science, and Political Economy, founded in Germany, are but two examples of this approach to the "dangerous classes."

Organized religion took a different approach. British evangelicals set up Sunday schools to improve the morals of working children, and in Germany, evangelical Protestants established nurseries for orphans and homeless children, women's societies to care for the sick and poor, and prison societies that prepared women to work in prisons. The Catholic Church attempted the same kind of work through a revival of its religious orders; dedicated priests and nuns used spiritual instruction and recreation to turn young male workers away from the moral vices of gambling and drinking and female workers from lives of prostitution.

Prison Reform

The increase in crime led to a rise in arrests. By the 1820s in most countries, the indiscriminate use of capital punishment, even for crimes against property, was increasingly being viewed as ineffective and was replaced by imprisonment. Although the British had shipped people convicted of serious offenses to their colonial territory of Australia, that practice began to slow down in the late 1830s when the colonists loudly objected. Incarceration, then, was the only alternative. Prisons served to isolate criminals from society, but a growing number of reformers questioned their purpose and effectiveness, especially when prisoners were subjected to harsh and even humiliating work as punishment. By the 1830s, European governments were seeking ways to reform their penal systems. Motivated by the desire not just to punish but to rehabilitate and transform criminals into new persons, the British and French sent missions to the United States in the early 1830s to examine how the two different systems then used in American prisons accomplished this goal. At the Auburn Prison in New York, for example, prisoners were separated at night but worked together in the same workshop during the day. At Walnut Street Prison in Philadelphia, prisoners were separated into individual cells.

After examining the American prisons, both the French and the British constructed prisons on the Walnut Street model with separate cells that isolated prisoners from one another. At Petite Roquette in France and Pentonville in Britain, prisoners wore leather masks while they exercised and sat in separate stalls when in chapel. Solitary confinement, it was believed, forced prisoners back on their own consciences, led to greater remorse, and increased the possibility that they would change their evil ways. One supporter of the separate-cell system noted:

> A few months in the solitary cell renders a prisoner strangely impressible. The chaplain can then make the brawny navvy cry like a child; he can work on his feelings in almost any way he pleases; he can, so to speak, photograph his thoughts, wishes and opinions on his patient's mind, and fill his mouth with his own phrases and language.[12]

As prison populations increased, however, solitary confinement proved expensive and less feasible. The French even returned to their custom of sending prisoners to French Guiana to handle the overload.

Prison reform and police forces were geared toward one primary end, the creation of a more disciplined society. Disturbed by the upheavals associated with revolutions and the social discontent wrought by industrialization and urbanization, the ruling elites sought to impose some order on society.

Culture in an Age of Reaction and Revolution: The Mood of Romanticism

Q **Focus Question:** What were the characteristics of Romanticism, and how were they reflected in literature, art, and music?

At the end of the eighteenth century, a new intellectual movement known as Romanticism emerged to challenge the Enlightenment's preoccupation with reason in discovering truth. The Romantics tried to balance the use of reason by stressing the importance of intuition, feeling, emotion, and imagination as sources of knowing. As one German Romantic put it, "It was my heart that counseled me to do it, and my heart cannot err."

The Characteristics of Romanticism

Romantic writers emphasized emotion, sentiment, and inner feelings in their works. An important model for Romantics was the tragic figure in *The Sorrows of the Young Werther,* a novel by the great German writer Johann Wolfgang von Goethe (1749–1832), who later rejected Romanticism in favor of Classicism. Werther was a Romantic figure who sought freedom in order to fulfill himself. Misunderstood and rejected by society, he continued to believe in his own worth through his inner feelings, but his deep love for a girl who did not love him finally led him to commit suicide. After Goethe's *Sorrows of the Young Werther,* numerous novels and plays appeared whose plots revolved around young maidens tragically carried off at an early age (twenty-three was most common) by disease (usually tuberculosis, at that time a protracted disease that was usually fatal) to the sorrow and despair of their male lovers.

Another important characteristic of Romanticism was **individualism,** an interest in the unique traits of each person. The Romantics' desire to follow their inner drives led them to rebel against middle-class conventions. Long hair, beards, and outrageous clothes served to reinforce the individualism that young Romantics were trying to express.

Sentiment and individualism came together in the Romantics' stress on the heroic. The Romantic hero was a solitary genius who was ready to defy the world and sacrifice his life for a great cause. In the hands of the British writer Thomas Carlyle (1795–1881), however, the Romantic hero did not destroy himself in ineffective protests against society but transformed society instead. In his historical works, Carlyle stressed that historical events were largely determined by the deeds of such heroes.

Many Romantics possessed a passionate interest in the past. This historical focus was manifested in many ways. In Germany, the Grimm brothers collected and published local fairy tales, as did Hans Christian Andersen in Denmark. The revival of medieval Gothic architecture left European countrysides adorned with pseudo-medieval castles and cities bedecked with grandiose neo-Gothic cathedrals, city halls, parliamentary buildings, and even railway stations. Literature, too, reflected this historical consciousness. The novels of Walter Scott (1771–1832) became European best-sellers in the first half of the nineteenth century. *Ivanhoe,* in which Scott tried to evoke the clash between Saxon and Norman knights in medieval England, became one of his most popular works.

American writers and poets made significant contributions to the movement of Romanticism. Although Edgar Allan Poe (1809–1849) was influenced by the German Romantic school of mystery and horror, many literary historians give him the credit for pioneering the modern short story. This selection from the conclusion of "The Fall of the House of Usher" gives a sense of the nature of so-called Gothic literature.

Edgar Allan Poe, "The Fall of the House of Usher"

No sooner had these syllables passed my lips, than—as if a shield of brass had indeed, at the moment, fallen heavily upon a floor of silver—I became aware of a distinct, hollow, metallic, and clangorous, yet apparently muffled, reverberation. Completely unnerved, I leaped to my feet; but the measured rocking movement of Usher was undisturbed. I rushed to the chair in which he sat. His eyes were bent fixedly before him, and throughout his whole countenance there reigned a stony rigidity. But, as I placed my hand upon his shoulder, there came a strong shudder over his whole person; a sickly smile quivered about his lips and I saw that he spoke in a low, hurried, and gibbering murmur, as if unconscious of my presence. Bending closely over him, I at length drank in the hideous import of his words.

"Not hear it?—yes, I hear it, and *have* heard it. Long-long-long-many minutes, many hours, many days, have I heard it—yet I dared not—oh, pity me, miserable wretch that I am!—I dared not—I *dared* not speak! *We have put her living in the tomb!* Said I not that my senses were acute? I now tell you that I heard her first feeble movements in the hollow coffin. I heard them—many, many days ago—yet I dared not—I *dared not speak!* And now—to-night . . . the rending of her coffin, and the grating of the iron hinges of her prison, and her struggles within the coppered archway of the vault! Oh whither shall I fly? Will she not be here anon? Is she not hurrying to upbraid me for my haste? Have I not heard her footstep on the stair? Do I not distinguish that heavy and horrible beating of her heart? MADMAN!"—here he sprang furiously to his feet, and shrieked out his syllables, as if in the effort he were giving up his soul—"MADMAN! I TELL YOU THAT SHE NOW STANDS WITHOUT THE DOOR!"

As if in the superhuman energy of his utterance there had been found the potency of a spell, the huge antique panels to which the speaker pointed threw slowly back, upon the instant, their ponderous and ebony jaws. It was the work of the rushing gust—but then without those doors there DID stand the lofty and enshrouded figure of the lady Madeline of Usher. There was blood upon her white robes, and the evidence of some bitter struggle upon every portion of her emaciated frame. For a moment she remained trembling and reeling to and fro upon the threshold, then, with a low moaning cry, fell heavily inward upon the person of her brother, and in her violent and now final death-agonies, bore him to the floor a corpse, and a victim to the terrors he had anticipated.

Q *What characteristics of Romanticism are revealed in Poe's tale? In what ways did Romanticism offer alternatives to the reigning influences of rationalism and industrialization?*

To the history-mindedness of the Romantics could be added an attraction to the bizarre and unusual. In an exaggerated form, this preoccupation gave rise to so-called **Gothic literature** (see the box above), chillingly evident in the short stories of horror by the American Edgar Allan Poe (1808–1849) and in *Frankenstein* by Mary Shelley (1797–1851). Shelley's novel was the story of a mad scientist who brings into being a humanlike monster who goes berserk. Some Romantics even sought the unusual in their own lives by pursuing extraordinary states of experience in dreams, nightmares, frenzies, and suicidal depression or by experimenting with cocaine, opium, and hashish to produce altered states of consciousness.

Romantic Poets

To the Romantics, poetry ranked above all other literary forms because they believed it was the direct expression of one's soul. The Romantic poets were viewed as seers who could reveal the invisible world to others. Their incredible sense of drama made some of them the most colorful figures of their era, living intense but short lives.

Percy Bysshe Shelley (1792–1822), expelled from school for advocating atheism, set out to reform the world. His *Prometheus Unbound*, completed in 1820, is a portrait of the revolt of human beings against the laws and customs that oppress them. He drowned in a storm in the Mediterranean. Lord Byron (1788–1824) dramatized himself as the melancholy Romantic hero that he had described in his work, *Childe Harold's Pilgrimage*. He participated in the movement for Greek independence and died in Greece fighting the Ottomans.

Love of Nature Romantic poetry gave full expression to one of the most important characteristics of Romanticism: love of nature, especially evident in the works of William Wordsworth (1770–1850). His experience of nature was almost mystical as he claimed to receive "authentic tidings of invisible things":

> *One impulse from a vernal wood*
> *May teach you more of man,*
> *Of Moral Evil and of good,*
> *Than all the sages can.*[13]

Neo-Gothic Revival: British Houses of Parliament. The Romantic movement of the first half of the nineteenth century led, among other things, to a revival of medieval Gothic architecture that left European cities bedecked with neo-Gothic buildings. After the Houses of Parliament in London burned down in 1834, they were replaced with new buildings of neo-Gothic design, as seen in this photograph.

To Wordsworth, nature contained a mysterious force that the poet could perceive and learn from. Nature served as a mirror into which humans could look to learn about themselves. Nature was, in fact, alive and sacred:

> *To every natural form, rock, fruit or flower,*
> *Even the loose stones that cover the high-way,*
> *I gave a moral life, I saw them feel,*
> *Or link'd them to some feeling: the great mass*
> *Lay bedded in a quickening soul, and all*
> *That I beheld, respired with inward meaning.*[14]

Other Romantics carried this worship of nature further into **pantheism** by identifying the great force in nature with God. The Romantics would have nothing to do with the deist God of the Enlightenment, the remote creator of the world-machine. As the German Romantic poet Friedrich Novalis said, "Anyone seeking God will find him anywhere."

Critique of Science The worship of nature also led Wordsworth and other Romantic poets to critique the mechanistic materialism of eighteenth-century science, which, they believed, had reduced nature to a cold object of study. Against that view of the natural world, Wordsworth offered his own vivid and concrete experience. To him, the scientists' dry, mathematical approach left no room for the imagination or for the human soul. The poet who left to the world "one single moral precept, one single affecting sentiment," Wordsworth said, did more for the world than scientists who were soon forgotten. The monster created by Frankenstein in Mary Shelley's Gothic novel symbolized well the danger of science when it tries to conquer nature. Many Romantics were convinced that the emerging industrialization would cause people to become alienated from their inner selves and the natural world around them.

Romanticism in Art

Like the literary arts, the visual arts were also deeply affected by Romanticism. Although their works varied widely, Romantic artists shared at least two fundamental characteristics. All artistic expression to them was a reflection of the artist's inner feelings; a painting should mirror the artist's vision of the world and be the instrument of his own imagination. Moreover, Romantic artists deliberately rejected the principles of Classicism. Beauty was not a timeless thing; its expression depended on one's culture and one's age. The Romantics abandoned classical restraint for warmth, emotion, and movement. Through an examination of three painters, we can see how Romanticism influenced the visual arts.

Friedrich The early life experiences of the German painter Caspar David Friedrich (1774–1840) left him with a lifelong preoccupation with God and nature. Friedrich painted landscapes with an interest that transcended the mere presentation of natural details. His portrayal of mountains shrouded in mist, gnarled trees bathed in moonlight, and the stark ruins of monasteries surrounded by withered trees all conveyed a feeling of mystery and mysticism. For Friedrich, nature was a manifestation of divine life, as is evident in *Man and Woman Gazing at the Moon*. To Friedrich, the artistic process depended on one's inner vision. He advised artists, "Shut your physical eye and look first at your picture with your spiritual eye; then bring to the light of day what you have seen in the darkness."

Turner Another artist who dwelled on nature and made landscape his major subject was the Englishman Joseph Malford William Turner (1775–1851). Turner was an incredibly prolific artist who produced more than 20,000 paintings, drawings, and watercolors. Turner's concern with nature manifested itself in innumerable landscapes

Caspar David Friedrich, *Man and Woman Gazing at the Moon.* The German artist Caspar David Friedrich sought to express in painting his own mystical view of nature. "The divine is everywhere," he once wrote, "even in a grain of sand." In this painting, two solitary wanderers are shown from the back gazing at the moon. Overwhelmed by the all-pervasive presence of nature, the two figures express the human longing for infinity.

and seascapes, sunrises and sunsets. He did not idealize nature or reproduce it with realistic accuracy, however. He sought instead to convey its moods by using a skilled interplay of light and color to suggest natural effects. In allowing his objects to melt into their surroundings, he anticipated the Impressionist painters of the second half of the nineteenth century (see Chapter 24). John Constable, a contemporary English Romantic painter, described Turner's paintings as "airy visions, painted with tinted steam."

Delacroix Eugène Delacroix (1798–1863) was the most famous French Romantic artist. Largely self-taught, he was fascinated by the exotic and had a passion for color. Both characteristics are visible in *The Death of Sardanapalus.* Significant for its use of light and its patches of interrelated color, this portrayal of the world of the last Assyrian king was criticized at the time for its garishness. Delacroix rejoiced in combining theatricality and movement with a daring use of color. Many of his works reflect his own belief that "a painting should be a feast to the eye."

Romanticism in Music

To many Romantics, music was the most Romantic of the arts because it enabled the composer to probe deeply into human emotions. One Romantic writer noted, "It has been rightly said that the object of music is the awakening of emotion. No other art can so sublimely arouse human

J. M. W. Turner, *Rain, Steam, and Speed–The Great Western Railway.* Although Turner began his artistic career by painting accurate representations of the natural world, he increasingly sought to create an atmosphere through the skillful use of light and color. In this painting, Turner eliminates specific details and uses general fields of color to convey the impression of a locomotive rushing toward the spectator.

Eugène Delacroix, *The Death of Sardanapalus.* Delacroix's *Death of Sardanapalus* was based on Lord Byron's verse account of the dramatic last moments of the decadent Assyrian king. Besieged by enemy troops and with little hope of survival, Sardanapalus orders that his harem women and prize horses go to their death with him. At the right, a guard stabs one of the women as the king looks on.

sentiments in the innermost heart of man."[15] Although music historians have called the eighteenth century the age of Classicism and the nineteenth the era of Romanticism, there was much carryover of classical forms from one century to the next. One of the greatest composers of all time, Ludwig van Beethoven, served as a bridge between Classicism and Romanticism.

Beethoven Beethoven (1770–1827) is one of the few composers to singlehandedly transform the art of music. Set ablaze by the events in France, a revolutionary mood burned brightly across Europe, and Beethoven, like other creative personalities, yearned to communicate his cherished beliefs. He said, "I *must* write, for what weighs on my heart, I *must* express." For Beethoven, music had to reflect his deepest inner feelings.

Born in Bonn, Beethoven came from a family of musicians who worked for the electors of Cologne. He became an assistant organist at the court by the age of thirteen and soon made his way to Vienna, the musical capital of Europe, where he studied briefly under Haydn. Beginning in 1792, this city became his permanent residence.

During his first major period of composing (1792–1800), his work was largely within the classical framework of the eighteenth century, and the influences of Haydn and Mozart are apparent. But with the composition of the Third Symphony (1804), also called the *Eroica*, which was originally intended for Napoleon, Beethoven broke through to the elements of Romanticism in his use of uncontrolled rhythms to create dramatic struggle and uplifted resolutions. E. T. A. Hoffman, a contemporary composer and writer, said, "Beethoven's music opens the flood gates of fear, of

terror, of horror, of pain, and arouses that longing for the eternal which is the essence of Romanticism. He is thus a pure Romantic composer."[16] Beethoven went on to write a vast quantity of works, but in the midst of this productivity and growing fame, he was more and more burdened by his growing deafness. One of the most moving pieces of music of all time, the chorale finale of his Ninth Symphony, was composed when Beethoven was totally deaf.

Berlioz Beethoven served as a bridge from the classical era to Romanticism; after him came a number of musical geniuses who composed in the Romantic style. The Frenchman Hector Berlioz (1803–1869) was one of the most outstanding. His father, a doctor in Grenoble, intended that his son should also study medicine. The young Berlioz eventually rebelled, however, maintaining to his father's disgust that he would be "no doctor or apothecary but a great composer." Berlioz managed to fulfill his own expectations, achieving fame in Germany, Russia, and Britain, although the originality of his work kept him from receiving much recognition in his native France.

Berlioz was one of the founders of program music, which was an attempt to use the moods and sound effects of instrumental music to depict the actions and emotions inherent in a story, an event, or even a personal experience. This development of program music was evident in his most famous piece, the first complete program symphony, known as the *Symphonie Fantastique*. In this work, Berlioz used music to evoke the passionate emotions of a tortured love affair, including a fifth movement in which he musically creates an opium-induced nightmare of a witches' gathering.

The Revival of Religion in the Age of Romanticism

After 1815, Christianity experienced a revival. In the eighteenth century, Catholicism had lost its attraction for many of the educated elite as even the European nobility flirted with the ideas of the Enlightenment. The restoration of the nobility brought a new appreciation for the Catholic faith as a force for order in society. This appreciation was greatly reinforced by the Romantic movement. The Romantics' attraction to the Middle Ages and their emphasis on emotion led them to their own widespread revival of Christianity.

Catholicism Catholicism, in particular, benefited from this Romantic enthusiasm for religion. Especially among German Romantics, there were many conversions to the Catholic faith. One of the most popular expressions of this Romantic revival of Catholicism was found in the work of the Frenchman François-René de Chateaubriand (1768–1848). His book *Genius of Christianity*, published in 1802, was soon labeled the "Bible of Romanticism." His defense of Catholicism was based not on historical, theological, or even rational grounds but largely on Romantic sentiment. As a faith, Catholicism echoed the harmony of all things. Its cathedrals brought one into the very presence of God; according to Chateaubriand, "You could not enter a Gothic church without feeling a kind of awe and a vague sentiment of the Divinity.... Every thing in a Gothic church reminds you of the labyrinths of a wood; every thing excites a feeling of religious awe, of mystery, and of the Divinity."[17]

Protestantism Protestantism also experienced a revival. That "awakening," as it was called, had already begun in the eighteenth century with the enthusiastic emotional experiences of Methodism in Britain and Pietism in Germany (see Chapter 17). Methodist missionaries from England and Scotland carried their messages of sin and redemption to liberal Protestant churches in France and Switzerland, winning converts to their strongly evangelical message. Germany, too, witnessed a Protestant awakening as enthusiastic evangelical preachers found that their messages of hellfire and their methods of emotional conversion evoked a ready response among people alienated by the highly educated establishment clergy of the state churches.

TIMELINE

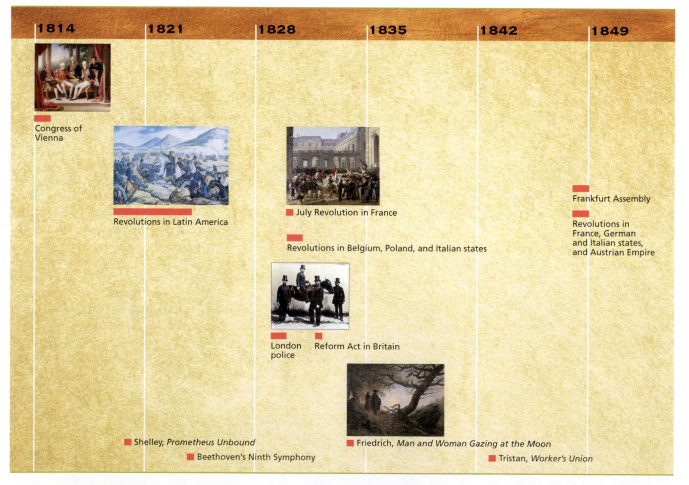

| 1814 | 1821 | 1828 | 1835 | 1842 | 1849 |

Congress of Vienna

Revolutions in Latin America

July Revolution in France

Revolutions in Belgium, Poland, and Italian states

Frankfurt Assembly

Revolutions in France, German and Italian states, and Austrian Empire

London police   Reform Act in Britain

Shelley, *Prometheus Unbound*

Beethoven's Ninth Symphony

Friedrich, *Man and Woman Gazing at the Moon*

Tristan, *Worker's Union*

CONCLUSION

In 1815, a conservative order was reestablished throughout Europe, and the cooperation of the great powers, embodied in the Concert of Europe, tried to ensure its durability. But the revolutionary waves of the 1820s and 1830s made it clear that the ideologies of liberalism and nationalism, unleashed by the French Revolution and now reinforced by the spread of the Industrial Revolution, were still alive and active. They faced enormous difficulties, however, as failed revolutions in Poland, Russia, Italy, and Germany all testify.

At the same time, reform legislation in Britain and successful revolutions in Greece, France, and Belgium demonstrated the continuing strength of these forces of change. In 1848, they erupted once more all across Europe. And once more they failed. But not all was lost. Both liberalism and nationalism would succeed in the second half of the nineteenth century, but in ways not foreseen by the idealistic liberals and nationalists, who were utterly convinced that their time had come when they manned the barricades in 1848.

NOTES

1. Quoted in Charles Breunig, *The Age of Revolution and Reaction, 1789–1850* (New York, 1970), p. 119.
2. Quoted in M. S. Anderson, *The Ascendancy of Europe, 1815–1914,* 2d ed. (London, 1985), p. 1.
3. Quotations from Burke can be found in Peter Viereck, *Conservatism* (Princeton, N.J., 1956), pp. 27, 114.
4. Quoted in René Albrecht-Carrié, *The Concert of Europe* (New York, 1968), p. 48.
5. Quoted in G. de Berthier de Sauvigny, *Metternich and His Times* (London, 1962), p. 105.
6. Quoted in S. Joan Moon, "Feminism and Socialism: The Utopian Synthesis of Flora Tristan," in Marilyn J. Boxer and Jean H. Quataert, eds., *Socialist Women* (New York, 1978), p. 38.
7. Quoted in Stanley Z. Pech, *The Czech Revolution of 1848* (Chapel Hill, N.C., 1969), p. 82.
8. Quoted in Clive Emsley, *Policing and Its Context, 1750–1870* (New York, 1984), p. 58.
9. Quoted in Clive Emsley, *Crime and Society in England, 1750–1900* (London, 1987), p. 173.
10. Quoted in Emsley, *Policing and Its Context,* p. 66.
11. Quoted in ibid., p. 102.
12. Quoted in Emsley, *Crime and Society in England,* p. 226.
13. William Wordsworth, "The Tables Turned," *Poems of Wordsworth,* ed. Matthew Arnold (London, 1963), p. 138.
14. William Wordsworth, *The Prelude* (Harmondsworth, England, 1971), p. 109.
15. Quoted in H. G. Schenk, *The Mind of the European Romantics* (Garden City, N.Y., 1969), p. 205.
16. Quoted in Siegbert Prawer, ed., *The Romantic Period in Germany* (London, 1970), p. 285.
17. Quoted in John B. Halsted, ed., *Romanticism* (New York, 1969), p. 156.

SUGGESTIONS FOR FURTHER READING

General Works   For a good survey of the entire nineteenth century, see **R. Gildea, *Barricades and Borders: Europe, 1800–1914,*** 3d ed. (Oxford, 2003), in the Short Oxford History of the Modern World series. Also valuable is **T. C. W. Blanning, ed., *Nineteenth Century: Europe 1789–1914*** (Oxford, 2000). For surveys of the period covered in this chapter, see **M. Broers, *Europe After Napoleon: Revolution, Reaction, and Romanticism, 1814–1848*** (New York, 1996); **M. Lyons, *Postrevolutionary Europe 1815–1856*** (New York, 2006); and **C. Breunig and M. Levinger, *The Age of Revolution and Reaction, 1789–1850,*** 3d ed. (New York, 2002).

There are also some useful books on individual countries that cover more than the subject of this chapter. These include **R. Magraw, *France, 1815–1914: The Bourgeois Century,*** rev. ed. (Oxford, 2006); **D. Saunders, *Russia in the Age of Reaction and Reform, 1801–1881*** (London, 1992); **D. Blackbourn, *The Long Nineteenth Century: A History of Germany, 1789–1918*** (New York, 1998); **A. Sked, *The Decline and Fall of the Habsburg Empire, 1815–1918,*** 2d ed. (London, 2001); **J. A. David, *Italy in the Nineteenth Century: 1796–1900*** (Oxford, 2001); **R. Carr, *Spain, 1808–1939*** (Oxford, 1991); and **N. McCord, *British History, 1815–1906*** (New York, 1991).

Europe, 1815–1830   On the peace settlement of 1814–1815, see **T. Chapman, *The Congress of Vienna*** (London, 1998). A concise summary of the international events of the entire nineteenth century can be found in **R. Bullen and F. R. Bridge, *The Great Powers and the European States System, 1815–1914,*** rev. ed. (London, 2004). See also **N. Rich, *Great Power Diplomacy, 1814–1914*** (New York, 1992). On the man whose conservative policies dominated this era, see the brief but good biography by **A. Palmer, *Metternich*** (New York, 1972). On the revolutions in Europe in 1830, see **C. Church, *Europe in 1830: Revolution and Political Change*** (Chapel Hill, N.C., 1983). On Great Britain's reform legislation, see **E. J. Evans, *Great Reform Act of 1832,*** 2d ed. (London, 1994). The Greek revolt is examined in detail in **D. Brewer, *Greek War of Independence*** (New York, 2001).

Revolutions of 1848   The best introduction to the revolutions of 1848 is **J. Sperber, *The European Revolutions, 1848–1851,*** 2d ed. (New York, 2005). Good accounts of the revolutions in individual countries include **R. J. Rath, *The Viennese Revolution of 1848*** (Austin, Tex., 1957); **I. Déak, *The Lawful Revolution: Louis Kossuth and the Hungarians, 1848–49*** (New York, 1979); **R. Stadelmann, *Social and Political History of the German 1848 Revolution*** (Athens, Ohio, 1975); and **P. Ginsborg, *Daniele Manin and the Venetian Revolution of 1848–49*** (New York, 1979). On Mazzini, see **D. M. Smith, *Mazzini*** (New Haven, Conn., 1994). On the ideologies connected to the revolutions of 1848, see **J. Gray, *Liberalism*** (Minneapolis, Minn., 1995), and **T. Baycroft, *Nationalism in Europe, 1789–1945*** (Cambridge, 1998).

An Ordered Society   On changes in the treatment of crime and punishment, see **M. Foucault, *Discipline and Punish: The Birth of the Prison*** (New York, 1977). The new police forces are examined in **C. Emsley, *Policing and Its Context, 1750–1870*** (New York, 1984), and **C. Emsley, *Crime and Society in England, 1750–1900,*** 3d ed. (London, 2005).

Romanticism   On the ideas of the Romantics, see
M. Cranston, *The Romantic Movement* (Oxford, 1994). On
Wordsworth and English Romanticism, see **J. Wordsworth,** *William
Wordsworth and the Age of English Romanticism* (New Brunswick,
N.J., 1987), and **S. Hebron,** *William Wordsworth* (New York, 2000).
For an introduction to the arts, see **W. Vaughan,** *Romanticism and
Art* (New York, 1994), and **I. Ciseri,** *Romanticism 1780–1860: The
Birth of a New Sensibility* (New York, 2003).

CENGAGENOW   CengageNOW is an integrated online suite of services and resources with proven ease of use and
efficient paths to success, delivering the results you want—NOW!

academic.cengage.com/login/

Enter CengageNOW using the access card that is available with
Western Civilization. CengageNOW will assist you in understanding the content in this chapter with lesson plans generated for
your needs. In addition, you can read the following documents,
and many more, online:

James Monroe, the Monroe Doctrine
Klemens von Metternich, excerpts from *Memoirs*
Louis Napoleon, campaign address

CHAPTER 22
AN AGE OF NATIONALISM
AND REALISM, 1850–1871

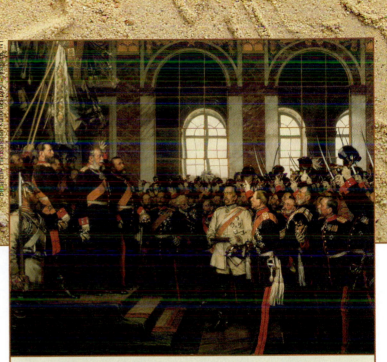

Proclamation of the German Empire in the Hall of Mirrors in the palace of Versailles

CHAPTER OUTLINE AND FOCUS QUESTIONS

The France of Napoleon III

Q What were the characteristics of Napoleon III's government, and how did his foreign policy contribute to the unification of Italy and Germany?

National Unification: Italy and Germany

Q What actions did Cavour and Bismarck take to bring about unification in Italy and Germany, respectively, and what role did war play in their efforts?

Nation Building and Reform: The National State in Midcentury

Q What efforts for reform occurred in the Austrian Empire, Russia, and Great Britain between 1850 and 1870, and how successful were they in alleviating each nation's problems?

Industrialization and the Marxist Response

Q What were the main ideas of Karl Marx?

Science and Culture in an Age of Realism

Q How did the belief that the world should be viewed realistically manifest itself in science, art, and literature in the second half of the nineteenth century?

CRITICAL THINKING

Q What was the relationship between nationalism and reform between 1850 and 1871?

ACROSS THE EUROPEAN continent, the revolutions of 1848 had failed. The forces of liberalism and nationalism appeared to have been decisively defeated as authoritarian governments reestablished their control almost everywhere in Europe by 1850. And yet within twenty-five years, many of the goals sought by the liberals and nationalists during the first half of the nineteenth century seemed to have been achieved. National unity became a reality in Italy and Germany, and many European states were governed by constitutional monarchies, even though the constitutional-parliamentary features were frequently facades.

All the same, these goals were not achieved by liberal and nationalist leaders but by a new generation of conservative leaders who were proud of being practitioners of *Realpolitik,* the "politics of reality." One reaction to the failure of the revolutions of 1848 had been a new toughness of mind as people prided themselves on being realistic in their handling of power. The new conservative leaders used armies and power politics to achieve their foreign policy goals. And they did not hesitate to manipulate liberal means to achieve conservative ends at home. Nationalism had failed as a revolutionary movement in 1848–1849, but between 1850 and 1871, these new leaders found a variety of ways to pursue nation building. One of the most successful was the Prussian Otto von Bismarck, who used both astute diplomacy and war to achieve the unification of Germany. On January 18, 1871, Bismarck and six hundred German princes, nobles, and generals filled the Hall of Mirrors in the palace of Versailles, outside Paris. The Prussian army had defeated the French, and the assembled notables were gathered for the proclamation of the Prussian king as the new emperor of a united German state. When the words "Long live His Imperial Majesty, the Emperor William!" rang out, the assembled guests took up the cry. One participant wrote, "A thundering cheer, repeated at least six times, thrilled through the room while the flags and standards waved over the head of the new emperor of Germany." European rulers who feared the power of the new German state were not so cheerful. "The balance of power has been entirely destroyed," declared the British prime minister. ◈

The France of Napoleon III

Q **Focus Question:** What were the characteristics of Napoleon III's government, and how did his foreign policy contribute to the unification of Italy and Germany?

After 1850, a new generation of conservative leaders came to power in Europe. Foremost among them was Napoleon III (1852–1870) of France, who taught his contemporaries how authoritarian governments could use liberal and nationalistic forces to bolster their own power. It was a lesson others quickly learned.

Louis Napoleon: Toward the Second Empire

Even after his election as the president of the French Republic, many of his contemporaries dismissed "Napoleon the Small" as a nonentity whose success was due only to his name. But Louis Napoleon was a clever politician who was especially astute at understanding the popular forces of his day. After his election, he was clear about his desire to have personal power. He wrote, "I shall never submit to any attempt to influence me.... I follow only the promptings of my mind and heart.... Nothing, nothing shall trouble the clear vision of my judgment or the strength of my resolution."[1]

Louis Napoleon was a patient man. For three years, he persevered in winning the support of the French people, and when the National Assembly rejected his wish to revise the constitution and be allowed to stand for reelection, Louis used troops to seize control of the government on December 1, 1851. After restoring universal male suffrage, Louis Napoleon asked the French people to restructure the government by electing him president for ten years (see the box on p. 667). By an overwhelming majority, 7.5 million yes votes to 640,000

no votes, they agreed. A year later, on November 21, 1852, Louis Napoleon returned to the people to ask for the restoration of the empire. This time, 97 percent responded affirmatively, and on December 2, 1852, Louis Napoleon assumed the title of Napoleon III (the first Napoleon had abdicated in favor of his son, Napoleon II, on April 6, 1814). The Second Empire had begun.

The Second Napoleonic Empire

The government of Napoleon III was clearly authoritarian in a Bonapartist sense. Louis Napoleon had asked, "Since France has carried on for fifty years only by virtue of the administrative, military, judicial, religious and financial organization of the Consulate and Empire, why should she not also adopt the political institutions of that period?"[2] As chief of state, Napoleon III controlled the armed forces, police, and civil service. Only he could introduce legislation and declare war. The Legislative Corps gave an

Emperor Napoleon III. On December 2, 1852, Louis Napoleon took the title of Napoleon III and then proceeded to create an authoritarian monarchy. As opposition to his policies intensified in the 1860s, Napoleon III began to liberalize his government. A disastrous military defeat at the hands of Prussia in 1870–1871, however, brought the collapse of his regime.

LOUIS NAPOLEON APPEALS TO THE PEOPLE

After his coup d'état on December 1, 1851, Louis Napoleon asked the French people to approve his actions. By making this appeal, the clever politician was demonstrating how universal male suffrage, considered a democratic and hence revolutionary device, could be used to bolster a basically authoritarian regime. This selection is from Louis Napoleon's proclamation to the French people in 1851.

Louis Napoleon, *Proclamation to the People* (1851)

Frenchmen! The present situation cannot last much longer. Each passing day increases the danger to the country. The [National] Assembly, which ought to be the firmest supporter of order, has become a center of conspiracies.... It attacks the authority that I hold directly from the people; it encourages all evil passions; it jeopardizes the peace of France: I have dissolved it and I make the whole people judge between it and me....

I therefore make a loyal appeal to the whole nation, and I say to you: If you wish to continue this state of uneasiness which degrades us and makes our future uncertain, choose another in my place, for I no longer wish an authority which is powerless to do good, makes me responsible for acts I cannot prevent, and chains me to the helm when I see the vessel speeding toward the abyss.

If, on the contrary, you still have confidence in me, give me the means to accomplish the great mission that I hold from you. This mission consists in bringing to a close the era of revolutions by satisfying the legitimate wants of the people and by protecting them against subversive passions. It consists, especially, in creating institutions that may survive men and that may be at length foundations on which something durable can be established.

Persuaded that the instability of authority and the preponderance of a single Assembly are permanent causes of trouble and discord, I submit to you the following fundamental bases of a constitution which the Assemblies will develop later.

1. A responsible chief elected for ten years.
2. Ministers dependent upon the executive power alone.
3. A Council of State composed of the most distinguished men to prepare the laws and discuss them before the legislative body.
4. A legislative body to discuss and vote the laws, elected by universal [male] suffrage....

This system, created by the First Consul [Napoleon I] at the beginning of the century, has already given France calm and prosperity; it will guarantee them to her again.

Such is my profound conviction. If you share it, declare that fact by your votes. If, on the contrary, you prefer a government without force, monarchical or republican, borrowed from I know not what past or from which chimerical future, reply in the negative....

If I do not obtain a majority of your votes, I shall then convoke a new assembly, and I shall resign to it the mandate that I received from you. But if you believe that the cause of which my name is the symbol, that is, France regenerated by the revolution of 1789 and organized by the Emperor, is forever yours, proclaim it by sanctioning the powers that I ask from you. Then France and Europe will be saved from anarchy, obstacles will be removed, rivalries will disappear, for all will respect the decree of Providence in the decision of the people.

Q *What were Louis Napoleon's arguments to the French people? Why did his arguments have such a strong popular appeal? Can Louis Napoleon be viewed as a precursor of modern authoritarian state politics? Why or why not?*

appearance of representative government since its members were elected by universal male suffrage for six-year terms. But they could neither initiate legislation nor affect the budget.

Early Domestic Policies The first five years of Napoleon III's reign were a spectacular success as he reaped the benefits of worldwide economic prosperity as well as of some of his own economic policies. Napoleon believed in using the resources of government to stimulate the national economy and took many steps to encourage industrial growth. Government subsidies were used to foster the construction of railroads, harbors, roads, and canals. The major French railway lines were completed during Napoleon's reign, and industrial expansion was evident in the tripling of iron production. In his concern to reduce tensions and improve the social welfare of the nation, Napoleon provided hospitals and free medicine for the workers and advocated better housing for the working class.

In the midst of this economic expansion, Napoleon III undertook a vast reconstruction of the city of Paris. Under the direction of Baron Haussmann, the medieval Paris of narrow streets and old city walls was destroyed and replaced by a modern Paris of broad boulevards, spacious buildings, circular plazas, public squares, an underground sewage system, a new public water supply, and gaslights. The new Paris served a military as well as an aesthetic purpose: broad streets made it more difficult for would-be insurrectionists to throw up barricades and easier for troops to move rapidly through the city to put down revolts.

Liberalization of the Regime In the 1860s, as opposition to some of the emperor's policies began to mount, Napoleon III liberalized his regime. He reached out to the working class by legalizing trade unions and granting them the right to strike. He also began to liberalize the political process. The Legislative Corps had been closely controlled during the 1850s. In the 1860s, opposition candidates were allowed greater freedom to campaign, and the Legislative Corps was permitted more say in affairs of state, including debate over the budget. Napoleon's liberalization policies did serve initially to strengthen the hand of the government. In a plebiscite in May 1870 on whether to accept a new constitution that might have inaugurated a parliamentary regime, the French people gave Napoleon another resounding victory. This triumph was short-lived, however. Foreign policy failures led to growing criticism, and war with Prussia in 1870 turned out to be the death blow for Napoleon III's regime (see "The Franco-Prussian War" later in this chapter).

Foreign Policy: The Mexican Adventure

Napoleon III was considerably less accomplished at dealing with foreign policy, especially his imperialistic adventure in Mexico. Seeking to dominate Mexican markets for French goods, the emperor sent French troops to Mexico in 1861 to join British and Spanish forces in protecting their interests in the midst of the upheaval caused by a struggle between liberal and conservative Mexican factions. Although the British and Spanish withdrew their troops after order had been restored, French forces remained, and in 1864, Napoleon III installed Archduke Maximilian of Austria, his handpicked choice, as the new emperor of Mexico. When the French troops were needed in Europe, Maximilian became an emperor without an army. He surrendered to liberal Mexican forces in May 1867 and was executed in June. His execution was a blow to the prestige of the French emperor.

Foreign Policy: The Crimean War

Napoleon III's participation in the Crimean War (1854–1856) was more rewarding. As heir to the Napoleonic empire, Napoleon III was motivated by the desire to free France from the restrictions of the peace settlements of 1814–1815 and to make France the chief arbiter of Europe.

The Ottoman Empire

The Crimean War was yet another attempt to answer the Eastern Question: Who would be the chief beneficiaries of the disintegration of the Ottoman Empire? In the seventeenth century, the Ottoman Empire had control of southeastern Europe but in 1699 had lost Hungary, Transylvania, Croatia, and Slovenia to the expanding Austrian Empire.

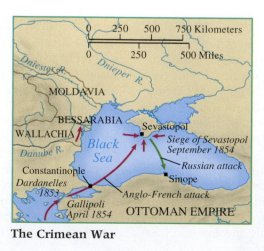

The Crimean War

The Russian Empire to its north also encroached on the Ottoman Empire by seizing the Crimea in 1783 and Bessarabia in 1812 (see Map 22.1).

By the beginning of the nineteenth century, the Ottoman Empire had entered a fresh period of decline. Nationalist revolts gained independence for Serbia in 1817 and Greece in 1830. The Russians had obtained a protectorate over the Danubian provinces of Moldavia and Wallachia in 1829.

As Ottoman authority over the outlying territories in southeastern Europe waned, European governments began to take an active interest in the empire's apparent demise. Russia's proximity to the Ottoman Empire and the religious bonds between the Russians and the Greek Orthodox Christians in Ottoman-dominated southeastern Europe naturally gave it special opportunities to enlarge its sphere of influence. Other European powers not only feared Russian ambitions but also had objectives of their own in the area. Austria craved more land in the Balkans, a desire that inevitably meant conflict with Russia, and France and Britain were interested in commercial opportunities and naval bases in the eastern Mediterranean.

War in the Crimea

War erupted between Russia and the Ottoman Empire in 1853 when the Russians demanded the right to protect Christian shrines in Palestine, a privilege that had already been extended to the French. When the Ottomans refused, the Russians invaded Moldavia and Wallachia. Failure to resolve the dispute by negotiations led the Ottoman Empire to declare war on Russia on October 4, 1853. The following year, on March 28, Great Britain and France declared war on Russia.

Why did Britain and France take that step? Concern over the prospect of an upset in the balance of power was clearly one reason. The British in particular feared that an aggressive Russia would try to profit from the obvious weakness of the Ottoman government by seizing Ottoman territory or the long-coveted Dardanelles. Such a move would make Russia the major power in eastern Europe and would enable the Russians to challenge British naval control of the eastern Mediterranean. Napoleon III felt that the Russians had insulted France, first at the Congress of Vienna and now by their insistence on replacing the French as the protectors of Christians living in the Ottoman Empire. The Russians assumed that they could count on support from the Austrians (since Russian troops had saved the Austrian government in 1849). However, the Austrian prime minister blithely explained, "We will astonish the world by our ingratitude," and Austria remained neutral. Since the Austrians had perceived that it was not in their best interest to intervene, Russia had to fight alone.

Legend:
- Ottoman Empire
- Regions winning independence
- Regions winning autonomous government
- Regions lost to Russia
- Regions lost to the Austrian Habsburg dynasty
- Regions lost to France

MAP 22.1 **Decline of the Ottoman Empire.** The decline in Ottoman fortunes began in 1699 with major losses to the Austrian Empire. The slide accelerated in the nineteenth century with nationalist revolts in the European provinces and defeat in the Crimean War. Being on the losing side of World War I would complete its destruction.
Q What is the relationship between distance from Constantinople and date of independence, and how can you explain it? 🌐 **View an animated version of this map or related maps at**
academic.cengage.com/history/spielvogel

The Crimean War was poorly planned and poorly fought. Britain and France decided to attack Russia's Crimean peninsula in the Black Sea. After a long siege and at a terrible cost in manpower for both sides, the main Russian fortress of Sevastopol fell in September 1855, six months after the death of Tsar Nicholas I. His successor, Alexander II, soon sued for peace. By the Treaty of Paris, signed in March 1856, Russia was forced to give up Bessarabia at the mouth of the Danube and accept the neutrality of the Black Sea. In addition, the principalities of Moldavia and Wallachia were placed under the protection of all five great powers.

The Crimean War proved costly to both sides. More than 250,000 soldiers died in the war, with 60 percent of the deaths coming from disease (especially cholera). Even more would have died on the British side if it had not been for the efforts of Florence Nightingale (1820–1910). Her insistence on strict sanitary conditions saved many lives and helped make nursing a profession of trained, middle-class women.

The Crimean War broke up long-standing European power relationships and effectively destroyed the Concert of Europe. Austria and Russia, the two chief powers maintaining the status quo in the first half of the nineteenth century, were now enemies because of Austria's unwillingness to support Russia in the war. Russia, defeated, humiliated, and weakened by the obvious failure of its serf-armies, withdrew from European affairs for the next two decades to set its house in order. Great Britain, disillusioned by its role in the war, also pulled back from Continental affairs. Austria, paying the price for its neutrality, was now without friends among the great powers. Not until the 1870s were new combinations formed to replace those that had disappeared, and in the meantime, the European international situation remained fluid. Leaders who were willing to pursue the "politics of reality" found themselves in a situation rife with opportunity. It was this new international situation that made possible the unification of Italy and Germany.

Florence Nightingale. Florence Nightingale is shown caring for wounded British soldiers following a battle in September 1854 in which the allies had defeated the Russians. After a British journalist, W. H. Russell, issued a scathing denunciation of the quality of medical care afforded to wounded British soldiers, the British government allowed Nightingale to take a group of nurses to the Crimean warfront. Through her efforts in the Crimean War, Nightingale helped make nursing an admirable profession for middle-class women.

National Unification: Italy and Germany

Q Focus Question: What actions did Cavour and Bismarck take to bring about unification in Italy and Germany, respectively, and what role did war play in their efforts?

The breakdown of the Concert of Europe opened the way for the Italians and the Germans to establish national states. Their successful unifications transformed the power structure of the European continent. Europe would be dealing with the consequences well into the twentieth century.

The Unification of Italy

In 1850, Austria was still the dominant power on the Italian peninsula. After the failure of the revolution of 1848–1849, a growing number of advocates for Italian unification focused on the northern Italian state of Piedmont as their best hope to achieve their goal. The royal house of Savoy ruled the kingdom of Piedmont, which also included the island of Sardinia (see Map 22.2). Although soundly defeated by the Austrians in 1848–1849, Piedmont under King Charles Albert had made a

valiant effort; it seemed reasonable that Piedmont would now assume the leading role in the cause of national unity. The little state seemed unlikely to supply the needed leadership, however, until the new king, Victor Emmanuel II (1849–1878), named Count Camillo di Cavour (1810–1861) as his prime minister in 1852.

The Leadership of Cavour Cavour was a liberal-minded nobleman who had made a fortune in agriculture and went on to make even more money in banking, railroads, and shipping. Cavour was a moderate who favored constitutional government. He was a consummate politician with the ability to persuade others of the rightness of his own convictions. After becoming prime minister in 1852, he pursued a policy of economic expansion, encouraging the building of roads, canals, and railroads and fostering business enterprise by expanding credit and stimulating investment in new industries. The growth in the Piedmontese economy and the subsequent increase in government revenues enabled Cavour to pour money into equipping a large army.

Cavour had no illusions about Piedmont's military strength and was well aware that he could not challenge Austria directly. He would need the French. In 1858, Cavour came to an agreement with Napoleon III. The emperor agreed to ally with Piedmont in driving the Austrians out of Italy. Once the Austrians were driven out, Italy would be reorganized. Piedmont would be extended into the kingdom of Upper Italy by adding Lombardy, Venetia, Parma, Modena, and part of the Papal States to its territory. In compensation for its efforts, France would receive the Piedmontese provinces of Nice and Savoy. A kingdom of Central Italy would be created for Napoleon III's cousin, Prince Napoleon, who would be married to the younger daughter of King Victor Emmanuel. This agreement between Napoleon and Cavour seemed to assure the French ruler of the opportunity to control Italy. Confident that the plan would work, Cavour provoked the Austrians into invading Piedmont in April 1859.

In the initial stages of fighting, it was the French who were largely responsible for defeating the Austrians in two major battles at Magenta and Solferino. It was also the French who made peace with Austria on July 11, 1859, without informing their Italian ally. Why did Napoleon withdraw so hastily? For one thing, he realized

FILM & HISTORY
The Charge of the Light Brigade (1936)

The charge of the Light Brigade was a disastrous incident that occurred during the Crimean War and was immortalized in a poem by Alfred, Lord Tennyson in 1854:

> *Forward the Light Brigade!*
> *Theirs not to reason why.*
> *Theirs but to do and die.*
> *Into the valley of Death*
> *Rode the six hundred.*

The film opens with the dedication "To the officers and men of the Light Brigade who died victorious in a gallant charge at Balaklava for Queen and Country." Most of this film, however, actually takes place in India with the 27th Lancers (a regiment of British cavalry). Captain (later Major) Geoffrey Vickers (Erroll Flynn) leads his men to the garrison fort of Chukoti, where he hears that the tribal warriors of the Surat Khan of Suristan (which in the film is located on India's northwestern frontier) are plotting to attack the fort. Vickers wants to attack the Khan, but his superior officers insist that there is no danger and order most of the forces in Chukoti to march off on maneuvers, much to Vickers's disgust. He is told, "When you've been soldiering as long as I have, you'll understand it's best to follow instructions regardless." But Vickers proves to be correct, and when the Khan's forces attack Chukoti, the small force left there is unable to repel the attack. The Khan orders the slaughter of all the men, women, and children in the fort. Vickers (who managed to escape) and the Lancers who lost their loved ones vow to take revenge, but the Khan flees from India. The 27th Lancers are then sent to the Crimea, where they learn that the Khan is with the Russian artillery on the Balaklava heights. Vickers countermands his orders in order to attack the heights at Balaklava and says to his men: "Surat Khan is on the field with the opposing Russian forces. The same Surat Khan who massacred the women and children of Chukoti. Show no mercy!" Thus, the Lancers' desire for revenge and their wish to teach the Khan that he can't kill women and children with impunity become the reason for the charge, even though it means a suicidal attack that costs the lives of most of the regiment. When the Light Brigade attacks, the Khan is killed, but so are Vickers and most of the six

The Charge of the Light Brigade

Warner Bros/The Kobal Collection

hundred members of the 27th Lancers. Thanks to Tennyson's poem and Hollywood's priorities, a historical military disaster is presented as a heroic triumph. In reality, the attack was a military blunder, and it resulted in a foolish waste of lives. But that was not much of an epitaph for brave men who followed orders; nor was it heroic enough to justify an epic film.

Although the charge of the Light Brigade did actually happen, almost all the rest of this film is fiction. The only real historical characters depicted are three British leaders, Lord Raglan, General Canrobert, and Lord Cardigan, who are shown in a war council during the Crimean War. No doubt, they were included to appease a British audience with some authentic detail. All the rest is blatantly false: after marching hundreds of miles through deserts and swampland, the 27th Lancers still wear impeccably clean uniforms. The cavalry charge at Balaklava did not bring about a British victory and did not justify the sacrifice of the troops. Nevertheless, we learn something about the values of the people who made the film. The movie exalts the civilized nature of British rule while depicting the indigenous peoples of India and "Suristan" as savages. Western civilization is treated as clearly superior. Made in the 1930s at the time of the Great Depression and the rise of totalitarian regimes, the film reassured Americans of Western values and reminded them that once again heroes would arise who would fight the barbarians.

---

that despite two losses, the Austrian army had not yet been defeated; the struggle might be longer and more costly than he had anticipated. Moreover, the Prussians were mobilizing in support of Austria, and Napoleon III had no desire to take on two enemies at once. As a result of Napoleon's peace with Austria, Piedmont received only Lombardy; Venetia remained under Austrian control. Cavour was furious at the French perfidy, but events in northern Italy now turned in his favor. Soon after the war with Austria had begun, some northern Italian

MAP 22.2 **The Unification of Italy.** Piedmont under the able guidance of Count Camillo di Cavour provided the nucleus for Italian unification. Alliances with France and Prussia, combined with the military actions of republican nationalists like Giuseppe Garibaldi, led to complete unification in 1870.

Q Of the countries shown on this map, which would likely, taking geographic factors and size of population into account, pose the greatest military threat to the new Italian state? **View an animated version of this map or related maps at** **academic.cengage.com/history/spielvogel**

Legend:
- Kingdom of Piedmont, before 1859
- To kingdom of Piedmont, 1859
- To kingdom of Piedmont, 1860
- To kingdom of Italy, 1866, 1870

states, namely, Parma, Modena, Tuscany, and part of the Papal States, had been taken over by nationalists. In plebiscites held in 1860, these states agreed to join Piedmont. Napoleon agreed to the annexations in return for Nice and Savoy.

The Efforts of Garibaldi Meanwhile, in southern Italy, a new leader of Italian unification had come to the fore. Giuseppe Garibaldi (1807–1882), a dedicated Italian patriot who had supported Mazzini and the republican cause of Young Italy, raised an army of a thousand Red Shirts, as his volunteers were called because of their distinctive dress, and on May 11, 1860, landed in Sicily, where a revolt had broken out against the Bourbon king of the Two Sicilies.

Although his forces were greatly outnumbered, Garibaldi's daring tactics won the day (see the box on p. 674). By the end of July 1860, most of Sicily had been pacified under Garibaldi's control. In August, Garibaldi and his forces crossed over to the mainland and began a victorious march up the Italian peninsula. Naples and the Two Sicilies fell in early September. At this point, Cavour reentered the scene. Aware that Garibaldi planned to march on Rome, Cavour feared that such a move would bring war with France as the defender of papal interests. Moreover, Garibaldi and his men favored a democratic republicanism; Cavour did not and acted quickly to

preempt Garibaldi. The Piedmontese army invaded the Papal States and, bypassing Rome, moved into the kingdom of Naples. Ever the patriot, Garibaldi chose to yield to Cavour's fait accompli rather than provoke a civil war and retired to his farm. Plebiscites in the Papal States and the Two Sicilies resulted in overwhelming support for union with Piedmont. On March 17, 1861, the new kingdom of Italy was proclaimed under a centralized government subordinated to the control of Piedmont and King Victor Emmanuel II (1861–1878) of the house of Savoy. Worn out by his efforts, Cavour died three months later.

Despite the proclamation of the new kingdom, the task of unification was not yet complete since Venetia in the north was still held by Austria and Rome was under papal control, supported by French troops. To attack either one meant war with a major European state, which the Italian army was not prepared to handle. It was the Prussian army that indirectly completed the task of Italian unification. In the Austro-Prussian War of 1866, the new Italian state became an ally of Prussia. Although the Italian army was defeated by the Austrians, Prussia's victory left the Italians with Venetia. In 1870, the Franco-Prussian War resulted in the withdrawal of French troops from Rome. The Italian army then annexed the city on September 20, 1870, and Rome became the new capital of the united Italian state.

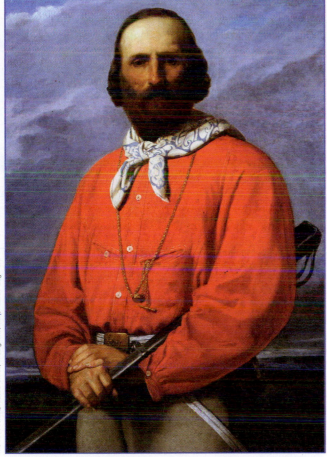

Garibaldi Arrives in Sicily. The Italian nationalists' dream of a united Italian state finally became a reality by 1870. An important figure in the cause of unification was Giuseppe Garibaldi, a determined Italian patriot. Garibaldi is shown here in his red shirt in a portrait done by Silvestro Lega.

The Unification of Germany

After the failure of the Frankfurt Assembly to achieve German unification in 1848–1849, German nationalists focused on Austria and Prussia as the only two states powerful enough to dominate German affairs. Austria had long controlled the existing Germanic Confederation, but Prussian power had grown, strongly reinforced by economic expansion in the 1850s. Prussia had formed the **Zollverein,** a German customs union, in 1834. By eliminating tolls on rivers and roads among member states, the *Zollverein* had stimulated trade and added to the prosperity of its member states. By 1853, all the German states except Austria had joined the Prussian-dominated customs union. A number of middle-class liberals now began to see Prussia in a new light; some even looked openly to Prussia to bring about the unification of Germany.

In 1848, Prussia had framed a constitution that at least had the appearance of constitutional monarchy in that it had established a bicameral legislature with the lower house elected by universal male suffrage. The voting population, however, was divided into three classes

CHRONOLOGY The Unification of Italy

Victor Emmanuel II	1849–1878
Count Cavour becomes prime minister of Piedmont	1852
Agreement with Napoleon III	1858
Austrian War	1859
Plebiscites in the northern Italian states	1860
Garibaldi's invasion of the kingdom of the Two Sicilies	1860
Kingdom of Italy is proclaimed	1861
Italy's annexation of Venetia	1866
Italy's annexation of Rome	1870

determined by the amount of taxes they paid, a system that allowed the biggest taxpayers to gain the most seats. Unintentionally, by 1859, this system had allowed control of the lower house to fall largely into the hands of the rising middle classes, whose numbers were growing as a result of continuing industrialization. Their desire was to have a real parliamentary system, but the king's executive power remained too strong; royal ministers answered for their actions only to the king, not the parliament. Nevertheless, the parliament had been granted important legislative and taxation powers on which it could build.

In 1861, King Frederick William IV died and was succeeded by his brother. King William I (1861–1888) had definite ideas about the Prussian army because of his own military training. He and his advisers believed that the army was in dire need of change if Prussia was to remain a great power. The king planned to double the size of the army and institute three years of compulsory military service for all young men.

Middle-class liberals in the parliament, while willing to have reform, feared compulsory military service because they believed the government would use it to inculcate obedience to the monarchy and strengthen the influence of the conservative-military clique in Prussia. When the Prussian legislature rejected the new military budget submitted to parliament in March 1862, William I appointed a new prime minister, Count Otto von Bismarck (1815–1898). Bismarck, regarded even by the king as too conservative, came to determine the course of modern German history. Until 1890, he dominated both German and European politics.

Bismarck Otto von Bismarck was born into the Junker class, the traditional, landowning aristocracy of Prussia, and remained loyal to it throughout his life. "I was born and raised as an aristocrat," he once said. As a university student, Bismarck indulged heartily in wine, women, and song yet managed to read widely in German history. After earning a law degree, he embarked on a career in the Prussian civil service but soon tired of bureaucratic, administrative routine and retired to manage his country

GARIBALDI AND ROMANTIC NATIONALISM

Giuseppe Garibaldi was one of the most colorful figures involved in the unification of Italy. Accompanied by only one thousand of his famous Red Shirts, the Italian soldier of fortune left Genoa on the night of May 5, 1860, for an invasion of the kingdom of the Two Sicilies. The ragged band entered Palermo, the chief city on the island of Sicily, on May 31. This selection is taken from an account by a correspondent for the *Times* of London, the Hungarian-born Nandor Eber.

London Times, June 13, 1860

PALERMO, May 31—Anyone in search of violent emotions cannot do better than set off at once for Palermo. However blasé he may be, or however milk-and-water his blood, I promise it will be stirred up. He will be carried away by the tide of popular feeling....

In the afternoon Garibaldi made a tour of inspection round the town. I was there, but find it really impossible to give you a faint idea of the manner in which he was received everywhere. It was one of those triumphs which seem to be almost too much for a man.... The popular idol, Garibaldi, in his red flannel shirt, with a loose colored handkerchief around his neck, and his worn "wide-awake" [a soft-brimmed felt hat], was walking on foot among those cheering, laughing, crying, mad thousands; and all his few followers could do was to prevent him from being bodily carried off the ground. The people threw themselves forward to kiss his hands, or, at least, to touch the hem of his garment, as if it contained the panacea for all their past and perhaps coming suffering. Children were brought up, and mothers asked on their knees for his blessing; and all this while the object of this idolatry was calm and smiling as when in the deadliest fire, taking up the children and kissing them, trying to quiet the crowd, stopping at every moment to hear a long complaint of houses burned and property sacked by the retreating soldiers, giving good advice, comforting, and promising that all damages should be paid for....

One might write volumes of horrors on the vandalism already committed, for every one of the hundred ruins has its story of brutality and inhumanity.... In these small houses a dense population is crowded together even in ordinary times. A shell falling on one, and crushing and burying the inmates, was sufficient to make people abandon the neighboring one and take refuge a little further on, shutting themselves up in the cellars. When the Royalists retired they set fire to those of the houses which had escaped the shells, and numbers were thus burned alive in their hiding places....

If you can stand the exhalation, try and go inside the ruins, for it is only there that you will see what the thing means and you will not have to search long before you stumble over the remains of a human body, a leg sticking out here, an arm there, a black face staring at you a little further on. You are startled by a rustle. You look round and see half a dozen gorged rats scampering off in all directions, or you see a dog trying to make his escape over the ruins.... I only wonder that the sight of these scenes does not convert every man in the town into a tiger and every woman into a fury. But these people have been so long ground down and demoralized that their nature seems to have lost the power of reaction.

Q *Why did Garibaldi become such a hero to the Italian people? How does Garibaldi's comportment as a political and military leader prefigure the conduct of later revolutionary military leaders and activists?*

estates. Comparing the civil servant to a musician in an orchestra, he responded, "I want to play the tune the way it sounds good to me or not at all.... My pride bids me command rather than obey."[3] In 1847, desirous of more excitement and power than he could find in the country, he reentered public life. Four years later, he began to build a base of diplomatic experience as the Prussian delegate to the parliament of the Germanic Confederation. This, combined with his experience as Prussian ambassador to Russia and later to France, gave him opportunities to acquire a wide knowledge of European affairs and to learn how to assess the character of rulers.

Because Bismarck succeeded in guiding Prussia's unification of Germany, it is often assumed that he had determined on a course of action that led precisely to that goal. That is hardly the case. Bismarck was a consummate politician and opportunist. He was not a political gambler but a moderate who waged war only when all other diplomatic alternatives had been exhausted and when he was reasonably sure that all the military and diplomatic advantages were on his side. Bismarck has often been portrayed as the ultimate realist, the foremost nineteenth-century practitioner of *Realpolitik.* He was also quite open about his strong dislike of anyone who opposed him. He said one morning to his wife, "I could not sleep the whole night; I hated throughout the whole night."

In 1862, Bismarck resubmitted the army appropriations bill to parliament along with a passionate appeal to his liberal opponents: "Germany does not look to Prussia's liberalism but to her power.... Not by speeches and majorities will the great questions of the day be decided—that was the mistake of 1848–1849—but by iron and blood."[4] His opponents were not impressed and rejected the bill once again. Bismarck went ahead, collected the taxes, and reorganized the army anyway, blaming the liberals for causing the breakdown of constitutional government. From 1862 to 1866, Bismarck governed Prussia by largely ignoring parliament. Unwilling to

The Art Archive/Culver Pictures

Otto von Bismarck. Otto von Bismarck played a major role in leading Prussia to achieve the unification of the German states into a new German Empire, proclaimed on January 18, 1871. Bismarck then became chancellor of the new Germany. This photograph of Bismarck was taken in 1874, when he was at the height of his power and prestige.

revolt, parliament did nothing. In the meantime, opposition to his domestic policy determined Bismarck on an active foreign policy, which in 1864 led to his first war.

The Danish War (1864)

In the three wars that he waged, Bismarck's victories were as much diplomatic and political as they were military. Before war was declared, Bismarck always saw to it that Prussia would be fighting only one power and that that opponent was isolated diplomatically.

The Danish War arose over the duchies of Schleswig and Holstein. In 1863, contrary to international treaty, the Danish government moved to incorporate the two duchies into Denmark. German nationalists were outraged since both duchies had large German populations and were regarded as German states. The diet of the Germanic Confederation urged its member states to send troops against Denmark, but Bismarck did not care to subject Prussian policy to the Austrian-dominated German parliament. Instead, he persuaded the Austrians to join Prussia in declaring war on Denmark on February 1, 1864. The Danes were quickly defeated

and surrendered Schleswig and Holstein to the victors (see Map 22.3). Austria and Prussia then agreed to divide the administration of the two duchies; Prussia took Schleswig while Austria administered Holstein. The plan was Bismarck's. By this time, Bismarck had come to the realization that for Prussia to expand its power by dominating the northern, largely Protestant part of the Germanic Confederation, Austria would have to be excluded from German affairs or, less likely, be willing to accept Prussian domination of Germany. The joint administration of the two duchies offered plenty of opportunities to create friction with Austria and provide a reason for war if it came to that. While he pursued negotiations with Austria, he also laid the foundations for the isolation of Austria.

The Austro-Prussian War (1866)

Bismarck had no problem gaining Russia's agreement to remain neutral in the event of an Austro-Prussian war because Prussia had been the only great power to support Russia's repression of a Polish revolt in 1863. Napoleon III was a thornier problem, but Bismarck was able to buy his neutrality with vague promises of territory in the Rhineland. Finally, Bismarck made an alliance with the new Italian state and promised it Venetia in the event of Austrian defeat.

With the Austrians isolated, Bismarck used the joint occupation of Schleswig-Holstein to goad the Austrians into a war on June 14, 1866. Many Europeans, including Napoleon III, expected a quick Austrian victory, but they overlooked the effectiveness of the Prussian military reforms of the 1860s. The Prussian breech-loading needle gun had a much faster rate of fire than the Austrian muzzleloader, and a superior network of railroads enabled the Prussians to mass troops quickly. At Königgrätz (Sadowa) on July 3, the Austrian army was defeated. Looking ahead, Bismarck refused to create a hostile enemy by burdening Austria with a harsh peace as the Prussian king wanted. Austria lost no territory except Venetia to Italy but was excluded from German affairs. The German states north of the Main River were organized into the North German Confederation, controlled by Prussia. The southern German states, largely Catholic, remained independent but were coerced into signing military agreements with Prussia. In addition to Schleswig and Holstein, Prussia annexed Hanover and Hesse-Cassel because they had openly sided with Austria.

The Austrian war was a turning point in Prussian domestic affairs. After the war, Bismarck asked the Prussian parliament to pass a bill of indemnity, retroactively legalizing the taxes he had collected illegally since 1862. Even most of the liberals voted in favor of the bill because they had been won over by Bismarck's successful use of military power. With his victory over Austria and the creation of the North German Confederation, Bismarck had proved Napoleon III's dictum that nationalism and authoritarian government could be combined. In using nationalism to win support from liberals and prevent governmental reform, Bismarck

MAP 22.3 **The Unification of Germany.** Count Otto von Bismarck, the Prussian prime minister, skillfully combined domestic policies with wars with Denmark, Austria, and France to achieve the creation of the German Empire in 1871.

Q From the perspective of Prussia's increasing its military power and ability to rule all parts of its lands, which was more important: formation of the North German Confederation or absorption of the South German Confederation? **View an animated version of this map or related maps at** academic.cengage.com/history/spielvogel

showed that liberalism and nationalism, the two major forces of change in the early nineteenth century, could be separated.

He showed the same flexibility in the creation of a new constitution for the North German Confederation. Each German state kept its own local government, but the king of Prussia was head of the confederation, and the chancellor (Bismarck) was responsible directly to the king. Both the army and foreign policy remained in the hands of the king and his chancellor. Parliament consisted of two bodies: the Bundesrat, or federal council, composed of delegates nominated by the states, and a lower house, the Reichstag, elected by universal male suffrage. Like Napoleon, Bismarck believed that the peasants and artisans who made up most of the population were conservative at heart and could be used to overcome the advantages of the liberals.

The Franco-Prussian War (1870–1871) Bismarck and William I had achieved a major goal by 1866. Prussia now dominated all of northern Germany, and Austria had been excluded from any significant role in German affairs. Nevertheless, unsettled business led to new international complications and further change. Bismarck realized that France would never be content with a strong German state to its east because of the potential threat to French security. At the same time, after a series of setbacks, Napoleon III needed a diplomatic triumph to offset his serious domestic problems. The French were not happy with the turn of events in Germany and looked for opportunities to humiliate the Prussians.

After a successful revolution had deposed Queen Isabella II, the throne of Spain was offered to Prince Leopold of Hohenzollern-Sigmaringen, a distant relative of the Hohenzollern king of Prussia. Bismarck welcomed

BISMARCK "GOADS" FRANCE INTO WAR

After his meeting with the French ambassador at Ems, King William I of Prussia sent a telegram to Bismarck with a report of their discussions. By editing the telegram from King William I before releasing it to the press, Bismarck made it sound as if the Prussian king had treated the ambassador in a demeaning fashion. Six days later, France declared war on Prussia.

The Abeken [Privy Councillor] Text, Ems, July 13, 1870

To the Federal Chancellor, Count Bismarck. His Majesty the King writes to me:

"M. Benedetti intercepted me on the Promenade in order to demand of me most insistently that I should authorize him to telegraph immediately to Paris that I shall obligate myself for all future time never again to give my approval to the candidacy of the Hohenzollerns should it be renewed. I refused to agree to this, the last time somewhat severely, informing him that one dare not and cannot assume such obligations *à tout jamais* [forever]. Naturally, I informed him that I had received no news as yet, and since he had been informed earlier than I by way of Paris and Madrid, he could easily understand why my government was once again out of the matter."

Since then His Majesty has received a dispatch from the Prince [father of the Hohenzollern candidate for the Spanish throne]. As His Majesty has informed Count Benedetti that he was expecting news from the Prince, His Majesty himself, in view of the above-mentioned demand and in consonance with the advice of Count Eulenburg and myself, decided not to receive the French envoy again but to inform him through an adjutant that His Majesty had now received from the Prince confirmation of the news which Benedetti had already received from Paris, and that he had nothing further to say to the Ambassador. His Majesty leaves it to the judgment of Your Excellency whether or not to communicate at once the new demand by Benedetti and its rejection to our ambassadors and to the press.

Bismarck's Edited Version

After the reports of the renunciation by the hereditary Prince of Hohenzollern had been officially transmitted by the Royal Government of Spain to the Imperial Government of France, the French Ambassador presented to His Majesty the King at Ems the demand to authorize him to telegraph to Paris that His Majesty the King would obligate himself for all future time never again to give his approval to the candidacy of the Hohenzollerns should it be renewed.

His Majesty the King thereupon refused to receive the French envoy again and informed him through an adjutant that His Majesty had nothing further to say to the Ambassador.

Q *What did Bismarck do to the Ems telegram? What does this affair tell us about Bismarck's motives and his concept of politics?*

---

this possibility for the same reason that the French objected to it. If Leopold were placed on the throne of Spain, France would be virtually encircled by members of the Hohenzollern dynasty. French objections caused King William I to force his relative to withdraw his candidacy. Bismarck was disappointed with the king's actions, but at this point, the French overreached themselves. Not content with their diplomatic victory, they pushed William I to make a formal apology to France and promise never to allow Leopold to be a candidate again. When Bismarck received a telegram from the king informing him of the French request, Bismarck edited it to make it appear even more insulting to the French, knowing that the French would be angry and declare war (see the box above). The French reacted as Bismarck expected they would and declared war on Prussia on July 15, 1870. The French prime minister remarked, "We go to war with a light heart."

Unfortunately for the French, a "light heart" was not enough. They proved no match for the better-led and better-organized Prussian forces. The southern German states honored their military alliances with Prussia and joined the war effort against the French. The Prussian armies advanced into France, and at Sedan on September 2, 1870, an entire French army and Napoleon III himself were captured. The Second French Empire collapsed, but the war was not yet over. After four months of bitter resistance, Paris finally capitulated on January 28, 1871, and an official peace treaty was signed in May. France had to pay an indemnity of 5 billion francs (about $1 billion) and give up the provinces of Alsace and Lorraine to the new German state, a loss that angered the French and left them burning for revenge.

Even before the war had ended, the southern German states had agreed to enter the North German Confederation. On January 18, 1871, in the Hall of Mirrors in Louis XIV's palace at Versailles, William I, with Bismarck standing at the foot of the throne, was proclaimed kaiser or emperor of the Second German Empire (the first was the medieval Holy Roman Empire). German unity had been achieved by the Prussian monarchy and the Prussian army. In a real sense, Germany had been merged into Prussia, not Prussia into Germany. German liberals also rejoiced. They had dreamed of unity and freedom, but the achievement of

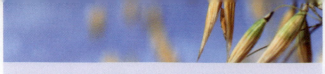

CHRONOLOGY The Unification of Germany

King William I of Prussia	1861–1888
Bismarck becomes minister-president of Prussia	1862
Danish War	1864
Austro-Prussian War	1866
Battle of Königgrätz	1866 (July 3)
Franco-Prussian War	1870–1871
Battle of Sedan	1870 (September 2)
Fall of Paris	1871 (January 28)
German Empire is proclaimed	1871 (January 18)

unity now seemed much more important. One old liberal proclaimed:

> I cannot shake off the impression of this hour. I am no devotee of Mars; I feel more attached to the goddess of beauty and the mother of graces than to the powerful god of war, but the trophies of war exercise a magic charm even upon the child of peace. One's view is involuntarily chained and one's spirit goes along with the boundless row of men who acclaim the god of the moment—success.[5]

The Prussian leadership of German unification meant the triumph of authoritarian, militaristic values over liberal, constitutional sentiments in the development of the new German state. With its industrial resources and military might, the new state had become the strongest power on the Continent. A new European balance of power was at hand.

Nation Building and Reform: The National State in Midcentury

Q Focus Question: What efforts for reform occurred in the Austrian Empire, Russia, and Great Britain between 1850 and 1870, and how successful were they in alleviating each nation's problems?

While European affairs were dominated by the unification of Italy and Germany, other states were also undergoing transformations (see Map 22.4). War, civil war, and changing political alignments served as catalysts for domestic reforms.

The Austrian Empire: Toward a Dual Monarchy

After the Habsburgs had crushed the revolutions of 1848–1849, they restored centralized, autocratic government to the empire. What seemed to be the only lasting result of the revolution of 1848 was the act of emancipation of September 7, 1848, that freed the serfs and eliminated all compulsory labor services. Nevertheless, the development of industrialization after 1850, especially

in Vienna and the provinces of Bohemia and Galicia, served to bring economic and social change to the empire in the form of an urban proletariat, labor unrest, and a new industrial middle class.

In 1851, the revolutionary constitutions were abolished, and a system of centralized autocracy was imposed on the empire. Under the leadership of Alexander von Bach (1813–1893), local privileges were subordinated to a unified system of administration, law, and taxation implemented by German-speaking officials. Hungary was subjected to the rule of military officers, and the Catholic Church was declared the state church and given control of education. Economic troubles and war, however, soon brought change. After Austria's defeat in the Italian war in 1859, the Emperor Francis Joseph (1848–1916) attempted to establish an imperial parliament (*Reichsrat*) with a nominated upper house and an elected lower house of representatives. Although the system was supposed to provide representation for the nationalities of the empire, the complicated formula used for elections ensured the election of a German-speaking majority, serving once again to alienate the ethnic minorities, particularly the Hungarians.

Ausgleich **of 1867** Only when military disaster struck again in the Austro-Prussian War did the Austrians deal with the fiercely nationalistic Hungarians. The result was the negotiated **Ausgleich,** or Compromise, of 1867, which created the Dual Monarchy of Austria-Hungary. Each part of the empire now had a constitution, its own bicameral legislature, its own governmental machinery for domestic affairs, and its own capital (Vienna for Austria and Buda—soon to be united with Pest, across the river—for Hungary). Holding the two states together were a single monarch (Francis Joseph was emperor of Austria and king of Hungary) and a common army, foreign policy, and system of finances. In domestic affairs, the Hungarians had become an independent nation. The *Ausgleich* did not, however, satisfy the other nationalities that made up the multinational Austro-Hungarian Empire (see Map 22.5). The dual monarchy simply enabled the German-speaking Austrians and Hungarian Magyars to dominate the minorities, especially the Slavic peoples (Poles, Croats, Czechs, Serbs, Slovaks, Slovenes, and Little Russians), in their respective states. As the Hungarian nationalist Louis Kossuth remarked, "Dualism is the alliance of the conservative, reactionary and any apparently liberal elements in Hungary with those of the Austrian Germans who despise liberty, for the oppression of the other nationalities and races."[6] The nationalities problem persisted until the demise of the empire at the end of World War I.

Imperial Russia

Russia's defeat in the Crimean War at the hands of the British and French revealed the blatant deficiencies behind the facade of absolute power and made it clear even to staunch conservatives that Russia was falling hopelessly behind the western European powers. Tsar Alexander II

MAP 22.4 **Europe in 1871.** By 1871, most of the small states of Europe had been absorbed into larger ones, leaving the major powers uncomfortably rubbing shoulders with one another. Meanwhile, the power equation was shifting: the German Empire increased in power while Austria-Hungary and the Ottoman Empire declined.

Q Of the great powers, which had the greatest overall exposure to the others in terms of shared borders and sea access?  **View an animated version of this map or related maps at** academic.cengage.com/history/spielvogel

(1855–1881), who came to power in the midst of the Crimean War, turned his energies to a serious overhaul of the Russian system.

Serfdom was the most burdensome problem in tsarist Russia. The continuing subjugation of millions of peasants to the land and their landlords was an obviously corrupt and failing system. Reduced to antiquated methods of production based on serf labor, Russian landowners were economically pressed and unable to compete with foreign agriculture. The serfs, who formed the backbone of the Russian infantry, were uneducated and consequently increasingly unable to deal with the more complex machines and weapons of war. Then, too, peasant dissatisfaction still led to local peasant revolts that disrupted the countryside.

Alexander II seemed to recognize the inevitable: "The existing order of serfdom," he told a group of Moscow nobles, "cannot remain unchanged. It is better to abolish serfdom from above than to wait until it is abolished from below."

Abolition of Serfdom On March 3, 1861, Alexander issued his emancipation edict (see the box on p. 681). Peasants could now own property, marry as they chose, and bring suits in the law courts. Nevertheless, the benefits of emancipation were limited. The government provided land for the peasants by purchasing it from the landowners, but the landowners often chose to keep the best lands. The Russian peasants soon found that they

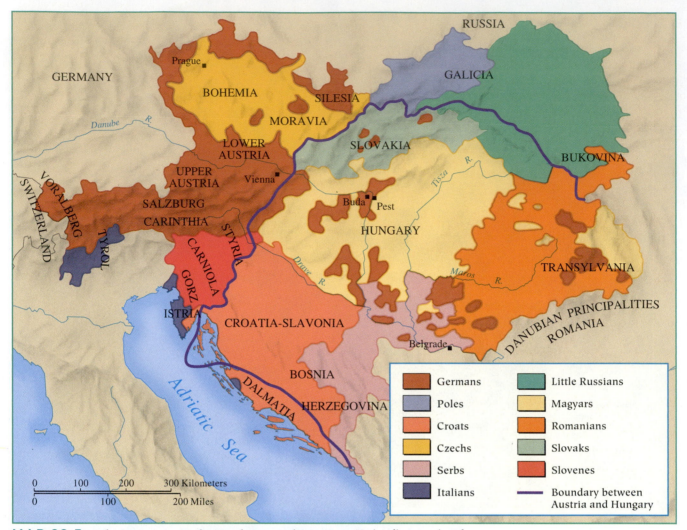

MAP 22.5 **Ethnic Groups in the Dual Monarchy, 1867.** Nationalism continued to be a problem in the Austrian Empire after the suppression of the 1848–1849 revolutions. Military defeats led Emperor Francis Joseph to create the Dual Monarchy, giving Hungary power over its domestic affairs. The demands of other ethnic minorities went largely unmet, however.

Q Which ethnic group was most widely dispersed throughout the Dual Monarchy?

View an animated version of this map or related maps at academic.cengage.com/history/spielvogel

had inadequate amounts of good arable land to support themselves, a situation that worsened as the peasant population increased rapidly in the second half of the nineteenth century.

Nor were the peasants completely free. The state compensated the landowners for the land given to the peasants, but the peasants were expected to repay the state in long-term installments. To ensure that the payments were made, peasants were subjected to the authority of their *mir,* or village commune, which was collectively responsible for the land payments to the government. In a very real sense, then, the village commune, not the individual peasants, owned the land the peasants were purchasing. And since the village communes were responsible for the payments, they were reluctant to allow peasants to leave their land. Emancipation, then, led not to a free, landowning peasantry along the Western model

but to an unhappy, land-starved peasantry that largely followed the old ways of farming.

Other Reforms Alexander II also attempted other reforms. In 1864, he instituted a system of **zemstvos,** or local assemblies, that provided a moderate degree of self-government. Representatives to the zemstvos were to be elected from the noble landowners, townspeople, and peasants, but the property-based system of voting gave a distinct advantage to the nobles. Zemstvos were given a limited power to provide public services, such as education, famine relief, and road and bridge maintenance. They could levy taxes to pay for these services, but their efforts were frequently disrupted by bureaucrats, who feared any hint of self-government. The hope of liberal nobles and other social reformers that the zemstvos would be expanded into a national parliament remained

EMANCIPATION: SERFS AND SLAVES

Although overall their histories have been quite different, Russia and the United States shared a common feature in the 1860s. They were the only states in the Western world that still had large enslaved populations (the Russian serfs were virtually slaves). The leaders of both countries issued emancipation proclamations within two years of each other. The first excerpt is taken from the Imperial Decree of March 3, 1861, which freed the Russian serfs. The second excerpt is from Abraham Lincoln's Emancipation Proclamation, issued on January 1, 1863.

Tsar Alexander II, Imperial Decree, March 3, 1861

By the grace of God, we, Alexander II, Emperor and Autocrat of all the Russias, King of Poland, Grand Duke of Finland, etc., to all our faithful subjects, make known:

Called by Divine Providence and by the sacred right of inheritance to the throne of our ancestors, we took a vow in our innermost heart to respond to the mission which is intrusted to us as to surround with our affection and our Imperial solicitude all our faithful subjects of every rank and of every condition, from the warrior, who nobly bears arms for the defense of the country to the humble artisan devoted to the works of industry; from the official in the career of the high offices of the State to the laborer whose plow furrows the soil. . . .

We thus came to the conviction that the work of a serious improvement of the condition of the peasants was a sacred inheritance bequeathed to us by our ancestors, a mission which, in the course of events, Divine providence called upon us to fulfill. . . .

In virtue of the new dispositions above mentioned, the peasants attached to the soil will be invested within a term fixed by the law with all the rights of free cultivators. . . .

At the same time, they are granted the right of purchasing their close, and, with the consent of the proprietors, they may acquire in full property the arable lands and other appurtenances which are allotted to them as a permanent holding. By the acquisition in full property of the quantity of land fixed, the peasants are free from their obligations toward the proprietors for land thus purchased, and they enter definitely into the condition of free peasants–landholders.

President Abraham Lincoln, Emancipation Proclamation, January 1, 1863

Now therefore, I, Abraham Lincoln, President of the United States, by virtue of the power in me vested as Commander-in-Chief of the Army and Navy of the United States in time of actual armed rebellion against the authority and government of the United States, and as a fit and necessary war measure for suppressing such rebellion, do, on this 1st day of January, A.D. 1863, and in accordance with my purpose to do so, . . . order and designate as the States and parts of States wherein the people thereof, respectively, are this day in rebellion against the United States the following, to wit:

Arkansas, Texas, Louisiana, . . . Mississippi, Alabama, Florida, Georgia, South Carolina, North Carolina, and Virginia. . . .

And by virtue of the power for the purpose aforesaid, I do order and declare that all persons held as slaves within said designated States and parts of States are, and henceforward shall be free; and that the Executive Government of the United States, including the military and naval authorities thereof, will recognize and maintain the freedom of said persons.

Q *What changes did Tsar Alexander's emancipation of the serfs initiate in Russia? What effect did Lincoln's Emancipation Proclamation have on the southern "armed rebellion"? What reason does each leader give for his action? Were they equally effective?*

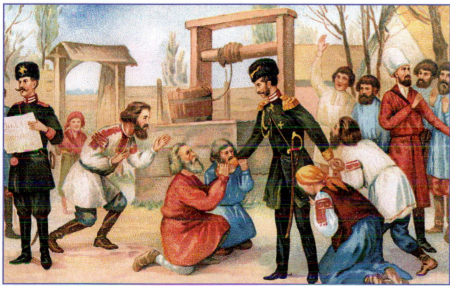

Emancipation of the Serfs. On March 3, 1861, Tsar Alexander II issued an edict emancipating the Russian serfs. This illustration shows at the left the tsar making his proclamation while at the right serfs express their gratitude to the tsar.

© Mary Evans Picture Library/The Image Works

Queen Victoria and Her Family. Queen Victoria, who ruled Britain from 1837 to 1901, married her German first cousin, Prince Albert of Saxe-Coburg-Gotha, in 1840 and subsequently gave birth to four sons and five daughters, who married into a number of European royal families. When she died at age eighty-one, she had thirty-seven great-grandchildren. Victoria is seated at the center of this 1881 photograph, surrounded by members of her family.

unfulfilled. The legal reforms of 1864, which created a regular system of local and provincial courts and a judicial code that accepted the principle of equality before the law, proved successful, however.

Even the autocratic tsar was unable to control the forces he unleashed by his reform program. Reformers wanted more and rapid change; conservatives opposed what they perceived as the tsar's attempts to undermine the basic institutions of Russian society. By 1870, Russia was witnessing an increasing number of reform movements. One of the most popular stemmed from the radical writings of Alexander Herzen (1812–1870), a Russian exile living in London, whose slogan, "Land and Freedom," epitomized his belief that the Russian peasant must be the chief instrument for social reform. Herzen believed that the peasant village commune could serve as an independent, self-governing body that would form the basis of a new Russia. Russian students and intellectuals who followed Herzen's ideas formed a movement called **populism** whose aim was to create a new society through the revolutionary acts of the peasants. The peasants' lack of interest in these revolutionary ideas, however, led some of the populists to resort to violent means to overthrow tsarist autocracy. One who advocated the use of violence to counteract the violent repression of the tsarist regime was Vera Zasulich (1849–1919). Daughter of a poor nobleman, she worked as a clerk before joining Land and Freedom, an underground populist organization advocating radical reform. In 1878, Zasulich shot and wounded the governor-general of Saint Petersburg. Put on trial, she was acquitted by a sympathetic jury.

Encouraged by Zasulich's successful use of violence against the tsarist regime, another group of radicals, known as the People's Will, succeeded in assassinating Alexander II in 1881. His son and successor, Alexander III (1881–1894), turned against reform and returned to the traditional methods of repression.

Great Britain: The Victorian Age

Like Russia, Britain was not troubled by revolutionary disturbances during 1848, although for quite different reasons. The Reform Act of 1832 had opened the door to political representation for the industrial middle class, and in the 1860s, Britain's liberal parliamentary system demonstrated once more its ability to make both social and political reforms that enabled the country to remain stable and prosperous.

One of the reasons for Britain's stability was its continuing economic growth. After 1850, middle-class prosperity was at last coupled with some improvements for the working classes. Real wages for laborers increased more than 25 percent between 1850 and 1870. The British feeling of national pride was well reflected in Queen Victoria, whose reign from 1837 to 1901 was the longest in English history. Her sense of duty and moral respectability reflected the attitudes of her age, which has ever since been known as the Victorian Age.

Politically, this was an era of uneasy stability as the aristocratic and upper-middle-class representatives who dominated Parliament blurred party lines by their internal strife and shifting positions. One political figure who stood out was Henry John Temple, Lord Palmerston (1784–1865), who was prime minister for most of the period from 1855 to 1865. Although a Whig, Palmerston was without strong party loyalty and found it easy to make political compromises. He was not a reformer, however, and opposed expanding the franchise. He said, "We should by such an arrangement increase the number of Bribeable Electors and overpower Intelligence and Property by Ignorance and Poverty."

Disraeli and the Reform Act of 1867 After Palmerston's death in 1865, the movement for the extension of the franchise only intensified. Although the Whigs

TABLE 22.1 Expansion of the British Electorate

Year	Number of Voters	Percentage of Total Population
1831	516,000	2.1
(Reform Act of 1832)		
1833	812,000	3.4
1866	1,364,000	4.7
(Reform Act of 1867)		
1868	2,418,000	8.4
1883	3,152,000	9.0
(Reform Act of 1884)		
1885	5,669,000	16.3

SOURCE: Chris Cook and Brendan Keith, *British Historical Facts, 1830–1900* (London, 1975), pp. 115, 232–233.

(now called the Liberals), who had been responsible for the Reform Act of 1832, talked about passing additional reform legislation, it was actually the Tories (now called the Conservatives) who carried it through. The Tory leader in Parliament, Benjamin Disraeli (1804–1881), was apparently motivated by the desire to win over the newly enfranchised groups to the Conservative Party. The Reform Act of 1867 was an important step toward the democratization of Britain. By lowering the monetary requirements for voting (taxes paid or income earned), it by and large enfranchised many male urban workers. The number of voters increased from about 1 million to slightly over 2 million (see Table 22.1). Although Disraeli believed that this would benefit the Conservatives, industrial workers helped produce a huge Liberal victory in 1868.

The extension of the right to vote had an important by-product as it forced the Liberal and Conservative Parties to organize carefully in order to manipulate the electorate. Party discipline intensified, and the rivalry between the Liberals and Conservatives became a regular feature of parliamentary life. In large part this was due to the personal and political opposition of the two leaders of these parties, William Gladstone (1809–1898) and Disraeli.

The Liberal Policies of Gladstone The first Liberal administration of William Gladstone, from 1868 to 1874, was responsible for a series of impressive reforms. Legislation and government orders opened civil service positions to competitive exams rather than patronage, introduced the secret ballot for voting, and abolished the practice of purchasing military commissions. The Education Act of 1870 attempted to make elementary schools available for all children (see Chapter 24). These reforms were typically liberal. By eliminating abuses and enabling people with talent to compete fairly, they sought to strengthen the nation and its institutions.

The United States: Slavery and War

By the mid-nineteenth century, American national unity was increasingly threatened by the issue of slavery. Both North and South had grown dramatically in population during the first half of the nineteenth century. But their development was quite different. The cotton economy and social structure of the South were based on the exploitation of enslaved black Africans and their descendants. The importance of cotton is evident from production figures. In 1810, the South produced a raw cotton crop of 178,000 bales worth $10 million. By 1860, it was generating 4.5 million bales of cotton with a value of $249 million. Fully 93 percent of southern cotton in 1850 was produced by a slave population that had grown dramatically in fifty years. Although new slave imports had been barred in 1808, there were 4 million Afro-American slaves in the South by 1860—four times the number sixty years earlier. The cotton economy and plantation-based slavery were intimately related, and the attempt to maintain them in the course of the first half of the nineteenth century led the South to become increasingly defensive, monolithic, and isolated. At the same time, the rise of an abolitionist movement in the North challenged the southern order and created an "emotional chain reaction" that led to civil war.

By the 1850s, the slavery question had caused the Whig Party to become defunct and the Democrats to split along North-South lines. The Kansas-Nebraska Act of 1854, which allowed slavery in the Kansas and Nebraska territories to be determined by popular sovereignty, created a firestorm in the North and led to the creation of a new sectional party. The Republicans were united by antislavery principles and were especially driven by the fear that the "slave power" of the South would attempt to spread the slave system throughout the country.

As polarization over the issue of slavery intensified, compromise became less feasible. When Abraham Lincoln, the man who had said in a speech in Illinois in 1858 that "this government cannot endure permanently half slave and half free," was elected president in November 1860, the die was cast. Lincoln carried only 2 of the 1,109 counties in the South; the Republicans were not even on the ballot in ten southern states. On December 20, 1860, a South Carolina convention voted to repeal the state's ratification of the U.S. Constitution. In February 1861, six more southern states did the same, and a rival nation—the Confederate States of America—was formed (see Map 22.6). In April, fighting erupted between North and South.

The Civil War The American Civil War (1861–1865) was an extraordinarily bloody struggle, a foretaste of the total war to come in the twentieth century. More than 600,000 soldiers died, either in battle or from deadly infectious diseases spawned by filthy camp conditions. Over a period of four years, the Union states of the North mobilized their superior assets and gradually wore down the Confederate forces of the South. As the war dragged on, it had the effect of radicalizing public opinion in the

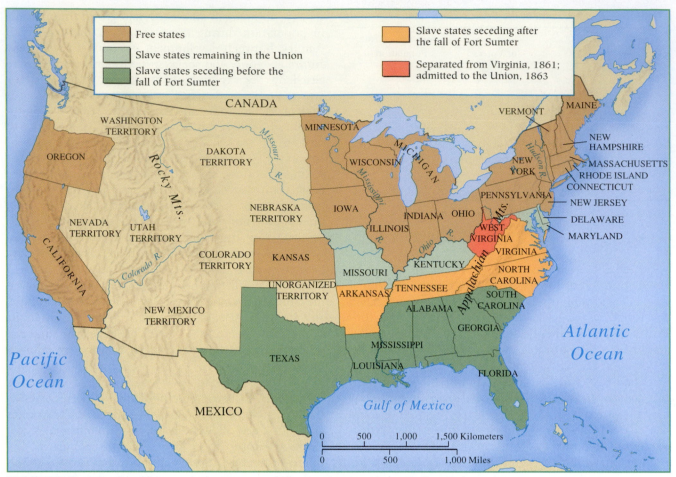

MAP 22.6   The United States: The West and the Civil War.   By 1860, the North had developed an economy based on industry and commerce, whereas the South had remained a primarily agrarian economy based on black slave labor. The question of the continuance of slavery itself and the expansion of slavery into western territories led to the Civil War, in which the South sought to create an independent country.

Q Why would its inhabitants want to create a separate state of West Virginia?

View an animated version of this map or related maps at academic.cengage.com/history/spielvogel

North. What began as a war to save the Union became a war against slavery. On January 1, 1863, Lincoln's Emancipation Proclamation made most of the nation's slaves "forever free" (see the box on p. 681). The increasingly effective Union blockade of the South, combined with a shortage of fighting men, made the Confederate cause desperate by the end of 1864. The final push of Union troops under General Ulysses S. Grant forced General Robert E. Lee's Confederate Army to surrender on April 9, 1865. Although problems lay ahead, the Union victory confirmed that the United States would be "one nation, indivisible."

The Emergence of a Canadian Nation

North of the United States, the process of nation building was also making progress. By the Treaty of Paris in 1763, Canada—or New France, as it was called—passed into the hands of the British. By 1800, most Canadians favored more autonomy, although the colonists disagreed on the

form this autonomy should take. Upper Canada (now Ontario) was predominantly English-speaking, whereas Lower Canada (now Quebec) was dominated by French Canadians. A dramatic increase in immigration to Canada from Great Britain (almost one million immigrants between 1815 and 1850) also fueled the desire for self-government.

In 1837, a number of Canadian groups rose in rebellion against British authority. Rebels in Lower Canada demanded separation from Britain, creation of a republic, universal male suffrage, and freedom of the press. Although the rebellions were crushed by the following year, the British government now began to seek ways to satisfy some of the Canadian demands. The American Civil War proved to be a turning point. Fearful of American designs on Canada during the war and eager to reduce the costs of maintaining the colonies, the British government finally capitulated to Canadian demands. In 1867, Parliament established the Canadian nation—the Dominion of Canada—with its own constitution. Canada now

CHRONOLOGY National States at Midcentury

France	
Louis Napoleon is elected president	1848
Coup d'état by Louis Napoleon	1851
Creation of the Second Empire	1852
Emperor Napoleon III	1852–1870
"Authoritarian empire"	1852–1860
Crimean War	1854–1856
Treaty of Paris	1856
"Liberal empire"	1860–1870
Austrian Empire	
Establishment of imperial parliament	1859
Ausgleich, Dual Monarchy	1867
Russia	
Tsar Alexander II	1855–1881
Emancipation edict	1861 (March 3)
Creation of zemstvos and legal reforms	1864
Great Britain	
Queen Victoria	1837–1901
Ministry of Palmerston	1855–1865
Reform Act	1867
First Liberal ministry of William Gladstone	1868–1874
United States	
Kansas-Nebraska Act	1854
Election of Lincoln and secession of South Carolina	1860
Outbreak of Civil War	1861
Surrender of Lee	1865 (April 9)
Canada	
Formation of the Dominion of Canada	1867

possessed a parliamentary system and ruled itself, although foreign affairs still remained under the control of the British government.

Industrialization and the Marxist Response

Q **Focus Question:** What were the main ideas of Karl Marx?

Between 1850 and 1871, Continental industrialization came of age. The innovations of the British Industrial Revolution—mechanized factory production, the use of coal, the steam engine, and the transportation revolution—all became regular features of economic expansion. Although marred periodically by economic depression (1857–1858) or recession (1866–1867), this was an age of considerable economic prosperity, particularly evident in the growth of domestic and foreign markets.

Industrialization on the Continent

The transformation of textile production from hand looms to power looms had largely been completed in Britain by the 1850s (for cotton) and 1860s (for wool). On the Continent, the period from 1850 to 1870 witnessed increased mechanization of the cotton and textile industries, although Continental countries still remained behind Britain. By 1870, hand looms had virtually disappeared in Britain, whereas in France there were still 200,000 of them, along with 80,000 power looms. Nevertheless, this period of industrial expansion on the Continent was fueled not so much by textiles as by the growth of railroads. Between 1850 and 1870, European railroad track mileage increased from 14,500 to almost 70,000. The railroads, in turn, stimulated growth in both the iron and coal industries.

Between 1850 and 1870, Continental iron industries made the transition from charcoal iron smelting to cokeblast smelting. Despite the dramatic increases in the production of pig iron, the Continental countries had not yet come close to surpassing British iron production. In 1870, the British iron industry produced half the world's pig iron—four times as much as Germany and five times as much as France. In the middle decades of the nineteenth century, the textile, mining, and metallurgical industries on the Continent also rapidly converted to the use of the steam engine.

An important factor in the expansion of markets was the elimination of barriers to international trade. Essential international waterways were opened up by the elimination of restrictive tolls. The Danube River in 1857 and the Rhine in 1861, for example, were declared freeways for all ships. The negotiation of trade treaties in the 1860s reduced or eliminated protective tariffs throughout much of western Europe.

Governments also played a role in first allowing and then encouraging the formation of joint-stock investment banks (see Chapter 20). These banks were crucial to Continental industrial development because they mobilized enormous capital resources for investment. In the 1850s and 1860s, they were very important in the promotion of railway construction, although railroads were not always a safe investment. During a trip to Spain to examine possibilities for railroad construction, the locomotive manufacturer George Stephenson reported, "I have been a month in the country, but have not seen during the whole of that time enough people of the right sort to fill a single train."[7] His misgivings proved to be well founded. In 1864, the Spanish banking system, which depended largely on investments in railway shares, collapsed.

Before 1870, capitalist factory owners remained largely free to hire labor on their own terms based on market forces. Although workers formed trade unions as organizations that would fight for improved working conditions and reasonable wages, the unions tended to represent only a small part of the industrial working class

Opening of the Suez Canal. Between 1850 and 1871, Continental Europeans built railways, bridges, and canals as part of the ever-spreading process of industrialization. A French diplomat, Ferdinand de Lesseps, was the guiding force behind the construction of the Suez Canal, which provided a link between the Mediterranean and Red seas. Work on the canal began in 1859 and was completed ten years later. As seen here, an elaborate ceremony marked the opening of the canal. A French vessel led the first convoy of ships through the canal. The banks are lined with curious local inhabitants.

and proved largely ineffective. Real change for the industrial proletariat would come only with the development of socialist parties and socialist trade unions. These emerged after 1870, but the theory that made them possible had already been developed by midcentury in the work of Karl Marx.

Marx and Marxism

The beginnings of Marxism can be traced to the 1848 publication of a short treatise titled *The Communist Manifesto,* written by two Germans, Karl Marx (1818–1883) and Friedrich Engels (1820–1895). Marx was born into a relatively prosperous middle-class family in Trier in western Germany. He descended from a long line of rabbis, although his father, a lawyer, had become a Protestant to keep his job. Marx enrolled at the University of Bonn in 1835, but his carefree student ways soon led his father to send him to the more serious-minded University of Berlin, where he encountered the ideas of the German philosopher Georg Wilhelm Friedrich Hegel. After receiving a Ph.D. in philosophy, Marx planned to teach at a university. Unable to obtain a position because of his professed atheism, Marx decided on a career in journalism and eventually became the editor of a liberal bourgeois newspaper in Cologne in 1842. After the newspaper was suppressed because of his radical views, Marx moved to Paris. There he met Friedrich Engels, who became his lifelong friend and financial patron.

Engels, the son of a wealthy German cotton manufacturer, had worked in Britain at one of his father's factories in Manchester. There he had acquired a firsthand knowledge of what he came to call the "wage slavery" of the British working classes, which he detailed in a damning indictment of industrial life titled *The Conditions of the Working Class in England,* written in 1844. Engels would contribute his knowledge of actual working conditions as well as monetary assistance to the financially strapped Marx.

In 1847, Marx and Engels joined a tiny group of primarily German socialist revolutionaries known as the Communist League. By this time, both Marx and Engels were enthusiastic advocates of the radical working-class movement and agreed to draft a statement of their ideas for the league. The resulting *Communist Manifesto,* published in German in January 1848, appeared on the eve of the revolutions of 1848. One would think from the opening lines of the preface that the pamphlet alone had caused this revolutionary upheaval: "A spectre is haunting Europe—the spectre of Communism. All the Powers of Old Europe have entered into a holy alliance to exorcise this spectre: Pope and Czar, Metternich and Guizot, French Radicals and German police spies."[8] In fact, *The Communist Manifesto* was known to only a few of Marx's friends. Although its closing words—"The proletarians have nothing to lose but their chains. They have a world to win. WORKING MEN OF ALL COUNTRIES, UNITE!"—were clearly intended to rouse the working classes to action, they passed unnoticed in 1848. The work, however, became one of the most influential political treatises in modern European history.

According to Engels, Marx's ideas were partly a synthesis of French and German thought. The French provided Marx with ample documentation for his assertion that a revolution could totally restructure society. They also provided him with several examples of socialism. From the German idealistic philosophers such as Hegel, Marx took the idea of dialectic: everything evolves, and all change in history is the result of conflicts between antagonistic elements. Marx was particularly impressed by Hegel, but he disagreed with Hegel's belief that history is determined by ideas manifesting themselves in historical forces. Instead, said Marx, the course of history is determined by material forces.

Ideas of *The Communist Manifesto* Marx and Engels began the *Manifesto* with the statement that "the history of all hitherto existing society is the history of class struggles." Throughout history, oppressed and oppressor have "stood in constant opposition to one another." In an

© Bettmann/CORBIS

Karl Marx. Karl Marx was a radical journalist who joined with Friedrich Engels to write *The Communist Manifesto*, which proclaimed the ideas of a revolutionary socialism. After the failure of the 1848 revolution in Germany, Marx fled to Britain, where he continued to write and became involved in the work of the first International Working Men's Association.

earlier struggle, the feudal classes of the Middle Ages were forced to accede to the emerging middle class or bourgeoisie. As the bourgeoisie took control in turn, its ideas became the dominant views of the era, and government became its instrument. Marx and Engels declared, "The executive of the modern State is but a committee for managing the common affairs of the whole bourgeoisie."[9] In other words, the government of the state reflected and defended the interests of the industrial middle class and its allies.

Although bourgeois society had emerged victorious out of the ruins of feudalism, Marx and Engels insisted that it had not triumphed completely. Now once again the members of the bourgeoisie were antagonists in an emerging class struggle, but this time they faced the **proletariat,** or the industrial working class. The struggle would be fierce; in fact, Marx and Engels predicted that the workers would eventually overthrow their bourgeois masters. After this victory, the proletariat would form a dictatorship to reorganize the means of production. Then

a classless society would emerge, and the state—itself an instrument of the bourgeoisie—would wither away since it no longer represented the interests of a particular class. Class struggles would then be over (see the box on p. 688). Marx believed that the emergence of a classless society would lead to progress in science, technology, and industry and to greater wealth for all.

After the failure of the revolutions of 1848, Marx went to London, where he spent the rest of his life. He continued his writing on political economy, especially his famous work, *Das Kapital* (Capital), only one volume of which he completed. After his death, the remaining volumes were edited by his friend Engels.

Organizing the Working Class   One of the reasons *Das Kapital* was not finished was Marx's own preoccupation with organizing the working-class movement. In *The Communist Manifesto*, Marx had defined the communists as "the most advanced and resolute section of the working-class parties of every country." Their advantage was their ability to understand "the line of march, the conditions, and the ultimate general results of the proletarian movement." Marx saw his role in this light and participated enthusiastically in the activities of the International Working Men's Association. Formed in 1864 by British and French trade unionists, this "First International" served as an umbrella organization for working-class interests. Marx was the dominant personality on the organization's General Council and devoted much time to its activities. Internal dissension within the ranks soon damaged the organization, and it failed in 1872. Although it would be revived in 1889, the fate of socialism by that time was in the hands of national socialist parties.

Science and Culture in an Age of Realism

Q **Focus Question:** How did the belief that the world should be viewed realistically manifest itself in science, art, and literature in the second half of the nineteenth century?

Between 1850 and 1870, two major intellectual developments are evident: the growth of scientific knowledge, with its rapidly increasing impact on the Western worldview, and the shift from Romanticism and its focus on the inner world of reality to Realism and its turning toward the outer, material world.

A New Age of Science

By the mid-nineteenth century, science was having an ever-greater impact on European life. The Scientific Revolution of the sixteenth and seventeenth centuries had fundamentally transformed the Western worldview and

THE CLASSLESS SOCIETY

In *The Communist Manifesto*, Karl Marx and Friedrich Engels projected the creation of a classless society as the end product of the struggle between the bourgeoisie and the proletariat. In this selection, they discuss the steps by which that classless society would be reached.

Karl Marx and Friedrich Engels, *The Communist Manifesto*

We have seen...that the first step in the revolution by the working class is to raise the proletariat to the position of ruling class.... The proletariat will use its political supremacy to wrest, by degrees, all capital from the bourgeoisie, to centralize all instruments of production in the hands of the State, i.e., of the proletariat organized as the ruling class; and to increase the total of productive forces as rapidly as possible.

Of course, in the beginning, this cannot be effected except by means of despotic inroads on the rights of property, and on the conditions of bourgeois production; by means of measures, therefore, which appear economically insufficient and untenable, but which, in the course of the movement, outstrip themselves, necessitate further inroads upon the old social order, and are unavoidable as a means of entirely revolutionizing the mode of production.

These measures will of course be different in different countries.

Nevertheless, in the most advanced countries, the following will be pretty generally applicable:

1. Abolition of property in land and application of all rents of land to public purposes.
2. A heavy progressive or graduated income tax.
3. Abolition of all right of inheritance....
5. Centralization of credit in the hands of the State, by means of a national bank with State capital and an exclusive monopoly.
6. Centralization of the means of communication and transport in the hands of the State.
7. Extension of factories and instruments of production owned by the State....
8. Equal liability of all to labor. Establishment of industrial armies, especially for agriculture.
9. Combination of agriculture with manufacturing industries; gradual abolition of the distinction between town and country, by a more equable distribution of the population over the country.
10. Free education for all children in public schools. Abolition of children's factory labor in its present form....

When, in the course of development, class distinctions have disappeared, and all production has been concentrated in the whole nation, the public power will lose its political character. Political power, properly so called, is merely the organized power of one class for oppressing another. If the proletariat during its contest with the bourgeoisie is compelled, by the force of circumstances, to organize itself as a class, if, by means of a revolution, it makes itself the ruling class, and, as such, sweeps away by force the old conditions of production, then it will, along with these conditions, have swept away the conditions for the existence of class antagonisms and of classes generally, and will thereby have abolished its own supremacy as a class.

In place of the old bourgeois society, with its classes and class antagonisms, we shall have an association, in which the free development of each is the condition for the free development of all.

Q *How did Marx and Engels define the proletariat? The bourgeoisie? Why did Marxists come to believe that this distinction was paramount for understanding history? What steps did Marx and Engels believe would lead to a classless society? Considering that Marx criticized early socialists as utopian and regarded his own socialism as scientific, why does his socialism appear equally utopian?*

---

led to a modern, rational approach to the study of the natural world. Even in the eighteenth century, however, these intellectual developments had remained the preserve of an educated elite and resulted in few practical benefits. Moreover, the technical advances of the early Industrial Revolution had depended little on pure science and much more on the practical experiments of technologically oriented amateur inventors. Advances in industrial technology, however, fed an interest in basic scientific research, which in the 1830s and afterward resulted in a rash of basic scientific discoveries that were soon converted into technological improvements that affected everybody.

The development of the steam engine was important in encouraging scientists to work out its theoretical foundations, a preoccupation that led to thermodynamics, the science of the relationship between heat and mechanical energy. The laws of thermodynamics were at the core of nineteenth-century physics. In biology, the Frenchman Louis Pasteur formulated the germ theory of disease, which had enormous practical applications in the development of modern scientific medical practices (see "A Revolution in Health Care" later in this chapter). In chemistry, in the 1860s, the Russian Dmitri Mendeleyev (1834–1907) classified all the material elements then known on the basis of their atomic weights and provided the systematic foundation for the periodic law. The Englishman Michael Faraday (1791–1867) discovered the phenomenon of electromagnetic induction and put together a primitive generator that laid the foundation for the use of electricity, although economically efficient generators were not built until the 1870s.

The steadily increasing and often dramatic material gains generated by science and technology led to a growing faith in the benefits of science. The popularity of scientific and technological achievement produced a widespread acceptance of the scientific method, based on observation, experiment, and logical analysis, as the only path to objective truth and objective reality. This in turn undermined the faith of many people in religious revelation and truth. It is no accident that the nineteenth century was an age of increasing secularization, particularly evident in the growth of **materialism,** the belief that everything mental, spiritual, or ideal was simply a result of physical forces. Truth was to be found in the concrete material existence of human beings and not, as the Romantics imagined, in revelations gained by feeling or intuitive flashes. The importance of materialism was strikingly evident in the most important scientific event of the nineteenth century, the development of the theory of organic evolution according to natural selection. On the theories of Charles Darwin could be built a picture of humans as material beings that were simply part of the natural world.

Charles Darwin and the Theory of Organic Evolution

Charles Darwin (1809–1882), like many of the great scientists of the nineteenth century, was a scientific amateur. Born into an upper-middle-class family, he studied theology at Cambridge University while pursuing an intense side interest in geology and biology. In 1831, at the age of twenty-two, his hobby became his vocation when he accepted an appointment as a naturalist to study animals and plants on an official Royal Navy scientific expedition aboard the H.M.S. *Beagle.* Its purpose was to survey and study the landmasses of South America and the South Pacific. Darwin's specific job was to study the structure of various forms of plant and animal life. He was able to observe animals on islands virtually untouched by external influence and compare them to animals on the mainland. As a result, Darwin came to discard the notion of a special creation and to believe that animals evolved over time and in response to their environment. When he returned to Britain, he eventually formulated an explanation for evolution in the principle of **natural selection,** a theory that he presented in 1859 in his celebrated book, *On the Origin of Species by Means of Natural Selection.*

The Theory of Evolution The basic idea of Darwin's book was that all plants and animals had evolved over a long period of time from earlier and simpler forms of life, a principle known as **organic evolution.** Darwin was important in explaining how this natural process worked. He took the first step from Thomas Malthus's theory of population: in every species, "many more individuals of each species are born than can possibly survive." This

results in a "struggle for existence." Darwin believed that "as more individuals are produced than can possibly survive, there must in every case be a struggle for existence, either one individual with another of the same species, or with the individuals of distinct species, or with the physical conditions of life." Those who succeeded in this struggle for existence had adapted better to their environment, a process made possible by the appearance of "variants." Chance variations that occurred in the process of inheritance enabled some organisms to be more adaptable to the environment than others, a process that Darwin called natural selection: "Owing to this struggle [for existence], variations, however slight, . . . if they be in any degree profitable to the individuals of a species, in their infinitely complex relations to other organic beings and to their physical conditions of life, will tend to the preservation of such individuals, and will generally be inherited by the offspring."[10] Those that were naturally selected for survival ("survival of the fit") survived. The unfit did not and became extinct. The fit who survived propagated and passed on the variations that enabled them to survive until, from Darwin's point of view, a new separate species emerged.

In *On the Origin of Species,* Darwin discussed plant and animal species only. He was not concerned with humans themselves and only later applied his theory of natural selection to humans. In *The Descent of Man,* published in 1871, he argued for the animal origins of human beings: "man is the co-descendant with other mammals of a common progenitor." Humans were not an exception to the rule governing other species (see the box on p. 690).

Darwin's ideas were highly controversial at first. Some people fretted that Darwin's theory made human beings ordinary products of nature rather than unique beings. Others were disturbed by the implications of life as a struggle for survival, of "nature red in tooth and claw." Was there a place in the Darwinian world for moral values? For those who believed in a rational order in the world, Darwin's theory seemed to eliminate purpose and design from the universe. Gradually, however, Darwin's theory was accepted by scientists and other intellectuals. In the process of accepting Darwin's ideas, some people even tried to apply them to society, yet another example of science's increasing prestige.

A Revolution in Health Care

The application of natural science to the field of medicine in the nineteenth century led to revolutionary breakthroughs in health care. The first steps toward a more scientific basis for medicine were taken in Paris hospitals during the first half of the nineteenth century. Clinical observation, consisting of an active physical examination of patients, was combined with the knowledge gained from detailed autopsies to create a new clinical medicine.

DARWIN AND THE DESCENT OF MAN

Darwin published his theory of organic evolution in 1859, followed twelve years later by *The Descent of Man*, in which he argued that human beings, like other animals, evolved from lower forms of life. The theory provoked a firestorm of criticism, especially from the clergy. One critic described Darwin's theory as a "brutal philosophy—to wit, there is no God, and the ape is our Adam."

Charles Darwin, *The Descent of Man*

The main conclusion here arrived at, and now held by many naturalists, who are well competent to form a sound judgment, is that man is descended from some less highly organized form. The grounds upon which this conclusion rests will never be shaken, for the close similarity between man and the lower animals in embryonic development, as well as in innumerable points of structure and constitution, both of high and of the most trifling importance,—the rudiments which he retains, and the abnormal reversions to which he is occasionally liable,—are facts which cannot be disputed. They have long been known, but until recently they told us nothing with respect to the origin of man. Now when viewed by the light of our knowledge of the whole organic world, their meaning is unmistakable. The great principle of evolution stands up clear and firm, when these groups of facts are considered in connection with others, such as the mutual affinities of the members of the same group, their geographical distribution in past and present times, and their geological succession. It is incredible that all these facts should speak falsely. He who is not content to look, like a savage, at the phenomena of nature as disconnected, cannot any longer believe that man is the work of a separate act of creation. He will be forced to admit that the close resemblance of the embryo of man to that, for instance, of a dog—the construction of his skull, limbs and whole frame on the same plan with that of other mammals, independently of the uses to which the parts may be put—the occasional reappearance of various structures, for instance of several muscles, which man does not normally possess . . .—and a crowd of analogous facts—all point in the plainest manner to the conclusion that man is the co-descendant with other mammals of a common progenitor. . . .

Man may be excused for feeling some pride at having risen, though not through his own exertions, to the very summit of the organic scale; and the fact of his having thus risen, instead of having been aboriginally placed there, may give him hope for a still higher destiny in the distant future. But we are not here concerned with hopes or fears, only with the truth as far as our reason permits us to discover it; and I have given the evidence to the best of my ability. We must, however, acknowledge, as it seems to me, that man with all his noble qualities, with sympathy which feels for the most debased, with benevolence which extends not only to other men but to the humblest living creature, with his god-like intellect which has penetrated into the movements and constitution of the solar system—with all these exalted powers—Man still bears in his bodily frame the indelible stamp of his lowly origin.

Q *What is Darwin's basic argument in* The Descent of Man? *Why did so many object to it? What forces in nineteenth-century European society do you think came together to stimulate Darwin's thinking and publication on this subject?*

Pasteur and Germs   The major breakthrough toward a scientific medicine occurred with the discovery of microorganisms, or germs, as the agents causing disease. The germ theory of disease was largely the work of Louis Pasteur (1822–1895). Pasteur was not a doctor but a chemist who approached medical problems in a scientific fashion. In 1857, Pasteur went to Paris as director of scientific studies at the École Normale, where experiments he conducted proved that microorganisms of various kinds were responsible for the process of fermentation, thereby launching the science of bacteriology.

Government and private industry soon perceived the inherent practical value of Pasteur's work. His examination of a disease threatening the wine industry led to the development in 1863 of a process—subsequently known as **pasteurization**—for heating a product to destroy the organisms causing spoilage. In 1877, Pasteur turned his attention to human diseases. His desire to do more than simply identify disease-producing organisms led him in 1885 to a preventive vaccination against rabies. In the 1890s, the principle of vaccination was extended to diphtheria, typhoid fever, cholera, and plague, creating a modern immunological science.

The work of Pasteur and the others who followed him in isolating the specific bacteriological causes of numerous diseases had a far-reaching impact. By providing a rational means of treating and preventing infectious diseases, they transformed the medical world. Both the practice of surgery and public health experienced a renaissance.

New Surgical Practices   Surgeons had already achieved a new professionalism by the end of the eighteenth century (see Chapter 17), but the discovery of germs and the introduction of anesthesia created a new environment for surgical operations. Surgeons had traditionally set broken bones, treated wounds, and amputated limbs, usually shattered in war. One major obstacle to more successful surgery was the inevitable postoperative infection, which was especially rampant in hospitals.

Joseph Lister (1827–1912), who developed the antiseptic principle, was one of the first people to deal with

ANESTHESIA AND MODERN SURGERY

Modern scientific medicine became established in the nineteenth century. Important to the emergence of modern surgery was the development of anesthetic agents that would block the patient's pain and enable surgeons to complete their surgery without the haste that had characterized earlier operations. This document is an eyewitness account of the first successful use of ether anesthesia, which took place at the Massachusetts General Hospital in 1846.

The First Public Demonstration of Ether Anesthesia, October 16, 1846

The day arrived; the time appointed was noted on the dial, when the patient was led into the operating-room, and Dr. Warren and a board of the most eminent surgeons in the State were gathered around the sufferer. "All is ready—the stillness oppressive." It had been announced "that a test of some preparation was to be made for which the astonishing claim had been made that it would render the person operated upon free from pain." These are the words of Dr. Warren that broke the stillness.

Those present were incredulous, and, as Dr. Morton had not arrived at the time appointed and fifteen minutes had passed, Dr. Warren said, with significant meaning, "I presume he is otherwise engaged." This was followed with a "derisive laugh," and Dr. Warren grasped his knife and was about to proceed with the operation. At that moment Dr. Morton entered a side door, when Dr. Warren turned to him and in a strong voice said, "Well, sir, your patient is ready." In a few minutes he was ready for the surgeon's knife, when Dr. Morton said, "Your patient is ready, sir."

Here the most sublime scene ever witnessed in the operating-room was presented, when the patient placed himself voluntarily upon the table, which was to become the altar of future fame. Not that he did so for the purpose of advancing the science of medicine, nor for the good of his fellow-men, for the act itself was purely a personal and self-ish one. He was about to assist in solving a new and important problem of therapeutics, whose benefits were to be given to the whole civilized world, yet wholly unconscious of the sublimity of the occasion or the art he was taking.

That was a supreme moment for a most wonderful discovery, and, had the patient died upon the operation, science would have waited long to discover the hypnotic effects of some other remedy of equal potency and safety, and it may be properly questioned whether chloroform would have come into use as it has at the present time.

The heroic bravery of the man who voluntarily placed himself upon the table, a subject for the surgeon's knife, should be recorded and his name enrolled upon parchment, which should be hung upon the walls of the surgical amphitheater in which the operation was performed. His name was Gilbert Abbott.

The operation was for a congenital tumor on the left side of the neck, extending along the jaw to the maxillary gland and into the mouth, embracing a margin of the tongue. The operation was successful; and when the patient recovered he declared he had suffered no pain. Dr. Warren turned to those present and said, "Gentlemen, this is no humbug."

Q *In what ways does this document demonstrate the impact that modern science had made on Western society by the middle of the nineteenth century? What forces conjoined to encourage the practical application and refinement of new scientific discoveries?*

---

this problem. Following the work of Pasteur, Lister perceived that bacteria might enter a wound and cause infection. His use of carbolic acid, a newly discovered disinfectant, proved remarkably effective in eliminating infections during surgery. Lister's discoveries dramatically transformed surgery wards as patients no longer succumbed regularly to what was called "hospital gangrene."

The second great barrier to large-scale surgery stemmed from the inability to lessen the pain of the patient. Alcohol and opiates had been used for centuries during surgical operations, but even their use did not allow unhurried operative maneuvers. After experiments with numerous agents, sulfuric ether was first used successfully in an operation at the Massachusetts General Hospital in 1846 (see the box above). Within a year, chloroform began to rival ether as an anesthetic agent.

New Public Health Measures   Although the great discoveries of bacteriology came after the emergence of the first public health movement, they significantly furthered its development. Based on the principle of preventive rather than curative medicine, the urban public health movement of the 1840s and 1850s was largely a response to the cholera epidemic (see Chapter 23). One medical man, in fact, called cholera "our best ally" in furthering public hygiene. The prebacteriological hygiene movement focused on providing clean water, adequate sewage disposal, and less crowded housing conditions. Bacterial discoveries led to greater emphasis on preventive measures, such as the pasteurization of milk, improved purification of water supplies, immunization against disease, and control of waterborne diseases. The public health movement also resulted in the government's hiring medical doctors not just to treat people but to deal with issues of public health as well.

New Medical Schools   The new scientific developments also had an important impact on the training of doctors for professional careers in health care. Although there were a few medical schools at the beginning of the

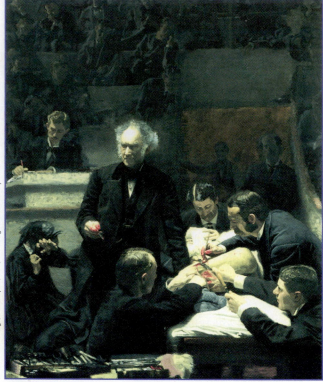

Thomas Eakins, *The Gross Clinic.* This painting, completed in 1875, shows Dr. Samuel Gross, one of the foremost surgeons in the United States, scalpel in hand, pausing midway in surgery on a young man's leg to discuss the operation with his students in the amphitheater of the Jefferson Medical College. Various tasks are performed by assistant doctors, including the anesthetist, who holds his cloth over the youth's face. Eakins's painting is a realistic portrayal of the new medical science at work.

nineteenth century, most medical instruction was still done by a system of apprenticeship. In the course of the nineteenth century, virtually every Western country founded new medical schools, but attempts to impose uniform standards on them through certifying bodies met considerable resistance. Entrance requirements were virtually nonexistent, and degrees were granted after several months of lectures. Professional organizations founded around midcentury, such as the British Medical Association in 1832, the American Medical Association in 1847, and the German Doctors' Society in 1872, attempted to elevate professional standards but achieved little until the end of the century. The establishment of the Johns Hopkins University School of Medicine in 1893, with its four-year graded curriculum, clinical training for advanced students, and use of laboratories for teaching purposes, provided a new model for medical training that finally became standard practice in the twentieth century.

Women and Medical Schools During most of the nineteenth century, medical schools in Europe and the United States were closed to female students. When

Harriet Hunt applied to Harvard Medical School, the male students drew up resolutions that prevented her admission:

> Resolved, that no woman of true delicacy would be willing in the presence of men to listen to the discussion of subjects that necessarily come under consideration of the students of medicine.
>
> Resolved, that we object to having the company of any female forced upon us, who is disposed to unsex herself, and to sacrifice her modesty by appearing with men in the lecture room.[11]

Elizabeth Blackwell (1821–1910) achieved the first major breakthrough for women in medicine. Although she had been admitted to the Geneva College of Medicine in New York by mistake, Blackwell's perseverance and intelligence won her the respect of her fellow male students. She received her M.D. degree in 1849 and eventually established a clinic in New York City.

European women experienced difficulties similar to Blackwell's. In Britain, Elizabeth Garret and Sophia Jex-Blake had to struggle for years before they were finally admitted to the practice of medicine. The unwillingness of medical schools to open their doors to women led to the formation of separate medical schools for women. The Female Medical College of Pennsylvania, established in 1850, was the first in the United States, and the London School of Medicine for Women was founded in 1874. But even after graduation from such institutions, women faced obstacles when they tried to practice as doctors. Many were denied licenses, and hospitals often closed their doors to them. In Britain, Parliament finally capitulated to pressure and passed a bill in 1876 giving women the right to take qualifying examinations. Soon women were entering medical schools in ever-larger numbers. By the 1890s, universities in Great Britain, Sweden, Denmark, Norway, Finland, Russia, and Belgium were admitting women to medical training and practice. Germany and Austria did not do so until after 1900. Even then, medical associations refused to accept women as equals in the medical profession. Women were not given full membership in the American Medical Association until 1915.

Science and the Study of Society

The importance of science in the nineteenth century perhaps made it inevitable that a scientific approach would be applied to the realm of human activity. The attempt to apply the methods of science systematically to the study of society was perhaps most evident in the work of the Frenchman Auguste Comte (1798–1857). His major work, titled *System of Positive Philosophy,* was published between 1837 and 1842 but had its real impact after 1850.

Comte created a system of "positive knowledge" based on a hierarchy of all the sciences. Mathematics was the foundation on which the physical sciences, earth sciences, and biological sciences were built. At the top was sociology, the science of human society, which for Comte incorporated economics, anthropology, history, and social psychology. Comte saw sociology's task as a difficult one. The discovery of the general laws of society would have to be based on the collection and analysis of data on humans and their social environment. Although his schemes were often complex and dense, Comte played an important role in the growing popularity of science and materialism in the mid-nineteenth century.

Realism in Literature

The belief that the world should be viewed realistically, frequently expressed after 1850, was closely related to the materialistic outlook. The term **Realism** was first employed in 1850 to describe a new style of painting and soon spread to literature.

The literary Realists of the mid-nineteenth century were distinguished by their deliberate rejection of Romanticism. The literary Realists wanted to deal with ordinary characters from real life rather than Romantic heroes in unusual settings. They also sought to avoid flowery and sentimental language by using careful observation and accurate description, an approach that led them to eschew poetry in favor of prose and the novel. Realists often combined their interest in everyday life with a searching examination of social questions.

The leading novelist of the 1850s and 1860s, the Frenchman Gustave Flaubert (1821–1880), perfected the Realist novel. His *Madame Bovary* (1857) was a straightforward description of barren and sordid small-town life in France. Emma Bovary, a woman of some vitality, is trapped in a marriage to a drab provincial doctor. Impelled by the images of romantic love she has read about in novels, she seeks the same thing for herself in adulterous affairs. Unfulfilled, she is ultimately driven to suicide, unrepentant to the end for her lifestyle. Flaubert's contempt for bourgeois society was evident in his portrayal of middle-class hypocrisy and smugness.

William Thackeray (1811–1863) wrote Britain's prototypical Realist novel, *Vanity Fair: A Novel Without a Hero*, in 1848. Thackeray deliberately flouted the Romantic conventions. A novel, Thackeray said, should "convey as strongly as possible the sentiment of reality as opposed to a tragedy or poem, which may be heroical." Perhaps the greatest of the Victorian novelists was Charles Dickens (1812–1870), whose realistic novels focusing on the lower and middle classes in Britain's early industrial age became extraordinarily successful. His descriptions of the urban poor and the brutalization of human life were vividly realistic (see the box on p. 694).

Realism in Art

In the first half of the nineteenth century, Romanticism in art had been paralleled by the classical school of painting, but both were superseded by the new mood of the mid-nineteenth century. In art, too, Realism became dominant after 1850, although Romanticism was by no means dead. Among the most important characteristics of Realism are a desire to depict the everyday life of ordinary people, be they peasants, workers, or prostitutes; an attempt at photographic realism; and an interest in the natural environment. The French became leaders in Realist painting.

Courbet Gustave Courbet (1819–1877) was the most famous artist of the Realist school. In fact, the word *Realism* was first coined in 1850 to describe one of his paintings. Courbet reveled in a realistic portrayal of everyday life. His subjects were factory workers, peasants, and the wives of saloon keepers. "I have never seen either angels or goddesses, so I am not interested in painting them," he exclaimed. One of his famous works, *The Stonebreakers*, painted in 1849, shows two road workers engaged in the deadening work of breaking stones to build a road. This representation of human misery was a scandal to those who objected to his "cult of ugliness." To Courbet, no subject was too ordinary, too harsh, or too ugly to interest him.

Gustave Courbet, *The Stonebreakers*. Realism, largely developed by French painters, aimed at a lifelike portrayal of the daily activities of ordinary people. Gustave Courbet was the most famous of the Realist artists. As is evident in *The Stonebreakers,* he sought to portray things as they really appear. He shows an old road builder and his young assistant in their tattered clothes, engrossed in their dreary work of breaking stones to construct a road. The use of browns and grays helps communicate the drudgery of their task.

REALISM: CHARLES DICKENS AND AN IMAGE OF HELL ON EARTH

Charles Dickens was one of Britain's greatest novelists. Though he realistically portrayed the material, social, and psychological milieu of his time, an element of Romanticism still pervaded his novels. This is evident in this selection from *The Old Curiosity Shop* in which his description of the English mill town of Birmingham takes on the imagery of Dante's Hell.

Charles Dickens, *The Old Curiosity Shop*

A long suburb of red brick houses,—some with patches of garden ground, where coal-dust and factory smoke darkened the shrinking leaves, and coarse rank flowers; and where the struggling vegetation sickened and sank under the hot breath of kiln and furnace, making them by its presence seem yet more blighting and unwholesome than in the town itself,—a long, flat, straggling suburb passed, they came by slow degrees upon a cheerless region, where not a blade of grass was seen to grow; where not a bud put forth its promise in the spring; where nothing green could live but on the surface of the stagnant pools, which here and there lay idly sweltering by the black roadside.

Advancing more and more into the shadow of this mournful place, its dark depressing influence stole upon their spirits, and filled them with a dismal gloom. On every side, and as far as the eye could see into the heavy distance, tall chimneys, crowding on each other, and presenting that endless repetition of the same dull, ugly form, which is the horror of oppressive dreams, poured out their plague of smoke, obscured the light, and made foul the melancholy air. On mounds of ashes by the wayside, sheltered only by a few rough boards, or rotten pent-house roofs, strange engines spun and writhed like tortured creatures; clanking their iron chains, shrieking in their rapid whirl from time to time as though in torment unendurable, and making the ground tremble with their agonies. Dismantled houses here and there appeared, tottering to the earth, propped up by fragments of others that had fallen down, unroofed, windowless, blackened, desolate, but yet inhabited. Men, women, children, wan in their looks and ragged in attire, tended the engines, fed their tributary fires, begged upon the road, or scowled half-naked from the doorless houses. Then came more of the wrathful monsters, whose like they almost seemed to be in their wildness and their untamed air, screeching and turning to the right and left, with the same interminable perspective of brick towers, never ceasing in their black vomit, blasting all things living or inanimate, shutting out the face of day, and closing in on all these horrors with a dense dark cloud.

But night-time in this dreadful spot!—night, when the smoke was changed to fire; when every chimney spurted up its flame; and places, that had been dark vaults all day, now shone red-hot, with figures moving to and fro within their blazing jaws, and calling to one another with hoarse cries—night, when the noise of every strange machine was aggravated by the darkness; when the people near them looked wilder and more savage; when bands of unemployed laborers paraded in the roads, or clustered by torchlight round their leaders, who told them in stern language of their wrongs, and urged them on by frightful cries and threats; when maddened men, armed with sword and firebrand, spurning the tears and prayers of women who would restrain them, rushed forth on errands of terror and destruction, to work no ruin half so surely as their own—night, when carts came rumbling by, filled with rude coffins (for contagious disease and death had been busy with the living crops); or when orphans cried, and distracted women shrieked and followed in their wake—night, when some called for bread, and some for drink to drown their cares; and some with tears, and some with staggering feet, and so with bloodshot eyes, went brooding home—night, which, unlike the night that Heaven sends on earth, brought with it no peace, nor quiet, nor signs of blessed sleep—who shall tell the terrors of the night to that young wandering child!

Q *What image of Birmingham do you get from this selection by Dickens? Why is it so powerful? What does the passage reveal about Dickens himself and the roles European writers played in the reform of nineteenth-century society?*

Millet Jean-François Millet (1814–1875) was preoccupied with scenes from rural life, especially peasants laboring in the fields, although his Realism still contained an element of Romantic sentimentality. In *The Gleaners*, his most famous work, three peasant women gather grain in a field, a centuries-old practice that for Millet showed the symbiotic relationship between humans and nature. Millet made landscape and country life an important subject matter for French artists, but he, too, was criticized by his contemporaries for crude subject matter and unorthodox technique.

Music: The Twilight of Romanticism

The mid-nineteenth century witnessed the development of a new group of musicians known as the New German School. It emphasized emotional content rather than abstract form and championed new methods of using music to express literary or pictorial ideas.

Liszt The Hungarian-born composer Franz Liszt (1811–1886) best exemplifies the achievements of the New German School. A child prodigy, he established

Jean-François Millet, *The Gleaners*. Jean-François Millet, another prominent French Realist painter, took a special interest in the daily activities of French peasants, although he tended to transform his peasants into heroic figures who dominated their environment. In *The Gleaners*, for example, the three peasant women who are engaged in the backbreaking work of gathering grain left after the harvest still appear as powerful figures, symbolizing the union of humans with the earth.

himself as an outstanding concert artist by the age of twelve. Liszt's performances and his dazzling personality made him the most highly esteemed virtuoso of his age. He has been called the greatest pianist of all time and has been credited with introducing the concept of the modern piano recital.

Liszt's compositions consist mainly of piano pieces, although he composed in other genres as well, including sacred music. He invented the term *symphonic poem* to refer to his orchestral works, which did not strictly obey traditional forms and were generally based on a literary or pictorial idea. Under the guidance of Liszt and the New German School, Romantic music reached its peak.

Wagner Although Liszt was an influential mentor to a number of young composers, he was most closely associated with his eventual son-in-law Richard Wagner (1813–1883). Building on the advances made by Liszt

and the New German School, Wagner ultimately realized the German desire for a truly national opera. Wagner was not only a composer but also a propagandist and writer in support of his unique conception of dramatic music. Called both the culmination of the Romantic era and the beginning of the avant-garde, Wagner's music may be described as a monumental development in classical music.

Believing that opera is the best form of artistic expression, Wagner transformed opera into "music drama" through his *Gesamtkunstwerk* ("total art work"), a musical composition for the theater in which music, acting, dance, poetry, and scenic design are synthesized into a harmonious whole. He abandoned the traditional divisions of opera, which interrupted the dramatic line of the work, and instead used a device called a leitmotiv, a recurring musical theme in which the human voice combined with the line of the orchestra instead of rising above it. His operas incorporate literally hundreds of leitmotivs in order to convey the story. For his themes, Wagner looked to myth and epic tales from the past. His most ambitious work was *The Ring of the Nibelung*, a series of four music dramas dealing with the mythical gods of the ancient German epic.

CONCLUSION

Between 1850 and 1871, the national state became the focus of people's loyalty. Wars, both foreign and civil, were fought to create unified nation-states. Political nationalism had emerged during the French revolutionary era and had become a powerful force of change during the first half of the nineteenth century, but its triumph came only after 1850. Associated initially with middle-class liberals, it would have great appeal to the broad masses as well by the end of the nineteenth century. In 1871, however, the political transformations stimulated by the force of nationalism were by no means complete. Significantly, large minorities, especially in the polyglot empires controlled by the Austrians, Turks, and Russians, had not achieved the goal of their own national states. Moreover, the nationalism that had triumphed by 1871 was no longer

the nationalism that had been closely identified with liberalism. Liberal nationalists had believed that unified nation-states would preserve individual rights and lead to a greater community of European peoples. Rather than unifying people, however, the new, loud, and chauvinistic nationalism of the late nineteenth century divided them as the new national states became embroiled in bitter competition after 1871.

Europeans, however, were hardly aware of nationalism's dangers in 1871. The spread of industrialization and the wealth of scientific and technological achievements were sources of optimism. After the revolutionary and military upheavals of the midcentury decades, many Europeans believed that they stood on the verge of a new age of progress.

TIMELINE

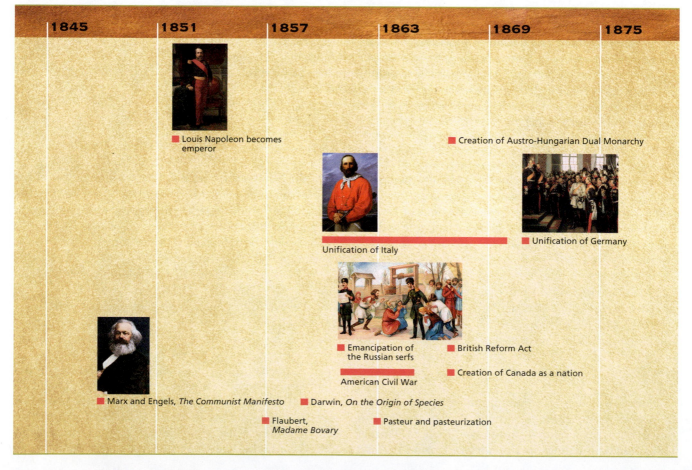

1845   1851   1857   1863   1869   1875

- Louis Napoleon becomes emperor
- Creation of Austro-Hungarian Dual Monarchy
- Unification of Italy
- Unification of Germany
- Emancipation of the Russian serfs
- British Reform Act
- American Civil War
- Creation of Canada as a nation
- Marx and Engels, *The Communist Manifesto*
- Darwin, *On the Origin of Species*
- Flaubert, *Madame Bovary*
- Pasteur and pasteurization

NOTES

1. Quoted in James F. McMillan, *Napoleon III* (New York, 1991), p. 37.
2. Quoted in Robert Gildea, *Barricades and Borders: Europe, 1800–1914*, 2d ed. (Oxford, 1996), p. 170.
3. Quoted in Otto Pflanze, *Bismarck and the Development of Germany: The Period of Unification, 1815–1871* (Princeton, N.J., 1963), p. 60.
4. Louis L. Snyder, ed., *Documents of German History* (New Brunswick, N.J., 1958), p. 202.
5. Quoted in Pflanze, *Bismarck and the Development of Germany*, p. 327.
6. Quoted in György Szabad, *Hungarian Political Trends Between the Revolution and the Compromise, 1849–1867* (Budapest, 1977), p. 163.
7. Quoted in Rondo Cameron, "Crédit Mobilier and the Economic Development of Europe," *Journal of Political Economy* 61 (1953): 470.
8. Karl Marx and Friedrich Engels, *The Communist Manifesto* (Harmondsworth, England, 1967), p. 79.
9. Ibid., pp. 79, 81, 82.
10. Charles Darwin, *On the Origin of Species* (New York, 1872), vol. 1, pp. 77, 79.
11. Quoted in Albert Lyons and R. Joseph Petrucelli, *Medicine: An Illustrated History* (New York, 1978), p. 569.

SUGGESTIONS FOR FURTHER READING

General Works   In addition to the general works on nineteenth-century Europe cited in Chapter 21, see three general surveys of the midcentury decades: **N. Rich, *The Age of Nationalism and Reform, 1850–1890,*** 2d ed. (New York, 1980); **E. Hobsbawm, *The Age of Capital, 1845–1875*** (London, 1975); and **J. A. S. Grenville, *Europe Reshaped, 1848–1878,*** 2d ed. (London, 2000).

The French Second Empire   For a good introduction to the French Second Empire, see **A. Plessis, *The Rise and Fall of the Second Empire, 1852–1871,*** trans. **J. Mandelbaum** (New York, 1985). Napoleon's role can be examined in **J. F. McMillan, *Napoleon III*** (New York, 1991). The Crimean War and its impact are examined in **C. Ponting, *The Crimean War*** (New York, 2004).

Unification of Italy and Germany   The unification of Italy can be examined in **F. Coppa, *The Origins of the Italian Wars of Independence*** (New York, 1992); **B. Derek and E. F. Biagini, *The Risorgimento and the Unification of Italy,*** 2d ed. (London, 2002); **D. M. Smith, *Cavour*** (London, 1985); and **H. Hearder, *Cavour*** (New York, 1994). The unification of Germany can be pursued first in **W. Carr, *The Origins of the Wars of German Unification*** (New York, 1991), and in two good biographies of Bismarck, **E. Crankshaw, *Bismarck*** (New York, 1981), and **E. Feuchtwanger, *Bismarck*** (London, 2002). See also the brief study by **B. Waller, *Bismarck,*** 2d ed. (Oxford, 1997). On the Franco-Prussian War, see **G. Wawro, *The Franco-Prussian War*** (Cambridge, 2003).

The National State   On the Austrian Empire, see **R. Okey, *The Habsburg Monarchy*** (New York, 2001). Imperial Russia is covered in **T. Chapman, *Imperial Russia, 1801–1905*** (London, 2001). On Victorian Britain, see **W. L. Arnstein, *Queen Victoria*** (New York, 2005), and **I. Machlin, *Disraeli*** (London, 1995). The definitive one-volume history of the American Civil War is **J. M. McPherson, *Battle Cry of Freedom: The Civil War Era*** in the Oxford History of the United States series (New York, 2003).

Economic Developments and Thought   In addition to the general works on economic development listed in Chapters 20 and 21, some specialized works on this period are worthwhile. These include **W. O. Henderson, *The Rise of German Industrial Power, 1834–1914*** (Berkeley, Calif., 1975), and **F. Crouzet, *The Victorian Economy*** (London, 1982). On Marx, a standard work is **D. McLellan, *Karl Marx: A Biography,*** 4th ed. (New York, 2006). See also **F. Wheen, *Karl Marx: A Life*** (New York, 2001), but it can be supplemented by the interesting and comprehensive work by **L. Kolakowski, *Main Currents of Marxism,*** 3 vols. (Oxford, 1978).

Science and Culture   For an introduction to the intellectual changes of the nineteenth century, see **O. Chadwick, *The Secularization of the European Mind in the Nineteenth Century*** (Cambridge, 1975). A detailed biography of Darwin can be found in **J. Bowlby, *Charles Darwin: A Biography*** (London, 1990). For an introduction to the transformation of medical practices in the nineteenth century, see the appropriate chapters in **L. N. Magner, *A History of Medicine*** (New York, 1992). On Realism, **J. Malpas, *Realism*** (Cambridge, 1997), is a good introduction.

CENGAGENOW   CengageNOW is an integrated online suite of services and resources with proven ease of use and efficient paths to success, delivering the results you want—NOW!
academic.cengage.com/login/
Enter CengageNOW using the access card that is available with *Western Civilization.* CengageNOW will assist you in understanding the content in this chapter with lesson plans generated for your needs. In addition, you can read the following documents, and many more, online:

Charles Darwin, *On the Origin of Species*
Otto von Bismarck, *Memoirs*
Abraham Lincoln and Stephen Douglas debates
The Emancipation of the Russian Serfs
Friedrich Engels and Karl Marx, *The Communist Manifesto*

WESTERN CIVILIZATION RESOURCES

Visit the *Western Civilization* Companion Web site for resources specific to this book:
academic.cengage.com/history/spielvogel
For a variety of tools to help you succeed in this course, visit the Western Civilization Resource Center. Enter the Resource Center using either your *CengageNOW* access card or your standalone access card for the *Wadsworth Western Civilization Resource Center.* Organized by topic, this Web site includes quizzes; images; primary source documents; interactive simulations, maps, and timelines; movie explorations; and a wealth of other resources.
http://westernrc.wadsworth.com/

CHAPTER 23
MASS SOCIETY IN AN "AGE OF PROGRESS," 1871–1894

Swimmers gather in front of concession stands at Coney Island

CHAPTER OUTLINE AND FOCUS QUESTIONS

The Growth of Industrial Prosperity

Q What was the Second Industrial Revolution, and what effects did it have on European economic and social life? What roles did socialist parties and trade unions play in improving conditions for the working classes?

The Emergence of a Mass Society

Q What is a mass society, and what were its main characteristics? What role were women expected to play in society and family life in the latter half of the nineteenth century, and how closely did patterns of family life correspond to this ideal?

The National State

Q What general political trends were evident in the nations of western Europe in the last decades of the nineteenth century, and how did these trends differ from the policies pursued in Germany, Austria-Hungary, and Russia?

CRITICAL THINKING

Q What was the relationship among economic, social, and political developments between 1871 and 1894?

IN THE LATE 1800s, Europe entered a dynamic period of material prosperity. Bringing with it new industries, new sources of energy, and new goods, a second Industrial Revolution transformed the human environment, dazzled Europeans, and led them to believe that their material progress meant human progress. Scientific and technological achievements, many naively believed, would improve humanity's condition and solve all human problems. The doctrine of progress became an article of great faith.

The new urban and industrial world created by the rapid economic changes of the nineteenth century led to the emergence of a mass society by the late nineteenth century. Mass society meant improvements for the lower classes, who benefited from the extension of voting rights, a better standard of living, and education. It also brought mass leisure. New work patterns established the "weekend" as a distinct time of recreation and fun, and new forms of mass transportation—railroads and streetcars—enabled even ordinary workers to make excursions to amusement parks. Coney Island was only 8 miles from central New York City; Blackpool in England was a short train ride from nearby industrial towns. With their Ferris wheels and other daring rides that threw young men and women together, amusement parks offered a whole new world of entertainment. Thanks to the railroad, seaside resorts, once the preserve of the wealthy, became accessible to more people for weekend visits, much to the disgust of one upper-class regular, who complained about the new "day-trippers": "They swarm upon the beach, wandering listlessly about with apparently no other aim than to get a mouthful of fresh air." Enterprising entrepreneurs in resorts like Blackpool welcomed the masses of new visitors, however, and built piers laden with food, drink, and entertainment to serve them.

The coming of mass society also created new roles for the governments of Europe's nation-states, which now fostered national loyalty, created national armies by conscription, and took more responsibility for public health and housing measures in their cities. By 1871, the national state had become the focus of Europeans' lives. Within many of these nation-states, the growth of the middle class had led to the triumph of liberal practices: constitutional governments, parliaments, and principles of equality. The period after 1871 also witnessed the growth of political democracy as the right to vote was extended to all adult males; women, though, would still have to fight for the same political rights. With political democracy came a new mass politics and a new mass press. Both would become regular features of the twentieth century. ◇

The Growth of Industrial Prosperity

Q **Focus Questions:** What was the Second Industrial Revolution, and what effects did it have on European economic and social life? What roles did socialist parties and trade unions play in improving conditions for the working classes?

At the heart of Europeans' belief in progress after 1871 was the stunning material growth produced by what historians have called the Second Industrial Revolution. The First Industrial Revolution had given rise to textiles, railroads, iron, and coal. In the second revolution, steel, chemicals, electricity, and petroleum led the way to new industrial frontiers.

New Products

The first major change in industrial development after 1870 was the substitution of steel for iron. New methods of rolling and shaping steel made it useful in the construction of lighter, smaller, and faster machines and engines, as well as railways, ships, and armaments. In 1860, Great Britain, France, Germany, and Belgium together produced 125,000 tons of steel; by 1913, the total was 32 million tons. Whereas in the early 1870s Britain had produced twice as much steel as Germany, by 1910,

German production was double that of Great Britain. Both had been surpassed by the United States in 1890.

Chemicals   Great Britain also fell behind in the new chemical industry. A change in the method of making soda enabled France and Germany to take the lead in producing the alkalies used in the textile, soap, and paper industries. German laboratories soon overtook the British in the development of new organic chemical compounds, such as artificial dyes. By 1900, German firms had cornered 90 percent of the market for dyestuffs and also led in the development of photographic plates and film.

Electricity   Electricity was a major new form of energy that proved to be of great value since it could be easily converted into other forms of energy, such as heat, light, and motion, and moved relatively effortlessly through space over wires. In the 1870s, the first commercially practical generators of electrical current were developed. By 1881, Britain had its first public power station. By 1910, hydroelectric power stations and coal-fired steam-generating plants enabled entire districts to be tied in to a single power distribution system that provided a common source of power for homes, shops, and industrial enterprises.

Electricity spawned a whole series of inventions. The invention of the lightbulb by the American Thomas Edison (1847–1931) and the Briton Joseph Swan (1828–1914) opened homes and cities to illumination by electric lights. A revolution in communications was fostered when Alexander Graham Bell (1847–1922) invented the telephone in 1876 and Guglielmo Marconi (1874–1937) sent the first radio waves across the Atlantic in 1901. Although most electricity was initially used for lighting, it was eventually put to use in transportation. The first electric railway was installed in Berlin in 1879. By the 1880s, streetcars and subways had appeared in major European cities and had begun to replace horse-drawn buses. Electricity also transformed the factory. Conveyor belts, cranes, machines, and machine tools could all be powered by electricity and located anywhere. In the First Industrial Revolution, coal had been the major source of energy. Countries without adequate coal supplies lagged behind in industrialization. Thanks to electricity, they could now enter the industrial age.

The Internal Combustion Engine   The development of the internal combustion engine had a similar effect. The first internal combustion engine, fired by gas and air, was produced in 1878. It proved unsuitable for widespread use as a source of power in transportation until the development of liquid fuels—petroleum and its distilled derivatives. An oil-fired engine was made in 1897, and by 1902, the Hamburg-Amerika Line had switched from coal to oil on its new ocean liners. By the end of the nineteenth century, some naval fleets had been converted to oil burners as well.

An Age of Progress. In the decades after 1871, the Second Industrial Revolution led many Europeans to believe that they were living in an age of progress when most human problems would be solved by scientific achievements. This illustration is taken from a special issue of the *Illustrated London News* celebrating the Diamond Jubilee of Queen Victoria in 1897. On the left are scenes from 1837, when Victoria came to the British throne; on the right are scenes from 1897. The vivid contrast underscored the magazine's conclusion: "The most striking . . . evidence of progress during the reign is the ever increasing speed which the discoveries of physical science have forced into everyday life. Steam and electricity have conquered time and space to a greater extent during the last sixty years than all the preceding six hundred years witnessed."

The development of the internal combustion engine gave rise to the automobile and the airplane. Gottlieb Daimler's invention of a light engine in 1886 was the key to the development of the automobile. In 1900, world production stood at nine thousand cars; by 1906, Americans had overtaken the initial lead of the French. It was an American, Henry Ford (1863–1947), who revolutionized the car industry with the mass production of the Model T. By 1916, Ford's factories were producing 735,000 cars a year. Air transportation began with the Zeppelin airship in 1900. In 1903, at Kitty Hawk, North Carolina, Wilbur and Orville Wright made the first flight in a fixed-wing plane powered by a gasoline engine. It took World War I to stimulate the aircraft industry, however, and the first regular passenger air service was not established until 1919.

New Markets

The growth of industrial production depended on the development of markets for the sale of manufactured goods. After 1870, the best foreign markets were already heavily saturated, forcing Europeans to take a renewed look at their domestic markets. As Europeans were the richest consumers in the world, those markets offered abundant possibilities. The dramatic population increases after 1870 (see "Population Growth" later in this chapter) were accompanied by a steady rise in national incomes. The leading industrialized nations, Britain and Germany, doubled or tripled their national incomes. Between 1850 and 1900, real wages increased by two-thirds in Britain and by one-third in Germany. As the prices of both food and manufactured goods declined due to lower transportation costs, Europeans could spend more on consumer products. Businesses soon perceived the value of using new techniques of mass marketing to sell the consumer goods made possible by the development of the steel and electrical industries. By bringing together a vast array of new products in one place, they created the department store (see the box on p. 701). The desire to own sewing machines, clocks, bicycles, electric lights, and typewriters rapidly created a new consumer ethic that became a crucial part of the modern economy.

Tariffs and Cartels Meanwhile, increased competition for foreign markets and the growing importance of domestic demand led to a reaction against free trade. To many industrial and political leaders, protective **tariffs** guaranteed domestic markets for the products of their own industries. That is why, after a decade of experimentation with free trade in the 1860s, Europeans returned to tariff protection.

THE DEPARTMENT STORE AND THE BEGINNINGS OF MASS CONSUMERISM

Domestic markets were especially important for the sale of the goods being turned out by Europe's increasing number of industrial plants. Techniques of mass marketing were developed to encourage people to purchase the new consumer goods. The Parisians pioneered the department store, and this selection is taken from a contemporary's account of the growth of these stores in the French capital city.

E. Lavasseur, *On Parisian Department Stores*

It was in the reign of Louis-Philippe that department stores for fashion goods and dresses, extending to material and other clothing, began to be distinguished. The type was already one of the notable developments of the Second Empire; it became one of the most important ones of the Third Republic. These stores have increased in number and several of them have become extremely large. Combining in their different departments all articles of clothing, toilet articles, furniture and many other ranges of goods, it is their special object so to combine all commodities as to attract and satisfy customers who will find conveniently together an assortment of a mass of articles corresponding to all their various needs. They attract customers by permanent display, by free entry into the shops, by periodic exhibitions, by special sales, by fixed prices, and by their ability to deliver the goods purchased to customers' homes, in Paris and to the provinces. Turning themselves into direct intermediaries between the producer and the consumer, even producing sometimes some of their articles in their own workshops, buying at lowest prices because of their large orders and because they are in a position to profit from bargains, working with large sums, and selling to most of their customers for cash only, they can transmit these benefits in lowered selling prices. They can even decide to sell at a loss, as an advertisement or to get rid of out-of-date fashions. Taking 5–6 percent on 100 million brings them in more than 20 percent would bring to a firm doing a turnover of 50,000 francs.

The success of these department stores is only possible thanks to the volume of their business and this volume needs considerable capital and a very large turnover. Now capital, having become abundant, is freely combined nowadays in large enterprises, although French capital has the reputation of being more wary of the risks of industry than of State or railway securities. On the other hand, the large urban agglomerations, the ease with which goods can be transported by the railways, the diffusion of some comforts to strata below the middle classes, have all favored these developments.

As example we may cite some figures relating to these stores, since they were brought to the notice of the public in the *Revue des Deux-Mondes.* . . .

Le Louvre, dating to the time of the extension of the rue de Rivoli under the Second Empire, did in 1893 a business of 120 million at a profit of 6.4 percent. *Le Bon-Marché,* which was a small shop when Mr. Boucicaut entered it in 1852, already did a business of 20 million at the end of the Empire. During the republic its new buildings were erected; Mme. Boucicaut turned it by her will into a kind of cooperative society, with shares and an ingenious organization; turnover reached 150 million in 1893, leaving a profit of 5 percent. . . .

According to the tax records of 1891, these stores in Paris, numbering 12, employed 1,708 persons and were rated on their site values at 2,159,000 francs; the largest had then 542 employees. These same stores had, in 1901, 9,784 employees; one of them over 2,000 and another over 1,600; their site value has doubled (4,089,000 francs).

Q *Did the invention of department stores respond to or create the new "consumer ethic" in industrialized societies? What was the new turn-of-the-century ethic? According to Lavasseur, what were the positive effects of department stores for Parisian society?*

During this same period, **cartels** were being formed to decrease competition internally. In a cartel, independent enterprises worked together to control prices and fix production quotas, thereby restraining the kind of competition that led to reduced prices. Cartels were especially strong in Germany, where banks moved to protect their investments by eliminating the "anarchy of competition." German businesses established cartels in potash, coal, steel, and chemicals.

Larger Factories The formation of cartels was paralleled by a move toward ever-larger manufacturing plants, especially in the iron and steel, machinery, heavy electrical equipment, and chemical industries. Although evident in Britain, France, and Belgium, the trend was most pronounced in Germany. Between 1882 and 1907, the number of people working in German factories with over one thousand employees rose from 205,000 to 879,000. This growth in the size of industrial plants led to pressure for greater efficiency in factory production at the same time that competition led to demands for greater economy. The result was a desire to streamline or rationalize production as much as possible. One way to accomplish this was by cutting labor costs through the mechanization of transport within plants, such as using electric cranes to move materials. Even more important, the development of precision tools enabled manufacturers to produce interchangeable parts, which in turn led to the creation of the assembly line for production. First used in the United States for small arms and clocks, the assembly line had moved to Europe by 1850. In the second half of the nineteenth century, it was used primarily in manufacturing nonmilitary goods, such as sewing machines, typewriters, bicycles, and eventually automobiles. Principles of scientific management were also introduced by 1900 to maximize workers' efficiency.

New Patterns in an Industrial Economy

The Second Industrial Revolution played a role in the emergence of basic economic patterns that have characterized much of modern European economic life. Although the period after 1871 has been described as an age of material prosperity, recessions and crises were still very much a part of economic life. Although some historians question the appropriateness of characterizing the period from 1873 to 1895 as a great **depression**, Europeans did experience a series of economic crises during those years. Prices, especially those of agricultural products, fell dramatically. Slumps in the business cycle reduced profits, although recession occurred at different times in different countries. France and Britain, for example, sank into depression in the 1880s while Germany and the United States were recovering from their depression of the 1870s. From 1895 until World War I, however, Europe overall experienced an economic boom and achieved a level of prosperity that encouraged people later to look back to that era as *la belle époque*—a golden age in European civilization.

German Industrial Leadership   After 1870, Germany replaced Great Britain as the industrial leader of Europe. Within two decades, Germany's superiority was evident in new areas of manufacturing, such as organic chemicals and electrical equipment, and increasingly apparent in its ever-greater share of worldwide trade. Why had industrial leadership passed from Britain to Germany?

Britain's early lead in industrialization gave it an established industrial plant and made it more difficult to shift to the new techniques of the Second Industrial Revolution. As later entrants to the industrial age, the Germans could build the latest and most efficient industrial plants. British entrepreneurs made the situation worse by their tendency to be suspicious of innovations and their reluctance to invest in new plants and industries. As one manufacturer remarked, "One wants to be thoroughly convinced of the superiority of a new method before condemning as useless a large plant that has hitherto done good service."[1] German managers, by contrast, were accustomed to change, and the formation of large cartels encouraged German banks to provide enormous sums for investment. Then, too, unlike the Germans, the British were not willing to encourage formal scientific and technical education.

After 1870, the relationship of science and technology grew closer. Newer fields of industrial activity, such as organic chemistry and electrical engineering, required more scientific knowledge than the commonsense tinkering once employed by amateur inventors. Companies began to invest capital in laboratory equipment for their own research or hired scientific consultants for advice. Nowhere was the relationship between science and technology more apparent than in Germany. In 1899, German technical schools were allowed to award doctorate degrees, and by 1900, they were turning out three to four thousand graduates a year. Many of these graduates made their way into industrial firms.

European Economic Zones   The struggle for economic (and political) supremacy between Great Britain and Germany should not cause us to overlook the other great polarization of the age. By 1900, Europe was divided into two economic zones. Great Britain, Belgium, France, the Netherlands, Germany, the western part of the Austro-Hungarian Empire, and northern Italy constituted an advanced industrialized core that had a high standard of living, decent systems of transportation, and relatively healthy and educated populations (see Map 23.1). Another part of Europe, the backward and little industrialized area to the south and east, consisting of southern Italy, most of Austria-Hungary, Spain, Portugal, the Balkan kingdoms, and Russia, was still largely agricultural and relegated by the industrial countries to the function of providing food and raw materials. The presence of Romanian oil, Greek olive oil, and Serbian pigs and prunes in western Europe served as reminders of an economic division of Europe that continued well into the twentieth century.

The growth of an industrial economy also led to new patterns for European agriculture. An abundance of grain and lower transportation costs caused the prices of farm commodities to plummet. Some countries responded with tariff barriers against lower-priced foodstuffs. Where agricultural labor was scarce and hence expensive, as in Britain and Germany, landowners introduced machines for threshing and harvesting. The slump in grain prices also led some countries to specialize in other food products. Denmark, for example, exported eggs, butter, and cheese; sugar beets predominated in Bohemia and northern France; fruit in Mediterranean countries; and wine in Spain and Italy. This age also witnessed the introduction of chemical fertilizers. Large estates could make these adjustments easily, but individual small farmers could not afford them and formed farm cooperatives that provided capital for making improvements and purchasing equipment and fertilizer.

The Spread of Industrialization   After 1870, industrialization began to spread beyond western and central Europe and North America. Especially noticeable was its rapid development in Russia (see Chapter 24) and Japan. In Japan, the imperial government took the lead in promoting industry. The government financed industries, built railroads, brought foreign experts to train Japanese employees in new industrial techniques,

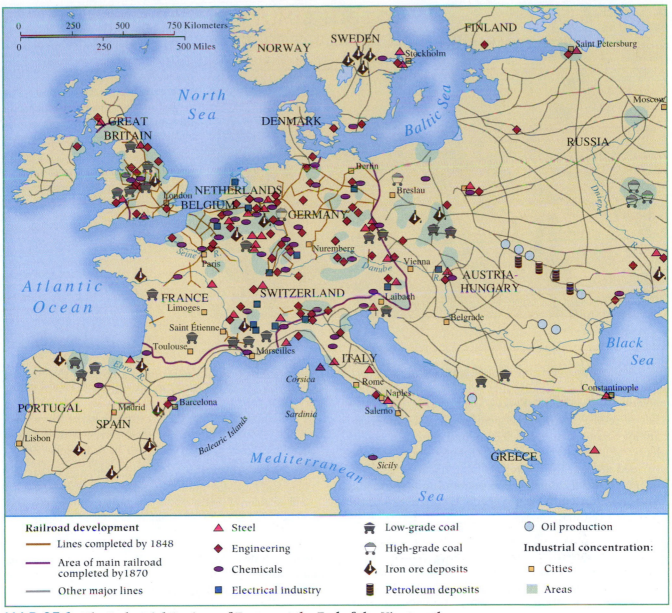

Railroad development
— Lines completed by 1848
— Area of main railroad completed by 1870
— Other major lines

▲ Steel
◆ Engineering
⬭ Chemicals
◼ Electrical industry

⛏ Low-grade coal
⛏ High-grade coal
⬥ Iron ore deposits
⬛ Petroleum deposits

◯ Oil production
Industrial concentration:
▢ Cities
▨ Areas

MAP 23.1 **The Industrial Regions of Europe at the End of the Nineteenth Century.** By the end of the nineteenth century, the Second Industrial Revolution—in steelmaking, electricity, petroleum, and chemicals—had spurred substantial economic growth and prosperity in western and central Europe; it also sparked economic and political competition between Great Britain and Germany.

Q Look back at Map 20.2. What parts of Europe not industrialized in 1850 had become industrialized in the ensuing decades? 🌐 **View an animated version of this map or related maps at** academic.cengage.com/history/spielvogel

and instituted a universal educational system based on applied science. By the end of the nineteenth century, Japan had developed key industries in tea, silk, armaments, and shipbuilding. Workers for these industries came from the large number of people who had abandoned their farms due to severe hardships in the countryside and fled to the cities, where they provided an abundant source of cheap labor.

As in Europe during the early decades of the Industrial Revolution, workers toiled for long hours in the coal mines and textile mills, often under horrendous conditions. Reportedly, coal miners employed on a small island in Nagasaki harbor worked naked in temperatures up to 130 degrees Fahrenheit. If they tried to escape, they were shot.

A World Economy The economic developments of the late nineteenth century, combined with the transportation revolution that saw the growth of marine transport and railroads, also fostered a true world economy. By 1900, Europeans were importing beef and wool from Argentina and Australia, coffee from Brazil, nitrates

The Art Archive/Private Collection/Laurie Platt Winfrey

A Textile Factory in Japan. The development of the factory forced workers to adjust to a new system of discipline in which they worked regular hours under close supervision. Shown here is one of the earliest industrial factories in Japan, the Tomioka silk factory, built in the 1870s. As can be seen by comparing this illustration to the one on p. 610, in Chapter 20, although women are doing the work in both factories, the managers are men.

from Chile, iron ore from Algeria, and sugar from Java. European capital was also invested abroad to develop railways, mines, electrical power plants, and banks. High rates of return, such as 11.3 percent on Latin American banking shares that were floated in London, provided plenty of incentive. Of course, foreign countries also provided markets for the surplus manufactured goods of Europe. With its capital, industries, and military might, Europe dominated the world economy by the end of the nineteenth century.

Women and Work: New Job Opportunities

The Second Industrial Revolution had an enormous impact on the position of women in the labor market. During the course of the nineteenth century, considerable controversy erupted over a woman's "right to work." Working-class organizations tended to reinforce the underlying ideology of domesticity: women should remain at home to bear and nurture children and should not be allowed in the industrial workforce. Working-class men argued that keeping women out of industrial work would ensure the moral and physical well-being of families. In reality, keeping women out of the industrial workforce simply made it easier to exploit them when they needed income to supplement their husbands' wages or to support their families when their husbands were unemployed. The desperate need to work at times forced women to do marginal work at home or labor as pieceworkers in sweatshops. "Sweating" referred to the subcontracting of piecework usually, but not exclusively, in the tailoring trades; it was done at home since it required few skills or equipment. Pieceworkers were poorly paid and worked long hours. The poorest-paid jobs for the cheapest goods were called "slop work."

In this description of the room of a London slopper, we see how precarious her position was:

> I then directed my steps to the neighborhood of Drury-lane, to see a poor woman who lived in an attic on one of the closest courts in that quarter. On the table was a quarter of an ounce of tea. Observing my eye to rest upon it, she told me it was all she took. "Sugar," she said, "I broke myself of long ago; I couldn't afford it. A cup of tea, a piece of bread, and an onion is generally all I have for my dinner, and sometimes I haven't even an onion, and then I sops my bread."[2]

Often excluded from factories and in need of income, many women had no choice but to work for the pitiful wages of the sweated industries.

White-Collar Jobs After 1870, however, new job opportunities for women became available. Although the growth of heavy industry in the mining, metallurgy, engineering, chemicals, and electrical sectors meant fewer jobs for women in manufacturing, the development of larger industrial plants and the expansion of government services created a large number of service or white-collar jobs. The increased demand for white-collar workers at relatively low wages, coupled with a shortage of male workers, led employers to hire women. Big businesses and retail shops needed clerks, typists, secretaries, file clerks, and salesclerks. The expansion of government services created opportunities for women to be secretaries and telephone operators and to take jobs in health and social services. Compulsory education necessitated more teachers, and the development of modern hospital services opened the way for an increase in nurses. Many of the new white-collar jobs were unexciting. The work was routine and, except for teaching and

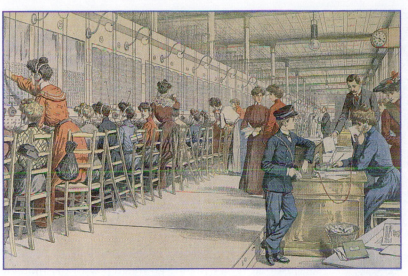

New Jobs for Women: The Telephone Exchange. The invention of the telephone in 1876 soon led to its widespread use. As is evident from this illustration of a telephone exchange in Paris in 1904, most of the telephone operators were women. This was but one of a number of new job opportunities for women created by the Second Industrial Revolution.

nursing, required few skills beyond basic literacy. Although there was little hope for advancement, these jobs had distinct advantages for the daughters of the middle classes and especially the upward-aspiring working classes. For some middle-class women, the new jobs offered freedom from the domestic patterns expected of them. Nevertheless, because middle-class women did not receive an education comparable to that of men, the careers they could pursue were limited. Thus, they found it easier to fill the jobs at the lower end of middle-class occupations, such as teaching and civil service jobs, especially in the postal service.

Most of the new white-collar jobs, however, were filled by working-class women who saw them as an opportunity to escape from the "dirty" work of the lower-class world. Studies in France and Britain indicate that the increase in white-collar jobs did not lead to a rise in the size of the female labor force, but resulted only in a shift from industrial jobs to the white-collar sector of the economy.

Prostitution Despite the new job opportunities, many lower-class women were forced to become prostitutes to survive. The rural, working-class girls who flocked into the cities in search of new opportunities were often naive and vulnerable. Employment was unstable, and wages were low. No longer protected by family or village community and church, some girls faced only one grim alternative—prostitution. In Paris, London, and many other large cities with transient populations, thousands of prostitutes plied their trade. One journalist estimated that there were 60,000 prostitutes in London in 1885. Most prostitutes were active for only a short time, usually from their late teens through their early twenties. Many eventually rejoined the regular workforce or married when they could.

In most European countries, prostitution was licensed and regulated by government and municipal authorities. Although the British government provided minimal regulation of prostitution, it did attempt to

enforce the Contagious Diseases Acts in the 1870s and 1880s by giving authorities the right to examine prostitutes for venereal disease. Prostitutes found to be infected were confined for some time to special institutions called lock hospitals, where they were given moral instruction. But opposition to the Contagious Diseases Acts soon arose from middle-class female reformers. Their leader was Josephine Butler (1828–1906), who objected to laws that punished women but not men who suffered from venereal disease. Known as the "shrieking sisters" because they discussed sexual matters in public, Butler and her fellow reformers were successful in gaining the repeal of the acts in 1886.

Organizing the Working Classes

In the first half of the nineteenth century, many workers had formed trade unions that had functioned primarily as mutual aid societies (see Chapter 20). In return for a small weekly payment, benefits were provided to assist unemployed workers. In the late nineteenth century, the desire to improve their working and living conditions led many industrial workers to form political parties and labor unions, often based on the ideas of Karl Marx (see Chapter 22). One of the most important of the working-class or socialist parties was formed in Germany in 1875.

Socialist Parties Under the direction of its two Marxist leaders, Wilhelm Liebknecht (1826–1900) and August Bebel (1840–1913), the German Social Democratic Party (SPD) espoused revolutionary Marxist rhetoric while organizing itself as a mass political party competing in elections for the Reichstag (the German parliament). Once in the Reichstag, SPD delegates worked to enact legislation to improve the condition of the working class. As August Bebel explained, "Pure negation would not be accepted by the voters. The masses demand that something should be done for today irrespective of what will happen on the morrow."[3] Despite government efforts to destroy it (see "Central and Eastern Europe: Persistence of

"Proletarians of the World, Unite." To improve their working and living conditions, many industrial workers, inspired by the ideas of Karl Marx, joined working-class or socialist parties. Pictured here is a socialist-sponsored poster that proclaims in German the closing words of *The Communist Manifesto:* "Proletarians of the World, Unite!"

the Old Order" later in this chapter), the SPD continued to grow. In 1890, it received 1.5 million votes and thirty-five seats in the Reichstag. When it received 4 million votes in the 1912 elections, it became the largest single party in Germany.

Socialist parties also emerged in other European states, although none proved as successful as the German Social Democrats. France had a variety of socialist parties, including a Marxist one. The leader of French socialism, Jean Jaurès (1859–1914), was an independent socialist who looked to the French revolutionary tradition rather than Marxism to justify revolutionary socialism. In 1905, the French socialist parties succeeded in unifying themselves into a single, mostly Marxist-oriented socialist party. Social democratic parties on the German model were founded in Belgium, Austria, Hungary, Bulgaria, Poland, Romania, and the Netherlands before 1900. The Marxist Social Democratic Labor Party had been organized in Russia by 1898.

As the socialist parties grew, agitation for an international organization that would strengthen their position against international capitalism also grew. In 1889, leaders of the various socialist parties formed the Second International, which was organized as a loose association of national groups. Although the Second International took some coordinated actions—May Day (May 1), for example, was made an international labor day to be marked by strikes and mass labor demonstrations—differences often wreaked havoc at the organization's congresses. Two issues proved particularly divisive: revisionism and nationalism.

Evolutionary Socialism Some Marxists believed in a pure **Marxism** that accepted the imminent collapse of capitalism and the need for socialist ownership of the means of production. The guiding light of the German Social Democrats, August Bebel, confided to another socialist that "every night I go to sleep with the thought that the last hour of bourgeois society strikes soon." Earlier, Bebel had said, "I am convinced that the fulfillment of our aims is so close, that there are few in this hall who will not live to see the day."[4] But a severe challenge to this orthodox Marxist position arose in the form of **evolutionary socialism,** also known as **revisionism.**

Most prominent among the evolutionary socialists was Eduard Bernstein (1850–1932), a member of the German Social Democratic Party who had spent years in exile in Britain, where he had been influenced by moderate English socialism and the British parliamentary system. In 1899, Bernstein challenged Marxist orthodoxy with a book titled *Evolutionary Socialism* in which he argued that some of Marx's ideas had turned out to be quite wrong (see the box on p. 707). The capitalist system had not broken down, said Bernstein. Contrary to Marx's assertion, the middle class was actually expanding, not declining. At the same time, the proletariat was not sinking further down; instead, its position was improving as workers experienced a higher standard of living. In the face of this reality, Bernstein discarded Marx's emphasis on class struggle and revolution. The workers, he asserted, must continue to organize in mass political parties and even work together with the other advanced elements in a nation to bring about change. With the extension of the right to vote, workers were in a better position than ever to achieve their aims through democratic channels. Evolution by democratic means, not revolution, would achieve the desired goal of socialism. German and French socialist leaders, as well as the Second International, condemned evolutionary socialism as heresy and opportunism. But many socialist parties, including the German Social Democrats, while spouting revolutionary slogans, followed Bernstein's revisionist, gradualist approach.

The Problem of Nationalism A second divisive issue for international socialism was nationalism. Marx and Engels had said that "the working men have no country" and that "national differences and antagonisms between peoples are daily more and more vanishing, owing to the

The Voice of Evolutionary Socialism: Eduard Bernstein

The German Marxist Eduard Bernstein was regarded as the foremost late-nineteenth-century theorist of Marxist revisionism. In his book *Evolutionary Socialism*, Bernstein argued that Marx had made some fundamental mistakes and that socialists needed to stress cooperation and evolution rather than class conflict and revolution.

Eduard Bernstein, *Evolutionary Socialism*

It has been maintained in a certain quarter that the practical deductions from my treatises would be the abandonment of the conquest of political power by the proletariat organized politically and economically. That is quite an arbitrary deduction, the accuracy of which I altogether deny.

I set myself against the notion that we have to expect shortly a collapse of the bourgeois economy, and that social democracy should be induced by the prospect of such an imminent, great, social catastrophe to adapt its tactics to that assumption. That I maintain most emphatically.

The adherents of this theory of a catastrophe base it especially on the conclusions of the *Communist Manifesto*. This is a mistake in every respect.

The theory which the *Communist Manifesto* sets forth of the evolution of modern society was correct as far as it characterized the general tendencies of that evolution. But it was mistaken in several special deductions, above all in the estimate of the time the evolution would take.... But it is evident that if social evolution takes a much greater period of time than was assumed, it must also take upon itself forms and lead to forms that were not foreseen and could not be foreseen then.

Social conditions have not developed to such an acute opposition of things and classes as is depicted in the *Manifesto*. It is not only useless, it is the greatest folly to attempt to conceal this from ourselves. The number of members of the possessing classes is today not smaller but larger. The enormous increase of social wealth is not accompanied by a decreasing number of large capitalists but by an increasing number of capitalists of all degrees. The middle classes change their character but they do not disappear from the social scale....

In all advanced countries we see the privileges of the capitalist bourgeoisie yielding step by step to democratic organizations. Under the influence of this, and driven by the movement of the working classes which is daily becoming stronger, a social reaction has set in against the exploiting tendencies of capital, a counteraction which, although it still proceeds timidly and feebly, yet does exist, and is always drawing more departments of economic life under its influence. Factory legislation, the democratizing of local government, and the extension of its area of work, the freeing of trade unions and systems of cooperative trading from legal restrictions, the consideration of standard conditions of labor in the work undertaken by public authorities—all these characterize this phase of the evolution.

But the more the political organizations of modern nations are democratized the more the needs and opportunities of great political catastrophes are diminished.... But is the conquest of political power by the proletariat simply to be by a political catastrophe? Is it to be the appropriation and utilization of the power of the State by the proletariat exclusively against the whole non-proletarian world?...

No one has questioned the necessity for the working classes to gain the control of government. The point at issue is between the theory of a social cataclysm and the question whether, with the given social development in Germany and the present advanced state of its working classes in the towns and the country, a sudden catastrophe would be desirable in the interest of the social democracy. I have denied it and deny it again, because in my judgment a greater security for lasting success lies in a steady advance than in the possibilities offered by a catastrophic crash.

Q *Based on this document, how would you define evolutionary socialism? What broader forces in nineteenth-century European society came together to promote this type of political thinking?*

---

development of the bourgeoisie."[5] They proved drastically wrong. Congresses of the Second International passed resolutions in 1907 and 1910 advocating joint action by workers of different countries to avert war but provided no real machinery to implement the resolutions. In truth, socialist parties varied from country to country and remained tied to national concerns and issues. Socialist leaders always worried that in the end, national loyalties might outweigh class loyalties among the masses. When World War I came in 1914, not only the working-class masses but even many of their socialist party leaders supported the war efforts of their national governments. Nationalism had proved a much more powerful force than socialism.

The Role of Trade Unions   Workers also formed trade unions to improve their working conditions. Attempts to organize the workers did not come until after unions had won the right to strike in the 1870s. Strikes proved necessary to achieve the workers' goals. A walkout by female workers in the match industry in 1888 and by dockworkers in London the following year led to the establishment of trade union organizations for both groups. By 1900, 2 million workers were enrolled in British unions, and by the outbreak of World War I, this number had risen to between 3 million and 4 million, although this was still less than one-fifth of the total workforce.

Trade unions failed to develop as quickly on the Continent as they had in Britain. In France, the union movement was from the beginning closely tied to socialist ideology. As there were a number of French socialist parties, the socialist trade unions remained badly splintered. Not until 1895 did French unions create a national organization called the General Confederation of Labor. Its decentralization and failure to include some of the more important individual unions, however, kept it weak and ineffective.

German trade unions, also closely attached to political parties, were first formed in the 1860s. Although there were liberal trade unions comprising skilled artisans and Catholic or Christian trade unions, the largest German trade unions were those of the socialists. By 1899, even the latter had accepted the practice of collective bargaining with employers. As strikes and collective bargaining achieved successes, German workers were increasingly inclined to forgo revolution for gradual improvements. By 1914, its 3 million members made the German trade union movement the second largest in Europe, after Great Britain's. Almost 85 percent of these 3 million belonged to socialist unions. Trade unions in the rest of Europe had varying degrees of success, but by the beginning of World War I, they had made considerable progress in bettering both the living and the working conditions of the laboring classes.

The Anarchist Alternative Despite the revolutionary rhetoric, socialist parties and trade unions gradually became less radical in pursuing their goals. Indeed, this lack of revolutionary fervor drove some people from Marxist socialism into **anarchism,** a movement that was especially prominent in less industrialized and less democratic countries.

Initially, anarchism was not a violent movement. Early anarchists believed that people were inherently good but had been corrupted by the state and society. True freedom could be achieved only by abolishing the state and all existing social institutions. In the second half of the nineteenth century, however, anarchists in Spain, Portugal, Italy, and Russia began to advocate using radical means to accomplish this goal. The Russian Michael Bakunin (1814–1876), for example, believed that small groups of well-trained, fanatical revolutionaries could perpetrate so much violence that the state and all its institutions would disintegrate. To revolutionary anarchists, that would usher in the anarchist golden age. The Russian anarchist Lev Aleshker wrote shortly before his execution:

Slavery, poverty, weakness, and ignorance—the external fetters of man—will be broken. Man will be at the center of nature. The earth and its products will serve everyone dutifully.

Weapons will cease to be a measure of strength and gold a measure of wealth; the strong will be those who are bold and daring in the conquest of nature, and riches will be the things that are useful. Such a world is called "Anarchy." It will have no castles, no place for masters and slaves. Life will be open to all. Everyone will take what he needs—this is the anarchist ideal. And when it comes about, men will live wisely and well. The masses must take part in the construction of this paradise on earth.[6]

After Bakunin's death in 1876, anarchist revolutionaries used assassination as their primary instrument of terror. The list of victims of anarchist assassins at the turn of the century included a Russian tsar (1881), a president of the French Republic (1894), the king of Italy (1900), and a president of the United States (1901). Despite anarchist hopes, these states did not collapse.

The Emergence of a Mass Society

Q **Focus Questions:** What is a mass society, and what were its main characteristics? What role were women expected to play in society and family life in the latter half of the nineteenth century, and how closely did patterns of family life correspond to this ideal?

The new patterns of industrial production, mass consumption, and working-class organization that we identify with the Second Industrial Revolution were only one aspect of the new **mass society** that emerged in Europe after 1870. A larger and vastly improved urban environment, new patterns of social structure, gender issues, mass education, and mass leisure were also important features of European society.

Population Growth

The European population increased dramatically between 1850 and 1910, rising from 270 million to over 460 million by 1910 (see Table 23.1). Between 1850 and 1880, the main cause of the population increase was a rising birthrate, at least in western Europe, but after 1880, a noticeable decline in death rates largely explains the increase in population. Although the causes of this decline have been debated, two major factors—medical discoveries and environmental conditions—stand out. Some historians have stressed the importance of developments in medical science. Smallpox vaccinations, for example, were compulsory in many European countries by the mid-1850s. More important were improvements in the urban environment in the second half of the nineteenth century that greatly reduced fatalities from such diseases as diarrhea, dysentery, typhoid fever, and cholera, which had been spread through contaminated water supplies and improper elimination of sewage. Improved nutrition also made a significant difference in the health of the

TABLE 23.1 European Populations, 1851–1911 (in thousands)

	1851	1881	1911
England and Wales	17,928	25,974	36,070
Scotland	2,889	3,736	4,761
Ireland	6,552	5,175	4,390
France	35,783	37,406	39,192
Germany	33,413	45,234	64,926
Belgium	4,530	5,520	7,424
Netherlands	3,309	4,013	5,858
Denmark	1,415	1,969	2,757
Norway	1,490	1,819	2,392
Sweden	3,471	4,169	5,522
Spain	15,455	16,622	19,927
Portugal	3,844	4,551	5,958
Italy	24,351	28,460	34,671
Switzerland	2,393	2,846	3,753
Austria	17,535	22,144	28,572
Hungary	18,192	15,739	20,886
Russia	68,500	97,700	160,700
Romania	—	4,600	7,000
Bulgaria	—	2,800	4,338
Greece	—	1,679	2,632
Serbia	—	1,700	2,912

SOURCE: Data from B. R. Mitchell, *European Historical Statistics, 1750–1970* (New York, 1975).

population. The increase in agricultural productivity combined with improvements in transportation facilitated the shipment of food supplies from areas of surplus to regions with poor harvests. Better nutrition and food hygiene were especially instrumental in the decline in infant mortality by 1900. The pasteurization of milk reduced intestinal disorders that had been a major cause of infant deaths.

Emigration

Although growing agricultural and industrial prosperity supported an increase in the European population, it could not do so indefinitely, especially in areas that had little industrialization and severe rural overpopulation. Some of the excess labor from underdeveloped areas migrated to the industrial regions of Europe (see Map 23.2). By 1913, more than 400,000 Poles were working in the heavily industrialized Ruhr region of western Germany, and thousands of Italian laborers had migrated to France. The industrialized regions of Europe, however, were not able to absorb the entire surplus population of heavily agricultural regions like southern Italy, Spain, Hungary, and Romania, where the land could not support the growing numbers of people. The booming economies of North America after 1898 and cheap shipping fares after 1900 led to mass emigration from southern and eastern Europe to North America at the beginning of the twentieth century. In 1880, about 500,000 people left Europe each year on average; between 1906 and 1910, annual departures increased to 1.3 million, many of them from southern and eastern Europe. Altogether, between 1846 and 1932, probably 60 million Europeans left Europe, half of them bound for the United States and most of the rest for Canada or Latin America (see Table 23.2).

It was not only economic motives that caused people to leave eastern Europe. Migrants from Austria and Hungary, for example, were not the dominant nationalities, the Germans and Magyars, but mostly their oppressed minorities, such as Poles, Slovaks, Serbs, Croats, Romanians, and Jews. Between 1880 and 1914, some 3.5 million Poles from Russia, Austria, and Germany went to the United States. Jews, who were severely persecuted, constituted 40 percent of the Russian emigrants to the United States between 1900 and 1913 and almost

TABLE 23.2 European Emigration, 1876–1910 (Average Annual Emigration to Non-European Countries per 100,000 Population)

	1876–1880	1881–1885	1886–1890	1891–1895	1896–1900	1901–1905	1906–1910
Europe	94	196	213	185	147	271	322
Ireland	650	1,422	1,322	988	759	743	662
Great Britain	102	174	162	119	88	127	172
Denmark	157	380	401	338	117	292	275
Norway	432	1,105	819	597	312	903	746
Sweden	301	705	759	587	249	496	347
Germany	108	379	207	163	47	50	44
Belgium	—	—	86	50	23	57	69
Netherlands	32	136	111	76	25	45	58
France	8	14	49	14	13	12	12
Spain	—	280	437	434	446	391	758
Portugal	258	356	423	609	417	464	694
Italy	396	542	754	842	974	1,706	1,938
Austria	48	90	114	182	182	355	469
Hungary	—	92	156	134	205	437	616
Russia	6	13	42	47	32	63	67

SOURCE: Robert Gildea, *Barricades and Borders: Europe, 1800–1914* (Oxford, 1987), p. 283.

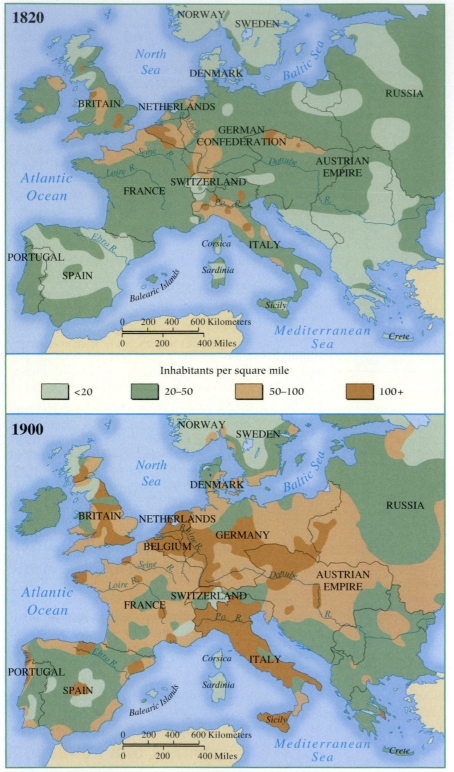

MAP 23.2 Population Growth in Europe, 1820–1900. European population increased steadily throughout the nineteenth century. Advances in medical science, hygiene, nutrition, living conditions, and standards of living help account for the population increase, even though emigration to the United States, South America, and other regions reduced the total growth numbers.

Q Which regions experienced the greatest population growth between 1820 and 1900, and how can you account for this? 🌐 **View an animated version of this map or related maps at** academic.cengage.com/history/spielvogel

12 percent of all emigrants to the United States during the first five years of the twentieth century.

Transformation of the Urban Environment

One of the most important consequences of industrialization and the population explosion of the nineteenth century was urbanization. In the course of the nineteenth century, urban dwellers came to make up an ever-increasing percentage of the European population. In 1800, they constituted 40 percent of the population in Britain, 25 percent in France and Germany, and only 10 percent in eastern Europe. By 1914, urban inhabitants had increased to 80 percent of the population in Britain, 45 percent in France, 60 percent in Germany, and 30 percent in eastern Europe. The size of cities also expanded dramatically, especially in industrialized countries. In 1800, there were 21 European cities with populations over 100,000; by 1900, there were 147. Between 1800 and 1900, London's population grew from 960,000 to 6.5 million and Berlin's from 172,000 to 2.7 million.

Urban populations grew faster than the general population primarily because of the vast migration from rural areas to cities. People were driven from the countryside to the cities by sheer economic necessity—unemployment, land hunger, and physical want. Urban centers offered something positive as well, usually mass employment in factories and later in service trades and professions. But cities also grew faster in the second half of the nineteenth century because health and living conditions in them were improving.

Improving Living Conditions In the 1840s, a number of urban reformers, such as Edwin Chadwick in Britain (see Chapter 20) and Rudolf Virchow and Solomon Neumann in Germany, had pointed to filthy living conditions as the primary cause

The Emigrants. In this painting done in 1880, C. J. Staniland presented a sentimental image of the scene faced by the tens of millions of Europeans who migrated to other parts of the world, especially the United States, Canada, and Latin America. Shown in the painting are people boarding a ship, saying farewell to family members and loved ones they might never see again. Ships were often crowded, making conditions uncomfortable during the journey.

of epidemic disease and urged sanitary reforms to correct the problem. Soon legislative acts created boards of health that brought governmental action to bear on public heath issues. Urban medical officers and building inspectors were authorized to inspect dwellings for public health hazards. New building regulations made it more difficult for private contractors to build shoddy housing. The Public Health Act of 1875 in Britain, for example, prohibited the construction of new buildings without running water and an internal drainage system. For the first time in Western history, the role of municipal governments had been expanded to include detailed regulations for the improvement of the living conditions of urban dwellers.

Essential to the public health of the modern European city was the ability to bring clean water into the city and to expel sewage from it. The accomplishment of those two tasks was a major engineering feat in the second half of the nineteenth century. The problem of fresh water was solved by a system of dams and reservoirs that stored the water and aqueducts and tunnels that carried it from the countryside to the city and into individual dwellings. Regular private baths became accessible to more people as gas heaters in the 1860s and later electric heaters made hot baths possible. The shower had appeared by the 1880s.

The treatment of wastewater was improved by building mammoth underground pipes that carried raw sewage far from the city for disposal. In the late 1860s, a number of German cities began to construct sewer systems. Frankfurt began its program after a lengthy public campaign enlivened by the slogan "From the toilet to the river in half an hour." London devised a system of five enormous sewers that discharged their loads 12 miles from the city, where the waste was chemically treated. Unfortunately, in many places, new underground sewers simply discharged their raw sewage into what soon became highly polluted lakes and rivers. Nevertheless, the development of pure water and sewerage systems dramatically improved the public health of European cities.

Housing Needs Middle-class reformers who denounced the unsanitary living conditions of the working classes also focused on their housing needs. Overcrowded, disease-ridden slums were viewed as dangerous not only to physical health but also to the political and moral health of the entire nation. V. A. Huber, the foremost early German housing reformer, wrote in 1861, "Certainly it would not be too much to say that the home is the communal embodiment of family life. Thus the purity of the dwelling is almost as important for the family as is the cleanliness of the body for the individual."[7] To Huber, good housing was a prerequisite for a stable family life and hence a stable society.

Early efforts to attack the housing problem emphasized the middle-class, liberal belief in the efficacy of private enterprise. Reformers such as Huber believed that the construction of model dwellings renting at a reasonable price would force other private landlords to elevate their housing standards. A fine example of this approach was the work of Octavia Hill, granddaughter of a celebrated social reformer (see the box on p. 713). With the financial assistance of a friend, she rehabilitated some old dwellings and constructed new ones to create housing for 3,500 tenants.

Other wealthy reformer-philanthropists took a different approach to the housing problem. In 1887, Lord Leverhulme began construction of a model village called Port Sunlight outside Liverpool for the workers at his soap factory. Port Sunlight offered pleasant living conditions in the belief that good housing would ensure a healthy and happy workforce. Yet another approach was the garden city. At the end of the nineteenth century,

Topical Press Agency/Getty Images

Working-Class Housing in London. Although urban workers experienced some improvements in the material conditions of their lives after 1871, working-class housing remained drab and depressing. This 1912 photograph of working-class housing in the East End of London shows rows of similar-looking buildings on treeless streets. Most often, these buildings had no yards or green areas.

Ebenezer Howard founded the British garden city movement, which advocated the construction of new towns separated from each other by open country that would provide the recreational areas, fresh air, and sense of community that would encourage healthy family life. Letchward Garden City, started in 1903, was the first concrete result of Howard's theory.

As the number and size of cities continued to mushroom, by the 1880s governments came to the conclusion—reluctantly—that private enterprise could not solve the housing crisis. In 1890, a British law empowered local town councils to collect new taxes and construct cheap housing for the working classes. London and Liverpool were the first communities to take advantage of their new powers. Similar activity had been set in motion in Germany by 1900. In 1894, the French government took a lesser step by providing easy credit for private contractors to build working-class housing. Everywhere, however, these lukewarm measures failed to do much to meet the real housing needs of the working classes. In Britain, for example, only 5 percent of all dwellings erected between 1890 and 1914 were constructed by municipalities under the Housing Act of 1890. Nevertheless, by the start of World War I, the need for planning had been recognized, and after the war, municipal governments moved into housing construction on a large scale. In housing, as in so many other areas of life in the late nineteenth century, the liberal principle that the government that governs least governs best had simply proved untrue. More and more, governments were stepping into areas of activity that they would never have touched earlier.

Redesigning the Cities Housing was but one area of urban reconstruction after 1870. As urban populations expanded in the nineteenth century, the older layout,

confining the city to a compact area enclosed by defensive walls, seemed restrictive and utterly useless. In the second half of the nineteenth century, many of the old defensive walls—worthless anyway from a military standpoint—were pulled down, and the areas were converted into parks and boulevards. In Vienna, for example, the great boulevards of the Ringstrasse replaced the old medieval walls. While the broad streets served a military purpose—the rapid deployment of troops to crush civil disturbances—they also offered magnificent views of the city hall, the university, and the parliament building, all powerful symbols of middle-class social values.

Like Vienna, many European urban centers were redesigned during the second half of the nineteenth century. The reconstruction of Paris after 1850 by Emperor Napoleon III was perhaps the most famous project and provided a model for other urban centers. The old residential districts in the central city, many of them working-class slums, were demolished and replaced with town halls, government office buildings, retail stores including the new department stores, museums, cafés, and theaters, all of which provided for the shopping and recreational pleasures of the middle classes.

As cities expanded and entire groups of people were displaced from urban centers by reconstruction, city populations spilled over into the neighboring villages and countrysides, which were soon incorporated into the cities. The construction of streetcar and commuter train lines by the turn of the century enabled both working-class and middle-class populations to live in their own suburban neighborhoods far removed from their places of work. Cheap, modern transportation essentially separated home and work for many Europeans.

Senator shall ha...
Immediately after they sh...
...tors of the first Class shall be vacated...
...the ninth Year; so that one third m...
...the Executive thereof may make...
...attained to the Age of thirty Years,
...be chosen...
...shall have no vote, unless they be e...
...ence of the Vice President; or when...
...on Oath or Affirmation. When th...
...members present...
...any Office of honor...

THE HOUSING VENTURE OF OCTAVIA HILL

Octavia Hill was a practical-minded British housing reformer who believed that workers and their families were entitled to happy homes. At the same time, she was convinced that the poor needed guidance and encouragement, not charity. In this selection, she describes her housing venture.

Octavia Hill, *Homes of the London Poor*

About four years ago I was put in possession of three houses in one of the worst courts of Marylebone. Six other houses were bought subsequently. All were crowded with inmates.

The first thing to be done was to put them in decent tenantable order. The set last purchased was a row of cottages facing a bit of desolate ground, occupied with wretched, dilapidated cow-sheds, manure heaps, old timber, and rubbish of every description. The houses were in a most deplorable condition—the plaster was dropping from the walls; on one staircase a pail was placed to catch the rain that fell through the roof. All the staircases were perfectly dark; the banisters were gone, having been burnt as firewood by tenants. The grates, with large holes in them, were falling forward into the rooms. The wash-house, full of lumber belonging to the landlord, was locked up; thus the inhabitants had to wash clothes, as well as to cook, eat and sleep in their small rooms. The dustbin, standing in the front part of the houses, was accessible to the whole neighborhood, and boys often dragged from it quantities of unseemly objects and spread them over the court. The state of the drainage was in keeping with everything else. The pavement of the back-yard was all broken up, and great puddles stood in it, so that the damp crept up the outer walls....

As soon as I entered into possession, each family had an opportunity of doing better: those who would not pay, or who led clearly immoral lives, were ejected. The rooms they vacated were cleansed; the tenants who showed signs of improvement moved into them, and thus, in turn, an opportunity was obtained for having each room distempered [painted] and papered. The drains were put in order, a large slate cistern was fixed, the wash-house was cleared of its lumber, and thrown open on stated days to each tenant in turn. The roof, the plaster, the woodwork were repaired; the staircase walls were distempered; new grates were fixed; the layers of paper and rag (black with age) were torn from the windows, and glass put in; out of 192 panes only eight were found unbroken. The yard and foot-path were paved.

The rooms, as a rule, were re-let at the same prices at which they had been let before; but tenants with large families were counseled to take two rooms, and for these much less was charged than if let singly: this plan I continue to pursue. In-coming tenants are not allowed to take a decidedly insufficient quantity of room, and no sub-letting is permitted....

The pecuniary result has been very satisfactory. Five percent has been paid on all the capital invested. A fund for the repayment of capital is accumulating. A liberal allowance has been made for repairs....

My tenants are mostly of a class far below that of mechanics. They are, indeed, of the very poor. And yet, although the gifts they have received have been next to nothing, none of the families who have passed under my care during the whole four years have continued in what is called "distress," except such as have been unwilling to exert themselves. Those who will not exert the necessary self-control cannot avail themselves of the means of livelihood held out to them. But, for those who are willing, some small assistance in the form of work has, from time to time, been provided—not much, but sufficient to keep them from want or despair.

Q *Did Octavia Hill's housing venture generate financial returns on her initial investment? What benefits did her tenants receive in turn? What feelings and beliefs about the lower classes are evident in Hill's account?*

Social Structure of the Mass Society

Historians generally agree that after 1871, the average person enjoyed an improving standard of living. The real wages of British workers, for example, probably doubled between 1871 and 1910. We should not allow this increase in the standard of living to mislead us, however. Great poverty did remain in Western society, and the gap between rich and poor was enormous. There were many different groups of varying wealth between the small group of the elite at the top and the large number of very poor at the bottom.

The Upper Classes At the top of European society stood a wealthy elite, constituting only 5 percent of the population but controlling between 30 and 40 percent of its wealth. In the course of the nineteenth century, aristocrats coalesced with the most successful industrialists, bankers, and merchants to form this new elite. Big business had produced this group of wealthy **plutocrats,** while aristocrats, whose income from landed estates declined, invested in railway shares, public utilities, government bonds, and businesses, sometimes on their own estates. Gradually, the greatest fortunes shifted into the hands of the upper middle class. In Great Britain, for example, landed aristocrats constituted 73 percent of the country's millionaires at midcentury, while commercial and financial magnates made up 14 percent. By the period 1900–1914, landowners had declined to 27 percent. The wealthiest person in Germany was not an aristocrat but Bertha Krupp, granddaughter of Alfred Krupp and heiress to the business dynasty left by her father Friedrich, who committed suicide in 1902.

Increasingly, aristocrats and plutocrats fused as the wealthy upper middle class purchased landed estates to join the aristocrats in the pleasures of country living and the aristocrats bought lavish town houses for part-time urban life. Common bonds were also forged when the sons of wealthy middle-class families were admitted to the elite schools dominated by the children of the aristocracy. At Oxford, the landed upper class made up 40 percent of the student body in 1870 but only 15 percent in 1910, while undergraduates from business families went from 7 to 21 percent during the same period. This educated elite, whether aristocratic or middle class in background, assumed leadership roles in government bureaucracies and military hierarchies. Marriage also served to unite the two groups. Daughters of tycoons acquired titles, while aristocratic heirs gained new sources of cash. Wealthy American heiresses were in special demand. When Consuelo Vanderbilt married the duke of Marlborough, the new duchess brought £2 million (approximately $10 million) to her husband.

It would be misleading, however, to assume that the alliance of the wealthy business elite and traditional aristocrats was always harmonious. In Germany, class lines were sometimes strictly drawn, especially if they were complicated by anti-Semitism. Albert Ballin, the wealthy director of the Hamburg-Amerika luxury liners, may have been close to Emperor William II, who entertained him on a regular basis, but the Prussian aristocracy snubbed Ballin because of his Jewish origins. Although the upper middle class was allowed into the bureaucracy of the German Empire, the diplomatic corps remained an aristocratic preserve.

The Middle Classes

The middle classes consisted of a variety of groups. Below the upper middle class was a level that included such traditional groups as professionals in law, medicine, and the civil service as well as moderately well-to-do industrialists and merchants. The industrial expansion of the nineteenth century also added new groups to this segment of the middle class. These included business managers and new professionals, such as the engineers, architects, accountants, and chemists who formed professional associations as the symbols of their newfound importance. A lower middle class of small shopkeepers, traders, manufacturers, and prosperous peasants provided goods and services for the classes above them.

Standing between the lower middle class and the lower classes were new groups of white-collar workers who were the product of the Second Industrial Revolution. They were the traveling sales representatives, bookkeepers, bank tellers, telephone operators, department store salesclerks, and secretaries. Although largely propertyless and often paid little more than skilled laborers, these white-collar workers were often committed to middle-class ideals and optimistic about improving their status.

The moderately prosperous and successful middle classes shared a common lifestyle and values that dominated nineteenth-century society. The members of the middle class were especially active in preaching their worldview to their children and to the upper and lower classes of their society. This was particularly evident in Victorian Britain, often considered a model of middle-class society. It was the European middle classes who accepted and promulgated the importance of progress and science. They believed in hard work, which they viewed as the primary human good, open to everyone and guaranteed to have positive results. They were also regular churchgoers who believed in the good conduct associated with traditional Christian morality. The middle class was concerned with propriety, the right way of doing things, which gave rise to an incessant number of books aimed at the middle-class market with such titles as *The Habits of Good Society* and *Don't: A Manual of Mistakes and Improprieties More or Less Prevalent in Conduct and Speech.*

The Lower Classes

Almost 80 percent of Europeans belonged to the lower classes. Many of them were landholding peasants, agricultural laborers, and sharecroppers, especially in eastern Europe. This was less true, however, in western and central Europe. About 10 percent of the British population worked in agriculture; in Germany, the figure was 25 percent. Many prosperous, landowning peasants shared the values of the middle class. Military conscription brought peasants into contact with the other groups of society, and state-run elementary schools forced the children of peasants to speak the national dialect and accept national loyalties.

The urban working class consisted of many different groups, including skilled artisans in such trades as cabinetmaking, printing, and jewelry making. Semiskilled laborers, who included such people as carpenters, bricklayers, and many factory workers, earned wages that were about two-thirds of those of highly skilled workers. At the bottom of the working-class hierarchy stood the largest group of workers, the unskilled laborers. They included day laborers, who worked irregularly for very low wages, and large numbers of domestic servants. One out of every seven employed persons in Great Britain in 1900 was a domestic servant. Most were women.

Urban workers did experience a real betterment in the material conditions of their lives after 1871. For one thing, urban improvements meant better living conditions. A rise in real wages, accompanied by a decline in many consumer costs, especially in the 1880s and 1890s, made it possible for workers to buy more than just food and housing. French workers in 1900, for example, spent 60 percent of their income on food, down from 75 percent in 1870. Workers' budgets now provided money for more clothes and even leisure at the same time that strikes and labor agitation were winning shorter (ten-hour) workdays and Saturday afternoons off.

"The Woman Question": The Role of Women

"The woman question" was the catchphrase used to refer to the debate over the role of women in society. In the nineteenth century, women remained legally inferior, economically dependent, and largely defined by family and household roles. Many women still aspired to the ideal of femininity popularized by writers and poets. Alfred, Lord Tennyson's poem *The Princess* expressed it well:

> Man for the field and woman for the hearth:
> Man for the sword and for the needle she:
> Man with the head and woman with the heart:
> Man to command and woman to obey;
> All else confusion.

Historians have pointed out that this traditional characterization of the sexes, based on gender-defined social roles, was elevated to the status of universal male and female attributes in the nineteenth century, due largely to the impact of the Industrial Revolution on the family. As the chief family wage earners, men worked outside the home, while women were left with the care of the family, for which they were paid nothing. Of course, the ideal did not always match reality, especially for the lower classes, where the need for supplemental income drove women to do sweatwork.

Marriage and Domesticity Throughout most of the nineteenth century, marriage was viewed as the only honorable and available career for most women. Though the middle class glorified the ideal of domesticity (see the box on p. 716), for most women, marriage was a matter of economic necessity. The lack of meaningful work and the lower wages paid to women made it difficult for single women to earn a living. Retiring to convents as in the past was no longer an option; many spinsters who could not find sufficiently remunerative work therefore elected to enter domestic service as live-in servants. Most women chose instead to marry, which was reflected in an increase in marriage rates and a decline in illegitimacy rates in the course of the nineteenth century.

Birthrates and Birth Control Birthrates also dropped significantly at this time. A very important factor in the evolution of the modern family was the decline in the number of offspring born to the average woman. The change was not necessarily due to new technological products. Although the invention of vulcanized rubber in the 1840s made possible the production of condoms and diaphragms, they were not widely used as effective contraceptive devices until World War I. Some historians maintain that the change in attitude that led parents to deliberately limit the number of offspring was more important than the method used. Although some historians attribute increased birth control to more widespread use of coitus interruptus, or male withdrawal before ejaculation, others have emphasized the ability of women to restrict family size through abortion and even infanticide or abandonment. That a change in attitude occurred was apparent in the emergence of a movement to increase awareness of birth control methods. Authorities prosecuted individuals who spread information about contraception for "depraving public morals" but were unable to stop them. In 1882 in Amsterdam, Dr. Aletta Jacob founded Europe's first birth control clinic. Initially, "family planning" was the suggestion of reformers who thought that the problem of poverty could be solved by reducing the number of children among the lower classes. In fact, the practice spread quickly among the propertied classes, rather than among the impoverished, a good reminder that considerable differences still remained between middle-class and working-class families.

The Middle-Class Family The family was the central institution of middle-class life. Men provided the family income, while women focused on household and child care. The use of domestic servants in many middle-class homes, made possible by an abundant supply of cheap labor, reduced the amount of time middle-class women had to spend on household work. At the same time, by reducing the number of children in the family, mothers could devote more time to child care and domestic leisure. The idea that leisure should be used for constructive purposes supported and encouraged the cult of middle-class domesticity.

The middle-class family fostered an ideal of togetherness. The Victorians created the family Christmas with its yule log, Christmas tree, songs, and exchange of gifts. In the United States, Fourth of July celebrations changed from drunken revels to family picnics by the 1850s. The education of middle-class females in domestic crafts, singing, and piano playing prepared them for their function of providing a proper environment for home recreation.

The new domestic ideal had an impact on child raising and children's play. Late-eighteenth-century thought, beginning with Rousseau, had encouraged a new view of children as unique beings, not small adults, which had carried over into the nineteenth century. They were entitled to a long childhood involved in activities with other children their own age. The early environment in which they were raised, it was thought, would determine how they turned out. And mothers were seen as the most important force in protecting children from the harmful influences of the adult world. New children's games and toys, including mass-produced dolls for girls, appeared in middle-class homes. The middle-class emphasis on the functional value of knowledge was also evident in these games.

OPPOSING VIEWPOINTS
ADVICE TO WOMEN: TWO VIEWS

Industrialization had a strong impact on middle-class women as gender-based social roles became the norm. Men worked outside the home to support the family, while women provided for the needs of their children and husband at home. In the first selection, *Woman in Her Social and Domestic Character* (1842), Elizabeth Poole Sanford gives advice to middle-class women on their proper role and behavior.

Although a majority of women probably followed the nineteenth-century middle-class ideal of women as keepers of the household and nurturers of husband and children, an increasing number of women fought for the rights of women. The second selection is taken from the third act of Henrik Ibsen's 1879 play *A Doll's House*, in which the character Nora Helmer declares her independence from her husband's control.

Elizabeth Poole Sanford, *Woman in Her Social and Domestic Character*

The changes wrought by Time are many. It influences the opinions of men as familiarity does their feelings; it has a tendency to do away with superstition, and to reduce every thing to its real worth.

It is thus that the sentiment for woman has undergone a change. The romantic passion which once almost deified her is on the decline; and it is by intrinsic qualities that she must now inspire respect. She is no longer the queen of song and the star of chivalry. But if there is less of enthusiasm entertained for her, the sentiment is more rational, and, perhaps, equally sincere; for it is in relation to happiness that she is chiefly appreciated.

And in this respect it is, we must confess, that she is most useful and most important. Domestic life is the chief source of her influence; and the greatest debt society can owe to her is domestic comfort; for happiness is almost an element of virtue; and nothing conduces more to improve the character of men than domestic peace. A woman may make a man's home delightful, and may thus increase his motives for virtuous exertion. She may refine and tranquilize his mind,—may turn away his anger or allay his grief. Her smile may be the happy influence to gladden his heart, and to disperse the cloud that gathers on his brow. And in proportion to her endeavors to make those around her happy, she will be esteemed and loved. She will secure by her excellence that interest and that regard which she might formerly claim as the privilege of her sex, and will really merit the deference which was then conceded to her as a matter of course....

Perhaps one of the first secrets of her influence is adaptation to the tastes, and sympathy in the feelings, of those around her. This holds true in lesser as well as in graver points. It is in the former, indeed, that the absence of interest in a companion is frequently most disappointing. Where want of congeniality impairs domestic comfort, the fault is generally chargeable on the female side. It is for woman, not for man, to make the sacrifice, especially in indifferent matters. She must, in a certain degree, be plastic herself if she would mold others....

Nothing is so likely to conciliate the affections of the other sex as a feeling that woman looks to them for support and guidance. In proportion as men are themselves superior, they are accessible to this appeal. On the contrary, they never feel interested in one who seems disposed rather to offer than to ask assistance. There is, indeed, something unfeminine in independence. It is contrary to nature, and therefore it offends. We do not like to see a woman affecting tremors, but still less do we like to see her acting the amazon. A really sensible woman feels her dependence. She does what she can; but she is conscious of inferiority, and therefore grateful for support. She knows that she is the weaker vessel, and that as such she should receive honor. In this view, her weakness is an attraction, not a blemish.

In every thing, therefore, that women attempt, they should show their consciousness of dependence. If they are learners, let them evince a teachable spirit; if they give an opinion, let them do it in an unassuming manner. There is something so unpleasant in female self-sufficiency that it not unfrequently deters instead of persuading, and prevents the adoption of advice which the judgment even approves.

Henrik Ibsen, *A Doll's House*

NORA (*Pause*): Does anything strike you as we sit here?

HELMER: What should strike me?

NORA: We've been married eight years; does it not strike you that this is the first time we two, you and I, man and wife, have talked together seriously?

HELMER: Seriously? What do you mean, *seriously?*

NORA: For eight whole years, and more—ever since the day we first met—we have never exchanged one serious word about serious things....

HELMER: Why, my dearest Nora, what have you to do with serious things?

NORA: There we have it! You have never understood me. I've had great injustice done to me, Torvald; first by Father, then by you.

HELMER: What! Your father *and* me? We, who have loved you more than all the world!

NORA (*Shaking her head*): You have never loved me. You just found it amusing to think you were in love with me.

HELMER: Nora! What a thing to say!

NORA: Yes, it's true, Torvald. When I was living at home with Father, he told me his opinions and mine were the same. If I had different opinions, I said nothing about them,

(continued)

(continued)

because he would not have liked it. He used to call me his doll-child and played with me as I played with my dolls. Then I came to live in your house.

HELMER: What a way to speak of our marriage!

NORA (*Undisturbed*): I mean that I passed from Father's hands into yours. You arranged everything to your taste and I got the same tastes as you; or pretended to—I don't know which—both, perhaps; sometimes one, sometimes the other. When I look back on it now, I seem to have been living here like a beggar, on handouts. I lived by performing tricks for you, Torvald. But that was how you wanted it. You and Father have done me a great wrong. It is your fault that my life has come to naught.

HELMER: Why, Nora, how unreasonable and ungrateful! Haven't you been happy here?

NORA: No, never. I thought I was, but I never was.

HELMER: Not—not happy! . . .

NORA: I must stand quite alone if I am ever to know myself and my surroundings; so I cannot stay with you.

HELMER: Nora! Nora!

NORA: I am going at once. I daresay [my friend] Christina will take me in for tonight.

HELMER: You are mad! I shall not allow it! I forbid it!

NORA: It's no use your forbidding me anything now. I shall take with me only what belongs to me; from you I will accept nothing, either now or later.

HELMER: This is madness!

NORA: Tomorrow I shall go home—I mean to what was my home. It will be easier for me to find a job there.

HELMER: On, in your blind inexperience—

NORA: I must try to gain experience, Torvald.

HELMER: Forsake your home, your husband, your children! And you don't consider what the world will say.

NORA: I can't pay attention to that. I only know that I must do it.

HELMER: This is monstrous! Can you forsake your holiest duties?

NORA: What do you consider my holiest duties?

HELMER: Need I tell you that? Your duties to your husband and children.

NORA: I have other duties equally sacred.

HELMER: Impossible! What do you mean?

NORA: My duties toward myself.

HELMER: Before all else you are a wife and a mother.

NORA: That I no longer believe. Before all else I believe I am a human being just as much as you are—or at least that I should try to become one. I know that most people agree with you, Torvald, and that they say so in books. But I can no longer be satisfied with what most people say and what is in books. I must think things out for myself and try to get clear about them.

Q *According to Elizabeth Sanford, what is the proper role of women? What forces in nineteenth-century European society merged to shape Sanford's understanding of "proper" gender roles? In Ibsen's play, what challenges does Nora Helmer make to Sanford's view of the proper role and behavior of wives? Why is her husband so shocked? Why did Ibsen title this play* A Doll's House?

One advice manual maintained that young children should learn checkers because it "calls forth the resources of the mind in the most gentle as well as the most successful manner."

Since the sons of the middle-class family were expected to follow careers like their father's, they were sent to schools where they were kept separate from the rest of society until the age of sixteen or seventeen. Sport was used in the schools to "toughen boys up," and their leisure activities centered around both national military concerns and character building. This combination was especially evident in the establishment of the Boy Scouts in Britain in 1908. Boy Scouts provided organized recreation for boys between the ages of twelve and eighteen; adventure was combined with the discipline of earning merit badges and ranks in such a way as to instill ideals of patriotism and self-sacrifice. Many men viewed such activities as a corrective to the possible dangers that female domination of the home posed for male development. As one scout leader wrote: "The REAL Boy Scout is not a sissy. [He] adores his mother [but] is not hitched to [her] apron strings." There was little organized recreational activity of this type for girls, although Robert Baden-Powell (1857–1941), the founder of the Boy Scouts, did encourage his sister to establish a girls' division as an afterthought. Its goal is evident from Agnes Baden-Powell's comment that "you do not want to make tomboys of refined girls, yet you want to attract, and thus raise, the slum girl from the gutter. The main object is to give them all the ability to be better mothers and Guides to the next generation."[8] Despite her comment, most organizations of this kind were for middle-class children, although some reformers tried to establish boys' clubs for working-class youths to reform them.

The new ideal of the middle-class woman as nurturing mother and wife who "determined the atmosphere of the household" through her character, not her work, frequently did not correspond to reality. In France, Germany, and even mid-Victorian Britain, relatively few families could actually afford to hire a host of servants. More often, middle-class families had one servant, usually a young working-class or country girl not used to middle-class lifestyles. Women, then, were often forced to work quite hard to maintain the expected appearance of the well-ordered

IMAGES OF EVERYDAY LIFE

The Middle-Class Family. Nineteenth-century middle-class moralists considered the family the fundamental pillar of a healthy society. The family was a crucial institution in middle-class life, and togetherness constituted one of the important ideals of the middle-class family. The painting below by William P. Frith, titled *Many Happy Returns of the Day,* shows grandparents, parents, and children taking part in a family birthday celebration for a little girl. The servant at the left holds the presents for the little girl. New games and toys also appeared for middle-class children. The illustration on the bottom right is taken from a book of games of 1889 and shows young girls playing a game called battledore and shuttlecock, which is described in the book as "a most convenient game because one solitary individual can find amusement as well as any number, provided there is a bat for each player. The object of the game is to keep the shuttlecock going as long as possible." The final illustration shows the cover of *The Scout,* a magazine of the scouting movement founded by Robert Baden-Powell. The cover shows one of the new scouts wearing his uniform and watching a ship at sea.

household. A German housekeeping manual makes this evident:

> It often happens that even high-ranking ladies help at home with housework, and particularly with kitchen chores, scrubbing, etc., so that, above all, the hands have good cause to become very rough, hard, and calloused. When these ladies appear in society, they are extremely upset at having such rough-looking hands. In order to perform the hardest and most ordinary chores . . . and, at the same time, to keep a soft hand like those fine ladies who have no heavier work to do than embroidering and sewing, always keep a piece of fresh bacon, rub your hands with it just before bedtime, and you will fully achieve your goal. You will, as a result, have the inconvenience of having to sleep with gloves on, in order not to soil the bed.[9]

Many middle-class wives, then, were caught in a no-win situation. Often, for the sake of the advancement of her husband's career, she was expected to maintain in public the image of the "idle" wife, freed from demeaning physical labor and able to pass her days in ornamental pursuits. In truth, it was frequently the middle-class woman who paid the price for this facade in a life of unpaid work, carefully managing the family budget and participating in housework that could never be done by only one servant girl. As one historian has argued, the reality of many middle-class women's lives was that "what appears at first glance to be idleness is revealed, on closer examination, to be difficult and tiresome work."

The Working-Class Family Hard work was, of course, standard fare for women in working-class families. Daughters in working-class families were expected to work until they married; even after marriage, they often did piecework at home to help support the family. For the children of the working classes, childhood was over by the age of nine or ten, when they became apprentices or were employed in odd jobs.

Between 1890 and 1914, however, family patterns among the working class began to change. High-paying jobs in heavy industry and improvements in the standard of living made it possible for working-class families to depend on the income of husbands and the wages of grown children. By the early twentieth century, some working-class mothers could afford to stay at home, following the pattern of middle-class women. At the same time, new consumer products, such as sewing machines, clocks, bicycles, and cast-iron stoves, spurred consumerism, focusing society on ever-higher levels of consumption.

Working-class families also followed the middle classes in limiting the size of their families. Children began to be viewed as dependents rather than as potential wage earners as child labor laws and compulsory education moved children out of the workforce and into schools. Improvements in public health, as well as advances in medicine and a better diet, resulted in a decline in infant mortality rates for the lower classes, especially noticeable in the cities after 1890, and made it easier for working-class families to choose to have fewer children. At the same time, strikes and labor agitation led to laws that reduced work hours to ten per day by 1900 and eliminated work on Saturday afternoons, which enabled working-class parents to devote more attention to their children and develop deeper emotional ties with them. Even working-class fathers became involved in their children's lives. One observer in the French town of Belleville in the 1890s noted that "the workingman's love for his children borders on being an obsession."[10] Interest in educating children as a way to improve their future also grew.

Education in the Mass Society

Mass education was a product of the mass society of the late nineteenth century. Being "educated" in the early nineteenth century meant attending a secondary school or possibly even a university. Secondary schools emphasized a classical education based on the study of Greek and Latin. Secondary and university education was primarily for the elite, the sons of government officials, nobles, or wealthier middle-class families. After 1850, secondary education was expanded as more middle-class families sought employment in public service and the professions or entry into elite scientific and technical schools.

At the beginning of the nineteenth century, European states showed little interest in primary education. Only in the German states was there a state-run system for it. In 1833, the French government created a system of state-run secular schools by instructing local government to establish an elementary school for both boys and girls. None of these primary schools required attendance, however, which tended to be irregular at best. In rural society, children were still expected to work in the fields. In industrializing countries like Britain and France, both employers and parents were eager to maintain the practice of child labor.

Universal Elementary Education In the decades after 1870, the functions of the state were extended to include the development of mass education in state-run systems. Most Western governments began to offer at least primary education to both boys and girls between the ages of six and twelve. In most countries, it was not optional. Austria had established free, compulsory elementary education in 1869. In France, an 1882 law made primary education compulsory for all children between six and thirteen. Elementary education was made compulsory in Britain in 1880, but it was not until 1902 that an act of Parliament brought all elementary schools under county and town control. States also assumed responsibility for the quality of teachers by establishing teacher-training schools. By 1900, many European states, especially in northern and western Europe, were providing state-financed primary schools, salaried and trained teachers, and free, compulsory elementary education for the masses.

Why did European states make this commitment to mass education? Liberals believed that education was important to personal and social improvement and also sought, as in France, to supplant Catholic education with moral and civic training based on secular values. Even conservatives were attracted to mass education as a means of improving the quality of military recruits and training people in social discipline. In 1875, a German military journal stated, "We in Germany consider education to be one of the principal ways of promoting the strength of the nation and above all military strength."[11]

Another incentive for mass education came from industrialization. In the early Industrial Revolution, unskilled labor was sufficient to meet factory needs, but the new firms of the Second Industrial Revolution demanded skilled labor. Both boys and girls with an elementary education had new possibilities of jobs beyond their villages or small towns, including white-collar jobs in railways, subway stations, post offices, banking and shipping firms, teaching, and nursing. To industrialists, then, mass education furnished the trained workers they needed.

Nevertheless, the chief motive for mass education was political. For one thing, the expansion of voting rights necessitated a more educated electorate. Even more important, however, mass compulsory education instilled patriotism and nationalized the masses, providing an opportunity for even greater national integration. As people lost their ties to local regions and even to religion, nationalism supplied a new faith. The use of a single national language created greater national unity than loyalty to a ruler did.

A nation's motives for universal elementary education largely determined what was taught in its elementary schools. Indoctrination in national values took on great importance. At the core of the academic curriculum were reading, writing, arithmetic, national history (especially geared to a patriotic view), geography, literature, and some singing and drawing. The education of boys and girls varied, however. Where possible, the sexes were separated. Girls did less math and no science but concentrated on such domestic skills as sewing, washing, ironing, and cooking, all prerequisites for providing a good home for husband and children. Boys were taught some practical skills, such as carpentry, and even some military drill. Most of the elementary schools also inculcated the middle-class virtues of hard work, thrift, sobriety, cleanliness, and respect for the family. For most students, elementary education led to apprenticeship and a job.

Female Teachers The development of compulsory elementary education created a demand for teachers, and most of them were female. In the United States, for example, women constituted two-thirds of all teachers by the 1880s. Many men viewed the teaching of children as an extension of women's "natural role" as nurturers of children. Moreover, females were paid lower salaries, in itself a considerable incentive for governments to encourage the establishment of teacher-training institutes for women. The first colleges for women were really teacher-training schools. In Britain, the women's colleges of Queen's and Bedford were established in the 1840s to provide teacher training for middle-class spinsters who needed to work. Barbara Bodichon (1827–1891), a pioneer in the development of female education, established her own school where girls were trained for economic independence as well as domesticity. Not until the beginning of the twentieth century, however, were women permitted to enter the male-dominated universities. In France, 3 percent of university students in 1902 were women; by 1914, their number had increased to 10 percent of the total.

Literacy and Newspapers The most immediate result of mass education was an increase in literacy. Compulsory elementary education and the growth of literacy

© Bettmann/CORBIS

A Women's College. Women were largely excluded from male-dominated universities before 1900. Consequently, the demand of women for higher education led to the establishment of women's colleges, most of which were primarily teacher-training schools. This photograph shows female medical students dissecting cadavers in anatomy class at the Women's Medical College of Philadelphia, Pennsylvania.

were directly related. In Germany, Great Britain, France, and the Scandinavian countries, adult illiteracy was virtually eliminated by 1900. Where there was less schooling, the story is very different. Adult illiteracy rates were 79 percent in Serbia, 78 percent in Romania, 72 percent in Bulgaria, and 79 percent in Russia. All of these countries had made only a minimal investment in compulsory mass education.

With the dramatic increase in literacy after 1871 came the rise of mass-circulation newspapers, such as the *Evening News* (1881) and *Daily Mail* (1896) in London, which sold millions of copies a day. Known as the "yellow press" in the United States, these newspapers shared some common characteristics. They were written in an easily understood style and tended toward the sensational. Unlike eighteenth-century newspapers, which were full of serious editorials and lengthy political analyses, these tabloids provided lurid details of crimes, jingoistic diatribes, gossip, and sports news. There were other forms of cheap literature as well. Specialty magazines, such as the *Family Herald* for the entire family, and women's magazines began in the 1860s. Pulp fiction for adults included the extremely popular westerns with their innumerable variations on conflicts between cowboys and Indians. Literature for the masses was but one feature of the new mass culture; another was the emergence of new forms of leisure.

Mass Leisure

In the preindustrial centuries, play or leisure activities had been closely connected to work patterns based on the seasonal or daily cycles typical of the life of peasants and artisans. The process of industrialization in the nineteenth century had an enormous impact on those traditional patterns. The factory imposed new work patterns that were determined by the rhythms of machines and clocks and removed work time completely from the family environment of farms and workshops. Work and leisure became opposites as leisure came to be viewed as what people did for fun when not on the job. In fact, the new leisure hours created by the industrial system—evening hours after work, weekends, and later a week or two in the summer—largely determined the contours of the new **mass leisure.**

New technology and business practices also determined the forms of leisure pursuits. New technology created novelties such as the Ferris wheel at amusement parks. The mechanized urban transportation systems of the 1880s meant that even the working classes were no longer dependent on neighborhood taverns but could make their way to athletic events, amusement parks, and dance halls. Likewise, railroads could take people to the beaches on weekends.

Music and Dance Halls

Music and dance halls appeared in the second half of the nineteenth century. The first music hall in London was constructed in 1849 for a lower-class audience. As is evident from one Londoner's observation, music halls were primarily for males:

> [They were a] popular place of Saturday night resort with working men, as at them they can combine the drinking of the Saturday night glass and smoking of the Saturday night pipe, with the seeing and hearing of a variety of entertainments, ranging from magnificent ballets and marvelous scenic illusions to inferior tumbling, and from well-given operatic selections to the most idiotic of the so-called comic songs.[12]

By the 1880s, there were five hundred music halls in London. Promoters gradually made them more respectable and broadened their fare to entice both women and children to attend the programs. The new dance halls, which were all the rage by 1900, were more strictly oriented toward adults. Contemporaries were often shocked by the sight of young people engaged in sexually suggestive dancing.

Mass Tourism

The upper and middle classes had created the first market for tourism, but as wages increased and workers were given paid vacations, tourism became another form of mass leisure. Thomas Cook (1808–1892) was a British pioneer of mass tourism. Secretary to a British temperance group, Cook had been responsible for organizing a railroad trip to temperance gatherings in 1841. This experience led him to offer trips on a regular basis after he found that he could make substantial profits by renting special trains, lowering prices, and increasing the number of passengers. In 1867, he offered tours to Paris and by the 1880s to Switzerland. Of course, overseas tours were for the industrial and commercial middle classes, but soon, thanks to savings clubs, even British factory workers were able to take weekend excursions.

Team Sports

Team sports had also developed into yet another form of mass leisure by the late nineteenth century. Sports were by no means a new activity. Unlike the old rural games, however, they were no longer chaotic and spontaneous activities but became strictly organized, with written rules and officials to enforce them. The rules were the products of organized athletic groups, such as the English Football Association (1863) and the American Bowling Congress (1895).

The new sports were not just for fun; like other forms of middle-class recreation, they were intended to provide training for people, especially adolescents. Not only could the participants develop individual skills, but they could also acquire a sense of teamwork useful for military service. These characteristics were already evident in the British public schools (which were really private boarding schools) in the 1850s and 1860s when such schools as Harrow, Uppingham, and Loretto placed organized sports at the center of the curriculum (see the box on p. 722). At Loretto, for example, education was supposed to instill "First—Character. Second—Physique. Third—Intelligence. Fourth—Manners. Fifth—Information."

THE FIGHT SONG: SPORTS IN THE ENGLISH PUBLIC SCHOOL

In the second half of the nineteenth century, organized sports were often at the center of the curriculum in English public schools. These sports were not just for leisure but were intended to instill character, strength, and teamwork. This "fight song" was written by H. B. Tristam for the rugby team at Loretto School.

H. B. Tristam, "Going Strong"

Sing Football the grandest of sports in the world,
And you know it yourself if your pluck's never curled,
If you've gritted your teeth and gone hard to the last,
And sworn that you'll never let anyone past.

Chorus
Keeping close upon the ball—we drive it through
*   them all,*
And again we go rushing along, along, along;
O the tackle and the run, and the matches we
*   have won,*

From the start to the finish going strong, strong,
*   strong, going strong!*

If you live to be a hundred you'll never forget
How they hacked in the scrum, how you payed back
*   the debt;*
The joy of the swing when you tackled your man,
The lust of the fray when the battle began.

Long hence when you look with a quivering eye
On the little white tassel you value so high;
You'll think of the matches you've played in and won,
And you'll long for the days that are over and done.

Q How would the singing of such songs and the virtues they express work to shape the boys' conceptions of proper male behavior, masculine values, and masculinity itself?

The new team sports rapidly became professionalized. In Britain, soccer had its Football Association in 1863 and rugby its Rugby Football Union in 1871. In the United States, the first national association to recognize professional baseball players was formed in 1863. By 1900, the National League and American League had a complete monopoly over professional baseball. The development of urban transportation systems made possible the construction of stadiums where thousands could attend, making mass spectator sports a big business. In 1872, some 2,000 people watched the British Soccer Cup Final. By 1885, the crowd had increased to 10,000 and by 1901 to 100,000. Professional teams became objects of mass adulation by crowds of urbanites who compensated for their lost sense of identity in mass urban areas by developing these new loyalties. Spectator sports even reflected class differences. Upper-class soccer teams in Britain viewed working-class teams as vicious and prone to "money-grubbing, tricks, sensational displays, and utter rottenness."

The sports cult of the late nineteenth century was mostly male oriented. Many men believed that females were not particularly suited for "vigorous physical activity," although it was permissible for middle-class women to indulge in less active sports such as croquet and lawn tennis. Eventually, some athletics crept into women's colleges and girls' public schools in England.

Standardized forms of amusement drew mass audiences. Although some authorities argued that the new amusements were important for improving people, in truth, they served primarily to provide entertainment and distract people from the realities of their work lives. The new mass leisure also represented a significant change from earlier forms of popular culture. Festivals and fairs had been based on active and spontaneous community participation, whereas the new forms of mass leisure were businesses, standardized for largely passive mass audiences and organized to make profits.

The National State

Q Focus Question: What general political trends were evident in the nations of western Europe in the last decades of the nineteenth century, and how did these trends differ from the policies pursued in Germany, Austria-Hungary, and Russia?

Within the major European states, considerable progress was made toward achieving such liberal practices as constitutions and parliaments, but it was largely in western European states that **mass politics** became a reality. Reforms encouraged the expansion of political democracy through voting rights for men and the creation of mass political parties. At the same time, however, these developments were strongly resisted in parts of Europe where the old political forces remained strong.

Western Europe: The Growth of Political Democracy

In general, parliamentary government was most firmly rooted in the western European states. Both Britain and France saw an expansion of the right to vote, but liberal reforms proved less successful in Spain and Italy.

Soccer Moments. Until 1863, football (soccer) in Britain was an aggressive sport with few set rules. One of the first things the new English Football Association did after it was established on October 26, 1863, was to set up fourteen rules of play. At the left, a sketch from a magazine called *The Graphic* shows a scene from an international soccer match in 1872. The two players with the ball have the rose of England on their shirts. At the right, another sketch from *The Graphic* shows the first match of the Ladies' Football Club in 1895.

Reform in Britain   By 1871, Great Britain had a functioning two-party parliamentary system, and the growth of political democracy became one of the preoccupations of British politics. Its cause was pushed along by the expansion of suffrage. Much advanced by the Reform Act of 1867 (see Chapter 22), the right to vote was further extended during the second ministry of William Gladstone (1880–1885) with the passage of the Reform Act of 1884. It gave the vote to all men who paid regular rents or taxes; by largely enfranchising agricultural workers, a group previously excluded, the act added another 2 million male voters to the electorate (see Table 22.1 on p. 683 in Chapter 22). Women were still denied the right to vote. The following year, the Redistribution Act eliminated historic boroughs and counties and established constituencies with approximately equal populations and one representative each. The payment of salaries to members of the House of Commons beginning in 1911 further democratized that institution by at least opening the door to people other than the wealthy. The British system of gradual reform through parliamentary institutions had become the way of British political life.

Gradual reform failed to solve the problem of Ireland, however. The Irish had long been subject to British rule, and the Act of Union of 1801 had united the English and Irish Parliaments. Like other unfree ethnic groups in Europe, the Irish developed a sense of national self-consciousness. They detested the absentee British landlords and their burdensome rents.

In 1870, William Gladstone attempted to alleviate Irish discontent by enacting limited land reform, but as Irish tenants continued to be evicted in the 1870s, the

Irish began to make new demands. In 1879, a group called the Irish Land League, which advocated independence, called on Parliament to at least institute land reform. Charles Parnell (1846–1891), a leader of the Irish representatives in Parliament, called for **home rule**, which meant self-government by having a separate Parliament but not complete independence. Soon Irish peasants were responding to British inaction with terrorist acts. When the British government reacted with more force, Irish Catholics began to demand independence.

The Liberal leader William Gladstone, continuing to hope for a peaceful solution to the "Irish question," introduced a home rule bill in 1886 that would have created an Irish Parliament without granting independence. But even this compromise was voted down in Parliament, especially by Conservative members who believed that concessions would only result in more violence. Gladstone tried again when he was prime minister in 1893 but experienced yet another defeat. The Irish question remained unresolved.

The Third Republic in France   The defeat of France by the Prussian army in 1870 brought the downfall of Louis Napoleon's Second Empire. French republicans initially set up a provisional government, but the victorious Otto von Bismarck intervened and forced the French to choose a government by universal male suffrage. The French people rejected the republicans and overwhelmingly favored the monarchists, who won 400 of the 630 seats in the new National Assembly. In response, on March 26, 1871, radical republicans formed an independent republican government in Paris known as the Commune.

© Scottish National Portrait Gallery, Edinburgh, Scotland/The Bridgeman Art Library

William Gladstone. Gladstone was one of the most prominent liberal leaders of the nineteenth century. He served four times as British prime minister. Although he began his political career as a Conservative, he soon switched to the Liberals. Gladstone was a brilliant political strategist who believed that religion could help stabilize society.

But the National Assembly refused to give up its power and decided to crush the revolutionary Commune. When vicious fighting broke out in April, many working-class men and women stepped forth to defend the Commune. At first, women's activities were the traditional ones: caring for the wounded soldiers and feeding the troops. Gradually, however, women expanded their activities to include taking care of weapons, working as scouts, and even setting up their own fighting brigades. Louise Michel (1830–1905), a schoolteacher, emerged as one of the leaders of the Paris Commune (see the box on p. 725). She proved tireless in forming committees for the defense of the revolutionary Commune.

All of these efforts were in vain, however. In the last week of May, government troops massacred thousands of the Commune's defenders. Estimates are that 20,000 were shot; another 10,000 (including Louise Michel) were shipped to the French penal colony of New Caledonia in the South Pacific. The brutal repression of the Commune bequeathed a legacy of hatred that continued to plague French politics for decades. The split between the middle and working classes, begun in the revolutionary hostilities of 1848–1849, had widened immensely. The harsh

punishment of women who participated in the revolutionary activity also served to discourage any future efforts by working-class women to improve their conditions.

Although a majority of the members of the monarchist-dominated National Assembly wished to restore a monarchy to France, inability to agree on who should be king caused the monarchists to miss their opportunity and led in 1875 to an improvised constitution that established a republican form of government as the least divisive compromise. This constitution established a bicameral legislature with an upper house, the Senate, elected indirectly and a lower house, the Chamber of Deputies, chosen by universal male suffrage; a president, selected by the legislature for a term of seven years, served as executive of the government. The Constitution of 1875, intended only as a stopgap measure, solidified the republic—the Third Republic—which lasted sixty-five years. New elections in 1876 and 1877 strengthened the hands of the republicans who managed by 1879 to institute ministerial responsibility and establish the power of the Chamber of Deputies. The prime minister or premier and his ministers were now responsible not to the president but to the Chamber of Deputies.

Although the government's moderation gradually encouraged more and more middle-class and peasant support, the position of the Third Republic remained precarious because monarchists, Catholic clergy, and professional army officers were still its enemies.

A major crisis in the 1880s, however, actually served to strengthen the republican government. General Georges Boulanger (1837–1891) was a popular military officer who attracted the public attention of all those discontented with the Third Republic: the monarchists, Bonapartists, aristocrats, and nationalists who favored a war of revenge against Germany. Boulanger appeared as the strong man on horseback, the savior of France. By 1889, just when his strength had grown to the point where many expected a coup d'état, he lost his nerve and fled France, a completely discredited man. In the long run, the Boulanger crisis served to rally support for the resilient republic.

Spain In Spain, a new constitution, drafted in 1875 under King Alfonso XII (1874–1885), established a parliamentary government dominated by two political groups, the Conservatives and the Liberals, whose members stemmed from the same small social group of great landowners allied with a few wealthy industrialists. Because suffrage was limited to the propertied classes, Liberals and Conservatives alternated in power but followed basically the same conservative policies. Spain's defeat in the Spanish-American War in 1898 and the loss of Cuba and the Philippines to the United States increased the discontent with the status quo. When a group of young intellectuals known as the Generation of 1898 called for political and social reforms, both Liberals and Conservatives attempted to enlarge the electorate and win the masses' support for their policies. The attempted reforms did little to allay the unrest, however, and the

A Leader of the Paris Commune

Louise Michel was a schoolteacher in Paris who took an interest in radical ideas. She became active among revolutionary groups in Paris in 1870 and then emerged as a leader of the Paris Commune in 1871. Exiled to New Caledonia after the crushing of the Commune, in 1880 she was allowed to return to France, where she became a heroic figure among radical groups. Later, she spent three years in prison and then lived much of the time in England in self-imposed exile. In her memoirs, Michel discusses what happened on March 18, 1871, when the National Assembly sent troops to seize cannons that had been moved earlier to the hills of Montmartre. She also reflected on her activities in the Commune.

Louise Michel, *Memoirs*

Learning that the Versailles soldiers [troops of the National Assembly] were trying to seize the cannon, men and women of Montmartre swarmed up the Butte in a surprise maneuver. Those people who were climbing believed they would die, but they were prepared to pay the price.

The Butte of Montmartre was bathed in the first light of day, through which things were glimpsed as if they were hidden behind a thin veil of water. Gradually the crowd increased. The other districts of Paris, hearing of the events taking place on the Butte of Montmartre, came to our assistance.

The women of Paris covered the cannon with their bodies. When their officers ordered the soldiers to fire, the men refused. The same army that would be used to crush Paris two months later decided now that it did not want to be an accomplice of the reaction. They gave up their attempt to seize the cannon from the National Guard. They understood that the people were defending the Republic by defending the arms that the royalists and imperialists would have turned on Paris in agreement with the Prussians. When we had won our victory, I looked around and noticed my poor mother, who had followed me to the Butte of Montmartre, believing that I was going to die.

On this day, the eighteenth of March, the people awakened. If they had not, it would have been the triumph of some king; instead it was a triumph of the people. The eighteenth of March could have belonged to the allies of kings, or to foreigners, or to the people. It was the people's....

During the entire time of the Commune, I only spent one night at my poor mother's. I never really went to bed during that time. I just napped a little whenever there was nothing better to do, and many other people lived the same way. Everybody who wanted deliverance gave himself totally to the cause.... During the Commune I went unhurt except for a bullet that grazed my wrist, although my hat was literally riddled with bullet holes.

Q *What does this account from the memoirs of the Parisian feminist Louise Michel tell you about new opportunities for political involvement that were available to female and male residents of European capital cities during the late nineteenth century?*

---

growth of industrialization in some areas resulted in more workers being attracted to the radical solutions of socialism and anarchism. When violence erupted in Barcelona in July 1909, the military forces brutally suppressed the rebels. The revolt and its repression made clear that reform would not be easily accomplished because the Catholic Church, the large landowners, and the army remained tied to a conservative social order.

Italy By 1870, Italy had emerged as a geographically united state with pretensions to great power status. Its internal weaknesses, however, gave that claim a particularly hollow ring. One Italian leader said after unification, "We have made Italy; now we must make Italians." But many Italians continued to put loyalty to their families, towns, and regions above their loyalty to the new state.

Sectional differences—a poverty-stricken south and an industrializing north—also weakened any sense of community. Most of the Italian leaders were northerners who treated southern Italians with contempt. The Catholic Church, which had lost control of the Papal States as a result of unification, even refused to accept the existence of the new state. Chronic turmoil between workers and industrialists undermined the social fabric. And few Italians felt empowered in the new Italy: only 2.5 percent of the people could vote for the legislative body. In 1882, the number was increased, but only to 10 percent. The Italian government was unable to deal effectively with these problems because of the extensive corruption among government officials and the lack of stability created by ever-changing government coalitions.

Central and Eastern Europe: Persistence of the Old Order

Germany, Austria-Hungary, and Russia pursued political policies that were quite different from those of the western European nations. The central European states (Germany and Austria-Hungary) had the trappings of parliamentary government, including legislative bodies and elections by universal male suffrage, but authoritarian forces, especially powerful monarchies and conservative social groups, remained strong. In eastern Europe, especially Russia, the old system of autocracy was barely touched by the winds of change.

Germany Despite unification, important divisions remained in German society that could not simply be papered over by the force of nationalism. These divisions were already evident in the new German constitution that provided for a federal system with a bicameral legislature. The Bundesrat, or upper house, represented the twenty-five states that made up Germany. Individual states, such as Bavaria and Prussia, kept their own kings, their own post offices, and even their own armies in peacetime. The lower house of the German parliament, the Reichstag, was elected on the basis of universal male suffrage, but it did not have ministerial responsibility. Ministers of government, the most important of which was the chancellor, were responsible not to the parliament but to the emperor. The emperor also commanded the armed forces and controlled foreign policy and internal administration. Though the creation of a parliament elected by universal male suffrage presented opportunities for the growth of a real political democracy, it failed to develop in Germany before World War I. The army and Bismarck were two major reasons why it did not.

The German (largely Prussian) army viewed itself as the defender of monarchy and aristocracy and sought to escape any control by the Reichstag by operating under a general staff responsible only to the emperor. Prussian military tradition was strong, and military officers took steps to ensure the loyalty of their subordinates to the emperor, which was easy as long as Junker landowners were officers. As the growth of the army made it necessary to turn to the middle class for officers, extreme care was taken to choose only sons "of honorable bourgeois families in whom the love for King and Fatherland, a warm heart for the soldier's calling, and Christian morality are planted and nurtured."

The policies of Otto von Bismarck, who served as chancellor of the new German state until 1890, often served to prevent the growth of more democratic institutions. At first, Bismarck worked with the liberals to achieve greater centralization of Germany through common codes of criminal and commercial law. The liberals also joined Bismarck in his attack on the Catholic Church, the so-called *Kulturkampf,* or "struggle for civilization." Like Bismarck, middle-class liberals distrusted Catholic loyalty to the new Germany. Bismarck's strong-arm tactics against the Catholic clergy and Catholic institutions proved counterproductive, however, and Bismarck welcomed an opportunity in 1878 to abandon the attack on Catholicism by making an abrupt shift in policy.

In 1878, Bismarck abandoned the liberals and began to persecute the socialists. When the Social Democratic Party elected twelve deputies to the Reichstag in 1877, Bismarck grew alarmed. He genuinely believed that the socialists' antinationalistic, anticapitalistic, and antimonarchical stance represented a danger to the empire. In 1878, Bismarck got parliament to pass a stringent antisocialist law that outlawed the Social Democratic Party and limited socialist meetings and publications, although socialist candidates were still permitted to run for the Reichstag. In addition to repressive measures, Bismarck also attempted to woo workers away from socialism by enacting social welfare legislation (see the box on p. 728). Between 1883 and 1889, the Reichstag passed laws that established sickness, accident, and disability benefits as well as old-age pensions financed by compulsory contributions from workers, employers, and the state. Bismarck's social security system was the most progressive the world had yet seen, although even his system left much to be desired, as the Social Democrats pointed out. A full pension, for example, was payable only at age seventy after forty-eight years of contributions. In the event of a male worker's death, no benefits were paid to his widow or children.

Both the repressive and the social welfare measures failed to stop the growth of socialism, however. The Social Democratic Party continued to grow. In his frustration, Bismarck planned still more repressive measures in 1890, but before he could carry them out, the new emperor, William II (1888–1918), eager to pursue his own policies, cashiered the aged chancellor.

Austria-Hungary   After the creation of the Dual Monarchy of Austria-Hungary in 1867, the Austrian part received a constitution that established a parliamentary system with the principle of ministerial responsibility. But Emperor Francis Joseph (1848–1916) largely ignored ministerial responsibility and proceeded to personally appoint and dismiss his ministers and rule by decree when parliament was not in session.

The problem of the minorities continued to trouble the empire. The ethnic Germans, who made up only one-third of Austria's population, governed Austria but felt increasingly threatened by the Czechs, Poles, and other Slavic groups within the empire. The difficulties in dealing with this problem were especially evident from 1879 to 1893 when Count Edward von Taaffe (1833–1895) served as prime minister. Taaffe attempted to "muddle through" by relying on a coalition of German conservatives, Czechs, and Poles to maintain a majority in parliament. But his concessions to national minorities, such as allowing the Slavic languages as well as German to be used in education and administration, antagonized the German-speaking Austrian bureaucracy and aristocracy, two of the basic pillars of the empire. Opposition to Taaffe's policies brought his downfall in 1893 but did not solve the **nationalities problem.** While the dissatisfied non-German groups demanded concessions, the ruling Austrian Germans resisted change.

What held the Austro-Hungarian Empire together was a combination of forces. Francis Joseph, the emperor, was one unifying factor. Although strongly anti-Hungarian, the cautious emperor made an effort to take a position above national differences. Loyalty to the Catholic Church also helped keep such national groups as Czechs, Slovaks, and Poles loyal to the Catholic Habsburg dynasty. Finally, although dominated by German-speaking officials, the large imperial bureaucracy served as a unifying force for the empire.

CHRONOLOGY National States of Europe, 1871–1894

Great Britain	
Second ministry of William Gladstone	1880–1885
Reform Act	1884
France	
Surrender of French provisional government to Germany	1871 (January 28)
Paris Commune	1871 (March–May)
Republican constitution (Third Republic)	1875
Boulanger is discredited	1889
Spain	
King Alfonso XII	1874–1885
New constitution	1875
Germany	
Bismarck as chancellor	1871–1890
Antisocialist law	1878
Social welfare legislation	1883–1889
Austria-Hungary	
Emperor Francis Joseph	1848–1916
Count Edward von Taaffe as prime minister	1879–1893
Russia	
Tsar Alexander III	1881–1894

Unlike Austria, Hungary had a working parliamentary system, but it was controlled by the great Magyar land-owners who dominated both the Hungarian peasantry and the other ethnic groups in Hungary. The Hungarians attempted to solve their nationalities problem by systematic Magyarization. The Magyar language was imposed on all schools and was the only language that could be used by government and military officials.

Russia   In Russia, the government made no concession whatever to liberal and democratic reforms, eliminating altogether any possibility of a mass politics. The assassination of Alexander II in 1881 convinced his son and successor, Alexander III (1881–1894), that reform had been a mistake, and he quickly instituted what he said were "exceptional measures." The powers of the secret police were expanded. Advocates of constitutional monarchy and social reform, along with revolutionary groups, were persecuted. Entire districts of Russia were placed under martial law if the government suspected the inhabitants of treason. The powers of the zemstvos, created by the reforms of Alexander II, were sharply curtailed.

Alexander also pursued a radical Russification program of the numerous nationalities that made up the Russian Empire. Russians themselves constituted only 40 percent of the population, which did not stop the tsar from banning the use of all languages except Russian in schools. The policy of Russification served primarily to anger national groups and create new sources of opposition to tsarist policies.

When Alexander III died, his weak son and successor Nicholas II (1894–1917), adopted his father's conviction that the absolute power of the tsars should be preserved: "I shall maintain the principle of autocracy just as firmly and unflinchingly as did my unforgettable father."[13] But conditions were changing, especially with the growth of industrialization, and the tsar's approach was not realistic in view of the new circumstances he faced.

Bismarck and William II.   In 1890, Bismarck sought to undertake new repressive measures against the Social Democrats. Disagreeing with this policy, Emperor William II forced him to resign. This political cartoon shows William II reclining on a throne made of artillery and cannonballs and holding a doll labeled "socialism." Bismarck bids farewell as Germany, personified as a woman, looks on with grave concern.

© Bettmann/CORBIS

BISMARCK AND THE WELFARE OF THE WORKERS

In his attempt to win workers away from socialism, Bismarck favored an extensive program of social welfare benefits, including old-age pensions and compensation for absence from work due to sickness, accident, and disability. This selection is taken from Bismarck's address to the Reichstag on March 10, 1884, in which he explained his motives for social welfare legislation.

Bismarck, *Address to the Reichstag*

The positive efforts began really only in the year...1881... with the imperial message...in which His Majesty William I said: "Already in February of this year, we have expressed our conviction that the healing of social ills is not to be sought exclusively by means of repression of Social Democratic excesses, but equally in the positive promotion of the welfare of the workers."

In consequence of this, first of all the insurance law against accidents was submitted.... And it reads..."But those who have, through age or disability, become incapable of working have a confirmed claim on all for a higher degree of state care than could have been their share heretofore...."

The worker's real sore point is the insecurity of his existence. He is not always sure he will always have work. He is not sure he will always be healthy, and he foresees some day he will be old and incapable of work. But also if he falls into poverty as a result of long illness, he is completely helpless with his own powers, and society hitherto does not recognize relief, even when he has worked ever so faithfully and diligently before. But ordinary poor relief leaves much to be desired, especially in the great cities where it is extraordinarily much worse than in the country.... We read in Berlin newspapers of suicide because of difficulty in making both ends meet, of people who died from direct hunger and have hanged themselves because they have nothing to eat, of people who announce in the paper they were tossed out homeless and have no income.... For the worker it is always a fact that falling into poverty and onto poor relief in a great city is synonymous with misery, and this insecurity makes him hostile and mistrustful of society. That is humanly not unnatural, and as long as the state does not meet him halfway, just as long will this trust in the state's honesty be taken from him by accusations against the government, which he will find where he wills; always running back again to the socialist quacks...and, without great reflection, letting himself be promised things, which will not be fulfilled. On this account, I believe that accident insurance, with which we show the way,...will still work on the anxieties and ill-feeling of the working class.

Q *What arguments does Bismarck advance for social welfare legislation? How did Bismarck benefit politically from these moves toward state protection of workers' interests? To what broader forces in nineteenth-century European social and political life is Bismarck responding through the formulation of these policies?*

CONCLUSION

The Second Industrial Revolution helped create a new material prosperity that led Europeans to believe they had ushered in a new age of progress. A major feature of this age was the emergence of a mass society. The lower classes in particular benefited from the right to vote, a higher standard of living, and new schools that provided them with a modicum of education. New forms of mass transportation, combined with new work patterns, enabled large numbers of people to enjoy weekend excursions to amusement parks and seaside resorts and to participate in new leisure activities.

By 1871, the national state had become the focus of people's lives. Liberal and democratic reforms brought new possibilities for greater participation in the political process, although women were still largely excluded from political rights. After 1871, the national state also began to expand its functions beyond all previous limits. Fearful of the growth of socialism and trade unions, governments attempted to appease the working masses by adopting such social insurance measures as protection against accidents, illness, and old age. These social welfare measures were narrow in scope and limited in benefits, but they signaled a new direction for state action to benefit the mass of its citizens. The enactment of public health and housing measures, designed to curb the worst ills of urban living, were yet another indication of how state power could be used to benefit the people.

This extension of state functions took place in an atmosphere of increased national loyalty. After 1871, Western nation-states increasingly sought to solidify the social order and win the active loyalty and support of their citizens by deliberately cultivating national feelings. Yet this policy contained potentially great dangers. As we shall see in the next chapter, nations had discovered once again that imperialistic adventures and military successes could arouse nationalistic passions and smother domestic political unrest. But they also found that nationalistic feelings could lead to intense international rivalries that made war almost inevitable.

TIMELINE

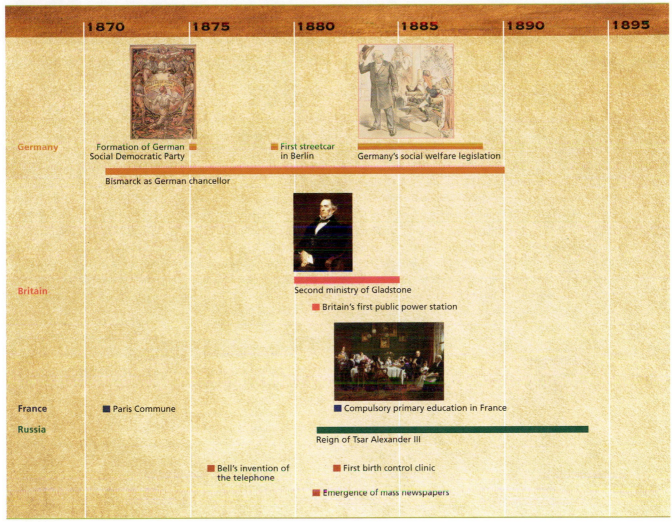

	1870	1875	1880	1885	1890	1895

Germany
- Formation of German Social Democratic Party
- First streetcar in Berlin
- Germany's social welfare legislation
- Bismarck as German chancellor

Britain
- Second ministry of Gladstone
- Britain's first public power station

France
- Paris Commune
- Compulsory primary education in France

Russia
- Reign of Tsar Alexander III
- Bell's invention of the telephone
- First birth control clinic
- Emergence of mass newspapers

NOTES

1. Quoted in David Landes, *The Unbound Prometheus: Technological Change and Industrial Development in Western Europe from 1750 to the Present* (Cambridge, 1969), p. 353.
2. Quoted in Barbara Franzoi, "... With the Wolf Always at the Door: Women's Work in Domestic Industry in Britain and Germany," in Marilyn J. Boxer and Jean H. Quataert, eds., *Connecting Spheres: Women in the Western World, 1500 to the Present* (New York, 1987), p. 151.
3. Quoted in W. L. Guttsman, *The German Social Democratic Party, 1875–1933* (London, 1981), p. 63.
4. Quoted in Leslie Derfler, *Socialism Since Marx: A Century of the European Left* (New York, 1973), p. 58.
5. Karl Marx and Friedrich Engels, *The Communist Manifesto* (Harmondsworth, England, 1967), p. 102.
6. Quoted in Paul Avrich, *The Russian Anarchists* (Princeton, N.J., 1971), p. 67.
7. Quoted in Nicholas Bullock and James Read, *The Movement for Housing Reform in Germany and France, 1840–1914* (Cambridge, 1985), p. 42.
8. Quoted in Gary Cross, *A Social History of Leisure Since 1600* (State College, Pa., 1990), pp. 116, 119.
9. Quoted in Sibylle Meyer, "The Tiresome Work of Conspicuous Leisure: On the Domestic Duties of the Wives of Civil Servants in the German Empire (1871–1918)," in Boxer and Quataert, *Connecting Spheres*, p. 161.
10. Quoted in Lenard R. Berlanstein, *The Working People of Paris, 1871–1914* (Baltimore, 1984), p. 141.
11. Quoted in Robert Gildea, *Barricades and Borders: Europe, 1800–1914,* 2d ed. (Oxford, 1996), pp. 240–241.
12. Quoted in Cross, *Social History of Leisure*, p. 130.
13. Quoted in Shmuel Galai, *The Liberation Movement in Russia, 1900–1905* (Cambridge, 1973), p. 26.

SUGGESTIONS FOR FURTHER READING

General Works In addition to the general works on the nineteenth century and individual European countries cited in Chapters 21 and 22, two more specialized works on the subject matter of this chapter are available in **N. Stone, *Europe Transformed, 1878–1919,*** 2d ed. (London, 1999), and **F. Gilbert and D. C. Large, *The End of the European Era, 1890 to the Present,*** 5th ed. (New York, 2002).

Second Industrial Revolution The subject of the Second Industrial Revolution is well covered in **D. Landes, *The Unbound Prometheus,*** cited in Chapter 20. For a fundamental survey of European industrialization, see **A. S. Milward and S. B. Saul, *The Development of the Economies of Continental Europe, 1850–1914***

(Cambridge, Mass., 1977). For an introduction to the development of mass consumerism in Britain, see **W. H. Fraser**, *The Coming of the Mass Market, 1850–1914* (Hamden, Conn., 1981). The impact of the new technology on European thought is imaginatively discussed in **S. Kern**, *The Culture of Time and Space, 1880–1918*, rev. ed. (Cambridge, Mass., 2003).

Socialism   For an introduction to international socialism, see **A. Lindemann**, *A History of European Socialism* (New Haven, Conn., 1983), and **L. Derfler**, *Socialism Since Marx: A Century of the European Left* (New York, 1973). On the emergence of German social democracy, see **W. L. Guttsman**, *The German Social Democratic Party, 1875–1933* (London, 1981). A good introduction to anarchism is **R. D. Sonn**, *Anarchism* (New York, 1992).

Migration   Demographic problems are examined in **T. McKeown**, *The Modern Rise of Population* (New York, 1976). On European emigration, see **L. P. Moch**, *Moving Europeans: Migration in Western Europe Since 1650* (Bloomington, Ind., 1993).

Housing Reform   For a good introduction to housing reform on the Continent, see **N. Bullock and J. Read**, *The Movement for Housing Reform in Germany and France, 1840–1914* (Cambridge, 1985). Working-class housing in Paris during its reconstruction is the subject of **A. L. Shapiro**, *Housing the Poor of Paris, 1850–1902* (Madison, Wis., 1985).

Social Classes   An interesting work on aristocratic life is **D. Cannadine**, *The Decline and Fall of the British Aristocracy* (New Haven, Conn., 1990). On the middle classes, see **P. Pilbeam**, *The Middle Classes in Europe, 1789–1914* (Basingstoke, England, 1990). On the working classes, see **L. Berlanstein**, *The Working People of Paris, 1871–1914* (Baltimore, 1984), and **R. Magraw**, *A History of the French Working Class* (Cambridge, Mass., 1992).

Women's Experiences   There are good overviews of women's experiences in the nineteenth century in **B. G. Smith**, *Changing Lives: Women in European History Since 1700,* rev. ed. (Lexington, Mass., 2005), and **M. J. Boxer and J. H. Quataert, eds.**, *Connecting Spheres: Women in the Western World, 1500 to the Present* (New York, 1987). The world of women's work is examined in **L. A. Tilly and J. W. Scott**, *Women, Work, and Family,* rev. ed. (New York, 1987). Important studies of women include **M. J. Peterson**, *Family, Love and Work in the Lives of Victorian Gentlewomen* (Bloomington, Ind., 1989); **B. G. Smith**, *Ladies of the Leisure Class: The Bourgeoises of Northern France in the Nineteenth Century* (Princeton, N.J., 1981); and **B. Franzoi**, *At the Very Least She Pays the Rent: Women and German Industrialization, 1871–1914* (Westport, Conn., 1985). For a new perspective on domestic life, see **J. Flanders**, *Inside the Victorian Home: A Portrait of Domestic Life in Victorian England* (New York, 2004). Prostitution is discussed in **J. R. Walkowitz**, *Prostitution and Victorian Society: Women, Class and the State* (Cambridge, 1980).

Mass Education and Leisure   On various aspects of education, see **M. J. Maynes**, *Schooling in Western Europe: A Social History* (Albany, N.Y., 1985). A concise and well-presented survey of leisure patterns is **G. Cross**, *A Social History of Leisure Since 1600* (State College, Pa., 1990).

Domestic Politics   The domestic politics of the period can be examined in the general works on individual countries listed in the bibliographies for Chapters 21 and 22. There are also specialized works on aspects of each country's history. On Britain, see **D. Read**, *The Age of Urban Democracy: England, 1868–1914* (New York, 1994). The Irish problem is covered in **O. MacDonagh**, *States of Mind: A Study of Anglo-Irish Conflict, 1780–1980* (London, 1983). For a detailed examination of French history during the Third Republic, see **J. M. Mayeur and M. Reberioux**, *The Third Republic from Its Origins to the Great War, 1871–1914* (Cambridge, 1988). On the Paris Commune, see **D. A. Shafer**, *The Paris Commune* (New York, 2005), and **C. J. Eichner**, *Surmounting the Barricades: Women in the Paris Commune* (Bloomington, Ind., 2004). On Germany, see **W. J. Mommsen**, *Imperial Germany, 1867–1918* (New York, 1995), and **E. Feuchtwanger**, *Imperial Germany, 1850–1918* (London, 2001).

CENGAGENOW   **CengageNOW is an integrated online suite of services and resources with proven ease of use and efficient paths to success, delivering the results you want—NOW!**
academic.cengage.com/login/
Enter CengageNOW using the access card that is available with *Western Civilization*. CengageNOW will assist you in understanding the content in this chapter with lesson plans generated for your needs. In addition, you can read the following documents, and many more, online:

   Ethel Snowden, selected chapters from *The Feminist Movement*

   Theodore Roosevelt, speeches

WESTERN CIVILIZATION RESOURCES

Visit the *Western Civilization* Companion Web site for resources specific to this book:

   academic.cengage.com/history/spielvogel

For a variety of tools to help you succeed in this course, visit the Western Civilization Resource Center. Enter the Resource Center using either your *CengageNOW* access card or your standalone access card for the *Wadsworth Western Civilization Resource Center*. Organized by topic, this Web site includes quizzes; images; primary source documents; interactive simulations, maps, and timelines; movie explorations; and a wealth of other resources.

   http://westernrc.wadsworth.com/

CHAPTER 24

AN AGE OF MODERNITY,
ANXIETY, AND IMPERIALISM,
1894–1914

Police prevent Emmeline Pankhurst and her two daughters from entering Buckingham Palace to present a petition to the king

CHAPTER OUTLINE
AND FOCUS QUESTIONS

Toward the Modern Consciousness: Intellectual and Cultural Developments

Q What developments in science, intellectual affairs, and the arts in the late nineteenth and early twentieth centuries "opened the way to a modern consciousness," and how did this consciousness differ from earlier worldviews?

Politics: New Directions and New Uncertainties

Q What gains did women make in their movement for women's rights? How did a new right-wing politics affect the Jews in different parts of Europe? What political problems did Great Britain, Italy, France, Austria-Hungary, Germany, and Russia face between 1894 and 1914, and how did they solve them?

The New Imperialism

Q What were the causes of the new imperialism that took place after 1880, and what effects did European imperialism have on Africa and Asia?

International Rivalry and the Coming of War

Q What was the Bismarckian system of alliances, and how successful was it at keeping the peace? What issues lay behind the international crises that Europe faced in the late nineteenth and early twentieth centuries?

CRITICAL THINKING

Q What is the connection between the "new imperialism" of the late nineteenth century and the causes of World War I?

MANY EUROPEANS after 1894 continued to believe they lived in an era of material and human progress. For some, however, progress entailed much struggle. Emmeline Pankhurst, who became the leader of the women's suffrage movement in Britain, said that her determination to fight for women's rights stemmed from a childhood memory: "My father bent over me, shielding the candle flame with his big hand and I heard him say, somewhat sadly, 'What a pity she wasn't born a lad.' " Eventually, Emmeline Pankhurst and her daughters marched and fought for women's right to vote. The struggle was often violent: "They came in bruised, hatless, faces scratched, eyes swollen, noses bleeding," one of the Pankhurst daughters recalled. Arrested and jailed in 1908, Pankhurst informed her judges: "If you had the power to send us to prison, not for six months, but for six years, or for our lives, the Government must not think they could stop this agitation. It would go on!" It did go on, and women in Britain did eventually receive the right to vote; to some, this was yet another confirmation of Europe's progress.

But the period after 1894 was not just a time of progress; it was also a time of great tension as imperialist adventures, international rivalries, and cultural uncertainties disturbed the apparent calm. After 1880, Europeans engaged in a great race for colonies around the world. This competition for lands abroad greatly intensified existing antagonisms among European states.

Ultimately, Europeans proved incapable of finding constructive ways to cope with their international rivalries. The development of two large alliance systems—the Triple Alliance and the Triple Entente—may have helped preserve peace for a time, but eventually the alliances made it easier for the European nations to be drawn into World War I. The alliances helped maintain a balance of power but also led to the creation of large armies, enormous military establishments, and immense arsenals. The alliances also generated tensions that were unleashed when Europeans rushed into the catastrophic carnage of World War I.

The cultural life of Europe in the decades before 1914 reflected similar dynamic tensions. The advent of mass education produced better-informed citizens but also made it easier for governments to stir up the masses by nationalistic appeals through the new mass journalism. At the same time, despite the appearance of progress, European philosophers, writers, and artists were creating modern cultural expressions that questioned traditional ideas and values and incited a crisis of confidence. Before 1914, many intellectuals had a sense of unease about the direction in which society was heading, accompanied by a feeling of imminent catastrophe. They proved remarkably prophetic. ◆

Toward the Modern Consciousness: Intellectual and Cultural Developments

Q Focus Question: What developments in science, intellectual affairs, and the arts in the late nineteenth and early twentieth centuries "opened the way to a modern consciousness," and how did this consciousness differ from earlier worldviews?

Before 1914, most Europeans continued to believe in the values and ideals that had been generated by the Scientific Revolution and the Enlightenment. *Reason, science,* and *progress* were still important buzzwords in the European vocabulary. The ability of human beings to improve themselves and achieve a better society seemed to be well demonstrated by a rising standard of living, urban improvements, and mass education. Such products of modern technology as electric lights, phonographs, and automobiles reinforced the popular prestige of science and the belief in the ability of the human mind to comprehend the universe through the use of reason. Near the end of the nineteenth century, however, a dramatic transformation in the realm of ideas and culture challenged many of these assumptions. A new view of the physical universe, an appeal to the irrational, alternative views of human nature, and radically innovative forms of literary and artistic expression shattered old beliefs and opened the way to a modern consciousness. These new ideas called forth a sense of confusion and anxiety that would become even more pronounced after World War I.

Developments in the Sciences: The Emergence of a New Physics

Science was one of the chief pillars supporting the optimistic and rationalistic view of the world that many Westerners shared in the nineteenth century. Supposedly based on hard facts and cold reason, science offered a certainty of belief in the orderliness of nature that was comforting to many people for whom traditional religious beliefs no longer had much meaning. Many naively believed that the application of already known scientific laws would give humanity a complete understanding of the physical world and an accurate picture of reality. The new physics dramatically altered that perspective.

Throughout much of the nineteenth century, Westerners adhered to the mechanical conception of the universe postulated by the classical physics of Isaac Newton. In this perspective, the universe was viewed as a giant machine in which time, space, and matter were objective realities that existed independently of the people observing them. Matter was thought to be composed of indivisible solid material bodies called atoms.

These views were first seriously questioned at the end of the nineteenth century. The French scientist Marie Curie (1867–1934) and her husband Pierre (1859–1906) discovered that the element radium gave off rays of radiation that apparently came from within the atom itself. Atoms were not simply hard, material bodies but small worlds containing such subatomic particles as electrons and protons that behaved in seemingly random and inexplicable fashion. Inquiry into the disintegrative process within atoms became a central theme of the new physics.

Building on this work, in 1900, a Berlin physicist, Max Planck (1858–1947), rejected the belief that a heated body radiates energy in a steady stream but maintained instead that energy is radiated discontinuously, in irregular packets that he called "quanta." The quantum theory raised fundamental questions about the subatomic realm of the atom. By 1900, the old view of atoms as the basic building blocks of the material world was being seriously questioned, and Newtonian physics was in trouble.

The Work of Einstein Albert Einstein (1879–1955), a German-born patent officer working in Switzerland, pushed these theories of thermodynamics into new terrain. In 1905, Einstein published a paper titled "The Electro-Dynamics of Moving Bodies" that contained his special theory of relativity. According to **relativity theory,** space and time are not absolute but relative to the observer, and both are interwoven into what Einstein called a four-dimensional space-time continuum. Neither space nor time had an existence independent of human experience. As Einstein later explained simply to a journalist, "It was formerly believed that if all material things disappeared out

AP Images

Marie Curie. Marie Curie was born in Warsaw, Poland, but studied at the University of Paris, where she received degrees in both physics and mathematics. She was the first woman to win two Nobel Prizes, one in 1903 in physics and another in chemistry in 1911. She is shown here in her Paris laboratory in 1921. She died of leukemia, a result of her laboratory work with radioactivity.

of the universe, time and space would be left. According to the relativity theory, however, time and space disappear together with the things."[1] Moreover, matter and energy reflected the relativity of time and space. Einstein concluded that matter was nothing but another form of energy. His epochal formula $E = mc^2$—each particle of matter is equivalent to its mass times the square of the velocity of light—was the key theory explaining the vast energies contained within the atom. It led to the atomic age.

Many scientists were unable to comprehend Einstein's ideas, but during a total eclipse of the sun in May 1919, scientists were able to demonstrate that light was deflected in the gravitational field of the sun, just as Einstein had predicted. This confirmed Einstein's general theory of relativity and opened the scientific and intellectual world to his ideas. The 1920s would become the "heroic age" of physics.

Toward a New Understanding of the Irrational

Intellectually, the decades before 1914 witnessed a combination of contradictory developments. Thanks to the

influence of science, confidence in human reason and progress still remained a dominant thread. At the same time, however, a small group of intellectuals attacked the idea of optimistic progress, dethroned reason, and glorified the irrational.

Nietzsche Friedrich Nietzsche (1844–1900) was one of the intellectuals who glorified the irrational. According to Nietzsche, Western bourgeois society was decadent and incapable of any real cultural creativity, primarily because of its excessive emphasis on the rational faculty at the expense of emotions, passions, and instincts. Reason, Nietzsche claimed, actually played little role in human life because humans were at the mercy of irrational life forces.

Nietzsche believed that Christianity should shoulder much of the blame for Western civilization's enfeeblement. The "slave morality" of Christianity, he believed, had obliterated the human impulse for life and had crushed the human will:

> I call Christianity the one great curse, the one enormous and innermost perversion....I call it the one immortal blemish of mankind....Christianity has taken the side of everything weak, base, ill-constituted, it has made an ideal out of opposition to the preservative instincts of strong life....Christianity is called the religion of pity.—Pity stands in antithesis to the basic emotions which enhance the energy of the feeling of life: it has a depressive effect. One loses force when one pities.[2]

How, then, could Western society be renewed? First, said Nietzsche, one must recognize that "God is dead." Europeans had killed God, he said, and it was no longer possible to believe in some kind of cosmic order. Eliminating God and hence Christian morality had liberated human beings and made it possible to create a higher kind of being Nietzsche called the superman: "I teach you the Superman. Man is something that is to be surpassed."[3] Superior intellectuals must free themselves from the ordinary thinking of the masses, create their own values, and lead the masses. Nietzsche rejected and condemned political democracy, social reform, and universal suffrage.

Bergson Another popular revolutionary against reason in the 1890s was Henri Bergson (1859–1941), a French philosopher whose lectures at the University of Paris made him one of the most important influences in French thought in the early twentieth century. Bergson accepted rational, scientific thought as a practical instrument for providing useful knowledge but maintained that it was incapable of arriving at truth or ultimate reality. To him, reality was the "life force" that suffused all things; it could not be divided into analyzable parts. Reality was a whole that could only be grasped intuitively and experienced directly. When we analyze it, we have merely a description, no longer the reality we have experienced.

Sorel Georges Sorel (1847–1922), a French political theorist, combined Bergson's and Nietzsche's ideas on the

Sigmund Freud. Freud was one of the intellectual giants of the nineteenth and twentieth centuries. Born in Moravia, Freud began to study medicine at the University of Vienna in 1873. After entering private practice, he began to study patients suffering from psychosomatic symptoms. This led him to his belief that unconscious forces strongly determine human behavior. This idea formed the foundation for twentieth-century psychoanalysis.

limits of rational thinking with his own passionate interest in **revolutionary socialism.** Sorel understood the political potential of the nonrational and advocated violent action as the only sure way to achieve the aims of socialism. To destroy capitalist society, he recommended the use of the **general strike,** envisioning it as a mythic image that had the power to inspire workers to take violent, heroic action against the capitalist order. Sorel also came to believe that the new socialist society would have to be governed by a small elite ruling body because the masses were incapable of ruling themselves.

Sigmund Freud and Psychoanalysis

Around the turn of the twentieth century, a Viennese doctor, Sigmund Freud (1856–1939), put forth a series of theories that undermined optimism about the rational nature of the human mind. Freud's thought, like the new physics and the irrationalism of Nietzsche, added to the uncertainties of the age. His major ideas were published in 1900 in *The Interpretation of Dreams,* which contained the basic foundation of what came to be known as **psychoanalysis.**

Role of the Unconscious   According to Freud, human behavior was strongly determined by the unconscious, by earlier experiences and inner forces of which people were largely oblivious. To explore the content of the unconscious, Freud relied not only on hypnosis but also on dreams, but the latter were dressed in an elaborate code that had to be deciphered if the content was to be properly understood.

But why did some experiences whose influence persisted in controlling an individual's life remain unconscious? According to Freud, the answer was repression (see the box on p. 735), a process by which unsettling experiences were blotted from conscious awareness but still continued to influence behavior because they had become part of the unconscious. To explain how repression worked, Freud elaborated an intricate theory of the inner life of human beings.

According to Freud, a human being's inner life was a battleground of three contending forces: the id, ego, and superego. The id was the center of unconscious drives and was ruled by what Freud termed the pleasure principle. As creatures of desire, human beings directed their energy toward pleasure and away from pain. The id contained all kinds of lustful drives and desires and crude appetites and impulses. The ego was the seat of reason and hence the coordinator of the inner life. It was governed by the reality principle. Although humans were dominated by the pleasure principle, a true pursuit of pleasure was not feasible. The reality principle meant that people rejected pleasure so that they might live together in society. The superego was the locus of conscience and represented the inhibitions and moral values that society in general and parents in particular imposed on people. The superego served to force the ego to curb the unsatisfactory drives of the id.

The human being was thus a battleground among id, ego, and superego. Ego and superego exerted restraining influences on the unconscious id and repressed or kept out of consciousness what they wanted to. The most important repressions, according to Freud, were sexual, and he went on to develop a theory of infantile sexual drives embodied in the Oedipus complex (Electra complex for females), or the infant's craving for exclusive possession of the parent of the opposite sex. Repression began in childhood, and psychoanalysis was accomplished through a dialogue between psychotherapist and patient in which the therapist probed deeply into memory in order to retrace the chain of repression all the way back to its childhood origins. By making the conscious mind aware of the unconscious and its repressed contents, the patient's psychic conflict was resolved.

Although many of Freud's ideas have been shown to be wrong in many details, he is still regarded as an important figure because of the impact his theories have had.

FREUD AND THE CONCEPT OF REPRESSION

Freud's psychoanalytical theories resulted from his attempt to understand the world of the unconscious. This excerpt is taken from a lecture given in 1909 in which Freud describes how he arrived at his theory of the role of repression. Although Freud valued science and reason, his theories of the unconscious produced a new image of the human being as governed less by reason than by irrational forces.

Sigmund Freud, *Five Lectures on Psychoanalysis*

I did not abandon [the technique of encouraging patients to reveal forgotten experiences], however, before the observations I made during my use of it afforded me decisive evidence. I found confirmation of the fact that the forgotten memories were not lost. They were in the patient's possession and were ready to emerge in association to what was still known by him; but there was some force that prevented them from becoming conscious and compelled them to remain unconscious. The existence of this force could be assumed with certainty, since one became aware of an effort corresponding to it if, in opposition to it, one tried to introduce the unconscious memories into the patient's consciousness. The force which was maintaining the pathological condition became apparent in the form of resistance on the part of the patient.

It was on this idea of resistance, then, that I based my view of the course of physical events in hysteria. In order to effect a recovery, it had proved necessary to remove these resistances. Starting out from the mechanism of cure, it now became possible to construct quite definite ideas of the origin of the illness. The same forces which, in the form of resistance, were now offering opposition to the forgotten material's being made conscious, must formerly have brought about the forgetting and must have pushed the pathogenic experiences in question out of consciousness. I gave the name of "repression" to this hypothetical process, and I considered that it was proved by the undeniable existence of resistance.

The further question could then be raised as to what these forces were and what the determinants were of the repression in which we now recognized the pathogenic mechanism of hysteria. A comparative study of the pathogenic situations which we had come to know through the cathartic procedure made it possible to answer this question. All these experiences had involved the emergence of a wishful impulse which was in sharp contrast to the subject's other wishes and which proved incompatible with the ethical and aesthetic standards of his personality. There had been a short conflict, and the end of this internal struggle was that the idea which had appeared before consciousness as the vehicle of this irreconcilable wish fell a victim to repression, was pushed out of consciousness with all its attached memories, and was forgotten. Thus, the incompatibility of the wish in question with the patient's ego was the motive for the repression; the subject's ethical and other standards were the repressing forces. An acceptance of the incompatible wishful impulse or a prolongation of the conflict would have produced a high degree of unpleasure; this unpleasure was avoided by means of repression, which was thus revealed as one of the devices serving to protect the mental personality.

Q *According to Freud, how did he discover the existence of repression? What function does repression perform? What forces in modern European society might have contributed to force individuals into repressive modes of thinking and acting?*

The Impact of Darwin

In the second half of the nineteenth century, scientific theories were sometimes wrongly applied to achieve other ends. The application of Darwin's principle of organic evolution to the social order came to be known as **social Darwinism.**

Social Darwinism   The most popular exponent of social Darwinism was the British philosopher Herbert Spencer (1820–1903). Using Darwin's terminology, Spencer argued that societies were organisms that evolved through time from a struggle with their environment. Progress came from "the struggle for survival," as the "fit"—the strong—advanced while the weak declined. As Spencer expressed it in 1896 in his book *Social Statics:*

> Pervading all Nature we may see at work a stern discipline which is a little cruel that it may be very kind.... Meanwhile, the well-being of existing humanity and the unfolding of it into this ultimate perfection, are both secured by the same beneficial though severe discipline to which the animate creation at large is subject. It seems hard that an unskillfulness, which with all his efforts he cannot overcome, should entail hunger upon the artisan. It seems hard that a laborer, incapacitated by sickness from competing with his stronger fellows, should have to bear the resulting privations. It seems hard that widows and orphans should be left to struggle for life or death. Nevertheless, when regarded not separately but in connection with the interests of universal humanity, these harsh fatalities are seen to be full of beneficence—the same beneficence which brings to early graves the children of diseased parents, and singles out the intemperate and the debilitated as the victims of an epidemic.[4]

The state should not intervene in this natural process.

Racism   Darwin's ideas were also applied to human society in an even more radical way by rabid nationalists and racists. In their pursuit of national greatness, extreme nationalists argued that nations, too, were engaged in a "struggle for existence" in which only the fittest survived. The German general Friedrich von Bernhardi argued in 1907:

> War is a biological necessity of the first importance, a regulative element in the life of mankind which cannot be dispensed with, since without it an unhealthy development will follow, which excludes every advancement of the race, and therefore all real civilization. "War is the father of all things." The sages of antiquity long before Darwin recognized this.[5]

Numerous nationalist organizations preached the same doctrine as Bernhardi. The Nationalist Association of Italy, for example, founded in 1910, declared that "we must teach Italy the value of international struggle. But international struggle is war? Well, then, let there be war! And nationalism will arouse the will for a victorious war, . . . the only way to national redemption."[6]

Racism, too, was dramatically revived and strengthened by new biological arguments. Perhaps nowhere was the combination of extreme nationalism and racism more evident and more dangerous than in Germany. The concept of the *Volk* (nation, people, or race) had been an underlying idea in German history since the beginning of the nineteenth century. One of the chief propagandists for German **volkish thought** at the turn of the twentieth century was Houston Stewart Chamberlain (1855–1927), an Englishman who became a German citizen. His book *The Foundations of the Nineteenth Century*, published in 1899, made a special impact on Germany. Modern-day Germans, according to Chamberlain, were the only pure successors of the "Aryans," who were portrayed as the true and original creators of Western culture. The Aryan race, under German leadership, must be prepared to fight for Western civilization and save it from the destructive assaults of such lower races as Jews, Negroes, and Orientals. Increasingly, Jews were singled out by German volkish nationalists as the racial enemy in biological terms and as parasites who wanted to destroy the Aryan race.

The Attack on Christianity

The growth of scientific thinking as well as the forces of modernization presented new challenges to the Christian churches. Industrialization and urbanization had an especially adverse effect on religious institutions. The mass migration of people from the countryside to the city meant a change from the close-knit, traditional ties of the village in which the church had been a key force to new urban patterns of social life from which the churches were often excluded. The established Christian churches had a weak hold on workers.

The political movements of the late nineteenth century were also hostile to the established Christian churches. Beginning during the eighteenth-century Enlightenment and continuing well into the nineteenth century, European governments, especially in predominantly Catholic countries, had imposed controls over church courts, religious orders, and appointments of the clergy. But after the failure of the revolutions of 1848, governments were eager to use the churches' aid in reestablishing order and therefore relaxed these controls.

Eventually, however, the close union of state authorities with established churches produced a backlash in the form of **anticlericalism,** especially in the liberal nation-states of the late nineteenth century. As one example, in the 1880s, the French republican government substituted civic training for religious instruction in order to undermine the Catholic Church's control of education. In 1901, Catholic teaching orders were outlawed, and four years later, in 1905, church and state were completely separated.

Science became one of the chief threats to all the Christian churches and even to religion itself in the nineteenth century. Darwin's theory of evolution, accepted by ever-larger numbers of educated Europeans, seemed to contradict the doctrine of divine creation. By seeking to suppress Darwin's books and to forbid the teaching of the evolutionary hypothesis, the churches often caused even more educated people to reject established religions.

The scientific spirit also encouraged a number of biblical scholars to apply critical principles to the Bible, leading to the so-called higher criticism. One of its leading exponents was Ernst Renan (1823–1892), a French Catholic scholar. In his *Life of Jesus*, Renan questioned the historical accuracy of the Bible and presented a radically different picture of Jesus. He saw Jesus not as the son of God but as a human being whose value lay in the example he provided by his life and teaching.

Response of the Churches One response of the Christian churches to these attacks was the outright rejection of modern ideas and forces. Protestant fundamentalist sects were especially important in maintaining a literal interpretation of the Bible. The Catholic Church under Pope Pius IX (1846–1878) also took a rigid stand against modern ideas. In 1864, Pope Pius issued a papal encyclical called the *Syllabus of Errors* in which he stated that it is "an error to believe that the Roman Pontiff can and ought to reconcile himself to, and agree with, progress, liberalism, and modern civilization." He condemned nationalism, socialism, religious toleration, and freedom of speech and press.

Rejection of the new was not the churches' only response, however. A religious movement called Modernism included an attempt by the churches to reinterpret Christianity in the light of new developments. The modernists viewed the Bible as a book of useful moral ideas, encouraged Christians to become involved in social reforms, and insisted that the churches must provide a greater sense of community. The Catholic Church condemned Modernism in 1907 and had driven it underground by the beginning of World War I.

Yet another response of the Christian churches to modern ideas was compromise, an approach especially evident in the Catholic Church during the pontificate of

Leo XIII (1878–1903). Pope Leo permitted the teaching of evolution as a hypothesis in Catholic schools and also responded to the challenges of modernization in the economic and social spheres. In his encyclical *De Rerum Novarum,* issued in 1891, he upheld the individual's right to private property but at the same time criticized "naked" capitalism for the poverty and degradation in which it had left the working classes. Much in socialism, he declared, was Christian in principle, but he condemned Marxist socialism for its materialistic and antireligious foundations. The pope recommended that Catholics form socialist parties and labor unions of their own to help the workers.

Other religious groups also made efforts to win support for Christianity among the working-class poor and to restore religious practice among the urban working classes. Sects of evangelical missionaries were especially successful; a prime example is the Salvation Army, founded in London in 1865 by William Booth, the army's first "general." The Salvation Army established food centers, shelters where the homeless could sleep, and "rescue homes" for women, but all these had a larger purpose, as Booth admitted: "It is primarily and mainly for the sake of saving the soul that I seek the salvation of the body."[7]

The Culture of Modernity: Literature

The revolution in physics and psychology was paralleled by a revolution in literature and the arts. Before 1914, writers and artists were rebelling against the traditional literary and artistic styles that had dominated European cultural life since the Renaissance. The changes that they produced have since been called **Modernism.**

Naturalism Throughout much of the late nineteenth century, literature was dominated by Naturalism. Naturalists accepted the material world as real and felt that literature should be realistic. By addressing social problems, writers could contribute to an objective understanding of the world. Although Naturalism was a continuation of Realism, it lacked the underlying note of liberal optimism about people and society that had been prevalent in the 1850s. The Naturalists were pessimistic about Europe's future and often portrayed characters caught in the grip of forces beyond their control.

The novels of the French writer Émile Zola (1840–1902) provide a good example of Naturalism. Against a backdrop of the urban slums and coalfields of northern France, Zola showed how alcoholism and different environments affected people's lives. He had read Darwin's *Origin of Species* and had been impressed by its emphasis on the struggle for survival and the importance of environment and heredity. These themes were central to his *Rougon-Macquart,* a twenty-volume series of novels on the "natural and social history of a family." Zola maintained that the artist must analyze and dissect life as a biologist would a living organism. He said, "I have simply done on living bodies the work of analysis which surgeons perform on corpses."

The second half of the nineteenth century was a golden age for Russian literature. The nineteenth-century realistic novel reached its high point in the works of Leo Tolstoy (1828–1910) and Fyodor Dostoevsky (1821–1881). Tolstoy's greatest work was *War and Peace,* a lengthy novel played out against the historical background of Napoleon's invasion of Russia in 1812. It is realistic in its vivid descriptions of military life and character portrayal. Each person is delineated clearly and analyzed psychologically. Upon a great landscape, Tolstoy imposed a fatalistic view of history that ultimately proved irrelevant in the face of life's enduring values of human love and trust.

Dostoevsky combined narrative skill and acute psychological and moral observation with profound insights into human nature. He maintained that the major problem of his age was a loss of spiritual belief. Western people were attempting to gain salvation through the construction of a materialistic paradise built only by human reason and human will. Dostoevsky feared that the failure to incorporate spirit would result in total tyranny. His own life experiences led him to believe that only through suffering and faith could the human soul be purified, views that are evident in his best-known works, *Crime and Punishment* and *The Brothers Karamazov.*

Symbolism At the turn of the century, a new group of writers, known as the Symbolists, reacted against Realism. Primarily interested in writing poetry, the Symbolists believed that an objective knowledge of the world was impossible. The external world was not real but only a collection of symbols that reflected the true reality of the individual human mind. Art, they believed, should function for its own sake instead of serving, criticizing, or seeking to understand society. In the works of such Symbolist poets as W. B. Yeats and Rainer Maria Rilke, poetry ceased to be part of popular culture because only through a knowledge of the poet's personal language could one hope to understand what the poem was saying (see the box on p. 738).

Modernism in the Arts

Since the Renaissance, artists had tried to represent reality as accurately as possible. By the late nineteenth century, however, artists were seeking new forms of expression.

Impressionism The preamble to modern painting can be found in **Impressionism,** a movement that originated in France in the 1870s when a group of artists rejected the studios and museums and went out into the countryside to paint nature directly. Camille Pissarro (1830–1903), one of Impressionism's founders, expressed what they sought:

> Precise drawing is dry and hampers the impression of the whole, it destroys all sensations. Do not define too closely the outlines of things; it is the brush stroke of the right

SYMBOLIST POETRY: ART FOR ART'S SAKE

Arthur Rimbaud was one of Symbolism's leading practitioners in France. Although his verses seem to have little real meaning, they were not meant to describe the external world precisely but to enchant the mind. Art was not meant for the masses but only for "art's sake." Rimbaud wrote, "By the alchemy of the words, I noted the inexpressible. I fixed giddiness."

Arthur Rimbaud, *The Drunken Boat*

As I floated down impassable rivers,
I felt the boatmen no longer guiding me.
After them came redskins who with war cries
Nailed them naked to the painted poles.

I was oblivious to the crew,
I who bore Flemish wheat and English cotton.
When the racket was finished with my boatmen,
The waters let me drift my own free way.

In the tide's furious pounding,
I, the other winter, emptier than children's minds,
I sailed! And the unmoored peninsulas
Have not suffered more triumphant turmoils.

The tempest blessed my maritime watches.
Lighter than a cork I danced on the waves,
Those eternal rollers of victims,
Ten nights, without regretting the lantern-foolish eye!

Sweeter than the bite of sour apples to a child,
The green water seeped through my wooden hull,
Rinsed me of blue wine stains and vomit,
Broke apart grappling iron and rudder.

And then I bathed myself in the poetry
Of the star-sprayed milk-white sea,
Devouring the azure greens; where, pale
And ravished, a pensive drowned one sometimes floats;

Where, suddenly staining the blueness, frenzies
And slow rhythms in the blazing of day,

Stronger than alcohol, vaster than our lyres,
The russet bitterness of love ferments. . . .

I have dreamed of the green night bedazzled
    with snow,
A kiss climbing slowly to the eyes of the sea,
The flow of unforgettable sap,
And the yellow-blue waking of singing phosphorous!

Long months I have followed, like maddened cattle,
The surge assaulting the rocks
Without dreaming that the Virgin's luminous feet
Could force a muzzle on the panting ocean!

I have struck against the shores of incredible Floridas
Mixing panther-eyed flowers like human skins!
Rainbows stretched like bridle reins
Under the ocean's horizon, toward sea-green troops!

I have seen the fermenting of monstrous marshes,
Nets where a whole Leviathan rots in the reeds!
The waters collapsing in the middle of the calm,
And horizons plunging toward the abyss!

Glaciers, silver suns, waves of pearl, charcoal skies,
Hideous beaches at the bottom of brown gulfs
Where giant serpents devoured by vermin
Tumble from twisted trees with black perfumes!

I would have liked to show the children those
    dolphins
On the blue waves, those golden singing fish.
— The froth of flowers lulled my voyagings,
Ineffable winds gave me wings by the moment. . . .

Q After reading Rimbaud's poem, what do you think Symbolism is? What strikes you as the goals or ambitions of the Symbolists in this era of artistic innovation and challenge to older forms of expression?

---

value and color which should produce the drawing. . . . Work at the same time upon sky, water, branches, ground, keeping everything going on an equal basis and unceasingly rework until you have got it. . . . Don't proceed according to rules and principles, but paint what you observe and feel. Paint generously and unhesitatingly, for it is best not to lose the first impression.[8]

Impressionists like Pissarro sought to put into their paintings their impressions of the changing effects of light on objects in nature.

Pissarro's suggestions are visibly portrayed in the work of Claude Monet (1840–1926). He was especially enchanted with water and painted many pictures in which he sought to capture the interplay of light, water, and atmosphere, especially evident in *Impression, Sunrise*. But the Impressionists did not just paint scenes from nature. Streets and cabarets, rivers, and busy boulevards—wherever people congregated for work and leisure—formed their subject matter.

Another important Impressionist painter was Berthe Morisot (1841–1895), who broke with the practice of women being only amateur artists and became a professional painter. Her dedication to the new style of painting won her the disfavor of the traditional French academic artists. Morisot believed that women had a special vision, which was, as she said, "more delicate than that of men." Her special touch is evident in the lighter colors and flowing brush strokes of *Young Girl by the*

Claude Monet, *Impression, Sunrise.* Impressionists rejected "rules and principles" and sought to paint what they observed and felt in order "not to lose the first impression." Monet entered this painting, *Impression, Sunrise*, in the first Impressionist show in 1874. He sought to capture his impression of the fleeting moments of sunrise through the simple interplay of light, water, and atmosphere.

Window. Near the end of her life, Morisot lamented the refusal of men to take her work seriously: "I don't think there has ever been a man who treated a woman as an equal, and that's all I would have asked, for I know I'm worth as much as they."[9]

Post-Impressionism   By the 1880s, a new movement known as **Post-Impressionism** arose in France and soon spread to other European countries. Post-Impressionism retained the Impressionist emphasis on light and color but revolutionized it even further by paying more attention to structure and form. Post-Impressionists sought to use both color and line to express inner feelings and produce a personal statement of reality rather than an imitation of objects. Impressionist paintings had retained a sense of realism, but the Post-Impressionists shifted from objective reality to subjective reality and in so doing began to withdraw from the artist's traditional task of depicting the external world. Post-Impressionism was the real beginning of modern art.

Berthe Morisot, *Young Girl by the Window.* Berthe Morisot came from a wealthy French family that settled in Paris when she was seven. The first female painter to join the Impressionists, she developed her own unique Impressionist style. Her gentle colors and strong use of pastels are especially evident in *Young Girl by the Window*, painted in 1878. Many of her paintings focus on women and domestic scenes.

Paul Cézanne, *Woman with Coffee Pot.* Post-Impressionists sought above all to express their inner feelings and capture on canvas their own vision of reality. In *Woman with Coffee Pot*, Paul Cézanne tried to relate the geometric shapes of his central female figure to the geometric shapes of the coffeepot and the rectangles of the door panels.

Paul Cézanne (1839–1906) was one of the most important Post-Impressionists. Initially, he was influenced by the Impressionists but soon rejected their work. In his paintings, such as *Woman with Coffee Pot*, Cézanne sought to express visually the underlying geometric structure and form of everything he painted. As Cézanne explained to one young painter: "You must see in nature the cylinder, the sphere, and the cone."

Another famous Post-Impressionist was a tortured and tragic figure, Vincent van Gogh (1853–1890). For van Gogh, art was a spiritual experience. He was especially interested in color and believed that it could act as its own form of language. Van Gogh maintained that artists should paint what they feel, which is evident in his *Starry Night.*

Vincent van Gogh, *The Starry Night.* The Dutch painter Vincent van Gogh was a major figure among the Post-Impressionists. His originality and power of expression made a strong impact on his artistic successors. In *The Starry Night*, painted in 1889, van Gogh's subjective vision was given full play as the dynamic swirling forms of the heavens above overwhelm the village below. The heavens seem alive with a mysterious spiritual force. Van Gogh painted this work in an asylum one year before he committed suicide.

Pablo Picasso, *Les Demoiselles d'Avignon.* Pablo Picasso, a major pioneer and activist of modern art, experimented with a remarkable variety of modern styles. *Les Demoiselles d'Avignon* (1907) was the first great example of Cubism, which one art historian has called "the first style of this century to break radically with the past." Geometric shapes replace traditional forms, forcing the viewer to re-create reality in his or her own mind. Picasso said of this painting, "I paint forms as I think them, not as I see them." The head at the upper right of the painting reflects Picasso's attraction to aspects of African art, as is evident from the Congo mask included at the left.

The Search for Individual Expression By the beginning of the twentieth century, the belief that the task of art was to represent "reality" had lost much of its meaning. By that time, psychology and the new physics had made it evident that many people were not sure what constituted reality anyway. Then, too, the development of photography gave artists another reason to reject visual realism. Invented in the 1830s, photography became popular and widespread after George Eastman produced the first Kodak camera for the mass market in 1888. What was the point of an artist doing what the camera did better? Unlike the camera, which could only mirror reality, artists could create reality. Individual consciousness became the source of meaning. Between 1905 and 1914, this search for individual expression produced a wide variety of schools of painting, all of which had their greatest impact after World War I.

In 1905, one of the most important figures in modern art was just beginning his career. Pablo Picasso (1881–1973) was from Spain but settled in Paris in 1904. Picasso was extremely flexible and painted in a remarkable variety of styles. He was instrumental in the development of a new style called **Cubism** that used geometric designs as visual stimuli to re-create reality in the viewer's mind. Picasso's 1907 work *Les Demoiselles d'Avignon* has been called the first Cubist painting.

The modern artist's flight from "visual reality" reached a high point in 1910 with the beginning of **abstract painting.** A Russian who worked in Germany, Wassily Kandinsky (1866–1944), was one of the founders of abstract painting. As is evident in his *Square with White Border,* Kandinsky sought to avoid representation altogether. He believed that art should speak directly to the soul. To do so, it must avoid any reference to visual reality and concentrate on color.

Modernism in Music

In the first half of the nineteenth century, the Romantics' attraction to exotic and primitive cultures had sparked a fascination with folk music, which became increasingly important as musicians began to look for ways to express their national identities. In the second half of the century, new flames of nationalistic spirit were fanned in both literary and musical circles.

Grieg One example of this new nationalistic spirit may be found in the Scandinavian composer Edvard Grieg (1843–1907), who remained a dedicated supporter of Norwegian nationalism throughout his life. Grieg's nationalism expressed itself in the lyric melodies found in the folk music of his homeland. Among his best-known works is the *Peer Gynt Suite* (1876), incidental music to a play by Henrik Ibsen. Grieg's music paved the way for the creation of a national music style in Norway.

Wassily Kandinsky, *Square with White Border.* One of the originators of abstract painting was the Russian Wassily Kandinsky, who sought to eliminate representation altogether by focusing on color and avoiding any resemblance to visual reality. In *Square with White Border,* Kandinsky used color "to send light into the darkness of men's hearts." He believed that color, like music, could fulfill a spiritual goal of appealing directly to the human senses.

Debussy The Impressionist movement in music followed its artistic counterpart by some thirty years. Impressionist music stressed elusive moods and haunting sensations and is distinct in its delicate beauty and elegance of sound. The composer most tangibly linked to the Impressionist movement was Claude Debussy (1862–1918), whose musical compositions were often inspired by the visual arts. One of Debussy's most famous works, *Prelude to the Afternoon of a Faun* (1894), was actually inspired by a poem, "Afternoon of a Faun," composed by his friend, the Symbolist poet Stéphane Mallarmé. But Debussy did not tell a story in music; rather, *Prelude to the Afternoon of a Faun* re-created in sound the overall feeling of the poem. Said Mallarmé upon hearing Debussy's piece, "I was not expecting anything like this. This music prolongs the emotion of my poem, and evokes the scene more vividly than color."[10]

Other composers adopted stylistic idioms that imitated presumably primitive forms in an attempt to express less refined and therefore more genuine feelings. A chief exponent of musical primitivism was Igor Stravinsky (1882–1971), one of the twentieth century's most important composers, both for his compositions and for his impact on other composers. He gained international fame as a ballet composer and together with the Ballet Russe, under the direction of Sergei Diaghilev (1872–1929), revolutionized the world of music with a series of ballets. The three most significant ballets Stravinsky composed for Diaghilev's company were *The Firebird* (1910), *Petrushka* (1911), and *The Rite of Spring* (1913). All three were based on Russian folk tales. *The Rite of Spring* proved to be a revolutionary piece in the development of music. At its premiere on May 29, 1913, the pulsating rhythms, sharp dissonances, and unusual dancing overwhelmed the Paris audience and caused a riot at the theater. Like the intellectuals of his time, Stravinsky sought a new understanding of irrational forces in his music, which became an important force in inaugurating a modern musical movement.

Politics: New Directions and New Uncertainties

Q Focus Questions: What gains did women make in their movement for women's rights? How did a new right-wing politics affect the Jews in different parts of Europe? What political problems did Great Britain, Italy, France, Austria-Hungary, Germany, and Russia face between 1894 and 1914, and how did they solve them?

The uncertainties in European intellectual and cultural life were paralleled by growing anxieties in European political life. The seemingly steady progress in the growth of liberal principles and **political democracy** after 1871 was soon slowed or even halted altogether after 1894. The new mass politics had opened the door to changes that many nineteenth-century liberals found unacceptable, and liberals themselves were forced to move in new directions. The appearance of a new right-wing politics based on racism added an ugly note to the already existing anxieties. With their newfound voting rights, workers elected socialists who demanded new reforms when they took their places in legislative bodies. Women, too, made new demands, insisting on the right to vote and using new tactics to gain it. In central and eastern Europe, tensions grew as authoritarian governments refused to meet the demands of reformers. And outside Europe, a new giant appeared in the Western world as the United States emerged as a great industrial power with immense potential.

The Movement for Women's Rights

In the 1830s, a number of women in the United States and Europe, who worked together in several reform movements, became frustrated by the apparent prejudices against females. They sought improvements for women by focusing on specific goals. Family and marriage laws were especially singled out because it was difficult for women to secure divorces and property laws gave husbands almost complete control over the property of their wives. These early efforts were not particularly successful, however. For example, women did not gain the right to their own property until 1870 in Britain, 1900 in Germany, and 1907 in France. Although the British legalized divorce in 1857, the French state permitted only a limited degree of divorce in 1884. In Catholic countries such as Spain and Italy, women had no success at all in achieving the right to divorce their husbands.

New Professions Divorce and property rights were only a beginning for the women's movement, however. Some middle- and upper-middle-class women gained access to higher education, and others sought entry into occupations dominated by men. The first to fall was teaching. Because medical training was largely closed to women, they sought alternatives through the development of nursing. One nursing pioneer was Amalie Sieveking (1794–1859), who founded the Female Association for the Care of the Poor and Sick in Hamburg, Germany. As she explained, "To me, at least as important were the benefits which [work with the poor] seemed to promise for those of my sisters who would join me in such a work of charity. The higher interests of my sex were close to my heart."[11] Sieveking's work was followed by the more famous British nurse, Florence Nightingale (1820–1910), whose efforts during the Crimean War, along with those of Clara Barton (1821–1912) in the American Civil War, transformed nursing into a profession of trained, middle-class "women in white."

The Right to Vote By the 1840s and 1850s, the movement for women's rights had entered the political arena with the call for equal political rights. Many feminists believed that the right to vote was the key to all other reforms to improve the position of women. The British women's movement was the most vocal and active in Europe, but it divided over tactics. The liberal Millicent Fawcett (1847–1929) organized a moderate group who believed that women must demonstrate that they would use political power responsibly if they wanted Parliament to grant them the right to vote. Another group, however, favored a more radical approach. Emmeline Pankhurst (1858–1928) and her daughters, Christabel and Sylvia,

founded the Women's Social and Political Union in 1903, which enrolled mostly middle- and upper-class women. Pankhurst's organization realized the value of the media and used unusual publicity stunts to call attention to its demands (see the box on p. 745). Derisively labeled "suffragettes" by male politicians, they pelted government officials with eggs, chained themselves to lampposts, smashed the windows of department stores on fashionable shopping streets, burned railroad cars, and went on hunger strikes in jail. In 1913, Emily Davison accepted martyrdom for the cause when she threw herself in front of the king's horse at the Epsom Derby horse race. **Suffragists** had one fundamental aim: the right of women to full citizenship in the nation-state.

Although few women elsewhere in Europe used the Pankhursts' confrontational methods, demands for women's rights were heard throughout Europe and the United States before World War I. Nevertheless, only in Finland, Norway, and some American states did women actually receive the right to vote before 1914. It would take the dramatic upheaval of World War I before male-dominated governments capitulated on this basic issue (see Chapter 25).

Efforts for Peace Women reformers took on other issues besides suffrage. In many countries, women supported peace movements. Bertha von Suttner (1843–1914) became the head of the Austrian Peace Society and protested against the growing arms race of the 1890s. Her novel *Lay Down Your Arms* became a best-seller and brought her the Nobel Peace Prize in 1905. Lower-class women also took up the cause of peace. In 1911, a group of female workers marched in Vienna and demanded, "We want an end to armaments, to the means of murder and we want these millions to be spent on the needs of the people."[12]

The New Woman Bertha von Suttner was but one example of the "new women" who were becoming more prominent at the turn of the century. These women renounced traditional feminine roles. Although some of them supported political ideologies such as socialism that flew in the face of the ruling classes, others simply sought new freedom outside the household and new roles other than those of wives and mothers.

Maria Montessori (1870–1952) was a good example of the "new woman." Breaking with tradition, she attended medical school at the University of Rome. Although often isolated by the male students, she persisted and in 1896 became the first Italian woman to receive a medical degree. Three years later, she undertook a lecture tour in Italy on the subject of the "new woman," whom she characterized as a woman who followed a rational, scientific perspective. In keeping with this ideal, Montessori put her medical background to work in a school for mentally handicapped children. She devised new teaching materials that enabled these children

IMAGES OF EVERYDAY LIFE

The Struggle for the Right to Vote. For many feminists, the right to vote came to represent the key to other reforms that would benefit women. In Britain, suffragists attracted attention to their cause by unusual publicity stunts. The photograph at the right shows the arrest of a suffragist who had chained herself to the railings of Buckingham Palace in London. Below is a photo of Emily Davison throwing herself under the king's horse at the Epsom Derby horse race. Shortly before her sacrificial action, she had written, "The glorious and indomitable Spirit of Liberty has but one further penalty within its power, the surrender of life itself, the supreme consummation of sacrifice."

to read and write and became convinced, as she later wrote, "that similar methods applied to normal students would develop or set free their personality in a marvelous and surprising way." Subsequently, she established a system of childhood education based on natural and spontaneous activities in which students learned at their own pace. By the 1930s, hundreds of Montessori schools had been established in Europe and the United States. As a professional woman and an unwed mother,

Montessori also embodied some of the freedoms of the "new woman."

Jews in the European Nation-State

Near the end of the nineteenth century, a revival of racism combined with extreme nationalism to produce a new right-wing politics aimed primarily at the Jews. Of course, anti-Semitism was not new to European civilization. Since

THE STRUGGLE FOR THE RIGHT TO VOTE

Emmeline Pankhurst, with the help of her daughters, was the leader of the women's movement for the right to vote in Britain at the end of the nineteenth century and the beginning of the twentieth century. Believing that peaceful requests were achieving little from the members of Parliament, Pankhurst came to advocate more forceful methods, as is evident in this selection from *My Own Story*, her autobiography published in 1914. Although this confrontational approach was abandoned during World War I, the British government granted women the right to vote in 1918 at the end of the war.

Emmeline Pankhurst, *My Own Story*

I had called upon women to join me in striking at the Government through the only thing that governments are really very much concerned about—property—and the response was immediate. Within a few days the newspapers rang with the story of the attack made on letter boxes in London, Liverpool, Birmingham, Bristol, and half a dozen other cities. In some cases the boxes, when opened by postmen, mysteriously burst into flame; in others the letters were destroyed by corrosive chemicals; in still others the addresses were rendered illegible by black fluids. Altogether it was estimated that over 5,000 letters were completely destroyed and many thousands more were delayed in transit.

It was with a deep sense of their gravity that these letter-burning protests were undertaken, but we felt that something drastic must be done in order to destroy the apathy of the men of England who view with indifference the suffering of women oppressed by unjust laws. As we pointed out, letters, precious though they may be, are less precious than human bodies and souls.... And so, in order to call attention to greater crimes against human beings, our letter burnings continued.

In only a few cases were the offenders apprehended, and one of the few women arrested was a helpless cripple, a woman who could move about only in a wheeled chair. She received a sentence of eight months in the first division, and, resolutely hunger striking, was forcibly fed with unusual brutality, the prison doctor deliberately breaking one of her teeth in order to insert a gag. In spite of her disabilities and her weakness the crippled girl persisted in her hunger strike and her resistance to prison rules, and within a short time had to be released. The excessive sentences of the other pillar box destroyers resolved themselves into very short terms because of the resistance of the prisoners, every one of whom adopted the hunger strike.

It was at this time, February, 1913, less than two years ago as I write these words, that militancy, as it is now generally understood by the public began—militancy in the sense of continued, destructive, guerrilla warfare against the Government through injury to private property. Some property had been destroyed before this time, but the attacks were sporadic, and were meant to be in the nature of a warning as to what might become a settled policy. Now we indeed lighted the torch, and we did it with the absolute conviction that no other course was open to us. We had tried every other measure, as I am sure that I have demonstrated to my readers, and our years of work and suffering and sacrifice had taught us that the Government would not yield to right and justice, what the majority of members of the House of Commons admitted was right and justice, but that the Government would, as other governments invariably do, yield to expediency. Now our task was to show the Government that it was expedient to yield to the women's just demands. In order to do that we had to make England and every department of English life insecure and unsafe. We had to make English law a failure and the courts farce comedy theatres; we had to discredit the Government and Parliament in the eyes of the world; we had to spoil English sports, hurt business, destroy valuable property, demoralize the world of society, shame the churches, upset the whole orderly conduct of life.

That is, we had to do as much of this guerrilla warfare as the people of England would tolerate. When they came to the point of saying to the Government: "Stop this, in the only way it can be stopped, by giving the women of England representation," then we should extinguish our torch.

Q   *What methods did Emmeline Pankhurst advocate be used to achieve the right to vote for women? Why did she feel justified in using these methods? Do you think she was justified? Why or why not?*

---

the Middle Ages, Jews had been portrayed as the murderers of Jesus and subjected to mob violence; their rights had been restricted, and they had been physically separated from Christians in quarters known as ghettos.

In the nineteenth century, as a result of the ideals of the Enlightenment and the French Revolution, Jews were increasingly granted legal equality in many European countries. The French revolutionary decrees of 1790 and 1791 emancipated the Jews and admitted them to full citizenship. After the revolutions of 1848, emancipation became a fact of life for Jews throughout western and central Europe. For many Jews, emancipation enabled them to leave the ghetto and become assimilated as hundreds of thousands of Jews entered what had been the closed worlds of parliaments and universities. In 1880, for example, Jews made up 10 percent of the population of the city of Vienna, Austria, but 39 percent of its medical students and 23 percent of its law students. A Jew could "leave his Jewishness behind," as the career of Benjamin Disraeli, who became prime minister of Great Britain, demonstrated. Many other Jews became successful bankers, lawyers, scientists, scholars, journalists, and stage performers.

Anti-Semitism in the Austrian Empire and Germany

These achievements represent only one side of the picture, however. In Austrian politics, for example, the Christian Socialists combined agitation for workers with a virulent **anti-Semitism.** They were most powerful in Vienna, where they were led by Karl Lueger, mayor of Vienna from 1897 to 1910. Imperial Vienna at the turn of the century was a brilliant center of European culture, but it was also the home of an insidious German nationalism that blamed Jews for the corruption of German culture. It was in Vienna between 1907 and 1913 that Adolf Hitler later claimed to have found his worldview, one that was largely based on violent German nationalism and rabid anti-Semitism.

Germany, too, had its right-wing anti-Semitic parties, such as Adolf Stocker's Christian Social Workers. These parties used anti-Semitism to win the votes of traditional lower-middle-class groups who felt threatened by the new economic forces of the times. These German anti-Semitic parties were based on race. In medieval times, Jews could convert to Christianity and escape from their religion. To modern racial anti-Semites, Jews were racially stained; this could not be altered by conversion. One could not be both a German and a Jew. Hermann Ahlwardt, an anti-Semitic member of the German Reichstag, made this clear in a speech to that body:

> The Jew is no German.... A Jew who was born in Germany does not thereby become a German; he is still a Jew. Therefore it is imperative that we realize that Jewish racial characteristics differ so greatly from ours that a common life of Jews and Germans under the same laws is quite impossible because the Germans will perish.[13]

After 1898, the political strength of the German anti-Semitic parties began to decline.

Persecution of Jews in Eastern Europe The worst treatment of Jews in the last two decades of the nineteenth century and the first decade of the twentieth occurred in eastern Europe, where 72 percent of the entire world Jewish population lived. Russian Jews were admitted to secondary schools and universities only under a quota system and were forced to live in certain regions of the country. Persecutions and **pogroms** (organized massacres) were widespread. Between 1903 and 1906, pogroms took place in almost seven hundred Russian towns and villages, mostly in the Ukraine. Hundreds of thousands of Jews decided to emigrate to escape the persecution. Between 1881 and 1899, an average of 23,000 Jews left Russia each year. Many of them went to the United States and Canada, although some (probably about 25,000) moved to Palestine, which soon became the focus for a Jewish nationalist movement called **Zionism.**

The Zionist Movement The emancipation of the nineteenth century had presented vast opportunities for some Jews but dilemmas for others. Did emancipation mean full assimilation, and did assimilation mean the disruption of traditional Jewish life? Many Jews paid the price willingly, but others questioned its value and advocated a different answer, a return to Palestine. For many Jews, Palestine, the land of ancient Israel, had long been the land of their dreams. During the nineteenth century, as nationalist ideas spread and Italians, Poles, Irish, Greeks, and others sought national emancipation, so did the idea of national independence capture the imagination of some Jews. A key figure in the growth of political Zionism was Theodor Herzl (1860–1904). In 1896, he published a book called *The Jewish State* (see the box on p. 747) in which he maintained that "the Jews who wish it will have their state." Financial support for the development of settlements in Palestine came from wealthy Jewish banking families who wanted a refuge in Palestine for persecuted Jews. Even settlements were difficult because Palestine was then part of the Ottoman Empire and Ottoman authorities were opposed to Jewish immigration. In 1891, one Jewish essayist pointed to the problems this would create:

Palestine

> We abroad are accustomed to believe that Erez Israel [the land of Israel] is almost totally desolate at present...but in reality it is not so.... Arabs, especially those in towns, see and understand our activities and aims in the country but keep quiet and pretend as if they did not know,...and they try to exploit us, too, and profit from the new guests while laughing at us in their hearts. But if the time comes and our people make such progress as to displace the people of the country...they will not lightly surrender the place.[14]

Despite the warnings, however, the First Zionist Congress, which met in Switzerland in 1897, proclaimed as its aim the creation of a "home in Palestine secured by public law" for the Jewish people. One thousand Jews migrated to Palestine in 1901, and the number rose to three thousand annually between 1904 and 1914; but on the eve of World War I, the Zionist dream remained just that.

The Transformation of Liberalism: Great Britain and Italy

In dealing with the problems created by the new mass politics, liberal governments often followed policies that

THE VOICE OF ZIONISM: THEODOR HERZL AND THE JEWISH STATE

The Austrian Jewish journalist Theodor Herzl wrote *The Jewish State* in the summer of 1895 in Paris while he was covering the Dreyfus case for his Vienna newspaper. During several weeks of feverish composition, he set out to analyze the fundamental causes of anti-Semitism and devise a solution to the "Jewish problem." In this selection, he discusses two of his major conclusions.

Theodor Herzl, *The Jewish State*

I do not intend to arouse sympathetic emotions on our behalf. That would be a foolish, futile, and undignified proceeding. I shall content myself with putting the following questions to the Jews: Is it true that, in countries where we live in perceptible numbers, the position of Jewish lawyers, doctors, technicians, teachers, and employees of all descriptions becomes daily more intolerable? True, that the Jewish middle classes are seriously threatened? True, that the passions of the mob are incited against our wealthy people? True, that our poor endure greater sufferings than any other proletariat?

I think that this external pressure makes itself felt everywhere. In our economically upper classes it causes discomfort, in our middle classes continual and grave anxieties, in our lower classes absolute despair.

Everything tends, in fact, to one and the same conclusion, which is clearly enunciated in that classic Berlin phrase: "Juden 'raus!" (Out with the Jews!)

I shall now put the Jewish Question in the curtest possible form: Are we to "get out" now? And if so, to what place?

Or, may we yet remain? And if so, how long?

Let us first settle the point of staying where we are. Can we hope for better days, can we possess our souls in patience, can we wait in pious resignation till the princes and peoples of this earth are more mercifully disposed toward us? I say that we cannot hope for a change in the current of feeling. And why not? Were we as near to the hearts of princes as are their other subjects, even so they could not protect us. They would only feed popular hatred of Jews by showing us too much favor. By "too much," I

really mean less than is claimed as a right by every ordinary citizen, or by every race. The nations in whose midst Jews live are all, either covertly or openly, Anti-Semitic....

The whole plan is in its essence perfectly simple, as it must necessarily be if it is to come within the comprehension of all.

Let the sovereignty be granted us over a portion of the globe large enough to satisfy the rightful requirements of a nation; the rest we shall manage for ourselves.

The creation of a new State is neither ridiculous nor impossible. We have in our day witnessed the process in connection with nations which were not in the bulk of the middle class, but poorer, less educated, and consequently weaker than ourselves. The Governments of all countries scourged by Anti-Semitism will be keenly interested in assisting us to obtain the sovereignty we want....

Palestine is our ever-memorable historic home. The very name of Palestine would attract our people with a force of marvelous potency. Supposing his Majesty the Sultan were to give us Palestine, we could in return undertake to regulate the whole finances of Turkey. We should there form a portion of the rampart of Europe against Asia, an outpost of civilization as opposed to barbarism. We should as a neutral State remain in contact with all Europe, which would have to guarantee our existence. The sanctuaries of Christendom would be safeguarded by assigning to them an extra-territorial status such as is well known to the law of nations. We should form a guard of honor about these sanctuaries, answering for the fulfillment of this duty with our existence. This guard of honor would be the great symbol of the solution of the Jewish Question after eighteen centuries of Jewish suffering.

Q *What forces in European society came together to intensify anti-Semitism in the late nineteenth century? What was the relationship between nationalism and Zionism at this time? Was Herzl's Zionism simply a reaction to Western anti-Semitism, or did other developments also contribute to his movement?*

---

undermined the basic tenets of liberalism. This was particularly true in Great Britain and Italy.

Great Britain   In Britain, the demands of the working-class movement caused Liberals to move away from their ideals. Liberals were forced to adopt significant social reforms due to the pressure of two new working-class organizations: trade unions and the Labour Party. Frustrated by the government's failure to enact social reform, trade unions began to advocate more radical change of the economic system, calling for "collective ownership and control over production, distribution, and exchange." This "new unionism" also led to the union organization of many steel factory workers and to new confrontations

in the streets of London as British workers struck for a minimum wage and other benefits.

At the same time, a movement for laborers emerged among a group of intellectuals known as the Fabian Socialists who stressed the need for the workers to use their right to vote to capture the House of Commons and pass legislation that would benefit the laboring class. Neither the Fabian Socialists nor the British trade unions were Marxist. They did not advocate class struggle and revolution but instead favored evolution toward a socialist state by democratic means. In 1900, representatives of the trade unions and Fabian Socialists coalesced to form the Labour Party. Although the new party won only one seat in 1900, it managed to elect twenty-nine members to the House of Commons in 1906.

The Liberals, who gained control of the House of Commons in that year and held the government from 1906 to 1914, perceived that they would have to enact a program of social welfare or lose the support of the workers. The policy of reform was especially advanced by David Lloyd George (1863–1945), a brilliant orator from Wales who had been deeply moved by the misery of Welsh coal miners. The Liberals abandoned the classical principles of *laissez-faire* and voted for a series of social reforms. The National Insurance Act of 1911 provided benefits for workers in case of sickness and unemployment, to be paid for by compulsory contributions from workers, employers, and the state. Additional legislation provided a small pension for retirees over seventy and compensation for workers injured on the job. To pay for the new program, Lloyd George increased the tax burden on the wealthy classes. Though both the benefits of the program and the tax increases were modest, they were the first hesitant steps toward the future British welfare state. Liberalism, which had been based on the principle that the government that governs least governs best, had been transformed.

In the effort to achieve social reform, Lloyd George was also forced to confront the power of the House of Lords. Composed of hereditary aristocrats, the House of Lords took a strong stance against Lloyd George's effort to pay for social reform measures by taxes, however modest, on the wealthy. The prime minister pushed through a law in 1911 that restricted the ability of the House of Lords to impede legislation enacted by the House of Commons. After 1911, the House of Lords became largely a debating society.

The Liberals also tried to solve the Irish problem (see Chapter 23). Parliament finally granted home rule in 1914, but the explosive situation in Ireland itself created more problems. Irish Protestants in northern Ireland, especially in the province of Ulster, wanted no part of an Irish Catholic state. The outbreak of World War I enabled the British government to sidestep the potentially explosive issue and to suspend Irish home rule for the duration of the war. Failure to deal decisively with the issue simply led to more problems later.

Italy Liberals had even greater problems in Italy. A certain amount of stability was achieved from 1903 to 1914 when the liberal leader Giovanni Giolitti served intermittently as prime minister. Giolitti was a master of using *trasformismo*, or **transformism,** a system in which old political groups were transformed into new government coalitions by political and economic bribery. In the long run, however, Giolitti's devious methods made Italian politics even more corrupt and unmanageable. When urban workers turned to violence to protest their living and working conditions, Giolitti tried to appease them with social welfare legislation and universal male suffrage in 1912. To strengthen his popularity, he also aroused nationalistic passions by conquering Libya. Despite his efforts, however, worker unrest continued, and in 1914 government troops had to be used to quell rioting workers.

France: Travails of the Third Republic

In the 1890s, the fragile Third Republic experienced yet another crisis, which was also evidence of the renewed anti-Semitism in Europe in the late nineteenth century. Early in 1895, Alfred Dreyfus, a Jew and a captain in the French general staff, was found guilty by a secret military court of selling army secrets and condemned to life imprisonment on Devil's Island. Evidence soon emerged that pointed to his innocence. Another officer, a Catholic aristocrat, was more obviously the traitor, but the army, a stronghold of aristocratic and Catholic officers, refused a new trial. Some right-wing journalists even used the case to push their own anti-Semitic views. Republic leaders, however, insisted on a new trial after a wave of intense public outrage. Although the new trial failed to set aside the guilty verdict, the government pardoned Dreyfus in 1899, and in 1906, he was finally fully exonerated.

One result of the Dreyfus affair was a change in government. Moderate republicans lost control to radical republicans who were determined to make greater progress toward a more democratic society by breaking the power of the Republic's enemies, especially the army and the Catholic Church. The army was purged of all high-ranking officers who had antirepublican reputations. Most of the Catholic religious orders that had controlled many French schools were forced to leave France. Moreover, church and state were officially separated in 1905, and during the next two years, the government seized church property and began to pay clerical salaries.

These changes ended the political threat from the right to the Third Republic, which by now commanded the loyalty of most French people. Nevertheless, problems remained. As a nation of small businessmen and farmers, the French lagged far behind Great Britain, Germany, and the United States in industrial activity. Moreover, a surge of industrialization after 1896 left the nation with the realization that little had been done to appease the discontent of the French working classes and their abysmal working conditions. Since only a quarter of the French wage earners worked in industry, there was little pressure for labor legislation from the French parliament. This made the use of strikes more appealing to the working classes. The brutal government repression of labor walkouts in 1911 only further alienated the working classes.

Growing Tensions in Germany

The new imperial Germany begun by Bismarck in 1871 continued as an "authoritarian, conservative, military-bureaucratic power state" during the reign of Emperor William II (1888–1918). Unstable and aggressive, the emperor was inclined to tactless remarks, as when he told the soldiers of a Berlin regiment that they must be prepared to shoot their fathers and mothers if he ordered them to do so. A small group of about twenty powerful men joined William in setting government policy.

By 1914, Germany had become the strongest military and industrial power on the Continent. New social configurations had emerged as more than 50 percent of German workers had jobs in industry while only 30 percent of the workforce was still in agriculture. Urban centers had mushroomed in number and size. The rapid changes in William's Germany helped produce a society torn between modernization and traditionalism.

The growth of industrialization led to even greater expansion for the Social Democratic Party. Despite the enactment of new welfare legislation to favor the working classes, William II was no more successful than Bismarck at slowing the growth of the Social Democrats. By 1912, it had become the largest single party in the Reichstag. At the same time, the party increasingly became less revolutionary and more revisionist in its outlook. Nevertheless, its growth frightened the middle and upper classes, who blamed labor for their own problems.

With the expansion of industry and cities came demands for more political participation and growing sentiment for reforms that would produce greater democratization. Conservative forces, especially the landowning nobility and representatives of heavy industry, two of the powerful ruling groups in Germany, tried to block it by supporting William II's activist foreign policy (see "New Directions and New Crises" later in this chapter). Expansionism, they believed, would divert people from further democratization.

The tensions in German society created by the conflict between modernization and traditionalism were also manifested in a new, radicalized, right-wing politics. A number of pressure groups arose to support nationalistic goals. Groups such as the Pan-German League stressed strong German nationalism and advocated imperialism as a tool to overcome social divisions and unite all classes. They were also anti-Semitic and denounced Jews as the destroyers of the national community.

Austria-Hungary: The Problem of the Nationalities

At the beginning of the 1890s, Austria-Hungary was still troubled by the problem of its numerous nationalities (see Chapter 23). The granting of universal male suffrage in 1907 served only to exacerbate the problem when nationalities that had played no role in the government now agitated in the parliament for autonomy. This led prime ministers after 1900 to ignore the parliament and rely increasingly on imperial emergency decrees to govern. Parliament itself became a bizarre forum in which, in the words of one incredulous observer, "about a score of men, all decently clad, were seated or standing, each at his little desk. Some made an infernal noise violently opening and shutting the lids of their desks. Others emitted a blaring sound from little toy trumpets; . . . still others beat snare drums."[15]

The threat the nationalities posed to the position of the dominant German minority in Austria also produced a backlash in the form of virulent German nationalism. As Austria industrialized in the 1870s and 1880s, two working-class parties came into existence, both strongly influenced by nationalism. The Social Democrats, although a Marxist party, supported the Austrian government, fearful that the autonomy of the different nationalities would hinder industrial development and prevent improvements for workers. Even more nationalistic, however, were the Christian Socialists, who, as we have seen, combined agitation for workers with a virulent anti-Semitism.

While subjugating their nationalities, the ruling Magyars in Hungary developed a movement for complete separation from Austria. In 1903, when they demanded that the Hungarian army be separated from the imperial army, Emperor Francis Joseph (as king of Hungary) responded quickly and forcefully. He threatened to impose universal male suffrage on Hungary, a move that would challenge Magyar domination of the minorities. Hungarian leaders fell into line, and the new Hungarian parliamentary leader, Count István Tisza, cooperated in maintaining the Dual Monarchy. Magyar rule in Hungary, he realized, was inextricably bound up with the Dual Monarchy; its death would only harm the rule of the Magyar landowning class.

Industrialization and Revolution in Imperial Russia

Starting in the 1890s, Russia experienced a massive surge of state-sponsored industrialism under the guiding hand of Sergei Witte (1849–1915), the minister for finance from 1892 to 1903. Count Witte saw industrial growth as crucial to Russia's national strength. Believing that railroads were a powerful weapon in economic development, Witte pushed the government toward a program of massive railroad construction. By 1900, some 35,000 miles of railroads had been built, including large parts of the 5,000-mile trans-Siberian line between Moscow and Vladivostok, on the Pacific Ocean. Witte also encouraged a system of protective tariffs to help Russian industry and persuaded Tsar Nicholas II (1894–1917) that foreign capital was essential for rapid industrial development. Witte's program made possible the rapid growth of a modern steel and coal industry in the Ukraine, making Russia by 1900 the fourth-largest producer of steel behind the United States, Germany, and Great Britain.

With industrialization came factories, an industrial working class, industrial suburbs around Saint Petersburg and Moscow, and the pitiful working and living conditions that accompanied the beginnings of industrialization everywhere. Socialist thought and socialist parties developed, although repression in Russia soon forced them to go underground and become revolutionary. The Marxist Social Democratic Party, for example, held its first congress in

© Underwood & Underwood/CORBIS

Nicholas II. The last tsar of Russia hoped to preserve the traditional autocratic ways of his predecessors. In this photograph, Nicholas II and his wife, Alexandra, are shown around 1907 with their four daughters and son on holiday on the deck of a ship.

lack of land, and laborers felt oppressed by their working and living conditions in Russia's large cities. The breakdown of the transport system caused by the Russo-Japanese War led to food shortages in the major cities of Russia. As a result, on January 9, 1905, a massive procession of workers went to the Winter Palace in Saint Petersburg to present a petition of grievances to the tsar. Troops foolishly opened fire on the peaceful demonstration, killing hundreds and launching a revolution (see the box on p. 751). This "Bloody Sunday" incited workers to call strikes and form unions; meanwhile, zemstvos demanded parliamentary government, ethnic groups revolted, and peasants burned the houses of landowners. After a general strike in October 1905, the government capitulated. Nicholas II issued the October Manifesto, in which he granted civil liberties and agreed to create a legislative assembly known as the Duma, elected directly by a broad franchise. This satisfied the middle-class moderates, who now supported the government's repression of a workers' uprising in Moscow at the end of 1905.

Minsk in 1898, but the arrest of its leaders caused the next one to be held in Brussels in 1903, attended by Russian émigrés. The Social Revolutionaries worked to overthrow the tsarist autocracy and establish peasant socialism. Having no other outlet for their opposition to the regime, they advocated political terrorism and attempted to assassinate government officials and members of the ruling dynasty. The growing opposition to the tsarist regime finally exploded into revolution in 1905.

The Revolution of 1905

As had happened elsewhere in Europe in the nineteenth century, defeat in war led to political upheaval at home. Russia's territorial expansion to the south and east, especially its designs on northern Korea, led to a confrontation with Japan. Japan made a surprise attack on the Russian eastern fleet at Port Arthur on February 8, 1904. In turn, Russia sent its Baltic fleet halfway around the world to the East, only to be defeated by the new Japanese navy at Tsushima Strait off the coast of Japan. Much to the astonishment of many Europeans, who could not believe that an Asian state was militarily superior to a great European power, the Russians admitted defeat and sued for peace in 1905.

In the midst of the war, the growing discontent of increased numbers of Russians rapidly led to upheaval. A middle class of business and professional people longed for liberal institutions and a liberal political system. Nationalities were dissatisfied with their domination by an ethnic Russian population that constituted only 40 percent of the empire's total population. Peasants were still suffering from

Failure of the Revolution But real constitutional monarchy proved short-lived. Under Peter Stolypin, who served as the tsar's chief adviser from late 1906 until his assassination in 1911, important agrarian reforms dissolved the village ownership of land and opened the door to private ownership by enterprising peasants. Nicholas II, however, was no friend of reform. Already by 1907, the tsar had curtailed the power of the Duma, and after Stolypin's murder, he fell back on the army and bureaucracy to rule Russia.

The Rise of the United States

Between 1860 and 1914, the United States made the shift from an agrarian to a mighty industrial nation. American heavy industry stood unchallenged in 1900. In that year, the Carnegie Steel Company alone produced more steel than Great Britain's entire steel industry. Industrialization also led to urbanization. While established cities, such as New York, Philadelphia, and Boston, grew even larger, other moderate-size cities, such as Pittsburgh, grew by leaps and bounds because of industrialization. Whereas 20 percent of Americans lived in cities in 1860, over 40 percent did in 1900. Four-fifths of the population growth in cities came from migration. Eight to 10 million Americans moved from rural areas into the cities, and 14 million foreigners came from abroad.

The United States had become the world's richest nation and greatest industrial power. Yet serious questions remained about the quality of American life. In

BLOODY SUNDAY

On January 9, 1905, a massive procession of workers led by a Russian Orthodox priest loyal to the tsar, Father Gregory Gapon, carried pictures of the tsar and a petition to present to him at his imperial palace in Saint Petersburg. Although the tsar was not even there, government officials ordered troops to fire on the crowd. This account is by the leader of the procession, Father Gapon.

An Account of Bloody Sunday

We were not more than thirty yards from the soldiers, being separated from them only by the bridge over the Tarakanovskii Canal, which here marks the border of the city, when suddenly, without any warning and without a moment's delay, was heard the dry crack of many rifle-shots. I was informed later on that a bugle was blown, but we could not hear it above the singing, and even if we had heard it we should not have known what it meant.

Vasiliev, with whom I was walking hand in hand, suddenly left hold of my arm and sank upon the snow. One of the workmen who carried the banners fell also. Immediately one of the two police officers to whom I had referred shouted out, "What are you doing? How dare you fire upon the portrait of the Tsar?" This, of course, had no effect, and both he and the other officer were shot down—as I learned afterwards, one was killed and the other dangerously wounded.

I turned rapidly to the crowd and shouted to them to lie down, and I also stretched myself out upon the ground. As we lay thus another volley was fired, and another, and yet another, till it seemed as though the shooting was continuous. The crowd first kneeled and then lay flat down, hiding their heads from the rain of bullets, while the rear rows of the procession began to run away. The smoke of the fire lay before us like a thin cloud, and I felt it stiflingly in my throat. An old man named Lavrentiev, who was carrying the Tsar's portrait, had been one of the first victims. Another old man caught the portrait as it fell from his hands and carried it till he too was killed by the next volley. With his last gasp the old man said, "I may die, but I will see the Tsar." One of the banner-carriers had his arm broken by a bullet. A little boy of ten years, who was carrying a church lantern, fell pierced by a bullet, but still held the lantern tightly and tried to rise again, when another shot struck him down. Both the smiths who had guarded me were killed, as well as all those who were carrying the icons and banners; and all these emblems now lay scattered on the snow....

Horror crept into my heart. The thought flashed through my mind, "And this is the work of our Little Father, the Tsar." Perhaps this anger saved me, for now I knew in very truth that a new chapter was opened in the book of the history of our people. I stood up, and a little group of workmen gathered round me again. Looking backward, I saw that our line, though still stretching away into the distance, was broken and that many of the people were fleeing. It was in vain that I called to them, and in a moment I stood there, the center of a few scores of men, trembling with indignation amid the broken ruins of our movement.

Q *What were the possible factors that led to the shooting of the demonstrators by the troops? According to this selection, who was responsible for the shooting? Was the author justified in holding them responsible? Why or why not? What impact, if any, might the violence of 1905 have had on the events of 1917?*

1890, the richest 9 percent of Americans owned an incredible 71 percent of all the wealth. Labor unrest over unsafe working conditions, strict work discipline, and periodic cycles of devastating unemployment led workers to organize. By the turn of the century, one national organization, the American Federation of Labor, emerged as labor's dominant voice. Its lack of real power, however, was reflected in its membership figures. In 1900, it included only 8.4 percent of the American industrial labor force.

During the so-called Progressive Era after 1900, an age of reform swept across the United States. State governments enacted economic and social legislation, such as laws that governed hours, wages, and working conditions, especially for women and children. The realization that state laws were ineffective in dealing with nationwide problems, however, led to a Progressive movement at the national level. The Meat Inspection Act and Pure Food and Drug Act provided for a limited degree of federal regulation of corrupt industrial practices. The presidency of Woodrow Wilson (1913–1921) witnessed the enactment of a graduated federal income tax and the establishment of the Federal Reserve System, which permitted the federal government to play a role in important economic decisions formerly made by bankers. Like European nations, the United States was slowly adopting policies that extended the functions of the state.

The Growth of Canada

Canada faced problems of national unity at the end of the nineteenth century. In 1870, the Dominion of Canada had four provinces: Quebec, Ontario, Nova Scotia, and New Brunswick. With the addition of two more—Manitoba and British Columbia—the following year, Canada stretched from the Atlantic to the Pacific.

Real unity was difficult to achieve, however, because of the distrust between the English-speaking majority and the French-speaking Canadians, living primarily in

CHRONOLOGY Politics, 1894–1914

Reign of Emperor William II	1888–1918
Reign of Tsar Nicholas II	1894–1917
Dreyfus affair in France	1895–1899
Theodor Herzl, *The Jewish State*	1896
Austrian Christian Socialists under Karl Lueger	1897–1910
First congress of Social Democratic Party in Russia	1898
Beginning of the Progressive Era in the United States	1900
Formation of Labour Party in Britain	1900
Pankhursts establish Women's Social and Political Union	1903
Ministries of Giovanni Giolitti in Italy	1903–1914
Russo-Japanese War	1904–1905
Revolution in Russia	1905
National Insurance Act in Britain	1911
Universal male suffrage in Italy	1912
Social Democratic Party becomes largest party in Germany	1912

Quebec. Wilfred Laurier, who became the first French Canadian prime minister in 1896, was able to reconcile the two groups. During his administration, industrialization boomed, especially the production of textiles, furniture, and railway equipment. Hundreds of thousands of immigrants, primarily from Europe, also flowed into Canada. Many settled on lands in the west, thus helping populate Canada's vast territories.

Canada, 1871

The New Imperialism

Q **Focus Question:** What were the causes of the new imperialism that took place after 1880, and what effects did European imperialism have on Africa and Asia?

In the 1880s, European states embarked on an intense scramble for overseas territory. This **"new imperialism,"** as some have called it, led Europeans to carve up Asia and Africa. What explains the mad scramble for colonies after 1880?

Causes of the New Imperialism

The existence of competitive nation-states after 1870 was undoubtedly a major determinant in the growth of the new imperialism. As European affairs grew tense, heightened competition spurred European states to acquire colonies abroad that provided ports and coaling stations for their navies. Great Britain, for example, often expanded into new regions not for economic reasons but to keep the French, Germans, or Russians from setting up bases that could harm British interests. Colonies were also a source of international prestige. Once the scramble for colonies began, failure to enter the race was perceived as a sign of weakness, totally unacceptable to an aspiring great power. As a British foreign minister wrote, "When I left the Foreign Office in 1880, nobody thought about Africa. When I returned to it in 1885, the nations of Europe were almost quarreling with each other as to the various portions of Africa which they should obtain."[16] Late-nineteenth-century imperialism was closely tied to nationalism.

Patriotic fervor was often used to arouse interest in imperialism. Newspapers and magazines often featured soldiers' letters that made imperialism seem a heroic adventure on behalf of one's country. Even plays were written to excite people about expanding abroad. Voluntary groups, such as geographic societies and naval leagues, fostered enthusiasm for imperial adventures.

The Role of Social Darwinism and Racism Imperialism was tied to social Darwinism and racism, too. As noted earlier, social Darwinists believed that in the struggle between nations, the fit are victorious and survive. Superior races must dominate inferior races by military force to show how strong and virile they are. As British professor of mathematics Karl Pearson argued in 1900, "The path of progress is strewn with the wrecks of nations; traces are everywhere to be seen of the [slaughtered remains] of inferior races.... Yet these dead people are, in very truth, the stepping stones on which mankind has arisen to the higher intellectual and deeper emotional life of today."[17] Others were equally blunt. One Englishman wrote, "To the development of the White Man, the Black Man and the Yellow must ever remain inferior, and as the former raised itself higher and yet higher, so did these latter seem to shrink out of humanity and appear nearer and nearer to the brutes."[18]

Religious Motives Some Europeans took a more religious or humanitarian approach to imperialism when they argued that Europeans had a moral responsibility to civilize ignorant peoples. This notion of the "white man's burden" (see the box on p. 754) helped at least the more idealistic individuals rationalize imperialism in their own minds. One British official declared that the British Empire "was under Providence, the greatest instrument for good that the world has seen." Thousands of Catholic and Protestant missionaries went abroad to seek converts to their faith. Nevertheless, the belief that the superiority

The first step towards lightening

The White Man's Burden

is through teaching the virtues of cleanliness.

Pears' Soap

is a potent factor in brightening the dark corners of the earth as civilization advances, while amongst the cultured of all nations it holds the highest place—it is the ideal toilet soap.

Soap and the White Man's Burden. The concept of the "white man's burden" included the belief that the superiority of their civilization obligated Europeans to impose their practices on supposedly primitive nonwhites. This advertisement for Pears' Soap clearly communicates the Europeans' view of their responsibility toward other peoples.

of their civilization obligated them to impose modern industries and new medicines on supposedly primitive nonwhites was yet another form of racism.

The Economic Motive

Some historians have emphasized an economic motivation for imperialism. There was a great demand for natural resources and products not found in Western countries, such as rubber, oil, and tin. Instead of just trading for these products, European investors advocated direct control of the areas where the raw materials were found. The large surpluses of capital that bankers and industrialists were accumulating often encouraged them to seek higher rates of profit in underdeveloped areas. All of these factors combined to create an **economic imperialism** whereby European finance dominated the economic activity of a large part of the world. This economic imperialism, however, was not necessarily the same thing as colonial expansion. Businesses invested where it was most profitable, not

necessarily where their own countries had colonial empires. For example, less than 10 percent of French foreign investments before 1914 went to French colonies; most of the rest went to Latin American and European countries. Even the British had more trade with Belgium than with all of Africa in the 1890s. It should also be remembered that much of the colonial territory that was acquired was mere wasteland from the perspective of industrialized Europe and cost more to administer than it produced economically. Only the search for national prestige could justify such losses.

Followers of Karl Marx were especially eager to argue that imperialism was economically motivated because they associated imperialism with the ultimate demise of the capitalist system. Marx had hinted at this argument, but it was one of his followers, the Russian V. I. Lenin (see Chapter 25), who in *Imperialism, the Highest Stage of World Capitalism* developed the idea that capitalism leads to imperialism. According to Lenin, as the capitalist system concentrates more wealth in ever-fewer hands, the possibility for investment at home is exhausted, and capitalists are forced to invest abroad, establish colonies, and exploit small, weak nations. In his view, then, the only cure for imperialism was the destruction of capitalism.

The Scramble for Africa

Europeans controlled relatively little of the African continent before 1880. Earlier, when their economic interests were more limited (in the case of Africa, primarily the slave trade), European states had generally been satisfied to deal with existing independent states rather than attempting to establish direct control over vast territories. For the most part, the Western presence in Africa had been limited to controlling the regional trade network and establishing a few footholds where the foreigners could carry on trade and missionary activity. During the last two decades of the nineteenth century, however, the quest for colonies became a scramble as all of the major European states engaged in a land grab.

South Africa During the Napoleonic wars, the British had established themselves in South Africa by taking control of Cape Town, originally founded by the Dutch. After the wars, the British encouraged settlers to come to what they called the Cape Colony. British policies disgusted the Boers or Afrikaners, as the descendants of the

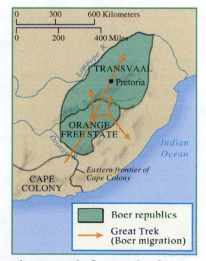

The Struggle for South Africa

OPPOSING VIEWPOINTS
WHITE MAN'S BURDEN VERSUS BLACK MAN'S BURDEN

One of the justifications for European imperialism was the notion that superior white peoples had the moral responsibility to raise ignorant native peoples to a higher level of civilization. The British poet Rudyard Kipling (1865–1936) captured this notion in his poem "The White Man's Burden." The Western justification of imperialism that was based on a sense of moral responsibility, evident in Rudyard Kipling's poem, was often hypocritical. Edward Morel, a British journalist who spent time in the Congo, pointed out the destructive effects of Western imperialism on Africans in his book *The Black Man's Burden*.

Rudyard Kipling, *The White Man's Burden*

Take up the White Man's burden—
Send forth the best ye breed—
Go bind your sons to exile
to serve your captives' needs;
To wait in heavy harness,
On fluttered folk and wild—
Your new-caught sullen peoples,
Half-devil and half-child.

Take up the White Man's burden—
In patience to abide,
To veil the threat of terror
And check the show of pride;
By open speech and simple,
An hundred times made plain
To seek another's profit,
And work another's gain.

Take up the White Man's burden—
The savage wars of peace—
Fill full the mouth of Famine
And bid the sickness cease;
And when your goal is nearest
The end for others sought,
Watch sloth and heathen Folly
Bring all your hopes to nought.

Take up the White Man's burden—
No tawdry rule of kings,
But toil of serf and sweeper—
The tale of common things.
The ports ye shall not enter,
The roads ye shall not tread,
Go mark them with your living,
And mark them with your dead.

Take up the White Man's burden—
And reap his old reward:
The blame of those ye better,
The hate of those ye guard—

The cry of hosts ye humour
(Ah, slowly!) toward the light—
'Why brought ye us from bondage,
Our loved Egyptian night?'

Take up the White Man's burden—
Ye dare not stoop to less—
Nor call too loud on Freedom
To cloak your weariness;
By all ye cry or whisper,
By all you leave or do,
The silent, sullen peoples
Shall weigh your gods and you.

Take up the White Man's burden—
Have done with childish days—
The lightly proferred laurel,
The easy, ungrudged praise.
Comes now, to search your manhood
Through all the thankless years,
Cold, edged with dear-bought wisdom,
The judgment of your peers!

Edward Morel, *The Black Man's Burden*

It is [the Africans] who carry the "Black man's burden." They have not withered away before the white man's occupation. Indeed . . . Africa has ultimately absorbed within itself every Caucasian and, for that matter, every Semitic invader, too. In hewing out for himself a fixed abode in Africa, the white man has massacred the African in heaps. The African has survived, and it is well for the white settlers that he has. . . .

What the partial occupation of his soil by the white man has failed to do; what the mapping out of European political "spheres of influence" has failed to do; what the Maxim [machine gun] and the rifle, the slave gang, labor in the bowels of the earth and the lash, have failed to do; what imported measles, smallpox and syphilis have failed to do; whatever the overseas slave trade failed to do; the power of modern capitalistic exploitation, assisted by modern engines of destruction, may yet succeed in accomplishing.

For from the evils of the latter, scientifically applied and enforced, there is no escape for the African. Its destructive effects are not spasmodic: they are permanent. In its permanence resides its fatal consequences. It kills not the body merely, but the soul. It breaks the spirit. It attacks the African at every turn, from every point of vantage. It wrecks his polity, uproots him from the land, invades his family life, destroys his natural pursuits and occupations, claims his whole time, enslaves him in his own home. . . .

In Africa, especially in tropical Africa, which a capitalistic imperialism threatens and has, in part, already

(continued)

(continued)

devastated, man is incapable of reacting against unnatural conditions. In those regions man is engaged in a perpetual struggle against disease and an exhausting climate, which tells heavily upon childbearing; and there is no scientific machinery for saving the weaker members of the community. The African of the tropics is capable of tremendous physical labors. But he cannot accommodate himself to the European system of monotonous, uninterrupted labor, with its long and regular hours, involving, moreover, as it frequently does, severance from natural surroundings and nostalgia, the condition of melancholy resulting from separation from home, a malady to which the African is specially prone. Climatic conditions forbid it. When the system is forced upon him, the tropical African droops and dies.

Nor is violent physical opposition to abuse and injustice henceforth possible for the African in any part of Africa. His chances of effective resistance have been steadily dwindling with the increasing perfectibility in the killing power of modern armament. . . .

Thus the African is really helpless against the material gods of the white man, as embodied in the trinity of imperialism, capitalistic exploitation, and militarism. . . .

To reduce all the varied and picturesque and stimulating episodes in savage life to a dull routine of endless toil for uncomprehended ends, to dislocate social ties and disrupt social institutions; to stifle nascent desires and crush mental development; to graft upon primitive passions the annihilating evils of scientific slavery, and the bestial imaginings of civilized man, unrestrained by convention or law; in fine, to kill the soul in a people—this is a crime which transcends physical murder.

Q *What arguments did Kipling make to justify European expansion in Africa and Asia? How does the selection by Edward Morel challenge or undermine Kipling's beliefs?*

Dutch colonists were called, and led them in 1835 to migrate north on the Great Trek to the region between the Orange and Vaal rivers (later known as the Orange Free State) and north of the Vaal River (the Transvaal). Hostilities between the British and the Boers continued, however. In 1877, the British governor of the Cape Colony seized the Transvaal, but a Boer revolt led the British government to recognize Transvaal as the independent South African Republic. These struggles between the British and the Boers did not prevent either white group from massacring and subjugating the Zulu and Xhosa peoples of the region.

In the 1880s, British policy in South Africa was largely determined by Cecil Rhodes (1853–1902). Rhodes founded both diamond and gold companies that monopolized production of these precious commodities and enabled him to gain control of a territory north of Transvaal that he named Rhodesia after himself. Rhodes was a great champion of British expansion. He said once, "If there be a God, I think what he would like me to do is to paint as much of Africa British red as possible." One of his goals was to create a series of British colonies "from the Cape to Cairo," all linked by a railroad. His imperialist ambitions led to his downfall in 1896, however, when the British government forced him to resign as prime minister of the Cape Colony after he conspired to overthrow the Boer government of the South African Republic without British approval. Although the British government had hoped to avoid war with the Boers, it could not stop extremists on both sides from precipitating a conflict. The Boer War dragged on from 1899 to 1902, when the Boers were overwhelmed by the larger British army. British policy toward the defeated Boers was remarkably conciliatory. Transvaal and the Orange Free State had representative governments by 1907, and in 1910, the Union of South Africa was created. Like

Canada, Australia, and New Zealand, it became a fully self-governing dominion within the British Empire.

Portuguese and French Possessions Before 1880, the only other European settlements in Africa had been made by the French and the Portuguese. The Portuguese had held on to their settlements in Angola on the west coast and Mozambique on the east coast. The French had started the conquest of Algeria in Muslim North Africa in 1830, although it was not until 1879 that French civilian rule was established there. The next year, 1880, the European scramble for possession of Africa began in earnest. By 1900, the French had added the huge area of French West Africa and Tunisia to their African empire. In 1912, they established a protectorate over much of Morocco; the rest was left to Spain.

Other British Possessions The British took an active interest in Egypt after the Suez Canal was opened by the French in 1869. Believing that the canal was their lifeline to India, the British sought to control the canal area. Egypt was a well-established state with an autonomous Muslim government, but that did not stop the British from landing an expeditionary force there in 1882. Although they claimed that their occupation was only temporary, they soon established a protectorate over Egypt. From Egypt, the British moved south into Sudan and seized it after narrowly averting a war with France. Not to be outdone, Italy joined in the imperialist scramble. Their humiliating defeat by the Ethiopians in 1896 only led the Italians to try again in 1911, when they invaded and seized Ottoman Tripoli, which they renamed Libya.

Belgium and Central Africa Central Africa was also added to the list of European colonies. Popular interest in

CHRONOLOGY The New Imperialism: Africa

Great Trek of the Boers	1835
Opening of the Suez Canal	1869
Leopold of Belgium establishes settlements in the Congo	1876
British seizure of Transvaal	1877
French conquest of Algeria	1879
British expeditionary force in Egypt	1882
Ethiopians defeat the Italians	1896
Battle of Omdurman in the Sudan	1898
Boer War	1899–1902
Union of South Africa	1910
Italians seize Tripoli	1911
French protectorate over Morocco	1912

the forbiddingly dense tropical jungles of Central Africa was first aroused in the 1860s and 1870s by explorers, such as the Scottish missionary David Livingstone and the British-American journalist Henry M. Stanley. But the real driving force for the colonization of Central Africa was King Leopold II (1865–1909) of Belgium, who rushed enthusiastically into the pursuit of empire in Africa: "To open to civilization," he said, "the only part of our globe where it has not yet penetrated, to pierce the darkness which envelops whole populations, is a crusade, if I may say so, a crusade worthy of this century of progress." Profit, however, was far more important to Leopold than progress; his treatment of the Africans was so brutal that even other Europeans condemned his actions. In 1876, Leopold created the International Association for the Exploration and Civilization of Central Africa and engaged Henry Stanley to establish Belgian settlements in the Congo. Alarmed by Leopold's actions, the French also moved into the territory north of the Congo River.

German Possessions Between 1884 and 1900, most of the rest of Africa was carved up by the European powers. Germany entered the ranks of the imperialist powers at this time. Initially, Bismarck had downplayed the significance of colonies, but as domestic political pressures for a German empire intensified, Bismarck became a political convert to colonialism. As he expressed it, "All this colonial business is a sham, but we need it for the elections." The Germans established colonies in South-West Africa, the Cameroons, Togoland, and Tanganyika.

Impact on Africa By 1914, Britain, France, Germany, Belgium, Spain, and Portugal had carved up the entire African continent (see Map 24.1). Only Liberia, founded by emancipated American slaves, and Ethiopia remained free states. Despite the humanitarian rationalizations about the "white man's burden," Africa had been

conquered by European states determined to create colonial empires (see the box on p. 754). Any peoples who dared to resist (with the exception of the Ethiopians, who defeated the Italians) were simply devastated by the superior military force of the Europeans. In 1898, Sudanese tribesmen attempted to defend their independence and stop a British expedition armed with the recently developed machine gun. In the ensuing Battle of Omdurman, the Sudanese were massacred. One observer noted, "It was not a battle but an execution.... The bodies were not in heaps—bodies hardly ever are; but they spread evenly over acres and acres. Some lay very composedly with their slippers placed under their heads for a last pillow; some knelt, cut short in the middle of a last prayer. Others were torn to pieces."[19] The battle casualties at Omdurman tell the story of the one-sided conflicts between Europeans and Africans: twenty-eight British deaths to 11,000 Sudanese. Military superiority was frequently accompanied by brutal treatment of blacks. Nor did Europeans hesitate to deceive the Africans to gain their way. One South African king, Lo Bengula, informed Queen Victoria about how he had been cheated:

> Some time ago a party of men came to my country, the principal one appearing to be a man called Rudd. They asked me for a place to dig for gold, and said they would give me certain things for the right to do so. I told them to bring what they could give and I would show them what I would give. A document was written and presented to me for signature. I asked what it contained, and was told that in it were my words and the words of those men. I put my hand to it. About three months afterwards I heard from other sources that I had given by that document the right to all the minerals of my country.[20]

Imperialism in Asia

Although Asia had been open to Western influence since the sixteenth century, not much of its immense territory had fallen under direct European control. The Dutch were established in the East Indies, the Spanish were in the Philippines, and the French and Portuguese had trading posts on the Indian coast. China, Japan, Korea, and Southeast Asia had largely managed to exclude Westerners. The British and the Russians, however, had acquired the most Asian territory.

The British in Asia It was not until the explorations of Australia by Captain James Cook between 1768 and 1771 that Britain took an active interest in the East. The availability of land for grazing sheep and the discovery of gold in Australia led to an influx of settlers who slaughtered many of the indigenous inhabitants. In 1850, the British government granted the various Australian colonies virtually complete self-government, and fifty years later, on January 1, 1901, all the colonies were unified into the Commonwealth of Australia. Nearby New Zealand, which the British had declared a colony in 1840, was granted dominion status in 1907.

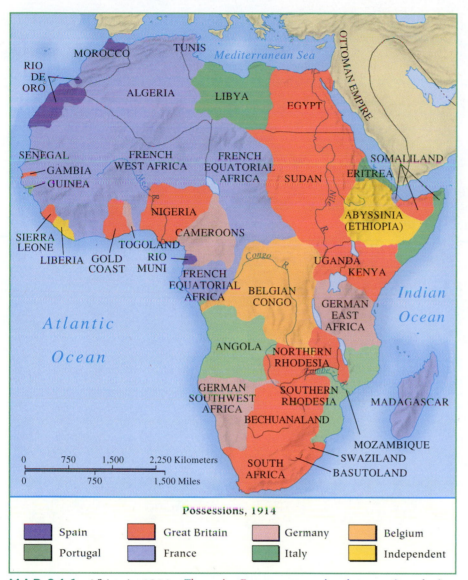

Possessions, 1914

Spain	Great Britain	Germany	Belgium
Portugal	France	Italy	Independent

MAP 24.1 **Africa in 1914.** The major European powers' rush to acquire colonies was motivated by a combination of factors: ports and fueling stations for navies, enhancement of international prestige, outlets for nationalist feelings, expression of social Darwinism, and a desire to "civilize" non-Europeans.

Q Of the two countries with the largest amount of territory in Africa, which one's colonies were more geographically concentrated, and what could be the benefits of this?

View an animated version of this map or related maps at academic.cengage.com/history/spielvogel

A private trading company known as the British East India Company had been responsible for subjugating much of India. In 1858, however, after a revolt of the sepoys, or Indian troops of the East India Company's army, had been crushed, the British Parliament transferred the company's powers directly to the government in London. In 1876, the title Empress of India was bestowed on Queen Victoria; Indians were now her colonial subjects.

Russian expansion in Asia was a logical outgrowth of its traditional territorial aggrandizement. Russian explorers had penetrated the wilderness of Siberia in the seventeenth century and reached the Pacific coast in 1637. In the eighteenth century, Russians established a

claim on Alaska, which they sold to the United States in 1867. Gradually, Russian settlers moved into cold and forbidding Siberia. Altogether, 7 million Russians settled in Siberia between 1800 and 1914, by which time 90 percent of the Siberian population was Slavic, not Asiatic.

The Russians also moved south, attracted by warmer climes and the crumbling Ottoman Empire. By 1830, the Russians had established control over the entire northern coast of the Black Sea and then pressed on into Central Asia, securing the trans-Caspian area by 1881 and Turkestan in 1885. These advances brought the Russians to the borders of Persia and Afghanistan, where the British also had interests because of their desire to protect their holdings in India. In 1907, the Russians and British agreed to make Afghanistan a buffer state between Russian Turkestan and British India and to divide Persia into two spheres of influence. Halted by the British in their expansion to the south, the Russians moved east in Asia. The Russian occupation of Manchuria and an attempt to move into Korea brought war with the new imperialist power, Japan. After losing the Russo-Japanese War in 1905, the Russians agreed to a Japanese protectorate in Korea, and their Asian expansion was brought to a temporary halt (see Map 24.2).

China The thrust of imperialism after 1880 led Westerners to move into new areas of Asia hitherto largely free of Western influence. By the nineteenth century, the ruling Manchu dynasty of the Chinese Empire was showing signs of decline. In 1842, the British had obtained (through war) the island of Hong Kong and trading rights in a number of Chinese cities. Other Western nations soon rushed in to gain similar trading privileges. Chinese attempts to resist this foreign encroachment led to military defeats and new demands. Only rivalry among the great powers themselves prevented the complete dismemberment of the Chinese Empire. Instead, Britain, France, Germany, Russia, the United States, and Japan established spheres of influence and long-term leases of Chinese territory. In 1899, urged along by the American secretary of state, John Hay, they agreed to an

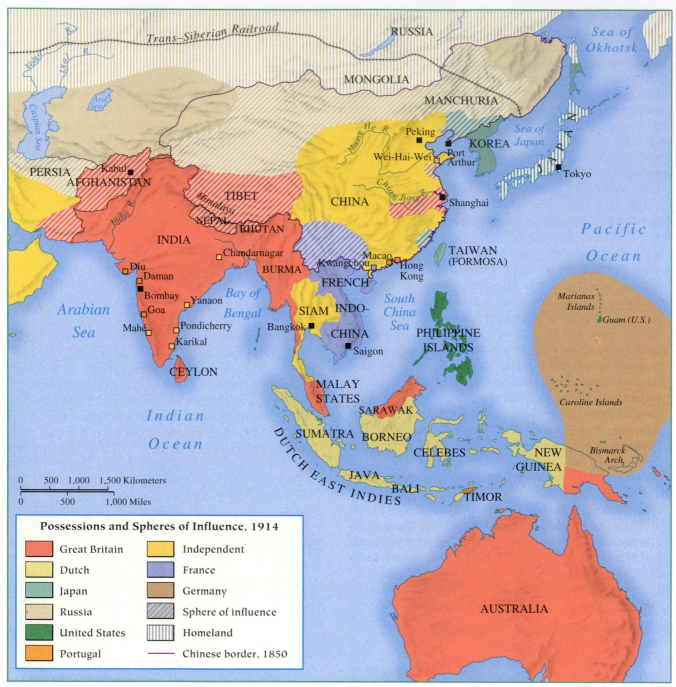

MAP 24.2 **Asia in 1914.** Asia became an important arena of international competition in the nineteenth and early twentieth centuries. Beset by economic stagnation and an inability to modernize, a weak China was unable to withstand the demands of the United States, European powers, and a Westernizing Japan. Britain, France, Russia, Japan, and the United States had direct or indirect control of nearly all of Asia by 1914.

Q Why would both Russia and Japan covet Manchuria? **View an animated version of this map or related maps at** academic.cengage.com/history/spielvogel

"open door" policy in which one country would not restrict the commerce of the other countries in its sphere of influence.

Japan and Korea Japan avoided Western intrusion until 1853–1854, when American naval forces under Commodore Matthew Perry forced the Japanese to grant the United States trading and diplomatic privileges. Japan, however, managed to avoid China's fate. Korea had also largely excluded Westerners. The fate of Korea was determined by the struggle first between China and Japan in 1894–1895 and later between Japan and Russia in 1904–1905. Japan's victories gave it clear superiority, and in 1910, Japan formally annexed Korea.

Britain obtains Hong Kong and trading rights from Chinese government	1842
Australian colonies receive self-government	1850
Mission of Commodore Perry to Japan	1853–1854
Rebellion of sepoys in India	1857–1858
French occupy Saigon	1858
Overthrow of the shogun in Japan	1867
Emperor Mutsuhito and the Meiji Restoration	1867–1912
Queen Victoria is made empress of India	1876
Russians in Central Asia (trans-Caspian area)	1881
Formation of Indian National Congress	1883
Japanese defeat of China	1894–1895
Spanish-American War; United States annexes Philippines	1898
"Open door" policy in China	1899
Boxer Rebellion in China	1900–1901
Commonwealth of Australia	1901
Commonwealth of New Zealand	1907
Russian-British agreement over Afghanistan and Persia	1907
Japan annexes Korea	1910
Overthrow of Manchu dynasty in China	1912

Southeast Asia In Southeast Asia, Britain established control over Burma (modern Myanmar) and the Malay States, and France played an active role in subjugating Indochina. The city of Saigon was occupied in 1858, and four years later, Cochin China was taken. In the 1880s, the French extended "protection" over Cambodia, Annam, Tonkin, and Laos and organized them into the Union of French Indochina. Only Siam (Thailand) remained free as a buffer state because of British-French rivalry.

American Imperialism The Pacific islands were also the scene of great power competition and witnessed the entry of the United States onto the imperialist stage. The Samoan Islands became the first important American colony; the Hawaiian Islands were the next to fall. Soon after Americans had made Pearl Harbor into a naval station in 1887, American settlers gained control of the sugar industry on the islands. When Hawaiian natives tried to reassert their authority, the U.S. Marines were brought in to "protect" American lives. Hawaii was annexed by the United States in 1898 during the era of American nationalistic fervor generated by the Spanish-American War. The American defeat of Spain encouraged Americans to extend their empire by acquiring Puerto Rico, Guam, and the Philippine Islands. Although the Filipinos hoped for independence, the Americans refused to grant it. As President William McKinley said, the United States had the duty "to educate the Filipinos and uplift and Christianize them," a remarkable statement in view of the fact that most of them had been Roman Catholics for centuries. It took three years and 60,000 troops to pacify the Philippines and establish American control.

Responses to Imperialism

When Europeans imposed their culture on peoples they considered inferior, how did the conquered peoples respond? Initial attempts to expel the foreigners only led to devastating defeats at the hands of Westerners, whose industrial technology gave them modern weapons of war with which to crush the indigenous peoples. Accustomed to rule by small elites, most people simply accepted their new governors, making Western rule relatively easy. The conquered peoples subsequently adjusted to foreign rule in different ways. Traditionalists sought to maintain their cultural traditions, but modernizers believed that adoption of Western ways would enable them to reform their societies and eventually challenge Western rule. Most people probably stood somewhere between these two extremes. Four examples illustrate different approaches to the question of how indigenous peoples responded to foreign rule.

Africa By the beginning of the twentieth century, a new class of African leaders had emerged. Educated in colonial schools and some even in the West, they were the first generation of Africans to know a great deal about the West and to write in the language of their colonial masters. Although this "new class" admired Western culture and even disliked the ways of their own countries, many came to resent the foreigners and their arrogant contempt for colonial peoples. Westerners had exalted democracy, equality, and political freedom, but these values were not applied in the colonies. There were few democratic institutions, and colonial peoples could hold only lowly jobs in the colonial bureaucracy. Equally important, the economic prosperity of the West never extended to the colonies. To many Africans, colonialism meant the loss of their farmlands or terrible jobs on plantations or in sweatshops and factories run by foreigners.

Although middle-class Africans did not suffer to the extent that poor peasants or workers on plantations did, they too had complaints. They usually qualified only for menial jobs in the government or business. The purported superiority of the Europeans over the natives was also expressed in a variety of ways. Segregated clubs, schools, and churches were set up as more European officials brought their wives and began to raise families. Europeans also had a habit of addressing natives by their first names or calling an adult male "boy."

Such conditions led many of the new urban educated class to have very complicated feelings about their colonial masters and the civilization they represented. Though willing to admit the superiority of many aspects of Western culture, these new intellectuals fiercely hated colonial rule and were determined to assert their own nationality and cultural destiny. Out of this mixture of hopes and resentments emerged the first stirrings of modern nationalism in Africa. During the first quarter of the twentieth century, in colonial societies across Africa, educated native peoples began to organize political parties and movements seeking the end of foreign rule.

China   The humiliation of China by the Western powers led to much antiforeign violence, but the Westerners used this lawlessness as an excuse to extort further concessions from the Chinese. A major outburst of violence against foreigners occurred in the Boxer Rebellion in 1900–1901. "Boxers" was the popular name given to Chinese who belonged to a secret organization called the Society of Harmonious Fists, whose aim was to push the foreigners out of China. The Boxers murdered foreign missionaries, Chinese who had converted to Christianity, railroad workers, foreign businessmen, and even the German envoy to Beijing. Response to the killings was immediate and overwhelming. An allied army consisting of British, French, German, Russian, American, and Japanese troops attacked Beijing, restored order, and demanded more concessions from the Chinese government. The imperial government was so weakened that the forces of the revolutionary leader Sun Yat-sen (1866–1925), who adopted a program of "nationalism, democracy, and socialism," overthrew the Manchu dynasty in 1912. The new Republic of China remained weak and ineffective, and China's travails were far from over.

Japan   In the late 1850s and early 1860s, it looked as if Japan would follow China's fate and be carved up into spheres of influence by aggressive Western powers. A remarkably rapid transformation, however, produced a very different result. Before 1868, the shogun, a powerful hereditary military governor assisted by a warrior nobility known as the samurai, exercised real power in Japan. The emperor's functions had become primarily religious. After the shogun's concessions to the Western nations, antiforeign sentiment led to a samurai revolt in 1867 and the restoration of the emperor as the rightful head of the government. The new emperor was the astute, dynamic, young Mutsuhito (1867–1912), who called his reign the Meiji (Enlightened Government). The new leaders who controlled the emperor now inaugurated a remarkable transformation of Japan that has since been known as the Meiji Restoration.

Recognizing the obvious military and industrial superiority of the West, the new leaders decided to modernize Japan by absorbing and adopting Western methods. Thousands of young Japanese were sent abroad to receive Western educations, especially in the social and

Japanese Expansion

natural sciences. A German-style army and a British-style navy were established. The Japanese copied the industrial and financial methods of the United States and developed a modern commercial and industrial system. A highly centralized administrative system copied from the French replaced the old system. Initially, the Japanese adopted the French principles of social and legal equality, but by 1890, they had created a political system that was democratic in form but authoritarian in practice.

In imitating the West, Japan also developed a powerful military state. Universal military conscription was introduced in 1872, and a modern peacetime army of 240,000 was eventually established. The Japanese avidly pursued the Western imperialistic model. They defeated China in 1894–1895, annexed some Chinese territory, and established their own sphere of influence in China. After they had defeated the Russians in 1905, the Japanese made Korea a colony under harsh rule. The Japanese had proved that an Asian power could play the "white man's" imperialistic game and provided a potent example to peoples in other regions of Asia and Africa.

India   The British government had been in control of India since the mid-nineteenth century. After crushing a major revolt in 1858, the British ruled India directly. Under Parliament's supervision, a small group of British civil servants directed the affairs of India's almost 300 million people.

The British brought order to a society that had been divided by civil wars for some time and created a relatively honest and efficient government. They also brought Western technology—railroads, banks, mines, industry, medical knowledge, and hospitals. The British introduced Western-style secondary schools and colleges where the Indian upper and middle classes and professional classes were educated so that they could serve as trained subordinates in the government and army.

But the Indian people paid a high price for the peace and stability brought by British rule. Due to population growth in the nineteenth century, extreme poverty was a way of life for most Indians; almost two-thirds of the population was malnourished in 1901. British industrialization brought little improvement for the masses. British manufactured goods destroyed local industries, and Indian wealth was used to pay British officials and a large army. The system of education served only the elite, upper-class Indians, and it was conducted only in the rulers' English language while 90 percent of the population remained illiterate. Even for the Indians who benefited the most from

The West and Japan. In their attempt to modernize, the Japanese absorbed and adopted Western methods. They were also influenced by Western culture as Western fashions became the rage in elite circles. Baseball was even imported from the United States. This painting shows Western-style stone houses in Tokyo and streets filled with people dressed in a variety of styles.

their Western educations, British rule was degrading. The best jobs and the best housing were reserved for Britons. Despite their education, the Indians were never considered equals of the British, whose racial attitudes were made quite clear by Lord Kitchener, one of Britain's foremost military commanders in India, when he said, "It is this consciousness of the inherent superiority of the European which has won for us India. However well educated and clever a native may be, and however brave he may prove himself, I believe that no rank we can bestow on him would cause him to be considered an equal of the British officer."[21] Such smug racial attitudes made it difficult for British rule, no matter how beneficent, ever to be ultimately accepted and led to the rise of an Indian nationalist movement. By 1883, when the Indian National Congress was formed, moderate, educated Indians were beginning to seek self-government. By 1919, in response to British violence and British insensitivity, Indians were demanding complete independence.

Results of the New Imperialism

By 1900, almost all the societies of Africa and Asia were either under full colonial rule or, as in the case of China and the Ottoman Empire, at a point of virtual collapse. Only a handful of states, such as Japan in East Asia, Thailand in Southeast Asia, Afghanistan and Persia in the Middle East, and mountainous Ethiopia in East Africa, managed to escape internal disintegration or subjection to colonial rule. For the most part, the exceptions were the result of good fortune rather than design. Thailand escaped subjugation primarily because officials in Britain and France found it more convenient to transform the country into a buffer state than to fight over it. Ethiopia and Afghanistan survived due to their remote location and mountainous terrain. Only Japan managed to avoid the common fate through a concerted strategy of political and economic reform. With the coming of imperialism, a global economy was finally established, and the domination of Western civilization over those of Africa and Asia appeared to be complete. At the same time, the competition for lands abroad also heightened the existing rivalries among European states.

International Rivalry and the Coming of War

Q **Focus Questions:** What was the Bismarckian system of alliances, and how successful was it at keeping the peace? What issues lay behind the international crises that Europe faced in the late nineteenth and early twentieth centuries?

Before 1914, Europeans had experienced almost fifty years of peace. There had been wars (including wars of conquest in the non-Western world), but none had involved the great powers. A series of crises had occurred that might easily have led to general war. One reason they did not is that until 1890, Bismarck of Germany exercised a restraining influence on the Europeans.

The Bismarckian System

Bismarck knew that the emergence of a unified Germany in 1871 had upset the balance of power established at Vienna in 1815. Fearing the French desire for revenge over their loss of Alsace-Lorraine in the Franco-Prussian War, Bismarck made an alliance in 1873 with the traditionally conservative powers Austria-Hungary and Russia. The Three Emperors' League, as it was called, failed to work very well, however, primarily because of Russian-Austrian rivalry in the Balkans.

The Balkans: Decline of Ottoman Power The problem in the Balkans was a by-product of the disintegration of the Ottoman Empire. As subject peoples in the Balkans clamored for independence, corruption and inefficiency weakened the Ottoman government. Only the interference of the great European powers, who were fearful of each other's designs on its territories, kept the Ottoman Empire alive. Complicating the situation was the rivalry between Russia and Austria, which both had designs on the Balkans. For Russia, the Balkans provided the shortest overland route to Constantinople and the Mediterranean. Austria viewed the Balkans as fertile ground for Austrian expansion. Although Germany had no real interests in the Balkans, Bismarck was fearful of the consequences of a war between Russia and Austria over the region and served as a restraining influence on both powers. Events in the Balkans, however, precipitated a new crisis.

In 1876, the Balkan states of Serbia and Montenegro declared war on the Ottoman Empire. Both were defeated, but Russia, with Austrian approval, attacked and defeated the Ottomans. By the Treaty of San Stefano in 1878, a large Bulgarian state, extending from the Danube in the north to the Aegean Sea in the south, was created. As Bulgaria was viewed as a Russian satellite, this Russian success caused the other great powers to call for a congress of European powers to discuss a revision of the treaty.

The Congress of Berlin, which met in the summer of 1878, was dominated by Bismarck. The congress effectively demolished the Treaty of San Stefano, much to Russia's humiliation. The new Bulgarian state was considerably reduced, and the rest of the territory was returned to Ottoman control. The three Balkan states of Serbia, Montenegro, and Romania, until then nominally under Ottoman control, were recognized as independent. The other Balkan territories of Bosnia and Herzegovina were placed under Austrian protection; Austria could occupy but not annex them.

New Alliances After the Congress of Berlin, the European powers sought new alliances to safeguard their security. Angered by the Germans' actions at the congress, the Russians had terminated the Three Emperors' League. Bismarck then made an alliance with Austria in 1879 that was joined by Italy in

1882. The Triple Alliance of 1882 committed Germany, Austria, and Italy to support the existing political order while providing a defensive alliance against France or "two or more great powers not members of the alliance." At the same time, Bismarck sought to remain on friendly terms with the Russians and signed the Reinsurance Treaty with Russia in 1887, hoping to prevent a French-Russian alliance that would threaten Germany with the possibility of a two-front war. The Bismarckian system of alliances, geared to preserving peace and the status quo, had worked, but in 1890, Emperor William II dismissed Bismarck and began to chart a new direction for Germany's foreign policy.

New Directions and New Crises

Emperor William II embarked on an activist foreign policy dedicated to enhancing German power by finding, as he put it, Germany's rightful "place in the sun." One of his changes in Bismarck's foreign policy was to drop the Reinsurance Treaty with Russia, which he viewed as being at odds with Germany's alliance with Austria. The ending of the alliance achieved what Bismarck had feared: it brought France and Russia together. Long isolated by Bismarck's policies, republican France leaped at the chance to draw closer to tsarist Russia, and in 1894, the two powers concluded a military alliance.

During the next ten years, German policies abroad caused the British to draw closer to France (see the box on p. 763). By 1907, a loose confederation of Great Britain, France, and Russia—known as the Triple Entente—stood opposed to the Triple Alliance of Germany, Austria-Hungary, and Italy. Europe was divided into two opposing camps that became more and more inflexible and unwilling to compromise. When the members of the two alliances became involved in a new series of crises between 1908 and 1913 over control of the remnants of the Ottoman Empire in the Balkans, the stage was set for World War I.

Crises in the Balkans, 1908–1913 The Bosnian Crisis of 1908–1909 initiated a chain of events that eventually spun out of control. Since 1878, Bosnia and Herzegovina had been under the protection of Austria, but in

The Balkans in 1878

Map legend:
- Ottoman Empire
- Bulgaria as amended by Congress of Berlin, 1878

THE EMPEROR'S BIG MOUTH

Emperor William II had the unfortunate tendency to stir up trouble by his often tactless public remarks. In this 1908 interview, for example, William intended to strengthen Germany's ties with Britain. His words had just the opposite effect and raised a storm of protest in both Britain and Germany.

Daily Telegraph Interview, October 28, 1908

His Majesty [William II] honored me with a long conversation, and spoke with impulsive and unusual frankness. "You English," he said, "are mad, mad, mad as March hares. What has come over you that you are so completely given over to suspicions quite unworthy of a great nation? What more can I do than I have done? I declared with all the emphasis at my command, in my speech at Guildhall, that my heart is set upon peace, and that it is one of my dearest wishes to live on the best of terms with England. Have I ever been false to my word? Falsehoods and prevarication are alien to my nature. My actions ought to speak for themselves, but you listen not to them but to those who misinterpret and distort them. That is a personal insult which I feel and resent. To be forever misjudged, to have my repeated offers of friendship weighed and scrutinized with jealous, mistrustful eyes, taxes my patience severely. I have said time after time that I am a friend of England, and your Press—or, at least, a considerable section of it—bids the people of England to refuse my proffered hand, and insinuates that the other holds a dagger. How can I convince a nation against its will?

"I repeat," continued his Majesty, "that I am a friend of England, but you make things difficult for me. My task is not of the easiest. The prevailing sentiment among large sections of the middle and lower classes of my own people is not friendly to England. I am, therefore, so to speak, in a minority in my own land, but it is a minority of the best elements as it is in England with respect to Germany. That is another reason why I resent your refusal to accept my pledged word that I am the friend of England. I strive without ceasing to improve relations, and you retort that I am your arch-enemy. You make it hard for me. Why is it?...

"But, you will say, what of the German Navy? Surely, that is a menace to England! Against whom but England are my squadrons being prepared? If England is not in the minds of those Germans who are bent on creating a powerful fleet, why is Germany asked to consent to such new and heavy burdens of taxation? My answer is clear. Germany is a young and growing Empire. She has a world-wide commerce, which is rapidly expanding, and to which the legitimate ambition of patriotic Germans refuses to assign any bounds. Germany must have a powerful fleet to protect that commerce, and her manifold interests in even the most distant seas. She expects those interests to go on growing, and she must be able to champion them manfully in any quarter of the globe. Germany looks ahead. Her horizons stretch far away. She must be prepared for any eventualities in the Far East. Who can foresee what may take place in the Pacific in the days to come, days not so distant as some believe, but days, at any rate, for which all European Powers with Far Eastern interests ought steadily to prepare? Look at the accomplished rise of Japan; think of the possible national awakening of China; and then judge of the vast problems of the Pacific. Only those Powers which have great navies will be listened to with respect, when the future of the Pacific comes to be solved; and, if for that reason only, Germany must have a powerful fleet. It may even be that England herself will be glad that Germany has a fleet when they speak together on the same side in the great debates of the future."

Q *What did William II mean to say? What did he actually say? What does this interview with William II reveal about the emperor's attitudes and character?*

1908, Austria took the drastic step of annexing these two Slavic-speaking territories. Serbia became outraged at this action because it dashed the Serbs' hopes of creating a large Serbian kingdom that would include most of the southern Slavs. This was why the Austrians had annexed Bosnia and Herzegovina. To the Austrians, a large Serbia would be a threat to the unity of the Austro-Hungarian Empire, with its large Slavic population. The Russians, as protectors of their fellow Slavs and desiring to increase their own authority in the Balkans, supported the Serbs and opposed the Austrian action. Backed by the Russians, the Serbs prepared for war against Austria. At this point, William II intervened and demanded that the Russians accept Austria's annexation of Bosnia and Herzegovina or face war with Germany. Weakened from their defeat in the Russo-Japanese War in 1904–1905, the Russians backed down. Humiliated, they vowed revenge.

European attention returned to the Balkans in 1912 when Serbia, Bulgaria, Montenegro, and Greece organized the Balkan League and defeated the Ottomans in the First Balkan War. When the victorious allies were unable to agree on how to divide the conquered Ottoman provinces of Macedonia and Albania, the Second Balkan War erupted in 1913. Greece, Serbia, Romania, and the Ottoman Empire attacked and defeated Bulgaria. As a result, Bulgaria obtained only a small part of Macedonia, and most of the rest was divided between Serbia and Greece (see Map 24.3). Yet Serbia's aspirations remained unfulfilled. The two Balkan wars left the inhabitants embittered and created more tensions among the great powers.

One of Serbia's major ambitions had been to acquire Albanian territory that would give it a port on the Adriatic. At the London Conference, arranged by Austria

CHRONOLOGY European Diplomacy

Three Emperors' League	1873
Serbia and Montenegro attack the Ottoman Empire	1876
Treaty of San Stefano	1878
Congress of Berlin	1878
Defensive alliance: Germany and Austria	1879
Triple Alliance: Germany, Austria, and Italy	1882
Reinsurance Treaty: Germany and Russia	1887
Military alliance: Russia and France	1894
Triple Entente: France, Britain, and Russia	1907
First Balkan War	1912
Second Balkan War	1913

at the end of the two Balkan wars, the Austrians had blocked Serbia's wishes by creating an independent Albania. The Germans, as Austrian allies, had supported this move. In their frustration, Serbian nationalists increasingly portrayed the Austrians as monsters who were keeping the Serbs from becoming a great nation. As Serbia's chief supporters, the Russians were also upset by the turn of events in the region. A feeling had grown among Russian leaders that they could not back down again in the event of a confrontation with Austria or Germany in the Balkans. One Russian military journal even stated early in 1914, "We are preparing for a war in the west. The whole nation must accustom itself to the idea that we arm ourselves for a war of annihilation against the Germans."

Austria-Hungary had achieved another of its aims, but it was still convinced that Serbia was a mortal threat to its empire and must at some point be crushed. Meanwhile, the French and Russian governments renewed their alliance and promised each other that they would not back down at the next crisis. Britain drew closer to France. By the

MAP 24.3 **The Balkans in 1913.** The First Balkan War (1912) liberated most of the region from Ottoman control; the Second Balkan War (1913) increased the size of Greece and Serbia at Bulgaria's expense. Russia supported the ambitions of fellow Slavs in Serbia, who sought to rule a large Slavic kingdom in the Balkans. Austria and its ally Germany opposed Serbia's ambitions.

Q Look at the map on p. 762. What territories had the Ottomans lost by the end of 1913? View an animated version of this map or related maps at academic.cengage.com/history/spielvogel beginning of 1914, the two armed camps viewed each other with suspicion. An American in Europe observed, "The whole of Germany is charged with electricity. Everybody's nerves are tense. It only needs a spark to set the whole thing off." The German ambassador to France noted at the same time that "peace remains at the mercy of an accident." The European "age of progress" was about to come to an inglorious and bloody end.

TIMELINE

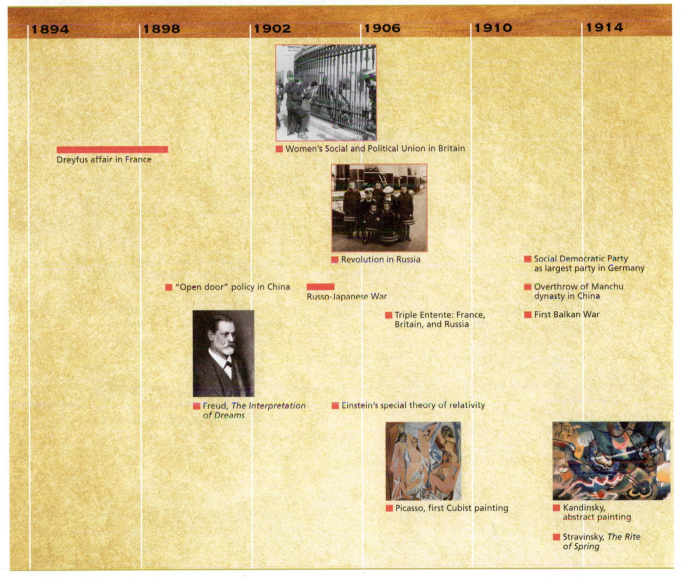

1894   1898   1902   1906   1910   1914

■ Women's Social and Political Union in Britain

Dreyfus affair in France

■ Revolution in Russia

■ Social Democratic Party as largest party in Germany

■ "Open door" policy in China

Russo-Japanese War

■ Overthrow of Manchu dynasty in China

■ Triple Entente: France, Britain, and Russia

■ First Balkan War

■ Freud, *The Interpretation of Dreams*

■ Einstein's special theory of relativity

■ Picasso, first Cubist painting

■ Kandinsky, abstract painting

■ Stravinsky, *The Rite of Spring*

CONCLUSION

What many Europeans liked to call their "age of progress" in the decades before 1914 was also an era of anxiety. Frenzied imperialist expansion had created vast European empires and spheres of influence around the globe. This feverish competition for colonies, however, had markedly increased the existing antagonisms among the European states. At the same time, the Western treatment of non-Western peoples as racial inferiors caused educated, non-Western elites in these colonies to initiate movements for national independence. Before these movements could be successful, however, the power that Europeans had achieved through their mass armies and technological superiority had to be weakened. The Europeans soon inadvertently accomplished this task for their colonial subjects by demolishing their own civilization on the battlegrounds of Europe.

The cultural revolutions before 1914 had also produced anxiety and a crisis of confidence in European civilization. A brilliant minority of intellectuals had created a modern consciousness that questioned most Europeans' optimistic faith in reason, the rational structure of nature, and the certainty of progress. The devastating experiences of World War I turned this culture of uncertainty into a way of life after 1918.

NOTES

1. Quoted in Arthur E. E. McKenzie, *The Major Achievements of Science* (New York, 1960), vol. 1, p. 310.
2. Friedrich Nietzsche, *Twilight of the Idols and the Anti-Christ*, trans. R. J. Hollingdale (New York, 1972), pp. 117–118.
3. Friedrich Nietzsche, *Thus Spake Zarathustra*, in *The Philosophy of Nietzsche* (New York, 1954), p. 6.
4. Herbert Spencer, *Social Statics* (New York, 1896), pp. 146, 150.
5. Friedrich von Bernhardi, *Germany and the Next War*, trans. Allen H. Powles (New York, 1914), pp. 18–19.
6. Quoted in Edward R. Tannenbaum, *1900: The Generation Before the Great War* (Garden City, N.Y., 1976), p. 337.
7. William Booth, *In Darkest England and the Way Out* (London, 1890), p. 45.
8. Quoted in John Rewald, *The History of Impressionism* (New York, 1961), pp. 456–458.
9. Quoted in Anne Higonnet, *Berthe Morisot's Images of Women* (Cambridge, Mass., 1992), p. 19.
10. Quoted in Craig Wright, *Listening to Music* (Saint Paul, Minn., 1992), p. 327.
11. Quoted in Catherine M. Prelinger, "Prelude to Consciousness: Amalie Sieveking and the Female Association for the Care of the Poor and the Sick," in John C. Fout, ed., *German Women in the Nineteenth Century: A Social History* (New York, 1984), p. 119.
12. Quoted in Bonnie G. Smith, *Changing Lives: Women in European History Since 1700* (Lexington, Mass., 1989), p. 379.
13. Quoted in Paul Massing, *Rehearsal for Destruction: A Study of Political Anti-Semitism in Imperial Germany* (New York, 1949), p. 147.
14. Quoted in Abba Eban, *Heritage: Civilization and the Jews* (New York, 1984), p. 249.
15. Quoted in John Merriman, *A History of Modern Europe* (New York, 1996), p. 953.
16. Quoted in ibid., p. 965.
17. Karl Pearson, *National Life from the Standpoint of Science* (London, 1905), p. 184.
18. Quoted in John Ellis, *The Social History of the Machine Gun* (New York, 1975), p. 80.
19. Quoted in ibid., p. 86.
20. Quoted in Louis L. Snyder, ed., *The Imperialism Reader* (Princeton, N.J., 1962), p. 220.
21. Quoted in K. M. Panikkar, *Asia and Western Dominance* (London, 1959), p. 116.

SUGGESTIONS FOR FURTHER READING

Intellectual and Cultural Developments   Two well-regarded studies of Freud are **P. D. Kramer, *Sigmund Freud: Inventor of the Modern Mind*** (New York, 2006), and **P. Gay, *Freud: A Life for Our Time,*** rev. ed. (New York, 2006). Nietzsche is examined in **L. Spinks, *Friedrich Nietzsche*** (London, 2003). On Bergson, see **S. Guerlac, *Thinking in Time: An Introduction to Henri Bergson*** (Ithaca, N.Y., 2006). The basic study on Sorel is **J. J. Roth, *The Cult of Violence: Sorel and the Sorelians*** (Berkeley, Calif., 1980). A useful study on the impact of Darwinian thought on religion is **J. Moore, *The Post-Darwinian Controversies: A Study of the Protestant Struggle to Come to Terms** with Darwin in Great Britain and America, 1870–1900* (Cambridge, 1979). Studies of the popular religion of the period include **T. A. Kselman, *Miracles and Prophesies in Nineteenth-Century France*** (New Brunswick, N.J., 1983), and **J. Sperber, *Popular Catholicism in Nineteenth-Century Germany*** (Princeton, N.J., 1984). Very valuable on modern art are **M. Powell-Jones, *Impressionism*** (London, 1994); **G. Crepaldi, *The Impressionists*** (New York, 2002); **B. Denvir, *Post-Impressionism*** (New York, 1992); and **T. Parsons, *Post-Impressionism: The Rise of Modern Art*** (London, 1992).

Politics: New Directions   The rise of feminism is examined in **J. Rendall, *The Origins of Modern Feminism: Women in Britain, France and the United States*** (London, 1985). On the "new woman," see **M. L. Roberts, *Disruptive Acts: The New Woman in Fin-de-Siècle France*** (Chicago, 2002), and **A. Richardson and C. Willis, eds., *The New Woman in Fiction and Fact,*** rev. ed. (New York, 2007). The subject of modern anti-Semitism is covered in **A. S. Lindemann, *Esau's Tears: Modern Anti-Semitism and the Rise of the Jews*** (New York, 1997). European racism is analyzed in **N. MacMaster, *Racism in Europe, 1870–2000*** (New York, 2001). Anti-Semitism in France is the subject of **L. Derfler, *The Dreyfus Affair*** (Westport, Conn., 2002). The problems of Jews in Russia are examined in **J. Frankel, *Prophecy and Politics: Socialism, Nationalism and the Russian Jews, 1862–1917*** (Cambridge, 1981). On Theodor Herzl, see **J. Kornberg, *Theodor Herzl: From Assimilation to Zionism*** (Bloomington, Ind., 1993). The beginnings of the Labour Party are examined in **R. J. H. Stewart, *Origins of the British Labour Party*** (New York, 2003). There are good introductions to the political world of William II's Germany in **T. A. Kohut, *Wilhelm II and the Germans: A Study in Leadership*** (New York, 1991), and **C. Clark, *Kaiser Wilhelm II*** (London, 2000). On Russia, see **A. Ascher, *Revolution of 1905: A Short History*** (Stanford, Calif., 2004).

The New Imperialism   For broad perspectives on imperialism, see **T. Smith, *The Pattern of Imperialism*** (Cambridge, 1981); **M. W. Doyle, *Empires*** (Ithaca, N.Y., 1986); and **P. Darby, *Three Faces of Imperialism: British and American Approaches to Asia and Africa, 1870–1970*** (New Haven, Conn., 1987). Different aspects of imperialism are covered in **A. Burton, *Burdens of History: British Feminists, Indian Women, and Imperial Culture, 1865–1915*** (Chapel Hill, N.C., 1994); **M. Strobel, *European Women and the Second British Empire*** (Bloomington, Ind., 1991); **N. Ferguson, *Empire: The Rise and Demise of the British World Order*** (New York, 2002), a broad survey that emphasizes how the British Empire gave rise to many aspects of the modern world; **P. J. Marshall, ed., *The Cambridge Illustrated History of the British Empire*** (Cambridge, 1996); and **T. Pakenham, *The Scramble for Africa*** (New York, 1991).

International Rivalry   Two fundamental works on the diplomatic history of the period are **W. L. Langer, *European Alliances and Alignments,*** 2d ed. (New York, 1966), and ***The Diplomacy of Imperialism,*** 2d ed. (New York, 1965). Also valuable are **N. Rich, *Great Power Diplomacy: 1814–1914*** (New York, 1991), and **C. J. Bartlett, *Peace, War and European Powers,*** rev. ed. (New York, 1996).

CengageNOW is an integrated online suite of services and resources with proven ease of use and efficient paths to success, delivering the results you want—NOW!

academic.cengage.com/login/

Enter CengageNOW using the access card that is available with *Western Civilization*. CengageNOW will assist you in understanding the content in this chapter with lesson plans generated for your needs. In addition, you can read the following documents, and many more, online:

King Leopold II of Belgium, letter to the minister of the Congo

Henry Morton Stanley, *How I Found Livingstone*

Sigmund Freud, excerpts from *The Interpretation of Dreams*

Friedrich Nietzsche, selected chapters from *Thus Spake Zarathustra*

Georges Sorel, "The Proletarian Strike"

Oliver Wendell Holmes, "Dissent in Lochner v. New York"

WESTERN CIVILIZATION RESOURCES

Visit the *Western Civilization* Companion Web site for resources specific to this book:

academic.cengage.com/history/spielvogel

For a variety of tools to help you succeed in this course, visit the Western Civilization Resource Center. Enter the Resource Center using either your *CengageNOW* access card or your standalone access card for the *Wadsworth Western Civilization Resource Center*. Organized by topic, this Web site includes quizzes; images; primary source documents; interactive simulations, maps, and timelines; movie explorations; and a wealth of other resources.

http://westernrc.wadsworth.com/

CHAPTER 25
THE BEGINNING OF THE TWENTIETH-CENTURY CRISIS:
WAR AND REVOLUTION

British troops wait for the signal to attack

CHAPTER OUTLINE
AND FOCUS QUESTIONS

The Road to World War I

Q What were the long-range and immediate causes of
World War I?

The War

Q What did the belligerents expect at the beginning of
World War I, and why did the course of the war turn out
to be so different from their expectations? How did
World War I affect the belligerents' governmental and
political institutions, economic affairs, and social life?

War and Revolution

Q What were the causes of the Russian Revolution of 1917,
and why did the Bolsheviks prevail in the civil war and
gain control of Russia?

The Peace Settlement

Q What were the objectives of the chief participants at the
Paris Peace Conference of 1919, and how closely did the
final settlement reflect these objectives?

CRITICAL THINKING

Q What was the relationship between World War I and the
Russian Revolution?

ON JULY 1, 1916, British and French infantry forces
attacked German defensive lines along a 25-mile front near
the Somme River in France. Each soldier carried almost 70
pounds of equipment, making it "impossible to move
much quicker than a slow walk." German machine guns
soon opened fire: "We were able to see our comrades
move forward in an attempt to cross No-Man's Land, only
to be mown down like meadow grass," recalled one British
soldier. "I felt sick at the sight of this carnage and remember weeping."[1] In one day, more than 21,000 British soldiers died. After six months of fighting, the British had
advanced 5 miles; one million British, French, and German
soldiers had been killed or wounded.

Philip Gibbs, an English war correspondent, described
what he saw in the German trenches that the British forces
overran: "Victory!...Some of the German dead were young
boys, too young to be killed for old men's crimes, and
others might have been old or young. One could not tell
because they had no faces, and were just masses of raw
flesh in rags of uniforms. Legs and arms lay separate without any bodies thereabout."[2]

World War I (1914–1918) was the defining event of
the twentieth century. It devastated the prewar economic,
social, and political order of Europe, and its uncertain

outcome served to prepare the way for an even more destructive war. Overwhelmed by the size of its battles, the number of its casualties, and the extent of its impact on all facets of European life, contemporaries referred to it simply as the Great War.

The Great War was all the more disturbing to Europeans because it came after a period that many believed to have been an age of progress. There had been international crises before 1914, but somehow Europeans had managed to avoid serious and prolonged military confrontations. When smaller European states had gone to war, as in the Balkans in 1912 and 1913, the great European powers had shown the ability to keep the conflict localized. Material prosperity and a fervid belief in scientific and technological progress had convinced many people that Europe stood on the verge of creating the utopia that humans had dreamed of for centuries. The historian Arnold Toynbee expressed what the pre–World War I era had meant to his generation:

> [It was expected] that life throughout the World would become more rational, more humane, and more democratic and that, slowly, but surely, political democracy would produce greater social justice. We had also expected that the progress of science and technology would make mankind richer, and that this increasing wealth would gradually spread from a minority to a majority. We had expected that all this would happen peacefully. In fact we thought that mankind's course was set for an earthly paradise.[3]

After 1918, it was no longer possible to maintain naive illusions about the progress of Western civilization. As World War I was followed by the destructiveness of World War II and the mass murder machines of totalitarian regimes, it became all too apparent that instead of a utopia, European civilization had become a nightmare. The Great War resulted not only in great loss of life and property but also in the annihilation of one of the basic intellectual precepts on which Western civilization had been thought to have been founded—the belief in progress. A sense of hopelessness and despair soon replaced blind faith in progress. World War I and the revolutions it spawned can properly be seen as the first stage in the crisis of the twentieth century. ◆

The Road to World War I

Q **Focus Question:** What were the long-range and immediate causes of World War I?

On June 28, 1914, the heir to the Austrian throne, Archduke Francis Ferdinand, was assassinated in the Bosnian city of Sarajevo. Although this event precipitated the confrontation between Austria and Serbia that led to World War I, war was not inevitable. Previous assassinations of European leaders had not led to war, and

European statesmen had managed to localize such conflicts. Although the decisions that European statesmen made during this crisis were crucial in leading to war, there were also long-range underlying forces that were propelling Europeans toward armed conflict.

Nationalism

In the first half of the nineteenth century, liberals had maintained that the organization of European states along national lines would lead to a peaceful Europe based on a sense of international fraternity. They had been very wrong. The system of nation-states that had emerged in Europe in the second half of the nineteenth century led not to cooperation but to competition. Rivalries over colonial and commercial interests intensified during an era of frenzied imperialist expansion, and the division of Europe's great powers into two loose alliances (Germany, Austria, and Italy and France, Great Britain, and Russia) only added to the tensions (see Map 25.1). The series of crises that tested these alliances in the early years of the new century had taught European states a dangerous lesson. Governments that had exercised restraint in order to avoid war wound up being publicly humiliated, whereas those that went to the brink of war to maintain their national interests had often been praised for having preserved national honor. In either case, by 1914, the major European states had come to believe that their allies were important and that their security depended on supporting those allies, even when they took foolish risks.

Diplomacy based on brinkmanship was especially frightening in view of the nature of the European state system. Each nation-state regarded itself as sovereign, subject to no higher interest or authority. Each state was motivated by its own self-interest and success. As Emperor William II of Germany remarked, "In questions of honor and vital interests, you don't consult others." Such attitudes made war an ever-present possibility, particularly since most statesmen considered war an acceptable way to preserve the power of their national states. And within each state, there were circles of political and military leaders who thought that war was inevitable and provided an opportunity to achieve their goals. In Germany, there were those who advocated the creation of a German empire by acquiring parts of Russia and possibly even parts of Belgium and France. France wished to regain control of Alsace-Lorraine, which had been seized by the Germans in the Franco-Prussian War. Austria-Hungary sought to prevent Serbia from creating a large Serbian state at the expense of its own multinational empire. Britain sought to preserve its world empire, and Russia felt compelled to maintain its great power status by being a protector of its fellow Slavic peoples in the Balkans.

Internal Dissent

The growth of nationalism in the nineteenth century had yet another serious consequence. Not all ethnic groups

MAP 25.1 **Europe in 1914.** By 1914, two alliances dominated Europe: the Triple Entente of Britain, France, and Russia and the Triple Alliance of Germany, Austria-Hungary, and Italy. Russia sought to bolster fellow Slavs in Serbia, whereas Austria-Hungary was intent on increasing its power in the Balkans and thwarting Serbia's ambitions. Thus, the Balkans became the flash point for World War I.

Q Which nonaligned nations were positioned between the two alliances?

View an animated version of this map or related maps at **academic.cengage.com/history/spielvogel**

---

had achieved the goal of nationhood. Slavic minorities in the Balkans and the Austrian Empire, for example, still dreamed of creating their own national states. So did the Irish in the British Empire and the Poles in the Russian Empire.

National aspirations, however, were not the only source of internal strife at the beginning of the twentieth century. Socialist labor movements had grown more powerful and were increasingly inclined to use strikes, even violent ones, to achieve their goals. Some conservative leaders, alarmed at the increase in labor strife and class division, even feared that European nations were on the verge of revolution. Did these statesmen opt for war in 1914 because they believed that "prosecuting an active foreign policy," as one leader expressed it, would smother "internal troubles"? Some historians have argued that the desire to suppress internal disorder may have encouraged some leaders to take the plunge into war in 1914.

Militarism

The growth of large mass armies after 1900 not only heightened the existing tensions in Europe but made it inevitable that if war did come, it would be highly destructive. Conscription had been established as a regular practice in most Western countries before 1914 (the United States and Britain were major exceptions).

European military machines had doubled in size between 1890 and 1914. With its 1.3 million men, the Russian army had grown to be the largest, but the French and Germans were not far behind with 900,000 each. The British, Italian, and Austrian armies numbered between 250,000 and 500,000 soldiers. Most European land armies were filled with peasants, since many young, urban working-class males were unable to pass the physical examinations required for military service.

Militarism, however, involved more than just large armies. As armies grew, so did the influence of military leaders, who drew up vast and complex plans for quickly mobilizing millions of men and enormous quantities of supplies in the event of war. Fearful that changes in these plans would cause chaos in the armed forces, military leaders insisted that their plans could not be altered. In the crises during the summer of 1914, the generals' lack of flexibility forced European political leaders to make decisions for military instead of political reasons.

The Outbreak of War: The Summer of 1914

Militarism, nationalism, and the desire to stifle internal dissent may all have played a role in the coming of World War I, but the decisions made by European leaders in the summer of 1914 directly precipitated the conflict. It was another crisis in the Balkans that forced this predicament on European statesmen.

Another Crisis in the Balkans As we have seen, states in southeastern Europe had struggled to free themselves from Ottoman rule in the course of the nineteenth and early twentieth centuries. But the rivalry between Austria-Hungary and Russia for domination of these new states created serious tensions in the region. The crises between 1908 and 1913 had only intensified the antagonisms. By 1914, Serbia, supported by Russia, was determined to create a large, independent Slavic state in the Balkans, but Austria, which had its own Slavic minorities to contend with, was equally set on preventing that possibility. Many Europeans perceived the inherent dangers in this combination of Serbian ambition bolstered by Russian opposition to Austria and Austria's conviction that Serbia's success would mean the end of its empire. The British ambassador to Vienna wrote in 1913:

> Serbia will some day set Europe by the ears, and bring about a universal war on the Continent.... I cannot tell you how exasperated people are getting here at the continual worry which that little country causes to Austria under encouragement from Russia.... It will be lucky if Europe succeeds in avoiding war as a result of the present crisis. The next time a Serbian crisis arises, ... I feel sure that Austria-Hungary will refuse to admit of any Russian interference in the dispute and that she will proceed to settle her differences with her little neighbor by herself.[4]

It was against this backdrop of mutual distrust and hatred between Austria-Hungary and Russia, on the one hand, and Austria-Hungary and Serbia, on the other, that the events of the summer of 1914 were played out.

Assassination of Francis Ferdinand The assassination of the Austrian Archduke Francis Ferdinand and his wife, Sophia, on June 28, 1914, was carried out by a Bosnian activist who worked for the Black Hand, a Serbian terrorist organization dedicated to the creation of a pan-Slavic kingdom. Although the Austrian government did not know whether the Serbian government had been directly involved in the archduke's assassination, it saw an opportunity to "render Serbia impotent once and for all by a display of force," as the Austrian foreign minister put it. Fearful of Russian intervention on Serbia's behalf, Austrian leaders sought the backing of their German allies. Emperor William II and his chancellor, Theobald von Bethmann-Hollweg, responded with the infamous "blank check," their assurance that Austria-Hungary could rely on Germany's "full support," even if "matters went to the length of a war between Austria-Hungary and Russia." Much historical debate has focused on this "blank check" extended to the Austrians. Did the Germans realize that an Austrian-Serbian war could lead to a wider war? If so, did they actually want one? Historians are still divided on the answers to these questions.

Strengthened by German support, Austrian leaders issued an ultimatum to Serbia on July 23. Austrian leaders made their demands so extreme that Serbia had little choice but to reject some of them in order to

	1914
Assassination of Archduke Francis Ferdinand	June 28
Austria's ultimatum to Serbia	July 23
Austria declares war on Serbia	July 28
Russia mobilizes	July 29
German ultimatum to Russia	July 31
Germany declares war on Russia	August 1
Germany declares war on France	August 3
German troops invade Belgium	August 4
Great Britain declares war on Germany	August 4

preserve its sovereignty. Austria then declared war on Serbia on July 28. Although both Germany and Austria had hoped to keep the war limited to Serbia and Austria in order to ensure Austria's success in the Balkans, these hopes soon vanished.

Declarations of War Still smarting from its humiliation in the Bosnian crisis of 1908, Russia was determined to support Serbia's cause. On July 28, Tsar Nicholas II ordered partial mobilization of the Russian army against Austria. At this point, the rigidity of the military war plans played havoc with diplomatic and political decisions. The Russian General Staff informed the tsar that their mobilization plans were based on a war against both Germany and Austria simultaneously. They could not execute partial mobilization without creating chaos in the army. Consequently, the Russian government ordered full mobilization of the Russian army on July 29, knowing that the Germans would consider this an act of war against them (see the box on p. 772). Germany responded to Russian mobilization with its own ultimatum that the Russians must halt their mobilization within twelve hours. When the Russians ignored it, Germany declared war on Russia on August 1.

At this stage of the conflict, German war plans determined whether France would become involved in the war. Under the guidance of General Alfred von Schlieffen, chief of staff from 1891 to 1905, the German General Staff had devised a military plan based on the

The Schlieffen Plan

"YOU HAVE TO BEAR THE RESPONSIBILITY FOR WAR OR PEACE"

After Austria declared war on Serbia on July 28, 1914, Russian support of Serbia and German support of Austria threatened to escalate the conflict in the Balkans into a wider war. As we can see in these last-minute telegrams between the Russians and the Germans, neither side was able to accept the other's line of reasoning.

Communications between Berlin and Saint Petersburg on the Eve of World War I

Emperor William II to Tsar Nicholas II, July 28, 10:45 P.M.

I have heard with the greatest anxiety of the impression which is caused by the action of Austria-Hungary against Servia [Serbia]. The inscrupulous agitation which has been going on for years in Servia, has led to the revolting crime of which Archduke Franz Ferdinand has become a victim. The spirit which made the Servians murder their own King and his consort still dominates that country. Doubtless You will agree with me that both of us, You as well as I, and all other sovereigns, have a common interest to insist that all those who are responsible for this horrible murder shall suffer their deserved punishment....

Your most sincere and devoted friend and cousin

(Signed)
Wilhelm

Tsar Nicholas II to Emperor William II, July 29, 1:00 P.M.

I am glad that You are back in Germany. In this serious moment I ask You earnestly to help me. An ignominious war has been declared against a weak country and in Russia the indignation which I full share is tremendous. I fear that very soon I shall be unable to resist the pressure exercised upon me and that I shall be forced to take measures which will lead to war. To prevent a calamity as a European war would be, I urge You in the name of our old friendship to do all in Your power to restrain Your ally from going too far.

(Signed)
Nicolas

Emperor William II to Tsar Nicholas II, July 29, 6:30 P.M.

I have received Your telegram and I share Your desire for the conservation of peace. However: I cannot—as I told You in my first telegram—consider the action of Austria-Hungary as an "ignominious war." Austria-Hungary knows from experience that the promises of Servia as long as they are merely on paper are entirely unreliable.... I believe that a direct understanding is possible and desirable between Your Government and Vienna, an understanding which I—as I have already telegraphed You—my Government endeavors to aid with all possible effort. Naturally military measures by Russia, which might be construed as a menace by Austria-Hungary, would accelerate a calamity which both of us desire to avoid and would undermine my position as mediator which—upon Your appeal to my friendship and aid—I willingly accepted.

(Signed)
Wilhelm

Emperor William II to Tsar Nicholas II, July 30, 1:00 A.M.

My Ambassador has instructions to direct the attention of Your Government to the dangers and serious consequences of a mobilization. I have told You the same in my last telegram. Austria-Hungary has mobilized only against Servia, and only a part of her army. If Russia, as seems to be the case, according to Your advice and that of Your Government, mobilizes against Austria-Hungary, the part of the mediator with which You have entrusted me in such friendly manner and which I have accepted upon Your express desire, is threatened if not made impossible. The entire weight of decision now rests upon Your shoulders, You have to bear the responsibility for war or peace.

(Signed)
Wilhelm

German Chancellor to German Ambassador at Saint Petersburg, July 31, URGENT

In spite of negotiations still pending and although we have up to this hour made no preparations for mobilization, Russia has mobilized her entire army and navy, hence also against us. On account of these Russian measures, we have been forced, for the safety of the country, to proclaim the threatening state of war, which does not yet imply mobilization. Mobilization, however, is bound to follow if Russia does not stop every measure of war against us and against Austria-Hungary within 12 hours, and notifies us definitely to this effect. Please to communicate this at once to M. Sasonof and wire hour of communication.

Q *How do the telegrams exchanged between William II and Nicholas II reveal why the Europeans foolishly went to war in 1914? What do they tell us about the nature of the relationship between these two monarchs?*

---

assumption of a two-front war with France and Russia, since the two powers had formed a military alliance in 1894. The Schlieffen Plan called for a minimal troop deployment against Russia while most of the German army would make a rapid invasion of western France by way of neutral Belgium. After the planned quick defeat of the French, the German army expected to redeploy to the east against Russia. Under the Schlieffen Plan, Germany could not mobilize its troops solely against Russia and therefore declared war on France on August 3 after issuing an ultimatum to Belgium on August 2 demanding the right of German troops to pass through Belgian territory. On August 4, Great Britain declared war on Germany, officially over this violation of Belgian neutrality but in fact over the British desire to maintain world power. As one British diplomat argued, if Germany and Austria were to win the war, "what would be the position of a friendless England?" By August 4, all the great powers of Europe were at war. Through all the maneuvering of the last few days before the war, one fact stands out—all the great powers seemed willing to risk war. They were not disappointed.

The War

Q **Focus Questions:** What did the belligerents expect at the beginning of World War I, and why did the course of the war turn out to be so different from their expectations? How did World War I affect the belligerents' governmental and political institutions, economic affairs, and social life?

Before 1914, many political leaders had become convinced that war involved so many political and economic risks that it was not worth fighting. Others had believed that "rational" diplomats could control any situation and prevent the outbreak of war. At the beginning of August 1914, both of these prewar illusions were shattered, but the new illusions that replaced them soon proved to be equally foolish.

1914–1915: Illusions and Stalemate

Europeans went to war in 1914 with remarkable enthusiasm (see the box on p. 774). Government propaganda had been successful in stirring up national antagonisms before the war. Now, in August 1914, the urgent pleas of governments for defense against aggressors fell on receptive ears in every belligerent nation. Most people seemed genuinely convinced that their nation's cause was just. Even domestic differences were temporarily shelved in the midst of war fever. Socialists had long derided "imperialist war" as a blow against the common interests that united the working classes of all countries. Nationalism, however, proved more powerful than working-class solidarity in the summer of 1914 as socialist parties everywhere dropped plans for strikes and workers expressed their readiness to fight for their country. The German Social Democrats, for example, decided that it was imperative to "safeguard the culture and independence of our own country."

The Excitement of War. World War I was greeted with incredible enthusiasm. Each of the major belligerents was convinced of the rightness of its cause. Everywhere in Europe, jubilant civilians sent their troops off to war with joyous fervor as is evident in the photograph at the top, showing French troops marching off to war. The photograph below shows a group of German soldiers marching off to battle with civilian support. The belief that the soldiers would be home by Christmas proved to be a pathetic illusion.

A new set of illusions fed the enthusiasm for war. Almost everyone in August 1914 believed that the war would be over in a few weeks. People were reminded that all European wars since 1815 had in fact ended in a matter of weeks, conveniently overlooking the American Civil War (1861–1865), which was the true prototype for World War I. The illusion of a short war was also

THE EXCITEMENT OF WAR

The incredible outpouring of patriotic enthusiasm that greeted the declaration of war at the beginning of August 1914 demonstrated the power that nationalistic feeling had attained at the beginning of the twentieth century. Many Europeans seemingly believed that the war had given them a higher purpose, a renewed dedication to the greatness of their nations. These selections are taken from three sources: the autobiography of Stefan Zweig, an Austrian writer; the memoirs of Robert Graves, a British writer; and a letter by a German soldier, Walter Limmer, to his parents.

Stefan Zweig, *The World of Yesterday*

The next morning I was in Austria. In every station placards had been put up announcing general mobilization. The trains were filled with fresh recruits, banners were flying, music sounded, and in Vienna I found the entire city in a tumult.... There were parades in the street, flags, ribbons, and music burst forth everywhere, young recruits were marching triumphantly, their faces lighting up at the cheering....

And to be truthful, I must acknowledge that there was a majestic, rapturous, and even seductive something in this first outbreak of the people from which one could escape only with difficulty. And in spite of all my hatred and aversion for war, I should not like to have missed the memory of those days. As never before, thousands and hundreds of thousands felt what they should have felt in peace time, that they belonged together. A city of two million, a country of nearly fifty million, in that hour felt that they were participating in world history, in a moment which would never recur, and that each one was called upon to cast his infinitesimal self into the glowing mass, there to be purified of all selfishness. All differences of class, rank, and language were flooded over at that moment by the rushing feeling of fraternity....

What did the great mass know of war in 1914, after nearly half a century of peace? They did not know war, they had hardly given it a thought. It had become legendary, and distance had made it seem romantic and heroic. They still saw it in the perspective of their school readers and of paintings in museums; brilliant cavalry attacks in glittering uniforms, the fatal shot always straight through the heart, the entire campaign a resounding march of victory—"We'll be home at Christmas," the recruits shouted laughingly to their mothers in August of 1914.... A rapid excursion into the romantic, a wild, manly adventure—that is how the war of 1914 was painted in the imagination of the simple man, and the younger people were honestly afraid that they might miss this most wonderful and exciting experience of their lives; that is why they hurried and thronged to the colors, and that is why they shouted and sang in the trains that carried them to the slaughter; wildly and feverishly the red wave of blood coursed through the veins of the entire nation.

Robert Graves, *Goodbye to All That*

I had just finished with Charterhouse and gone up to Harlech, when England declared war on Germany. A day or two later I decided to enlist. In the first place, though the papers predicted only a very short war—over by Christmas at the outside—I hoped that it might last long enough to delay my going to Oxford in October, which I dreaded. Nor did I work out the possibilities of getting actively engaged in the fighting, expecting garrison service at home, while the regular forces were away. In the second place, I was outraged to read of the Germans' cynical violation of Belgian neutrality. Though I discounted perhaps twenty per cent of the atrocity details as wartime exaggeration, that was not, of course, sufficient.

Walter Limmer, Letter to His Parents

In any case I mean to go into this business.... That is the simple duty of every one of us. And this feeling is universal among the soldiers, especially since the night when England's declaration of war was announced in the barracks. We none of us got to sleep till three o'clock in the morning, we were so full of excitement, fury, and enthusiasm. It is a joy to go to the Front with such comrades. We are bound to be victorious! Nothing else is possible in the face of such determination to win.

Q *What do these excerpts reveal about the motivations of people to join and support World War I? Do the excerpts reveal anything about the power of nationalism in Europe in the early twentieth century?*

---

bolstered by another illusion, the belief that in an age of modern industry, war could not be conducted for more than a few months without destroying a nation's economy. Both the soldiers who exuberantly boarded the trains for the war front in August 1914 and the jubilant citizens who bombarded them with flowers when they departed believed that the warriors would be home by Christmas.

Then, too, war held a fatal attraction for many people. To some, war was an exhilarating release from humdrum bourgeois existence, from a "world grown old and cold and weary," as one poet wrote. To some, war meant a glorious adventure, as a young German student wrote to his parents: "My dear ones, be proud that you live in such a time and in such a nation and that you...have the privilege of sending those you love into so glorious a battle."[5] And finally, some believed that the war would have a redemptive effect, that millions would abandon their petty preoccupations with material life, ridding the nation of selfishness and sparking a national

Farthest German advance, September 1914

German offensive, March–July 1918

German advances

Winter, 1914–1915

Armistice line, November 1918

Allied advances

MAP 25.2 **The Western Front, 1914–1918.** The Western Front was the site of massive carnage: millions of soldiers died in offensives and counteroffensives as they moved battle lines a few miles at a time in France and Belgium from 1914 to 1917. Soldiers in the trenches were often surrounded by the rotting bodies of dead comrades. **Q** What is the approximate distance between the armistice line near Sedan and the closest approach of the Germans to Paris? ● **View an animated version of this map or related maps at** academic.cengage.com/history/spielvogel

rebirth based on self-sacrifice, heroism, and nobility. All of these illusions about war died painful deaths on the battlefields of World War I.

War in the West German hopes for a quick end to the war rested on a military gamble. The Schlieffen Plan had called for the German army to make a vast encircling movement through Belgium into northern France that would sweep around Paris and surround most of the French army. But the plan suffered a major defect from the beginning; it called for a strong right flank for the encircling of Paris, but German military leaders, concerned about a Russian invasion in the east, had moved forces from the right flank to strengthen the German army in the east.

On August 4, German troops crossed into Belgium and by the first week of September had reached the Marne River, only 20 miles from Paris. The Germans seemed on the verge of success but had underestimated the speed with which the British would be able to mobilize and put troops into battle in France. An unexpected counterattack by British and French forces under the French commander General Joseph Joffre stopped the Germans at the First Battle of the Marne (September 6–10) east of Paris (see Map 25.2). The German troops fell back, but the exhausted French army was unable to pursue its advantage. The war quickly turned into a stalemate as neither the Germans nor the French could dislodge the other from the trenches they had begun to dig for shelter. Two lines of trenches soon extended from the English Channel to the frontiers of Switzerland. The Western Front had become bogged down in trench warfare, which kept both sides in virtually the same positions for four years.

War in the East In contrast to the west, the war in the east was marked by much more mobility, although the cost in lives was equally enormous. At the beginning of the war, the Russian army moved into eastern Germany but was decisively defeated at the Battles of Tannenberg on August 30 and the Masurian Lakes on September 15 (see Map 25.3). These battles established the military reputations of the commanding general, Paul von Hindenburg, and his chief of staff, General Erich Ludendorff. The Russians were no longer a threat to German territory.

The Austrians, Germany's allies, fared less well initially. They had been defeated by the Russians in Galicia and thrown out of Serbia as well. To make matters worse, the Italians broke their alliance with the Germans and Austrians and entered the war on the Allied side by attacking Austria in May 1915. By this time, the Germans had come to the aid of the Austrians. A German-Austrian army defeated and routed the Russian army in Galicia and pushed the Russians back 300 miles into their own territory. Russian casualties stood at 2.5 million killed, captured, or wounded; the Russians had almost been knocked out of the war. Buoyed by their success, the Germans and Austrians, joined by the Bulgarians in September 1915, attacked and eliminated Serbia from the war.

MAP 25.3 **The Eastern Front, 1914–1918.** Russia made early gains but then was pushed far back into its own territory by the German army. After the Bolsheviks seized power, they negotiated the Treaty of Brest-Litovsk, which extracted Russia from the war at the cost of substantial Russian territory (see Map 25.4).

Q What is the approximate average distance between the farthest advances of Russia into Germany and the farthest advances of Germany into Russia?

View an animated version of this map or related maps at academic.cengage.com/history/spielvogel

Map legend:

- ·—·— Russian advances, 1914–1916
- ······ Deepest German penetration
- —— Brest-Litovsk boundary, 1918
- ⚓ Battle site
- (CRIMEA) Regions of national states

General Photographic Agency/Getty Images

Impact of the Machine Gun. Trench warfare on the Western Front stymied military leaders, who had expected to fight a war based on movement and maneuver. Their efforts to effect a breakthrough by sending masses of men against enemy lines were the height of folly in view of the brutal efficiency of the machine gun. This photograph shows a group of German soldiers in their machine-gun nest.

1916–1917: The Great Slaughter

The successes in the east enabled the Germans to move back to the offensive in the west. The early trenches dug in 1914 had by now become elaborate systems of defense. Both lines of trenches were protected by barbed wire entanglements 3 to 5 feet high and 30 yards wide, concrete machine-gun nests, and mortar batteries, supported further back by heavy artillery. Troops lived in holes in the ground, separated from each other by a "no-man's land."

The unexpected development of trench warfare baffled military leaders, who had been trained to fight wars of movement and maneuver. But public outcries for action put them under heavy pressure. The only plan generals could devise was to attempt a breakthrough by throwing masses of men against enemy lines that had first been battered by artillery barrages. Once the decisive breakthrough had been achieved, they thought, they could then return to the war of movement that they knew best. Periodically, the high command on either side would order an offensive that would begin with an artillery barrage to flatten the enemy's barbed wire and leave the enemy in a state of shock. After "softening up" the enemy in this fashion, a mass of soldiers would climb out of their trenches with fixed bayonets and try to work their way toward the enemy trenches. The attacks rarely worked; the machine gun put hordes of men advancing unprotected across open fields at a severe disadvantage. In 1916 and 1917, millions of young men were killed in the search for the elusive breakthrough. In the German offensive at Verdun in 1916, the British campaign on the Somme in 1916, and the French attack in Champagne in 1917, the senselessness of trench warfare became all too obvious. In ten months at Verdun, 700,000 men lost their lives over a few square miles of terrain.

Daily Life in the Trenches Warfare in the trenches of the Western Front produced unimaginable horrors (see the box on p. 778). Many participants commented on the cloud of confusion that covered the battlefields. When attacking soldiers entered "no-man's land," the noise, machine-gun fire, and exploding artillery shells often caused them to panic and lose their bearings; they went forward only because they were carried on by the momentum of the soldiers beside them. Rarely were battles as orderly as they were portrayed on military maps and in civilian newspapers.

Battlefields were hellish landscapes of barbed wire, shell holes, mud, and injured and dying men. The introduction of poison gas in 1915 produced new forms of injuries, as one British writer described:

> I wish those people who write so glibly about this being a holy war could see a case of mustard gas . . . could see the poor things burnt and blistered all over with great mustard-colored suppurating blisters with blind eyes all sticky . . . and stuck together, and always fighting for breath, with voices a mere whisper, saying that their throats are closing and they know they will choke.[6]

Soldiers in the trenches also lived with the persistent presence of death. Since combat went on for months, they had to carry on in the midst of countless bodies of dead men or the remains of men dismembered by artillery barrages. Many soldiers remembered the stench of decomposing bodies and the swarms of rats that grew fat in the trenches.

Soldiers on the Western Front did not spend all of their time on the front line or in combat when they were on the front line. An infantryman spent one week out of every month in the front-line trenches, one week in the reserve lines, and the remaining two weeks somewhere behind the lines. Daily life in the trenches was predictable. Thirty minutes before sunrise, troops had to "stand to" or be ready to repel any attack. If no attack was forthcoming that day, the day's routine consisted of breakfast followed by inspection, sentry duty, restoration of the trenches, care of personal items, or whiling away the time as best they could. Soldiers often recalled the boredom of life in the dreary, lice-ridden, muddy or dusty trenches.

At many places along the opposing lines of trenches, a "live and let live" system evolved based on the realization that neither side was going to drive out the

Victims of the Machine Gun. Masses of men weighed down with equipment and advancing slowly across open land made magnificent targets for opponents armed with machine guns. This photograph shows French soldiers moving across a rocky terrain, all open targets for their enemies manning the new weapons.

Hulton Archive/Getty Images

THE REALITY OF WAR: TRENCH WARFARE

The romantic illusions about the excitement and adventure of war that filled the minds of so many young men who marched off to battle (see the box on p. 774) quickly disintegrated after a short time in the trenches on the Western Front. This description of trench warfare is taken from the most famous novel that emerged from World War I, Erich Maria Remarque's *All Quiet on the Western Front*, written in 1929. Remarque had fought in the trenches in France.

Erich Maria Remarque, *All Quiet on the Western Front*

We wake up in the middle of the night. The earth booms. Heavy fire is falling on us. We crouch into corners. We distinguish shells of every caliber.

Each man lays hold of his things and looks again every minute to reassure himself that they are still there. The dug-out heaves, the night roars and flashes. We look at each other in the momentary flashes of light, and with pale faces and pressed lips shake our heads.

Every man is aware of the heavy shells tearing down the parapet, rooting up the embankment and demolishing the upper layers of concrete.... Already by morning a few of the recruits are green and vomiting. They are too inexperienced....

The bombardment does not diminish. It is falling in the rear too. As far as one can see it spouts fountains of mud and iron. A wide belt is being raked.

The attack does not come, but the bombardment continues. Slowly we become mute. Hardly a man speaks. We cannot make ourselves understood.

Our trench is almost gone. At many places it is only eighteen inches high, it is broken by holes, and craters, and mountains of earth. A shell lands square in front of our post. At once it is dark. We are buried and must dig ourselves out....

Towards morning, while it is still dark, there is some excitement. Through the entrance rushes in a swarm of fleeing rats that try to storm the walls. Torches light up the confusion. Everyone yells and curses and slaughters. The madness and despair of many hours unloads itself in this outburst. Faces are distorted, arms strike out, the beasts scream; we just stop in time to avoid attacking one another....

Suddenly it howls and flashes terrifically, the dug-out cracks in all its joints under a direct hit, fortunately only a light one that the concrete blocks are able to withstand. It rings metallically, the walls reel, rifles, helmets, earth, mud, and dust fly everywhere. Sulphur fumes pour in.... The recruit starts to rave again and two others follow suit. One jumps up and rushes out, we have trouble with the other two. I start after the one who escapes and wonder whether to shoot him in the leg—then it shrieks again, I fling myself down and when I stand up the wall of the trench is plastered with smoking splinters, lumps of flesh, and bits of uniform. I scramble back.

The first recruit seems actually to have gone insane. He butts his head against the wall like a goat. We must try tonight to take him to the rear. Meanwhile we bind him, but so that in case of attack he can be released.

Suddenly the nearer explosions cease. The shelling continues but it has lifted and falls behind us, our trench is free. We seize the hand-grenades, pitch them out in front of the dug-out and jump after them. The bombardment has stopped and a heavy barrage now falls behind us. The attack has come.

No one would believe that in this howling waste there could still be men; but steel helmets now appear on all sides out of the trench, and fifty yards from us a machine-gun is already in position and barking.

The wire-entanglements are torn to pieces. Yet they offer some obstacle. We see the storm-troops coming. Our artillery opens fire. Machine-guns rattle, rifles crack. The charge works its way across. Haie and Kropp begin with the hand-grenades. They throw as fast as they can, others pass them, the handles with the strings already pulled. Haie throws seventy-five yards, Kropp sixty, it has been measured, the distance is important. The enemy as they run cannot do much before they are within forty yards.

We recognize the distorted faces, the smooth helmets: they are French. They have already suffered heavily when they reach the remnants of the barbed-wire entanglements. A whole line has gone down before our machine-guns; then we have a lot of stoppages and they come nearer.

I see one of them, his face upturned, fall into a wire cradle. His body collapses, his hands remain suspended as though he were praying. Then his body drops clean away and only his hands with the stumps of his arms, shot off, now hang in the wire.

Q   *What does this excerpt from Erich Maria Remarque reveal about the realities of trench warfare? Would the surviving front-line victims of the war have been able to describe or explain their experiences there to those left behind on the home front? What effect would that have on postwar European society?*

---

other anyway. The "live and let live" system resulted in arrangements such as not shelling the latrines or attacking during breakfast. Some parties even worked out agreements to make noise before lesser raids so that the opposing soldiers could retreat to their bunkers.

On both sides, troops produced their own humorous magazines to help pass the time and fulfill the need to laugh in the midst of their daily madness. The British trench magazine, the *B.E.F. Times*, devoted one of its issues to defining military terms. A typical definition was

FILM & HISTORY
PATHS OF GLORY (1957)

Paths of Glory, directed by Stanley Kubrick, is a powerful antiwar film made in 1957 and based on the novel with the same name by Humphrey Cobb. Set in France in 1916, the film deals with the time during World War I when the Western Front had become bogged down in brutal trench warfare. The novel was based loosely on a true story of five French soldiers who were executed for mutiny. In the film, General George Broulard (Adolphe Menjou) of the French General Staff suggests to his subordinate, General Mireau (George Macready), that he launch what would amount to a suicidal attack on the well-defended Ant Hill. Mireau refuses until Broulard mentions the possibility of a promotion, at which point Mireau abruptly changes his mind and accepts the challenge. He walks through the trenches preparing his men with the stock question: "Hello there soldier, are you ready to kill more Germans?" Mireau persuades Colonel Dax (Kirk Douglas) to mount the attack, despite Dax's protest that it will be a disaster. Dax proves to be right. None of the French soldiers reach the German lines, and one-third of the troops are not even able to leave their trenches because of enemy fire. To avoid blame for the failure, General Mireau accuses his men of cowardice, and three of them (one from each company, chosen in purely arbitrary fashion) are brought before a hastily arranged court-martial. Dax defends his men but to no avail. The decision has already been made, and the three men are shot in front of the assembled troops. As General Broulard cynically comments, "One way to maintain discipline is to shoot a man now and then." After the execution, when General Broulard offers Dax a promotion, Dax responds, "Would you like me to suggest what you can do with that promotion?" Replies Broulard, "You're an idealist; I pity you." But Dax has the last word: "I pity you for not seeing the wrongs you have done." The film ends with the troops being ordered back to the front.

The film realistically portrays the horrors of trench warfare in World War I—the senseless and suicidal attacks through no-man's land against well-entrenched machine-gun

Colonel Dax (Kirk Douglas) begins to lead his men out of the trenches to attack Ant Hill.

batteries. The film is also scathing in its portrayal of military leaders. The generals are shown drinking cognac in the palaces they requisitioned for their headquarters while the troops live in the mud and filth of the trenches. Both generals are portrayed as arrogant, ego-driven individuals who think nothing of the slaughter of their men in battle. The men condemned to die for cowardice are scapegoats sacrificed to cover up the mistakes of their superior officers who are determined to pursue "paths of glory" to advance themselves. The film's portrayal of the military executions was not accurate, however. The French army did not choose individuals at random for punishment, although it did execute some soldiers on charges of cowardice, as did the armies of the other belligerents.

This realistic indictment of war and the military elites offended some countries. French authorities saw it as an insult to the honor of the army and did not allow it to be shown in France until 1975. The military regime of Francisco Franco in Spain also banned the film for its antimilitary content. Kubrick himself went on to make two other antiwar films, capturing the Vietnam War in *Full Metal Jacket* and the Cold War in *Dr. Strangelove* (see the Film and History feature on p. 921).

"DUDS—These are of two kinds. A shell on impact failing to explode is called a dud. They are unhappily not as plentiful as the other kind, which often draws a big salary and explodes for no reason. These are plentiful away from the fighting areas."[7] Soldiers' songs also captured a mixture of the sentimental and the frivolous (see the box on p. 781).

The Widening of the War

As another response to the stalemate on the Western Front, both sides looked for new allies that might provide a winning advantage. The Ottoman Empire had already come into the war on Germany's side in August 1914. Russia, Great Britain, and France declared war on the

IMAGES OF EVERYDAY LIFE

Life in the Trenches. The slaughter of millions of men in the trenches of World War I created unimaginable horrors for the participants. For the sake of survival, many soldiers learned to harden themselves against the stench of decomposing bodies and the sight of bodies horribly dismembered by artillery barrages, as is evident in the photograph at the top left. Life in the trenches could also be boring as soldiers whiled away the time as best they could when they were not fighting. Shown in the photograph at the top right is a group of German soldiers in their trench reading and writing letters during a lull in the fighting. The introduction of poison gas in 1915 led quickly to the use of protective gas masks. The bottom photograph shows Austrian soldiers in their trench demonstrating how to use the gas masks.

Hulton Archive/Getty Images

Three Lions/Getty Images

Hulton Archive/Getty Images

THE SONGS OF WORLD WAR I

On the march, in bars, in trains, and even in the trenches, the soldiers of World War I spent time singing. The songs sung by soldiers of different nationalities varied considerably. A German favorite, "The Watch on the Rhine," focused on heroism and patriotism. British war songs often partook of black humor, as in "The Old Barbed Wire." An American favorite was the rousing "Over There," written by the professional songwriter George M. Cohan.

From "The Watch on the Rhine"

There sounds a call like thunder's roar,
Like the crash of swords, like the surge of waves.
To the Rhine, the Rhine, the German Rhine!
Who will the stream's defender be?
    Dear Fatherland, rest quietly
    Sure stands and true the Watch,
    The Watch on the Rhine.

To heaven he gazes.
Spirits of heroes look down.
He vows with proud battle-desire:
O Rhine! You will stay as German as my breast!
    Dear Fatherland, [etc.]

Even if my heart breaks in death,
You will never be French.
As you are rich in water
Germany is rich in hero's blood.
    Dear Fatherland, [etc.]

So long as a drop of blood still glows,
So long a hand the dagger can draw,
So long an arm the rifle can hold—
Never will an enemy touch your shore.
    Dear Fatherland, [etc.]

From "The Old Barbed Wire"

If you want to find the old battalion,
I know where they are,
I know where they are.
If you want to find a battalion,
I know where they are,
They're hanging on the old barbed wire.
I've seen 'em, I've seen 'em,

Hanging on the old barbed wire,
I've seen 'em,
Hanging on the old barbed wire.

George M. Cohan, "Over There"

Over There
Over There
Send the word
Send the word
Over There
That the Yanks are coming
The Yanks are coming,
The drums rum-tuming everywhere.
So prepare,
Say a prayer
Send the word
Send the word
To beware.
We'll be over.
We're coming over
And we won't come back
Till it's over
Over There.

Johnnie get your gun
Get your gun
Get your gun
Take it on the run
On the run
On the run
Hear them calling you and me
Every son of liberty
Hurry right away
No delay, go today
Make your Daddy glad
To have had such a lad
Tell your sweetheart not to pine
To be proud her boy's in line.

Q Based on their war songs, what ideas or themes do you believe maintained the will of soldiers on all sides to fight? How do you think the lyrics and performances of these songs worked to shape the psychology of the singers?

Ottoman Empire in November. Although the forces of the British Empire attempted to open a Balkan front by landing forces at Gallipoli, southwest of Constantinople, in April 1915, the entry of Bulgaria into the war on the side of the Central Powers (as Germany, Austria-Hungary, and the Ottoman Empire were called) and a disastrous campaign at Gallipoli caused them to withdraw. The Italians, as we have seen, entered the war on the Allied side after France and Britain promised to further their acquisition of Austrian territory. In the long run, however, Italian military incompetence forced the Allies to come to the assistance of Italy.

A Global Conflict The war that originated in Europe rapidly became a world conflict. In the Middle East, a British officer who came to be known as Lawrence of Arabia (1888–1935) incited Arab princes to revolt against their Ottoman overlords in 1917. In 1918,

French African Troops. The French drafted more than 170,000 West African soldiers to fight in Europe. Shown here are some French African troops who fought in France on the Western Front. The French also drafted African soldiers from their North African colonies and Madagascar.

British forces from Egypt destroyed the rest of the Ottoman Empire in the Middle East. For their Middle East campaigns, the British mobilized forces from India, Australia, and New Zealand.

The Allies also took advantage of Germany's preoccupations in Europe and lack of naval strength to seize German colonies in Africa and Asia. In the battles in Africa, Allied governments drew on mainly African soldiers, but some states, especially France, also recruited African troops to fight in Europe. The French drafted more than 170,000 West African soldiers, many of whom fought in the trenches on the Western Front. About 80,000 Africans were killed or injured in Europe. They were often at a distinct disadvantage due to the unfamiliar terrain and climate.

Hundreds of thousands of Africans were also used for labor, especially for carrying supplies and building roads and bridges. In East Africa, both sides drafted African laborers as carriers for their armies. More than 100,000 of these laborers died from disease and starvation caused by neglect.

In East Asia and the Pacific, Japan joined the Allies on August 23, 1914, primarily to seize control of German territories in Asia. The Japanese took possession of German territories in China, as well as the German-occupied islands in the Pacific. New Zealand and Australia quickly joined the Japanese in conquering the German-held parts of New Guinea.

Entry of the United States The United States tried to remain neutral in the Great War but found it more difficult to do so as the war dragged on. Although there was considerable sentiment for the British side in the conflict, the immediate cause of American involvement grew out of the naval conflict between Germany and Great Britain. Only once did the German and British naval forces engage in direct combat—at the Battle of Jutland on May 31, 1916, when the Germans won an inconclusive victory.

Britain used its superior naval power to maximum effect, however, by imposing a naval blockade on Germany. Germany retaliated with a counterblockade enforced by the use of unrestricted submarine warfare. At the beginning of 1915, the German government declared the area around the British Isles a war zone and threatened to torpedo any ship caught in it. Strong American protests over the German sinking of passenger liners, especially the British ship *Lusitania* on May 7, 1915, when more than one hundred Americans lost their lives, forced the German government to modify its policy of unrestricted submarine warfare starting in September 1915 and to briefly suspend unrestricted submarine warfare a year later.

In January 1917, however, eager to break the deadlock in the war, the Germans decided on another military gamble by returning to unrestricted submarine warfare. German naval officers convinced Emperor William II that the use of unrestricted submarine warfare could starve the British into submission within five months. When the emperor expressed concern about the Americans, he was told not to worry. The Americans, the chief of the German Naval Staff said, were "disorganized and undisciplined." The British would starve before the Americans could act. And even if the Americans did intervene, Admiral Holtzendorff assured the emperor, "I give your Majesty my word as an officer, that not one American will land on the Continent."

The return to unrestricted submarine warfare brought the United States into the war on April 6, 1917. Although American troops did not arrive in Europe in large numbers until the following year, the entry of the United States into the war in 1917 gave the Allied Powers a psychological boost when they needed it. The year 1917 was not a good one for them. Allied offensives on the Western Front were disastrously defeated. The Italian armies were smashed in October, and in November, the Bolshevik Revolution in Russia led to Russia's withdrawal from the war (see "The Russian Revolution" later in this chapter). The cause of the Central Powers looked favorable, although war weariness in the Ottoman Empire, Bulgaria, Austria-Hungary, and Germany was beginning to take its toll. The home front was rapidly becoming a cause for as much concern as the war front.

A New Kind of Warfare

By the end of 1915, airplanes had appeared on the battlefront for the first time in history. At first, planes were used to spot the enemy's position, but planes soon began to attack ground targets, especially enemy communications. Fights for control of the air occurred and increased over time. At first, pilots fired at each other with hand-held pistols, but later machine guns were mounted on the noses of planes, which made the skies considerably more dangerous.

The Germans also used their giant airships—the zeppelins—to bomb London and eastern England. This caused little damage but frightened many people. Germany's enemies, however, soon found that zeppelins, which were filled with hydrogen gas, quickly became raging infernos when hit by antiaircraft guns.

Tanks   Tanks were also introduced to the battlefields of Europe in 1916. The first tank—a British model—used caterpillar tracks, which enabled it to move across rough terrain. Armed with mounted guns, tanks could attack enemy machine-gun positions as well as enemy infantry. But the first tanks were not very effective, and it was not until 1918, with the introduction of the British Mark V model, that tanks had more powerful engines and greater maneuverability. They could now be used in large numbers, and coordinated with infantry and artillery, they became effective instruments in pushing back the retreating German army.

The tank came too late to have a great effect on the outcome of World War I, but the lesson was not lost on those who realized the tank's potential for creating a whole new kind of warfare. In World War II (see Chapter 27), lightning attacks that depended on tank columns and massive air power enabled armies to cut quickly across battle lines and encircle entire enemy armies. It was a far cry from the trench warfare of World War I.

The Home Front: The Impact of Total War

The prolongation of World War I made it a **total war** that affected the lives of all citizens, however remote they might be from the battlefields. World War I transformed the governments, economies, and societies of the European belligerents in fundamental ways. The need to organize masses of men and matériel for years of combat (Germany alone had 5.5 million men in active units in 1916) led to increased centralization of government powers, economic regimentation, and manipulation of public opinion to keep the war effort going.

Total War: Political Centralization and Economic Regimentation   As we have seen, the outbreak of World War I was greeted with a rush of patriotism; even socialists went enthusiastically into the fray. As the war dragged on, governments realized, however, that more than patriotism would be needed. Since the war was expected to be short, little thought had been given to economic problems and long-term wartime needs. Governments had to respond quickly, however, when the war machines failed to achieve their knockout blows and made ever-greater demands for men and matériel.

The extension of government power was a logical outgrowth of these needs. Most European countries had already devised some system of mass conscription or military draft. It was now carried to unprecedented heights as countries mobilized tens of millions of young men for that elusive breakthrough to victory. Even countries that traditionally relied on volunteers (Great Britain had the largest volunteer army in modern history—one million men—in 1914 and 1915) were forced to resort to conscription, especially to ensure that skilled workers did not enlist but remained in factories that were crucial to the production of munitions. In 1916, despite widespread resistance to this extension of government power, compulsory military service was introduced in Great Britain.

Throughout Europe, wartime governments expanded their powers over their economies. Free market capitalistic systems were temporarily shelved as governments experimented with price, wage, and rent controls, the rationing of food supplies and materials, the regulation of imports and exports, and the nationalization of transportation systems and industries. Some governments even moved toward compulsory employment. In effect, to mobilize the entire resources of their nations for the war effort, European nations had moved toward planned economies directed by government agencies. Under total war mobilization, the distinction between soldiers at war and civilians at home was narrowed. In the view of political leaders, all citizens constituted a national army dedicated to victory. As the American president, Woodrow Wilson, expressed it, the men and women "who remain to till the soil and man the factories are no less a part of the army than the men beneath the battle flags."

Not all European nations made the shift to total war equally well. Germany had the most success in developing a planned economy. At the beginning of the war, the government asked Walter Rathenau, head of the German General Electric Company, to use his business methods to organize the War Raw Materials Board, which would allocate strategic raw materials to produce the goods that were most needed. Rathenau made it possible for the German war machine to be effectively supplied. The Germans were much less successful with the rationing of food, however. Even before the war, Germany had to import about 20 percent of its food supply. The British blockade of Germany and a decline in farm labor made food shortages inevitable. Daily food rations in Germany were cut from 1,350 calories in 1916 to 1,000 by 1917, barely adequate for survival. As a result of a poor potato harvest in the winter of 1916–1917, turnips became the basic staple for the poor. An estimated 750,000 German civilians died of hunger during World War I.

The German war government was eventually consolidated under military authority. The two popular military heroes of the war, General Paul von Hindenburg, chief of the General Staff, and Erich Ludendorff, deputy chief of staff, came to control the government by 1916 and virtually became the military dictators of Germany. In 1916, Hindenburg and Ludendorff decreed a system of complete mobilization for total war. In the Auxiliary Service Law of December 2, 1916, they required all male noncombatants between the ages of seventeen and sixty to work only in jobs deemed crucial to the war effort.

Germany, of course, had an authoritarian political system before the war began. France and Britain did not, but even in those countries, the power of the central government was dramatically increased. At first, Great Britain tried to fight the war by continuing its liberal tradition of limited government interference in the economy. The pressure of circumstances, however, forced the British government to take a more active role in

economic matters. The need to ensure an adequate production of munitions led to the creation in July 1915 of the Ministry of Munitions under a dynamic leader, David Lloyd George. The Ministry of Munitions took numerous steps to ensure that private industry would produce war matériel at limited profits. It developed a vast bureaucracy of 65,000 clerks to oversee munitions plants. Beginning in 1915, it was given the power to take over plants manufacturing war goods that did not cooperate with the government. The British government also rationed food supplies and imposed rent controls.

The French were less successful than the British and Germans in establishing a strong war government during much of the war. For one thing, the French faced a difficult obstacle in organizing a total war economy. German occupation of northeastern France cost the nation 75 percent of its coal production and almost 80 percent of its steelmaking capacity. Then, too, the relationship between civil and military authorities in France was extraordinarily strained. For the first three years of the war, military and civil authorities struggled over who would oversee the conduct of the war. Not until the end of 1917 did the French war government find a strong leader in Georges Clemenceau. Declaring that "war is too important to be left to generals," Clemenceau established clear civilian control of a total war government.

The three other major belligerents—Russia, Austria-Hungary, and Italy—had much less success than Britain, Germany, and France in mobilizing for total war. The autocratic empires of Russia and Austria-Hungary had backward economies that proved incapable of turning out the quantity of war matériel needed to fight a modern war. The Russians, for example, conscripted millions of men but could arm only one-fourth of them. Unarmed Russian soldiers were sent into battle anyway and advised to pick up rifles from their dead colleagues. With their numerous minorities, both the Russian and Austro-Hungarian empires found it difficult to achieve the kind of internal cohesion needed to fight a prolonged total war. Italy, too, lacked both the public enthusiasm and the industrial resources needed to wage a successful total war.

Public Order and Public Opinion   As the Great War dragged on and both casualties and privations worsened, internal dissatisfaction replaced the patriotic enthusiasm that had marked the early stages of the war. By 1916, there were numerous signs that civilian morale was beginning to crack under the pressure of total war.

The first two years of the war witnessed only a few scattered strikes, but thereafter strike activity increased dramatically. In 1916, 50,000 German workers carried out a three-day work stoppage in Berlin to protest the arrest of a radical socialist leader. In France and Britain, the number of strikes increased significantly. Even worse was the violence that erupted in Ireland when members of the Irish Republican Brotherhood and Citizens Army occupied government buildings in Dublin on Easter Sunday

© Bettmann/CORBIS

The Wartime Leaders of Germany.   Over the course of the war, the power of central governments was greatly enlarged in order to meet the demands of total war. In Germany, the two military heroes of the war, Paul von Hindenburg (left) and Erich Ludendorff (right), became virtual military dictators by 1916. The two are shown here with Emperor William II (center), whose power declined as the war dragged on.

(April 24) in 1916. British forces crushed the Easter Rebellion and then condemned its leaders to death.

Internal opposition to the war came from two major sources in 1916 and 1917, liberals and socialists. Liberals in both Germany and Britain sponsored peace resolutions calling for a negotiated peace without any territorial acquisitions. They were largely ignored. Socialists in Germany and Austria also called for negotiated settlements. By 1917, war morale had so deteriorated that more dramatic protests took place. Mutinies in the Italian and French armies were put down with difficulty. Czech leaders in the Austrian Empire openly called for an independent democratic Czech state. In April 1917, some 200,000 workers in Berlin went out on strike for a week to protest the reduction of bread rations. Only the threat of military force and prison brought them back to their jobs. Despite the strains, all of the belligerent countries except Russia survived the stresses of 1917 and fought on.

War governments also fought back against the growing opposition to the war. Authoritarian regimes, such as those of Germany, Russia, and Austria-Hungary, had always relied on force to subdue their populations. Under the pressures of the war, however, even parliamentary regimes resorted to an expansion of police powers to stifle internal dissent. At the very beginning of the war, the British Parliament passed the Defence of the Realm Act, which allowed the public authorities to arrest dissenters as traitors. The act was later extended to authorize public officials to censor newspapers by deleting objectionable material and even to suspend newspaper publication. In France, government authorities had initially been lenient about public opposition to the war. But by 1917, they began to fear that open opposition to the war might weaken the French will to fight. When Georges Clemenceau became premier near the end of 1917, the lenient French policies came to an end, and basic civil liberties were suppressed for the duration of the war. The editor of an antiwar newspaper was even executed on a charge of treason.

Wartime governments made active use of propaganda to arouse enthusiasm for the war. At the beginning, public officials needed to do little to achieve this goal. The British and French, for example, exaggerated German atrocities in Belgium and found that their citizens were only too willing to believe these accounts. But as the war dragged on and morale sagged, governments were forced to devise new techniques to stimulate declining enthusiasm. In one British recruiting poster, for example, a small daughter asked her father, "Daddy, what did you do in the Great War?" while her younger brother played with toy soldiers and cannons.

The Social Impact of Total War Total war made a significant impact on European society, most visibly by bringing an end to unemployment. The withdrawal of millions of men from the labor market to fight, combined with the heightened demand for wartime products, led to jobs for everyone able to work.

British Recruiting Poster. As the conflict persisted month after month, governments resorted to active propaganda campaigns to generate enthusiasm for the war. In this British recruiting poster, the government tried to pressure men into volunteering for military service. By 1916, the British were forced to adopt compulsory military service.

The cause of labor also benefited from the war. The enthusiastic patriotism of workers was soon rewarded with a greater acceptance of trade unions. To ensure that labor problems would not disrupt production, war governments in Britain, France, and Germany not only sought union cooperation but also for the first time allowed trade unions to participate in making important government decisions on labor matters. In return, unions cooperated on wage limits and production schedules. Labor gained two benefits from this cooperation: it opened the way to the collective bargaining practices that became more widespread after World War I and increased the prestige of trade unions, enabling them to attract more members.

World War I also created new roles for women. With so many men off fighting at the front, women were called on to take over jobs and responsibilities that had not been open to them before. These included certain clerical jobs that only small numbers of women had held earlier. In Britain, for example, the number of women who worked in banking rose from 9,500 to almost 64,000 in the course of the war, while the number of women in commerce rose

Women Workers in a British Munitions Factory. World War I created new job opportunities for women. They were now employed in jobs that had earlier been considered beyond their capacity. As seen in this picture, this included factory work in heavy industry. These British women are working in an arms factory weighing shells during the war. Between 1913 and 1917, female metalworkers increased from 5 to 28 percent of the total labor force.

from a half million to almost one million. Overall, 1,345,000 women in Britain obtained new jobs or replaced men during the war. Women were also now employed in jobs that had been considered "beyond the capacity of women." These included such occupations as chimney sweeps, truck drivers, farm laborers, and, above all, factory workers in heavy industry (see the box on p. 787). In France, 684,000 women worked in armaments plants for the first time; in Britain, the figure was 920,000. Thirty-eight percent of the workers in the Krupp armaments works in Germany in 1918 were women.

Male resistance, however, often made it difficult for women to enter these new jobs, especially in heavy industry. One Englishwoman who worked in a munitions factory recalled her experience: "I could quite see it was hard on the men to have women coming into all their pet jobs and in some cases doing them a good deal better. I sympathized with the way they were torn between not wanting the women to undercut them, and yet hating them to earn as much."[8] While male workers expressed concern that the employment of females at lower wages would depress their own wages, women began to demand equal-pay legislation. The French government passed a law in July 1915 that established a minimum wage for women homeworkers in textiles, an industry that had grown dramatically because of the need for military uniforms. In 1917, the government decreed that men and women should receive equal rates for piecework. Despite the noticeable increase in women's wages that resulted from government regulations, women's industrial wages still were not equal to men's wages by the end of the war.

Even worse, women had achieved little real security about their place in the workforce. Both men and women seemed to think that many of the new jobs for women were only temporary, an expectation quite evident in the British poem "War Girls," written in 1916:

There's the girl who clips your ticket for the train,
And the girl who speeds the lift from floor to floor,
There's the girl who does a milk-round in the rain,
And the girl who calls for orders at your door.
Strong, sensible, and fit,
They're out to show their grit,
And tackle jobs with energy and knack.
No longer caged and penned up,
They're going to keep their end up
Till the khaki soldier boys come marching back.[9]

At the end of the war, governments moved quickly to remove women from the jobs they had encouraged them to take earlier. By 1919, there were 650,000 unemployed women in Britain, and wages for women who were still employed were also lowered. The work benefits for women from World War I seemed to be short-lived.

Nevertheless, in some countries, the role played by women in the wartime economies did have a positive impact on the women's movement for social and political emancipation. The most obvious gain was the right to vote, given to women in Germany and Austria immediately after the war (in Britain already in January 1918). The Nineteenth Amendment to the U.S. Constitution gave women in the United States the right to vote in 1920. Contemporary media, however, tended to focus on the more noticeable yet in some ways more superficial social emancipation of upper- and middle-class women. In ever-larger numbers, these young women took jobs, had their own apartments, and showed their new independence by smoking in public and wearing shorter dresses, cosmetics, and boyish hairstyles.

In one sense, World War I had been a great social leveler. Death in battle did not distinguish between classes. Although all social classes suffered casualties in battle, two groups were especially hard-hit. Junior officers

WOMEN IN THE FACTORIES

During World War I, women were called on to assume new job responsibilities, including factory work. In this selection, Naomi Loughnan, a young, upper-middle-class woman, describes the experiences in a munitions plant that considerably broadened her perspective on life.

Naomi Loughnan, "Munition Work"

We little thought when we first put on our overalls and caps and enlisted in the Munition Army how much more inspiring our life was to be than we had dared to hope. Though we munition workers sacrifice our ease we gain a life worth living. Our long days are filled with interest, and with the zest of doing work for our country in the grand cause of Freedom. As we handle the weapons of war we are learning great lessons of life. In the busy, noisy workshops we come face to face with every kind of class, and each one of these classes has something to learn from the others. . . .

Engineering mankind is possessed of the unshakable opinion that no woman can have the mechanical sense. If one of us asks humbly why such and such an alteration is not made to prevent this or that drawback to a machine, she is told, with a superior smile, that a man has worked her machine before her for years, and that therefore if there were any improvement possible it would have been made. As long as we do exactly what we are told and do not attempt to use our brains, we give entire satisfaction, and are treated as nice, good children. Any swerving from the easy path prepared for us by our males arouses the most scathing contempt in their manly bosoms. . . . Women have, however, proved that their entry into the munition world has increased the output. Employers who forget things personal in their patriotic desire for large results are enthusiastic over the success of women in the shops. But their workmen have to be handled with the utmost tenderness and caution lest they should actually imagine it was being suggested that women could do their work equally well, given equal conditions of training—at least where muscle is not the driving force. . . .

The coming of the mixed classes of women into the factory is slowly but surely having an educative effect upon the men. "Language" is almost unconsciously becoming subdued. There are fiery exceptions who make our hair stand up on end under our close-fitting caps, but a sharp rebuke or a look of horror will often straighten out the most savage. . . . It is grievous to hear the girls also swearing and using disgusting language. Shoulder to shoulder with the children of the slums, the upper classes are having their eyes opened at last to the awful conditions among which their sisters have dwelt. Foul language, immorality, and many other evils are but the natural outcome of overcrowding and bitter poverty. . . . Sometimes disgust will overcome us, but we are learning with painful clarity that the fault is not theirs whose actions disgust us, but must be placed to the discredit of those other classes who have allowed the continued existence of conditions which generate the things from which we shrink appalled.

Q *What did Naomi Loughnan learn about men and lower-class women while working in the munitions factory? What did she learn about herself? What can one conclude about the effects of total war on European women?*

---

who led the charges across the "no-man's land" that separated the lines of trenches experienced death rates that were three times higher than regular casualty rates. Many of these junior officers were members of the aristocracy (see the box on p. 788). The unskilled workers and peasants who made up the masses of soldiers mowed down by machine guns also suffered heavy casualties. The fortunate ones were the skilled laborers who gained exemptions from military service because they were needed at home to train workers in the war industries.

The burst of patriotic enthusiasm that marked the beginning of the war deceived many into believing that the war was creating a new sense of community that meant the end of the class conflict that had marked European society at the end of the nineteenth and beginning of the twentieth centuries. David Lloyd George, who became the British prime minister in 1916, wrote in September 1914 that "all classes, high and low, are shedding themselves of selfishness. . . . It is bringing a new outlook to all classes. . . . We can see for the first time the fundamental things that matter in life, and that have been obscured from our vision by the . . . growth of prosperity."[10] Lloyd George's optimistic opinion proved to be quite misguided, however. The Great War did not eliminate the class conflict that had characterized pre-1914 Europe, and this became increasingly apparent as the war dragged on.

The economic impact of the war was felt unevenly. One group of people who especially benefited were the owners of the large industries manufacturing the weapons of war. Despite public outrage, governments rarely limited the enormous profits made by the industrial barons. In fact, in the name of efficiency, wartime governments tended to favor large industries when scarce raw materials were allocated. Small firms considered less essential to the war effort even had to shut down because of a lack of resources.

Inflation also caused inequities. The combination of full employment and high demand for scarce consumer goods caused prices to climb. Many skilled workers were able to earn wages that enabled them to keep up with inflation, but this was not true for unskilled workers or those in nonessential industries. Only in Great Britain did the wages of workers outstrip prices. Everywhere else in Europe, people experienced a loss of purchasing power.

WAR AND THE FAMILY

John Mott was a captain in the British army. He came from an aristocratic family with a strong military tradition. He married Muriel Backhouse in 1907, and they had three sons before he was called up for service in World War I. These excerpts are taken from four of Mott's letters to his wife and a letter informing her of her husband's death during the Gallipoli campaign. The human experience of World War I was made up of millions of stories like that of John Mott and his family.

One Family's War

1 July [1915]

My darling Childie,

I hope you got home safely. I have been promised that I shall know the ship we go on tomorrow. But it will be no good writing to Gibraltar as we should get there before the letter. Try Malta as that goes over land. If you get overdrawn go and see Cox. Goodbye Darling. Don't worry I shall come back alright. Your devoted husband John F. Mott

13 July

Mediterranean field force, Mudros
My darling Childie,

This island is very hot indeed but beastly windy. We have absolutely no news from the Front. Troops are pouring out now and I expect we shall be in it next week.

We have all gone through our little bout of diarrhea. I was not too bad and only had pains in my stomach otherwise I am very well indeed.

Everyone is standing the heat very well. The Brigadier has a tent but everybody else is out in the blazing sun.

31 July

My darling Childie,

I got more letters from you today dated 5th, 6th, 7th. I had no idea till I read the letter that they could do all that about writs. I would never have left things in such a muddle, I only hope you can get straight.

Yesterday I left here at 5:30 am to go to the trenches with the Brigadier. We had an awful day, and I am not at all keen to go into that lot at all events. We sailed over in a trawler and had a long walk in the open under shrapnel fire. It was not very pleasant. Then we got to the communications trenches and had a mile and a half of them to go up. When we got to the fire trenches the stink was awful. Arms and legs of Turks sticking out of the trench parapets and lying dead all round. In one place the bottom of the trench was made up by dead Turks, but this has been abandoned as the place was too poisonous.

Our battle ships have been shelling very heavily so there may be an attack on. I must write to my mother tonight. All my love and kisses for ever

Your loving husband
John F. Mott

6 August

My darling Childie,

We are off today just as we stand up, with four days rations. I can't say where we are going but we shall see spots. I shall not get a chance to write again for a bit as we shall be on the move. I expect you have got a map of the place by now and perhaps you will hear where we have gone.

Very good to get away. All my love and kisses for ever

Your loving husband
John F. Mott
Best love to all kids and baby

Pte A Thompson
6 Batt Y and L Red Cross Hospital

We landed on the 6th of Aug and took 2 hills and at daybreak on the 7th advanced across an open plain to the left of Salt Lake and got an awful shelling. We came to a small hill which was flat on top and it was about 2 hundred yards further on where the Capt was hit. They gave us it worse than ever when we got on there and I might have been happen 50 yds away when I saw the Capt and about 5 men fall badly hit. I could not say whether it was shrapnel or common shell but I think it was most probably shrapnel as they use that mostly. It was that thick that no one could get to the Capt at the time and I don't think he lived very long, well he could not the way they were hit and was afterwards buried when things had quietened down in the evening and a cross was put on his grave with an inscription and he got as good a burial as could be given out there. Well I think I have told you all I know about Capt Mott. I only wishe I could have given you better news, so I will close with Kind Regards

Yours Obediently,
Pte Thompson

Q What do these letters tell you about the ordinary officer's perspective on the war? How great do you think the gulf was between front line and home front? What does the tone of Private Thompson's final letter suggest about the ordinary soldier's experience of battle and the effects of such service on fighting men?

Many middle-class people were hit especially hard by inflation. They included both those who lived on fixed incomes, such as retired people on pensions, and professional people, such as clerks, lesser civil servants, teachers, small shopkeepers, and members of the clergy, whose incomes remained stable at a time when prices were rising. By the end of the war, many of these people were actually doing less well economically than skilled workers. Their discontent would find expression after the war.

War and Revolution

Q **Focus Question:** What were the causes of the Russian Revolution of 1917, and why did the Bolsheviks prevail in the civil war and gain control of Russia?

By 1917, total war was creating serious domestic turmoil in all of the European belligerent states. Most countries were able to prop up their regimes and convince their people to continue the war for another year, but others were coming close to collapse. In Austria, for example, a government minister warned that "if the monarchs of the Central Powers cannot make peace in the coming months, it will be made for them by their peoples." Russia, however, was the only belligerent that actually experienced the kind of complete collapse in 1917 that others were predicting might happen throughout Europe. Out of Russia's collapse came the Russian Revolution, whose impact would be widely felt in Europe for decades to come.

The Russian Revolution

After the Revolution of 1905 had failed to bring any substantial changes to Russia, Tsar Nicholas II relied on the army and bureaucracy to uphold his regime. But World War I magnified Russia's problems and severely challenged the tsarist government. The tsar, possessed of a strong sense of moral duty to his country, was the only European monarch to take personal charge of the armed forces, despite a lack of training for such an awesome responsibility. Russian industry was unable to produce the weapons needed for the army. Ill-led and ill-armed, Russian armies suffered incredible losses. Between 1914 and 1916, 2 million soldiers were killed while another 4 to 6 million were wounded or captured.

The tsarist government was unprepared for the tasks that it faced in 1914. The surge of patriotic enthusiasm that greeted the outbreak of war was soon dissipated by a government that distrusted its own people. Although the middle classes and liberal aristocrats still hoped for a constitutional monarchy, they were sullen over the tsar's revocation of the political concessions made during the Revolution of 1905. Peasant discontent flourished as conditions worsened. The concentration of Russian industry in a few large cities made workers' frustrations all the more evident and dangerous. In the meantime, Nicholas was increasingly insulated from events by his wife, Alexandra.

This German-born princess was a well-educated woman who had fallen under the influence of Rasputin, a Siberian peasant whom the tsarina regarded as a holy man because he alone seemed able to stop the bleeding of her hemophiliac son, Alexis. Rasputin's influence made him a power behind the throne, and he did not hesitate to interfere in government affairs. As the leadership at the top experienced a series of military and economic disasters, the middle class, aristocrats, peasants, soldiers, and workers grew more and more disenchanted with the tsarist regime. Even conservative aristocrats who supported the monarchy felt the need to do something to reverse the deteriorating situation. For a start, they assassinated Rasputin in December 1916. By then it was too late to save the monarchy, and its fall came quickly at the beginning of March 1917.

The March Revolution At the beginning of March, a series of strikes broke out in the capital city of Petrograd (formerly Saint Petersburg). Here the actions of working-class women helped change the course of Russian history. Weeks earlier, the government had introduced bread rationing in the city after the price of bread skyrocketed. Many of the women who stood in the lines waiting for bread were also factory workers who put in twelve-hour days. The number of women working in Petrograd factories had doubled since 1914. The Russian government had become aware of the volatile situation in the capital from police reports, one of which stated:

> Mothers of families, exhausted by endless standing in line at stores, distraught over their half-starving and sick children, are today perhaps closer to revolution than [the liberal opposition leaders] and of course they are a great deal more dangerous because they are the combustible material for which only a single spark is needed to burst into flame.[11]

On March 8, a day celebrated since 1910 as International Women's Day, about ten thousand Petrograd women marched through the city shouting "Peace and bread" and "Down with autocracy." Soon the women were joined by other workers, and together they called for a general strike that succeeded in shutting down all the factories in the city on March 10. The tsarina wrote to Nicholas at the battlefront that "this is a hooligan movement. If the weather were very cold they would all probably stay at home." Believing his wife, Nicholas told his military commanders, "I command you tomorrow to stop the disorders in the capital, which are unacceptable in the difficult time of war with Germany and Austria."[12] The troops were ordered to disperse the crowds, shooting them if necessary. Initially, the troops cooperated, but soon significant numbers of the soldiers joined the demonstrators. The situation was now out of the tsar's control. The Duma, or legislature, which the tsar had tried to dissolve, met anyway and on March 12 declared that it was assuming governmental responsibility. It established a provisional government on March 15; the tsar abdicated the same day.

In just one week, the tsarist regime had fallen apart. Although no particular group had been responsible for the outburst, the moderate Constitutional Democrats were responsible for establishing the provisional government. They represented primarily a middle-class and liberal aristocratic minority. Their program consisted of a liberal agenda that included working toward a parliamentary democracy and passing reforms that provided universal suffrage, civil equality, and an eight-hour workday.

The Women's March in Petrograd. After the imposition of bread rationing in Petrograd, ten thousand women engaged in mass demonstrations and demanded "Peace and bread" for the families of soldiers. This photograph shows the women marching through the streets of Petrograd on March 8, 1917.

The provisional government also faced another authority, the **soviets,** or councils of workers' and soldiers' deputies. The soviet of Petrograd had been formed in March 1917; around the same time, soviets sprang up spontaneously in army units and towns. The soviets represented the more radical interests of the lower classes and were largely composed of socialists of various kinds. Among them was the Marxist Social Democratic Party, which had formed in 1898 but divided in 1903 into two factions known as the Mensheviks and the **Bolsheviks.** The Mensheviks wanted the Social Democrats to be a mass electoral socialist party based on a Western model. Like the Social Democrats of Germany, they were willing to cooperate temporarily in a parliamentary democracy while working toward the ultimate achievement of the socialist state.

The Bolsheviks were a small faction of Russian Social Democrats who had come under the leadership of Vladimir Ulianov, known to the world as V. I. Lenin (1870–1924). Born in 1870, Lenin received a legal education and became a lawyer. In 1887, he turned into a dedicated enemy of tsarist Russia when his older brother was executed for planning to assassinate the tsar. Lenin's search for a revolutionary faith led him to Marxism, and in 1894 he moved to Saint Petersburg, where he helped organize an illegal group known as the Union for the Liberation of the Working Class. Arrested for this activity, Lenin was shipped to Siberia. After his release, he chose to go into exile in Switzerland and eventually assumed the leadership of the Bolshevik wing of the Russian Social Democratic Party.

Under Lenin's direction, the Bolsheviks became a party dedicated to a violent revolution that would destroy the capitalist system. He believed that a "vanguard" of activists must form a small party of well-disciplined professional revolutionaries to accomplish the task. Between 1900 and 1917, Lenin spent most of his time in Switzerland. The outbreak of war in 1914 gave him hope that all of Europe was ripe for revolution, and when the provisional government was formed in March 1917, he believed that an opportunity for the Bolsheviks to seize power in Russia had come. A few weeks later, with the connivance of the German High Command, who hoped to create disorder in Russia, Lenin, his wife, and a small group of his followers were shipped to Russia in a "sealed train" by way of Finland.

Lenin's arrival in Russia opened a new stage in the Russian Revolution. In his "April Theses," issued on April 20, Lenin presented a blueprint for revolutionary action based on his own version of Marxist theory. According to Lenin, it was not necessary for Russia to experience a bourgeois revolution before it could move toward socialism, as orthodox Marxists had argued. Instead, Russia could move directly into socialism. In the April Theses, Lenin maintained that the soviets of soldiers, workers, and peasants were ready-made instruments of power. The Bolsheviks must work toward gaining control of these groups and then use them to overthrow the provisional government. At the same time, the Bolsheviks articulated the discontent and aspirations of the people, promising an end to the war, the redistribution of all land to the peasants, the transfer of factories and industries from

Lenin and Trotsky. V. I. Lenin and Leon Trotsky were important figures in the success of the Bolsheviks in seizing power in Russia. On the left, Lenin is seen addressing a rally in Moscow in 1917. On the right, Trotsky, who became commissar of war in the new regime, is shown haranguing his troops.

capitalists to committees of workers, and relegation of government power from the provisional government to the soviets. Three simple slogans summed up the Bolshevik program: "Peace, land, bread," "Worker control of production," and "All power to the soviets."

In late spring and early summer, while the Bolsheviks set about winning over the masses to their program and gaining a majority in the Petrograd and Moscow soviets, the provisional government struggled to gain control of Russia against almost overwhelming obstacles. Peasants began land reform by seizing property on their own in March. The military situation was also deteriorating. The Petrograd soviet had issued its Army Order No. 1 in March to all Russian military forces, encouraging them to remove their officers and replace them with committees composed of "the elected representatives of the lower ranks" of the army. Army Order No. 1 led to the collapse of all discipline and created military chaos. When the provisional government attempted to initiate a new military offensive in July, the army simply dissolved as masses of peasant soldiers turned their backs on their officers and returned home to join their families in seizing land.

The Bolshevik Revolution In July 1917, Lenin and the Bolsheviks were falsely accused of inciting an attempt to overthrow the provisional government, and Lenin was forced to flee to Finland. But the days of the provisional government were numbered. In July 1917, Alexander Kerensky, a Socialist Revolutionary, had become prime minister in the provisional government. In September, when General Lavr Kornilov attempted to march on Petrograd and seize power, Kerensky released Bolsheviks

from prison and turned to the Petrograd soviet for help. Although General Kornilov's forces never reached Petrograd, Kerensky's action had strengthened the hands of the Petrograd soviet and had shown Lenin how weak the provisional government really was.

By the end of October, the Bolsheviks had achieved a slight majority in the Petrograd and Moscow soviets. The number of party members had also grown from 50,000 to 240,000. Reports of unrest abroad had convinced Lenin that "we are on the threshold of a world proletarian revolution," and he tried to persuade his fellow Bolsheviks that the time was ripe for the overthrow of the provisional government. Although he faced formidable opposition within the Bolshevik ranks, he managed to gain support for his policy. With Leon Trotsky (1877–1940), a fervid revolutionary, as chairman of the Petrograd soviet, the Bolsheviks were in a position to seize power in the name of the soviets. During the night of November 6, pro-soviet and pro-Bolshevik forces took control of Petrograd under the immensely popular slogan "All power to the soviets." The provisional government quickly collapsed with little bloodshed. The following night, the all-Russian Congress of Soviets, representing local soviets from all over the country, affirmed the transfer of power. At the second session, on the night of November 8, Lenin announced the new Soviet government, the Council of People's Commissars, with himself as its head.

One immediate problem the Bolsheviks faced was the Constituent Assembly, which had been initiated by the provisional government and was scheduled to meet in

SOLDIER AND PEASANT VOICES

In 1917, Russia experienced a cataclysmic upheaval as two revolutions overthrew the tsarist regime and then the provisional government that replaced it. Peasants, workers, and soldiers poured out their thoughts and feelings on these events, some of them supporting the Bolsheviks and others denouncing the Bolsheviks for betraying their socialist revolution. These selections are taken from two letters, the first from a soldier and the second from a peasant. Both are addressed to Bolshevik leaders.

Letter from a Soldier in Leningrad to Lenin, January 6, 1918

Bastard! What the hell are you doing? How long are you going to keep on degrading the Russian people? After all, it's because of you they killed the former minister ... and so many other innocent victims. Because of you, they might kill even other former ministers belonging to the [Socialist Revolutionary] party because you call them counterrevolutionaries and even monarchists.... And you, you Bolshevik gang leader hired either by Nicholas II or by Wilhelm II, are waging this pogrom propaganda against men who may have done time with you in exile.

Scoundrel! A curse on you from the politically conscious Russian proletariat, the conscious ones and not the kind who are following you—that is, the Red Guards, the tally clerks, who, when they are called to military service, all hide at the factories and now are killing ... practically their own father, the way the soldiers did in 1905 when they killed their own, or the way the police and gendarmes did in [1917]. That's who they're more like. They're not pursuing the ideas of socialism because they don't understand them (if they did they wouldn't act this way) but because they get paid a good salary both at the factory and in the Red Guards. But not all the workers are like that—there are very politically aware ones and the soldiers—again not all of them—are like that but only former policemen, constables, gendarmes and the very very ignorant ones who under the old regime tramped with hay on one foot and straw on the other because they couldn't tell their right foot from their left and they are pursuing not the ideas of socialism that you advocate but to be able to lie on their cots in the barracks and do absolutely nothing not even be asked to sweep the floor, which is already piled with several inches of filth. And so the entire proletariat of Russia is following you, by count fewer than are against you, but they are only physically or rather technically stronger than the majority, and

that is what you're abusing when you disbanded the Constituent Assembly the way Nicholas II disbanded the Duma. You point out that counterrevolutionaries gathered there. You lie, scoundrel, there wasn't a single counterrevolutionary and if there was then it was you, the Bolsheviks, which you proved by your actions when you encroached on the gains of the revolution: you are shutting down newspapers, even socialist ones, arresting socialists, committing violence and deceiving the people; you promised loads but did none of it.

Letter from a Peasant to the Bolshevik Leaders, January 10, 1918

TO YOU!

Rulers, plunderers, rapists, destroyers, usurpers, oppressors of Mother Russia, citizens Lenin, Trotsky, Uritsky, Zinoviev, Spiridonova, Antonov, Lunacharsky, Krylenko, and Co. [leaders of the Bolshevik party]:

Allow me to ask you how long you are going to go on degrading Russia's millions, its tormented and exhausted people. Instead of peace, you signed an armistice with the enemy, and this gave our opponent a painful advantage, and you declared war on Russia. You moved the troops you had tricked to the Russian-Russian front and started a fratricidal war. Your mercenary Red Guards are looting, murdering, and raping everywhere they go. A fire has consumed all our dear Mother Russia. Rail transport is idle, as are the plants and factories; the entire population has woken up to find itself in the most pathetic situation, without bread or kerosene or any of the other essentials, unclothed and unshod in unheated houses. In short: hungry and cold.... You have strangled the entire press, and freedom with it, you have wiped out the best freedom fighters, you have destroyed all Russia. Think it over, you butchers, you hirelings of the Kaiser [William II]. Isn't your turn about up, too? For all you are doing, we, politically aware Great Russians, are sending you butchers, you hirelings of the Kaiser, our curse. May you be damned, you accursed one, you bloodthirsty butchers, you hirelings of the Kaiser—don't think you're in the clear, because the Russian people will sober up and that will be the end of you. I'm writing in red ink to show that you are bloodthirsty.... I'm writing these curses, a Great Russian native of Orel Province, peasant of Mtsensk Uezd.

Q *What arguments do the writers of these letters use against Lenin and the Bolsheviks? Why do they feel so betrayed by the Bolsheviks?*

January 1918. Elections to the assembly by universal suffrage had resulted in a defeat for the Bolsheviks, who had only 225 delegates compared to the 420 garnered by the Socialist Revolutionaries. But no matter. Lenin simply broke the Constituent Assembly by force. "To hand over power," he said, "to the Constituent Assembly would

again be compromising with malignant bourgeoisie" (see the box above).

But the Bolsheviks (soon renamed the Communists) still had a long way to go. Lenin, ever the opportunist, realized the importance of winning mass support as quickly as possible by fulfilling Bolshevik promises. In his first law, issued on the new regime's first day in power, Lenin declared the land nationalized and turned it over to local rural land committees. In effect, this action merely ratified the peasants' seizure of the land and assured the Bolsheviks of peasant support, especially against any attempt by the old landlords to restore their power. Lenin also met the demands of urban workers by turning over control of the factories to committees of workers. To Lenin, however, this was merely a temporary expedient.

The new government also introduced a number of social changes. Alexandra Kollontai (1872–1952), who had become a supporter of revolutionary socialism while in exile in Switzerland, took the lead in pushing a Bolshevik program for women's rights and social welfare reforms. As minister of social welfare, she tried to provide health care for women and children by establishing "palaces for the protection of maternity and children." Between 1918 and 1920, the new regime enacted a series of reforms that made marriage a civil act, legalized divorce, decreed the equality of men and women, and permitted abortions. Kollontai was also instrumental in establishing a women's bureau, known as Zhenotdel, within the Communist Party. This bureau sent men and women to all parts of the Russian Empire to explain the new social order. Members of Zhenotdel were especially eager to help women with matters of divorce and women's rights. In the eastern provinces, several Zhenotdel members were brutally murdered by angry males who objected to any kind of liberation for their wives and daughters. Much to Kollontai's disappointment, many of these Communist social reforms were later undone as the Communists came to face more pressing matters, including the survival of the new regime.

Lenin had also promised peace, and that, he realized, was not an easy task because of the humiliating losses of Russian territory that it would entail. There was no real choice, however. On March 3, 1918, the new Communist government signed the Treaty of Brest-Litovsk with Germany and gave up eastern Poland, the Ukraine, Finland, and the Baltic provinces. To his critics, Lenin argued that it made no difference since the spread of socialist revolution throughout Europe would make the treaty largely irrelevant. In any case, he had promised peace to the Russian people, but real peace did not occur, for the country soon lapsed into civil war.

Civil War There was great opposition to the new Bolshevik regime, not only from groups loyal to the tsar but also from bourgeois and aristocratic liberals and anti-Leninist socialists, including Mensheviks and Socialist Revolutionaries. In addition, thousands of Allied troops were eventually sent to different parts of Russia in the hope of bringing Russia back into the Great War.

Between 1918 and 1921, the Bolshevik (Red) Army was forced to fight on many fronts (see Map 25.4). The first serious threat to the Bolsheviks came from Siberia, where a White (anti-Bolshevik) force under Admiral Alexander Kolchak pushed westward and advanced almost to the Volga River before being stopped. Attacks also came from the Ukrainians in the southeast and from the

MAP 25.4   The Russian Revolution and Civil War. The Russian Civil War lasted from 1918 to 1921. A variety of disparate groups, including victorious powers from World War I, sought to either overthrow the Bolsheviks or seize Russian territory. Lack of cohesion among their enemies helped the Bolsheviks triumph, but at the cost of much hardship and bloodshed.

Q How did the area under Bolshevik control make it easier for the Bolsheviks to defeat the White forces? View an animated version of this map or related maps at academic.cengage.com/history/spielvogel

Baltic regions. In mid-1919, White forces under General Anton Denikin, probably the most effective of the White generals, swept through the Ukraine and advanced almost to Moscow. At one point in late 1919, three separate White armies seemed to be closing in on the Bolsheviks but were eventually pushed back. By 1920, the major White forces had been defeated, and the Ukraine was retaken. The next year, the Communist regime regained control over the independent nationalist governments in the Caucasus: Georgia, Russian Armenia, and Azerbaijan.

The royal family was yet another victim of the civil war. After the tsar had abdicated, he, his wife, and their five children had been taken into custody. They were moved in August 1917 to Tobolsk in Siberia and in April 1918 to Ekaterinburg, a mining town in the Urals. On the night of July 16, members of the local soviet murdered the tsar and his family and burned their bodies in a nearby mine shaft.

How had Lenin and the Bolsheviks triumphed over what seemed at one time to be overwhelming forces? For one thing, the Red Army became a well-disciplined and formidable fighting force, thanks largely to the organizational genius of Leon Trotsky. As commissar of war, Trotsky reinstated the draft and even recruited and gave commands to former tsarist army officers. Trotsky insisted on rigid discipline; soldiers who deserted or refused to obey orders were summarily executed. The Red Army also had the advantage of interior lines of defense and was able to move its troops rapidly from one battlefront to the other.

The disunity of the anti-Communist forces seriously weakened their efforts. Political differences created distrust among the Whites and prevented them from cooperating effectively with each other. Some Whites, such as Admiral Kolchak, insisted on restoring the tsarist regime, but others understood that only a more liberal and democratic program had any chance of success. Since the White forces were forced to operate on the fringes of the Russian Empire, it was difficult enough to achieve military cooperation. Political differences made it virtually impossible.

The Whites' inability to agree on a common goal contrasted sharply with the Communists' single-minded sense of purpose. Inspired by their vision of a new socialist order, the Communists had the advantage of possessing the determination that comes from revolutionary fervor and revolutionary convictions.

The Communists also succeeded in translating their revolutionary faith into practical instruments of power. A policy of war communism, for example, was used to ensure regular supplies for the Red Army. War communism included the nationalization of banks and most industries, the forcible requisition of grain from peasants, and the centralization of state administration under Bolshevik control. Another Bolshevik instrument was "revolutionary terror." Although the old tsarist secret police had been abolished, a new Red secret police—known as the Cheka—replaced it. The Red Terror instituted by the Cheka aimed at nothing less than the destruction of all opponents of the new regime. "Class enemies"—the bourgeoisie—were especially singled out, at least according to a Cheka officer:

CHRONOLOGY The Russian Revolution

	1917
March of women in Petrograd	March 8
General strike in Petrograd	March 10
Establishment of provisional government	March 15
Tsar abdicates	March 15
Formation of Petrograd soviet	March
Lenin arrives in Russia	April 3
Lenin's "April Theses"	April 20
Failed attempt to overthrow provisional government	July
Bolsheviks gain majority in Petrograd soviet	October
Bolsheviks overthrow provisional government	November 6–7
	1918
Lenin disbands Constituent Assembly	January
Treaty of Brest-Litovsk	March 3
Civil war	1918–1921

"The first questions you should put to the accused person are: To what class does he belong, what is his origin, what was his education, and what is his profession? These should determine the fate of the accused." In practice, however, the Cheka promulgated terror against members of all classes, including the proletariat, if they opposed the new regime. Thousands were executed. The Red Terror added an element of fear to the Bolshevik regime.

Finally, the intervention of foreign armies enabled the Communists to appeal to the powerful force of Russian patriotism. Although the Allied Powers had initially intervened in Russia to encourage the Russians to remain in the war, the end of the war on November 11, 1918, had made that purpose inconsequential. Nevertheless, Allied troops remained, and Allied countries did not hide their anti-Bolshevik feelings. At one point, British, American, French, and (in Siberia) Japanese forces were stationed on Russian soil. These forces rarely engaged in pitched battles, however, nor did they pursue a common strategy, although they did give material assistance to the anti-Bolsheviks. This intervention by the Allies enabled the Communist government to appeal to patriotic Russians to fight the attempts of foreigners to control their country. Allied interference was never substantial enough to make a military difference in the civil war, but it did serve indirectly to help the Bolshevik cause.

By 1921, the Communists had succeeded in retaining control of Russia (though not without an enormous loss of life and destruction in the country; see Chapter 27). In the course of the civil war, the Bolshevik regime had also transformed Russia into a bureaucratically centralized state dominated by a single party. It was also a state that was largely hostile to the Allied Powers that had sought to assist the Bolsheviks' enemies in the civil war. To most historians, the Russian Revolution is unthinkable without the total war of World War I, for only the collapse of Russia made it possible for a radical minority like the Bolsheviks to seize the reins of power. In turn, the Russian Revolution had an impact on the course of World War I.

The Last Year of the War

For Germany, the withdrawal of the Russians from the war in March 1918 offered renewed hope for a favorable outcome. The victory over Russia persuaded Ludendorff and most German leaders to make one final military gamble—a grand offensive in the west to break the military stalemate. The German attack was launched in March and lasted into July. The German forces succeeded in advancing 40 miles to the Marne River, within 35 miles of Paris. But an Allied counterattack, led by the French General Ferdinand Foch and supported by the arrival of 140,000 fresh American troops, defeated the Germans at the Second Battle of the Marne on July 18. Ludendorff's gamble had failed. Having used up his reserves, Ludendorff knew that defeat was now inevitable. With the arrival of one million more American troops on the Continent, Allied forces began making a steady advance toward Germany.

On September 29, 1918, General Ludendorff informed German leaders that the war was lost. Unwilling to place the burden of defeat on the army, Ludendorff demanded that the government sue for peace at once. When German officials discovered that the Allies were unwilling to make peace with the autocratic imperial government, they instituted reforms to set up a liberal government. But these constitutional reforms came too late for the exhausted and angry German people. On November 3, naval units in Kiel mutinied, and within days, councils of workers and soldiers, German versions of the Russian soviets, were forming throughout northern Germany and taking over the supervision of civilian and military administrations. William II capitulated to public pressure and left the country on November 9, while the socialists under Friedrich Ebert announced the establishment of a republic. Two days later, on November 11, 1918, an armistice agreed to by the new German government went into effect. The war was over, but the revolutionary forces set in motion by the war were not yet exhausted.

The Casualties of the War World War I devastated European civilization. Between 8 and 9 million soldiers died on the battlefields; another 22 million were wounded. Many of those who survived later died from war injuries or suffered the loss of arms or legs or other forms of mutilation. The birthrate in many European countries declined noticeably as a result of the death or maiming of so many young men. World War I also created a "lost generation" of war veterans who had become accustomed to violence and who would form the postwar bands of fighters who supported Mussolini and Hitler in their bids for power (see Chapter 27).

CHRONOLOGY World War I

1914	
Battle of Tannenberg	August 26–30
First Battle of the Marne	September 6–10
Battle of Masurian Lakes	September 15
Russia, Great Britain, and France declare war on Ottoman Empire	November
1915	
Battle of Gallipoli begins	April 25
Italy declares war on Austria-Hungary	May 23
Entry of Bulgaria into the war	September
1916	
Battle of Verdun	February 21–December 18
Battle of Jutland	May 31
Somme offensive	July 1–November 19
1917	
Germany returns to unrestricted submarine warfare	January
United States enters the war	April 6
The Champagne offensive	April 16–29
1918	
Last German offensive	March 21–July 18
Second Battle of the Marne	July 18
Allied counteroffensive	July 18–November 10
Armistice between Allies and Germany	November 11
1919	
Paris Peace Conference begins	January 18
Peace of Versailles	June 28

Nor did the killing affect only soldiers. Untold numbers of civilians died from war, civil war, or starvation. In 1915, after an Armenian uprising against the Ottoman government, the government retaliated with fury by killing Armenian men and expelling women and children. Within seven months, 600,000 Armenians had been killed, and 500,000 had been deported. Of the latter, 400,000 died while marching through the deserts and swamps of Syria and Iraq. By September 1915, an estimated one million Armenians were dead, the victims of genocide.

Revolutionary Upheavals in Germany and Austria-Hungary

Like Russia, Germany and Austria-Hungary experienced political revolution as a result of military defeat. In November 1918, when Germany began to disintegrate in a convulsion of mutinies and mass demonstrations (known as the November Revolution), only the Social Democrats were numerous and well organized enough to pick up the pieces. But the German socialists had divided into two groups during the war. A majority of the Social Democrats still favored parliamentary democracy as a gradual approach to social democracy and the elimination of the capitalist system. A minority of German socialists, however, disgusted with the Social Democrats' support of the war, had formed their own Independent Social Democratic Party in 1916. In 1918, the more radical members of the Independent Socialists favored an immediate social revolution carried out by the councils of soldiers, sailors, and workers. Led by Karl Liebknecht and Rosa Luxemburg, these radical, left-wing socialists formed the German Communist Party in December 1918. In effect, two parallel governments were established in Germany: the parliamentary republic proclaimed by the majority Social Democrats and the revolutionary socialist republic declared by the radicals.

Unlike Russia's Bolsheviks, Germany's radicals failed to achieve control of the government. By ending the war on November 11, the moderate socialists had removed a major source of dissatisfaction. When the radical socialists (now known as Communists) attempted to seize power in Berlin in January 1919, Friedrich Ebert and the moderate socialists called on the regular army and groups of antirevolutionary volunteers known as Free Corps to crush the rebels. The victorious forces brutally murdered Liebknecht and Luxemburg. A similar attempt at Communist revolution in the city of Munich in southern Germany was also crushed by the Free Corps and the regular army. The German republic had been saved, but only because the moderate socialists had relied on the traditional army—in effect, the same conservatives who had dominated the old imperial regime. Moreover, this "second revolution" of January 1919, bloodily crushed by the republican government, created a deep fear of communism among the German middle classes. All too soon, this fear would be cleverly manipulated by a politician named Adolf Hitler.

Austria-Hungary, too, experienced disintegration and revolution. In 1914, when it attacked Serbia, the imperial regime had tried to crush the nationalistic forces that it believed were destroying the empire. By 1918, those same nationalistic forces had brought the complete breakup of the Austro-Hungarian Empire. As war weariness took hold of the empire, ethnic minorities increasingly sought to achieve national independence. This desire was further encouraged by Allied war aims that included calls for the independence of the subject peoples. By the time the war ended, the Austro-Hungarian Empire had been replaced by the independent republics of Austria, Hungary, and Czechoslovakia and a new southern Slavic monarchical state that eventually came to be called Yugoslavia. Other regions clamored to join Italy, Romania, and a reconstituted Poland. Rivalries among the nations that succeeded Austria-Hungary would weaken eastern Europe for the next eighty years. Ethnic pride and national statehood proved far more important to these states than class differences. Only in Hungary was there an attempt at social

revolution when Béla Kun established a Communist state. It was crushed after a brief five-month existence.

The Peace Settlement

Q Focus Question: What were the objectives of the chief participants at the Paris Peace Conference of 1919, and how closely did the final settlement reflect these objectives?

In January 1919, the delegations of the victorious Allied nations gathered in Paris to conclude a final settlement of the Great War. Over the years, the reasons for fighting World War I had been transformed from selfish national interests to idealistic principles. At the end of 1917, after they had taken over the Russian government, Lenin and the Bolsheviks had publicly revealed the contents of secret wartime treaties found in the archives of the Russian foreign ministry. The documents made it clear that European nations had gone to war primarily to achieve territorial gains.

Peace Aims

The American president, Woodrow Wilson, however, attempted at the beginning of 1918 to shift the discussion of war aims to a higher ground. Wilson submitted to the U.S. Congress an outline known as the "Fourteen Points" that he believed justified the enormous military struggle. Later, Wilson spelled out additional steps for a truly just and lasting peace. Wilson's proposals included "open covenants of peace, openly arrived at" instead of secret diplomacy; the reduction of national armaments to a "point consistent with domestic safety"; and the self-determination of people so that "all well-defined national aspirations shall be accorded the utmost satisfaction." Wilson characterized World War I as a people's war waged against "absolutism and militarism," two scourges of liberty that could only be eliminated by creating democratic governments and a "general association of nations" that would guarantee the "political independence and territorial integrity to great and small states alike" (see the box on p. 797). As the spokesman for a new world order based on democracy and international cooperation, Wilson was enthusiastically cheered by many Europeans when he arrived in Europe for the peace conference.

Wilson soon found, however, that other states at the Paris Peace Conference were guided by considerably more pragmatic motives. The secret treaties and agreements, for example, that had been made before the war could not be totally ignored, even if they did conflict with the principle of self-determination enunciated by Wilson. National interests also complicated the deliberations of the Paris Peace Conference. David Lloyd George, prime minister of Great Britain, had won a decisive electoral victory in December 1918 on a platform of making the Germans pay for this dreadful war.

OPPOSING VIEWPOINTS
THREE VOICES OF PEACEMAKING

When the Allied powers met in Paris in January 1919, it soon became apparent that the victors had different opinions on the kind of peace they expected. The first selection is a series of excerpts from the speeches of Woodrow Wilson in which the American president presented his idealistic goals for a peace based on justice and reconciliation.

The French leader Georges Clemenceau had a vision of peacemaking quite different from that of Woodrow Wilson. The French sought revenge and security. In the selection from his book *Grandeur and Misery of Victory*, Clemenceau revealed his fundamental dislike and distrust of Germany.

Yet a third voice of peacemaking was heard in Paris in 1919, although not at the peace conference. W. E. B. Du Bois, an African American writer and activist, had organized the Pan-African Congress to meet in Paris during the sessions of the Paris Peace Conference. The goal of the Pan-African Congress was to present a series of resolutions that promoted the cause of Africans and people of African descent. As can be seen in the selection presented here, the resolutions did not call for immediate independence for African nations.

Woodrow Wilson, Speeches

May 26, 1917

We are fighting for the liberty, the self-government, and the undictated development of all peoples, and every feature of the settlement that concludes this war must be conceived and executed for that purpose. Wrongs must first be righted and then adequate safeguards must be created to prevent their being committed again. . . .

No people must be forced under sovereignty under which it does not wish to live. No territory must change hands except for the purpose of securing those who inhabit it a fair chance of life and liberty. No indemnities must be insisted on except those that constitute payment for manifest wrongs done. No readjustments of power must be made except such as will tend to secure the future peace of the world and the future welfare and happiness of its peoples.

And then the free peoples of the world must draw together in some common covenant, some genuine and practical cooperation that will in effect combine their force to secure peace and justice in the dealings of nations with one another.

April 6, 1918

We are ready, whenever the final reckoning is made, to be just to the German people, deal fairly with the German power, as with all others. There can be no difference between peoples in the final judgment, if it is indeed to be a righteous judgment. To propose anything but justice, even-handed and dispassionate justice, to Germany at any time, whatever the outcome of the war, would be to renounce and dishonor our own cause. For we ask nothing that we are not willing to accord.

January 3, 1919

Our task at Paris is to organize the friendship of the world, to see to it that all the moral forces that make for right and justice and liberty are united and are given a vital organization to which the peoples of the world will readily and gladly respond. In other words, our task is no less colossal than this, to set up a new international psychology, to have a new atmosphere.

Georges Clemenceau, *Grandeur and Misery of Victory*

War and peace, with their strong contrasts, alternate against a common background. For the catastrophe of 1914 the Germans are responsible. Only a professional liar would deny this. . . .

What after all is this war, prepared, undertaken, and waged by the German people, who flung aside every scruple of conscience to let it loose, hoping for a peace of enslavement under the yoke of a militarism, destructive of all human dignity? It is simply the continuance, the recrudescence, of those never-ending acts of violence by which the first savage tribes carried out their depredations with all the resources of barbarism. . . .

I have sometimes penetrated into the sacred cave of the Germanic cult, which is, as every one knows, the *Bierhaus* [beer hall]. A great aisle of massive humanity where there accumulate, amid the fumes of tobacco and beer, the popular rumblings of a nationalism upheld by the sonorous brasses blaring to the heavens the supreme voice of Germany, *Deutschland über alles! Germany above everything!* Men, women, and children, all petrified in reverence before the divine stoneware pot, brows furrowed with irrepressible power, eyes lost in a dream of infinity, mouths twisted by the intensity of willpower, drink in long draughts the celestial hope of vague expectations. These only remain to be realized presently when the chief marked out by Destiny shall have given the word. There you have the ultimate framework of an old but childish race.

Pan-African Congress

Resolved

That the Allied and Associated Powers establish a code of law for the international protection of the natives of Africa. . . .

(continued)

(continued)

The Negroes of the world demand that hereafter the natives of Africa and the peoples of African descent be governed according to the following principles:

1. The Land: the land and its natural resources shall be held in trust for the natives and at all times they shall have effective ownership of as much land as they can profitably develop....

3. Labor: slavery and corporal punishment shall be abolished and forced labor except in punishment for crime....

5. The State: the natives of Africa must have the right to participate in the government as fast as their

development permits, in conformity with the principle that the government exists for the natives, and not the natives for the government.

Q *How did the peacemaking aims of Wilson and Clemenceau differ? How did their different views affect the deliberations of the Paris Peace Conference and the nature of the final peace settlement? How and why did the views of the Pan-African Congress differ from those of Wilson and Clemenceau?*

France's approach to peace was primarily determined by considerations of national security. Georges Clemenceau, the feisty premier of France, believed that the French people had borne the brunt of German aggression and deserved revenge and security against future German aggression (see the box on p. 797). Clemenceau wanted a demilitarized Germany, vast German reparations to pay for the costs of the war, and a separate Rhineland as a buffer state between France and Germany—demands that Wilson viewed as vindictive and contrary to the principle of national self-determination.

Yet another consideration affected the negotiations at Paris: the fear that Bolshevik revolution would spread from Russia to other European countries. This concern led the Allies to enlarge and strengthen such eastern European states as Poland, Czechoslovakia, and Romania at the expense of both Germany and Bolshevik Russia.

Although twenty-seven nations were represented at the Paris Peace Conference, the most important decisions were made by Wilson, Clemenceau, and Lloyd George. Italy was considered one of the so-called Big Four powers but played a much less important role than the other three countries. Germany, of course, was not invited to attend, and Russia could not because of its civil war.

In view of the many conflicting demands at the conference table, it was inevitable that the Big Three would quarrel. Wilson was determined to create a "league of nations" to prevent future wars. Clemenceau and Lloyd George were equally determined to punish Germany. In the end, only compromise made it possible to achieve a peace settlement. On January 25, 1919, the conference adopted the principle of the League of Nations. The details of its structure were left for later sessions, and Wilson willingly agreed to make compromises on territorial arrangements to guarantee the establishment of the League, believing that a functioning League could later rectify bad arrangements. Clemenceau also compromised to obtain some

guarantees for French security. He renounced France's desire for a separate Rhineland and instead accepted a defensive alliance with Great Britain and the United States. Both states pledged to help France if it was attacked by Germany.

The Treaty of Versailles

The final peace settlement of Paris consisted of five separate treaties with the defeated nations—Germany, Austria, Hungary, Bulgaria, and the Ottoman Empire. The Treaty of Versailles with Germany, signed on June 28, 1919, was by far the most important. The Germans considered it a harsh peace, conveniently overlooking that the Treaty of Brest-Litovsk, which they had imposed on Bolshevik Russia, was even more severe. The Germans

Lee Jackson/Topical Press Agency/Getty Images

The Big Four at Paris. Shown here are the Big Four at the Paris Peace Conference: David Lloyd George of Britain, Vittorio Orlando of Italy, Georges Clemenceau of France, and Woodrow Wilson of the United States. Although Italy was considered one of the Big Four powers, Britain, France, and the United States (the Big Three) made the major decisions at the peace conference.

were particularly unhappy with Article 231, the so-called **War Guilt Clause,** which declared Germany (and Austria) responsible for starting the war and ordered Germany to pay **reparations** for all the damage to which the Allied governments and their people were subjected as a result of the war "imposed upon them by the aggression of Germany and her allies." Reparations were a logical consequence of the wartime promises that Allied leaders had made to their people that the Germans would pay for the war effort. The treaty did not establish the amount to be paid but left that to be determined later by a reparations commission (see Chapter 26).

The military and territorial provisions of the treaty also rankled the Germans, although they were by no means as harsh as the Germans claimed. Germany had to reduce its army to 100,000 men, cut back its navy, and eliminate its air force. German territorial losses included the cession of Alsace and Lorraine to France and sections of Prussia to the new Polish state. German land west and as far as 30 miles east of the Rhine was established as a demilitarized zone and stripped of all armaments or fortifications to serve as a barrier to any future German military moves westward against France. Outraged by the "dictated peace," the new German government vowed to resist rather than accept the treaty, but it had no real alternative. Rejection meant a renewal of the war, and as the army pointed out, that was no longer practicable.

The Middle East in 1919

The Other Peace Treaties

The separate peace treaties made with the other Central Powers extensively redrew the map of eastern Europe. Many of these changes merely ratified what the war had already accomplished. The empires that had controlled eastern Europe for centuries had been destroyed or weakened, and a number of new states appeared on the map of Europe (see Map 25.5).

Both the German and Russian empires lost considerable territory in eastern Europe, and the Austro-Hungarian Empire disappeared altogether. New nation-states emerged from the lands of these three empires: Finland, Latvia, Estonia, Lithuania, Poland, Czechoslovakia, Austria, and Hungary. Territorial rearrangements were also made in the Balkans. Romania acquired additional lands from Russia, Hungary, and Bulgaria. Serbia formed the nucleus of the new state of Yugoslavia.

Although the Paris Peace Conference was supposedly guided by the principle of self-determination, the mixtures of peoples in eastern Europe made it impossible to draw boundaries along neat ethnic lines. Compromises had to be made, sometimes to satisfy the national interest of the victors. France, for example, had lost Russia as its major

ally on Germany's eastern border and wanted to strengthen and expand Poland, Czechoslovakia, Yugoslavia, and Romania as much as possible so that those states could serve as barriers against Germany and Communist Russia. As a result of compromises, virtually every eastern European state was left with a minorities problem that could lead to future conflicts. Germans in Poland; Hungarians, Poles, and Germans in Czechoslovakia; and Serbs, Croats, Slovenes, Macedonians, and Albanians in Yugoslavia all became sources of later conflict.

The centuries-old Ottoman Empire was dismembered by the peace settlement after the war. To gain Arab support against the Ottomans during the war, the Allies had promised to recognize the independence of Arab states in the Middle Eastern lands of the Ottoman Empire. But the imperialist habits of Europeans died hard. After the war, France took control of Lebanon and Syria, and Britain received Iraq and Palestine. Officially, both acquisitions were called **mandates.** Since Woodrow Wilson had opposed the outright annexation of colonial territories by the Allies, the peace settlement had created a system of mandates whereby a nation officially administered a territory on behalf of the League of Nations. The system of mandates could not hide the fact that the principle of national self-determination at the Paris Peace Conference was largely for Europeans.

The peace settlement negotiated at Paris soon came under attack, not only by the defeated Central Powers but also by others who felt that the peacemakers had been shortsighted. Some people agreed, however, that the settlement was the best that could be achieved under the circumstances. They believed that self-determination had served reasonably well as a central organizing principle, and the establishment of the League of Nations gave some hope that future conflicts could be resolved peacefully. Yet within twenty years, Europe would again be engaged in deadly conflict. As some historians have suggested, perhaps a lack of enforcement, rather than the structure of the settlement, may account for the failure of the peace of 1919.

Successful enforcement of the peace necessitated the active involvement of its principal architects, especially in helping the new German state develop a peaceful and democratic republic. The failure of the U.S. Senate to ratify the Treaty of Versailles, however, meant that the United States never joined the League of Nations. The Senate also rejected Wilson's defensive alliance with Great Britain and France. Already by the end of 1919, the United States was pursuing policies intended to limit its direct involvement in future European wars.

This retreat had dire consequences. American withdrawal from the defensive alliance with Britain and France led Britain to withdraw as well. By removing itself

MAP 25.5 **Europe in 1919.** The victorious allies met to determine the shape and nature of postwar Europe. At the urging of U.S. President Woodrow Wilson, many nationalist aspirations of former imperial subjects were realized with the creation of several new countries from the prewar territory of Austria-Hungary, Germany, and Russia.

Q What new countries emerged, and what countries gained territory when Austria-Hungary was dismembered? 🌐 **View an animated version of this map or related maps at** academic.cengage .com/history/spielvogel

from European affairs, the United States forced France to stand alone facing its old enemy, leading the embittered nation to take strong actions against Germany that only intensified German resentment. By the end of 1919, it appeared that the peace established mere months earlier was already beginning to unravel.

CONCLUSION

World War I shattered the liberal and rational assumptions of late-nineteenth- and early-twentieth-century European society. The incredible destruction and the deaths of almost 10 million people undermined the whole idea of progress. New propaganda techniques had manipulated entire populations into sustaining their involvement in a meaningless slaughter.

World War I was a total war that involved a mobilization of resources and populations and increased government centralization of power over the lives of its citizens. Civil liberties, such as freedom of the press, speech, assembly, and movement, were circumscribed in the name of national security. Governments' need to plan the production and distribution of goods and to ration consumer goods restricted economic freedom. Although the late nineteenth and early twentieth centuries had witnessed the extension of government authority into such areas as mass education, social welfare legislation, and mass conscription, World War I made the practice of strong central authority a way of life.

Finally, World War I ended the age of European hegemony over world affairs. In 1917, the Russian Revolution laid the foundation for the creation of a new Eurasian power, the Soviet Union, and the United States had entered the war. The waning of the European age was not evident to all, however, for it was clouded by American isolationism and the withdrawal of the Soviets from world affairs while they nurtured the growth of their own socialist system. These developments, though temporary, created a political vacuum in Europe that all too soon was filled by the revival of German power.

TIMELINE

	1914	1915	1916	1917	1918	1919	1920	1921

Europe
- Assassination of Archduke Francis Ferdinand
- Battle of Verdun
- United States enters the war
- First Battle of the Marne
- Easter Rebellion in Ireland
- Surrender of Germany
- Ministry of Munitions in Britain
- Second Battle of the Marne
- Complete mobilization for total war in Germany
- November Revolution in Germany

Russia
- Bolshevik Revolution
- Civil war in Russia

NOTES

1. Martin Gilbert, *The First World War: A Complete History* (New York, 1994), p. 259.
2. Quoted in ibid., p. 264.
3. Arnold Toynbee, *Surviving the Future* (New York, 1971), pp. 106–107.
4. Quoted in Joachim Remak, "1914—The Third Balkan War: Origins Reconsidered," *Journal of Modern History* 43 (1971): 364–365.
5. Quoted in Robert G. L. Waite, *Vanguard of Nazism* (New York, 1969), p. 22.
6. Quoted in J. M. Winter, *The Experience of World War I* (New York, 1989), p. 142.
7. Quoted in ibid., p. 137.
8. Quoted in Gail Braybon, *Women Workers in the First World War: The British Experience* (London, 1981), p. 79.
9. Quoted in Catherine W. Reilly, ed., *Scars upon My Heart: Women's Poetry and Verse of the First World War* (London, 1981), p. 90.
10. Quoted in Robert Paxton, *Europe in the Twentieth Century*, 2d ed. (New York, 1985), p. 110.
11. Quoted in William M. Mandel, *Soviet Women* (Garden City, N.Y., 1975), p. 43.
12. Quoted in Mark D. Steinberg, *Voices of Revolution, 1917* (New Haven, Conn., 2001), p. 55.

SUGGESTIONS FOR FURTHER READING

General Works on Twentieth-Century Europe   A number of general works on European history in the twentieth century provide a context for understanding both World War I and the Russian Revolution. Especially valuable is **N. Ferguson**, *The War of the World: Twentieth-Century Conflict and the Descent of the West* (New York, 2006). See also **R. Paxton**, *Europe in the Twentieth Century,* 4th ed. (New York, 2004); **H. James**, *Europe Reborn: A History, 1914–2000* (London, 2003); **E. D. Brose**, *History of Europe in the Twentieth Century* (Oxford, 2004); and **M. Mazower**, *The Dark Continent: Europe's Twentieth Century* (New York, 2000).

Causes of World War I   The historical literature on the causes of World War I is enormous. Good starting points are **J. Joll and G. Martel**, *The Origins of the First World War,* 3d ed. (London, 2006), and **A. Mombauer**, *The Origins of the First World War: Controversies and Consensus* (London, 2002). The role of each great power has been reassessed in a series of books on the causes of World War I. They include **V. R. Berghahn**, *Germany and the Approach of War in 1914,* 2d ed. (London, 1993); **Z. S. Steiner**, *Britain and the Origins of the First World War,* 2d ed. (New York, 2003); **R. Bosworth**, *Italy and the Approach of the First World War* (New York, 1983); **J. F. Keiger**, *France and the Origins of the First World War* (New York, 1984); and **D. C. B. Lieven**, *Russia and the Origins of the First World War* (New York, 1984). On the role of militarism, see **D. Hermann**, *The Arming of Europe and the Making of the First World War* (New York, 1997). On the events leading to war, see **D. Fromkin**, *Europe's Last Summer: Who Started the Great War in 1914?* (New York, 2004).

World War I   The best brief account of World War I is **H. Strachan**, *The First World War* (New York, 2003). Strachan has also completed the first volume of a massive three-volume study, *First World War: To Arms* (New York, 2003). Two additional accounts of World War I are **M. Gilbert**, *The First World War* (New York, 1994), and the lavishly illustrated book by **J. M. Winter**, *The Experience of World War I* (New York, 1989). See also the brief work by **N. Heyman**, *World War I* (Westport, Conn., 1997). There is an excellent collection of articles in **H. Strachan**, *The Oxford Illustrated History of the First World War* (New York, 1998). See also **J. Keegan**, *An Illustrated History of the First World War* (New York, 2001), and **S. Audoin-Rouzeau and A. Becker**, *14–18: Understanding the Great War* (New York, 2002). On the global nature of World War I, see **M. S. Neiberg**, *Fighting the Great War: A Global History* (Cambridge, Mass., 2005), and **J. H. Morrow Jr.**, *The Great War: An Imperial History* (London, 2004). The use of poison gas is examined in **L. F. Haber**, *The Poisonous Cloud: Chemical Warfare in the First World War* (Oxford, 1986). The war at sea is examined in **R. Hough**, *The Great War at Sea, 1914–18* (Oxford, 1984). **B. Tuchman**, *The Guns of August* (New York, 1962), is a magnificently written account of the opening days of the war, although scholars do not always agree with the author's conclusions. For an interesting perspective on World War I and the beginnings of the modern world, see **M. Eksteins**, *Rites of Spring: The Great War and the Birth of the Modern Age* (Boston, 1989). For a new interpretation, see **D. Stevenson**, *Cataclysm: The First World War as Political Tragedy* (New York, 2004).

Women in World War I   On the role of women in World War I, see **S. Grayzel**, *Women and the First World War* (London,

2002); **J. M. Winter and R. M. Wall**, eds., *The Upheaval of War: Family, Work and Welfare in Europe, 1914–1918* (Cambridge, 1988); **G. Braybon and P. Summerfield**, *Women's Experiences in Two World Wars* (London, 1987); and **M. R. Higonnet, J. Jensen, S. Michel, and M. C. Weitz**, *Behind the Lines: Gender and the Two World Wars* (New Haven, Conn., 1987).

The Russian Revolution   A good introduction to the Russian Revolution can be found in **R. A. Wade**, *The Russian Revolution, 1917,* 2d ed. (Cambridge, 2005), and **S. Fitzpatrick**, *The Russian Revolution, 1917–1932,* 2d ed. (New York, 2001). See also **R. Pipes**, *The Russian Revolution* (New York, 1990). For a study that puts the Russian Revolution into the context of World War I, see **P. Holquist**, *Making War, Forging Revolution* (Cambridge, Mass., 2002). There is a good analysis as well as a good collection of the thoughts and experiences of ordinary Russian people in 1917 in **M. D. Steinberg**, *Voices of Revolution, 1917* (New Haven, Conn., 2001). On Lenin, see **R. Service**, *Lenin: A Biography* (Cambridge, Mass., 2000). On social reforms, see **W. Goldman**, *Women, the State and Revolution* (Cambridge, 1993). A comprehensive study of the Russian civil war is **W. B. Lincoln**, *Red Victory: A History of the Russian Civil War* (New York, 1989).

The Peace Settlement   On the Paris Peace Conference, see **M. MacMillan**, *Paris 1919: Six Months That Changed the World* (New York, 2002), and **E. Goldstein**, *The First World War Peace Settlements* (London, 2002). On the effect of World War I on the multinational empires existing before World War I, see **A. Roshwald**, *Ethnic Nationalism and the Fall of Empires: Central Europe, Russia, and the Middle East, 1914–1923* (New York, 2001).

CENGAGENOW   CengageNOW is an integrated online suite of services and resources with proven ease of use and efficient paths to success, delivering the results you want—NOW!

academic.cengage.com/login/

Enter CengageNOW using the access card that is available with *Western Civilization.* CengageNOW will assist you in understanding the content in this chapter with lesson plans generated for your needs. In addition, you can read the following documents, and many more, online:

Entente Cordiale, *Declaration of Understanding*
Siegfried Sassoon, poems "Attack" and "Dreamers"
Treaty of Versailles

WESTERN CIVILIZATION RESOURCES

Visit the *Western Civilization* Companion Web site for resources specific to this book:

academic.cengage.com/history/spielvogel

For a variety of tools to help you succeed in this course, visit the Western Civilization Resource Center. Enter the Resource Center using either your *CengageNOW* access card or your standalone access card for the *Wadsworth Western Civilization Resource Center.* Organized by topic, this Web site includes quizzes; images; primary source documents; interactive simulations, maps, and timelines; movie explorations; and a wealth of other resources.

http://westernrc.wadsworth.com/

CHAPTER 26
THE FUTILE SEARCH FOR STABILITY: EUROPE BETWEEN THE WARS, 1919–1939

CHAPTER OUTLINE AND FOCUS QUESTIONS

An Uncertain Peace

Q What was the impact of World War I, and what problems did European countries face in the 1920s?

The Democratic States

Q How did France, Great Britain, and the United States respond to the various crises, including the Great Depression, that they faced in the interwar years? How did World War I affect Europe's colonies in Asia and Africa?

The Authoritarian and Totalitarian States

Q Why did many European states experience a retreat from democracy in the interwar years? What are the characteristics of totalitarian states, and to what degree were these characteristics present in Fascist Italy, Nazi Germany, and Stalinist Russia?

The Expansion of Mass Culture and Mass Leisure

Q What new dimensions in mass culture and mass leisure emerged during the interwar years, and what role did these activities play in the totalitarian states?

Cultural and Intellectual Trends in the Interwar Years

Q What were the main cultural and intellectual trends in the interwar years?

CRITICAL THINKING

Q Why have some historians called the 1920s both an age of anxiety and a period of hope?

Men are served in a soup line in Berlin in 1930

ONLY TWENTY YEARS after the Treaty of Versailles, Europeans were again at war. Yet in the 1920s, many people assumed that the world was about to enter a new era of international peace, economic growth, and political democracy. In all of these areas, the optimistic hopes of the 1920s failed to be realized. After 1919, most people wanted peace but were unsure how to maintain it. The League of Nations, conceived as a new instrument to provide for collective security, failed to work well. New treaties that renounced the use of war looked good on paper but had no means of enforcement. Then, too, virtually everyone favored disarmament, but few could agree on how to achieve it.

Europe faced serious economic and social hardships after World War I. The European economy did not begin to recover from the war until 1922, and even then it was beset by financial problems left over from the war and, most devastating of all, the severe depression that began at the end of 1929. The Great Depression brought misery to millions of people. Begging for food on the streets became widespread, especially when soup kitchens were unable to keep up with the demand. Larger and larger numbers of people were homeless and moved from place to place looking for work and shelter. In the United States, the homeless set up shantytowns they derisively named "Hoovervilles" after the U.S. president, Herbert Hoover. Some of the destitute saw but one solution; as one unemployed person expressed it, "Today, when I am experiencing this for the first time, I think that I should prefer to do away with myself, to take gas, to jump into the river, or leap from some high place . . . Would I really come to such a decision? I do not know. Animals die, plants wither, but men always go on living." Social unrest spread rapidly, and some unemployed staged hunger marches to get attention. In democratic countries, more and more people began to listen to and vote for radical voices calling for extreme measures.

According to Woodrow Wilson, World War I had been fought to make the world safe for democracy, and for a while after 1919, political democracy seemed well on its way. But hope soon faded as authoritarian regimes spread into Italy and Germany and across eastern Europe. ◆

An Uncertain Peace

Q **Focus Question:** What was the impact of World War I, and what problems did European countries face in the 1920s?

Four years of devastating war had left many Europeans with a profound sense of despair and disillusionment. The Great War indicated to many people that something was dreadfully wrong with Western values. In *The Decline of the West*, the German writer Oswald Spengler (1880–1936) reflected this disillusionment when he emphasized the decadence of Western civilization and posited its collapse.

The Impact of World War I

The enormous suffering and the deaths of almost 10 million people shook traditional society to its foundations and undermined the whole idea of progress. New propaganda techniques had manipulated entire populations into maintaining their involvement in a senseless slaughter. How did Europeans deal with such losses? In France, for example, probably two-thirds of the population were in mourning over the deaths of these young people.

An immediate response was the erection of war memorials accompanied by ceremonies to honor the dead. Battlefields also became significant commemorative sites with memorial parks, large monuments, and massive cemeteries, including ossuaries or vaults where the bones of thousands of unidentified soldiers were interred. Virtually all belligerent countries adopted national ceremonies for the burial of an Unknown Soldier, a telling reminder of the brutality of World War I. Moreover, businesses, schools, universities, and other corporate bodies all set up their own war memorials.

It is impossible to calculate the social impact of the mourning for the lost soldiers. One French mother explained, "No matter how proud as Frenchwomen we poor mothers may be of our sons, we nevertheless carry wounds in our hearts that nothing can heal. It is strongly contrary to nature for our children to depart before us." Another Frenchman wrote, "Why should the old people remain alive, when the children who might have initiated the most beautiful era in French history march off to the sacrifice."[1]

World War I created a lost generation of war veterans who had become accustomed to violence. In the course of the war, extreme violence and brutality became a way of life and a social reality. As one Frenchman recounted: "Not only did war make us dead, impotent or blind. In the midst of beautiful actions, of sacrifice and self-abnegation, it also awoke in us, . . . ancient instincts of cruelty and barbarity. At times, I, who have never punched anyone, who loathes disorder and brutality, took pleasure in killing."[2] After the war, some veterans became pacifists, but for many veterans, the violence of the war became a starting point for the use of violence in the new political movements of the 1920s and 1930s (see "The Authoritarian and Totalitarian States" later in this chapter). These men were fiercely nationalistic and eager to restore the national interests they felt had been betrayed in the peace treaties.

The Search for Security

The peace treaties at the end of World War I had tried to fulfill the nineteenth-century dream of nationalism by redrawing boundaries and creating new states. Nevertheless, this peace settlement had left many nations unhappy. Conflicts over disputed border regions poisoned mutual relations in eastern Europe for years, and many Germans viewed the Peace of Versailles as a dictated peace and vowed to seek its revision.

U.S. President Woodrow Wilson had recognized that the peace treaties contained unwise provisions that could serve as new causes for conflicts and had placed many of his hopes for the future in the League of Nations. The League, however, was not particularly effective in maintaining the peace. The failure of the United States to join the League and the subsequent American determination to be less involved in European affairs undermined the effectiveness of the League from its beginning. Moreover, the League's sole weapon for halting aggression was economic sanctions.

The weakness of the League of Nations and the failure of both the United States and Great Britain to honor their promises to form defensive military alliances with France left France embittered and alone. Before World War I, France's alliance with Russia had served to threaten Germany with the possibility of a two-front war. But Communist Russia was now a hostile power. To compensate, France built a network of alliances in eastern Europe with Poland and the members of the so-called Little Entente (Czechoslovakia, Romania, Yugoslavia). Although these alliances looked good on paper as a way to contain Germany and maintain the new status quo, they overlooked the fundamental military weaknesses of those nations. Poland and the Little Entente states were no real substitutes for Russia.

The French Policy of Coercion (1919–1924)

France's search for security between 1919 and 1924 was founded primarily on a strict enforcement of the Treaty of Versailles. This tough policy toward Germany began with the issue of reparations, the payments that the Germans were supposed to make to compensate for the "damage done to the civilian population of the Allied and Associated Powers and to their property," as the treaty asserted. In April 1921, the Allied Reparations Commission settled on a sum of 132 billion marks ($33 billion) for German reparations, payable in annual installments of 2.5 billion (gold) marks. Allied threats to occupy the Ruhr valley, Germany's chief industrial and mining center, led the new German republic to accept the reparations settlement and make its first payment in 1921. By the following year, however, facing financial problems, the German government announced that it was unable to pay any more. Outraged by what they considered Germany's violation of the peace settlement, the French government sent troops to occupy the Ruhr valley. Because the Germans would not pay reparations, the French would collect reparations in kind by operating and using the Ruhr mines and factories.

Both Germany and France suffered from the French occupation of the Ruhr. The German government adopted a policy of passive resistance that was largely financed by printing more paper money, but this only intensified the inflationary pressures that had already appeared in Germany by the end of the war. The German mark soon became worthless. In 1914, a dollar was worth 4.2 marks; by November 1, 1923, the rate had reached 130 billion to the dollar, and by the end of November, it had snowballed to an incredible 4.2 trillion marks to the dollar. Economic disaster fueled political upheavals as Communists staged uprisings in October 1923, and Adolf Hitler's band of Nazis attempted to seize power in Munich in November (see "Hitler and Nazi Germany" later in this chapter). But the French were hardly victorious. The cost of the French occupation was not offset by the gains. Meanwhile, pressure from the United States and Great Britain against the French policy forced the French to agree to a new conference of experts to reassess the reparations problem. By the time the conference did its work in 1924, both France and Germany were opting to pursue a more conciliatory approach toward each other.

The Hopeful Years (1924–1929)

The formation of new governments in both Great Britain and France opened the door to conciliatory approaches

The Little Entente

to Germany and the reparations problem. At the same time, a new German government led by Gustav Stresemann (1878–1929) ended the policy of passive resistance and committed Germany to carry out most of the provisions of the Treaty of Versailles while seeking a new settlement of the reparations question. At the same time, the German government stabilized the currency and ended the extreme inflation by issuing a new temporary currency, the Rentenmark, equal to 3 trillion old marks.

In August 1924, an international commission produced a new plan for reparations. Named the Dawes Plan after the American banker who chaired the commission, it reduced reparations and stabilized Germany's payments on the basis of its ability to pay. The Dawes Plan also granted an initial $200 million loan for German recovery, which opened

Three Lions/Getty Images

The Effects of Inflation. The inflationary pressures that had begun in Germany at the end of World War I intensified during the French occupation of the Ruhr. By the early 1920s, the value of the German mark had fallen precipitously. This photograph shows German children using bundles of worthless money as building blocks. The wads of money were cheaper than toys.

the door to heavy American investments in Europe that helped usher in a new era of European prosperity between 1924 and 1929.

The Spirit of Locarno

With prosperity came new efforts at European diplomacy. A spirit of international cooperation was fostered by the foreign ministers of Germany and France, Gustav Stresemann and Aristide Briand (1862–1932), who concluded the Treaty of Locarno in 1925. This guaranteed Germany's new western borders with France and Belgium. Although Germany's new eastern borders with Poland were conspicuously absent from the agreement, a clear indication that Germany did not accept those borders as permanent, the Locarno pact was viewed by many as the beginning of a new era of European peace. On the day after the pact was concluded, the headline in the *New York Times* ran "France and Germany Ban War Forever," and the *London Times* declared, "Peace at Last."[3]

Germany's entry into the League of Nations in March 1926 soon reinforced the new spirit of conciliation engendered at Locarno. Two years later, similar optimistic attitudes prevailed in the Kellogg-Briand pact, drafted by the American secretary of state Frank B. Kellogg and the French foreign minister Aristide Briand. Sixty-three nations eventually agreed to the pact, in which they pledged "to renounce war as an instrument of national policy." Nothing was said, however, about what would be done if anyone violated the treaty.

The spirit of Locarno was based on little real substance. Germany lacked the military power to alter its western borders even if it wanted to. And the issue of disarmament soon proved that even the spirit of Locarno could not induce nations to cut back on their weapons. The League of Nations Covenant had suggested the "reduction of national armaments to the lowest point consistent with national safety." Germany, of course, had been disarmed with the expectation that other states would do likewise. Numerous disarmament conferences, however, failed to achieve anything substantial as states proved unwilling to trust their security to anyone but their own military forces. When a world disarmament conference finally met in Geneva in 1932, the issue was already dead.

Coexistence with Soviet Russia

One other hopeful sign in the years between 1924 and 1929 was the new coexistence of the West with Soviet Russia. By the beginning of 1924, Soviet hopes for Communist revolutions in Western states had largely dissipated. In turn, these states had realized by then that the Bolshevik regime could not be ousted. By 1924, Germany, Britain, France, and Italy, as well as several smaller European countries, had established full diplomatic relations with Soviet Russia. Nevertheless, Western powers remained highly suspicious of Soviet intentions.

The Great Depression

After World War I, most European states hoped to return to the liberal ideal of a market economy based on private enterprise and largely free of state intervention. But the war had vastly strengthened business cartels and labor unions, making some government regulation of these powerful organizations appear necessary. Then, too, the economic integration of Europe before 1914 that had been based on free trade was soon undermined by a wave of protectionism and trade barriers, and reparations and war debts had further damaged the postwar international economy. Consequently, the prosperity that did occur between 1924 and 1929 was uncommonly fragile, and the dream of returning to a self-regulating market economy was mere illusion. Then, to dash the dream altogether, along came the Great Depression.

Causes

Two factors played an important role in bringing on the Great Depression: a downturn in domestic economies and an international financial crisis caused by the collapse of the American stock market in 1929. Already in the mid-1920s, prices for agricultural goods were beginning to decline rapidly due to overproduction of basic commodities, such as wheat. In 1925, states in central and eastern Europe began to impose tariffs to close their markets to other countries' goods. An increase in the use of oil and hydroelectricity led to a slump in the coal industry even before 1929.

Furthermore, much of Europe's prosperity between 1924 and 1929 had been built on American bank loans to Germany. Twenty-three billion new marks had been invested in German municipal bonds and German industries since 1924. Already in 1928 and 1929, American investors had begun to pull money out of Germany in order to invest in the booming New York stock market. The crash of the American stock market in October 1929 led panicky American investors to withdraw even more of their funds from Germany and other European markets. The withdrawal of funds seriously weakened the banks of Germany and other central European states. The Credit-Anstalt, Vienna's most prestigious bank, collapsed on May 31, 1931. By that time, trade was slowing down, industrialists were cutting back production, and unemployment was increasing as the ripple effects of international bank failures had a devastating impact on domestic economies.

Unemployment

Economic depression was by no means a new phenomenon in European history. But the depth of the economic downturn after 1929 fully justifies the "Great Depression" label. During 1932, the worst year of the depression, one British worker in four was unemployed, and 6 million Germans—40 percent of the German labor force—were out of work. Between 1929 and 1932, industrial production plummeted almost 50 percent in the United States and nearly as much in

The Great Depression: Bread Lines in Paris. The Great Depression devastated the European economy and had serious political repercussions. Because of its more balanced economy, France did not feel the effects of the depression as quickly as other European countries. By 1931, however, even France was experiencing lines of unemployed people at free-food centers.

Hartingue/Roger Viollet/Getty Images

Germany. The unemployed and homeless filled the streets of cities throughout the advanced industrial countries (see the box on p. 808).

Social and Political Repercussions   The economic crisis also had unexpected social repercussions. Women were often able to secure low-paying jobs as servants, house-cleaners, or laundresses while many men remained unemployed, either begging on the streets or staying at home to do household tasks. Many unemployed men, resenting this reversal of traditional gender roles, were open to the shrill cries of demagogues with simple solutions to the economic crisis. High unemployment rates among young males often led them to join gangs that gathered in parks or other public places, arousing fear among local residents.

Governments seemed powerless to deal with the crisis. The classical liberal remedy for depression, a deflationary policy of balanced budgets, which involved cutting costs by lowering wages and raising tariffs to exclude other countries' goods from home markets, only served to worsen the economic crisis and create even greater mass discontent. This in turn led to serious political repercussions. Increased government activity in the economy was one reaction, even in countries like the United States that had a strong *laissez-faire* tradition. Another effect was a renewed interest in Marxist doctrines, since Marx had predicted that capitalism would destroy itself through over-production. Communism took on new popularity, especially among workers and intellectuals. Finally, the Great Depression increased the attractiveness of simplistic dictatorial solutions, especially from a new authoritarian movement known as **fascism.** Everywhere in Europe, democracy seemed on the defensive in the 1930s.

The Democratic States

Q **Focus Questions:** How did France, Great Britain, and the United States respond to the various crises, including the Great Depression, that they faced in the interwar years? How did World War I affect Europe's colonies in Asia and Africa?

Woodrow Wilson proclaimed that World War I had been fought to make the world safe for democracy, and in 1919, there seemed to be some justification for that claim. Four major European states and a host of minor ones had functioning political democracies. In a number of nations, universal male suffrage had even been replaced by universal suffrage as male politicians rewarded women for their contributions to World War I by granting them the right to vote (except in Italy, France, and Spain, where women had to wait until the end of World War II). Women also began to enter political life as deputies to parliamentary bodies. In the new German republic, for example, almost 10 percent of the deputies elected to the Reichstag in 1919 were women, although the number dropped to 6 percent by 1926.

Great Britain

After World War I, Great Britain went through a period of painful readjustment and serious economic difficulties. During the war, Britain had lost many of its markets for industrial products, especially to the United States and Japan. The postwar decline of such staple industries as coal, steel, and textiles led to a rise in unemployment, which reached the 2 million mark in 1921. The continuing wartime coalition government led by Liberal David Lloyd George proved unable to change this situation.

THE GREAT DEPRESSION: UNEMPLOYED AND HOMELESS IN GERMANY

In 1932, Germany had 6 million unemployed workers, many of them wandering aimlessly through the country, begging for food and seeking shelter in city lodging houses for the homeless. The Great Depression was an important factor in the rise to power of Adolf Hitler and the Nazis. This selection presents a description of the unemployed homeless in 1932.

Heinrich Hauser, "With Germany's Unemployed"

An almost unbroken chain of homeless men extends the whole length of the great Hamburg-Berlin highway.... All the highways in Germany over which I have traveled this year presented the same aspect....

Most of the hikers paid no attention to me. They walked separately or in small groups, with their eyes on the ground. And they had the queer, stumbling gait of barefooted people, for their shoes were slung over their shoulders. Some of them were guild members—carpenters...milkmen... and bricklayers...—but they were in a minority. Far more numerous were those whom one could assign to no special profession or craft—unskilled young people, for the most part, who had been unable to find a place for themselves in any city or town in Germany, and who had never had a job and never expected to have one. There was something else that had never been seen before—whole families that had piled all their goods into baby carriages and wheelbarrows that they were pushing along as they plodded forward in dumb despair. It was a whole nation on the march.

I saw them—and this was the strongest impression that the year 1932 left with me—I saw them, gathered into groups of fifty or a hundred men, attacking fields of potatoes. I saw them digging up the potatoes and throwing them into sacks while the farmer who owned the field watched them in despair and the local policeman looked on gloomily from the distance. I saw them staggering toward the lights of the city as night fell, with their sacks on their backs. What did it remind me of? Of the War, of the worst periods of starvation in 1917 and 1918, but even then people paid for the potatoes....

I saw that the individual can know what is happening only by personal experience. I know what it is to be a tramp. I know what cold and hunger are.... But there are two things that I have only recently experienced—begging and spending the night in a municipal lodging house.

I entered the huge Berlin municipal lodging house in a northern quarter of the city....

Distribution of spoons, distribution of enameled-ware bowls with the words "Property of the City of Berlin" written on their sides. Then the meal itself. A big kettle is carried. Men with yellow smocks have brought it in and men with yellow smocks ladle out the food. These men, too, are homeless and they have been expressly picked by the establishment and given free food and lodging and a little pocket money in exchange for their work about the house.

Where have I seen this kind of food distribution before? In a prison that I once helped to guard in the winter of 1919 during the German civil war. There was the same hunger then, the same trembling, anxious expectation of rations. Now the men are standing in a long row, dressed in their plain nightshirts that reach to the ground, and the noise of their shuffling feet is like the noise of big wild animals walking up and down the stone floor of their cages before feeding time. The men lean far over the kettle so that the warm steam from the food envelops them and they hold out their bowls as if begging and whisper to the attendant, "Give me a real helping. Give me a little more." A piece of bread is handed out with every bowl.

My next recollection is sitting at a table in another room on a crowded bench that is like a seat in a fourth-class railway carriage. Hundreds of hungry mouths make an enormous noise eating their food. The men sit bent over their food like animals who feel that someone is going to take it away from them. They hold their bowl with their left arm part way around it, so that nobody can take it away, and they also protect it with their other elbow and with their head and mouth, while they move the spoon as fast as they can between their mouth and the bowl.

Q *Why did Hauser compare the scene he describes from 1932 with conditions in the years 1917 and 1918? How did the growing misery of many ordinary Germans promote the rise of extremist political parties like the Nazis?*

By 1923, British politics experienced a major transformation when the Labour Party surged ahead of the Liberals as the second most powerful party in Britain after the Conservatives. In fact, after the elections of November 1923, a Labour-Liberal agreement enabled Ramsay MacDonald (1866–1937) to become the first Labour prime minister of Britain. Dependent on Liberal support, MacDonald rejected any extreme social or economic experimentation. His government lasted only ten months, however, as the Conservative Party's charge that his administration was friendly toward communism proved to be a highly successful campaign tactic.

Under the direction of Stanley Baldwin (1867–1947) as prime minister, the Conservatives guided Britain during an era of renewed prosperity from 1925 to 1929. This prosperity, however, was relatively superficial. British exports in the 1920s never compensated for the overseas investments lost during the war, and even in these so-called prosperous years, unemployment remained at a startling 10 percent level. Coal miners were especially affected by the decline of the antiquated and

THE STRUGGLES OF A DEMOCRACY: UNEMPLOYMENT AND SLUMS IN GREAT BRITAIN

During the 1920s and 1930s, Britain struggled with the problems of economic depression. Unemployment was widespread, especially after the onset of the Great Depression. Even after Britain began to recover in the late 1930s, many Britons still lived in wretched conditions. These selections reflect Britain's economic and social problems.

Men Without Work: A Report Made to the Pilgrim Trust, 1938

A week's notice may end half a lifetime's service, with no prospects, if he is elderly, but the dole, followed by a still further reduction in his means of livelihood when the old age pension comes. We take as an example a shoe laster from Leicester, who had worked thirty-seven years with one firm. "When I heard the new manager going through and saying: 'The whole of this side of this room, this room, and this room is to be stopped,' I knew it would be uphill work to get something." He went on to describe to us how he had not been able to bring himself to tell his wife the bad news when he got home, how she had noticed that something was wrong, how confident she had been that he would get work elsewhere, but how he had known that the chances were heavily against him. For months and indeed often for years such men go on looking for work, and the same is true of many casual laborers. There were in the sample old men who have not a remote chance of working again but yet make it a practice to stand every morning at six o'clock at the works gates in the hope that perhaps they may catch the foreman's eye.

George Orwell, "A Woman in the Slums"

As we moved slowly through the outskirts of the town we passed row after row of little grey slum houses.... At the back of one of the houses a young woman was kneeling on the stones, poking a stick up the leaden wastepipe which ran from the sink inside, and which I suppose was blocked....She had a round pale face, the usual exhausted face of the slum girl who is twenty-five and looks forty, thanks to miscarriages and drudgery; and it wore, for the second in which I saw it, the most desolate, hopeless expression I have ever seen. It struck me then that we are mistaken when we say that "It isn't the same for them as it would be for us," and that people bred in the slums can imagine nothing but the slums. For what I saw in her face was not the ignorant suffering of an animal. She knew well enough what was happening to her— understood as well as I did how dreadful a destiny it was to be kneeling there in the bitter cold, on the slimy stones of a slum backyard, poking a stick up a foul drain-pipe.

Q *What economic and social problems are described in these documents? What do these pieces tell you about the quality of life and politics in Great Britain during the interwar years?*

---

inefficient British coal mines, which also suffered from a world glut of coal. Attempts by mine owners to lower coal miners' wages led to a national strike (the General Strike of 1926) by miners and sympathetic trade unions. A compromise settled the strike, but many miners refused to accept the settlement and were eventually forced back to work at lower wages for longer hours.

In 1929, just as the Great Depression was beginning, a second Labour government came into power, but its failure to solve the nation's economic problems caused it to fall in 1931. A National Government (a coalition of Liberals and Conservatives) claimed credit for bringing Britain out of the worst stages of the depression, primarily by using the traditional policies of balanced budgets and protective tariffs. By 1936, unemployment had dropped to 1.6 million after reaching a depression high of 3 million in 1932 (see the box above).

British politicians largely ignored the new ideas of a Cambridge economist, John Maynard Keynes (1883–1946), who published his *General Theory of Employment, Interest and Money* in 1936. He condemned the traditional view that in a free economy, depressions should be left to work themselves out. Instead, Keynes argued that unemployment stemmed not from overproduction but from a decline in demand and that demand could be increased by public works, financed, if necessary, through deficit spending to stimulate production.

France

After the defeat of Germany, France had become the strongest power on the European continent. Its greatest need was to rebuild the devastated areas of northern and eastern France. The conservative National Bloc government, led by Raymond Poincaré (1860–1934), sought to use German reparations for this purpose, which resulted in Poincaré's hard-line policy toward Germany and the Ruhr invasion. When Poincaré's conservative government was forced to raise taxes in 1924 to pay for the cost of the Ruhr fiasco, his National Bloc was voted out of power and replaced by the so-called Cartel of the Left.

The Cartel of the Left was a coalition government formed by two French leftist parties, the Radicals and the Socialists. These parties shared a belief in antimilitarism, anticlericalism, and the importance of education. But despite their name, the Radicals were a democratic party of small property owners, whereas the Socialists were nominally committed to Marxist socialism. Although they cooperated to win elections, their differences on economic and financial issues made their efforts to solve France's financial problems between 1924 and 1926 largely futile. The failure of the Cartel of the Left led to the return of Raymond Poincaré, whose government from 1926 to 1929 stabilized the French economy during a period of relative prosperity.

France began to feel the full effects of the Great Depression in 1932, and that economic instability soon had political repercussions. During a nineteen-month period in 1932 and 1933, six different cabinets were formed as France faced political chaos. During the same time, French right-wing groups, adhering to policies similar to those of the Fascists in Italy and the Nazis in Germany, marched through French streets in numerous demonstrations. The riots of February 1934, fomented by a number of French right-wing leagues, frightened many into believing that the extremists intended to seize power. These fears began to drive the leftist parties together despite their other differences and led in 1936 to the formation of the Popular Front.

The first Popular Front government was formed in June 1936 and was a coalition of the Socialists and Radicals. The Socialist leader, Léon Blum (1872–1950), served as prime minister. The Popular Front succeeded in initiating a program for workers that some have called the French New Deal. It established the right of collective bargaining, a forty-hour workweek, two-week paid vacations, and minimum wages. The Popular Front's policies failed to solve the problems of the depression, however. By 1938, the French were experiencing a serious decline of confidence in their political system that left them unprepared to deal with their aggressive Nazi enemy to the east.

The Scandinavian States

The Scandinavian states were particularly successful in coping with the Great Depression. Socialist parties had grown steadily in the late nineteenth and early twentieth centuries and between the wars came to head the governments of Sweden, Denmark, Norway, and Finland. These Social Democratic governments encouraged the development of rural and industrial cooperative enterprises. Ninety percent of the Danish milk industry, for example, was organized on a cooperative basis by 1933. Privately owned and managed, Scandinavian cooperatives seemed to avoid the pitfalls of either Communist or purely capitalist economic systems.

Social Democratic governments also greatly expanded social services. Not only did Scandinavian governments increase old-age pensions and unemployment insurance, but they also provided such novel forms of assistance as subsidized housing, free prenatal care, maternity allowances, and annual paid vacations for workers. To achieve their social welfare states, the Scandinavian governments required high taxes and large bureaucracies, but these did not prevent both private and cooperative enterprises from prospering. Indeed, between 1900 and 1939, Sweden experienced a greater rise in real wages than any other European country.

The United States

After Germany, no Western nation was more affected by the Great Depression than the United States. By the end of 1932, industrial production was down almost 50 percent. By 1933, there were 15 million unemployed. Under these circumstances, the Democrat Franklin Delano Roosevelt (1882–1945) won the 1932 presidential election by a landslide.

Roosevelt and his advisers pursued a policy of active government intervention in the economy that came to be known as the New Deal. The first New Deal created a variety of agencies designed to bring relief, recovery, and reform. To support the nation's banks, the Federal Deposit Insurance Corporation was established; it insured the safety of bank deposits up to $5,000. The Federal Emergency Relief Administration provided funds to help states and local communities meet the needs of the destitute and the homeless. The Civilian Conservation Corps employed over 2 million people on reforestation projects and federal road and conservation projects.

By 1935, it was becoming apparent that the initial efforts of Roosevelt's administration had produced only a slow recovery at best. As his policies came under more and more criticism by people who advocated more radical change, Roosevelt inaugurated new efforts that collectively became known as the Second New Deal. These included a stepped-up program of public works, such as the Works Progress Administration (WPA), established in 1935. This government organization employed between 2 and 3 million people who worked at building bridges, roads, post offices, and airports. The Roosevelt administration was also responsible for social legislation that launched the American welfare state. In 1935, the Social Security Act created a system of old-age pensions and unemployment insurance. The National Labor Relations Act of 1935 encouraged the rapid growth of labor unions.

The New Deal provided some social reform measures that perhaps averted the possibility of social revolution in the United States. It did not, however, solve the unemployment problems of the Great Depression. After partial recovery between 1933 and 1937, the economy experienced another downturn during the winter of 1937–1938. In May 1937, American unemployment still stood at 7 million; by the following year, it had increased to 11 million. Only World War II and the subsequent growth of armaments industries brought American workers back to full employment.

European States and the World: The Colonial Empires

World War I and the Great Depression also had an impact on Europe's colonial empires. Despite the war, the Allied nations had managed to keep their colonial empires

CHRONOLOGY The Democratic States

Great Britain

First Labour Party government	1924
Conservative Party government	1924–1929
General strike	1926
Second Labour Party government	1929–1931
Beginnings of National Government coalition	1931

France

Cartel of the Left	1924–1926
Poincaré's government	1926–1929
Formation of the Popular Front	1936

United States

Election of Franklin D. Roosevelt	1932
Beginning of the New Deal	1933
Second New Deal	1935

intact. Great Britain and France had even added to their empires by dividing up many of Germany's colonial possessions and, as we have seen, taking control of large parts of the Middle East through a system of mandates.

Although Europe had emerged from World War I relatively intact, its political and social foundations and its self-confidence had been severely undermined. In Asia and Africa, a rising tide of unrest against European political domination began to emerge. That unrest took a variety of forms but was most notably displayed in increasing worker activism, rural protest, and a rising sense of national fervor. In areas of Asia and Africa, the discontent fostered by the war and later by the Great Depression led to movements for change.

The Middle East

For the countries of the Middle East, the period between the two world wars was a time of transition. With the fall of the Ottoman and Persian empires, new modernizing regimes emerged in Turkey and Iran. A fiercely independent government was established in Saudi Arabia in 1932. Iraq, too, gained its independence from Britain in the same year. Elsewhere in the Middle East, European influence remained strong; the British and French maintained their mandates in Syria, Lebanon, Jordan, and Palestine.

Although Britain and France had made plans to divide up Ottoman territories in the Middle East, Colonel Mustafa Kemal (1881–1938) led Turkish forces in creating a new republic of Turkey in 1923. Kemal wanted to modernize Turkey along Western lines. The trappings of a democratic system were put in place, although the new president did not tolerate opposition. In addition to introducing a state-run industrial system, Kemal also westernized Turkish culture. The Turkish language was now written using the Latin alphabet. Popular education was introduced, and old aristocratic titles were abolished. All Turkish citizens were

forced to adopt family names, in the European style (Kemal himself adopted the name Atatürk, meaning "Father Turk"). Atatürk made Turkey a secular republic and broke the power of the Islamic religion. New laws gave women equal rights with men in all aspects of marriage and inheritance, and in 1934, women received the right to vote. Education and the professions were now open to citizens of both sexes. By and large, the Turkish republic was the product of Atatürk's determined efforts to use nationalism and Western ways to create a modern Turkish nation.

India

By the time of World War I, the Indian people had already begun to refer to Mohandas Gandhi as India's "Great Soul," or Mahatma. Gandhi (1869–1948) set up a movement based on nonviolent resistance whose aim was to force the British to improve the lot of the poor and grant independence to India. When the British tried to suppress Indian calls for independence, Gandhi called on his followers to follow a peaceful policy of **civil disobedience** by refusing to obey British regulations. Gandhi also began to manufacture his own clothes and dressed in a simple *dhoti* or loincloth made of coarse homespun cotton. He adopted the spinning wheel as a symbol of India's resistance to imports of British textiles. Although the British resisted Gandhi's movement, in 1935 they granted India internal self-government. Independence, however, would have to wait until after World War II.

Africa

Black Africans who fought in World War I in the armies of the British and the French hoped for independence after the war. As one newspaper in the Gold Coast put it, if African volunteers who fought on European battlefields were "good enough to fight and die in the Empire's cause, they were good enough to have a share in the government of their countries." This feeling was shared by many. The peace settlement after World War I, then, turned out be a great disappointment. Germany was stripped of its African colonies, but they were awarded to the British and the French to administer as mandates for the League of Nations.

After World War I, Africans became more active politically. Africans who had fought in World War I had learned new ideas in the West about freedom and nationalism. Even in Africa itself, missionary schools had often taught their African pupils about liberty and equality. As more Africans became aware of the enormous gulf between Western ideals and practices, they decided to seek reform. Independence remained but a dream.

Protest took different forms. In Nigeria and South Africa, workers created trade unions that tried to gain benefits for workers. But there were also incidents of violent protest. In British Nigeria in 1929, a group of women protested the high taxes that were levied on the goods they were selling in the markets. During the riot that ensued, women cried for all white men to leave their country. The British killed fifty women and ended the riot. Although colonial powers responded to these protest movements with force, they also began to make some

Nehru and Gandhi. Mahatma Gandhi (on the right), India's "Great Soul," became the emotional leader of India's struggle for independence from British colonial rule. Unlike many other nationalist leaders, Gandhi rejected the materialistic culture of the West and urged his followers to return to the native traditions of the Indian village. To illustrate his point, Gandhi dressed in the simple Indian *dhoti* rather than in the Western fashion favored by many of his colleagues. With Gandhi, Jawaharlal Nehru (on the left) was a leading figure in the Indian struggle for independence. Unlike Gandhi, however, his goal was to transform India into a modern industrial society.

reforms in the hope of satisfying indigenous peoples. Reforms, however, were too few and too late, and by the 1930s, an increasing number of African leaders were calling for independence, not reform.

The clearest calls came from a new generation of young African leaders who had been educated in Europe and the United States. Those who went to the United States were especially influenced by the pan-African ideas of W. E. B. Du Bois (1868–1963) and Marcus Garvey (1887–1940). Du Bois, an African American educated at Harvard, was the leader of a movement that tried to make all Africans aware of their own cultural heritage. Garvey, a Jamaican who lived in Harlem in New York, also stressed the need for the unity of all Africans. Leaders and movements in individual African nations also appeared. In his book *Facing Mount Kenya,* Jomo Kenyatta (1894–1978) of Kenya, who had been educated in Great Britain, argued that British rule was destroying the traditional culture of the peoples of black Africa.

The Authoritarian and Totalitarian States

Q **Focus Questions:** Why did many European states experience a retreat from democracy in the interwar years? What are the characteristics of totalitarian states, and to what degree were these characteristics present in Fascist Italy, Nazi Germany, and Stalinist Russia?

The apparent triumph of liberal democracy in 1919 proved extremely short-lived. By 1939, only two major states (Great Britain and France) and several minor ones

(the Low Countries, the Scandinavian states, Switzerland, and Czechoslovakia) remained democratic. What had happened to Woodrow Wilson's claim that World War I had been fought to make the world safe for democracy? Actually, World War I turned out to have had the opposite effect.

The Retreat from Democracy

The postwar expansion of the electorate made mass politics a reality and seemed to enhance the spread of democracy in Europe. But the war itself had created conditions that led the new mass electorate to distrust democracy and move toward a more radicalized politics.

Many postwar societies were badly divided, especially along class lines. During the war, to maintain war production, governments had been forced to make concessions to trade unions and socialist parties, which strengthened the working class after the war. At the same time, the position of many middle-class people had declined as consumer industries had been curtailed during the war and war bonds, which had been purchased by the middle classes as their patriotic contribution to the war effort, sank in value and even became worthless in some countries.

Gender divisions also weakened social cohesion. After the war, as soldiers returned home, women were forced out of jobs they had taken during the war, jobs that many newly independent women wanted to retain. The loss of so many men during the war had also left many younger women with no marital prospects and widows with no choice but to find jobs in the labor force. At the same time, fears about a declining population because of the war led many male political leaders to encourage women to return to their traditional roles as

AP Images/Max Desfor

wives and mothers. Many European countries outlawed abortions and curtailed the sale of birth control devices while providing increased welfare benefits to entice women to remain at home and bear children.

The Great Depression served to deepen social conflict. Larger and larger numbers of people felt victimized, first by the war, and now by socioeconomic conditions that seemed beyond their control. Postwar politics became more and more polarized as people reverted to the wartime practice of dividing into friends and enemies, downplaying compromise and emphasizing conflict. Moderate centrist parties that supported democracy soon found themselves with fewer and fewer allies as people became increasingly radicalized politically, supporting the extremes of left-wing communism or right-wing fascism. In the 1920s, Italy had become the first Fascist state while the Soviet Union moved toward a repressive **totalitarian state.** In the 1930s, a host of other European states adopted authoritarian structures of various kinds.

The dictatorial regimes between the wars assumed both old and new forms. Dictatorship was not a new phenomenon, but the modern totalitarian state was. The totalitarian regimes, whose best examples can be found in Stalinist Russia and Nazi Germany, extended the functions and power of the central state far beyond what they had been in the past. The immediate origins of totalitarianism can be found in the total warfare of World War I when governments, even in the democratic states, exercised controls over economic, political, and personal freedom in order to achieve victory.

The modern totalitarian state expected the active loyalty and commitment of citizens to the regime's goals. It used modern mass **propaganda** techniques and high-speed modern communications to conquer the minds and hearts of its subjects. The total state aimed to control not only the economic, political, and social aspects of life but the intellectual and cultural aspects as well. But that control also had a purpose: the active involvement of the masses in the achievement of the regime's goals, whether they be war, a socialist state, or a thousand-year Reich.

The modern totalitarian state was to be led by a single leader and a single party. It ruthlessly rejected the liberal ideal of limited government power and constitutional guarantees of individual freedoms. Indeed, individual freedom was to be subordinated to the collective will of the masses, organized and determined for them by a leader or leaders. Modern technology also gave total states unprecedented police controls to enforce their wishes on their subjects.

Totalitarianism is an abstract term, and no state followed all its theoretical implications. The fascist states—Italy and Nazi Germany—as well as Stalin's Soviet Union have all been labeled totalitarian, although their regimes exhibited significant differences and met with varying degrees of success. Totalitarianism transcended traditional political labels. Fascism in Italy and Nazism in Germany grew out of extreme rightist preoccupations with nationalism and, in the case of Germany, with racism. Communism in the Soviet Union emerged out of Marxist socialism, a radical leftist program. Thus, totalitarianism could and did exist in what were perceived as extreme right-wing and left-wing regimes. This fact helped bring about a new concept of the political spectrum in which the extremes were no longer seen as opposites on a linear scale but came to be viewed as similar to each other in at least some respects.

Fascist Italy

In the early 1920s, in the wake of economic turmoil, political disorder, and the general insecurity and fear stemming from World War I, Benito Mussolini burst onto the Italian scene with the first fascist movement in Europe.

Impact of World War I   As a new European state after 1870, Italy faced a number of serious problems that were only magnified when it became a belligerent in World War I. An estimated 700,000 Italian soldiers died, and the treasury reckoned the cost of the war at 148 billion lire, twice the sum of all government expenditures between 1861 and 1913. Italy did gain some territory, namely, Trieste, and a new northern border that included the formerly Austrian South Tyrol area. Italy's demands for Fiume and Dalmatia on the Adriatic coast were rejected, however, which gave rise to the myth that Italy had been cheated of its just rewards by the other victors. The war created immense domestic confusion. Inflation undermined middle-class security. Demobilization of the troops created high unemployment and huge groups of dissatisfied veterans. The government proved unable to deal effectively with these problems.

Gained Italian Territory

The Birth of Fascism   Benito Mussolini (1883–1945) was an unruly and rebellious child who ultimately received a diploma as an elementary school teacher. After an unsuccessful stint as a teacher, Mussolini became a socialist and gradually became well known in Italian socialist circles. In 1912, he obtained the important position of editor of *Avanti* (Forward), the official socialist daily newspaper. After editorially switching his position from ardent neutrality, the socialist position, to intervention in World War I, he was expelled from the Socialist Party.

In 1919, Mussolini laid the foundations for a new political movement that came to be called fascism after the name of his group, the *Fascio di Combattimento* (League of Combat). It received little attention in the elections of 1919, but political stalemate in Italy's parliamentary system and strong nationalist sentiment saved Mussolini and the Fascists.

The new parliament elected in November quickly proved incapable of governing Italy. Three major parties, the Socialists, Liberals, and Popolari (or Christian Democrats, a new Catholic party formed in January 1919), were unable to form an effective coalition. The Socialists, who had now become the largest party, spoke theoretically of the need for revolution, which alarmed conservatives, who quickly associated them with Bolsheviks or Communists. Thousands of industrial and agricultural strikes in 1919 and 1920 created a climate of class warfare and continual violence. Mussolini shifted quickly from leftist to rightist politics and began to gain support from middle-class industrialists fearful of working-class agitation and large landowners who objected to the agricultural strikes. Mussolini also perceived that Italians were angry over Italy's failure to receive more fruits of victory in the form of territorial acquisitions after World War I. He realized then that anticommunism, antistrike activity, and nationalist rhetoric combined with the use of brute force might help him obtain what he had been unable to achieve in free elections.

In 1920 and 1921, bands of armed Fascists called *squadristi* were formed and turned loose in attacks on Socialist offices and newspapers. Strikes by trade unionists and Socialist workers and peasant leagues were broken up by force. At the same time, Mussolini entered into a political alliance with the Liberals under then Prime Minister Giovanni Giolitti. No doubt, Giolitti and the Liberals believed that the Fascists could be used to crush socialism temporarily and then be dropped. In this game of mutual deceit, Mussolini soon proved to be the more skillful player. By allying with the government coalition, he gained respectability and a free hand for his violent *squadristi*. Mussolini's efforts were rewarded when the Fascists won thirty-five parliamentary seats, or 7 percent of the total, in the election of May 1921.

The use of violence was crucial to Mussolini's plans. By 1921, the black-shirted Fascist squads numbered 200,000 and had become a regular feature of Italian life. World War I veterans and students were especially attracted to the *squadristi* and relished the opportunity to use unrestrained violence. Administering large doses of castor oil to unwilling victims became one of their favorite tactics.

Mussolini and the Fascists believed that these terrorist tactics would eventually achieve political victory. They deliberately created conditions of disorder knowing that fascism would flourish in such an environment. The Fascists construed themselves as the party of order and drew the bulk of their support from the middle and upper classes; white-collar workers, professionals and civil servants, landowners, merchants and artisans, and students made up almost 60 percent of the membership of the Fascist Party. The middle-class fear of socialism, Communist revolution, and disorder made the Fascists attractive.

As the Italian political situation deteriorated further, Mussolini and the Fascists were emboldened to plan a march on Rome in order to seize power. In a speech in Naples to Fascist Blackshirts on October 24, 1922, Mussolini exclaimed, "Either we are allowed to govern, or we will seize power by marching on Rome" to "take by the throat the miserable political class that governs us."[4] Bold words, but in truth the planned march on Rome was a calculated bluff to frighten the government into giving them power. The bluff worked, and the government capitulated even before the march occurred. On October 29, 1922, King Victor Emmanuel III (1900–1946) made Mussolini prime minister of Italy. Twenty-four hours later, the Fascist Blackshirts were allowed to march into Rome in order to create the myth that they had gained power by an armed insurrection after a civil war.

Mussolini and the Italian Fascist State Since the Fascists constituted but a small minority in parliament, the new prime minister was forced to move slowly. In the summer of 1923, Mussolini began to prepare for a national election that would consolidate the power of his Fascist government and give him a more secure base from which to govern. In July 1923, parliament enacted the Acerbo Law, which stipulated that any party winning at least 25 percent of the votes in the next national election would automatically be allotted two-thirds of the seats in parliament. The national elections that were subsequently held on April 6, 1924, resulted in an enormous victory for the Fascists. They won 65 percent of the votes and garnered 374 seats out of a total of 535 in parliament. Although the elections were conducted in an atmosphere of Fascist fraud, force, and intimidation, the size of the victory indicated the growing popularity of Mussolini and his Fascists.

By 1926, Mussolini had established his Fascist dictatorship. Press laws gave the government the right to suspend any publications that fostered disrespect for the Catholic Church, the monarchy, or the state. The prime minister was made "head of government" with the power to legislate by decree. A police law empowered the police to arrest and confine anybody for nonpolitical or political crimes without due process of law. The government was given the power to dissolve political and cultural associations. In 1926, all anti-Fascist parties were outlawed. A secret police, known as the OVRA, was also established. By the end of 1926, Mussolini ruled Italy as *Il Duce,* the leader.

Mussolini conceived of the Fascist state as totalitarian: "Fascism is totalitarian, and the Fascist State, the synthesis and unity of all values, interprets, develops and gives strength to the whole life of the people"[5] (see the box on p. 816). Mussolini did try to create a police state, but police activities in Italy were never as repressive, efficient, or savage as those of Nazi Germany. Likewise, the Italian Fascists' attempt to exercise control over all forms of mass media, including newspapers, radio, and cinema, so that they could use propaganda as an instrument to

Mussolini, the Iron Duce. One of Mussolini's favorite images of himself was that of the Iron Duce—the strong leader who is always right. Consequently, he was often seen in military-style uniforms and military poses. This photograph shows Mussolini in one of his numerous uniforms with his Blackshirt bodyguards giving the Fascist salute.

integrate the masses into the state, failed to achieve its major goals. Most commonly, Fascist propaganda was disseminated through simple slogans, such as "Mussolini is always right," plastered on walls all over Italy.

Mussolini and the Fascists also attempted to mold Italians into a single-minded community by pursuing a Fascist educational policy and developing Fascist organizations. Because the secondary schools maintained considerable freedom from Fascist control, the regime relied more and more on the activities of youth organizations, known as the Young Fascists, to indoctrinate the young people of the nation in Fascist ideals. By 1939, about 6.8 million children, teenagers, and young adults of both sexes, or 66 percent of the population between eight and eighteen, were enrolled in some kind of Fascist youth group. Activities for these groups included unpopular Saturday afternoon marching drills and calisthenics, seaside and mountain summer camps, and competitions. An underlying motif for all of these activities was the Fascist insistence on militarization. Beginning in the 1930s, all male groups were given some kind of pre-military exercises to develop discipline and provide training for war. Results were mixed. Italian teenagers, who liked neither military training nor routine discipline of any kind, simply refused to attend Fascist youth meetings on a regular basis.

The Fascist organizations hoped to create a new Italian, hardworking, physically fit, disciplined, intellectually sharp, and martially inclined. In practice, the Fascists largely reinforced traditional social attitudes in Italy, as is evident in their policies regarding women. The Fascists portrayed the family as the pillar of the state and women as the basic foundation of the family. "Woman into the home" became the Fascist slogan. Women were to be homemakers and baby producers, "their natural and fundamental mission in life," according to Mussolini, who viewed population growth as an indicator of national strength. To Mussolini, female emancipation was "unfascist." Employment outside the home was an impediment distracting women from conception. "It forms an independence and consequent physical and moral habits contrary to child bearing."[6] A practical consideration also underlay the Fascist attitude toward women: eliminating women from the job market reduced male unemployment figures in the depression economy of the 1930s.

In the 1930s, the Fascists translated their attitude toward women into law with a series of enactments aimed at encouraging larger families. Families with many offspring were offered supplementary pay, loans, prizes, and subsidies, and mothers of many children received gold medals. A national "Mother and Child" holiday was celebrated on December 24, with prizes awarded for fertility. Also in the 1930s, decrees were passed that set quotas on the employment of women, but they were not successful in accomplishing their goal.

Despite the instruments of repression, the use of propaganda, and the creation of numerous Fascist organizations, Mussolini failed to attain the degree of totalitarian control achieved in Hitler's Germany or Stalin's Soviet Union. Mussolini and the Fascist Party never really destroyed the old power structure. Some institutions, including the armed forces and the monarchy, were never absorbed into the Fascist state and managed to maintain their independence. Mussolini had boasted that he would

THE VOICE OF ITALIAN FASCISM

In 1932, an article on fascism appeared in the *Italian Encyclopedia.* Attributed to Mussolini, it was largely written by the philosopher Giovanni Gentile. Mussolini had always argued that fascism was based only on the need for action, not on doctrines, but after its success, he felt the need to summarize the basic political and social ideas of fascism. These excerpts are taken from that article.

Benito Mussolini, "The Political and Social Doctrine of Fascism"

Above all, Fascism...believes neither in the possibility nor the utility of perpetual peace. It thus repudiates the doctrine of Pacifism—born of a renunciation of struggle and an act of cowardice in the face of sacrifice. War alone brings up to its highest tension all human energy and puts the stamp of nobility upon the peoples who have the courage to meet it. All other trials are substitutes, which never really put men into the position where they have to make the great decision—the alternative of life or death. Thus a doctrine which is founded upon this harmful postulate of peace is hostile to Fascism.... Thus the Fascist accepts life and loves it, knowing nothing of and despising suicide: he rather conceives of life as duty and struggle and conquest....

Fascism is the complete opposite of Marxian socialism, the materialist conception of history; according to which the history of human civilization can be explained simply through the conflict of interests among the various social groups and by the change and development in the means and instruments of production. That the changes in the economic field have their importance no one can deny; but that these factors are sufficient to explain the history of humanity excluding all others is an absurd delusion. Fascism, now and always, believes in holiness and in heroism; that is to say, in actions influenced by no economic motive, direct or indirect....

After Socialism, Fascism combats the whole complex system of democratic ideology, and repudiates it, whether in its theoretical premises or in its practical application. Fascism denies that the majority, by the simple fact that it is a majority, can direct human society; it denies that numbers alone can govern by means of a periodical consultation, and it affirms the immutable, beneficial, and fruitful inequality of mankind, which can never be permanently leveled through the mere operation of a mechanical process such as universal suffrage.

The foundation of Fascism is the conception of the State, its character, its duty and its aim. Fascism conceives of the State as an absolute, in comparison with which all individuals or groups are relative, only to be conceived of in their relation to the State.... The Fascist state organizes the nation, but leaves a sufficient margin of liberty to the individual; the latter is deprived of all useless and possibly harmful freedom, but retains what is essential; the deciding power in the question cannot be the individual, but the State alone....

For Fascism, the growth of empire, that is to say the expansion of the nation, is an essential manifestation of vitality, and its opposite a sign of decadence. Peoples which are rising, or rising again after a period of decadence, are always imperialist; any renunciation is a sign of decay and of death. Fascism is the doctrine best adapted to represent the tendencies and the aspirations of a people, like the people of Italy, who are rising again after many centuries of abasement and foreign servitude. But Empire demands discipline, the coordination of all forces and a deeply felt sense of duty and sacrifice.

Q *In Mussolini's view, what were the basic principles of Italian Fascism? Why might such principles have appealed to a broad public in the aftermath of World War I?*

---

help the workers and peasants, but instead he generally allied himself with the interests of the industrialists and large landowners at the expense of the lower classes.

Even more indicative of Mussolini's compromise with the traditional institutions of Italy was his attempt to gain the support of the Catholic Church. In the Lateran Accords of February 1929, Mussolini's regime recognized the sovereign independence of a small enclave of 109 acres within Rome, known as Vatican City, which had remained in the church's possession since the unification of Italy in 1870; in return, the papacy recognized the Italian state. The Lateran Accords also guaranteed the church a large grant of money and recognized Catholicism as the "sole religion of the state." In return, the Catholic Church urged Italians to support the Fascist regime.

In all areas of Italian life under Mussolini and the Fascists, there was a noticeable dichotomy between Fascist ideals and practice. The Italian Fascists promised much but delivered considerably less, and they were soon overshadowed by a much more powerful fascist movement to the north.

Hitler and Nazi Germany

In 1923, a small rightist party, known as the Nazis, led by an obscure Austrian rabble-rouser named Adolf Hitler, tried to seize power in southern Germany in conscious imitation of Mussolini's march on Rome in 1922. Although the attempt failed, Hitler and the Nazis achieved sudden national prominence. Within ten years, they had taken over complete power.

Weimar Germany After Germany's defeat in World War I, a German democratic state known as the Weimar

CHRONOLOGY Fascist Italy

Creation of *Fascio di Combattimento*	1919
Squadristi violence	1920–1921
Fascists win thirty-five seats in Parliament	1921
Mussolini is made prime minister	1922
Acerbo Law	1923
Electoral victory for Fascists	1924
Establishment of Fascist dictatorship	1925–1926
Lateran Accords with Catholic Church	1929

Republic had been established. From its beginnings, the Weimar Republic was plagued by problems. One problem was that it had no outstanding political leaders. In 1925, Paul von Hindenburg, the World War I military hero, was elected president. Hindenburg was a traditional military man, monarchist in sentiment, who at heart was not in favor of the republic. The young republic also suffered politically from attempted uprisings and attacks from both the left and the right.

The Weimar Republic also faced serious economic difficulties. The runaway inflation of 1922 and 1923 had serious social repercussions. Widows, orphans, the retired elderly, army officers, teachers, civil servants, and others who lived on fixed incomes all watched their monthly stipends become worthless and their lifetime savings disappear. Their economic losses increasingly pushed the middle class to the rightist parties that were hostile to the republic. To make matters worse, after a period of prosperity from 1924 to 1929, Germany faced the Great Depression. Unemployment increased to nearly 4.4 million by December 1930. The depression paved the way for social discontent, fear, and extremist parties. The political, economic, and social problems of the Weimar Republic provided an environment in which Hitler and the Nazis were able to rise to power.

The Emergence of Adolf Hitler Born in 1889, Adolf Hitler was the son of an Austrian customs official. He was a total failure in secondary school and eventually made his way to Vienna to become an artist. Though he was rejected by the Vienna Academy of Fine Arts, Hitler stayed on in Vienna to live the bohemian lifestyle of an artist. In his autobiography, *Mein Kampf* (My Struggle), Hitler characterized his years in Vienna from 1908 to 1913 as an important formative period in his life: "In this period there took shape within me a world picture and a philosophy which became the granite foundation of all my acts. In addition to what I then created, I have had to learn little, and I have had to alter nothing."[7]

In Vienna, then, Hitler established the basic ideas of an ideology from which he never deviated for the rest of his life. At the core of Hitler's ideas was racism, especially anti-Semitism (see the box on p. 818). His hatred of the Jews lasted to the very end of his life. Hitler also became

an extreme German nationalist who learned from the mass politics of Vienna how political parties could effectively use propaganda and terror. Finally, in his Viennese years, Hitler also came to a firm belief in the need for struggle, which he saw as the "granite foundation of the world."

In 1913, Hitler moved to Munich, still without purpose and with no real future in sight. World War I saved him: "Overpowered by stormy enthusiasm, I fell down on my knees and thanked Heaven from an overflowing heart for granting me the good fortune of being permitted to live at this time."[8] As a dispatch runner on the Western Front, Hitler distinguished himself by his brave acts. At the end of the war, finding again that his life had no purpose or meaning, he returned to Munich and decided to enter politics and found, at last, his true profession.

The Rise of the Nazis Hitler joined the obscure German Workers' Party, one of a number of right-wing extreme nationalist parties in Munich. By the summer of 1921, Hitler had assumed total control of the party, which he renamed the National Socialist German Workers' Party, or Nazi for short (from the first two syllables of its German name). His idea was that the party's name would distinguish the Nazis from the socialist parties while gaining support from both working-class and nationalist circles. Hitler worked assiduously to develop the party into a mass political movement with flags, badges, uniforms, its own newspaper, and its own police force or militia known as the SA, the *Sturmabteilung*, or Storm Troops. The SA was used to defend the party in meeting halls and to break up the meetings of other parties. Hitler's own oratorical skills were largely responsible for attracting an increasing number of followers. By 1923, the party had grown from its early hundreds into a membership of 55,000, plus another 15,000 in the SA.

When it appeared that the Weimar Republic was on the verge of collapse in the fall of 1923, the Nazis and other right-wing leaders in the south German state of Bavaria decided to march on Berlin to overthrow the Weimar government. When his fellow conspirators reneged, Hitler and the Nazis decided to act on their own by staging an armed uprising in Munich on November 8. The so-called Beer Hall Putsch was quickly crushed. Hitler was arrested, put on trial for treason, and sentenced to prison.

During his brief stay in prison, Hitler wrote *Mein Kampf,* an autobiographical account of his movement and its underlying ideology. Extreme German nationalism, virulent anti-Semitism, and vicious anti-communism are linked together by a social Darwinian theory of struggle that stresses the right of superior nations to **Lebensraum** (living space) through expansion and the right of superior individuals to secure authoritarian leadership over the masses. What is perhaps most remarkable about *Mein Kampf* is its

ADOLF HITLER'S HATRED OF THE JEWS

A believer in Aryan racial supremacy, Adolf Hitler viewed the Jews as the archenemies of the Aryans. He believed that the first task of a true Aryan state would be the elimination of the Jewish threat. This is why Hitler's political career both began and ended with a warning against the Jews. In this excerpt from his autobiography, *Mein Kampf*, Hitler describes how he came to be an anti-Semite when he lived in Vienna in his early twenties.

Adolf Hitler, *Mein Kampf*

My views with regard to anti-Semitism thus succumbed to the passage of time, and this was my greatest transformation of all....

Once, as I was strolling through the Inner City [of Vienna], I suddenly encountered an apparition in a black caftan and black hair locks. Is this a Jew? was my first thought.

For, to be sure, they had not looked like that in Linz. I observed the man furtively and cautiously, but the longer I stared at this foreign face, scrutinizing feature for feature, the more my first question assumed a new form:

Is this a German?

As always in such cases, I now began to try to relieve my doubts by books. For a few pennies I bought the first anti-Semitic pamphlets of my life....

Yet I could no longer very well doubt that the objects of my study were not Germans of a special religion, but a people in themselves; for since I had begun to concern myself with this question and to take cognizance of the Jews, Vienna appeared to me in a different light than before. Wherever I went, I began to see Jews, and the more I saw, the more sharply they became distinguished in my eyes from the rest of humanity....

In a short time I was made more thoughtful than ever by my slowly rising insight into the type of activity carried on by the Jews in certain fields.

Was there any form of filth or profligacy, particularly in cultural life, without at least one Jew involved in it?...

Sometimes I stood there thunderstruck.

I didn't know what to be more amazed at: the agility of their tongues or their virtuosity at lying.

Gradually I began to hate them.

Q *What was Hitler's attitude toward the Jews? Why do you think such crazed views became acceptable (or at least tolerable) to large numbers of ordinary Germans in the aftermath of World War I?*

---

elaboration of a series of ideas that directed Hitler's actions once he took power. That others refused to take Hitler and his ideas seriously was one of his greatest advantages.

Hitler's New Tactics The Beer Hall Putsch proved to be a major turning point in Hitler's career. Rather than discouraging him, his trial and imprisonment reinforced his faith in himself and in his mission. He now clearly

Hitler and the Blood Flag Ritual. In developing his mass political movement, Adolf Hitler used ritualistic ceremonies as a means of binding party members to his own person. Here Hitler is shown touching the "blood flag," which had supposedly been stained with the blood of Nazis killed during the Beer Hall Putsch, to an SS banner while the SS standard-bearer makes a "blood oath" of allegiance: "I vow to remain true to my Führer, Adolf Hitler. I bind myself to carry out all orders conscientiously and without reluctance. Standards and flags shall be sacred to me." The SS originated as Hitler's personal bodyguard and later became a secret police force and instrument of terror in the Nazi state.

understood the need for a change in tactics. If the Nazis could not overthrow the Weimar Republic by force, they would have to use constitutional means to gain power. This implied the formation of a mass political movement that would actively compete for votes with the other political parties.

After his release from prison, Hitler set about organizing the Nazi Party for the lawful takeover of power. His position on leadership in the party was quite clear. There was to be no discussion of ideas in the party, and the party was to follow the *Führerprinzip*, the leadership principle, which entailed nothing less than a single-minded party under one leader. As Hitler expressed it, "A good National Socialist is one who would let himself be killed for his Führer at any time."[9]

In the late 1920s, Hitler reorganized the Nazi Party on a regional basis and expanded it to all parts of Germany. By 1929, the Nazis had a national party organization. The party also grew from 27,000 members in 1925 to 178,000 by the end of 1929. Especially noticeable was the youthfulness of the regional, district, and branch leaders of the Nazi organization. Many were under thirty and were fiercely committed to Hitler because he gave them the kind of active politics they sought. Rather than democratic debate, they wanted brawls in beer halls, enthusiastic speeches, and comradeship in the building of a new Germany. One new young Nazi member expressed his excitement about the party:

> For me this was the start of a completely new life. There was only one thing in the world for me and that was service in the movement. All my thoughts were centered on the movement. I could talk only politics. I was no longer aware of anything else. At the time I was a promising athlete; I was very keen on sport, and it was going to be my career. But I had to give this up too. My only interest was agitation and propaganda.[10]

Such youthful enthusiasm gave Nazism the aura of a "young man's movement" and a sense of dynamism that the other parties could not match.

By 1929, the Nazi Party had also made a significant shift in strategy. Between 1925 and 1927, Hitler and the Nazis had pursued an urban strategy geared toward winning workers from the socialists and Communists. But failure in the 1928 elections, when the Nazis gained only 2.6 percent of the vote and twelve seats in the Reichstag (parliament), convinced Hitler of the need for a change. By 1929, the party began to pursue middle-class and lower-middle-class votes in small towns and rural areas, especially in northern, central, and eastern Germany.

Germany's economic difficulties paved the way for the Nazis' rise to power. Unemployment rose dramatically, from 4.35 million in 1931 to 6 million by the winter of 1932. The economic and psychological impact of the Great Depression made the radical solutions offered by extremist parties appear more attractive. Already in the Reichstag elections of September 1930, the Nazis polled 18 percent of the vote and gained 107 seats in the Reichstag, making the Nazi Party one of the largest in Germany.

By 1930, Chancellor Heinrich Brüning (1885–1970) had found it impossible to form a working parliamentary majority in the Reichstag and relied on the use of emergency decrees by President Hindenburg to rule. In a real sense, then, parliamentary democracy was already dying in 1930, three years before Hitler destroyed it.

The Nazi Seizure of Power Hitler's quest for power from late 1930 to early 1933 depended on the political maneuvering around President Hindenburg. Nevertheless, the elections from 1930 through 1932 were indirectly responsible for the Nazis' rise to power since they showed the importance of the Nazi Party. The party itself grew dramatically during this period, from 289,000 members in September 1930 to 800,000 by 1932. The SA also rose to 500,000 members.

The Nazis proved very effective in developing modern electioneering techniques. In their election campaigns, party members pitched their themes to the needs and fears of different social groups. But even as they were making blatant appeals to class interests, the Nazis were denouncing conflicts of interest and maintaining that they stood above classes and parties. Hitler, in particular, claimed to stand above all differences and promised to create a new Germany free of class differences and party infighting. His appeal to national pride, national honor, and traditional militarism struck chords of emotion in his listeners.

Elections, however, proved to have their limits. In the elections of July 1932, the Nazis won 230 seats, making them the largest party in the Reichstag. But four months later, in November, they declined to 196 seats. It became apparent to many Nazis that they would not gain power simply by the ballot box. Hitler saw clearly, however, that the Reichstag after 1930 was not all that important, since the government ruled by decree with the support of President Hindenburg. Increasingly, the right-wing elites of Germany—the industrial magnates, landed aristocrats, military establishment, and higher bureaucrats—came to see Hitler as the man who had the mass support to establish a right-wing, authoritarian regime that would save Germany and their privileged positions from a Communist takeover. These people almost certainly thought that they could control Hitler and, like many others, may well have underestimated his abilities. Under pressure from these elites, President Hindenburg agreed to allow Hitler to become chancellor (on January 30, 1933) and form a new government.

Within two months, Hitler had laid the foundations for the Nazis' complete control over Germany. One of Hitler's important cohorts, Hermann Göring (1893–1946), had been made minister of the interior and hence head of the police of the Prussian state, the largest of the federal states in Germany. He used his power to purge the police of non-Nazis and to establish an auxiliary police force composed of SA members. This action legitimized Nazi terror. On the day after a fire broke out in the Reichstag building (February 27), supposedly set by the Communists, Hitler was also able to convince President Hindenburg to issue a decree that gave the government emergency powers. It suspended all basic rights of citizens for the full duration of the emergency, thus enabling the Nazis to arrest and imprison anyone without redress.

The crowning step of Hitler's legal seizure of power came on March 23 when a two-thirds majority of the Reichstag passed the Enabling Act, which empowered the government to dispense with constitutional forms for four years while it issued laws that would deal with the country's problems. In effect, Hitler became a dictator appointed by the parliamentary body itself.

With their new source of power, the Nazis acted quickly to enforce *Gleichschaltung,* the coordination of all institutions under Nazi control. The civil service was purged of Jews and democratic elements, concentration camps were established for opponents of the new regime, the autonomy of the federal states was eliminated, trade unions were dissolved and swallowed up by the gigantic Labor Front, and all political parties except the Nazis were abolished. By the end of the summer of 1933, within seven months of being appointed chancellor, Hitler and the Nazis had established the foundations for a totalitarian state.

Why had this seizure of power been so quick and easy? The Nazis were not only ruthless in their use of force but ready to take control. The depression had weakened what little faith the Germans had in their democratic state. But negative factors alone cannot explain the Nazi success. To many Germans, the Nazis offered a national awakening. "Germany awake," one of the many Nazi slogans, had a powerful appeal to a people psychologically crushed by their defeat in World War I. The Nazis presented a strong image of a dynamic new Germany that was above parties and above classes.

By the end of 1933, there were only two sources of potential danger to Hitler's authority: the armed forces and the SA within his own party. The SA, under the leadership of Ernst Röhm, openly criticized Hitler and spoke of the need for a "second revolution" and the replacement of the regular army by the SA. Neither the army nor Hitler favored such a possibility. Hitler solved both problems simultaneously on June 30, 1934, by having Röhm and a number of other SA leaders killed in return for the army's support in allowing Hitler to succeed Hindenburg when the president died. When Hindenburg died on August 2, 1934, the office of president was abolished, and Hitler became sole ruler of Germany. Public officials and soldiers were all required to take a personal oath of loyalty to Hitler as the "Führer of the German Reich and people." The Third Reich had begun.

The Nazi State (1933–1939) Having smashed the parliamentary state, Hitler now felt that the real task was at hand: to develop the "total state." Hitler's aims had not been simply power for power's sake or a tyranny based on personal ambition. He had larger ideological goals. The development of an Aryan racial state that would dominate Europe and possibly the world for generations to come required a massive movement in which the German people would be actively involved, not passively cowed by force. Hitler stated:

> We must develop organizations in which an individual's entire life can take place. Then every activity and every need of every individual will be regulated by the collectivity represented by the party. There is no longer any arbitrary will, there are no longer any free realms in which the individual belongs to himself.... The time of personal happiness is over.[11]

The Nazis pursued the creation of this totalitarian state in a variety of ways. Mass demonstrations and spectacles were employed to integrate the German nation into a collective fellowship and to mobilize it as an instrument for

Hugo Jaeger/Time & Life Pictures/Getty Images

The Nazi Mass Spectacle. Hitler and the Nazis made clever use of mass spectacles to rally the German people behind the Nazi regime. These mass demonstrations evoked intense enthusiasm, as is evident in this photograph of Hitler arriving at the Bückeberg near Hamelin for the Harvest Festival in 1937. Almost one million people were present for the celebration.

PROPAGANDA AND MASS MEETINGS IN NAZI GERMANY

Propaganda and mass rallies were two of the chief instruments that Hitler used to prepare the German people for the tasks he set before them. In the first selection, taken from a speech to a crowd at Nuremberg, Hitler describes the kind of mystical bond he hoped to create through his mass rallies. In the second excerpt, a Hamburg schoolteacher provides her impression of a Hitler rally.

Adolf Hitler, Speech at the Nuremberg Party Rally, 1936

Do we not feel once again in this hour the miracle that brought us together? Once you heard the voice of a man, and it struck deep into your hearts; it awakened you, and you followed this voice. Year after year you went after it, though him who had spoken you never even saw. You heard only a voice, and you followed it. When we meet each other here, the wonder of our coming together fills us all. Not everyone of you sees me, and I do not see everyone of you. But I feel you, and you feel me. It is the belief in our people that has made us small men great, that has made us poor men rich, that has made brave and courageous men out of us wavering, spiritless, timid folk; this belief made us see our road when we were astray; it joined us together into one whole! . . . You come, that . . . you may, once in a while, gain the feeling that now we are together; we are with him and he with us, and we are now Germany!

A Teacher's Impression of a Hitler Rally, 1932

The April sun shone hot like in summer and turned everything into a picture of gay expectation. There was immaculate order and discipline, although the police left the whole square to the stewards and stood on the sidelines. Nobody spoke of "Hitler," always just "the Führer," "the Führer says," "the Führer wants," and what he said and wanted seemed right and good. The hours passed, the sun shone, expectations rose. In the background, at the edge of the track there were columns of carriers like ammunition carriers. . . . Aeroplanes above us. Testing of the loudspeakers, buzzing of the cine-cameras. It was nearly 3 P.M. "The Führer is coming!" A ripple went through the crowds. Around the speaker's platform one could see hands raised in the Hitler salute. A speaker opened the meeting, abused the "system," nobody listened to him. A second speaker welcomed Hitler and made way for the man who had drawn 120,000 people of all classes and ages. There stood Hitler in a simple black coat and looked over the crowd, waiting—a forest of swastika pennants swished up, the jubilation of this moment was given vent in a roaring salute. Main theme: Out of parties shall grow a nation, the German nation. He censured the "system" ("I want to know what there is left to be ruined in this state!"). "On the way here Socialists confronted me with a poster, 'Turn back, Adolf Hitler.' Thirteen years ago I was a simple unknown soldier. I went my way. I never turned back. Nor shall I turn back now." Otherwise he made no personal attacks, nor any promises, vague or definite. His voice was hoarse after all his speaking during the previous days. When the speech was over, there was roaring enthusiasm and applause. Hitler saluted, gave his thanks, the Horst Wessel song sounded out across the course. Hitler was helped into his coat. Then he went.—How many look up to him with touching faith! as their helper, their savior, their deliverer from unbearable distress—to him who rescues the Prussian prince, the scholar, the clergyman, the farmer, the worker, the unemployed, who rescues them from the parties back into the nation.

Q *In Hitler's view, what would mass meetings accomplish for his movement? How do mass rallies further the development of nationalism?*

Hitler's policies. These mass demonstrations, especially the Nuremberg party rallies that were held every September and the Harvest Festivals celebrated at the Bückeberg near Hamelin every fall, combined the symbolism of a religious service with the merriment of a popular amusement. They had great appeal and usually evoked mass enthusiasm and excitement (see the box above).

Some features of the state apparatus of Hitler's total state seem contradictory. One usually thinks of Nazi Germany as having an all-powerful government that maintained absolute control and order. In truth, Nazi Germany was the scene of almost constant personal and institutional conflict, which resulted in administrative chaos. Incessant struggle characterized relationships within the party, within the state, and between party and state. By fostering rivalry within the party and between party and state, Hitler became the ultimate decision maker.

In the economic sphere, Hitler and the Nazis also established control, but industry was not nationalized, as the left wing of the Nazi Party wanted. Hitler felt that it was irrelevant who owned the means of production so long as the owners recognized their master. Although the regime pursued the use of public works projects and "pump-priming" grants to private construction firms to foster employment and end the depression, there is little doubt that rearmament did far more to solve the unemployment problem. Unemployment, which had stood at 6 million in 1932, dropped to 2.6 million in 1934 and less than 500,000 in 1937. The regime claimed full credit for solving Germany's economic woes, and the improved economy was an important factor in convincing many Germans to accept the new regime, despite its excesses.

The German Labor Front under Robert Ley regulated the world of labor. The Labor Front was a state-controlled union. To control all laborers, it used the workbook. Every salaried worker had to have one in order to hold a job. Only by submitting to the policies of the Nazi-controlled Labor Front could a worker obtain and retain a workbook. The Labor Front also sponsored activities to keep the workers happy (see "Mass Leisure" later in this chapter).

For those who needed coercion, the Nazi total state had its instruments of terror and repression. Especially important was the SS (the *Schutzstaffeln,* or Protection Squads). Originally created as Hitler's personal bodyguard, the SS, under the direction of Heinrich Himmler (1900–1945), came to control all of the regular and secret police forces. Himmler and the SS functioned on the basis of two principles: terror and ideology. Terror included the instruments of repression and murder: the secret police, criminal police, concentration camps, and later the execution squads and death camps for the extermination of the Jews (see Chapter 27). For Himmler, the SS was a crusading order whose primary goal was to further the Aryan master race. SS members, who constituted a carefully chosen elite, were thoroughly indoctrinated in racial ideology.

Other institutions, such as the Catholic and Protestant churches, primary and secondary schools, and universities, were also brought under the control of the Nazi totalitarian state. Nazi professional organizations and leagues were formed for civil servants, teachers, women, farmers, doctors, and lawyers. Because the early indoctrination of the nation's youth would lay the foundation for a strong totalitarian state, youth organizations, the *Hitler Jugend* (Hitler Youth) and its female counterpart, the *Bund Deutscher Mädel* (German Girls Association), were given special attention. The oath required of Hitler Youth members demonstrates the dedication expected of youth in the Nazi state: "In the presence of this blood banner, which represents our Führer, I swear to devote all my energies and my strength to the savior of our country, Adolf Hitler. I am willing and ready to give up my life for him, so help me God."

Women played a crucial role in the Aryan racial state as bearers of the children who would bring about the triumph of the Aryan race. To the Nazis, the differences between men and women were quite natural. Men were warriors and political leaders; women were destined to be wives and mothers. Motherhood was also exalted in an annual ceremony on August 12, Hitler's mother's birthday, when Hitler awarded the German Mother's Cross to a select group of German mothers. Those with four children received a bronze cross, those with six a silver cross, and those with eight or more a gold cross.

Nazi ideas determined employment opportunities for women. The Nazis hoped to drive women out of heavy industry or other jobs that might hinder them from bearing healthy children, as well as certain professions, including university teaching, medicine, and law, which were considered inappropriate for women, especially married women. The Nazis encouraged women

CHRONOLOGY Nazi Germany

Hitler as Munich politician	1919–1923
Beer Hall Putsch	1923
Nazis win 107 seats in Reichstag	1930 (September)
Hitler is made chancellor	1933 (January 30)
Reichstag fire	1933 (February 27)
Enabling Act	1933 (March 23)
Purge of the SA	1934 (June 30)
Hindenburg dies; Hitler as sole ruler	1934 (August 2)
Nuremberg laws	1935
Kristallnacht	1938 (November 9–10)

to pursue professional occupations that had direct practical application, such as social work and nursing. In addition to restrictive legislation against females, the Nazi regime pursued its campaign against working women with such poster slogans as "Get hold of pots and pans and broom and you'll sooner find a groom!" Nazi policy toward female workers remained inconsistent, however. Especially after the rearmament boom and increased conscription of males for military service resulted in a labor shortage, the government encouraged women to work, even in areas previously dominated by males.

The Nazi total state was intended to be an Aryan racial state. From its beginning, the Nazi Party reflected Hitler's strong anti-Semitic beliefs. Once in power, the Nazis translated anti-Semitic ideas into anti-Semitic policies. Already on April 1, 1933, the new Nazi government initiated a two-day boycott of Jewish businesses. A series of laws soon followed that excluded "non-Aryans" (defined as anyone "descended from non-Aryans, especially Jewish parents or grandparents") from the legal profession, civil service, judgeships, the medical profession, teaching positions, cultural and entertainment enterprises, and the press.

In September 1935, the Nazis announced new racial laws at the annual party rally in Nuremberg. These "Nuremberg laws" excluded German Jews from German citizenship and forbade marriages and extramarital relations between Jews and German citizens. The "Nuremberg laws" essentially separated Jews from the Germans politically, socially, and legally and were the natural extension of Hitler's stress on the preservation of a pure Aryan race.

Another considerably more violent phase of anti-Jewish activity took place in 1938 and 1939; it was initiated on November 9–10, 1938, the infamous *Kristallnacht,* or Night of Shattered Glass. The assassination of a third secretary in the German embassy in Paris by a young Polish Jew became the excuse for a Nazi-led destructive rampage against the Jews in which synagogues were burned, seven thousand Jewish businesses were destroyed, and at least one hundred Jews were killed.

Anti-Semitism in Nazi Germany. At the core of Hitler's ideology was an intense anti-Semitism. Soon after seizing power, Hitler and the Nazis began to translate their anti-Semitic ideas into anti-Semitic policies. This photograph shows one example of Nazi action against the Jews as Germans are seen passing by the broken windows of a Jewish shop in Berlin the morning after *Kristallnacht,* the Night of Shattered Glass, when thousands of Jewish businesses were destroyed.

claimed as many as 5 million lives. Industrial collapse paralleled the agricultural disaster. By 1921, industrial output was at only 20 percent of its 1913 levels. Russia was exhausted. As Leon Trotsky said: "The collapse of the productive forces surpassed anything of the kind that history had ever seen. The country, and the government with it, were at the very edge of the abyss."[12]

The New Economic Policy In March 1921, Lenin pulled Russia back from the abyss by establishing his **New Economic Policy** (NEP). The NEP was a modified version of the old capitalist system. Peasants were now allowed to sell their produce openly, and retail stores as well as small industries that employed fewer than twenty employees could now operate under private ownership; heavy industry, banking, and mines remained in the hands of the government. In 1922, Lenin and the Communists formally created a new state called the Union of Soviet Socialist Republics, known by its initials as the USSR and commonly called the Soviet Union. Already in that year, a revived market and good harvest had brought the famine to an end; Soviet agriculture climbed to 75 percent of its prewar level. Industry, especially state-owned heavy industry, fared less well and continued to stagnate. Only coal production had reached prewar levels by 1926. Overall, the NEP had saved the Soviet Union from complete economic disaster even though Lenin and other leading Communists intended it to be only a temporary, tactical retreat from the goals of communism.

In the meantime, Lenin and the Communists were strengthening their one-party state. The number of bureaucrats increased dramatically and soon constituted a new elite with the best jobs, food, and dwellings. Even Lenin issued warnings about the widening power of the bureaucracy that he had helped create.

Moreover, 30,000 Jewish males were rounded up and sent to concentration camps. *Kristallnacht* also led to further drastic steps. Jews were barred from all public buildings and prohibited from owning, managing, or working in any retail store. Finally, under the direction of the SS, Jews were encouraged to "emigrate from Germany." After the outbreak of World War II, the policy of emigration was replaced by a more gruesome one.

The Soviet Union

Yet another example of totalitarianism was to be found in the Soviet Union. The civil war in Russia had come to an end by the beginning of 1921. It had taken an enormous toll of life, but the Red Terror and the victories of the Red Army had guaranteed the survival of the Communist regime. During the civil war, Lenin had pursued a policy of "war communism." Under this policy of expedience, the government had nationalized transportation and communication facilities as well as banks, mines, factories, and businesses that employed more than ten workers. The government had also assumed the right to requisition the food of peasants, who often resisted fiercely, though without much success. Hunger led to an untold number of deaths in the countryside. Added to this problem was drought, which caused a great famine between 1920 and 1922 that

The Struggle for Power Between 1922 and 1924, Lenin suffered a series of strokes that finally led to his death on January 21, 1924. Although Communist control theoretically rested on a principle of collective leadership, Lenin had in fact provided one-man rule. His death inaugurated a struggle for power among the members of the Politburo, the institution that had become the leading organ of the party.

Time & Life Pictures/Getty Images

Stalin Signing a Death Warrant.   Terror played an important role in the authoritarian system created by Joseph Stalin. Here Stalin is shown signing what is supposedly a death warrant in 1933. As the terror increased in the late 1930s, Stalin signed such orders every day.

In 1924, the Politburo of seven members was severely divided over the future direction of the nation. The Left, led by Leon Trotsky, wanted to end the NEP and launch the Soviet Union on the path of rapid industrialization, primarily at the expense of the peasantry. This same group wanted to carry the revolution on, believing that the survival of the Russian Revolution ultimately depended on the spread of communism abroad. Another group in the Politburo, called the Right, rejected the cause of world revolution and wanted instead to concentrate on constructing a socialist state. Believing that too rapid industrialization would worsen the living standards of the Soviet peasantry, this group also favored a continuation of Lenin's NEP.

These ideological divisions were underscored by an intense personal rivalry between Leon Trotsky and Joseph Stalin. Trotsky had been a key figure in the success of the Bolshevik Revolution and the Red Army. In 1924, he held the post of commissar of war and was the leading spokesman for the Left in the Politburo. Joseph Stalin (1879–1953) had joined the Bolsheviks in 1903 and had come to Lenin's attention after staging a daring bank robbery to obtain funds for the Bolshevik cause. Stalin, who was neither a dynamic speaker nor a forceful writer, was content to hold the dull bureaucratic job of party general secretary while other Politburo members held party positions that enabled them to display their brilliant oratorical abilities. He was a good organizer (his fellow Bolsheviks called him "Comrade Card-Index"), and the other members of the Politburo soon found that the position of party secretary was really the most important in the party hierarchy. The general secretary

appointed the regional, district, city, and town party secretaries. In 1922, for example, Stalin had made some ten thousand appointments, many of them trusted followers whose holding of key positions proved valuable in the struggle for power. Although Stalin at first refused to support either the Left or the Right in the Politburo, he finally came to favor the goal of "socialism in one country" rather than world revolution.

Stalin used his post as party general secretary to gain complete control of the Communist Party. Trotsky was expelled from the party in 1927. Eventually, he made his way to Mexico, where he was murdered in 1940, no doubt on Stalin's orders. By 1929, Stalin had succeeded in eliminating the Old Bolsheviks of the revolutionary era from the Politburo and establishing a dictatorship so powerful that the Russian tsars of old would have been envious.

The Stalinist Era (1929–1939)   The Stalinist era marked the beginning of an economic, social, and political revolution that was more sweeping in its results than the revolutions of 1917. Stalin made a significant shift in economic policy in 1928 when he launched his first five-year plan. Its real goal was nothing less than the transformation of the Soviet Union from an agricultural country into an industrial state virtually overnight. Instead of consumer goods, the first five-year plan emphasized maximum production of capital goods and armaments and succeeded in quadrupling the production of heavy machinery and doubling oil production. Between 1928 and 1937, during the first two five-year plans, steel production increased from 4 to 18 million tons per year, and hard coal output went from 36 to 128 million tons.

The social and political costs of industrialization were enormous. Little provision was made for absorbing the expanded labor force into the cities. Though the industrial labor force increased by millions between 1932 and 1940, total investment in housing actually declined after 1929; as a result, millions of workers and their families lived in pitiful conditions. Real wages in industry also declined by 43 percent between 1928 and 1940, and strict laws limited workers' freedom of movement. To inspire and pacify the workers, government propaganda stressed the need for sacrifice to create the new socialist state. Soviet labor policy stressed high levels of achievement, typified by the Stakhanov cult. Alexei Stakhanov was a coal miner who mined 102 tons of coal in one shift, exceeding the norm by 1,300 percent. He was held up as an example to others, even though the event had been contrived for publicity purposes.

Rapid industrialization was accompanied by an equally rapid collectivization of agriculture. Stalin believed that the capital needed for industrial growth could be

THE FORMATION OF COLLECTIVE FARMS

Accompanying the rapid industrialization of the Soviet Union was the collectivization of agriculture, a feat that involved nothing less than transforming Russia's 26 million family farms into 250,000 collective farms (*kolkhozes*). This selection provides a firsthand account of how the process worked.

Max Belov, *The History of a Collective Farm*

General collectivization in our village was brought about in the following manner: Two representatives of the [Communist] Party arrived in the village. All the inhabitants were summoned by the ringing of the church bell to a meeting at which the policy of general collectivization was announced.... The upshot was that although the meeting lasted two days, from the viewpoint of the Party representatives nothing was accomplished.

After this setback the Party representatives divided the village into two sections and worked each one separately. Two more officials were sent to reinforce the first two. A meeting of our section of the village was held in a stable which had previously belonged to a kulak. The meeting dragged on until dark. Suddenly someone threw a brick at the lamp, and in the dark the peasants began to beat the Party representatives who jumped out the window and escaped from the village barely alive. The following day seven people were arrested. The militia was called in and stayed in the village until the peasants, realizing their helplessness, calmed down....

By the end of 1930 there were two kolkhozes in our village. Though at first these collectives embraced at most only 70 percent of the peasant households, in the months that followed they gradually absorbed more and more of them.

In these kolkhozes the great bulk of the land was held and worked communally, but each peasant household owned a house of some sort, a small plot of ground and perhaps some livestock. All the members of the kolkhoz were required to work on the kolkhoz a certain number of days each month; the rest of the time they were allowed to work on their own holdings. They derived their income partly from what they grew on their garden strips and partly from their work in the kolkhoz.

When the harvest was over, and after the farm had met its obligations to the state and to various special funds (for instance, seed, etc.) and had sold on the market whatever undesignated produce was left, the remaining produce and the farm's monetary income were divided among the kolkhoz members according to the number of "labor days" each one had contributed to the farm's work.... It was in 1930 that the kolkhoz members first received their portions out of the "communal kettle." After they had received their earnings, at the rate of 1 kilogram of grain and 55 kopecks per labor day, one of them remarked, "You will live, but you will be very, very thin."

In the spring of 1931 a tractor worked the fields of the kolkhoz for the first time. The tractor was "capable of plowing every kind of hard soil and virgin soil," as Party representatives told us at the meeting in celebration of its arrival. The peasants did not then know that these "steel horses" would carry away a good part of the harvest in return for their work....

By late 1932 more than 80 percent of the peasant households...had been collectivized.... That year the peasants harvested a good crop and had hopes that the calculations would work out to their advantage and would help strengthen them economically. These hopes were in vain. The kolkhoz workers received only 200 grams of flour per labor day for the first half of the year; the remaining grain, including the seed fund, was taken by the government. The peasants were told that industrialization of the country, then in full swing, demanded grain and sacrifices from them.

Q   What was the purpose of collectivizing Soviet agriculture? According to Belov, why did the peasants of his village assault the Communist Party representatives? What was the result of their protest?

gained by creating agricultural surpluses through eliminating private farms and pushing people onto collective farms (see the box above). By eliminating private property, a Communist ideal would also be achieved.

By 1930, some 10 million peasant households had been collectivized; by 1934, the Soviet Union's 26 million family farms had been collectivized into 250,000 units. This was done at tremendous cost since Stalin did not hesitate to starve the peasants, especially in the Ukraine, to force them to comply with the policy of collectivization. Stalin himself supposedly told Winston Churchill during World War II that 10 million peasants died during the artificially created famines of 1932 and 1933. The only concession Stalin made to the peasants was to allow each household to have one tiny, privately owned garden plot.

Stalin's program of rapid industrialization entailed additional costs as well. To achieve his goals, Stalin strengthened the party bureaucracy under his control. Those who resisted were sent into forced labor camps in Siberia. Stalin's desire for sole control of decision making also led to purges of the Old Bolsheviks. Between 1936 and 1938, the most prominent Old Bolsheviks were put on trial and condemned to death. During this same time, Stalin undertook a purge of army officers, diplomats, union officials, party members, intellectuals, and numerous ordinary citizens. One old woman was sent to Siberia for saying, "If people prayed, they would work better." Estimates are that 8 million Russians were arrested; millions died in Siberian forced labor camps. This gave Stalin the distinction of being one of the greatest mass

CHRONOLOGY The Soviet Union

New Economic Policy begins	1921
Death of Lenin	1924
Trotsky is expelled from the Communist Party	1927
First five-year plan begins	1928
Stalin's dictatorship is established	1929
Height of Stalin's purges	1936–1938

murderers in human history. The Stalinist bloodbath made what some Western intellectuals had hailed as the "new civilization" much less attractive by the late 1930s.

Disturbed by a rapidly declining birthrate, Stalin also reversed much of the permissive social legislation of the early 1920s. Advocating complete equality of rights for women, the Communists had made divorce and abortion easy to obtain while also encouraging women to work outside the home and liberate themselves sexually. After Stalin came to power, the family was praised as a miniature collective in which parents were responsible for inculcating values of duty, discipline, and hard work. Abortion was outlawed, and divorced fathers who did not support their children were fined heavily. A new divorce law of June 1936 imposed fines for repeated divorces, and homosexuality was declared a criminal activity. The regime now praised motherhood and urged women to have large families as a patriotic duty. But by this time, many Soviet women worked in factories and spent many additional hours waiting in line to purchase increasingly scarce consumer goods. Despite the change in policy, no dramatic increase in the birthrate occurred.

The Stalinist era did witness some positive changes in the everyday lives of Soviet citizens. To create leaders for the new Communist society, Stalin began a program to enable workers, peasants, and young Communists to receive higher education, especially in engineering. There was also tremendous growth in part-time schools where large numbers of adults took courses to become literate so that they could advance to technical school or college. Increasing numbers of people saw education as the key to better jobs and upward mobility in Soviet society. One woman of peasant background recounted: "In Moscow I had a burning desire to study. Where or what wasn't important; I wanted to study." For what purpose? "We had a saying at work: 'Without that piece of paper [the diploma] you are an insect; with it, a human being.' My lack of higher education prevented me from getting decent wages."[13]

Authoritarianism in Eastern Europe

A number of other states in Europe were not totalitarian but did have conservative authoritarian governments. These states adopted some of the trappings of totalitarian states, especially wide police powers, but their greatest concern was not the creation of a mass movement aimed at the establishment of a new kind of society but rather the defense of the existing social order. Consequently, the **authoritarian state** tended to limit the participation of the masses and was content with passive obedience rather than active involvement in the goals of the regime. A number of states in eastern Europe adopted this kind of authoritarian government.

Nowhere had the map of Europe been more drastically altered by World War I than in eastern Europe. The new states of Austria, Poland, Czechoslovakia, and Yugoslavia adopted parliamentary systems, and the preexisting kingdoms of Romania and Bulgaria gained new parliamentary constitutions in 1920. Greece became a republic in 1924. Hungary's government was parliamentary in form but was controlled by its landed aristocrats. At the beginning of the 1920s, political democracy seemed well established, but almost everywhere in eastern Europe, parliamentary governments soon gave way to authoritarian regimes.

Several problems helped create this situation. Eastern European states had little tradition of liberalism or parliamentary politics and no substantial middle class to support them. Then, too, these states were largely rural and agrarian. Much of the land was still dominated by large landowners who feared the growth of agrarian peasant parties with their schemes for land redistribution. Ethnic conflicts also threatened to tear these countries apart. Fearful of land reform, Communist agrarian upheaval, and ethnic conflict, powerful landowners, the churches, and even some members of the small middle class looked to authoritarian governments to maintain the old system.

Eastern Europe After World War I

Already in the 1920s, some eastern European states began to move away from political democracy toward authoritarian structures. A military coup d'état established an authoritarian regime in Bulgaria in 1923. Poland established an authoritarian regime in 1926 when Marshal Joseph Pilsudski (1867–1935) created a military dictatorship. In Yugoslavia, King Alexander I (1921–1934) abolished the constitution and imposed a royal dictatorship in 1929. During the 1930s, all of the remaining parliamentary regimes except Czechoslovakia succumbed to authoritarianism. Eastern European states were increasingly attracted to the authoritarian examples of Fascist Italy and Nazi Germany.

CHRONOLOGY The Authoritarian States

Eastern Europe

A military coup d'état establishes authoritarian regime in Bulgaria	1923
Pilsudski creates military dictatorship in Poland	1926
Alexander I creates royal dictatorship in Yugoslavia	1929
Gömbös is made prime minister in Hungary	1932
Dictatorship of General Metaxas in Greece	1936
Carol II crushes Iron Guard and imposes authoritarian rule in Romania	1938

Spain

Dictatorship of Primo de Rivera	1923–1930
Creation of Spanish Republic	1931
Spanish Civil War	1936–1939
Dictatorship of Franco	1939–1975

Although Admiral Miklós Horthy (1868–1957) had ruled Hungary as "regent" since 1919, the appointment of Julius Gömbös (1886–1936) as prime minister in 1932 brought Hungary even closer to Italy and Germany. Romania witnessed the development of a strong fascist movement led by Corneliu Codreanu (1899–1938). Known as the Legion of the Archangel Michael, it possessed its own paramilitary squad called the Iron Guard. As Codreanu's fascist movement grew and became Romania's third largest political party, King Carol II (1930–1940) responded in 1938 by ending parliamentary rule, crushing the leadership of the legion, and imposing authoritarian rule. In Greece, General John Metaxas (1871–1941) imposed a dictatorship in 1936.

Only Czechoslovakia, with its substantial middle class, liberal tradition, and strong industrial base, maintained its political democracy. Thomas Masaryk (1850–1937), an able and fair leader who served as president from 1918 to 1935, was able to maintain an uneasy but stable alliance of reformist socialists, agrarians, and Catholics.

Dictatorship in the Iberian Peninsula

Parliamentary regimes also failed to survive in both Spain and Portugal. Both countries were largely agrarian, illiterate, and dominated by powerful landlords and Catholic clergy.

Spain's parliamentary monarchy was unable to deal with the social tensions generated by the industrial boom and inflation that accompanied World War I. Supported by King Alfonso XIII (1886–1931), General Miguel Primo de Rivera (1870–1930) led a successful military coup in September 1923 and created a personal dictatorship that lasted until 1930. But a faltering economy because of the Great Depression led to the collapse of Primo de Rivera's regime in January 1930 as well as to a widespread lack of support for the monarchy. Alfonso XIII left Spain in 1931, and a new Spanish republic was instituted, governed by a coalition of democrats and reformist socialists. Political turmoil ensued as control of the government passed from leftists to rightists until the Popular Front, an antifascist coalition composed of democrats, socialists, and the revolutionary left, took over in 1936. The Popular Front was unacceptable, however, to senior army officers. Led by General Francisco Franco (1892–1975), Spanish military forces revolted against the government and inaugurated a brutal and bloody civil war that lasted three years.

The Spanish Civil War The conflict between Franco's right-wing military rebels and the left-wing republic government of the Popular Front was complicated by foreign intervention. Franco's forces were aided by arms, money, and men from the fascist regimes of Italy and Germany. Hitler used the Spanish Civil War as an opportunity to test the new weaponry of his revived air force. The Popular Front appealed to democratic states for assistance, but only the Soviet Union provided trucks, planes, and tanks. The involvement of the Soviet Union caused the governments of France, Great Britain, and the United States to adopt a policy of neutrality. Nevertheless, international brigades of volunteers joined the republican side, including the Abraham Lincoln Brigade from the United States.

Gradually, Franco's forces wore down the Popular Front, and after they captured Madrid on March 28, 1939, the Spanish Civil War finally came to an end. The war had been a brutal one. Probably 400,000 people died in the war, only one-fourth of them on the battlefield. Civilians died from air raids, disease, and bloody reprisals by both sides against their enemies and their supporters. Another 200,000 people were executed in the years following Franco's victory.

The Franco Regime General Franco soon established a dictatorship that lasted until his death in 1975. It was not a fascist government, although it was unlikely to oppose the Fascists in Italy or the Nazis in Germany. The fascist movement in Spain, known as the Falange and led by José Antonio Primo de Rivera, son of the former dictator, contributed little to Franco's success and played a minor role in the new regime. Franco's government, which favored large landowners, business, and the Catholic clergy, was yet another example of a traditional, conservative, authoritarian regime.

Portugal In 1910, the Portuguese had overthrown their monarchy and established a republic. Severe inflation after World War I, however, undermined support for the republic and helped intensify political instability. In 1926, a group of army officers seized power, and by the early 1930s, the military junta's finance minister, Antonio Salazar (1889–1970), had become the strongman of the regime. Salazar controlled the Portuguese government for the next forty years.

The Expansion of Mass Culture and Mass Leisure

Q **Focus Question:** What new dimensions in mass culture and mass leisure emerged during the interwar years, and what role did these activities play in the totalitarian states?

The Roaring Twenties was the name given to the decade known for the exuberance of its popular culture. Berlin, the capital of Germany, became the entertainment center of Europe with its theaters, cabarets, cinemas, and jazz clubs. The Roaring Twenties was especially known for its dance crazes. People danced in clubs and dance halls, at home, and in the streets, doing the Charleston, the Bunny Hug, and a variety of other dances. Josephine Baker (1906–1975), an American singer and dancer, became especially well known in Europe, appearing at European clubs featuring American "Negro" jazz music. One critic said, "She dances for hours without the slightest trace of tiredness." She became a wonderful symbol of the popular "flapper," the unconventional and lively young woman of the 1920s.

So popular was jazz, a musical form that had originated with African American musicians in the United States, that the 1920s also were known as the Jazz Age. Admired for its improvised qualities and forceful rhythms, jazz spread throughout the Western world as King Oliver, Bix Beiderbecke, Jelly Roll Morton, and others wrote and played some of the greatest jazz music of the time.

Radio and Movies

A series of technological inventions in the late nineteenth century had prepared the way for a revolution in mass communications. Especially important was Marconi's discovery of "wireless" radio waves. But it was not until June 16, 1920, that a radio broadcast (of a concert by soprano Nellie Melba from London) for a mass audience was attempted. Permanent broadcasting facilities were then constructed in the United States, Europe, and Japan during 1921 and 1922, and mass production of radios (receiving sets) also began. In 1926, when the British Broadcasting Corporation (BBC) was made into a public corporation, there were 2.2 million radios in Great Britain. By the end of the 1930s, there were 9 million.

The technical foundation for motion pictures had already been developed in the 1890s when short movies were produced as novelties for music halls. Shortly before World War I, full-length features, such as the Italian film *Quo Vadis* and the American film *Birth of a Nation,* were released, and it quickly became apparent that cinema was a new form of entertainment for the masses.

Sasha/Getty Images

The Charleston. Dancing became the rage during the Roaring Twenties, and the Charleston was the most popular and enduring dance of the decade. This photograph shows a couple dancing the Charleston in a scene from a London musical, *Just a Kiss,* performed in 1926.

By 1939, about 40 percent of adults in the more advanced industrial countries were attending the movies once a week. That figure increased to 60 percent by the end of World War II.

Mass forms of communication and entertainment were not new, but the increased size of audiences and the ability of radio and cinema, unlike the printed word, to provide an immediate shared experience added new dimensions to mass culture. Favorite film actors and actresses became stars who then became the focus of public adoration and scrutiny. Sensuous actresses such as Marlene Dietrich, whose appearance in the early sound film *The Blue Angel* catapulted her to fame, popularized new images of women's sexuality.

Of course, radio and movies could also be used for political purposes. Hitler had said that "without motor cars, sound films, and wireless, no victory of National Socialism." Radio seemed to offer great opportunities for reaching the masses, especially when it became apparent that the emotional harangues of a demagogue such as Hitler had just as much impact on people when heard on radio as in person. The Nazi regime encouraged radio listening by urging manufacturers to produce cheap radios that could be bought on the installment plan. The Nazis also erected loudspeaker pillars in the streets to encourage communal radio listening, especially to broadcasts of mass meetings.

Film, too, had propaganda potential, a possibility not lost on Joseph Goebbels (1897–1945), the propaganda minister of Nazi Germany. Believing that film constituted one of the "most modern and scientific means of influencing the masses," Goebbels created a special film section in his Propaganda Ministry and encouraged the production of both documentaries and popular feature films that carried the Nazi message. *Triumph of the Will*, for example, was a documentary of the 1934 Nuremberg party rally that forcefully conveyed the power of National Socialism to viewers. Both Fascist Italy and Nazi Germany controlled and exploited the content of newsreels shown in movie theaters.

Mass Leisure

Mass leisure activities had developed at the turn of the century, but new work patterns after World War I dramatically expanded the amount of free time available to take advantage of them. By 1920, the eight-hour day had become the norm for many office and factory workers in northern and western Europe.

Sports Professional sporting events for mass audiences became an especially important aspect of mass leisure. Attendance at association football (soccer) games increased dramatically, and the inauguration of the World Cup contest in 1930 added to the nationalistic rivalries that began to surround such mass sporting events. Increased attendance also made the 1920s and 1930s a great era of stadium building. For the 1936 Olympics, the Germans built a stadium in Berlin that seated 140,000 people.

Tourism Travel opportunities also added new dimensions to mass leisure activities. The military use of aircraft during World War I spurred improvements in planes that made civilian air travel a reality. The first regular international airmail service began in 1919, and regular passenger service soon followed. Although air travel remained the preserve of the wealthy or the adventurous, trains, buses, and private cars made excursions to beaches or resorts more popular and more affordable. Beaches, such as the one at Brighton in England, were increasingly mobbed by crowds of people from all social classes, a clear reflection of the growth of democratic politics.

Organized Mass Leisure in Italy and Germany Mass leisure provided totalitarian regimes with new ways to control their populations. Mussolini's Italy created the *Dopolavoro* (Afterwork) as a vast national recreation agency. The *Dopolavoro* was responsible for establishing clubhouses with libraries, radios, and athletic facilities in virtually every town and village. In some places, they included auditoriums for plays and films, as well as travel agencies that arranged tours, cruises, and resort vacations on the Adriatic at reduced rates. *Dopolavoro* groups introduced many Italians to various facets of mass culture and mass leisure with activities such as band concerts, movies, choral groups, roller skating, and ballroom dancing. Essentially, the *Dopolavoro* enabled the Italian government to provide recreational activities and supervise them as well. By doing so, the state imposed new rules and regulations on previously spontaneous activities, thus breaking down old group solidarities and enabling these groups to be guided by the goals of the state.

The Nazi regime adopted a program similar to the *Dopolavoro* in its *Kraft durch Freude* (Strength Through Joy). The purpose of *Kraft durch Freude* was to coordinate the free time of the working class by offering a variety of leisure time activities, including concerts, operas, films, guided tours, and sporting events (see the box on p. 831). Especially popular were inexpensive vacations, much like modern package tours, such as cruises to Scandinavia or the Mediterranean or, more likely for workers, short trips to various sites in Germany. Some 130,000 workers took cruises in 1938; 7 million took short trips.

More and more, mass culture and mass leisure had the effect of increasing the homogeneity of national populations, a process that had begun in the nineteenth century with the development of the national state and mass politics. Local popular culture was increasingly replaced by national and even international culture as new forms of mass production and consumption brought similar styles of clothing and fashion to people throughout Europe.

Cultural and Intellectual Trends in the Interwar Years

Q **Focus Question:** What were the main cultural and intellectual trends in the interwar years?

The artistic and intellectual innovations of the pre–World War I period, which had shocked many Europeans, had been the preserve primarily of a small group of avant-garde artists and intellectuals. In the 1920s and 1930s, they became more widespread as artists and intellectuals continued to work out the implications of the ideas developed before 1914. But what made the prewar avant-garde culture acceptable in the 1920s and the 1930s? Perhaps the most important factor was the impact of World War I.

To many people, the experiences of the war seemed to confirm the prewar avant-garde belief that human beings were violent and irrational animals who were incapable of creating a sane and rational world. The Great Depression of the late 1920s and early 1930s, as well as the growth of fascist movements based on violence and the degradation of individual rights, only added to the uncertainties generated by the Great War. The crisis of

FILM & HISTORY
TRIUMPH OF THE WILL (1934)

Probably the best-known films of Nazi Germany today are the documentaries, in particular those of Leni Riefenstahl. Riefenstahl was an actress who turned to directing in 1932. Adolf Hitler liked her work and invited her to make a film about the 1934 Nuremberg party rally. In filming this party day of unity—as it was called—Hitler was trying to demonstrate, in the wake of the purge of the SA on June 30, that the Nazi Party was strongly united behind its leader. Hitler provided the film's title, *Triumph des Willens* (Triumph of the Will).

Much of the film's success was due to careful preparation. Riefenstahl was assisted by a crew of 172 people. Good camera work was coordinated with the physical arrangements for the rally to produce a spectacle that was manipulated for cinematic purposes from beginning to end. As one critic remarked, "The Rally was planned not only as a spectacular mass meeting, but as a spectacular propaganda film." To add to the dramatic effect, Riefenstahl used a number of techniques, including moving cameras (one was even mounted on Hitler's Mercedes), telephoto lenses for unusual perspectives, aerial photographs, and music carefully synchronized with each scene. The result is an effective piece of propaganda aimed at conveying to viewers the power of National Socialism.

The movie begins with introductory titles that are almost religious in character:

> *Twenty years after the outbreak of the World War,*
> *Sixteen years after the beginning of Germany's suffering,*
> *Nineteen months after the beginning of the rebirth of Germany,*
> *Adolf Hitler flew to Nuremberg to review his faithful followers.*

The rest of the film is devoted to scenes from the six days of the party rally: the dramatic opening when Hitler is greeted with thunderous applause; the major speeches of party leaders; an outdoor rally of Labor Service men who perform pseudo-military drills with their shovels; a Hitler Youth rally in which Hitler tells thousands of German boys, "in you Germany will live"; military exercises; and massive ceremonies with thousands of parading SA and SS men. The film ends with Hitler's closing speech in which

A scene from *Triumph of the Will* of one of the many mass rallies at Nuremberg.

he reviews the struggle of the Nazi Party to take control of Germany. The screen fades to black as the crowd sings "The Horst Wessel Lied," a famous Nazi anthem.

Throughout the film, Hitler is shown in messianic terms—his descent from the clouds at the beginning, his motorcades through the streets with him standing like a god in an open car as thousands of people cheer, and his many appearances at the rally where he commands the complete adulation of the masses assembled before him. In his speeches, Hitler emphasized the power of the new German state: "It is our will that this state shall endure for a thousand years." He also stressed the need for unity: "We want to be one people, one nation, and with one leader." As Rudolf Hess, Hitler's deputy, summed up at the end of the film: "The Party is Hitler. Hitler is Germany just as Germany is Hitler."

Considerable controversy has surrounded the film. Riefenstahl was accused by many of using art to promote a murderous and morally corrupt regime. In Germany, under postwar denazification laws, the film can be shown only for educational purposes. Yet Riefenstahl always maintained, against all the evidence, that it was "a pure historical film." To a viewer today, however, the film is obviously a propaganda piece. The speeches seem tedious and the ideas simplistic, but to watch thousands of people responding the way they did is a terrible reminder of how Hitler used mass spectacles to achieve his goal of educating the German people to his new authoritarian state.

MASS LEISURE: STRENGTH THROUGH JOY

In November 1933, the German Labor Front established an organization called *Kraft durch Freude* (Strength Through Joy), whose purpose was to organize the leisure time of workers in the interests of the Nazi regime. These excerpts are taken from the reports of the Social Democratic Party's contact men in Germany and give a fairly accurate account of the attitudes of the German workers toward the *Kraft durch Freude* (KdF) program.

Reports of the SOPADE (Social Democratic Party in Exile)

Central Germany, April 1939

While Beauty of Labor [another Labor Front organization] makes no impressions whatsoever... Strength Through Joy is not without impact. However, workers' wages are only barely sufficient for essentials and nobody can afford a trip to Madeira, 150 Reichsmarks per person—300 RM with the wife. Even the shorter trips produce so many additional expenses that they often double the cost. But some people like them nonetheless. Anybody who has never made a trip in his life and sees the sea for the first time is much impressed. The effect is: "The Nazis have done some good things after all." The enthusiasm is, however, greater on the first trip. On the second, many are put off by the crowds.

Berlin, February 1938

Strength Through Joy is very popular. The events appeal to the yearning of the little man who wants an opportunity to get out and about himself and to take part in the pleasures of the "top people." It is a clever appeal to the petty bourgeois inclinations of the unpolitical workers. For such a man it really means something to have been on a trip to Scandinavia, or even if he only went to the Black Forest or the Harz Mountains, he imagines that he has thereby climbed up a rung on the social ladder.

Bavaria, April 1939

On the group tours there is a sharp social differentiation. The "top people" only go on big trips where there will be a more select clientele. The big mass trips are for the proletariat. People now look for places where there are no KdF visitors. "Not visited by KdF" is now a particular asset for summer vacations. A landlord in a mountain village in Upper Bavaria wrote in his prospects: "Not visited by KdF tourists." The Labor Front, which was sent the prospectus by someone, took the landlord to court. He had to withdraw the prospectus and was not allowed to receive summer guests. Nevertheless, information about summer Pensions [boardinghouses] which are not used by KdF is becoming more and more widespread.

Q *Based on these documents, what were the attitudes of ordinary Germans toward the Nazi regime's Strength Through Joy program? What do the content and tone of these reports tell you about the nature of public support for Nazism?*

---

confidence in Western civilization ran deep and was well captured in the words of the French poet Paul Valéry in the early 1920s:

> The storm has died away, and still we are restless, uneasy, as if the storm were about to break. Almost all the affairs of men remain in a terrible uncertainty. We think of what has disappeared, and we are almost destroyed by what has been destroyed; we do not know what will be born, and we fear the future.... Doubt and disorder are in us and with us. There is no thinking man, however shrewd or learned he may be, who can hope to dominate this anxiety, to escape from this impression of darkness.[14]

Political and economic uncertainties were paralleled by social insecurities. The war had served to break down many traditional middle-class attitudes, especially toward sexuality. In the 1920s, women's physical appearance changed dramatically. Short skirts, short hair, the use of cosmetics that were once thought to be the preserve of prostitutes, and the new practice of suntanning gave women a new image. This change in physical appearance, which stressed more exposure of a woman's body, was also accompanied by frank discussions of sexual matters. In England in 1918, Marie Stopes published *Married Love*, which emphasized sexual pleasure in marriage and soon became a best-seller. In 1926, the Dutch physician Theodore van de Velde published *Ideal Marriage: Its Physiology and Technique*. Translated into a number of languages, it became an international best-seller. Van de Velde described female and male anatomy, discussed birth control techniques, and glorified sexual pleasure in marriage. New ideas on sexuality and birth control were also spread to the working classes by family planning clinics, such as those of Margaret Sanger in the United States and Marie Stopes in Britain.

Nightmares and New Visions: Art and Music

Uncertainty also pervaded the cultural and intellectual achievements of the interwar years. Postwar artistic trends were largely a working out of the implications of prewar developments. Abstract painting, for example, became ever more popular as many pioneering artists of the early twentieth century matured in the decades after the war. In addition, prewar fascination with the absurd and the unconscious contents of the mind seemed even more appropriate after the nightmare landscapes of World War I battlefronts. This gave rise to both the Dada movement and Surrealism, although it was German

Otto Dix, _The War._   In _The War_, Otto Dix used the traditional format of a triptych—a three-paneled painting usually used as an altarpiece—to demonstrate the devastating effects of World War I. In the left panel, soldiers march off to battle, while the results of the battlefield are shown in the center and right panels in the contorted and mutilated bodies riddled with bullets. The coffinlike bottom panel is filled with dead soldiers. Dix portrayed himself in the right panel as a ghostlike soldier towing a fellow soldier from battle.

Expressionist artists who best captured directly the disturbingly destructive effects of World War I.

German Expressionists   Although Expressionism as a movement began before World War I, the war itself had a devastating impact on a group of German Expressionist artists who focused on the suffering and shattered lives caused by the war. George Grosz (1893–1959), one of these artists, expressed his anger in this way: "Of course, there was a kind of mass enthusiasm at the start.... And then after a few years when everything bogged down, when we were defeated, when everything went to pieces, all that remained, at least of me and most of my friends, were disgust and horror."[15] Another German artist who gave visual expression to the horrors of World War I was Otto Dix (1891–1969), who had also served in the war and was well versed in its effects. In _The War_, he gave a graphic presentation of the devastating effects of the Great War.

The Dada Movement   **Dadaism** attempted to enshrine the purposelessness of life. Tristan Tzara (1896–1945), a Romanian-French poet and one of the founders of Dadaism, expressed the Dadaist contempt for the Western tradition in a lecture in 1922: "The acts of life have no beginning or end. Everything happens in a completely idiotic way.... Like everything in life, Dada is useless." Revolted by the insanity of life, the Dadaists tried to give it expression by creating "anti-art." The 1918 Berlin Dada Manifesto maintained that "Dada is the international expression of our times, the great rebellion of artistic movements."

In the hands of Hannah Höch (1889–1978), Dada became an instrument to comment on women's roles in the new mass culture. Höch was the only female member of the Berlin Dada Club, which featured the use of photomontage. Her work was part of the first Dada show in Berlin in 1920. In _Dada Dance,_ she seemed to criticize the "new woman" by making fun of the way women were inclined to follow new fashion styles. In other works, however, she created positive images of the modern woman and expressed a keen interest in new freedoms for women.

Surrealism   Perhaps more important as an artistic movement was **Surrealism,** which sought a reality beyond the material, sensible world and found it in the world of the unconscious through the portrayal of fantasies, dreams, or nightmares. Employing logic to portray the illogical, the Surrealists created disturbing and evocative images. The Spaniard Salvador Dalí (1904–1989) became the high priest of Surrealism and in his mature phase became a master of representational Surrealism. In _The Persistence of Memory,_ Dalí portrayed recognizable objects divorced from their normal context. By placing these objects into unrecognizable relationships, Dalí created a disturbing world in which the irrational had become tangible.

Hannah Höch, *Cut with the Kitchen Knife Dada Through the Last Weimar Beer Belly Cultural Epoch of Germany.* Hannah Höch, a prominent figure in the postwar Dada movement, used photomontage to create images that reflected on women's issues. In *Cut with the Kitchen Knife* (1919), she combined pictures of German political leaders with sports stars, Dada artists, and scenes from urban life. One major theme emerged: the confrontation between the anti-Dada world of German political leaders and the Dada world of revolutionary ideals. Höch associated women with Dada and the new world.

Functionalism in Modern Architecture

The move to **functionalism** in modern architecture also became more widespread in the 1920s and 1930s. First conceived near the end of the nineteenth century, functionalism meant that buildings, like the products of machines, should be "functional" or useful, fulfilling the purpose for which they were constructed. Art and engineering were to be unified, and all unnecessary ornamentation was to be stripped away. Functionalism was based on the architects' belief that art had a social function and could help create a new civilization.

The United States was a leader in these pioneering architectural designs. Unprecedented urban growth and the absence of restrictive architectural traditions allowed for new building methods, especially in the relatively "new city" of Chicago. The Chicago School of the 1890s, led by Louis H. Sullivan (1856–1924), used reinforced concrete, steel frames, and electric elevators to build skyscrapers virtually free of external ornamentation. One of Sullivan's most successful pupils was Frank Lloyd Wright (1867–1959), who became known for innovative designs in domestic architecture. Wright's private houses, built chiefly for wealthy patrons, featured geometric structures with long lines, overhanging roofs, and severe planes of brick and stone. The interiors were open spaces that included cathedral ceilings and built-in furniture and lighting fixtures. Wright pioneered the modern American house.

Especially important in the spread of functionalism was the Bauhaus School of art, architecture, and design, founded in 1919 at Weimar, Germany, by the Berlin architect Walter Gropius (1883–1969). The Bauhaus teaching staff consisted of architects, artists, and designers who worked together to blend the study of fine arts (painting and sculpture) with the applied arts (printing, weaving,

Salvador Dalí, *The Persistence of Memory.* Surrealism was another important artistic movement between the wars. Influenced by the theories of Freudian psychology, Surrealists sought to reveal the world of the unconscious, or the "greater reality" that they believed existed beyond the world of physical appearances. As is evident in this 1931 painting, Salvador Dalí sought to portray the world of dreams by painting recognizable objects in unrecognizable relationships.

and furniture making). Gropius urged his followers to foster a new union of arts and crafts to create the buildings and objects of the future. Gropius's own buildings were often unornamented steel boxes with walls of windows, reflecting his belief that the "sensibility of the artist must be combined with the knowledge of the technician to create new forms in architecture and design."

A Popular Audience

Important to the development of artistic expression between the wars was the search for a new popular audience. To attract a wider audience, artists and musicians began to involve themselves in the new mass culture. The German Kurt Weill (1900–1950), for example, had been a struggling composer of classical music before he turned to jazz rhythms and other popular musical idioms for the music for *The Threepenny Opera*. Some artists even regarded art as a means to transform society and located their studios in poor, working-class neighborhoods. Theater proved especially attractive as postwar artists sought to make an impact on popular audiences. The German director Erwin Piscator began his directing career by offering plays to workers on picket lines. Piscator hoped to reach workers by experimental drama with political messages. Like many other artists, however, he became frustrated by his failure to achieve a mass audience.

The postwar acceptance of modern art forms was by no means universal. Many traditionalists denounced what they considered degeneracy and decadence in the arts. Nowhere was this more evident than in the totalitarian states of Nazi Germany and the Soviet Union.

Walter Gropius, The Bauhaus. Walter Gropius was one of Europe's pioneers in modern architecture. When the Bauhaus moved to Dessau in 1925, Gropius designed a building for its activities. His straightforward use of steel, reinforced concrete, and rows of windows reflects the move to functionalism in modern architecture.

Art in Totalitarian Regimes

In the 1920s, Weimar Germany was one of the chief European centers for modern arts and sciences. Hitler and the Nazis rejected modern art as "degenerate" or "Jewish" art. In an address at the premiere of the Great German Art Exhibition in the newly opened House of German Art in July 1937, Hitler proclaimed, "The people regarded this art [modern art] as the outcome of an impudent and unashamed arrogance or of a simply shocking lack of skill; . . . these achievements—which might have been produced by untalented children of from eight to ten years old—could never be valued as an expression of our own times or of the German future."[16] Hitler and the Nazis believed that they had laid the foundation for a new and genuine German art, which would glorify the strong, the healthy, and the heroic—all supposedly attributes of the Aryan race. The new German art was actually the old nineteenth-century genre art with its emphasis on realistic scenes of everyday life.

So, too, was the art produced by the school of "socialist realism" in the Soviet Union. After the bold experimentalism of the 1920s, the Stalinist era imposed a stifling uniformity on artistic creativity. Like German painting, Soviet painting was expected to focus on a nineteenth-century pictorial style aimed at realistic presentation. Both the new German art and socialist realism were intended to inculcate social values useful to the ruling regimes.

A New Style in Music

At the beginning of the twentieth century, a revolution in music parallel to the revolution in art had begun with the work of Igor Stravinsky (see Chapter 24). But Stravinsky still wrote music in a definite key. The Viennese composer Arnold Schönberg (1874–1951) began to experiment with a radically new style by creating musical pieces in which tonality is completely abandoned, a system that he called atonal music. Since the use of traditional forms was virtually impossible in atonal music, Schönberg created a new system of composition—twelve-tone composition—which used a scale of twelve notes independent of any tonal key. Resistance to modern music was even greater than to modern painting, and atonal music did not begin to win favor until after World War II.

The Search for the Unconscious in Literature

The interest in the unconscious, heightened by the impact of World War I and evident in Surrealism, was also apparent in the new literary techniques that emerged in the 1920s. One of its most visible manifestations was the "stream-of-consciousness" technique in which the writer presented an interior monologue, or a report of the innermost thoughts of each character. One example of this genre was written by the Irish exile James Joyce (1882–1941). His *Ulysses,* published in 1922, told the story of one day in the life of ordinary people in

HESSE AND THE UNCONSCIOUS

The novels of Hermann Hesse made a strong impact on young people, first in Germany in the 1920s and then in the United States in the 1960s after they had been translated into English. Many of these young people shared Hesse's fascination with the unconscious and his dislike of modern industrial civilization. This excerpt from *Demian* spoke directly to many of them.

Hermann Hesse, *Demian*

The following spring I was to leave the preparatory school and enter a university. I was still undecided, however, as to where and what I was to study. I had grown a thin mustache, I was a full-grown man, and yet I was completely helpless and without a goal in life. Only one thing was certain: the voice within me, the dream image. I felt the duty to follow this voice blindly wherever it might lead me. But it was difficult and each day I rebelled against it anew. Perhaps I was mad, as I thought at moments; perhaps I was not like other men? But I was able to do the same things the others did; with a little effort and industry I could read

Plato, was able to solve problems in trigonometry or follow a chemical analysis. There was only one thing I could not do: wrest the dark secret goal from myself and keep it before me as others did who knew exactly what they wanted to be—professors, lawyers, doctors, artists, however long this would take them and whatever difficulties and advantages this decision would bear in its wake. This I could not do. Perhaps I would become something similar, but how was I to know? Perhaps I would have to continue my search for years on end and would not become anything, and would not reach a goal. Perhaps I would reach this goal but it would turn out to be an evil, dangerous, horrible one.

I wanted only to try to live in accord with the promptings which came from my true self. Why was that so very difficult?

Q *How does Hesse's interest in the unconscious appear in this excerpt? Why was a dislike of mechanized society particularly intense after World War I?*

Dublin by following the flow of their inner dialogue. Disconnected ramblings and veiled allusions pervade Joyce's work.

Another famous writer who used her own stream-of-consciousness technique was Virginia Woolf (1882–1942). Woolf belonged to a group of intellectuals and artists, known as the Bloomsbury Circle, who sought to create new artistic and literary forms. In her novels *Mrs. Dalloway* and *Jacob's Room*, Woolf used the inner monologues of her main characters to reveal their world of existence. Woolf came to believe that for a woman to be a writer, she would need to have her own income to free herself from the expected roles of wife and mother.

The German writer Hermann Hesse (1877–1962) dealt with the unconscious in a different fashion. His novels reflected the influence of both Carl Jung's psychological theories and Eastern religions and focused among other things on the spiritual loneliness of modern human beings in a mechanized urban society. *Demian* was a psychoanalytic study of incest, and *Steppenwolf* mirrored the psychological confusion of modern existence. Hesse's novels made a large impact on German youth in the 1920s (see the box above). He won the Nobel Prize for literature in 1946.

The Unconscious in Psychology: Carl Jung

The growing concern with the unconscious also led to greater popular interest in psychology. The full impact of Sigmund Freud's thought was not felt until after World War I. The 1920s witnessed a worldwide acceptance of his ideas. Freudian terms, such as *unconscious, repression, id, ego,* and *Oedipus complex,* entered the common

vocabulary. Popularization of Freud's ideas led to the widespread misconception that an uninhibited sex life was necessary for a healthy mental life. Despite such misconceptions, psychoanalysis did develop into a major profession, especially in the United States. But Freud's ideas did not go unchallenged, even by his own pupils. One of the most prominent challenges came from Carl Jung.

A disciple of Freud, Carl Jung (1856–1961) came to believe that Freud's theories were too narrow and reflected Freud's own personal biases. Jung's study of dreams—his own and those of others—led him to diverge sharply from Freud. Whereas for Freud the unconscious was the seat of repressed desires or appetites, for Jung it was an opening to deep spiritual needs and ever-greater vistas for humans.

Jung viewed the unconscious as twofold: a "personal unconscious" and, at a deeper level, a "collective unconscious." The collective unconscious was the repository of memories that all human beings share and consisted of archetypes, mental forms or images that appear in dreams. The archetypes are common to all people and have a special energy that creates myths, religions, and philosophies. To Jung, the archetypes proved that mind was only in part personal or individual because their origin was buried so far in the past that they seemed to have no human source. Their function was to bring the original mind of humans into a new, higher state of consciousness.

The "Heroic Age of Physics"

The prewar revolution in physics initiated by Max Planck and Albert Einstein continued in the interwar period.

In fact, Ernest Rutherford (1871–1937), one of the physicists responsible for demonstrating that the atom could be split, dubbed the 1920s the "heroic age of physics." By the early 1940s, seven subatomic particles had been distinguished, and a sufficient understanding of the atom had been achieved to lay the foundations for the development of a sophisticated new explosive device, the atomic bomb.

The new picture of the universe that was unfolding continued to undermine the old scientific certainties of classical physics. Classical physics had rested on the fundamental belief that all phenomena could be predicted if they could be completely understood; thus, the weather could be accurately predicted if we knew everything about the wind, sun, and water. In 1927, the German physicist Werner Heisenberg (1901–1976) upset this belief when he posited the **uncertainty principle.** In essence, Heisenberg argued that no one could determine the path of an electron because the very act of observing the electron with light affected the electron's location. The uncertainty principle was more than an explanation for the path of an electron, however; it was a new worldview. Heisenberg shattered confidence in predictability and dared to propose that uncertainty was at the root of all physical laws.

TIMELINE

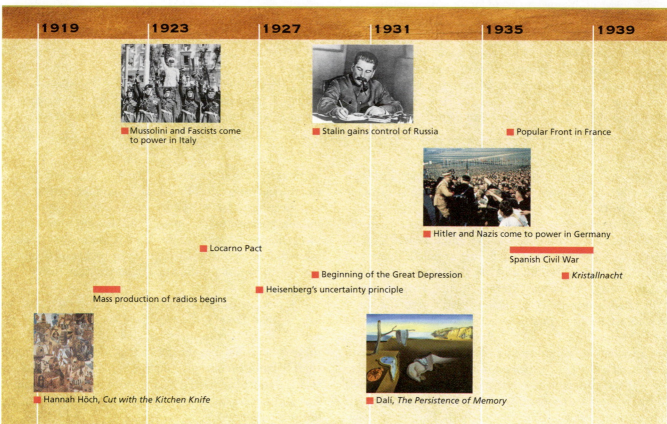

1919	1923	1927	1931	1935	1939

Mussolini and Fascists come to power in Italy

Stalin gains control of Russia

Popular Front in France

Hitler and Nazis come to power in Germany

Spanish Civil War

Locarno Pact

Beginning of the Great Depression

Kristallnacht

Heisenberg's uncertainty principle

Mass production of radios begins

Hannah Höch, *Cut with the Kitchen Knife*

Dalí, *The Persistence of Memory*

CONCLUSION

The devastation wrought by World War I destroyed the liberal optimism of the prewar era. Yet many in the 1920s still hoped that the progress of Western civilization, so seemingly evident before 1914, could somehow be restored. These hopes proved largely unfounded as plans for economic reconstruction gave way to inflation and to the even more devastating Great Depression at the end of the 1920s. Likewise, confidence in political democracy was soon shattered by the rise of authoritarian governments that not only restricted individual freedoms and the rule of law but, in the cases of Italy, Germany, and the Soviet Union, sought even greater control over the lives of their subjects in order to manipulate and guide them to achieve the goals of their totalitarian regimes. For many people, despite the loss of personal freedom, these mass movements offered some sense of security in a world that seemed fraught with uncertainty.

But the seeming security of these mass movements gave rise to even greater uncertainty as Europeans, after a brief twenty-year interlude of peace, again plunged into war, this time on a scale even more horrendous than that of World War I. The twentieth-century crisis, begun in 1914, seemed only to be worsening in 1939, and Western civilization itself appeared to be in great danger.

NOTES

1. Quoted in Stéphane Audoin-Rouzeau and Annette Becker, *14–18: Understanding the Great War,* trans. Catherine Temerson (New York, 2002), pp. 212–213.

2. Quoted in ibid., p. 41.

3. Quoted in Robert Paxton, *Europe in the Twentieth Century,* 2d ed. (New York, 1985), p. 237.

4. Quoted in Denis Mack Smith, *Mussolini* (New York, 1982), p. 51.

5. Benito Mussolini, "The Doctrine of Fascism," in Adrian Lyttleton, ed., *Italian Fascisms from Pareto to Gentile* (London, 1973), p. 42.

6. Quoted in Alexander De Grand, "Women Under Italian Fascism," *Historical Journal* 19 (1976): 958–959.

7. Adolf Hitler, *Mein Kampf,* trans. Ralph Manheim (Boston, 1943), p. 22.

8. Ibid., p. 161.

9. Quoted in Joachim Fest, *Hitler,* trans. Richard Winston and Clara Winston (New York, 1974), p. 241.

10. Quoted in Jeremy Noakes and Geoffrey Pridham, eds., *Nazism, 1919–1945* (Exeter, England, 1983), vol. 1, pp. 50–51.

11. Quoted in Jackson J. Spielvogel, *Hitler and Nazi Germany: A History,* 5th ed. (Upper Saddle River, N.J., 2005), p. 84.

12. Irving Howe, ed., *The Basic Writings of Trotsky* (London, 1963), p. 162.

13. Quoted in Sheila Fitzpatrick, *Everyday Stalinism. Ordinary Life in Extraordinary Times: Soviet Russia in the 1930s* (New York, 1999), p. 87.

14. Paul Valéry, *Variety,* trans. Malcolm Cowley (New York, 1927), pp. 27–28.

15. Quoted in Matthis Eberle, *World War I and the Weimar Artists: Dix, Grosz, Beckmann, Schlemmer* (New Haven, Conn., 1985), p. 54.

16. Norman H. Baynes, ed., *The Speeches of Adolf Hitler, 1922–1939* (Oxford, 1942), vol. 1, p. 591.

SUGGESTIONS FOR FURTHER READING

General Works For a general introduction to the interwar period, see **M. Kitchen, *Europe Between the Wars: A Political History,*** 2d ed. (London, 2006), and the general survey by **R. Paxton, *Europe in the Twentieth Century,*** 4th ed. (New York, 2004). On Europe in the 1930s, see **P. Brendon, *The Dark Valley*** (New York, 2002). On European security issues after the Peace of Paris, see **S. Marks, *The Illusion of Peace: Europe's International Relations, 1918–1933,*** 2d ed. (New York, 2003). The best study on the problem of reparations is **M. Trachtenberg, *Reparations in World Politics*** (New York, 1980), which paints a positive view of French policies. On the Great Depression, see **C. P. Kindleberger, *The World in Depression, 1929–39,*** rev. ed. (Berkeley, Calif., 1986).

The Democratic States On Great Britain, see **B. B. Gilbert, *Britain, 1914–1945*** (London, 1996). France is covered in **A. P. Adamthwaite, *Grandeur and Misery: France's Bid for Power in Europe, 1914–1940*** (London, 1995).

Fascism and Fascist Italy For general studies of fascist movements, see **S. Payne, *A History of Fascism*** (Madison, Wis., 1996), and **R. O. Paxton, *The Anatomy of Fascism*** (New York, 2004). The best biographies of Mussolini are **D. Mack Smith, *Mussolini*** (New York, 1982), and **R. J. B. Bosworth, *Mussolini*** (London, 2002). On Fascist Italy, see **R. J. B. Bosworth, *Mussolini's Italy: Life Under the Fascist Dictatorship*** (New York, 2006).

Nazi Germany On the Weimar Republic, see **P. Bookbinder, *Weimar Germany*** (New York, 1996), and **R. Henig, *The Weimar Republic, 1919–1933*** (New York, 1998). Two brief but sound surveys of Nazi Germany are **J. J. Spielvogel, *Hitler and Nazi Germany: A History,*** 5th ed. (Upper Saddle River, N.J., 2005), and **W. Benz, *A Concise History of the Third Reich,*** trans. T. Dunlap (Berkeley, Calif., 2006). A more detailed examination can be found in **M. Burleigh, *The Third Reich: A New History*** (New York, 2000), and **K. P. Fischer, *Nazi Germany: A New History*** (New York, 1995). On the rise of the Nazis to power, see **R. J. Evans, *The Coming of the Third Reich*** (New York, 2004), the first volume in a projected three-volume history of Nazi Germany. The second volume is ***The Third Reich in Power: 1933–1939*** (New York, 2005). The best biography of Hitler is **I. Kershaw, *Hitler, 1889–1936: Hubris*** (New York, 1999), and ***Hitler: Nemesis*** (New York, 2000). Two recent works that examine the enormous literature on Hitler are **J. Lukacs, *The Hitler of History*** (New York, 1997), and **R. Rosenbaum, *Explaining Hitler*** (New York, 1998). On women, see **C. Koonz, *Mothers in the Fatherland: Women, the Family, and Nazi Politics*** (New York, 1987). The Hitler Youth is examined in **M. Kater, *The Hitler Youth*** (Cambridge, Mass., 2004). The books on the Holocaust cited in Chapter 27 contain background information on Nazi anti-Jewish policies between 1933 and 1939, but see especially **S. Friedländer, *Nazi Germany and the Jews,*** vol. 1: ***The Years of Persecution, 1933–1939*** (New York, 1997).

Authoritarian States Starting points for the study of eastern Europe are **J. Rothschild, *East Central Europe Between the Two World Wars,*** rev. ed. (New York, 1993), and **J. R. Lampe, *Balkans into Southeastern Europe: A Century of War and Transition*** (London, 2006). On the Spanish Civil War, see **F. J. R. Salvado, *The Spanish Civil War*** (New York, 2005); **A. Beevor, *The Battle for Spain: The Spanish Civil War*** (New York, 2006); and **H. Graham, *The Spanish Civil War: A Very Short Introduction*** (Oxford, 2005).

The Stalinist Era The collectivization of agriculture in the Soviet Union is examined in **S. Fitzpatrick, *Stalin's Peasants: Resistance and Survival in the Russian Village After Collectivization*** (New York, 1995); industrialization is covered in **H. Kuromiya, *Stalin's Industrial Revolution: Politics and Workers, 1928–1932*** (New York, 1988). On Stalin, see **R. Service, *Stalin: A Biography*** (Cambridge, Mass., 2006); **S. S. Montefiore, *Stalin: The Court of the Red Tsar*** (New York, 2004); and **R. W. Thurston, *Life and Terror in Stalin's Russia*** (New Haven, Conn., 1996). On everyday life in the Stalinist era, see **S. Fitzpatrick, *Everyday Stalinism*** (Oxford, 1999).

Society and Culture The use of cinema for propaganda purposes is well examined in **D. Welch, *Propaganda and the German Cinema*** (New York, 1985). Gender issues are discussed in **S. K. Kent, *Making Peace: The Reconstruction of Gender in Interwar Britain*** (Princeton, N.J., 1993); **S. Pedersen, *Family, Dependence, and the Origins of the Welfare State: Britain and France, 1914–1945*** (New York, 1994); and **M. L. Roberts, *Civilization Without Sexes: Reconstructing Gender in Postwar France, 1917–1927*** (Chicago, 1994). On the cultural and intellectual environment of Weimar Germany, see **P. Gay, *Weimar Culture: The***

Outsider as Insider (New York, 1968), and **R. Metzger and C. Brandstetter,** *Berlin: The Twenties* (New York, 2007). For a study of Carl Jung, see **D. Bair,** *Jung: A Biography* (New York, 2003).

 CengageNOW is an integrated online suite of services and resources with proven ease of use and efficient paths to success, delivering the results you want—NOW!

academic.cengage.com/login/

Enter CengageNOW using the access card that is available with *Western Civilization.* CengageNOW will assist you in understanding the content in this chapter with lesson plans generated for your needs. In addition, you can read the following documents, and many more, online:

Adolf Hitler, speech

CHAPTER 27

THE DEEPENING OF THE EUROPEAN CRISIS: WORLD WAR II

Adolf Hitler salutes military leaders and soldiers during a military rally.

CHAPTER OUTLINE AND FOCUS QUESTIONS

Prelude to War (1933–1939)

Q What were Hitler's foreign policy goals, and what steps did he take to achieve them between 1933 and 1939? How did Japan's policies lead to war in Asia?

The Course of World War II

Q What were the main events of World War II in Europe and in Asia, and why were the Allies ultimately victorious?

The New Order

Q How was the Nazi empire organized? What was the Holocaust, and what role did it play in Nazi policy?

The Home Front

Q What were conditions like on the home front for Japan and the major Western nations involved in World War II?

Aftermath of the War

Q What were the costs of World War II? How did the Allies' visions of postwar Europe differ, and how did these differences contribute to the emergence of the Cold War?

CRITICAL THINKING

Q What was the relationship between World War I and World War II, and how did the ways in which the wars were fought differ?

ON FEBRUARY 3, 1933, only four days after he had been appointed chancellor of Germany, Adolf Hitler met secretly with Germany's leading generals. He revealed to them his desire to remove the "cancer of democracy," create a new authoritarian leadership, and forge a new domestic unity. All Germans would need to realize that "only a struggle can save us and that everything else must be subordinated to this idea." Youth especially must be trained and their wills strengthened "to fight with all means." Since Germany's living space was too small for its people, Hitler said, Germany must rearm and prepare for "the conquest of new living space in the east and its ruthless Germanization." Even before he had consolidated his power, Hitler had a clear vision of his goals, and their implementation meant another European war. World War II was clearly Hitler's war. Although other countries may have helped make the war possible by not resisting Hitler's Germany earlier, it was Nazi Germany's actions that made World War II inevitable.

World War II was more than just Hitler's war, however. This chapter will focus on the European theater of war, but both European and American armies were also involved in fighting around the world. World War II consisted of two conflicts: one provoked by the ambitions of

Germany in Europe, the other by the ambitions of Japan in Asia. By 1941, with the involvement of the United States in both wars, the two had merged into one global conflict.

Although World War I has been described as a total war, World War II was even more so and was fought on a scale unknown in history. Almost everyone in the warring countries was involved in one way or another: as soldiers; as workers in wartime industries; as ordinary citizens subject to invading armies, military occupation, or bombing raids; as refugees; or as victims of mass extermination. The world had never witnessed such widespread willful death and destruction. ◆

Prelude to War (1933–1939)

Q Focus Questions: What were Hitler's foreign policy goals, and what steps did he take to achieve them between 1933 and 1939? How did Japan's policies lead to war in Asia?

Only twenty years after the "war to end all war," Europe plunged back into the nightmare of total war. The efforts at collective security in the 1920s—the League of Nations, the attempts at disarmament, the pacts and treaties—all proved meaningless in light of the growth of Nazi Germany and its deliberate scrapping of the postwar settlement in the 1930s. Still weary from the last war, France and Britain refused to accept the possibility of another war. The Soviet Union, treated as an outcast by the Western powers, had turned in on itself, and the United States had withdrawn into its traditional isolationism. The small successor states to Austria-Hungary were too weak to oppose Germany. Thus, the power vacuum in the heart of Europe encouraged a revived and militarized Germany to acquire the living space that Hitler claimed Germany needed for its rightful place in the world.

The Role of Hitler

World War II in Europe began in the mind of Adolf Hitler, who believed that only the Aryans were capable of building a great civilization. But to Hitler, the Germans, in his view the leading group of Aryans, were threatened from the east by a large mass of inferior peoples, the Slavs, who had learned to use German weapons and technology. Germany needed more land to support a larger population and be a great power. Hitler was a firm believer in the doctrine of *Lebensraum* (living space), espoused by Karl Haushofer, a professor of geography at the University of Munich. The doctrine of *Lebensraum* maintained that a nation's power depended on the amount and kind of land it occupied. Already in the 1920s, in the second volume of *Mein Kampf*, Hitler had indicated where a National Socialist regime would find this land: "And so we National Socialists . . . take up where we broke off six hundred years ago. We stop the endless

German movement to the south and west, and turn our gaze toward the land in the east. . . . If we speak of soil in Europe today, we can primarily have in mind only Russia and her vassal border states."[1]

In Hitler's view, the Russian Revolution had created the conditions for Germany's acquisition of land to its east. Imperial Russia had been strong only because of its German leadership. The seizure of power by the Bolsheviks (who, in Hitler's mind, were Jewish) had left Russia weak and vulnerable. Once it had been conquered, the land of Russia could be resettled by German peasants, and the Slavic population could be used as slave labor to build the Aryan racial state that would dominate Europe for the next thousand years. Hitler's conclusion was clear: Germany must prepare for its inevitable war with the Soviet Union. Hitler's ideas were by no means secret. He had spelled them out in *Mein Kampf*, a book readily available to anyone who wished to read it (see the box on p. 841).

Hitler and the Nazis were neither the first Europeans nor the first Germans to undertake European conquest and world power. A number of elite circles in Germany before World War I had argued that Germany needed to annex lands to its south, east, and west if it wished to compete with the large states and remain a great power. The defeat in World War I destroyed this dream of world power, but the traditional conservative elites in the German military and the Foreign Office supported Hitler's foreign policy until 1937, largely because it accorded with their own desires for German expansion. But, as they realized too late, Nazi policy went far beyond previous German goals. Hitler's desire to create an Aryan racial empire led to slave labor and even mass extermination on a scale that would have been incomprehensible to previous generations of Germans.

Although Hitler had defined his goals, he had no prearranged timetable for achieving them. During his rise to power, he had demonstrated the ability to be both ideologue and opportunist. After 1933, a combination of military and diplomatic situations, organizational chaos in the administration of Germany, and economic pressures, especially after 1936, caused Hitler periodically to take steps that seemed to contradict the foreign policy goals of *Mein Kampf*. But he always returned to his basic ideological plans for racial supremacy and empire. He was certain of one thing: only he had the ability to accomplish these goals, and his fears for his health pushed him to fulfill his mission as quickly as possible. His impatience would become a major cause of his own undoing.

The "Diplomatic Revolution" (1933–1936)

Between 1933 and 1936, Hitler and Nazi Germany achieved a "diplomatic revolution" in Europe. When Hitler became chancellor of Germany on January 30, 1933, Germany's position in Europe seemed weak. The Versailles treaty had created a demilitarized zone on Germany's western border that would allow the French to move into

HITLER'S FOREIGN POLICY GOALS

Adolf Hitler was a firm believer in the geopolitical doctrine of *Lebensraum*, which advocated that nations must find sufficient living space to be strong. This idea was evident in *Mein Kampf*, but it was explained in even more detail in a treatise that Hitler wrote in 1928. It was not published in his lifetime.

Hitler's *Secret Book*, 1928

I have already dealt with Germany's various foreign policy possibilities in this book. Nevertheless I shall once more briefly present the possible foreign policy goals so that they may yield a basis for the critical examination of the relations of these individual foreign policy aims to those of other European states.

1. Germany can renounce setting a foreign policy goal altogether. This means that in reality she can decide for anything and need be committed to nothing at all.... [Hitler rejects this alternative.]
2. Germany desires to effect the sustenance of the German people by peaceful economic means, as up to now. Accordingly even in the future she will participate most decisively in world industry, export and trade.... From a folkish standpoint setting this foreign policy aim is calamitous, and it is madness from the point of view of power politics.
3. Germany establishes the restoration of the borders of the year 1914 as her foreign policy aim. This goal is insufficient from a national standpoint, unsatisfactory from a military point of view, impossible from a folkish standpoint with its eye on the future, and mad from the viewpoint of its consequences....
4. Germany decides to go over to a clear, far-seeing territorial policy. Thereby she abandons all attempts at world-industry and world-trade and instead concentrates all her strength in order, through the allotment of sufficient living space for the next hundred years to our people, also to prescribe a path of life. Since this territory can be only in the East, the obligation to be a naval power also recedes into the background. Germany tries anew to champion her interests through the formation of a decisive power on land.

This aim is equally in keeping with the highest national as well as folkish requirements. It likewise presupposes great military power means for its execution, but does not necessarily bring Germany into conflict with all European great powers. As surely as France here will remain Germany's enemy, just as little does the nature of such a political aim contain a reason for England, and especially for Italy, to maintain the enmity of the World War.

Q *According to Hitler, what were Germany's possible foreign policy goals? Which one did Hitler prefer? Why? What were the consequences of his decisions in this realm?*

---

the heavily industrialized parts of Germany in the event of war. To Germany's east, the smaller states, such as Poland and Czechoslovakia, had defensive treaties with France. The Versailles treaty had also limited Germany's army to 100,000 troops with no air and limited naval forces.

The Germans were not without advantages, however. Germany was the most populous European state after the Soviet Union and still possessed a great industrial capacity. Hitler was also well aware that Great Britain and France, dismayed by the costs and losses of World War I, wanted to avoid another war. Hitler knew that France posed a threat to an unarmed Germany, but he believed that if he could keep the French from acting against Germany in his first years, he could remove the restrictions imposed on Germany by Versailles and restore its strength.

Hitler's ability to rearm Germany and fulfill his expansionist policies depended initially on whether he could convince others that his intentions were peaceful. Posing as a man of peace in his public speeches, Hitler emphasized that Germany wished only to revise the unfair provisions of Versailles by peaceful means and achieve Germany's rightful place among the European states. During his first two years in office, Hitler pursued a prudent foreign policy without unnecessary risks. His dramatic action in October 1933, when he withdrew Germany from the Geneva Disarmament Conference and the League of Nations, was done primarily for domestic political reasons, to give the Germans the feeling that their country was no longer dominated by other European states.

German Rearmament By the beginning of 1935, Hitler had become convinced that Germany could break some of the provisions of the Treaty of Versailles without serious British and French opposition. Hitler had come to believe, based on their responses to his early actions, that both states wanted to maintain the international status quo, but without using force. Consequently, he decided to announce publicly what had been going on secretly for sometime—Germany's military rearmament. On March 9, 1935, Hitler announced the creation of a new air force and, one week later, the introduction of a military draft that would expand Germany's army from 100,000 to 550,000 troops.

Hitler's unilateral repudiation of the disarmament clauses of the Versailles treaty brought a swift reaction as France, Great Britain, and Italy condemned Germany's action and warned against future aggressive steps. But nothing concrete was done. Even worse, Britain subsequently moved toward open acceptance of Germany's right to rearm when it agreed to the Anglo-German Naval Pact on June 18, 1935. This treaty allowed Germany to build a navy that would be 35 percent of the size of the British navy, with equality in submarines. The British were starting a policy of **appeasement,** based on the belief that if European states satisfied the reasonable demands of dissatisfied powers, the latter would be content, and stability and peace would be achieved in Europe. British appeasement was grounded in large part on Britain's desire to avoid another war, but it was also fostered by British statesmen who believed that Nazi Germany offered a powerful bulwark against Soviet communism.

Occupation of the Rhineland On March 7, 1936, buoyed by his conviction that the Western democracies had no intention of using force to maintain all aspects of the Treaty of Versailles, Hitler sent German troops into the demilitarized Rhineland. According to the Versailles treaty, the French had the right to use force against any violation of the demilitarized Rhineland. But France would not act without British support, and the British viewed the occupation of German territory by German troops as another reasonable action by a dissatisfied power. The London *Times* noted that the Germans were only "going into their own back garden." The French and British response only reinforced Hitler's growing conviction that they were weak nations unwilling to use force to defend the old order. At the same time, since the German generals had opposed his plan, Hitler became even more convinced of his own superior abilities. Many Germans expressed fresh enthusiasm for a leader who was restoring German honor.

New Alliances Meanwhile, Hitler gained new allies. In October 1935, Benito Mussolini had committed Fascist Italy to imperial expansion by invading Ethiopia. Angered by French and British opposition to his invasion, Mussolini welcomed Hitler's support and began to draw closer to the German dictator he had once called a buffoon. The joint intervention of Germany and Italy on behalf of General Francisco Franco in the Spanish Civil War in 1936 also drew the two nations closer together. In October 1936, Mussolini and Hitler concluded an agreement that recognized their common political and economic interests, and one month later, Mussolini referred publicly to the new Rome-Berlin Axis. Also in November 1936, Germany and Japan (the rising military power in the East) concluded the Anti-Comintern Pact and agreed to maintain a common front against communism.

By the end of 1936, Hitler and Nazi Germany had achieved a "diplomatic revolution" in Europe. The Treaty of Versailles had been virtually scrapped, and Germany was once more a "world power," as Hitler proclaimed. Hitler had demonstrated a great deal of diplomatic skill in taking advantage of Europeans'

burning desire for peace. He had used the tactic of peaceful revision as skillfully as he had used the tactic of legality in his pursuit of power in Germany. By the end of 1936, Nazi power had increased enough that Hitler could initiate an even more daring foreign policy. As Hitler perceived, if the Western states were so afraid of war that they resisted its use when they were strong and Germany was weak, then they would be even more reluctant to do so now that Germany was strong. Although many Europeans still wanted to believe that Hitler desired peace, his moves had actually made war more possible.

The Path to War in Europe (1937–1939)

On November 5, 1937, at a secret conference with his military leaders in Berlin, Adolf Hitler revealed his future aims. Germany's ultimate goal, he assured his audience, must be the conquest of living space in the east. Although this might mean war with France and Great Britain, Germany had no alternative if the basic needs of the German people were to be met. First, however, Germany must deal with Austria and Czechoslovakia and secure its eastern and southern flanks.

Ongoing Rearmament In the meantime, Hitler had continued Germany's rearmament at an ever-quickening pace. Expenditures on rearmament rose dramatically: in 1933, 1 billion Reichsmarks; in 1935, 5 billion; in 1937, 9.5 billion; and in 1939, 30 billion. Important to rearmament was the planning for a new type of warfare known as **Blitzkrieg,** or "lightning war." Hitler and some of his military commanders wanted to avoid the trench warfare of World War I and conceived a lightning warfare that depended on mechanized columns and massive air power to cut quickly across battle lines and encircle and annihilate entire armies. Blitzkrieg meant the quick defeat of an enemy and also determined much of Hitler's rearmament program: the construction of a large air force (Luftwaffe) and immense numbers of tanks and armored trucks to carry infantry. The tanks, mechanized infantry, and mobile artillery formed the new panzer divisions that, with air force support, would lead the Blitzkrieg attack. At the same time, the number of men in the German armed services rose from 550,000 in 1935 to 4.5 million in 1939. Naval rearmament also proceeded after the Anglo-German Naval Pact of 1935.

Union with Austria By the end of 1937, Hitler was convinced that neither the French nor the British would provide much opposition to his plans. Neville Chamberlain (1869–1940), who had become prime minister of Britain in May 1937, was a strong advocate of appeasement and believed that the survival of the British Empire depended on an accommodation with Germany. Chamberlain had made it known to Hitler in November 1937 that he would not oppose changes in central Europe, provided that they were executed peacefully.

Hitler Arrives in Vienna. By threatening to invade Austria, Hitler forced the Austrian government to capitulate to his wishes. Austria was annexed to Germany. Shown here is the triumphal arrival of Hitler in Vienna on March 13, 1938. Sitting in the car beside Hitler is Arthur Seyss-Inquart, Hitler's new handpicked governor of Austria.

Bildarchiv Preussischer Kulturbesitz/Art Resource, NY

Hitler decided to move first on Austria. By threatening Austria with invasion, Hitler coerced the Austrian chancellor, Kurt von Schuschnigg (1897–1977), into putting an Austrian Nazi in charge of the government. When German troops marched unopposed into Austria on March 12, 1938, they did so on the "legal basis" of the new Austrian chancellor's request for German troops to assist in establishing law and order. One day later, on March 13, after his triumphal return to his native land, Hitler formally annexed Austria to Germany. Great Britain's ready acknowledgment of Hitler's action and France's inability to respond due to a political crisis only increased the German dictator's contempt for Western weakness.

The annexation of Austria improved Germany's strategic position in central Europe and put Germany in position for Hitler's next objective, the destruction of Czechoslovakia (see Map 27.1). On May 30, 1938, Hitler had already told his generals that it was his "unalterable decision to smash Czechoslovakia by military action in the near future."[2] This goal might have seemed unrealistic since democratic Czechoslovakia was quite prepared to defend itself and was well supported by pacts with France and Soviet Russia. Nevertheless, Hitler believed that France and Britain would not use force to defend Czechoslovakia.

Czechoslovakia   In the meantime, Hitler had stepped up his demands on the Czechs. Initially, the Germans had asked for autonomy for the Sudetenland, the mountainous northwestern border area of Czechoslovakia that was home to 3 million ethnic Germans. As Hitler knew, the Sudetenland also contained Czechoslovakia's most important frontier defenses and considerable industrial

resources as well. But on September 15, 1938, Hitler demanded the cession of the Sudetenland to Germany and expressed his willingness to risk "world war" to achieve his objective. By that time, Hitler was convinced that France and Britain would not use force to defend Czechoslovakia. On paper, the Czech republic seemed well protected by a pact with France. Yet the French made it clear that they would act only if the British supported them. The British refused to do so, and on September 29, at the hastily arranged Munich Conference, the British, French, Germans, and Italians (neither the Czechs nor the Russians were invited) reached an agreement that essentially met all of Hitler's demands. German troops were allowed to occupy the Sudetenland as the Czechs, abandoned by their Western allies, stood by helplessly. The Munich Conference was the high point of Western appeasement of Hitler. When Chamberlain returned to England from Munich, he boasted that the Munich agreement meant "peace for our time." Hitler had promised Chamberlain that he had made his last demand; all other European problems could be settled by negotiation. Like many German politicians, Chamberlain had believed Hitler's assurances (see the box on p. 845).

In fact, Munich confirmed Hitler's perception that the Western democracies were weak and would not fight. Increasingly, Hitler was convinced of his own infallibility, and he had by no means been satisfied at Munich. Already at the end of October 1938, Hitler told his generals to prepare for the final liquidation of the Czechoslovakian state. Using the internal disorder that he had deliberately fostered as a pretext, Hitler occupied the Czech lands (Bohemia and Moravia) while the Slovaks, with Hitler's encouragement, declared their independence of the Czechs and became a puppet state (Slovakia) of Nazi

MAP 27.1 **Changes in Central Europe, 1936–1939.** Hitler's main objectives in the late 1930s were the reoccupation of the Rhineland, incorporation into a greater Germany of lands that contained German people (Austria and the Sudetenland), and the acquisition of *Lebensraum* (living space) in eastern Europe for the expansion of the German people. **Q** What aspects of Czechoslovakia's location would have made it difficult for France and Britain to come directly to its aid in 1938? ❧ **View an animated version of this map or related maps at academic.cengage.com/history/spielvogel**

Germany. On the evening of March 15, 1939, Hitler triumphantly declared in Prague that he would be known as the greatest German of them all.

Poland   At last, the Western states reacted vigorously to Hitler's threat. After all, the Czechs were not Germans crying for reunion with Germany. Hitler's naked aggression made clear that his promises were utterly worthless. When Hitler began to demand the return to

Germany of Danzig, which had been made a free city by the Treaty of Versailles to serve as a seaport for Poland, Britain recognized the danger and offered to protect Poland in the event of war. At the same time, both France and Britain, realizing that only the Soviet Union was powerful enough to help contain Nazi aggression, began political and military negotiations with Joseph Stalin and the Soviets. The West's distrust of Soviet communism, however, made an alliance unlikely.

OPPOSING VIEWPOINTS
THE MUNICH CONFERENCE: TWO VIEWS

At the Munich Conference, the leaders of France and Great Britain capitulated to Hitler's demands on Czechoslovakia. Although the British prime minister, Neville Chamberlain, defended his actions at Munich as necessary for peace, another British statesman, Winston Churchill, characterized the settlement at Munich as "a disaster of the first magnitude."

Winston Churchill, Speech to the House of Commons, October 5, 1938

I will begin by saying what everybody would like to ignore or forget but which must nevertheless be stated, namely, that we have sustained a total and unmitigated defeat, and that France has suffered even more than we have.... The utmost my right honorable Friend the Prime Minister... has been able to gain for Czechoslovakia and in the matters which were in dispute has been that the German dictator, instead of snatching his victuals from the table, has been content to have them served to him course by course.... And I will say this, that I believe the Czechs, left to themselves and told they were going to get no help from the Western Powers, would have been able to make better terms than they have got....

We are in the presence of a disaster of the first magnitude which has befallen Great Britain and France. Do not let us blind ourselves to that....

And do not suppose that this is the end. This is only the beginning of the reckoning. This is only the first sip, the first foretaste of a bitter cup which will be proffered to us year by year unless by a supreme recovery of moral health and martial vigor, we arise again and take our stand for freedom as in the olden time.

Neville Chamberlain, Speech to the House of Commons, October 6, 1938

That is my answer to those who say that we should have told Germany weeks ago that, if her army crossed the border of Czechoslovakia, we should be at war with her. We had no treaty obligations and no legal obligations to Czechoslovakia.... When we were convinced, as we became convinced, that nothing any longer would keep the Sudetenland within the Czechoslovakian State, we urged the Czech Government as strongly as we could to agree to the cession of territory, and to agree promptly.... It was a hard decision for anyone who loved his country to take, but to accuse us of having by that advice betrayed the Czechoslovakian State is simply preposterous. What we did was to save her from annihilation and give her a chance of new life as a new State, which involves the loss of territory and fortifications, but may perhaps enable her to enjoy in the future and develop a national existence under a neutrality and security comparable to that which we see in Switzerland today. Therefore, I think the Government deserve the approval of this House for their conduct of affairs in this recent crisis which has saved Czechoslovakia from destruction and Europe from Armageddon.

Q *What were the opposing views of Churchill and Chamberlain on the Munich Conference? Why did they disagree so much? With whom do you agree? Why?*

Meanwhile, Hitler pressed on in the belief that the West would not really fight over Poland. He ordered his generals to prepare for the invasion of Poland on September 1, 1939. To preclude an alliance between the West and the Soviet Union, which would create the danger of a two-front war, Hitler, ever the opportunist, negotiated his own nonaggression pact with Stalin and shocked the world with its announcement on August 23, 1939. A secret protocol to the treaty created German and Soviet spheres of influence in eastern Europe: Finland, the Baltic states (Estonia, Latvia, and Lithuania), and eastern Poland would go to the Soviet Union, while Germany would acquire western Poland. The treaty with the Soviet Union gave Hitler the freedom to attack Poland. He told his generals: "Now Poland is in the position in which I wanted her.... I am only afraid that at the last moment some swine or other will yet submit to me a plan for mediation."[3] He need not have worried. On September 1, German forces invaded Poland; two days later, Britain and France declared war on Germany. Two weeks later, on September 17, Germany's newfound ally, the Soviet Union, sent its troops into eastern Poland. Europe was again at war.

The Path to War in Asia

The war in Asia arose from the ambitions of Japan, whose rise to the status of world power had been swift. Japan had defeated China in 1895 and Russia in 1905 and had taken over many of Germany's eastern and Pacific colonies in World War I. By 1933, the Japanese Empire included Korea, Formosa (Taiwan), Manchuria, and the Marshall, Caroline, and Mariana islands in the Pacific.

By the early 1930s, Japan was experiencing severe internal tensions. Its population had exploded from 30 million in 1870 to 80 million by 1937. Much of Japan's ability to feed its population and to pay for industrial raw materials depended on the manufacture of heavy industrial goods (especially ships) and textiles. But in the 1930s, Western nations established tariff barriers to protect their own economies from the effects of the depression. Japan was devastated, both economically and politically.

Hitler Declares War. Adolf Hitler believed that it was necessary for Germany to gain living space through conquest in the east. This policy meant war. Hitler's nonaggression pact with the Soviet Union on August 23, 1939, paved the way for his invasion of Poland on September 1. On that day, Hitler spoke to the German Reichstag and announced the outbreak of war.

seizure, which caused Japan to withdraw from the League. During the next several years, Japan consolidated its hold on Manchuria, which it renamed Manchukuo, and then began to expand its control in North China. By the mid-1930s, militant elements connected with the government and the armed forces were effectively in control of Japanese politics.

For the moment, the prime victim of Tokyo's militant strategy was China. When clashes between Chinese and Japanese troops broke out, the Chinese Nationalist leader, Chiang Kai-shek (1887–1975), sought to appease Tokyo by granting Japan the authority to administer areas in North China. But as Japan moved steadily southward, popular protests in Chinese cities against Japanese aggression intensified. When Chinese and Japanese forces clashed at the Marco Polo Bridge, south of Beijing, in July 1937, China refused to apologize, and hostilities spread.

Japan had not planned to declare war on China, but neither side would compromise, and the 1937 incident eventually turned into a major conflict. The Japanese advanced up the Yangtze valley and seized the Chinese capital of Nanjing, raping and killing thousands of innocent civilians in the process. But Chiang Kai-shek refused to capitulate and moved his government upriver to Hankou. Japanese strategists had hoped to force Chiang to join a Japanese-dominated new order in East Asia, comprising Japan, Manchuria, and China. This aim was part of a larger plan to seize Soviet Siberia with its rich resources and create a new "Monroe Doctrine for Asia," in which Japan would guide its Asian neighbors on the path to development and prosperity.

During the late 1930s, Japan began to cooperate with Nazi Germany on the assumption that the two countries would ultimately launch a joint attack on the Soviet Union and divide up its resources between them. But when Germany surprised the world by signing a nonaggression pact with the Soviets in August 1939, Japanese strategists were compelled to reevaluate their long-term objectives. Japan was not strong enough to defeat the Soviet Union alone, so the Japanese began to shift their gaze southward to the vast resources of Southeast Asia—the oil of the Dutch East Indies, the rubber and tin of Malaya, and the rice of Burma and Indochina.

A move southward, of course, would risk war with the European colonial powers, especially Britain and France, as well as with the other rising power in the Pacific, the United States. When the Japanese occupied

Although political power had been concentrated in the hands of the emperor and his cabinet, Japan had also experienced a slow growth of political democracy with universal male suffrage in 1924 and the emergence of mass political parties. The economic crises of the 1930s stifled this democratic growth. Right-wing patriotic societies allied themselves with the army and navy to push a program of expansion at the expense of China and the Soviet Union, while the navy hoped to make Japan self-sufficient in raw materials by conquering British Malaya and the Dutch East Indies. In 1935, Japan began to construct a modern naval fleet, and after 1936, the armed forces exercised much influence over the government.

Japanese Goals in East Asia In September 1931, Japanese soldiers had seized Manchuria, an area of northeastern China that had natural resources Japan needed. Eventually, worldwide protests against the Japanese action led the League of Nations to condemn the Japanese

CHRONOLOGY Prelude to War, 1933–1939

Japan seizes Manchuria	September 1931
Hitler becomes chancellor	January 30, 1933
Hitler announces a German air force	March 9, 1935
Hitler announces military conscription	March 16, 1935
Anglo-German Naval Pact	June 18, 1935
Mussolini invades Ethiopia	October 1935
Hitler occupies demilitarized Rhineland	March 7, 1936
Mussolini and Hitler intervene in the Spanish Civil War	1936
Rome-Berlin Axis	October 1936
Anti-Comintern Pact (Japan and Germany)	November 1936
Japan invades China	1937
Germany annexes Austria	March 13, 1938
Munich Conference: Germany occupies Sudetenland	September 29, 1938
Germany occupies the rest of Czechoslovakia	March 1939
German-Soviet Nonaggression Pact	August 23, 1939
Germany invades Poland	September 1, 1939
Britain and France declare war on Germany	September 3, 1939
Soviet Union invades Poland	September 17, 1939

Indochina in July 1941, the Americans responded by cutting off sales of vital scrap iron and oil to Japan. Japan's military leaders decided to preempt any further American response by attacking the American naval fleet in the Pacific.

The Course of World War II

Q Focus Question: What were the main events of World War II in Europe and in Asia, and why were the Allies ultimately victorious?

Nine days before he attacked Poland, Hitler made clear to his generals what was expected of them: "When starting and waging a war it is not right that matters, but victory. Close your hearts to pity. Act brutally. Eighty million people must obtain what is their right. . . . The wholesale destruction of Poland is the military objective. Speed is the main thing. Pursuit until complete annihilation."[4] Hitler's remarks set the tone for what became the most destructive war in human history.

Victory and Stalemate

Unleashing an early form of Blitzkrieg, or "lightning war," Hitler stunned Europe with the speed and efficiency of the German attack. Moving into Poland with about 1.5 million troops from two fronts, German forces used armored columns or panzer divisions (a **panzer division** was a strike force of about three hundred tanks with accompanying forces and supplies) supported by airplanes to break quickly through the Polish lines and encircle the outnumbered and poorly equipped Polish armies. The coordinated air and ground assaults included the use of Stuka dive bombers; as they descended from the skies, their sirens emitted a blood-curdling shriek, adding a frighteningly destructive element to the German attack. Regular infantry units, still on foot with their supplies drawn by horses, then marched in to hold the

A Japanese Victory in China. After consolidating its authority over Manchuria, Japan began to expand into northern China. Direct hostilities between Japanese and Chinese forces began in 1937. This photograph shows victorious Japanese forces in January 1938 riding under the arched Chungshan Gate in Nanjing after they had conquered the Chinese capital city. By 1939, Japan had conquered most of eastern China.

Keystone/Getty Images

newly conquered territory. Soon afterward, Soviet military forces attacked eastern Poland. Within four weeks, Poland had surrendered. On September 28, 1939, Germany and the Soviet Union officially divided Poland between them.

Hitler's Attack in the West   Although Hitler's hopes of avoiding a war in the west were dashed when France and Britain declared war on September 3, he was confident that he could control the situation. Expecting another war of attrition and economic blockade, Britain and France refused to go on the offensive. Between 1930 and 1935, France had built a series of concrete and steel fortifications armed with heavy artillery—known as the Maginot Line—along its border with Germany. Now France was quite happy to remain in its defensive shell.

After a winter of waiting (called the "phony war"), Hitler resumed the war on April 9, 1940, with another Blitzkrieg, this time against Denmark and Norway. The invasion of Norway was dramatic; the Nazis landed troops at key positions along the coast and dropped paratroopers into airfields and major cities. The British landed a force of almost 50,000 troops but were eventually driven out. Norway surrendered on June 9, and Germany's northern flank was now secure.

One month later, on May 10, the Germans launched their attack on the Netherlands, Belgium, and France. The Netherlands fell in five days. The Dutch city of Rotterdam was devastated by bombing and quickly became a symbol of ruthless Nazi destruction of civilian life. The German forces pushed into Belgium as if to move into France as they had done in World War I, but this was only a trick. The Germans now unleashed their main assault through Luxembourg and the Ardennes, a move that was completely unexpected by the French and British forces. German panzer divisions broke through the weak French defensive positions there, outflanking the Maginot Line, raced across northern France, and reached the English Channel on May 21, splitting the Allied armies. The main Belgian army surrendered on May 28, and the other British and French forces were trapped at Dunkirk. At this point Hitler stopped the advance of the German armored units and ordered the Luftwaffe (the German air force) to destroy the Allied army on the beaches of Dunkirk. The Luftwaffe was ineffective in bombing the Allied forces, however, and by the time Hitler ordered his armored units to advance again, the British had rebuilt their defenses sufficiently to allow for a gigantic evacuation of 350,000 French and British troops by a fleet of small ships. The "miracle of Dunkirk" saved a well-trained army to fight another day.

On June 5, the Germans launched another offensive into southern France. Five days later, Benito Mussolini, believing that the war was over and eager to grab some of the spoils, declared war on France and invaded from the south. Dazed by the speed of the German offensive, the French were never able to mount an adequate resistance and surrendered on June 22. German armies occupied about three-fifths of France while the French hero of World War I, Marshal Henri Pétain (1856–1951), established an authoritarian regime (known as Vichy France) over the remainder. The Allies regarded the Pétain government as a Nazi puppet state, and a French government-in-exile took up residence in Britain. Germany was now in control of western and central Europe, but Britain still had not been defeated.

The Problem of Britain   The German victories in Denmark and Norway had led to a change of government in Britain. Growing dissatisfaction with the apostle of appeasement, Neville Chamberlain, led a member of his own party to say to the prime minister, "You have sat too long for any good you have been doing. Depart, I say, and let us have done with you. In the name of God go!"[5] Chamberlain resigned, and on May 10, 1940, Winston Churchill (1874–1965), a longtime advocate of a hard-line policy toward Nazi Germany, became prime minister. Churchill was confident that he could guide Britain to ultimate victory. "I thought I knew a great deal about it all," he later wrote, "and I was sure I should not fail." Churchill proved to be an inspiring leader who rallied the British people with stirring speeches. Hitler had hoped that the British could be persuaded to make peace so that he could fulfill his long-awaited opportunity to gain living space in the east. Led by the stubbornly determined Churchill, who believed there could be no compromise with Nazism, the British refused, and Hitler was forced to prepare for an invasion of Britain, a prospect that he faced with little confidence.

As Hitler realized, an amphibious invasion of Britain would be possible only if Germany gained control of the air. At the beginning of August 1940, the Luftwaffe launched a major offensive against British air and naval bases, harbors, communication centers, and war industries. The British fought back doggedly, supported by an effective radar system that gave them early warning of German attacks. Moreover, the Ultra intelligence operation, which had broken German military codes, gave the British air force information about the specific targets of German air attacks. Nevertheless, the British air force suffered critical losses by the end of August and was probably saved by Hitler's change of strategy. In September, in retaliation for a British attack on Berlin, Hitler ordered a shift from military targets to massive bombing of cities to break British morale. The British rebuilt their air strength quickly and were soon inflicting major losses on Luftwaffe bombers. By the end of September, Germany had lost the Battle of Britain, and the invasion of Britain had to be postponed.

At this point, Hitler pursued the possibility of a Mediterranean strategy, which would involve capturing Egypt and the Suez Canal and closing the Mediterranean to British ships, thereby shutting off Britain's supply of oil. Hitler's commitment to the Mediterranean was never wholehearted, however. His initial plan was to let the Italians, whose role was to secure the Balkan and

Mediterranean flanks, defeat the British in North Africa, but this strategy failed when the British routed the Italian army. Although Hitler then sent German troops to the North African theater of war, his primary concern lay elsewhere: he had already reached the decision to fulfill his lifetime obsession with the acquisition of living space in the east.

Invasion of the Soviet Union   Already at the end of July 1940, Hitler had told his army leaders to begin preparations for the invasion of the Soviet Union. Although he had no desire for a two-front war, Hitler became convinced that Britain was remaining in the war only because it expected Soviet support. If the Soviet Union were smashed, Britain's last hope would be eliminated. Moreover, Hitler had convinced himself that the Soviet Union, with its Jewish-Bolshevik leadership and a pitiful army, could be defeated quickly and decisively. Although the invasion of the Soviet Union was scheduled for spring 1941, the attack was delayed because of problems in the Balkans.

Hitler had already obtained the political cooperation of Hungary, Bulgaria, and Romania. Mussolini, however, who liked to think of the Balkans as being within the Italian sphere of influence, became considerably upset over Germany's gains in southeastern Europe. To ensure the extension of Italian influence in that region, Mussolini launched an attack on Greece on October 28, 1940. But the Italians were militarily unprepared, and their invasion was quickly stopped. Hitler was furious because the disastrous invasion of Greece exposed his southern flank to British air bases in Greece. To secure his Balkan flank, Hitler first invaded Yugoslavia on April 6, 1941. After its surrender on April 17, he smashed Greece in six days. Now reassured, Hitler turned to the east and invaded the Soviet Union, believing that the Soviets could still be decisively defeated before winter set in.

On June 22, 1941, Nazi Germany launched its attack on the Soviet Union, by far the largest invasion the Germans had yet attempted. The German force consisted of 180 divisions, including 20 panzer divisions, 8,000 tanks, and 3,200 airplanes. German troops were stretched out along an 1,800-mile front (see Map 27.2). The Soviets had 160 infantry divisions but were able to mobilize another 300 divisions out of reserves within half a year. Hitler had badly miscalculated the Soviets' potential power.

The German troops advanced rapidly, capturing 2 million Soviet soldiers. By November, one German army group had swept through the Ukraine while a second was besieging Leningrad; a third approached within 25 miles of Moscow, the Soviet capital. But despite their successes, the Germans had failed to achieve their primary objective. They did not eliminate the Soviet army, nor did the Soviet state collapse in a few months, as Hitler thought it would.

An early winter and unexpected Soviet resistance brought the German advance to a halt. Armor and transport vehicles stalled in temperatures of 30 below

© Artmedia/HIP/The Image Works

German Troops in the Soviet Union.   At first, the German attack on the Soviet Union was enormously successful, leading one German general to remark in his diary: "It is probably no overstatement to say that the Russian campaign has been won in the space of two weeks." This picture shows German troops firing on Soviet positions.

zero. Hitler's commanders wished to withdraw and regroup for the following spring, but Hitler refused. Fearing the disintegration of his lines, he insisted that there would be no retreat. A Soviet counterattack in December 1941 by an army supposedly exhausted by Nazi victories came as an ominous ending to the year. Although the Germans managed to hold on and reestablish their lines, a war diary kept by a member of Panzer Group Three described their desperate situation: "Discipline is breaking down. More and more soldiers are heading west on foot without weapons. . . . The road is under constant air attack. Those killed by bombs are no longer being buried. All the hangers-on (cargo troops, Luftwaffe, supply trains) are pouring to the rear in full flight."[6] By December 1941, another of Hitler's decisions—the declaration of war on the United States—had probably made his defeat inevitable and turned another European conflict into a global war.

The War in Asia

On December 7, 1941, Japanese carrier-based aircraft attacked the United States naval base at Pearl Harbor in the Hawaiian Islands. The same day, other units launched

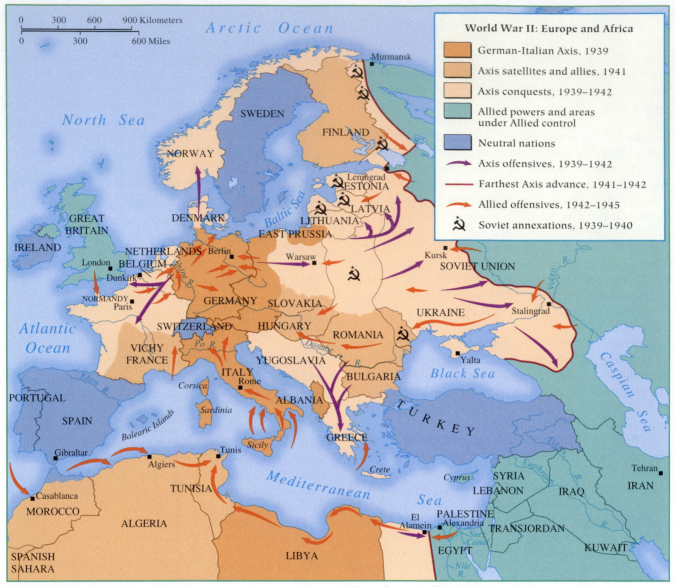

MAP 27.2 **World War II in Europe and North Africa.** With its fast and effective military, Germany quickly overwhelmed much of western Europe. Hitler had overestimated his country's capabilities, however, and underestimated those of his foes. By late 1942, his invasion of the Soviet Union was failing, and the United States had become a major factor in the war. The Allies successfully invaded Italy in 1943 and France in 1944.

Q Which countries were neutral, and how did geography help make their neutrality an option?

View an animated version of this map or related maps at **academic.cengage.com/history/spielvogel**

additional assaults on the Philippines and began advancing toward the British colony of Malaya. The next day, the United States declared war on Japan. Three days later, Hitler declared war on the United States, although he was by no means required to do so by his loose alliance with Japan. This action enabled President Franklin D. Roosevelt to overcome strong American isolationist sentiment and bring the United States into the European conflict.

Shortly after the American entry into the war, Japanese forces invaded the Dutch East Indies and occupied a number of islands in the Pacific Ocean (see Map 27.3). In some cases, as on the Bataan peninsula and the island

of Corregidor in the Philippines, resistance was fierce, but by the spring of 1942, almost all of Southeast Asia and much of the western Pacific had fallen into Japanese hands. Tokyo declared the creation of the Great East Asia Co-Prosperity Sphere, encompassing the entire region under Japanese tutelage, and announced its intention to liberate the colonial areas of Southeast Asia from Western colonial rule. For the moment, however, Japan needed the resources of the region for its war machine and placed the countries under its rule on a wartime basis.

Japanese leaders had hoped that their lightning strike at American bases would destroy the U.S. Pacific Fleet

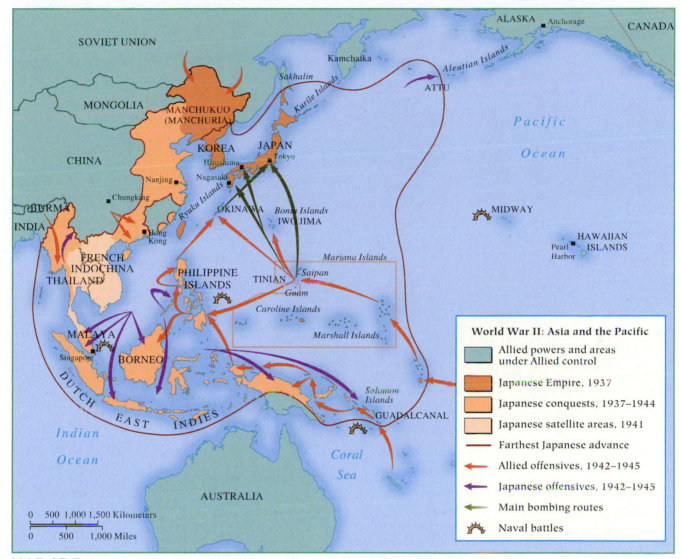

MAP 27.3 **World War II in Asia and the Pacific.** In 1937, Japan invaded northern China, beginning its effort to create a "Great East Asia Co-Prosperity Sphere." Further expansion induced America to end iron and oil sales to Japan. Deciding that war with the United States was inevitable, Japan engineered a surprise attack on Pearl Harbor. **Q** Why was control of the islands in the western Pacific of great importance both to the Japanese and to the Allies? ◉ **View an animated version of this map or related maps at** academic.cengage.com/history/spielvogel

and persuade the Roosevelt administration to accept Japanese domination of the Pacific. The American people, in the eyes of Japanese leaders, had been made soft by material indulgence. But Tokyo had miscalculated. The attack on Pearl Harbor galvanized American opinion and won broad support for Roosevelt's war policy. The United States now joined with European nations and Nationalist China in a combined effort to defeat Japan and bring to an end its hegemony in the Pacific.

The Turning Point of the War (1942–1943)

The entry of the United States into the war created a coalition (the Grand Alliance) that ultimately defeated the Axis powers (Germany, Italy, Japan). Nevertheless, the three major Allies—Britain, the United States, and the Soviet Union—had to overcome mutual suspicions before they could operate as an effective alliance. Two factors aided that process. First, Hitler's declaration of war on the United States made it easier for the Americans to accept the British and Soviet contention that the defeat of Germany should be the first priority of the United States. For that reason, the United States increased the quantity of trucks, planes, and other arms that it sent to the British and Soviets. Also important to the alliance was the tacit agreement of the three chief Allies to stress military operations while ignoring political differences and larger strategic issues concerning any postwar settlement. At the beginning of 1943, the Allies agreed to fight until the Axis powers surrendered unconditionally. Although this

The Air War. Air power played a major role in the battles of World War II. Because his supply lines in North Africa were extended, the German general Erwin Rommel was forced to rely heavily on transport aircraft to keep his forces supplied. This photograph shows a group of German aircraft at an airfield in Libya during the summer of 1941. In the background are the three-engine Junkers Ju-52s used for transporting reinforcements and supplies. Two Messerschmidt fighter planes are in the foreground.

principle of **unconditional surrender** might have discouraged dissident Germans and Japanese from overthrowing their governments in order to arrange a negotiated peace, it also had the effect of cementing the Grand Alliance by making it nearly impossible for Hitler to divide his foes.

Defeat was far from Hitler's mind at the beginning of 1942, however. As Japanese forces advanced into Southeast Asia and the Pacific after crippling the American naval fleet at Pearl Harbor, Hitler and his European allies continued the war in Europe against Britain and the Soviet Union. Until the fall of 1942, it appeared that the Germans might still prevail on the battlefield.

After the British defeat of Italian troops in North Africa, Hitler sent General Erwin Rommel, whom he described as "the most daring general of armored forces in the German army," with the German Afrika Korps to Libya in February 1941. Leading a combined force of Germans and Italians, Rommel attacked on March 30 and by the end of May had reached the Egyptian frontier, where he was finally forced to halt. Reinforcements in North Africa in 1942 enabled the Afrika Korps to break though the British defenses in Egypt, capture Tobruk in June, and begin an advance toward Alexandria.

The Germans were also continuing their success in the Battle of the North Atlantic as their submarines continued to attack Allied ships carrying supplies to Great Britain. In the spring of 1942, a renewed German offensive in the Soviet Union led to the capture of the entire Crimea, causing Hitler to boast in August 1942:

> As the next step, we are going to advance south of the Caucasus and then help the rebels in Iran and Iraq against the English. Another thrust will be directed along the Caspian Sea toward Afghanistan and India. Then the English will run out of oil. In two years we'll be on the borders of India. Twenty to thirty elite German divisions will do. Then the British Empire will collapse.[7]

But this would be Hitler's last optimistic outburst. By the fall of 1942, the war had turned against the Germans.

In North Africa, British forces had stopped Rommel's troops at El Alamein in the summer of 1942 and then forced them back across the desert. In November 1942, British and American forces invaded French North Africa and forced the German and Italian troops to surrender in May 1943. By that time, new detection devices had enabled the Allies to destroy increasing numbers of German submarines in the shipping war in the Atlantic.

Battle of Stalingrad On the Eastern Front, the turning point of the war occurred at Stalingrad. After the capture of the Crimea, Hitler's generals wanted him to concentrate on the Caucasus and its oil fields, but Hitler decided that Stalingrad, a major industrial center on the Volga, should be taken first.

A GERMAN SOLDIER AT STALINGRAD

The Soviet victory at Stalingrad was a major turning point in World War II. This excerpt comes from the diary of a German soldier who fought and died in the Battle of Stalingrad. His dreams of victory and a return home with medals were soon dashed by the realities of Soviet resistance.

Diary of a German Soldier

Today, after we'd had a bath, the company commander told us that if our future operations are as successful, we'll soon reach the Volga, take Stalingrad and then the war will inevitably soon be over. Perhaps we'll be home by Christmas.

July 29. The company commander says the Russian troops are completely broken, and cannot hold out any longer. To reach the Volga and take Stalingrad is not so difficult for us. The Führer knows where the Russians' weak point is. Victory is not far away....

August 10. The Führer's orders were read out to us. He expects victory of us. We are all convinced that they can't stop us.

August 12. This morning outstanding soldiers were presented with decorations.... Will I really go back to Elsa without a decoration? I believe that for Stalingrad the Führer will decorate even me....

September 4. We are being sent northward along the front toward Stalingrad. We marched all night and by dawn had reached Voroponovo Station. We can already see the smoking town. It's a happy thought that the end of the war is getting nearer. That's what everyone is saying....

September 8. Two days of non-stop fighting. The Russians are defending themselves with insane stubbornness. Our regiment has lost many men....

September 16. Our battalion, plus tanks, is attacking the [grain storage] elevator, from which smoke is pouring—the grain in it is burning, the Russians seem to have set light to it themselves. Barbarism. The battalion is suffering heavy losses....

October 10. The Russians are so close to us that our planes cannot bomb them. We are preparing for a decisive attack. The Führer has ordered the whole of Stalingrad to be taken as rapidly as possible....

October 22. Our regiment has failed to break into the factory. We have lost many men; every time you move you have to jump over bodies....

November 10. A letter from Elsa today. Everyone expects us home for Christmas. In Germany everyone believes we already hold Stalingrad. How wrong they are. If they could only see what Stalingrad has done to our army....

November 21. The Russians have gone over to the offensive along the whole front. Fierce fighting is going on. So, there it is—the Volga, victory and soon home to our families! We shall obviously be seeing them next in the other world.

November 29. We are encircled. It was announced this morning that the Führer has said: "The army can trust me to do everything necessary to ensure supplies and rapidly break the encirclement."

December 3. We are on hunger rations and waiting for the rescue that the Führer promised....

December 14. Everybody is racked with hunger. Frozen potatoes are the best meal, but to get them out of the ice-covered ground under fire from Russian bullets is not so easy....

December 26. The horses have already been eaten. I would eat a cat; they say its meat is also tasty. The soldiers look like corpses or lunatics, looking for something to put in their mouths. They no longer take cover from Russian shells; they haven't the strength to walk, run away and hide. A curse on this war!

Q *What did this soldier believe about the Führer? Why? What was the source of his information? Why is the battle for Stalingrad considered a major turning point in World War II?*

The German advance on Stalingrad encountered fierce resistance, but Hitler was determined to capture the city named after the Soviet dictator. Stalin had issued a war order called "Not a Step Back." Although the Germans destroyed much of the city, the Soviet troops used the bombed-out buildings and factories as well-fortified defensive positions. A deadly and brutal street-by-street conflict evolved during September, October, and November, in which both sides took severe losses. On November 8, Hitler announced that the German Sixth Army had taken Stalingrad, but in fact, on November 19 and 20, the Soviets attacked German positions north and south of Stalingrad, and by November 23 they had surrounded the German forces. Hitler commanded General Friedrich von Paulus to stand firm with his Sixth Army and forbade attempts to break out of the encirclement. Winter privations and Soviet attacks, however, forced the Germans to surrender on February 2, 1943 (see the box above). The entire German Sixth Army of 300,000 men was lost. By February 1943, German forces in the Soviet Union were back to their positions of June 1942. By the spring of 1943, even Hitler knew that the Germans would not defeat the Soviet Union.

Battle of Midway The tide of battle in Asia also turned dramatically in 1942. In the Battle of the Coral Sea on May 7–8, 1942, American naval forces stopped the Japanese advance and temporarily relieved Australia of the threat of invasion. On June 4, at the Battle of Midway Island, American planes destroyed all four of the attacking

Crossing the Rhine. After landing at Normandy, Allied forces liberated France and prepared to move into Germany. Makeshift bridges enabled the Allies to cross the Rhine in some areas and advance deeper into Germany. Units of the U.S. Seventh Army of General Patch are shown here crossing the Rhine at Worms on a pontoon bridge constructed by battalions of engineers alongside the ruins of the old bridge.

Japanese aircraft carriers and established American naval superiority in the Pacific. The victory was especially remarkable in that almost all of the American planes were shot down in the encounter. By the fall of 1942, Allied forces were beginning to gather for offensive operations in three areas: from Burma into South China; through the Indonesian islands, where troops commanded by the American general Douglas MacArthur would proceed by a process of "island hopping"; and across the Pacific where combined U.S. Army, Marine, and Navy forces would mount attacks against Japanese-held islands. After a series of bitter engagements in the waters off the Solomon Islands from August to November 1942, Japanese fortunes began to fade.

The Last Years of the War

By the beginning of 1943, the tide of battle had turned against Germany, Italy, and Japan, but it would take a long time to achieve the goal of unconditional surrender of the three Axis powers. After the Axis forces had surrendered in Tunisia on May 13, 1943, the Allies crossed the Mediterranean and carried the war to Italy, an area that Winston Churchill had called the "soft underbelly" of Europe. After taking Sicily, Allied troops began the invasion of mainland Italy in September. In the meantime, after the ouster and arrest of Benito Mussolini, a new Italian government offered to surrender to Allied forces. But Mussolini was liberated by the Germans in a daring raid and then set up as the head of a puppet German state in northern Italy while German troops moved in and occupied much of Italy. The new defensive lines established by the Germans in the hills south of Rome were so effective that the Allied advance up the Italian peninsula was a painstaking affair accompanied by heavy casualties. Rome did not fall to the Allies until June 4, 1944. By that time, the Italian war had assumed a secondary role anyway as the Allies opened their long-awaited "second front" in western Europe two days later.

Allied Advances in the West   Since the autumn of 1943, the Allies had been planning a cross-channel invasion of France from Britain. A series of Allied deceptions managed to trick the Germans into believing that the invasion would come on the flat plains of northern France. Instead, the Allies, under the direction of the American general, Dwight D. Eisenhower (1890–1969), landed five assault divisions on the Normandy beaches on June 6 in history's greatest amphibious invasion. Three airborne divisions were also sent to secure the flanks of the areas where the troops went ashore. Putting 150,000 troops ashore in one day required the support of more than 7,000 naval ships. An initially indecisive German response enabled the Allied forces to establish a beachhead. Within three months, they had landed 2 million men and a half-million vehicles that pushed inland and broke through the German defensive lines.

After the breakout, Allied troops moved south and east and liberated Paris by the end of August. Supply problems as well as a last-minute, desperate (and unsuccessful) offensive by German troops in the Battle of the Bulge slowed the Allied advance. Nevertheless, by March 1945, Allied armies had crossed the Rhine River and advanced further into Germany. At the end of April, Allied forces in northern Germany moved toward the Elbe River, where they finally linked up with the Soviets.

Soviet Offensive in the East   The Soviets had come a long way since the Battle of Stalingrad in 1943. In the summer of 1943, Hitler's generals had urged him to build an "east wall" based on river barriers to halt the Soviets. Instead, Hitler gambled on taking the offensive by making use of newly developed heavy tanks. German forces were soundly defeated by the Soviets at the Battle of

Germany and the Soviet Union divide Poland	September 1939
Blitzkrieg against Denmark and Norway	April 1940
Blitzkrieg against Belgium, Netherlands, and France	May 1940
Churchill becomes British prime minister	May 10, 1940
France surrenders	June 22, 1940
Battle of Britain	Fall 1940
Nazi seizure of Yugoslavia and Greece	April 1941
Germany invades the Soviet Union	June 22, 1941
Japanese attack on Pearl Harbor	December 7, 1941
Battle of the Coral Sea	May 7–8, 1942
Battle of Midway Island	June 4, 1942
Allied invasion of North Africa	November 1942
Soviets win Battle of Stalingrad	February 2, 1943
Axis forces surrender in North Africa	May 13, 1943
Battle of Kursk	July 5–12, 1943
Invasion of mainland Italy	September 1943
Allied invasion of France	June 6, 1944
Hitler commits suicide	April 30, 1945
Germany surrenders	May 7, 1945
Atomic bomb dropped on Hiroshima	August 6, 1945
Japan surrenders	August 14, 1945

Kursk (July 5–12), the greatest tank battle of World War II. The Germans lost eighteen of their best panzer divisions. Soviet forces now began a relentless advance westward. The Soviets had reoccupied the Ukraine by the end of 1943 and lifted the siege of Leningrad and moved into the Baltic states by the beginning of 1944. Advancing along a northern front, Soviet troops occupied Warsaw in January 1945 and entered Berlin in April. Meanwhile, Soviet troops swept along a southern front through Hungary, Romania, and Bulgaria.

In January 1945, Adolf Hitler had moved into a bunker 55 feet under Berlin to direct the final stages of the war. Hitler continued to arrange his armies on worn-out battle maps as if it still made a difference. In his final political testament, Hitler, consistent to the end in his rabid anti-Semitism, blamed the Jews for the war: "Above all I charge the leaders of the nation and those under them to scrupulous observance of the laws of race and to merciless opposition to the universal poisoner of all peoples, international Jewry."[8] Hitler committed suicide on April 30, two days after Mussolini had been shot by partisan Italian forces. On May 7, German commanders surrendered. The war in Europe was over.

Defeat of Japan   The war in Asia continued. Beginning in 1943, American forces had gone on the offensive and advanced their way, slowly at times, across the Pacific.

American forces took an increasing toll of enemy resources, especially at sea and in the air. When President Harry Truman (Roosevelt had died on April 12, 1945) and his advisers became convinced that American troops might suffer heavy casualties in the invasion of the Japanese homeland, they made the decision to drop the newly developed atomic bomb on Hiroshima and Nagasaki. The Japanese surrendered unconditionally on August 14. World War II was finally over.

The New Order

Q **Focus Questions:** How was the Nazi empire organized? What was the Holocaust, and what role did it play in Nazi policy?

The initial victories of the Germans and the Japanese gave them the opportunity to create new orders in Europe and Asia. Although both countries presented positive images of these new orders for publicity purposes, in practice both followed policies of ruthless domination of their subject peoples.

The Nazi Empire

After the German victories in Europe, Nazi propagandists created glowing images of a new European order based on "equal chances" for all nations and an integrated economic community. This was not Hitler's conception of a European New Order. He saw the Europe he had conquered simply as subject to German domination. Only the Germans, he once said, "can really organize Europe."

The Nazi empire stretched across continental Europe from the English Channel in the west to the outskirts of Moscow in the east. In no way was this empire organized systematically or governed efficiently. Some states—Spain, Portugal, Switzerland, Sweden, and Turkey—remained neutral and outside the empire. Germany's allies—Italy, Romania, Bulgaria, Hungary, and Finland—kept their independence but found themselves increasingly restricted by the Germans as the war progressed. The remainder of Europe was largely organized in one of two ways. Some areas, such as western Poland, were directly annexed by Nazi Germany and made into German provinces. Most of occupied Europe was administered by German military or civilian officials, combined with varying degrees of indirect control from collaborationist regimes. Competing lines of authority by different offices in occupied Europe made German occupation inefficient.

Racial considerations played an important role in how conquered peoples were treated in the **Nazi New Order.** German civil administrations were established in Norway, Denmark, and the Netherlands because the Nazis considered their peoples Aryan, racially akin to the Germans and hence worthy of more lenient treatment. "Inferior" Latin peoples, such as the occupied French, were given

HITLER'S PLANS FOR A NEW ORDER IN THE EAST

Hitler's nightly monologues to his postdinner guests, which were recorded by the Führer's private secretary, Martin Bormann, reveal much about the New Order he wished to create. On the evening of October 17, 1941, he expressed his views on what the Germans would do with their newly conquered territories in the east.

Hitler's Secret Conversations, October 17, 1941

In comparison with the beauties accumulated in Central Germany, the new territories in the East seem to us like a desert.... This Russian desert, we shall populate it.... We'll take away its character of an Asiatic steppe, we'll Europeanize it. With this object, we have undertaken the construction of roads that will lead to the southernmost point of the Crimea and to the Caucasus. These roads will be studded along their whole length with German towns, and around these towns our colonists will settle.

As for the two or three million men whom we need to accomplish this task, we'll find them quicker than we think. They'll come from Germany, Scandinavia, the Western countries and America. I shall no longer be here to see all that, but in twenty years the Ukraine will already be a home for twenty million inhabitants besides the natives. In three hundred years, the country will be one of the loveliest gardens in the world.

As for the natives, we'll have to screen them carefully. The Jew, that destroyer, we shall drive out.... We shan't settle in the Russian towns, and we'll let them fall to pieces without intervening. And, above all, no remorse on this subject! We're not going to play at children's nurses; we're absolutely without obligations as far as these people are concerned. To struggle against the hovels, chase away the fleas, provide German teachers, bring out newspapers—very little of that for us! We'll confine ourselves, perhaps, to setting up a radio transmitter, under our control. For the rest, let them know just enough to understand our highway signs, so that they won't get themselves run over by our vehicles.... There's only one duty: to Germanize this country by the immigration of Germans, and to look upon the natives as Redskins. If these people had defeated us, Heaven have mercy! But we don't hate them. That sentiment is unknown to us. We are guided only by reason....

All those who have the feeling for Europe can join in our work.

In this business I shall go straight ahead, cold-bloodedly. What they may think about me, at this juncture, is to me a matter of complete indifference. I don't see why a German who eats a piece of bread should torment himself with the idea that the soil that produces this bread has been won by the sword.

Q *What new order did Hitler envision in the east? What would its achievement have meant for the peoples of eastern Europe?*

---

military administrations. By 1943, however, as Nazi losses continued to multiply, all the occupied territories of northern and western Europe were ruthlessly exploited for material goods and workers for Germany's war needs.

Plans for an Aryan Racial Empire Because the conquered lands in the east contained the living space for German expansion and were populated in Nazi eyes by racially inferior Slavic peoples, Nazi administration there was considerably more ruthless. Hitler's racial ideology and his plans for an Aryan racial empire were so important to him that he and the Nazis began to implement their racial program soon after the conquest of Poland. Heinrich Himmler, a strong believer in Nazi racial ideology and the leader of the SS, was put in charge of German resettlement plans in the east. Himmler's task was to evacuate the inferior Slavic peoples and replace them with Germans, a policy first applied to the new German provinces created from the lands of western Poland. One million Poles were uprooted and dumped in southern Poland. Hundreds of thousands of ethnic Germans (descendants of Germans who had migrated years earlier from Germany to various parts of southern and eastern Europe) were encouraged to colonize the designated areas in Poland. By 1942, 2 million ethnic Germans had been settled in Poland.

The invasion of the Soviet Union inflated Nazi visions of German colonization in the east. Hitler spoke to his intimate circle of a colossal project of social engineering after the war, in which Poles, Ukrainians, and Soviets would become slave labor and German peasants would settle on the abandoned lands and Germanize them (see the box above). Nazis involved in this kind of planning were well aware of the human costs. Himmler told a gathering of SS officers that although the destruction of 30 million Slavs was a prerequisite for German plans in the east, "whether nations live in prosperity or starve to death interests me only insofar as we need them as slaves for our culture. Otherwise it is of no interest."[9]

Economic Exploitation Economically, the Nazi New Order meant the ruthless exploitation of conquered Europe's resources. In eastern Europe, economic exploitation was direct and severe. The Germans seized raw materials, machines, and food, leaving only enough to maintain local peoples at a bare subsistence level. Although the Germans adopted legal formalities in their economic exploitation of western Europe, military supplies and important raw materials were taken outright. As Nazi policies created drastic shortages of food, clothing, and shelter, many Europeans suffered severely.

Use of Foreign Workers Labor shortages in Germany led to a policy of ruthless mobilization of foreign labor for Germany. After the invasion of the Soviet Union, the 4 million Soviet prisoners of war captured by the Germans became a major source of heavy labor, but it was wasted by allowing 3 million of them to die from neglect. In 1942, a special office was created to recruit labor for German farms and industries. By the summer of 1944, 7 million foreign workers were laboring in Germany and constituted 20 percent of Germany's labor force. At the same time, another 7 million workers were supplying forced labor in their own countries on farms, in industries, and even in military camps. Forced labor often proved counterproductive, however, because it created economic chaos in occupied countries and disrupted industrial production that could have helped Germany. Even worse for the Germans, the brutal character of Germany's recruitment policies often led more and more people to resist the Nazi occupation forces.

Resistance Movements

German policies toward conquered peoples quickly led to the emergence of resistance movements throughout Europe, especially in the east, where brutality toward the native peoples produced a strong reaction. In the Ukraine and the Baltic states, for example, the Germans were initially hailed as liberators from Communist rule, but Hitler's policies of treating Slavic peoples as subhumans only drove those peoples to support and join guerrilla forces.

Resistance Movements in Nazi-Occupied Europe Resistance movements were formed throughout Europe. Active resisters committed acts of sabotage against German installations, assassinated German officials, spread anti-German newspapers, wrote anti-German sentiments on walls, and spied on German military positions for the Allies. Some anti-Nazi groups from occupied countries, such as the Free French movement under Charles de Gaulle, created governments-in-exile in London. In some countries, resistance groups even grew strong enough to take on the Germans in pitched battles. In Yugoslavia, for example, Josip Broz, known as Tito (1892–1980), led a band of guerrillas against German occupation forces. By 1944, his partisan army numbered 250,000, including 100,000 women.

After the invasion of the Soviet Union in 1941, Communists throughout Europe assumed leadership roles in underground resistance movements. This sometimes led to conflict with other local resistance groups who feared the postwar consequences of Communist power. Charles de Gaulle's Free French movement, for example, thwarted the attempt of French Communists to dominate the major French resistance groups.

Women, too, joined resistance movements in large numbers throughout Nazi-occupied Europe. Women served as message carriers, planted bombs in Nazi headquarters, assassinated Nazi officers, published and spread anti-German underground newspapers, spied on German military movements and positions, and used shopping baskets to carry weapons, medicines, and money to help their causes. In Norway, women smuggled Jews into neutral Sweden. In Greece, wives dressed their husbands as women to save them when the Nazis sought to stop acts of sabotage by vicious reprisals in which all the males of a village were executed.

Resistance in Germany Germany had its resistance movements, too, although the increased control of the SS over everyday life made resistance both dangerous and ineffectual. The White Rose movement involved an attempt by a small group of students and one professor at the University of Munich to distribute pamphlets denouncing the Nazi regime as lawless, criminal, and godless. Its members were caught, arrested, and promptly executed. Likewise, Communist resistance groups were mostly crushed by the Gestapo (the secret police).

Only one plot against Hitler and the Nazi regime came remotely close to success. It was the work primarily of a group of military officers and conservative politicians who were appalled at Hitler's warmongering and sickened by the wartime atrocities he had encouraged. One of their number, Colonel Count Claus von Stauffenberg (1907–1944), believed that only the elimination of Hitler would bring the overthrow of the Nazi regime. On July 20, 1944, a bomb planted by Stauffenberg in Hitler's East Prussian headquarters exploded, but it failed to kill the dictator. The plot was then quickly uncovered and crushed. Five thousand people were executed, and Hitler remained in control of Germany.

The Holocaust

There was no more terrifying aspect of the Nazi New Order than the deliberate attempt to exterminate the Jewish people of Europe. Racial struggle was a key element in Hitler's ideology and meant to him a clearly defined conflict of opposites: the Aryans, creators of human cultural development, against the Jews, parasites who were trying to destroy the Aryans. At a meeting of the Nazi Party in 1922, Hitler proclaimed, "There can be no compromise—there are only two possibilities: either victory of the Aryan or annihilation of the Aryan and the victory of the Jew."[10] Although Hitler later toned down his anti-Semitic message when his party sought mass electoral victories, anti-Semitism was a recurring theme in Nazism and resulted in a wave of legislative acts against the Jews between 1933 and 1939 (see Chapter 26).

Early Nazi Policy By the beginning of 1939, Nazi policy focused on promoting the "emigration" of German Jews from Germany. At the same time, Hitler had given ominous warnings about the future of European Jewry. When he addressed the German Reichstag on January 30, 1939, he stated:

> I have often been a prophet in life and was generally laughed at. During my struggle for power, the Jews primarily received with laughter my prophecies that I would someday assume

FILM & HISTORY
EUROPA, EUROPA (1990)

Directed by Agnieszka Holland, *Europa, Europa* (known as *Hitlerjunge Salomon* [Hitler Youth Salomon] in Germany) is a harrowing story of one Jewish boy's escape from the horrors of Nazi persecution. It is based on the memoirs of Salomon Perel, a German Jew of Polish background who survived by pretending to be a pure Aryan. The film begins in 1938 during Kristallnacht when the family of Solly (a nickname for Salomon Perel) is attacked in their hometown of Peine, Germany. Solly's sister is killed, and the family moves back to Poland. When the Nazis invade Poland, Solly (Marco Hofschneider) and his brother are sent east, but the brothers become separated and Solly is placed in a Soviet orphanage in Grodno in the eastern part of Poland occupied by the Soviets.

For two years Solly becomes a dedicated Communist youth, but when the Germans invade in 1941, he falls into their hands and quickly assumes a new identity in order to survive. He becomes Josef "Jupp" Peters, supposedly the son of German parents from Latvia. Fluent in both Russian and German, Solly/Jupp becomes a translator for the German forces. After an unintended act of bravado, he is rewarded by being sent to a Hitler Youth school where he lives in fear of being exposed as a Jew because of his circumcised penis. He manages to survive the downfall of Nazi Germany and at the end of the war makes his way with his brother, who has also survived, to Palestine. Throughout much of the movie, Solly/Jupp lives in constant fear that his true identity as a Jew will be recognized, but his luck, charm, and resourcefulness enable him to survive a series of extraordinary events.

Although there is no way of knowing if each detail of this movie is historically accurate (and a few are absurdly inaccurate, such as a bombing run by a plane that was not developed until after the war), overall the story has the ring of truth. The fanaticism of both the Soviet and the Nazi officials who indoctrinate young people seems real. The scene in the Hitler Youth school on how to identify a Jew is realistic, even when it is made ironic by the instructor's choice of Solly/Jupp to demonstrate the characteristics of a true Aryan. The movie also realistically portrays the fearful world in which Jews had to live under the Nazis before the war and the horrible conditions of the Jewish

Salomon Perel/Josef Peters (Marco Hofschneider) as a Hitler Youth member

ghettos in Polish cities during the war. The film shows how people had to fight for their survival in a world of ideological madness, when Jews were killed simply for being Jews. The attitudes of the German soldiers also seem real. Many are shown following orders and killing Jews based on the beliefs in which they have been indoctrinated. But the movie also portrays some German soldiers whose humanity did not allow them to kill Jews. One homosexual soldier discovers that Solly/Jupp is a Jew when he tries—unsuccessfully—to have sex with him. The soldier then becomes the boy's protector until he himself is killed in battle.

Many movies have been made about the horrible experiences of Jews during World War II, but this one is quite different from most of them. It might never have been made except for the fact that Salomon Perel, who was told by his brother not to tell his story because no one would believe it, was inspired to write his memoirs after a 1985 reunion with his former Hitler Youth group leader. This passionate and intelligent film is ultimately a result of that encounter.

---

the leadership of the state and thereby of the entire Volk and then, among many other things, achieve a solution of the Jewish problem.... Today I will be a prophet again: if international finance Jewry within Europe and abroad should succeed once more in plunging the peoples into a world war, then the consequence will be not the Bolshevization of the world and therewith a victory of Jewry, but on the contrary, the destruction of the Jewish race in Europe.[11]

At the time, emigration was still the favored policy. Once the war began in September 1939, the so-called Jewish

problem took on new dimensions. For a while, there was discussion of the Madagascar Plan, which aspired to the mass shipment of Jews to the island of Madagascar, off the eastern coast of Africa. When war contingencies made this plan impracticable, an even more drastic policy was conceived.

The SS and the *Einsatzgruppen* Heinrich Himmler and the SS organization closely shared Adolf Hitler's racial ideology. The SS was given responsibility for what the

Les Films Du Losange/CCC Filmkunst/The Kobal Collection

The Holocaust: Activities of the *Einsatzgruppen*. The activities of the mobile killing units known as the *Einsatzgruppen* were the first stage in the mass killings of the Holocaust. This picture shows the execution of a Jew by a member of one of these SS killing squads. Onlookers include members of the German army, the German Labor Service, and even Hitler Youth. When it became apparent that this method of killing was inefficient, it was replaced by the death camps.

Nazis called their **Final Solution** to the Jewish problem—the annihilation of the Jewish people. Reinhard Heydrich (1904–1942), head of the SS's Security Service, was given administrative responsibility for the Final Solution. After the defeat of Poland, Heydrich ordered the special strike forces (***Einsatzgruppen***) that he had created to round up all Polish Jews and concentrate them in ghettos established in a number of Polish cities.

In June 1941, the *Einsatzgruppen* were given new responsibilities as mobile killing units. These SS death squads followed the regular army's advance into the Soviet Union. Their job was to round up Jews in their villages and execute and bury them in mass graves, often giant pits dug by the victims themselves before they were shot. The leader of one of these death squads described the mode of operation:

The unit selected for this task would enter a village or city and order the prominent Jewish citizens to call together all Jews for the purpose of resettlement. They were requested to hand over their valuables to the leaders of the unit, and shortly before the execution to surrender their outer clothing. The men, women, and children were led to a place of execution which in most cases was located next to a more deeply excavated anti-tank ditch. Then they were shot, kneeling or standing, and the corpses thrown into the ditch.[12]

Such regular killing created morale problems among the SS executioners. During a visit to Minsk in the Soviet Union, SS leader Himmler tried to build morale by pointing out that "he would not like it if Germans did such a thing gladly. But their conscience was in no way impaired, for they were soldiers who had to carry out every order unconditionally. He alone had responsibility before God and Hitler for everything that was happening, . . . and he was acting from a deep understanding of the necessity for this operation."[13]

The Death Camps Although it has been estimated that as many as one million Jews were killed by the *Einsatzgruppen*, this approach to solving the Jewish problem was soon perceived as inadequate. Instead, the Nazis opted for the systematic annihilation of the European Jewish population in specially built death camps. The plan was simple. Jews from countries occupied by Germany (or sympathetic to Germany) would be rounded up, packed like cattle into freight trains, and shipped to Poland, where six extermination centers were built for this purpose (see Map 27.4). The largest and most infamous was Auschwitz-Birkenau. Technical assistance for the construction of the camps was provided by experts from the T-4 program, which had been responsible for the extermination of 80,000 alleged racially unfit mental and physical defectives in Germany between 1938 and 1941. Based on their experiences, medical technicians chose Zyklon B (the commercial name for hydrogen cyanide) as the most effective gas for quickly killing large numbers of people in gas chambers designed to look like shower rooms to facilitate the cooperation of the victims. After gassing, the corpses would be burned in specially built crematoria.

To inform party and state officials of the general procedures for the Final Solution, a conference was held at Wannsee, outside Berlin, on January 20, 1942. Reinhard Heydrich outlined the steps that would now be taken to "solve the Jewish question." He explained how "in the course of the practical implementation of the final solution Europe is to be combed through from west to east" for Jews, who would then be brought "group by group, into so-called transit ghettos, to be transported from there farther to the east." The conference then worked out all of the bureaucratic details so that party and state officials would cooperate fully in the final elimination of the Jews.

By the spring of 1942, the death camps were in operation. Although initial priority was given to the

MAP 27.4 The Holocaust.
Hitler used the fiction of the Aryan race, to which Germans supposedly belonged, to help radicalize the German people and justify his hatred of Jews. Hitler's "Final Solution" to the "Jewish problem" was mass execution of Europe's Jews in death camps.

Q Which region lost the largest number of Jews in the camps, and what helps explain this?

View an animated version of this map or related maps at academic.cengage.com/ history/spielvogel

Map legend:
- ⚡Dachau Concentration camp
- ⚡Treblinka Death camp
- 277,000 Estimated Jewish death toll (per country)

elimination of the ghettos in Poland, by the summer of 1942, Jews were also being shipped from France, Belgium, and the Netherlands. In 1943, there were shipments of Jews from the capital cities of Berlin, Vienna, and Prague and from Greece, southern France, Italy, and Denmark. Even as the Allies were making important advances in 1944, Jews were being shipped from Greece and Hungary. These shipments depended on the cooperation of Germany's Transport Ministry, and despite desperate military needs, the Final Solution had priority in using railroad cars for the transportation of Jews to the death camps. Even the military argument that Jews could be used to produce armaments was overridden by the demands of extermination.

A harrowing experience awaited the Jews when they arrived at one of the six death camps. Rudolf Höss, commandant at Auschwitz-Birkenau, described it:

> We had two SS doctors on duty at Auschwitz to examine the incoming transports of prisoners. The prisoners would be marched by one of the doctors who would make spot decisions as they walked by. Those who were fit for work were sent into the camp. Others were sent immediately to the extermination plants. Children of tender years were invariably exterminated since by reason of their youth they were unable to work. . . . At Auschwitz we endeavored to fool the victims into thinking that they were to go through a delousing process. Of course, frequently they realized our true intentions and we sometimes had riots and difficulties due to that fact.[14]

About 30 percent of the arrivals at Auschwitz were sent to a labor camp; the remainder went to the gas chambers (see the box on p. 862). After they had been gassed, the bodies were burned in the crematoria. The victims' goods and even their bodies were used for economic gain. Female hair was cut off, collected, and turned into mattresses or cloth. Some inmates were also subjected to cruel and painful "medical" experiments. The Germans killed between 5 and 6 million Jews, more than 3 million of them in the death camps. Virtually 90 percent of the Jewish populations of Poland, the Baltic countries, and Germany were exterminated. Overall, the Holocaust was responsible for the death of nearly two out of every three European Jews.

The Other Holocaust The Nazis were also responsible for the deliberate death by shooting, starvation, or

The Holocaust: The Extermination Camp at Auschwitz. After his initial successes in the east, Hitler set in motion the machinery for the physical annihilation of Europe's Jews. Shown here is a group of Hungarian Jews arriving at Auschwitz. Hungarian Jews were not rounded up and shipped to the death camps until 1944, at the time when the Allies were making significant advances in the war. In fact, between May 2 and July 9, 1944, more than 430,000 Hungarian Jews were deported to Auschwitz.

overwork of at least another 9 to 10 million people. Because the Nazis also considered the Gypsies of Europe (like the Jews) a race containing alien blood, they were systematically rounded up for extermination. About 40 percent of Europe's one million Gypsies were killed in the death camps. The leading elements of the "subhuman" Slavic peoples—the clergy, intelligentsia, civil leaders, judges, and lawyers—were arrested and deliberately killed. Probably, an additional 4 million Poles, Ukrainians, and Belorussians lost their lives as slave laborers for Nazi Germany, and at least 3 to 4 million Soviet prisoners of war were killed in captivity. The Nazis also singled out homosexuals for persecution, and thousands lost their lives in concentration camps.

The New Order in Asia

Once Japan's takeover was completed, Japanese war policy in the occupied areas in Asia became essentially defensive, as Japan hoped to use its new possessions to meet its needs for raw materials, such as tin, oil, and rubber, as well as to serve as an outlet for Japanese manufactured goods. To provide a structure for the arrangement, Japanese leaders set up the Great East Asia Co-Prosperity Sphere as a self-sufficient community designed to provide mutual benefits to the occupied areas and the home country.

The Japanese conquest of Southeast Asia had been accomplished under the slogan "Asia for the Asians." Japanese officials in occupied territories quickly promised that independent government would be established under Japanese tutelage. Such governments were eventually established in Burma, the Dutch East Indies, Vietnam, and the Philippines.

In fact, however, real power rested with Japanese military authorities in each territory, and the local Japanese military command was directly subordinated to the army general staff in Tokyo. The economic resources of the colonies were exploited for the benefit of the Japanese war machine, while natives were recruited to serve in local military units or were conscripted to work on public works projects. In some cases, the people living in the occupied areas were subjected to severe hardships.

Like German soldiers in occupied Europe, Japanese military forces often had little respect for the lives of their subject peoples. In their conquest of Nanjing, China, in 1937, Japanese soldiers had spent several days killing, raping, and looting. Almost 800,000 Koreans were sent overseas, most of them as forced laborers, to Japan. Tens of thousands of Korean women were forced to serve as

THE HOLOCAUST: THE CAMP COMMANDANT AND THE CAMP VICTIMS

The systematic annihilation of millions of men, women, and children in extermination camps makes the Holocaust one of the most horrifying events in history. The first document is taken from an account by Rudolf Höss, commandant of the extermination camp at Auschwitz-Birkenau. In the second document, a French doctor explains what happened to the victims at one of the crematoria described by Höss.

Commandant Höss Describes the Equipment

The two large crematoria, Nos. I and II, were built during the winter of 1942–43.... They each...could cremate c. 2,000 corpses within twenty-four hours.... Crematoria I and II both had underground undressing and gassing rooms which could be completely ventilated. The corpses were brought up to the ovens on the floor above by lift. The gas chambers could hold c. 3,000 people.

The firm of Topf had calculated that the two smaller crematoria, III and IV, would each be able to cremate 1,500 corpses within twenty-four hours. However, owing to the wartime shortage of materials, the builders were obliged to economize and so the undressing rooms and gassing rooms were built above ground and the ovens were of a less solid construction. But it soon became apparent that the flimsy construction of these two four-retort ovens was not up to the demands made on it. No. III ceased operating altogether after a short time and later was no longer used. No. IV had to be repeatedly shut down since after a short period in operation of 4–6 weeks, the ovens and chimneys had burnt out. The victims of the gassing were mainly burnt in pits behind crematorium IV.

The largest number of people gassed and cremated within twenty-four hours was somewhat over 9,000.

A French Doctor Describes the Victims

It is mid-day, when a long line of women, children, and old people enter the yard. The senior official in charge... climbs on a bench to tell them that they are going to have a bath and that afterward they will get a drink of hot coffee. They all undress in the yard.... The doors are opened and an indescribable jostling begins. The first people to enter the gas chamber begin to draw back. They sense the death which awaits them. The SS men put an end to this pushing and shoving with blows from their rifle butts beating the heads of the horrified women who are desperately hugging their children. The massive oak double doors are shut. For two endless minutes one can hear banging on the walls and screams which are no longer human. And then—not a sound. Five minutes later the doors are opened. The corpses, squashed together and distorted, fall out like a waterfall.... The bodies which are still warm pass through the hands of the hairdresser who cuts their hair and the dentist who pulls out their gold teeth.... One more transport has just been processed through No. IV crematorium.

Q *What equipment does Höss describe? What process does the French doctor describe? It there any sympathy for the victims in either account? Why or why not? How could such a horrifying process have been allowed to occur?*

"comfort women" (prostitutes) for Japanese troops. In construction projects to help their war effort, the Japanese also made extensive use of labor forces composed of both prisoners of war and local peoples. In building the Burma-Thailand railway in 1943, for example, the Japanese used 61,000 Australian, British, and Dutch prisoners of war and almost 300,000 workers from Burma, Malaya, Thailand, and the Dutch East Indies. By the time the railway was completed, 12,000 Allied prisoners of war and 90,000 native workers had died from the inadequate diet and appalling working conditions in an unhealthy climate.

The Home Front

Q Focus Question: What were conditions like on the home front for Japan and the major Western nations involved in World War II?

World War II was even more of a total war than World War I. Fighting was much more widespread and covered most of the globe. Economic mobilization was more extensive; so too was the mobilization of women. The number of civilians killed was far higher; almost 20 million died as a result of bombing raids, mass extermination policies, and attacks by invading armies.

The Mobilization of Peoples

The home fronts of the major belligerents varied considerably, based on national circumstances.

Great Britain The British mobilized their resources more thoroughly than their allies or even Germany. By the summer of 1944, fully 55 percent of the British people were in the armed forces or civilian "war work." The British were especially determined to make use of women. Most women under forty years of age were called on to do war work of some kind. By 1944, women held almost 50 percent of the civil service positions, and the number of women in agriculture doubled as "land girls" performed agricultural labor usually undertaken by men.

Women in the Factories. Although only the Soviet Union used women in combat positions, the number of women working in industry increased dramatically in most belligerent countries. British women are shown here in a British munitions factory during World War II, probably in 1943.

The government encouraged the "Dig for Victory" campaign to increase food production. Fields normally reserved for athletic events were turned over to citizens to plant gardens in "Grow Your Own Food" campaigns. Even with 1.4 million new gardens in 1943, Britain still faced a shortage of food as German submarines continued to sink hundreds of British merchant vessels. Food rationing, with its weekly allotments of bacon, sugar, fats, and eggs, intensified during the war as the British became accustomed to a diet dominated by bread and potatoes. For many British people, hours after work were spent in such wartime activities as "Dig for Victory," the Civil Defence, or the Home Guard. The Home Guard had been founded in 1940 to fight off German invaders. Even elderly people were expected to help manufacture airplane parts in their homes.

During the war, the British placed much emphasis on a planned economy. In 1942, the government created a ministry for fuel and power to control the coal industry and a ministry for production to oversee supplies for the armed forces. Although controls and bureaucratic "red tape" became unpopular, especially with businesspeople, most British citizens seemed to accept that total war required unusual governmental interference in people's lives. The British did make substantial gains in manufacturing war matériel. Tank production quadrupled between 1940 and 1942, and the production of aircraft grew from 8,000 in 1939 to 26,000 in 1943 and 1944.

The Soviet Union World War II had an enormous impact on the Soviet Union. Known to the Soviets as the Great Patriotic War, the German-Soviet war witnessed the greatest land battles in history as well as incredible ruthlessness. To Nazi Germany, it was a war of oppression

and annihilation that called for merciless measures. Two out of every five persons killed in World War II were Soviet citizens.

The shift to a war footing necessitated only limited administrative change in the Soviet Union. As the central authority, the dictator Joseph Stalin simply created a system of "supercentralization," by which he directed military and political affairs. All civil and military organizations were subjected to the control of the Communist Party and the Soviet police.

The initial defeats of the Soviet Union led to drastic emergency mobilization measures that affected the civilian population. Leningrad, for example, experienced nine hundred days of siege, during which its inhabitants became so desperate for food that they ate dogs, cats, and mice. As the German army made its rapid advance into Soviet territory, the factories in the western part of the Soviet Union were dismantled and shipped to the interior—to the Urals, western Siberia, and the Volga region. Machines were placed on the bare ground, and walls went up around them as workers began their work. The Kharkov Tank Factory produced its first twenty-five T-34 tanks only ten weeks after the plant had been rebuilt.

This widespread military, industrial, and economic mobilization created yet another industrial revolution for the Soviet Union. Stalin labeled it a "battle of machines," and the Soviets won, producing 78,000 tanks and 98,000 artillery pieces. Fifty-five percent of Soviet national income went for war matériel, compared to 15 percent in 1940. As a result of the emphasis on military goods, Soviet citizens experienced incredible shortages of both food and housing. Civilian food consumption fell by 40 percent during the war; in the Volga area, the Urals, and Siberia, workers lived in dugouts or dilapidated barracks.

Soviet women played a major role in the war effort. Women and girls worked in industries, mines, and railroads. Women constituted between 26 and 35 percent of the laborers in mines and 48 percent in the oil industry. Overall, the number of women working in industry increased almost 60 percent. Soviet women were also expected to dig antitank ditches and work as air-raid wardens. In addition, the Soviet Union was the only country in World War II to use women as combatants. Soviet women functioned as snipers and also as aircrews in bomber squadrons. The female pilots who helped defeat the Germans at Stalingrad were known as the "Night Witches."

Soviet peasants were asked to bear enormous burdens. Not only did the peasants furnish 60 percent of the military forces, but at the same time, they were expected to feed the Red Army and the Soviet people under very trying conditions. The German occupation in the early months of the war resulted in the loss of 47 percent of the country's grain-producing regions. Although new land was opened in the Urals, Siberia, and Soviet Asia, a shortage of labor and equipment hindered the effort to expand agricultural production. Because farm tractors and trucks were requisitioned to carry guns for the military, women and children were literally harnessed to do the plowing, and everywhere peasants worked long hours on collective farms for no pay. In 1943, the Soviet harvest was only 60 percent of its 1940 figure, a shortfall that meant extreme hardship for many people.

Total mobilization produced victory for the Soviet Union. Stalin and the Communist Party had quickly realized after the start of the German invasion that the Soviet people would not fight for Communist ideology but would do battle to preserve "Mother Russia." Government propaganda played on patriotic feelings. In a speech on the anniversary of the Bolshevik Revolution in November 1941, Stalin rallied the Soviet people by speaking of the country's past heroes, including the famous tsars of imperial Russia.

The United States The home front in the United States was quite different from those of its two chief wartime allies, largely because the United States faced no threat of war in its own territory. Although the economy and labor force were slow to mobilize, eventually the United States became the arsenal of the Allied powers, producing the military equipment they needed. The mobilization of the United States also had a great impact on American social and economic developments.

The immediate impact of mobilization was a dramatic expansion of the American economy, which ultimately brought an end to the Great Depression. Old factories were converted from peacetime goods to war goods, and many new factories were built. Massive amounts of government money also financed new industries, such as chemicals and electronics. A new government Office of Scientific Research and Development provided funds for contracts with universities and scientists to create such new products as rocket engines. The Manhattan Project for the development of an atomic bomb, which employed 130,000 people and cost $2 billion, involved the cooperation of scientists, defense contractors, and the federal government.

American industry supplied not only the U.S. armed forces but also the other Allies with the huge quantities of tanks, trucks, jeeps, and airplanes needed to win the war. During the war years, gross national product (GNP) rose by 15 percent a year. During the high point of war production in the United States in November 1943, the nation was constructing six ships a day and $6 billion worth of other military equipment a month. The production of airplanes increased from 6,000 in 1939 to over 96,000 in 1944.

Industrial mobilization led to an increased government role in the economy. The federal bureaucracy grew dramatically with the establishment of a War Production Board, which allocated resources and managed production; a War Labor Board, which settled labor disputes; and an Office of Price Administration, which controlled prices and rationed scarce goods, such as gasoline, rubber, and meat.

The mobilization of the American economy also caused social problems. The construction of new factories created boomtowns where thousands came to work but then faced a shortage of houses, health facilities, and schools. The dramatic expansion of small towns into large cities often brought a breakdown in traditional social mores, especially evident in the growth of teenage prostitution. Economic mobilization also led to a widespread movement of people, which in turn created new social tensions. Sixteen million men and women were enrolled in the military, and another 16 million, mostly wives and sweethearts of the servicemen or workers looking for jobs, also relocated. Over one million African Americans migrated from the rural South to the industrial cities of the North and West, looking for jobs in industry. The presence of African Americans in areas where they had not lived before led to racial tensions and sometimes even racial riots. In Detroit in June 1943, white mobs roamed the streets attacking African Americans. Many of the one million African Americans who enlisted in the military, only to be segregated in their own battle units, were angered by the way they were treated. Some became militant and prepared to fight for their civil rights.

Japanese Americans were treated even more shabbily. On the West Coast, 110,000 Japanese Americans, 65 percent of whom had been born in the United States, were removed to camps encircled by barbed wire and required to take loyalty oaths. Although public officials claimed that this policy was necessary for security reasons, no similar treatment of German Americans or Italian Americans ever took place. The racism inherent in this treatment of Japanese Americans was evident when the California governor, Culbert Olson, said, "You know, when I look out at a group of Americans of German or Italian descent, I can tell whether they're loyal or not. I can tell how they think and even perhaps what they are thinking. But it is impossible for me to do this with inscrutable orientals, and particularly the Japanese."[15]

Germany In August 1914, Germans had enthusiastically cheered their soldiers marching off to war. In September 1939, the streets were quiet. Many Germans were apathetic or, even worse for the Nazi regime, had a foreboding of disaster. Hitler was very aware of the importance of the home front. He believed that the collapse of the home front in World War I had caused Germany's defeat, and in his determination to avoid a repetition of that experience, he adopted economic policies that may indeed have cost Germany the war.

To maintain the morale of the home front during the first two years of the war, Hitler refused to convert production from consumer goods to armaments. Blitzkrieg allowed the Germans to win quick victories, after which they could plunder the food and raw materials of conquered countries in order to avoid diverting resources away from the civilian economy. After the German defeats on the Soviet front and the American entry into the war, the economic situation changed. Early in 1942, Hitler finally ordered a massive increase in armaments production and the size of the army. Hitler's personal architect, Albert Speer, was made minister for armaments and munitions in 1942. By eliminating waste and rationalizing procedures, Speer was able to triple the production of armaments between 1942 and 1943 despite the intense Allied air raids. Speer's urgent plea for a total mobilization of resources for the war effort went unheeded, however. Hitler, fearful of civilian morale problems that would undermine the home front, refused any dramatic cuts in the production of consumer goods. A total mobilization of the economy was not implemented until 1944, when schools, theaters, and cafés were closed and Speer was finally permitted to use all remaining resources for the production of a few basic military items. By that time, it was in vain. Total war mobilization was too little and too late in July 1944 to save Germany from defeat.

The war produced a reversal in Nazi attitudes toward women. Nazi resistance to female employment declined as the war progressed and more and more men were called up for military service. Nazi magazines now proclaimed, "We see the woman as the eternal mother of our people, but also as the working and fighting comrade of the man."[16] But the number of women working in industry, agriculture, commerce, and domestic service increased only slightly. The total number of employed women in September 1944 was 14.9 million, compared to 14.6 in May 1939. Many women, especially those of the middle class, resisted regular employment, particularly in factories. Even the introduction of labor conscription for women in January 1943 failed to achieve much as women found ingenious ways to avoid the regulations.

Japan Wartime Japan was a highly mobilized society. To guarantee its control over all national resources, the government set up a planning board to control prices, wages, the utilization of labor, and the allocation of resources. Traditional habits of obedience and hierarchy, buttressed by the concept of imperial divinity, were emphasized to encourage citizens to sacrifice their resources, and sometimes their lives, for the national cause. Especially important was the code of *bushido*, or the way of the warrior, the old code of morality of the samurai, who had played a prominent military role in medieval and early modern Japanese history. The code of *bushido* was revived during the nationalistic fervor of the 1930s. Based on an ideal of loyalty and service, the code emphasized the obligation to honor and defend emperor, country, and family and to sacrifice one's life if one failed in this sacred mission. The system culminated in the final years of the war when young Japanese were encouraged to volunteer en masse to serve as pilots in suicide missions (known as *kamikaze*, "divine wind") against U.S. battleships.

Women's rights, too, were to be sacrificed to the greater national cause. Already by 1937, Japanese women were being exhorted to fulfill their patriotic duty by bearing more children and by espousing the slogans of the Greater Japanese Women's Association. Nevertheless, Japan was extremely reluctant to mobilize women on behalf of the war effort. General Hideki Tojo, prime minister from 1941 to 1944, opposed female employment, arguing that "the weakening of the family system would be the weakening of the nation. . . . We are able to do our duties only because we have wives and mothers at home."[17] Female employment increased during the war, but only in areas where women traditionally worked, such as the textile industry and farming. Instead of using women to meet labor shortages, the Japanese government brought in Korean and Chinese laborers.

Front-Line Civilians: The Bombing of Cities

Bombing was used in World War II in a variety of ways: against nonhuman military targets, against enemy troops, and against civilian populations. The use of bombs made World War II as devastating for civilians as for front-line soldiers (see the box on p. 866). A small number of bombing raids in the last year of World War I had given rise to the argument, expressed in 1930 by the Italian general Giulio Douhet, that the public outcry generated by the bombing of civilian populations would be an effective way to coerce governments into making peace. Consequently, European air forces began to develop long-range bombers in the 1930s.

Luftwaffe Attacks The first sustained use of civilian bombing contradicted Douhet's theory. Beginning in early September 1940, the German Luftwaffe subjected London and many other British cities and towns to nightly air raids, making the Blitz (as the British called the German air raids) a national experience. Londoners took the first heavy blows and set the standard for the rest of the British

THE BOMBING OF CIVILIANS

The home front became a battle front when civilian populations became the targets of mass bombing raids. Many people believed that mass bombing could effectively weaken the morale of the people and shorten the war. Rarely did it achieve its goal. In these selections, British, German, and Japanese civilians relate their experiences during bombing raids.

London, 1940

Early last evening, the noise was terrible. My husband and Mr. P. were trying to play chess in the kitchen. I was playing draughts with Kenneth in the cupboard.... Presently I heard a stifled voice "Mummy! I don't know what's become of my glasses." "I should think they are tied up in my wool." My knitting had disappeared and wool seemed to be everywhere! We heard a whistle, a bang which shook the house, and an explosion.... Well, we straightened out, decided draughts and chess were no use under the circumstances, and waited for a lull so we could have a pot of tea.

Hamburg, 1943

As the many fires broke through the roofs of the burning buildings, a column of heated air rose more than two and a half miles high and one and a half miles in diameter.... This column was turbulent, and it was fed from its base by in-rushing cooler ground-surface air. One and one half miles from the fires this draught increased the wind velocity from eleven to thirty-three miles per hour. At the edge of the area the velocities must have been appreciably greater, as trees three feet in diameter were uprooted. In a short time the temperature reached ignition point for all combustibles, and the entire area was ablaze. In such fires complete burn-out occurred; that is, no trace of combustible material remained, and only after two days were the areas cool enough to approach.

Hiroshima, August 6, 1945

I heard the airplane; I looked up at the sky, it was a sunny day, the sky was blue.... Then I saw something drop—and pow!—a big explosion knocked me down. Then I was unconscious—I don't know for how long. Then I was conscious but I couldn't see anything.... Then I see people moving away and I just follow them. It is not light like it was before, it is more like evening. I look around; houses are all flat!...I follow the people to the river. I couldn't hear anything, my ears are blocked up. I am thinking a bomb has dropped!...I didn't know my hands were burned, nor my face.... My eyes were swollen and felt closed up.

Q *What common elements do you find in these three different descriptions of bombing raids? What effect did aerial bombing have on the nature of modern warfare?*

---

population by refusing to panic. One British woman expressed well what many others apparently felt:

> It was a beautiful summer night, so warm it was incredible, and made more beautiful than ever by the red glow from the East, where the docks were burning. We stood and stared for a minute, and I tried to fix the scene in my mind, because one day this will be history, and I shall be one of those who actually saw it. I wasn't frightened any more.[18]

But London morale was helped by the fact that German raids were widely scattered over a very large city. Smaller communities were more directly affected by the devastation. On November 14, 1940, for example, the Luftwaffe destroyed hundreds of shops and 100 acres of the city center of Coventry. The destruction of smaller cities did produce morale problems as wild rumors of heavy casualties spread quickly in these communities. Nevertheless, morale was soon restored. In any case, war production in these areas seems to have been little affected by the raids.

The Bombing of Germany The British failed to learn from their own experience, however, and soon proceeded to bomb German cities. Churchill and his advisers believed that destroying German communities would break civilian morale and bring victory. Major bombing raids began in 1942 under the direction of Arthur Harris, the wartime leader of the British air force's Bomber Command, which was rearmed with four-engine heavy bombers capable of taking the war into the center of occupied Europe. On May 31, 1942, Cologne became the first German city to be subjected to an attack by one thousand bombers.

With the entry of the Americans into the war, the bombing strategy changed. American planes flew daytime missions aimed at the precision bombing of transportation facilities and war industries, while the British Bomber Command continued nighttime saturation bombing of all German cities with populations over 100,000. Bombing raids added an element of terror to circumstances already made difficult by growing shortages of food, clothing, and fuel. Germans especially feared the incendiary bombs, which created firestorms that swept destructive paths through the cities. Four raids on Hamburg in August 1943 produced temperatures of 1,800 degrees Fahrenheit, obliterated half the city's buildings, and killed thousands of civilians. The ferocious bombing of Dresden from February 13 to 15, 1945, created a firestorm that may have killed as many as 35,000 inhabitants and refugees. Even some Allied leaders began

IMAGES OF EVERYDAY LIFE

The Impact of Total War. World War II was a total war for civilians as political leaders came to see the bombing of civilians as a legitimate way to demoralize the population and end a war. The result of this policy is evident in these three scenes of life between 1941 and 1945. In the first photograph (top left), a group of refugees walk past a bombed tenement building, where 800 people died and 800 more were injured during a German bombing raid in March 1941 on Clydebank near Glasgow in Scotland. Only 7 of the city's 12,000 houses were left undamaged; 35,000 of the 47,000 inhabitants became homeless overnight. The raid on Clydebank was Scotland's only severe bombing experience. The city was attacked because of its proximity to nearby shipyards that were refitting ships to serve in the war. The second photograph (bottom left) shows the devastation in Dresden, Germany, as a result of British and American bombing raids on February 13 and 14, 1945. An area of 2.5 square miles in the city was destroyed, and as many as 35,000 people died. The most devastating destruction of civilians came near the end of World War II when the United States dropped atomic bombs on the Japanese cities of Hiroshima and Nagasaki. The panoramic view of Hiroshima after the bombing in the third photograph shows the incredible devastation produced by the atomic bomb.

Keystone/Getty Images

© Bettmann/CORBIS

J. R. Eyerman//Time & Life Pictures/Getty Images

to criticize what they saw as the unnecessary terror bombing of German cities. Urban dwellers became accustomed to living in air-raid shelters, usually cellars in businesses or houses. Occupants of shelters could be crushed to death, however, if the shelters were hit directly or die by suffocation from the effects of high-explosive bombs. Not until 1943 did Nazi leaders begin to evacuate women and children to rural areas. But evacuation created its own problems since people in country villages were often hostile to the urban newcomers.

Germany suffered enormously from the Allied bombing raids. Millions of buildings were destroyed, and possibly half a million civilians died in the raids. Nevertheless, it is highly unlikely that Allied bombing sapped the morale of the German people. Instead, Germans, whether pro-Nazi or anti-Nazi, fought on stubbornly, often driven simply by a desire to live. Nor did the bombing destroy Germany's industrial capacity. The Allied Strategic Bombing survey revealed that the production of war matériel actually increased between 1942 and 1944. Even in 1944 and 1945, Allied raids cut German production of armaments by only 7 percent. Nevertheless, the widespread destruction of transportation systems and fuel supplies made it extremely difficult for the new matériel to reach the German military. Because of strong German air defenses, air raids were also costly for the Allies. Nearly 40,000 Allied planes were destroyed, and 160,000 airmen lost their lives.

The destruction of German cities from the air did accomplish one major goal. There would be no stab-in-the-back myth after World War II as there had been after World War I. The loss of the war could not be blamed on the collapse of the home front. Many Germans understood that the home front had been a battlefront, and they had fought on their front just as the soldiers had on theirs.

The Bombing of Japan: The Atomic Bomb The bombing of civilians eventually reached a new level with the dropping of the first atomic bomb on Japan. Fearful of German attempts to create a superbomb through the use of uranium, the American government pursued a dual strategy. While sabotaging German efforts, the United States and Britain recruited scientists, including many who had fled from Germany, to develop an atomic bomb. Working under the direction of J. Robert Oppenheimer at a secret laboratory in Los Alamos, New Mexico, Allied scientists built and tested the first atomic bomb by the summer of 1945. A new era in warfare was about to begin.

Japan was especially vulnerable to air raids because its air force had been virtually destroyed in the course of the war, and its crowded cities were built of flimsy materials. Attacks on Japanese cities by the new American B-29 Superfortresses, the biggest bombers of the war, had begun on November 24, 1944. By the summer of 1945, many of Japan's factories had been destroyed, along with one-fourth of its dwellings. After the Japanese government decreed the mobilization of all people between the ages of thirteen and sixty into a "people's volunteer corps," President Truman and his advisers feared that Japanese fanaticism might mean a million American casualties. This concern led them to drop the atomic bomb on Hiroshima (August 6) and Nagasaki (August 9). The destruction was incredible. Of 76,000 buildings near the hypocenter of the explosion in Hiroshima, 70,000 were flattened; 140,000 of the

city's 400,000 inhabitants died by the end of 1945. By the end of 1950, another 50,000 had perished from the effects of radiation.

Aftermath of the War

Q **Focus Questions:** What were the costs of World War II? How did the Allies' visions of postwar Europe differ, and how did these differences contribute to the emergence of the Cold War?

World War II was the most destructive war in history. Much had been at stake. Nazi Germany followed a worldview based on racial extermination and the enslavement of millions in order to create an Aryan racial empire. The Japanese, fueled by extreme nationalist ideals, also pursued dreams of empire in Asia that led to mass murder and untold devastation. Fighting the Axis powers in World War II required the mobilization of millions of ordinary men and women in the Allied countries who rose to the occasion and struggled to preserve a different way of life. As Winston Churchill once put it, "War is horrible, but slavery is worse."

The Costs of World War II

The costs of World War II were enormous. At least 21 million soldiers died. Civilian deaths were even greater and are now estimated at around 40 million, of whom more than 28 million were Russian and Chinese. The Soviet Union experienced the greatest losses: 10 million soldiers and 19 million civilians. In 1945, millions of people around the world faced starvation; in Europe, 100 million people depended on food relief of some kind.

Millions of people had also been uprooted by the war and became "displaced persons." Europe alone may have had 30 million displaced persons, many of whom found it hard to return home. After the war, millions of Germans were expelled from the Sudetenland in Czechoslovakia, and millions more were ejected from former eastern German territories that were turned over to Poland, all of which seemed reasonable to people who had suffered so much at the hands of the Germans. In Asia, millions of Japanese were returned from the former Japanese empire to Japan, while thousands of Korean forced laborers returned to Korea.

Everywhere cities lay in ruins. In Europe, physical devastation was especially bad in eastern and southeastern Europe as well as in the cities of western and central Europe. In Asia, China had experienced extensive devastation from eight years of conflict. So too had the Philippines, while large parts of the major cities in Japan had been destroyed in air raids. At the same time, millions of tons of shipping were now underneath the seas; factories, farms, transportation systems, bridges, and dams were in ruins. The total monetary cost of the war has been estimated at $4 trillion. The economies of most belligerents, with the exception of the United States, were left drained and on the brink of disaster.

The Allied War Conferences

The total victory of the Allies in World War II was succeeded not by true peace but by a new conflict known as the **Cold War** that dominated European and world politics for more than forty years. The Cold War stemmed from military, political, and ideological differences, especially between the Soviet Union and the United States, that became apparent at the Allied war conferences held in the last years of the war. Although Allied leaders were mostly preoccupied with how to end the war, they also were strongly motivated by differing and often conflicting visions of postwar Europe.

The Conference at Tehran Stalin, Roosevelt, and Churchill, the leaders of the Big Three of the Grand Alliance, met at Tehran (the capital of Iran) in November 1943 to decide the future course of the war. Their major tactical decision concerned the final assault on Germany. Churchill had wanted British and American forces to follow up their North African and Italian campaigns by an indirect attack on Germany through the Balkans. Stalin and Roosevelt, however, overruled Churchill and argued successfully for an American-British invasion of the Continent through France, which they scheduled for the spring of 1944. The acceptance of this plan had important consequences. It meant that Soviet and British-American forces would meet in defeated Germany along a north-south dividing line and that, most likely, eastern Europe would be liberated by Soviet forces. The Allies also agreed to a partition of postwar Germany, but differences over questions like the frontiers of Poland were carefully set aside. Roosevelt was pleased with the accord with Stalin. Harry Hopkins, one of Roosevelt's advisers at the conference, remarked:

> We really believed in our hearts that this was the dawn of the new day.... We were absolutely certain that we had won the first great victory of the peace—and by "we," I mean all of us, the whole civilized human race. The Russians had proved that they could be reasonable and far-seeing and there wasn't any doubt in the minds of the President or any of us that we could live with them and get along with them peacefully for as far into the future as any of us could imagine.[19]

The Yalta Conference By the time of the conference at Yalta in the Ukraine in February 1945, the defeat of Germany was a foregone conclusion. The Western powers, which had earlier believed that the Soviets were in a weak position, were now faced with the reality of 11 million Red Army soldiers taking possession of eastern and much of central Europe. Stalin was still operating under the notion of spheres of influence. He was deeply suspicious of the Western powers and desired a buffer to protect the Soviet Union from possible future Western aggression. At the same time, however, Stalin was eager to obtain economically important resources and strategic military positions. Roosevelt by this time was moving away from the notion of spheres of influence to the ideal of self-determination. He called for "the end of the system of unilateral action, exclusive alliances, and spheres of influence." The Grand Alliance approved the "Declaration on Liberated Europe." This was a pledge to

The Victorious Allied Leaders at Yalta. Even before World War II ended, the leaders of the Big Three of the Grand Alliance, Churchill, Roosevelt, and Stalin (seated, left to right), met in wartime conferences to plan the final assault on Germany and negotiate the outlines of the postwar settlement. At the Yalta meeting (February 5–11, 1945), the three leaders concentrated on postwar issues. The American president, who died two months later, was already a worn-out man at Yalta.

assist liberated European nations in the creation of "democratic institutions of their own choice." Liberated countries were to hold free elections to determine their political systems.

At Yalta, Roosevelt sought Soviet military help against Japan. The atomic bomb was not yet assured, and American military planners feared the possible loss of as many as one million men in amphibious assaults on the Japanese home islands. Roosevelt therefore agreed to Stalin's price for military assistance against Japan: possession of Sakhalin and the Kurile Islands as well as two warm-water ports and railroad rights in Manchuria.

The creation of the United Nations was a major American concern at Yalta. Roosevelt hoped to ensure the participation of the Big Three powers in a postwar international organization before difficult issues divided them into hostile camps. After a number of compromises, both Churchill and Stalin accepted Roosevelt's plans for a United Nations organization and set the first meeting for San Francisco in April 1945.

The issues of Germany and eastern Europe were treated less decisively. The Big Three reaffirmed that Germany must surrender unconditionally and created four occupation zones. Churchill, over the objections of the Soviets and Americans, insisted that the French be given one occupation zone, carved out of the British and American zones. German reparations were set at $20 billion. A compromise was also worked out with regard to Poland. It was agreed that a provisional government would be established with members of both the Lublin Poles, who were Polish Communists living in exile in the Soviet Union, and the London Poles, who were non-Communists exiled in Britain. Stalin also agreed to free elections in the future to determine a new government. But the issue of free elections in eastern Europe caused a serious rift between the Soviets and the Americans. The principle was that eastern European governments would be freely elected, but they were also supposed to be pro-Soviet. As Churchill expressed it, "The Poles will have their future in their own hands, with the single limitation that they must honestly follow in harmony with their allies, a policy friendly to Russia."[20] This attempt to reconcile two irreconcilable goals was doomed to failure, as soon became evident at the next conference of the Big Three powers.

Intensifying Differences   Even before the conference at Potsdam took place in July 1945, Western relations with the Soviets were deteriorating rapidly. The Grand Alliance had been one of necessity in which disagreements had been subordinated to the pragmatic concerns of the war. The Allied powers' only common aim was the defeat of Nazism. Once this aim had all but been accomplished, the many differences that troubled East-West relations came to the surface. Each side

committed acts that the other viewed as unbecoming of "allies."

From the perspective of the Soviets, the United States' termination of Lend-Lease aid before the war was over and its failure to respond to the Soviet request for a $6 billion loan for reconstruction exposed the Western desire to keep the Soviet state weak. On the American side, the Soviet Union's failure to fulfill its Yalta pledge on the "Declaration on Liberated Europe" as applied to eastern Europe set a dangerous precedent. This was evident in Romania as early as February 1945, when the Soviets engineered a coup and installed a new government under the Communist Petra Groza, called the "Little Stalin." One month later, the Soviets sabotaged the Polish settlement by arresting the London Poles and their sympathizers and placing the Soviet-backed Lublin Poles in power. To the Americans, the Soviets seemed to be asserting control of eastern European countries under puppet Communist regimes (see Map 27.5).

The Potsdam Conference   The Potsdam Conference of July 1945 consequently began under a cloud of mistrust. Roosevelt had died on April 12 and had been succeeded by Harry Truman. During the conference, Truman received word that the atomic bomb had been successfully tested. Some historians have argued that this knowledge resulted in Truman's stiffened resolve against the Soviets. Whatever the reasons, there was a new coldness in the relations between the Soviets and Americans. At Potsdam, Truman demanded free elections throughout eastern Europe. Stalin responded, "A freely elected government in any of these East European countries would be anti-Soviet, and that we cannot allow."[21] After a bitterly fought and devastating war, Stalin sought absolute military security. To him, it could be gained only by the presence of Communist states in eastern Europe. Free elections might result in governments hostile to the Soviets. By the middle of 1945, only an invasion by Western forces could undo developments in eastern Europe, and after the world's most destructive conflict had ended, few people favored such a policy.

Emergence of the Cold War

The Soviets did not view their actions as dangerous expansionism but as legitimate security maneuvers. Was it not the West that had attacked the East? When Stalin sought help against the Nazis in the 1930s, had not the West turned a deaf ear? But there was little sympathy in the West for Soviet fears and even less trust in Stalin. When the American secretary of state, James Byrnes, proposed a twenty-five-year disarmament of Germany, the Soviet Union rejected it. In the West, many saw this as proof of Stalin's plans to expand in central Europe and

MAP 27.5 **Territorial Changes After World War II.** In the last months of World War II, the Red Army occupied much of eastern Europe. Stalin sought pro-Soviet satellite states in the region as a buffer against future invasions from western Europe, whereas Britain and the United States wanted democratically elected governments. Soviet military control of the territory settled the question.

Q Which country gained the greatest territory at the expense of Germany? **View an animated version of this map or related maps at** academic.cengage.com/history/spielvogel

create a Communist East German state. When Byrnes responded by announcing that American troops would be needed in Europe for an indefinite time and made moves that foreshadowed the creation of an independent West Germany, the Soviets saw this as a direct threat to Soviet security in Europe.

As the war slowly receded into the past, the reality of conflicting ideologies had reappeared. Many in the West interpreted Soviet policy as part of a worldwide Communist conspiracy. The Soviets, for their part, viewed Western, especially American, policy as nothing less than global capitalist expansionism or, in Leninist terms, economic imperialism. Vyacheslav

Molotov, the Russian foreign minister, referred to the Americans as "insatiable imperialists" and "warmongering groups of adventurers."[22] In March 1946, in a speech to an American audience, former British prime minister Winston Churchill declared that "an iron curtain" had "descended across the continent," dividing Germany and Europe into two hostile camps. Stalin branded Churchill's speech a "call to war with the Soviet Union" (see the box on p. 872). Only months after the world's most devastating conflict had ended, the world seemed once again bitterly divided. Would the twentieth-century crisis of Western civilization never end?

EMERGENCE OF THE COLD WAR: CHURCHILL AND STALIN

Less than a year after the end of World War II, the major Allies that had fought together to destroy Hitler's Germany had divided into two hostile camps. These excerpts, taken from Winston Churchill's speech to an American audience on March 5, 1946, and Joseph Stalin's reply to Churchill only nine days later, reveal the divisions in the Western world that marked the beginning of the Cold War.

Churchill's Speech at Fulton, Missouri, March 5, 1946

From Stettin in the Baltic to Trieste in the Adriatic, an iron curtain has descended across the continent. Behind that line lie all the capitals of the ancient states of central and eastern Europe. Warsaw, Berlin, Prague, Vienna, Budapest, Belgrade, Bucharest, and Sofia, all these famous cities and the populations around them lie in the Soviet sphere and all are subject, in one form or another, not only to Soviet influence but to a very high and increasing measure of control from Moscow....

The Russian-dominated Polish Government has been encouraged to make enormous and wrongful inroads upon Germany, and mass expulsions of millions of Germans on a scale grievous and undreamed of are now taking place. The Communist parties, which were very small in all these eastern states of Europe, have been raised to preeminence and power far beyond their numbers and are seeking everywhere to obtain totalitarian control. Police governments are prevailing in nearly every case, and so far, except in Czechoslovakia, there is no true democracy.... Whatever conclusions may be drawn from these facts—and facts they are—this is certainly not the liberated Europe we fought to build up. Nor is it one which contains the essentials of permanent peace.

Stalin's Reply to Churchill, March 14, 1946

In substance, Mr. Churchill now stands in the position of a firebrand of war. And Mr. Churchill is not alone here. He has friends not only in England but also in the United States of America.

In this respect, one is reminded remarkably of Hitler and his friends. Hitler began to set war loose by announcing his racial theory, declaring that only people speaking the German language represent a fully valuable nation. Mr. Churchill begins to set war loose, also by a racial theory, maintaining that only nations speaking the English language are fully valuable nations, called upon to decide the destinies of the entire world.

The German racial theory brought Hitler and his friends to the conclusion that the Germans, as the only fully valuable nation, must rule over other nations. The English racial theory brings Mr. Churchill and his friends to the conclusion that nations speaking the English language, being the only fully valuable nations, should rule over the remaining nations of the world.

Q   *What do the statements of Churchill and Stalin tell us about the origins and rhetoric of the Cold War? Why might it be said that both sides in this global conflict persistently misunderstood the other?*

CONCLUSION

Between 1933 and 1939, Europeans watched as Adolf Hitler rebuilt Germany into a great military power. For Hitler, military power was an absolute prerequisite for the creation of a German racial empire that would dominate Europe and the world for generations to come. If Hitler had been successful, the Nazi New Order, built on authoritarianism, racial extermination, and the brutal oppression of peoples, would have meant a triumph of barbarism and the end of freedom and equality, which, however imperfectly realized, had become important ideals in Western civilization.

The Nazis lost, but only after tremendous sacrifices and costs. Much of European civilization lay in ruins, and the old Europe had disappeared forever. Europeans, who had been accustomed to dominating the world at the beginning of the twentieth century, now watched helplessly at mid-century as the two new superpowers created by the two world wars took control of their destinies. Even before the last battles had been fought, the United States and the Soviet Union had arrived at different visions of the postwar European world. No sooner had the war ended than their differences gave rise to a new and potentially even more devastating conflict known as the Cold War. Yet even though Europeans seemed merely pawns in the struggle between the two superpowers, they managed to stage a remarkable recovery of their own civilization.

TIMELINE

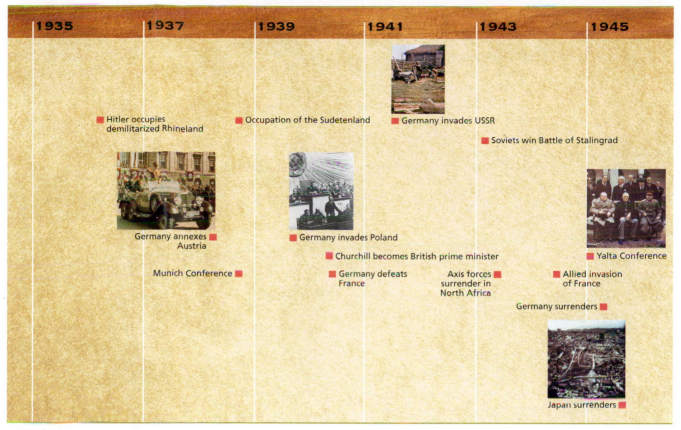

1935 — Hitler occupies demilitarized Rhineland

1937

Germany annexes Austria

Munich Conference

1939 — Occupation of the Sudetenland

Germany invades Poland

Churchill becomes British prime minister

Germany defeats France

1941 — Germany invades USSR

Soviets win Battle of Stalingrad

Axis forces surrender in North Africa

1943

Allied invasion of France

Germany surrenders

1945 — Yalta Conference

Japan surrenders

NOTES

1. Adolf Hitler, *Mein Kampf,* trans. Ralph Manheim (Boston, 1971), p. 654.
2. *Documents on German Foreign Policy* (London, 1956), ser. D, vol. 2, p. 358.
3. Ibid., vol. 7, p. 204.
4. Quoted in Norman Rich, *Hitler's War Aims* (New York, 1973), vol. 1, p. 129.
5. Quoted in Williamson Murray and Allan Millett, *A War to Be Won: Fighting the Second World War* (Cambridge, Mass., 2000), p. 66.
6. Quoted in ibid., p. 137.
7. Albert Speer, *Spandau,* trans. Richard Winston and Clara Winston (New York, 1976), p. 50.
8. *Nazi Conspiracy and Aggression* (Washington, D.C., 1946), vol. 6, p. 262.
9. International Military Tribunal, *Trial of the Major War Criminals* (Nuremberg, 1947–1949), vol. 22, p. 480.
10. Adolf Hitler, *My New Order,* ed. Raoul de Roussy de Sales (New York, 1941), pp. 21–22.
11. Quoted in Lucy Dawidowicz, *The War Against the Jews* (New York, 1975), p. 106.
12. *Nazi Conspiracy and Aggression,* vol. 5, pp. 341–342.
13. Quoted in Raul Hilberg, *The Destruction of the European Jews,* rev. ed. (New York, 1985), vol. 1, pp. 332–333.
14. *Nazi Conspiracy and Aggression,* vol. 6, p. 789.
15. Quoted in John Campbell, *The Experience of World War II* (New York, 1989), p. 170.
16. Quoted in Claudia Koonz, "Mothers in the Fatherland: Women in Nazi Germany," in Renate Bridenthal and Claudia Koonz, eds., *Becoming Visible: Women in European History* (Boston, 1977), p. 466.
17. Quoted in Campbell, *The Experience of World War II,* p. 143.
18. Quoted in ibid., p. 177.
19. Quoted in Robert E. Sherwood, *Roosevelt and Hopkins: An Intimate History* (New York, 1948), p. 870.
20. Quoted in Norman Graebner, *Cold War Diplomacy, 1945–1960* (Princeton, N.J., 1962), p. 117.
21. Quoted in ibid., p. 117.
22. Quoted in Wilfried Loth, *The Division of the World, 1941–1955* (New York, 1988), p. 81.

SUGGESTIONS FOR FURTHER READING

Prelude to War   On the causes of World War II, see **A. J. Crozier, *Causes of the Second World War*** (Oxford, 1997). For a good collection of essays, see **J. A. Maiolo, ed., *The Origins of World War II: The Debate Continues*** (New York, 2003). On the origins of the war in the Pacific, see **A. Iriye, *The Origins of the Second World War in Asia and the Pacific*** (London, 1987). The basic study of Germany's prewar foreign policy can be found in **G. Weinberg, *The Foreign Policy of Hitler's Germany: Diplomatic Revolution in Europe, 1933–36*** (Chicago, 1970), and ***The Foreign Policy of Hitler's Germany: Starting World War II, 1937–1939*** (Chicago, 1980).

General Works   General works on World War II include the comprehensive work by **G. Weinberg, *A World at Arms: A Global History of World War II,*** 2d ed. (Cambridge, 2005), and **J. Campbell, *The Experience of World War II*** (New York, 1989).

For briefer histories, see **J. Plowright**, *Causes, Course, and Outcomes of World War II* (New York, 2007), and **M. J. Lyon**, *World War II: A Short History,* 4th ed. (Upper Saddle River, N.J., 2004). On Hitler's attack on Poland, see **A. B. Rossino**, *Hitler Strikes Poland: Blitzkrieg, Ideology, and Atrocity* (Lawrence, Kans., 2003). The Eastern Front is covered in **O. Bartov**, *The Eastern Front, 1941–45: German Troops and the Barbarisation of Warfare* (London, 1986). See also **D. Glantz and J. M. House**, *When Titans Clashed: How the Red Army Stopped Hitler* (Lawrence, Kans., 1995). For a good military history of World War II, see **W. Murray and A. Millett**, *A War to Be Won: Fighting the Second World War* (Cambridge, Mass., 2000). See also **R. Overy's** *Why the Allies Won* (New York, 1996) on the reasons for the Allies' military victory. On the experiences of ordinary soldiers, see **P. Addison and A. Calder, eds.,** *Time to Kill: The Soldiers' Experience of War in the West, 1939–1945* (London, 1997), and **S. G. Fritz**, *Frontsoldaten: The German Soldier in World War Two* (Lexington, Ky., 1995). On the impact of the war on civilians, see **J. Bourke**, *The Second World War: A People's History* (Oxford, 2003). On the war in the Atlantic, see **D. F. White**, *Bitter Ocean: The Battle of the Atlantic, 1939–1945* (New York, 2006). On the end of Nazi Germany, see **J. Fest,** *Inside Hitler's Bunker: The Last Days of the Third Reich,* trans. **M. B. Dembo** (New York, 2004).

The New Order   A standard work on the German New Order in Russia is **A. Dallin**, *German Rule in Russia, 1941–1945,* rev. ed. (London, 1985). On Poland, see **P. T. Rutherford**, *Prelude to the Final Solution: The Nazi Program for Deporting Ethnic Poles, 1939–1941* (Lawrence, Kans., 2007). On foreign labor, see **U. Herbert**, *Hitler's Foreign Workers: Enforced Foreign Labor in Germany Under the Third Reich,* trans. **W. Templer** (Cambridge, 1997). Resistance movements in Europe are covered in **J. Semelin,** *Unarmed Against Hitler: Civilian Resistance in Europe, 1939–1943,* trans. **S. Husserl-Kapit** (Westport, Conn., 1993). A fundamental study on resistance in Germany is **H. Mommsen,** *Alternatives to Hitler: German Resistance Under the Third Reich,* trans. **A. McGeoch** (Princeton, N.J., 2003). There is a good collection of articles in **W. Benz and W. H. Pehle, eds.,** *Encyclopedia of German Resistance to the Nazi Movement* (New York, 1997). On women in resistance movements, see **M. Rossiter,** *Women in the Resistance* (New York, 1986).

The Holocaust   The best studies of the Holocaust include **R. Hilberg**, *The Destruction of the European Jews,* rev. ed., 3 vols. (New York, 1985); **S. Friedländer**, *The Years of Extermination: Nazi Germany and the Jews, 1939–1945* (New York, 2007); and **L. Yahil**, *The Holocaust* (Oxford, 1990). For brief studies, see **J. Fischel**, *The Holocaust* (Westport, Conn., 1998); **R. S. Botwinick,** *A History of the Holocaust,* 3d ed. (Upper Saddle River, N.J., 2004); and **D. Dwork and R. J. van Pelt**, *Holocaust: A History* (New York, 2002). Other Nazi atrocities are examined in **R. C. Lukas,** *Forgotten Holocaust: The Poles Under German Occupation, 1939–44,* 2d ed. (Lexington, Ky., 2001).

The Home Front   General studies on the impact of total war include **J. Costello**, *Love, Sex and War: Changing Values, 1939–1945* (London, 1985); **P. Summerfield**, *Women Workers in the Second World War: Production and Patriarchy in Conflict*
(London, 1984); and **M. R. Marrus**, *The Unwanted: European Refugees in the Twentieth Century* (New York, 1985). On the impact of the war on the home front from an economic perspective, see **M. Harrison, ed.,** *The Economics of World War II: Six Great Powers in International Comparison* (Cambridge, 1998). On the home front in Germany, see **E. R. Beck,** *Under the Bombs: The German Home Front, 1942–1945* (Lexington, Ky., 1986); **M. Kitchen,** *Nazi Germany at War* (New York, 1995); and **J. Stephenson,** *The Nazi Organisation of Women* (London, 1981). On the home front in Britain, see **A. Marwick,** *The Home Front* (London, 1976), and **S. Rose,** *Which People's War? National Identity and Citizenship in Britain, 1939–1945* (Oxford, 2003). The Soviet Union during the war is examined in **M. Harrison and J. Barber,** *The Soviet Home Front 1941–1945* (London, 1991). On the American home front, see the collection of essays in **K. P. O'Brien and L. H. Parsons,** *The Home-Front War: World War II and American Society* (Westport, Conn., 1995).

The Bombing Campaigns   On the Allied bombing campaign against Germany, see **R. Neillands,** *The Bomber War: The Allied Air Offensive Against Nazi Germany* (New York, 2005), and **J. Friedrich:** *The Fire: The Bombing of Germany,* trans. **A. Brown** (New York, 2006). One aspect of the German bombing of Britain is covered in **M. Gaskin,** *Blitz: The Story of December 29, 1940* (Boston, 2005). On the use of the atomic bomb in Japan, see **M. Gordin,** *Five Days in August: How World War II Became a Nuclear War* (Princeton, N.J., 2006).

CENGAGENOW   CengageNOW is an integrated online suite of services and resources with proven ease of use and efficient paths to success, delivering the results you want—NOW!
academic.cengage.com/login/
Enter CengageNOW using the access card that is available with *Western Civilization.* CengageNOW will assist you in understanding the content in this chapter with lesson plans generated for your needs. In addition, you can read the following documents, and many more, online:

   Adolf Hitler, Proclamation to the German Nation
   Winston Churchill, speeches
   Charles de Gaulle, Tunis speech
   Nuremberg Trials, excerpts

WESTERN CIVILIZATION RESOURCES

Visit the *Western Civilization* Companion Web site for resources specific to this book:
academic.cengage.com/history/spielvogel
For a variety of tools to help you succeed in this course, visit the Western Civilization Resource Center. Enter the Resource Center using either your *CengageNOW* access card or your standalone access card for the *Wadsworth Western Civilization Resource Center.* Organized by topic, this Web site includes quizzes; images; primary source documents; interactive simulations, maps, and timelines; movie explorations; and a wealth of other resources.
http://westernrc.wadsworth.com/

CHAPTER 28
COLD WAR AND A NEW WESTERN WORLD, 1945–1965

Children play amid the ruins of Warsaw, Poland, at the end of World War II

CHAPTER OUTLINE
AND FOCUS QUESTIONS

Development of the Cold War

Q Why were the United States and the Soviet Union suspicious of each other after World War II, and what events between 1945 and 1949 heightened the tensions between the two nations? How and why did the Cold War become a global affair after 1949?

Europe and the World: Decolonization

Q Why and how did the European colonies in Africa, the Middle East, and Asia gain independence between 1945 and 1965?

Recovery and Renewal in Europe

Q What were the main developments in the Soviet Union, Eastern Europe, and Western Europe between 1945 and 1965?

The United States and Canada: A New Era

Q What were the main political developments in North America between 1945 and 1965?

Postwar Society and Culture in the Western World

Q What major changes occurred in Western society and culture between 1945 and 1965?

CRITICAL THINKING

Q What were the similarities and differences in the political, social, and economic history of Eastern Europe and Western Europe between 1945 and 1965?

THE END OF WORLD WAR II in Europe had been met with great joy. One visitor to Moscow reported, "I looked out of the window [at 2 A.M.], almost everywhere there were lights in the window—people were staying awake. Everyone embraced everyone else, someone sobbed aloud." But after the victory parades and celebrations, Europeans awoke to a devastating realization: their civilization was in ruins. Some wondered if Europe would ever regain its former prosperity and importance. Winston Churchill wrote, "What is Europe now? A rubble heap, a charnel house, a breeding ground of pestilence and hate." There was ample reason for his pessimism. Almost 40 million people (soldiers and civilians) had been killed during the preceding six years. Massive air raids and artillery bombardments had reduced many of the great cities of Europe to heaps of rubble. The Polish capital of Warsaw had been almost completely obliterated. An American general described Berlin: "Wherever we looked we saw desolation. It was like a city of the dead."

Suffering and shock were visible in every face. Dead bodies still remained in canals and lakes and were being dug out from under bomb debris." Millions of Europeans faced starvation as grain harvests were only half of what they had been in 1939. Millions were also homeless. In the parts of the Soviet Union that had been occupied by the Germans, almost 25 million people were without homes. The destruction of bridges, roads, and railroads had left transportation systems paralyzed. Untold millions of people had been uprooted by the war; now they became "displaced persons," trying to find food and then their way home. Eleven million prisoners of war had to be returned to their native countries while 15 million Germans and Eastern Europeans were driven out of countries where they were no longer wanted. Yet despite the chaos, Europe was soon on the road to a remarkable recovery. Already by 1950, Europe's industrial and agricultural output was 30 percent above prewar levels.

World War II had cost Europe more than physical destruction, however. European supremacy in world affairs had also been destroyed. After 1945, the colonial empires of the European nations disintegrated, and Europe's place in the world changed radically. As the Cold War conflict between the world's two superpowers—the United States and the Soviet Union—intensified, the European nations were divided into two armed camps dependent on one or the other of these two major powers. The United States and the Soviet Union, whose rivalry raised the specter of nuclear war, seemed to hold the survival of Europe and the world in their hands. ◆

Development of the Cold War

Q Focus Questions: Why were the United States and the Soviet Union suspicious of each other after World War II, and what events between 1945 and 1949 heightened the tensions between the two nations? How and why did the Cold War become a global affair after 1949?

Even before World War II had ended, the two major Allied powers—the United States and the Soviet Union—had begun to disagree on the nature of the postwar European world. Unity had been maintained during the war because of the urgent need to defeat the Axis powers, but once they were defeated, the differences between the Americans and Soviets again surged to the front.

Confrontation of the Superpowers

Considerable historical debate has been waged about who was responsible for starting the Cold War. Both the United States and the Soviet Union took steps at the end of World War II that were unwise or might have been avoided. Both nations, however, were working within a framework conditioned by the past. Ultimately, the rivalry between the two superpowers stemmed from their different historical perspectives and their irreconcilable political ambitions. Intense competition for political and military supremacy had long been a regular feature of Western civilization. The United States and the Soviet

Union were the heirs of that European tradition of power politics, and it should not surprise us that two such different systems would seek to extend their way of life to the rest of the world. Because of its need to feel secure on its western border, the Soviet Union was not prepared to give up the advantages it had gained in Eastern Europe from Germany's defeat. But neither were American leaders willing to give up the power and prestige the United States had gained throughout the world. Suspicious of each other's motives, the United States and the Soviet Union soon raised their mutual fears to a level of intense competition (see the box on p. 877). Between 1945 and 1949, a number of events embroiled the two countries in continual conflict.

Disagreement over Eastern Europe   Eastern Europe was the first area of disagreement. The United States and Great Britain had championed self-determination and democratic freedom for the liberated nations of Eastern Europe. Joseph Stalin, however, fearful that the Eastern European nations would return to traditional anti-Soviet attitudes if they were permitted free elections, opposed the West's plans. Having liberated Eastern Europe from the Nazis, the Red Army proceeded to install pro-Soviet governing regimes in Poland, Romania, Bulgaria, and Hungary. These pro-Soviet governments satisfied Stalin's desire for a buffer zone against the West, but the local populations and their sympathizers in the West saw the regimes as an expansion of Stalin's empire. Only another war could change this situation, and few people wanted another armed conflict.

The Truman Doctrine   A civil war in Greece provided another arena for confrontation between the superpowers. In 1946, the Communist People's Liberation Army and the anti-Communist forces supported by the British were fighting each other for control of Greece. Great Britain had initially assumed primary responsibility for promoting postwar reconstruction in the eastern Mediterranean, but in 1947 ongoing postwar economic problems caused the British to withdraw from the active role they had been playing in both Greece and Turkey. President Harry Truman of the United States, alarmed by British weakness and the possibility of Soviet expansion into the eastern Mediterranean, responded with the **Truman Doctrine** (see the box on p. 878). The Truman Doctrine said, in essence, that the United States would provide money to countries that claimed they were threatened by Communist expansion. If the Soviets were not stopped in Greece, the United States would have to face the spread of communism throughout the free world. As Dean Acheson, the American secretary of state, explained, "Like apples in a barrel infected by disease, the corruption of Greece would infect Iran and all the East . . . likewise Africa . . . Italy . . . France. . . . Not since Rome and Carthage had there been such a polarization of power on this earth."[1] In March 1947, Truman requested $400 million in economic and military aid for Greece and Turkey from the U.S. Congress.

OPPOSING VIEWPOINTS

WHO STARTED THE COLD WAR? AMERICAN AND SOVIET PERSPECTIVES

Although the United States and the Soviet Union had cooperated during World War II to defeat the Germans and Japanese, differences began to appear as soon as victory became certain. The year 1946 was an especially important turning point in the relationship between the two new superpowers. George Kennan, an American diplomat regarded as an expert on Soviet affairs, was asked to write an analysis of one of Stalin's speeches. His U.S. Foreign Service dispatch, which came to be known as the Long Telegram, was sent to U.S. embassies, U.S. State Department officials, and military leaders. The Long Telegram gave a strong view of Soviet intentions. A response to Kennan's position was written by Nikolai Novikov, a former Soviet ambassador to the United States. His response was read by Vyacheslav Molotov, the Soviet foreign minister, but historians are not sure if Stalin or other officials also read it and were influenced by it.

George Kennan, The Long Telegram, February 1946

At the bottom of [the Soviet] neurotic view of world affairs is a traditional and instinctive Russian sense of insecurity. Originally, this was the insecurity of a peaceful agricultural people trying to live on a vast exposed plain in the neighborhood of fierce nomadic peoples. To this was added, as Russia came into contact with the economically advanced West, the fear of more competent, more powerful, more highly organized societies.... For this reason they have always feared foreign penetration, feared direct contact between the Western world and their own.... And they have learned to seek security only in patient but deadly struggle for total destruction of rival power, never in compacts and compromises with it....

In summary, we have here a political force committed fanatically to the belief that with the United State there can be no permanent modus vivendi, that it is desirable and necessary the internal harmony of our society be disrupted, our traditional way of life be destroyed, the international authority of our state be broken, if Soviet power is to be secure.... In addition it has an elaborate and far-flung apparatus for exertion of its influence in other countries, an apparatus of amazing flexibility and versatility, managed by people whose experience and skill in underground methods are presumably without parallel in history. Finally, it is seemingly inaccessible to considerations of reality in its basic reactions.... This is admittedly not a pleasant picture.... But I would like to record my conviction that

the problem is within our power to solve—and that without recourse to any general conflict.... I think we may approach calmly and with good heart the problem of how to deal with Russia ... [but] we must have the courage and self-confidence to cling to our own methods and conceptions of human society. After all, the greatest danger that can befall us in coping with this problem of Soviet communism is that we shall allow ourselves to become like those with whom we are coping.

Nikolai Novikov, Telegram, September 27, 1946

One of the stages in the achievement of dominance over the world by the United States is its understanding with England concerning the partial division of the world on the basis of mutual concessions. The basic lines of the secret agreement between the United States and England regarding the division of the world consist, as shown by facts, in their agreement on the inclusion of Japan and China in the sphere of influence of the United States in the Far East.... The American policy in China is striving for the complete economic and political submission of China to the control of American monopolistic capital....

Obvious indications of the U.S. effort to establish world dominance are also to be found in the increase in military potential in peacetime and in the establishment of a large number of naval and air bases both in the United States and beyond its borders....

Careful note should be taken of the fact that the preparation by the United States for a future war is being conducted with the prospect of war against the Soviet Union, which in the eyes of American imperialists is the main obstacle in the path of the United States to world domination. This is indicated by facts such as the tactical training of the American army for war with the Soviet Union as the future opponent, the placing of American strategic bases in regions from which it is possible to launch strikes on Soviet territory, intensified training and strengthening of Arctic regions as close approaches to the USSR, and attempts to prepare Germany and Japan to use those countries in a war against the USSR.

Q *In Kennan's view, what was the Soviet policy after World War II? What did he believe determined that policy, and how did he think the United States should respond? In Novikov's view, what was the goal of U.S. foreign policy, and how did he believe the Americans planned to achieve it? Why was it so difficult to achieve a common ground between the two positions?*

The Marshall Plan The proclamation of the Truman Doctrine was followed in June 1947 by the European Recovery Program, better known as the **Marshall Plan.** Intended to rebuild prosperity and stability, this program included $13 billion for the economic recovery of war-torn Europe. Underlying it was the belief that Communist aggression fed off economic turmoil. General George C. Marshall had noted in a commencement speech at

THE TRUMAN DOCTRINE

By 1947, the battle lines had been clearly drawn in the Cold War. This selection is taken from a speech by President Harry Truman to the U.S. Congress in which he justified his request for aid to Greece and Turkey. Truman expressed the urgent need to contain the expansion of communism.

President Harry Truman, Address to Congress, March 12, 1947

The peoples of a number of countries of the world have recently had totalitarian regimes forced upon them against their will. The Government of the United States has made frequent protests against coercion and intimidation, in violation of the Yalta agreement, in Poland, Romania, and Bulgaria. I must also state that in a number of other countries there have been similar developments.

At the present moment in world history nearly every nation must choose between alternative ways of life. The choice is too often not a free one.

One way of life is based upon the will of the majority, and is distinguished by free institutions, representative government, free elections, guaranties of individual liberty, freedom of speech and religion, and freedom from political oppression.

The second way of life is based upon the will of a minority forcibly imposed upon the majority. It relies upon terror and oppression, a controlled press and radio, fixed elections, and the suppression of personal freedoms.

I believe that it must be the policy of the United States to support free peoples who are resisting attempted subjugation by armed minorities or by outside pressures.

I believe that we must assist free people to work out their own destinies in their own way.

I believe that our help should be primarily through economic and financial aid which is essential to economic stability and orderly political processes.... I therefore ask the Congress for assistance to Greece and Turkey in the amount of $400 million.

Q *How did President Truman defend his request for aid to Greece and Turkey? Did this decision play a role in intensifying the Cold War? Why or why not?*

Harvard, "Our policy is not directed against any country or doctrine but against hunger, poverty, desperation and chaos."[2] Nevertheless, the Marshall Plan, which did not include the Soviet Union, helped speed up the division of Europe into two competing blocs. According to the Soviet view, the Marshall Plan aimed at the "construction of a bloc of states bound by obligations to the USA, and to guarantee the American loans in return for the relinquishing by the European states of their economic and later also their political independence."[3] To some scholars, the Marshall Plan encouraged Stalin to push for even greater control of Eastern Europe to safeguard Soviet interests.

The American Policy of Containment By 1947, the split in Europe between East and West had become a fact of life. At the end of World War II, the United States had favored a quick end to its commitments in Europe. But American fears of Soviet aims caused the United States to play an increasingly important role in European affairs. In an article in *Foreign Affairs* in July 1947, George Kennan, a well-known American diplomat with much knowledge of Soviet affairs, advocated a policy of **containment** against further aggressive Soviet moves. Kennan favored the "adroit and vigilant application of counter-force at a series of constantly shifting geographical and political points, corresponding to the shifts and maneuvers of Soviet policy." After the Soviet blockade of Berlin in 1948, containment of the Soviet Union became formal American policy.

Contention over Germany The fate of Germany also became a source of heated contention between East and West. Besides **denazification** and the partitioning of Germany (and Berlin) into four occupied zones, the Allied powers had agreed on little else with regard to the conquered nation. The Soviets, hardest hit by the war, took reparations from Germany in the form of booty. The technology-starved Soviets dismantled and removed to the Soviet Union 380 factories from the western zones of Berlin before transferring their control to the Western powers. By the summer of 1946, two hundred chemical, paper, and textile factories in the Soviets' East German zone had likewise been shipped to the Soviet Union. At the same time, the German Communist Party was reestablished under the control of Walter Ulbricht (1893–1973) and was soon in charge of the political reconstruction of the Soviet zone in eastern Germany.

At the same time, the British, French, and Americans gradually began to merge their zones economically and by February 1948 were making plans for the unification of these three western sections of Germany and the formal creation of a West German federal government. The Soviets responded with a blockade of West Berlin that allowed neither trucks nor trains to enter the three western zones of Berlin. The Soviets hoped to secure economic control of all Berlin and force the Western powers to halt the creation of a separate West German state.

The Western powers faced a dilemma. Direct military confrontation seemed dangerous, and no one wished to risk World War III. Therefore, an attempt to break through the blockade with tanks and trucks was ruled out. But how could the 2.5 million people in the three western zones of Berlin be kept alive when the whole city

FILM & HISTORY
THE THIRD MAN (1949)

Directed by Carol Reed, *The Third Man* is a classic thriller set in post–World War II Vienna. It is based on a novel by Graham Greene, who also wrote the screenplay for the movie. When he arrives in Vienna, Holly Martins (Joseph Cotton), an out-of-work American writer of pulp-fiction Westerns, learns that his old school friend Harry Lime (Orson Welles), who had offered him a job in Vienna, has recently died in a traffic accident. But the circumstances surrounding Lime's death are suspicious. With the help of Lime's girlfriend, Anna Schmidt (Alida Valli), Martins sets out to determine what really happened. Eventually, he finds that Lime did not really die but has gone underground in the Russian sector of Vienna to avoid capture by the British Major Calloway (Trevor Howard). British authorities

Harry Lime (Orson Welles) tries to avoid capture.

have ascertained that Lime is responsible for a number of black-market activities, which are common in postwar Vienna. Lime, however, has been involved in the heinous sale of watered-down penicillin that has led to pain and death for many children. When Lime and Martins finally meet, Lime justifies his activities with the cynical words:

> Don't be so gloomy. After all it's not that awful. Like the fella says, in Italy for 30 years under the Borgias they had warfare, terror, murder, and bloodshed, but they produced Michelangelo, Leonardo da Vinci, and the Renaissance. In Switzerland they had brotherly love— they had 500 years of democracy and peace, and what did that produce? The cuckoo clock.

Martins agrees to help the British authorities track down Lime, who tries without success to escape through the massive sewers underneath the cobblestone streets of Vienna.

The Third Man is a thriller, but it also serves to give viewers a picture of the bleakness of postwar Europe. Carol Reed had worked for a British wartime documentary group and insisted that the movie be shot completely on location in Vienna, where piles of rubble and bomb craters still stood alongside architectural masterpieces. The movie accurately reflects the different points-of-view between Americans and Europeans at the end of World War II. The United States began to experience an economic boom, and most Americans had a great deal of hope about the future. Europeans in contrast, were world-weary and disillusioned. Many lived, as in Vienna, in a joyless world, reflected in the words of Anna Schmidt when Martins asks her about Lime's untimely death: "I don't know anything anymore, except that I want to be dead, too."

The Third Man also reflected the growing uncertainties and paranoia associated with the emerging Cold War in Europe. Bombed-out Vienna was divided into four zones, each with its group of suspicious officials from the four powers—the United States, Britain, France, and the Soviet Union. The inner city was jointly administered by the four powers. As the authorities spar over the details of governing Vienna, Holly Martins is never quite sure who to trust in this new world of confused loyalties. In the film, the Russians are trying to take Anna Schmidt back to her native Czechoslovakia, a clear indication of the growing Soviet power in Eastern Europe. And Major Calloway is obviously suspicious of his Russian counterparts. Vienna itself is a forlorn city where black marketers control the economy and the underground sewer system serves as a route for travel between the closed sectors of the city.

was inside the Soviet zone? The solution was the Berlin Air Lift.

It was an enormous task. Western Allied air forces worked around the clock for almost a year to supply the city of Berlin with foodstuffs as well as the coal, oil, and gasoline needed to heat the city's dwellings and run its power stations, sewer plants, and factories. At the peak, 13,000 tons of supplies were being flown to Berlin daily. Altogether the Western powers shipped 2.3 million tons of food on 277,500 flights. Seventy-three Allied airmen lost their lives due to accidents. The Soviets, also not wanting war, did not interfere and finally lifted the blockade in May 1949. The blockade of Berlin had severely increased tensions between the United States and the Soviet Union and brought about the separation of Germany into two states. At the end of May, a constitution was drafted for a Federal Republic of Germany (West Germany). Konrad Adenauer was elected as the new German chancellor in September 1949. A month later, the separate German Democratic Republic was established in East Germany. Berlin remained a divided city and the source of much contention between East and West.

The Berlin Air Lift

New Military Alliances The Soviet Union also detonated its first atomic bomb in 1949, and all too soon, both superpowers were involved in an escalating arms race that resulted in the construction of ever more destructive nuclear weapons. Soon the search for security took the form of **mutual deterrence,** the belief that an arsenal of nuclear weapons prevented war by assuring that if one nation launched its nuclear weapons in a preemptive first strike, the other nation would still be able to respond and devastate the attacker. Therefore, the assumption was that neither side would risk using the massive arsenals that had been assembled.

The search for security in the uncertain atmosphere of the Cold War also led to the formation of military alliances. The North Atlantic Treaty Organization (**NATO**) was formed in April 1949 when Belgium, Britain,

Denmark, France, Iceland, Italy, Luxembourg, the Netherlands, Norway, and Portugal signed a treaty with the United States and Canada. All the powers agreed to provide mutual assistance if any one of them was attacked. A few years later West Germany, Greece, and Turkey joined NATO.

The Eastern European states soon followed suit. In 1949, they formed the Council for Mutual Economic Assistance (COMECON) for economic cooperation. Then in 1955, Albania, Bulgaria, Czechoslovakia, East Germany, Hungary, Poland, Romania, and the Soviet Union organized a formal military alliance in the **Warsaw Pact.** As had happened so many times before, Europe was divided into hostile alliance systems (see Map 28.1).

Globalization of the Cold War

The Cold War soon spread from Europe to the rest of the world. In 1949, the victory of the Chinese Communists in the Chinese civil war brought a new Communist regime and intensified American fears about the spread of communism. Shortly thereafter, the Korean War turned the Cold War into a worldwide struggle, eventually leading to a system of military alliances around the globe.

The Korean War The removal of Korea from Japanese control had been one of the stated objectives of the Allies in World War II, and on the eve of the Japanese

The Berlin Air Lift. During the Berlin Air Lift, the United States and its Western allies flew 13,000 tons of supplies daily to Berlin and thus were able to break the Soviet land blockade of the city. In this photograph, residents of West Berlin watch an American plane arrive with supplies for the city.

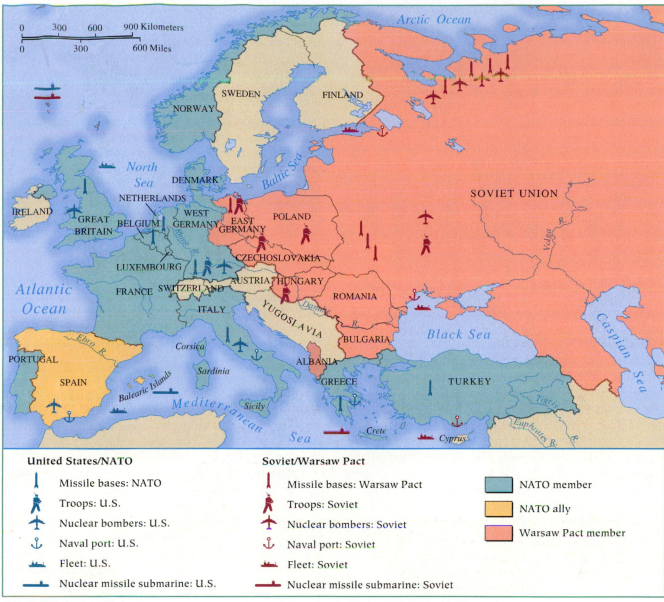

United States/NATO

- ⚔ Missile bases: NATO
- 🚶 Troops: U.S.
- ✈ Nuclear bombers: U.S.
- ⚓ Naval port: U.S.
- 🚢 Fleet: U.S.
- ⛴ Nuclear missile submarine: U.S.

Soviet/Warsaw Pact

- ⚔ Missile bases: Warsaw Pact
- 🚶 Troops: Soviet
- ✈ Nuclear bombers: Soviet
- ⚓ Naval port: Soviet
- 🚢 Fleet: Soviet
- ⛴ Nuclear missile submarine: Soviet

- ▮ NATO member
- ▮ NATO ally
- ▮ Warsaw Pact member

MAP 28.1   The New European Alliance Systems in the 1950s and 1960s.   With the United States as its leader, NATO was formed in 1949 to counter the perceived military threat of the Soviet Union and its Eastern European satellites, which formally created the Warsaw Pact in 1955. Soviet and American troops, each backed by nuclear weapons, directly faced each other, heightening Cold War tensions.

Q Which NATO countries shared a border with one or more Warsaw Pact countries?

🌐 **View an animated version of this map or related maps at academic.cengage.com/history/spielvogel**

surrender in August 1945, the Soviet Union and the United States agreed to divide the country into two separate occupation zones at the 38th parallel. They originally planned to hold national elections after the restoration of peace to reunify Korea under an independent government. But as U.S.-Soviet relations deteriorated, two separate governments emerged in Korea, a Communist one in the north (Democratic People's Republic of Korea or North Korea) and an anti-Communist one (Republic of Korea or South Korea) in the south.

Tensions between the two governments ran high along the dividing line, and on June 25, 1950, with the apparent approval of Joseph Stalin, North Korean troops invaded South Korea. The Americans, seeing this as yet another example of Communist aggression and expansion, gained the support of the United Nations and intervened by sending American troops to turn back the invasion. By September, United Nations forces (mostly Americans and South Koreans) under the command of General Douglas MacArthur marched northward across the 38th parallel with the aim of unifying Korea under a single non-Communist government. But Mao Zedong (1893–1976), the leader of Communist China, sent Chinese forces into the fray and forced MacArthur's troops back to South Korea.

To many Americans, the Chinese intervention in Korea was clear evidence that China intended to promote communism throughout Asia. In

The Korean War

fact, China's decision to enter the war was probably motivated in large part by the fear that hostile U.S. forces might be stationed on the Chinese frontier. When two more years of fighting failed to produce a conclusive victory, an armistice was finally signed in 1953. The boundary line between North and South Korea remained roughly at the 38th parallel. To many Americans, the policy of containing communism had succeeded in Asia, just as it had earlier in Europe, though at the cost of losing more than 50,000 men in the war. The Chinese invasion also hardened Western attitudes against the new Chinese government and led to China's isolation from the major capitalist powers for two decades. As a result, China was forced to rely almost entirely on the Soviet Union, with which it had signed a pact of friendship and cooperation in early 1950.

The First Vietnam War

A struggle began in French Indochina after World War II, when Ho Chi Minh's Indochinese Communist Party formed a multiparty nationalist alliance called the Vietminh Front and seized power in northern and central Vietnam. When negotiations broke down between Ho's government and the returning French, war broke out in December 1946.

For three years, the Vietminh gradually increased in size and effectiveness. What had begun as an anticolonial struggle by Ho Chi Minh's Vietminh Front against the French soon became entangled in the Cold War as both the United States and the new Communist government in China began to intervene in the conflict in the early 1950s. China began to provide military assistance to the Vietminh to protect its own borders from hostile forces. The Americans supported the French but pressured the French government to prepare for an eventual transition to a non-Communist government in Vietnam.

At the Geneva Conference in 1954, with the French public tired of fighting the "dirty war" in Indochina, the French agreed to a peace settlement with Ho Chi Minh's Vietminh. Vietnam was temporarily divided into a

northern Communist half (known as the Democratic Republic of Vietnam) and a non-Communist southern half based in Saigon (known eventually as the Republic of Vietnam). Elections were to be held in two years to create a unified government.

Escalation of the Cold War

The Korean and Vietnamese experiences seemed to confirm American fears of Communist expansion and reinforced American determination to contain Soviet power. In the mid-1950s, the administration of President Dwight D. Eisenhower (1890–1969) adopted a policy of massive retaliation, which advocated the full use of American nuclear bombs to counteract even a Soviet ground attack in Europe, although there was no evidence that Stalin ever planned such an attack. Meanwhile, American military alliances were extended around the world. Eisenhower claimed, "The freedom we cherish and defend in Europe and in the Americas is no different from the freedom that is imperiled in Asia." The Central Treaty Organization (CENTO) of Great Britain, Iran, Iraq, Pakistan, Turkey, and the United States was intended to prevent the Soviet Union from expanding at the expense of its southern neighbors. In addition, Australia, Britain, France, New Zealand, Pakistan, the Philippines, Thailand, and the United States formed the Southeast Asia Treaty Organization (SEATO). By the mid-1950s, the United States found itself allied militarily with forty-two states around the world.

Despite the escalation of the Cold War, hopes for a new era of peaceful coexistence also appeared. The death of Stalin in 1953 caused some people in the West to think that the new Soviet leadership might be more flexible in its policies. But this optimism proved premature. A summit conference at Geneva in 1955 between President Eisenhower and Nikolai Bulganin, then leader of the Soviet government, produced no real benefits. A year later, all talk of **rapprochement** between East and West temporarily ceased when the Soviet Union used its armed forces to crush Hungary's attempt to assert its independence from Soviet control.

Another Berlin Crisis

A crisis over Berlin also added to the tension in the late 1950s. In August 1957, the Soviet Union had launched its first intercontinental ballistic missile (ICBM) and, shortly thereafter, *Sputnik I,* the first space satellite. Fueled by partisan political debate, fears of a "missile gap" between the United States and the Soviet Union seized the American public. Nikita Khrushchev (1894–1971), the new leader of the Soviet Union, attempted to take advantage of the American frenzy over missiles to solve the problem of West Berlin. Khrushchev had said that Berlin was like "the testicles of the West: every time I want to make the West scream, I squeeze on Berlin."[4] West Berlin had remained a "Western island" of prosperity in the midst of the relatively poverty-stricken East Germany. Many East Germans also managed to escape East Germany by fleeing through West Berlin.

In November 1958, Khrushchev announced that unless the West removed its forces from West Berlin within six months, he would turn over control of the access routes to Berlin to the East Germans. Unwilling to accept an ultimatum that would have abandoned West Berlin to the Communists, Eisenhower and the West stood firm, and Khrushchev eventually backed down.

The crisis was revived when John F. Kennedy (1917–1963) became the American president. During a summit meeting in Vienna in June 1961, Khrushchev threatened Kennedy with another six-month ultimatum over West Berlin. Kennedy left Vienna convinced of the need to deal firmly with the Soviet Union, and Khrushchev was forced once again to back off. Frustrated, Khrushchev conspired with Walter Ulbricht, the East German leader, to build a wall around West Berlin to cut off the flow of refugees to the West. On August 31, 1961, East German workers under military supervision began the construction of the Berlin Wall. Within a few months, more than 100 miles of wall, topped by numerous watchtowers, surrounded West Berlin. Since access from West Germany into West Berlin was still permitted, the Americans acquiesced and accepted the wall's existence. The Berlin Wall became a powerful symbol of a divided Europe. And Khrushchev, determined to achieve some foreign policy success, soon embarked on an even more dangerous venture in Cuba.

The Cuban Missile Crisis   The Cold War confrontation between the United States and the Soviet Union reached frightening levels during the Cuban Missile Crisis. In 1959, a left-wing revolutionary named Fidel Castro (b. 1927) had overthrown the Cuban dictator Fulgencio Batista and established a Soviet-supported totalitarian regime. In 1961, an American-supported attempt to invade Cuba via the Bay of Pigs and overthrow Castro's regime ended in utter failure. The next year, in 1962, the Soviet Union decided to station nuclear missiles in Cuba.

The United States was not prepared to allow nuclear weapons within such close striking distance of the American mainland, even though it had placed nuclear weapons in Turkey within easy range of the Soviet Union. Khrushchev was quick to point out that "your rockets are in Turkey. You are worried by Cuba...because it is 90 miles from the American coast. But Turkey is next to us."[5] When U.S. intelligence discovered that a Soviet fleet carrying missiles was heading to Cuba, President Kennedy decided to blockade Cuba and prevent the fleet from reaching its destination. This approach to the problem had the benefit of delaying confrontation and giving each side time to find a peaceful solution (see the box on p. 884). Khrushchev agreed to turn back the fleet if Kennedy pledged not to invade Cuba. In a conciliatory letter to Kennedy, Khrushchev wrote:

> We and you ought not to pull on the ends of the rope in which you have tied the knot of war, because the more the two of us pull, the tighter that knot will be tied. And a moment may come when that knot will be tied too tight that even he who tied it will not have the strength to untie it....Let us not only relax the forces pulling on the ends of the rope, let us take measures to untie that knot. We are ready for this.[6]

The Cuban Missile Crisis brought the world frighteningly close to nuclear war. Indeed, in 1992, a high-ranking Soviet officer revealed that short-range rockets armed with nuclear devices would have been used against American troops if the United States had invaded Cuba, an option that President Kennedy fortunately had rejected. The intense feeling that the world might have been annihilated in a few days had a profound influence on both sides. A hotline communication system between Moscow and Washington was installed in 1963 to expedite rapid communication between the two superpowers in a time of crisis. In the same year, the two powers agreed to ban nuclear tests in the atmosphere, a step that served to lessen the tensions between the two nations.

Europe and the World: Decolonization

Q **Focus Question:** Why and how did the European colonies in Africa, the Middle East, and Asia gain independence between 1945 and 1965?

As we saw in Chapter 26, movements for independence had begun in earnest in Africa and Asia in the years between the wars. After World War II, these movements grew even louder. The ongoing subjugation of peoples by colonial powers seemed at odds with the goals the Allies had pursued in overthrowing the repressive regimes of Germany, Italy, and Japan. Then, too, indigenous peoples everywhere took up the call for national self-determination and expressed their determination to fight for independence.

The Cuban Missile Crisis from Khrushchev's Perspective

The Cuban Missile Crisis was one of the sobering experiences of the Cold War. It led the two superpowers to seek new ways to lessen the tensions between them. This version of the events is taken from the memoirs of Nikita Khrushchev.

Nikita Khrushchev, *Khrushchev Remembers*

I will explain what the Caribbean crisis of October 1962, was all about.... At the time that Fidel Castro led his revolution to victory and entered Havana with his troops, we had no idea what political course his regime would follow.... All the while the Americans had been watching Castro closely. At first they thought that the capitalist underpinnings of the Cuban economy would remain intact. So by the time Castro announced that he was going to put Cuba on the road toward Socialism, the Americans had already missed their chance to do any thing about it by simply exerting their influence: there were no longer any forces left which could be organized to fight on America's behalf in Cuba. That left only one alternative—invasion!...

After Castro's crushing victory over the counterrevolutionaries we intensified our military aid to Cuba.... We were sure that the Americans would never reconcile themselves to the existence of Castro's Cuba. They feared, as much as we hoped, that a Socialist Cuba might become a magnet that would attract other Latin American countries to Socialism.... It was clear to me that we might very well lose Cuba if we didn't take some decisive steps in her defense.... We had to think up some way of confronting America with more than words. We had to establish a tangible and effective deterrent to American interference in the Caribbean. But what exactly? The logical answer was missiles. We knew that American missiles were aimed against us in Turkey and Italy, to say nothing of West Germany.... My thinking went like this: if we installed the missiles secretly and then if the United States discovered the missiles were there after they were already poised and ready to strike, the Americans would think twice before trying to liquidate our installations by military means.... I want to make one thing absolutely clear: when we put our ballistic missiles in Cuba we had no desire to start a war. On the contrary, our principal aim was only to deter America from starting a war....

President Kennedy issued an ultimatum, demanding that we remove our missiles and bombers from Cuba.... We sent the Americans a note saying that we agreed to remove our missiles and bombers on the condition that the President give us his assurance that there would be no invasion of Cuba by the forces of the United States or anybody else. Finally Kennedy gave in and agreed to make a statement giving us such an assurance.... It had been, to say the least, an interesting and challenging situation. The two most powerful nations of the world had been squared off against each other, each with its finger on the button. You'd have thought that war was inevitable. But both sides showed that if the desire to avoid war is strong enough, even the most pressing dispute can be solved by compromise. And a compromise over Cuba was indeed found. The episode ended in a triumph of common sense.... It was a great victory for us, though, that we had been able to extract from Kennedy a promise that neither America nor any of her allies would invade Cuba.... The Caribbean crisis was a triumph of Soviet foreign policy and a personal triumph in my own career as a statesman and as a member of the collective leadership. We achieved, I would say, a spectacular success without having to fire a single shot!

Q *According to his memoirs, why did Khrushchev decide to install missiles in Cuba? Why did he later agree to remove them? What did each side "lose" and what did each side "win" in the Cuban Missile Crisis?*

The ending of the European colonial empires did not come easy, however. In 1941, Churchill had said, "I have not become His Majesty's Chief Minister in order to preside over the liquidation of the British Empire." Britain and France in particular seemed reluctant to let go of their colonies, but for a variety of reasons both eventually gave in to the obvious: the days of empire were over.

During the war, the Japanese had already humiliated the Western states by overrunning their colonial empires. In addition, colonial soldiers who had fought on behalf of the Allies were well aware that Allied war aims included the principle of self-determination for the peoples of the world. Equally important to the process of **decolonization** after the war, the power of the European states had been destroyed by the exhaustive struggles of World War II. The greatest colonial empire builder, Great Britain, no longer had the energy or the wealth to maintain its colonial empire. Given the combination of circumstances, a rush of decolonization swept the world. Between 1947 and 1962, virtually every colony achieved independence and attained statehood. Although some colonial powers willingly relinquished their control, others had to be driven out by national wars of liberation. Decolonization was a difficult and even bitter process, but it created a new world as the non-Western states ended the long era of Western domination.

Africa: The Struggle for Independence

After World War II, Europeans reluctantly realized that colonial rule in Africa would have to come to an end, but little had been done to prepare Africans for self-rule. Political organizations that had been formed by Africans before the war to gain their rights became formal political parties with independence as their goal. In the Gold Coast, Kwame Nkrumah (1909–1972) formed the Convention People's Party, the first African political party in black Africa. In the late 1940s, Jomo Kenyatta (1894–1978) founded the Kenya African National Union, which focused on economic issues but also sought self-rule for Kenya.

For the most part, these political activities were nonviolent and were led by Western-educated African intellectuals. Their constituents were primarily merchants, urban professionals, and members of labor unions. But the demand for independence was not restricted to the cities. In Kenya, for example, the widely publicized Mau Mau movement among the Kikuyu peoples used terrorism to demand *uhuru* (Swahili for "freedom") from the British. Mau Mau terrorism alarmed the European population and convinced the British in 1959 to promise eventual independence.

A similar process was occurring in Egypt, which had been a protectorate of Great Britain since the 1880s. In 1918, a formal political party called the Wafd was formed to promote Egyptian independence. Although Egypt gained its independence in 1922, it still remained under British control. Egyptian intellectuals, however, were opposed as much to the Egyptian monarchy as to the British, and in 1952, an army coup overthrew King Farouk and set up an independent republic.

In North Africa, the French, who were simply not strong enough to maintain control of their far-flung colonial empire, granted full independence to Morocco and Tunisia in 1956 (see Map 28.2). Since Algeria was home to 2 million French settlers, however, France chose to retain its dominion there. But a group of Algerian nationalists organized the National Liberation Front (FLN) and in 1954 initiated a guerrilla war to liberate their homeland (see the box on p. 887). The French people became so divided over this war that their leader, Charles de Gaulle, accepted the inevitable and granted Algerian independence in 1962.

In areas such as South Africa, where the political system was dominated by European settlers, the transition to independence was more complicated. In South Africa, political activity by local blacks began with the formation of the African National Congress (ANC) in 1912. At first, it was a group of intellectuals whose goal was to gain economic and political reforms, including full equality for educated Africans, within the framework of the existing system. The ANC's efforts, however, met with little success. At the same time, by the 1950s, South African whites were strengthening the laws separating whites and blacks, creating a system of racial segregation in South Africa known as **apartheid.** When blacks demonstrated against the apartheid laws, the white government brutally repressed the demonstrators. After the arrest of Nelson Mandela (b. 1918), the ANC leader, in 1962, members of the ANC called for armed resistance to the white government.

Algerian Independence. Although the French wanted to retain control of their Algerian colony, a bloody war of liberation finally led to Algeria's freedom. This photograph shows a group of Algerians celebrating the announcement of independence on July 3, 1962.

When both the British and the French decided to let go of their colonial empires, most black African nations achieved their independence in the late 1950s and 1960s. The Gold Coast, now renamed Ghana and under the guidance of Kwame Nkrumah, was first in 1957. Nigeria, the Belgian Congo (renamed Zaire), Kenya, Tanganyika (later, when joined with Zanzibar, renamed Tanzania), and others soon followed. Seventeen new African nations emerged in 1960. Another eleven followed between 1961 and 1965. By the late 1960s, only parts of southern Africa and the Portuguese possessions of Mozambique and Angola remained under European rule. After a series of brutal guerrilla wars, the Portuguese finally gave up their colonies in the 1970s.

Conflict in the Middle East

Although Turkey, Iran, Saudi Arabia, and Iraq had become independent states between the two world wars, the end of World War II led to the emergence of other

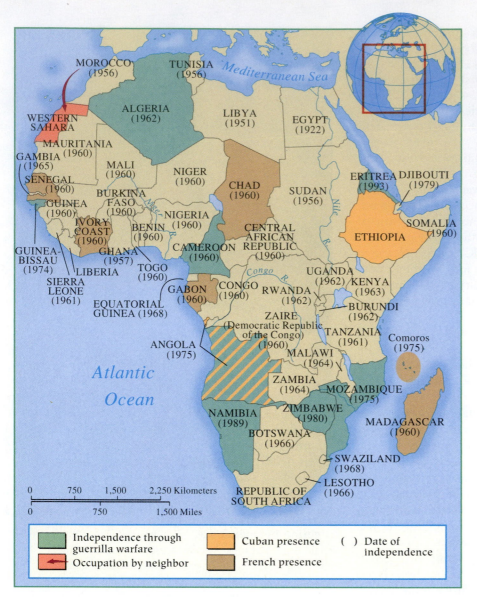

MAP 28.2 **Decolonization in Africa.** By the late 1950s, Britain and France had decided to allow independence for most of their African colonies, although France fought hard before relinquishing Algeria. Most of the new states had difficulty promoting economic growth and dealing with internal ethnic animosities.

Q Of the countries that gained independence from 1975 onward, what is a significant characteristic shared by a majority of them? View an animated version of this map or related maps at **academic.cengage.com/history/spielvogel**

Map labels:
MOROCCO (1956)
TUNISIA (1956)
Mediterranean Sea
WESTERN SAHARA
ALGERIA (1962)
LIBYA (1951)
EGYPT (1922)
MAURITANIA (1960)
GAMBIA (1965)
MALI (1960)
NIGER (1960)
SENEGAL (1960)
BURKINA FASO (1960)
CHAD (1960)
SUDAN (1956)
ERITREA (1993)
DJIBOUTI (1979)
GUINEA (1960)
NIGERIA (1960)
CENTRAL AFRICAN REPUBLIC (1960)
SOMALIA (1960)
IVORY COAST (1960)
BENIN (1960)
GUINEA-BISSAU (1974)
GHANA (1957)
LIBERIA
TOGO (1960)
CAMEROON (1960)
ETHIOPIA
SIERRA LEONE (1961)
EQUATORIAL GUINEA (1968)
GABON (1960)
CONGO (1960)
RWANDA (1962)
UGANDA (1962)
KENYA (1963)
BURUNDI (1962)
ZAIRE (Democratic Republic of the Congo) (1960)
TANZANIA (1961)
Comoros (1975)
ANGOLA (1975)
MALAWI (1964)
Atlantic Ocean
ZAMBIA (1964)
MOZAMBIQUE (1975)
NAMIBIA (1989)
ZIMBABWE (1980)
MADAGASCAR (1960)
BOTSWANA (1966)
SWAZILAND (1968)
LESOTHO (1966)
REPUBLIC OF SOUTH AFRICA
Congo R.
Nile R.
Niger R.

0   750   1,500   2,250 Kilometers
0   750   1,500 Miles

Legend:
- Independence through guerrilla warfare
- Occupation by neighbor
- Cuban presence
- French presence
- ( ) Date of independence

independent states in the Middle East. Jordan, Syria, and Lebanon, all European mandates before the war, became independent (see Map 28.3 on p. 888). Sympathy for the idea of Arab unity led to the formation of the Arab League in 1945, but different points of view among its members prevented it from achieving anything of substance.

The Question of Palestine   The one issue on which all Muslim states in the area could agree was the question of Palestine. As tensions between Jews and Arabs intensified in that mandate during the 1930s, the British reduced Jewish immigration into the area and firmly rejected Jewish proposals for an independent state in Palestine. The Zionists, who wanted Palestine as a home for Jews, were not to be denied, however. Many people had been shocked at the end of World War II when they learned about the Holocaust, and sympathy for the Jewish cause grew dramatically. As a result, the Zionists turned for support to the United States, and in March 1948, the

Truman administration approved the concept of an independent Jewish state in Palestine, even though only about one-third of the local population were Jews. When a United Nations resolution divided Palestine into a Jewish state and an Arab state, the Jews in Palestine acted. On May 14, 1948, they proclaimed the state of Israel.

Its Arab neighbors saw the new state as a betrayal of the Palestinian people, 90 percent of whom were Muslim. Outraged at the lack of Western support for Muslim interests in the area, several Arab countries invaded the new Jewish state. The invasion failed, but both sides remained bitter. The Arab states refused to recognize the existence of Israel.

Nasser and Pan-Arabism   In Egypt, a new leader arose who would play an important role in the Arab world and the Arab-Israeli conflict. Colonel Gamal Abdel Nasser (1918–1970) seized control of the Egyptian government in 1954 and two years later nationalized the Suez Canal Company, which had been under British and French

FRANTZ FANON AND THE WRETCHED OF THE EARTH

Born on the island of Martinique, Frantz Fanon (1925–1961) studied psychiatry in France. His work as head of a psychiatric hospital in Algeria led him to favor violence as a necessary instrument to overthrow Western imperialism, which to Fanon was itself rooted in violence. *The Wretched of the Earth,* published in 1961, provided an argument for national liberation movements in the Third World. In the last part of the book, Fanon discussed the problem of mental disorders that arose from Algeria's war of national liberation.

The Wretched of the Earth: Colonial War and Mental Disorders, Series B

We have here brought together certain cases or groups of cases in which the event giving rise to the illness is in the first place the atmosphere of total war which reigns in Algeria.

Case No. 1: The murder by two young Algerians, thirteen and fourteen years old respectively, of their European playmate.

We had been asked to give expert medical advice in a legal matter. Two young Algerians thirteen and fourteen years old, pupils in a secondary school, were accused of having killed one of their European schoolmates. They admitted having done it. The crime was reconstructed, and photos were added to the record. Here one of the children could be seen holding the victim while the other struck at him with a knife. The little defendants did not go back on their declarations. We had long conversations with them. We here reproduce the most characteristic of their remarks:

The boy fourteen years old:

This young defendant was in marked contrast to his school fellow. He was already almost a man, and an adult in his muscular control, his appearance, and the content of his replies. He did not deny having killed either. Why had he killed? He did not reply to the question but asked me had I ever seen a European in prison. Had there ever been a European arrested and sent to prison after the murder of an Algerian? I replied that in fact I had never seen any Europeans in prison.

"And yet there are Algerians killed every day, aren't there?"

"Yes."

"So why are only Algerians found in the prisons? Can you explain that to me?"

"No. But tell me why you killed this boy who was your friend."

"I'll tell you why. You've heard tell of the Rivet business?" [Rivet was a village near Algiers where in 1956 the French militia dragged forty men from their own beds and afterward murdered them.]

"Yes."

"Two of my family were killed then. At home, they said that the French had sworn to kill us all, one after the other. And did they arrest a single Frenchman for all those Algerians who were killed?"

"I don't know."

"Well, nobody at all was arrested. I wanted to take to the mountains, but I was too young. So [my friend] and I said we'd kill a European."

"Why?"

"In your opinion, what should we have done?"

"I don't know. But you are a child and what is happening concerns grown-up people."

"But they kill children too."

"That is no reason for killing your friend."

"Well, kill him I did. Now you can do what you like."

"Had your friend done anything to harm you?"

"Not a thing."

"Well?"

"Well, there you are."

Q *What does this document tell you about some of the fundamental characteristics of European colonial regimes? What broader forces, perhaps liberated or focused by World War II, could have contributed to the uprisings and to the crimes the colonized committed against the colonizers in the postwar period?*

---

administration. Seeing a threat to their route to the Indian Ocean, the British and French launched a joint attack on Egypt to protect their investment. They were joined by Israel, whose leaders had grown exasperated at sporadic Arab commando raids on Israeli territory and now decided to strike back. But the Eisenhower administration in the United States, concerned that the attack smacked of a revival of colonialism, joined with the Soviet Union, its Cold War enemy, and supported Nasser. Together, they brought about the withdrawal of foreign forces from Egypt and of Israeli troops from the Sinai peninsula.

Nasser emerged from the conflict as a powerful leader and now began to promote Pan-Arabism, or Arab unity. In March 1958, Egypt formally united with Syria in the United Arab Republic (UAR), and Nasser was named president of the new state. Egypt and Syria hoped that the union would eventually include all Arab states, but many other Arab leaders were suspicious of Pan-Arabism. Oil-rich Arab states such as Iraq and Saudi Arabia feared that they would be asked to share their vast oil revenues with the poorer states of the Middle East. Indeed, in Nasser's view, through Arab unity, this wealth could be used to improve the standard of living in the area. In 1961, Nasser's plans and the UAR came to an end when military leaders seized control of Syria and withdrew it from its union with Egypt.

MAP 28.3 **Decolonization in the Middle East.** Under the control of the Ottoman Empire prior to World War I, much of the Middle East was ruled directly or indirectly by the British and French after the war. Britain, the main colonial power, granted independence to most of its holdings in the first years after World War II, although it did maintain control of small states in the Persian Gulf and Arabian Sea region until 1971.

Q Which countries are major oil producers?

View an animated version of this map or related maps at academic.cengage.com/history/spielvogel

The Arab-Israeli Dispute The breakup of the UAR did not end the dream of Pan-Arabism. At a meeting of Arab leaders held in Jerusalem in 1964, Egypt took the lead in forming the Palestine Liberation Organization (PLO) to represent the interests of the Palestinians. The PLO believed that only the Palestinian peoples (and not Jewish immigrants from abroad) had the right to form a state in Palestine. A guerrilla movement called al-Fatah, led by the PLO political leader Yasir Arafat (1929–2004), began to launch terrorist attacks on Israeli territory, prompting the Israeli government to raid PLO bases in Jordan in 1966.

During the 1960s, the dispute between Israel and other states in the Middle East intensified. Essentially alone except for the sympathy of the United States and a few Western European countries, Israel adopted a policy of immediate retaliation against any hostile act by the PLO and its Arab neighbors. By the spring of 1967, Nasser in Egypt had stepped up his military activities and imposed a blockade against Israeli shipping through the Gulf of Aqaba. Learning that an attack was imminent, on June 5, 1967, Israel launched preemptive air strikes against Egypt and several of its Arab neighbors. Israeli

warplanes bombed seventeen Egyptian airfields and wiped out most of the Egyptian air force. Israeli armies then broke the blockade at the head of the Gulf of Aqaba and occupied the Sinai peninsula. Other Israeli forces seized Jordanian territory on the West Bank of the Jordan River, occupied all of Jerusalem (formerly divided between Israel and Jordan), and attacked Syrian military positions in the Golan Heights area along the Israeli-Syrian border. In this brief Six-Day War, as it is called, Israel devastated Nasser's forces and tripled the size of its territory. The new Israel aroused even more bitter hatred among the Arabs. Furthermore, another million Palestinians now lived inside Israel's new borders, most of them on the West Bank.

Asia: Nationalism and Communism

In Asia, the United States initiated the process of decolonization in 1946 when it granted independence to the Philippines (see Map 28.4). Britain soon followed suit with India. But ethnic and religious differences made the process both difficult and violent.

At the end of World War II, the British negotiated with both the Indian National Congress, which was mostly Hindu, and the Muslim League. British India's Muslims and Hindus were bitterly divided and unwilling to accept a single Indian state. Britain soon realized that British India would have to be divided into two countries, one Hindu (India) and one Muslim (Pakistan). Pakistan would actually consist of two regions separated by more than 1,000 miles.

Among Congress leaders, only Mahatma Gandhi objected to the division of India. A Muslim woman, critical of his opposition to partition, asked him, "If two brothers were living together in the same house and wanted to separate and live in two different houses, would you object?" "Ah," Gandhi replied, "if only we could separate as two brothers. But we will not. It will be an orgy of blood. We shall tear ourselves asunder in the womb of the mother who bears us."[7]

On August 15, 1947, India and Pakistan became independent. But Gandhi had been right. The flight of millions of Hindus and Muslims across the new borders led to violence, and over a million people were killed—including Gandhi, who was assassinated on January 30, 1948, by a Hindu militant. India's new beginning had not been easy.

Other areas of Asia also achieved independence. In 1948, Britain granted independence to Ceylon (modern Sri Lanka) and Burma (modern Myanmar). When the Dutch failed to reestablish control over the Dutch East Indies, Indonesia emerged as an independent nation in 1949. The French effort to remain in Indochina led to a bloody struggle with the Vietminh, led by Ho Chi Minh, the Communist and nationalist leader of the Vietnamese. After their defeat in 1954, the French granted independence to Laos and Cambodia, and Vietnam was temporarily divided in anticipation of elections in 1956

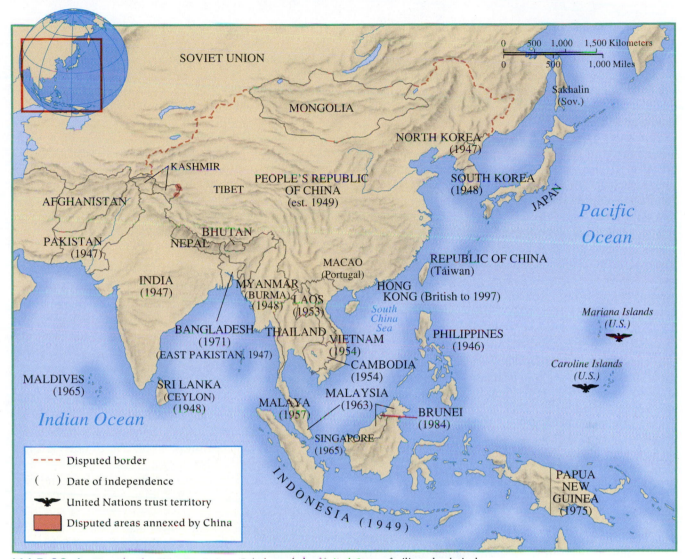

MAP 28.4 **Decolonization in Asia.** Britain and the United States facilitated relatively peaceful transitions to independence for their possessions in Asia. France fought hard to hold Indochina but left after major military defeats. Cold War tensions in Asia led to both the Korean War and the Vietnam War.

Q What two neighboring countries' presence helps explain why Korea has had difficulty maintaining complete independence throughout much of its history? 🐢 **View an animated version** of this map or related maps at academic.cengage.com/history/spielvogel

that would decide its fate. But the elections were never held, and the division of Vietnam by Communist and pro-Western regimes eventually led to the Second Vietnam War (see Chapter 29).

China Under Communism At the end of World War II, two Chinese governments existed side by side. The Nationalist government of Chiang Kai-shek, based in southern and central China, was supported by the Americans. The Communists, under the leadership of Mao Zedong, had built a strong base in North China. Their People's Liberation Army included nearly one million troops.

When efforts to form a coalition government in 1946 failed, full-scale war between the Nationalists and the Communists broke out. In the countryside, millions of peasants were attracted to the Communists by promises of land, and many joined Mao's army. By 1948, the People's Liberation Army had surrounded Beijing. The following spring, the Communists crossed the Yangtze and occupied Shanghai. During the next few months, Chiang's government and 2 million of his followers fled to the island of Taiwan, off the coast of mainland China. On October 1, 1949, Mao mounted the rostrum of the Gate of Heavenly Peace in Beijing and made a victory statement to the thousands gathered in the square before him. The Chinese people have stood up, he said, and no one will be able to humiliate us again.

The newly victorious Communist Party, under the leadership of its chairman, Mao, had a long-term goal of building a socialist society. In 1955, the Chinese government collectivized all private farmland and nationalized most industry and commerce. When the collective farms failed to increase food production, Mao began a more radical program, known as the Great Leap Forward, in 1958. Existing collective farms, normally the size of the traditional village, were combined into vast "people's communes," each containing more than 30,000 people. Mao hoped this program would mobilize the people for a massive effort to speed up economic growth and reach the final stage of communism—the classless society—before the end of the twentieth century. But the Great Leap Forward was a disaster. Bad weather and peasant hatred of the new system combined to drive food production downward. Despite his failures, Mao was not yet ready to abandon his dream of a totally classless society, and in 1966 he launched China on a new forced march toward communism (see Chapter 29).

Decolonization and Cold War Rivalries

The process of decolonization also became embroiled in Cold War politics. As independent nations emerged in Asia and Africa, they often found themselves caught in the rivalry between the United States and the Soviet Union. In Vietnam, for example, the division of the country in 1954 left the northern half under the Communist leader Ho Chi Minh supported by the Soviet Union. Meanwhile, South Vietnam was kept afloat by American financial and military aid. The Second Vietnam War resulted from the American perception that it needed to keep communism from expanding, while Ho Chi Minh saw the struggle between North and South as an attempt to overthrow Western colonial masters (the Americans had simply replaced the French) and achieve self-determination for the Vietnamese people.

Many new nations tried to stay neutral in the Cold War. Under the leadership of Jawaharlal Nehru (1889–1964), for example, India took a neutral stance in the Cold War and sought to provide leadership to all newly independent nations in Asia and Africa. India's neutrality put it at odds with the United States, which during the 1950s was trying to mobilize all nations against what it viewed as the menace of international communism.

Often, however, new nations found it difficult to remain nonaligned. In Indonesia, for example, which achieved its independence from the Dutch in 1950, President Sukarno (1901–1970), who was highly suspicious of the West, nationalized foreign-owned enterprises and sought economic aid from China and the Soviet Union while relying for domestic support on the Indonesian Communist Party. The army and conservative Muslims resented Sukarno's increasing reliance on the Communists, overthrew him in 1965, and established a military government under General Suharto. Suharto (b. 1921) restored good relations with the West and sought foreign investment to repair the country's ravaged economy.

Recovery and Renewal in Europe

Q **Focus Question:** What were the main developments in the Soviet Union, Eastern Europe, and Western Europe between 1945 and 1965?

The barbarism of the Nazis seemed to challenge the very foundation of European civilization. But Europe made a remarkable recovery, and within a few years after the defeat of Germany and Italy, economic revival brought renewed growth to European society, although major differences remained between Western and Eastern Europe.

The Soviet Union: From Stalin to Khrushchev

World War II devastated the Soviet Union. To create a new industrial base, Stalin returned to the method that he had used in the 1930s—the acquisition of development capital from Soviet labor. Working hard for little pay, poor housing, and precious few consumer goods, Soviet laborers were expected to produce goods for export with little in return for themselves. The incoming capital from abroad could then be used to purchase machinery and Western technology. The loss of millions of men in the war meant that much of this tremendous workload fell upon Soviet women. Almost 40 percent of heavy manual labor was performed by women.

Economic recovery in the Soviet Union was nothing less than spectacular. By 1947, industrial production had attained prewar levels; three years later, it had surpassed them by 40 percent. New power plants, canals, and giant factories were built, and new industries and oil fields were established in Siberia and Soviet Central Asia. Stalin's five-year plan of 1946 reached its goals in less than five years.

Stalin's Policies Although Stalin's economic policy was successful in promoting growth in heavy industry, primarily for the benefit of the military, consumer goods were scarce. The development of thermonuclear weapons in 1953, MIG fighters from 1950 to 1953, and the first space satellite (*Sputnik*) in 1957 may have elevated the Soviet state's reputation as a world power abroad, but domestically, the Soviet people were shortchanged. Heavy industry grew at a rate three times that of personal consumption. Moreover, the housing shortage was acute. A British military attaché in Moscow reported that "all houses, practically without exception, show lights from every window after dark. This seems to indicate that every room is both a living room by day and a bedroom by night. There is no place in overcrowded Moscow for the luxury of eating and sleeping in separate rooms."[8]

When World War II ended in 1945, Stalin had been in power for more than fifteen years. During that time, he had removed all opposition to his rule and remained the undisputed master of the Soviet Union. Other leading members of the Communist Party were completely obedient to his will. Increasingly distrustful of competitors,

*Immediately after they
the oath Year ...
... the Executive thereof may me*

KHRUSHCHEV DENOUNCES STALIN

Three years after the death of Stalin, the new Soviet premier, Nikita Khrushchev, addressed the Twentieth Congress of the Communist Party and denounced the former Soviet dictator for his crimes. This denunciation was the beginning of a policy of de-Stalinization.

Nikita Khrushchev, Address to the Twentieth Party Congress, February 1956

Comrades, ... quite a lot has been said about the cult of the individual and about its harmful consequences.... The cult of the person of Stalin ... became at a certain specific stage the source of a whole series of exceedingly serious and grave perversions of Party principles, of Party democracy, of revolutionary legality.

Stalin absolutely did not tolerate collegiality in leadership and in work and ... practiced brutal violence, not only toward everything which opposed him, but also toward that which seemed to his capricious and despotic character, contrary to his concepts.

Stalin abandoned the method of ideological struggle for that of administrative violence, mass repressions and terror.... Arbitrary behavior by one person encouraged and permitted arbitrariness in others. Mass arrests and deportations of many thousands of people, execution without trial and without normal investigation created conditions of insecurity, fear and even desperation.

Stalin showed in a whole series of cases his intolerance, his brutality and his abuse of power.... He often chose the path of repression and annihilation, not only against actual enemies, but also against individuals who had not committed any crimes against the Party and the Soviet government....

Many Party, Soviet and economic activists who were branded in 1937–8 as "enemies" were actually never enemies, spies, wreckers and so on, but were always honest communists; they were only so stigmatized, and often, no longer able to bear barbaric tortures, they charged themselves (at the order of the investigative judges-falsifiers) with all kinds of grave and unlikely crimes.

This was the result of the abuse of power by Stalin, who began to use mass terror against the Party cadres.... Stalin put the Party and the NKVD [the secret police] up to the use of mass terror when the exploiting classes had been liquidated in our country and when there were no serious reasons for the use of extraordinary mass terror. The terror was directed ... against the honest workers of the Party and the Soviet state....

Stalin was a very distrustful man, sickly suspicious.... Everywhere and in everything he saw "enemies," "two-facers" and "spies." Possessing unlimited power, he indulged in great willfulness and choked a person morally and physically. A situation was created where one could not express one's own will. When Stalin said that one or another would be arrested, it was necessary to accept on faith that he was an "enemy of the people." What proofs were offered? The confession of the arrested.... How is it possible that a person confesses to crimes that he had not committed? Only in one way—because of application of physical methods of pressuring him, tortures, bringing him to a state of unconsciousness, deprivation of his judgment, taking away of his human dignity.

Q *According to Khrushchev, what were Stalin's crimes? What purposes, political and historical, do you think Khrushchev intended his denunciation of Stalin to serve?*

Stalin exercised sole authority and pitted his subordinates against one another.

Stalin's morbid suspicions fueled the constantly increasing repression that was a characteristic of his regime. In 1946, the government decreed that all literary and scientific works must conform to the political needs of the state. Along with this anti-intellectual campaign came political terror. A new series of purges seemed imminent in 1953 when a number of Jewish doctors were implicated in a spurious plot to kill high-level party officials. Only Stalin's death on March 5, 1953, prevented more bloodletting.

Khrushchev's Rule A new collective leadership succeeded Stalin until Nikita Khrushchev emerged as the chief Soviet policy maker. Khrushchev had been responsible for ending the system of forced-labor camps, a regular feature of Soviet life under Stalin. At the Twentieth Congress of the Communist Party in 1956, Khrushchev condemned Stalin for his "administrative violence, mass repression, and terror" (see the box above).

Once in power, Khrushchev took steps to undo some of the worst features of Stalin's repressive regime. A certain degree of intellectual freedom was now permitted; Khrushchev said that "readers should be given the chance to make their own judgments" regarding the acceptability of controversial literature and that "police measures shouldn't be used."[9] In 1962, he allowed the publication of Alexander Solzhenitsyn's novel *A Day in the Life of Ivan Denisovich*, a grim portrayal of the horrors of the forced-labor camps. Most important, Khrushchev extended the process of **de-Stalinization** by reducing the powers of the secret police and closing some of the Siberian prison camps. Nevertheless, Khrushchev's revelations about Stalin at the Twentieth Congress caused turmoil in Communist ranks everywhere and encouraged a spirit of rebellion in Soviet satellite countries in Eastern Europe. Soviet troops reacted by crushing an uprising in Hungary in 1956, and Khrushchev and the Soviet leaders, fearful of further undermining the basic foundations of the regime, downplayed their de-Stalinization campaign.

Economically, Khrushchev tried to place more emphasis on light industry and consumer goods. Attempts to increase agricultural output by growing corn and cultivating vast lands east of the Ural Mountains proved less successful and damaged Khrushchev's reputation within the Party. These failures, combined with increased military spending, hurt the Soviet economy. The industrial growth rate, which had soared in the early 1950s, now declined dramatically from 13 percent in 1953 to 7.5 percent in 1964.

Khrushchev's personality also did not endear him to the higher Soviet officials, who frowned at his tendency to crack jokes and play the clown. Nor were the higher members of the Party bureaucracy pleased when Khrushchev tried to curb their privileges. Foreign policy failures caused additional damage to Khrushchev's reputation among his colleagues. His rash plan to place missiles in Cuba was the final straw. While he was on vacation in 1964, a special meeting of the Soviet Politburo voted him out of office (because of "deteriorating health") and forced him into retirement. Although a group of leaders succeeded him, real power came into the hands of Leonid Brezhnev (1906–1982), the "trusted" supporter of Khrushchev who had engineered his downfall.

Eastern Europe: Behind the Iron Curtain

At the end of World War II, Soviet military forces remained in all the lands they had liberated from the Nazis in Eastern Europe and the Balkans except for Greece, Albania, and Yugoslavia. All of the occupied states came to be part of the Soviet sphere of influence and, after 1945, experienced similar political developments. Between 1945 and 1947, one-party Communist governments became firmly entrenched in East Germany, Bulgaria, Romania, Poland, and Hungary. In Czechoslovakia, which had some tradition of democratic institutions, the Communists did not achieve their goals until 1948. In the elections of 1946, the Communist Party of Czechoslovakia had become the largest party. But it was not all-powerful and shared control of the government with the non-Communist parties. When it appeared that the latter might win new elections early in 1948, the Communists seized control of the government on February 25. All other parties were dissolved, and Klement Gottwald, the leader of the Communists, became the new president of Czechoslovakia.

Albania and Yugoslavia Albania and Yugoslavia were exceptions to this progression of Soviet dominance in Eastern Europe. Both had had strong Communist resistance movements during the war, and in both countries, the Communist Party simply took over power when the war ended. In Albania, local Communists established a rigidly Stalinist regime that grew increasingly independent of the Soviet Union.

In Yugoslavia, Josip Broz Tito, leader of the Communist resistance movement, seemed to be a loyal Stalinist. After the war, however, he moved toward the establishment of an independent Communist state in Yugoslavia. Stalin hoped to take control of Yugoslavia, just as he had done in other Eastern European countries, but Tito refused to capitulate to Stalin's demands and gained the support of the people by portraying the struggle as one of Yugoslav national freedom. In 1958, the Yugoslav party congress asserted that Yugoslav Communists did not see themselves as deviating from communism, only Stalinism. They considered their way closer to the Marxist-Leninist ideal. This included a more decentralized economic and political system in which workers could manage themselves and local communes could exercise some political power.

Khrushchev's Visit to Yugoslavia. The leadership of Nikita Khrushchev appeared for a while to open the door to more flexible Soviet policies. In 1955, he visited Yugoslavia in an attempt to improve relations with a Communist state that had deviated from Soviet policies. Khrushchev is shown here making a conciliatory speech with Marshal Tito, the leader of Yugoslavia, looking on.

Time & Life Pictures (Ralph Crane)/Getty Images

Between 1948 and Stalin's death in 1953, the Eastern European satellite states followed a policy of **Stalinization.** They instituted Soviet-type five-year plans with emphasis on heavy industry rather than consumer goods. They began to collectivize agriculture. They eliminated all non-Communist parties and established the institutions of repression—secret police and military forces. But communism—a foreign import—had not developed deep roots among the peoples of Eastern Europe. Moreover, Soviet economic exploitation of Eastern Europe resulted in harsh living conditions for most people. The Soviets demanded reparations from their defeated wartime enemies Bulgaria, Romania, and Hungary—often in the form of confiscated plants and factories removed to the Soviet Union—and forced all of the Eastern European states to trade with the Soviet Union to the latter's advantage.

Upheaval in Eastern Europe After Stalin's death, many Eastern European states began to pursue a new, more nationalistically oriented course as the new Soviet leaders, including Khrushchev, interfered less in the internal affairs of their satellites. But in the late 1950s, the Soviet Union also made it clear, particularly in Poland and Hungary, that it would not allow its Eastern European satellites to become independent of Soviet control.

In 1956, after the circulation of Khrushchev's denunciation of Stalin, protests—especially by workers—erupted in Poland. In response, the Polish Communist Party adopted a series of reforms in October 1956 and elected Wladyslaw Gomulka (1905–1982) as first secretary. Gomulka declared that Poland had the right to follow its own socialist path. Fearful of Soviet armed response, however, the Poles compromised. Poland pledged to remain loyal to the Warsaw Pact, and the Soviets agreed to allow Poland to follow its own path to socialism.

The developments in Poland in 1956 inspired national Communists in Hungary to seek the same kinds of reforms and independence. Intense debates eventually resulted in the ouster of the ruling Stalinist and the selection of Imry Nagy (1896–1958) as the new Hungarian leader. Internal dissent, however, was not directed simply against the Soviets but against communism in general, which was viewed as a creation of the Soviets, not the Hungarians. The Stalinist secret police had also bred much terror and hatred. This dissatisfaction, combined with economic difficulties, created a situation ripe for revolt. To quell the rising rebellion, Nagy declared Hungary a free nation on November 1, 1956. He promised free elections, and the mood of the country made it clear that this could mean the end of Communist rule in Hungary. But Khrushchev was in no position at home to allow a member of the Communist flock to fly the coop. Just three days after Nagy's declaration, the Red Army invaded the capital city of Budapest (see the box on p. 894). The Soviets reestablished control over the country, and János Kádár (1912–1989), a reform-minded cabinet minister, replaced Nagy and worked with the

CHRONOLOGY The Soviet Union and Satellite States in Eastern Europe

Death of Stalin	1953
Khrushchev's denunciation of Stalin	1956
Attempt at reforms in Poland	1956
Hungarian revolt is crushed	1956
Berlin Wall is built	1961
Brezhnev replaces Khrushchev	1964

Soviets to quash the revolt. By collaborating with the Soviet invaders, Kádár saved many of Nagy's economic reforms. The developments in Poland and Hungary in 1956 discouraged any similar upheavals elsewhere in Eastern Europe.

Western Europe: The Revival of Democracy and the Economy

All the countries of Western Europe faced similar kinds of problems at the end of World War II. They needed to rebuild their economies, re-create their democratic institutions, and contend with the growth of Communist parties.

The important role that Communists had played in the resistance movements against the Nazis gained them a new respectability and strength once the war was over. Communist parties did well in elections in Italy and France in 1946 and 1947 and even showed strength in some countries, such as Belgium and the Netherlands, where they had not been much of a political factor before the war. But Communist success was short-lived. After the hardening of the divisions in the Cold War, their advocacy of Soviet policies hurt the Communist parties at home, and support began to dwindle. Only in France and Italy, where social inequities remained their focus, did Communist parties retain significant support—about 25 percent of the vote.

As part of their electoral strategy, Communist parties had often joined forces with other left-wing parties, such as the Social Democrats. Socialist parties had also fared well immediately after the war as the desire to overthrow the old order led to the abandonment of conservative politics. But support for the socialists soon waned. In France, for example, socialists won 23 percent of the vote in 1945 but 18 percent in 1946 and only 12.6 percent in 1962. The Cold War also hurt the cause of socialism. Socialist parties had originally been formed in the late nineteenth century as Marxist parties, and their identification with Communist parties in postwar coalitions cost them dearly. In the late 1950s, many socialist parties on the Continent perceived the need to eliminate their old doctrinal emphasis on class struggle and began to call for social justice and liberty. Although they advocated economic and social planning, they no longer demanded the elimination of the capitalist system.

SOVIET REPRESSION IN EASTERN EUROPE: HUNGARY, 1956

Developments in Poland in 1956 inspired the Communist leaders of Hungary to begin to remove their country from Soviet control. But there were limits to Khrushchev's tolerance, and he sent Soviet troops to crush Hungary's movement for independence. The first selection is a statement by the Soviet government justifying the use of Soviet troops; the second is a brief and tragic final statement from Imry Nagy, the Hungarian leader.

Statement of the Soviet Government, October 30, 1956

The Soviet Government regards it as indispensable to make a statement in connection with the events in Hungary.

The course of the events has shown that the working people of Hungary, who have achieved great progress on the basis of their people's democratic order, correctly raise the question of the necessity of eliminating serious shortcomings in the field of economic building, the further raising of the material well-being of the population, and the struggle against bureaucratic excesses in the state apparatus.

However, this just and progressive movement of the working people was soon joined by forces of black reaction and counterrevolution, which are trying to take advantage of the discontent of part of the working people to undermine the foundations of the people's democratic order in Hungary and to restore the old landlord and capitalist order.

The Soviet Government and all the Soviet people deeply regret that the development of events in Hungary has led to bloodshed. On the request of the Hungarian People's Government the Soviet Government consented to the entry into Budapest of the Soviet Army units to assist the Hungarian People's Army and the Hungarian authorities to establish order in the town.

The Last Message of Imry Nagy, November 4, 1956

This fight is the fight for freedom by the Hungarian people against the Russian intervention, and it is possible that I shall only be able to stay at my post for one or two hours. The whole world will see how the Russian armed forces, contrary to all treaties and conventions, are crushing the resistance of the Hungarian people. They will also see how they are kidnapping the Prime Minister of a country which is a Member of the United Nations, taking him from the capital, and therefore it cannot be doubted at all that this is the most brutal form of intervention. I should like in these last moments to ask the leaders of the revolution, if they can, to leave the country. I ask that all that I have said in my broadcast, and what we have agreed on with the revolutionary leaders during meetings in Parliament, should be put in a memorandum, and the leaders should turn to all the peoples of the world for help and explain that today it is Hungary and tomorrow, or the day after tomorrow, it will be the turn of other countries because the imperialism of Moscow does not know borders, and is only trying to play for time.

Q *Based on this selection, what was the Soviet Union's policy toward its Eastern European satellite states in the 1950s? Compare this policy to Soviet policy in Eastern Europe in the late 1980s (see Chapter 29). What impact did this change in policy have on Eastern Europe?*

By 1950, moderate political parties had made a remarkable comeback in Western Europe. Especially important was the rise of Christian Democratic parties. The new Christian Democrats were not connected to the prewar church-based parties that had been advocates of church interests and had crusaded against both liberal and socialist causes. The new Christian Democrats were sincerely interested in democracy and in significant economic reforms. They were especially strong in Italy and Germany and played a particularly important role in achieving Europe's economic restoration.

Western European countries recovered relatively rapidly from the devastation of World War II. The Marshall Plan played a significant role in this process. Between 1947 and 1950, European countries received $9.4 billion to be used for new equipment and raw materials. By 1950, industrial output in Europe was 30 percent above prewar levels. Between 1947 and 1950, steel production alone expanded by 70 percent. And this economic recovery continued well into the 1950s and 1960s. Those years were a time of dramatic economic growth and prosperity in Western Europe, which experienced virtually full employment.

France: The Domination of de Gaulle The history of France for nearly a quarter century after the war was dominated by one man—Charles de Gaulle (1890–1970)—who possessed an unshakable faith that he had a historic mission to reestablish the greatness of the French nation. During the war, de Gaulle had assumed leadership of some resistance groups and played an important role in ensuring the establishment of a French provisional government after the war. The declaration of the Fourth Republic, with a return to a parliamentary system based on parties that de Gaulle considered weak, led him to withdraw from politics. Eventually, he formed the French Popular Movement, a decidedly rightist organization. It blamed the parties for France's political mess and called for an even stronger presidency, a goal that de Gaulle finally achieved in 1958.

The fragile political stability of the Fourth Republic had been badly shaken by the Algerian crisis. The French

Charles de Gaulle. As president, Charles de Gaulle sought to revive the greatness of the French nation. He is shown here dressed in his military uniform during a formal state ceremony on a visit to Quebec, Canada, in July 1967.

army had suffered defeat in Indochina in 1954 and was determined to resist Algerian demands for independence. But a strong antiwar movement among French intellectuals and church leaders led to bitter divisions that opened the door to the possibility of civil war in France. The panic-stricken leaders of the Fourth Republic offered to let de Gaulle take over the government and revise the constitution.

In 1958, de Gaulle immediately drafted a new constitution for the Fifth Republic that greatly enhanced the power of the president, who would now have the right to choose the prime minister, dissolve parliament, and supervise both defense and foreign policy. De Gaulle had always believed in strong leadership, and the new Fifth Republic was by no means a democratic system. As the new president, de Gaulle sought to return France to the position of a great power. He believed that playing a pivotal role in the Cold War might enhance France's stature. For that reason, he pulled France out of the NATO high command. He increased French prestige among Third World countries by consenting to Algerian independence despite strenuous opposition from the army. With an eye toward achieving the status of a world power, de Gaulle invested heavily in the nuclear arms race. France exploded its first nuclear bomb in 1960.

Despite his successes, de Gaulle did not really achieve his ambitious goals of world power. Although his successors maintained that France was the "third nuclear power" after the United States and the Soviet Union, in truth France was too small for such global ambitions.

Although the cost of the nuclear program increased the defense budget, de Gaulle did not neglect the French economy. Economic decision making was centralized. Between 1958 and 1968, the French gross national product increased by 5.5 percent annually, faster than the U.S. economy was growing. By the end of de Gaulle's era, France was a major industrial producer and exporter, particularly in such areas as automobiles and armaments. Nevertheless, problems remained. The **nationalization** (government ownership) of traditional industries, such as coal, steel, and railroads, led to large government deficits. The cost of living increased faster than in the rest of Europe. Consumer prices were 45 percent higher in 1968 than they had been ten years earlier.

Increased dissatisfaction with the inability of de Gaulle's government to deal with these problems soon led to more violent action. In May 1968, a series of student protests, followed by a general strike by the labor unions, shook the government. Although de Gaulle managed to restore order, the events of May 1968 seriously undermined the French people's respect for their aloof and imperious president. Tired and discouraged, de Gaulle resigned from office in April 1969 and died within a year.

West Germany: A Reconceived Nation Already by the end of 1945, the Western powers occupying Germany (the United States, Britain, and France) had allowed the reemergence of political parties in their zones. Three major parties came forth: the Social Democrats (SPD), the Christian Democrats (CDU), and the Free Democrats (FDP). Over the next three years, the occupation forces gradually allowed the political parties to play greater roles in their zones.

As a result of the pressures of the Cold War, the unification of the three Western zones into the Federal Republic of Germany became a reality in 1949. Konrad Adenauer (1876–1967), the leader of the CDU who served as chancellor from 1949 to 1963, became the "founding hero" of the Federal Republic. Adenauer sought respect for West Germany by cooperating with the United States and the other Western European nations. He was especially desirous of reconciliation with France, Germany's longtime enemy. The beginning of the Korean War in June 1950 had unexpected repercussions for West Germany. The fear that South Korea might fall to the Communist forces of the north led many Germans and Westerners to worry about the security of West Germany and led to calls for the rearmament of West Germany. Although many people, concerned about a revival of German militarism, condemned this proposal, Cold War tensions were decisive. West Germany rearmed in 1955 and became a member of NATO.

Adenauer's chancellorship is largely associated with the resurrection of the West German economy, often referred to as the "economic miracle." It was largely guided by the minister of finance, Ludwig Erhard (1897–1977), who pursued a policy of a new currency, free markets, low taxes, and elimination of controls, which, combined with American financial aid, led to rapid economic growth. Although West Germany had only 75 percent of the population and 52 percent of the territory of prewar Germany, by 1955 the West German gross national product exceeded that of prewar Germany. Real wages doubled between 1950 and 1965 even though work hours were cut by 20 percent. Unemployment fell from 8 percent in 1950 to 0.4 percent in 1965. To maintain its economic expansion, West Germany even imported hundreds of thousands of "guest workers," primarily from Italy, Spain, Greece, Turkey, and Yugoslavia.

Throughout its postwar existence, West Germany was troubled by its Nazi past. The surviving major Nazi leaders had been tried and condemned as war criminals at war crimes trials held in Nuremberg in 1945 and 1946. As part of the denazification of Germany, the victorious Allies continued war crimes trials of lesser officials, but these diminished as the Cold War brought about a shift in attitudes. By 1950, German courts had begun to take over the war crimes trials, and the German legal machine persisted in prosecuting cases. Beginning in 1953, the West German government also began to make payments to Israel and to Holocaust survivors and their relatives in order to make some restitution for the crimes of the Nazi era.

Adenauer resigned in 1963, after fourteen years of firmly guiding West Germany through its postwar recovery. Adenauer had wanted no grand experimentation at home or abroad; he was content to give Germany time to regain its equilibrium. Ludwig Erhard succeeded Adenauer and largely continued his policies. But an economic downturn in the mid-1960s opened the door to the rise of the Social Democrats, and in 1969, they became the leading party.

Great Britain: The Welfare State

The end of World War II left Britain with massive economic problems. In elections held immediately after the war, the Labour Party overwhelmingly defeated Churchill's Conservative Party. The Labour Party had promised far-reaching reforms, particularly in the area of social welfare, and in a country with a tremendous shortage of consumer goods and housing, its platform was quite appealing. The new Labour government, with Clement Attlee (1883–1967) as prime minister, proceeded to enact reforms that created a modern **welfare state.**

The establishment of the British welfare state began with the nationalization of the Bank of England, the coal and steel industries, public transportation, and public utilities, such as electricity and gas. In the area of social welfare, the new government enacted the National Insurance Act and the National Health Service Act in 1946.

The British Welfare State: Free Milk at School. The creation of the welfare state was a prominent social development in postwar Europe. The desire to improve the health of children led to welfare programs that provided free food for young people. Pictured here are boys at a grammar school in England during a free milk break.

The insurance act established a comprehensive **social security** program and nationalized medical insurance, thereby enabling the state to subsidize the unemployed, the sick, and the aged. The health act created a system of **socialized medicine** that required doctors and dentists to work with state hospitals, although private practices could be maintained. This measure was especially costly for the state, but within a few years, 90 percent of medical practitioners were participating. The British welfare state became the model for most European states after the war.

The cost of building a welfare state at home forced the British to reduce expenses abroad. This meant the dismantling of the British Empire and the reduction of military aid to such countries as Greece and Turkey. It was not a belief in the morality of self-determination but economic necessity that brought an end to the British Empire.

Continuing economic problems, however, brought the Conservatives back into power from 1951 to 1964. Although they favored private enterprise, the Conservatives accepted the welfare state and even extended it when they undertook an ambitious construction program to improve British housing. Although the British economy had recovered from the war, it had done so at a slower rate than other European countries. Moreover, the slow rate of recovery masked a long-term economic decline caused by a variety of factors. The demands of British trade unions for wages that rose faster than productivity were a problem in the late 1950s and 1960s. The unwillingness of the British to invest in modern industrial machinery and to adopt new methods also did not help.

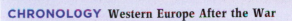

Underlying the immediate problems, however, was a deeper issue. As a result of World War II, Britain had lost much of its prewar revenues from abroad but was left with a burden of debt from its many international commitments. Britain was no longer a world power.

Italy: Weak Coalition Government   After the war, Italy faced a period of heavy reconstruction. Only Germany had sustained more physical destruction. The monarchy was abolished when 54 percent of Italian voters rejected the royal house, and in June 1946, Italy became a democratic republic.

In the first postwar parliamentary elections, held in April 1948, the Christian Democrats, still allied with the Catholic Church, emerged as the leading political party. Alcide de Gasperi (1881–1954) served as prime minister from 1948 to 1953, an unusually long span of time for an Italian government. Like pre-Fascist governments, postwar Italian coalitions, largely dominated by the Christian Democrats, were famous for their instability and short lives. Although the Italian Communist Party was one of Italy's three largest parties, it was largely excluded from all of these government coalitions. It did, however, manage to gain power in a number of provinces and municipalities in the 1960s. The Christian Democrats were able to maintain control by keeping the support of the upper and middle classes and the southern peasantry.

Italy, too, experienced an "economic miracle" after the war, although it was far less publicized than Germany's. In 1945, Italy's industrial production was only 20 percent of prewar levels, and agricultural output was about 50 percent. The Marshall Plan helped stabilize the postwar Italian economy. Especially during the late 1950s and early 1960s, Italy made rapid strides in economic growth. The production of electrical appliances, cars, and office machinery made the most significant leap. As in other Western welfare states, the Italian economy combined private enterprise with government management, particularly of heavy industry. In 1965, for example, the government controlled 60 percent of Italy's steel production. The major economic problem continued to be the backwardness of southern Italy, a region that possessed 36 percent of the total population but generated only 25 percent of the national income. In the 1960s, millions of Italians from the south migrated to the more prosperous north.

Western Europe: The Move Toward Unity

As we have seen, the divisions created by the Cold War led the nations of Western Europe to form the North Atlantic Treaty Organization in 1949. But military unity was not the only kind of unity fostered in Europe after 1945. The destructiveness of two world wars caused many thoughtful Europeans to consider the need for some form of European unity. National feeling was still too powerful, however, for European nations to give up their political

Welfare state emerges in Great Britain	1946
Italy becomes a democratic republic	1946
Alcide de Gasperi becomes prime minister of Italy	1948
Konrad Adenauer becomes chancellor of West Germany	1949
Formation of European Coal and Steel Community	1951
West Germany joins NATO	1955
Suez Crisis	1956
Formation of EURATOM	1957
Formation of European Economic Community (Common Market)	1957
Charles de Gaulle assumes power in France	1958
Erhard becomes chancellor of Germany	1963

sovereignty. Consequently, the desire for a sense of solidarity was forced to focus primarily on the economic arena, not the political one.

In 1951, France, West Germany, the Benelux countries (Belgium, Netherlands, and Luxembourg), and Italy formed the European Coal and Steel Community (ECSC). Its purpose was to create a common market for coal and steel products among the six nations by eliminating tariffs and other trade barriers. The success of the ECSC encouraged its members to proceed further, and in 1957 they created the European Atomic Energy Community (EURATOM) to further European research on the peaceful uses of nuclear energy.

In the same year, these six nations signed the Rome Treaty, which created the European Economic Community (EEC), also known as the Common Market. The EEC eliminated customs barriers for the six member nations and created a large free-trade area protected from the rest of the world by a common external tariff. By promoting free trade, the EEC also encouraged cooperation and standardization in many aspects of the six nations'

European Economic Community, 1957

economies. All the member nations benefited economically. By the 1960s, the EEC nations had become an important trading bloc. With a total population of 165 million, the EEC became the world's largest exporter and purchaser of raw materials. Only the United States surpassed the EEC in steel production.

The United States and Canada: A New Era

Q **Focus Question:** What were the main political developments in North America between 1945 and 1965?

At the end of World War II, the United States was one of the world's two superpowers. As the Cold War with the Soviet Union intensified, the United States worked hard to prevent the spread of communism throughout the world. American domestic political life after 1945 was played out against a background of American military power abroad.

American Politics and Society in the 1950s

Between 1945 and 1970, the ideals of Franklin Roosevelt's New Deal largely determined the patterns of American domestic politics. The New Deal had brought basic changes to American society, including a dramatic increase in the role and power of the federal government, the rise of organized labor as a significant force in the economy and politics, the beginning of a welfare state, and a grudging realization of the need to deal fairly with the concerns of minorities.

The New Deal tradition was bolstered by the election of three Democratic presidents—Harry Truman in 1948, John Kennedy in 1960, and Lyndon Johnson in 1964. Even the election of a Republican president, Dwight Eisenhower, in 1952 and 1956 did not change the basic direction of American politics. As Eisenhower stated, "Should any political party attempt to abolish Social Security and eliminate labor laws and farm programs, you would not hear of that party again in our political history."

The economic boom after World War II fueled confidence in the American way of life. A shortage of consumer goods during the war had left Americans with both extra income and a pent-up desire to buy these goods after the war. Then, too, the growth of labor unions brought higher wages that enabled more and more workers to buy consumer goods. Between 1945 and 1973, real wages grew 3 percent a year on average, the most prolonged advance in American history.

Prosperity was not the only characteristic of the early 1950s. Cold War confrontations abroad had repercussions at home. The takeover of China by Mao Zedong's Communist forces in 1949 and Communist North Korea's invasion of South Korea in 1950 led to a fear that Communists had infiltrated the United States. President Truman's attorney general warned that Communists "are everywhere—in factories, offices, butcher stores, on street corners, in private businesses. And each carried in himself the germ of death for society." A demagogic senator from Wisconsin, Joseph R. McCarthy, helped intensify the "Red Scare" with his exposés of supposed Communists in high government positions.

McCarthy went too far when he attacked alleged "Communist conspirators" in the U.S. Army and was censured by Congress in 1954. Very quickly, his anti-Communist crusade came to an end.

Decade of Upheaval: America in the 1960s

During the 1960s, the United States experienced a period of upheaval that brought to the fore problems that had been glossed over in the 1950s. The 1960s began on a youthful and optimistic note. At age forty-three, John F. Kennedy became the youngest elected president in the history of the United States. His own administration, cut short by an assassin's bullet on November 22, 1963, focused primarily on foreign affairs. Kennedy's successor, Lyndon B. Johnson (1908–1973), who won a new term as president in a landslide in 1964, used his stunning mandate to pursue what he called the Great Society, heir to the welfare state first begun in the New Deal. Johnson's programs included health care for the elderly, a "war on poverty" to be fought with food stamps and the new Job Corps, the new Department of Housing and Urban Development to deal with the problems of the cities, and federal assistance for education.

Civil Rights Movement Johnson's other domestic passion was equal rights for African Americans. The civil rights movement had its beginnings in 1954 when the U.S. Supreme Court took the dramatic step of striking down the practice of racially segregating public schools. An eloquent Baptist minister named Martin Luther King Jr. (1929–1968) became the leader of a growing movement for racial equality, and by the early 1960s, a number of groups, including King's Southern Christian Leadership Conference (SCLC), were organizing sit-ins and demonstrations across the South to end racial segregation. In August 1963, King led the March on Washington for Jobs and Freedom to dramatize African Americans' desire for equal rights and opportunities. This march and King's impassioned plea for racial equality had an electrifying effect on the American people. By the end of that year, 52 percent of Americans called civil rights the most significant national issue; eight months earlier, only 4 percent had done so.

President Johnson took up the cause of civil rights. As a result of his initiative, Congress passed the Civil Rights Act of 1964, which created the machinery to end segregation and discrimination in the workplace and all public places. A voting rights act the following year made it easier for blacks to vote in southern states. But laws alone could not guarantee the Great Society, and Johnson soon faced bitter social unrest, both from African Americans and from the burgeoning movement opposing the Vietnam War.

In the North and the West, African Americans had had voting rights for many years, but local patterns of segregation led to higher unemployment rates for blacks than for whites and left African Americans segregated in

The Civil Rights Movement. In the early 1960s, Martin Luther King Jr. and his Southern Christian Leadership Conference organized a variety of activities to pursue the goal of racial equality. He is shown here with his wife Coretta (right) and Rosa Parks and Ralph Abernathy (far left) leading a march against racial discrimination in 1965.

huge urban ghettos. In these ghettos, the call for action by radical black leaders, such as Malcom X of the Black Muslims, attracted more attention than the nonviolent appeals of Martin Luther King. Malcom X's advice was straightforward: "If someone puts a hand on you, send him to the cemetery."

In the summer of 1965, race riots broke out in the Watts district of Los Angeles. Thirty-four people died and more than one thousand buildings were destroyed. Cleveland, San Francisco, Chicago, Newark, and Detroit likewise exploded in the summers of 1966 and 1967. After the assassination of Martin Luther King in 1968, more than one hundred cities experienced riots. The combination of riots and extremist comments by radical black leaders led to a "white backlash" and a severe division of the American population.

The Development of Canada

Canada experienced many of the same developments as the United States in the postwar years. For twenty-five years after World War II, prosperous Canada set out on a new path of industrial development. Canada had always had a strong export economy based on its abundant natural resources. Now it also developed electronic, aircraft, nuclear, and chemical engineering industries on a large scale. Much of the Canadian growth, however, was financed by capital from the United States, which led to American ownership of Canadian businesses. Although many Canadians welcomed the economic growth, others feared American economic domination.

Canadians also worried about playing a secondary role politically and militarily to their neighboring superpower. Canada agreed to join NATO in 1949 and even sent military forces to fight in Korea the following year.

At the same time, to avoid subordination to the United States, Canada actively supported the United Nations. Nevertheless, concerns about the United States did not keep Canada from maintaining a special relationship with its southern neighbor. The North American Air Defense Command (NORAD), formed in 1957, maintained close cooperation between the air forces of the two countries for the defense of North America against missile attack.

After 1945, the Liberal Party continued to dominate Canadian politics until 1957, when John Diefenbaker (1895–1979) achieved a Conservative Party victory. But major economic problems returned the Liberals to power, and under Lester Pearson (1897–1972), they created Canada's welfare state by enacting a national social security system (the Canada Pension Plan) and a national health insurance program.

Postwar Society and Culture in the Western World

Q **Focus Question:** What major changes occurred in Western society and culture between 1945 and 1965?

During the postwar era, Western society and culture witnessed remarkably rapid change. Computers, television, jet planes, contraceptive devices, and new surgical techniques all dramatically and quickly altered the pace and nature of human life. The rapid changes in postwar society, fueled by scientific advances and rapid economic growth, led many to view it as a new society. As part of this new society, blacks demanded civil rights, the welfare state came into being, women argued for equal rights with men, and a dazzling array of new cultural expressions emerged.

The Structure of European Society

The structure of European society was altered after 1945. Especially noticeable were the changes in the middle class. Such traditional middle-class groups as businesspeople and professionals in law, medicine, and the universities were greatly augmented by a new group of managers and technicians as large companies and government agencies employed increasing numbers of white-collar supervisory and administrative personnel. In both Eastern and Western Europe, the new managers and experts were very much alike. Everywhere their positions depended on specialized knowledge acquired from some form of higher education. Everywhere they focused on the effective administration of their organizations. Because their positions usually depended on their skills, they took steps to ensure that their own children would be educated.

A Society of Consumers
Changes also occurred among the traditional lower classes. Especially noticeable was the dramatic shift of people from rural to urban areas. The number of people working in agriculture declined dramatically, yet the size of the industrial labor force remained the same. In West Germany, industrial workers made up 48 percent of the labor force throughout the 1950s and 1960s. Thereafter, the number of industrial workers began to dwindle as white-collar and service jobs increased. At the same time, a substantial increase in their real wages enabled the working classes to aspire to the consumption patterns of the middle class, leading to what some observers have called the **consumer society.** Buying on the installment plan, introduced in the 1930s, became widespread in the 1950s and gave workers a chance to imitate the middle class by buying such products as televisions, washing machines, refrigerators, vacuum cleaners, and stereos. But the most visible symbol of mass consumerism was the automobile. Before World War II, cars were reserved mostly for the European upper classes. In 1948, there were 5 million cars in all of Europe, but by 1957, the number had tripled. By the 1960s, there were almost 45 million cars.

Mass Leisure
Rising incomes, combined with shorter working hours, created an even greater market for mass leisure activities. Between 1900 and 1960, the workweek was reduced from sixty hours to a little more than forty hours, and the number of paid holidays increased. In the 1960s, German and Italian workers received between thirty-two and thirty-five paid holidays a year. All aspects of popular culture—music, sports, media—became commercialized and offered opportunities for leisure activities, including concerts, sporting events, and television viewing.

Another visible symbol of mass leisure was the growth of mass tourism. Before World War II, mostly the upper and middle classes traveled for pleasure. After the war, the combination of more vacation time, increased prosperity, and the flexibility provided by

Television in the Consumer Society. Buying on the installment plan made it possible for consumers to purchase a wide variety of new products. Televisions were one of the most popular. By 1956, fully 80 percent of all American families owned a television set. Many families considered a television a necessity, not a luxury. Television advertising also encouraged even more consumption in the new consumer society.

package tours with their lower rates and less expensive lodgings enabled millions to expand their travel possibilities. By the mid-1960s, 100 million tourists were crossing European boundaries each year.

Creation of the Welfare State

One of the most noticeable social developments in postwar Europe was the creation of the welfare state. In one sense, the welfare state represented another extension of the power of the state over the lives of its citizens, a process that had increased dramatically as a result of two world wars. Yet the goal of the welfare state was to make it possible for people to live better and more meaningful lives. Advocates of the welfare state believed that by eliminating poverty and homelessness, providing medical services for all, ensuring dignity for older people, and extending educational opportunities for all who wanted them, the state would satisfy people's material needs and thereby free them to achieve happiness.

Social welfare schemes were not new to Europe. Beginning in the late nineteenth century, some states had provided for the welfare of the working class by instituting old-age pensions, medical insurance, and unemployment compensation. But these efforts were piecemeal and were by no means based on a general belief that society had a responsibility to care for all of its citizens.

The new postwar social legislation greatly extended earlier benefits and created new ones as well. Of course, social welfare benefits differed considerably from country to country in quantity and quality as well as in how they were paid for and managed. Nevertheless, there were some common trends. In many countries, already existing benefits for sickness, accidents, unemployment, and old age were simply extended to cover more people and provide larger payments. Men were generally eligible for old-age pensions at age sixty-five and women at sixty.

Affordable health care for all people was another goal of the welfare state, although the methods of achieving this goal varied. In some countries, medical care was free to all people with some kind of insurance, but in others, people had to contribute toward the cost of their medical care. The amount ranged from 10 to 25 percent of the total cost.

Another feature of welfare states was the use of **family allowances,** which were instituted in some countries to provide a minimum level of material care for children. Most family allowance programs provided a fixed amount per child. Family allowances were also conceived in large part as a way to increase the population after the decline suffered during the war. The French, for example, increased the amount of aid for each new child after the first one.

Welfare states also sought to remove class barriers to opportunity by expanding the number of universities and providing scholarship aid to allow everyone to attend these institutions of higher learning. Overall, European states moved toward free tuition or modest fees for university attendance. These policies did not always achieve their goals, however. In the early 1960s, most students in Western European universities still came from privileged backgrounds. In Britain, 25 percent of university students came from working-class backgrounds; in France, the figure was only 17.6 percent.

The welfare state dramatically increased the amount of money states expended on social services. In 1967, such spending constituted 17 percent of the gross national product of the major European countries; by the 1980s, it absorbed 40 to 50 percent. To some critics, these figures proved that the welfare state had produced a new generation of citizens overly dependent on the state. But most people favored the benefits, and most leaders were well aware that it was political suicide to advocate curtailing or seriously lowering those benefits.

Gender Issues in the Welfare State   Gender issues also influenced the form that the welfare state took in different countries. One general question dominated the debate: Should women be recognized in a special category as mothers, or should they be regarded as individuals? William Beveridge, the economist who drafted the report that formed the basis for the British welfare

state, said that women had "vital work to do in ensuring the adequate continuance of the British race." "During marriage," he said, "most women will not be gainfully employed. The small minority of women who undertake paid employment or other gainful employment or other gainful occupations after marriage require special treatment differing from that of single women."[10] Accordingly, the British welfare system was based on the belief that women should stay home with their children: women received subsidies for children, but married women who worked were given few or no benefits. Employers were also encouraged to pay women lower wages to discourage them from joining the workforce. Thus, the British welfare system encouraged the dependence of wives on their husbands. So did the West German system. The West German government passed laws that discouraged women from working. In keeping its women at home, West Germany sought to differentiate itself from neighboring Communist countries in Eastern Europe and the Soviet Union, where women were encouraged to work outside the home. At the same time, to help working women raise families, Communist governments also provided day-care facilities, as well as family subsidies and maternity benefits.

France sought to maintain the individual rights of women in its welfare system. The French government recognized women as equal to men and thus as entitled to the same welfare benefits as men for working outside the home. At the same time, wanting to encourage population growth, the government provided incentives for women to stay home and bear children as well as day-care and after-school programs for working mothers.

Women in the Postwar Western World

Despite their enormous contributions to the war effort, women were removed from the workforce at the end of World War II to provide jobs for the soldiers returning home. After the horrors of war, people seemed willing for a while to return to traditional family practices. Female participation in the workforce declined, and birthrates began to rise, creating a "baby boom." This increase in the birthrate did not last, however, and birthrates, and thus the size of families, began to decline by the end of the 1950s. Largely responsible for this decline was the widespread practice of birth control. Invented in the nineteenth century, the condom was already in wide use, but the development in the 1960s of oral contraceptives, known as birth control pills or simply "the pill," provided a reliable means of birth control that quickly spread to all Western countries.

Women in the Workforce   The trend toward smaller families no doubt contributed to the change in the character of women's employment in both Europe and the United States as women experienced considerably more years when they were not involved in rearing children. The most important development was the increased number of married women in the workforce. At the beginning of the twentieth century, even working-class wives tended to stay at home if they could afford to do so. In the postwar period, this was no longer the case. In the United States, for example, in 1900, married women made up about 15 percent of the female labor force; by 1970, their number had increased to 62 percent. The percentage of married women in the female labor force in Sweden increased from 47 to 66 percent between 1963 and 1975. Figures for the Soviet Union and its satellites were even higher. In 1970, fully 92.5 percent of all women in the Soviet Union held jobs, compared to around 50 percent in France and West Germany. The industrial development of the Soviet Union relied on female labor.

But the increased number of women in the workforce did not change some old patterns. Working-class women in particular still earned salaries lower than those of men for equal work. In the 1960s, women earned only 60 percent of men's wages in Britain, 50 percent in France, and 63 percent in West Germany. In addition, women still tended to enter traditionally female jobs. As one Swedish female guidance counselor remarked in 1975, "Every girl now thinks in terms of a job. This is progress. They want children, but they don't pin their hopes on marriage. They don't intend to be housewives for some future husband. But there has been no change in their vocational choices."[11] Many European women also still faced the double burden of earning income on the one hand and raising a family and maintaining the household on the other. Such inequities led increasing numbers of women to rebel.

Suffrage and the Search for Liberation The participation of women in the two world wars helped them achieve one of the major aims of the nineteenth-century women's movement—the right to vote. Already after World War I, many governments acknowledged the contributions of women to the war effort by granting them **suffrage.** Sweden, Great Britain, Germany, Poland, Hungary, Austria, and Czechoslovakia did so in 1918, followed by the United States in 1920. Women in France and Italy did not obtain the right to vote until 1945. After World War II, European women tended to fall back into the traditional roles expected of them, and little was heard of feminist concerns.

A women's liberation movement would arise in the late 1960s (see Chapter 29), but much of the theoretical foundation for the emergence of the postwar women's liberation movement was evident in the earlier work of Simone de Beauvoir (1908–1986). Born into a Catholic middle-class family and educated at the Sorbonne in Paris, she supported herself as a teacher and later as a novelist and writer. She maintained a lifelong relationship (but not marriage) with Jean-Paul Sartre. Her involvement in the existentialist movement, the leading intellectual movement of the time (see "The Philosophical

Dilemma: Existentialism" later in this chapter), led to her involvement in political causes. De Beauvoir believed that she lived a "liberated" life for a twentieth-century European woman, but for all her freedom, she still came to perceive that as a woman she faced limits that men did not. In 1949, she published her highly influential work *The Second Sex,* in which she argued that as a result of male-dominated societies, women had been defined by their differences from men and consequently received second-class status: "What peculiarly signalizes the situation of woman is that she—a free and autonomous being like all human creatures—nevertheless finds herself living in a world where men compel her to assume the status of the Other."[12] De Beauvoir took an active role in the French women's movement of the 1970s, and her book was a major influence on both sides of the Atlantic (see the box on p. 903).

Postwar Art and Literature

Many artists and writers struggled to understand the horrors of World War II. The German philosopher Theodor Adorno believed that "to write poetry after Auschwitz is barbaric."

Art Jean Dubuffet (1901–1985) was a French artist who adopted an intentionally raw style of art to depict the atrocities wrought by global conflict and genocide. Dubuffet consciously rejected notions of beauty to capture the effects of war. Borrowing from the art of children and the psychologically distressed, Dubuffet developed *Art Brut,* a gritty style that suggested no formal training. He created numerous portraits that caricatured Nazi sympathizers and French revolutionaries alike.

Although Dubuffet remained in Paris during the war years, many artists and writers, particularly the Surrealists, fled to the United States to avoid persecution for their revolutionary ideas. Following the war, the United States dominated the art world, much as it did the world of popular culture (see "The Americanization of the World" later in this chapter). New York City replaced Paris as the artistic center of the West. The Guggenheim Museum, the Museum of Modern Art, and the Whitney Museum of Modern Art, together with New York's numerous art galleries, promoted modern art and helped determine artistic tastes throughout much of the world. One of the styles that became synonymous with the emergence of the New York art scene was **Abstract Expressionism.**

Dubbed "action painting" by one critic, Abstract Expressionism was energetic and spontaneous, qualities evident in the enormous canvases of Jackson Pollock (1912–1956). In such works as *Lavender Mist* (1950), paint seems to explode, enveloping the viewer with emotion and movement. Pollock's swirling forms and seemingly chaotic patterns broke all conventions of form and structure. His drip paintings, with their total abstraction, were extremely influential with other artists,

THE VOICE OF THE WOMEN'S LIBERATION MOVEMENT

Simone de Beauvoir was an important figure in the emergence of the postwar women's liberation movement. This excerpt is taken from her influential book *The Second Sex*, in which she argued that women have been forced into a position subordinate to men.

Simone de Beauvoir, *The Second Sex*

Now, woman has always been man's dependent, if not his slave; the two sexes have never shared the world in equality. And even today woman is heavily handicapped, though her situation is beginning to change. Almost nowhere is her legal status the same as man's and frequently it is much to her disadvantage. Even when her rights are legally recognized in the abstract, long-standing custom prevents their full expression in the mores. In the economic sphere men and women can almost be said to make up two castes; other things being equal, the former hold the better jobs, get higher wages, and have more opportunity for success than their new competitors. In industry and politics men have a great many more positions and they monopolize the most important posts. In addition to all this they enjoy a traditional prestige that the education of children tends in every way to support, for the present enshrines the past—and in the past all history has been made by men. At the present time, when women are beginning to take part in the affairs of the world, it is still a world that belongs to men—they have no doubt of it at all and women have scarcely any. To decline to be the Other, to refuse to be a party to a deal—this would be for women to renounce all the advantages conferred upon them by their alliance with the superior caste. Man-the-sovereign will provide woman-the-liege with material protection and will undertake the moral justification of her existence; thus she can evade at once both economic risk and the metaphysical risk of a liberty in which ends and aims must be contrived without assistance. Indeed, along with the ethical urge of each individual to affirm his subjective existence, there is also the temptation to forgo liberty and become a thing. This is an inauspicious road, for he who takes it—passive, lost, ruined—becomes henceforth the creature of another's will, frustrated in his transcendence and deprived of every value. But it is an easy road; on it one avoids the strain involved in undertaking an authentic existence. When man makes of woman the *Other* he may, then, expect her to manifest deep-seated tendencies toward complicity. Thus woman may fail to lay claim to the status of subject because she lacks definite resources, because she feels the necessary bond that ties her to man regardless of reciprocity, and because she is often very well pleased with her role as the *Other*.

Now, what peculiarly signalizes the situation of woman is that she—a free and autonomous being like all human creatures—nevertheless finds herself living in a world where men compel her to assume the status of the Other.

Q *What factors or values do you think informed de Beauvoir's implicit call for a new history of women? Why was she outraged by the neglect of women in the Western historical consciousness?*

and he eventually became a celebrity. Inspired by Native American sand painters, Pollock painted with the canvas on the floor. He explained, "On the floor I am more at ease. I feel nearer, more a part of the painting, since this way I can walk around in, work from four sides and be literally *in* the painting. When I am in the painting, I am not aware of what I am doing. There is pure harmony."

The 1950s and early 1960s saw the emergence of **Pop Art,** which took images of popular culture and transformed them into works of fine art. Several British art students, known as the Independent Group, incorporated science fiction and American advertising techniques into their exhibitions. "This Is Tomorrow," an exhibit held in 1956 at the Whitechapel Gallery in London, was the group's crowning achievement. It featured environments inspired by advertisements as well as mural-sized reproductions of movie characters like Robby the Robot.

Andy Warhol (1930–1987), who began as an advertising illustrator, became the most famous of the American Pop artists. Warhol adapted images from commercial art, such as Campbell's soup cans, and photographs of celebrities such as Marilyn Monroe. Derived from mass culture, these works were mass-produced and deliberately "of the moment," expressing the fleeting whims of popular culture. The detached style of Warhol's silk-screened prints put Pop Art at odds with the aggressive, painterly techniques of the Abstract Expressionists.

Literature The most significant new trend in postwar literature was called the "Theater of the Absurd." This new convention in drama began in France in the 1950s, although its most famous proponent was the Irishman Samuel Beckett (1906–1990), who lived in France. In Beckett's *Waiting for Godot* (1952), the action on stage is not realistic. Two men wait incessantly for the appearance of someone, with whom they may or may not have an appointment. No background information on the two men is provided. During the course of the play, nothing seems to be happening. The audience is never told if what they are watching is real or not. Unlike traditional theater, suspense is maintained not by having the audience wonder what is going to happen next but by having them ask, what is happening now?

The Theater of the Absurd reflected its time. The postwar period was a time of disillusionment with ideological beliefs in politics or religion. A sense of the

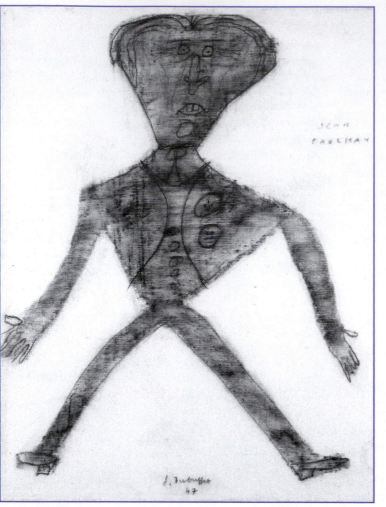

Jean Dubuffet, *Portrait of Jean Paulhan.* In 1947, Jean Dubuffet exhibited more than seventy portraits of his friends and collaborators at the Galerie René Drouin in Paris. The subjects of Dubuffet's portraits were both Nazi sympathizers and fighters against the German occupation. Jean Paulhan, the subject of this portrait, was a well-known critic and writer. Paulhan, who promoted Dubuffet's work, had led an underground movement to resist Nazi propaganda during World War II.

world's meaninglessness underscored the desolate worldview of absurdist drama and literature. This can be seen in Günter Grass's novel *The Tin Drum,* published in 1959, which reflected postwar Germany's preoccupation with the seeming incomprehensibility of Nazi Germany.

The Philosophical Dilemma: Existentialism

The sense of meaninglessness that inspired the Theater of the Absurd also underscored the philosophy of **existentialism.** It was born largely of the desperation caused by two world wars and the breakdown of traditional values. Existentialism reflected the anxieties of the twentieth century and became especially well known after World War II through the works of two Frenchmen, Jean-Paul Sartre (1905–1980) and Albert Camus (1913–1960).

The central point of the existentialism of Sartre and Camus was the absence of God in the universe. The death of God, though tragic, meant that humans had no preordained destiny and were utterly alone in the universe, with no future and no hope. As Camus expressed it:

> A world that can be explained even with bad reasons is a familiar world. But, on the other hand, in a universe suddenly divested of illusions and lights, man feels an alien, a stranger. His exile is without remedy since he is deprived of the memory of a lost home or the hope of a promised land. This divorce between man and his life, the actor and his setting, is properly the feeling of absurdity.[13]

According to Camus, then, the world was absurd and without meaning; humans, too, are without meaning and purpose. Reduced to despair and depression, humans have but one source of hope—themselves.

Though the world might be absurd, Camus argued, it could not be absurd unless people judged it to be so. People are unique in the world, and their kind of being is quite different from that of all others. In the words of Sartre, human "existence precedes essence." Humans are beings who first exist and then define themselves. They determine what they will be. According to Sartre, "Man is nothing else but what he makes of himself. Such is the first principle of existentialism." People, then, must take full responsibility for what they are. They create their values and give their lives meaning. And this can only be done by their involvement in life. Only through one's acts can one determine one's values.

Existentialism, therefore, involved an ethics of action, of involvement in life. But people could not define themselves without their involvement with others. Thus, existentialism's ethical message was just as important as its philosophy of being. Essentially, the message of existentialism was one of authenticity. Individuals true to themselves refused to be depersonalized by their society. As one author noted, "Existentialism is the struggle to discover the human person in a depersonalized age."

The Revival of Religion

Existentialism was one response to the despair generated by the apparent collapse of civilized values in the twentieth century. The revival of religion was another. Ever since the Enlightenment of the eighteenth century, Christianity and religion had been on the defensive. But a number of religious thinkers and leaders attempted to bring new life to Christianity in the twentieth century.

Hans Namuth/Photo Researchers, Inc.

Jackson Pollock Painting. After World War II, Abstract Expressionism moved to the center of the artistic mainstream. One of its best-known practitioners was the American Jackson Pollock, who achieved his ideal of total abstraction in his drip paintings. He is shown here at work in his Long Island studio. Pollock found it easier to cover his large canvases with spontaneous patterns of color when he put them on the floor.

One expression of this religious revival was the attempt by such theologians as the Protestant Karl Barth (1886–1968) and the Catholic Karl Rahner (1904–1984) to infuse traditional Christian teachings with new life. In numerous writings, Barth attempted to reinterpret the religious insights of the Reformation era for the modern world. To Barth, the sinful and hence imperfect nature of human beings meant that humans could know religious truth not through reason but only through the grace of God. Rahner attempted to revitalize traditional Catholic theology by incorporating aspects of modern thought. He was careful, however, to emphasize the continuity between ancient and modern interpretations of Catholic doctrine.

In the Catholic Church, an attempt at religious renewal also came from a charismatic pope. Pope John XXIII (1881–1963) reigned as pope for only a short time

(1958–1963) but sparked a dramatic revival of Catholicism when he summoned the twenty-first ecumenical council of the Catholic Church. Known as Vatican II, the council liberalized a number of Catholic practices. For example, the liturgy of the Mass, the central feature of Catholic worship, was now to be spoken in the vernacular, not in Latin. New avenues of communication with other Christian faiths were also opened for the first time since the Reformation.

The Explosion of Popular Culture

Since World War II, popular culture has played an increasingly important role in helping Western people define themselves. At one level, popular culture is but the history of the ever-changing whims of mass taste, but on another level, "it is a history of how modern society has created images of itself and expressed its fantasies, its fears, its ambitions."[14]

Culture as a Consumer Commodity   The history of popular culture is also the history of the economic system that supports it, for this system manufactures, distributes, and sells the images that people consume as popular culture. As popular culture and its economic support system become increasingly intertwined, industries of leisure emerge. As one historian of popular culture has argued, "Industrial societies turn the provision of leisure into a commercial activity, in which their citizens are sold entertainment, recreation, pleasure, and appearance as commodities that differ from the goods at the drugstore only in the way they are used."[15] Modern popular culture is therefore inextricably tied to the mass consumer society in which it has emerged.

The Americanization of the World   The United States has been the most influential force in shaping popular culture in the West and, to a lesser degree, the rest of the world. Through movies, music, advertising, and television, the United States has spread its particular form of consumerism and the American dream to millions around the world. Already in 1923, the New York *Morning Post* noted that "the film is to America what the flag was once to Britain. By its means Uncle Sam may hope some day...to Americanize the world."[16] In movies, television, and popular music, the impact of American popular culture on the Western world is pervasive.

Motion pictures were the primary vehicle for the diffusion of American popular culture in the years immediately following the war, and they continued to dominate both European and American markets in the next decades (40 percent of Hollywood's income in the 1960s came from the European market). Nevertheless, the existence of a profitable art-house circuit in America and Europe enabled European filmmakers to make films whose themes and avant-garde methods were quite different from those of Hollywood. Italy and Sweden, for example, developed a tradition of "national cinema" that reflected "specific cultural traits in a mode in which they could be successfully exported." The 1957 film *The Seventh Seal,* by the Swedish director Ingmar Bergman (1918–2007), was a good example of the successful European art film. Bergman's films caused him to be viewed as "an artist of comparable stature to a novelist or playwright." So too were François Truffaut (1932–1984) in France and Federico Fellini (1920–1993) in Italy; such directors gloried in experimenting with subject matter and technique and produced films dealing with more complex and daring themes than Hollywood would attempt.

Although developed in the 1930s, television did not become readily available until the late 1940s. By 1954, there were 32 million sets in the United States as television became the centerpiece of middle-class life. In the 1960s, as television spread around the world, American networks unloaded their products on Europe and the Third World at extraordinarily low prices. For instance, the British Broadcasting Corporation (BBC) could buy American programs for one-tenth the cost per viewer of producing its own. Only the establishment of quota systems prevented American television from completely inundating these countries.

The United States has dominated popular music since the end of World War II. Jazz, blues, rhythm and blues, and rock-and-roll have been by far the most popular music forms in the Western world—and much of the non-Western world—during this time. All of them originated in the United States, and all are rooted in African American musical innovations. These forms later spread around the globe, inspiring local artists who then transformed the music in their own way. Often these transformed models then returned to the United States to inspire American artists. This was certainly the case with rock-and-roll. Through the 1950s, American figures such as Chuck Berry, Little Richard, and Elvis Presley inspired the Beatles and other British performers, who then led an "invasion" of the United States in the 1960s, creating a sensation and in part sparking new rockers in America. Rock music itself developed in the 1950s. In 1952, white disk jockeys began playing rhythm and blues and traditional blues music performed by African Americans to young white audiences. The music was popular with this audience, and record companies began recording watered-down white "cover" versions of this music. It was not until performers such as Elvis Presley mixed white "folkabilly" with rhythm and blues that rock-and-roll became popular with the larger white audience.

The Beatles. Although rock-and-roll originated in the United States, it inspired musical groups around the world. This was certainly true of Britain's Beatles, who caused a sensation among young people when they came to the United States in the 1960s. Here the Beatles are shown during a performance on *The Ed Sullivan Show.*

AP Images

TIMELINE

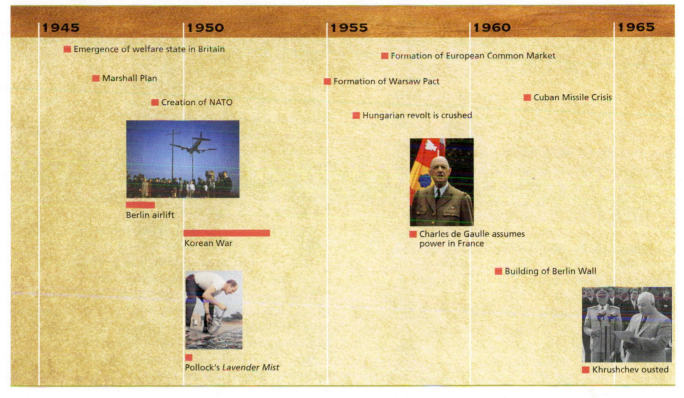

1945	1950	1955	1960	1965

- Emergence of welfare state in Britain
- Marshall Plan
- Creation of NATO
- Formation of European Common Market
- Formation of Warsaw Pact
- Cuban Missile Crisis
- Hungarian revolt is crushed

Berlin airlift

Korean War

Charles de Gaulle assumes power in France

Building of Berlin Wall

Pollock's *Lavender Mist*

Khrushchev ousted

CONCLUSION

At the end of a devastating world war, a new kind of conflict erupted in the Western world as two of the victors, the United States and the Soviet Union, emerged as superpowers and began to argue over the political organization of a Europe liberated from Nazi Germany. Europeans, whether they wanted to or not, were forced to become supporters of one side or the other. The Western world was soon divided between supporters of a capitalistic West and adherents of a Communist East. Western Europe emerged as a new community in the 1950s and the 1960s and staged a remarkable economic recovery, while Eastern Europe seemed to stagnate under the control of the Soviet Union. Regardless of their economic differences, however, both Western and Eastern Europeans were well aware that their future still depended on the conflict between the two superpowers.

In addition to the Cold War conflict, the postwar era was also characterized by decolonization. After World War II, the colonial empires of the European states were largely dissolved, and the liberated territories of Africa, Asia, and the Middle East emerged as sovereign states. All too soon, these newly independent nations often found themselves caught in the Cold War rivalry between the United States and the Soviet Union. After the United States fought in Korea to prevent the spread of communism, the ideological division that had begun in Europe quickly spread to the rest of the world.

NOTES

1. Quoted in Joseph M. Jones, *The Fifteen Weeks (February 21–June 5, 1947)*, 2d ed. (New York, 1964), pp. 140–141.
2. Quoted in Walter Laqueur, *Europe in Our Time* (New York, 1992), p. 111.
3. Quoted in Wilfried Loth, *The Division of the World, 1941–1955* (New York, 1988), pp. 160–161.
4. Quoted in William I. Hitchcock, *The Struggle for Europe: The Turbulent History of a Divided Continent, 1945–2002* (New York, 2003), p. 215.
5. Quoted in Peter Lane, *Europe Since 1945: An Introduction* (Totowa, N.J., 1985), p. 248.
6. Quoted in Robert F. Kennedy, *Thirteen Days: A Memoir of the Cuban Missile Crisis* (New York, 1969), pp. 89–90.
7. Quoted in Larry Collins and Dominique Lapierre, *Freedom at Midnight* (New York, 1975), p. 252.
8. R. Hilton, *Military Attaché in Moscow* (London, 1949), p. 41.
9. Nikita Khrushchev, *Khrushchev Remembers*, trans. Strobe Talbott (Boston, 1970), p. 77.
10. Quoted in Bonnie G. Smith, *Changing Lives: Women in European History Since 1700* (Lexington, Mass., 1989), p. 513.
11. Quoted in Hilda Scott, *Sweden's "Right to Be Human": Sex-Role Equality—The Goal and the Reality* (London, 1982), p. 125.
12. Simone de Beauvoir, *The Second Sex*, trans. H. M. Parshley (New York, 1961), p. xxviii.

13. Quoted in Henry Grosshans, *The Search for Modern Europe* (Boston, 1970), p. 421.
14. Richard Maltby, ed., *Passing Parade: A History of Popular Culture in the Twentieth Century* (Oxford, 1989), p. 8.
15. Ibid.
16. Quoted in ibid., p. 11.

SUGGESTIONS FOR FURTHER READING

General Works   For a well-written survey on Europe since 1945, see **T. Judt**, *Postwar: A History of Europe Since 1945* (New York, 2005). See also **W. I. Hitchcock**, *The Struggle for Europe: The Turbulent History of a Divided Continent, 1945–2002* (New York, 2003), and **W. Laqueur**, *Europe in Our Time* (New York, 1992).

Cold War   There is a detailed literature on the Cold War. A good account is **J. L. Gaddis**, *The Cold War: A New History* (New York, 2005). See also **J. W. Langdon**, *A Hard and Bitter Peace: A Global History of the Cold War* (Englewood Cliffs, N.J., 1995). Two brief works on the Cold War are **J. H. Mason**, *The Cold War* (New York, 1996), and **J. Smith**, *The Cold War, 1945–1991* (Oxford, 1998). For an illustrated history, see **J. Isaacs and T. Downing**, *Cold War: An Illustrated History, 1945–1991* (Boston, 1998). On the Berlin Wall and the Cold War in Germany, see **F. Taylor**, *The Berlin Wall: A World Divided, 1961–1989* (New York, 2006). For a good introduction to the arms race, see **E. M. Bottome**, *The Balance of Terror: A Guide to the Arms Race,* rev. ed. (Boston, 1986). On the Cuban Missile Crisis, see **D. Munton and D. A. Welch**, *The Real Thirteen Days: A Concise History of the Cuban Missile Crisis* (Oxford, 2006).

Decolonization   On decolonization after World War II, see **R. F. Betts**, *Decolonization,* 2d ed. (London, 2004). To put the subject into a broader context, see **D. Newsom**, *Imperial Mantle: The United States, Decolonization and the Third World* (Bloomington, Ind., 2001).

Soviet Union and Eastern Europe   On the Khrushchev years, see **W. Taubman**, *Khrushchev: The Man and His Era* (New York, 2004). For a general study of the Soviet satellites in Eastern Europe, see **J. Rothschild**, *Return to Diversity: A Political History of East Central Europe Since World War II,* 3d ed. (New York, 1999), and **M. Pittaway**, *Brief Histories: Eastern Europe 1945–2000* (London, 2003).

Postwar Western Europe   The rebuilding of postwar Europe is examined in **D. W. Ellwood**, *Rebuilding Europe: Western Europe, America, and Postwar Reconstruction* (London, 1992), and **M. A. Schain**, ed., *The Marshall Plan: Fifty Years After* (New York, 2001). On the building of common institutions in Western Europe, see **S. Henig**, *The Uniting of Europe: From Discord to Concord* (London, 1997). For surveys of West Germany, see **H. A. Turner**, *Germany from Partition to Reunification* (New Haven, Conn., 1992), and **T. G. Ash**, *In Europe's Name: Germany and the Enduring Balance* (New York, 1993). France under de Gaulle is examined in **J. Jackson**, *Charles de Gaulle* (London, 2003), and

D. J. Mahoney, *De Gaulle: Statesmanship, Grandeur, and Modern Democracy* (Westport, Conn., 1996). On Britain, see **K. O. Morgan**, *The People's Peace: British History, 1945–1990* (Oxford, 1992). On Italy, see **P. Ginsborg**, *A History of Contemporary Italy: Society and Politics, 1943–1988* (New York, 1990).

Postwar Society and Culture   On the welfare state, see **A. de Swann**, *In Care of the State: Health Care, Education, and Welfare in Europe and the United States in the Modern Era* (New York, 1988). On women and the welfare state, see **R. Cleave et al.**, *Gender and the Welfare State* (New York, 2003), and **D. Sainsbury**, ed., *Gendering Welfare States* (London, 1994). On Simone de Beauvoir, see **T. Keefe**, *Simone de Beauvoir* (New York, 1998). More general works that include much information on the contemporary period are **B. G. Smith**, *Changing Lives: Women in European History Since 1700* (Lexington, Mass., 2005), and **F. Thebaud**, ed., *A History of Women in the West,* vol. 5, *Toward a Cultural Identity in the Twentieth Century* (Cambridge, Mass., 1994). A classic work on existentialism is **W. Barrett**, *Irrational Man* (Garden City, N.Y., 1962), but see also **T. Flynn**, *Existentialism: A Very Short History,* 5th ed. (Oxford, 2006). On the arts, see **A. Marwick**, *Arts in the West Since 1945* (Oxford, 2002), and **D. Anfam**, *Abstract Expressionism* (New York, 1990). An excellent survey of twentieth-century popular culture is **R. Maltby**, ed., *Passing Parade: A History of Popular Culture in the Twentieth Century* (Oxford, 1989).

CENGAGENOW   CengageNOW is an integrated online suite of services and resources with proven ease of use and efficient paths to success, delivering the results you want—NOW!

academic.cengage.com/login/

Enter CengageNOW using the access card that is available with *Western Civilization.* CengageNOW will assist you in understanding the content in this chapter with lesson plans generated for your needs. In addition, you can read the following documents, and many more, online:

> Winston Churchill, The Sinews of Peace
> McCarran International Security Act

WESTERN CIVILIZATION RESOURCES

Visit the *Western Civilization* Companion Web site for resources specific to this book:

academic.cengage.com/history/spielvogel

For a variety of tools to help you succeed in this course, visit the Western Civilization Resource Center. Enter the Resource Center using either your *CengageNOW* access card or your standalone access card for the *Wadsworth Western Civilization Resource Center.* Organized by topic, this Web site includes quizzes; images; primary source documents; interactive simulations, maps, and timelines; movie explorations; and a wealth of other resources.

http://westernrc.wadsworth.com/

CHAPTER 29
PROTEST AND STAGNATION:
THE WESTERN WORLD, 1965–1985

A barricade of overturned cars in Paris on May 11, 1968

CHAPTER OUTLINE AND FOCUS QUESTIONS

A Culture of Protest

Q What were the goals of the revolt in sexual mores, the youth protest and student revolts, the feminist movement, and the antiwar protests? To what extent were their goals achieved?

A Divided Western World

Q What were the major political developments in the Soviet Union, Eastern Europe, Western Europe, and the United States between 1965 and 1985?

The Cold War: The Move to Détente

Q What were the main events in the Cold War between 1965 and 1985, and how important was the role of détente in those events?

Society and Culture in the Western World

Q What were the major social and cultural developments in the Western world between 1965 and 1985?

CRITICAL THINKING

Q What are the similarities and differences between the feminist movement of the nineteenth century and the post–World II feminist movement?

BETWEEN 1945 AND 1965, Europe not only overcame the devastating effects of World War II but actually experienced an economic recovery that seemed nothing less than miraculous to many people. Economic growth and virtually full employment continued so long that the first post–World War II recession in 1973 came as a shock to Western Europe.

In 1968, Europe had experienced a different kind of shock. May 1968 is now remembered as a historic month because of events in Paris, where a student revolt occurred. It erupted at the University of Nanterre outside Paris but soon spread to the Sorbonne, the main campus of the University of Paris, where about five hundred students gathered for demonstrations and demanded a greater voice in the administration of the university. The authorities decided to react with force and arrested a number of the demonstrators, although as one police officer said, "to tell the truth, we were not enthusiastic about it if we could avoid it, knowing too well, from experience, that our interventions created more problems than they solved." Indeed, students fought back, prying up paving stones from the streets to use as weapons. On May 3, eighty policemen and about three hundred students were hurt; almost six hundred were arrested. Demonstrations then spread to other universities, which served to embolden the students in Paris. On the night of May 10, barricades, formed by overturning cars, went up in the streets of Paris. When police moved in to tear down the barricades, violence ensued. One eyewitness recounted: "A young girl came rushing out into the street practically naked and was manhandled from one cop to another; then beaten like the other wounded students." Students expanded the scale of their protests by inviting workers to support them. Half of France's workforce went on strike in May 1968. After de Gaulle's government instituted a hefty wage hike, the workers returned to work, and the police repressed the remaining student protesters.

The year 1968 saw widespread student protests around the world, and for a brief moment, students and radicals everywhere believed the time had come for a complete renovation of society and government. But the moment passed, and the Western world was left with the new order created in the twenty years after World War II. In Eastern Europe, the crushing of Czechoslovakia in 1968 by Soviet troops left Eastern Europeans with little choice but to continue as Soviet satellites. In Western Europe, democracies continued to evolve. But everywhere, resignation and stagnation seemed to prevail as the new order established in the Western world during the twenty years after World War II appeared to have become permanent: a prosperous, capitalistic West and an impoverished Communist East. ◆

A Culture of Protest

Q **Focus Questions:** What were the goals of the revolt in sexual mores, the youth protest and student revolts, the feminist movement, and the antiwar protests? To what extent were their goals achieved?

In the late 1960s, the Western world was rocked by a variety of protest movements relating to sexual mores, education, and women's rights as well as a strong antiwar movement against the Second Vietnam War (see "The Second Vietnam War" later in this chapter). Although many of the dreams of the protesters were not immediately realized, the forces they set in motion helped to transform Western society.

A Revolt in Sexual Mores

The **permissive society** was a label used by critics to describe the new society of postwar Europe. World War I had opened the first significant crack in the rigid code of manners and morals of the nineteenth century. The 1920s had witnessed experimentation with drugs, the appearance of pornography, and a new sexual freedom (police in Berlin, for example, issued cards that permitted female and male homosexual prostitutes to practice their trade). But these indications of a new attitude appeared mostly in major cities and touched only small numbers of

people. After World War II, changes in manners and morals were far more extensive and far more noticeable.

Sweden took the lead in the propagation of the so-called sexual revolution of the 1960s. Sex education in the schools and the decriminalization of homosexuality were but two aspects of Sweden's liberal legislation. The rest of Europe and the United States soon followed Sweden's example. A gay rights movement emerged in California in 1969 and had spread to France, Italy, and Britain by 1970.

The introduction of the birth control pill, which became widely available by the mid-1960s, gave people more freedom in sexual behavior. Meanwhile, sexually explicit movies, plays, and books broke new ground in the treatment of once-hidden subjects. Cities like Amsterdam, which allowed open prostitution and the public sale of pornography, attracted thousands of curious tourists.

The new standards were evident in the breakdown of the traditional family. Divorce rates increased dramatically, especially in the 1960s, and premarital and extramarital sexual experiences also rose substantially. A survey in the Netherlands in 1968 revealed that 78 percent of men and 86 percent of women had engaged in extramarital sex. The appearance of *Playboy* magazine in the 1950s had also already added a new dimension to the sexual revolution for adult males. Along with photographs of nude women, *Playboy* offered well-written articles on various aspects of masculinity. *Playboy*'s message was clear: men were encouraged to seek sexual gratification outside marriage.

Youth Protest and Student Revolt

The decade of the 1960s also saw the emergence of a drug culture, especially among young people. For most college and university students, marijuana was the recreational drug of choice. For young people more interested in mind expansion into higher levels of consciousness, Timothy Leary, who had done psychedelic research at Harvard on the effects of LSD (lysergic acid diethylamide), became the high priest of hallucinogenic experiences.

New attitudes toward sex and the use of drugs were only two manifestations of a growing youth movement in the 1960s that questioned authority and fostered rebellion against the older generation. Spurred on by the Second Vietnam War and a growing political consciousness, the youth rebellion became a youth protest movement by the second half of the 1960s (see the box on p. 912).

Before World War II, higher education had largely remained the preserve of Europe's wealthier classes. After the war, European states began to foster greater equality of opportunity in higher education by reducing or eliminating fees, and universities experienced an influx of students from the middle and lower classes. Enrollments grew dramatically; in France, 4.5 percent of young people attended a university in 1950. By 1965, the figure had increased to 14.5 percent.

But there were problems. Classrooms with too many students, professors who paid little attention to their

IMAGES OF EVERYDAY LIFE

Youth Culture in the 1960s. Protest was an integral part of the growing youth movement in the 1960s. Young people questioned authority and fostered rebellion in an attempt to change the social thinking of an older generation. The photograph at the bottom left shows a group of young protesters facing the bayonets of the National Guardsmen who had been called in by Governor Ronald Reagan to restore order on the Berkeley campus of the University of California during an antiwar rally. The "love-in" at the top left shows another facet of the youth movement. In the 1960s, a number of outdoor public festivals for young people combined music, drugs, and sex. Flamboyant dress, face painting, free-form dancing, and drugs were vital ingredients in creating an atmosphere dedicated to "love and peace." A popular slogan was "Make Love, Not War." Shown here are dozens of hippies dancing around a decorated bus at a "love-in" during the Summer of Love, 1967. Many young people were excited about creating a new culture based on love and community. In the photograph below right, a member of the Diggers, a communal group in San Francisco, is shown feeding a flower child.

© Henry Diltz/CORBIS

© Ted Streshinsky/CORBIS

© Ted Streshinsky/CORBIS

students, and administrators who acted in an authoritarian fashion led to student resentment. In addition, despite changes in the curriculum, students often felt that the universities were not providing an education relevant to the realities of the modern age. This discontent led to an outburst of student revolts in the late 1960s (see the box on p. 913). In part, these protests were an extension of the spontaneous disruptions in American universities

"THE TIMES THEY ARE A-CHANGIN'": THE MUSIC OF YOUTHFUL PROTEST

In the 1960s, the lyrics of rock and folk music reflected the rebellious mood of many young people. Bob Dylan (b. 1941) expressed the feelings of the younger generation. His song "The Times They Are A-Changin'," released in 1964, has been called an "anthem for the protest movement."

Bob Dylan, "The Times They Are A-Changin'"

Come gather round people
Wherever you roam
And admit that the waters
Around you have grown
And accept it that soon
You'll be drenched to the bone
If your time to you
Is worth savin'
Then you better start swimmin'
Or you'll sink like a stone
For the times they are a-changin'

Come writers and critics
Who prophesize with your pen
And keep your eyes wide
The chance won't come again
And don't speak too soon
For the wheel's still in spin
And there's no tellin' who
That it's namin'
For the loser now
Will be later to win
For the times they are a-changin'

Come senators, congressmen
please heed the call
Don't stand in the doorway
Don't block up the hall

For he that gets hurt
Will be he who has stalled
There's a battle outside
And it is ragin'
It'll soon shake your windows
And rattle your walls
For the times they are a-changin'

Come mothers and fathers
Throughout the land
And don't criticize
What you can't understand
Your sons and your daughters
Are beyond your command
Your old road
Is rapidly agin'
Please get out of the new one
If you can't lend your hand
For the times they are a-changin'

The line it is drawn
The curse it is cast
The slow one now
Will later be fast
As the present now
Will later be past
The order is
Rapidly fadin'
And the first one now
Will later be last
For the times they are a-changin'

Q *What caused the student campus revolts of the 1960s? What and whom does Dylan identify in this song as the problem?*

---

in the mid-1960s, which were often sparked by student opposition to the Second Vietnam War. Perhaps the most famous student revolt occurred in France in 1968, as we saw in the introduction to this chapter.

The French revolt spurred student protests elsewhere in Europe, although none of them succeeded in becoming mass movements. In West Berlin, university students led a protest against Axel Springer, leader of Germany's largest newspaper establishment. Many German students were motivated by a desire to destroy what they considered to be the corrupt old order and were especially influenced by the ideas of the German American social philosopher Herbert Marcuse (1898–1979). In *One-Dimensional Man*, published in 1964, Marcuse argued that capitalism had undermined the dissatisfaction of the oppressed masses by encouraging the consumption of material things. He proposed that a small cadre of unindoctrinated students could liberate the masses from the control of the capitalist ruling class. But the German students' attempt at revolutionary violence backfired as angry Berliners supported police repression of the students.

The student protest movement reached its high point in 1968, although scattered incidents lasted into the early 1970s. There were several reasons for the student radicalism. Some students were genuinely motivated by the desire to reform the university. Others were protesting the Second Vietnam War, which they viewed as a product of Western imperialism. They also attacked other aspects of Western society, such as its materialism, and expressed concern about becoming cogs in the large and impersonal bureaucratic jungles of the modern world. For many students, the calls for democratic decision making within the universities were a reflection of their deeper concerns about the direction of Western society. Although the student revolts fizzled out in the 1970s, the larger issues they raised were increasingly revived in the 1990s.

1968: THE YEAR OF STUDENT REVOLTS

The outburst of student upheavals in the late 1960s reached its high point in 1968. These two very different selections illustrate some of the issues that prompted university students to occupy campus buildings and demand reforms.

A Student Manifesto in Search of a Real and Human Educational Alternative, University of British Columbia, June 1968

Today we as students are witnessing a deepening crisis within our society. We are intensely aware, in a way perhaps not possible for the older generation, that humanity stands on the edge of a new era. Because we are young, we have insights into the present and visions of the future that our parents do not have. Tasks of an immense gravity wait solution in our generation. We have inherited these tasks from our parents. We do not blame them so much for that . . . but we do blame them for being unwilling to admit that there are problems or for saying that it is we who have visited these problems on ourselves because of our perversity, ungratefulness and unwillingness to listen to "reason."

Much of the burden of solving the problems of the new era rests on the university. We have been taught to look to it for leadership. While we know that part of the reason for the university is to render direct services to the community, we are alarmed at its servility to industry and government as to what and how it teaches. We are scandalized that the university fails to realize its role in renewing and vivifying those intellectual and moral energies necessary to create a new society—one in which a sense of personal dignity and human community can be preserved.

Student Inscriptions on the Walls of Paris, May and June 1968

The dream is the reality.
May 1968. World revolution is the order of the day.
I decree a state of permanent happiness.
To be free in 1968 is to take part.
Take the trip every day of your life.
Make love, not war.
No exams.
The mind travels farther than the heart but it doesn't go as far.
Run, comrade, the old are behind you!
Don't make a revolution in the image of your confused and hide-bound university.
Exam = servility, social promotion, hierarchic society.
Love each other.
SEX. It's good, said Mao, but not too often.
Alcohol kills. Take LSD.
Are you consumers or participants?
Professors, you are as old as your culture; your modernism is only the modernization of the police.
Live in the present.
Revolution, I love you.
Long live direct democracy!

Q *Based on these selections, what do you believe were the key problems or causes that motivated the student protesters of this era? Did the student revolts resolve any of the issues raised, or are their complaints still relevant today?*

The Feminist Movement

By the late 1960s, women began to assert their rights and speak as feminists. Along with the student upheavals of the late 1960s came renewed interest in **feminism,** or the women's liberation movement, as it was now called. Increasingly, women protested that the acquisition of political and legal equality had not brought true equality with men:

> We are economically oppressed: in jobs we do full work for half pay, in the home we do unpaid work full time. We are commercially exploited by advertisement, television, and the press; legally, we often have only the status of children. We are brought up to feel inadequate, educated to narrower horizons than men. This is our specific oppression as women. It is as women that we are, therefore, organizing.[1]

These were the words of a British Women's Liberation Workshop in 1969.

An important contributor to the growth of the women's movement in the 1960s was Betty Friedan (1921–2006). A journalist and the mother of three children, Friedan grew increasingly uneasy with her attempt to fulfill the traditional role of the "ideal housewife and mother." In 1963, she published *The Feminine Mystique,* in which she analyzed the problems of middle-class American women in the 1950s and argued that women were being denied equality with men. She wrote, "The problem that has no name—which is simply the fact that American women are kept from growing to their full human capacities—is taking a far greater toll on the physical and mental health of our country than any known disease."[2]

The Feminine Mystique became a best-seller and propelled Friedan into a newfound celebrity. In 1966, she founded the National Organization for Women (NOW), whose stated goal was to take "action to bring women into full participation in the mainstream of American society *now,* exercising all the privileges and responsibilities thereof in truly equal partnership with men." Friedan's voice was also prominent in calling for the addition to the U.S. Constitution of an amendment guaranteeing equal rights for women.

Women's Liberation Movement. In the late 1960s, as women began once again to assert their rights, a revived women's liberation movement emerged. Feminists in the movement maintained that women themselves must alter the conditions of their lives. During this women's liberation rally, some women climbed the statue of Admiral Farragut in Washington, D.C., to exhibit their signs.

Antiwar Protests

One of the major issues that mobilized youthful European protesters was the U.S. war in Vietnam, which they viewed as an act of aggression and imperialism. In 1968, demonstrations broke out in universities in Italy, France, and Britain. In London, 30,000 demonstrators took to the streets protesting America's war in Vietnam. But student protests in Europe also backfired in that they provoked a reaction from people who favored order over the lawlessness of privileged young people. As Pier Paolo Pasolini, an Italian poet and intellectual, wrote: "Now all the journalists of the world are licking your arses . . . but not me, my dears. You have the faces of spoiled brats, and I hate you, like I hate your fathers. . . . When yesterday at Valle Giulia [in Rome] you beat up the police, I sympathized with the police because they are the sons of the poor."[3]

Antiwar protests also divided the American people after President Lyndon Johnson sent American troops to war in Vietnam. As the war dragged on and a military draft ensued, protests escalated. Teach-ins, sit-ins, and the occupation of buildings at universities alternated with more radical demonstrations that led to violence. The killing of four student protesters at Kent State University in 1970 by the Ohio National Guard caused a reaction, and the antiwar movement began to decline. By that time, however, antiwar demonstrations had worn down the willingness of many Americans to continue the war. The combination of antiwar demonstrations and ghetto riots in the cities also heightened the appeal of a call for "law and order," used by Richard Nixon, the Republican presidential candidate in 1968.

A Divided Western World

Q Focus Question: What were the major political developments in the Soviet Union, Eastern Europe, Western Europe, and the United States between 1965 and 1985?

Between 1945 and 1965, economic recovery had brought renewed growth to Europe. Nevertheless, the political divisions between Western and Eastern Europe remained; so did disparities in prosperity.

Stagnation in the Soviet Union

Between 1964 and 1982, significant change in the Soviet Union seemed highly unlikely. The man in charge, Leonid Brezhnev (1906–1982), lived by the slogan "No experimentation." Brezhnev had entered the ranks of the Party leadership under Stalin and, after the overthrow of Khrushchev in 1964, had become head of both the Communist Party and the state. He was optimistic, yet reluctant to reform. Overall, the Brezhnev years were relatively calm, although the **Brezhnev Doctrine**—the right of the Soviet Union to intervene if socialism was threatened in another socialist state—became an article of faith and led to the use of Soviet troops in Czechoslovakia in 1968 (see the box on p. 915).

The Brezhnev Years Brezhnev benefited from the more relaxed atmosphere associated with **détente** (see "The Cold War: The Move to Détente" later in this chapter). The Soviets had reached a rough parity with the United States in nuclear arms and enjoyed a sense of external security that seemed to allow for a relaxation of authoritarian rule. The regime permitted more access to Western styles of music, dress, and art, although dissenters were still punished. Andrei Sakharov, for example, who had played an important role in the development of the Soviet hydrogen bomb, was placed under house arrest for his defense of human rights.

In his economic policies, Brezhnev continued to emphasize heavy industry. Overall industrial growth declined, although the Soviet production of iron, steel, coal, and cement surpassed that of the United States. Two problems bedeviled the Soviet economy. The government's insistence on vigorous central planning led to a huge, complex bureaucracy that discouraged efficiency and reduced productivity. Moreover, the Soviet system,

THE BREZHNEV DOCTRINE

In the summer of 1968, when the new Communist Party leaders in Czechoslovakia were seriously considering proposals for reforming the Stalinist system there, the Warsaw Pact nations met under the leadership of Soviet Party leader Leonid Brezhnev to assess the threat to the Communist camp. Shortly thereafter, military forces of several Soviet bloc nations entered Czechoslovakia and imposed a new government subject to the Soviet Union. The move was justified by the principle that came to be known as the Brezhnev Doctrine.

A Letter to Czechoslovakia

To the Central Committee of the Communist Party of Czechoslovakia

Warsaw, July 15, 1968

Dear comrades!

On behalf of the Central Committees of the Communist and Workers' Parties of Bulgaria, Hungary, the German Democratic Republic, Poland, and the Soviet Union, we address ourselves to you with this letter, prompted by a feeling of sincere friendship based on the principles of Marxism-Leninism and proletarian internationalism and by the concern of our common affairs for strengthening the positions of socialism and the security of the socialist community of nations.

The development of events in your country evokes in us deep anxiety. It is our firm conviction that the offensive of the reactionary forces, backed by imperialists, against your Party and the foundations of the social system in the Czechoslovak Socialist Republic, threatens to push your country off the road of socialism and that consequently it jeopardizes the interests of the entire socialist system....

We neither had nor have any intention of interfering in such affairs as are strictly the internal business of your Party and your state, nor of violating the principles of respect, independence, and equality in the relations among the Communist Parties and socialist countries....

At the same time we cannot agree to have hostile forces push your country from the road of socialism and create a threat of severing Czechoslovakia from the socialist community.... This is the common cause of our countries, which have joined in the Warsaw Treaty to ensure independence, peace, and security in Europe, and to set up an insurmountable barrier against aggression and revenge.... We shall never agree to have imperialism, using peaceful or nonpeaceful methods, making a gap from the inside or from the outside in the socialist system, and changing in imperialism's favor the correlation of forces in Europe....

That is why we believe that a decisive rebuff of the anticommunist forces, and decisive efforts for the preservation of the socialist system in Czechoslovakia are not only your task but ours as well....

We express the conviction that the Communist Party of Czechoslovakia, conscious of its responsibility, will take the necessary steps to block the path of reaction. In this struggle you can count on the solidarity and all-round assistance of the fraternal socialist countries.

Q *How does Leonid Brezhnev justify the Soviet invasion of Czechoslovakia in 1968? Is his argument persuasive?*

---

based on guaranteed employment and a lack of incentives, bred apathy, complacency, absenteeism, and drunkenness. Agricultural problems added to Soviet economic woes. Bad harvests in the mid-1970s, caused by a series of droughts, heavy rains, and early frosts, forced the Soviet government to buy grain from the West, particularly the United States. To their chagrin, the Soviets were increasingly dependent on capitalist countries.

By the 1970s, the Soviet Union had developed a ruling system that depended on patronage as a major avenue of advancement. Those who aspired to rise in the Communist Party and the state bureaucracy needed the support of successful Party leaders. At the same time, Party and state leaders—as well as leaders of the army and the secret police (KGB)—were granted awards and material privileges. Brezhnev was unwilling to tamper with the Party leadership and state bureaucracy despite the inefficiency and corruption that the system encouraged.

By 1980, the Soviet Union was ailing. A declining economy, a rise in infant mortality rates, a dramatic surge in alcoholism, and a deterioration in working conditions all gave impetus to a decline in morale and a growing perception that the system was foundering. Within the Party, a small group of reformers emerged who understood the real condition of the Soviet Union. One member of this group was Yuri Andropov (1914–1985), head of the KGB and successor to Brezhnev after the latter's death in November 1982. But Andropov was already old and in poor health when he came to power, and he was unable to make any substantive changes. His most significant move may have been his support for a young reformer, Mikhail Gorbachev, who was climbing the rungs of the Party ladder. When Party leaders chose Gorbachev as Party secretary in March 1985, a new era began (see Chapter 30).

Conformity in Eastern Europe

As we saw in Chapter 28, the attempt of the Poles and Hungarians to gain their freedom from Soviet domination had been repressed in 1956. This year of discontent had consequences, however. Soviet leaders now recognized that Moscow could maintain control over its satellites in Eastern Europe only by granting them leeway

to adopt domestic policies appropriate to local conditions. As a result, Eastern European Communist leaders now adopted reform programs to make socialism more acceptable to their subject populations.

In Poland, continued worker unrest led to the rise of the independent labor movement called Solidarity. Led by Lech Walesa (b. 1943), Solidarity represented 10 million of Poland's 35 million people. With the support of the workers, many intellectuals, and the Catholic Church, Solidarity was able to win a series of concessions. The Polish government seemed powerless to stop the flow of concessions until December 1981, when it arrested Walesa and other Solidarity leaders, outlawed the union, and imposed military rule.

The government of János Kádár (1912–1989) in Hungary enacted the most far-reaching reforms in Eastern Europe. In the early 1960s, Kadar legalized small private enterprises, such as retail stores, restaurants, and artisan shops. His economic reforms were termed "Communism with a capitalist facelift." Under his leadership, Hungary moved slowly away from its strict adherence to Soviet dominance and even established fairly friendly relations with the West.

The Prague Spring   Czechoslovakia did not share in the thaw of the mid-1950s and remained under the rule of Antonin Novotny (1904–1975), who had been placed in power by Stalin himself. By the late 1960s, however, Novotny had alienated many members of his own party and was particularly resented by Czechoslovakia's writers, such as the playwright Vaclav Havel (b. 1936). A writers' rebellion late in 1967, in fact, led to Novotny's resignation.

CHRONOLOGY The Soviet Bloc

Era of Brezhnev	1964–1982
Rule of Ceaușescu in Romania	1965–1989
Prague Spring	1968
Honecker succeeds Ulbricht in East Germany	1971
Emergence of Solidarity in Poland	1980
Gorbachev comes to power in the Soviet Union	1985

In January 1968, Alexander Dubček (1921–1992) was elected first secretary of the Communist Party and soon introduced a number of reforms, including freedom of speech and the press, freedom to travel abroad, and a relaxation of secret police activities. Dubček hoped to create "communism with a human face." A period of euphoria erupted that came to be known as the "Prague Spring."

It proved short-lived. The euphoria had led many to call for more far-reaching reforms, including neutrality and withdrawal from the Soviet bloc. To forestall the spreading of this "spring" fever, the Red Army invaded Czechoslovakia in August 1968 and crushed the reform movement. Gustav Husák (1913–1991), a committed nonreformist, replaced Dubček, abolished his reforms, and reestablished the old order.

Repression in East Germany and Romania

Elsewhere in Eastern Europe, Stalinist policies continued to hold sway. In the early 1950s, the ruling Communist government in East Germany, led by Walter Ulbricht, had consolidated its position and become a faithful Soviet satellite. Industry was nationalized and agriculture collectivized. After a workers' revolt in 1953 was crushed by Soviet tanks, a steady flight of East Germans to West Germany ensued, primarily through the divided city of Berlin. This exodus of mostly skilled laborers created economic problems and led the East German government in 1961 to build the infamous Berlin Wall separating West from East Berlin, as well as equally fearsome barriers along the entire border with West Germany.

After building the wall, East Germany succeeded in developing the strongest economy among the Soviet Union's Eastern European satellites. In 1971, Ulbricht was succeeded by Erich Honecker (1912–1992), a party hard-liner who made use of the Stasi, the secret police, to rule with an iron fist for the next eighteen years. By 1989, there was one Stasi officer for every 165 people in East Germany. Prosperity (by 1980, East Germany had the tenth-largest economy in the world) and repression were the two mainstays of East Germany's stability.

© Bettmann/CORBIS

Soviet Invasion of Czechoslovakia, 1968.   The attempt of Alexander Dubček, the new first secretary of the Communist Party, to liberalize Communist rule in Czechoslovakia failed when Soviet troops invaded and crushed the reform movement. This photograph shows a Czech youth climbing aboard a Russian tank during demonstrations near the Prague radio station on August 21.

Repression was also an important part of Romania's postwar history. By 1948, with Soviet assistance, the Communist People's Democratic Front had assumed complete power in Romania. In 1965, leadership of the Communist government passed into the hands of Nicolae Ceaușescu (1918–1989), who with his wife, Elena, established a rigid and dictatorial regime. Ceaușescu ruled Romania with an iron grip, using a secret police force—the Securitate—as his personal weapon against dissent.

Western Europe: The Winds of Change

After two decades of incredible economic growth, Europe experienced severe economic recessions in 1973–1974 and 1979–1983. Both inflation and unemployment rose dramatically. A substantial increase in the price of oil in 1973 was a major cause for the first downturn. But other factors were present as well. A worldwide recession had led to a decline in demand for European goods, and in Europe itself, the reconstruction of many European cities after their devastation in World War II had largely been completed. The economies of the Western European states recovered in the course of the 1980s, although problems remained.

West Germany

After the Adenauer era, West German voters moved politically from the center-right politics of the Christian Democrats to center-left politics, and in 1969, the Social Democrats became the leading party. By forming a ruling coalition with the small Free Democratic Party (FPD), the Social Democrats remained in power until 1982. The first Social Democratic chancellor was Willy Brandt (1913–1992). Brandt was especially successful with his "opening toward the east" (known as *Ostpolitik*), for which he received the Nobel Peace Prize in 1972. On March 19, 1971, Brandt met with Walter Ulbricht, the leader of East Germany, and worked out the details of a treaty that was signed in 1972. This agreement did not establish full diplomatic relations with East Germany but did call for "good neighborly" relations. As a result, it led to greater cultural, personal, and economic contacts between West and East Germany. Despite this success, the discovery of an East German spy among Brandt's advisers caused his resignation in 1974.

His successor, Helmut Schmidt (b. 1918), was more of a technocrat than a reform-minded socialist and concentrated primarily on the economic problems largely brought about by high oil prices between 1973 and 1975. Schmidt was successful in eliminating a deficit of 10 billion marks in three years. In 1982, when the coalition of Schmidt's Social Democrats with the Free Democrats fell apart over the reduction of social welfare expenditures, the Free Democrats joined with the Christian Democratic Union of Helmut Kohl (b. 1930) to form a new government.

Great Britain: Thatcher and Thatcherism

Between 1964 and 1979, the Conservative and Labour Parties alternated in power. Neither could solve the problem of fighting between Catholics and Protestants in Northern Ireland. Violence increased as the Irish Republican Army (IRA) staged a series of dramatic terrorist acts in response to the suspension of Northern Ireland's parliament in 1972 and the establishment of direct rule by London. Nor was either party able to deal with Britain's ailing economy. Failure to modernize made British industry less and less competitive. Moreover, Britain was hampered by frequent labor strikes, many of them caused by conflicts between rival labor unions.

In 1979, after Britain's economic problems had seemed to worsen during five years under a Labour government, the Conservatives returned to power under Margaret Thatcher (b. 1925). She became the first woman to serve as prime minister in British history (see the box on p. 918). Thatcher pledged to lower taxes, reduce government bureaucracy, limit social welfare, restrict union power, and end inflation. The "Iron Lady," as she was called, did break the power of the labor unions. Although she did not eliminate the basic components of the

Margaret Thatcher. Great Britain's first female prime minister, Margaret Thatcher was a strong leader who dominated British politics in the 1980s. This picture of Thatcher was taken during a meeting with French president François Mitterrand in 1986.

MARGARET THATCHER: ENTERING A MAN'S WORLD

In 1979, Margaret Thatcher became the first woman to serve as Britain's prime minister and went on to be its longest-serving prime minister as well. In this excerpt from her autobiography, Thatcher describes how she was interviewed by Conservative Party officials when they first considered her as a possible candidate for Parliament. Thatcher ran for Parliament for the first time in 1950; she lost but did increase the Conservative vote total in the district by 50 percent over the previous election.

Margaret Thatcher, *The Path to Power*

And, as always with me, there was politics. I immediately joined the Conservative Association and threw myself into the usual round of Party activities. In particular, I thoroughly enjoyed what was called the " '39–'45" discussion group, where Conservatives of the war generation met to exchange views and argue about the political topics of the day.... It was as a representative of the Oxford University Graduate Conservative Association (OUGCA) that I went to the Llandudno Conservative Party Conference in October 1948.

It had originally been intended that I should speak at the Conference, seconding an OUGCA motion deploring the abolition of university seats. At that time universities had separate representation in Parliament, and graduates had the right to vote in their universities as well as in the constituency where they lived. (I supported separate university representation, but not the principle that graduates should have more than one vote....) It would have been my first Conference speech, but in the end the seconder chosen was a City man, because the City seats were also to be abolished.

My disappointment at this was, however, very quickly overcome and in a most unexpected way. After one of the debates, I found myself engaged in one of those speculative conversations which young people have about their future prospects. An Oxford friend, John Grant, said he supposed that one day I would like to be a Member of Parliament. "Well, yes," I replied, "but there's not much hope of that. The chances of my being selected are just nil at the moment." I might have added that with no private income of my own there was no way I could have afforded to be an MP on the salary then available. I had not even tried to get on the Party's list of approved candidates.

Later in the day, John Grant happened to be sitting next to the Chairman of the Dartford Conservative Association, John Miller. The Association was in search of a candidate. I learned afterwards that the conversation went something like this: "I understand that you're still looking for a candidate at Dartford?"...

"That's right. Any suggestions?"

"Well, there's a young woman, Margaret Roberts, that you might look at. She's very good."

"Oh, but Dartford is a real industrial stronghold. I don't think a woman would do at all."

"Well, you know best of course. But why not just look at her?"

And they did. I was invited to have lunch with John Miller and his wife, Phee, and the Dartford Woman's Chairman, Mrs. Fletcher, on the Saturday on Llandudno Pier. Presumably, and in spite of any reservations about the suitability of a woman candidate for their seat, they liked what they saw. I certainly got on well with them....

I did not hear from Dartford until December, when I was asked to attend an interview at Palace Chambers, Bridge Street.... Very few outside the political arena know just how nerve-racking such occasions are. The interviewee who is not nervous and tense is very likely to perform badly: for, as any chemist will tell you, the adrenaline needs to flow if one is to perform at one's best....

I found myself short-listed, and was asked to go to Dartford itself for a further interview.... As one of five would-be candidates, I had to give a fifteen-minute speech and answer questions for a further ten minutes.

It was the questions which were more likely to cause me trouble. There was a good deal of suspicion of woman candidates, particularly in what was regarded as a tough industrial seat like Dartford. This was quite definitely a man's world into which not just angels feared to tread....

The most reliable sign that a political occasion has gone well is that you have enjoyed it. I enjoyed that evening at Dartford, and the outcome justified my confidence. I was selected.

Q *In this account, is Margaret Thatcher's being a woman more important to her or to others? Why would this disparity exist?*

---

social welfare system, she did use austerity measures to control inflation. "Thatcherism," as her economic policy was termed, improved the British economic situation, but at a price. The south of England, for example, prospered, but the old industrial areas of the Midlands and north declined and were beset by high unemployment, poverty, and sporadic violence. Cutbacks in education seriously undermined the quality of British education, long regarded as among the world's finest.

In the area of foreign policy, Thatcher, like Ronald Reagan in the United States, took a hard-line approach toward communism. She oversaw a large military buildup aimed at replacing older technology and reestablishing Britain as a world police officer. In 1982, when Argentina attempted to take control of the Falkland Islands (one of Britain's few remaining colonial outposts; known to Argentines as the Malvinas) 300 miles off its coast, the British successfully rebuffed the Argentines, although at considerable economic cost and the loss of 255 lives. The Falklands War, however, did generate popular support for Thatcher, as many in Britain reveled in memories of the nation's glorious imperial past. In truth, however, in a world still dominated by two superpowers—the United States and the Soviet Union—Britain was no longer a world power.

Uncertainties in France

The worsening of France's economic situation in the 1970s brought a shift to the left politically. By 1981, the Socialists had become the dominant party in the National Assembly, and the Socialist leader, François Mitterrand (1916–1995), was elected president. His first concern was with France's economic difficulties. In 1982, Mitterrand froze prices and wages in the hope of reducing the huge budget deficit and high inflation. He also passed a number of liberal measures to aid workers: an increased minimum wage, expanded social benefits, a mandatory fifth week of paid vacation for salaried workers, a thirty-nine-hour workweek, and higher taxes for the rich. Mitterrand's administrative reforms included both centralization (nationalization of banks and industry) and decentralization (granting local governments greater powers). The party's victory had convinced the Socialists that they could enact some of their more radical reforms. Consequently, the government nationalized the steel industry, major banks, the space and electronics industries, and important insurance firms.

The Socialist policies largely failed, however, and within three years, a decline in support for the Socialists caused the Mitterrand government to turn portions of the economy back over to private enterprise. Some economic improvement in the late 1980s enabled Mitterrand to win a second seven-year term in the 1988 presidential elections.

Confusion in Italy

In the 1970s and 1980s, Italy continued to practice the politics of coalitions that had characterized much of its history. Italy witnessed the installation of its fiftieth postwar government in 1991, and its new prime minister, Giulio Andreotti, had already served six times in that office. Italian governments continued to consist of coalitions mostly led by the Christian Democrats.

In the 1980s, even the Communists had been included briefly in the government. The Italian Communists had become advocates of **Eurocommunism,** basically an attempt to broaden communism's support by dropping its Marxist ideology. Although its popularity declined in the 1980s, the Communist Party still garnered 26 percent of the vote in 1987. The Communists also won a number of local elections and took charge of municipal governments in several cities, including Rome and Naples, for a brief time.

In the 1970s, Italy suffered from a severe economic recession. The Italian economy, which depended on imported oil as its chief source of energy, was especially vulnerable to the steep increase in oil prices in 1973. Parallel to the economic problems was a host of political

and social problems: student unrest, mass strikes, and terrorist attacks. In 1978, a former prime minister, Aldo Moro, was kidnapped and killed by the Red Brigades, a terrorist organization. Then, too, there was the all-pervasive and corrupting influence of the Mafia, which had always been an important factor in southern Italy but spread to northern Italy as well in the 1980s. Italy survived the crises of the 1970s and in the 1980s began to experience remarkable economic growth. But severe problems remained.

The European Community

After 1970, Western European states continued to pursue the goal of integrating their economies. Beginning with six states in 1957, the European Economic Community expanded in 1973 when Great Britain, Ireland, and Denmark joined what its members now renamed the European Community (EC). Greece joined in 1981, followed by Spain and Portugal in 1986. The economic integration of the members of the EC led to cooperative efforts in international and political affairs as well. The foreign ministers of the twelve members consulted frequently and provided a common front in negotiations on important issues.

The United States: Turmoil and Tranquillity

With the election of Richard Nixon (1913–1994) as president in 1968, American politics made a shift to the right. Nixon ended American involvement in Vietnam by 1973 by gradually withdrawing American troops. Politically, he pursued a "southern strategy," carefully calculating that "law and order" issues and a slowdown in racial desegregation would appeal to southern whites. The South, which had once been a Democratic stronghold, began to form a new allegiance to the Republican Party. The Republican strategy also gained support among white Democrats in northern cities, where court-mandated busing to achieve racial integration had led to a backlash among whites.

As president, Nixon was paranoid about conspiracies and began to use illegal methods to gather intelligence on his political opponents. One of the president's advisers explained that their intention was to "use the available federal machinery to screw our political enemies." Nixon's zeal led to the Watergate scandal—the attempted bugging of Democratic National Headquarters, located in the Watergate apartment and hotel complex in Washington, D.C. Although Nixon repeatedly lied to the American public about his involvement in the affair, secret tapes of his own conversations in the White House revealed the truth. On August 9, 1974, Nixon resigned the presidency rather than face possible impeachment and then trial by the U.S. Congress.

Economic Problems   After Watergate, American domestic politics focused on economic issues. Vice President Gerald Ford (1913–2006) became president when Nixon resigned, only to lose in the 1976 election to the former governor of Georgia, Jimmy Carter (b. 1924). Both Ford and Carter faced severe economic problems. The period from 1973 to the mid-1980s was one of economic stagnation, which came to be known as **stagflation**—a combination of high inflation and high unemployment. In part, the economic downturn stemmed from a dramatic change in oil prices. Oil was considered a cheap and abundant source of energy in the 1950s, and Americans had grown dependent on imported oil from the Middle East. But an oil embargo and price increases by the Organization of Petroleum Exporting Countries (OPEC) as a result of the Arab-Israeli War in 1973 quadrupled oil prices. Additional price hikes increased oil prices twentyfold by the end of the 1970s, encouraging inflationary tendencies throughout the economy.

By 1980, the Carter administration faced two devastating problems. High inflation and a noticeable decline in average weekly earnings were causing a drop in American living standards. At the same time, a crisis abroad had erupted when fifty-three Americans were taken hostage by the Iranian government of Ayatollah Khomeini. Carter's inability to gain the release of the hostages led to perceptions at home that he was a weak president. His overwhelming loss to Ronald Reagan (1911–2004) in the election of 1980 enabled the chief exponent of right-wing Republican policies to assume the presidency and initiate a new political order.

The Reagan Revolution   The Reagan Revolution, as it has been called, consisted of a number of new policies. Reversing decades of increased spending on social welfare, Reagan cut back on the welfare state by reducing spending on food stamps, school lunch programs, and job programs. At the same time, his administration fostered the largest peacetime military buildup in American history. Total federal spending rose from $631 billion in 1981 to over $1 trillion by 1986. But instead of raising taxes to pay for the new expenditures, which far outweighed the budget cuts in social areas, Reagan convinced Congress to rely on "supply-side economics." Massive tax cuts would supposedly stimulate rapid economic growth and produce new revenues. Much of the tax cut went to the wealthy. Reagan's policies seemed to work in the short run as the United States experienced an economic upturn that lasted until the end of the 1980s. The spending

policies of the Reagan administration, however, also produced record government deficits, which loomed as an obstacle to long-term growth. In the 1970s, the total deficit was $420 billion. Between 1981 and 1987, Reagan's budget deficits were three times that amount.

Canada

In 1963, during a major economic recession, the Liberals had been returned to power in Canada. The most prominent Liberal government was that of Pierre Trudeau (1919–2000), who came to power in 1968. Although French Canadian in background, Trudeau was dedicated to Canada's federal union, and in 1968, his government passed the Official Languages Act that allowed both English and French to be used in the federal civil service. Although Trudeau's government vigorously pushed an industrialization program, high inflation and Trudeau's efforts to impose the will of the federal government on the powerful provincial governments alienated voters and weakened his government. Economic recession in the early 1980s brought Brian Mulroney (b. 1939), leader of the Progressive Conservative Party, to power in 1984.

The Cold War: The Move to Détente

Q **Focus Question:** What were the main events in the Cold War between 1965 and 1985, and how important was the role of détente in those events?

The Cuban Missile Crisis led to the lessening of tensions between the United States and the Soviet Union. But within another year the United States had been drawn into a new confrontation that had an important impact on the Cold War—the Second Vietnam War.

The Second Vietnam War

After Vietnamese forces had defeated their French colonial masters in 1954, Vietnam had been divided. A strongly nationalistic regime in the north under Ho Chi Minh (1890–1969) received Soviet aid, while American sponsors worked to establish a pro-Western regime in South Vietnam. President John F. Kennedy maintained Eisenhower's policy of providing military and financial aid to the regime of Ngo Dinh Diem, the autocratic ruler of South Vietnam. But the Kennedy administration grew increasingly disenchanted with the Diem regime, which was corrupt and seemed incapable of gaining support from the people. From the American point of view, this lack of support simply undermined the ability of the South Vietnamese government to deal with the Vietcong, the South Vietnamese Communist guerrillas backed by the North Vietnamese. In November 1963, the U.S. government supported a military coup that overthrew the Diem regime.

FILM & HISTORY
DR. STRANGELOVE, OR: HOW I LEARNED TO STOP WORRYING AND LOVE THE BOMB (1964)

In 1964, director Stanley Kubrick released *Dr. Strangelove, Or: How I Learned to Stop Worrying and Love the Bomb,* a black comedy about the Cold War and nuclear weapons. The film begins when a general in the U.S. Air Force, Jack D. Ripper (Sterling Hayden), orders a nuclear attack on the Soviet Union because he believes that Communists are secretly poisoning American drinking water with fluoride. The situation becomes critical when efforts to call off Ripper's air strike fail. The Soviet Union, in an attempt to deter such an attack, has created the "Doomsday Device," a computerized defense system that will destroy the earth if triggered. This system, however, is irreversible, and unless Ripper's men are stopped, the entire planet will be consumed by nuclear holocaust.

Numerous communications lapses occur throughout the film, as it satirizes the leadership protocol each nation has implemented to oversee its nuclear arsenal. The president of the United States (Peter Sellers) and the Soviet premier lack the means to fully prevent the pending nuclear war. Meanwhile, the mysterious Dr. Strangelove (also played by Peter Sellers), a German physicist and adviser to the president, suggests how accidents and misunderstandings could easily cause the destruction of our planet. Even Dr. Strangelove's plan to repopulate the planet fails, as he relies on Nazi ideals and prejudices to select those who will survive.

Kubrick based the film on Peter George's 1958 novel *Red Alert,* a thriller about accidental nuclear war. Written at a time when more than 34,000 nuclear weapons existed, the film pokes fun at military and political leaders and the posturing that resulted from the Cold War arms race. Although it is a parody, *Dr. Strangelove* accurately portrayed American paranoia and policies during the Cold War. Senator Joseph McCarthy and the House Un-American Activities Committee (HUAC) sought out anyone who might be conspiring against America or promoting Communist ideals, and the threat of nuclear attack prompted the creation of numerous bomb shelters and contingency plans. Schoolchildren were trained to hide under their desks in the event of a disaster, and a telephone hotline connected Moscow and Washington, D.C., to ensure communications between the two superpowers.

The military showdown in *Dr. Strangelove* paralleled actual events, in particular the Cuban Missile Crisis of 1962. In the film, General Turgidson (George C. Scott) suggests that a preemptive nuclear strike would catch the Soviets by surprise. "We would therefore prevail," declares Turgidson, "and suffer only modest and acceptable civilian casualties from their remaining force which would be badly damaged and uncoordinated." Turgidson believed that "acceptable" casualties would number "no more than 10 to 20 million killed," an irreverent jab at President Kennedy's advisers, who in 1962 recommended attacking Cuba despite the threat of nuclear missiles. The Doomsday

General Turgidson (George C. Scott) with the president (Peter Sellers)

Dr. Strangelove (Peter Sellers)

(continued)

(continued)

Device of *Dr. Strangelove* also mocked the superpowers' attempts at deterrence. Nikita Khrushchev claimed that by placing missiles in Cuba, the Soviets would deter the United States from starting war, and the fictional Doomsday Device was intended to produce a similar effect.

As Dr. Strangelove explained, "Deterrence is the art of producing in the mind of the enemy...the fear to attack." Hailed by one film critic as "arguably the best political satire of the century," *Dr. Strangelove* evoked the fear and anxiety of the Cold War.

The new military government seemed even less able to govern the country, and by early 1965, the Vietcong, their ranks now swelled by military units infiltrating from North Vietnam, were on the verge of seizing control of the entire country. In desperation, President Lyndon Johnson decided to launch bombing raids on the north and to send U.S. combat troops to South Vietnam to prevent a total defeat of the anti-Communist government in Saigon and keep the Communist regime of the north from uniting the entire country under its control. Although nationalism played a powerful role in this conflict, American policy makers saw it in terms of a **domino theory** concerning the spread of communism. If the Communists succeeded in Vietnam, so the argument went, all the other countries in Asia freeing themselves from colonial domination would fall, like dominoes, to communism.

The Vietnam War

Despite their massive superiority in equipment and firepower, U.S. forces failed to prevail over the persistence of the North Vietnamese and especially the Vietcong. These guerrilla forces were extremely effective against American troops. Natives of Vietnam, they were able to live off the land, disappear among the people, and attack when least expected. Many South Vietnamese villagers were so opposed to their own government that they sheltered and supported the Vietcong.

The growing number of American troops sent to Vietnam soon produced a persistent antiwar movement in the United States, especially among college students of draft age. As described earlier, a similar movement also arose in Europe. Although Europeans had generally acquiesced in American leadership of the Cold War, some Europeans recognized the importance of Europe's playing its own role in foreign affairs. Under President Charles de Gaulle, France grew especially critical of U.S. involvement in Vietnam. De Gaulle believed that the Vietnamese should be allowed to live in their own unified country and in 1965 called the United States "the greatest danger in the world today to peace." After President Johnson escalated the American war effort, antiwar protests broke out all over France in 1966 and 1967 and soon spread throughout Europe.

The mounting destruction and increasing brutalization of the war, brought into American homes every evening on television, also turned American public opinion against the war. Finally, in 1973, President Richard Nixon reached an agreement with North Vietnam

The Second Vietnam War. Between 1965 and 1973, U.S. troops fought against Vietcong guerrillas and North Vietnamese regular forces until they were finally withdrawn as a result of the Paris Agreement reached in January 1973. Shown here are U.S. troops after a Vietcong attack. The helicopter that is arriving would soon remove the American wounded from the battlefield.

that allowed the United States to withdraw its forces. Within two years, Vietnam had been forcibly reunited by Communist armies from the North.

Despite the success of the North Vietnamese Communists, the domino theory proved unfounded. A noisy rupture between Communist China and the Soviet Union put an end to the idea of a monolithic communism directed by Moscow. Under President Nixon, American relations with China were resumed. New nations in Southeast Asia also managed to avoid Communist governments. Above all, Vietnam helped show the limitations of American power. By the end of the Second Vietnam War, a new era in American-Soviet relations, known as **détente,** had begun to emerge.

China and the Cold War

The Johnson administration had sent U.S. combat troops to South Vietnam in 1965 in an effort to prevent the expansion of communism in Southeast Asia. The primary concern of the United States, however, was not the Soviet Union but Communist China. By the mid-1960s, U.S. officials viewed the Soviet Union as an essentially conservative power, more concerned with protecting its vast empire than with expanding its borders. Mao Zedong's attempt to create a totally classless society had received much attention, and, despite his failures with the Great Leap Forward (see Chapter 28), he now launched China on an even more dramatic forced march toward communism.

The Great Proletarian Cultural Revolution

Mao was convinced that only an atmosphere of constant revolutionary fervor could enable the Chinese to overcome the past and achieve the final stage of communism. Accordingly, in 1966 he unleashed the Red Guards, revolutionary units composed of unhappy Communist Party members and discontented young people who were urged to take to the streets to cleanse Chinese society of impure elements guilty of taking the capitalist road. Schools, universities, factories, and even government ministries were all subject to the scrutiny of the Red Guards. This so-called Great Proletarian Cultural Revolution (literally, the Chinese name translates as "great revolution to create a proletarian culture") lasted for ten years, from 1966 to 1976. Red Guards set out across the nation to eliminate the "four olds"—old ideas, old culture, old customs, and old habits (see the box on p. 924). They destroyed temples, books written by foreigners, and jazz records. They tore down street signs and replaced them with ones carrying revolutionary names. Destruction of property was matched by vicious attacks on individuals who had supposedly deviated from Mao's

thought. Those accused were humiliated at public meetings where they were forced to admit their "crimes." Many were brutally beaten, often to death.

Mao found, however, that it was not easy to maintain a constant mood of revolutionary enthusiasm. Key groups, including Party members, urban professionals, and many military officers, did not share Mao's desire for "permanent revolution." People began to turn against the movement, and in September 1976, when Mao died, a group of practical-minded reformers seized power from the radicals and adopted a more rational approach to China's problems.

U.S.-China Relations For years U.S. policy toward Communist China was determined by American fears of Communist expansion in Asia. Already in 1950, the Truman administration had adopted a new national policy that implied that the United States would take whatever steps were necessary to stem expansion of communism in the region, a policy that Truman invoked

The Great Proletarian Cultural Revolution. The Cultural Revolution, which began in 1966, was a massive effort by Mao Zedong and his radical supporters to eliminate rival elements within the Chinese Communist Party and achieve the final stage of communism—a classless society. Shown here in front of a picture of Chairman Mao Zedong is a group of Chinese children in uniform holding Mao's *Little Red Book* (a collection of Mao's thoughts that became a sort of bible for Chinese Communists) during the Cultural Revolution in 1968.

THE FURY OF THE RED GUARDS

In 1966, Mao Zedong unleashed the fury of the Red Guards on all levels of society, exposing anti-Maoist elements, suspected "capitalists," and those identified with the previous ruling class. In this excerpt, Nien Cheng, the widow of an official of Chiang Kai-shek's regime, describes a visit by Red Guards to her home during the height of the Cultural Revolution.

Nien Cheng, *Life and Death in Shanghai*

Suddenly the doorbell began to ring incessantly. At the same time, there was furious pounding of many fists on my front gate, accompanied by the confused sound of hysterical voices shouting slogans. The cacophony told me that the time of waiting was over and that I must face the threat of the Red Guards and the destruction of my home....

Outside, the sound of voices became louder. "Open the gate! Open the gate! Are you all dead? Why don't you open the gate?" Someone was swearing and kicking the wooden gate. The horn of the truck was blasting too....

I stood up to put the book on the shelf. A copy of the Constitution of the People's Republic caught my eye. Taking it in my hand and picking up the bunch of keys I had ready on my desk, I went downstairs.

At the same moment, the Red Guards pushed open the front door and entered the house. There were thirty or forty senior high school students, aged between fifteen and twenty, led by two men and one woman much older.

The leading Red Guard, a gangling youth with angry eyes, stepped forward and said to me, "We are the Red Guards. We have come to take revolutionary action against you!"

Though I knew it was futile, I held up the copy of the Constitution, and said calmly, "It's against the Constitution of the People's Republic of China to enter a private house without a search warrant."

The young man snatched the document out of my hand and threw it on the floor. With his eyes blazing, he said, "The Constitution is abolished. It was a document written by the Revisionists within the Communist Party. We recognize only the teachings of our Great Leader Chairman Mao."...

Another young man used a stick to smash the mirror hanging over the blackwood chest facing the front door.

Mounting the stairs, I was astonished to see several Red Guards taking pieces of my porcelain collection out of their padded boxes. One young man had arranged a set of four Kangxi wine cups in a row on the floor and was stepping on them. I was just in time to hear the crunch of delicate porcelain under the sole of his shoe. The sound pierced my heart. Impulsively I leapt forward and caught his leg just as he raised his foot to crush the next cup. He toppled. We fell in a heap together.... The other Red Guards dropped what they were doing and gathered around us, shouting at me angrily for interfering in their revolutionary activities.

The young man whose revolutionary work of destruction I had interrupted said angrily, "You shut up! These things belong to the old culture. They are useless toys of the feudal emperors and the modern capitalist class and have no significance to us, the proletarian class. They cannot be compared to the cameras and binoculars, which are useful for our struggle in time of war. Our Great Leader Chairman Mao taught us, 'If we destroy, we cannot establish.' The old culture must be destroyed to make way for the new socialist culture."

Q *What were the tactics of the Red Guards? To what degree did they succeed in remaking the character of the Chinese people?*

---

when he sent troops to Korea in 1950 (see "The Korean War" in Chapter 28). The Second Vietnam War raised additional concerns about Communist China's intentions.

President Richard Nixon, however, opened a new door in American relations when he visited China and met with Mao Zedong in 1972. Despite Nixon's reputation as a devout anti-Communist, the visit was a success as the two leaders agreed to put aside their most bitter differences in an effort to reduce tensions in Asia. During the 1970s, Chinese-American relations continued to improve. In 1979, diplomatic ties were established between the two countries, and by the end of the 1970s, China and the United States had forged a "strategic relationship" in which they would cooperate against the threat of Soviet intervention in Asia.

The Practice of Détente

By the 1970s, American-Soviet relations had entered a new phase known as détente, marked by a reduction of tensions between the two superpowers. An appropriate symbol of détente was the Antiballistic Missile Treaty, signed in 1972, in which the two nations agreed to limit their systems for launching antiballistic missiles (ABMs). The U.S. objective in pursuing the treaty was to make it unlikely that either superpower could win a nuclear exchange by launching a preemptive strike against the other. U.S. officials believed that a policy of "equivalence," in which there was a roughly equal power balance on each side, was the best way to avoid a nuclear confrontation.

In 1975, the Helsinki Agreements provided yet another example of reduced tensions between the superpowers. Signed by the United States, Canada, and all European nations, these accords recognized all borders that had been established in Europe since the end of World War II, thereby acknowledging the Soviet sphere of influence in Eastern Europe. The Helsinki Agreements also committed the signatory powers to recognize and protect the human rights of their citizens.

The Limits of Détente

This protection of human rights became one of the major foreign policy goals of the next American president, Jimmy Carter. Although hopes ran high for the continuation of détente, the Soviet invasion of Afghanistan in 1979, undertaken to restore a pro-Soviet regime, hardened relations between the United States and the Soviet Union. President Carter canceled American participation in the 1980 Olympic Games in Moscow and placed an embargo on the shipment of American grain to the Soviet Union.

The early administration of President Ronald Reagan witnessed a return to the harsh rhetoric, if not all of the harsh practices, of the Cold War. Calling the Soviet Union an "evil empire," Reagan began a military buildup that stimulated a renewed arms race. In 1982, the Reagan administration introduced the nuclear-tipped cruise missile, whose ability to fly at low altitudes made it difficult to detect. President Reagan also became an ardent proponent of the Strategic Defense Initiative (SDI), nicknamed "Star Wars." Its purpose was to create a space shield that could destroy incoming missiles.

By providing military support to the anti-Soviet insurgents in Afghanistan, the Reagan administration helped maintain a Vietnam-like war in Afghanistan that would embed the Soviet Union in its own quagmire. Like the Second Vietnam War, the conflict in Afghanistan resulted in heavy casualties and demonstrated that the influence of a superpower was limited in the face of strong nationalist, guerrilla-type opposition.

Society and Culture in the Western World

Q **Focus Question:** What were the major social and cultural developments in the Western world between 1965 and 1985?

Dramatic social and cultural developments accompanied political and economic changes after 1965. Scientific and technological achievements revolutionized people's lives, while at the same time environmental problems were becoming increasingly apparent. Intellectually and culturally, the Western world after 1965 was notable for its diversity and innovation. New directions led some observers to speak of a postmodern cultural world.

The World of Science and Technology

Before World War II, theoretical science and technology were largely separated. Pure science was the domain of university professors who were far removed from the practical technological concerns of technicians and engineers. But during World War II, university scientists were recruited to work for their governments and develop new weapons and practical instruments of war. British physicists played a crucial role in the development of an improved radar system in 1940 that helped defeat the German air force in the Battle of Britain. German scientists created self-propelled rockets and jet airplanes to keep Hitler's hopes alive for a miraculous turnaround in the war. The computer, too, was a wartime creation. The British mathematician Alan Turing designed a primitive computer to assist British intelligence in breaking the secret codes of German ciphering machines. The most famous product of wartime scientific research was the atomic bomb, created by a team of American and European scientists under the guidance of the American physicist J. Robert Oppenheimer. Obviously, most wartime devices were created for destructive purposes, but merely to mention computers and jet airplanes demonstrates that they could easily be adapted for peacetime uses.

The sponsorship of research by governments and the military during World War II created a new scientific model. Science had become very complex, and only large organizations with teams of scientists, huge laboratories, and complex equipment could undertake such large-scale projects. Such facilities were so expensive that they could only be provided by governments and large corporations.

There was no more stunning example of how the new scientific establishment operated than the space race of the 1960s. The announcement by the Soviets in 1957 that they had sent the first space satellite, *Sputnik,* into orbit around the earth caused the United States to launch a gigantic project to land a manned spacecraft on the moon within a decade. Massive government funds financed the scientific research and technological advances that attained this goal in 1969, an achievement that was greeted by some with great expectations for the future of humanity. One *New York Times* editorialist wrote:

> It will take years, decades, perhaps centuries, for man to colonize even the moon, but that is the end inherent in Armstrong's first step on extraterrestrial soil. Serious and hardheaded scientists envision, even in the not remote future, lunar communities capable of growing into domed cities subsisting on hydroponically grown food, of developing the moon's resources, and eventually of acquiring a breathable atmosphere and a soil capable of being farmed. What with the dire threats of population explosion at best and nuclear explosion at worst, the human race, as Sir Bernard Lovell warns, may find itself sometime in the 21st century "having to consider how best to insure the survival of the species."[4]

The Computer The alliance of science and technology has led to an accelerated rate of change that has become a fact of life in Western society. One product of this alliance—the computer—may be the most revolutionary of all the technological inventions of the twentieth century. Early computers, which required thousands of vacuum tubes to function, were large and took up considerable space. An important figure in the development of the early computer was Grace Hopper (1906–1992), a career Navy officer. Hopper was instrumental in inventing COBOL, a computer language that enabled computers to respond to words as well as numbers.

On the Moon. The first landing on the moon in 1969 was one of the great technological achievements of the twentieth century. The picture shows astronaut James Irwin shortly after the he raised the American flag during a moonwalk in 1971. The lunar module and lunar rover are also visible in the picture.

Courtesy of NASA

The development of the transistor and then the silicon chip produced a revolutionary new approach to computers. In 1971, the invention of the microprocessor, a machine that combines the equivalent of thousands of transistors on a single, tiny silicon chip, opened the road for the development of the personal computer.

New Conception of the Universe After World War II, a number of physicists continued to explore the implications of Einstein's revolution in physics and raised fundamental questions about the nature of reality. To some physicists, quantum and relativity theory described the universe as a complicated web of relations in which there were no isolated building blocks. Thus, the universe was not a "collection of physical objects" but a complicated web of relations between "various parts of a unified whole." Moreover, this web of relations that is the universe also included the human observer. Human beings could not be objective observers of objects detached from themselves because the very act of observation made them participants in the process. These speculations implied that the old Newtonian conception of the universe as a machine was an outdated tool for understanding the nature of the universe.

Dangers of Science and Technology Despite the marvels that were produced by the alliance of science and technology, some people came to question the underlying assumption of this alliance—that scientific knowledge gave human beings the ability to manipulate the environment for their benefit. They maintained that some technological advances had far-reaching side effects damaging to the environment. For example, the chemical fertilizers that were touted for producing larger crops

wreaked havoc with the ecological balance of streams, rivers, and woodlands. *Small Is Beautiful,* written by the British economist E. F. Schumacher (1911–1977), was a fundamental critique of the dangers of the new science and technology (see the box on p. 927). The proliferation of fouled beaches and dying forests and lakes made environmentalism one of the important issues of the late twentieth century.

The Environment and the Green Movements

By the 1970s, serious ecological problems had become all too apparent. Air pollution, produced by nitrogen oxide and sulfur dioxide emissions from road vehicles, power plants, and industrial factories, was causing respiratory illnesses and having corrosive effects on buildings and monuments. Many rivers, lakes, and seas had become so polluted that they posed serious health risks. Dying forests and disappearing wildlife alarmed more and more people. A nuclear power disaster at Chernobyl in the Ukrainian Soviet Socialist Republic in 1986 made Europeans even more aware of potential environmental hazards. The opening of Eastern Europe after the revolutions of 1989 (see Chapter 30) brought to the world's attention the incredible environmental destruction of that region caused by unfettered industrial pollution. Environmental concerns forced the major political parties in Europe to advocate new regulations for the protection of the environment.

Growing ecological awareness also gave rise to the Green movements and Green parties that emerged throughout Europe in the 1970s. The origins of these movements were by no means uniform. Some came from the antinuclear movement; others arose out of such causes as women's liberation and concerns for foreign workers. Most started at the local level and then gradually expanded to include activities at the national level, where they became formally organized as political parties. Green parties competed successfully in Sweden, Austria, and Switzerland. Most visible was the Green Party in Germany, which was officially organized in 1979 and by 1987 had elected forty-two delegates to the West German parliament. In 1998, when the Green Party became a coalition partner with the Socialists under Gerhard Schroeder, one of the Green Party members, Joschka Fischer, became the nation's foreign minister.

Although the Green movements and parties have played an important role in making people aware of ecological problems, they have not replaced the traditional political parties, as some political analysts in the mid-1980s forecast. For one thing, the coalitions that made up the Greens found it difficult to agree on all issues and tended to splinter into different cliques. Moreover, traditional political parties co-opted the

The Limits of Modern Technology

Although science and technology have produced an amazing array of achievements in the postwar world, some voices have been raised in criticism of their sometimes destructive aspects. In 1975, in his book *Small Is Beautiful,* the British economist E. F. Schumacher examined the effects modern industrial technology has had on the earth's resources.

E. F. Schumacher, *Small Is Beautiful*

Is it not evident that our current methods of production are already eating into the very substance of industrial man? To many people this is not at all evident. Now that we have solved the problem of production, they say, have we ever had it so good? Are we not better fed, better clothed, and better housed than ever before—and better educated? Of course we are: most, but by no means all, of us: in the rich countries. But this is not what I mean by "substance." The substance of man cannot be measured by Gross National Product. Perhaps it cannot be measured at all, except for certain symptoms of loss. However, this is not the place to go into the statistics of these symptoms, such as crime, drug addiction, vandalism, mental breakdown, rebellion, and so forth. Statistics never prove anything.

I started by saying that one of the most fateful errors of our age is the belief that the problem of production has been solved. This illusion, I suggested, is mainly due to our inability to recognize that the modern industrial system, with all its intellectual sophistication, consumes the very basis on which it has been erected. To use the language of the economist, it lives on irreplaceable capital which it cheerfully treats as income. I specified three categories of such capital: fossil fuels, the tolerance margins of nature, and the human substance. Even if some readers should refuse to accept all three parts of my argument, I suggest that any one of them suffices to make my case.

And what is my case? Simply that our most important task is to get off our present collision course. And who is there to tackle such a task? I think every one of us.... To talk about the future is useful only if it leads to action *now.* And what can we do *now,* while we are still in the position of "never having had it so good"? To say the least...we must thoroughly understand the problem and begin to see the possibility of evolving a new life-style, with new methods of production and new patterns of consumption: a lifestyle designed for permanence. To give only three preliminary examples: in agriculture and horticulture, we can interest ourselves in the perfection of production methods which are biologically sound, build up soil fertility, and produce health, beauty and permanence. Productivity will then look after itself. In industry, we can interest ourselves in the evolution of small-scale technology, relatively non-violent technology, "technology with a human face," so that people have a chance to enjoy themselves while they are working, instead of working solely for their pay packet and hoping, usually forlornly, for enjoyment solely during their leisure time.

Q *What was Schumacher's critique of modern technology? To what extent has this critique been substantiated by developments since 1975?*

---

environmental issues of the Greens. More and more European governments began to sponsor projects to safeguard the environment and clean up the worst sources of pollution.

Postmodern Thought

The term *Postmodern* covers a variety of artistic and intellectual styles and ways of thinking prominent since the 1970s. In the broadest sense, **Postmodernism** rejects the modern Western belief in an objective truth and instead focuses on the relative nature of reality and knowledge. Human knowledge is defined by a number of factors that must be constantly revised and tested by human experiences.

While existentialism wrestled with notions of meaning and existence, a group of French philosophers in the 1960s attempted to understand how meaning and knowledge operate through the study of language and signs. In the early twentieth century, the Swiss language scholar Ferdinand de Saussure (1857–1913) gave birth to structuralism by asserting that the very nature of signs is arbitrary and that language is a human construct. And though the external world has existed for ages, de Saussure believed that humans possessed no capacity for knowledge until language was devised. Language employs signs to denote meaning and, according to de Saussure, possesses two components: the *signifier,* the expression of a concept, and the *signified,* its meaning. For de Saussure, meaning seeks expression in language, although the reliance on language for knowledge suggested that such meaning is learned rather than preexisting.

Jacques Derrida (1930–2004) drew on the ideas of de Saussure to demonstrate how dependent Western culture is on binary oppositions. In Western thought, one set of oppositions is generally favored over the other (in the case of de Saussure, speech was favored over writing), but Derrida showed that the privileged depends on the inferior. Rather than reversing the opposition and claiming that writing surpasses speech, for example, Derrida showed that spelling often altered pronunciation. This indebtedness to written language demonstrates that oral speech is not superior. **Poststructuralism,** or **deconstruction,** which Derrida formulated, believes that culture is created and can therefore be analyzed in a variety of ways, according to the manner in which people create their own meaning. Hence, there is no fixed truth or universal meaning.

Michel Foucault (1926–1984) likewise drew upon de Saussure and Derrida to explore relationships of power. Believing that "power is exercised, rather than possessed," Foucault argued that the diffusion of power and oppression marks all relationships. For example, any act of teaching entails components of assertion and submission, as the student adopts the ideas of the one in power. Therefore, all norms are culturally produced and entail some degree of power struggle. In establishing laws of conduct, society not only creates ideal behavior from those who conform, but it also invents a subclass of individuals who do not conform. In *The History of Sexuality*, Foucault suggested that homosexuality was produced by cultures attempting to define and limit homosexual acts. Yet in seeking to control and delineate homosexuality, those in power established the grounds on which it could be defined and practiced. As such, power ultimately requires resistance for it to exist; otherwise, it loses all meaning.

Trends in Art, Literature, and Music

Beginning in the 1960s and continuing well into the 1980s, styles emerged that some have referred to as "Postmodern." Postmodernism tends to move away from the futurism or "cutting-edge" qualities of Modernism. Instead it favors "tradition," whether that means using earlier styles of painting or elevating traditional crafts to the level of fine art. Weavers, potters, glassmakers, metalsmiths, and furniture makers have gained respect as artists. Postmodern artists and architects frequently blur the distinction between the arts, creating works that include elements of film, performance, popular culture, sculpture, and architecture.

Art   In the 1960s and 1970s, artists often rejected the notion of object-based artworks. Instead, performances and installations that were either too fleeting or too large to appear in the traditional context of a museum were produced. Allen Kaprow (1927–2006) suggested that "happenings," works of art rooted in performance, grew out of Jackson Pollock's process of action painting. Rather than producing abstract paintings, however, Kaprow created events that were not scripted but chance occurrences. These "happenings" often included audience participation. Kaprow's emphasis on the relationship of art to its surroundings was continued in the "land art" of the early 1970s. In one such example, *Spiral Jetty* (1970), Robert Smithson (1938–1973) used a bulldozer to move more than 6,000 tons

Art © Estate of Robert Smithson/Licensed by VAGA, New York, NY/Photo © George Steinmetz/CORBIS

Robert Smithson, *Spiral Jetty*.   Built on an abandoned industrial site, *Spiral Jetty* disappears and reappears according to the rise and fall of the Great Salt Lake's water level. As seen in this 2002 photograph, the surface has become encrusted in salt as drought has lowered the lake level. Robert Smithson filmed the construction of *Spiral Jetty*, carefully noting the various geological formations included in his creation. Earthworks like *Spiral Jetty* increased in number as the welfare of the world's ecosystems became a growing concern in the 1960s and 1970s.

Charles Moore, *Piazza d'Italia.* Dedicated to the Italian communities of New Orleans, *Piazza d'Italia* includes a schematic map of Italy on its pavement. The architect, Charles Moore, combined elements from Italy's rich cultural past, such as Roman columns and Renaissance Baroque colonnades, with modern materials like neon lighting and stainless steel to create an eclectic Postmodern plaza.

of earth into a 1,500-foot-long corkscrew in Utah's Great Salt Lake. Responding to the founding of the Environmental Protection Agency as well as to the cycles of nature, Smithson's artwork resembled a science-fiction wasteland while challenging notions of traditional fine art.

Postmodernism's eclectic mixing of past tradition with Modernist innovation became increasingly evident in architecture. Robert Venturi (b. 1925) argued that architects should look as much to the commercial strips of Las Vegas as to the historical styles of the past for inspiration. Venturi advocated an architecture of "complexity and contradiction" as appropriate for the diversity of experiences offered by contemporary life. One example is provided by Charles Moore (1929–1993). His *Piazza d'Italia* (1976–1980) in New Orleans is an outdoor plaza that combines classical columns with stainless steel and neon lights. This blending of modern-day materials with historical reference distinguished the Postmodern architecture of the late 1970s and 1980s from the Modernist glass box.

Another Postmodern response to Modernism can be seen in a return to Realism in the arts, a movement called Photorealism. Some Photorealists paint or sculpt with such minute attention to detail that their paintings appear to be photographs and their sculptures living human beings. Their subjects are often ordinary individuals, stuck in ordinary lives, demonstrating the Postmodern emphasis on low culture and the commonplace rather than the ambitious nature of high art. These works were often pessimistic or cynical.

Literature Postmodernism was also evident in literature. In the Western world, the best examples were found in Latin America, in a literary style called "magic realism," and in central and Eastern Europe. Magic realism combined realistic events with dreamlike or fantastic backgrounds. One of the finest examples of magic realism can be found in the novel *One Hundred Years of Solitude,* by Gabriel García Márquez (b. 1928), who won the Nobel Prize for Literature in 1982. The novel is the story of the fictional town of Macondo as seen by several generations of the Buendias, its founding family. The author slips back and forth between fact and fantasy. Villagers are not surprised when a local priest rises into the air and floats. Yet, when wandering Gypsies introduce these villagers to magnets, telescopes, and magnifying glasses, the villagers are dumbfounded by what they see as magic. According to the author, fantasy and fact depend on one's point of view.

The European center of Postmodernism is well represented by the work of the Czech writer Milan Kundera (b. 1929). Like the magic realists of Latin America, Kundera also blended fantasy with realism. Unlike the magic realists, Kundera used fantasy to examine moral issues and remained optimistic about the human condition. Indeed, in his novel, *The Unbearable Lightness of Being* (1984), Kundera does not despair because of the political repression in his native Czechoslovakia that he so aptly describes but allows his characters to use love as a way to a better life. The human spirit can be lessened but not destroyed.

Music Like modern art, modern music has focused on variety and radical experimentation. Also like modern art, modern classical music witnessed a continuation of prewar developments. Some composers, the neo-classicists, remained closely tied to nineteenth-century Romantic music, although they occasionally incorporated some twentieth-century developments, such as atonality and dissonance. Their style was strongly reminiscent of Stravinsky (see Chapter 24).

The major musical trend since the war, however, has been serialism. Inspired mostly by the twelve-tone music of Schönberg (see Chapter 26), serialism is a compositional procedure in which an order of succession is set for specific values: pitch (for tones of the tempered scale), loudness (for dynamic levels), and units of time (for rhythm). By predetermining the order of succession, the composer restricts his or her intuitive freedom as the work to some extent creates itself. However, the mechanism the composer initially establishes could generate unanticipated musical events, thereby creating new and exciting compositions. Serialist composition diminishes the role of intuition and emotion in favor of intellect and mathematical precision. The first recognized serialist was the Frenchman Olivier Messiaen (1908–1992). Significantly, Messiaen was influenced in part by Indian and Greek music, plainchant, folk music, and birdsongs. Most critics have respected serialism, although the public has been largely indifferent, if not hostile, to it.

An offshoot of serialism that has won popular support, but not the same critical favor, is minimalism. Like serialism, this style uses repeated patterns and series and steady pulsation with gradual changes occurring over time. But whereas serialism is often atonal, minimalism is usually tonal and more harmonic. Perhaps the most successful minimalist composer is Philip Glass (b. 1937), who demonstrated in *Einstein on the Beach* that minimalist music could be adapted to full-scale opera. Like other modern American composers, Glass found no contradiction in moving between the worlds of classical music and popular music. His *Koyaanisqatsi* was used as background music to a documentary film on the disintegrative forces in Western society. In 2002, Glass composed the score for the highly acclaimed film *The Hours,* starring Nicole Kidman who won an Academy Award for her portrayal of the English writer Virginia Woolf (see Chapter 26).

Popular Culture: Image and Globalization

The period from 1967 to 1973 was probably the true golden age of rock. During this brief period, much experimentation in rock music took place, as it did in society in general. Straightfoward rock-and-roll competed with a new hybrid blues rock, created in part by British performers such as the Rolling Stones, who were in turn inspired by African American blues artists. Many musicians also experimented with non-Western musical sounds, such as Indian sitars. Some of the popular music of the 1960s also focused on social issues. It was against the Vietnam War and materialism and promoted "peace and love" as alternatives to the prevailing "establishment" culture.

The same migration of a musical form from the United States to Britain and back to the United States that characterized the golden age of rock also occurred when the early punk movement in New York spread to Britain in the mid-1970s after failing to make an immediate impact in the United States. The more influential British punk movement of 1976–1979 was also fueled by an economic crisis that had resulted in large numbers of unemployed and undereducated young people. Punk was not simply a proletarian movement, however. Many of its supporters, performers, and promoters were British art school graduates who applied avant-garde experimentation to the movement. Punk rockers such as Britain's Sex Pistols rejected most social conventions and preached anarchy and rebellion. They often wore tattered clothes and pins in their cheeks, symbolizing their rejection of a materialistic and degenerate culture. Pure punk was short-lived, partly because its intense energy quickly burned out (as did many of its performers) and partly because, as ex-punk Mick Hucknall said, "the biggest mistake of the punks was that they rejected music." Offshoots of punk proliferated through the 1980s, however, especially in Eastern Europe, with groups named Crisis, Sewage, and Dead Organism.

The introduction of the video music channel MTV in the early 1980s radically changed the music scene by making image as important as sound in selling records. Artists like Michael Jackson became superstars by treating the music video as an art form. Jackson's videos often were short films with elaborate staging and special effects set to music. Technological advances became prevalent in the music of the 1980s with the advent of the synthesizer, an electronic piano that produced computerized sounds. Some performers replaced ensembles of guitar, bass, and drums with synthesizers, creating a futuristic and manufactured sound.

Paralleling the rise of the music video was the emergence of rap or hip-hop. Developed in New York City in the late 1970s and early 1980s, rap combined rhymed lyrics with disco beats and turntable manipulations. One scholar noted that hip-hop "also encompassed break dancing, graffiti art, and new styles of language and fashion." Early rap groups like Public Enemy and Grandmaster Flash and the Furious Five instilled social commentaries into their songs, using the popularity of hip-hop to raise awareness about social conditions in American cities (see the box on p. 931).

The Growth of Mass Sports Sports became a major product of both popular culture and the leisure industry. The development of satellite television and various electronic breakthroughs helped make sports a global

GRANDMASTER FLASH AND THE FURIOUS FIVE: "THE MESSAGE"

In the 1982 hit single "The Message," Grandmaster Flash and the Furious Five added depth to rap music. No longer novelty or dance music, hip-hop began tackling serious social issues like the harsh realities of ghetto life. More and more rappers began to use music as a means of social protest and commentary. "The Message" tells of a boy who shunned education in favor of a flashy but criminal lifestyle. The story has a tragic ending when the boy dies in prison, as the chorus equates life in the ghetto to a jungle.

"The Message"

A child is born, with no state of mind
Blind to the ways of mankind
God is smiling on you but he's frowning too
Cause only God knows what you'll go through
You'll grow in the ghetto, living second rate
And your eyes will sing a song of deep hate
The places you play and where you stay
Looks like one great big alleyway
You'll admire all the number book takers
Thugs, pimps, pushers and the big money makers
Driving big cars, spending twenties and tens
And you wanna grow up to be just like them

Smugglers, scramblers, burglars, gamblers
Pickpockets, peddlers and even pan-handlers
You say I'm cool, I'm no fool
But then you wind up dropping out of high school
Now you're unemployed, all null 'n' void
Walking around like you're Pretty Boy Floyd
Turned stickup kid, look what you done did
Got send up for an eight year bid
Now you man is took and you're a Maytag
Spend the next two years as an undercover fag
Being used and abused, and served like hell
Till one day you was found hung dead in a cell
It was plain to see that your life was lost
You was cold and your body swung back and forth
But now your eyes sing the sad sad song
Of how you lived so fast and died so young

It's like a jungle sometimes, it makes me wonder
How I keep from goin' under

Q What differences and similarities do you see between the lyrics of "The Message" and those of Bob Dylan's "The Times They Are A-Changin' " on p. 912, and what do they tell you about the differences and similarities between the decades of the 1960s and the 1980s?

---

phenomenon. The Olympic Games could now be broadcast around the globe from anywhere in the world. Sports were a cheap form of entertainment since fans did not have to leave their homes to enjoy athletic competitions. In fact, some sports organizations initially resisted television, fearing that it would hurt ticket sales. Soon, however, the tremendous revenues possible from television contracts overcame this hesitation. As sports television revenue escalated, many sports came to receive the bulk of their yearly revenue from television contracts. The Olympics, for example, are now funded primarily by American television. These contracts are paid for by advertising sponsors, mostly for products to be consumed while watching the sport: beer, soda, and snack foods.

Sports became big politics as well as big business. Football (soccer) remained the dominant world sport and more than ever became a vehicle for nationalist sentiment and expression. The World Cup is the most watched event on television. Although the sport can be a positive outlet for national and local pride, all too often it has been marred by violence as nationalistic energies have overcome rational behavior.

The most telling example of the potent mix of politics and sport continued to be the Olympic Games. When the Soviets entered Olympic competition in 1952, the Olympics began to take on Cold War implications and became known as the "war without weapons." The Soviets saw the Olympics as a way to stimulate nationalist spirit, as well as to promote the Communist system as the best path for social progress. The Soviets led the Olympics in terms of total medals won between 1956 and 1988. The nature of the Olympics, with their daily medal count by nation and elaborate ceremonies and rituals such as the playing of the national anthem of the winning athletes and the parade of nations, virtually ensured the politicization of the games originally intended to foster international cooperation through friendly competition.

The political nature of the games found expression in other ways as well. In 1956, six nations withdrew from the games to protest the Soviet crushing of the Hungarian uprising. In 1972, twenty-seven African nations threatened to pull out of the Munich Olympics because of apartheid in South Africa. Also at the Munich Games, the Palestinian terrorist group Black September seized eleven Israeli athletes as hostages, all of whom died in a confrontation at an airport. The United States led a boycott of the 1980 Moscow Games to protest the Soviet invasion of Afghanistan, and the Soviets responded by boycotting the Los Angeles Games in 1984.

As sports assumed a prominent position in the social life of the world, the pressures and rewards to not just compete but win intensified. Fueled by advertising endorsements, the scientific study of sport led to aerodynamic helmets for cyclists, skintight bodysuits for skiers and swimmers, and improved nutritional practices in all sports. Such technological advances, however, also increased the manner in which athletes might break the rules. From steroids to blood doping, some have used medical supplements to illegally enhance their conditioning. Mandatory drug testing in the Olympics, Tour de France, and World Cup attempts to level the playing field and avoid repercussions such as occurred when reports of steroid abuse prompted a governmental investigation of Major League Baseball.

Popular Culture: Increasingly Global Media critic and theorist Marshall McLuhan predicted in the 1960s that advances in mass communications technology, such as satellites and electronics, would eventually lead to a shrinking of the world, a lessening of cultural distinctions, and a breaking down of cultural barriers, all of which would in time transform the world into a single "global village." McLuhan was optimistic about these developments, and his ideas became quite popular at the time. Many critics have since argued that McLuhan was too utopian about the benefits of technological progress and maintain that the mass media that these technological breakthroughs created are still controlled by a small number of multinational corporations that "colonize the rest of the world, sometimes benignly, sometimes not." They argue that this has allowed Western popular culture to disrupt the traditional cultures of less developed countries and inculcate new patterns of behavior as well as new desires and new dissatisfactions. Cultural contacts, however, often move in two directions. While the world has been "Americanized" to a great extent, formerly unfamiliar ways of life and styles of music have also come into the world of the West (see Chapter 30).

TIMELINE

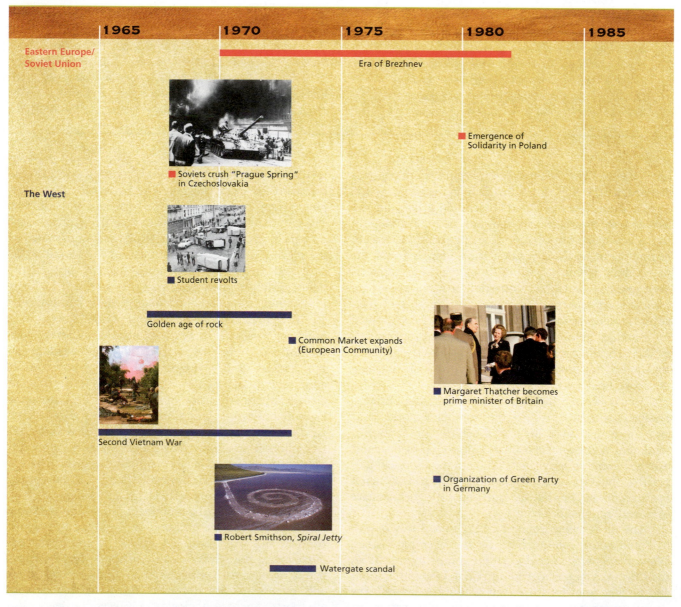

1965   1970   1975   1980   1985

Eastern Europe/ Soviet Union

Era of Brezhnev

Soviets crush "Prague Spring" in Czechoslovakia

Emergence of Solidarity in Poland

The West

Student revolts

Golden age of rock

Common Market expands (European Community)

Margaret Thatcher becomes prime minister of Britain

Second Vietnam War

Organization of Green Party in Germany

Robert Smithson, *Spiral Jetty*

Watergate scandal

CONCLUSION

The late 1960s experienced a rash of protest as women actively sought equality of rights with men and numerous groups of students and radicals protested the war in Vietnam and unsatisfactory university conditions. The women's movement gained momentum in the 1970s and 1980s, but the student upheavals were not a "turning point in the history of postwar Europe," as some people thought at the time. In the 1970s and 1980s, student rebels would become middle-class professionals, and revolutionary politics would remain mostly a memory.

In the 1970s, the Cold War took a new direction as the Soviet Union and the United States moved, if ever fitfully, toward a lessening of tensions, while the United States restored diplomatic ties with China by the end of the 1970s. There were renewed tensions in the Cold War between the United States and the Soviet Union in the early 1980s, but as we shall see in the next chapter, a dramatic shift in Soviet leadership would soon bring an unexpected end to the Cold War.

Between 1965 and 1985, the Western world remained divided between a prosperous capitalistic West and a stagnant Eastern Europe. The division seemed permanent at the time, but dramatic changes in the Soviet Union would soon bring an end to the new order created as a result of World War II.

NOTES

1. Quoted in Marsha Rowe et al., *Spare Rib Reader* (Harmondsworth, England, 1982), p. 574.
2. Betty Friedan, *The Feminine Mystique* (New York, 1963), p. 10.
3. Quoted in Tony Judt, *Postwar: A History of Europe Since 1945* (New York, 2005), p. 390.
4. "To Walk the Moon," *New York Times,* July 20, 1969.

SUGGESTIONS FOR FURTHER READING

General Works   For a well-written survey on Europe between 1965 and 1985, see **T. Judt, *Postwar: A History of Europe Since 1945*** (New York, 2005). Additional general surveys of contemporary European history are listed in Chapter 28.

A Culture of Protest   On the sexual revolution of the 1960s, see **D. Allyn, *Make Love, Not War: The Sexual Revolution—An Unfettered History*** (New York, 2000). On the turbulent 1960s, see **A. Marwick, *The Sixties: Social and Cultural Transformation in Britain, France, Italy, and the United States*** (Oxford, 1999), and **T. H. Anderson, *The Sixties*** (London, 1998). On the women's liberation movement, see **C. Duchen, *Women's Rights and Women's Lives in France, 1944–1968*** (New York, 1994); **D. Meyer, *The Rise of Women in America, Russia, Sweden, and Italy,*** 2d ed. (Middletown, Conn., 1989); and **K. C. Berkeley, *The Women's Liberation Movement in America*** (Westport, Conn., 1999).

Soviet Union and Eastern Europe   On the Brezhnev era in the Soviet Union, see **E. Bacon, ed., *Brezhnev Remembered*** (New York, 2003). On events in Eastern Europe, see the surveys listed in Chapter 28. On the Czech upheaval in 1968, see **K. Williams, *The Prague Spring and Its Aftermath: Czechoslovak Politics, 1968–1970*** (Cambridge, 1997).

Western Europe   For general works on Western Europe and individual countries, see the works cited in Chapter 28. More specific works dealing with the period 1965–1985 include **E. J. Evans, *Thatcher and Thatcherism*** (New York, 1997);

P. A. Hall, *Governing the Economy: The Politics of State Intervention in Britain and France* (New York, 1986); **D. S. Bell, *François Mitterrand*** (Cambridge, 2005); and **R. J. Dalton, *Politics in West Germany*** (Glenview, Ill., 1989).

The Cold War: The Move to Détente   For general studies on the Cold War, see the works listed in Chapter 28. A detailed analysis of American-Soviet relations in the 1970s and 1980s is available in **R. Garthoff, *Détente and Confrontation: American-Soviet Relations from Nixon to Reagan*** (Washington, D.C., 1985). On the Second Vietnam War, see **M. Hall, *The Vietnam War,*** 2d ed. (London, 2007). On China's cultural revolution, see **R. MacFarquhar and M. Schoenhals, *Mao's Last Revolution*** (Cambridge, Mass., 2006); the brief biography of Mao Zedong by **J. Spence, *Mao Zedong*** (New York, 1999); and **T. Cheek, *Mao Zedong and China's Revolutions: A Brief History*** (Boston, 2002).

Society and Culture   On the development of the Green parties, see **M. O'Neill, *Green Parties and Political Change in Contemporary Europe*** (Aldershot, England, 1997), and **D. Richardson and C. Rootes, eds., *The Green Challenge: The Development of the Green Parties in Europe*** (London, 1995). A physicist's view of science is contained in **J. Ziman, *The Force of Knowledge: The Scientific Dimension of Society*** (Cambridge, 1976). A physicist's view of a new conception of reality is **D. Bohm, *Wholeness and the Implicate Order*** (London, 2002). The space race is examined in **W. A. McDougall, *The Heavens and the Earth: A Political History of the Space Age*** (New York, 1987). For a general view of postwar thought and culture, see **J. A. Winders, *European Culture Since 1848: From Modern to Postmodern and Beyond,*** rev. ed. (New York, 2001). On Postmodernism, see **C. Butler, *Postmodernism: A Very Short Introduction*** (Oxford, 2002). The cultural impact of sports is examined in **R. Mandell, *Sport: A Cultural History*** (New York, 1999), and **T. Collins and W. Vamplew, *Mud, Sweat and Beers: A Cultural History of Sport and Alcohol*** (London, 2002).

CengageNOW is an integrated online suite of services and resources with proven ease of use and efficient paths to success, delivering the results you want—NOW!

academic.cengage.com/login/

Enter CengageNOW using the access card that is available with *Western Civilization*. CengageNOW will assist you in understanding the content in this chapter with lesson plans generated for your needs. In addition, you can read the following documents, and many more, online:

Brezhnev Doctrine

CHAPTER 30
AFTER THE FALL: THE WESTERN WORLD
IN A GLOBAL AGE (SINCE 1985)

Boris Yeltsin waves the Russian tricolor flag before a crowd of supporters.

CHAPTER OUTLINE AND FOCUS QUESTIONS

Toward a New Western Order

Q What reforms did Gorbachev institute in the Soviet Union, and what role did he play in the demise of the Soviet Union? What are the major political developments in Eastern Europe, Western Europe, and North America since 1985?

After the Cold War: New World Order or Age of Terrorism?

Q How and why did the Cold War end? What are the main issues in the struggle with terrorism?

New Directions and New Problems in Western Society

Q What are the major developments in the women's movement since 1985, and what problems have immigrants created for European society?

Western Culture Today

Q What major Western cultural trends have emerged since 1985?

The Digital Age

Q What is the Digital Age, and what are its products, results, and dangers?

Toward a Global Civilization

Q What is globalization, and what are the main ways in which globalization is manifesting in the twenty-first century?

CRITICAL THINKING

Q In thinking about the problems in the Western world and our world since 1985, what solutions would you propose if you were the president of the United States?

BY 1985, AFTER FOUR DECADES of the Cold War, Westerners had become accustomed to a new division of Europe between West and East that seemed to be permanent. A prosperous Western Europe allied with the United States stood opposed to a still-struggling Eastern Europe that remained largely subject to the Soviet Union. The division of Germany symbolized the new order, which seemed so well established. Yet within a few years, a revolutionary upheaval in the Soviet Union and Eastern Europe brought an end to the Cold War and to the division of postwar Europe. Even the Soviet Union ceased to exist as a nation.

On August 19, 1991, a group of Soviet leaders opposed to reform arrested Mikhail Gorbachev, the president of the Soviet Union, and tried to seize control of the government. Hundreds of thousands of Russians, led by Boris Yeltsin, poured into the streets of Moscow and Leningrad to resist the attempted coup. Some army units, sent out to enforce the wishes of the rebels, defected to Yeltsin's side, and within days, the rebels were forced to surrender. This failed attempt to seize power had unexpected results as Russia and many of the other Soviet republics declared their independence. By the end of 1991, the Soviet Union—one of the largest empires in world history—had come to an end, and a new era of cooperation between the successor states in the old Soviet Union and the nations of the West had begun.

As the world adjusted to the transformation from Cold War to post–Cold War sensibilities, other changes shaped the Western outlook. The demographic face of European countries changed as massive numbers of immigrants created more ethnically diverse populations. New artistic and intellectual currents, the continued advance of science and technology, the emergence of a Digital Age, the surge of the women's liberation movement—all spoke of a vibrant, ever-changing world. At the same time, a devastating terrorist attack on the World Trade Center in New York City and the Pentagon outside Washington, D.C., in 2001 made the Western world vividly aware of its vulnerability to international terrorism. But most important of all, Western nations, like all nations on the planet, have become aware of the political and economic interdependence of the world's nations and the global nature of our twenty-first-century problems. ◆

Toward a New Western Order

Q **Focus Questions:** What reforms did Gorbachev institute in the Soviet Union, and what role did he play in the demise of the Soviet Union? What are the major political developments in Eastern Europe, Western Europe, and North America since 1985?

Between 1945 and 1985, a new political order following the devastation of World War II had seemingly left the Western world divided permanently between a prosperous, capitalistic West and an impoverished, Communist East. But in the late 1980s and early 1990s, the Soviet Union and its Eastern European satellite states underwent a revolutionary upheaval that dramatically altered the European landscape (see Map 30.1) and left many Europeans with both new hopes and new fears.

The Revolutionary Era in the Soviet Union

By 1980, it was becoming apparent to a small number of reformers in the Communist Party that the Soviet Union was seriously ailing. When one of these young reformers, Mikhail Gorbachev, was chosen as Party secretary in March 1985, a new era began in the Soviet Union.

The Gorbachev Era Born into a peasant family in 1931, Mikhail Gorbachev combined farm work with school and received the Order of the Red Banner for his agricultural efforts. This award and his good school record enabled him to study law at the University of Moscow. After receiving his law degree in 1955, he returned to his native southern

Russia, where he eventually became first secretary of the Party in the city of Stavropol (he had joined the Party in 1952) and then first secretary of the regional Party committee. In 1978, Gorbachev was made a member of the Party's Central Committee in Moscow. Two years later, he became a full member of the ruling Politburo and secretary of the Central Committee. In March 1985, Party leaders elected him general secretary of the Party, and he became the new leader of the Soviet Union.

Educated during the years of reform under Khrushchev, Gorbachev seemed intent on taking earlier reforms to their logical conclusions. He had said to his wife on achieving power, "We cannot go on living like this."[1] By the 1980s, Soviet economic problems were obvious. Rigid, centralized planning had led to mismanagement and stifled innovation. Although the Soviets still excelled in space exploration, they had fallen behind the West in high technology, especially in the development and production of computers for private and public use. Most noticeable to the Soviet people was the decline in the standard of living. In February 1986, at the Twenty-Seventh Congress of the Communist Party, Gorbachev made clear the need for changes in Soviet society: "The practical actions of the Party and state agencies lag behind the demands of the times and of life itself.... Problems grow faster than they are solved. Sluggishness, ossification in the forms, and methods of management decrease the dynamism of work.... Stagnation begins to show up in the life of society."[2] Thus, from the start, Gorbachev preached the need for radical reforms.

The cornerstone of Gorbachev's radical reforms was **perestroika,** or "restructuring" (see the box on p. 938). At first, this meant only a reordering of economic policy as Gorbachev called for the beginning of a market economy with limited free enterprise and some private property. Gorbachev soon perceived, however, that in the Soviet system, the economic sphere was intimately tied to the social and political spheres. Attempting to reform the economy without political or social reform would be doomed to failure. One of the most important instruments of *perestroika* was **glasnost,** or "openness." Soviet citizens and officials were encouraged to discuss openly the strengths and weaknesses of the Soviet Union. *Pravda,* the official newspaper of the Communist Party, began to include reports of official corruption, sloppy factory work, and protests against government policy. The arts also benefited from the new policy. Previously banned works were now published, and music based on Western styles, such as jazz and rock, began to be performed openly.

Political reforms were equally revolutionary. At the Communist Party conference in 1988, Gorbachev called for the creation of a new Soviet parliament, the Congress of People's Deputies, whose members were to be chosen in competitive elections. It convened in 1989, the first such meeting in Russia since 1918. Early in 1990, Gorbachev legalized the formation of other political parties and struck Article 6, which had guaranteed the "leading role" of the Communist Party, from the Soviet constitution. At the

MAP 30.1 The New Europe. The combination of an inefficient economy and high military spending had led to stagnation in the Soviet Union by the early 1980s. Mikhail Gorbachev came to power in 1985, unleashing political, economic, and nationalist forces that led to independence for the former Soviet republics and also for Eastern Europe. **Q** Compare this map with Map 28.1. What new countries had emerged by the early twenty-first century? View an animated version of this map or related maps at academic.cengage.com/history/spielvogel

same time, Gorbachev attempted to consolidate his power by creating a new state presidency. The new position was a consequence of the separation of the state from the Communist Party. Hitherto, the position of first secretary of the Party had been the most important post in the Soviet Union, but as the Communist Party became less closely associated with the state, the powers of this office diminished correspondingly. In March 1990, Gorbachev became the Soviet Union's first president.

One of Gorbachev's most serious problems stemmed from the nature of the nation he led. The Union of Soviet Socialist Republics was a truly multiethnic country, containing 92 nationalities and 112 recognized languages. Previously, the iron hand of the Communist Party, centered in Moscow, had kept a lid on the centuries-old ethnic tensions that had periodically erupted. As Gorbachev released this iron grip, tensions resurfaced, a by-product of *glasnost* that Gorbachev had not anticipated. Ethnic groups took advantage of the new openness to protest what they perceived as ethnically motivated slights. When violence erupted, the Soviet army, in disrepair since its ill-fated

decade-long foray into Afghanistan, had difficulty controlling the situation.

The years 1988 to 1990 also witnessed the appearance of nationalist movements in the republics that made up the Soviet Union. Many were motivated by ethnic concerns, with calls for sovereignty and independence from the Russian-based rule centered in Moscow. These movements sprang up first in Georgia in late 1988 and then in Latvia, Estonia, Moldavia, Uzbekistan, Azerbaijan, and Lithuania. On March 11, 1990, the Lithuanian Supreme Council proclaimed Lithuania an independent state.

The End of the Soviet Union During 1990 and 1991, Gorbachev struggled to deal with Lithuania and the other problems unleashed by his reforms. On the one hand, he tried to appease conservatives who complained about the growing disorder within the Soviet Union. On the other hand, he tried to accommodate the liberal forces, especially those in the Soviet republics, who increasingly favored a new kind of decentralized Soviet federation. In particular, Gorbachev labored to cooperate more closely

GORBACHEV AND *PERESTROIKA*

After assuming the leadership of the Soviet Union in 1985, Mikhail Gorbachev worked to liberalize and restructure the country. His policies opened the door to rapid changes in Eastern Europe and in Soviet-American relations at the end of the 1980s. In his book *Perestroika*, Gorbachev explained some of his "New Thinking."

Mikhail Gorbachev, *Perestroika*

The fundamental principle of the new political outlook is very simple: *nuclear war cannot be a means of achieving political, economic, ideological or any other goals.* This conclusion is truly revolutionary, for it means discarding the traditional notions of war and peace. It is the political function of war that has always been a justification for war, a "rational" explanation. Nuclear war is senseless; it is irrational. There would be neither winners nor losers in a global nuclear conflict: world Civilization would inevitably perish....

But military technology has developed to such an extent that even a non-nuclear war would now be comparable with a nuclear war in its destructive effect. That is why it is logical to include in our category of nuclear wars this "variant" of an armed clash between major powers as well.

Thereby, an altogether different situation has emerged. A way of thinking and a way of acting, based on the use of force in world politics, have formed over centuries, even millennia. It seems they have taken root as something unshakable. Today, they have lost all reasonable grounds.... For the first time in history, basing international politics on moral and ethical norms that are common to all humankind, as well as humanizing interstate relations, has become a vital requirement....

There is a great thirst for mutual understanding and mutual communication in the world. It is felt among politicians, it is gaining momentum among the intelligentsia, representatives of culture, and the public at large. And if the Russian word "perestroika" has easily entered the international lexicon, this is due to more than just interest in what is going on in the Soviet Union. Now the whole world needs restructuring, i.e., progressive development, a fundamental change.

People feel this and understand this. They have to find their bearings, to understand the problems besetting mankind, to realize how they should live in the future. The restructuring is a must for a world overflowing with nuclear weapons; for a world ridden with serious economic and ecological problems; for a world laden with poverty, backwardness and disease; for a human race now facing the urgent need of ensuring its own survival.

We are all students, and our teacher is life and time. I believe that more and more people will come to realize that through RESTRUCTURING in the broad sense of the word, the integrity of the world will be enhanced. Having earned good marks from our main teacher—life—we shall enter the twenty-first century well prepared and sure that there will be further progress.

Q *How revolutionary was Gorbachev's rejection of nuclear war? What impact did this idea of restructuring have on communism and the Soviet Union's ability to reform itself?*

---

with Boris Yeltsin (1931–2007), who had been elected president of the Russian Republic in June 1991.

By 1991, the conservative leaders of the traditional Soviet institutions—the army, government, KGB, and military industries—had grown increasingly worried about the impending dissolution of the Soviet Union and its impact on their own fortunes. On August 19, 1991, a group of these discontented rightists arrested Gorbachev and attempted to seize power. Gorbachev's unwillingness to work with the conspirators and the brave resistance in Moscow of Yeltsin and thousands of Russians who had grown accustomed to their new liberties caused the coup to disintegrate rapidly. The actions of these right-wing plotters, however, served to accelerate the very process they had hoped to stop—the disintegration of the Soviet Union.

Despite desperate pleas by Gorbachev, the Soviet republics soon moved for complete independence. Ukraine voted for independence on December 1, 1991, and a week later, the leaders of Russia, Ukraine, and Belarus announced that the Soviet Union had "ceased to exist" and would be replaced by the new and voluntary Commonwealth of Independent States. Gorbachev resigned on December 25, 1991, and turned over his responsibilities as commander in chief to Boris Yeltsin, the president of Russia. By the end of 1991, one of the largest empires in world history had evaporated, and a new era had begun in its lands.

The New Russia A new power struggle soon ensued within Russia, by far the largest of the former Soviet republics. Yeltsin was committed to introducing a free market economy as quickly as possible, but the transition was not easy. Economic hardships and social disarray, made worse by a dramatic rise in the activities of organized crime mobs, led increasing numbers of Russians to support both former Communists and hard-line nationalists who tried to place new limits on Yeltsin's powers. Yeltsin fought back and pushed ahead with plans for a new Russian constitution that would abolish the Congress of People's Deputies, create a two-chamber parliament, and establish a strong presidency. A hard-line parliamentary minority resisted and in early October took the offensive, urging their supporters to take over government offices. Yeltsin responded by ordering military forces to storm the parliament building and arrest

assertive role in international affairs. Fighting in Chechnya continued throughout 2000, nearly reducing the republic's capital city of Grozny to ruins. In July 2001, Putin launched reforms, which included the unrestricted sale and purchase of land and tax cuts aimed at boosting economic growth and budget revenues. Although Russia soon experienced a budget surplus and a growing economy, serious problems remained. The economy continued to rely on exports of natural gas, oil, and metals, all products whose prices can fluctuate wildly. Most disturbing was the large number of people—possibly 40 percent—who still lived in poverty.

President Putin has attempted to deal with the chronic problems in Russian society by centralizing his control over the system and by silencing critics—notably in the Russian media.

Yeltsin Resists a Right-Wing Coup. In August 1991, the attempt of right-wing plotters to overthrow Mikhail Gorbachev and seize power in the Soviet Union was thwarted by the efforts of Boris Yeltsin, president of the Russian Republic, and his supporters. Yeltsin (holding papers) is shown here atop a tank in front of the Russian parliament building in Moscow, urging the Russian people to resist the conspirators.

his hard-line opponents. Yeltsin used his victory to consolidate his power in parliamentary elections held in December.

During the mid-1990s, Yeltsin sought to implement reforms that would set Russia on a firm course toward a pluralistic political system and a market economy. But the new post-Communist Russia remained as fragile as ever. Growing economic inequality and rampant corruption aroused widespread criticism and shook the confidence of the Russian people in the superiority of the capitalist system over the one that had existed under Communist rule. A nagging war in the Caucasus—where the Muslim people of Chechnya sought national independence from Russia—drained the government's budget and exposed the decrepit state of the once vaunted Red Army. Yeltsin won reelection as president in 1996, although his precarious health raised serious questions about his ability to govern.

The Putin Era At the end of 1999, Yeltsin suddenly resigned and was replaced by Vladimir Putin (b. 1952), a former member of the KGB. Putin vowed to bring an end to the rampant corruption and inexperience that permeated Russian political culture and to strengthen the role of the central government in managing the affairs of state. During the succeeding months, the parliament approved his proposal to centralize power in the hands of the federal government in Moscow.

Putin also vowed to return the breakaway state of Chechnya to Russian authority and to adopt a more

Although he has been criticized in the West for these moves, many Russians today have a sense of unease about the decline of social order and express sympathy with Putin's attempts to restore a sense of pride and discipline in Russian society.

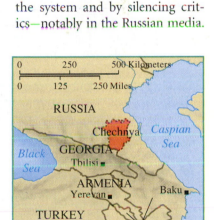

Chechnya

Eastern Europe: The Revolutions of 1989 and the Collapse of the Communist Order

Stalin's postwar order had imposed Communist regimes throughout Eastern Europe. The process of sovietization seemed so complete that few people believed that the new order could be undone. But discontent with their Soviet-style regimes always simmered beneath the surface of these satellite states, and after Mikhail Gorbachev made it clear that his government would not intervene militarily, the Communist regimes fell quickly in the revolutions of 1989.

The Fall Martial law had not solved Poland's problems after it had been imposed in 1981, and in 1988, new demonstrations led the Polish regime to agree to free parliamentary elections—the first free elections in Eastern Europe in forty years. Bowing to the inevitable, the military regime allowed the newly elected Solidarity coalition to form a new government, thus ending forty-five years of Communist rule. The Soviet Union, in line with Gorbachev's new policy of nonintervention, also took no action to reverse the verdict in Poland. In December 1990, Lech Walesa, the head of Solidarity, was chosen as the new Polish president.

In Hungary, the economy had sagged by the late 1980s, and in 1989, the Communist regime, aware of growing dissatisfaction, began to undertake reforms. But they came too late as new political parties called for Hungary to become a democratic republic. After elections in March 1990, a new coalition government was formed that committed Hungary to democratic government.

Czechoslovakia, too, found a peaceful way to a new political system. Government attempts to suppress mass demonstrations in Prague and other cities in 1988 and 1989 only led to more and larger demonstrations. In December 1989, as demonstrations continued, the Communist government, lacking any real support, collapsed. President Gustav Husák resigned and at the end of December was replaced by Vaclav Havel (b. 1936), a dissident playwright who had played an important role in bringing the Communist government down. Havel set out on a goodwill tour to various Western countries where he proved to be an eloquent spokesman for Czech democracy and a new order in Europe (see the box on p. 941).

Czechoslovakia's revolutionary path was considerably less violent than Romania's, where opposition grew as the dictator Nicolae Ceaușescu rejected the reforms in Eastern Europe promoted by Gorbachev. Ceaușescu's extreme measures to reduce Romania's external debt led to economic difficulties. Although he was successful in reducing foreign debt, the sharp drop in living standards that resulted from those hardship measures angered many Romanians. A small incident became the spark that ignited heretofore suppressed flames of discontent. The ruthless crushing of a demonstration in Timisoara in December 1989 led to other mass demonstrations. After the dictator was booed at a mass rally on December 21, the army refused to support any more repression. Ceaușescu and his wife were captured on December 22 and tried and executed on Christmas Day. Leadership now passed into the hands of the hastily formed National Salvation Front.

After the Fall   The fall of Communist governments in Eastern Europe during the revolutions of 1989 brought a wave of euphoria to Europe. The new structures meant an end to a postwar European order that had been imposed on unwilling peoples by the victorious forces of the Soviet Union. In 1989 and 1990, new governments throughout Eastern Europe worked diligently to scrap the remnants of the old system and introduce the democratic procedures and market systems they believed would revitalize their scarred lands. But this process proved to be neither simple nor easy.

Most Eastern European countries had little or even no experience with democratic systems. Then, too, ethnic divisions, which had troubled these areas before World War II and had been forcibly submerged under Communist rule, reemerged with a vengeance. Finally, the rapid conversion to market economies also proved painful. The adoption of "shock-therapy" austerity measures produced much suffering. Unemployment, for example, climbed to over 13 percent in Poland in 1992.

Nevertheless, by the beginning of the twenty-first century, many of these states, especially Poland and the Czech Republic, were making a successful transition to both free markets and democracy. In Poland, Aleksander Kwasniewski (b. 1954), although a former Communist, was elected president in November 1995 and pushed Poland toward an increasingly prosperous free market economy. Current president Lech Kaczyński (b. 1949) is emphasizing the need to combine modernization with tradition. In Czechoslovakia, the shift to non-Communist rule was complicated by old problems, especially ethnic issues. Czechs and Slovaks disagreed over the makeup of the new state but were able to agree to a peaceful division of the country. On January 1, 1993, Czechoslovakia split into the Czech Republic and Slovakia. Vaclav Havel was elected the first president of the new Czech Republic. In Romania,

© Peter Turnley/CORBIS

A Romanian Revolutionary.   The revolt against Communist rule in Eastern Europe in 1989 came last to Romania. It was also more violent as the government at first tried to stem the revolt by massacring demonstrators. This picture shows a young Romanian rebel waving the national flag with the Communist emblem cut out of the center. He is on a balcony overlooking the tanks, soldiers, and citizens filling Palace Square in Bucharest.

VACLAV HAVEL: THE CALL FOR A NEW POLITICS

In attempting to deal with the world's problems, some European leaders have pointed to the need for a new perspective, especially a moral one, if people are to live in a sane world. These two excerpts are taken from speeches by Vaclav Havel, who was elected president of Czechoslovakia at the end of 1989. The first is from his inaugural address as president on January 1, 1990; the second is from a speech given to the U.S. Congress.

Vaclav Havel, Address to the People of Czechoslovakia, January 1, 1990

But all this is still not the main problem [the environmental devastation of the country by its Communist leaders]. The worst thing is that we live in a contaminated moral environment. We fell morally ill because we became used to saying something different from what we thought. We learned not to believe in anything, to ignore each other, to care only about ourselves. Concepts such as love, friendship, compassion, humility, or forgiveness lost their depth and dimensions, and for many of us they represented only psychological peculiarities, or they resembled gone-astray greetings from ancients, a little ridiculous in the era of computers and spaceships. Only a few of us were able to cry out loud that the powers that be should not be all-powerful, and that special farms, which produce ecologically pure and top-quality food just for them should send their produce to schools, children's homes and hospitals if our agriculture was unable to offer them to all. The previous regime—armed with its arrogant and intolerant ideology—reduced man to a force of production and nature to a tool of production. In this it attacked both their very substance and their mutual relationship. It reduced gifted and autonomous people, skillfully working in their own country, to nuts and bolts of some monstrously huge, noisy, and stinking machine, whose real meaning is not clear to anyone.

Vaclav Havel, Speech to Congress, February 21, 1990

For this reason, the salvation of this human world lies nowhere else than in the human heart, in the human power to reflect, in human meekness and in human responsibility.

Without a global revolution in the sphere of human consciousness, nothing will change for the better in the sphere of our being as humans, and the catastrophe toward which this world is headed—be it ecological, social, demographic or a general breakdown of civilization—will be unavoidable . . . .

We are still a long way from that "family of man." In fact, we seem to be receding from the ideal rather than growing closer to it. Interests of all kinds—personal, selfish, state, nation, group, and if you like, company interests—still considerably outweigh genuinely common and global interests. We are still under the sway of the destructive and vain belief that man is the pinnacle of creation and not just a part of it and that therefore everything is permitted . . . .

In other words, we still don't know how to put morality ahead of politics, science and economics. We are still incapable of understanding that the only genuine backbone of all our actions, if they are to be moral, is responsibility.

Responsibility to something higher than my family, my country, my company, my success—responsibility to the order of being where all our actions are indelibly recorded and where and only where they will be properly judged.

The interpreter or mediator between us and this higher authority is what is traditionally referred to as human conscience.

Q *How different is Havel's view of politics from the views of mainstream politicians? What broader forces working in modern European society do you believe shaped Havel's thinking? How can Havel's view of our common humanity and responsibility to conscience help revitalize Western civilization?*

---

the current president, Traian Băsescu (b. 1951), leads a country that is just beginning to show economic growth and the rise of a middle class.

The revival of the post–Cold War Eastern European states is evident in their desire to join both NATO and the European Union (EU), the two major Cold War institutions of Western European unity. In 1997, Poland, the Czech Republic, and Hungary became full members of NATO. In 2004, ten nations—including Hungary, Poland, the Czech Republic, Slovenia, Estonia, Latvia, and Lithuania—joined the EU, and Romania and Bulgaria joined in 2007.

Yet not all are convinced that inclusion in European integration is a good thing. Eastern Europeans fear that their countries will be dominated by investment from their prosperous neighbors, while their counterparts in Western Europe are concerned about a possible influx of low-wage workers from the new member countries.

The Reunification of Germany

Perhaps the most dramatic events took place in East Germany, where a persistent economic slump and the ongoing oppressiveness of the regime of Erich Honecker led to a flight of refugees and mass demonstrations against the regime in the summer and fall of 1989. After more than half a million people flooded the streets of East Berlin on November 4, shouting, "The wall must go!" the German Communist government soon capitulated to popular pressure and on November 9 opened the entire border with the West. Hundreds of thousands of Germans swarmed across the border, mostly to visit and return. The Berlin Wall, long a symbol of the Cold War, became the site of massive celebrations as thousands of people used sledgehammers to tear it down. By December, new political parties had emerged, and on March 18, 1990, in East Germany's first

© Reuters (David Brauchili)/CORBIS

And the Wall Came Tumbling Down. The Berlin Wall, long a symbol of Europe's Cold War divisions, became the site of massive celebrations after the East German government opened its border with the West. The activities include spontaneous acts of demolition as Germans used sledgehammers and crowbars to tear down parts of the wall. In this photograph, a demonstrator pounds away at the Berlin Wall as East German border guards observe from above.

free elections ever, the Christian Democrats won almost 50 percent of the vote.

The Christian Democrats supported rapid monetary unification, and on July 1, 1990, the economies of West and East Germany were united, with the West German deutsche mark becoming the official currency of the two countries. And after months of political negotiations between West and East German officials as well as the original four postwar occupying powers (the United States, Great Britain, France, and the Soviet Union), political reunification was achieved on October 3, 1990. What had seemed almost impossible at the beginning of 1989 had become a reality by the end of 1990.

The Disintegration of Yugoslavia

From its beginning in 1919, Yugoslavia had been an artificial creation. The peace treaties at the end of World War I combined Serbs, Croats, and Slovenes into a new

south Slav state called Yugoslavia (known until 1929 as the Kingdom of the Slavs, Croats, and Slovenes). After World War II, the dictatorial Marshal Tito had managed to hold the six republics and two autonomous provinces that constituted Yugoslavia together. After his death in 1980, no strong leader emerged, and his responsibilities passed to a collective state presidency and the League of Communists of Yugoslavia. At the end of the 1980s, Yugoslavia was caught up in the reform movements sweeping through Eastern Europe. The League of Communists collapsed, and new parties quickly emerged.

The Yugoslav political scene was complicated by the development of separatist movements. In 1990, the republics of Slovenia, Croatia, Bosnia-Herzegovina, and Macedonia began to lobby for a new federal structure of Yugoslavia that would fulfill their separatist desires. Slobodan Milošević (1941–2006), who had become the leader of the Serbian Communist Party in 1987 and had managed to stay in power by emphasizing his Serbian nationalism, rejected these efforts. He asserted that these republics could be independent only if new border arrangements were made to accommodate the Serb minorities in those republics who did not want to live outside the boundaries of a Greater Serbian state. Serbs constituted 11.6 percent of Croatia's population and 32 percent of Bosnia-Herzegovina's in 1981.

After negotiations among the six republics failed, Slovenia and Croatia declared their independence in June 1991. Milošević's government sent the Yugoslavian army, which it controlled, into Slovenia, without much success. In September 1991, it began a full assault against Croatia. Increasingly, the Yugoslavian army was becoming the Serbian army, while Serbian irregular forces played a growing role in military operations. Before a cease-fire was arranged, the Serbian forces had captured one-third of Croatia's territory in brutal and destructive fighting.

A Child's Account of the Shelling of Sarajevo

When Bosnia declared its independence in March 1992, Serbian army units and groups of Bosnian Serbs went on the offensive and began to shell the capital city of Sarajevo. One of its residents was Zlata Filipovic, the ten-year-old daughter of a middle-class lawyer. Zlata was a fan of MTV and pizza, but when the Serbs began to shell Sarajevo from the hills above the city, her life changed dramatically, as is apparent in this excerpt from her diary.

Zlata Filipovic, *Zlata's Diary, A Child's Life in Sarajevo*

April 3, 1992: Daddy came back . . . all upset. He says there are terrible crowds at the train and bus stations. People are leaving Sarajevo.

April 4, 1992: There aren't many people in the streets. I guess it's fear of the stories about Sarajevo being bombed. But there's no bombing . . . .

April 5, 1992: I'm trying hard to concentrate so I can do my homework (reading), but I simply can't. Something is going on in town. You can hear gunfire from the hills.

April 6, 1992: Now they're shooting from the Holiday Inn, killing people in front of the parliament . . . . Maybe we'll go to the cellar . . .

April 9, 1992: I'm not going to school. All the schools in Sarajevo are closed . . . .

April 14, 1992: People are leaving Sarajevo. The airport, train and bus stations are packed . . . .

April 18, 1992: There's shooting, shells are falling. This really is WAR. Mommy and Daddy are worried, they sit up late at night, talking. They're wondering what to do, but it's hard to know . . . . Mommy can't make up her mind— she's constantly in tears. She tries to hide it from me, but I see everything.

April 21, 1992: It's horrible in Sarajevo today. Shells falling, people and children getting killed, shooting. We will probably spend the night in the cellar.

April 26, 1992: We spent Thursday night with the Bobars again. The next day we had no electricity. We had no bread, so for the first time in her life Mommy baked some.

April 28, 1992: SNIFFLE! Everybody has gone. I'm left with no friends.

April 29, 1992: I'd write to you much more about the war if only I could. But I simply don't want to remember all these horrible things.

Q *How do you think Zlata Filipovic was able to deal with the new conditions in her life?*

The War in Bosnia The recognition of independent Bosnia-Herzegovina, Slovenia, and Croatia by many European states and the United States early in 1992 did not stop the Serbs from turning their guns on Bosnia. By mid-1993, Serbian forces had acquired 70 percent of Bosnian territory (see the box above). The Serbian policy of "**ethnic cleansing**"—killing or forcibly removing Bosnian Muslims from their lands—revived memories of Nazi atrocities during World War II. This account by one Muslim survivor from the town of Srebrenica is eerily reminiscent of the activities of the Nazi *Einsatzgruppen* (see Chapter 27):

> When the truck stopped, they told us to get off in groups of five. We immediately heard shooting next to the trucks . . . . About ten Serbs with automatic rifles told us to lie down on the ground face first. As we were getting down, they started to shoot, and I fell into a pile of corpses. I felt hot liquid running down my face. I realized that I was only grazed. As they continued to shoot more groups, I kept on squeezing myself in between dead bodies.[3]

Almost 8,000 men and boys were killed in the Serbian massacre at Srebrenica. Nevertheless, despite worldwide outrage, European governments failed to take a decisive and forceful stand against these Serbian activities. By 1995, some 250,000 Bosnians (mostly civilians) had been killed, and 2 million others were left homeless.

Renewed offensives by mostly Muslim Bosnian government army forces and by the Croatian army regained considerable territory that had been lost to Serbian forces. Air strikes by NATO bombers, strongly advocated by U.S. President Bill Clinton, were launched in retaliation for Serb attacks on civilians and weakened the Serb military positions. All sides were now encouraged by the United States to end the war and met in Dayton, Ohio, in November 1995 for negotiations. A formal peace treaty was signed in Paris on December 14 that split Bosnia into a loose union of a Serb republic (with 49 percent of the land) and a Muslim-Croat federation (with 51 percent of the land). NATO agreed to send a force of 60,000 troops (20,000 American troops made up the largest single contingent) that would monitor the frontier between the new political entities (see Map 30.2).

The War in Kosovo Peace in Bosnia, however, did not bring peace to the remnants of Yugoslavia. A new war erupted in 1999 over Kosovo, which had been made an autonomous province within Yugoslavia in 1974. Kosovo's inhabitants were mainly ethnic Albanians who were allowed to keep their Albanian language. But Kosovo also had a Serbian minority who considered Kosovo a sacred territory because it contained the site where Serbian forces had been defeated by the Ottoman Turks in the fourteenth century in a battle that became a defining moment in Serbian history (see Chapter 12).

In 1989, Yugoslav president Milošević, who had become an ardent Serbian nationalist, stripped Kosovo of its autonomous status and outlawed any official use of the Albanian language. In 1993, some groups of ethnic

The War in Bosnia. By mid-1993, irregular Serb forces had overrun much of Bosnia-Herzegovina amid scenes of untold suffering. This photograph shows a woman running past the bodies of victims of a mortar attack on Sarajevo on August 21, 1992. Three mortar rounds landed, killing at least three people.

MAP 30.2 The Lands of the Former Yugoslavia, 1995. By 1991, resurgent nationalism and the European independence wave overcame the forces that held Yugoslavia together. Independence declarations by Slovenia, Croatia, and Bosnia-Herzegovina brought war with the Serbian-dominated rump Yugoslavia of Slobodan Milošević.

Q What aspects of Slovenia's location help explain why its war of liberation was briefer and less bloody than others in the former Yugoslavia? **View an animated version of this map or related maps at** academic.cengage.com/history/spielvogel

Albanians founded the Kosovo Liberation Army (KLA) and began a campaign against Serbian rule in Kosovo. When Serb forces began to massacre ethnic Albanians in an effort to crush the KLA, the United States and its NATO allies sought to arrange a settlement. After months of negotiations, the Kosovo Albanians agreed to a peace plan that would have given the ethnic Albanians in Kosovo broad autonomy for a three-year interim period. When Milošević refused to sign the agreement, the United States and its NATO allies began a bombing campaign that forced the Yugoslavian government into compliance.

The Aftermath Since 1991, Yugoslavia had been embroiled in an appalling and destructive war, largely caused by the policies of Slobodan Milošević. By 2000, the Serbian people had finally tired of the violence and in the fall elections ousted Milošević from power. The new Serbian government under Vojislav Kostunica (b. 1944) moved quickly to cooperate with the international community and begin rebuilding the Serbian economy. On June 28, 2001, the Serbian government agreed to allow Milošević to be put on trial by an international tribunal for crimes against humanity for his ethnic cleansing policies throughout Yugoslavia's disintegration. He died in prison in 2006 before his trial could be completed.

The fate of Bosnia and Kosovo has not yet been finally determined. In Bosnia, 30,000 NATO troops remain, trying to keep the peace between the Serb republic and the Muslim-Croat federation. More than thirty international organizations are at work rebuilding schools, roads, and sewers, but only the presence of NATO troops keeps old hatreds from erupting again.

In Kosovo, NATO military forces were brought in to maintain an uneasy peace, while United Nations officials worked to create democratic institutions and the European Union provided funds for rebuilding the region's infrastructure. These efforts are ongoing but are made difficult by the festering hatred between Kosovo Albanians and the remaining Serbs.

The last political vestiges of Yugoslavia ceased to exist in 2004 when the Kostunica government officially renamed the truncated country Serbia and Montenegro. Two years later, Montenegrans voted in favor of independence. Thus, by 2006, all six republics cobbled together to form Yugoslavia in 1918 were once again independent nations.

Western Europe and the Search for Unity

With the revolutions of 1989, Western Europe was faced with new political possibilities and challenges. Germany was once again united, delighting the Germans but frightening their neighbors. At the same time, new opportunities for thinking of all of Europe as a political entity also emerged. Eastern Europe was no longer cut off from Western Europe by the Iron Curtain of the Cold War.

Germany Restored With the end of the Cold War, West Germany faced a new challenge. Chancellor Helmut Kohl had benefited greatly from an economic boom in the mid-1980s. Gradually, however, discontent with the Christian Democrats increased, and by 1988, their political prospects seemed diminished. But unexpectedly, the 1989 revolution in East Germany led to the reunification of the two Germanies, leaving the new Germany, with its 79 million people, the leading power in Europe. Reunification, which was accomplished during Kohl's administration and owed much to his efforts, brought rich political dividends to the Christian Democrats. In the first all-German federal election, Kohl's Christian Democrats won 44 percent of the vote, while their coalition partners, the Free Democrats, received 11 percent.

But the excitement over reunification soon dissipated as new problems arose. All too soon, the realization set in that the revitalization of eastern Germany would take far more money than was originally thought, and Kohl's government was soon forced to face the politically undesirable task of raising taxes substantially. Moreover, the virtual collapse of the economy in eastern Germany led to extremely high levels of unemployment and severe discontent. One reason for the problem was the government's decision to establish a 1:1 ratio between the East and West German marks. This policy raised salaries for East German workers, but it increased labor costs and caused many companies to hire workers abroad.

East Germans were also haunted by another memory from their recent past. The opening of the files of the secret police (the Stasi) showed that millions of East Germans had spied on their neighbors and colleagues, and even their spouses and parents, during the Communist era. A few senior Stasi officials were put on trial for their past actions but many Germans preferred simply to close the door on an unhappy period in their lives.

As the century neared its close, then, Germans struggled to cope with the challenge of building a new, united nation. To reduce the debt incurred because of economic reconstruction in the east, the government threatened to cut back on many of the social benefits West Germans had long been accustomed to receiving. This in turn sharpened resentments that were already beginning to emerge between western and eastern Germany.

In 1998, voters took out their frustrations at the ballot box. Helmut Kohl's conservative coalition was defeated in new elections, and a new prime minister, Social Democrat Gerhard Schroeder (b. 1944), came into office. But Schroeder had little success at solving Germany's economic woes, and as a result of elections in 2005, Angela Merkel (b. 1954), leader of the Christian Democrats, became the first female chancellor in German history.

Post-Thatcher Britain While Margaret Thatcher dominated British politics in the 1980s, the Labour Party, beset by divisions between its moderate and radical wings, offered little effective opposition. Only in 1990 did Labour's

FILM & HISTORY
THE LIVES OF OTHERS (2006)

Directed by Florian Henckel von Donnersmarck, *The Lives of Others,* which won the Academy Award for Best Foreign Film, is a German film (*Das Leben der Anderen*) that brilliantly re-creates the depressing debilitation of East German society under its Communist regime, and especially the Stasi, its secret police. Georg Dreyman (Sebastian Koch) is a successful playwright in the German Democratic Republic (East Germany). Although he is a dedicated socialist who has not offended the authorities, they try to determine whether he is completely loyal by wiretapping his apartment, where he lives with his girlfriend, Christa-Maria Sieland (Martina Gedeck), an actress

Georg Dreyman (Sebastian Koch) examines his Stasi files.

in some of Dreyman's plays. Captain Gerd Wiesler (Ulrich Mühe) of the Stasi takes charge of the spying operation. He is the epitome of the perfect functionary—a cold, calculating, dedicated professional who is convinced he is building a better society and is only too eager to fight the "enemies of socialism." But in the course of listening to the everyday details of Dreyman's life, Wiesler begins to develop a conscience and becomes sympathetic to the writer. After a close friend of Dreyman's commits suicide, Dreyman turns against the Communist regime and writes an article on the alarming number of suicides in East German society for *Der Spiegel,* a West German magazine. Lieutenant Colonel Grubitz (Ulrich Tukur), Wiesler's boss, suspects that Dreyman is the author. His girlfriend is brought in for questioning and provides some damning information about Dreyman's involvement. Horrified by what she has done, she commits suicide, but Wiesler, who is now determined to save Dreyman, fudges his reports and protects him from being arrested. Wiesler's boss suspects what Wiesler has done and demotes him. The film ends after the fall of the Berlin Wall when the new German government opens the Stasi files. When Dreyman reads his file, he realizes how Wiesler saved him and writes a book dedicated to him.

The film brilliantly re-creates the stifling atmosphere of East Germany under Communist rule. The Stasi had about 90,000 employees but also recruited a network of hundreds of thousands of informers who submitted secret reports on their friends, family, bosses, and coworkers: Some volunteered the information, but as the film makes clear, others were bribed or blackmailed into working with the authorities. As the movie demonstrates, the Stasi were experts at wiretapping dwellings and compiling detailed written reports about what they heard, including conversations, arguments, jokes, and even sexual activities. Ironically, Ulrich Mühe, who plays Captain Wiesler in the film, was an East German who himself had been spied on by the Stasi.

The Lives of Others has been praised by East Germans for accurately depicting the drab environment of their country and the role of the Stasi in fostering a society riddled by secrecy, fear, and the abuse of power. The dangers of governments that monitor their citizens are apparent and quite relevant in an age of Patriot Acts designed to fight terrorism. The police state is revealed for what it is, a soulless and hollow world with no redeeming features or values.

---

fortunes seem to revive when Thatcher's government attempted to replace local property taxes with a flat-rate tax payable by every adult to a local authority. Though Thatcher maintained that this would make local government more responsive to its electors, many argued that this was nothing more than a poll tax that would enable the rich to pay the same rate as the poor. In 1990, after antitax riots broke out, Thatcher's once remarkable popularity fell to an all-time low. At the end of November, a revolt within her own party caused Thatcher to resign as Britain's longest-serving prime minister. She was replaced by John Major, whose Conservative Party won a narrow victory in the general elections held in April 1992. His government, however, failed to capture the imagination of most Britons. In new elections on May 1, 1997, the Labour Party won a landslide victory. The new prime

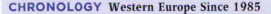

minister, Tony Blair (b. 1953), was a moderate whose youthful energy immediately instilled new vigor into the political scene. Adopting centrist policies reminiscent of those followed by President Bill Clinton in the United States (see "The United States: Move to the Center" later in this chapter), his party dominated the political arena into the new century. Blair was one of the prominent leaders in forming an international coalition against terrorism after the terrorist attack on the United States in 2001. Three years later, his support of the U.S. war in Iraq, when a majority of Britons opposed it, caused his popularity to plummet, although the failure of the Conservative Party to field a popular candidate kept him in power until the summer of 2007, when he stepped down and allowed the new Labour leader Gordon Brown (b. 1951) to become prime minister.

France: A Move to the Right Although François Mitterrand was able to win a second term as president in 1988, France's economic decline continued. In 1993, French unemployment stood at 10.6 percent, and in the elections in March of that year, the Socialists won only 28 percent of the vote as a coalition of conservative parties gained 80 percent of the seats in the National Assembly. The move to the right in France was strengthened when the conservative mayor of Paris, Jacques Chirac (b. 1932), was elected president in 1995 and reelected in 2002.

By 1995, resentment against foreign-born residents had become a growing political reality. Spurred by rising rates of unemployment and large numbers of immigrants from North Africa (often identified in the public mind with terrorist actions committed by militant groups based in the Middle East), many French voters advocated restrictions on all new immigration. Chirac himself pursued a plan of sending illegal immigrants back to their home countries. He said, "France cannot accept all of the wretched of the earth" (see the box on p. 887).

In the fall of 2005, however, antiforeign sentiment provoked a backlash of its own, as young Muslims in the crowded suburbs of Paris rioted against dismal living conditions and the lack of employment opportunities for foreign residents in France. After the riots subsided, government officials promised to adopt measures to respond to the complaints, but tensions between the Muslim community and the remainder of the French population have become a chronic source of social unrest throughout the country—an unrest that Nicolas Sarkozy (b. 1955), elected as president in 2007, has promised to address.

Corruption in Italy Corruption has continued to trouble Italian politics after 1985. In 1993, hundreds of politicians and business leaders were under investigation for their involvement in a widespread scheme to use political bribes to secure public contracts. Public disgust with political corruption became so intense that in April 1996, Italian voters took the unusual step of giving control of the government to a center-left coalition that included the Communists. In recent years, Silvio Berlusconi, owner of

CHRONOLOGY Western Europe Since 1985

First all-German federal election	1990
Victory of Conservative Party under John Major in Britain	1992
Conservative victory in France	1993
Creation of European Union	1994
Jacques Chirac becomes president of France	1995
Election of Tony Blair in Britain	1997
Gerhard Schroeder becomes chancellor of Germany	1998
Reelection of Chirac	2002
Angela Merkel becomes chancellor of Germany	2005
Romano Prodi becomes prime minister of Italy	2006
Election of Nicolas Sarkozy in France	2007

a media empire, has dominated Italian politics, even though he became a politician primarily in order to protect his own business interests. He lost to Socialist Romano Prodi (b. 1939) in a close election in 2006.

The Unification of Europe

With the addition of Austria, Finland, and Sweden in 1995, the European Community (EC) had grown to fifteen members (see Map 30.3). The EC was primarily an economic union, not a political one. By 2000, it contained 370 million people and constituted the world's largest single trading entity, transacting one-fourth of the world's commerce. In 1986, the EC had created the Single Europe Act, which had opened the door by 1992 to a truly united internal market, thereby eliminating all barriers to the exchange of people, goods, services, and capital. This was followed by a proposal for a monetary union and a common currency. The Treaty on European Union (also called the Maastricht Treaty after the city in the Netherlands where the agreement was reached) represented an attempt to create a true economic and monetary union of all EC members. On January 1, 1994, the EC renamed itself the European Union (EU). One of its first goals was to introduce a common currency, called the euro, adopted by twelve EU nations early in 1999. On June 1, 1999, a European Central Bank was created, and by January 2007, the euro had officially replaced thirteen national currencies.

Goals In addition to having a single internal market for its members and a common currency, the EU also established a common agricultural policy, under which subsidies are provided to farmers to enable them to sell their goods competitively on the world market. The policy also provides aid to the EU's poorest regions as well as subsidies for job training, education, and modernization. The end of national passports gave millions of Europeans greater flexibility in travel.

The European Union has been less successful in setting common foreign policy goals, primarily because

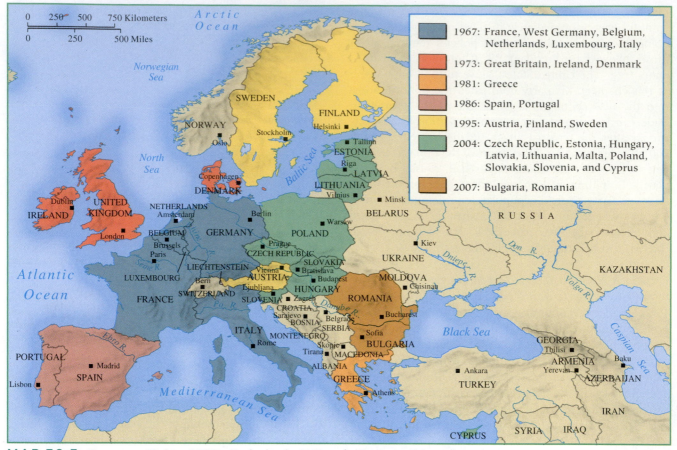

MAP 30.3 **European Union, 2007.** Beginning in 1967 as the European Economic Community, also known as the Common Market, the union of European states seeking to integrate their economies has gradually grown from six members to twenty-seven in 2007. By 2002, the European Union had achieved two major goals—the creation of a single internal market and a common currency—although it has been less successful at working toward common political and foreign policy goals.

Q What additional nations do you think will eventually join the European Union?

View an animated version of this map or related maps at **academic.cengage.com/history/spielvogel**

individual nations still see foreign policy as a national prerogative and are reluctant to give it up to an overriding institution. Although EU foreign ministers meet periodically, they usually do not draw up a uniform policy. Nevertheless, the EU did create a military force of 60,000, chiefly used for humanitarian and peacekeeping purposes. Indeed, the focus of the EU is on peaceful conflict resolution, not making war.

Problems As successful as the European Union has been, problems still exist. Europeans are often divided on the EU. Some oppose it because the official representatives of the EU are not democratically accountable to the people. Moreover, many Europeans do not regard themselves as "Europeans" but remain committed to a national identity. Despite these problems, a majority—although not a large one—of the members remain committed to the EU. In a poll taken in the fall of 2001, some 54 percent of Europeans said that membership in the EU was a "good thing."

Toward a United Europe At the beginning of the twenty-first century, the EU has established a new goal: to incorporate into the union the states of eastern and southeastern Europe. Many of these states are considerably poorer than the older members, which raised the possibility that adding these nations might weaken the EU itself. To lessen the danger, EU members established a set of qualifications that focus on demonstrating a commitment both to market capitalism and to democracy, including not only the rule of law but also respect for minorities and human rights. Hence, joining the EU might well add to the stability of these nations and make possible the dream of a united Europe. In May 2004, the EU took the plunge and added ten new members: Cyprus, the Czech Republic, Estonia, Hungary, Latvia, Lithuania, Malta, Poland, Slovakia, and Slovenia. Their addition enlarged the population of the EU to 455 million people. In January 2007, the EU expanded again as Bulgaria and Romania joined the union.

The United States: Move to the Center

After twelve years of Republican administrations, the Democratic Party captured the U.S. presidency in the elections in November 1992. The inability of George H. W. Bush (b. 1924), Ronald Reagan's successor, to deal with the deficit problem, as well as an economic downturn, enabled Democrat Bill Clinton (b. 1946) to become president. The new president was a southerner who claimed to be a "new Democrat"—one who favored fiscal responsibility and a more conservative social agenda—a clear indication that the rightward drift in American politics had not been reversed by his victory. During his first term in office, Clinton reduced the budget deficit and signed a bill turning the welfare program back to the states while pushing measures to provide job opportunities for those Americans removed from the welfare rolls. By seizing the center of the American political agenda, Clinton was able to win reelection in 1996, although the Republican Party now held a majority in both houses of Congress.

Clinton's political fortunes were helped considerably by a lengthy economic revival. At the same time, a steady reduction in the annual government budget deficit strengthened confidence in the performance of the national economy. Much of Clinton's second term, however, was overshadowed by charges of presidential misconduct stemming from the president's affair with a White House intern. After a bitter partisan struggle, the U.S. Senate acquitted the president on two articles of impeachment brought by the House of Representatives. But Clinton's problems helped the Republican candidate, George W. Bush (b. 1946), win the presidential election in 2000. Although Bush lost the popular vote to Al Gore, he narrowly won the electoral vote after a highly controversial victory in the state of Florida decided ultimately by the U.S. Supreme Court.

The first four years of Bush's administration were largely occupied with the war on terrorism and the U.S.-led war on Iraq. The Department of Homeland Security was established after the 2001 terrorist assaults to help protect the United States from future terrorist acts. At the same time, Bush pushed tax cuts through Congress that mainly favored the wealthy and helped produce record deficits reminiscent of the Reagan years. Environmentalists were especially disturbed by the Bush administration's efforts to weaken environmental laws and impose regulations to benefit American corporations. In November 2004, after a highly negative political campaign, Bush was narrowly elected to a second term. From 2005 to 2007, Bush's popularity plummeted drastically as discontent grew over the Iraq War and financial corruption in the Republican Party, as well as the administration's poor handling of relief efforts after Hurricane Katrina.

Contemporary Canada

The government of Brian Mulroney, who came to power in 1984, sought greater privatization of Canada's state-run corporations and negotiated a free trade agreement with the United States. Bitterly resented by many Canadians, the agreement cost Mulroney's government much of its popularity. In 1993, the ruling Conservatives were overwhelmingly defeated, and the Liberal leader, Jean Chrétien (b. 1934), became prime minister. Chrétien's conservative fiscal policies, combined with strong economic growth, enabled his government to have a budgetary surplus by the late 1990s and led to another Liberal victory in the elections of 1997. Charges of widespread financial corruption in the government, however, led to a Conservative victory early in 2006, and Stephen Harper (b. 1959) became the new prime minister.

Mulroney's government had been unable to settle the ongoing crisis over the French-speaking province of Quebec. In the late 1960s, the Parti Québécois, headed by René Lévesque, ran on a platform of Quebec's secession from the Canadian union. To pursue their dream of separation, some underground separatist groups even resorted to terrorist bombings. In 1976, the Parti Québécois won Quebec's provincial elections and in 1980 called for a referendum that would enable the provincial government to negotiate Quebec's independence from the rest of Canada. Quebec voters narrowly rejected the plan in 1995, however, and debate over the province's status continues to divide Canada.

Quebec

After the Cold War: New World Order or Age of Terrorism?

Q **Focus Questions:** How and why did the Cold War end? What are the main issues in the struggle with terrorism?

Even before the collapse of the Soviet Union, there had been tantalizing signs of a thaw in the Cold War. China and the United States had decided in 1979 to establish mutual diplomatic relations, a consequence of Beijing's decision to focus on domestic reform and stop supporting wars of national liberation in Asia. Six years later, the ascent of Mikhail Gorbachev to leadership, culminating in the demise of the Soviet Union in 1991, brought a final end to almost half a century of bitter rivalry between the world's two superpowers.

The End of the Cold War

The accession of Mikhail Gorbachev to power in the Soviet Union in 1985 eventually brought a dramatic

AP Images/Ira Schwartz

Reagan and Gorbachev. The willingness of Mikhail Gorbachev and Ronald Reagan to dampen the arms race was a significant factor in ending the Cold War confrontation between the United States and the Soviet Union. Reagan and Gorbachev are shown here standing before Saint Basil's Cathedral during Reagan's visit to Moscow in 1988.

aware that their large military budgets made it difficult for them to solve their serious social problems.

The years 1989 and 1990 were a crucial period in the ending of the Cold War. As described earlier, the postwar settlements came unstuck as a mostly peaceful revolutionary upheaval swept through Eastern Europe. Gorbachev's policy of allowing greater autonomy for the Communist regimes of Eastern Europe meant that the Soviet Union would no longer militarily support Communist governments that faced internal revolt. The unwillingness of the Soviet regime to use force to maintain the status quo, as it had in Hungary in 1956 and in Czechoslovakia in 1968, opened the door to the overthrow of the Communist regimes. The reunification of Germany on October 3, 1990, marked the end of one of the most prominent legacies of the Cold War.

The Persian Gulf War provided the first major opportunity for testing the new relationship between the United States and the Soviet Union in the post–Cold War era. In early August 1990, Iraqi military forces suddenly occupied the small neighboring country of Kuwait, in the northeastern corner of the Arabian peninsula at the head of the Persian Gulf. The Iraqi invasion of Kuwait sparked an international outcry, and an international force led by the United States liberated Kuwait and destroyed a substantial part of Iraq's armed forces in the early months of 1991.

The Gulf War was the first important military conflict in the post–Cold War period. Although Gorbachev tried to persuade Iraq to withdraw its forces from Kuwait before the war began, overall the Soviets played a minor role in the crisis and supported the American action. By the end of 1991, the Soviet Union had disintegrated, making any renewal of global rivalry between the superpowers impossible and leaving the United States as the world's leading military power. With the end of superpower rivalry and the collapse of the Soviet Union in 1991, attention focused on the new post–Cold War era. Many observers were optimistic. U.S. president George H. W. Bush looked forward to a new era of peace and international cooperation that he called the "New World Order." Others predicted the beginning of a new "American century," characterized by the victory of liberal democratic values and free market capitalism.

But the voices of optimism began to fade as it became clear that forces were now being released that had long been held in check by the ideological rigidities of the Cold War. The age of conflict that had long characterized the twentieth century was not at an end but was simply beginning to take a different form.

end to the Cold War. Gorbachev was willing to rethink many of the fundamental assumptions underlying Soviet foreign policy, and his "New Thinking," as it was called, opened the door to a series of stunning changes. For one, Gorbachev initiated a plan for arms limitation that led in 1987 to an agreement with the United States to eliminate intermediate-range nuclear weapons (the INF Treaty). Both sides had incentives to dampen the expensive arms race. Gorbachev hoped to make extensive economic and internal reforms, and the United States had serious deficit problems. During the Reagan years, the United States had moved from being a creditor nation to being the world's biggest debtor nation. By 1990, both countries were becoming

This was soon apparent around the world. In Southeast Asia, even before the end of the Cold War, former allies in China, Vietnam, and Cambodia turned on each other in a conflict that joined territorial ambitions with deep-seated historical suspicions based on the memory of past conflicts. The pattern was repeated elsewhere: in Africa, where several nations erupted into civil war during the late 1980s and 1990s; in the Balkans, where Yugoslavia broke apart in a bitter conflict not yet completely resolved; and in the Middle East, where disputes in Palestine and the Persian Gulf have grown in strength and erupted into open war.

An Age of Terrorism?

Acts of terror by individuals and groups opposed to governments have become a frightening aspect of modern Western society and indeed of all the world. In 1996, President Clinton called terrorism "the enemy of our generation," and since the end of Cold War, it has often seemed as though terrorism has replaced communism as the West's number one enemy.

Already during the late 1970s and 1980s, concern about terrorism was often at the top of foreign policy agendas in the United States and many European countries. Small bands of terrorists used assassination; indiscriminate killing of civilians, especially by bombing; the taking of hostages; and the hijacking of airplanes to draw attention to their demands or to destabilize governments in the hope of achieving their political goals. Terrorist acts garnered considerable media attention. When Palestinian terrorists kidnapped and killed eleven Israeli athletes at the Munich Olympic Games in 1972, hundreds of millions of people watched the drama unfold on television.

Motivations for terrorist acts varied considerably. Left- and right-wing terrorist groups flourished in the late 1970s and early 1980s. Left-wing groups, such as the Baader-Meinhof gang (also known as the Red Army Faction) in Germany and the Red Brigades in Italy, consisted chiefly of affluent middle-class young people who denounced the injustices of capitalism and supported acts of revolutionary terrorism in an attempt to bring down the system. Right-wing terrorist groups, such as the New Order in Italy and the Charles Martel Club in France, used bombings to foment disorder and bring about authoritarian regimes. These groups received little or no public support, and authorities were able to crush them fairly quickly.

But terrorist acts also stemmed from militant nationalists who wished to create separatist states. Because they received considerable support from local populations sympathetic to their cause, these terrorist groups could maintain their activities over a long period of time. Most prominent was the Irish Republican Army (IRA), which resorted to vicious attacks against the ruling government and innocent civilians in Northern Ireland. Over a period of twenty years, IRA terrorists were responsible for the deaths of two thousand people in Northern Ireland; three-fourths of the victims were civilians.

Although left- and right-wing terrorist activities declined in Europe in the 1980s, international terrorism remained commonplace. Angered over the loss of their territory to Israel in 1967, some militant Palestinians responded with a policy of terrorist attacks against Israel's supporters. Palestinian terrorists operated throughout European countries, attacking both Europeans and American tourists; vacationers at airports in Rome and Vienna were massacred by Palestinian terrorists in 1985. State-sponsored terrorism was often an integral part of international terrorism. Militant governments, especially in Iran, Libya, and Syria, assisted terrorist organizations that made attacks on Europeans and Americans. On December 21, 1988, Pan American flight 103 from Frankfurt to New York exploded over Lockerbie, Scotland, killing all 258 passengers and crew members. A massive investigation finally revealed that the bomb responsible for the explosion had been planted by two Libyan terrorists who were connected to terrorist groups based in Iran and Syria.

Terrorist Attack on the United States

One of the most destructive acts of terrorism occurred on September 11, 2001, in the United States. Four groups of terrorists hijacked four commercial jet airplanes after takeoff from Boston, Newark, and Washington, D.C. The hijackers flew two of the airplanes directly into the towers of the World Trade Center in New York City, causing these buildings, as well as a number of surrounding buildings, to collapse. A third hijacked plane slammed into the Pentagon near Washington, D.C. The fourth plane, apparently headed for Washington, crashed instead in an isolated area of Pennsylvania, apparently as the result of an attempt by a group of heroic passengers to overcome the hijackers. In total, nearly three thousand people were killed, including everyone aboard the four airliners.

These coordinated acts of terror were carried out by hijackers connected to an international terrorist organization known as al-Qaeda ("the Base"), run by Osama bin Laden (b. 1957). A native of Saudi Arabia, bin Laden used an inherited fortune to set up terrorist training camps in Afghanistan, under the protection of the nation's militant fundamentalist Islamic rulers known as the Taliban. Bin Laden was also suspected of directing earlier terrorist attacks against the United States, including the bombing of two U.S. embassies in Africa in 1998 and an attack on a naval ship, the U.S.S. *Cole*, in 2000.

War in Afghanistan U.S. president George W. Bush vowed to wage a lengthy war on terrorism and worked to create a coalition of nations to assist in ridding the world of al-Qaeda and other terrorist groups. In October 2001, United States and NATO air forces began bombing Taliban-controlled command centers, airfields, and al-Qaeda hiding places in Afghanistan. On the ground, Afghan forces opposed to the Taliban, assisted by U.S. special forces, pushed the Taliban out of the capital city of Kabul and seized

Terrorist Attack on the World Trade Center in New York City. On September 11, 2001, hijackers flew two commercial jetliners into the twin towers of the World Trade Center. Shown at the left are the two towers in the New York skyline before the attack. The middle picture shows the second of the two jetliners about to hit one of the towers while smoke billows from the site of the first attack. In the scene below, firefighters are making their way through what was left of the 110-story towers after the collapse.

control of nearly all of the country by the end of November. A multiethnic government was installed but faced problems from renewed Taliban activity. The country's history of bitter internecine warfare among various tribal groups presents a severe challenge to the new government as well.

War in Iraq In 2002, President George Bush, charging that Iraqi dictator Saddam Hussein had not only provided support to bin Laden's terrorist organization but also sought to develop weapons of mass destruction, threatened to invade Iraq and remove him from power. Both claims were widely doubted by other member states at the United Nations. As a result, the United States was forced to attack Iraq with little world support. Moreover, the plan to attack upset many Arab leaders and fanned anti-American sentiment throughout the Muslim world.

In March 2003, a largely American-led army invaded Iraq. The Iraqi army was quickly defeated, and in the months that followed, occupation forces sought to restore stability to the country while setting forth plans to lay the foundations of a future democratic society. But although Saddam Hussein was later captured by U.S. troops, Saddam's supporters, foreign terrorists, and Islamic militants continued to battle the American-led forces.

American efforts focused on training an Iraqi military force capable of defeating the insurgents and establishing an Iraqi government that could hold free elections and create a democracy. Establishing a new government was difficult, however, because there were differences among the three major groups in Iraqi society: Shi'ite Muslims, Sunni Muslims, and ethnic Kurds. Although a new Iraqi government came into being, it has been unable to establish a unified state. By 2006, violence had increased dramatically and Iraq seemed to be descending into a widespread civil war, especially between the Shi'ites, who control southern Iraq, and the Sunnis, who control central Iraq. In 2007, President Bush increased the number of U.S. troops in the hope of lessening the violence.

The West and Islam

One of the major sources of terrorist activity against the West, especially the United States, has come from some parts of the Muslim world. No doubt, the ongoing Israeli-Palestinian conflict, in which the United States has steadfastly supported Israel, helped give rise to anti-Western and especially anti-U.S. feeling among many Muslims. In 1979, a revolution in Iran that led to the overthrow of the shah and the creation of a new Islamic government led by

Ayatollah Khomeini, also fed anti-Western sentiment. In the eyes of the ayatollah and his followers, the United States was the "great Satan," the powerful protector of Israel, and the enemy of Muslim peoples everywhere. Furthermore, the United States was blamed for the corruption of Iranian society under the shah.

The involvement of the United States in the liberation of Kuwait in the Persian Gulf War in 1991 also had unexpected consequences in the relationship of Islam and the West. During that war, U.S. forces were stationed in Saudi Arabia, the location of many sacred Islamic sites. The presence of American forces was considered an affront to Islam by anti-Western Islamic groups, especially that of Osama bin Laden and his followers. These anti-Western attitudes came to be shared by a number of Islamic groups in other parts of the world.

The U.S. attack on Iraq in 2003 has further inflamed some Islamic groups against the West. Although there was no evidence of a relationship between al-Qaeda terrorists and the regime of Saddam Hussein, this claim was one of the excuses used by the United States to launch a preemptive war against Iraq. Although many Iraqis welcomed the overthrow of Saddam, the deaths of innocent civilians and the torturing of prisoners by American soldiers in prisons in Iraq served to deepen anti-American sentiment in the Arab world.

New Directions and New Problems in Western Society

Q **Focus Question:** What are the major developments in the women's movement since 1985, and what problems have immigrants created for European society?

Dramatic social developments have accompanied political and economic changes since 1985. New opportunities for women have emerged, and a reinvigorated women's movement has sought to bring new meaning to the principle of equality with men. New problems for Western society have also arisen with a growing reaction against foreign workers and immigrants.

Transformation in Women's Lives

It is estimated that parents need to average 2.1 children to ensure a natural replacement of a country's population. In many European countries, the population stopped growing in the 1960s, and the trend has continued since then. By the 1990s, birthrates were down drastically; among the nations of the European Union, the average number of children per mother was 1.4. Spain's rate of 1.15 was among the lowest in the world in 2002.

At the same time, the number of women in the workforce continued to rise. In Britain, for example, women made up 44 percent of the labor force in 1990, up from 32 percent in 1970. Moreover, women were entering new employment areas. Greater access to universities and professional schools enabled women to take jobs in law, medicine, government, business, and education. In the Soviet Union, for example, about 70 percent of doctors and teachers were women. Nevertheless, economic inequality still often prevailed; women received lower wages than men for comparable work and found fewer opportunities for advancement to management positions.

The Women's Movement Feminists in the women's liberation movement came to believe that women themselves must transform the fundamental conditions of their lives. They did so in a variety of ways. First, they formed numerous "consciousness-raising" groups to heighten awareness of women's issues. Women got together to share their personal experiences and become aware of the many ways that male dominance affected their lives. This consciousness-raising helped many women become activists.

Women also sought and gained a measure of control over their own bodies by insisting that they had a right to both contraception and abortion. In the 1960s and 1970s, hundreds of thousands of European women worked, often successfully, to repeal the laws that outlawed contraception and abortion. In 1968, a French law permitted the sale of contraceptive devices, and in the 1970s, French feminists began to call for the legalization of abortion. One group of 343 prominent French women even signed a manifesto declaring that they had had abortions. In 1979, abortion became legal in France. Even in Catholic countries, where the church remained adamantly opposed to abortion, legislation allowing contraception and abortion was passed in the 1970s and 1980s.

As more women became activists, they also became involved in new issues. In the 1980s and 1990s, women faculty in universities concentrated on developing new cultural attitudes through the new academic field of women's studies. Courses in women's studies, which stressed the role and contributions of women in history, mushroomed in both American and European colleges and universities.

Other women began to try to affect the political environment by allying with the antinuclear movement. In 1982, a group of women protested American nuclear missiles in Britain by chaining themselves to the fence of an American military base. Thousands more joined in creating a peace camp around the military compound. Enthusiasm ran high; one participant said: "I'll never forget that feeling; it'll live with me forever.... We walked round, and we clasped hands.... It was for women; it was for peace; it was for the world."[4]

Some women joined the ecological movement. As one German writer who was concerned with environmental issues said, it is women "who must give birth to children, willingly or unwillingly, in this polluted world of ours." Especially prominent were the female members of the Green Party in Germany (see "The Environment and the Green Movements" in Chapter 29), which

An Antinuclear Protest. Women were active participants in the antinuclear movement of the 1980s. Shown here are some of the ten thousand antinuclear protesters who linked hands to form a human chain around the 9-mile perimeter of the U.S. Air Force base at Greenham Common, England, on December 13, 1982. They were protesting the planned siting of ninety-six U.S. cruise missiles at the base.

France, and people from the Caribbean, India, and Pakistan to Great Britain. Overall, there were probably 15 million guest workers in Europe in the 1980s. They constituted 17 percent of the labor force in Switzerland and 10 percent in Germany.

Although these workers had been recruited for economic reasons, they often found themselves unwelcome socially and politically. Many foreign workers complained that they received lower wages and inferior social benefits. Moreover, their concentration in certain cities or certain sections of cities often created tensions with the local native populations. Foreign workers, many of them nonwhites, constituted almost one-fifth of the population in the German cities of Frankfurt, Munich, and Stuttgart. Having become

supported environmental issues and elected forty-two delegates to the West German parliament in 1987. Among the delegates was Petra Kelly (b. 1947), one of the founders of the German Green Party and a tireless campaigner for the preservation of the environment as well as human rights and equality.

Women in the West have also reached out to work with women from the rest of the world in international conferences to change the conditions of their lives. Between 1975 and 1995, the United Nations held conferences in Mexico City, Copenhagen, Nairobi, and Beijing. These meetings made clear that women from Western and non-Western countries had different priorities. Whereas women from Western countries spoke about political, economic, cultural, and sexual rights, women from developing countries in Latin America, Africa, and Asia focused on bringing an end to the violence, hunger, and disease that haunt their lives. Despite these differences, the meetings were an indication of how women in both developed and developing nations were organizing to make people aware of women's issues.

Guest Workers and Immigrants

As the economies of the Western European countries revived in the 1950s and 1960s, a severe labor shortage encouraged them to rely on foreign workers. Government and businesses actively recruited so-called **guest workers** to staff essential jobs. Scores of Turks and eastern and southern Europeans came to Germany, North Africans to

settled in their new countries, many wanted to stay, even after the end of the postwar boom in the early 1970s led to mass unemployment. Moreover, as guest workers settled permanently in their host countries, additional family members migrated to join them. Although they had little success in getting guest workers already there to leave, some European countries passed legislation or took other measures to restrict new immigration. In 1991, thousands of Albanians fled their homeland after its Communist government began to fall apart, but when they arrived in Italy, the Italian authorities forcibly evicted them and sent them back to Albania.

In the 1980s, there was an influx of other refugees, especially to West Germany, which had liberal immigration laws that permitted people seeking asylum for political persecution to enter the country. During the 1970s and 1980s, West Germany absorbed over a million refugees from Eastern Europe and East Germany. In 1986 alone, 200,000 political refugees from Pakistan, Bangladesh, and Sri Lanka entered the country. Other parts of Europe saw a similar influx of foreigners. Between 1992 and 2002, London and the southeast region of England witnessed an increase of 700,000 new foreigners, primarily from Yugoslavia, Southeast Asia, the Middle East, and Africa. A survey in 1998 found that English was not the first language of one-third of inner-city children in London.

The arrival of so many foreigners strained not only the social services of European countries but also the patience of many native residents who opposed making their countries ethnically diverse. Antiforeign sentiment, especially in a time of growing unemployment, increased and was encouraged by new right-wing political parties that catered to people's complaints. Thus, the National Front in France, organized by Jean-Marie Le Pen, and the Republican Party in Germany, led by Franz Schönhuber, a former SS officer, advocated restricting all new immigration and limiting the assimilation of settled immigrants. Although these parties had only limited success in elections, even that modest accomplishment encouraged traditional conservative and even moderately conservative parties to adopt more nationalistic policies. Occasionally, an antiforeign party was quite successful. Jorg Haider, whose Freedom Party received 27 percent of the vote in 1999, cushioned his rejection of foreigners by appealing to Austrian nationalism and attacking the European Union: "We Austrians should answer not to the European Union, not to Maastricht, not to some international idea or other, but to this our Homeland."[5] Even more frightening than the growth of these right-wing political parties were the organized campaigns of violence in the early 1990s, especially against African and Asian immigrants, by radical, right-wing groups (see the box on p. 956).

Even nations that have been especially tolerant in opening their borders to immigrants and seekers of asylum are changing their policies. In the Netherlands, 19 percent of the people have a foreign background, representing almost 180 nationalities. In 2004, however, the Dutch government passed tough new immigration laws, including a requirement that newcomers pass a Dutch language and culture test before being admitted to the Netherlands.

One other effect of the influx of foreigners into Europe is religious—a dramatic increase in the number of Muslims. Although Christians still constitute a majority (though many no longer practice their faith), the number of Muslims has mushroomed in France, Britain, Belgium, the Netherlands, and Germany. It has been estimated that at least 15 million Muslims were living in European Union nations at the beginning of the twenty-first century.

Western Culture Today

Q **Focus Question:** What major Western cultural trends have emerged since 1985?

Western culture has expanded to most parts of the world, although some societies see it as a challenge to their own culture and national identity. At the same time, other societies are also strongly influencing Western cultural expressions, making recent Western culture a reflection of the evolving global response to the rapid changes in human society today.

Varieties of Religious Life

Despite the revival of religion after World War II, church attendance in Europe and the United States declined dramatically in the 1960s and 1970s as a result of growing secular attitudes. Yet even though the numbers of regular churchgoers in established Protestant and Catholic churches continued to decline, the number of fundamentalist churches and churchgoers has been growing, especially in the United States.

Fundamentalism was originally a movement within Protestantism that arose early in the twentieth century. Its goal was to maintain a strict traditional interpretation of the Bible and the Christian faith, especially in opposition to the theory of Darwinian evolution and secularism. In the 1980s and 1990s, fundamentalists became involved in a struggle against so-called secular humanism, godless communism, legalized abortion, and homosexuality. Especially in the United States, fundamentalists organized politically to elect candidates who supported their views. This so-called Christian right played an influential role in electing both Ronald Reagan and George W. Bush to the presidency.

The Growth of Islam Fundamentalism, however, was not unique to Protestantism. In Islam, the term *fundamentalism* is used to refer to a return to traditional Islamic values, especially in opposition to a perceived weakening of moral values due to the corrupting influence of Western ideas and practices. After the Iranian Revolution of 1979, the term was also applied to militant Islamic movements, such as the Taliban in Afghanistan, who favored militant action against Western influence.

Despite the wariness of Islamic radicalism in the aftermath of the September 11, 2001 terrorist attacks on the United States, Islam is growing in both Europe and the United States, thanks primarily to the migration of people from Muslim countries. As Muslim communities became established in France, Germany, Britain, Italy, and Spain during the 1980s and 1990s, they built mosques for religious worship and religious education. In the United States, the states of California and New York each have more than two hundred mosques.

Pope John Paul II Although changes have also occurred in the Catholic Church, much of its history in the 1980s and 1990s was dominated by the charismatic Pope John Paul II (1920–2005). Karol Wojtyla, who had been the archbishop of Krakow in Poland before his elevation to the papacy in 1978, was the first non-Italian to be elected pope since the sixteenth century. Although he alienated a number of people by reasserting traditional Catholic teaching on such issues as birth control, women in the priesthood, and clerical celibacy, John Paul's numerous travels around the world helped strengthen the Catholic Church throughout the non-Western world. A strong believer in social justice, John Paul was a powerful figure in reminding Europeans of their spiritual heritage and the need to temper the pursuit of materialism with spiritual concerns. He also condemned nuclear weapons and constantly reminded leaders and laity of their obligations to prevent war (see the box on p. 957).

VIOLENCE AGAINST FOREIGNERS IN GERMANY

As the number of foreign guest workers and immigrants increased in Europe, violent attacks against them also escalated. Especially in the former East Germany, where unemployment rose dramatically after reunification, gangs of neo-Nazi youth have perpetrated violent attacks on foreigners. This document is taken from a German press account of an attack on guest workers from Vietnam and Mozambique who had originally been recruited by the East German government.

Knud Pries, "East Germans Have Yet to Learn Tolerance," October 6, 1991

The police headquarters in Dresden, the capital of Saxony, announced that "a political situation" had developed in the town of Hoyerswerda. Political leaders and the police needed to examine the problem and corresponding measures should be taken: "In the near future the residents of the asylum hostel will be moved."

The people of Hoyerswerda prefer to be more direct, referring to the problem of *Neger* (niggers) and *Fidschis* (a term for Asian foreigners). The loudmouths of the neofascist gangs make the message clear: "Niggers Go Home!"

It looks as if some Germans have had enough of bureaucratic officialese. What is more, they will soon make sure that no more foreign voices are heard in Hoyerswerda.

The municipality in northern Saxony has a population of just under 70,000, including 70 people from Mozambique and Vietnam who live in a hostel for foreigners and about 240 asylum-seekers in a hostel at the other end of town.

The "political situation" was triggered by an attack by a neo-Nazi gang on Vietnamese traders selling their goods on the market square on 17 September. After being dispersed by the police the Faschos carried out their first attack on the hostel for foreigners.

The attacks then turned into a regular evening "hunt" by a growing group of right-wing radicals, some of them minors, who presented their idea of a clean Germany by roaming the streets armed with truncheons, stones, steel balls, bottles and Molotov cocktails. Seventeen people were injured, some seriously.

After the police stepped in on a larger scale the extremists moved across the town to the asylum hostel. To begin with, only the gang itself and onlookers were outside the building, but on the evening of 22 September members of the "Human Rights League" and about 100 members of "autonomous" groups turned up to help the foreigners who had sought refuge in the already heavily damaged block of flats.

A large police contingent, reinforced by men from Dresden and the Border Guard, prevented the situation from becoming even more critical. Two people were seriously injured. The mob was disbanded with the help of dogs, tear gas and water-cannons.

Thirty-two people were arrested, and blank cartridge guns, knives, slings and clubs were seized. On 23 September, a police spokesman announced that the situation was under control. It seems doubtful whether things will stay this way, since the pogroms have become an evening ritual. Politicians and officials are racking their brains about how to grapple with the current crisis and the basic problem. One thing is clear: without a massive intervention by the police the problem cannot even be contained. But what then?

Saxony's Interior Minister, Rudolf Krause, initially recommended that the hostels concerned should be "fenced in," but then admitted that this was "not the final solution." Providing the Defense Ministry approves, the "provisional solution" will be to move the foreigners to a barracks in Kamenz.

Even if this operation is completed without violence it would represent a shameful success for the right-wing radicals. Although the Africans and Asians still living in Hoyerswerda will have to leave at the end of November anyway once the employment contracts drawn up in the former [East Germany] expire, they are unwilling to endure the terror that long. "Even if we're going anyway—they want all foreigners to go now," says the 29-year-old Martinho from Mozambique.

His impression is that the gangs of thugs are doing something for which others are grateful: "The neighbors are glad when the skinheads arrive."

Interior Minister Krause feels that the abuse of asylum laws, the social problems in East Germany and an historically rooted deficit explain this situation: "The problem is that we were unable in the past to practice the tolerance needed to accept alien cultures."

Q *What forces in modern western and central Europe came together to promote the rise of neo-Nazi groups and their attacks against foreign minorities in European communities? Why does toleration seem to be absent from many of the communities in the former East Germany?*

Art and Music in the Age of Commerce: The 1980s and 1990s

Throughout the 1980s and 1990s, the art and music industries increasingly adopted the techniques of marketing and advertising. With large sums of money invested in artists and musicians, pressure mounted to achieve critical and commercial success. Negotiating the distinction between art and popular culture was essential since many equated merit with sales or economic value.

POPE JOHN PAUL II: AN APPEAL FOR PEACE

Pope John Paul II became the spiritual leader of the Catholic Church in 1978. He made numerous trips to all parts of the globe, addressing a variety of spiritual and social issues. He made a point of speaking directly to as many lay groups as possible, often focusing on one of his chief themes, the desire for peace.

Pope John Paul II, *Speeches*

Today peace has become, throughout the world, a preoccupation not only for those responsible for the destiny of nations but even more so for broad sections of the population and innumerable individuals who generously and tenaciously dedicate themselves to creating an outlook of peace and to establishing genuine peace between peoples and nations. This is comforting. But there is no hiding the fact that in spite of the efforts of all men and women of good will, there are still serious threats to peace in the world. Some of these threats take the form of divisions within various nations; others stem from deep-rooted and acute tensions between opposing nations and blocs within the world community. In reality, the confrontations that we witness today are distinguished from those of past history by certain new characteristics. In the first place they are worldwide: even a local conflict is often an expression of tensions originating elsewhere in the world. In the same way, it often happens that a conflict has profound effects far from where it broke out. Another characteristic is totality: present day tensions mobilize all the forces of the nations involved; moreover, selfish monopolization and even hostility are to be found today as much in the way economic life is run and in the technological application of science as in the way that the mass media or military resources are utilized . . . .

Elsewhere, fear of a precarious peace, military and political imperatives, and economic and commercial interests lead to the establishment of arms stockpiles or to the sale of weapons capable of appalling destruction. The arms race, then, prevails over the great tasks of peace, which ought to unite peoples in new solidarity; it fosters sporadic but murderous conflicts and builds up the gravest threats. It is true that at first sight the cause of peace seems to be handicapped to a crippling extent.

But we must reach peace. Peace, as I said earlier, is threatened when uncertainty, doubt, and suspicion reign, and violence makes good use of this. Do we really want peace? Then we must dig deep within ourselves, and going beyond the divisions we find within us and between us, we must find the areas in which we can strengthen our conviction that human beings' basic driving forces and the recognition of their real nature carry them toward openness to others, mutual respect, community, and peace. The course of this laborious search for the objective and universal truth about humanity, and the result of the search, will develop men and women of peace and dialogue, people who draw both strength and humility from a truth that they realize they must serve and not make use of for partisan interests.

Q *What lessons did Pope John Paul II seek to teach here and what do these lessons tell you about the objectives of institutionalized religion in modern times?*

The Visual Arts In the art world, Neo-Expressionism reached its zenith in the mid-1980s. The economic boom and free spending of the Reagan years contributed to a thriving art scene in the United States. Neo-Expressionist artists like Anselm Kiefer and Jean-Michel Basquiat (1960–1988) became increasingly popular as the art market soared.

Born in Germany in 1945, Kiefer combines aspects of Abstract Expressionism, collage, and German Expressionism to create works that are stark and haunting. His *Departure from Egypt* (1984) is a meditation on Jewish history and its descent into the horrors of Nazism. Kiefer hoped that a portrayal of Germany's atrocities could free Germans from their past and bring some good out of evil. Another example of Neo-Expressionism can be seen in the work of Basquiat. The son of Haitian and Puerto Rican immigrants, Basquiat first made his name as a graffiti artist in New York City and became an overnight success during the 1980s art market boom.

While some critics dismissed Basquiat's paintings as a fad, other artists were criticized for employing controversy to market their art. In the mid-1980s, the photographers Andres Serrano and Robert Mapplethorpe became the focal point of a debate about censorship in the arts. Mapplethorpe was known for his portraits of male nudes that often featured homoerotic imagery, while Serrano created photographs of objects submerged in bodily fluids, including a crucifix immersed in urine. Though these images were often visually beautiful, they became the subject of heated debates because both artists received financial aid from a government agency, the National Endowment for the Arts (NEA). Senator Jesse Helms urged the U.S. Congress to dissolve the NEA for supporting indecency, and its budget was reduced considerably.

Music As artists and musicians became increasingly disenchanted with the excesses of the Reagan era, they also began to question the consumerism that had seemingly homogenized popular culture. The emergence of "grunge" music in the early 1990s reflected this attitude, as rock bands like Nirvana, Sonic Youth, and Pearl Jam rejected the materialism of the previous decade. Employing distortion and amplified feedback in their music, grunge artists often sang of disillusion and angst. Rather than conforming to the mass-produced norms of the fashion industry, these musicians typically

Jean-Michel Basquiat, *Self Portrait,* **1986.** In his paintings, Basquiat combined Abstract Expressionist brushwork with the popular culture of urban life. He dabbled with hip-hop and included references to comic book characters, jazz musicians, and sports heroes in his work.

The Technological World

Electronic mail, or e-mail, is a form of computerized communication that became popular in the mid-1990s. As the capacity of computers to transmit data increased, e-mail messages could carry document and image attachments, making them a workable and speedier alternative to conventional postal mail. The Worldwide Web, or Internet, is another computerized system for information exchange. A network of smaller, interlinking Web pages, the Internet includes sites devoted to news, commerce, entertainment, and academic scholarship. As computer processors have become more powerful, these Web sites now possess video and music capabilities in addition to text-based documents.

Advances in telecommunications led to cellular or mobile phones. Though cellular phones existed in the 1970s and 1980s, it was not until the digital components of these devices were reduced in size in the 1990s that cell phones became truly portable. Cell phones have since become enormously important, and not only for communication. Indeed, many nations have become financially dependent on their sales for economic growth. For example, the Nokia Corporation of Finland is largely responsible for the country's fiscal stability. Sales of Nokia phones, approximately $25 billion, nearly equal the total Finnish budget. The ubiquity of cell phones and their ability to transfer data electronically have made text messaging a recent global communications craze. Text and instant messaging have revolutionized written language, as shorthand script has replaced complete sentences for the purposes of relaying brief messages.

In 2001, Apple Computer Company introduced the iPod, a portable digital music player. The pocket-sized device has since revolutionized the music industry, as downloading music from the Internet has surpassed the purchasing of albums from record stores. In fact, album sales declined by nearly 25 percent from 2000 to 2006, while digital-single sales have risen 2,930 percent in the past four years. In April 2007, Apple sold its 100 millionth iPod, an indication of the iPod's status as a worldwide cultural phenomenon.

Music and Art in the Digital Age

Whereas the iPod altered the way in which we listen to, store, and access music, innovations in digital technology have changed the sound and production of music. In the

wore ripped jeans and weathered flannel attire to protest the excesses of capitalism.

Hip-hop continued to gain popularity following the success of Grandmaster Flash and the Furious Five. In the early 1990s, rappers like Dr. Dre and Snoop Doggy Dogg created "gangsta rap," an offshoot of hip-hop with raw lyrics praising violence, drugs, and promiscuous sex. By the late 1990s, teen and preteen consumers steered the music industry back to pop music, generating millions of dollars of sales in the process. Many pop acts became successful as music turned away from grunge and gangsta rap. Instead, musicians and audiences favored the light-hearted music that made Ricky Martin and Britney Spears famous. Drawing from rhythm and blues, Latin music, and hip-hop, these artists used catchy dance beats and extravagant music videos to market their work.

The Digital Age

Q **Focus Question:** What is the Digital Age, and what are its products, results, and dangers?

Since the invention of the microprocessor in 1971, the capabilities of computers have continued to grow, resulting in today's "Information" or "Digital Age." Beginning in the 1980s, computer companies like Apple and Microsoft competed to create more powerful computers. By the 1990s, the booming technology industry had made Microsoft founder Bill Gates the richest man in the world. Much of this success was due to several innovations within computers that made them essential devices for communication, information, and entertainment.

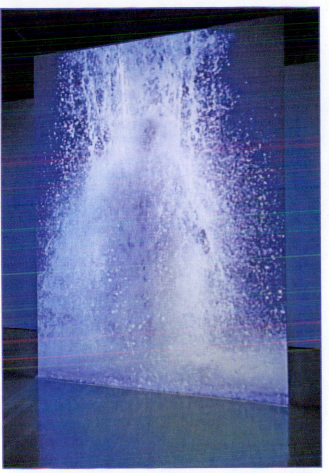

Bill Viola, *The Crossing*, 1996. In this video piece, Viola projected two films on each side of a 16-foot-high screen. On one side, a man is inundated with water, while on the other side, he is consumed by flames. The events occur in slow motion and, when experienced in conjunction with the sound of the deluge and/or flames, evoke feelings of spiritual regeneration.

late-1990s, musicians like Moby and Fatboy Slim became internationally famous for creating music layered with synthesizers, distorted guitars, and simulated drum beats. These artists sampled earlier soul music to create albums and film scores.

Many visual artists have also adopted digital effects in producing artworks that fuse photography, sculpture, and cinema. Bill Viola (b. 1951) was one of the first artists to exclusively employ video in his exhibits. By projecting films in a gallery space, Viola created powerful sensory experiences. He evoked mystical sensations with his allusions to rebirth and mysticism, contrasting light, sound, and focus with techniques of slow motion and editing.

Matthew Barney (b. 1967) has received critical attention for his multimedia presentations. His *Cremaster Series* (1994–2002) is an elaborate spectacle consisting of feature-length films, still photography, sculpture, and written texts that explore themes of creation, mythological fantasy, and social identity. In *Cremaster,* Barney produced an event that bewildered viewers with hybrid characters and seemingly unrelated plotlines. Critics consider this hybrid work important for its fusion of technology and art, suggesting that its confusion mimics that of the contemporary world.

Video Games While record sales have struggled worldwide, the video game industry has skyrocketed. In 2007, it was projected that global sales of video games would outnumber those of the music industry. With faster data processors fueling enhanced graphics in such video game consoles as the PlayStation 3 and Xbox 360, higher levels of realism have been developed. Despite the popularity of video games, many questions have arisen about their role in childhood obesity as well as neurological disorders. In June 2007, the American Medical Association heard testimony concerning video game addiction. Though video game manufacturers reject the claim, some psychologists fear that learning disabilities and dependency can result from excessive gaming.

Film: Fantasy and Epics The films, video games, and literature of the late 1990s and early 2000s made fantasy and historical epics internationally popular. The successful adaptation of the *Lord of the Rings* trilogy and Harry Potter series indicated the manner in which mythology, magic, and medieval fantasies appeal to contemporary sensibilities. At the heart of these epic motion pictures, *Troy* and *Gladiator* included, is a mythical struggle between good and evil that is governed by a moral sense of right and wrong, love, and companionship. Yet these romanticized tales also featured non-Western cultures as Japanese animé and martial arts films increased in worldwide popularity. The computer animation and digitized special effects of these movies reflect the impact of computers on the film industry as it too enters the Digital Age.

Reality in the Digital Age

Advances in communication and information during the Digital Age have led many to believe that world cultures are becoming increasingly interdependent and homogenized. Many contemporary artists have questioned the effects of the computer age on identity and material reality. According to some, the era of virtual reality, or what French philosopher Jean Baudrillard has termed "hyperreality," has displaced cultural uniqueness and bodily presence.

The Body and Identity in Contemporary Art By focusing on bodily experience and cultural norms, contemporary artists have attempted to restore that which has been lost in the Digital Age. Kiki Smith (b. 1954), an American artist born in Germany, creates sculptures of the human body that often focus on anatomical processes. These works, commonly made of wax or plaster, question the politics surrounding the body, including AIDS and domestic abuse, while reconnecting to bodily experiences.

Contemporary artists also continue to explore the interaction between the Western and non-Western world, particularly with the **multiculturalism** generated by

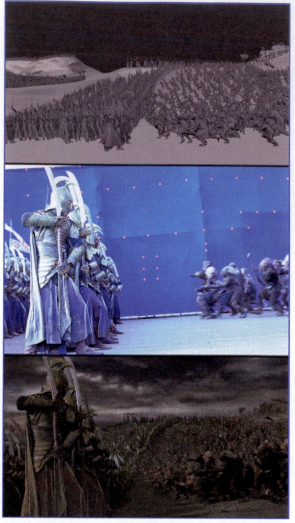

Lord of the Rings. In *The Lord of the Rings*, British writer J. R. R. Tolkien created a fantasy world in Middle Earth that has enchanted readers for decades. Beginning in 2000, Tolkien's work was brought to the screen in a series of three films. As seen in these stills from the studio that produced the films, computer graphics were used to create the special effects that re-created Tolkien's fantasy world.

global migrations (see "The Social Challenges of Globalization" later in this chapter). For example, the art of Yinka Shonibare (b. 1962), a Nigerian-born artist who resides in England, investigates the notion of hybrid identity, as he creates clothing and tableaux that fuse European designs with African traditions.

Multiculturalism in Literature The interaction of East and West has also preoccupied numerous authors since the late-1990s. Jhumpa Lahiri (b. 1967) has received international attention for writings that explore contemporary Indian life. Lahiri won the Pulitzer Prize for her collection of stories, *Interpreter of Maladies* (1999), while her first novel, *The Namesake* (2003), chronicled the lives of Indian immigrants in the United States. Both works examine generation gaps, particularly the alienation and unique

synthesis that can accompany cross-cultural exchange. The success of Lahiri's work and other novels such as Arthur Golden's *Memoirs of a Geisha* (1997) indicates how, in the Digital Age, Western peoples remain interested in other cultures and traditions. This emergence of a global culture has become part of the new globalism at the beginning of the twenty-first century.

Toward a Global Civilization

Q **Focus Question:** What is globalization, and what are the main ways in which globalization is manifesting in the twenty-first century?

Multiculturalism in literature reminds us that more and more people are becoming aware of the political, economic, and social interdependence of the world's nations and the global nature of our contemporary problems. We are coming to understand that destructive forces generated in one part of the world soon affect the entire world. Smokestack pollution in one nation can produce acid rain in another. Oil spills and dumping of wastes in the ocean have an impact on the shores of many nations. As crises of food, water, energy, and natural resources proliferate, one nation's solutions often become other nations' problems. The new globalism includes the recognition that the challenges that seem to threaten human existence today are global. In October 2001, in response to the terrorist attacks of September 11, British prime minister Tony Blair said, "We are realizing how fragile are our frontiers in the face of the world's new challenges. Today, conflict rarely stays within national boundaries."

As we saw in the discussion of the Digital Age, an important part of global awareness is the technological dimension. The growth of new technology has made possible levels of world communication that simply did not exist before. At the same time that Osama bin Laden and al-Qaeda were denouncing the forces of modernization, they were doing so by using advanced telecommunication systems that have only recently been developed. The technology revolution has tied peoples and nations closely together and contributed to **globalization,** the term that is frequently used today to describe the process by which peoples and nations have become more interdependent. Economically, globalization has taken the form of a **global economy.**

The Global Economy

Especially since the 1970s, the world has developed a global economy in which the production, distribution, and sale of goods are accomplished on a worldwide scale. Several international institutions have contributed to the rise of the global economy. Soon after the end of World War II, the United States and other nations established the World Bank and the International Monetary Fund (IMF). The World Bank is a group of five international organizations, largely controlled by developed countries, which provides grants, loans, and advice for economic

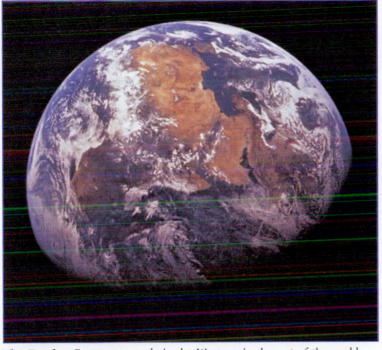

The Earth. For many people in the West, as in the rest of the world, the view of the earth from outer space fostered an important sense of global unity. The American astronaut Russell Schweickart wrote, "From where you see it, the thing is a whole, and it is so beautiful." In a similar reaction, Yuri Gagarin, the first Soviet cosmonaut, remarked, "What strikes me, is not only the beauty of the continents . . . but their closeness to one another . . . their essential unity."

development to developing countries. The goal of the IMF, which was also founded in 1945, is to oversee the global financial system by supervising exchange rates and offering financial and technical assistance to developing nations. Today, 185 countries are members of the IMF. Critics have argued that both the World Bank and the IMF push inappropriate Western economic practices on non-Western nations that only aggravate the poverty and debt of developing nations.

Another reflection of the new global economic order is the **multinational corporation** or **transnational corporation** (a company that has divisions in more than two countries). Prominent examples of multinational corporations include Siemens, General Motors, ExxonMobil, Mitsubishi, and the Sony Corporation. These companies are among the 200 largest multinational corporations, which are responsible for more than half of the world's industrial production. In 2000, 142 of the leading 200 multinational corporations were headquartered in three countries—the United States, Japan, and Germany. In addition, these super corporations dominate much of the world's investment capital, technology, and markets. A recent comparison of corporate sales and national gross domestic product disclosed that only 49 of the world's largest economies are nations; the remaining 51 are corporations. For this reason, some observers believe that economic globalization is more appropriately labeled "corporate globalization."

Another important component of economic globalization is free trade. In 1947, talks led to the General Agreement on Tariffs and Trade (GATT), a global trade organization that was replaced in 1995 by the World Trade Organization (WTO). Made up of more than 150 member nations, the WTO arranges trade agreements and settles trade disputes. Yet many critics charge that the WTO has ignored environmental and health concerns, harmed small and developing countries, and created an ever-growing gap between rich and poor nations.

Globalization and the Environmental Crisis

Taking a global perspective at the beginning of the twenty-first century has led many people to realize that everywhere on the planet human beings are interdependent in regard to the air they breathe, the water they drink, the food they consume, and the climate that affects their lives. At the same time, however, human activities are creating environmental challenges that threaten the very foundation of human existence on earth (see the box on p. 962).

One problem is population growth. As of July 2006, the world population was estimated at more than 6.5 billion people, only eighteen years after passing the 5 billion mark. At its current rate of growth, the world population could reach 12.8 billion by 2050, according to the United Nations' long-range population projections. The result has been an increased demand for food and other resources that has put great pressure on the earth's ecosystems. At the same time, the failure to grow enough food for more and more people has created a severe problem as an estimated 1 billion people worldwide today suffer from hunger. Every year, more than 8 million people die of hunger, many of them young children.

Another problem is the pattern of consumption, as the wealthy nations of the Northern Hemisphere consume vast quantities of the planet's natural resources. The United States, with just 6 percent of the planet's people, consumes 30 to 40 percent of its resources. The spread of these consumption patterns to other parts of the world raises serious questions about the ability of the planet to sustain itself and its population.

Yet another threat to the environment is **global warming**, which has the potential to create a global crisis. Virtually all of the world's scientists agree that the **greenhouse effect**, the warming of the earth because of the buildup of carbon dioxide in the atmosphere, is contributing to devastating droughts and storms, the melting of the polar ice caps, and rising sea levels that could inundate coastal regions in the second half of the twenty-first century. Also alarming is the potential loss of biodiversity. Seven out of ten biologists believe that the planet is now experiencing an alarming extinction of both plant and animal species.

A WARNING TO HUMANITY

As human threats to the environment grew, world scientists began to organize and respond to the crisis. One such group, founded in 1969, was the Union of Concerned Scientists, a nonprofit organization of professional scientists and private citizens, now with more than 200,000 members. In November 1992, the Union of Concerned Citizens published an appeal from 1,700 of the world's leading scientists. The first selection is taken from this "Warning to Humanity."

Earlier, in 1988, in response to the threat of global warming, the United Nations established an Intergovernmental Panel on Climate Change (IPCC) to study the most up-to-date scientific information on global warming and climate change. In 2007, more than 2,500 scientists from more than 130 countries contributed to the group's most recent report, "Climate Change 2007: The Fourth Assessment Report," to be released in November 2007. The second selection is taken from the Web page that summarizes the basic findings of the 2007 report.

"World Scientists' Warning to Humanity," 1992

Human beings and the natural world are on a collision course. Human activities inflict harsh and often irreversible damage on the environment and on critical resources. If not checked, many of our current practices put at serious risk the future that we wish for human society and the plant and animal kingdoms, and may so alter the living world that it will be unable to sustain life in the manner that we know. Fundamental changes are urgent if we are to avoid the collision our present course will bring about. The environment is suffering critical stress:

The Atmosphere
Stratospheric ozone depletion threatens us with enhanced ultraviolet radiation at the earth's surface, which can be damaging or lethal to many life forms. Air pollution near ground level, and acid precipitation, are already causing widespread injury to humans, forests, and crops.

Water Resources
Heedless exploitation of depletable ground water supplies endangers food production and other essential human systems. Heavy demands on the world's surface waters have resulted in serious shortages in some 80 countries, containing 40% of the world's population. Pollution of rivers, lakes, and ground water further limits the supply.

Oceans
Destructive pressure on the oceans is severe, particularly in the coastal regions which produce most of the world's food fish. The total marine catch is now at or above the estimated maximum sustainable yield. Some fisheries have already shown signs of collapse.

Soil
Loss of soil productivity, which is causing extensive land abandonment, is a widespread by-product of current practices in agriculture and animal husbandry. Since 1945, 11% of the earth's vegetated surface has been degraded—an area larger than India and China combined—and per capita food production in many parts of the world is decreasing.

Forests
Tropical rain forests, as well as tropical and temperate dry forests, are being destroyed rapidly. At present rates, some critical forest types will be gone in a few years, and most of the tropical rain forest will be gone before the end of the next century. With them will go large numbers of plant and animal species.

Living Species
The irreversible loss of species, which by 2100 may reach one-third of all species now living, is especially serious. We are losing the potential they hold for providing medicinal and other benefits, and the contribution that genetic diversity of life forms gives to the robustness of the world's biological systems and to the astonishing beauty of the earth itself.

Much of this damage is irreversible on a scale of centuries, or permanent. Other processes appear to pose additional threats. Increasing levels of gases in the atmosphere from human activities, including carbon dioxide released from fossil fuel burning and from deforestation, may alter climate on a global scale.

Warning
We the undersigned, senior members of the world's scientific community, hereby warn all humanity of what lies ahead. A great change in our stewardship of the earth and the life on it is required, if vast human misery is to be avoided and our global home on this planet is not to be irretrievably mutilated.

"Findings of the IPCC Fourth Assessment Report," 2007

Human Responsibility for Climate Change
The report finds that it is "very likely" that emissions of heat-trapping gases from human activities have caused "most of the observed increase in globally averaged temperatures since the mid-20th century." Evidence that human activities are the major cause of recent climate change is even stronger than in prior assessments.

Warming Is Unequivocal
The report concludes that it is "unequivocal" that Earth's climate is warming, "as is now evident from observations of increases in global average air and ocean temperatures, widespread melting of snow and ice, and rising global mean sea level." The report also confirms that the current

(continued)

(continued)

atmospheric concentration of carbon dioxide and methane, two important heat-trapping gases, "exceeds by far the natural range over the last 650,000 years." Since the dawn of the industrial era, concentrations of both gases have increased at a rate that is "very likely to have been unprecedented in more than 10,000 years."

Additional IPCC Findings on Recent Climate Change

Rising Temperatures

- Eleven of the last 12 years rank among the 12 hottest years on record (since 1850, when sufficient worldwide temperature measurements began).
- Over the last 50 years, "cold days, cold nights, and frost have become less frequent, while hot days, hot nights, and heat waves have become more frequent."

Increasingly Severe Weather (storms, precipitation, drought)

- The intensity of tropical cyclones (hurricanes) in the North Atlantic has increased over the past 30 years, which correlates with increases in tropical sea surface temperatures.
- Storms with heavy precipitation have increased in frequency over most land areas. Between 1900 and 2005, long-term trends show significantly increased precipitation in eastern parts of North and South America, northern Europe, and northern and central Asia.
- Between 1900 and 2005, the Sahel (the boundary zone between the Sahara desert and more fertile regions of Africa to the south), the Mediterranean, southern Africa, and parts of southern Asia have become drier, adding stress to water resources in these regions.
- Droughts have become longer and more intense, and have affected larger areas since the 1970s, especially in the tropics and subtropics.

Q   *What problems and challenges do these two reports present? What do these two reports have in common? How do they differ?*

The Social Challenges of Globalization

Since 1945, tens of millions of people have migrated from one part of the world to another. These migrations have occurred for many reasons. Persecution for political reasons caused many people from Pakistan, Bangladesh, Sri Lanka, and Eastern Europe to seek refuge in Western European countries, while brutal civil wars in Asia, Africa, the Middle East, and Europe led millions of refugees to seek safety in neighboring countries. Most people who have migrated, however, have done so to find jobs. Latin Americans seeking a better life have migrated to the United States, while guest workers from Turkey, southern and eastern Europe, North Africa, India, and Pakistan have migrated to more prosperous Western European lands. In 2005, nearly 200 million people, about 3 percent of the world's population, lived outside the country where they were born.

As discussed earlier, the migration of millions of people has created a social backlash in many countries. Foreign workers have often become scapegoats when countries face economic problems. Political parties in France and Norway have called for the removal of blacks and Arabs in order to protect the ethnic purity of their nations, while in Asian countries, there is animosity against other Asian ethnic groups. The problem of foreigners has also led to a more general attack on globalization itself as being responsible for a host of social ills that are undermining national sovereignty.

Another challenge of globalization is the wide gap between rich and poor nations. The rich nations, or **developed nations,** are located mainly in the Northern Hemisphere. They include countries such as the United States, Canada, Germany, and Japan, which have well-organized industrial and agricultural systems, advanced technologies, and effective educational systems. The poor nations, or **developing nations,** are located mainly in the Southern Hemisphere. They include many nations in Africa, Asia, and Latin America, which often have primarily agricultural economies with little technology. A serious problem in many developing nations is the explosive population growth, which has led to severe food shortages often caused by poor soil but also by economic factors. Growing crops for export to developed countries, for example, may lead to enormous profits for large landowners but leaves many small farmers with little land on which to grow food.

Civil wars have also created food shortages. War not only disrupts normal farming operations, but warring groups try to limit access to food to destroy their enemies. In the Sudan, 1.3 million people starved when combatants of a civil war in the 1980s prevented food from reaching them. As unrest continued during the early 2000s in Darfur, families were forced to leave their farms. As a result, an estimated 70,000 people starved by mid-2004.

New Global Movements and New Hopes

As the heirs of Western civilization have become aware that the problems humans face are not just national but global, they have responded to this challenge in different ways. One approach has been to develop grassroots social movements, including environmental, women's and men's liberation, human potential, appropriate-technology, and nonviolence movements. "Think globally, act locally" is frequently the slogan of these grassroots groups. Related to the emergence of these social movements is the growth of nongovernmental organizations (NGOs). According to one analyst, NGOs are an important instrument in the cultivation of global perspectives: "Since NGOs by definition are identified with interests that transcend national boundaries, we expect all NGOs to define problems in global terms, to take account of human interests and needs as they are found in all parts of the planet."[6] NGOs are often represented at the United Nations and include professional, business, and cooperative organizations; foundations; religious, peace, and disarmament groups; youth and women's organizations; environmental and human rights groups; and research institutes. The number of international NGOs increased from 176 in 1910 to 37,000 in 2000.

And yet hopes for global approaches to global problems have also been hindered by political, ethnic, and religious disputes. Pollution of the Rhine River by factories along its banks provokes angry disputes among European nations, and the United States and Canada have argued about the effects of acid rain on Canadian forests. The collapse of the Soviet Union and its satellite system seemed to provide an enormous boost to the potential for international cooperation on global issues, but it has had almost the opposite effect. The bloody conflict in the former Yugoslavia indicates the dangers inherent in the rise of nationalist sentiment among various ethnic and religious groups in Eastern Europe. The widening gap between the wealthy nations in the Northern Hemisphere and the poor,

developing nations in the Southern Hemisphere threatens global economic stability. Many conflicts begin with regional issues and then develop into international concerns. International terrorist groups seek to wreak havoc around the world.

Thus, even as the world becomes more global in culture and interdependent in its mutual relations, centrifugal forces are still at work attempting to redefine the political, cultural, and ethnic ways in which the world is divided. Such efforts are often disruptive and can sometimes work against measures to enhance our human destiny.

Many lessons can be learned from the history of Western civilization, but one of them is especially clear. Lack of involvement in the affairs of one's society can lead to a sense of powerlessness. In an age that is often crisis-laden and chaotic, an understanding of our Western heritage and its lessons can be instrumental in helping us create new models for the future. For we are all creators of history, and the future of Western and indeed world civilization depends on us.

TIMELINE

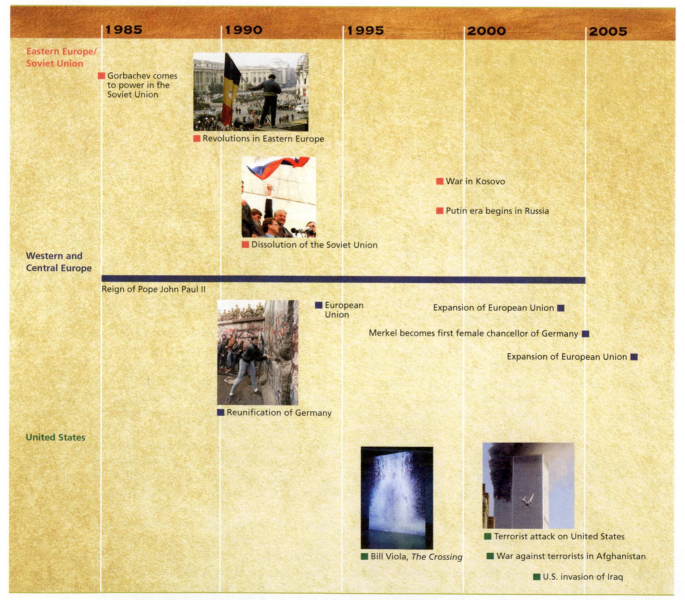

	1985	1990	1995	2000	2005

Eastern Europe/ Soviet Union

■ Gorbachev comes to power in the Soviet Union

■ Revolutions in Eastern Europe

■ Dissolution of the Soviet Union

■ War in Kosovo

■ Putin era begins in Russia

Western and Central Europe

Reign of Pope John Paul II

■ European Union

■ Expansion of European Union ■

Merkel becomes first female chancellor of Germany ■

■ Expansion of European Union ■

■ Reunification of Germany

United States

■ Bill Viola, *The Crossing*

■ Terrorist attack on United States

■ War against terrorists in Afghanistan

■ U.S. invasion of Iraq

NOTES

1. Quoted in Tony Judt, *Postwar: A History of Europe Since 1945* (New York, 2005), p. 585.
2. Mikhail Gorbachev, "Report to the 27th Party Congress," February 25, 1986, in *Current Soviet Policies* 9 (1986): 10.
3. Quoted in William I. Hitchcock, *The Struggle for Europe: The Turbulent History of a Divided Continent, 1945–2002* (New York, 2003), pp. 399–400.
4. Quoted in Renate Bridenthal, "Women in the New Europe," in Renate Bridenthal, Susan Mosher Stuard, and Merry E. Weisner, eds., *Becoming Visible: Women in European History,* 3d ed. (Boston, 1998), pp. 564–565.
5. Quoted in Judt, *Postwar Europe,* p. 743.
6. Elise Boulding, *Women in the Twentieth-Century World* (New York, 1977), pp. 186–187.

SUGGESTIONS FOR FURTHER READING

General Works   For a well-written survey on Europe from 1985 to 2004, see **T. Judt**, *Postwar: A History of Europe Since 1945* (New York, 2005). Additional general surveys of contemporary European history are listed in Chapter 28.

Toward a New Western Order   Different aspects of the revolutionary upheaval in the Soviet Union and its aftermath are covered in **M. Kramer,** *Collapse of the Soviet Union* (Boulder, Colo., 2007); **S. Lovell,** *Destination in Doubt: Russia Since 1989* (London, 2006); **M. McCauley,** *Gorbachev* (London, 2000); **G. W. Breslauer,** *Gorbachev and Yeltsin as Leaders* (Cambridge, 2002); and **M. Garcelon,** *Revolutionary Passage: From Soviet to Post-Soviet Russia, 1985–2000* (Philadelphia, 2005). On Eastern Europe, see **G. Stokes,** *The Walls Came Tumbling Down: The Collapse of Communism in Eastern Europe* (Oxford, 1993), and **P. Kenney,** *The Burden of Freedom: Eastern Europe Since 1989* (London, 2006). For general works on Western Europe and individual countries, see the works cited in Chapters 28 and 29. On the recent history of these countries, see **P. O'Dochartaigh,** *Germany Since 1945* (New York, 2004); **B. Thomaneck and J. K. Thomaneck,** *Division and Reunification of Germany* (London, 2000); and **M. Temple,** *Blair* (London, 2006), on the era of Tony Blair in Britain.

After the Cold War   On the end of the Cold War, see **S. Dockrill,** *The End of the Cold War Era* (London, 2005), and **J. L. Gaddis,** *The Cold War: A New History* (New York, 2005). On terrorism, see **W. Laqueur,** *History of Terrorism* (New York, 2001); **C. E. Simonsen and J. R. Spendlove,** *Terrorism Today: The Past, The Players, The Future,* 3d ed. (Upper Saddle River, N.J., 2006); and **T. R. Mockaitis,** *The "New" Terrorism: Myth and Reality* (New York, 2006).

New Directions and New Problems in Western Society   The changing role of women is examined in **C. Duchen,** *Feminism in France* (London, 1986), and **R. Rosen,** *The World Split Open: How the Modern Women's Movement Changed America* (New York, 2001).

The problems of guest workers and immigrants are examined in **W. Laqueur,** *The Last Days of Europe: Epitaph for an Old Continent* (New York, 2007), and **R. Chin,** *Guest Worker Question in Germany* (Cambridge, 2007).

The Digital Age   For a comprehensive examination of the Digital Age, see **M. Castells,** *The Information Age,* 3 vols. (Oxford, 1996–1998). On the role of the Internet in our global age, see **M. Castells,** *The Internet Galaxy* (Oxford, 2001). On the role of the media in the Digital Age, see **R. W. McChesney and E. S. Herman,** *The Global Media* (New York, 1997), and **J. R. Dominick,** *Dynamics of Mass Communication: Media in the Digital Age* (New York, 2006). On art, see **B. Wands,** *Art of the Digital Age* (London, 2007).

Toward a Global Civilization   Useful books on different facets of the new global civilization include **M. B. Steger,** *Globalization: A Very Short Introduction* (New York, 2003); **J. H. Mittelman,** *The Globalization Syndrome* (Princeton, N.J., 2000); **M. Waters,** *Globalization,* 2d ed. (London, 2001); **P. O'Meara et al., eds.,** *Globalization and the Challenges of the New Century* (Bloomington, Ind., 2000); **R. Gilpin,** *Global Political Economy* (Princeton, N.J., 2001); **A. Hoogvelt,** *Globalization and the Postcolonial World,* 2d ed. (Baltimore, 2001); and **H. French,** *Vanishing Borders* (New York, 2000) on globalization and the environment.

CENGAGENOW   CengageNOW is an integrated online suite of services and resources with proven ease of use and efficient paths to success, delivering the results you want—NOW!
academic.cengage.com/login/
Enter CengageNOW using the access card that is available with *Western Civilization.* CengageNOW will assist you in understanding the content in this chapter with lesson plans generated for your needs. In addition, you can read the following documents, and many more, online:

Maastricht Accords, excerpts

WESTERN CIVILIZATION RESOURCES

Visit the *Western Civilization* Companion Web site for resources specific to this book:
academic.cengage.com/history/spielvogel
For a variety of tools to help you succeed in this course, visit the Western Civilization Resource Center. Enter the Resource Center using either your *CengageNOW* access card or your standalone access card for the *Wadsworth Western Civilization Resource Center.* Organized by topic, this Web site includes quizzes; images; primary source documents; interactive simulations, maps, and timelines; movie explorations; and a wealth of other resources.
http://westernrc.wadsworth.com/

GLOSSARY

abbess   the head of a convent or monastery for women.

abbot   the head of a monastery.

absolutism   a form of government in which the sovereign power or ultimate authority rested in the hands of a monarch who claimed to rule by divine right and was therefore responsible only to God.

Abstract Expressionism   a post–World War II artistic movement that broke with all conventions of form and structure in favor of total abstraction.

abstract painting   an artistic movement that developed early in the twentieth century in which artists focused on color to avoid any references to visual reality.

aediles   Roman officials who supervised the public games and the grain supply of the city of Rome.

Agricultural (Neolithic) Revolution   the shift from hunting animals and gathering plants for sustenance to producing food by systematic agriculture that occurred gradually between 10,000 and 4000 B.C. (the Neolithic or "New Stone" Age).

agricultural revolution   the application of new agricultural techniques that allowed for a large increase in productivity in the eighteenth century.

anarchism   a political theory that holds that all governments and existing social institutions are unnecessary and advocates a society based on voluntary cooperation.

anticlericalism   opposition to the power of the clergy, especially in political affairs.

anti-Semitism   hostility toward or discrimination against Jews.

apartheid   the system of racial segregation practiced in the Republic of South Africa until the 1990s, which involved political, legal, and economic discrimination against nonwhites.

appeasement   the policy, followed by the European nations in the 1930s, of accepting Hitler's annexation of Austria and Czechoslovakia in the belief that meeting his demands would assure peace and stability.

Arianism   a Christian heresy that taught that Jesus was inferior to God. Though condemned by the Council of Nicaea in 325, Arianism was adopted by many of the Germanic peoples who entered the Roman Empire over the next centuries.

aristocracy   a class of hereditary nobility in medieval Europe; a warrior class who shared a distinctive lifestyle based on the institution of knighthood, although there were social divisions within the group based on extremes of wealth.

audiencias   advisory groups to viceroys in Spanish America.

Ausgleich   the "Compromise" of 1867 that created the dual monarchy of Austria-Hungary. Austria and Hungary each had its own capital, constitution, and legislative assembly but were united under one monarch.

authoritarian state   a state that has a dictatorial government and some other trappings of a totalitarian state but does not demand that the masses be actively involved in the regime's goals as totalitarian states do.

auxiliaries   troops enlisted from the subject peoples of the Roman Empire to supplement the regular legions composed of Roman citizens.

balance of power   a distribution of power among several states such that no single nation can dominate or interfere with the interests of another.

Baroque   an artistic movement of the seventeenth century in Europe that used dramatic effects to arouse the emotions and reflected the search for power that was a large part of the seventeenth-century ethos.

benefice   in the Christian church, a position, such as a bishopric, that consisted of both a sacred office and the right of the holder to the annual revenues from the position.

bicameral legislature   a legislature with two houses.

Black Death   the outbreak of plague (mostly bubonic) in the mid-fourteenth century that killed from 25 to 50 percent of Europe's population.

Blitzkrieg   "lightning war." A war conducted with great speed and force, as in Germany's advance at the beginning of World War II.

Bolsheviks   a small faction of the Russian Social Democratic Party who were led by Lenin and dedicated to violent revolution; they seized power in Russia in 1917 and were subsequently renamed the Communists.

bourgeoisie (burghers)   inhabitants (merchants and artisans) of boroughs and burghs (towns).

boyars   the Russian nobility.

Brezhnev Doctrine   the doctrine, enunciated by Leonid Brezhnev, that the Soviet Union had a right to intervene if socialism was threatened in another socialist state; used to justify moving Soviet troops into Czechoslovakia in 1968.

Burschenschaften   student societies in the German states dedicated to fostering the goal of a free, united Germany.

caliph   the secular leader of the Islamic community.

capital   material wealth used or available for use in the production of more wealth.

cartel   a combination of independent commercial enterprises that work together to control prices and limit competition.

Cartesian dualism   Descartes's principle of the separation of mind and matter (and mind and body) that enabled scientists to view matter as something separate from themselves that could be investigated by reason.

celibacy   complete abstinence from sexual activity. Many early Christians viewed celibacy as the surest way to holiness.

censors   Roman officials chosen every five years to assess property holdings to determine taxes, military service, and officeholding.

centuriate assembly   the chief popular assembly of the Roman Republic. It passed laws and elected the chief magistrates.

chansons de geste   a form of vernacular literature in the High Middle Ages that consisted of heroic epics focusing on the deeds of warriors.

chivalry   the ideal of civilized behavior that emerged among the nobility in the eleventh and twelfth centuries under the influence of the church; a code of ethics knights were expected to uphold.

Christian (northern) humanism   an intellectual movement in northern Europe in the late fifteenth and early sixteenth centuries that combined the interest in the classics of the Italian Renaissance with an interest in the sources of early Christianity, including the New Testament and the writings of the church fathers.

civic humanism   an intellectual movement of the Italian Renaissance that saw Cicero, who was both an intellectual and a statesman, as the ideal and held that humanists should be involved in government and use their rhetorical training in the service of the state.

civil disobedience   a policy of peaceful protest against laws or government policies in order to achieve political change.

civilization   a complex culture in which large numbers of humans share a variety of common elements, including cities; religious, political, military, and social structures; writing; and significant artistic and intellectual activity.

civil rights the basic rights of citizens, including equality before the law, freedom of speech and press, and freedom from arbitrary arrest.

Cold War the ideological conflict between the Soviet Union and the United States after World War II.

collective farms large farms created in the Soviet Union by Stalin by combining many small holdings into large farms worked by the peasants under government supervision.

collective security the use of an international army raised by an association of nations to deter aggression and keep the peace.

coloni free tenant farmers who worked as sharecroppers on the large estates of the Roman Empire (singular: *colonus*).

Columbian Exchange the reciprocal importation and exportation of plants and animals between Europe and the Americas.

commercial capitalism beginning in the Middle Ages, an economic system in which people invested in trade and goods in order to make profits.

common law law common to the entire kingdom of England; imposed by the king's courts beginning in the twelfth century to replace the customary law used in county and feudal courts that varied from place to place.

commune in medieval Europe, an association of townspeople bound together by a sworn oath for the purpose of obtaining basic liberties from the lord of the territory in which the town was located; also, the self-governing town after receiving its liberties.

conciliarism a movement in fourteenth- and fifteenth-century Europe that held that final authority in spiritual matters resided with a general church council, not the pope; it emerged in response to the Avignon papacy and the Great Schism and was used to justify the summoning of the Council of Constance (1414–1418).

condottieri leaders of bands of mercenary soldiers in Renaissance Italy who sold their services to the highest bidder.

confession one of the seven sacraments of the Catholic Church; it provided for the forgiveness of one's sins.

conquistadors "conquerors." Leaders in the Spanish conquests in the Americas, especially Mexico and Peru, in the sixteenth century.

conscription a military draft.

conservatism an ideology based on tradition and social stability that favored the maintenance of established institutions, organized religion, and obedience to authority and resisted change, especially abrupt change.

consuls the chief executive officers of the Roman Republic. Two were chosen annually to administer the government and lead the army in battle.

consumer society Western society that emerged after World War II as the working classes adopted the consumption patterns of the middle class and payment plans, credit cards, and easy credit made consumer goods such as appliances and automobiles affordable.

containment a policy adopted by the United States in the Cold War. Its goal was to use whatever means, short of all-out war, to limit Soviet expansion.

Continental System Napoleon's effort to bar British goods from the Continent in the hope of weakening Britain's economy and destroying its capacity to wage war.

cosmopolitanism the quality of being sophisticated and having wide international experience.

cottage industry a system of textile manufacturing in which spinners and weavers worked at home in their cottages using raw materials supplied to them by capitalist entrepreneurs.

council of the plebs a council only for plebeians. After 287 B.C., however, its resolutions were binding on all Romans.

Crusade in the Middle Ages, a military campaign in defense of Christendom.

Cubism an artistic style developed at the beginning of the twentieth century, especially by Pablo Picasso, that used geometric designs to re-create reality in the viewer's mind.

cultural relativism the belief that no culture is superior to another because culture is a matter of custom, not reason, and derives its meaning from the group holding it.

cuneiform "wedge-shaped." A system of writing developed by the Sumerians that consisted of wedge-shaped impressions made by a reed stylus on clay tablets.

curiales city councilors in Roman cities who played an important role in governing the vast Roman Empire.

Dadaism an artistic movement in the 1920s and 1930s by artists who were revolted by the senseless slaughter of World War I and used their "anti-art" to express contempt for the Western tradition.

de-Christianization a policy, adopted in the radical phase of the French Revolution, aimed at creating a secular society by eliminating Christian forms and institutions from French society.

decolonization the process of becoming free of colonial status and achieving statehood; it occurred in most of the world's colonies between 1947 and 1962.

deconstruction (poststructuralism) a system of thought, formulated by Jacques Derrida, that holds that culture is created in a variety of ways, according to the manner in which people create their own meaning. Hence, there is no fixed truth or universal meaning.

deism belief in God as the creator of the universe who, after setting it in motion, ceased to have any direct involvement in it and allowed it to run according to its own natural laws.

demesne the part of a manor retained under the direct control of the lord and worked by the serfs as part of their labor services.

denazification after World War II, the Allied policy of rooting out any traces of Nazism in German society by bringing prominent Nazis to trial for war crimes and purging any known Nazis from political office.

depression a very severe, protracted economic downturn with high levels of unemployment.

de-Stalinization the policy of denouncing and undoing the most repressive aspects of Stalin's regime; begun by Nikita Khrushchev in 1956.

détente the relaxation of tension between the Soviet Union and the United States that occurred in the 1970s.

developed nations a term used to refer to rich nations, primarily in the Northern Hemisphere, that have well-organized industrial and agricultural systems, advanced technologies, and effective educational systems.

developing nations a term used to refer to poor nations, mainly in the Southern Hemisphere, that are primarily farming nations with little technology and serious population problems.

dialectic logic, one of the seven liberal arts that made up the medieval curriculum. In Marxist thought, the process by which all change occurs through the clash of antagonistic elements.

Diaspora the scattering of Jews throughout the ancient world after the Babylonian captivity in the sixth century B.C.

dictator in the Roman Republic, an official granted unlimited power to run the state for a short period of time, usually six months, during an emergency.

diocese the area under the jurisdiction of a Christian bishop; based originally on Roman administrative districts.

direct representation a system of choosing delegates to a representative assembly in which citizens vote directly for the delegates who will represent them.

divination the practice of seeking to foretell future events by interpreting divine signs, which could appear in various forms, such as in entrails of animals, in patterns in smoke, or in dreams.

divine-right monarchy a monarchy based on the belief that monarchs receive their power directly from God and are responsible to no one except God.

domino theory the belief that if the Communists succeeded in Vietnam, other countries in Southeast and East Asia would also fall (like dominoes) to communism; cited as a justification for the U.S. intervention in Vietnam.

Donatism a Christian heresy that argued that the sacraments of the church were not valid if administered by an immoral priest.

dualism the belief that the universe is dominated by two opposing forces, one good and the other evil.

dynastic state a state in which the maintenance and expansion of the interests of the ruling family is the primary consideration.

economic imperialism   the process in which banks and corporations from developed nations invest in underdeveloped regions and establish a major presence there in the hope of making high profits; not necessarily the same as colonial expansion in that businesses invest where they can make a profit, which may not be in their own nation's colonies.

economic liberalism   the idea that government should not interfere in the workings of the economy.

Einsatzgruppen   in Nazi Germany, special strike forces in the SS that played an important role in rounding up and killing Jews.

empiricism   the practice of relying on observation and experiment.

enclosure movement   in the eighteenth century, the fencing in of the old open fields, combining many small holdings into larger units that could be farmed more efficiently.

encomienda   in Spanish America, a form of economic and social organization in which a Spaniard was given a royal grant that enabled the holder of the grant to collect tribute from the Indians and use them as laborers.

encyclical   a letter from the pope to all the bishops of the Roman Catholic Church.

enlightened absolutism   an absolute monarchy in which the ruler follows the principles of the Enlightenment by introducing reforms for the improvement of society, allowing freedom of speech and the press, permitting religious toleration, expanding education, and ruling in accordance with the laws.

Enlightenment   an eighteenth-century intellectual movement, led by the philosophes, that stressed the application of reason and the scientific method to all aspects of life.

entrepreneur   one who organizes, operates, and assumes the risk in a business venture in the expectation of making a profit.

Epicureanism   a philosophy founded by Epicurus in the fourth century B.C. that taught that happiness (freedom from emotional turmoil) could be achieved through the pursuit of pleasure (intellectual rather than sensual pleasure).

equestrians   a group of extremely wealthy men in the late Roman Republic who were effectively barred from high office but sought political power commensurate with their wealth; called equestrians because many had gotten their start as cavalry officers (*equites*).

ethnic cleansing   the policy of killing or forcibly removing people of another ethnic group; used by the Serbs against Bosnian Muslims in the 1990s.

Eucharist   a Christian sacrament in which consecrated bread and wine are consumed in celebration of Jesus' Last Supper; also called the Lord's Supper or communion.

Eurocommunism   a form of communism that dropped its Marxist ideology. It was especially favored in Italy.

evolutionary socialism   a socialist doctrine espoused by Eduard Bernstein who argued that socialists should stress cooperation and evolution to attain power by democratic means rather than by conflict and revolution.

exchequer   the permanent royal treasury of England. It emerged during the reign of King Henry II in the twelfth century.

excommunication   in the Catholic Church, a censure depriving a person of the right to receive the sacraments of the church.

existentialism   a philosophical movement that arose after World War II that emphasized the meaninglessness of life, born of the desperation caused by two world wars.

family allowances   one aspect of the welfare state whereby the state provides a minimum level of material assistance for children.

fascism   an ideology or movement that exalts the nation above the individual and calls for a centralized government with a dictatorial leader, economic and social regimentation, and forcible suppression of opposition; in particular, the ideology of Mussolini's Fascist regime in Italy.

federates   German troops enlisted in groups to fight as allies for the Romans.

feminism   the belief in the social, political, and economic equality of the sexes; also, organized activity to advance women's rights.

fief   a landed estate granted to a vassal in exchange for military services.

Final Solution   the attempted physical extermination of the Jewish people by the Nazis during World War II.

folk culture   the traditional arts and crafts, literature, music, and other customs of the people; something that people make, as opposed to modern popular culture, which is something people buy.

free trade   the unrestricted international exchange of goods with low or no tariffs.

Führerprinzip   in Nazi Germany, a leadership principle based on the belief in a single-minded party (the Nazis) under one leader (Hitler).

functionalism   the idea that the function of an object should determine its design and materials.

general strike   a strike by all or most workers in an economy; espoused by Georges Sorel as the heroic action that could be used to inspire the workers to destroy capitalist society.

genocide   the deliberate extermination of a people.

gentry   well-to-do English landowners below the level of the nobility. They played an important role in the English Civil War of the seventeenth century.

geocentric conception   the belief that the earth was at the center of the universe and that the sun and other celestial objects revolved around the earth.

glasnost   "openness." Mikhail Gorbachev's policy of encouraging Soviet citizens to openly discuss the strengths and weaknesses of the Soviet Union.

global economy   an interdependent economy in which the production, distribution, and sale of goods is accomplished on a worldwide scale.

globalization   a term referring to the trend by which peoples and nations have become more interdependent; often used to refer to the development of a global economy and culture.

global warming   the increase in the temperature of the earth's atmosphere caused by the greenhouse effect.

good emperors   the five emperors who ruled from 96 to 180 (Nerva, Trajan, Hadrian, Antoninus Pius, and Marcus Aurelius), a period of peace and prosperity for the Roman Empire.

Gothic   a term used to describe the art and especially architecture of Europe in the twelfth, thirteenth, and fourteenth centuries.

Gothic literature   a form of literature used by Romantics to emphasize the bizarre and unusual, especially evident in horror stories.

Great Schism   the crisis in the late medieval church when there were first two and then three popes; ended by the Council of Constance (1414–1418).

greenhouse effect   the warming of the earth caused by the buildup of carbon dioxide in the atmosphere as a result of human activity.

guest workers   foreign workers working temporarily in European countries.

guild   an association of people with common interests and concerns, especially people working in the same craft. In medieval Europe, guilds came to control much of the production process and to restrict entry into various trades.

gymnasium   in classical Greece, a place for athletics; in the Hellenistic Age, a secondary school with a curriculum centered on music, physical exercise, and literature.

heliocentric conception   the belief that the sun, not the earth, is at the center of the universe.

Hellenistic   literally, "imitating the Greeks"; the era after the death of Alexander the Great when Greek culture spread into the Near East and blended with the culture of that region.

helots   serfs in ancient Sparta who were permanently bound to the land that they worked for their Spartan masters.

heresy   the holding of religious doctrines different from the official teachings of the church.

Hermeticism   an intellectual movement beginning in the fifteenth century that taught that divinity is embodied in all aspects of nature; it included works on alchemy and magic as well as theology and philosophy. The tradition continued into the seventeenth century and influenced many of the leading figures of the Scientific Revolution.

hetairai   highly sophisticated courtesans in ancient Athens who offered intellectual and musical entertainment as well as sex.

hieroglyphics a pictorial system of writing used in ancient Egypt.

high culture the literary and artistic culture of the educated and wealthy ruling classes.

Holocaust the mass slaughter of European Jews by the Nazis during World War II.

home rule in the United Kingdom, self-government by having a separate parliament but not complete independence.

hoplites heavily armed infantry soldiers in ancient Greece who entered battle in a phalanx formation.

Huguenots French Calvinists.

humanism an intellectual movement in Renaissance Italy based on the study of the Greek and Roman classics.

iconoclast a member of an eighth-century Byzantine movement against the use of icons (pictures of sacred figures), which it condemned as idolatry.

ideology a political philosophy such as conservatism or liberalism.

imperium in the Roman Republic, the right to command troops that belonged to the chief executive officers (consuls and praetors); a military commander was known as an *imperator*. In the Roman Empire, the title *imperator* (emperor) came to be used for the ruler.

Impressionism an artistic movement that originated in France in the 1870s. Impressionists sought to capture their impressions of the changing effects of light on objects in nature.

indirect representation a system of choosing delegates to a representative assembly in which citizens do not choose the delegates directly but instead vote for electors who choose the delegates.

individualism emphasis on and interest in the unique traits of each person.

indulgence in Christian theology, the remission of part or all of the temporal punishment in purgatory due to sin; granted for charitable contributions and other good deeds. Indulgences became a regular practice of the Christian church in the High Middle Ages, and their abuse was instrumental in sparking Luther's reform movement in the sixteenth century.

infanticide the practice of killing infants.

inflation a sustained rise in the price level.

intendants royal officials in seventeenth-century France who were sent into the provinces to execute the orders of the central government.

interdict in the Catholic Church, a censure by which a region or country is deprived of receiving the sacraments.

intervention, principle of the idea, after the Congress of Vienna, that the great powers of Europe had the right to send armies into countries experiencing revolution to restore legitimate monarchs to their thrones.

isolationism a foreign policy in which a nation refrains from making alliances or engaging actively in international affairs.

Janissaries an elite core of eight thousand troops personally loyal to the sultan of the Ottoman Empire.

jihad "striving in the way of the Lord." In Islam, the attempt to achieve personal betterment, although it can also mean fair, defensive fighting to preserve one's life and one's faith.

joint-stock company a company or association that raises capital by selling shares to individuals who receive dividends on their investment while a board of directors runs the company.

joint-stock investment bank a bank created by selling shares of stock to investors. Such banks potentially have access to much more capital than private banks owned by one or a few individuals.

justification the primary doctrine of the Protestant Reformation, teaching that humans are saved not through good works but by the grace of God, bestowed freely through the sacrifice of Jesus.

Kulturkampf "culture conflict." The name given to Bismarck's attack on the Catholic Church in Germany, which has come to refer to conflict between church and state anywhere.

laissez-faire "let (them) do (as they please)." An economic doctrine that holds that an economy is best served when the government does not interfere but allows the economy to self-regulate according to the forces of supply and demand.

latifundia large landed estates in the Roman Empire (singular: *latifundium*).

lay investiture the practice in which someone other than a member of the clergy chose a bishop and invested him with the symbols of both his temporal office and his spiritual office; led to the Investiture Controversy, which was ended by compromise in the Concordat of Worms in 1122.

Lebensraum "living space." The doctrine, adopted by Hitler, that a nation's power depends on the amount of land it occupies; thus, a nation must expand to be strong.

legitimacy, principle of the idea that after the Napoleonic wars, peace could best be reestablished in Europe by restoring legitimate monarchs who would preserve traditional institutions; guided Metternich at the Congress of Vienna.

Leninism Lenin's revision of Marxism that held that Russia need not experience a bourgeois revolution before it could move toward socialism.

liberal arts the seven areas of study that formed the basis of education in medieval and early modern Europe. Following Boethius and other late Roman authors, they consisted of grammar, rhetoric, and dialectic or logic (the *trivium*) and arithmetic, geometry, astronomy, and music (the *quadrivium*).

liberalism an ideology based on the belief that people should be as free from restraint as possible. Economic liberalism is the idea that the government should not interfere in the workings of the economy. Political liberalism is the idea that there should be restraints on the exercise of power so that people can enjoy basic civil rights in a constitutional state with a representative assembly.

limited liability the principle that shareholders in a joint-stock corporation can be held responsible for the corporation's debts only up to the amount they have invested.

limited monarchy (constitutional monarchy) a system of government in which the monarch is limited by a representative assembly and by the duty to rule in accordance with the laws of the land.

major domus the chief officer of the king's household in the Frankish kingdom.

mandates a system established after World War I whereby a nation officially administered a territory (mandate) on behalf of the League of Nations. Thus, France administered Lebanon and Syria as mandates, and Britain administered Iraq and Palestine.

Mannerism a sixteenth-century artistic movement in Europe that deliberately broke down the High Renaissance principles of balance, harmony, and moderation.

manor an agricultural estate operated by a lord and worked by peasants who performed labor services and paid various rents and fees to the lord in exchange for protection and sustenance.

Marshall Plan the European Recovery Program, under which the United States provided financial aid to European countries to help them rebuild after World War II.

Marxism the political, economic, and social theories of Karl Marx, which included the idea that history is the story of class struggle and that ultimately the proletariat will overthrow the bourgeoisie and establish a dictatorship en route to a classless society.

mass education a state-run educational system, usually free and compulsory, that aims to ensure that all children in society have at least a basic education.

mass leisure forms of leisure that appeal to large numbers of people in a society, including the working classes; emerged at the end of the nineteenth century to provide workers with amusements after work and on weekends; used during the twentieth century by totalitarian states to control their populations.

mass politics a political order characterized by mass political parties and universal male and (eventually) female suffrage.

mass society a society in which the concerns of the majority—the lower classes—play a prominent role; characterized by extension of voting rights, an improved standard of living for the lower classes, and mass education.

materialism the belief that everything mental, spiritual, or ideal is an outgrowth of physical forces and that truth is found in concrete material existence, not through feeling or intuition.

mercantilism an economic theory that held that a nation's prosperity depended on its supply of gold and silver and that the total volume of trade is unchangeable; its adherents therefore advocated that the government play an active role in the economy by encouraging exports and discouraging imports, especially through the use of tariffs.

Mesolithic Age the period from 10,000 to 7000 B.C., characterized by a gradual transition from a food-gathering and hunting economy to a food-producing economy.

metics resident foreigners in ancient Athens who were not permitted full rights of citizenship but did receive the protection of the laws.

Middle Passage the journey of slaves from Africa to the Americas as the middle leg of the triangular trade.

militarism a policy of aggressive military preparedness; in particular, the large armies based on mass conscription and complex, inflexible plans for mobilization that most European nations had before World War I.

millenarianism the belief that the end of the world is at hand and the kingdom of God is about to be established on earth.

ministerial responsibility a tenet of nineteenth-century liberalism that held that ministers of the monarch should be responsible to the legislative assembly rather than to the monarch.

mir a peasant village commune in Russia.

mobilization the organization of troops and supplies for service in time of war.

Modern Devotion a movement founded by Gerard Groote in the fourteenth century, aimed at a practical mysticism based on leading lives serving the needs of fellow human beings.

Modernism the artistic and literary styles that emerged in the decades before 1914 as artists rebelled against traditional efforts to portray reality as accurately as possible (leading to Impressionism and Cubism) and writers explored new forms.

monasticism a movement that began in early Christianity whose purpose was to create communities of men and women who practiced a communal life dedicated to God as a moral example to the world around them.

monk a man who chooses to live a communal life divorced from the world in order to dedicate himself totally to the will of God.

monogamy the practice of being married to one person at a time.

monotheism the doctrine or belief that there is only one God.

multiculturalism a term referring to the connection of several cultural or ethnic groups within a society.

multinational corporation a company with divisions in more than two countries.

mutual deterrence the belief that nuclear war could best be prevented if both the United States and the Soviet Union had sufficient nuclear weapons so that even if one nation launched a preemptive first strike, the other could respond and devastate the attacker.

mystery religions religions that involve initiation into secret rites that promise intense emotional involvement with spiritual forces and a greater chance of individual immortality.

mysticism the immediate experience of oneness with God.

nationalism a sense of national consciousness based on awareness of being part of a community—a "nation"—that has common institutions, traditions, language, and customs and that becomes the focus of the individual's primary political loyalty.

nationalities problem the dilemma faced by the Austro-Hungarian Empire in trying to unite a wide variety of ethnic groups (Austrians, Hungarians, Poles, Croats, Czechs, Serbs, Slovaks, and Slovenes, among others) in an era when nationalism and calls for self-determination were coming to the fore.

nationalization the process of converting a business or industry from private ownership to government control and ownership.

nation in arms the people's army raised by universal mobilization to repel the foreign enemies of the French Revolution.

nation-state a form of political organization in which a relatively homogeneous people inhabits a sovereign state, as opposed to a state containing people of several nationalities.

NATO the North Atlantic Treaty Organization, a military alliance formed in 1949 in which the signatories (Belgium, Canada, Denmark, France, Great Britain, Iceland, Italy, Luxembourg, the Netherlands, Norway, Portugal, and the United States) agreed to provide mutual assistance if any one of them was attacked; later expanded to include other nations.

natural laws a body of laws or specific principles held to be derived from nature and binding on all human societies even in the absence of written laws governing such matters.

natural rights certain inalienable rights to which all people are entitled, including the right to life, liberty, and property; freedom of speech and religion; and equality before the law.

natural selection Darwin's idea that organisms that are most adaptable to their environment survive and pass on the variations that enabled them to survive, while less adaptable organisms become extinct; "survival of the fittest."

Nazi New Order the Nazis' plan for their conquered territories; it included the extermination of Jews and others considered inferior, ruthless exploitation of resources, German colonization in the east, and the use of Poles, Russians, and Ukrainians as slave labor.

Neoclassicism a late-eighteenth-century artistic movement that emerged in France. It sought to recapture the dignity and simplicity of the classical style of ancient Greece and Rome.

Neoplatonism a revival of Platonic philosophy in the third century A.D., associated with Plotinus; a similar revival in the Italian Renaissance, associated with Marsilio Ficino, who attempted to synthesize Christianity and Platonism.

nepotism the appointment of family members to important political positions; derived from the regular appointment of nephews (Greek, *nepos*) by Renaissance popes.

New Economic Policy a modified version of the old capitalist system introduced in the Soviet Union by Lenin in 1921 to revive the economy after the ravages of the civil war and war communism.

new imperialism the revival of imperialism after 1880 in which European nations established colonies throughout much of Asia and Africa.

new monarchies the governments of France, England, and Spain at the end of the fifteenth century, whose rulers succeeded in reestablishing or extending centralized royal authority, suppressing the nobility, controlling the church, and insisting on the loyalty of all peoples living in their territories.

nobiles "nobles." The small group of families from both patrician and plebeian origins who produced most of the men who were elected to office in the late Roman Republic.

nominalist a member of a school of thought in medieval Europe that, following Aristotle, held that only individual objects are real and that universals are only names created by humans.

nuclear family a family group consisting only of a father, a mother, and one or more children.

nuns women who withdrew from the world and joined a religious community; the female equivalent of monks.

old regime (old order) the political and social system of France in the eighteenth century before the Revolution.

oligarchy rule by a few.

optimates "best men." Aristocratic leaders in the late Roman Republic who generally came from senatorial families and wished to retain their oligarchical privileges.

orders (estates) the traditional tripartite division of European society based on heredity and quality rather than wealth or economic standing, first established in the Middle Ages and continuing into the eighteenth century; traditionally consisted of those who pray (the clergy), those who fight (the nobility), and those who work (all the rest).

organic evolution Darwin's principle that all plants and animals have evolved over a long period of time from earlier and simpler forms of life.

Paleolithic Age the period of human history when humans used simple stone tools (c. 2,500,000–10,000 B.C.).

pantheism a doctrine that equates God with the universe and all that is in it.

panzer division in the German army under Hitler, a strike force of about three hundred tanks and accompanying forces and supplies.

papal curia the administrative staff of the Catholic Church, composed of cardinals who assist the pope in running the church.

pasteurization a process developed by Louis Pasteur for heating a product to destroy the microorganisms that might cause spoilage.

paterfamilias the dominant male in a Roman family whose powers over his wife and children were theoretically unlimited, though they were sometimes circumvented in practice.

patriarchal family a family in which the husband dominates his wife and children.

patriarchy a society in which the father is supreme in the clan or family; more generally, a society dominated by men.

patricians great landowners who became the ruling class in the Roman Republic.

patronage the practice of awarding titles and making appointments to government and other positions to gain political support.

Pax Romana "Roman peace." A term used to refer to the stability and prosperity that Roman rule brought to the Mediterranean world and much of western Europe during the first and second centuries A.D.

Pentateuch the first five books of the Hebrew Bible (Genesis, Exodus, Leviticus, Numbers, and Deuteronomy).

perestroika "restructuring." A term applied to Mikhail Gorbachev's economic, political, and social reforms in the Soviet Union.

perioikoi in ancient Sparta, free inhabitants but not citizens who were required to pay taxes and perform military service.

permissive society a term applied to Western society after World War II to reflect the new sexual freedom and the emergence of a drug culture.

Petrine supremacy the doctrine that the bishop of Rome (the pope), as the successor of Saint Peter (traditionally considered the first bishop of Rome), should hold a preeminent position in the church.

phalanstery a self-sustaining cooperative community, as advocated by Charles Fourier in the early nineteenth century.

phalanx a rectangular formation of tightly massed infantry soldiers.

philosophes intellectuals of the eighteenth-century Enlightenment who believed in applying a spirit of rational criticism to all things, including religion and politics, and who focused on improving and enjoying this world, rather than on the afterlife.

Pietism a movement that arose in Germany in the seventeenth century whose goal was to foster a personal experience of God as the focus of true religious experience.

plebeians the class of Roman citizens that included nonpatrician landowners, craftspeople, merchants, and small farmers in the Roman Republic. Their struggle for equal rights with the patricians dominated much of the Republic's history.

plebiscita laws passed by the council of the plebs.

pluralism the practice of holding several church offices simultaneously; a problem of the late medieval church.

plutocrats members of the wealthy elite.

pogroms organized massacres of Jews.

polis an ancient Greek city-state encompassing both an urban area and its surrounding countryside; a small but autonomous political unit where all major political and social activities were carried out centrally.

political democracy a form of government characterized by universal suffrage and mass political parties.

politiques a group who emerged during the French Wars of Religion in the sixteenth century, placed politics above religion, and believed that no religious truth was worth the ravages of civil war.

polytheism belief in or worship of more than one god.

Pop Art an artistic movement of the 1950s and 1960s in which artists took images of popular culture and transformed them into works of fine art. Andy Warhol's painting of Campbell's soup cans is one example.

popular culture as opposed to high culture, the unofficial written and unwritten culture of the masses, much of which was traditionally passed down orally and centered on public and group activities such as festivals. In the modern age, the term refers to the entertainment, recreation, and pleasures that people purchase as part of the mass consumer society.

populares "favoring the people." Aristocratic leaders in the late Roman Republic who tended to use the people's assemblies in an effort to break the stranglehold of the *nobiles* on political offices.

popular sovereignty the doctrine that government is created by and subject to the will of the people, who are the source of all political power.

populism a political philosophy or movement that supports the rights and power of ordinary people in their struggle against the privileged elite.

portolani charts of landmasses and coastlines made by navigators and mathematicians in the thirteenth and fourteenth centuries.

Post-Impressionism an artistic movement that began in France in the 1880s. Post-Impressionists sought to use color and line to express inner feelings and produce a personal statement of reality.

Postmodernism a term used to cover a variety of artistic and intellectual styles and ways of thinking prominent since the 1970s.

praetor a Roman executive official responsible for the administration of the law.

praetorian guard the military unit that served as the personal bodyguard of the Roman emperors.

predestination the belief, associated with Calvinism, that God, as a consequence of his foreknowledge of all events, has predetermined those who will be saved (the elect) and those who will be damned.

prefect during the reign of Napoleon, an official appointed by the central government to oversee all aspects of a local government.

price revolution the dramatic rise in prices (inflation) that occurred throughout Europe in the sixteenth and early seventeenth centuries.

primogeniture an inheritance practice in which the eldest son receives all or the largest share of the parents' estate.

principate the form of government established by Augustus for the Roman Empire; it continued the constitutional forms of the Republic and consisted of the *princeps* ("first citizen") and the senate, although the *princeps* was clearly the dominant partner.

procurator the head of the Holy Synod, the chief decision-making body for the Russian Orthodox Church.

proletariat the industrial working class. In Marxism, the class that will ultimately overthrow the bourgeoisie.

propaganda a program of distorted information put out by an organization or government to spread its policy, cause, or doctrine.

psychoanalysis a method developed by Sigmund Freud to resolve a patient's psychic conflict.

purgatory defined by the Catholic Church as the place where souls went after death to be purged of punishment for sins committed in life.

Puritans English Protestants inspired by Calvinist theology who wished to remove all traces of Catholicism from the Church of England.

quadrivium arithmetic, geometry, astronomy, and music; four of the seven liberal arts (the others made up the *trivium*) that formed the basis of medieval and early modern education.

quaestors Roman officials responsible for the administration of financial affairs.

querelles des femmes "arguments about women." A centuries-old debate about the nature of women that continued during the Scientific Revolution as those who argued for the inferiority of women found additional support in the new anatomy and medicine.

rapprochement the rebuilding of harmonious relations between nations.

rationalism a system of thought based on the belief that human reason and experience are the chief sources of knowledge.

Realism a nineteenth-century school of painting that emphasized the everyday life of ordinary people, depicted with photographic accuracy.

realist a subscriber to the medieval European school of thought that held, following Plato, that the individual objects we perceive are not real but merely manifestations of universal ideas existing in the mind of God.

Realpolitik "politics of reality." Politics based on practical concerns rather than theory or ethics.

real wages, income, and prices wages, income, and prices that have been adjusted for inflation.

reason of state the principle that a nation should act on the basis of its long-term interests and not merely to further the dynastic interests of its ruling family.

Reconquista in Spain, the reconquest of Muslim lands by Christian rulers and their armies.

relativity theory Einstein's theory that, among other things, (1) space and time are not absolute but are relative to the observer and interwoven into a four-dimensional space-time continuum and (2) matter is a form of energy ($E = mc^2$).

relics the bones of Christian saints or objects intimately associated with saints that were considered worthy of veneration.

Renaissance the "rebirth" of classical culture that occurred in Italy between c. 1350 and c. 1550; also, the earlier revivals of classical culture that occurred under Charlemagne and in the twelfth century.

rentier a person who lives on income from property and is not personally involved in its operation.

reparations payments made by a defeated nation after a war to compensate another nation for damage sustained as a result of the war; required from Germany after World War I.

revisionism a socialist doctrine that rejected Marx's emphasis on class struggle and revolution and argued instead that workers should work through political parties to bring about gradual change.

revolution a fundamental change in the political and social organization of a state.

revolutionary socialism a socialist doctrine that violent action was the only way to achieve the goals of socialism.

rhetoric the art of persuasive speaking; in the Middle Ages, one of the seven liberal arts.

risorgimento a movement in Italy in the nineteenth century aimed at the creation of a united Italian republic.

Rococo an eighteenth-century artistic movement that emphasized grace, gentility, lightness, and charm.

Romanesque a term used to describe the art and especially architecture of Europe in the eleventh and twelfth centuries.

Romanticism a nineteenth-century intellectual and artistic movement that rejected the emphasis on reason of the Enlightenment. Instead, Romantics stressed the importance of intuition, feeling, emotion, and imagination as sources of knowing.

sacraments rites considered imperative for a Christian's salvation. By the thirteenth century, these consisted of the Eucharist or Lord's Supper, baptism, marriage, penance, extreme unction, holy orders, and confirmation of children; Protestant reformers of the sixteenth century generally recognized only two—baptism and communion (the Lord's Supper).

salons gatherings of philosophes and other notables to discuss the ideas of the Enlightenment; so called from the elegant drawing rooms (salons) where they met.

sans-culottes "without breeches." The common people, who did not wear the fine clothes of the upper classes and played an important role in the radical phase of the French Revolution.

satrap a governor with both civil and military duties in the ancient Persian Empire, which was divided into satrapies, or provinces, each administered by a satrap.

scholasticism the philosophical and theological system of the medieval schools, which emphasized rigorous analysis of contradictory authorities; often used to try to reconcile faith and reason.

scientific method a method of seeking knowledge through inductive principles, using experiments and observations to develop generalizations.

Scientific Revolution the transition from the medieval worldview to a largely secular, rational, and materialistic perspective that began in the seventeenth century and was popularized in the eighteenth.

scriptoria writing rooms for the copying of manuscripts in medieval monasteries.

scutage in the fourteenth century, a money payment for military service that replaced the obligation of military service in the lord-vassal relationship.

secularization the process of becoming more concerned with material, worldly, temporal things and less with spiritual and religious things.

self-determination the doctrine that the people of a given territory or a particular nationality should have the right to determine their own government and political future.

senate the leading council of the Roman Republic; composed of about three hundred men (senators) who served for life and dominated much of the political life of the Republic.

separation of powers a doctrine enunciated by Montesquieu in the eighteenth century that separate executive, legislative, and judicial powers serve to limit and control each other.

serf a peasant who is bound to the land and obliged to provide labor services and pay various rents and fees to the lord; considered unfree but not a slave because serfs could not be bought and sold.

skepticism a doubtful or questioning attitude, especially about religion.

social Darwinism the application of Darwin's principle of organic evolution to the social order; led to the belief that progress comes from the struggle for survival as the fittest advance and the weak decline.

socialism an ideology that calls for collective or government ownership of the means of production and the distribution of goods.

socialized medicine health services for all citizens provided by government assistance.

social security government programs that provide social welfare measures such as old-age pensions and sickness, accident, and disability insurance.

Socratic method a form of teaching that uses a question-and-answer format to enable students to reach conclusions by using their own reasoning.

Sophists wandering scholars and professional teachers in ancient Greece who stressed the importance of rhetoric and tended toward skepticism and relativism.

soviets councils of workers' and soldiers' deputies formed throughout Russia in 1917 that played an important role in the Bolshevik Revolution.

sphere of influence a territory or region over which an outside nation exercises political or economic influence.

squadristi in Italy in the 1920s, bands of armed Fascists used to create disorder by attacking Socialist offices and newspapers.

stagflation a combination of high inflation and high unemployment that was prevalent in the United States and elsewhere from 1973 to the mid-1980s.

Stalinization the adoption by Eastern European Communist countries of features of the economic, political, and military policies implemented by Stalin in the Soviet Union.

Stoicism a philosophy founded by Zeno in the fourth century B.C. that taught that happiness could be obtained by accepting one's lot and living in harmony with the will of God, thereby achieving inner peace.

subinfeudation the practice whereby a lord's greatest vassals subdivided their fiefs and had vassals of their own, who in turn subdivided their fiefs, and so on down to simple knights, whose fiefs were too small to subdivide.

suffrage the right to vote.

suffragists advocates of extending the right to vote to women.

sultan "holder of power." A title taken by Turkish leaders who took command of the Abbasid Empire in 1055.

surplus value in Marxism, the difference between a product's real value and the wages of the worker who produced the product.

Surrealism an artistic movement that arose between World War I and World War II. Surrealists portrayed recognizable objects in unrecognizable relationships in order to reveal the world of the unconscious.

syncretism the combining of different forms of belief or practice, as, for example, when two gods are regarded as different forms of the same underlying divine force and are fused together.

tariffs duties (taxes) imposed on imported goods, usually to raise revenue and to discourage imports and protect domestic industries.

tetrarchy rule by four; the system of government established by Diocletian (284–305) in which the Roman Empire was divided into two parts, each ruled by an "Augustus" assisted by a "Caesar."

theocracy a government ruled by a divine authority.

Third Estate one of the traditional tripartite divisions (orders) of European society based on heredity and quality rather than wealth or economic standing, first established in the Middle Ages and continuing into the eighteenth century; consisted of all who were not members of the clergy or nobility (the first two estates).

three-field system in medieval agriculture, the practice of dividing the arable land into three fields so that one could lie fallow while the others were planted in winter grains and spring crops.

tithe a portion of one's harvest or income, paid by medieval peasants to the village church.

Torah the body of law in Hebrew Scripture, contained in the Pentateuch (the first five books of the Hebrew Bible).

totalitarian state a state characterized by government control over all aspects of economic, social, political, cultural, and intellectual life, the subordination of the individual to the state, and insistence that the masses be actively involved in the regime's goals.

total war warfare in which all of a nation's resources, including civilians at home as well as soldiers in the field, are mobilized for the war effort.

trade union an association of workers in the same trade, formed to help members secure better wages, benefits, and working conditions.

transformism the theory that societies evolve gradually.

transnational corporation another term for "a multinational corporation," or a company with divisions in more than two countries.

transubstantiation a doctrine of the Roman Catholic Church that during the Eucharist, the substance of the bread and wine is miraculously transformed into the body and blood of Jesus.

trench warfare warfare in which the opposing forces attack and counterattack from a relatively permanent system of trenches protected by barbed wire; characteristic of World War I.

triangular trade a pattern of trade in early modern Europe that connected Europe, Africa, and the Americas in an Atlantic economy.

tribunes of the plebs beginning in 494 B.C., Roman officials who were given the power to protect plebeians against arrest by patrician magistrates.

trivium grammar, rhetoric, and dialectic or logic; three of the seven liberal arts (the others made up the *quadrivium*) that were the basis of medieval and early modern education.

Truman Doctrine the doctrine, enunciated by Harry Truman in 1947, that the United States would provide economic aid to countries that said they were threatened by Communist expansion.

tyrant in an ancient Greek *polis* (or an Italian city-state during the Renaissance), a ruler who came to power in an unconstitutional way and ruled without being subject to the law.

ultraroyalists in nineteenth-century France, a group of aristocrats who sought to return to a monarchical system dominated by a landed aristocracy and the Catholic Church.

uncertainty principle a principle in quantum mechanics, posited by Heisenberg, that holds that one cannot determine the path of an electron because the very act of observing the electron would affect its location.

unconditional surrender complete, unqualified surrender of a belligerent nation.

utopian socialists intellectuals and theorists in the early nineteenth century who favored equality in social and economic conditions and wished to replace private property and competition with collective ownership and cooperation.

vassalage the granting of a fief, or landed estate, in exchange for providing military services to the lord and fulfilling certain other obligations such as appearing at the lord's court when summoned and making a payment on the knighting of the lord's eldest son.

vernacular the everyday language of a region, as distinguished from a language used for special purposes. For example, in medieval Paris, French was the vernacular, but Latin was used for academic writing and for classes at the University of Paris.

viceroy the administrative head of the provinces of New Spain and Peru in the Americas.

volkish **thought** the belief that German culture is superior and that the German people have a universal mission to save Western civilization from "inferior" races.

war communism Lenin's policy of nationalizing industrial and other facilities and requisitioning the peasants' produce during the civil war in Russia.

war guilt clause the clause in the Treaty of Versailles that declared that Germany (with Austria) was responsible for starting World War I and ordered Germany to pay reparations for the damage the Allies had suffered as a result of the war.

Warsaw Pact a military alliance, formed in 1955, in which Albania, Bulgaria, Czechoslovakia, East Germany, Hungary, Poland, Romania, and the Soviet Union agreed to provide mutual assistance.

welfare state a sociopolitical system in which the government assumes primary responsibility for the social welfare of its citizens by providing such things as social security, unemployment benefits, and health care.

wergeld "money for a man." In early Germanic law, a person's value in monetary terms, paid by a wrongdoer to the family of the person who had been injured or killed.

world-machine Newton's conception of the universe as one huge, regulated, and uniform machine that operated according to natural laws in absolute time, space, and motion.

zemstvos local assemblies established in Russia in 1864 by Tsar Alexander II.

ziggurat a massive stepped tower on which a temple dedicated to the chief god or goddess of a Sumerian city was built.

Zionism an international movement that called for the establishment of a Jewish state or a refuge for Jews in Palestine.

Zollverein the customs union of all the German states except Austria, formed by Prussia in 1834.

Zoroastrianism a religion founded by the Persian Zoroaster in the seventh century B.C., characterized by worship of a supreme god, Ahuramazda, who represents the good against the evil spirit, identified as Ahriman.

Abbasid uh-BAH-sid *or* AB-uh-sid
Abd al-Rahman ub-duh-rahkh-MAHN
Abu al-Abbas uh-BOOL-uh-BUSS
Abu Bakr ah-bu-BAHK-ur
Achaemenid ah-KEE-muh-nud
Adenauer, Konrad AD-uh-now-ur
aediles EE-dylz
Aeolians ee-OH-lee-unz
Aeschylus ESS-kuh-luss
Aetius ay-EE-shuss
Afrikaners ah-fri-KAH-nurz
Agesilaus uh-jess-uh-LAY-uss
Agincourt AH-zhen-koor
Ahlwardt, Hermann AHL-vart
Ahuramazda uh-HOOR-uh-MAHZ-duh
Aix-la-Chapelle ex-lah-shah-PELL
Akhenaten ah-kuh-NAH-tun
Akkadians uh-KAY-dee-unz
Alaric AL-uh-rik
Alberti, Leon Battista al-BAYR-tee
Albigensians al-buh-JEN-see-unz
Albuquerque, Afonso de AL-buh-kur-kee, ah-FAHN-soh day
Alcibiades al-suh-BY-uh-deez
Alcuin AL-kwin
Alemanni al-uh-MAH-nee
al-Fatah al-FAH-tuh
al-Hakim al-hah-KEEM
Alia, Ramiz AH-lee-uh, rah-MEEZ
al-Khwarizmi al-KHWAR-iz-mee
Allah AH-lah
al-Ma'mun al-muh-MOON
al-Sadat, Anwar al-suh-DAHT, ahn-wahr
Amenhotep ah-mun-HOH-tep
Andreotti, Giulio ahn-dray-AH-tee, JOOL-yoh
Andropov, Yuri ahn-DRAHP-awf, YOOR-ee
Anjou AHN-zhoo
Antigonid an-TIG-uh-nid
Antigonus Gonatus an-TIG-oh-nuss guh-NAH-tuss
Antiochus an-TY-uh-kuss
Antonescu, Ion an-tuh-NESS-koo, YON
Antoninus Pius an-tuh-NY-nuss PY-uss
apella uh-PELL-uh
Apollonius ap-uh-LOH-nee-uss
appartement uh-par-tuh-MUNH
Aquinas, Thomas uh-KWY-nuss
Arafat, Yasir ah-ruh-FAHT, yah-SEER
aratrum uh-RAH-trum
Archimedes ahr-kuh-MEE-deez
Argonautica ahr-guh-NAWT-uh-kuh
Aristarchus ar-iss-TAR-kus
Aristotle AR-iss-tot-ul
Arsinoë ahr-SIN-oh-ee
artium baccalarius ar-TEE-um bak-uh-LAR-ee-uss
artium magister ar-TEE-um muh-GISS-ter
Aryan AR-ee-un
Ashkenazic ash-kuh-NAH-zik
Ashurbanipal ah-shur-BAH-nuh-pahl

Ashurnasirpal ah-shur-NAH-zur-pahl
asiento ah-SYEN-toh
Asoka uh-SOH-kuh
assignat ah-see-NYAH
Assyrians uh-SEER-ee-unz
Astell, Mary AST-ul
Atahualpa ah-tuh-WAHL-puh
Atatürk, Kemal ah-tah-TIRK, kuh-MAHL
Attalid AT-uh-lid
audiencias ow-dee-en-SEE-uss
Auerstadt OW-urr-shtaht
augur AW-gurr
Augustine AW-guh-steen
Aurelian aw-REEL-yun
Auschwitz-Birkenau OWSH-vitz-BEER-kuh-now
Ausgleich OWSS-glykh
auspices AWSS-puh-sizz
Austerlitz AWSS-tur-litz
Australopithecines aw-stray-loh-PITH-uh-synz
Austrasia au-STRY-zhuh
Autun oh-TUNH
Avicenna av-i-SENN-uh
Avignon ah-veen-YONH
Azerbaijan az-ur-by-JAN
Baader-Meinhof BAH-durr-MYN-huff
Babeuf, Gracchus bah-BUFF, GRAK-uss
Bach, Johann Sebastian BAKH, yoh-HAHN suh-BASS-chun
Baden-Powell, Robert BAD-un-POW-ul
Bakunin, Michael buh-KOON-yun
Balboa, Vasco Nuñez de bal-BOH-uh, BAHS-koh NOON-yez day
Ballin, Albert BAH-leen
Banque de Belgique BAHNK duh bel-ZHEEK
Barbarossa bar-buh-ROH-suh
Baroque buh-ROHK
Barth, Karl BAHRT
Bastille bass-STEEL
Batista, Fulgencio bah-TEES-tuh, full-JEN-see-oh
Bauhaus BOW-howss
Bayle, Pierre BELL, PYAYR
Beauharnais, Josephine de boh-ar-NAY, zhoh-seff-FEEN duh
Beauvoir, Simone de boh-VWAR, see-MUHN duh
Bebel, August BAY-bul, ow-GOOST
Beccaria, Cesare buh-KAH-ree-uh, CHAY-zuh-ray
Bede BEED
Beguines bay-GEENZ
Beiderbecke, Bix BY-der-bek, BIKS
Beijing bay-ZHING
Belarus bell-uh-ROOSS
Belgioioso, Cristina bell-joh-YOH-soh
Belisarius bell-uh-SAH-ree-uss
benefice BEN-uh-fiss
Bergson, Henri BERG-son, AHN-ree
Berlioz, Hector BAYR-lee-ohz
Berlusconi, Silvio bayr-loo-SKOH-nee, SEEL-vee-oh
Bernhardi, Friedrich von bayrn-HAR-dee, FREED-reekh fun
Bernini, Gian Lorenzo bur-NEE-nee, ZHAHN loh-RENT-zoh

Bernstein, Eduard BAYRN-shtyn, AY-doo-art
Bethman-Hollweg, Theobald von BET-mun-HOHL-vek,
  TAY-oh-bahlt fun
Blanc, Louis BLAHNH, LWEE
Blitzkrieg BLITZ-kreeg
Blum, Léon BLOOM, LAY-ohnh
Boccaccio, Giovanni boh-KAH-choh, joe-VAH-nee
Bodichon, Barbara boh-di-SHOHNH
Boer BOOR *or* BOR
Boethius boh-EE-thee-uss
Boleyn, Anne BUH-lin *or* buh-LIN
Bolívar, Simón buh-LEE-var, see-MOHN
Bologna buh-LOHN-yuh
Bolsheviks BOHL-shuh-viks
Bora, Katherina von BOH-rah, kat-uh-REE-nuh fun
Bosnia BAHZ-nee-uh
Bossuet, Jacques baw-SWAY, ZHAHK
Botta, Giuseppe BOH-tah, joo-ZEP-pay
Botticelli, Sandro bot-i-CHELL-ee, SAHN-droh
Boulanger, Georges boo-lahnh-ZHAY, ZHORZH
boule BOOL
Bracciolini, Poggio braht-choh-LEE-nee, POH-djoh
Brahe, Tycho BRAH, TY-koh
Bramante, Donato brah-MAHN-tay, doh-NAH-toh
Brandt, Willy BRAHNT, VIL-ee
Brasidas BRASS-i-duss
Brest-Litovsk BREST-li-TUFFSK
Brétigny bray-tee-NYEE
Brezhnev, Leonid BREZH-neff, lee-oh-NYEET
Briand, Aristide bree-AHNH, ah-ruh-STEED
Broz, Josip BRAWZ, yaw-SEEP
Brumaire broo-MAYR
Brunelleschi, Filippo BROO-nuh-LESS-kee, fee-LEE-poh
Brüning, Heinrich BROO-ning, HYN-rikh
Bückeberg BOOK-uh-bayrk
Bulganin, Nicolai bool-GAN-yin, nyik-uh-LY
Bund Deutscher Mädel BOONT DOIT-chuh MAY-dul
Bundesrat BOON-duhs-raht
Burckhardt, Jacob BOORK-hart, YAK-ub
Burschenschaften BOOR-shun-shahf-tuhn
bushido BOO-shee-doh
Cabral, Pedro kuh-BRAL
cahiers de doléances ka-YAY duh doh-lay-AHNSS
Calais ka-LAY
Calas, Jean ka-LAH, ZHAHNH
Caligula kuh-LIG-yuh-luh
caliph KAY-liff
caliphate KAY-luh-fayt
Callicrates kuh-LIK-ruh-teez
Calonne, Charles de ka-LUNN, SHAHRL duh
Cambyses kam-BY-seez
Camus, Albert ka-MOO, ahl-BAYR
Canaanites KAY-nuh-nytss
Capet, Hugh ka-PAY, YOO
Capetian kuh-PEE-shun
Caracalla kuh-RAK-uh-luh
Caraffa, Gian Pietro kuh-RAH-fuh, JAHN PYAY-troh
carbonari kar-buh-NAH-ree
Carolingian kar-uh-LIN-jun
carruca kuh-ROO-kuh
Carthage KAR-thij
Carthaginian kar-thuh-JIN-ee-un
Cartier, Jacques kar-TYAY, ZHAK
Cassiodorus kass-ee-uh-DOR-uss
Castiglione, Baldassare ka-steel-YOH-nay, bal-duh-SAH-ray
Castro, Fidel KASS-troh, fee-DELL
Çatal Hüyük chaht-ul hoo-YOOK
Catharism KA-thuh-riz-um
Catullus kuh-TULL-uss

Cavendish, Margaret KAV-un-dish
Cavour, Camillo di kuh-VOOR, kuh-MEEL-oh dee
Ceauşescu, Nicolae chow-SHES-koo, nee-koh-LY
celibacy SELL-uh-buh-see
cenobitic sen-oh-BIT-ik
Cereta, Laura say-REE-tuh, LOW-ruh
Cézanne, Paul say-ZAHN
Chaeronea ker-uh-NEE-uh
Chaldean kal-DEE-un
Chandragupta Maurya chun-druh-GOOP-tuh MOWR-yuh
chanson de geste shahn-SAWNH duh ZHEST
Charlemagne SHAR-luh-mayn
Chateaubriand, François-René de shah-TOH-bree-AHNH,
  frahnh-SWAH-ruh-NAY duh
Châtelet, marquise du shat-LAY, mahr-KEEZ duh
Chauvet shoh-VAY
Cheka CHEK-uh
Chiang Kai-shek CHANG ky-SHEK
Chirac, Jacques shee-RAK, ZHAHK
Chrétien, Jean kray-TYEN, ZHAHNH
Chrétien de Troyes kray-TYEN duh TRWAH
Cicero SIS-uh-roh
ciompi CHAHM-pee
Cistercians sis-TUR-shunz
Claudius KLAW-dee-uss
Cleisthenes KLYSS-thuh-neez
Clemenceau, Georges kluh-mahn-SOH, ZHORZH
Clovis KLOH-viss
Codreanu, Corneliu kaw-dree-AH-noo, kor-NELL-yoo
cognomen kahg-NOH-mun
Colbert, Jean-Baptiste kohl-BAYR, ZHAHN-bap-TEEST
Colonia Agrippinensis kuh-LOH-nee-uh uh-grip-uh-
  NEN-suss
colonus kuh-LOH-nuss
Columbanus kah-lum-BAY-nuss
comitia centuriata kuh-MISH-ee-uh sen-choo-ree-AH-tuh
Commodus KAHM-uh-duss
Comnenus kahm-NEE-nuss
Comte, Auguste KOHNT, ow-GOOST
concilium plebis kahn-SILL-ee-um PLEE-biss
Concordat of Worms kun-KOR-dat uv WURMZ *or*
  VORMPS
Condorcet, Marie-Jean de kohn-dor-SAY, muh-REE-
  ZHAHNH duh
condottieri kahn-duh-TYAY-ree
consul KAHN-sull
Contarini, Gasparo kahn-tuh-REE-nee, GAHS-puh-roh
conversos kohn-VAYR-sohz
Copernicus, Nicolaus kuh-PURR-nuh-kuss, nee-koh-
  LOW-uss
Córdoba KOR-duh-buh
Corinth KOR-inth
Corpus Hermeticum KOR-pus hur-MET-i-koom
Corpus Iuris Civilis KOR-pus YOOR-iss SIV-i-liss
corregidores kuhr-reg-uh-DOR-ayss
Cortés, Hernán kor-TAYSS *or* kor-TEZ, hayr-NAHN
Corvinus, Matthias kor-VY-nuss, muh-THY-uss
Courbet, Gustave koor-BAY, goo-STAHV
Crassus KRASS-uss
Crécy kray-SEE
Crédit Mobilier kray-DEE moh-bee-LYAY
Croatia kroh-AY-shuh
Croesus KREE-suss
Cruz, Juana Inés de la Sor KROOZ, HWAH-nuh ee-NAYSS
  day lah SAWR
cum manu koom MAH-noo
Curie, Marie kyoo-REE
Cyaxares si-AK-suh-reez
Cypselus SIP-suh-luss

d'Albret, Jeanne   dahl-BRAY, ZHAHN
d'Este, Isabella   DESS-tay, ee-suh-BELL-uh
d'Holbach, Paul   dawl-BAHK
Daimler, Gottlieb   DYM-lur, GUHT-leeb
Dalí, Salvador   dah-LEE *or* DAH-lee
Danton, Georges   dahn-TAWNH, ZHORZH
Darius   duh-RY-uss
Darmstadt   DARM-shtaht
dauphin   DAW-fin
David, Jacques-Louis   dah-VEED, ZHAHK-LWEE
de Champlain, Samuel   duh sham-PLAYN
de Gaulle, Charles   duh GOHL, SHAHRL
De Rerum Novarum   day RAYR-um noh-VAR-um
Debelleyme, Louis-Maurice   duh-buh-LAYM, LWEE-moh-REESS
Debussy, Claude   duh-bus-SEE, KLOHD
décades   day-KAD
Decameron   dee-KAM-uh-run
decarchies   DEK-ar-keez
decemviri   duh-SEM-vuh-ree
Deffand, marquise du   duh-FAHNH, mar-KEEZ doo
Delacroix, Eugène   duh-lah-KRWAH, oo-ZHEN
Démar, Claire   DAY-mar
Demosthenes   duh-MAHSS-thuh-neez
Denikin, Anton   dyin-YEE-kin, ahn-TOHN
Descartes, René   day-KART, ruh-NAY
Dessau   DESS-ow
dhoti   DOH-tee
Diaghilev, Sergei   DYAHG-yuh-lif, syir-GAY
Dias, Bartholomeu   DEE-ush, bar-toh-loh-MAY-oo
Diaspora   dy-ASS-pur-uh
Diderot, Denis   DEE-droh, duh-NEE
Diocletian   dy-uh-KLEE-shun
Disraeli, Benjamin   diz-RAY-lee
Djoser   ZHOH-sur
Dollfuss, Engelbert   DAHL-fooss
Domesday Book   DOOMZ-day book
Domitian   doh-MISH-un
Donatello, Donato di   doh-nuh-TELL-oh, doh-NAH-toh dee
Donatus   duh-NAY-tus
Donatist   DOH-nuh-tist
Dopolavoro   duh-puh-LAH-vuh-roh
Dorians   DOR-ee-unz
Doryphoros   doh-RIF-uh-rohss
Dostoevsky, Fyodor   dus-tuh-YEF-skee, FYUD-ur
Douhet, Giulio   doo-AY, JOOL-yoh
Dreyfus, Alfred   DRY-fuss
Dubček, Alexander   DOOB-chek
Du Bois, W. E. B.   doo-BOISS
Dufay, Guillaume   doo-FAY, gee-YOHM
Duma   DOO-muh
Dürer, Albrecht   DOO-rur, AHL-brekht
Ebert, Friedrich   AY-bert, FREE-drikh
ecclesia   ek-KLEE-zee-uh
Eckhart, Meister   EK-hart, MY-stur
Einsatzgruppen   YN-zahtz-groop-un
Einstein, Albert   YN-styn *or* Yn-shtyn
Ekaterinburg   i-kat-tuh-RIN-burk
encomienda   en-koh-MYEN-dah
Engels, Friedrich   ENG-ulz, FREE-drikh
Enki   EN-kee
Enlil   EN-lil
Entente Cordiale   ahn-TAHNT kor-DYAHL
Epaminondas   i-PAM-uh-NAHN-duss
ephor   EFF-ur
Epicureanism   ep-i-kyoo-REE-uh-ni-zum
Epicurus   ep-i-KYOOR-uss
episcopos   i-PIS-kuh-puss
equestrians   i-KWES-tree-unz

equites   EK-wuh-teez
Erasistratus   er-uh-SIS-truh-tuss
Erasmus, Desiderius   i-RAZZ-mus, dez-i-DEER-ee-uss
Eratosthenes   er-uh-TAHSS-thuh-neez
eremitical   er-uh-MIT-i-kul
Erhard, Ludwig   AYR-hart, LOOD-vik
Estonia   ess-TOH-nee-uh
Etruscans   i-TRUSS-kunz
Euclid   YOO-klid
Euripides   yoo-RIP-i-deez
exchequer   EKS-chek-ur
Execrabilis   ek-suh-KRAB-uh-liss
Eylau   Y-low
Falange   fuh-LANJ
fasces   FASS-eez
Fascio di Combattimento   FASH-ee-oh dee com-bat-ee-MEN-toh
Fatimid   FAT-i-mid
Fedele, Cassandra   FAY-duh-lee
Feltre, Vittorino da   FELL-tray, vee-tor-EE-noh dah
Ficino, Marsilio   fee-CHEE-noh, mar-SIL-yoh
Fischer, Joschka   FISH-ur, YUSH-kah
Flaubert, Gustave   floh-BAYR, goo-STAHV
Fleury, Cardinal   floo-REE
Floreal   floh-ray-AHL
fluyt   FLYT
Foch, Ferdinand   FUSH, fayr-di-nawnh
Fontainebleau   fawnh-ten-BLOH
Fontenelle, Bernard de   fawnt-NELL, bayr-NAHR duh
Fouquet, Nicolas   foo-KAY, nee-koh-LAH
Fourier, Charles   foo-RYAY, SHAHRL
Francesca, Piero della   frahn-CHESS-kuh, PYAY-roh del-luh
Frequens   FREE-kwenss
Freud, Sigmund   FROID, SIG-mund *or* ZIG-munt
Friedan, Betty   free-DAN
Friedland   FREET-lahnt
Friedrich, Caspar David   FREED-rikh, kass-PAR dah-VEET
Frimaire   free-MAYR
Froissart, Jean   frwah-SAR, ZHAHNH
Fronde   FROHND
Fructidor   FROOK-ti-dor
fueros   FWYA-rohss
Führerprinzip   FYOOR-ur-prin-TSEEP
gabelle   gah-BELL
Gaiseric   GY-zuh-rik
Galba   GAHL-buh
Galilei, Galileo   GAL-li-lay, gal-li-LAY-oh
Gama, Vasco da   GAHM-uh, VAHSH-koh dah
Gandhi, Mohandas (Mahatma)   GAHN-dee, moh-HAHN-dus (mah-HAHT-muh)
Garibaldi, Giuseppe   gar-uh-BAHL-dee, joo-ZEP-pay
Gasperi, Alcide de   GAHSS-pe-ree, ahl-SEE-day day
Gatti de Gamond, Zoé   gah-TEE duh gah-MOHNH, zoh-AY
Gaugamela   gaw-guh-MEE-luh
Gelasius   juh-LAY-shuss
gens   GENZ
Gentileschi, Artemisia   jen-tuh-LESS-kee, ar-tuh-MEE-zhuh
Geoffrin, Marie-Thérèse de   zhoh-FRANH, ma-REE-tay-RAYZ duh
Germinal   jayr-mee-NAHL
gerousia   juh-ROO-see-uh
Gesamtkunstwerk   guh-ZAHMT-koonst-vayrk
Gierek, Edward   GYER-ek
Gilgamesh   GILL-guh-mesh
Giolitti, Giovanni   joh-LEE-tee, joe-VAHN-nee
Giotto   JOH-toh
Girondins   juh-RAHN-dinz
glasnost   GLAHZ-nohst
Gleichschaltung   glykh-SHAHL-toonk

Goebbels, Joseph   GUR-bulz
Goethe, Johann Wolfgang von   GUR-tuh, yoh-HAHN VULF-
   gahnk fun
Gömbös, Julius   GUM-buhsh
Gomulka, Wladyslaw   goh-MOOL-kuh, vlah-DIS-lahf
gonfaloniere   gun-fah-loh-NYAY-ray
Gonzaga, Gian Francesco   gun-DZAH-gah, JAHN frahn-
   CHES-koh
Gorbachev, Mikhail   GOR-buh-chof, meek-HAYL
Göring, Hermann   GUR-ing
Gottwald, Clement   GUT-vald
Gouges, Olympe   GOOZH, oh-LAMP
Gracchus, Tiberius and Gaius   GRAK-us, ty-BEER-ee-uss
   and GY-uss
grandi   GRAHN-dee
Grieg, Edvard   GREEG, ED-vart
Groote, Gerard   GROH-tuh
Gropius, Walter   GROH-pee-uss, VAHL-tuh
Grossdeutsch   GROHS-doich
Groza, Petra   GRO-zhuh, PET-ruh
Guicciardini, Francesco   gwee-char-DEE-nee, frahn-
   CHESS-koh
Guindorf, Reine   GWIN-dorf, RY-nuh
Guise   GEEZ
Guizot, François   gee-ZOH, frahnh-SWAH
Gustavus Adolphus   goo-STAY-vus uh-DAHL-fuss
Gutenberg, Johannes   GOO-ten-bayrk, yoh-HAH-nuss
Guzman, Gaspar de   goos-MAHN, gahs-PAR day
Habsburg   HAPS-burg
Hadrian   HAY-dree-un
Hagia Sophia   HAG-ee-uh soh-FEE-uh
hajj   HAJ
Hammurabi   ham-uh-RAH-bee
Handel, George Friedrich   HAN-dul
Hankou   HAHN-kow
Hannibal   HAN-uh-bul
Hanukkah   HAH-nuh-kuh
Harappa   huh-RAP-uh
Hardenberg, Karl von   HAR-den-berk, KARL fun
Harun al-Rashid   huh-ROON ah-rah-SHEED
hastati   hahs-TAH-tee
Hatshepsut   hat-SHEP-soot
Haushofer, Karl   HOWSS-hoh-fuh
Haussmann, Baron   HOWSS-mun
Havel, Vaclav   HAH-vul, VAHT-slahf
Haydn, Franz Joseph   HY-dun, FRAHNTS YO-zef
hegemon   HEJ-uh-mun
Hegira   hee-JY-ruh
Heisenberg, Werner   HY-zun-bayrk, VAYR-nur
heliaea   HEE-lee-ee
Hellenistic   hel-uh-NIS-tik
helots   HEL-uts
Herculaneum   hur-kyuh-LAY-nee-um
Herodotus   huh-ROD-uh-tuss
Herophilus   huh-ROF-uh-luss
Herzegovina   HURT-suh-guh-VEE-nuh
Herzen, Alexander   HAYRT-sun
Herzl, Theodor   HAYRT-sul, TAY-oh-dor
Hesiod   HEE-see-ud
Hesse, Hermann   HESS-uh
hetairai   huh-TY-ree
Heydrich, Reinhard   HY-drikh, RYN-hart
hieroglyph   HY-uh-roh-glif
Hildegard of Bingen   HIL-duh-gard uv BING-un
Hindenburg, Paul von   HIN-den-boork, POWL fun
Hiroshima   hee-roh-SHEE-muh
Hitler Jugend   HIT-luh YOO-gunt

Ho Chi Minh   HOH CHEE MIN
Höch, Hannah   HEKH
Hohenstaufen   hoh-en-SHTOW-fen
Hohenzollern   hoh-en-TSULL-urn
Hohenzollern-Sigmaringen   hoh-en-TSULL-urn-zig-mah-
   RING-un
Holtzendorf   HOHLT-sen-dorf
Homo sapiens   HOH-moh SAY-pee-unz
Honecker, Erich   HOH-nek-uh
Honorius   hoh-NOR-ee-uss
hoplites   HAHP-lyts
Horace   HOR-uss
Horthy, Miklós   HOR-tee, MIK-lohsh
Höss, Rudolf   HESS
Hoxha, Enver   HAW-jah
Huayna Inca   WY-nuh INK-uh
Huguenots   HYOO-guh-nots
Husák, Gustav   HOO-sahk, goo-STAHV
Ibn Sina   ib-un SEE-nuh
Ictinus   ik-TY-nuss
Ignatius of Loyola   ig-NAY-shuss uv loi-OH-luh
Il Duce   eel DOO-chay
Île-de-France   EEL-de-fronhss
illustrés   ee-loo-STRAY
illustrissimi   ee-loo-STREE-see-mee
imperator   im-puh-RAH-tur
imperium   im-PEER-ee-um
intendant   anh-tahnh-DAHNH *or* in-TEN-dunt
Isis   Y-sis
Issus   ISS-uss
ius civile   YOOSS see-VEE-lay
ius gentium   YOOSS GEN-tee-um
ius naturale   YOOSS nah-too-RAH-lay
Jacobin   JAK-uh-bin
Jacquerie   zhak-REE
Jadwiga   yahd-VEE-guh
Jagiello   yahg-YEL-oh
Jahn, Friedrich Ludwig   YAHN, FREED-rikh LOOD-vik
Jaurès, Jean   zhaw-RESS, ZHAHNH
Jena   YAY-nuh
jihad   ji-HAHD
Joffre, Joseph   ZHUFF-ruh
Journal des Savants   zhoor-NAHL day sah-VAHNH
Judaea   joo-DEE-uh
Judas Maccabaeus   JOO-dus mak-uh-BEE-uss
Jung, Carl   YOONG
Junkers   YOONG-kers
Jupiter Optimus Maximus   JOO-puh-tur AHP-tuh-muss
   MAK-suh-muss
Justinian   juh-STIN-ee-un
Juvenal   JOO-vuh-nul
Ka'ba   KAH-buh
Kádár, János   KAH-dahr, YAH-nush
kamikaze   kah-mi-KAH-zay
Kandinsky, Wassily   kan-DIN-skee, vus-YEEL-yee
Kangxi   GANG-zhee
Kant, Immanuel   KAHNT, i-MAHN-yoo-el
Karlowitz   KARL-oh-vits
Karlsbad   KARLSS-baht
Kaunitz, Wenzel von   KOW-nits, VENT-sul fun
Kenyatta, Jomo   ken-YAHT-uh, JOH-moh
Kerensky, Alexander   kuh-REN-skee
Keynes, John Maynard   KAYNZ
Khanbaliq   khahn-bah-LEEK
Khomeini, Ayatollah   khoh-MAY-nee
Khrushchev, Nikita   KHROOSH-chawf, nuh-KEE-tuh
Khubilai Khan   KOO-bluh KAHN

Kikuya   ki-KOO-yuh
Kleindeutsch   KLYN-doich
Kohl, Helmut   KOHL, HEL-moot
koiné   koi-NAY
Kolchak, Alexander   kul-CHAHK
Kollantai, Alexandra   kul-lun-TY
Königgrätz   kur-nig-GRETS
Kornilov, Lavr   kor-NYEE-luff, LAH-vur
Kosciuszko, Thaddeus   kaw-SHOOS-koh, tah-DAY-oosh
Kosovo   KAWSS-suh-voh
Kossuth, Louis   KAWSS-uth *or* KAW-shoot
Kostunica, Vojislav   kuh-STOO-nit-suh, VOH-yee-slav
kouros   KOO-rohss
Koyaanisqatsi   koh-YAH-niss-kaht-si
Kraft durch Freude   KRAHFT doorkh FROI-duh
Kreditanstalt   kray-deet-AHN-shtalt
Kristallnacht   kri-STAHL-nahkht
Krupp, Alfred   KROOP
Kuchuk-Kainarji   koo-CHOOK-ky-NAR-jee
kulaks   KOO-lahks
Kulturkampf   kool-TOOR-kahmpf
Kun, Béla   KOON, BAY-luh
Kundera, Milan   koon-DAYR-uh, MEE-lahn
Kursk   KOORSK
Kwasniewski, Aleksander   kwahsh-NYEF-skee
la belle époque   lah BEL ay-PUK
Lafayette, marquis de   lah-fay-ET, mar-KEE duh
laissez-faire   less-ay-FAYR
Lamarck, Jean-Baptiste   lah-MARK, ZHAHNH-bah-TEEST
Lancaster   LAN-kas-tur
La Rochefoucauld-Liancourt, duc de   lah-RUSH-foo-koh-
    lee-ahnh-KOOR, dook duh
Las Navas de Tolosa   lahss nah-vahss day toh-LOH-suh
latifundia   lat-i-FOON-dee-uh
Latium   LAY-shee-um
Latvia   LAT-vee-uh
Launay, marquis de   loh-NAY, mar-KEE duh
Laurier, Wilfred   LOR-ee-ay
Lavoisier, Antoine   lah-vwah-ZYAY
Lazar   lah-ZAR
Lebensraum   LAY-benz-rowm
Les Demoiselles d'Avignon   lay dem-wah-ZEL dah-vee-
    NYOHNH
Lespinasse, Julie de   less-pee-NAHSS, zhoo-LEE duh
Le Tellier, François Michel   luh tel-YAY, frahnh-SWAH
    mee-SHEL
Lévesque, René   luh-VEK, ruh-NAY
Leviathan   luh-VY-uh-thun
Leyster, Judith   LESS-tur
Licinius   ly-SIN-ee-uss
Liebenfels, Lanz von   LEE-bun-felss, LAHNts fun
Liebknecht, Karl   LEEP-knekht
Liebknecht, Wilhelm   LEEP-knekht, VIL-helm
Lindisfarne   LIN-dis-farn
Lionne, Hugues de   LYUNN, OOG duh
List, Friedrich   LIST, FREED-rikh
Liszt, Franz   LIST, FRAHNTS
Lithuania   lith-WAY-nee-uh
Livy   LIV-ee
Li Zicheng   lee zee-CHENG
L'Ouverture, Toussaint   loo-vayr-TOOR, too-SANH
Louvois   loo-VWAH
Lucretius   loo-KREE-shus
Luddites   LUD-yts
Ludendorff, Erich   LOO-dun-dorf
Lueger, Karl   LOO-gur
Luftwaffe   LOOFT-vahf-uh

l'uomo universale   LWOH-moh OO-nee-ver-SAH-lay
Lützen   LOOT-sun
Luxemburg, Rosa   LOOK-sum-boork
Lyons   LYOHNH
Maastricht   MAHSS-trikht
Machiavelli, Niccolò   mahk-ee-uh-VEL-ee, nee-koh-LOH
Maginot Line   MA-zhi-noh lyn
Magna Graecia   MAG-nuh GREE-shuh
Magyars   MAG-yarz
Maimonides   my-MAH-nuh-deez
Maistre, Joseph de   MESS-truh
maius imperium   MY-yoos im-PEE-ree-um
Malaya   muh-LAY-uh
Mallarmé, Stéphane   mah-lahr-MAY, stay-FAHN
Malleus Maleficarum   mal-EE-uss mal-uh-FIK-uh-rum
Malthus, Thomas   MAWL-thuss
Manchukuo   man-CHOO-kwoh
Manetho   MAN-uh-thoh
Mao Zedong   mow zee-DAHNG
Marcus Aurelius   MAR-kuss aw-REE-lee-uss
Marcuse, Herbert   mar-KOO-zuh
Marie Antoinette   muh-REE an-twuh-NET
Marius   MAR-ee-uss
Marquez, Gabriel Garcia   mar-KEZ
Marseilles   mar-SAY
Marsiglio of Padua   mar-SIL-yoh uv PAD-juh-wuh
Masaccio   muh-ZAH-choh
Masaryk, Thomas   MAS-uh-rik
Mästlin, Michael   MEST-lin
Matteotti, Giacomo   mat-tay-AHT-tee, JAHK-uh-moh
Maxentius   mak-SEN-shuss
Maximian   mak-SIM-ee-un
Maya   MY-uh
Mazarin   maz-uh-RANH
Mazzini, Giuseppe   maht-SEE-nee, joo-ZEP-pay
Medes   MEEDZ
Megasthenes   muh-GAS-thuh-neez
Mehmet   meh-MET
Meiji   MAY-jee
Mein Kampf   myn KAHMPF
Melanchthon, Philip   muh-LANK-tun
Menander   muh-NAN-dur
Mendeleyev, Dmitri   men-duh-LAY-ef, di-MEE-tree
Mensheviks   MENS-shuh-viks
Mercator, Gerardus   mur-KAY-tur, juh-RAHR-dus
Merian, Maria Sibylla   MAY-ree-un
Merovingian   meh-ruh-VIN-jee-un
Mesopotamia   mess-uh-puh-TAY-mee-uh
Messiaen, Olivier   meh-SYANH, oh-lee-VYAY
Messidor   MESS-i-dor
mestizos   mess-TEE-ZOHZ
Metaxas, John   muh-tahk-SAHSS
Metternich, Klemens von   MET-ayr-nikh, KLAY-menss fun
Michel, Louise   mee-SHEL
Michelangelo   my-kuh-LAN-juh-loh
Mieszko   MYESH-koh
Millet, Jean-François   mi-YEH, ZHAHNH-frahnh-SWAH
Milošević, Slobodan   mi-LOH-suh-vich, sluh-BOH-dahn
Miltiades   mil-TY-uh-deez
Mirandola, Pico della   mee-RAN-doh-lah, PEE-koh DELL-uh
missi dominici   MISS-ee doh-MIN-i-chee
Mitterrand, François   MEE-tayr-rahnh, frahnh-SWAH
Moctezuma   mahk-tuh-ZOO-muh
Mohács   MOH-hach
Mohenjo-Daro   mo-HEN-jo-DAH-roh
Moldavia   mohl-DAY-vee-uh

Moldova mohl-DOH-vuh
Molière, Jean-Baptiste mohl-YAYR, ZHAHNH-bah-TEEST
Molotov, Vyacheslav MAHL-uh-tawf, vyich-chiss-SLAHF
Monet, Claude moh-NEH, KLOHD
Montaigne, Michel de mahn-TAYN, mee-SHELL duh
Montefeltro, Federigo da mahn-tuh-FELL-troh, fay-day-REE-goh dah
Montesquieu MOHN-tess-kyoo
Montessori, Maria mahn-tuh-SOR-ee
Morisot, Berthe mor-ee-ZOH, BAYRT
Mozambique moh-zam-BEEK
Mozart, Wolfgang Amadeus MOH-tsart, VULF-gahng ah-muh-DAY-uss
Muawiya moo-AH-wee-yah
Mudejares moo-theh-KHAH-rayss
Mughal MOO-gul
Muhammad moh-HAM-mud *or* moo-HAM-mud
Mühlberg MOOL-bayrk
mulattoes muh-LAH-tohz
Müntzer, Thomas MOON-tsur
Murad moo-RAHD
Muslim MUZ-lum
Mutsuhito moo-tsoo-HEE-toh
Myanmar MYAN-mahr
Mycenaean my-suh-NEE-un
Nabonidas nab-uh-NY-duss
Nabopolassar nab-uh-puh-LASS-ur
Nagasaki nah-gah-SAH-kee
Nagy, Imry NAHJ, IM-ray
Nanjing nan-JING
Nantes NAHNT
Nasser, Gamal Abdel NAH-sur, juh-MAHL ahb-DOOL
Navarre nuh-VAHR
Nebuchadnezzar neb-uh-kud-NEZZ-ur
Nehru, Jawaharlal NAY-roo, juh-WAH-hur-lahl
Nero NEE-roh
Nerva NUR-vuh
Neumann, Balthasar NOI-mahn, BAHL-tuh-zahr
Neumann, Solomon NOI-mahn
Neustria NOO-stree-uh
Nevsky, Alexander NYEF-skee
Newcomen, Thomas NYOO-kuh-mun *or* nyoo-KUM-mun
Ngo Dinh Diem GOH din DYEM
Nicias NISS-ee-uss
Nietzsche, Friedrich NEE-chuh *or* NEE-chee, FREED-rikh
Nimwegen NIM-vay-gun
Ninhursaga nin-HUR-sah-guh
Nivose nee-VOHZ
Nkrumah, Kwame en-KROO-muh, KWAH-may
nobiles no-BEE-layz
Nogarola, Isotta NOH-guh-roll-uh, ee-ZAHT-uh
nomen NOH-mun
Novalis, Friedrich noh-VAH-lis, FREED-rikh
Novotny, Antonin noh-VAHT-nee, AHN-toh-nyeen
novus homo NOH-vuss HOH-moh
Nystadt NEE-shtaht
Octavian ahk-TAY-vee-un
Odoacer oh-doh-AY-sur
Olivares oh-lee-BAH-rayss
optimates ahp-tuh-MAH-tayz
Oresteia uh-res-TY-uh
Osama bin Laden oh-SAH-muh bin LAH-dun
Osiris oh-SY-russ
Ostara oh-STAH-ruh
Ostpolitik OHST-paw-li-teek
ostrakon AHSS-truh-kahn
Ostrogoths AHSS-truh-gahthss

Ovid OH-vid
Oxenstierna, Axel OOK-sen-shur-nah, AHK-sul
Pachakuti pah-chah-KOO-tee
Paleologus pay-lee-AWL-uh-guss
Panaetius puh-NEE-shuss
Pankhurst, Emmeline PANK-hurst
papal curia PAY-pul KYOOR-ee-uh
Papen, Franz von PAH-pun, FRAHNTS fun
Paracelsus par-uh-SELL-suss
Parlement par-luh-MAHNH
Parti Québécois par-TEE kay-bek-KWA
Pascal, Blaise pass-KAHL, BLEZ
Pasteur, Louis pas-TOOR, LWEE
paterfamilias pay-tur-fuh-MEEL-yus
Pensées pahn-SAY
Pentateuch PEN-tuh-took
Pepin PEP-in *or* pay-PANH
perestroika per-uh-STROI-kuh
Pergamum PURR-guh-mum
Pericles PER-i-kleez
perioeci per-ee-EE-see
Pétain, Henri pay-TANH, AHN-ree
Petite Roquette puh-TEET raw-KET
Petrarch PEE-trark *or* PET-trark
Petronius pi-TROH-nee-uss
phalansteries fuh-LAN-stuh-reez
philosophe fee-loh-ZAWF
Phintys FIN-tiss
Phoenicians fuh-NEE-shunz
Photius FOH-shuss
Picasso, Pablo pi-KAH-soh
Pietism PY-uh-tiz-um
Pilsudski, Joseph peel-SOOT-skee
Piscator, Erwin PIS-kuh-tor, AYR-vin
Pisistratus puh-SIS-truh-tuss
Pissarro, Camille pee-SAH-roh, kah-MEEL
Pizan, Christine de pee-ZAHN, kris-TEEN duh
Pizarro, Francesco puh-ZAHR-oh, frahn-CHESS-koh
Planck, Max PLAHNK
Plantagenet plan-TAJ-uh-net
Plassey PLA-see
Plato PLAY-toh
Plautus PLAW-tuss
plebiscita pleb-i-SEE-tuh
Pluviose ploo-VYOHZ
Poincaré, Raymond pwanh-kah-RAY, ray-MOHNH
polis POH-liss
politiques puh-lee-TEEKS
Pollaiuolo, Antonio pohl-ly-WOH-loh
Poltava pul-TAH-vuh
Polybius puh-LIB-ee-uss
Pombal, marquis de pum-BAHL, mar-KEE duh
Pompadour, madame de POM-puh-door, ma-DAM duh
Pompeii pahm-PAY
Pompey PAHM-pee
pontifex maximus PAHN-ti-feks MAK-si-muss
populares PAWP-oo-lahr-ayss
populo grasso PAWP-oo-loh GRAH-soh
Postumus PAHS-choo-muss
Potsdam PAHTS-dam
Poussin, Nicholas poo-SANH, NEE-koh-lah
Praecepter Germaniae PREE-sep-tur gayr-MAHN-ee-ee
praenomen pree-NOH-mun
praetor PREE-tur
Prairial pray-RYAL
Pravda PRAHV-duh
Primo de Rivera PREE-moh day ri-VAY-ruh

primogeniture   pree-moh-JEN-i-choor
princeps   PRIN-keps *or* PRIN-seps
principes   prin-KI-payz *or* prin-SI-payz
Principia   prin-KIP-ee-uh *or* prin-SIP-ee-uh
Procopius   pruh-KOH-pee-uss
procurator   PROK-yuh-ray-tur
Ptolemaic   tahl-uh-MAY-ik
Ptolemy   TAHL-uh-mee
Pugachev, Emelyan   poo-guh-CHAWF, yim-yil-YAHN
Punic   PYOO-nik
Putin, Vladimir   POO-tin
Pyrrhic   PEER-ik
Pyrrhus   PEER-uss
Pythagoras   puh-THAG-uh-russ
Qianlong   CHAN-lung
Qing   CHING
quadrivium   kwah-DRIV-ee-um
quaestors   KWES-turs
querelle des femmes   keh-REL day FAHM
Quesnay, François   keh-NAY, frahnn-SWAH
Quetzelcoatl   KWET-sul-koh-AHT-ul
Qur'an   kuh-RAN *or* kuh-RAHN
Racine, Jean-Baptiste   ra-SEEN, ZHAHNH-buh-TEEST
Rahner, Karl   RAH-nur
Rameses   RAM-uh-seez
Raphael   RAFF-ee-ul
Rasputin   rass-PYOO-tin
Rathenau, Walter   RAH-tuh-now,VAHL-tuh
Realpolitik   ray-AHL-poh-lee-teek
Realschule   ray-AHL-shoo-luh
Reichsrat   RYKHSS-raht
Reichstag   RYKHSS-tahk
Rembrandt van Rijn   REM-brant vahn RYN
Renan, Ernst   re-NAHNH
Ricci, Matteo   REE-chee, ma-TAY-oh
Richelieu   REESH-uh-lyoo
Ricimer   RISS-uh-mur
Rikstag   RIKS-tahk
Rilke, Rainer Maria   RILL-kuh, RY-nuh mah-REE-uh
Rimbaud, Arthur   ram-BOH, ar-TOOR
risorgimento   ree-SOR-jee-men-toe
Robespierre, Maximilien   ROHBZ-pyayr, mak-see-meel-YENH
Rococo   ruh-KOH-koh
Rocroi   roh-KRWAH
Röhm, Ernst   RURM
Rommel, Erwin   RAHM-ul
Romulus Augustulus   RAHM-yuh-luss ow-GOOS-chuh-luss
Rossbach   RAWSS-bahkh
Rousseau, Jean-Jacques   roo-SOH, ZHAHNH-ZHAHK
Rudel, Jaufré,   roo-DEL, zhoh-FRAY
Rurik   ROO-rik
Ryswick   RYZ-wik
Sacrosancta   sak-roh-SANK-tuh
Saint-Just   sanh-ZHOOST
Saint-Simon, Henri de   sanh-see-MOHNH, ahnh-REE duh
Sakharov, Andrei   SAH-kuh-rawf, ahn-DRAY
Saladin   SAL-uh-din
Salazar, Antonio   SAL-uh-zahr
Sallust   SAL-ust
Samnites   SAM-nytss
San Martín, José de   san mar-TEEN, hoh-SAY day
sans-culottes   sahnh-koo-LUT *or* sanz-koo-LAHTSS
Sartre, Jean-Paul   SAR-truh, ZHAHNH-POHL
satrap   SAY-trap
satrapy   SAY-truh-pee
Satyricon   sat-TEER-i-kahn

Schaumburg-Lippe   SHOWM-boorkh-LEE-puh
Schleswig-Holstein   SHLESS-vik-HOHL-shtyn
Schlieffen, Alfred von   SHLEE-fun
Schliemann, Heinrich   SHLEE-mahn, HYN-rikh
Schmidt, Helmut   SHMIT, HEL-moot
Schönberg, Arnold   SHURN-bayrk, AR-nawlt
Schönborn   SHURN-bawn
Schönerer, Georg von   SHURN-uh-ruh, GAY-ork fun
Schröder, Gerhard   SHRUR-duh, GAYR-hahrt
Schuschnigg, Karl von   SHOOSH-nik
Schutzmannschaft   SHOOTS-mun-shahft
Scipio Aemilianus   SEE-pee-oh ee-mil-YAY-nuss
Scipio Africanus   SEE-pee-oh af-ree-KAY-nuss
scriptoria   skrip-TOR-ee-uh
Ségur   say-GOO-uh
Sejm   SAYM
Seleucid   suh-LOO-sid
Seleucus   suh-LOO-kuss
Seljuk   SEL-jook
Seneca   SEN-uh-kuh
Sephardic   suh-FAHR-dik
Septimius Severus   sep-TIM-ee-uss se-VEER-uss
serjents   sayr-ZHAHNH
Sforza, Ludovico   SFORT-sah, loo-doh-VEE-koh
Shalmaneser   shal-muh-NEE-zur
Shang   SHAHNG
Shari'a   shah-REE-uh
Sieveking, Amalie   SEE-vuh-king, uh-MAHL-yuh
Sieyès, Abbé   syay-YESS, ab-BAY
signoria   seen-YOR-ee-uh
sine manu   sy-nee-MAY-noo
Slovenia   sloh-VEE-nee-uh
Société Générale   soh-see-ay-TAY zhay-nay-RAHL
Socrates   SAHK-ruh-teez
Solon   SOH-lun
Solzhenitsyn, Alexander   sohl-zhuh-NEET-sin
Somme   SUM
Sophocles   SAHF-uh-kleez
Sorel, Georges   soh-RELL, ZHORZH
Spartacus   SPAR-tuh-kuss
Spartiates   spar-tee-AH-teez
Speer, Albert   SHPAYR
Speransky, Michael   spyuh-RAHN-skee
Spinoza, Benedict de   spi-NOH-zuh
squadristi   skwah-DREES-tee
Srebrenica   sreb-bruh-NEET-suh
stadholder   STAD-hohl-dur
Staël, Germaine de   STAHL, zhayr-MEN duh
Stakhanov, Alexei   stuh-KHAH-nuf, uh-LEK-say
Stasi   SHTAH-see
Stauffenberg, Claus von   SHTOW-fen-berk, KLOWSS fun
Stein, Heinrich von   SHTYN, HYN-rikh fun
Stilicho   STIL-i-koh
Stoicism   STOH-i-siz-um
Stolypin, Peter   stuh-LIP-yin
strategoi   strah-tay-GOH-ee
Stravinsky, Igor   struh-VIN-skee, EE-gor
Stresemann, Gustav   SHTRAY-zuh-mahn, GOOS-tahf
Strozzi, Alessandra   STRAWT-see
Struensee, John Frederick   SHTROO-un-zay
Sturmabteilung   SHTOORM-ap-ty-loonk
Sudetenland   soo-DAY-tun-land
Suger   soo-ZHAYR
Suharto   soo-HAHR-toh
Sukarno   soo-KAHR-noh
Suleiman   soo-lay-MAHN
Sulla   SULL-uh

Sumerians soo-MER-ee-unz *or* soo-MEER-ee-unz
Summa Theologica SOO-muh tay-oh-LOG-jee-kuh
Suppululiumas suh-PIL-oo-LEE-uh-muss
Suttner, Bertha von ZOOT-nuh
Symphonie Fantastique SANH-foh-nee fahn-tas-TEEK
Taaffe, Edward von TAH-fuh
Tacitus TASS-i-tuss
taille TY
Talleyrand, Prince tah-lay-RAHNH
Tanzania tan-zuh-NEE-uh
Tenochtitlán tay-nawch-teet-LAHN
Tertullian tur-TULL-yun
Thales THAY-leez
Theocritus thee-AHK-ruh-tuss
Theodora thee-uh-DOR-uh
Theodoric thee-AHD-uh-rik
Theodosius thee-uh-DOH-shuss
Theognis thee-AHG-nuss
Thermidor TAYR-mi-dor
Thermopylae thur-MAHP-uh-lee
Thiers, Adolphe TYAYR, a-DAWLF
Thucydides thoo-SID-uh-deez
Thutmosis thoot-MOH-suss
Tiberius ty-BEER-ee-uss
Tiglath-pileser TIG-lath-py-LEE-zur
Tirpitz, Admiral von TEER-pits
Tisza, István TISS-ah, ISHT-vun
Tito TEE-toh
Titus TY-tuss
Tlaxcala tuh-lah-SKAH-lah
Tojo, Hideki TOH-joh, hee-DEK-ee
Tokugawa Ieyasu toh-koo-GAH-wah ee-yeh-YAH-soo
Tolstoy, Leo TOHL-stoy
Topa Inca TOH-puh INK-uh
Torah TOR-uh
Tordesillas tor-day-SEE-yass
Trajan TRAY-jun
Trevithick, Richard TREV-uh-thik
triarii tri-AR-ee-ee
Tristan, Flora TRISS-tun
trivium TRIV-ee-um
Trotsky, Leon TRAHT-skee
Troyes TRWAH
Trudeau, Pierre troo-DOH, PYAYR
Trufaut, François troo-FOH, frahnh-SWAH
Tsara, Tristan TSAHR-rah, TRISS-tun
Tübingen TOO-bing-un
Tyche TY-kee
Uccello, Paolo oo-CHEL-oh, POW-loh
uhuru oo-HOO-roo
Ulbricht, Walter OOL-brikkt, VAHL-tuh
Umayyads oo-MY-adz
Unam Sanctam OO-nahm SAHNK-tahm
universitas yoo-nee-VAYR-see-tahss
Uzbekistan ooz-BEK-i-stan
Valens VAY-linz
Valentinian val-en-TIN-ee-un
Valéry, Paul vah-lay-REE, POHL
Valois val-WAH
Van de Velde, Theodore vahn duh VELL-duh, TAY-oh-dor
van Eyck, Jan vahn YK *or* van AYK, YAHN
van Gogh, Vincent van GOH *or* vahn GOK
Vasa, Gustavus VAH-suh, GUSS-tuh-vuss
Vega, Lope de VAY-guh, LOH-pay day
Vendée vahnh-DAY

Vendemiaire vahnh-duh-MYAYR
Venetia vuh-NEE-shuh
Ventose vahnh-TOHZ
Verdun vur-DUN
Vergerio, Pietro Paolo vur-JEER-ee-oh, PYAY-troh POW-loh
Versailles vayr-SY
Vesalius, Andreas vuh-SAY-lee-uss, ahn-DRAY-uss
Vespasian vess-PAY-zhun
Vespucci, Amerigo vess-POO-chee, ahm-ay-REE-goh
Vesuvius vuh-SOO-vee-uss
Vichy VISH-ee
Vierzehnheiligen feer-tsayn-HY-li-gen
Virchow, Rudolf FEER-khoh, ROO-dulf
Virgil VUR-jul
Visconti, Giangaleazzo vees-KOHN-tee, jahn-gah-lay-AH-tsoh
Visigoths VIZ-uh-gathz
Voilquin, Suzanne vwahl-KANH, soo-ZAHN
Volk FULK
Volkschulen FULK-shoo-lun
Voltaire vohl-TAYR
Wafd WAHFT
Wagner, Richard VAG-nur, RIKH-art
Walesa, Lech vah-WENT-sah, LEK
Wallachia wah-LAY-kee-uh
Wallenstein, Albrecht von VAHL-en-shtyn, AWL-brekht
Wannsee VAHN-zay
Watteau, Antoine wah-TOH, AHN-twahn
Weill, Kurt VYL
Weizsäcker, Richard von VYTS-zek-ur, RIKH-art
wergeld WURR-geld
Windischgrätz, Alfred VIN-dish-grets
Winkelmann, Maria VINK-ul-mahn
Witte, Sergei VIT-uh, syir-GYAY
Wittenberg VIT-ten-bayrk
Wojtyla, Karol voy-TEE-wah, KAH-rul
Wollstonecraft, Mary WULL-stun-kraft
Würzburg VOORTS-boork
Wyclif, John WIK-lif
Xavier, Francis ZAY-vee-ur
Xerxes ZURK-seez
Xhosa KHOH-suh
Ximenes khee-MAY-ness
Yahweh YAH-way
Yangtze YANG-tsee
Yeats, William Butler YAYTS
Yeltsin, Boris YELT-sun
yishuv YISH-uv
Zasulich, Vera tsah-SOO-likh
Zemsky Sobor ZEM-skee suh-BOR
zemstvos ZEMPST-vohz
Zeno ZEE-noh
Zenobia zuh-NOH-bee-uh
zeppelin ZEP-puh-lin
Zeus ZOOSS
Zhenotdel zhen-ut-DELL
Zhivkov, Todor ZHIV-kuff, toh-DOR
ziggurat ZIG-uh-rat
Zimmermann, Dominikus TSIM-ur-mahn, doh-MEE-nee-kuss
Zinzendorf, Nikolaus von TSIN-sin-dorf, NEE-koh-LOWSS fun
Zola, Émile ZOH-lah, ay-MEEL
zollverein TSOHL-fuh-ryn
Zoroaster ZOR-oh-ass-tur
Zwingli, Ulrich TSFING-lee, OOL-rikh

INDEX

Italicized page numbers show the locations of illustrations

Abstract Expressionism, 902–3
Abstract painting, 740, 831
Acerbo Law (Italy), 814
Acheson, Dean, 876
Adenauer, Konrad, 880, 895–96
Administration. *See* Government
Adrianople
    Treaty of, 638
Advertising, 956
Afghanistan, 757, 761, 925, 951–52
Africa
    after WWI, 811–12
    Belgian colonies, 755–56
    British colonies, 753, 755
    decolonization, 884–85, 886 (map)
    French colonies, 755, 756
    Germans colonies, 756
    imperialism, 753, 755–56, 759–60
    Italians in, 755
    movements to end foreign rule, 759–60
    in 1914, 757 (map)
    Portuguese colonies, 755
    WWI, 781–82
    WWII, 850 (map), 852. *See also specific countries*
African Americans
    civil rights movement, 898–99
    migration to North, 864
    slavery, 683–84
    during WWII, 864
African National Congress (ANC) (South Africa), 885
Afrikaners, 753, 754
Agricultural revolution, 605
Agriculture
    in Britain, 620
    in Eastern Europe, 893
    in nineteenth century, 709
    in Soviet Union, 823, 824–25
    in U.S., 615–16
Ahlwardt, Hermann, 746
Airforce, in WWII, 842, 848, *852*, 865–66
Airplanes, 700, 783, 829
Aix-la-Chapelle
    Congress of, 636
Alaska, 757
Albania/Albanians, 763–64, 892, 943–44, 945, 954
Aleshker, Lev, 708

Alexander I (Russia), 597, 640
Alexander I (Yugoslavia), 826
Alexander II (Russia), 669, 679–80, 681, 682, 727
Alexander III (Russia), 682, 727
Alexandra (Russia), 789
Alfonso XII (Spain), 724
Alfonso XIII (Spain), 827
Algeria, 649, 755, 885, 887, 894–95
Alliances
    of Cold War, 880
    of Nazi Germany, 842
    WWI, 769
    WWII, 851. *See also specific wars and pacts*
Allied Powers (WWI), 782, 794, 795, 850 (map)
Allies (WWII), 848, 850 (map), 852, 854, 866–68, 869–70, 871 (map)
All Quiet on the Western Front (Remarque), 778
Al-Qaeda, 951
Alsace-Lorraine, 677, 761, 769
Amalgamated Society of Engineers, 628
American Federation of Labor, 751
Americanization, 905–6
American Medical Association, 692
American Revolution, 572–75
Amiens, Peace of, 597
Amsterdam, 910
Amusement parks, 608, 698–99, 721
Anarchism, 708
Andersen, Hans Christian, 657
Andreotti, Giulio, 919
Andropov, Yuri, 915
Anesthesia, 691
Anglo-German Naval Pact, 841
Angola, 755, 885
Animé, 959
Annam, 759
Antiballistic Missile Treaty, 924
Anticlericalism, 736
Anti-Comintern Pact, 842
Anti-Corn Law League, 648
Anti-Semitism
    in Austrian Empire, 746
    in Germany, 736, 746, 822–23
    Herzl's analysis in *The Jewish State*, 747
    of Hitler/Nazi Germany, 817, 857
Antiwar protests, 914
Apartheid, 885

Appeasement, 842, 843
Apple Computer Company, 958–59
Apprenticeships, 624–25
"April Theses" (Lenin), 790
Aqaba, Gulf of, 888
Arab League, 886
Arabs
    and Israel, 886–87, 888. *See also* Islam
Arafat, Yasir, 888
Architecture
    Bauhaus School, 833
    Chicago School, 833
    functionalism, 833
    Gothic, 657, *658*
    Postmodernism, 929
Ardennes, 848
Argentina, 636
Aristocracy. *See* Nobility
Arkwright, Richard, 606, 607
Armed forces. *See* Military
Armenia, 795
Arms. *See* Weapons and warfare
Army
    Prussian, 673, 674
Art
    abstract painting, 740
    after WWII, 902–3
    contemporary, 960
    Cubism, 739–40
    Dadaism, 832
    in Digital Age, 959
    Expressionism, 832
    Impressionism, 737–39
    interwar years, 831–34
    Modernism, 737–40
    of Nazi Germany, 833–34
    Neo-Expressionism, 957
    Pop Art, 903
    Post-Impressionism, 739
    Postmodernism, 928–29
    Realism, 693–94
    Romanticism, 659–60
    of Soviet Union, 834
    Surrealism, 832, *834*
Art Brut, 902
Articles of Confederation, 573
Artisans and craftspeople
    in Britain, 623, 628
    in France, 576
    Luddites, 628
Aryan race, 736, 820, 822, 840, 855–56, 857

Asia
  decolonization of, 888–89
  imperialism in, 756–59
  in 1914, 758
  WWII, 845–47, 851 (map). *See also
    specific countries*
"Asia for Asians," 861
Assembly line, 701–2
Atatürk, 811
Athletics. *See* Sports
Atomic bomb, 836, 855, 864, 868,
    880, 925
Atoms, 732, 836
Atonal music, 834
Attlee, Clement, 896
Auerstadt, Battle of, 597
Auschwitz-Birkenau, 859, 860, *861*
Ausgleich, 678
Austerlitz, Battle of, 597
Australia, 756, 782
Austria
  after WWI, 796
  annexation by Nazi Germany,
    842–43
  Concert of Europe, 636
  emigration, 709 (table)
  Napoleonic Wars, 597
  population, 709 (table)
  war with France (1792), 584
Austria-Hungary
  and the Balkans, 762–65, 771
  breakup of, 796
  ethnic groups of, 680 (map), 726, 749
  formation of, 678
  under Francis Joseph I, 678, 726
  nationalism, 749
  Three Emperors' League, 761–62
  Triple Alliance, 762
  women's right to vote, 786
  before WWI, 769
  WWI, 769, 771, 775, 784
Austrian Empire
  after Congress of Vienna, 634 (map)
  Ausgleich, 678
  and Crimean War, 668
  diversity in, 640
  emancipation of serfs, 678
  imperial parliament, 678
  Italian territory, 639, 652, 670–71
  Italian War, 673, 678
  Ottoman Empire territories to, 668
  repression in, 640
  revolutions of 1848, 651–52
  Schleswig-Holstein, 675
  war with Prussia (1866), 672, 675–76
Austrian Peace Society, 743
Austro-Prussian War, 672, 675–76
Authoritarianism, 826–27
Autocracy
  of Austrian Empire, 678
  of Napoleon, 595
  of Russian tsars, 640, 727
Automobiles, 700, 900
Awakening, 662

Axis powers, 850 (map), 851, 854
Azerbaijan, 794, 937

Baby boom, 901
Bach, Alexander von, 678
Baden-Powell, Robert, 717
Baines, Edward, 606
Bakunin, Michael, 708
Balance of power
  after Crimean War, 668
  Congress of Vienna, 634–35
Baldwin, Stanley, 808
Balkan League, 763
Balkans
  Bosnian Crisis, 762–65
  crisis (1914), 771
  in 1878, 762 (map)
  in 1913, 764 (map)
  Ottoman Empire, 762. *See also specific
    countries*
Balkan Wars, 763
Ballet, 741
Ballin, Albert, 714
Banking, 615, 685
Barney, Matthew, 959
Barth, Karl, 905
Barton, Clara, 743
Baseball, 722
Basescu, Traian, 941
Basquiat, Jean-Michel, 957, *958*
Bastille, fall of, 571, 579–80
Batista, Fulgencio, 883
Battles. *See specific battles*
Baudrillard, Jean, 959–60
Bauhaus School, 833, *834*
Bay of Pigs invasion, 883
BBC (British Broadcasting Corporation),
    828, 906
Beatles, *906*
Beauty, 659
Beauvoir, Simone de, 902, 904
Bebel, August, 705, 706
Beckett, Samuel, 903
Beer Hall Putsch, 817
Beethoven, Ludwig van, 661
Belgioioso, Christina, 652
Belgium
  Africa, 755–56
  banking, 615
  emigration, 709 (table)
  independence, 647
  industrialization, 615
  population, 709 (table)
  WWI, 772–73, 775
  WWII, 848
Bell, Alexander Graham, 699
Belorussians, 861
Bergman, Ingmar, 906
Bergson, Henri, 733
Berlin
  Olympics (1936), 829
  police force, 655
  population, 710
  Soviet blockade and air lift, 878–80

Berlin Wall, 882–83, 941, *942*
Berlioz, Hector, 661
Berlusconi, Silvio, 947
Bernhardi, Friedrich von, 736
Bernstein, Eduard, 706, 707
Bessarabia, 668, 669
Bethmann-Hollweg, Theobald von, 771
Beveridge, William, 901
Bible
  nineteenth century criticism, 736
Bill of Rights (U.S.), 574, 642
Birth control, 715, 831, 901, 910, 953
Birth of a Nation, 828
Birthrates
  current trends, 953
  in nineteenth century, 618, 715
Bismarck, Otto von, 666, 673–77, 726, *727,*
    756, 761–62
The Black Man's Burden (Morel),
    754–55
Blacks. *See* Africa; African Americans;
    Slavery
Blackwell, Elizabeth, 692
Blair, Tony, 947, 960
Blanc, Louis, 644, 648
Blitzkrieg, 842, 847
Blood flag ritual, *818*
Bloody Sunday, 750, 751
Bloomsbury Circle, 835
Blues music, 906
Blum, Léon, 810
Bobbies, 655, 656
Bodichon, Barbara, 720
Boers, 753, 755
Boer War, 755
Bohemia
  German occupation, 843
  revolution of 1848, 651. *See also*
    Czechoslovakia
Bolívar, Simón, 636
Bolsheviks, 790–94, 824, 825
Booth, William, 737
Borodino, Battle at, 600
Bosnia-Herzegovina
  NATO peacekeepers in, 945
  separatist movement, 942
  war in, 943, *944*
Bosnian Crisis, 762–65
Boulanger, Georges, 724
Bourban dynasty, 639. *See also
    specific rulers*
Bourgeoisie, 576–77, 687
Bowling Congress, 721
Boxer Rebellion, 760
Boy Scouts, 717, *718*
Brandt, Willy, 917
Brest-Litovsk, Treaty of, 793
Brezhnev, Leonid, 892, 914–15
Brezhnev Doctrine, 914, 915
Briand, Aristide, 806
Bright, John, 648
Brinkmanship, 769
Britain. *See* England (Great Britain)
Britain, Battle of, 848

British Broadcasting Corporation (BBC), 828, 906
British East India Company, 757
Brothers Karmazov (Dostoevsky), 737
Brown, Gordon, 947
Brüning, Heinrich, 819
Bulganin, Nikolai, 882
Bulgaria
    authoritarian state after WWI, 826
    Balkan League, 763
    Balkan Wars, 763
    EU membership, 948
    illiteracy rates, 721
    population, 709 (table)
    Treaty of San Stefano, 762
    WWI, 775, 781
Bulge, Battle of, 854
Bureaucracy
    in Austria-Hungary, 726
    in France, 596
    in Russia/Soviet Union, 641, 914
    in U.S., 864. *See also* Government
Burke, Edmund, 635
Burma, 759, 888
Burschenschaften, 640, 641
Bush, George H. W., 949, 950
Bush, George W., 949, 952
Bushido, 865
Butler, Josephine, 705
Byrnes, James, 870
Byron, Lord, 658

Calendars, 590–91
Calonne, Charles de, 577
Cambodia, 759, 888
Camus, Albert, 903–4
Canada, 684–85, 751–52, 899, 920, 949
Canals, 605
Cape Town, 753
Capital, 605
Capitalism, 737, 753, 912
Carbonari, 639
Carlyle, Thomas, 657
Carnegie Steel Company, 750
Carol II (Romania), 827
Cars, 700, 900
Cartel of the Left (France), 809–10
Cartels, 701
Carter, Jimmy, 920, 925
Cartwright, Edmund, 607
Castro, Fidel, 883
Catholic Church
    and Austrian Empire, 678
    and fascist Italy, 816
    and French Revolution, 583
    Germany's *Kulturkampf,* 726
    Lateran Accords, 816
    and Napoleon, 595
    Romantic Era revival, 662
    Vatican II, 905
Cavour, Camillo di, 670–72
Ceausescu, Nicolae , 917, 940
Cell phones, 958

Central America, 636. *See also specific countries*
Central planning, 914
Central Powers, 721, 781, 783
Central Treaty Organization (CENTO), 882
Ceylon, 888
Cézanne, Paul, 739, *740*
Chadwick, Edwin, 621–22
Chamberlain, Houston Stewart, 736
Chamberlain, Neville, 842, 843, 845, 848
Champagne offensive, *777*
The Charge of the Light Brigade (film), 671
Charities, 737
Charles X (France), 639, 646
Charles Albert (Piedmont), 652, 670
Charles Martel Club, 951
Chartism, 628, 629
Chateaubriand, François-René de, 662
Chechnya, 939
Cheka, 794
Chemical industry, 699
Chernobyl disaster, 926
Chiang Kai-shek, 846, 889
Chicago School, of architecture, 833
Childe Harold's Pilgrimage (Byron), 658
Child labor, 624–25, 626, 627, 629–30
Children
    in nineteenth century, 715, 717. *See also* Education
Chile, 636
China
    after WWII, 868
    Boxer Rebellion, 760
    British in, 757
    and Cold War, 923–24
    communist takeover, 889–90
    Great Leap Forward, 890
    Great Proletarian Cultural Revolution, 923
    Japan's invasion of, 846
    Korean War, 882
    open door policy, 757–58
    U.S. relations with, 923–24
    war with Japan (1894–1895), 758, 760
Chirac, Jacques, 947
Cholera, 622, 669
Chrétien, Jean, 949
Christian Democrats, 894
Christian Democrats (CDU) (Germany), 895, 917, 942, 945
Christian Democrats (Italy), 897, 919
Christianity/Christians
    Nietzsche on, 733
    nineteenth century threats, 736–37
    Romantic revival, 662. *See also specific groups*
Christian Socialists (Austria), 746
Christian Social Workers (Germany), 746
Church and state, relationship between, 642
Churches and cathedrals
    Nazi control, 822_. *See also specific religions*

Churchill, Winston, 845, 848, 869, 870, 871, 872, 884
Cities and towns
    in nineteenth century, 619–22, 710–12
Citizenship
    of Jews, 745, 822
    of women, 743
Civil Code (Napoleon), 595, 639
Civil Constitution of the Clergy, 583
Civil disobedience, 811
Civilian Conservation Corps, 810
Civil liberties, 642
Civil Rights Act (1964) (U.S.), 898
Civil rights movement (U.S.), 898–99
Civil wars
    Greece, 876
    Russia, 793–95
    Spain, 827
    U.S., 683–84
Class conflict, 786–87. *See also* Social structure
Classical economics, 642
Clemenceau, Georges, 784, 797, 798
Clergy, 575, 583
Clinton, Bill, 943, 949, 951
Coal mines, 624, 627, 808–9
Coal Mines Act (1842) (Britain), 630
Cobden, Richard, 648
COBOL, 925
Cochin China, French occupation of, 759
Cockerill, John, 613
Codreanu, Corneliu, 827
Cohan, George M., 781
Cold War
    Berlin Wall, 841, *842,* 882–83
    China, 923–24
    Churchill's "iron curtain" speech, 871, 872
    containment policy, 878
    Cuban Missile Crisis, 883, 884
    and decolonization, 890
    détente, 914, 923, 924–25
    domino theory, 922
    and Eastern Europe, 876
    emergence of, 869, 870–72, 877
    end of, 949–51
    escalation (1950s), 882
    German occupation zones, 878–80
    grain embargo, 925
    Korean War, 880–82
    Marshall Plan, 877–78
    military alliances, 880
    Olympic Games, 925, 931
    Truman Doctrine, 876, 878
    Vietnam, 882, 920, 922–23
Collectivization, 824, 825
Cologne, 866
Colonies and colonization
    Africa, 753–56, 759–60
    after WWI, 810–12
    Asia, 756–59, 760
    British, 572–73, 606, 618
    Spanish, 636

COMECON (Council for Mutual Economic Assistance), 880
Commerce. *See* Trade
Committee of Public Safety, 585–88, 591–92
Common Market, 897
Commonwealth of Independent States, 938
Communism
  domino theory, 922
  Greek civil war, 876
  Marxism, 686–87, 688
  Red Scare in U.S., 898
  Truman Doctrine, 876
  in Western Europe after WWII, 893. *See also* Soviet Union
The Communist Manifesto (Marx and Engels), 686–87, 688
Communist Party (China), 889–90, 923
Communist Party (Germany), 796, 878
Communist Party (Indonesia), 890
Communist Party (Italy), 919, 947
Communist Party (Russia), 792, 793, 794–95, 915, 936
Competition, 644
Compromise of 1867, 678
Compulsory education, 719
Computers, 925–26, 958
Comte, Auguste, 692–93
Concentration camps, 859–60
Concert of Europe, 636
The Conditions of the Working Class in England (Engels), 686
Coney Island, 698–99
Confederate States of America, 683–84
Congo, 756, 885
Congress of Berlin, 762
Congress of People's Deputies, 936, 938
Congress of Vienna, 632, 633–35
Conscription, 770, 783
Conservatism
  after Napoleonic Wars, 635–41
  Burke's contributions, 635
  de Maistre's contributions, 635
Conservative Party (Britain), 683, 808–9, 946
Conservative Party (Canada), 899
Constantine (Russia), 641
Constituent Assembly (Russia), 791–92
Constitution(s)
  Austria-Hungary, 726
  France, 578, 580, 583, 584, 592, 594, 648, 649, 666, 724, 895
  Germany, 651, 726
  Prussia, 673
  Russia, 938
  Spain, 639, 724
  U.S., 574, 653, 913
Consumer goods, 700
Consumer society, 900, 905
Consumption, 626, 962
Contagious Diseases Acts (Great Britain), 705
Containment policy, 878
Continental System, 598

Contraception, 715, 831, 901, 910, 953
Convention People's Party (Gold Coast), 885
Cook, James, 756
Cook, Thomas, 721
Cooperatives, 644–45
Coral Sea, Battle of, 853
Corn Law (1815) (Britain), 639, 648
Cort, Henry, 608
Cotton industry, 607, 615, 624–25, 683
Cotton-spinning mills, 605
Council for Mutual Economic Assistance (COMECON), 880
Courbet, Gustave, 693
Crafts people. *See* Artisans and craftspeople
Crédit Mobilier, 615
Cremaster (Barney), 959
Crimea, 852
Crime and punishment, 655–57
Crime and Punishment (Dostoevsky), 737
Crimean War, 668–69, 671
Croatia/Croats, 942, 943
Crompton, Samuel, 607
Crops. *See* Agriculture
The Crossing (Viola), 959
Crystal Palace, 611, *612*
Cuba, 724
Cuban Missile Crisis, 883, 884
Cubism, 739–40
Culture
  popular, 905–6, 930–32. *See also* Art; Music
Curie, Marie, 732, *733*
Curie, Pierre, 732
Cut with the Kitchen Knife (Höch), 833
Cyprus, 948
Czechoslovakia
  break up of, 940
  collapse of communism, 940
  communist takeover, 892
  displacement of Germans after WWII, 868
  establishment of, 796
  German occupation, 843–44
  invasion by Soviet bloc nations (1968), 915
  Little Entente, 805
  political democracy under Masaryk, 827
  Prague Spring, 916
Czech people, 651–52
Czech Republic, 940, 948

Dada Dance (Höch), 832
Dadaism, 832
Daily Mail, 721
Daimler, Gottlieb, 700
Dalí, Salvador, 832, *834*
Dalmatia, 813
Dance halls, 721, 828
Dancing, 828
Danish War, 675
Danton, Georges, 584, 585
Danzig, 844

Darwin, Charles, 689, 690, 735, 736
Das Kapital (Marx and Engels), 687
Davison, Emily, 743
Dawes Plan, 805–6
A Day in the Life of Ivan Denisovich (Solzhenitsyn), 891
Dayton agreement, 943
Death camps, 859–60
The Death of Sardanapalus (Delacroix), 660, *661*
Death rates
  eighteenth century, 618
  of infants, 709, 719, 915
  nineteenth century, 708
Debelleyme, Louis-Maurice, 655
Debussy, Claude, 740–41
Decembrist Revolt, 641
De-Christianization, 590–91
Declaration of Independence, 574
Declaration of Pillnitz, 584
Declaration of the Rights of Man and the Citizen (France), 580, 581
Declaration of the Rights of Woman and the Female Citizen (France), 580, 581–82
Decolonization, 883–90
Deconstruction, 927
Defense of the Realm Act (Great Britain), 785
Defoe, Daniel, 606–7
Delacroix, Eugène, 660, *661*
Demian (Hesse), 835
Democracy
  Chartism, 628
  in nineteenth century (late), 722–25, 742
  retreat from after WWI, 812–13
  in U.S., 573–74
Democratic Party (U.S.), 683, 949
Les Demoiselles d'Avignon (Picasso), 740, *742*
Denazification, 878
Denikin, Anton, 794
Denmark
  emigration, 709 (table)
  industrial cooperatives after WWI, 810
  population, 709 (table)
  war with Prussia, 675
  WWII, 848
Department stores, 701
Departure from Egypt (Kiefer), 957
Depressions
  1842, 626
  1873–1895, 702
  Great, 803–4, 806–7, 809, 810
De Rerum Novarum (Leo XIII), 737
Derrida, Jacques, 927
The Descent of Man (Darwin), 689, 690
Despotism, 596–97
Détente, 914, 923, 924–25
Deterrence, mutual, 880
Developed nations, 964
Developing nations, 964
Diaghilev, Sergei, 741
Dickens, Charles, *693*, 694
Dictatorships, 813

Diefenbaker, John, 899
Diet/food
    in nineteenth century Britain, 621
Dietrich, Marlene, 828
Digital Age, 958–60
Diplomacy. See Foreign policy
"Diplomatic revolution" (Nazi Germany),
    840–42
Directory (France), 592–93
Diseases/illnesses
    cholera, 622
    in nineteenth century, 622
    prevention of, 708–9
    smallpox, 618, 708. See also Medicine
Disraeli, Benjamin, 683
Divorce
    increase in (1960s), 910
    legalization of, 743
    Napoleonic Code, 595
    in Soviet Union, 826
Dix, Otto, 832
A Doll's House (Ibsen), 716–17
Domesticity, 715
Domestic servants, 714
Domino theory, 922
Dopolavoro, 829
Dostoevsky, Fyodor, 737
Dr. Strangelove (film), 921–22
Draft (military), 770, 783
Drama
    "Theater of the Absurd," 903
Dresden, WWII bombing, 866, 867
Dreyfus affair, 748
Drugs, illegal, 910
The Drunken Boat (Rimbaud), 738
Dual Monarch. See Austria-Hungary
Dubcek, Alexander, 916
Du Bois, W. E. B., 797–97, 812
Dubuffet, Jean, 902, 903
Duma (Russia), 750
Dunkirk, miracle of, 848
Dutch. See Netherlands
Dutch East Indies, 846, 850, 861, 862, 888
The Duties of Man (Mazzini), 652
Dylan, Bob, 912

Eakins, Thomas, 692
Eastern Europe
    authoritarianism after WWI, 826–27
    Cold War disagreement over, 876
    collapse of communism, 939–42
    in EU, 948
    Soviet control, 870, 892–93. See also
        specific countries
Easter Rebellion, 785
East Germany, 880, 916, 917, 941–42, 945
East India Company, 757
Eastman, George, 739
Eber, Nandor, 674
Ebert, Friedrich, 795, 796
EC (European Community), 919, 947
Economic imperialism, 753
Economics
    Keynesian, 809

liberalism, 642
supply-side, 920
Economy
    of France, 919, 947
    global, 703–4, 961–62
    of Great Britain, 896–97, 918
    industrial, 702
    of Italy, 897, 919
    in nineteenth century, 702
    of Russia (1990s), 939
    of Soviet Union, 914–15
    of U.S., 920
    of West Germany, 896
Edison, Thomas, 699
Education
    in England, 630, 683
    in nineteenth century, 717, 719–21
    in Soviet Union, 826
    of women, 720. See also Schools
Education Act (1870) (Britain), 683
EEC (European Economic Community),
    897, 919
Ego, 734
Egypt (modern)
    British in, 755, 885
    decolonization, 885
    under Nasser, 886–88
    Six-Day War, 888
    Suez Canal, 686, 755
Einsatzgruppen, 859
Einstein, Albert, 732–33
Einstein on the Beach (Glass), 930
Eisenhower, Dwight D., 854, 882, 887, 898
Ekaterinburg, Russia, 794
El Alamein, Battle of, 852
Elba, 600
Elections. See Voting and voting rights
Electricity, 699
Elementary education, 719–20
e-mail, 958
Emancipation Proclamation, 681, 684
The Emigrants (Staniland), 711
Emigration
    from Ireland, 619
    in nineteenth century, 709–10
Employment. See Labor/labor force
Enabling Act (Germany), 820
Engels, Friedrich, 686–87, 688
Engines
    internal combustion, 699
    steam, 607–8, 615
England (Great Britain)
    after WWI, 807–9
    after WWII, 896–97
    agriculture, 620
    and American Revolutionary War,
        572–73
    appeasement policy, 842, 843
    Australia, 756
    Blair era, 947
    Canada, 684–85
    China, 757
    cities, 619–20
    Concert of Europe, 636

Congress of Vienna, 633–35
conservatism, 638–39
Corn Law (1815), 639, 648
Crimean War, 668–69
decolonization, 884, 885
depressions, 702
education, 719
Education Act (1870), 683
emigration, 709 (table)
Falklands War, 918–19
Gladstone's second ministry, 723
Great Depression, 809
Great Exhibition (1851), 611–13
housing, 712
immigrants, 954
imperialism, 752, 753, 755, 756, 757
India, 618, 757, 760–61, 811, 888
Industrial Revolution, 605–12
in Iraq, 799
and Ireland, 723, 748, 785
Labour Party, 747–48, 808, 809
Liberal Party, 683, 747–48
literature, 657, 693
medicine, 692
and Napoleon, 598
New Zealand, 756
Northern Ireland, 917
in Palestine, 799
Paris Peace Conference, 798
Parliament, 648
Peterloo Massacre, 639
police force, 655, 656
Poor Law Act (1834), 625, 648
population, 709 (table)
prostitution, 705
public health, 711
reforms, 647–48, 682–83, 723, 747–48
social structure, 622–23
South Africa, 753, 755
sports, 721–22
steel production, 699
Suez Canal, 755, 886–87
Thatcher era, 917–19, 945–46
trade unions, 627–28, 707–8, 747
Triple Entente, 762
Victorian Age, 682–83
welfare state, 896, 901
women's rights, 743, 744, 745
WWI, 773, 781–82, 783, 784, 785, 786
WWII, 845, 848–49, 852, 862–63,
    865–66, 869–70. See also specific rulers
Entertainment and leisure
    amusement parks, 608, 698–99, 721
    interwar period, 829
    of nineteenth century, 721–22
    travel, 721, 829, 900
Entrepreneurs, 605, 606, 622–23
Environmentalism, 926–27, 953–54
Environmental issues, 962, 963–64
Equality
    in France, 580, 591
    of women, 913, 953
Erhard, Ludwig, 896
Eroica (Beethoven), 661

Essay on the Principles of Population (Malthus), 642
Estates-General (France), 577, 578
Estonia, 948
Ethiopia, 755, 756, 761, 842
Ethnic cleansing, 943
EURATOM (European Atomic Energy Community), 897
Eurocommunism, 919
Europa, Europa (film), 858
Europe
    after WWII, 871 (map)
    emigration, 709 (table)
    in nineteenth century, 634 (map), 679 (map)
    in 1914, 770 (map)
    in 1919, 800 (map)
    in 1936–1939, 844 (map)
    in 1980s, 937 (map)
    population, 709 (table), 710 (map)
    in 2007, 948 (map). *See also specific countries*
European Atomic Energy Community (EURATOM), 897
European Coal and Steel Community (ECSC), 897
European Community (EC), 919, 947
European Economic Community (EEC), 897, 919
European Recovery Program (Marshall Plan), 877–78, 894, 897
European Union (EU), 941, 947–48
European Union, Treaty on, 947
Evangelical Christians, 737
Evening News, 721
Evolution, 689, 690, 736, 737
Evolutionary socialism, 706
Evolutionary Socialism (Bernstein), 706, 707
Existentialism, 902, 903–4, 927
Expressionism, 832
Extermination camps, 859–60
Eylau, Battle of, 597

Fabian Socialists (Great Britain), 747
Facing Mount Kenya (Kenyatta), 812
Factories
    electrification of, 699
    during Industrial Revolution, 609–11
    during nineteenth century, 701–2
    during WWI, 787
Factory Act (1833) (Britain), 625, 629–30
"Factory Rules" (Foundry and Engineering Works of the Royal Overseas Trading Company, Berlin), 611
Fairy tales, 657
Falklands War, 918–19
"The Fall of the House of Usher" (Poe), 658
Family allowances, 901
Family Herald, 721
Family structure
    in nineteenth century, 715, 717–19. *See also* Children; Marriage

Famine
    in Germany during WWI, 784
    in Ireland, 619
    in Russia, 750, 823, 825
    in Sudan, 964
Fanon, Frantz, 887
Faraday, Michael, 688
Farming. *See* Agriculture
Farouk (Egypt), 885
Fascio di Combattimento, 813–14
Fascism, 807, 813–16, 827. *See also* Nazi Germany
Fawcett, Millicent, 743
Federal Deposit Insurance Corporation (FDIC), 810
Federal Emergency Relief Administration, 810
Federalists, 653
Federal Republic of Germany, 880, 895–96, 900, 901, 912, 917
Federal Reserve System, 751
Fellini, Federico, 906
Female Association for the Care of the Poor and Sick, 743
The Feminine Mystique (Friedan), 913
Feminism, 743, 913, 953
Ferdinand I (Austria), 651, 652
Ferdinand I (Italy), 636
Ferdinand VII (Spain), 636, 639
Fertilizer, 702, 926
Festivals, 590
Feudalism, 576, 580
Fichte, Johann Gottlieb, 599
Fielden, Joshua, 622
Fifth Republic (France), 894
Filipovic, Zlata, 943
Films, 828–29, 905–6, 959. *See also specific films*
Final Solution, 859–60
Finland, 793
The Firebird (Stravinsky), 741
First Balkan War, 763
First Estate, 575, 578
First Vietnam War, 882
Fischer, Joschka, 926
Five Lectures on Psychoanalysis (Freud), 735
Flappers, 828
Flaubert, Gustave, 693
Flying shuttle, 607
Foch, Ferdinand, 795
Food. *See* Diet/food
Football (soccer), 721, 722, *723,* 829, 931
Football Association, 721
Forced labor camps, 891
Ford, Gerald, 920
Ford, Henry, 700
Foreign policy
    appeasement, 842
    balance of power, 634–35
    Brezhnev Doctrine, 914, 915
    brinkmanship, 769
    containment policy, 878

    détente, 914, 923, 924–25
    France, 668
    massive retaliation, 882
    Monroe Doctrine, 637
    mutual deterrence, 880
    rapprochement, 882
    Truman Doctrine, 876, 878
Foucault, Michel, 928
The Foundations of the Nineteenth Century (Chamberlain), 736
Fourier, Charles, 644
"Fourteen Points" (Wilson), 796
Fourth Republic (France), 894–95
France
    African colonies, 755, 756
    after WWI, 804–5, 806, 809–10
    after WWII, 894–95
    and American Revolutionary War, 572–73, 575
    anticlericalism, 736
    banking, 615
    Cartel of the Left, 809–10
    and Catholic Church, 595, 639
    Chirac era, 947
    Concert of Europe, 636
    Congress of Vienna, 634–35
    Constitution of 1795, 592
    Crimean War, 668–69
    decolonization, 885
    depressions, 702
    Directory, 592–93
    Dreyfus affair, 748
    education, 719, 720
    in eighteenth century, 587 (map)
    emigration, 709 (table)
    Estates-General, 577, 578
    Fifth Republic, 894
    Fourth Republic, 894–95
    Great Depression, *807,* 810
    housing, 712
    immigrants, 964
    Indochina, 759, 882
    and industrialization, 613–14, 615, 647, 748
    in Italian War of Independence, 670–71
    Jews in, 745
    in Mexico, 668
    in Middle East, 799
    military, 586, 770
    military alliance with Russia, 762
    Mitterand era, 919, 947
    monarchy, 577, 583, 646–47
    under Napoleon Bonaparte, 594–600
    under Napoleon III, 649, 666–69, 670, 675, 676, 677
    National Bloc, 809
    National Front, 955
    Paris Peace Conference, 798
    parlements (France), 577
    police force, 655
    Popular Front, 810
    population, 709 (table)
    poverty in, 577

prisons, 657
Restoration, 639
revolution of 1830 (July revolution), 646, *647*
revolution of 1848, 648–49
Second Republic, 649
slavery, 591
socialism, 706
student revolt, 909–10, 912
Suez Canal crisis, 886–87
Third Republic, 723–24, 748–49
trade unions, 708
Triple Entente, 762
university attendance, 910
war with Austria (1792), 584
war with Prussia (1870), 672, 676–78
welfare state, 901
women's movement, 902, 953
before WWI, 769
WWI, 772, 775, 782, 784, 785, 786, 804
WWII, 845, 848, 857. *See also* French Revolution; *specific rulers*
Francis I (Austria), 632
Francis Ferdinand (Austria), 769, *771*
Francis Joseph I (Austria), 652, 678, 726, 749
Franco, Francisco, 827
Franco-Prussian War, 672, 676–78
Frankenstein (Shelley), 658
Frankfurt Assembly, 651, 673
Frederick William II (Prussia), 583–84
Frederick William III (Prussia), 640
Frederick William IV (Prussia), 649, 651, 673
Free Democrats (FDP) (Germany), 895, 917, 945
Freedom of press, 597
Free trade, 615, 700, 962
French Revolution
abolishment of feudalism, 580
background to, 575–77
and Catholic Church, 583
Civil Constitution of the Clergy, 583
Committee of Public Safety, 585–88, 591–92
de-Christianization, 590–91
Declaration of Pillnitz, 584
Declaration of the Rights of Man and the Citizen, 580, 581
events of, 577–93
execution of Louis XVI, 584–85
expansion during, 587
fall of Bastille, 571, 579–80
Great Fear, 580
impact of, 571–72
Legislative Assembly, 583, 584
National Assembly, 578–79, 580, 583
National Convention, 584–85, 590, 591, 592
peasant rebellions, 580
Reign of Terror, 586–88, 591
Thermidorean Reaction, 592
women's role, 580, 582, 588–90
Freud, Sigmund, 734–35, 835

Friedan, Betty, 913
Friedland, Battle of, 597
Friedrich, Caspar David, 659, *660*
Frith, William P., 718
Führerprinzip, 819
Functionalism, 833
Fundamentalism, 955

Gagern, Heinrich von, 641
Galicia, 775
Gallipoli, Battle of, 781
Games
children's, 715, *718. See also* Sports
Gamond, Zoé Gatti de, 645
Gandhi, Mohandas (Mahatma), 811, *812,* 888
García Márquez, Gabriel, 929
Garibaldi, Giuseppe, 672, *673,* 674
Garvey, Marcus, 812
Gasperi, Alcide de, 897
Gates, Bill, 958
GATT (General Agreement on Tariffs and Trade), 962
Gaulle, Charles de, 857, 885, 894–95, 922
Gays and lesbians, 910, 928
Gender roles
during Great Depression, 807
in Italy under fascism, 815
in nineteenth century, 704, 715–19
and welfare programs, 901
and WWI, 785–86, 812–13
General Agreement on Tariffs and Trade (GATT), 962
General Theory of Employment, Interest and Money (Keynes), 809
Geneva Conference (1954), 882
Genius of Christianity (Chateaubriand), 662
Genocide, 795
Gentile, Giovanni, 816
George, David Lloyd, 748, 784, 787, 796, 798, 807
Germaine de Staël, 597
German Democratic Republic, 880, 916, 917, 941–42, 945
Germanic Confederation, 640, 673, 675
Germany
African colonies, 756, 811
after WWI, 795–96, 798–99, 800, 805, 806
banking, 615
Burschenschaften, 640, 641
chemical industry, 699
Dawes Plan, 805–6
depressions, 702
education, 719, 720
emigration, 709 (table)
factories, 701
Great Depression, 806–7, 808
Green Party, 926, 954
immigrants, 954–55
and industrialization, 613–14, 615, 702, 749
military, 770
nationalism in, 599, 644, 736, 749

neo-Nazi groups, 956
in nineteenth century, 725–26, 748–49
November Revolution, 795–96
occupation zones, 870, 878
police force, 655
population, 709 (table)
Reinsurance Treaty with Russia, 762
reunification of, 941–42, 945
revolution of 1848, 649, 650–51
social class, 714
Social Democratic Party, 705–6, 726, 749, 795–96, 895, 917, 945
steel production, 699
Three Emperors' League, 761–62
trade unions, 708
Treaty of Versailles, 798–99, 805, 840–41, 842
Triple Alliance, 762
unification of, 673–78
Weimar Republic, 816–17
women's right to vote, 786
before WWI, 749, 769
WWI, 771–73, 775, 782, 783–84, 795
WWII reparations, 870, 878. *See also* Nazi Germany
Germs, 690
Gesamtkunstwerk, 695
Gestapo, 857
Ghana, 885
Ghettos, 745
Giolitti, Giovanni, 748, 814
Girondins, 584–85
Gladstone, William, 683, 723, *724*
Glasgow, 867
Glasnost, 936, 937
Glass, Philip, 930
The Gleaners (Millet), 694, *695*
Gleichschaltung, 820
Global economy, 961–62
Globalization, 932, 960–65
Global warming, 962, 963–64
Goebbels, Joseph, 829
Goethe, Johann Wolfgang von, 657
Gold Coast, 885
Golden, Arthur, 960
Gömbös, Julius, 827
Gomulka, Wladyslaw, 893
Goodbye to All That (Graves), 774
Gorbachev, Mikhail, 915, 935, 936–38, 949–50
Gore, Al, 949
Göring, Hermann, 819–20
Gothic architecture, 657, *659*
Gothic literature, 658
Gottwald, Klement, 892
Government
France, 583, 592, 596, 649
and industrialization, 606, 614–15
U.S., 573–74. *See also* Bureaucracy
Goya, Francisco, 599
Grand Alliance, 851–52
Grand Empire (France), 597, 598 (map)

Grandmaster Flash and the Furious
Five, 931
Grand National Consolidated
Trades Union, 627
Grant, Ulysses S., 684
Grass, Günter, 903
Graves, Robert, 774
Great Britain. *See* England (Great Britain)
Great Depression, 803–4, 806–7, 809, 810
Great East Asia Co-Prosperity Sphere,
850, 861
Great Exhibition (1851), 611–13
Great Fear, 580
Great Leap Forward, 890
Great Proletarian Cultural Revolution, 923
Great Society, 898
Great War. *See* World War I
Greece (modern)
Balkan League, 763
civil war, 876
independence of, 638, 668
under Metaxas, 827
population, 709 (table)
revolt against Ottoman Empire, 638
WWII, 849, 857
Greenhouse effect, 962
Green movements, 926–27, 953–54
Grieg, Edvard, 740
Grimm brothers, 657
Gropius, Walter, 833, *834*
The Gross Clinic (Eakins), *692*
Grossdeutsch, 651
Gross national product (GNP)
France, 895
U.S., 864
Grosz, George, 832
Groza, Petra, 870
Grunge music, 957–58
Guam, 759
Guest workers, 954–55
Guizot, François, 647
Gulf War (1991), 950, 953
Gypsies, 861

Haider, Jorg, 955
Hamburg, 866
Hamilton, Alexander, 653
Hanover, 675
Hardenberg, Karl von, 599, 640
Hargreaves, James, 607
Harkort, Fritz, 613
Harper, Stephen, 949
Harpers Ferry arsenal, 616
Harris, Arthur, 866
Harry Potter, 959
Hasák, Gustav, 916
Hauser, Heinrich, 808
Haushofer, Karl, 840
Haussmann, Baron, 667
Havel, Vaclav, 916, 940, 941
Hawaiian Islands, 759
Hay, John, 757–58
Haydn, Franz Joseph, 661
Health care. *See* Medicine

Hegel, Georg Wilhelm Friedrich, 686
Heisenberg, Werner, 836
Helena (Saint), 600
Helsinki Agreements, 924
Herzegovina, under Austrian control, 762.
See also Bosnia-Herzegovina
Herzen, Alexander, 682
Herzl, Theodor, 746, 747
Hesse, Hermann, 835
Hesse-Cassel, 675
Heydrich, Reinhard, 859
Hill, Octavia, 711, 713
Himmler, Heinrich, 822, 856, 858, 859
Hindenburg, Paul von, 775, 784, 817,
819, 820
Hindus, 888
Hip-hop, 930, 931, 958
Hippies, 911
Hiroshima, 855, 866, *867*, 868
History of Sexuality (Foucault), 928
*History of the Cotton Manufacture in Great
Britain* (Baines), 606
Hitler, Adolf
anti-Semitism, 817, 857
assassination attempt, 857
background of, 817
as chancellor, 819
Mein Kampf, 817–18, 840
New Order, 855, 856
speech at the Nuremberg party rally, 821
suicide of, 855
WWII influence, 840
WWI service, 817. *See also* Nazi
Germany
Hitler Youth, 822, 858
Höch, Hannah, 832, *833*
Ho Chi Minh, 882, 888, 890, 920
Hohenstaufen dynasty, 676–77
Holidays, 590, 715
Hollywood, 905–6
Holocaust, 857–61, 862, 896
Homeland Security Department (U.S.), 949
Homes of the London Poor (Hill), 713
Homosexuality, 910, 928
Honecker, Erich, 916
Hong Kong, 757
Hopkins, Harry, 869
Hopper, Grace, 925
Horthy, Miklós, 827
Hospitals, 690–91
Höss, Rudolf, 862
House of Commons (England), 639,
648, 723
House of Lords (England), 748
Housing
in nineteenth century, 620, 711–12
Howard, Ebenezer, 712
Huber, V. A., 711
Human rights, 925
Hungary
after WWI, 796
authoritarian state under Horthy, 827
collapse of communism, 940
communist under Kádár, 893, 916

emigration, 709 (table)
EU membership, 948
Magyars in, 727, 749
minority groups in, 653
nationalism, 644, 749
population, 709 (table)
revolt (1956), 893, 894
revolution of 1848, 651, 652. *See also*
Austria-Hungary
Hunt, Harriet, 692
Husák, Gustav, 940
Hygiene, 620, 691, 709

Ibsen, Henrik, 716–17, 740
Id, ego, superego, 734
Ideal Marriage (van de Velde), 831
Ideology, 635
Illegal drugs, 910
Illiteracy, 721
Illness. *See* Diseases/illnesses
IMF (International Monetary Fund), 961
Immigrants and immigration
in Europe, 954–55
in France, 947
social challenges, 962, 964
in U.S., 617
Imperialism
motives for, 752–53
"new" (late nineteenth century),
752–61. *See also* Colonies and
colonization
Impression, Sunrise (Monet), *739*
Impressionism, 737–39, 740–41
Income, national, 700
Independent Group, 903
Independent Social Democratic Party
(Germany), 796
India
British colony, 757, 760–61
Cold War neutrality, 890
Gandhi, 811
independence of, 888
Indian National Congress, 761
and industrialization, 618
Indian National Congress, 761, 888
Individualism, 657
Indochina, 759, 847, 882, 888–89, 895
Indonesia, 888, 890
Industrial economy, 702
Industrialization
in France, 613–14, 615, 647, 748
in Germany, 613–14, 615, 702, 749
in India, 618
in Japan, 702–3
in Russia/Soviet Union, 618, 749,
824–25
and social structure, 622–23
spread of, 613–18, 614 (map), 702–3
in U.S., 615–18
and women, 616–17, 625. *See also*
Manufacturing
Industrial Revolution
in Britain, 605–12
in continental Europe, 613–18

impact of, 605
Marxist response, 685–87
Second, 699–705
social impact, 618–30
spread of, 613–18, 614 (map)
in U.S., 615–18
working conditions, 604–5
Industry. *See* Manufacturing
Infant mortality, 709, 719, 915
Infection, 690–91
Inflation
in Germany after WWI, 805, 817
during Industrial Revolution, 626
in U.S., 920
during WWI, 787–88
INF (Intermediate-Range Nuclear Forces) Treaty, 950
Intercontinental ballistic missiles (ICBMs), 882
Intergovernmental Panel on Climate Change (IPCC), 963–64
Intermediate-Range Nuclear Forces (INF) Treaty, 950
Internal combustion engine, 699
International Monetary Fund (IMF), 961
International Working Men's Association, 687
Internet, 958
The Interpretation of Dreams (Freud), 734
Interpreter of Maladies (Lahiri), 960
Intervention, principle of, 636, 638
iPod, 958–59
Iran
revolution (1979), 952–53
U.S. hostage crisis, 920
Iraq
British control, 799
Gulf War (1991), 950
independence of, 811
Iraq War, 947, 949, 952, 953
Ireland
Easter Rebellion, 785
emigration, 709 (table)
famine, 619
home rule, 723, 748
population, 619, 709 (table)
Irish Republican Army (IRA), 917, 951
Iron, 699
Iron Guard, 827
Iron industry, 608, 615, 685
Irrationality, 733–34
Isabella II (Spain), 676
Islam
growth of, 955
Shi'ite-Sunni division, 952. *See also* Muslims
Israel (modern)
formation of, 886
Munich Olympics, 931, 951
Six-Day War, 888
Italy/Italians
African colonies, 755
after WWII, 897
Albanian refugees, 954

corruption in (1980s–1990s), 947
Dopolavoro, 829
emigration, 709 (table)
fascism, 813–16
French in, 593–94
Giolitti's ministries, 748
nationalism, 736
in nineteenth century, 639, 725, 748
population, 709 (table)
revolts, 636, 647
revolutions of 1848, 652
Rome-Berlin Axis, 842
Triple Alliance, 762
unification, 652, 670–72
voting rights, 748
war with Austria (1859), 673
WWI, 775, 781, 782, 813
WWII, 849, 852, 854
Ivanhoe (Scott), 657

Jackson, Andrew, 654
Jackson, Michael, 930
Jacob, Aletta, 715
Jacobins, 583
Japan
annexation of Korea, 758
industrialization, 702–3
invasion of China (1937), 846
Manchuria, 846
Meiji Restoration, 760
and Nazi Germany, 846
overthrow of shogun, 760
textile factory, *704*
war with China (1894–1895), 758, 760
war with Russia (1904–1905), 750
WWI, 782
before WWII, 845–47
WWII, 849–51, 853–54, 855, 861–62, 865, 868
Japanese Americans, internment during WWII, 864–65
Jaurès, Jean, 706
Jazz, 828
Jefferson, Thomas, 574, 653
Jena, Battle of, 597
Jesus of Nazareth, 736
The Jewish State (Herzl), 746, 747
Jews and Judaism
emigration to U.S., 709–10
Holocaust, 857–61, 862, 896
in nineteenth century, 744–46
Zionism, 746, 886. *See also* Anti-Semitism
Israel (modern)
John XXIII (Pope), 905
John Paul II (Pope), 955, 957
Johns Hopkins University School of Medicine, 692
Johnson, Lyndon, 898, 914, 922
Joint-stock investment banks, 615, 685
Jordan, 811, 888
Josephine de Beauharnais, 593, *596*
Joyce, James, 834–35
Judaism. *See* Jews and Judaism

July Revolution, 646, *647*
Jung, Carl, 835
Jutland, Battle of, 782

Kaczynski, Lech , 940
Kádár, János, 893, 916
Kamikaze, 865
Kandinsky, Wassily, 740, *742*
Kansas-Nebraska Act (1854) (U.S.), 683
Kaprow, Allen, 928
Karlsbad Decrees, 640
Kay-Shuttleworth, James, 621
Kellogg-Briand pact, 806
Kelly, Petra, *954*
Kemal, Mustafa, 811
Kennan, George, 877, 878
Kennedy, John F., 883, 898, 920
Kent State University, 914
Kenya, 885
Kenya African National Union, 885
Kenyatta, Jomo, 812, 885
Keynes, John Maynard, 809
KGB, 915
Khomeini, Ayatollah, 920, 953
Khrushchev, Nikita, 882–83, 884, 891–92, 893
Kiefer, Anselm, 957
King, Martin Luther, 898, 899
Kingdom of Two Sicilies, 639, 672
Kings. *See* Monarchs and monarchies; *specific rulers*
Kipling, Rudyard, 754
Kleindeutsch, 651
Kohl, Helmut, 917, 945
Kolchak, Alexander, 793
Kollontai, Alexandra, 793
Königgrätz, Battle of, 675
Korea
division after WWII, 881
Japanese in, 757, 758, 760, 861–62
WWII, 861–62
Korean War, 880–82, 895
Kosovo, war in, 943–44
Kosovo Liberation Army (KLA), 945
Kossuth, Louis, 651, 652, 678
Kostunica, Vojislav, 945
Koyaanisqatsi (Glass), 930
Kraft durch Freude, 829, 831
Kristallnacht, 822–23
Krupp, Bertha, 714
Kubrick, Stanley, 779, 921
Kulturkampf, 726
Kun, Béla, 796
Kundera, Milan, 929
Kurile Islands, 870
Kursk, Battle of, 854–55
Kuwait, 950, 953
Kwasniewski, Aleksander, 940

Labor Front (Nazi Germany), 821–22, 831
Labor/labor force
in Great Britain, 747–48
guest workers, 954–55

Labor/labor force (*continued*)
and industrialization, 609–11, 616–18,
623, 627–28
and socialism, 705–6
working conditions, 623–25
work week, 900
and WWI, 785. *See also* Trade unions
Labour Party (Great Britain), 747–48, 808,
809, 896, 945–47
Lafayette, marquis de, 575
Lahiri, Jhumpa, 960
Laibach, Congress of, 636
Laissez-faire, 642, 807
Land art, 928–29
Languages
nineteenth century distribution,
645 (map)
Postmodern thought, 927
Laos, 759, 888
The Last Conquest of Ireland (Mitchel), 619
Lateran Accords, 816
Latin America, 636–38, 637 (map). *See also*
specific countries
Latvia, 799, 845, 937, 941, 948
Laurier, Wilfred, 752
Lavasseur, E., 701
Lavender Mist (Pollock), 902–3
Law
Napoleonic Code, 595, 639. *See also*
specific laws
Law enforcement, 654–56
Lawrence of Arabia, 781
Lay Down Your Arms (von Suttner), 743
League of Communists, 942
League of Nations, 798, 799, 804, 806,
841, 846
Learning. *See* Education
Leary, Timothy, 910
Lebanon, 799
Lebensraum, 817, 840, 841
Lee, Robert E., 684
Legislation. *See* Law
Legislative Assembly (France), 583, 584
Legislative Corps (France), 666–67, 668
Legitimacy, principle of, 633–34
Leisure. *See* Entertainment and leisure
Lend-Lease aid, 870
Lenin, V. I., 753, 790–93, 823
Leningrad, seize of, 855, 863
Leo XIII (Pope), 737
Leopold (Belgium), 647
Leopold II (Austria), 583–84
Leopold II (Belgium), 756
Leopold of Hohenzollern-Sigmaringen,
676–77
Le Pen, Jean-Marie, 955
Lesbians and gays, 910, 928
Lesseps, Ferdinand de, 686
Letchward Garden City, 712
Lévesque, René, 949
Ley, Robert, 821–22
Liberalism, 642–44
Liberal Party (Britain), 683, 747–48
Liberal Party (Canada), 899

Liberia, 756
Libya, 748, 755
Liebknecht, Karl, 796
Liebknecht, Wilhelm, 705
Life of Jesus (Renan), 736
Life on the Mississippi (Twain), 617
Lightbulb, 699
Limmer, Walter, 774
Lincoln, Abraham, 681, 683, 684
List, Friedrich, 615
Lister, Joseph, 690–91
Liszt, Franz, 694–95
Literacy, 720–21
Literature
after WWII, 903
Gothic, 658
"magic realism," 929
Modernism, 737
multiculturalism, 960
Naturalism, 737
Postmodernism, 929
Realism, 693
realism, 693
Romanticism, 657
Russian, 737, 891
stream-of-consciousness, 834–35
Symbolism, 737. *See also specific writers*
and works
Lithuania, 799, 845, 937, 941, 948
Little Entente, *804*, 805
The Lives of Others (film), 946
Living conditions, 620–22, 710–11
Livingstone, David, 756
Locarno, Treaty of, 806
Locomotives, 608
Lombardy, 634, 639, 652, 671
London
housing, *712*
music halls, 721
newspapers, 721
in nineteenth century, 619–20, 710, 711
police, 655
population, 710
sewers, 711
Vietnam war protests in, 914
WWII bombing, 865–66
London Conference, 763–64
London Times, 674
The Long Telegram (Kennan), 877
Looms, 607
The Lord of the Rings (film), *960*
Lorraine, 677, 761, 769
Loughnan, Naomi, 787
Louis XVI (France), 579, 580, 583, 584–85
Louis XVIII (France), 600, 639
Louis Napoleon (France), 649, 666–69
Louis-Philippe (France), 646–47, 648
Loyalists, 572
Luddites, 628
Ludendorff, Erich, 775, 784, 795
Lueger, Karl, 746
Luftwaffe, 842, 848, 865–66
Lusitania, 782
Luxembourg, 848

Luxemburg, Rosa, 796
Lyons, and Reign of Terror, 586

Maastricht Treaty, 947
MacArthur, Douglas, 854, 881
Macaulay, Thomas Babington, 650
MacDonald, Ramay, 808
Macedonia/Macedonians
and Balkan wars, 763
Machine guns, *776, 777*
Madame Bovary (Flaubert), 693
Madison, James, 653
Mafia, 919
Magazines, 721
Magenta, Battle of, 670
"Magic realism," 929
Maginot Line, 848
Magyars, 678, 727, 749
Maistre, Joseph de, 635
Major, John, 946
Malaya, 846, 850
Malay States, 759
Malcolm X, 899
Malta, 948
Malthus, Thomas, 642, 689
Man and Woman Gazing at the Moon
(Friedrich), *660*
Manchuria, 757, 846
Mandates, 799
Mandela, Nelson, 885
Manhattan Project, 864, 868
Manufacturing
decline after WWII, 900. *See also*
Industrialization
Many Happy Returns of the Day (Frith), 718
Mao Zedong, 882, 889–90, 923–24
Mapplethorpe, Robert, 957
March Revolution, 789–91
Marconi, Guglielmo, 699
Marcuse, Herbert, 912
Markets, 606–7, 700
Marne, First Battle of, 775
Marne, Second Battle of, 795
Márquez, Gabriel García, 929
Marriage
in nineteenth century, 715
Married Love (Stopes), 831
Marseilles, 585, 586
Marshall, John, 605, 653–54
Marshall Plan, 877–78, 894, 897
Martín, José de San, 636, *638*
Marx, Karl, 686–87, 688, 753
Marxism, 686–87, 688, 706, 790, 807
Masaryk, Thomas, 827
Massachusetts, mill towns, 617
Mass culture, 828–29
Mass education, 719–21
Massive retaliation, 882
Mass leisure, 720–21, 900
Mass politics, 722–27
Mass society, emergence of, 708–22
Masurian Lakes, Battle of, 775
Materialism, 689
Maximilian (Archduke of Austria), 668

May Day, 706
Mazzini, Giuseppe, 652, 653
McCarthy, Joseph R., 898
McKinley, William, 759
McLuhan, Marshall, 932
Meat Inspection Act (U.S.), 751
Medical schools, 691–92
Medicine
    affordable health care, 901
    anesthesia, 691
    in nineteenth century, 689–92
    socialized program in Great Britain, 896
Meiji Restoration, 760
Mein Kampf (Hitler), 817–18, 840
Memoirs (Metternich), 635
Memoirs (Michel), 725
Memoirs of a Geisha (Golden), 960
Mendeleyev, Dmitri, 688
Mensheviks, 790, 793
Merkel, Angela, 945
Messiaen, Olivier, 930
Metaxas, John, 827
Methodism, 610–11, 662
Metternich, Prince Klemens von, 633–34, 635, 636, 640, 651
Mexico
    French troops in, 668
    independence, 636
Michel, Louise, 724, 725
Microsoft, 958
Middle class
    in France, 576
    and industrialization, 622–23
    in nineteenth century, 714, 715, 717–19
    in Prussia, 673
Middle East
    after WWI, 811
    decolonization of, 885–89
    in 1919, 799 (map). *See also* Arabs
    specific countries
Midway, Battle of, 853–54
Militarism, 770
Military
    conscription, 770, 783
    Nazi Germany, 841
    Prussian, 673, 674
    Red Army, 794. *See also* Weapons
        and warfare
    specific branches
    specific wars and battles
Mill, John Stuart, 643–44
Millet, Jean-François, 694, *695*
Milligen, J. G., 588
Milosevic, Slobodan , 942, 943, 945
Minimalism, in music, 930
Minimum wage, 786
Ministerial responsibility, 639, 643
Minority groups
    after WWI, 799
    in Austria-Hungary, 680 (map), 726, 749
    in Hungary, 653
    before WWI, 769–70. *See also specific*
        groups
Mir, 680

Missionaries
    evangelicals, 737
Mitchel, John, 619
Mitterand, François, 919, 947
Mobilization, 771–73, 783–84
Modena, 672
Modernism, 736–41
Moldavia, 638, 668, 669
Molotov, Vyacheslav, 871
Monarchs and monarchies
    France, 577, 583, 646–47
    Russia, 727
Monet, Claude, 738, *739*
Monroe Doctrine, 637
Montenegro, 762, 763, 945
Montessori, Maria, 743–44
Moon landing, *926*
Moore, Charles, 929
Morality
    Christian, 714, 733
Moravia, 843
Morel, Edward, 754–55
Morisot, Berthe, 738–39, *740*
Moro, Aldo, 919
Morocco, 755, 885
Mortality rates. *See* Death rates
Mott, John, 788
Mountain, 584–85
Movies, 828–29, 905–6, 959. *See also*
    specific movies
Mozambique, 755, 885
Mozart, Wolfgang Amadeus, 661
MTV, 930
Mule, 607
Mulroney, Brian, 920, 949
Multiculturalism, 960
Multinational corporations, 961–62
Munich Conference, 843, 845
Munich Olympics, 931, 951
"Munition Work" (Loughnan), 787
Music
    atonal style, 834
    in Digital Age, 959
    grunge, 957–58
    Impressionism, 740–41
    and iPod, 958–59
    jazz, 828
    minimalism, 930
    modern, 930
    Modernism, 740–43
    primitivism, 741
    punk movement, 930
    rap/hip-hop, 930, 931, 958
    rock-and-roll, 906, 930
    Romanticism, 660–61, 694–96
    serialism, 930
    songs of WWI, 781
    Threepenny Opera, 833. *See also specific*
        composers
Music halls, 721
Music videos, 930
Muslims
    in European Union, 955
    in France, 947

    in India, 888
    in Palestine, 886
    and U.S., 952–53. *See also* Islam
Mussolini, Benito, 813–16, 829, 842, 848, 849, 854, 855
Mutsuhito, 760
Mutual deterrence, 880
Myanmar, 759, 888
My Own Story (Pankhurst), 745

Nagasaki, 855, 868
Nagy, Imry, 893, 894
The Namesake (Lahiri), 960
Nanjing, Japanese conquest of, 846, 861
Naples
    under unified Italy, 672
Napoleon Bonaparte
    bureaucracy, 596
    and Catholic Church, 595
    Civil Code, 595, 639
    coup of 1799, 594
    domestic policies, 594–95
    European response to, 597–99
    fall of, 599–600
    Grand Empire, 597–98
    military career, 592, 593–94
    portraits of, *595, 596*
    rise of, 593–94
Napoleonic Wars, 597
Napoleon III (France), 649, 666–69, 670, 675, 676, 677
Nasser, Gamal Abdel, 886–88
National Assembly (France), 578–79, 580, 583, 724
National Bloc (France), 809
National cemeteries, 804
National Convention (France), 584–85, 590, 591, 592
National Front (France), 955
National income, 700
National Insurance Act (Great Britain), 748
Nationalism
    in Austria-Hungary, 749
    of Belgians, 647
    in Germany, 599, 644, 736, 749
    in India, 761
    in Italy, 647
    and Napoleon, 598–99
    in nineteenth century, 644
    in Poland, 647
    and social Darwinism, 736
    and socialism, 706–7
    and WWI, 769, 773, 774
Nationalization, 783, 793, 821, 895
National Liberation Front (FLN), 885
National Organization of Women (NOW), 913
National Salvation Front (Romania), 940
National Socialist German Workers' Party, 817. *See also* Nazi Germany
National System of Political Economy (List), 615

NATO. *See* North Atlantic Treaty Organization (NATO)
Naturalism, 737
Natural selection, 689
Navy
    British, 598, 782
Nazi Germany
    administration of empire, 855–57
    Allied bombing of, 866–68
    art, 833–34
    Austria annexation, 842–43
    Beer Hall Putsch, 817
    blood flag ritual, *818*
    in Czechoslovakia, 843–44
    "diplomatic revolution," 840–42
    economic exploitation, 856
    emergence of, 813
    Enabling Act, 820
    foreign workers, 857
    and Germany, 846
    home front, 865
    Kristallnacht, 822–23
    Luftwaffe, 842, 848, 865–66
    mass leisure, 829, 831
    New Order, 855–56
    nonaggression pact with Soviets, 845
    Nuremberg laws, 822
    Poland invasion, 844–45, 847–48
    propaganda of, 821, 828–29, 830, 855
    racism, 855–56
    rearmament, 841–42
    Reichstag fire, 820
    resistance movements, 857
    Rhineland occupation, 842
    rise of, 817–19
    SA purge, 820
    seizure of power, 819–20
    SS (*Schutzstaffeln*), 822, 856, 858–59
    in Sudetenland, 843
    "total state" development, 820–23
    women in, 822. *See also* World War II
Nehru, Jawaharlal, 812, 890
Neo-Expressionism, 957
Netherlands
    Congress of Vienna, 634
    emigration, 709 (table)
    immigration laws, 955
    population, 709 (table)
    WWII, 848
New Deal, 810, 898
New Economic Policy (NEP) (Soviet Union), 823, 824
New German School, 694–95
New Guinea, 782
New Harmony, Indiana, 644
New imperialism, 752–61
New Lanark, Scotland, 644
New Order (Italy), 951
New Order (Nazi Germany), 855–56
Newspapers, 721
New Zealand, 756, 782
Ngo Dinh Diem, 920
NGOs (non-governmental organizations), 964

Nice, 670
Nicholas I (Russia), 641, *642*, 652, 669
Nicholas II (Russia), 727, 749, *750*, 771, 772, 789, 794
Nietzsche, Friedrich, 733
Nigeria, 811–12, 885
Nightingale, Florence, 669, *670*, 743
9/11/01, 951, *952*
Ninth Symphony (Beethoven), 661
Nixon, Richard, 914, 919–20, 922–23, 924
Nkrumah, Kwame, 885
Nobility
    in England, 623, 713
    in France, 575, 576–77, 596, 639
    in nineteenth century, 713–14
Nokia Corporation, 958
Non-governmental organizations (NGOs), 964
NORAD (North American Air Defense Command), 899
Normandy, invasion of, 854
North Africa
    WWII, 850 (map), 852. *See also specific countries*
North America
    eighteenth century, 573 (map). *See also specific countries*
North American Air Defense Command (NORAD), 899
North Atlantic, Battle of, 852
North Atlantic Treaty Organization (NATO)
    Afghanistan, 951
    Bosnian War, 943
    Canadian membership, 899
    formation of, 880
    Kosovo peacekeeping troops, 945
    in 1950s-1960s, 881 (map)
    West German membership, 895
Northern Ireland, 917, 951
Northern Union, 640–41
North German Confederation, 675, 676, 677
North Korea, 882. *See also* Korea
Norway
    emigration, 709 (table)
    immigrants, 964
    music, 740
    population, 709 (table)
    WWII, 848, 857
Notre-Dame Cathedral, 590
Novalis, Friedrich, 659
November Revolution, 795–96
Novikov, Nikolai, 877
Novotny, Antonin, 916
Nuclear arms
    Antiballistic Missile Treaty, 924
    Cuban Missile Crisis, 883, 884
    France, 895
    Intermediate-Range Nuclear Forces (INF) Treaty, 950
    massive retaliation, 882
    Strategic Defense Initiative (SDI), 925
Nuclear power, Chernobyl disaster, 926

Nuremberg laws, 822
Nuremberg trials, 896
Nursing, 669, *670*, 743

Occupation zones, in Germany, 870, 878
October Manifesto, 750
Office of Price Administration (U.S.), 864
Oil crisis, 920
The Old Curiosity Shop (Dickens), 694
Old order, 577
Olson, Culbert, 864
Olympic Games, 829, 925, 931
Omdurman, Battle of, 756
One-Dimensional Man (Marcuse), 912
One Hundred Years of Solitude (Márquez), 929
On Liberty (Mill), 643
On Parisian Department Stores (Lavasseur), 701
On the Origin of Species by Means of Natural Selection (Darwin), 689, 737
On the Subjection of Women (Mill), 644
OPEC (Organization of Petroleum Exporting Countries), 920
Open door policy, 757–58
Opera, 695–96
Oppenheimer, J. Robert, 868, 925
Orange Free State, 755
Organic evolution, 689, 690
Organization of Petroleum Exporting Countries (OPEC), 920
The Organization of Work (Blanc), 644
Origin of Species by Means of Natural Selection (Darwin), 689, 737
Orlando, Vittorio, *798*
Orwell, George, 809
Ostpolitik, 917
Ottoman Empire
    Armenian genocide, 795
    and the Balkans, 762
    Balkan Wars, 763
    Crimean War, 668–69
    decline of, 668, 669 (map)
    end of, 799
    Greek revolt against, 638
    war with Russia, 638
    WWI, 779, 781–82
Ouverture, Toussaint L', 591
Overpopulation, 962
"Over There" (Cohan), 781
Owen, Robert, 627, 644
Oxford University, 714

Painting. *See* Art
Painting with White Border (Kadinsky), 740
Pakistan, 888
Palestine
    British control, 799
    and Crimean War, 668
    Jewish state in, 886
    and Zionist movement, 746
Palestine Liberation Organization (PLO), 888
Palestinians, 951

Palmerston, Lord, 682
Pan-African Congress, 797–98, 812
Pan American flight, 951
Pan-Arabism, 887–88
Pankhurst, Emmeline, 731, 743, 745
Pantheism, 659
Panzer divisions, 847, 849
Paolini, Pier Paola, 914
Papacy. *See Names of specific Popes*
Papal encyclicals, 736, 737
Papal States, 639, 672
Paris
    fall of (1871), 678
    liberation (WWII), 854
    in nineteenth century, 620
    reconstruction under Napoleon III,
        667, 712
    student revolt (1968), 909–10, 912
Paris, Treaty of
    (1763), 684
    (1783), 573
    (1856), 669
Paris Commune, 584, 585, 723–24
Paris Peace Conference, 796–98
Parlements (France), 577
Parliament (England), 648
Parma, 672
Parnell, Charles, 723
Pasteur, Louis, 688, 690
Pasteurization, 690
Paths of Glory (film), 779
The Path to Power (Thatcher), 918
Patriots, 572
Peace settlements and treaties. *See specific
    names*
Peace societies, 743
Pearl Harbor, 849–50
Pearson, Karl, 752
Pearson, Lester, 899
Peasants
    in France, 576
    in nineteenth century, 714
    in Russia, 679–80, 682, 825, 864. *See also
        Serfs and serfdom*
Peel, Robert, 648, 655
Peer Gynt Suite (Grieg), 740
Pen, Jean-Marie Le, 955
People's Charter, 628
People's Liberation Army (China), 889
People's Will (Russia), 682
Perestroika, 936, 938
Permissive society, 910
Perry, Matthew, 758
Persia, 757
Persian Gulf War, 950, 953
The Persistence of Memory (Dalí),
    832, *834*
Peru
    revolt against Spain, 636
Pétain, Henri, 848
Peterloo Massacre, 639
Petrograd, 789, 790
Petrushka (Stravinsky), 741
Phalansteries, 644

Philippines, 724, 759, 868
Philosophes, 577
Philosophy
    existentialism, 902, 903–4, 927. *See also
        specific philosophers*
Photography, 739, 929, 957
Physics, 732–33, 835–36, 926
Piazza d'Italia (Moore), 929
Picasso, Pablo, 739–40, *742*
Piecework, 704
Piedmont, 639, 652, 670–72
Pillnitz, Declaration of, 584
Pilsudski, Joseph, 826
Piscator, Erwin, 833
Pissarro, Camille, 737–38
Pius VII (Pope), 595
Pius IX (Pope), 652, 736
Planck, Max, 732
Playboy magazine, 910
PLO (Palestine Liberation
    Organization), 888
Plutocrats, 713–14
Poe, Edgar Allan, 658
Poetry
    Romanticism, 658–59
    Symbolism, 737, 738
Pogroms, 746
Poincaré, Raymond, 809, 810
Poland
    after WWII, 870
    authoritarian state after WWI, 826
    collapse of communism, 939–40
    communist reforms (1956), 893
    Congress of Vienna, 633–34
    EU membership, 948
    German invasion of, 844–45
    nationalism, 647
    Solidarity movement, 916
    Treaty of Brest-Litovsk, 793
    uprising (1830), 647
    WWII, 847–48, 856, 861
Police forces, 654–55, 656
Politburo, 823–24
Political democracy. *See* Democracy
Political liberalism, 642–44
Political rights
    of African Americans, 898–99
    of women, 644, 731, 743–44
Political structure. *See* Government
Pollock, Jackson, 902–3, *905*
Poor Law Act (1834) (Britain), 625, 648
Pop Art, 903
Popes. *See Names of specific Popes*
Popular culture, 905–6, 930–32
Popular Front (France), 810
Popular Front (Spain), 827
Population
    and industrialization, 618
    Ireland (1781–1845), 619
    Malthus on, 642
    in nineteenth century, 618, 708–9
Population growth, 962
Populism, 682
Portrait of Jean Paulhan (Dubuffet), *903*

Port Sunlight, 711
Portugal
    African colonies, 755, 885
    emigration, 709 (table)
    population, 709 (table)
    under Salazar, 827–28
Post-Impressionism, 739
Postmodernism, 927–30
Poststructuralism, 927
Potsdam Conference, 870
Poverty, 577, 625, 656
Power (political), 928
Power loom, 607
Prague Spring, 916
Prefects, 596
Prelude to the Afternoon of a Faun
    (Debussy), 741
Presley, Elvis, 906
Preventive medicine, 691
Pries, Knud, 956
Primitivism, in music, 741
Primo de Rivera, Antonio, 827
Primo de Rivera, Miguel, 827
The Princess (Tennyson), 715
Principle of intervention, 636, 638
Principle of legitimacy, 633–34
Principles of Political Economy
    (Ricardo), 642
Prisoners of war, WWII, 857, 862
Prison reform, 656–57
Proclamation to the People (Louis
    Napoleon), 667
Prodi, Romano, 947
Progressive Era (U.S.), 751
Proletariat, 687
Prometheus Unbound (Shelley), 658
Propaganda, 813, 821, 828–29
Property rights, 574, 595
Prostitution, 705
Protestants and Protestantism
    Romantic Era revival, 662
Protest movements, 910–14, 953, *954*
Prussia
    Concert of Europe, 636
    and Congress of Vienna, 633–35,
        634 (map)
    Danish War, 675
    and German unification, 673–78
    Napoleonic Wars, 597
    reform in, 599, 640
    revolution of 1848, 649, 651
    Schleswig-Holstein, 675
    war with Austrian Empire (1866), 672
    war with France (1870), 672, 676–78
Psychoanalysis, 734–35
Psychology, 734–35, 835
Public Health Act (Great Britain), 711
Public health movement, 691, 710–11
Public works, 810
Puddling, 608
Puerto Rico, 759
Punk movement, 930
Pure Food and Drug Act (U.S.), 751
Putin, Vladimir, 939

Quadruple Alliance, 633, 636
Quakers, 622
Quantum theory, 732, 926
Quebec, 751–52, 949
Queens. *See* Monarchs and monarchies; *specific rulers*
Quo Vadis (film), 828

Racism
    apartheid, 885
    of Hitler and Nazi Germany, 817, 855–56
    and imperialism, 752
    and social Darwinism, 735–36
Radcliffe, William, 622
Radio, 699, 828–29
Radium, 732
Rahner, Karl, 905
Railroads, 608–9, 614, 685, 749
Rain, Steam, and Speed- The Great Western Railway (Turner), *660*
Rap music, 930, 931, 958
Rapprochement, 882
Rasputin, 789
Rathenau, Walter, 783
Reagan, Ronald, 920, 925, 950
Realism, 693–96, 834, 929
Realpolitik, 665, 674
Real wage growth
    U.S., 898
    West Germany, 896
Reason, 733
Rebellions. *See* Revolts and revolutions
Recessions, 917, 919
Recreation. *See* Entertainment and leisure
Red Army, 794
Red Army Faction, 951
Red Brigades, 919, 951
Red Guards, 923, 924
Redistribution Act (Great Britain), 723
Red Scare, 898
Red Shirts, 672, 674
Red Terror, 794
Reflections on the Revolution in France (Burke), 635
Reform Acts (Britain)
    (1832), 648, 682
    (1867), 683, 723
Reform and reformers
    in England (Great Britain), 647–48, 682–83, 723, 747–48
    and industrialization, 628–29
    of prisons, 656–57
    in Prussia, 599, 640
    in Russia, 678–82
    urban, 621–22
Reichstag, 820
Reign of Terror, 586–88, 591
Reinsurance Treaty, 762
Relativity theory, 732–33, 926
Religion
    after WWII, 905
    current trends, 955
    fundamentalism, 955

and imperialism, 752–53. *See also specific religions*
Remarque, Erich Maria, 778
Reminiscences (Schurz), 650–51
Renan, Ernst, 736
Reparations, 799, 805, 870, 878
Report on the Condition of the Labouring Population of Great Britain (Chadwick), 621–22
Repression, 734, 735
Republican Party (U.S.), 653, 683, 919
Resistance movements, against Nazis, 857
Revisionism, 706
Revolts and revolutions
    American, 572–75
    in Eastern Europe (1989), 939–40
    of 1848, 648–53, 651–52
    in Germany, 649, 650–51, 795–96
    in Greece, 638
    in Hungary, 893, 894
    in Italy, 636, 647
    in Russia, 750, 789–93
    in Saint Domingue, 591
    sexual, 910
    in Spain, 639
    of students, 909–10, 912. *See also* French Revolution
        Industrial Revolution
Revolutionary socialism, 734
The Revolutionary Tribunal (Milligen), 588
Revolutionary War (U.S.), 572–73
Rhineland, 842
Rhodes, Cecil, 755
Ricardo, David, 642
Right-wing groups, 955, 956
Rimbaud, Arthur, 738
The Ring of the Nibelung (Wagner), 696
Risorgimento, 652
The Rite of Spring (Stravinsky), 741
Roads
    in Britain, 605
    in U.S., 616
Roaring Twenties, 828, 831
Robespierre, Maximilien, 585, 589, 591, *592*
Robins, Thomas, *610*
Rock-and-roll, 906, 930
Rocket, 608
Röhm, Ernst, 820
Roman Catholic Church. *See* Catholic Church
Romania
    after WWI, 799
    collapse of communism, 940
    communist, 917
    EU membership, 948
    fascism, 827
    illiteracy rates, 721
    independence of, 762
    Little Entente, 805
    population, 709 (table)
Romanov dynasty, 634
Romanticism, 657–62, 694–96
Rome
    Italy's annexation of, 672

Rome-Berlin Axis, 842
Rommel, Erwin, 852
Roosevelt, Franklin Delano, 810, 850, 855, 869, 870
Rotterdam, 848
Rougon-Macquart (Zola), 737
Royal Albert Bridge, *610*
Ruhr valley, 805
Russia
    under Alexander III, 682, 727
    anarchism, 708
    art, 740
    and the Balkans, 762, 763, 764, 771
    Bloody Sunday, 750, 751
    Chechnya, 939
    civil war, 793–95
    Concert of Europe, 636
    Congress of Vienna, 633–35
    Crimean War, 668–69
    Decembrist Revolt, 641
    emigration, 709 (table)
    famines, 750, 823
    illiteracy rates, 721
    imperialism, 757
    and industrialization, 618, 749
    Jews in, 746
    literature, 737
    military, 770
    military alliance with France, 762
    music, 741
    Napoleonic Wars, 597, 599–600
    Northern Union, 640–41
    October Manifesto, 750
    peasants, 679–80, 682
    Polish territory, 634, 647
    population, 709 (table)
    Putin era, 939
    reform, 678–82
    Reinsurance Treaty with Germany, 762
    Revolution (1905), 750
    Revolution (1917–1918), 789–93
    serfdom, 679–80
    Social Democratic Labor Party, 706
    Three Emperors' League, 761–62
    Triple Entente, 762
    Turkish war, 638
    war with Russia (1904–1905), 750
    women's rights, 793
    before WWI, 769
    WWI, 771, 772, 775, 782–83, 784, 789
    Yeltsin era, 938–39. *See also* Soviet Union
        specific rulers
Russification, 727
Russo-Japanese War, 750
Rutherford, Ernest, 836

SA (*Sturmabteilung*), 817, 820
Sadler's Committee report, 626
Saigon, French occupation of, 759
Saint Domingue (Haiti), 591
Saint Helena, 600
Saint Petersburg, 789
Saint-Simon, comte de, 645
Sakhalin Islands, 870

Sakharov, Andrei, 914
Salazar, Antonio, 827–28
Saltaire, England, *620*
Salvation Army, 737
Sanford, Elizabeth Poole, 716
Sanger, Margaret, 831
Sanitary conditions, 620–22
Sans-culottes, 584
San Stefano, Treaty of, 762
Sardinia, 634 (map), 670
Sarkozy, Nicolas, 947
Sartre, Jean-Paul, 903–4
Saudi Arabia, 811
Saussure, Ferdinand de, 927
Saxony, 634
Scandinavia
    after WWI, 810. *See also specific*
        countries
Schleswig-Holstein, 675
Schlieffen Plan, 771–73, 775
Schmidt, Helmut, 917
Schönberg, Arnold, 834, 930
Schönhuber, Franz, 955
Schools
    Montessori, 743–44
    in nineteenth century, 719
    universities, 720, 901, 910–13. *See also*
        Education
Schroeder, Gerhard, 926, 945
Schumacher, E. F., 926, 927
Schurz, Carl, 650–51
Schuschnigg, Kurt von, 843
Schutzmannschaft, 655
Science
    in nineteenth century, 687–93
    Romantic poet's critique of, 659
    before WWI, 732–33
    since WWII, 925–26
Scientific method, 689
Scotland
    New Lanark cooperative, 644
    population, 709 (table)
    WWII, 867
Scott, Walter, 657
Scripture. *See* Bible
SEATO (Southeast Asia Treaty
    Organization), 882
Second Balkan War, 763
Second Empire (France), 666–69
Second Estate, 575, 578
Second German Empire, 677–78
Second Industrial Revolution, 699–705
Second International, 706, 707
The Second Sex (de Beauvoir), 902, 904
Second Vietnam War, 890, 912, 914, 920,
    922–23
Secret Book (Hitler), 841
Secret police, 794, 893, 915, 916, 917, 945
Secret societies
    in Italy, 639
Sedan, Battle of, 677
Ségur Law, 575
Self-determination, 796, 799, 884
Self-Portrait (Basquiat), *958*

Separation of church and state, 642
Sepoys, revolt of, 757
September 11, 2001, 951, *952*
Serbia
    and Bosnian Crisis, 763–65
    illiteracy rates, 721
    independence of, 668, 762
    population, 709 (table)
    war with Ottoman Empire, 762
    WWI, 769, 771, 775
Serbs, 771, 942, 943, 945
Serfs and serfdom
    emancipation in Austrian Empire, 678
    emancipation in Russia, 679–80, 681
    in Russia, 679–80, 681. *See also* Peasants
Serialism, 930
Serrano, Andres, 957
Servants, 623
The Seventh Seal (film), 906
Sewers, 620, 622, 711
Sex and sexuality
    extramarital sex, 910
    in Roaring Twenties, 831
Sexual revolution, 910
Shelley, Mary, 658, 659
Shelley, Percy Bysshe, 658
Shi'ite Muslims, 952
Ships, 699
Shogun, overthrow of, 760
Shonibare, Yinka, 960
Siam, 759
Siberia, 757
Sicily
    revolution of 1848, 652
    WWII, 854
Sieveking, Amalie, 743
Sieyès, Abbè, 578
Six-Day War, 888
Slater, Samuel, 616
Slavery
    in France, 591
    in U.S., 683–84
Slavic peoples, 856, 861. *See also specific*
    groups
Slovakia, 843–44, 940, 948
Slovenia, 942, 948
Small is Beautiful (Schumacher), 926, 927
Smallpox, 618, 708
Smith, Kiki, 960
Smithson, Robert, 928–29
Soccer, 721, 722, *723*, 829, 931
Social class. *See* Social structure
Social contract, 574, 705–6
Social Darwinism, 734–35, 752
Social Democratic Labor Party
    (Russia), 706
Social Democratic Party (Russia), 749–50,
    790
Social Democratic Party (SPD)
    (Germany), 705–6, 726, 749, 795–96,
    895, 917, 945
Socialism
    early, 644–46
    evolutionary, 706

    in France, 810, 919
    Leo XIII on, 737
    and nationalism, 706–7
    political parties, 705–6
    revolutionary, 734
    in Russia, 749–50
    in Western Europe after WWII, 893
    and WWI, 773, 785
Socialized medicine, 896
Social security
    Germany, 726
    Great Britain, 896
    in U.S., 810
Social Security Act (U.S.), 810
Social Statics (Spencer), 735
Social structure
    class conflict, 786–87
    in France, 575–77
    and industrialization, 622–23
    in nineteenth century, 713–19
    post-WWII, 900
Social welfare programs. *See* Welfare state
Society, scientific approach to,
    692–93
Society of Thirty, 578
Solferino, Battle of, 670
Solidarity movement, 916, 940
Solomon Islands, 854
Solzhenitsyn, Alexander, 891
Somme offensive, 777
Sorel, Georges, 733–34
The Sorrows of the Young Werther
    (Goethe), 657
South Africa, 753–54, 885
Southeast Asia. *See specific countries*
Southeast Asia Treaty Organization
    (SEATO), 882
Southern Christian Leadership Conference
    (SCLC), 898
South Korea, 882
South Tyrol, 813
Soviets, 790
Soviet Union
    Afghanistan invasion, 925
    Allied war conferences, 869–70
    art, 834
    Brezhnev era, 914–15
    coexistence with after WWI, 806
    coup attempt (1991), 938, *939*
    creation of, 823
    economy, 823
    end of, 935–36, 937–38
    Gorbachev era, 936–38, 949–50
    Hitler's view of, 840
    industrialization, 824
    Khrushchev era, 891–92
    nonaggression pact with Nazi Germany,
        845
    Poland, 845, 848, 870
    under Stalin, 824–26, 890–91
    women in, 826, 902
    WWII, 845, 849, 852–53, 854–55, 857,
        863–64, 869–70. *See also* Cold War;
        Russia

Space exploration, 890, 925, *926*
Spain
    after WWI, 827
    Civil War, 827
    emigration, 709 (table)
    under Franco, 827
    in nineteenth century, 724–25
    Popular Front, 827
    population, 709 (table)
    revolt, 639
    war with U.S., 724, 759
Spanish-American War, 724, 759
Speer, Albert, 865
Spencer, Herbert, 735
Speransky, Michael, 640
Spinning jenny, 607
Spiral Jetty (Smithson), 928–29
Spirituality. *See* Religion
Sports
    interwar period, 829
    in nineteenth century, 717, 721–22
    Olympic Games, 829, 925, 931
    since WWII, 930–32
Sputnik, 890, 925
Squadristi violence, 814
Square with White Border (Kandinsky), *742*
Srebrenica, massacre at, 943
Sri Lanka, 888
SS (*Schutzstaffeln*), 822, 856, 858–59
Stagflation, 920
Stalin, Joseph, 824–26, 863, 864, 869, 870,
    872, 881, 882
Stalingrad, Battle of, 852–53
Stalinization, 893
Standard of living, 625–27
Staniland, C. J., *711*
Stanley, Henry M., 756
Starry Night (Van Gogh), 739, *741*
Stasi, 945
Stauffenberg, Claus von, 857
Steamboats, 616
Steam engines, 607–8, 615
Steam-powered locomotives, 608
Steel, 699, 749, 750
Stein, Heinrich von, 599, 640
Stephenson, George, 608, 685
Steppenwolf (Hesse), 835
Stocker, Adolf, 746
Stock market, 806
Stolypin, Peter, 750
The Stonebreakers (Courbet), 693
Stopes, Marie, 831
Strategic Defense Initiative (SDI), 925
Stravinsky, Igor, 741, 834
Streetcars, 699
Stresemann, Gustav, 805, 806
Strikes, 627, 707, 734, 748, 750, 770, 784,
    789, 809, 814
Strutt, Jedediah, 622
Student protests, 909–13
Student societies, 640, 641
Submarines, 782, 842
Subways, 699
Sudan, 755, 756, 964

Sudetenland, 843, 868
Suez Canal, *686*, 755, 886–87
Suffrage movements, 743, 744, 745,
    786, 902
Suffragists, 743
Suharto, 890
Sukarno, 890
Sullivan, Louis H., 833
Sunday school, 656
Sunni Muslims, 952
Sun Yat-sen, 760
Superego, 734
Supply-side economics, 920
Supreme Court (U.S.), 653–54
Surgeons, 690–91
Surrealism, 832, *834*, 902
Suttner, Bertha von, 743
Swan, Joseph, 699
Sweatshops, 704
Sweden
    emigration, 709 (table)
    population, 709 (table)
    sexual revolution, 910
Switzerland, 709 (table)
Syllabus of Errors (Pius IX), 736
Symbolism, 737, 738
Symphonic poem, 695
Symphonie Fantastique (Berlioz), 661
Syria/Syrians
    French control, 799
    in United Arab Republic, 887
System of Positive Philosophy (Comte), 692

Taaffe, Edward von, 726
Taiwan, 889
Taliban, 951–52
Tanks, 783, 863
Tannenberg, Battle of, 775
Tanzania, 885
Tariffs, 614–15, 639, 700, 749
Taxation
    in England/Great Britain, 946
    in France, 596
    in U.S., 573, 920
Taylor, Harriet, 644
Teachers, 720
Tehran Conference, 869
Telephones, 699, *705*, 958
Television, *900,* 906, 930–31
Ten Hours Act (1847) (Britain), 630
Tennis Court Oath, 578–79
Tennyson, Alfred Lord, 671, 715
Terrorism, 885, 949, 951–52
Textiles
    child labor, 624–25, 626
    in Japan, *704*
    in nineteenth century, 607, *610, 615,* 685
    in U.S., 616
Thackeray, William, 693
Thailand, 759, 761
Thatcher, Margaret, 917–19
Theater. *See* Drama
"Theater of the Absurd," 903
Thermidorean Reaction, 592

Thiers, Adolphe, 647, 648
Third Coalition, 597
Third Estate, 575–77, 578–79
The Third Man (film), 879
The Third of May (Goya), 599
Third Reich. *See* Nazi Germany
Third Republic (France), 723–24, 748
Third Symphony (Beethoven), 661
Three Emperors' League, 761–62
Threepenny Opera, 833
The Tin Drum (Grass), 903
Tisza, Istvàn, 749
Tito, Josip Broz, 857, 892, 942
Tojo, Hideki, 865
Tolstoy, Leo, 737
Tonkin, 759
Tories (England), 638–39, 683
Totalitarianism, 813
Total war, 783
Tourism, 721, 829, 900
Towns. *See* Cities and towns
Toys, 715
Trade
    European Economic Community, 897
    with Latin America, 637–38
    in nineteenth century, 700–701, 703–4
Trade unions
    in Britain, 627–28
    in nineteenth century, 685–86, 707–8
    in U.S., 751
Trafalgar, Battle of, 598
Transformism, 748
Transnational corporations, 961–62
Transportation
    airplanes, 700, 783, 829
    automobiles, 700, 900
    and industrialization, 608–9, 616
    internal combustion engine, 699
    railroads, 608–9, 614, 685, 749
    streetcars, 699
    subways, 699
    in U.S., 616. *See also* Roads
Transvaal, British seizure of, 755
Travel, 721, 829, 900
Treaties. *See specific treaty names*
Trench warfare, 775, 777–78, 780
Trevithick, Richard, 608
Trieste, 813
Triple Alliance, 762, 770 (map)
Triple Entente, 762, 770 (map)
Tripoli, Italian seizure of, 755
Tristan, Flora, 645–46
Triumph of the Will (film), 829, 830
Troppau, Congress of, 636
Trotsky, Leon, 791, 794, 823, 824
Trudeau, Pierre, 920
Truffaut, François, 906
Truman, Harry, 855, 868, 870, 886, 898
Truman Doctrine, 876, 878
Tsars. *See Names of specific tsars*
Tunisia, 755, 885
Turing, Alan, 925
Turkestan, 757
Turkey, 811, 876, 878, 880, 883

Turks. *See* Ottoman Empire
Turner, Joseph Malford William, 659–60
Tuscany, 672
Twain, Mark, 617
Tzara, Tristan, 832

Ukraine
    Chernobyl disaster, 926
    independence, 938
    under Soviet rule, 794
    Treaty of Brest-Litovsk, 793
    WWII, 849, 855, 861
Ulbricht, Walter, 878, 883, 916, 917
Ulm, Battle of, 597
Ultraroyalists, 639
Ulysses (Joyce), 835
Unbearable Lightness of Being
    (Kundera), 929
Uncertainty principle, 836
Unconditional surrender, 852
Unconscious, 734, 834–35
Unemployment
    in France, 947
    in Germany, 808, 817, 819, 821, 896
    during Great Depression, 806–7, 808
    Keynes on, 809
    in U.S., 810
Union of Concerned Scientists, 963
Union of Soviet Socialist Republics
    (USSR). *See* Soviet Union
Unions. *See* Trade unions
United Arab Republic (UAR), 887
United Kingdom. *See* England (Great
    Britain)
United Nations, 870, 881, 886, 954
United States of America
    after WWII, 898–99
    Americanization, 905–6
    art, 902–3
    Articles of Confederation, 573
    birth of, 573–74
    Bush (George W.) presidency, 949
    Carter presidency, 920, 925
    China, 757–58
    civil rights movement, 898–99
    Civil War, 683–84
    Clinton presidency, 949
    Constitution, 574, 653
    Cuban Missile Crisis, 883
    Declaration of Independence, 574
    depressions, 702, 803–4, 806–7, 810
    in 1860, 684 (map)
    government, 573–74
    Hawaiian Islands, 759
    imperialism, 759
    industrialization, 615–18
    Iraq War, 949, 952
    jazz, 828
    Korean War, 880–82
    medicine, 692
    and Muslim world, 952–53
    New Deal, 810, 898
    Nixon presidency, 914, 919–20,
        922–23, 924

Paris Peace Conference, 797, 798
prisons, 657
Progressive Era, 751
Reagan presidency, 920, 925, 950
Red Scare, 898
rise of, 750–51
rock-and-roll, 906
September 11, 2001, 951, *952*
slavery, 683–84
Spanish-American War, 724, 759
sports, 722
Supreme Court, 653–54
trade unions, 751
Vietnam War, 890, 912, 914, 920,
    922–23
voting rights, 654, 786
war for independence, 572–73
Watergate, 919–20
WWI, 782–83, 795
WWII, 849–51, 854, 855, 864–65, 866,
    868, 869–70
youth protests, 911. *See also* Cold War
Universal elementary education, 719–20
Universe, nature of, 926
Universities, 720, 901, 910–13
Upper classes
    in nineteenth century, 713–14. *See also*
    Nobility
Urbanization, 710–12, 750
USSR. *See* Soviet Union
Utopian socialists, 644–46

Vaccination, 690
Valéry, Paul, 831
Vanderbilt, Consuelo, 714
Van de Velde, Theodore, 831
Van Gogh, Vincent, 739, *741*
Vanity Fair
    A Novel Without a Hero (Thackeray), 693
Vatican City, 816
Vatican II, 905
Venetia, 639, 652, 671, 672
Venezuela, 636
Venturi, Robert, 929
Verdun, Battle of, 777
Verona, Congress of, 636
Versailles, Palace of, 580, 582
Versailles, Treaty of, 798–99, 805,
    840–41, 842
Vichy France, 848
Victor Emmanuel II (Italy), 670, 672
Victor Emmanuel III (Italy), 814
Victoria (Great Britain), 682–83, 757
Video games, 959
Vienna
    Jews in, 745, 746
    in nineteenth century, 620
    revolution of 1848, 651
    Ringstrasse, 712
Vienna, Congress of, 632, 633–35
Vienna settlement, 640
Vienna summit (1961), 883
Vietcong, 920, 922
Vietnam, 882, 888–89

Vietnam War, First, 882
Vietnam War, Second, 890, 912, 914, 920,
    922–23
Viola, Bill, 959
Volkish thought, 736
Voting and voting rights
    in Britain, 648, 723
    in France, 649
    in U.S., 654, 898
    for women, 743, 744, 745, 786, 902

Wages
    in U.S., 898
    in West Germany, 896
Wagner, Richard, 695–96
Waiting for Godot (Beckett), 903
Walesa, Lech, 916, 940
Wallachia, 638, 668, 669
The War (Dix), 832
War and Peace (Tolstoy), 737
War communism, 794
War crimes, 896
Warfare. *See* Weapons and warfare
War Guilt Clause, 799
Warhol, Andy, 903
War Labor Board (U.S.), 864
War memorials, 804
War of 1812, 653
"War on poverty," 898
Wars. *See specific wars*
Warsaw
    Duchy of, 597
    Soviet occupation, 855
Warsaw Pact, 880, 881 (map)
Washington, George, 572, 573
Wastewater treatment, 711
Water, 711
Water frame, 607
Watergate, 919–20
Waterloo, Battle of, 600
Waterways, 685
Watt, James, 607
Watts riots, 899
Weapons and warfare
    atomic bomb, 836, 855, 864, 868, 880,
        925
    Austro-Prussian War, 675
    machine guns, *776, 777*
    of Red Army, 794
    WWI, 775, *776*, 777–78, 780,
        782, 783
    WWII, 842, 855, 864, 868. *See also*
        Nuclear arms
Weill, Kurt, 833
Weimar Republic, 816–17
Welfare state
    in Canada, 899
    in Europe after WWII, 900–901
    in France, 901
    gender issues, 901
    in Germany, 726
    in Great Britain, 748, 896–97, 901
    in Scandinavia, 810
    in U.S., 898, 920

West Germany , 880, 895–96, 900, 901, 912, 917

Westphalia, 634

Whig Party (U.S.), 683

Whigs (Britain), 639, 647

White-collar jobs, 704–5, 714

"The White Man's Burden" (Kipling), 754

White Rose movement, 857

White Russians, 793–94

William I (Netherlands), 634

William I (Prussia), 673, 677

William II (Germany), 726, *727*, 748–49, 762, 763, 769, 772, 782, 795

Wilson, Woodrow, 751, 783, 796, 797, 798, 799, 804

Windischgrätz, Alfred, 651–52

Witte, Sergei, 749

Woman in Her Social and Domestic Character (Sanford), 716

"A Woman in the Slums" (Orwell), 809

Woman with Coffee Pot (Cézanne), 739, *740*

Women
    after WWII, 901–2
    artists, 738–39
    education of, 720
    of French Revolution, 580, 582, 588–89
    and industrialization, 616–17, 625
    medical school admittance, 692
    in Napoleonic France, 595
    in Nazi Germany, 822
    in Roaring Twenties, 831
    socialists, 644–46
    in Soviet Union, 826
    in trade unions, 707–8
    voting rights, 743, 744, 745, 786, 902
    in workforce, 704–5, 901–2, 953
    during WWI, 785–86
    during WWII, 857, 862, 864, 865. *See also* Gender roles

Women's liberation movement, 902, 904, 953–54

Women's rights, 644, 731, 743–44

Women's Social and Political Union, 743

Women's suffrage, 743, 744, 745, 786, 902

Woolf, Virginia, 835

Wordsworth, William, 628, 658–59

Workers. *See* Labor/labor force

Worker's Union (Tristan), 646

Work hours, 719

Workhouses, 625

Working class
    in nineteenth century, 714–15, 719
    religious practice, 737. *See also* Labor/labor force

Working conditions, 623–25

Works Progress Administration (WPA), 810

Work week, 900

World Bank, 961

World Cup, 829

The World of Yesterday (Zweig), 774

World Trade Organization (WTO), 962

World War I
    African campaigns, 781–82
    casualties, 795
    declarations of war, 771–73
    eastern front, 775, 776 (map)
    end of, 795
    Europe after, 800 (map)
    events leading up to, 761–65, 769–70
    home front, 783–88
    impact of, 768–69, 785–88, 795, 804
    in 1914–1915, 773–75
    in 1916–1917, 777–79
    in 1918, 795
    Paris Peace Conference, 796–98
    peace treaties, 798–99, 804
    people's excitement over/opinion of, 773–75, 784–85
    soldiers' experiences, 768, 777–79, 780, 788
    U.S. entry, 782–83
    western front, 775, 775 (map)

World War II
    aftermath, 868–71, 875–76
    Asian-Pacific theatre, 849–51, 853–54, 855
    atomic bomb, 855, 864, 868
    Battle of Britain, 848
    casualties, 868
    costs of, 868–69
    declarations of, 845
    end of, 855
    European theatre, 847–49, 850 (map), 852–53, 854–55
    events leading up to, 840–47

Hitler's role in, 839, 840

Holocaust, 857–61, 862

home front, 862–68

Nazi invasion of France, 848

Nazi invasion of Greece, 849

Nazi invasion of Soviet Union, 849

Nazi invasion of Yugoslavia, 849

Normandy invasion, 854

in North Africa, 850 (map), 852

Pearl Harbor, 849–50

Soviet offensive (1943), 854–55

territorial changes after, 871 (map)

turning point (1942–1943), 851–54

U.S. entry, 849–51

The Wretched of the Earth (Fanon), 887

Wright, Frances, 644

Wright, Frank Lloyd, 833

Wright, Wilbur and Orville, 700

WTO (World Trade Organization), 962

Yalta Conference, 869–70

Yeltsin, Boris, 935–36, 938–39

Young Fascists, 815

Young Girl by the Window (Morisot), 739, *740*

Young Italy, 652, 653

Youth organizations
    Italy's Young Fascists, 815
    Nazi, 822

Youth protest movements, 910–13

Yugoslavia
    authoritarian state after WWI, 826
    break up of, 942–45
    establishment of, 796
    Little Entente, 805
    under Tito, 892
    WWII, 857

Zaire, 885

Zasulich, Vera, 682

Zemstvos, 680, 727, 750

Zeppelins, 783

Zhenotdel, 793

Zionism, 746, 886

Zola, Émile, 737

Zollverein, 673

Zweig, Stefan, 774